COMPARATIVE ECONOMIC SYSTEMS

COMPARATIVE ECONOMIC SYSTEMS

Allan G. Gruchy
University of Maryland

Competing Ways to Stability, Growth, and Welfare

Second Edition

Houghton Mifflin Company

Boston   Atlanta   Dallas   Geneva, Illinois
Hopewell, New Jersey   Palo Alto   London

Copyright © 1977
by Houghton Mifflin Company.
Copyright © 1966
by Allan G. Gruchy as *Comparative Economic Systems: Competing Ways to Stability and Growth*

All rights reserved. No part of this work may be reproduced or transmitted in any form or by any means, electronic or mechanical, including photocopying and recording, or by any information storage or retrieval system, without permission in writing from the publisher.

Printed in the U.S.A.

Library of Congress Catalogue Card Number: 76-10899

ISBN: 0-395-18606-4

To A.G.G., Jr., and K.A.G., whose generation may find something of value in this study, as they press their search for peaceful international coexistence and an equitable sharing of world income.

Contents

Preface   xv

Part One: Introduction   1

Chapter 1
The Nature of Economic Systems   3

The General Concept of System   4
The Concept of Economic System   6
The Economic System as a Dynamic Process   9
The Definition of Economic System   11
The Scope of Comparative Economics   11
The Natural and Social Environments of Economic Systems   12
The Structure and Functioning of Economic Systems   14
Economic Coordination, Intervention, and Planning   17
The Performance of Economic Systems   18
Economic Systems, Goals, and Convergence   20
The Classification of Economic Systems   22
Comparative Economic Systems and the Science of Economics   24
Selected Bibliography   26

Part Two: The Capitalist Economies   29

Chapter 2
The Model of the Mature Capitalist Economy   31

The Essence of Capitalism   32
The Evolution of the Capitalist Economy   35
The Model of Perfect Competition   36
Economic Analysis and Perfect Competition   38
The Limitations of the Model of Perfect Competition   40
Hypothetical and Actual Competition   42
The Idealized Model of the Regulated Mature Capitalist Economy   44

The Functioning of the Regulated Mixed Capitalist Economy   47
Mature Capitalist Economies in Practice   49
Functional Developments in Mature Capitalism   51
The Idealized Model of Guided or Planned Capitalism   54
Planned Capitalism in Practice   56
Selected Bibliography   58

Chapter 3
The Mature American Economy   59

The Structure of the American Economy   59
The Structural Aspects of American Manufacturing   61
The Structural Aspects of American Agriculture   62
Labor and the Structure of American Capitalism   64
Government and the Structure of the American Economy   67
The Evolution of the Capitalist Economic System   69
The American Economy, 1961–1965   69
The High-Pressure Economy, 1966–1968   74
Economic Developments in the United States, 1969–1973   77
Mandatory Wage and Price Controls   79
The External Sector and the End of Price Controls   82
Economic Developments in the United States since 1973   83
The Mature American Economy in Retrospect and Prospect   85
Improving the American Economy in the Short Run   86
The Mix of Short-Term and Medium-Term Economic Policies   88
National Programming and the Coordination of Economic Policies   89
Major Problems of the Mature American Economy   92
The Future of the Mature American Economy   95
Selected Bibliography   98

Chapter 4
The Mature British Capitalist Economy   99

"The Middle Way"   99
The Structure of the Mature British Economy   100
The Functioning of the Mature British Economy   103
The Reaction to Britain's Postwar Economic Problems   105
The Conservative Party and Private Enterprise   106
The Performance of the British Capitalist Economy, 1951–1963   108
Weaknesses of the Domestic Economy   112
British Economic Policy, 1951–1963   113
The Development of a National Incomes Policy   115
National Economic Development Council   118
The Conservative Party's Economic Program, 1970–1974   120
The British Economic Crisis, 1973–1974   124
Supply Management in the British Economy   126
Demand Management in the United Kingdom   128
The United Kingdom and the European Economic Community   131
The Search for a Viable British Economy   132
Selected Bibliography   134

Chapter 5
West Germany's Social Market Economy   136

The Development of the West German Economy since 1948   136
The Post–World War II West German Economy   137
Industry and Banking in West Germany   138
Agriculture and Labor in West Germany   142
West Germany's Foreign Trade   145

The Model of the Social Market Economy   146
The Performance of West Germany's Social Market Economy, 1953–1963   148
From Neoliberalism to Interventionism   152
West German Economic Performance, 1963–1972   155
West Germany's External Sector   159
West German Fiscal Policy   160
West German Monetary Policy   162
West German Incomes Policy   164
West German Antirecession Policy, 1973–1975   167
The Future of the West German Social Market Economy   170
Selected Bibliography   172

Chapter 6
The French Planned Economy   174

Major Features of the French Economy   176
French National Planning   181
The Organizational Structure of French Planning   182
The Theory of French National Planning   185
The Performance of the French Planned Economy, 1953–1963   187
Performance of the French Economy, 1964–1972   189
French Economic Performance, 1973–1975   191
Demand and Supply Management and National Planning   193
Short-Run Demand and Supply Management, 1963–1973   194
French Price Policy   195
Short-Term Monetary Policy   196
Foreign Exchange Policy   198
Short-Run Fiscal Policy   199
French Incomes Policies   201
Medium-Term French Planning   202
Medium-Term French Demand and Supply Management   206
Medium-Term Monetary and Fiscal Management   207

Demand and Supply Management and Long-Term French Development   209
The Concerted Economy in Retrospect and Prospect   211
The Labor Movement and French Planning   213
Economic Interest Groups and French Planning   214
Planning in the New Society   215
Selected Bibliography   217

Chapter 7
The Capitalist Economies: In Retrospect and Prospect   219

The Emergence of the High-Pressure Economy   220
Short-Run Problems of High-Pressure Western Economies   221
Incomes Policy and National Priorities in Industrial Economies   222
The Performance of the Western Capitalist Economies   224
Long-Term Trends in the Western Capitalist Economies   228
The Unfinished Business of the Capitalist Economies   229
Industrial Democracy in the Western Industrial Countries   231
Western Industrial Nations and Multinational Corporations   233
National Priorities and Directed Capitalism   235
Selected Bibliography   237

Part Three: The Democratic Socialist Economies   239

Chapter 8
The Model of the Democratic Socialist Economy   241

The Marxian Socialist Model   242
The Fabian Socialist Model   244
The Model of a Partial Democratic Socialist Society   245
The Model of Partial Democratic Socialism in Transition   247
Selected Bibliography   250

Chapter 9
The Norwegian Socialist Economy 251

The Pattern of the Scandinavian Economies 252
Norwegian Economic Trends, 1945–1973 253
The Planned Norwegian Economy 255
The Performance of the Norwegian Economy, 1963–1972 259
The Performance of the Norwegian Economy since 1972 261
Private Business in the Planned Norwegian Economy 263
Private Investment in the Planned Norwegian Economy 266
The Control of Private Investment 268
Norwegian Price Policy 269
Norwegian Organized Labor 271
Collective Bargaining in Norway 272
Norwegian Wage Policy 276
Agriculture in the Planned Norwegian Economy 277
The External Sector 279
The Norwegian Tax System 281
Fiscal Planning and Long-Term National Objectives 282
Monetary and Credit Policy 284
The Control of Borrowing Abroad 287
Price and Incomes Policies 289
The Norwegian Planned Economy: An Evaluation 292
Critics of National Economic Planning 293
Selected Bibliography 296

Chapter 10
The Swedish Socialist Economy 298

The Swedish Welfare State 299
The Swedish Industrialized Economy 301
The Financial System 305
The Planned Swedish Economy 307
The Performance of the Swedish Economy, 1963–1972 309
Swedish Economic Performance, 1973–1975 312
Short-Run Demand and Supply Management 315
Medium-Term Demand and Supply Management 318
Sweden's 1973–1977 Economic Survey 322
Long-Term Supply and Demand Management 324
Trends in Swedish Incomes Policy 326
Industrial Democracy in Sweden 328
Environmental Protection 331
Regional Development Policy 333
The Critics of Swedish National Economic Planning 334
The Swedish and Other Mixed Economies 335
Selected Bibliography 337

Chapter 11
The British Socialist Economy 339

British Socialism, 1945–1964 340
Criticism of Labour's Postwar National Planning 341
The British Socialist Economy, 1964–1970 342
Short-Term Demand and Supply Management 345
The Failure of Short-Run Demand and Supply Management 346
Medium-Term Demand and Supply Management 349
The National Plan and the Action Program 353
The Economic Assessment for 1969–1972 354
The Third Labour Government and the British Economy, 1974–1975 356
British National Planning: An Evaluation 359
The British Socialist Economy: In Retrospect and Prospect 360
Selected Bibliography 365

Chapter 12
The Mature Democratic Socialist Economies: In Retrospect and Prospect 366

The Performance of the Democratic Socialist Economies 366

The British, Norwegian, and Swedish
Socialist Economies: A Comparison   370
The Future of British Socialism   373
The Nature of Scandinavian Socialism   376
The Future of Scandinavian Socialism   379
Democratic Socialism and the Welfare
State   382
The Western Planned and Unplanned
Economies: An Evaluation   386
The Dynamics of Partial Democratic
Socialism   389
Selected Bibliography   392

Part Four: The Communist Economies   393

Chapter 13
The Four Models of the Communist Economy   395

The Spectrum of Communist
Economies   399
The Mobilized Command Economy   400
The Orthodox Command Economy   402
The Reformed Post-Stalinist Command
Economy   403
Extensive and Intensive Development in the
Orthodox and Reformed Command
Economies   405
The Decentralized, Market-Oriented
Communist Economy   407
The Future of Communist Economic Reform
and Development   410
Selected Bibliography   413

Chapter 14
The Soviet Economy   414

The Evolution of the Soviet Economy   415
The Soviet Planned Economy   419
The Administrative Apparatus of Soviet
National Planning   423
The Three Types of Soviet Plans   426
Industrial Subplans   429
The Unity of Soviet Planning   431
The Balance Method of Soviet Annual
National Planning   431

Soviet Real and Financial Planning   435
Soviet Annual Planning   436
The Ninth Five-Year Plan, 1971–1975   438
Major Ninth-Plan Targets   441
Performance under the Ninth Plan,
1971–1975   441
The Tenth Five-Year Plan, 1976–1980   444
The Deficiencies of Soviet Annual Materials
Planning   445
Input-Output Planning in the Soviet
Union   446
Efficiency in Soviet National Planning   454
The Future of Soviet Planning   456
Selected Bibliography   459

Chapter 15
The Soviet Economy (Continued)   460

The Annual Output Plan   461
Soviet Industry and Economic
Accountability   464
Wages and Salaries   464
The Wholesale Price System   466
The Profitability of Enterprises   467
Investment in Soviet Industry   468
Industrial Management in the Planned Soviet
Economy   470
Unofficial Managerial Practices   472
New Directions in Soviet Management   475
The Soviet Economic Reforms of 1965   476
Soviet Industrial Management since
1965   479
The New Industrial Associations   481
Agriculture in the Soviet Economy   482
The Role of Collective Farms   484
The Annual Revenues of Collective
Farms   486
The Private Sector in Soviet
Agriculture   487
Soviet Agricultural Policy, 1953–1964   488
The End of the Machine Tractor
Stations   490
Soviet Agricultural Policy since 1964   491
Agriculture in the Soviet Union and the
United States   493
Labor in the Soviet Economy   497
The Labor Plan   499

Microeconomic Aspects of Soviet Wage Policy   501
Macroeconomic Aspects of Soviet Wage Policy   503
Trends in Soviet Labor Policy   504
The Soviet Manpower Problem   506
The Soviet Distribution System   507
Prices of Consumer Goods   510
Consumer Welfare in the Soviet Union since 1964   512
Soviet Foreign Trade   514
The Soviet Financial System   516
The Real and Financial Flows   518
The State Fiscal Budget   520
The Performance of the Soviet Economy   521
Selected Bibliography   526

Chapter 16
The Communist Economies of the Comecon Bloc   527

The Comecon Bloc   527
The Structure and Performance of the Comecon Bloc   530
The Progress of Economic Reform in the Comecon Bloc   534
The Czechoslovakian Economic Reforms   535
Hungarian Economic Reforms   538
✓ Economic Reform in East Germany, Romania, and Bulgaria   541
Comecon Economic Reform: In Retrospect and Prospect   543
The Comecon Bloc and Economic Integration   544
Selected Bibliography   546

Chapter 17
The Yugoslav Socialist Market Economy   547

The Ideological Basis of Yugoslav Communism   548
The Yugoslav Political System   550
The Yugoslav Economy   551
Industry in the Planned Yugoslav Economy   553
The Yugoslav Monetary System   556
Labor in Yugoslavia   557
Transformation of the Yugoslav Economy after 1945   558
The Performance of the Yugoslav Economy, 1964–1975   560
Economic Planning in Yugoslavia   562
The 1971–1975 Economic and Social Plan   563
Annual Planning in Yugoslavia   564
Short- and Medium-Term Supply and Demand Management   565
Yugoslav Monetary and Fiscal Policies   566
Price Control and Incomes Policy   568
Long-Term Supply and Demand Management   570
The Yugoslav Economy: An Evaluation   572
Selected Bibliography   575

Part Five: The Less Developed Economies   577

Chapter 18
The Model of the Less Developed Economy   579

The Major Features of the Low-Income Developing Economy   580
The Model of the Less Developed Economy   584
Major Problems in the Less Developed Economies   586
The Growth Strategy of the Less Developed Economies   587
Population Growth and Poverty   589
The Future of the Less Developed Economies   592
Selected Bibliography   595

Chapter 19
The Chinese Communist Economy   596

China and World Communism   596

Communist China as a Less Developed Country   598
The Political Structure of Communist China   600
The Structure of the Chinese Communist Economy   602
The Decentralized Planned Chinese Economy   605
The Performance of the Chinese Economy since 1949   607
Industry in the Chinese Communist Economy   612
Agriculture in Communist China   615
China's Agricultural Prospects   617
The Chinese Price and Wage Systems   619
The Chinese Monetary and Fiscal Systems   622
Mainland China's Domestic and Foreign Trade   623
The Future of the Chinese Economy   627
Selected Bibliography   630

Chapter 20
The Indian Economy and the Third World   632

The Ideological Basis of the Indian Economy   633
The Indian Economy   636
Agriculture and Industry in the Indian Economy   636
The Planned Indian Economy   639
The Construction of India's Five-Year Plans   640
Indian Financial Planning   642
India's Five-Year Plans, 1951–1979   644
The Performance of the Indian Economy, 1962–1970   646
The Indian Economy, 1971–1975   647
Demand and Supply Management in the Indian Economy   649
Monetary and Other Aspects of Economic Management   650
Long-Term Demand and Supply Management and Structural Change   652
The Planned Indian Economy: An Evaluation   653
Selected Bibliography   657

Part Six: Conclusion   659

Chapter 21
Economic Systems in the Crucible   661

The Static and Dynamic Aspects of Economic Systems   661
The Spectrum Model   663
The General Theory of Economic Systems   666
The Convergence of Economic Systems   667
Interpretations of the Convergence Theory   668
The Future of Economic Systems   671
The No-Growth Society   672
The Zero Population Growth Society   673
Economic Systems and International Planning   674
Selected Bibliography   677

Index   678

Preface

In the decade since the first edition of this study appeared, economic and social trends have confirmed the author's view that little progress has been made in constructing a general theory of economic systems. Because the nations that make up economic systems have such diverse ideological, cultural, and economic characteristics, they can be classified only loosely as capitalist, socialist, or communist, or as developed and developing countries. The emphasis in the analyses of the various countries included in this study is not on tracing their historical development, but on surveying each country's economic development over the past few decades, as well as its current economic situation, and its economic and social trends and prospects. Since the world's economic systems are now in a state of great economic and political uncertainty, it is important to draw attention to the problems associated with future trends and prospects.

In this new edition, attention is directed toward a number of problems that have become especially important throughout the world since the quarter century of post-World War II prosperity came to an end in the early 1970s. The international economic and financial system is still on a very weak foundation, and nations now need to be more concerned with the determination of national goals and priorities, domestic and international planning, wage-price policy, the distribution of income, and the control of the economic power of large industrial corporations and trade unions. The developing countries of the Third World present a special challenge to the West because of their continuing problems of overpopulation and low per-capita economic growth, or because of their strategic importance as suppliers of oil or other important commodities.

This study of comparative economic systems emphasizes the fact that the world's major nations now stand on the threshold of a new era. In the coming post-industrial society, there will be a demand for a fresh approach to the construction and application of economic and social policies and programs. In the western nations, current economic concerns include recessions, inflation, poverty, and discrimination, as well as individual alienation, job dissatisfaction, and the search for a better lifestyle. These national and individual concerns have seriously shaken the confidence of the general populace in their traditional economic systems, and have posed the question: Where do we go from here?

This book explains that in the effort to find a satisfactory answer to this question, a number of nations, including France, Holland, Norway, Sweden, and Belgium, have turned to some forms of national planning that are essentially democratic in nature. Other countries, such as the United States and West Germany, have not gone beyond limited intervention in grappling with this question.

In the communist sphere, events of the last decade point to a similar lack of confidence on the people's part in their inherited economic systems. The once dominant position of the Soviet Union has been greatly eroded, and this study explains how communist countries such as Yugoslavia, Poland, Hungary, Czechoslovakia, and Mainland China are searching for alternatives to the highly centralized Stalinist type of economy that would be more responsive to the basic aspirations of the people in these countries.

Like the western nations, the eastern nations are now in a crucible of great ferment and change, and it is difficult to predict what will emerge from it. While some convergence among different economic systems has occurred in recent decades as a result of the responses of nations to the major late twentieth-century economic and social problems, there are still powerful forces at work to impede this convergence. It is clear that there are now no discernible trends toward any one basic type of economic system that will predominate worldwide.

In the preparation of this revised study of comparative economic systems I have benefited greatly from my contacts with Dr. Norton T. Dodge, whose Cremona Foundation studies of the Soviet Union have been particularly useful in analyzing the operations of the Soviet economic system. I have also drawn heavily upon another faculty associate, Mr. Yi Tsien, whose very deep understanding of economic and political developments in the People's Republic of China has contributed greatly to my appreciation of the importance of that rising world power. In addition I am indebted to the following reviewers for their many worthwhile suggestions for the improvement of this study: Dr. K. Laurence Chang of Case Western Reserve University, Dr. Paul Marer of Indiana University, and Dr. Robert C. Stuart of Rutgers University. I remain responsible, however, for whatever interpretations are presented here. I again have called upon my wife, Florence, for her very able editorial advice and assistance in the preparation of this new edition.

Allan G. Gruchy
College Park, Maryland

COMPARATIVE ECONOMIC SYSTEMS

Part One
Introduction

1
The Nature of Economic Systems

Chapter 1
The Nature of Economic Systems

One of the unique economic developments of the first half of the twentieth century has been the emergence of a large number of different types of national economies. When the twentieth century began, the world was dominated by the capitalistic system, with its center of gravity in Western Europe. During World War I, the first break in the dominance of the monolithic capitalist system occurred when the Soviet socialist system was established in 1917. In the interwar period 1919–1939, fascist regimes were founded in such major nations as Germany, Italy, and Japan. After the Second World War, a number of economies of the Soviet type were established in Central Europe and the Far East. The demise of colonialism after 1945 witnessed the establishment of socialist India and the rise of many developing countries in Africa and Asia. By 1976, the 144 members of the United Nations included a large assortment of nations at different stages of economic development and with widely varying cultural, historical, and ideological backgrounds.

Before the Second World War, economists had expressed little interest in different types of national economies. While the Soviet Union had made considerable progress in the years 1917–1939, it did not pose much of a challenge to the Western capitalist economies at the beginning of the Second World War. The fascist economies of Germany, Italy, and Japan were frequently regarded as deviants from the capitalist system rather than representatives of a distinctly different type of economic system. Since 1945, the spread of authoritarian socialism or communism to Central Europe and to Mainland China, the emergence of socialist India, the development of market socialism in Yugoslavia, and the rise of the less developed countries have led economists to pay increasing attention to the problems of diverse national economies. This new interest has taken the form of a concern with the field of comparative economic systems or comparative economic studies. The 144 members of the United Nations can be loosely divided into four major groups. The first cluster, composed of major Western European nations, the United States, Canada, and Australia, share a common capitalist orientation. The second group of authoritarian socialist or communist countries includes the Soviet Union, the Central European countries, the People's Republic of China, and some small Asiatic countries. A third much smaller group of countries—India, Israel, Norway, Sweden, and the United Kingdom (when the British Labour party is in office)—are examples of democratic partial or limited socialism. The fourth group, composed of newly developing countries of Africa and Asia have enough features in common to warrant being considered members of a Third World, in the view of some comparative economists.[1]

The General Concept of System

The development of the field of comparative economic systems has underlined the importance of the concept of the economic system. Conventional economists have traditionally given little attention to the concept, because they have taken as given the technological and institutional framework within which the market system operates. These economists have devoted their time to the analysis of the various parts of the total economic system and to the behavior of producers and consumers in these sectors. For this reason, conventional economics is frequently described as "market economics" and not "systems economics." When economists in recent decades turned to the comparison of economic systems, they soon recognized the importance of inquiring into how the concept of the economic system was being used. Early investigators of economic systems tended to develop a holistic approach, in which the similarities and dissimilarities of total economic systems, or "isms" such as capitalism, socialism, and communism were studied.[2] When mainstream economists turned to the study of economic systems after World War II, they avoided the broad holistic approach and substituted a particularistic approach to the analysis of economic systems. These economists tended to look at all economic systems from the single point of view of a perfectly competitive economy, and were unwilling to admit the existence of any special field of comparative economic systems. By contrast, economists with a more holistic approach take economics beyond the traditional scope of orthodox economics, making room for a field of comparative economic systems that is not included in the traditional study of economics.[3]

[1] In much economic literature reference is made to the three worlds of the capitalist, the communist or authoritarian socialist, and the less developed countries. No separate place is made for countries like Sweden, Norway, India, and the United Kingdom (when the British Labour party is in office), which provide examples of partial or limited democratic socialism. If four different groups or classes of economic systems are recognized, then one can speak of four and not three worlds or spheres of influence.

[2] This approach was used in the first textbook on comparative economic systems by W. N. Loucks and J. W. Hoot, *Comparative Economic Systems*, New York: Harper and Brothers, 1938.

[3] Disagreement abounds among economists as to whether or not there exists a separate field of comparative economic systems that is not covered by the scope of economics as viewed by conventional economists. Some conventional economists assert that there is no such separate field, and that what now passes for "comparative economic systems" is only a "botanical classification of national economies into a few loosely labeled boxes." See the views of the Inter-University Committee on Comparative Economics as expressed in the Foreword to *The Three Worlds of Economics* by L. G. Reynolds, New Haven: Yale University Press, 1971, p. ix. Other economists like B. Ward seem to prefer to leave this question unanswered, whereas economists like L. G. Reynolds call for a broader definition of economics which would make room for the study of "the curious variety of national economies throughout the world." See B. Ward,

The concept of "system" is used in many different ways, as shown by referring to number, cosmic, river, economic, or political systems. All types of systems have the common characteristic of being orderly, systematic, or regular in nature. In other words, they display a unity, pattern, or orderly arrangement of constituent items. In the most general terms, a system is an interdependent or interacting complex or pattern of items which make up a unified whole. All systems are mental constructs, which may be either real or imaginary. Sir Thomas More's Utopia exemplifies a concept of an imaginary social system, whereas the concept of finance or monopoly capitalism is a concept of a real or actual economic system. When economists in recent years turned their attention from individual to collective economic decision making and to a consideration of social rather than individual preferences, they invented "artificial" economic systems based on class, coalition, and team theories, in which equilibrium is achieved through various voting procedures rather than through the use of a price system.[4] These imaginary economic systems are explanatory devices designed to explain the problems of balance, efficiency, and incentive in real economic systems.

"Organization and Comparative Economics: Some Approaches" in *Comparison of Economic Systems* edited by A. Eckstein, Berkeley: University of California Press, 1971, p. 130; and L. G. Reynolds, *op. cit.*, pp. 328–329.

[4] These artificial economic systems are discussed in Edward Ames, *The Emerging Theory of Comparative Economic Systems*, Working Paper No. 63, Stony Brook, N.Y.: Economic Research Bureau, State University of New York at Stony Brook, April 1972, pp. 1–15; and "The Theory of Planning-Discussion," *American Economic Review*, Vol. LXI, May 1971, pp. 436–437. A very considerable literature on imaginary economic systems, in which equilibria are arrived at without the use of market prices, has appeared in recent years. See J. M. Buchanan and G. Tullock, *The Calculus of Consent*, 1971, and J. Marschak and R. Radner, *Economic Theory of Teams*, 1971.

The term *system* has played a vital role in the evolution of the various sciences. Not until the data of the external world could be placed in a system was science born. In such sciences as physics, chemistry, and botany the first step in developing the science was to classify the observed data. Thus botany was placed on the path to becoming a science when the Swedish botanist Carl von Linne in the eighteenth century worked out the system of binomial nomenclature for the classification of plants. Physicists developed the metric system of weights and measures based on the meter and the kilogram; chemists created the system or table of elements or atomic weights, with hydrogen being assigned an atomic weight of one. The progress of the natural, biological, and social sciences has been a record of improving the methods of systematizing data, and laying the foundation for the development of an expanding body of scientific generalizations based upon the regularities observed in the physical, biological, and cultural worlds.

All systems have a structure and a way of operating, functioning, or proceeding. These systems may be divided between those that are static and those that are dynamic. Static systems are mechanisms or equilibria, whereas dynamic systems are evolutionary processes or developmental complexes. Number systems, the decimal and metric systems, the Newtonian system of mechanics, and the systems of physics and chemistry are, in general, static in nature: they do not deal with change, growth, and development but relate instead to items at rest, or in equilibrium, or approaching equilibrium.

In contrast, biological and cultural systems are dynamic in nature, emphasizing change and development. The change inherent in biological and cultural systems may be gradual and imperceptible, or it may be rapid and quantum in nature. The kind of change observed in the biological world, such as the growth of an animal or plant, is gradual and imperceptible. In some circumstances, however, as when a biological mutation appears in animal or plant life, the biological change is a unique one or a quantum leap change. In the cultural world, while certain changes are gradual, others may be irregular or major. When the capitalist system changed from laissez-faire capitalism to welfare capitalism in the United States, or from laissez-faire capitalism to democratic partial socialism in Sweden, these economic transitions involved major alterations in the structure and functioning of these economic systems over a number of decades.

Developmental or evolutionary systems raise questions that are not brought up by static or mechanistic systems. The former call attention to the forces operating to change these systems in fundamental ways, and to the directions in which these changing systems are moving. In the biological world, scientists inquire into the causes of the emergence of biological mutations, but they do not ask where biological evolution is going because the concept of purpose or objective has no place in the biological world. The situation is quite different in the social or cultural world. There social scientists want to know why economic and political systems change, and what the goals or objectives are of the individuals and groups in a position to influence the course of economic and political development. Although not all cultural development is subject to human direction, a considerable part is, as evidenced by the planning carried on in varying degrees in most nations.

The Concept of Economic System

In the eighteenth century, social scientists like Jean Marie Condorcet constructed hypothetical social systems that were used as aids in explaining the nature of the real social world. These early social scientists believed that society was governed by laws similar to the laws of the physical world, and that a *social mathematics* could be devised for use in the construction of a mathematical model of human phenomena in the form of a social system. At a later time, Leon Walras and Vilfredo Pareto based their pure economics on the concept of a perfectly competitive exchange economy that can be expressed in mathematical terms. Their generalized view of the economic system as a purely competitive exchange economy was an abstraction drawn from the real world of the competitive capitalist system that prevailed in Western Europe in much of the nineteenth century. This view of the economic system continues to be the starting point of conventional economics, and is used in the field of comparative economic systems by those analysts who take the hypothetical model of the perfectly competitive economy as their point of departure for the investigation of actual existing economic systems.

The view of the economic system as a perfectly competitive economy is based upon the concept of an equilibrium in which all parts of the economy are harmoniously related to one another. Frictions or discrepancies may be introduced into the abstract, purely competitive, model in order to make it more realistic, but the functioning of this model in a theoretical way always eliminates these frictions in order to restore an equilibrium condition in the long run. The equilibrium model of a perfectly competitive economy is static in the sense that nothing occurs that would alter the fundamental structure and functioning of the competitive economic system. Such a model does not open the door to the possibility of a dynamic development or evolution from a perfectly competitive economic system to an economic system that is dominated by monopolistic or oligopolistic business enterprise. The equilibrium view of the economic system makes no allowance for dynamic technological and institutional changes that in the course of the process of industrialization may convert the small-scale competitive economy into a large-scale noncompetitive economy.

The equilibrium approach to the study of economic systems has received strong support from the development in recent years of the science of organization, or *organization theory*.[5] This theory deals with the principles that govern organizational behavior and focuses on the organization of productive human groups. The group may be an industrial enterprise, a cooperative, a government department, or a whole economy.[6] The basic approach of organization theorists is the equilibrium approach, which inquires into the sources of disequilibrium in organizations, and indicates how this disequilibrium may be removed in order to achieve optimal performance. The sources of disequilibrium may be either structural or functional. They are structural when some part of the organization's structure prevents its optimal functioning. For example, the hierarchical structure of an industrial organization may prevent the close contact between the managers and the workers that would lead to optimal performance. In some circumstances, the structure may be overcentralized, while in other cases it may be overdecentralized. The solution, as the organization theorist understands the problem, is to find the balance between the top and the bottom of the organization, or between its center (managers) and its periphery (workers), which results in the creation of an optimal structure.

The sources of organizational disequilibrium are functional when the organization's operations create conflict, low morale, lack of incentive, inefficiency, or failure to achieve organizational goals. The problem may be one of unsatisfactory communication, some deficiency in the information system, or a lack of individual incentive. In these situations, the search is for optimal communication, information, or incentive systems that would both satisfy the wants of individuals and also enable the organization to achieve its goals.

The organization theorist is concerned with balance and efficiency. Like the supply-and-demand theorist in conventional economics, the organization theorist thinks in terms of a two-part or two-phase equilibrium model. He observes that in every organization there is a center and a periphery, a hierarchical top and bottom, or a center of authority and control and outlying individuals who are expected to respond to orders from the center of authority. As in all equilibrium theories—of which organization theory is but one type—the problem of optimizing performance arises. The best is achieved when the two parts or phases of the organization are placed in such harmonious relations that the goals of the organization and its participants are reached. The overriding goal of the organization is survival; there are, however, subsidiary goals, such as efficient output, high morale, strong individual incentives, or good communication, which contribute to organizational survival. The equilibrium or optimum performance is

---

[5] The science of organization developed rapidly after 1950, when the attention of behavioral scientists was turned to the problems of large-scale organization in economic, governmental, and military activities. It cuts across many social sciences and incorporates the recent developments in game, team, decision, information, communication, and motivational theory. A good survey of the status of organization theory is presented in Mason Haire (ed.), *Modern Organization Theory*, New York: John Wiley, 1964; and James G. March (ed.), *Handbook of Organizations*, Chicago: Rand McNally, 1965. See also Kenneth E. Boulding, "General Systems Theory—The Skeleton of Science," *Management Science*, Vol. 2, No. 3, April 1956, pp. 197–208.

[6] An *organization* is defined as "any group of persons plus the system of roles defining their interactions with one another." Stanley H. Udy, Jr., "The Comparative Analysis of Organizations," *Handbook of Organizations*, p. 678.

attained, for instance, when the goals of the organization and of the individuals who participate in its affairs coincide, or when the flow of information between the center and the periphery of the organization results in agreement on a course of action.

From development and application of organization theory has stemmed the concept of a universal science of organization that would provide an understanding of organization in all human circumstances. Many organization theorists seek to construct an organization model universal in nature, and general enough to provide an analytical framework for the study of all types of real or actual organizations. This search for generality in organization theory has led to the construction of many mathematical organization models.[7] While these models throw some light on the logical structure and functioning of organizations, they are frequently very unrealistic and have little bearing on actual organizations in the real world. This situation results when mathematical models of organization gain in generality but lose in concreteness and realism.

Some comparative economists, following the lead of the organization theorists, have attempted to mathematicize the study of comparative economic systems. Janos Kornai has constructed a mathematical model or general schema designed to apply to all types of concrete economic systems.[8] This systemic model is a two-sector one, with the control sector assigned to administrative or planning activities and the producing sector to marketing activities. In the control sector are administrative or planning units that issue orders to the producing units or firms in the market sector of the model. Neither the control unit nor the producing unit seeks to optimize its activities; rather, each unit works out compromises between the specialized interests of all the participants. Adapting the principles of organization theory to his systemic model, Kornai ties together all organizational units and their individual participants in his general economic system with a web of information flows, decision rules, and response functions. He asserts that his two-sector system model can be applied to either capitalist or socialist economies. Many comparative economists, however, have found Kornai's mathematical model too general to be very useful for the study of the world's diverse economic systems.

The organization theory discussed above has been applied not only to organizations of many types in a particular social system but also to these organizations in different social systems. Comparative economists have applied organization theory to a wide assortment of economic systems and to their various sectors. They have made studies of hierarchical organization, efficiency, communication, information, and individual incentive in industrial enterprises, farm organizations, and retail establishments in capitalist, socialist, and communist countries. They have also analyzed the problems of total economic systems when they have inquired into the problems of national planning. These problems

---

[7] This point is developed in William H. Starbuck, "Mathematics and Organization Theory," *Handbook of Organizations*, pp. 335–386. T. C. Koopmans and J. M. Montias develop a conceptual framework in which economic systems are analyzed in terms of mathematical representations of the environment, system, actions, outcomes, and norms. See their "On the Description and Comparison of Economic Systems, *Comparison of Economic Systems*, pp. 27–40.

[8] Janos Kornai, *Anti-Equilibrium*, Amsterdam: North Holland, 1971. In the mathematical treatment of centralization and decentralization in economic processes, Leonid Hurwicz constructs a model "of rather general nature so that a variety of economic structures can be regarded as its special cases." L. Hurwicz, "Centralization and Decentralization in Economic Processes," *Comparison of Economic Systems*, p. 81.

deal with such matters as collective decision making in planned and unplanned economies and the balance between centralization and decentralization. In these comparative studies, economists have sought to uncover sources of disequilibrium and a less than optimal performance, and then to suggest an equilibrium solution which would bring about an optimal performance. The limitations of the comparative study of economic systems from the organization point of view are the same as those of studies in the field of general organization theory. These studies are basically static in nature, and do not deal with the long-run changes and development that affect all human organizations in the course of their existence. They ignore the many important economic, social, and political parameters outside the specific system or organization that frequently very profoundly affect its functioning.

The Economic System as a Dynamic Process

At the same time that the view of the economic system as a static equilibrium was being developed by orthodox economists in the nineteenth century, various heterodox economists were working out a view of the economic system as a dynamic evolving process. Karl Marx believed the capitalist system of Western Europe to be an evolving process that was going through a number of developmental stages. He studied the forces influencing the course of economic development, which he saw as propelling capitalism into socialism, and socialism eventually into communism. At a later date, the German historical school and the institutional school of economists, led by Thorstein Veblen, Werner Sombart, and John A. Hobson, theorized about the capitalist system in terms of an evolving process that was substituting monopolistic capitalism for competitive capitalism.

In more recent times, John K. Galbraith, Gunnar Myrdal, and other heterodox economists have approached the advanced industrial economies in the Western world as economic systems that are moving into a new postindustrial era. This view of the economic system as a developing process calls attention to the dynamic forces that bring about changes in the economy's structure and functioning. The process model emphasizes the change, development, conflict, and disharmony that occur as large-scale industry supplants small-scale industry, as free market prices are replaced by administered prices, and as the public sector becomes increasingly important in the nation's economic activities.

An important distinction between the equilibrium and process models of the eco- supplants small-scale industry, as free market reduced to mathematical terms, whereas the latter cannot. While there is a mathematics of static predictable equilibrium, there is no mathematics of the evolving process. There is no mathematics of dynamic unpredictable change that can be incorporated into an evolutionary process model of the economic system.[9] According to the equilibrium view of the economic system, which is patterned after the physical universe, the recurring regularities of economic activity resemble the recurring regularities of the physical world. Both types of regularities are subject to mathematical treatment and to the formulation of laws, principles, or generalizations that reflect a certain level of orderliness or logical arrangement. The laws of diminishing utility, supply and demand, and decreasing returns provide good examples of the regularities that

[9] This point is developed by Gunnar Myrdal in his analysis of the problem of the realism of economic models in *Asian Drama, An Inquiry into the Poverty of Nations*, Vol. III, New York: Pantheon, 1968, pp. 1961–1968.

The nature of economic systems

are applicable to the economic activities covered by the static equilibrium view of the economic system. In contrast, according to the theory that the economic system is an evolving process, no such economic regularities are revealed. No similar laws of the development of capitalist or socialist economies explain the process of long-run economic development or industrialization. One can, however, uncover historical patterns of economic development or industrialization that throw some light on the nature of the economic system as an evolving process.

The evolution of the advanced industrial economies has not been a haphazard or formless development. On the contrary, as Galbraith, Myrdal, and other investigators of the evolving industrial economies have explained, a logic or pattern inheres in the process of industrialization. In many ways, the industrialization of the United States, the major Western European countries, and the Soviet Union has followed a similar path. The application of the modern industrial technology to the production process in these countries has in each case resulted in the emergence of large-scale hierarchical industrial enterprises, the separation of the managers and the managed, the growth of a large public sector, the decline of the free competitive-market system, the spread of intervention or national planning, and the dominance of producer over consumer interests. In all these countries, consumers are endeavoring to domesticate the advanced industrial economy so that it will primarily serve their interests rather than the interests of industrial managers or distant government planners. In all advanced industrial economies, the process of industrialization is leading at different rates, however, to the emergence of a postindustrial society in which there may be more concern with the social costs of economic growth and the need to achieve a life-style of high quality.

The two concepts of the economic system as a static balance or equilibrium and a dynamic or evolutionary process are not contradictory or mutually exclusive, but complementary. Economic reality, like all forms of reality, can be viewed either at one point in time or over a period of time. Analysis of the economic system at a given point in time results in the equilibrium approach, in which the economist examines the current structure and functioning of the economic system. Taking the technological and institutional framework of the economic system as given, the equilibrium economist is mainly concerned with the parts, traits, or components of the economic system and how they are interrelated. He or she investigates the allocation of scarce economic resources by the market system in the private sector and by government action in the public sector. Given the existing economic system, the equilibrium economist inquires into what is produced, how it is produced, and who gets what is produced.

In contrast, these problems are not of special interest to the evolutionary economists, who deal instead with the development or evolution of the economic system over time. The latter economists want to know what forces determine the total economic system, what stages of development the economic system has gone through, and in what direction it may be moving. A full understanding of economic systems requires the use of both the equilibrium and process approaches to the study of these systems. A specialist in the field of comparative economic systems has aptly summarized the situation: "It seems clear that these two approaches to the study of economic systems should be considered complementary rather than alternative approaches. On the one hand, the sectoral [or partial] approach needs a view of the entire system, because the characteristics of a given sector in a particular country are determined by the system of which it is a part. On the other hand, sectoral comparisons enhance our understanding of the respective systems as a whole. Thus both approaches—and a synthesis of the results—are necessary."[10]

The Definition of Economic System

Definitions of the term *economic system* reflect the special interests of those who make these definitions. Among standard or conventional economists who are interested in narrowing the scope of economics until it is essentially no more than the "science of choice" or the "science of efficiency," there exists a strong preference for using the term *economic organization* in place of the term economic system.[11] At a conference on the scope, method, and theory of comparative economic systems held in 1968, a number of the participants wanted to get away from what they described as the grand concept of economic systems. In their search for a "system-free" term, they considered substituting the term economic organization for the term economic system. In their own words, "In general, we believe the new circumstances invite approaches to the comparison of economic systems that altogether avoid prior classification according to the grand 'isms' and instead start from comparisons of organizational arrangements for specific economic functions."[12]

This emphasis on "organization" rather than "system" leads to a definition of an economic system as a complex of organizational arrangements involving participants engaged, according to rules and orders, in the production, distribution, and consumption of goods and services. According to this definition, an economic system may be viewed as a static set of organizational arrangements by means of which the nation determines what shall be produced, how it shall be produced, and for whom it shall be produced. For example, Gregory Grossman states that "The set of institutions that characterizes a given economy comprises its economic system."[13] This definition covers no new ground and is essentially the same as that found in most standard economics textbooks. This definition is based on the view of the economic system as a static balance or equilibrium, which takes no account of the forces that lead to the evolution of economic systems or to the basic changes in their structure and functioning. If allowance is to be made for these dynamic forces, then the definition of an economic system presented above should be altered to state that an economic system is an evolving complex of organizations of participants concerned with the disposal of scarce resources for the satisfaction of private and collective wants. This definition makes it quite clear that the field of comparative economic systems includes the study of these systems from both the equilibrium and the process points of view.

The Scope of Comparative Economics

An understanding of the scope of comparative economics can be attained by inquiring into the kind of problems studied by analysts of comparative economic systems. When economists investigate the nature and functioning of various economic systems, they use four different bases of comparison. The first basis relates to the background forces or factors that broadly influence economic systems,

[10] M. Bornstein, "An Integration," *Comparison of Economic Systems*, p. 353.

[11] R. A. Mundell, *Man and Economics*, New York: McGraw-Hill, 1968, p. 1; and C. R. McConnell, *Economics: Principles, Problems, and Policies*, New York: McGraw-Hill, 1960, p. 25.

[12] T. C. Koopmans and J. M. Montias, *op. cit.*, p. 27. For a similar approach, but of a nonmathematical nature, see R. A. Dahl and C. E. Lindbloom, *Politics, Economics, and Welfare*, New York: Harper and Brothers, 1953, pp. 3-24.

[13] G. Grossman, *Economic Systems*, Englewood Cliffs, N.J.: Prentice-Hall, 1967, p. 3.

while the second basis deals with the narrower question of the nature of the economic systems and how they function. The third basis of comparison is the quality of performance of the various economic systems, as seen in the light of their own individual and collective goals or the goals of other systems. The fourth basis is concerned with the directions in which economic systems may be moving, and with the main features of the emerging phases in the evolution of these systems.

Comparative studies of economic systems may be either interspatial or intertemporal. Interspatial or transnational comparisons cut across different existing national economies and investigate either total economic systems or specific sectors or components of these systems at the same point in time. For example, a comparative appraisal may be made of the Soviet communistic and American capitalistic systems; or a comparison may be made of some particular components of these two systems, such as their industrial enterprises, agricultural sectors, or labor markets. Intertemporal comparisons analyze economic systems over various time periods. Some intertemporal comparisons study the same economic system at different time periods, such as the Soviet Union in 1928 and 1968. Other intertemporal studies compare different economic systems: the Soviet Union of 1970 may be contrasted with the United States at a similar level of development but at some earlier time. For some purposes, such as the study of problems of economic growth, it makes more sense to compare the Soviet Union of 1970 with the United States of 1930 or 1940.

Comparisons of economic systems also raise the question of exogenous and endogenous factors that influence the structure and functioning of these systems. Exogenous factors, according to orthodox economists, are external factors, such as new technologies, ideologies, and political developments. In the standard view of economics, these exogenous social and cultural factors should be investigated by social scientists other than economists. Endogenous factors, on the other hand, are internal to the economic system and concern such matters as production techniques, types of markets, size of industrial enterprises, and labor markets. These factors, dealing with the internal operations of the economic system, are the items with which conventional economics is usually concerned. The comparative economist broadens the scope of economics to include the social and cultural setting within which the economic system functions. Comparisons of economic systems thus include investigations of both the exogenous and the endogenous determinants of economic systems.

The Natural and Social Environments of Economic Systems

Comparative economists find it important to compare the natural environments of different economic systems. They point out that geographical location, area, population, resource endowment, and climate have much to do with the level of development and the economic growth rate of a country. Where a nation has a large area and is richly endowed with natural resources, as in the case of the United States, the Soviet Union, and the People's Republic of China, a high degree of self-sufficiency can be associated with a high level of economic development. Both the Soviet Union and the People's Republic of China have been able to pursue autarkic economic policies that could not be successfully adopted by small East European, African, Asiatic, and Latin American countries with very limited natural resources. Access to the sea is important for those nations that need to engage in extensive foreign trade if they are to achieve a rapid rate of economic growth. Geographical proximity, for example, has been a factor in the development of the European Common Market in Western Europe and the Council for Mutual Economic Assistance in Eastern Europe. An important element in Yugoslavia's breakaway from Stalinist domination after 1948 was its geographical location, which permitted the development of an extensive East-West trade. The location and limited availability of natural resources in Poland, Czechoslovakia, Hungary, and other Central European communist countries have contributed to many of the economic problems that have developed in these countries since the end of the Second World War.

A major factor influencing the nature of economic systems is their historico-cultural conditions. Each nation is an historico-cultural continuum, which constitutes an overall framework for the nation's economic system. If one asks why the American society is an open democratic society, whereas the Soviet society is to a great extent a closed authoritarian society, he or she must inquire into the very different cultural and historical backgrounds of these two countries, which include a wide variety of accumulated traditions, customs, attitudes, beliefs, and values.

Another related factor that contributes to the shaping of a nation's economic system is its institutional complex. This complex of institutional arrangements constitutes the nation's social organization and reveals its class structure and its economic, legal, and political arrangements. Many of the socio-cultural conditions that existed before 1917 in the Soviet Union and before 1949 in the People's Republic of China were preserved after the old regimes were abolished. Since the democratic way of life was never well established in either pre-1917 Russia or pre-1949 China, it is not surprising that neither country today accepts the Western version of democracy. Western social and cultural conditions have given rise to a Western view of life that is in many respects not duplicated in the East.

The social and cultural influences that help to determine the nature of a nation's economic system come to a head in its *ideology*. An ideology is a complex of attitudes, beliefs, and values that guides individuals and groups in their efforts to adjust to the natural and cultural environment. An ideology may be economic, political, legal, or religious in nature. It provides a framework by the aid of which individuals interpret the world around them and set goals for themselves. Since an ideology incorporates beliefs and values, it is a stimulus to action.

In the field of comparative economic systems, the important ideologies relate to economic, social, and political matters. One can compare, for instance, the capitalist ideology of the United States and the communist ideology of the Soviet Union. Both ideologies have much to do with the kinds of economic and political systems that have evolved in these two countries. Some economic and political ideologies are very clearly delineated, as in the case of the official Marxist-Leninist Soviet ideology; in the Western democracies, however, there exist no such neatly stated official ideologies. The dominant political and economic ideology of the United States is the result of an accumulation over a long period of time of attitudes, beliefs, and values relating to such matters as the government and its role, the ownership of property, the role of the free competitive markets, and consumer and worker freedoms. No one group, however, speaks for the entire nation; thus there is no official American ideology. Since each major interest group, such as business, labor, agriculture, and consumer interests, puts forth its own version of the American economic and political ideology, many versions of the so-called American capitalist ideology exist cheek by jowl. When a number of the nation's major interest groups hold similar ideological positions, a dominant national ideology emerges. This dominant ideology may be challenged by the ideologies of minority interest groups, such as blacks, ethnic groups, and workers outside traditional trade unions. In some countries, a revolutionary or insurgent ideology successfully challenges the ruling ideology, as in Cuba, where Fidel Castro's Marxist ideology replaced Fulgencio Batista's fascist ideology.

Ideology and economic and political power go hand in hand. In the Soviet Union, the ideology of the Communist party Politburo dominates the country and shapes the nation's economic system, because political and economic power are concentrated in the hands of the fourteen members of the Politburo. In the United States, the capitalist ideology has the backing of powerful business interests, especially the large industrial corporations. While many interest groups in the United States have much in common ideologically, most of them accepting such basic capitalist tenets as a preference for democratic government, private property, and consumer and occupational freedom, there are, nevertheless, many ideological variations associated with large and small business, farmers, organized workers, and consumers. Where a nation has an official ideology, as in the case of the Soviet Union, the People's Republic of China, and other communist countries, the impact of this ideology on the economic system can be more easily established. In countries with no official ideology, such as the United States and the major Western European countries, the role of ideology as a system determinant is much less clear cut.

In any comparison of economic systems, an important consideration is the level of the development of these systems. The achievements of different economic systems can be compared in terms of rates of economic growth, amount of per capita income, proportions of Gross National Product taken up by consumption and investment, and employment and output in the primary, secondary, and tertiary economic activities.[14] A close relationship exists between a nation's level of economic development and the structure and functioning of its economic system. A comparison of the mature and less developed economies reveals considerable differences with respect to the size of public and private sectors and of business enterprises, reliance upon foreign trade, availability of managerial expertise, and the role of the labor market. While certain structural and functional features of economic systems are usually found at particular levels of economic development, a given level of economic development is not necessarily associated with one specific type of economic system. For example, a nation with a well-developed economy may have a planned or unplanned capitalist system, a democratic partial socialist system, or an authoritarian communist system. The United States, France, Sweden, and the Soviet Union, which have advanced industrial economies, fall into these different categories or classes of economic systems.

The Structure and Functioning of Economic Systems

Comparisons of different economic systems draw attention to the similarities and dissimilarities in the structure and functioning of these systems. The structure of an economic system is made up of its component parts or organizations, such as households, industrial enterprises, farms, agricultural cooperatives, trade unions, banks and other financial institutions, and government departments and agencies. From a broader point of view, the structure of an economic system may be divided into private and public sectors. Differences in the structure of Western and Eastern

[14] S. Kuznets, *Modern Economic Growth: Rate, Structure, and Spread,* New Haven: Yale University Press, 1966.

economies are related to the matter of ownership, which is largely private in the West and public in the East. In the Western capitalist economies, individuals or groups own houses, factories, farms, and urban land, while this is generally not true in the Eastern economies.

Comparative economists are more interested in the functioning than the ownership of the component parts of the economic system. The emergence of market socialism in Yugoslavia and theoretical discussions of this type of socialism in other Central European communist countries point up the importance of how economic systems work and not of who owns the means of production. In both capitalism and market socialism, the bulk of the workers do not own the factories and other means of production. Nor is the legal ownership of the means of production a crucial matter. Most significant is the way in which the economy operates and for whose benefit. In both capitalist and socialist types of economic systems, the same basic questions arise. Does the economic system take care of consumer needs? Who makes the basic decisions with regard to investment, production, and pricing? How are profits shared? It is possible for market socialism in Yugoslavia and private capitalism in the United States to operate in fundamentally the same manner, even though public ownership dominates in the former country and private ownership in the latter.

All economic systems are made up of two basic flows: the real product flow and the financial or income-expenditure flow. The real flow is concerned with the combining of land, labor, and capital in producing units in order to create a flow of real goods and services. This is the realm of production economics, where the matters of concern include the organization of producing units, selecting production techniques, and getting the most physical output with the minimum use of raw materials, semiprocessed materials, and productive equipment. Interest in the economy's real product flow centers in industrial technology and the techniques of production that result from improvements in science and technology. In this area, *efficiency* means *physical,* not *financial,* efficiency. The production expert seeks to achieve the maximum physical output with the minimum real cost as measured in terms of raw materials, use of capital, and hours of labor. In primitive economies, where no monetary system exists, the real flow of goods is not accompanied by any financial or income-expenditure flow. Those responsible for production in such an economy seek to maximize the output of physical goods with the available supply of raw materials, equipment, and labor without the use of a financial system.

In nonprimitive economies, the real product flow is accompanied by a financial flow which involves the receiving of incomes by the owners of property and labor and the spending of these incomes on the output of the real flow. The nation's financial flow arises from the real flow when business people, workers, farmers, and government officials produce real goods, while exchanging the use of labor and property for incomes in the form of profits, dividends, wages, rent, interest, and taxes (which constitute government income). The basic problem in any economy with a financial flow as well as a real flow is to coordinate these two flows in order to achieve the national goals. In a democratic country, these goals include a high and sustained growth rate, full employment, price stability, a fair sharing of the national income, environmental protection, and a lifestyle of high quality.

In integrating an economy's two basic flows, three questions arise. (1) What kinds and amounts of goods shall be produced? (2) How shall these goods be produced? (3) How shall these goods be distributed among the households and other organizations that have claims on them? The kinds and amounts of goods to be produced are basically matters of individual and collective preferences or valuations. The economy's private sector is primarily concerned with the provision of goods and services that meet the needs of individuals; the latter, in turn, express their preferences through spending in the private market places. The public sector provides collective goods that are not obtainable in the private markets; these goods may be consumed by individuals acting either separately or collectively.

Nations vary widely in the ways in which individual and collective preferences for goods and services are met. In a perfectly competitive economy, individuals and groups are in theory free to express their preferences in the private sector through spending in the market place. In fact, however, the economies of the advanced industrial nations are far from being fully competitive, as their political systems are subject to the strong influences of lobbyists who represent sectional rather than national interests. In this situation, the preferences of the minority of individuals and groups with considerable economic and political power frequently take precedence over the preferences of the majority with little or no economic and political power.

In democratic, partially socialist countries, like Sweden and Norway, where the private enterprise system is regulated through a national planning program, and the political system is less subject to the pressures of lobbying groups than in the unplanned Western nations, the economic system is less manipulated by powerful interest groups; and the general majority are in a better position to have their preferences for goods and services satisfied. In authoritarian socialist nations, like the Soviet Union and other communist countries, the preferences of the ruling clique or oligarchy take precedence over the individual and collective preferences of the general population. Even here the situation may change, as we have seen in the case of the Soviet Union, where after the death of Stalin in 1953 investment in the consumer-goods industries was stepped up and the variety and quality of consumer goods were considerably improved.

The question of how an economy's goods and services shall be produced is a matter of the efficient allocation of the nation's scarce economic resources. Nations are constantly on the alert to improve the ways in which their scarce economic resources may be allocated. In the Western nations, new production techniques are adopted, large-scale industry is substituted for small-scale industry, and experiments are made in the methods of operating hierarchical business enterprises and in rewarding the participants in these enterprises. The communist countries have in recent decades sought to improve the efficiency of their resource allocation systems by decentralizing planning, providing for more flexibility in the decision making of industrial enterprises, establishing more rational prices, changing the success indicators of the state enterprises, improving incentive systems, and, in Yugoslavia, substituting market socialism for administrative socialism.

The allocation of economic resources can be carried on through a market system with its pricing and other financial arrangements, through a plan or command system based on administrative orders, or through some combination of these two. In the United States, the allocation of resources has been made very largely with the aid of a market system, supported, however, by a significant amount of government intervention. At the opposite extreme, the Soviet Union has allocated its economic resources primarily with the help of a command or administrative system and, until recently, with a very limited reliance upon the market system. In all patterns of resource allocation, there exist similar problems relating to production techniques, large and small-scale enterprise, hierarchical organizations, the structure of authority and the locus of decision making, personal incentives, and centralization versus decentralization.

In the operation of an economy, the allocation of economic resources is closely associated with the distribution of national income. A nation's income distribution pattern is important because of its relation to personal incentives, which in turn are connected with the size of the national output of goods and services. Just as resource allocation patterns vary widely among nations, so also do income distribution patterns. This distribution may be left largely to the forces of the market place, as in the United States; or it may be determined mainly by the requirements of some national plan, as in the Soviet Union. In a perfectly competitive economy, personal income is determined by the freely operating forces of the market place. In the advanced Western industrialized economies, where competition has been partly replaced by oligopoly, personal income is determined to an increasing extent by government action rather than by the competitive forces of the market mechanism. As competition has retreated, transfer incomes have been given to those who have been disadvantaged by the decline of competitive industry.

In the Eastern communist countries, personal incomes are largely determined by the authorities in charge of planning, who fix the prices of both commodities and the factors of production, including labor. Within the communist planned framework, however, a wide variation exists between planned wage differentials. In the Soviet Union, differentials are large, whereas in the People's Republic of China they are much smaller. Differences in the patterns of income distribution among nations reflect the economic and social priorities established by these nations. In the more consumer-oriented Western democracies, the national income pattern reflects the preference for allowing consumers to enjoy a rising standard of living. In the less consumer-oriented Eastern communist countries, however, the national income distribution pattern is designed to elevate investment over consumption by curbing personal incomes and reducing the claims of households on the national output of goods and services.

Economic Coordination, Intervention, and Planning

In all nations, the problem arises of improving the coordination of the economy's real and financial flows so as to satisfy individual and collective wants more efficiently. In a perfectly competitive economy, no problem of overall national economic coordination would exist, since the economy's real and financial flows would be automatically meshed by the self-correcting forces of the market system. Any deviation from a balanced and efficient coordination of these two flows would soon be eliminated by the economy's equilibrating forces. In advanced industrial economies, where competition has been extensively replaced by oligopolistic enterprise, the economy's self-correcting forces have largely been replaced by self-reinforcing forces, and the coordination of the economy's real and financial flows has at times been unsatisfactory. This coordination has been accompanied by recurring economic recessions, irregular economic growth rates, structural unemployment, urban decay, chronic poverty, and environmental deterioration. As a consequence of the changes in the structure and functioning of the modern industrial economy since the turn of the century, the coordination of the real and financial flows is no longer left only to the working out of the private market forces.

In the United States, the United Kingdom, West Germany, and other Western industrialized nations, government intervention in economic affairs has been practiced since 1929 on a wide and increasing scale. Some Western countries, like France, the Netherlands, Norway, and Sweden, have gone beyond intervention to adopt national planning. In all these nations, efforts have been made to coordinate the economy's real financial flows with the aid of a variety of economic policies; prominent among these have been fiscal, monetary, price, foreign exchange, investment, and incomes policies. The Western nations that have adopted indicative democratic national planning have coordinated their real and financial flows by using annual and four- or five-year national economic budgets, which project Gross National Product and its consumption and investment uses over a given plan period.

The Soviet Union and other communist countries have coordinated their real and financial flows by means of target or blueprint national planning. In general, this planning has remained highly centralized, but in recent decades it has become considerably decentralized in Yugoslavia and Hungary. The economic policy mixes used by Western and Eastern economies reflect the extent to which these economies rely upon free markets or administrative plans in their efforts to achieve a satisfactory overall national economic coordination.

The Performance of Economic Systems

A matter of great interest to comparative economists is the performance of different economic systems. Comparisons of this performance may be made for two reasons. Economists may be interested in comparing the performance of different economic systems in order to find ways of improving their own economic system. Thus American economists may analyze noncapitalist economic systems to determine whether some feature can be borrowed from these other systems that would improve the capitalist system. Or economists may evaluate the performance of different economic systems so as to decide whether a particular system is superior to other systems. Any such evaluation, which aims at appraisal of economic systems, is beset by many difficulties. What is meant by a "total appraisal of an economic system"? Does such an appraisal go beyond economic welfare to include social welfare? Some economists, like John K. Galbraith, have moved in this direction by analyzing an economic system in terms of its contribution to the achievement of a lifestyle of high quality. Not only is it difficult to define "a lifestyle of high quality," but it is also hard for any such definition to apply both to the Soviet Union, the People's Republic of China, and other communist countries as well as to the capitalist countries.

The performance of an economic system raises the question of how well it achieves its individual and social goals or preferences. The general concept of performance relates to the accomplishment of some goal or goals with skill or efficiency. An economic system can be said to perform poorly when it suffers from recession, low production, and high unemployment, or well when it has a high and sustained rate of economic growth and a rising standard of living. The performance-goal relationship is important because the economic system's goals supply the criteria by which performance is measured or evaluated. For example, where the national goals include full employment, efficient production, and a sustained and adequate rate of economic growth, these goals become criteria of performance evaluation.

Judging or evaluating an economic system's performance is sometimes difficult because the criteria of performance are not always easily established. Criteria of economic equality, stability, and security can be rather easily constructed because there is a quantitative basis for these criteria which permits some kind of measurement. The degree of economic instability can be measured by variations in the statistics of prices, output, and employment; economic insecurity can be determined by taking account of the levels of personal income and employment; and, in the case of economic inequality, Lorenz curves can be used to reveal the degree of inequality in the distribution of income and wealth. When, however, economists turn to other performance criteria, they find that these criteria do not have a quantitative basis, and so do not permit ready measurement. Such criteria as economic freedom, equality of opportunity, progressiveness of the economy, or adaptability to change have qualitative features that do not readily lend themselves to quantitative measurement.

Not only is it difficult to evaluate the performance of any one economic system, but it is even harder to compare the performances of a number of different economic systems. In the first place, national data vary in terms of reliability, availability, and coverage. A second difficulty is that the world's major economic systems, such as those of the United States and the Soviet Union, are at different stages of development. A recent study revealed that in 1960 the productivity of labor and capital was much lower in the Soviet Union than in the United States; but this study failed to indicate how much of the lower Soviet productivity resulted from the defects of the Soviet economic system, and how much from the less developed condition of that system.[15] Furthermore, in all countries the efficiency of labor and capital is affected by the interplay of economic and political factors whose influence cannot readily be measured.

Evsey Domar points out that "we do not know where the influence of noneconomic factors ends and true inefficiency begins. It seems that governments or ruling circles of all countries enjoy their own political systems well enough to be willing to pay high economic prices for maintaining them."[16] As long as these conditions prevail, attempts to measure the comparative efficiencies of different economic systems will meet with many serious obstacles.

Comparisons of the performance of economic systems are most meaningful when these systems have similar cultural and ideological foundations, and they are at about the same stage of development. For this reason, a comparative study of the advanced industrial economies of Western Europe and the United States can tell us a great deal about the performance of these economies. Where there are marked differences in their economic performance, economists look for economic reasons for these differences. Similarly, a comparative study of the Soviet economy and the Central European communist economic systems can throw much light on the differences in the performance of these economies.

Special problems arise when one attempts to compare the performance of two economies like the American and Soviet economies, which are at different stages of development and which have marked cultural and ideological differences. Soviet national goals tend to be highly collectivistic; American national goals are much more individualistic. Collective purposes, such as rapid industrialization and militarization, are of great concern to the authoritarian Soviet leaders. In the United States and other democratic Western nations, however, individual purposes, such as consumer sovereignty and occupational freedom, bulk large among national goals. All advanced nations are in general agreement on the de-

---

[15] A. Bergson, "Comparative Productivity and Efficiency in the Soviet Union and the United States," *Comparison of Economic Systems*, p. 179. E. D. Domar's criticism of Bergson's methodology is given in "On the Measurement of Comparative Efficiency," *Comparison of Economic Systems*, pp. 228-233.

[16] E. D. Domar, *op. cit.*, p. 228.

sirability of achieving certain goals, such as economic efficiency, sustained economic growth, price stability and freedom from economic fluctuations, full employment, and extensive social security. A fair sharing of the national income is a widely held national goal, but nations differ in their interpretation of how far they should go in securing this goal. Socialist Sweden has a more equitable sharing of national income than does capitalist America. In the Soviet Union, definite limits are placed on variation in personal incomes, but the government keeps the standard of living of most citizens low by promoting heavy industrial investment and curbing personal consumption.

The achieving of national goals raises a number of important problems. Some national goals are in conflict with each other, as in the case of full employment and price stability. The higher the level of employment sought by a given nation, the more difficult it is to prevent inflation and to secure price stability. Consumer freedom—the freedom to spend income as one wishes—conflicts with enlarging social security, which is obtained by taxing productive individuals and transferring a part of their income to individuals who are no longer productive. In the democratic nations, rapid and high economic growth can sometimes be secured only at the cost of considerable economic instability. Where economic goals are in conflict, nations must decide what kinds of tradeoffs will be made among these competing national goals. Decisions about these tradeoffs reflect the values that are held by people and that cannot be reduced to any common denominator applicable to all nations. The mixture of goals sought by a nation is a matter of value preferences, which are difficult to analyze in terms of any rational calculus. To comprehend what guides the world's various economic systems, the economist needs to understand the nature of the goals and values that dominate these systems, but in many cases he or she cannot prove that one nation's goals or values are superior or inferior to those of another nation.

It is also important to note that the national goals that guide the performance of economic systems change over time. Today in the Western world, emphasis on economic growth and efficiency is being replaced to some extent by concern with securing a lifestyle of higher quality, environmental protection, the elimination of race and sex discrimination, and greater participation of the public in the shaping of economic and social activities. Many individuals in the United States and other advanced industrialized nations are prepared to accept lower economic growth and less economic efficiency in exchange for more urban amenities, more protection of the natural environment, less individual and class discrimination, and an organization of the economic system in which individuals have more influence on the operation of this system and the determination of its goals. Some groups now advocate the eventual adoption of such national goals as zero economic growth (ZEG) and zero population growth (ZPG). They believe that the future welfare of all nations depends upon stabilizing the world's population and output of goods and services at levels and with a distribution that will be optimum in terms of human welfare.[17] These worldwide goals could very well be prominent in the postindustrial society that appears to be emerging among the Western industrialized nations.

Economic Systems, Goals, and Convergence

An important aspect of the comparative study of economic systems is the directions in

[17] These problems are analyzed in Donella H. Meadows and others, *Limits to Growth: A Report for the Club of Rome's Project on the Predicament of Mankind,* New York: Universe Books, 1972, and Paul R. Ehrlich, *The Population Bomb,* New York: Ballantine Books, 1968.

which these systems are moving. As an evolving process, every major economic system is passing through some phase or stage in its development. New scientific developments and new attitudes and values on the part of the participants in an economic system are constantly weakening old institutional arrangements and changing national goals. People are by nature exploratory individuals who are prepared to experiment with new ways of adjusting to the environment and of achieving individual and collective goals. The regulated capitalist and democratic socialist economies of Western Europe are now moving towards a new service economy in which the private and public service industries are becoming increasingly important. In the United States, more than half the nation's labor force now finds employment in the private and public service sectors; similar trends exist in Western Europe. The United States is now a mass-consumption economy dominated by the service sector, while the major Western European countries are close behind the United States.

The *service economy* may be defined as a postindustrial economy in which consumers have much discretionary spending power, the public sector is expanding rapidly because of the growing demand for services that cannot be supplied by private industry, and the number of white-collar workers is increasing more rapidly than the number of blue-collar workers. In a society where there is a great deal of discretionary personal income and consumers spend much of their incomes on services, these services contribute a great deal to the lifestyle of high quality which becomes the goal of the general public in the postindustrial society.

Like the mature industrial economies of the West, the communist economies of the Soviet Union and Central Europe have undergone very significant secular developments in the past half century. Much of the logic of industrialization that applies to the mature Western economies is also relevant to the less advanced Eastern communist economies. In the Soviet Union, the process of industrialization has created large state enterprises; problems relating to the hierarchical organization of economic activity have made their appearance; education has been directed towards the provision of increasing numbers of white-collar workers; and agriculture has declined in relation to industry. The thaw that came after Stalin's death in 1953 sparked an interest in expanding consumer welfare. Since 1928, the Soviet Union has passed through two stages of development. Under Stalin extensive development took place during the years 1928–1953, when the national economy was operated on the basis of highly centralized national planning that subordinated consumer-goods industries to investment-goods industries.

Since 1953, there has been a period of intensive development in which national planning has been considerably decentralized, economic growth has proceeded in a more balanced manner, and more attention has been given to enlarging the supply of consumer goods and services. Where intensive development is the main concern, emphasis is placed not upon securing more growth from extra inputs of labor and capital but upon achieving additional growth, largely as the result of improving the productivity or efficiency of the current supply of labor and capital. Extensive economic development has special application to underdeveloped countries, whereas intensive development relates to a more mature, sophisticated economy, such as the Soviet economy of today. Similar economic trends have also occurred in Poland, Hungary, and Rumania. In Yugoslavia the decentralization of economic activity has proceeded much further than in the Soviet Union.

In both the Western and Eastern economies, long-range developments are constantly at work propelling these economies towards new stages in which significant structural and functional changes occur. The presence of these secular developmental trends in these economies brings up the question of their possible convergence toward some common industrial pattern. According to the convergence hypothesis, industrial technology, urbanization, and affluence "create pressures toward the establishing of similar institutions for organizing economic and political decision-making."[18] Theorists of convergence like John K. Galbraith select the "logic of modern technology" as the major single causal factor that fosters the development of similarities in economic systems.[19] It is widely agreed that the process of industrialization has fostered the development of common structural and functional features among industrialized nations. As has already been explained, the economies of the Soviet Union and the United States have much in common in their structure and functioning. Also, in recent years, the Soviet Union and other communist countries have retreated to some extent from a highly centralized command economy and have moved towards a limited form of market socialism in which market forces are permitted to influence the allocation of economic resources. At the same time, the United States and other Western nations have curbed the free play of market forces, and have introduced considerable intervention and sometimes national planning into their economic affairs.

Comparative economists ask whether these trends in convergence will move the world's advanced industrial nations towards some common type of economic system. More specifically, are such countries as the United States and the Soviet Union, which in some cases use the same modern industrial technology, converging towards the same basic kind of economic system? Two kinds of factors besides geographical and historical conditions may have a significant influence on the nature of a country's economic system: technology and ideology. Economists like Galbraith emphasize the extent to which the logic of modern industrial technology fosters the development of similarities in economic and political organizations. Other economists have pointed out that while the American and Soviet economies have important common features, they are sustained by widely different ideologies that will continue to act as constraints upon any tendency to develop a common or uniform economic system.

The Classification of Economic Systems

Comparative economists do not all take the same typological or classificatory approach to the study of economic systems. Some adopt a dualistic position, while others use a three- or a four-model approach. Gregory Grossman observes that there are three coordination mechanisms in societies: tradition, the market mechanism, and command or plan.[20] Economic systems can then be classified as traditional, market, or command economies. Since he is only concerned with modern economic systems, Grossman focuses his attention on market and command economies, for each of which he constructs an abstract or hypothetical systemic model. In effect, Grossman's typological approach is a dualistic one, which takes as its starting point what he describes as the perfect-competition model of pure capitalism and then moves on to the pure or absolute command model of authoritarian socialism or communism.[21]

Between the two extremes of free market

---

[18] B. Ward, *op. cit.*, p. 126.
[19] J. K. Galbraith, *The New Industrial State*, Boston: Houghton Mifflin, 1967, pp. 388–392.

[20] G. Grossman, *op. cit.*, p. 13.
[21] G. Grossman, "Notes for a Theory of the Command Economy," *Soviet Studies*, Vol. XV, No. 2, Oct. 1963, p. 102.

and absolute command economies Grossman places actual economies with different mixtures of market and plan. These actual economies, however, cluster around either the Western capitalist market model or the Soviet command model. Following his two-model approach, Grossman places the United States, the major Western European countries, and Yugoslavia in the market category, while the Soviet Union, all Eastern European communist countries except Yugoslavia, and the People's Republic of China are placed in the command category.

Lloyd G. Reynolds substitutes a three-model approach for Grossman's two-model approach.[22] He observes that the less developed countries do not fit into either the free-market or the pure command systemic categories. Since these underdeveloped countries share many common economic features, Reynolds finds it helpful to weave these features into a pattern that applies to all less developed nations. He therefore adds a third systemic category to Grossman's two-system approach. Other comparative economists follow Reynolds in dividing the world of economic systems into three parts: "West," for the developed capitalist countries; "South," for the less developed noncommunist countries; and "East," for the communist countries. Since Yugoslavia does not fit into this threefold classification, it is usually given special separate treatment.

In the 1930s and 1940s, comparative economists frequently used a four-model approach, which placed the world's economic systems in the capitalist, fascist, socialist, and communist categories.[23] With the decline in the importance of fascist nations after the Second World War, less attention was paid to the role of fascist economic systems. A new fourth systemic category made its appearance after 1945 when the less developed countries became independent and developed a somewhat common economic and political pattern. Since 1945, the less-developed-country systemic category has usually replaced the fascist category of economic systems in studies of comparative economic systems.

In this study of comparative economic systems, the four-model approach is used. The model of the mature capitalist economy combines the major common features of the economic systems of such countries as the United States, the United Kingdom, West Germany, France, and Japan. The model of the mature democratic socialist economies draws upon the postwar experiences of Sweden, Norway, and the United Kingdom when the British Labour party is in office. The model of the developed authoritarian socialist communist economies is illustrated by taking account of the Soviet, Central European, and Yugoslavian economies. The fourth systemic category deals with the less developed economies. This model relates to the actual economies of the People's Republic of China, India, and African and Latin American countries.

Clearly, comparative economists do not agree on the one best typological approach to the study of economic systems. Those comparative economists with a conventional approach to the nature and scope of economics tend to adopt a two-model stance, because their view of the world emphasizes the importance of competitive and noncompetitive economies. Comparative economists with a broader and less orthodox view of the nature and scope of economics find that the two-model typological approach oversimplifies the nature of the world of economic systems. Since economists are far from agreeing on the nature and scope of economics, one cannot expect them to agree on the proper typological approach to the comparative study of economic systems. Economists with a strong empirical bias will find more systemic categories useful for analytical purposes than will

[22] L. G. Reynolds, op. cit., pp. 22–27.
[23] See, for example, W. N. Loucks and J. W. Hoot, *Comparative Economic Systems*, 1938.

The nature of economic systems

economists who search for formal models of economic systems and the general principles of organization that apply to all such systems. The lack of agreement among comparative economists on the proper typological approach to the study of comparative economic systems should not constitute a reason for discouragement. The history of the development of the field of comparative economic systems reveals that the various typological approaches used by comparative economists have in their own special ways contributed a great deal to this development.

Comparative Economic Systems and the Science of Economics

The study of comparative economic systems has raised many important questions about the usefulness for comparative studies of the conventional economics that is found in standard economics textbooks. This economics has in recent decades grown narrower in scope and more technical in method at the very time that a widespread interest has developed in the problems of the world's competing economic systems. As has already been explained, in the past quarter of a century there has been added to the capitalist and socialist worlds the world of the less developed countries or, as it is commonly called, the Third World. It is when comparative economists come to explain socialist economics and the economics of the Third World that they are not entirely satisfied with what traditional economics has to offer in the field of economic analysis. Conventional economics was first developed to explain the capitalist world. The critics of this kind of economics point out that it was designed to explain a world in which the emphasis was on the spontaneous, uncontrolled interplay of independent consumers and producers. In the socialist world and the Third World of the less developed countries deliberate economic control is emphasized rather than economic spontaneity. Comparative economists assert than an economics constructed to explain economic spontaneity is not well prepared to explain deliberate economic control. An explanation of such control in the socialist world and the Third World requires going beyond the exchange or market system to inquire into the nature of the social and political framework which underlies the economic system. This necessitates enlarging the scope of economics and analyzing what is taken as "given" by conventional economists.

Two matters are taken as given by conventional economists but not by comparative economists: (1) the creation of human wants, and (2) the social and cultural framework of the economic system which includes technology and society's institutional complex.[24] The equilibrium economics of conventional economists says nothing about the generation of human wants and the impact of technology and social institutions on the structure and functioning of the economic system. What the conventional economists ignore becomes important when economic systems are viewed as evolving processes. As has already been discussed, this is the approach of the comparative economists who are dissatisfied with what is covered by orthodox economics.

Many comparative economists call for a widening of the scope of economic analysis. They agree with Lloyd G. Reynolds who points out that "It is time that our definitions

[24] Lionel Robbins, a well-known exponent of conventional economics, explains that in this kind of economics human "Ends as such do not form part of this subject-matter [of economics]. Nor does the technical and social environment." According to this interpretation, economics is in essence "the study of the disposal of scarce commodities" and has nothing to do with the total system within which this disposal is carried on. See L. Robbins, *An Essay on the Nature and Significance of Economic Science*, 2d. ed. London: Macmillan, 1937, p. 38.

of economics were revised to correspond with our practice."[25] This practice has opened up the frontiers for research on many matters that do not fit into the scope of economics as it is viewed by conventional economists; these matters include technological change and its diffusion, the process of industrialization, investment in the human factor, the institutional obstacles of economic growth, and the role of ideology in economic affairs. Much of this frontier research goes beyond economic factors to the study of noneconomic factors which influence the structure and functioning of economic systems.

The important distinction here is not between economic and noneconomic factors, but between factors that affect economic activity and those that do not. The study of comparative economic systems points to the need for a new political economy that extends far beyond the narrow scope of the market economics inherited from the nineteenth century. In this new political economy, the theory of resource allocation remains a central consideration, but it is associated with a theory of the total economic system as an evolving process. Since there is no one universal economic system, the new political economy explains resource allocation in different economico-political settings, which can be reduced for analytical purposes to a few major systemic types, such as the capitalist, democratic socialist, communist, and less developed economic systems.

If economics is to be defined in a way that broadens its scope and provides room for the study of comparative economic systems as more than a limited exercise in the field of applied conventional economics, the conventional definition of economics needs to be modified. This can be done by defining *economics* as the study of the allocation of scarce resources within the evolving sociocultural framework. Economics then becomes the study of the world's evolving complexes of cultural relations that are concerned with the disposal of scarce resources for the satisfaction of individual and collective wants.[26] As a cultural or social science, economics studies the different parts of an evolving multisystem world which provide mankind with supplies of goods and services.

The conventional view of economics holds that the study of comparative economic systems should involve no more than enlarging the boundaries of such long-established areas of economic study as money and banking, public finance, industrial organization, and labor markets to include accounts of what goes on in these areas in various foreign countries. According to this conventional view, the study of comparative economic systems falls into the field of applied conventional economics, which deals only with the historical manifestations of economic scarcity. The theoretical study of economic scarcity is reserved by conventional economists for the field of pure economics which has nothing to do with the comparative study of economic systems.

Many comparative economists, however, are not satisfied with placing the study of comparative economic systems in the field of applied conventional economics, because this

[25] L. G. Reynolds, *op. cit.*, p. 329. While Reynolds expresses an interest in a definition of economics that is broader than the conventional Robbinsian definition, he himself provides no new definition. Morris Bornstein combines comparative economic systems and comparative economics under the comprehensive label of "comparative economic studies," but this approach does not address itself to the question of how economics should be redefined so as to make room for the study of comparative economic systems as more than a mere adjunct to conventional economics. See M. Bornstein, *op. cit.*, p. 353.

[26] For an analysis of economics from this point of view, see Allan G. Gruchy, *Modern Economic Thought, The American Contribution*, New York: Prentice-Hall, 1947, p. 541; and *Contemporary Economic Thought, The Contribution of Neo-Institutional Economics*, Clifton, N.J.: Augustus M. Kelley, 1972, p. 287.

field excludes from the scope of economics much analysis that can contribute to an understanding of the world's different economic systems. These comparative economists do not propose to abandon the study of the economizing or optimizing aspect of human behavior. They agree that the theory of resource allocation will always have a central place in the science of economics, but for them the major question is, what should go along with this theory of resource allocation? They do not object to the narrowing or technicalizing of economics on the ground that this trend leads to "bad" or "wrong" economics. On the contrary, these comparative economists are well aware of the many contributions of economic specialists in recent decades. They protest only that this trend in specialization leads to a narrowing of economics at the very time when what is needed is a broadening of economics to lay the foundation for a comprehensive understanding of different economic systems.

Selected Bibliography

AMES, EDWARD. *The Emerging Theory of Comparative Economic Systems.* Working Paper No. 63, Economic Research Bureau, State University of New York at Stony Brook, New York, April 1972.

BOULDING, KENNETH E. "General Systems Theory—The Skeleton of Science." *Management Science*, 2, No. 3 (April 1956), 197–208.

BUCHANAN, JAMES M., and GORDON TULLOCK. *The Calculus of Consent.* University of Michigan Press, Ann Arbor, 1962.

DAHL, ROBERT A., and CHARLES E. LINDBLOOM. *Politics, Economics, and Welfare.* Harper and Brothers, New York, 1953.

ECKSTEIN, ALEXANDER, ed. *Comparison of Economic Systems.* University of California Press, Berkeley, 1971.

EHRLICH, PAUL R. *The Population Bomb.* Ballantine Books, New York, 1969.

GALBRAITH, JOHN KENNETH. *The New Industrial State.* Houghton Mifflin Company, Boston, 1967.

GROSSMAN, GREGORY. *Economic Systems.* Prentice-Hall, Inc., Englewood Cliffs, N.J., 1967.

———. "Notes for a Theory of the Command Economy." *Soviet Studies*, XV (Oct. 1963), 101–123.

GRUCHY, ALLAN G. *Contemporary Economic Thought: The Contribution of Neo-Institutional Economics.* Augustus M. Kelley, Clifton, N.J., 1972.

———. *Modern Economic Thought, The American Contribution.* Prentice-Hall, Inc., New York, 1947.

HAIRE, MASON, ed. *Modern Organization Theory.* John Wiley, New York, 1964.

KORNAI, JANOS. *Anti-Equilibrium.* North Holland Publishing Company, Amsterdam, 1971.

LOUCKS, WILLIAM N., and J. WELDON HOOT. *Comparative Economic Systems.* Harper and Brothers, New York, 1938.

MCCONNELL, CAMPBELL R. *Economics: Principles, Problems, and Policies*, 2d. ed. McGraw-Hill Book Company, New York, 1960.

MARCH, JAMES G., ed. *Handbook of Organizations.* Rand McNally, Chicago, 1965.

MARSCHAK, JACOB, and R. RADNER. *Economic Theory of Teams.* Yale University Press, New Haven, 1972.

MEADOWS, DONELLA H., and others. *Limits to Growth.* Universe Books, New York, 1972.

MUNDELL, ROBERT A. *Man and Economics.* McGraw-Hill Book Company, New York, 1968.

MYRDAL, GUNNAR. *Asian Drama, An Inquiry into the Poverty of Nations,* III. Pantheon Books, New York, 1968.

REYNOLDS, LLOYD G. *The Three Worlds of Economics.* Yale University Press. New Haven, 1971.

ROBBINS, LIONEL. *An Essay on the Nature and Significance of Economic Science.* 2d. ed. Macmillan and Company, Ltd., London, 1937.

STARBUCK, WILLIAM H. "Mathematics and Organization Theory." In *Handbook of Organizations*, ed. James G. March.

UDY, STANLEY H., JR. "The Comparative Analysis of Organizations." In *Handbook of Organizations*, ed. James G. March.

Part Two
The Capitalist Economies

2
The Model of the Mature Capitalist Economy

3
The Mature American Economy

4
The Mature British Capitalist Economy

5
West Germany's Social Market Economy

6
The French Planned Economy

7
The Capitalist Economies: in Retrospect and Prospect

Chapter 2
The Model of the Mature Capitalist Economy

The private-enterprise or capitalist economic system before World War II was the world's dominant type of economic system. In recent decades, however, the emergence of the Soviet Union as a major world power has altered the political and economic balance of the world, and the communist or authoritarian socialist system is now seriously challenging the supremacy of the capitalist system. The capitalist system is still dominant in much of Western Europe and North America—largely because it is associated with nations such as the United States, Canada, the United Kingdom, France, and West Germany, which enjoy high standards of living. No matter what its ultimate future, clearly, the capitalist system will continue for a long time to be a potent factor in the affairs of mankind.

Unlike the democratic socialist and the communist systems, which have a short historical record, modern capitalism is the product of a long period of economic development. Some students of capitalism find the origins of this system in Graeco-Roman times, while others go no further back than the era of the medieval cities of Venice, Florence, Genoa, and Amsterdam. The evolution of capitalism may be divided into a number of stages or phases. Werner Sombart analyzed capitalism in terms of the three stages of early capitalism (1200–1750), full capitalism (1750–1914), and late (1914 and after) capitalism. A more recent student of capitalism, Joseph A. Schumpeter, divided the evolution of this system into four phases: early capitalism (from Graeco-Roman times to 1550), mercantilistic capitalism (1550–1800), intact capitalism (1800–1898), and modern capitalism (since 1898).

The current stage of modern capitalism is of special interest to students of comparative economic systems. Both the technological and the organizational bases of capitalism have undergone many important changes since 1885. In the past three-quarters of a century, the large-scale assembly line has replaced the small-scale factory system in many industries; and currently, further technological change is taking the form of automation or the widespread introduction of machines to run other machines. The organizational basis of capitalism has also changed. The single proprietorship and the partnership have been reduced in importance by the spread of the corporate form of business enterprise, as business has moved from a small-scale to a large-scale basis. The growth of large-scale corporate enterprise has been accompanied by large-scale developments in the fields of banking, insurance, and trade union activity. While these changes in the capitalist system have been revolutionary in their impact and have had important repercussions in the worlds of business, labor, and government, nothing indicates that the evolution of capitalism will not continue to be accompanied by further very fundamental changes in both industrial technology and economic organization.

The Essence of Capitalism

Throughout all its stages of development the feature of capitalism that has remained constant is its ideological or psychological basis. Max Weber calls this feature capitalism's "basic attitude or orientation toward world activity."[1] The essence of this attitude lies in the view that the individual business person is the ultimate factor in economic life. His or her initiative constitutes the mainspring of capitalist economic activity and must be relied upon to provide guidance for the nation's economic system. This was the position adopted by Werner Sombart in 1935 when he wrote that "capitalistic business is typically private, so that economic initiative is lodged with enterprises which are activated by the quest for private gain. These enterprises, subject to little regulation from the outside, assume the full risk of failure but enjoy also the unrestricted chance of success. Their activity keeps the economic machinery in motion."[2] The keynote of this definition of capitalism is its emphasis upon private business initiative in the pursuit of profits through the use of private property. As Sombart saw it, in the capitalist system there is much occupational specialization, functional separation, and decentralization of economic decision making. What holds the system together is not decision making by the state, but the "economic initiative lodged with business enterprises." The many private business enterprises, not public or state enterprise, keep "the economy in motion."

Joseph A. Schumpeter, writing after the depression of the 1930s and after the emergence of the state as an important factor in the economic life of capitalist nations, observed that "A society is called capitalist if it entrusts its economic process to the guidance of the private businessman. This may be said to imply, first, private ownership of nonpersonal means of production such as land, mines, industrial plant and equipment; and, second, production for private account, i.e., production by private initiative for private profit."[3]

Schumpeter's definition calls attention to the three essentials of the capitalist system. First, under capitalism, property is primarily in private hands. Exceptions to this rule occur, as witness the government-owned power projects in the United States and the state ownership of railroads, coal mines, and public utilities in the United Kingdom. However, in both the United States and the United King-

---

[1] Max Weber, *The Theory of Social and Economic Organization*, New York, Oxford University Press, 1947, p. 15.

[2] Werner Sombart, "Capitalism," *Encyclopedia of the Social Sciences,* Vol. 3, 1958, pp. 198–199.

[3] Joseph A. Schumpeter, "Capitalism," *Encyclopaedia Britannica*, Vol. 4, 1958, p. 801.

dom, as in other capitalist countries, the bulk of the means of production are still privately owned. Publicly owned industries under capitalism remain islands of public ownership in a sea of private ownership. Concessions are made to public ownership when private enterprise is unwilling to finance a project, when an industry is sick or is unable to cope with economic instabilities and maladjustments, or when the government considers an economic activity to be of such strategic importance that the national interest calls for the exclusion of private enterprise. In general, since under capitalism private ownership of property is preferred to public ownership, a great deal of encouragement and support is given to the preservation of the institution of private property.

It should be clearly understood, however, that the mere existence of private property on a wide basis in an economic system does not necessarily mean that this system is capitalist in nature. Private property in land, mines, and factories was preserved under both Hitler in Germany and Mussolini in Italy, and yet the German and Italian economic systems of the 1930s and 1940s did not constitute examples of capitalist private enterprise or democratic capitalism. Similarly, the private ownership of property has been, or is, the main form of property ownership in all the fascist nations of the period following the First World War. In democratic socialist nations, such as Norway, Sweden, and India, private ownership of property continues to be the main form of property ownership. The nationalization of private property in land, mines, and factories is no longer a prime consideration in the economic thinking of the labor or democratic socialist parties of Western Europe. The most recent development in Western democratic socialistic thinking points in the direction of a kind of socialism or laborism, which is solidly based on the continued and widespread private ownership of the means of production.

The second essential of a capitalist system is the use of private property for the accumulation of private gains or profits. Those who own land or capital are free to use such property for profit-making purposes. Profits are not an assured income. Those who own property run the risk of making a profit or of incurring a loss. Those who make a profit do so because they have succeeded in meeting consumer preferences. Consequently, no conflict may arise between making private profits and expanding social welfare. On the contrary, under capitalism, social welfare is held to be enlarged in most situations where private profit making is carried on.

It should be noted, however, that an economic system may exist in which private profits constitute a major source of income, but at the same time the system is not essentially capitalist. Under both fascism and partially democratic socialism of the Scandinavian type, the private profit-making activity is preserved. No attempts were made to eliminate private profits as a source of personal income in Peron's Argentina or Batista's Cuba, but these authoritarian systems were obviously not examples of capitalism. Furthermore, private profit making still goes on in socialist India, Israel, and Sweden, even though these countries have moved a considerable distance away from the capitalist model of economic activity.

The third essential of capitalism is that the owners of private property and the makers of private profits must be the same individuals and groups who are also primarily responsible for the level and direction of the national economy. Economic initiative in the main must spring not from the state, but from individuals and private groups. It is quite permissible to say that there are capitalist elements in both fascist and socialist systems, and that the totalitarian economies of Argentina, Chile, and Egypt and the democratic socialist economies of India, Israel and Sweden are mixed economies. But these economies are not in the final analysis capitalist, because in them the state, rather than private citizens as individuals or groups, is ultimately responsible for the level and direction of economic activity. Under modern controlled or welfare capitalism, the government can influence to a considerable degree the level and direction of economic activity. But its efforts in these directions are only supplemental. In the American, Canadian, British (under the Conservative party), and West German economies, the basic decisions relating to investment, production, and consumption are today made by individuals and groups in private markets and not by governmental authorities.

We can conclude that the dividing line between capitalism and other economic systems, such as democratic, partial socialism, communism, and fascism, is not found in the private ownership of property or in the making of private profits. It lies rather in the area of private economic initiative. When much of this initiative is taken out of private hands, as in Argentina and Chile today and also in India and Sweden, some system other than capitalism is in operation. The usual way of transferring economic initiative and responsibility from private to public hands is to set up a program for national economic planning under which the general level and direction of the nation's economic activity become primarily a state and not a private matter. Much initiative may still be left to individuals and private groups, as is true today in many authoritarian regimes and in countries with limited or partial socialism, but in these countries the final arbiter in economic affairs is the government.

The United States is today a capitalist country, because it has in operation no centralized national economic planning program to which private enterprise is subservient. True, the government carries on considerable piecemeal planning and attempts to influence the level of business activity through changes in fiscal, monetary, and other economic policies. But the major determinant of economic activity in the American capitalist system, as in all mature capitalist systems, is private and not public economic decision making.

Under capitalism, the government can go a long way in expanding the area of public decision making without destroying the essentially capitalist nature of the nation's economy. But at some point in the expansion of government enterprise the scales are tipped in favor of public initiative and against private initiative and responsibility; the economic system then ceases to be essentially capitalist. This point is obviously reached when private planning becomes secondary to public or national planning.

It was temporarily reached in the United Kingdom in the period 1945–1951 when the British Labour party launched its program for national planning. In those early postwar years, private enterprise continued to be vigorous and to play an important role in Britain's economic affairs. However, it was gradually fitted into a national planning program in which the British Labour government became more and more responsible for the nation's major economic decisions relating to levels of investment, production, and employment. From 1945 to 1951 and again from 1964 to 1970 the United Kingdom had a limited form of democratic socialism that combined important features of both socialist and capitalist economic systems. When the British Conservative party regained political power late in 1951, capitalism replaced socialism in the United Kingdom; national economic planning was largely abandoned, and the importance of private economic decision making in maximizing the nation's output of goods and services was reemphasized—until the pendulum swung back to democratic, partial socialism with the Labour party's 1964 victory.

The Evolution of the Capitalist Economy

Before capitalism could become established in Western Europe, a number of conditions had to be met, the first being a well-established capitalist attitude or spirit that would not only nourish business enterprise, but would also provide it with the necessary drive. Before capitalism could become well established, however, it was necessary for a dominant economic group to become imbued with the capitalist spirit; such a spirit would not only sanction the making of profits and the accumulation of private wealth, but would also ensure that considerable status was attached to the function of the entrepreneur. No such capitalist attitude existed on a widespread basis during the Middle Ages. As cities appeared after 1100, however, this outlook found a little fertile ground, but its growth was slow. Not until after the Protestant Reformation of the sixteenth century did the capitalist spirit become entrenched in Western Europe. In the seventeenth and eighteenth centuries, it continued to find wider and wider acceptance. And, finally in the second half of the nineteenth century, the capitalist attitude reached the pinnacle of its development.

Similarly, capitalism could not develop in Western Europe so long as the necessary economic, legal, and political institutions were absent. These capitalist institutions include the modern institution of private property, the right of inheritance, freedom of contract, a free market system, a wage system, a credit system, and a laissez-faire type of democratic government. None of these institutions existed to any appreciable degree before 1200. In the medieval era, business enterprise, trade, and industry were relegated to such an inferior position that capitalism was unable to emerge.

After 1200, the institutional structure of Western Europe began to change slowly in ways that favored the spread of capitalist enterprise. The movement became accelerated after the Protestant Reformation of 1500–1550 successfully challenged the monolithic power of the Roman Catholic Church. Between 1550 and 1775, contract took the place of status in many economic relationships; both land and labor became commodities that were available for sale and purchase in free markets; and the use of credit became well established. In the century from 1775 to 1875, capitalist institutions were perfected to such an extent that the golden era of competitive capitalism was ushered in. After 1875, competitive capitalism gave way to monopoly or finance capitalism. By 1929, the operations of the free-competitive-market system were extensively restricted by big business and high finance. In 1929, after the depression set in, the public soon came to demand a far-reaching regulation of monopoly capitalism. By 1939, monopoly capitalism had been converted into controlled or welfare capitalism.

As we shall see, it took many centuries to develop the capitalist system—a development which has not yet come to an end. Not surprisingly, therefore, the capitalist system is today a highly complicated system with considerable vitality and flexibility. In its long period of growth, the capitalist system has adjusted to many new developments in the realms of geographical discovery, nation building, and international politics. It has displayed a remarkable power to adjust without losing its basic identity. It should also be noted that capitalism flourished as an aspect of Western European culture. The progress of this culture and of capitalism went hand in hand. Today capitalism in its well-developed form is found only in countries which have an industrial society, such as the United States, Canada, Australia, the United Kingdom, West Germany, and other Continental countries.

The capitalist system is but one aspect of a highly complex cultural system; thus we should not be surprised to find that many of the less well-developed nations of the world, lacking advanced cultures, do not turn to the capitalist system in their efforts to achieve rapid industrialization, full employment, and an improved level of living.

The Model of Perfect Competition

During the second half of the nineteenth century, economists theorized about the competitive capitalism that had developed in the first half of that century. They sought to extract the fundamental principles that governed the operations of the competitive capitalist system. As a result of these endeavors, there emerged the concept of a perfectly competitive economic system, the central institution of which is the free market or exchange system. In developing this concept, economists made a number of basic assumptions about the structure and functioning of the competitive economic system; these assumptions enabled students to think in terms of achieving a stable equilibrium in the market place.[4]

The structural assumptions provide the institutional framework within which the perfectly competitive exchange economy is supposed to function. In the world of perfect competition, property is privately owned, wealth can be inherited, contracts may be legally enforced, and there is free entry into all lines of economic activity. Production is small scale; all firms are managed by their owners; no trade unions exist; and the government is a minor factor, concerned only with performing a few basic duties such as enforcing contracts, preserving the peace, protecting property, providing money, and collecting taxes. These basic assumptions are accompanied by a number of other assumptions relating to the participants in the activities of the perfectly competitive economy. Owner operators of the business firms, workers, and consumers are rational individuals who have free access to information about market conditions. These participants all function according to the maximization principle. They seek maximum profits, wages, or consumer utility, with a minimum expenditure of resources, human effort, or personal income.

The working of the model of the perfectly competitive economic system is based upon the concept of complete laissez faire. The forces at work in the market system are impersonal in nature, and find expression through the operations of this system. Prices are fully free to respond to changes in supply and demand conditions. The price system has two basic functions: to allocate scarce economic resources among alternative uses of these resources and to ration the output of goods and services among consumers. In the allocative process, competing business people combine scarce supplies of land, labor, and capital in order to produce the output that will maximize profits. In the rationing process, each consumer or household unit spends its limited income on the variety of goods and services that brings maximum satisfaction. Business firms have freedom of enterprise that permits them to move freely into and out of various lines of economic activity, while consumers have freedom of choice that enables them to alter the range of goods and services that they want from business people. An equilibrium situation is achieved when the operators of individual firms can no longer change the pattern of resource use so as to enlarge profits, and consumers can no longer alter their spending patterns so as to increase their utilities or satisfactions.

In the model of perfect competition, the

---

[4] These basic assumptions are elaborated in Robert Dorfman, *The Price System*, Englewood Cliffs, N.J.: Prentice-Hall, 1964, pp. 2–10. See also Paul A. Samuelson, *Economics*, 8th ed., New York: McGraw-Hill, 1970, pp. 37–41.

free market system not only coordinates production by bringing producers and consumers together, but it also distributes income according to the marginal contribution of each participant in the community's economic system. In Alfred Marshall's economy of perfect competition, business people earn normal profits that are just sufficient to induce them to remain in their line of economic activity.[5] Workers receive normal, competitively determined wages equal to the value of their marginal product; capital owners likewise receive a return in the form of interest.[6] Personal incomes can give rise to accumulated wealth, which may be inherited; by assumption, however, personal incomes can never be the source of large accumulations of wealth that are passed on from generation to generation. It is assumed that the incomes earned by producers in the small-scale competitive firms would be so small as to provide only for consumption needs and small amounts of investment. In the perfectly competitive economy, income earned is income spent for either consumption or investment purposes. There are no fluctuations in economic activity since supply creates its own demand. Savings and investment are in balance, and a general equilibrium prevails throughout the competitive system. Any tendency towards deviation from equilibrium is eliminated by the competitive economy's self-correcting forces.

In the general equilibrium situation of the perfectly competitive economy, the maximizing of producers' profits and consumers' satisfactions is accompanied by the most efficient use of the nation's scarce economic resources. Static efficiency is achieved at a given time, when no reallocation of scarce economic resources can provide a mix of output that will enlarge producer profits or consumer satisfactions. In the model of perfect competition, no room exists for dynamic efficiency which arises from economic growth and development. By assumption, nothing can lead to developments that will in any fundamental way alter the structure and functioning of the competitive economic system. For example, the small-scale competitive firms do not devote funds to research and development that result in dynamic and disruptive technological change. In the model of the perfectly competitive economy, there can be no technological innovations that replace small-scale production with large-scale production, that convert competition into monopoly or oligopoly, and that permit limited personal wealth to grow into massive personal wealth. While the technology of production may be altered in minor ways, no dynamic technological developments, by assumption, can change the basics of the perfectly competitive economy.

Since income and wealth are assumed to be widely distributed in the perfectly competitive economic system, the government need not be concerned with any kind of redistributive action that would lead to setting up schemes for transferring income from one class to another. Since disruptive dynamic technological change is excluded from the world of pure competition, there is no concern with the large social costs of economic growth or industrialization. In the nineteenth century, when Cournot, Walras, Pareto, and other economists constructed their model of perfect competition, they paid no attention to the complications created by the external diseconomies of rapid economic growth and widespread industrialization.

---

[5] Alfred Marshall, *Principles of Economics*, Book VI, "The Distribution of the National Income," 8th ed., New York: Macmillan, 1948.

[6] In the model of the perfectly competitive economy, it is assumed that the business firms operate with constant returns to scale. Only in this situation do the marginal contributions of the factors of production exhaust the total product that is to be distributed among the production factors. In cases of increasing returns to scale, the summation of all factors' marginal products exceeds total output; under decreasing returns to scale, total output exceeds the summation of each factor's marginal product.

The perfectly competitive economic system is an atomistic laissez faire system in which no problems of economic policy, market power, or producer sovereignty arise. Producers, workers, and consumers have no market power. The individual producer cannot influence the market price for his product. He carries on no advertising campaigns because he cannot influence consumer demand for undifferentiated products. In the perfectly competitive economy, what is produced is turned out in response to the preferences of consumers who individually cast dollar "votes" for various goods and services.[7] Goods produced by small-scale competing firms are undifferentiated products that can be easily produced by other firms and that in the long run are sold at uniform prices. Consumer sovereignty becomes important because consumers' preferences for goods and services ultimately guide the activities of the laissez faire, atomistic world of perfect competition. This consumer guidance of the economic system is achieved without any special effort or power on the part of individual consumers, for it results from the automatic working of the competitive market system and not from consumers' intervention in the community's marketing activities.

Economic Analysis and Perfect Competition

Economists find the model of the perfectly competitive economy useful for two important reasons. First, this model focuses attention on the problems of allocative efficiency or the optimal use of scarce economic resources. In the operations of all economic systems, whether capitalist or socialist, one of the basic matters of interest is the efficient allocation of the available scarce resources. The managers of the private capitalist firm and the socialist state enterprise both seek to achieve the most efficient use of the land, labor, and capital made available to them. In attaining this goal, the same general principle is applicable to the capitalist and socialist enterprises: production should be expanded until the marginal cost of the last unit turned out is equal to the selling price of the product. In market socialism, where production is directed by the free forces of the competitive market system in response to consumer preferences, the managers of the competing state enterprises in a given industry, if they desire maximum efficiency and profitability, will perform just like their counterparts in the model of the perfectly competitive economy.[8] If a competing socialist manager stops producing when his marginal cost is below his selling price, he could expand production further and still add to his efficiency and profitability. With output enlarged to the point where marginal cost and selling price are equal, the efficiency and profitability of the firm are maximized, and consumers purchase a socially desirable output.

As has already been explained, one of the criteria of performance by which economic systems may be evaluated is efficiency in the use of resources. This is a matter of concern in the mature capitalist economy of the Western world, the democratic socialist countries, the communist countries of the east, and the less developed countries. The efficiency criterion, however, is not always high on the list of national priorities. In the early years of Stalin's

[7] As Samuelson explains, "What things will be produced is determined by the dollar *votes* of consumers—not every 2 years at the polls, but every day in their decisions to purchase this item and not that." *Economics*, p. 40.

[8] For a discussion of pricing in market socialism, see Daniel R. Fusfeld, *Economics*, Ch. 29, "Market Socialism," Lexington, Mass.: D. C. Heath, 1972, pp. 546–558. Fusfeld explains that in market socialism "The price-making rule is that prices must clear the market. This makes the individual [socialist] enterprise a price taker in the same sense as the firm in the purely competitive model of self-adjusting markets. . . . Prices must equal costs of production at the margin (P = MC)." *Economics*, pp. 550 and 557.

regime in the Soviet Union, allocative efficiency was sacrificed to the goals of rapid industrialization and militarization. Only after the Second World War did the Soviet leaders, having reached high levels of industrialization and militarization, give special attention to achieving the goal of the optimal use of economic resources. This change of emphasis in Soviet national goals was made necessary by the shift from the extensive development of the Soviet economy to its intensive development.

At present, the less developed countries of Africa, Asia, and Latin America are more concerned with rapid economic growth than with the most efficient use of their scarce resources. Like the Soviet Union in the 1920s and 1930s, these young nations are mobilizing their human and natural resources with the aid of campaigns of exhortation and persuasion, backed up by strong nationalistic appeals, which have rapid economic growth as their main goal. Lacking trained technical personnel, expert political administrators, and well-educated industrial managers, the less developed countries are prepared for the time being to sacrifice the most efficient use of resources to a program of rapid economic development. Such a national program merely postpones the day when there will be a greater concern in these countries with allocative efficiency.

The choice between allocative efficiency and rapid mobilization may also be seen as the choice between balanced and unbalanced economic growth. When a country has lagged in its economic development and is classified as less developed, it can either grow slowly in a balanced manner or grow more rapidly in an unbalanced way. Slow balanced growth is based upon using the market system to give expression to consumer preferences, to permit consumers to decide how much of their incomes they will consume or save, and to achieve a market-determined and balanced growth of all sectors of the economy. Slow balanced growth also implies the presence of consumer freedom in a democratic political situation, where the voters determine the national priorities in a free democratic manner.

Rapid unbalanced growth is forced growth, in which a highly centralized government bureaucracy curbs consumer choice and real consumption, arbitrarily raises the level of investment in plant and equipment, and favors the sectors of the economy that turn out producers' goods rather than consumers' goods. Agriculture and the light consumer industries are sacrificed to heavy industries, and the high level of investment supports a high level of economic growth. Since rapid industrialization sacrifices the present generation of consumers in the interest of a future generation, a high degree of regimentation is frequently necessary to make certain that this sacrifice is put into effect. This combination of rapid industrialization and government regimentation is to be observed in the communist and less developed countries, where forced, unbalanced growth is usually the accepted goal of the minority with a monopoly of political power. In the democratic Western countries, balanced growth has been a slow process extending over two centuries. In order to avoid this slow growth process, governments in the less developed countries find it necessary to sacrifice allocative efficiency to rapid economic mobilization in the early stages of economic development.

The second reason why the model of the perfectly competitive economy is of great interest to economists is that this model is consumer oriented. In this model, allocative efficiency is tied in with consumer and occupational freedoms. Consumers are free to express their preferences in the market place, and workers are free to choose among the available occupational alternatives. Consumer and occupational freedoms constitute one of the main criteria by which economic systems may be evaluated. An economic system with much consumer and occupational freedom is preferred by most voters in democratic countries to a system in which much less of these freedoms exists. In the actual economic systems throughout the world, much concern with consumer and occupational freedom is expressed, although the intensity of this concern varies widely among different economic systems. In the Stalinist era from 1924 to 1945, very little consumer and occupational freedom existed. In those years, both allocative efficiency and consumer and occupational freedom were sacrificed to the achievement of rapid economic growth and a strong military posture. Likewise, today in the less developed countries, the goal of rapid economic development and sometimes the goal of building up a strong military position have shunted aside concern with consumer and occupational freedoms. In recent years, however, an opposite trend has developed in Yugoslavia, other Central European countries, and the Soviet Union, where increasing attention is being given to consumer and worker welfare.

The Limitations of the Model of Perfect Competition

While the model of the perfectly competitive economy is very useful for purposes of economic analysis, it has some serious limitations as an analytical device or aid. These limitations arise because of the nonevolutionary nature of this model. It cannot account for economic evolution and the various eras through which the capitalist system has passed since competitive capitalism declined rapidly in the fourth quarter of the nineteenth century. The basic assumptions of the competitive model dispense with all factors that could lead to fundamental changes in the structure and functioning of the competitive economic system. The industrial technology in a world of perfect competition is assumed to be unchanging and to give rise to no monopolistic or oligopolistic business enterprise. Nor is there any reason for the emergence of collective action in the form of business people's trade associations, labor unions, or cooperatives in the perfectly competitive economy.

Obviously, the model of perfect competition, when constructed in the nineteenth century, was designed to explain a particular era in the evolution of the private enterprise system. With the technological and institutional parameters of the competitive model taken by orthodox economists as given or fixed, this model necessarily excluded all factors that might create the economic disequilibrium, disharmony, and imbalances out of which large-scale corporate or oligopolistic capitalism would emerge after 1875.[9] One of the factors that led to the rise of the large-scale business enterprises and labor unions was the scientific advance and the subsequent shift from small-scale to large-scale industrial technology in the late decades of the nineteenth century and the early decades of the twentieth century.[10]

After 1875, the model of the perfectly competitive economy became progressively less a reflection of the actual economic system in the real world of large-scale production and oligopolistic enterprise. The problem today is how to achieve allocative efficiency and consumer and occupational freedoms in the

[9] Lionel Robbins, *An Essay on the Nature and Significance of Economic Science,* London: Macmillan, 1937. Robbins explains that "It follows from the argument of the preceding sections that the subject matter of economics is essentially a series of relationships.... Ends as such do not form part of this subject matter. Nor does the technical and social environment" (p. 38).

[10] On the impact of technological change on the structure and functioning of the American economic system, see John K. Galbraith, *The New Industrial State,* Boston: Houghton Mifflin, 1967. Galbraith points out that "In explaining the intricate complex of economic change, technology, having an initiative of its own, is the logical point at which to break in. But technology not only causes change, it is a response to change.... Though it requires extensive organization it is also the result of organization" (p. 20).

modern large-scale, mature capitalist economic system. Since the free competitive system has been eliminated or severely restricted in a large part of the advanced industrial economies, achieving the efficiency and freedom goals is no longer a matter of merely relying upon the free play of the impersonal competitive market forces. Other means, such as antitrust action, government intervention, or national planning, must be used to induce the large industrial enterprise to allocate land, labor, and capital efficiently and to meet consumer preferences. Securing these goals in the mature capitalist economy is largely a matter of controlling the use of market power by large economic interest groups.

Another major limitation of the model of perfect competition is that it provides no explanation of the rise and spread of market power after 1875. As we have seen, market power or the power to influence the price and wage determining processes is not possessed by the participants in the activities of the perfectly competitive economic system. This is the case because market power is associated only with large-scale business and labor organizations, which by definition are excluded from the model of perfect competition. When reference is made to imperfections in the market structure of the competitive economy, these imperfections are only of the kind that the self-correcting forces of the competitive economy can eliminate in the long run. The large-scale business firm or labor union is not to be regarded as an imperfection or frictional element in the purely competitive economic system, since the competitive or laissez faire market forces cannot eliminate these large-scale organizations that have appeared as a result of the use of the assembly-line or mass-production industrial technology. Samuelson and other mainstream economists point out that competition cannot be counted on to weaken or domesticate the oligopolistic imperfections of the American economic system that arise from bigness in economic life.

Only government action backed up by public watchfulness and support can, in these economists' opinion, effectively dilute the market power found in the advanced industrial economies.

Besides being of a nonevolutionary nature and failing to deal with the problem of market power, the model of perfect competition suffers from other serious limitations. The economists who constructed this model in the nineteenth century said little or nothing about the problems of external diseconomies, environmental deterioration, discrimination and poverty, the appropriate role of economic growth, and the impact of affluence on the quality of life that are so widely discussed today in the advanced capitalist economies. This was the case partly because the underlying assumption of the model of perfect competition is that all producers and consumers are rational individuals. Their individual rationality is assumed to lead to social rationality. These rational individuals would not pollute the land, air, and water and in other ways harm the natural environment, nor would they destroy the social amenities of the urban centers. Furthermore, rational individuals would not discriminate on the basis of race, color, or sex in their employment or purchasing activities. The competitive market would take no account of racial, sex, or other differences in individuals that did not affect labor productivity. In addition, in the perfectly competitive economy, no poverty would exist, since the impersonal forces of the competitive economy would prevent the development of large inequalities in the relative distribution of income.

By contrast with the hypothetical world of pure competition, there are in the real world large inequalities in the distribution of personal income and wealth ownership. As opposed to assumptions concerning the world of perfect competition, in the real world those individuals who receive large incomes also accumulate large amounts of wealth. While income and wealth inequalities in the Western world have not increased significantly since the end of the Second World War, in the period 1875–1929 the growth of large-scale capitalism was accompanied by increasing inequalities in income distribution and wealth ownership. Nothing in the model of perfect competition explains the growth of these inequalities after 1875. In addition, the unregulated large-scale capitalist economy before World War II suffered from chronic unemployment and poverty, extensive racial and sex discrimination, and environmental deterioration. Not until the government intervened extensively were some of the worse aspects of these major economic and social problems eliminated. Even yet, much remains to be done concerning these problems that have no place in the model of perfect competition.

These deficiencies or limitations of the model of the perfectly competitive economic system have not led economists to abandon this model, since it continues to be useful as a heuristic device. Instead, these limitations have made economists realize the need to broaden the scope of economic analysis to include studies of factors not incorporated in the competitive model. These limitations have led economists to see the importance of constructing other models of the economic system that reflect the nature of the real economic world of the last quarter of the twentieth century more closely than does the model of perfect competition. As a consequence of the realization of the limitations of the model of perfect competition, economists after 1929 supplemented this model with a new model of the idealized mature capitalist or mixed economy that is the foundation of what John Maurice Clark described as the system of "workable competition."[11]

[11] John M. Clark, "Toward a Concept of Workable Competition," *American Economic Review*, Vol. XXX, June 1940, pp. 241–256.

Standard economics textbook writers explain that "Most of our attention will be devoted to the special features of economic life found in twentieth-century industrial nations (with the exception of the Soviet system) . . . in almost all the countries under consideration there has been a steady increase in the economic functions of government. Ours is a 'mixed economy' in which both public and private institutions exercise economic control . . . in the real world, competition is nowhere near 'perfect'. . . . The most serious deviation from perfect competition comes from *monopoly* elements. . . . The problem is one of achieving reasonably effective 'workable competition'."[12] The modern mixed industrial economic system is so fundamentally different from the small-scale competitive economy of the middle nineteenth century in terms of structure and functioning that economists have found it necessary to construct a new idealized model of the mixed capitalist economy that provides the point of departure for their analysis of the problems of the modern industrial economy and their economic policy proposals for handling these problems.

Hypothetical and Actual Competition

The model of a perfectly competitive economy was regarded by many economists in the nineteenth century and the first quarter of the twentieth century as a close approximation of the actual economic systems of the Western capitalist nations. Orthodox economists then generally believed that while the actual economic systems in Western Europe and the United States deviated in a number of important ways from the model of perfect competition, forces were, nevertheless, at work constantly moving these actual capitalist systems

[12] P. A. Samuelson, *Economics*, pp. 37, 43, and 44.

towards the hypothetical model of perfect competition. Many economists before the beginning of the Great Depression in 1929 thought that self-correcting market forces would prevent large and permanent deviations from the ideal of a perfectly competitive economic system. Belief in the efficacy of these self-correcting forces went hand in hand with the position that the market system was still flexible enough to permit these forces to preserve what was taken to be the essentially competitive nature of the American and British capitalist economies. These self-correcting forces would place definite limits on booms and recessions which would be short-lived. Recessions were regarded as a necessary catharsis that would periodically eliminate the accumulated obstacles to the good functioning of what was asserted to be a still basically competitive economy.

The model of a perfectly competitive economy lost much of its relevance to the real economic world after 1929. Some economists, such as Henry Simon and other members of the Chicago school of economists, still believed in the possibility of reestablishing a highly competitive economy. By the end of the 1930s, however, the majority of economists agreed with John M. Keynes that self-correcting forces could not be relied upon to maintain a competitive economy at a full-employment level.[13] This was the case because by the 1930s the self-correcting forces of the market system had been largely replaced by self-reinforcing forces, which had pushed the advanced industrial system down to a less-than-full-employment level of equilibrium. This depressed equilibrium could be long lasting unless the government intervened with appropriate fiscal and monetary measures. Other economists, such as Adolf A. Berle and Gardiner C. Means, went beyond Keynes to point out that besides the emergence of self-reinforcing forces, there had occurred major structural changes in the economies of Western Europe and the United States which by 1929 had substituted "oligopoly" capitalism for "competitive" capitalism.[14]

Since the model of the perfectly competitive economy in the opinion of many economists no longer reflects conditions in the real economic world, this model is now presented in standard economics textbooks as a purely hypothetical or abstract model, useful only as a teaching tool or heuristic device. In his widely used textbook, Samuelson explains that the concept of "perfect competition" is now reduced by economists to the status of a technical term that does not adequately describe "our less-than-perfect-competition system."[15] For Samuelson, as for other orthodox economics textbook authors, the model of perfect competition is only an ideal system with which our actual mature capitalist system can be compared with the aim of improving its working. In order to make the ideal of perfect competition useful as a guide for concrete economic policy making, it has to be modified or altered in various ways. What such modifications amount to is

[13] Keynes concluded his study of the mature capitalist economic system with the observation that "The outstanding faults of the economic society in which we live are its failure to provide for full employment and its arbitrary and inequitable distribution of wealth and incomes." *The General Theory of Employment, Interest and Money,* New York: Harcourt, Brace, 1936, p. 372.

[14] For Berle's and Means's views on the emergence of "corporate" capitalism and changes in the structure and functioning of the economic system, see A. A. Berle, Jr., and G. C. Means, *The Modern Corporation and Private Property,* New York: Macmillan, 1933; and C. F. Ware and G. C. Means, *The Modern Economy in Action,* New York: Harcourt, Brace, 1936.

[15] P. A. Samuelson, *op. cit.,* p. 39. See also C. R. McConnell, *Economics: Principles, Problems and Policies,* 2d. ed., New York: McGraw-Hill, 1963, pp. 10 and 392.

substituting the concept of "workable competition" for the concept of perfect competition.[16]

Samuelson's concept of workable competition makes room for some degree of monopolistic imperfection in the market system, the emergence of large-scale industry, and considerable market power possessed by big business and large labor unions. His concept of workable competition, as well as that of other conventional economists, is applicable not to a perfectly competitive economy but to a mature capitalist economy. When Samuelson and other mainstream economists make recommendations for the improvement of the working of the American and other Western mature capitalist economies, such proposals are guided by a view of an idealized model of the regulated mature capitalist economy.[17]

The Idealized Model of the Regulated Mature Capitalist Economy

In each era in the development of the capitalist system, economists have made generalizations about the economic systems in the various capitalist countries. These generalizations have been used in the construction of a model that is representative of the actual capitalist economies that are being investigated. Today, economists in the Western democracies are concerned with generalizing about the examples of mature large-scale capitalism that are found in Western Europe, the United States, Canada, Australia, New Zealand, Japan, and the Union of South Africa. An analysis of the structure and functioning of the economic systems of these capitalist countries reveals that they have many common features, on the basis of which one can construct a representative or idealized model of the mixed capitalist economy. This model is a theoretical or idealized one, which the advocates of mature capitalism can hold up as the ideal system towards which they would like to see all actual mature capitalist economies move. Actual or concrete mature capitalist economies, such as the American, British, German, and French economies, differ in a number of important ways from the theoretical model of mature capitalism that guides the analytical work of economists.

Nevertheless, in spite of these differences, economists use this theoretical model as a point of departure or benchmark in their analysis of the actual mixed economies. In the idealized version of the mixed economy or the system of workable competition, large business units and labor unions are induced by government action to function as though they were operating in a world of perfect competition. In the industrial heartland of the mixed economy, competition among many small-scale producers has been replaced by competition "among the few" or "oligopolistic" competition.[18] If unregulated, this oligopolistic competition results in administered prices, large surplus profits, and restricted output. To make oligopolistic competition "workable" or "reasonably effective," in the sense of restoring prices to competitive levels and providing for a socially desirable scale of output, the

---

[16] P. A. Samuelson, *op. cit.*, pp. 506–509.

[17] A minority of economists who want to restore a small-scale competitive economic system adhere to the idealized model of a perfectly competitive economy, and use it to guide their policy recommendations and proposals. They do not make use of the Keynesian model of a regulated mixed economy. For this minority position, see Milton Friedman, *Capitalism and Freedom,* Chicago: University of Chicago Press, 1962.

[18] Oligopolistic competition is a term now widely used to describe the functioning of the large-scale mixed economy. See, for example, Organisation for Economic Co-operation and Development, OECD Surveys, *United Kingdom,* Paris, Nov. 1970, p. 14.

government has to intervene with the aim of fostering market competition.

One of the major differences between the idealized mature capitalist economy and the idealized perfectly competitive economy relates to the structures of these two hypothetical economies. Whereas the perfectly competitive economy is a small-scale economic system, the major structural feature of the idealized mature capitalist economy is the presence of a limited number of large-scale industrial enterprises. Reflecting the makeup of the actual mixed economies, the idealized mixed economy is one in which agriculture accounts for a very small part of the nation's total output. Manufacturing, the major public utilities, and construction account for about one-third of total national output, while the private and public service industries provide between one-half and two-thirds of that output. Table 2-1 contrasts the origins of gross domestic product in the highly industrialized economies of the United States and the United Kingdom with the origins of this product in the less developed economies of India and Kenya. While the latter two economies are primarily agricultural, the American and British economies are primarily industrial.

From an analysis of the advanced industrial economies of such countries as the United States, the United Kingdom, Germany, France, and Japan we find that the structures of these economies have many common features. We can, therefore, construct an idealized model of a mature capitalist economy; from this model the various capitalist economies may deviate to some extent, but in general they conform to it. This idealized model has an industrial core or heartland in which a limited number of large oligopolistic enterprises play a crucial role in the nation's economic affairs. These dominating enterprises typically appear in the primary metal, chemical, machinery, oil, automobile, rubber, mining, power, and transportation industries. Surrounding the mature economy's industrial core are the middle-sized and small-scale industries, such as the food, apparel, lumber, furniture, leather products, textile, printing, and stone and glass

Table 2-1

Gross Domestic Product by Origins in Selected Countries, 1973 (in percent)

Origins of Gross Domestic Product	United States	United Kingdom	India[1]	Kenya
Agriculture, forestry, and fishing	4.4	2.7	42.2	28.2
Mining and manufacturing	26.8	28.3	14.4	12.5
Construction and public utilities	7.1	9.0	5.9	6.5
Private and public service industries	61.7	60.0	37.5	52.8
Total Gross Domestic Product	100.0	100.0	100.0	100.0

[1] 1971

Source: United Nations, *Monthly Bulletin of Statistics*, October 1976.

industries. In each industry represented in the mature capitalist economy's core, there is a high degree of concentration.[19] Typically, a few large industrial enterprises, some of a conglomerate nature, account for more than half the total sales of each industry. Besides having membership in specialized industrial associations, these industrial enterprises are usually united in a confederation of industries that speaks for big industry in its dealings with the government, organized labor, and the public. In the industrial core of the idealized mixed economy, big business works closely with the highly concentrated commercial banking system.

In the hypothetical model of the mature capitalist economy, the organization of the labor market very closely follows the organizational pattern of industry. The largest and most powerful labor unions, such as the steel, transportation, communications, coal mining, and automobile workers' unions, are found in the economy's industrial heartland, where they match their market power against that of the large industrial enterprises. Organized labor becomes progressively weaker as it moves outside the industrial core into the areas of middle-sized and small-scale competitive industry. It is least effective in terms of market power in the peripheral competitive areas of agriculture, personal services, retailing, and small-scale manufacturing.

In the hypothetical model of the mature capitalist economy, the agricultural sector, as in actual industrial economies, is a highly protected remnant of the once predominantly competitive, nineteenth-century capitalist economy. Import regulations protect domestic farm markets. Output controls and price support schemes are manipulated with the aim of assuring parity incomes to the farm population. Until recent years, efforts were made to avoid the accumulation of large surpluses of agricultural products, since attempts to export such surpluses only spoil the international markets for these products. In the model of mature capitalism, the strong economic position of the agricultural sector stands in marked contrast to the very weak position of the consumer sector. Consumers, for the most part, remain unorganized and without market power. Efforts to strengthen the consumer interest with the aid of councils, cooperatives, and government agencies dealing with consumer affairs do not confer upon consumers the power and influence possessed by big business and organized labor.

In the idealized model of oligopolistic capitalism, the public sector is large and of increasing importance. The governments at all levels purchase a large part of the nation's Gross National Product and employ a significant part of the total labor force. What has occurred in the United States in the past half century is typical of all the mature capitalist economies. Between 1929 and 1975, government purchases of goods and services in the United States increased from 8 to 22 percent of Gross National Product, while government employment at all levels increased from 10 to 19 percent of nonagricultural wage and salary workers. By the middle of the 1950s, the United States had become a service economy, with more than half of the labor force employed in the private and public service industries.[20] While the government owns or

---

[19] Industrial concentration in the United States and other major industrial countries is analyzed in *Hearings before the Subcommittee on Antitrust and Monopoly, Economic Concentration*, S. Res. 233, Parts 7 and 7A, Washington, D.C., April 2–17, 1968. A similar pattern of industrial concentration is found in all major Western European countries, the United States, and Japan.

[20] In 1965, 55 percent of total employment in the United States was provided by private and public service industries. Victor R. Fuchs, *The Service Economy*, New York: National Bureau of Economic Research, 1968, p. 2. Fuchs argues that the service economy will weaken the influence of the large industrial corporations because the expanding service industries are small-scale and more competitive

regulates certain basic industries, such as the railroads, communications, and power production, it leaves the bulk of industry in private hands and relies upon private enterprise to provide the major portion of the nation's total output of goods and services.

The Functioning of the Regulated Mixed Capitalist Economy

In the idealized version of mature capitalism the price system, because of the presence of monopolistic imperfections, would not efficiently allocate scarce economic resources to meet the preferences of consumers in the absence of government intervention. Nor could laissez faire economic policies be counted upon to weaken these imperfections to the point where market prices would reflect consumer wants, and would also accurately measure the real social costs of meeting these wants. Consequently, in the idealized model of the mature mixed economy constructed by standard Keynesian economists, the government intervenes in the nation's economic activities in order for the economy to perform in a socially satisfactory manner. The government does not directly interfere with the operations of private economic organizations. Instead, it pursues a policy of vigilance, being always on the alert to prevent developments that would undermine the competitiveness of the private enterprise economy. Antitrust action is one of the main devices used to ensure that large industrial enterprises operate like small-scale competitive firms. Samuelson explains that "Government regulation and government antitrust laws are the principal weapons a mixed economy uses to improve the working of the price system."[21] Vigorous enforcement is proposed to maintain freedom of entry into oligopolistic industries, to forestall collusion among large business firms, to prevent the development of excess production capacity, and to keep selling prices close to marginal costs and output at a socially desirable level.

In the idealized model of the regulated mature capitalist economy, the large labor unions do not restrict the supply of skilled labor in order to achieve a strong bargaining position from which to demand excessive wage rate increases. Since the large industrial corporations are induced not to restrict output and not to raise prices above a competitive level, labor unions are expected to be willing to accept wage rate increases in line with the annual national improvement in output per manhour.

The voluntary wage and price guidelines that the government announces for the guidance of business and organized labor seek to achieve price stability by relating increases in wage rates and prices to amounts warranted by improvements in national productivity.[22] The economists who relate their analyses to the idealized model of the mixed economy assert that in their system of workable competition the acceptance of these guidelines by business and organized labor would curb domestic inflation, and would also keep the nation's economy competitive in the international economy. Since domestic prices would not get out of line with prices in other countries, imports and exports of goods and services would be such as to maintain a satisfactory balance of current international payments.

In the hypothetical model of the mature

---

than the durable consumer-goods industries, such as the automobile and home appliance industries. See his "The First Service Economy," *The Public Interest*, No. 2, Winter, 1966, pp. 7-17.

[21] P. A. Samuelson, *op. cit.*, p. 498.

[22] Voluntary wage and price guidelines were first proposed by the Council of Economic Advisers in 1962. For a detailed discussion of these guidelines, see *Economic Report of the President*, Jan. 1962, pp. 185-190. A number of the major Western European countries have announced similar wage and price guidelines.

capitalist economy, the microeconomic adjustments in the nation's industrial core are accompanied by various macroeconomic adjustments that are the concern of the central government. The government is responsible for taking steps to achieve whatever annual rate of economic growth is established as the national goal. With the aid of appropriate fiscal and monetary policies, the government sees to it that saving and investment are kept in balance at a level that supports the nation's economic growth goal. With high and sustained economic growth, cyclical unemployment is no longer a major problem; but structural unemployment remains, requiring special programs. The government is also concerned about securing a pattern of income distribution that is regarded by the public as being fair.

Since the price system in the mixed economy does not guarantee everyone an adequate or health-and-decency standard of living, distributive justice requires placing a floor under personal incomes in the form of a guaranteed minimum income. This minimum income would assure that no family fell below some designated poverty line.[23] The income distribution resulting from the operation of the price mechanism of the idealized mixed capitalist economy is supplemented by old-age pension payments, unemployment benefits, minimum wage rates, and social welfare payments, in conformity with prevailing public views about distributive justice. Another concern of the government is with the diseconomies or social costs of economic growth, which include environmental deterioration and the loss of urban amenities.

The general aim of government intervention in the idealized model of the regulated mature capitalist economy is for this economy in its operations to approximate the ideal of a perfectly competitive economy. The market power of large business units and labor unions is to be progressively reduced to the point where consumer interests rather than producer interests dominate the program for national economic guidance. The combination of microeconomic and macroeconomic policies seeks to prevent the misallocation of economic resources, remove the obstacles to the achievement of economic stability, secure the economies of mass production, and promote a more equal distribution of income. The key to such success is the domestication of the large industrial enterprises and the large labor unions with the aid of a program for workable or effective competition. This idealized version of the operation of a mature capitalist economy leads to "directed" or "regulated" capitalism, but not to "planned" capitalism.

In the theoretical model of the mixed capitalist economy that is the concern of orthodox Keynesian economists, the government intervenes in economic activities, but does not pursue a program for national planning. It supplements and facilitates the private enterprise system, which, however, remains the pivot around which the nation's economic activities revolve. The responsibility for the good working of the regulated mature capitalist economy is taken to be a "shared responsibility" of government and private enterprise. As the Council of Economic Advisers expressed it, "In our system of free competitive enterprise and shared responsibility, we do not rely on Government alone for the achievement of inflation-free economic growth. On the contrary, that achievement requires a blending of suitable private actions and public policies."[24]

Like all other models of economic systems,

---

[23] The war on poverty was begun in 1964 during the Johnson Administration with the setting of a poverty level at $3,000 per annum for a family of four persons. This level has been raised in step with the rising cost of living. The poverty program was a part of the Great Society program, which is discussed in the *Economic Report of the President,* Jan. 1964, p. 77.

[24] *Economic Report of the President,* Jan. 1960, p. iv.

the idealized model of regulated mature capitalism has an inner logic that is supposed to lead to the establishment of an equilibrium position. Just like perfect competition, the workable competition of the directed. mature mixed economy is expected to result in full employment, balanced economic growth, economic stability, and a fair sharing of the national income. Since these desirable ends would not be achieved by the unregulated mixed economy, the government is assigned the responsibility of supplementing the operations of the mixed economy.

Government intervention of this kind raises the question of how far such intervention must proceed in order to secure the objective of a full-employment, growing economy. The idealized model of regulated mature capitalism that has directed the analyses of many standard economists in the United States and the United Kingdom in recent decades places some very definite limits on government intervention in economic affairs. Intervention in the form of the direct control of individual prices and wage rates is used only as a last resort; preferable is indirect intervention through fiscal and monetary policies that induce producers and consumers to act in ways held to be socially beneficial. Furthermore, neither private business nor organized labor is brought in as an active participant in the formulation of government policy.[25] Instead, in constructing a tax or credit policy or proposing a wage or price guideline, the government does not call for the active collaboration of the nation's major economic interest groups.

The interventionist approach in the idealized model of the regulated mixed economy is thoroughly manipulative, for the government, acting through the central bank and the treasury, seeks to maneuver the economy into a managed equilibrium position. In this managed equilibrium, workable or effective competition is expected to prevail among the large industrial enterprises and labor unions. This interventionist approach in regulated mature capitalism is a compensatory one in which the government offsets or compensates for the tendencies of the mature capitalist economy to misallocate resources, to charge monopolistic prices, and to restrict the output of goods and services.

Finally, to manipulation and compensation are added persuasion and exhortation. The government calls upon the two sides of industry to be guided by "the consumer and the national interest" in their price- and wage-determining activities. In the idealized version of the controlled mixed economy, what is acceptable to most mainstream economists in the United States is government intervention that never goes beyond antitrust action, legislation affecting trade unions, and presidential and congressional pressures in collective bargaining to serve the national interest. An incomes or wage-price policy is held to be generally quite ineffective since it can only temporarily suppress inflation, and in addition, if maintained beyond the short run, becomes "increasingly distortive of pricing and inequitable as between those who do and those who do not comply."[26]

Mature Capitalist Economies in Practice

A survey of the functioning of the actual mature capitalist economies of the Western

---

[25] For example, when the Kennedy Administration announced wage and price guideposts in 1962, these guideposts were constructed without the collaboration of business, organized labor, and the government. Likewise, when wage rates and prices were frozen by the Nixon Administration in August 1971, this action was taken without the cooperation of business and organized labor. As the federal government explained, the wage and price freeze of August 1971 was "dramatically" announced to the nation. *Economic Report of the President,* Jan. 1972, pp. 22–24.

[26] P. A. Samuelson, *op. cit.*, p. 815.

world reveals that they have deviated significantly from the idealized model of the mixed mature capitalist economy that many economists have accepted as a desirable policy goal. These deviations have been both structural and functional. The structural developments of recent decades in the major Western nations have not been favorable to the establishment of a system of workable competition. In the United States, the antitrust program has not prevented the increasing concentration of industry. A study of corporate mergers since 1948 by the Federal Trade Commission reveals that industrial concentration has reached new heights and shows no sign of coming to an early end. This study shows that the 200 largest manufacturing corporations that owned 42.4 percent of total manufacturing corporation assets in 1947 owned 60.9 percent in 1967.[27] Between 1948 and 1968, the 200 largest manufacturing corporations of 1968 made at least 3,864 acquisitions of other corporations with combined assets of $50 billion. In recent years, many of these mergers have been conglomerate (rather than horizontal or vertical) mergers between corporations operating in different markets. The future course of industrial concentration remains uncertain. While there was a considerable increase in concentration from 1948 to 1968, there was a decline in overall concentration from the early 1930s to the late 1940s, and then a return to the level of the 1930s by the late 1960s.[28]

Industrial concentration has in recent decades grown rapidly in Western Europe and Japan, where it has frequently been encouraged by national policy in order to meet competition from the United States and the European Common Market. While governments in the United Kingdom, France, Germany, Italy, and the Scandinavian countries have since 1945 eliminated certain restrictive or monopolistic business practices, such as resale price maintenance and collective price agreements, these governments have at the same time fostered programs to substitute large industrial producing enterprises for small family-owned firms. The proconcentration industrial policies of the major Western European countries have been the opposite of the anticoncentration policy officially endorsed in the United States.[29]

A new post–World War II development has been the expansion of the large multinational industrial enterprises that escape much of the regulation of industry imposed by national governments. The rise of the multinational corporation has increased the size of industrial corporations and has enlarged their market power. Direct investment abroad by American corporations increased from $11.8 billion in 1950 to $70.8 billion in 1969. The bulk of this increase in foreign investment was made by a limited number of large industrial corporations. In 1957, of the 1,542 American firms with overseas investments, only 79 accounted for 69 percent of total American direct overseas investments. In 1962, 46 British firms accounted for 71 percent of total British manufacturing assets in foreign countries.[30] The market power possessed by the

---

[27] Subcommittee on Antitrust and Monopoly, *Hearings, Economic Concentration*, S. Res. 40, part 8A, Washington, D.C., 1969, p. 192.

[28] M. A. Adelman, "The Two Faces of Economic Concentration," *The Public Interest*, Fall 1970, pp. 122-123.

[29] Studies of the European Common Market show that "Intensified competition has led in many industries to a tendency toward—usually national—concentration as a means of counteracting 'foreign' competition," especially in the United Kingdom, France, Germany, and Italy." W. J. Karssen, "Concentration in the Automobile Industry of the E.E.C.," *Economic Concentration*, Part 7A, p. 3922. See also Andrew Shonfield, *Modern Capitalism, The Changing Balance of Public and Private Power*, New York: Oxford University Press, 1965, for concentration in France, Germany, and the United Kingdom.

[30] S. Hymer and R. Rowthorn, "Multinational Corporations and International Oligopoly: The Non-American Challenge," in *The International Corpo-

large multinational corporation is very considerable, since it operates across national boundaries, and has a wide choice of sources of raw materials and credit, labor supplies, and export markets. The idealized model of regulated mature capitalism that runs through standard economics textbooks makes no place for the large multinational industrial corporations, nor does it explain how such corporations may be fitted into a system of workable competition.

Functional Developments in Mature Capitalism

The functional developments of recent decades in the advanced industrial systems of the major Western capitalist nations have also not been favorable to the establishment in those countries of a system of effective competition. Efforts to increase competition, to get prices down to competitive levels, and to keep wage-rate increases in line with the improvement in productivity have not met with much success. In boom periods, all mature capitalist economies continue to suffer from a disruptive race for income, each major economic interest group tending to be dissatisfied with its share of the national income. Each group feels relatively deprived, so that it acts to enlarge its portion of the national income by resorting to the use of market power.

Efforts by governments in the Western democracies directed at voluntary acceptance of their wage and price guidelines by the major economic interest groups have not been successful. Organized labor has usually refused to accept wage and price guidelines on the grounds that while a precise guideline for wage increases has been established, no precise guideline for the control of profits has also been provided. Organized labor in the United States, the United Kingdom, and other mature capitalist countries has refused to limit demands for wage-rate increases to the annual improvement in national productivity. Organized labor has insisted at least upon wage-rate increases that make allowance for both productivity improvement and inflation. Business has reacted to these demands in boom periods by passing wage increases on to consumers in higher prices. Farmers have followed suit by demanding higher farm price supports. When uncontrolled, the incomes race leads to a round of inflationary wage and price increases that redistribute incomes arbitrarily, raise export prices, and lead to international balance-of-payments difficulties.

The governments in a number of the Western democracies first responded to the problem of the incomes race by calling for voluntary wage and price restraint. This was in accordance with the view widely held by Keynesian economists that persuasion and admonition, coupled with fiscal and monetary policies, would be sufficient to curb strong inflationary tendencies in the full-employment, high-growth economy. When appeals for voluntary wage and price restraint failed, the nonsocialist governments in France, the Netherlands, Denmark, and the United States turned to mandatory price controls, usually in the form of general price and wage freezes. By the middle of 1972, the British Conservative government was under heavy pressure to impose mandatory price and wage controls, which, however, had been adopted without much success by the British Labour government in 1966 and 1967.

By 1972, it was widely believed in the mature capitalist economies that a strong incomes policy, combined with fiscal and monetary measures, is essential for the good functioning of those economies. It is now also generally accepted that no incomes policy can be successful unless it is constructed and carried out with the close cooperation of all concerned economic interest groups. Both Walter

---

ration, edited by C. P. Kindleberger, Cambridge, Mass.: The M.I.T. Press, 1970, pp. 75–76.

W. Heller and Arthur M. Okun, former Chairmen of the Council of Economic Advisers, argue in support of a national incomes policy. Heller concludes that "in spite of their imperfections and the dents and scars they bear . . . the [wage and price] guideposts have served us tolerably well."[31] Okun emphasizes the point that wage and price "standards should be developed only after the fullest consultation with business and labor."[32] A Working Party of the Organisation for Economic Co-operation and Development, after surveying incomes policies in many Western European countries, agreed with Heller and Okun.[33]

Another way in which actual mixed capitalist economies have significantly deviated from the idealized model of these economies relates to the distribution of wealth and income. Those economists who accept the model of workable competition as the goal towards which the Western mature capitalist economies should move believe that a system of workable competition would tend to reduce the inequalities of wealth ownership and income distribution. According to their argument, if monopolistic imperfections could be removed from the market system, large surplus incomes would be eliminated and a more equitable sharing of national income and wealth would ensue.

This notion of a movement towards a fairer sharing of income and wealth lay behind the discussion of a "people's capitalism" that was popular in the 1950s. The increasing number of corporate stockholders was accepted as evidence that the capitalist system was becoming more a people's economic system and less the system of special monopolistic interests.[34] The available evidence with respect to wealth ownership and income distribution in Western Europe and the United States does not support the view that as capitalism matures there is a marked trend towards a significantly fairer sharing of income and wealth. A recent study of the American distribution of income concludes that income distribution has been basically unchanged since 1945.[35]

As Table 2-2 shows, the lowest fifth of American families, which received 5 percent of total before-tax personal income in 1947, had increased this share to only 5.4 percent in 1972. The top fifth of these families, which received 43 percent of total before-tax personal income in 1947, was still receiving 41 percent in 1972. The bottom 60 percent of families, which received one-third of total personal incomes in 1947, was receiving very little more in 1972. The concentration of wealth, which had decreased to some extent in the 1930s and 1940s, increased in the 1950s and was stable in the 1960s. At present, the top 10 percent of all families in the United States receive 29 percent of total pretax income and own 56 percent of all personal wealth, while the bottom 10 percent receive 1 percent of total pretax income and own no net wealth. Although millions of people in the United States own corporation stocks, the bulk of these stocks is owned by a very small

---

[31] Walter W. Heller, *New Dimensions of Political Economy,* New York: W. W. Norton, 1966, p. 46.

[32] A. M. Okun, *The Political Economy of Prosperity,* New York: W. W. Norton, 1970, p. 105.

[33] Organisation for Economic Co-operation and Development, *Policies for Price Stability,* Paris, 1962, pp. 46–47.

[34] The number of individual corporate shareowners in the United States which was 12,940,000 in 1951 increased to 30,850,000 in 1970.

[35] Lester C. Thurow and Robert E. B. Lucas, *The American Distribution of Income: A Structural Problem,* Joint Committee Print, 92d Congress, 2d Session, Joint Economic Committee, Washington, D.C., March 17, 1972, p. 7. See also Herman P. Miller, *Rich Man, Poor Man,* New York: Crowell, 1971. In both the United States and Great Britain, incomes and wealth are still distributed very unevenly but considerably less so than fifty or sixty years ago, as is pointed out in Robert J. Lampman, *The Share of Wealth-Holders in National Wealth, 1922–1956,* New York: National Bureau of Economic Research, 1962, pp. 210–217.

Table 2–2
Percentage Shares of Aggregate Before-Tax Income Going to Families in the United States

	1947	1956	1972
Lowest fifth	5.0	5.0	5.4
Second fifth	11.8	12.4	11.9
Middle fifth	17.0	17.8	17.5
Fourth fifth	23.1	23.7	23.9
Highest fifth	43.0	41.2	41.4

Source: U.S. Bureau of the Census, *Current Population Reports*.

minority of all stockholders. In 1962, the top 20 percent of wealth holders owned 97 percent of all publicly held corporate stock. In the major Western European countries, similarly large inequalities in income distribution and wealth ownership are found.

A factor contributing to the further growth of large-scale industry in the United States and other industrialized countries, and making it increasingly difficult to achieve the idealized system of workable competition, is that the managers of large business firms take a greater interest in maximum sales than in maximum profits. The mainstream or conventional economists who have developed the concept of workable competition have assumed that the managers of oligopolistic enterprises would be profit maximizers rather than sales maximizers.[36] According to the profit-maximizing principle, if a firm can make more profits by restricting its output, it will curb output in order to maximize profits.

In recent years, a number of economists have questioned the extent to which the managers of large business firms are profit maximizers. These economists have concluded that the managers of large business firms are now sales maximizers more frequently than profit maximizers. As William J. Baumol puts it, "I am prepared to generalize from these observations and assert that the typical oligopolist's objectives can usefully be characterized, approximately, as sales maximization subject to a minimum profit restraint."[37] The managers or technostructure of the large business enterprise increase their prestige in the business world, their managerial reputations, their market power, and their salaries by enlarging their firm's share of the market and by securing for it a more dominant position in the industry. Some economists assert that size is always on the side of market power, and the larger the firm the more market power it comes to possess.[38] The larger the firm the better it can deal with the government, the labor unions, the bankers, and the producers of raw materials. According to this interpretation, both technological change and the motivation of corporate managers are strong forces that contribute to the growing concentration of industry in the mature capitalist economy.

For these reasons, many economists now conclude that the antitrust program may delay, but cannot in the long run prevent, the further concentration of industry. These economists also argue that it is not possible to establish a system of workable competition

---

[36] The standard economics textbooks analyze the operations of the typical oligopolist in terms of the maximum-profit equilibrium. See P. A. Samuelson, *op. cit.*, p. 490. Robert Dorfman states that "A plausible hypothesis, though one very hard to explain, is that the price leaders [in an oligopoly industry] act like monopolists on behalf of the entire industry. That is, they recognize the industry demand curve and the cost curves of the average firm, and attempt to set a price that will afford such a firm the largest possible profits." R. Dorfman, *Prices and Markets*, Englewood Cliffs, N.J.: Prentice-Hall, 1967, p. 109.

[37] William J. Baumol, *Business Behavior, Value and Growth*, New York: Macmillan, 1959, p. 49.

[38] Galbraith explains that "It is clear, first of all, that industrial planning is in unabashed alliance with size.... Size is the general servant of technology, not the special servant of profits." John K. Galbraith, *op. cit.*, pp. 31 and 33.

through vigorous antitrust action accompanied by government persuasion and public vigilance. They believe that some other way of domesticating large-scale industrial enterprise and getting the mature capitalist economy to serve society more effectively should be tried. These economists advocate that the idealized model of the regulated mixed capitalist economy should now be reconstructed to provide a new model that would be more useful as a guide to national economic policy formulation in the closing quarter of the twentieth century. This new model of the mature capitalist economy substitutes the concept of guided or planned capitalism for the concept of regulated or controlled capitalism.

The Idealized Model of Guided or Planned Capitalism

The idealized version of the regulated mature capitalist economy that emerged from the Keynesian Revolution of the 1940s and 1950s, and that dominated standard economics in the quarter century after World War II, has since the 1950s lost much of its appeal as a national goal in a number of the Western democracies. Governments in these countries have in recent decades been searching for a more workable economic system than the one envisioned by post–World War II mainstream Keynesian economists in the United States and Great Britain. These governments have found that the Keynesian interventionist program has not been successful since 1945 in coping with the major problems of the high-pressure, full-employment economy. This postwar experience with limited intervention has caused some mature capitalist economies to move towards an economic system in which there is more and not less government intervention and national economic guidance. Capitalist countries such as France, the Netherlands, Japan, Belgium, Denmark and Italy already do considerable national economic planning. In the early 1960s, the possibility of introducing something resembling French indicative planning was considered by the British Conservative government; in 1962 it established the National Economic Development Council. This Council proposed a five-year plan for the United Kingdom, but a change in government occurred in 1964 before the proposal could be acted upon.[39]

The capitalist economic system continued to change in the post–World War II period. The welfare capitalism of the 1930s and 1940s was followed by what is described as guided or planned capitalism. Immediately after the Second World War, national planning was adopted in the United Kingdom, the Scandinavian countries, France, and the Netherlands. When the period of extreme scarcities came to an end in the early 1950s, formal national planning was abandoned in the United Kingdom and Denmark, but it was maintained in France, the Netherlands, Norway, and Sweden. Japan also adopted national planning in the postwar period. While experiences with democratic national planning have varied widely in different countries, there has been a widespread tendency towards more intervention and planning in the advanced industrial economies. Some economists have interpreted this development as a post-Keynesian development in which a shift from regulated to guided or planned capitalism has taken place. Economists like Gunnar Myrdal, John K. Galbraith,

[39] Planning proposals were discussed in the *Fourth Report* of the Council on Prices, Productivity and Incomes, London, July 1961. The National Economic Development Council published a five-year national economic budget in 1963 which was to serve as a guidepost for economic policy formulation. The National Economic Development Council, *Growth of the United Kingdom Economy, 1961–1966*, London, 1963.

Gerhard Colm, and Adolf Lowe have transferred their attention from the model of the regulated capitalist economy to the model of the planned capitalist economy.[40] In the work of these economists, the latter model has become the point of departure for their economic analyses and policy proposals.

The concept of the idealized model of planned capitalism is democratic and indicative. It is to be distinguished from the blueprint, target planning of the Eastern communist countries, where the plan is imposed by central planning authorities. Western planning is termed *indicative* because, while it sets out national economic and social goals, it leaves cooperation on the part of business people and workers on a voluntary basis. The present structure of the mature capitalist economy is by and large accepted on the ground that modern technology requires large industrial enterprises. With respect to the functioning of the mixed economy, under the idealized model of planned capitalism, government intervention is more coordinated than it is in the other model of regulated capitalism.[41]

For formal planning of economic activities, three prerequisites must be met: (1) the country must have a government planning body; (2) it must construct annual and longer-term national economic budgets; and (3) it must have a system of economic controls to achieve the goals set forth in these budgets.

The program for national planning is based on the annual and longer-term national economic budgets, which are quantitative projections of the Gross National Product and its uses for private and public consumption and investment over the plan period. Fiscal, monetary, price, and wage policies are coordinated with the budget to achieve the national goals. Since planned capitalism is a democratic system, provision is made in the idealized model for the participation of all economic and social interest groups in the selection of national priorities. This is accomplished through a national economic and social council, with representation from the various interest groups; this council informs the government about the public's preferences and advises on problems relating to implementation.

The success of a program for national economic planning depends upon the support from the nation's economic and social interest groups. Therefore, the approach used is no longer the Keynesian manipulative, compensatory one in which little collaboration takes place between the government and the private interest groups; it is replaced by the post-Keynesian anticipatory, participatory, and collaborative method.

In indicative national planning, the government does not react to problems but endeavors to anticipate them. The 1970 report of the National Goals Research Staff states that "What clearly emerges from these debates which have been subsumed under the label of a search for balanced growth is a dissatisfaction with the old ways of decisionmaking. The implication is that we wish to shift from a

---

[40] The current type of capitalism is also referred to as "managerial" capitalism. See Robin Marris, *The Economic Theory of "Managerial" Capitalism,* New York: The Free Press, 1964; and Michael D. Reagan, *The Managed Economy,* New York: Oxford University Press, 1963.

[41] The distinction between intervention and planning is more a matter of degree than of kind. As intervention increases in scope, at some point it takes on an overall character and may be described as "planning." Myrdal draws a distinction between uncoordinated and coordinated intervention and describes the latter as planning. As he puts it, "Coordination leads to planning, or, rather, it *is* planning, as the term has come to be understood in the western world. Coordination of measures of intervention implies a reconsideration of them all from the point of view of how they combine to serve the development goals of the entire national community, as these goals become determined by the political process that provides the basis for power." Gunnar Myrdal, *Beyond the Welfare State,* New Haven: Yale University Press, p. 63.

reactive mode of dealing with problems that have forced themselves on us to an anticipatory mode in which we either attempt to prevent their occurrence or are prepared to deal with them as they emerge. The latter mode is necessary and desirable in times of rapid change because of the inertia of large systems."[42] The technology, population, and knowledge explosions of the past quarter century have underlined the necessity for assessment and planning, if nations are to make satisfactory adjustments to the rapid changes of the last quarter of this century. Regulated capitalism suffers from the fact that regulation or intervention emphasizes the need for short-run economic stability to the neglect of consideration of long-term issues. What is now required for satisfactory national economic and social guidance is what Gunnar Myrdal describes as the "long view" or "long time horizon".[43]

Planned Capitalism in Practice

The nearest approaches to successful national planning in the democratic countries are found in France, Japan, Sweden, Norway, and the Netherlands, where such planning has been the accepted government policy since the early post–World War II years. In these five countries, the indicative national planning programs of the past quarter century have received the support of all or a number of the major economic interest groups, which have worked closely with the nation's planning authorities. In Norway and Sweden, the national planning has been carried on by democratic socialist governments, whereas in France, Japan, and the Netherlands the dominant political party has been a capitalist or nonsocialist party. National planning has also been practiced in France continuously since the early postwar years under the guidance of nonsocialist governments. The labor movement in France, unlike that of the Netherlands, has not actively supported the national planning program, because this program has been dominated by private business interests. In Japan, where the trade union movement is very weak, the national planning has also been largely the work of a government-business coalition, with the large business and banking firms playing the major role in the nation's planning activity.

Among actual economic systems, the nearest approach to the idealized model of planned capitalism appears in the Netherlands, where the traditions of public participation and collaboration in national planning are well established among all classes of the population. The Netherlands Central Planning Bureau constructs annual national economic budgets, which become the foundation of the government's annual national plans. The Economic and Social Council, with representatives from organized business, labor, farmers, and the public, enables all classes to participate in the national planning process. While national planning has not solved all economic problems in the Netherlands—not, for example, wage and price inflation—that country has enjoyed a high level of prosperity since 1945, and national planning has become a widely accepted way of operating its economy.

In the United Kingdom, national planning

---

[42] National Goals Research Staff, *Toward Balanced Growth: Quantity with Quality,* Washington, D.C., 1970, p. 31. The report of the staff approved the use of national economic budgets for the reason that this budget "is essential for developing policy since it quantitatively renders the consequences of [national] choices on available resources" (p. 160 fn.).

[43] Mydral explains that "America as a civilization has its interests focused upon the immediate, the concrete, and the experimental in a remarkable way. In all the sciences, including the social ones, America has had to rely upon European thought for philosophy and theory, for the comprehensive grip of things and events, and for the long view." Gunnar Myrdal, *Challenge to Affluence,* New York: Pantheon Books, 1962, p. 83.

has been tried twice by the Labour party. In the first planning period, 1945–1951, the planning was overshadowed by the postwar problems of reconstruction and return to a peacetime economy. In the second planning period, 1964–1970, not much was done to put national planning into practice, since the Labour government's energies were concentrated on inflation and the international balance-of-payments difficulties. The postwar Conservative governments in the United Kingdom have repudiated planning as a means of providing national economic guidance. The United States, West Germany, Canada, and other capitalist countries have likewise shunned formal national economic planning. These countries, however, have pushed intervention far beyond the limited Keynesian countercyclical program with its emphasis on deficit financing in recession periods.

In the United States, West Germany, and Canada, councils of economic experts have been established to advise the government on the formulation and coordination of economic policies. For the first time in peacetime circumstances, the United States imposed a general freeze on wages and prices in August 1971; many circles later called for a similar action in the United Kingdom. In these and other mature capitalist countries, governments have moved beyond Keynesian fiscal and monetary policies to consider developing an incomes or wage-price policy; and it is widely conceded in business, labor, and government circles that the control of administered inflation requires the supplementing of fiscal and monetary policies with some kind of incomes policy.[44]

While most of the major capitalist countries continue to cling to regulated rather than to planned capitalism, and so do not move close to the idealized model of guided capitalism, they are nevertheless under strong pressure to expand their intervention in economic and social affairs. The dominant issue in the affluent Western democracies in the closing quarter of this century will be national priorities. The vital question is: for what purposes should economic growth be encouraged? Or, to put it another way, how should affluence be used to achieve a lifestyle of high quality? The issue of national priorities focuses attention on the problems of environmental deterioration, rural and urban poverty, center-city decay, race and sex discrimination, the plight of the less developed countries, federal-state revenue sharing, tax reform and income inequalities, population control, and participation of all classes in public decision making.[45] It should not be surprising if efforts to deal with these and other issues in the next quarter century should result in much actual planning that is not overtly recognized as such in those capitalist countries officially opposed to national planning.

---

[44] The Committee for Economic Development, one of the most prestigious of private business organizations in the United States, has stated that "On balance of considerations, we believe that the United States should include voluntary wage-price policies among its policy tools for reconciling price stability and high employment." Committee for Economic Development, *Further Weapons against Inflation, Measures to Supplement General Fiscal and Monetary Measures,* New York, 1970, pp. 55–56.

[45] For a good statement of the national agenda of unfinished business in the United States, see the National Goals Research Staff report on *Toward Balanced Growth: Quantity with Quality,* and the U.S. Department of Health, Education, and Welfare, *Toward a Social Report,* Washington, D.C., 1969.

Selected Bibliography

BAUMOL, WILLIAM J. *Business Behavior, Value and Growth*. The Macmillan Company, New York, 1959.

BERLE, ADOLF A., JR., and G. C. MEANS. *The Modern Corporation and Private Property*. The Macmillan Company, New York, 1933.

CLARK, JOHN M. "Toward a Concept of Workable Competition." *American Economic Review*, XXX (June 1940), 241–256.

COMMITTEE FOR ECONOMIC DEVELOPMENT. *Further Weapons against Inflation*. New York, 1970.

COUNCIL ON PRICES, PRODUCTIVITY AND INCOMES. *Fourth Report*. London, 1961.

DORFMAN, ROBERT. *Prices and Markets*. Prentice-Hall, Inc., Englewood Cliffs, N.J., 1967.

———. *The Price System*. Prentice-Hall, Inc., Englewood Cliffs, N.J., 1964.

Economic Report of the President. 1960, 1962, 1964, and 1972.

FRIEDMAN, MILTON. *Capitalism and Freedom*. University of Chicago Press, Chicago, 1962.

FUCHS, VICTOR R. "The First Service Economy." *The Public Interest*, Winter 1966, 7–17.

———. *The Service Economy*. National Bureau of Economic Research, New York, 1968.

HELLER, WALTER W. *New Dimensions of Political Economy*. W. W. Norton and Company, Inc., New York, 1966.

HYMER, S., and R. ROWTHORN. "Multinational Corporations and International Oligopoly: The Non-American Challenge." In *The International Corporation*, edited by C. P. Kindleberger. M.I.T. Press, Cambridge, Mass., 1970.

KEYNES, JOHN MAYNARD. *The General Theory of Employment, Interest and Money*. Harcourt, Brace, New York, 1936.

LAMPMAN, ROBERT J. *The Share of Wealth-Holders in National Wealth, 1922–1956*. National Bureau of Economic Research, New York, 1962.

MARRIS, ROBIN. *The Economic Theory of Managerial Capitalism*. Free Press of Glencoe, New York, 1964.

MILLER, HERMAN P. *Rich Man, Poor Man*. Crowell, New York, 1964.

MYRDAL, GUNNAR. *Beyond the Welfare State*. Yale University Press, New Haven, 1960.

———. *Challenge to Affluence*. Pantheon Books, New York, 1962.

NATIONAL ECONOMIC DEVELOPMENT COUNCIL. *Growth of the United Kingdom Economy, 1961–1966*. London, 1963.

NATIONAL GOALS RESEARCH STAFF. *Toward Balanced Growth: Quantity with Quality*. Washington, D.C., 1970.

OKUN, ARTHUR M. *Equality and Efficiency*. Brookings Institution, Washington, D.C., 1975.

———. *The Political Economy of Prosperity*. Brookings Institution, Washington, D.C., 1970.

ORGANISATION FOR ECONOMIC CO-OPERATION AND DEVELOPMENT. *OECD Surveys, United Kingdom*, Paris, 1970.

———. *Policies for Price Stability*. Paris, 1962.

REAGAN, MICHAEL D. *The Managed Economy*. Oxford University Press, New York, 1963.

SAMUELSON, PAUL A. *Economics*. 8th. ed. McGraw-Hill Book Company, New York, 1970.

SCHUMPETER, JOSEPH A. "Capitalism." *Encyclopaedia Britannica*, 4, 1958.

SENATE SUBCOMMITTEE ON ANTITRUST AND MONOPOLY. *Hearings, Economic Concentration*, S. Res. 40, Part 8A, Washington, D.C., 1969.

———. *Hearings, Economic Concentration*. S. Res. 233, Parts 7 and 7A, Washington, D.C., April 1968.

SHONFIELD, ANDREW. *Modern Capitalism*. Oxford University Press, New York, 1965.

SOMBART, WERNER. "Capitalism." *Encyclopedia of the Social Sciences*, 3, 195–208.

THUROW, LESTER C., and ROBERT E. B. LUCAS. *The American Distribution of Income: A Structural Problem*. Joint Economic Committee, Washington, D.C., 1972.

U.S. DEPARTMENT OF HEALTH, EDUCATION, AND WELFARE. *Toward a Social Report*. Washington, D.C., 1969.

WARE, CAROLINE F., and GARDINER C. MEANS. *The Modern Economy in Action*. Harcourt, Brace, New York, 1936.

WEBER, MAX. *The Theory of Social and Economic Organization*. Oxford University Press, New York, 1947.

Chapter 3
The Mature American Economy

The Structure of the American Economy

Before we proceed to an analysis of the functioning of the mature American economy, we may find helpful an overall view of the structure of this complicated economic system. This structure acts as a bridge between the nation's economic resources and the many wants of its population. With the aid of many millions of individuals, business enterprises, and government units, land, labor, and capital are converted into final goods and services to meet the diverse private and public needs of ultimate consumers. The structure of an economic system is important, because it provides the framework within which business, labor, agriculture, and the government operate. This structure may be altered or modified over time, but at any given point in time the existing structure must be taken as being relatively fixed. This is especially true of the Western capitalist countries in which private enterprise plays a major role, and in which economic change usually comes quite slowly. The structure of an economic system may be the end product of many years' evolution, as in the case of the mature American economy; or it may be an institutional arrangement that is largely built up in a few generations, as in the case of the Soviet Union. Whether it is of old or recent origin, the structure or organizational basis of an economic system acts as a cultural imperative that canalizes the flow of the nation's economic activity.

The United States, less than one-half the size of the Soviet Union (8.6 million square miles), had in 1974 a population of 212 million, compared with the Soviet population of 252 million. It has a very extensive agricultural area (1.2 billion acres), with a favorable climate, and like the Soviet Union, has large mineral resources. The United States possesses more than one-third of the world's coal reserves, 15 percent of its copper reserves, 10 percent of its oil reserves and 8 percent of its iron ore reserves. The $1,499 billion Gross National Product (1975) provides the American people with one of the highest per capita Gross National Products in the world. Sweden and Switzerland, with the highest standards of living in Western Europe in 1975, had per capita Gross National Products of $6,880 and $6,970 respectively as compared with the United States per capita GNP in that year of $6,600. The Soviet Union's per capita GNP is estimated to have been $2,030, or only 33 percent of American per capita GNP in 1973.

The United States is the world's foremost industrialized nation. In 1973, agriculture accounted for only 3.6 percent of national income, whereas manufacturing contributed 34.1 percent. Not only is the American economy highly industrialized, but it also devotes more of its resources than do other economies to the production of services. In 1973, the provision of services of many kinds (professional, commercial, governmental, and personal) accounted for 54.7 percent of the national income. As a capitalist economy reaches an advanced stage of economic growth, productive capacities are increasingly shifted from industry to the activities providing private and public services.

Table 3-1, which shows the origins of the United States national income, reveals that very significant changes in the origins of national income have occurred in the last two decades. Income from agriculture in relation to other incomes has been cut in half, while more limited relative declines have been registered for manufacturing and public utilities. The development of major significance is the relative increase in incomes from service activities of all types. By 1973, the American service economy was well established. The old mass-consumption economy, which had stressed the acquisition of houses, automobiles, and household appliances, has now been replaced by an economy in which increasing amounts of discretionary personal income are spent on private and public services.

Table 3-1

U.S. National Income by Origins (Percentage Distribution) in 1950 and 1973

	1950	1973
Agriculture	7.3	3.6
Manufacturing	38.7	34.1
Public utilities	8.6	7.6
Services	45.4	54.7
Total national income	100.0	100.0

Source: *Statistical Abstract of the United States*, 1974.

The American economic system has almost 13 million business units (single proprietorships, partnerships, and corporations). In 1972, there were 9.6 million nonagricultural businesses and 3.3 million farms and other agricultural enterprises. The American business system has a tripartite form, in which there is a central core of five hundred to six hundred large-scale oligopolistic industrial enterprises, surrounded by an area of middle-sized business enterprises, and then an outlying area of many small-scale competitive enterprises. The large-scale core of the economic system includes the major industries with high concentration ratios. For example, in this central area of the economy is the motor vehicles industry in which the four largest firms accounted in 1972 for 93 percent of the industry's total shipments. Here also are the steel, petroleum, aluminum, aircraft, and television industries, with high concentration ratios. In these industries, shipments by the eight largest firms varied from 57 to 87 percent of the total industry shipments.[1]

The two hundred largest manufacturing

[1] *Statistical Abstract of the United States*, 1971, pp. 720-721.

corporations in the American economy's central core or heartland were reported in 1967 to account for 42 percent of the total value added by all manufacturing companies. In the area of middle-sized industry are found enterprises with highly differentiated products, such as the cigarette, drug, pharmaceutical, and food products industries. In the outlying competitive area are the highly competitive small-scale economic activities, such as farming, the service trades, small-scale retailing, and various branches of manufacturing such as the textile, furniture, wood products, and clothing industries. These industries are the vestigial remnants of the highly competitive capitalism of the mid-nineteenth century.

The Structural Aspects of American Manufacturing

The unique feature of the industrial structure of the United States is the small number of large industrial enterprises that hold the major portion of the assets of manufacturing corporations, and that receive the major portion of the net profits of these corporations.[2] Most of the five hundred large manufacturing corporations that dominate the American economy evolved in recent years from mergers rather than from internal growth. When a corporation expands by the latter method, it uses its own or borrowed financial resources in order to expand its productive capacity. The merger procedure entails the acquisition of the financial assets of already existing companies.

In the United States the growth of large-scale industrial enterprise has been fostered by three merger movements. The first movement took place during the period 1897–1903,

[2] The problems of industrial concentration are summarized in Willard F. Mueller, *A Primer on Monopoly and Competition*, New York: Random House, 1970.

the second in the years 1925–1930; the third, current merger movement has been in process since the 1950s. This merger movement is distinguished from the two earlier ones by the fact that it has been largely a matter of conglomerate mergers. The horizontal and vertical mergers of the first two merger movements took place between direct competitors in the same or related industries; in contrast, the conglomerate mergers have frequently been between noncompeting companies, as in the case of a copper company merging with a coal concern or an electronics company with a steel enterprise. Above all, the conglomerate merger enlarges the area in which the merged corporations can use their power to influence market, labor, and other conditions.

Today the advanced industrial American economy is highly concentrated. Table 3-2 indicates that the two hundred largest manufacturing corporations have continued to increase their control of the nation's productive capacity.[3] The one hundred largest corpora-

Table 3-2

Shares of American Manufacturing Corporation Assets Held by the 100 and 200 Largest Corporations, 1947–1967 (In Percent)

Year	100 largest corporations	200 largest corporations
1929	39.7	47.7
1947	39.3	47.2
1950	39.8	47.7
1955	44.2	53.1
1960	46.4	56.2
1965	46.5	56.6
1967	49.3	60.9

Source: Federal Trade Commission, *Economic Report on Corporate Mergers*, 1969, p. 173.

[3] A comprehensive recent analysis of the corporate merger movement is presented in Federal Trade Commission, *Economic Report on Corporate Mergers*, 1969, Part 8 A, Appendix to Part 8, Hearings before the Senate Subcommittee on Antitrust and Monopoly on *Economic Concentration*, 1969.

tions in 1967 controlled a slightly bigger percent of total manufacturing corporation assets than did the two hundred largest manufacturing corporations in 1947. The latter corporations, which held 47.2 percent of total manufacturing corporations' assets in 1947, increased this percent to 60.9 in 1968. By that year, the top eighty-seven manufacturing corporations, each with assets of over $1 billion, controlled 46 percent of the total assets of manufacturing corporations and received 50 percent of the net profits of these corporations. In 1968, 2,500 of the 194,593 manufacturing corporations controlled 86 percent of the assets of manufacturing corporations and earned 88 percent of the profits of all these corporations. In recent decades, furthermore, the downward movement among the top five hundred largest industrial corporations has declined, so that these corporations are now more likely than their predecessors to remain at the top.[4]

The increase in overall concentration of American industry has not been accompanied by a similar increase in market or individual industry concentration, which is measured by the percent of the industry's total sales accounted for by the four or eight largest firms in the industry. In general, industry concentration in the producer-goods industries, such as the gypsum, primary copper, explosives, and ball and bearing industries, has in recent decades fallen; at the same time, concentration has risen in the consumer-goods industries, such as the soap, cereal, automobile, and domestic laundry equipment industries. Whereas individual industry or market concentration has not significantly increased in recent decades, aggregate concentration has increased because of the many conglomerate mergers that have occurred since 1950. These mergers have extended the control of the two hundred largest industrial corporations over many different industries, without at the same time increasing the degree of concentration within many of these industries. One must conclude that a few hundred large industrial corporations now carry on the great bulk of the nation's manufacturing activities. In all likelihood, the nation's top five hundred corporations will hold or even expand their share of total industrial activity in the next several decades. These corporations in the industrial core of the nation's economy possess tremendous economic power, and can exercise a very considerable influence on the direction taken by the American economy.

The Structural Aspects of American Agriculture

The structure of the American economy today reflects the fact that agriculture is declining in a number of ways. This does not, however, mean that agricultural production has been falling off in recent decades. On the contrary, the index of farm output shows that in the past twenty years total farm output has increased 52 percent. But this increased output has been obtained since 1950 with 4 million fewer farmers and agricultural workers cultivating approximately the same amount of land. Table 3-3 reveals that in the years 1920–1973 farm population fell from 30.1 to 4.5 percent of total population; the number of farms declined 3.7 million; and agricultural employment was more than cut in half, falling from 10.3 million in 1930 to 3.4 million in 1973. Technological progress in agriculture, such as increased mechanization, improvements in plant and animal breeding, the use of antibiotics, and the increased use of improved fertilizers raised the index of output per man-hour in agriculture (1967=100) from 37.7 in 1950 to 133 in 1973.

---

[4] N. R. Collins and L. E. Preston, "The Size Structure of the Largest Industrial Firms," *American Economic Review*, Vol. LI, Dec. 1961, p. 1001.

Table 3-3
Selected Indicators of U.S. Agricultural Development, 1920-1973

Year	Farm population as percent of total population	Land area in farms (mil. acres)	Number of farms (in 1000s)	Average size of farms (in acres)	Agricultural employment (in 1000s)	Index of farm output (1967 = 100)	Index of farm output per man-hour (1967 = 100)
1920	30.1	956	6,518	148	—	—	—
1930	24.9	987	6,546	151	10,340	52	26.0
1940	23.2	1,065	6,103	174	9,540	60	27.0
1950	15.3	1,161	5,389	216	7,507	73	37.7
1959	9.4	1,123	3,711	303	5,836	88	61.5
1973	4.5	1,090	2,821	383	3,452	116	133.0

Source: *Statistical Abstract of the United States,* 1974.

The productivity of American agriculture has increased so rapidly that until the early 1970s a major problem was the overproduction of farm products. In recent years, recurring agricultural deficits in the Soviet Union, the People's Republic of China, and India, as well as the rising standards of living in the Soviet Union, Western Europe, and Japan, have combined to wipe out surpluses of wheat, corn, and soy beans in the United States. With world population continuing to increase and nations advancing to higher standards of living, agricultural surpluses in the United States could very well be much less of a problem in the future than in the 1950s and 1960s. A new era may be emerging, in which agricultural products, like oil and other raw materials, may be rather consistently in short supply. In any such era, the American farm sector would be very favorably situated since it is the source of large supplies of agricultural products, much of which are exported.

Although the private owner-operated farm continues to dominate American agriculture, strong forces are at work to make it difficult for the small farmer to remain in business. Increasingly, a limited number of large farms is producing the bulk of farm output. According to the most recent statistics (1969), 2.2 percent of the nation's farms, each having two thousand or more acres, hold 42.8 percent of all farm land. Only 13.4 percent of all farms account for 68.3 percent of total farm land owned. The distribution of farm sales reveals the same situation. In 1969, approximately 12.8 percent of the farms, each having gross sales of $40,000 or more per year, accounted for 57.1 percent of total farm sales. Approximately 32 percent of all farms accounted for 78 percent of total farm sales.

Not only is a growing number of large farms accounting for the bulk of farm production and sales, but also corporate farming is making significant inroads into small-scale private farming. With respect to a number of products, farming is rapidly duplicating the industrial system as it becomes a part of an integrated production-market system. Large food processing corporations, industrial conglomerates, and giant grocery chains in certain agricultural lines control everything from the production of the crop to the selling of the final product; or they are contracting with small-scale private producers for their agricultural output, as in the case of vegetable, fruit, and poultry producers. For those farmers who sell their entire output to one processor, the fate of many chicken farmers who have become "poultry peons" bodes ill for their future. While corporate farms now account for only 7 percent of total food production, they dominate the markets for poultry, fruits, vegetables, and feedlot cattle. Individual farmers are now dominant only in the production of corn, wheat, and other grains, but even in these areas the need exists for a large investment in land, buildings, and farm equipment that is beyond the reach of the small farmer.

The growth of large-scale business, the spread of labor unionism, and the decline of agriculture since 1918 have led to efforts to strengthen the economic position of the agricultural sector. Some progress has been made in the area of cooperative action. In 1915, the 5,149 agricultural marketing cooperatives had a membership of only 592,000. By 1971, 5,263 cooperatives had increased their membership to 3,130,000, with annual sales of over $16 billion. The success of the cooperative movement, however, has been restricted to only a small area of the nation's agricultural sector. The bulk of the sales of producers' cooperatives are made by dairy, livestock, fruit, and vegetable cooperatives. The great majority of farmers who produce such basic crops as wheat, corn, and cotton have had no great success with producers' cooperatives as a device by means of which their market position could be strengthened. They have been forced, therefore, to turn to politics as a means of improving their economic position.

The first step towards a strong political position capable of influencing the Congress to provide aid to agriculture was made with the enlargement of the membership of the three major farm organizations: the National Grange, the American Farm Bureau Federation, and the National Farmers' Union. Much of the economic and political power of American agriculture stems today from these three farm organizations, which in 1971 had a combined membership totalling 3,132,117 and equal to one-third of all the nation's farm population. This organized one-third has succeeded in offsetting to some extent the economic power of both big business and organized labor. Since farmers have not been able to strengthen their economic position satisfactorily by using their own devices, they have turned to the Congress for parity price programs, crop controls, commodity loans, soil bank programs, and other arrangements designed to improve farm prices and incomes.

Labor and the Structure of American Capitalism

The structure of employment in the United States has undergone major changes since the end of the Second World War as a consequence of technological progress, the automation of industry, and the shift from a mass consumption economy to a service economy. The occupational structure of the nation's work force has been greatly changed in the past two decades, as is revealed by the occupation statistics presented in Table 3–4. White-collar occupations have increased in importance as manual occupations have declined. The employment of professional, technical, clerical, service, and sales workers increased 116 percent between 1950 and 1974; at the same time, the employment of factory operatives and unskilled laborers increased only 14 percent. The contrast between the employment of professional and technical workers and unskilled laborers in 1950 and 1974 is striking. The number of professional and technical workers almost trebled in those two decades, increasing from 4.5 to 12.5 million, while the number of unskilled

Table 3-4
Employed Persons by Occupations in the United States, 1950 and 1974

Occupations	1950	1974	Percent increase or decrease in 1974 over 1950
White-collar workers	22,373,000	41,590,000	+86
Professional and technical workers	4,490,000	12,446,000	+148
Blue-collar workers	23,336,000	29,182,000	+25
Operatives	12,146,000	13,749,000	+14
Laborers	3,520,000	4,072,000	+16
Service workers	6,535,000	11,353,000	+74
Farm workers	7,408,000	3,066,000	−59

Source: *Statistical Abstract of the United States*, 1974, p. 350.

workers increased only 16 percent in the same period.

There has been a strong trend away from jobs requiring heavy, unskilled labor towards those that require considerable education and training. The expanding occupational groups have been those in which employment has been relatively stable through recessions. Since unemployment and occupation are closely related, workers in skilled occupations have relatively lower unemployment rates than workers in unskilled activities. In 1974, married men had an unemployment rate of only 2.7 percent, as compared with a rate of 5.6 percent for all workers. In the same year, workers of both sexes from sixteen to nineteen years of age had an unemployment rate of 16 percent, whereas men and women over twenty years had unemployment rates of 3.8 and 5.5 percent, respectively. The main burden of unemployment falls on young and unskilled workers and on the nonwhite workers, whose unemployment rate in 1974 was twice that of white workers (5 percent).

One of the most striking structural changes in the American economy since 1929 has been the expansion of trade union membership. In 1929, only about 10 percent of the nation's wage earners belonged to labor unions, whereas today one-third of all wage and salary workers are union members. With the growth of industrial unionism and the spread of union membership after 1936, the large labor union came to be the key institution in the world of labor. Today, three unions—the teamsters', automobile workers', and steel workers' unions—have each a membership of more than one million. Many of the nation's unions are gathered into two large organizations, the American Federation of Labor and the Congress of Industrial Organizations, which have been united since 1955, and now act as the spokesman for 82 percent of all union members.

It is not surprising that the post–World War II American economy has been described as a *laboristic* economy.[5] It is laboristic, not in the sense that organized labor directs the nation's economy, but rather in the sense that neither business nor the government can any longer ignore the economic and political power of organized labor in making their economic decisions. In 1972, the nation's 177 trade unions

[5] Sumner Slichter, *The American Economy, Its Problems and Prospects*, New York: Alfred A. Knopf, 1950, pp. 7-13.

had a total membership of 20.8 million. This means that approximately one out of every four members of the nation's total civilian labor force (which includes employers as well as workers) is a member of a trade union. The big growth in union membership took place between 1929 and 1945. Whereas in 1933, union membership included only 5.2 percent of the total civilian labor force, by 1947, union membership covered 23.9 percent of this force. Since 1947, there has not been much change in the ratio of organized to unorganized workers; union membership appears to have become stabilized at a little less than one-quarter of the nation's total civilian labor force. With more workers going into the white-collar occupations, which are difficult to unionize, the prospects for a further expansion of union membership are not good.

Concentration of membership in a few large unions has for many years been an important feature of the American labor movement. In 1972, six of the largest unions, out of a total of 177 unions, accounted for 34 percent of total union membership, while the fifteen largest unions enrolled 56 percent of all union members. The large unions, such as the automobile and steel workers' unions, play a major role in determining the nation's wage pattern. In their collective bargaining activities, these large unions establish patterns of wage increases that become guidelines for the smaller unions in their wage negotiations. Also, innovations such as the guaranteed annual wage, the tying of wage increases to improvements in productivity and to the changes in the cost of living, and joint consultation on such matters as the introduction of new equipment have come mainly from the large unions.

While the trade unions are not strengthening their hold on the total civilian labor force, they are undergoing a process of consolidation within their own ranks. The appearance of the conglomerate corporation in industry since 1950 has stimulated a corresponding development in the union world. When the American Federation of Labor and the Congress of Industrial Organizations were merged in 1955, it was then hoped that the 135 national unions affiliated with the two groups could be reduced to about 50. By 1972, the AFL-CIO still had 116 member unions. Among these unions, however, a tendency towards conglomeration has recently developed. The steel workers have now reached a dominant position in all the basic metals industries since they merged with the mine, mill, and smelter workers. Planned mergers among unions of the chemical workers open the door to further mergers with the steel workers' union, which already has a sizable chemical-worker membership. Other proposed mergers, such as the one between the communications workers, the postal workers, and the letter carriers, point in the direction of a possible comprehensive conglomerate "communications union," which would include all craftsmen, technicians, and workers doing similar or related work in the telephone, telegraph, broadcasting, and newspaper industries. The proposed merger of the teamsters', brewery workers', and dock workers' unions could also give rise to a conglomerate transportation workers' union.

Such actual and proposed trade union mergers under unified leadership seek economy in administration and a concentration of strength that would enable the unions to cope with large conglomerate industrial corporations on more nearly equal terms. As in the United Kingdom, in the United States strong trends towards the modernization of the union movement and towards the combining of existing unions may be observed. If these trends go far enough, the union structure in the United States could eventually duplicate that of Germany, Sweden, and Norway, where a small number of large unions dominate the labor world. Such a development could prepare the way in the United States for the centralized collective bargaining which has been so successfully carried on in the Scandinavian countries.

Government and the Structure of the American Economy

Another significant change in the structure of the American economy is the expansion of the federal, state, and local governments as factors in the nation's economic life. Up to 1929, the role of government in the United States was kept restricted by the general acceptance of the laissez-faire approach in the fields of both economics and politics. With the rise of the welfare state after 1929, however, the role of government has been very considerably increased, and the number of government units and of their employees has risen rapidly. In 1929, total federal, state, and local government employment accounted for 9.8 percent of the total nonagricultural wage and salary workers. By 1975, this employment absorbed 14.8 million workers, or 19 percent of the total wage and salary workers. Today, the 59,519 federal, state, and local government units constitute one of the nation's major sources of employment. These units together hire more workers than does any other economic activity except manufacturing and wholesale and retail trade.

Other measures of the economic significance of the 59,519 government units are the contributions of these units to the national income and the portion of GNP that is annually purchased by these government units. Table 3–5 indicates that in the forty–four-year period, 1929–1973, the percentage contribution of the federal, state, and local governments to total national income more than doubled. This contribution, which was 5.8 percent of total national income in 1929, rose to 15.5 percent in 1973. The federal, state, and local governments have become increasingly important as consumers of goods and services since 1929. In that year, these governments purchased a little more than one-tenth of the Gross National Product, but by 1975 they were taking up more than one-fifth of this product. When the local, state, and central governments of a country employ 19 percent of its nonagricultural workers, account for 15 percent of its national income, and purchase 22 percent of its GNP, obviously these governments are in a strategic position to influence the level and direction of the country's economic activities.

In the past thirty years, the federal government has become an especially important factor in the nation's economic life. In 1929, the federal government employed only a little more than a half-million workers, but by 1974 the number of such workers had increased to close to 2.8 million. The expansion of the welfare state and the new international position of the United States have placed a heavy burden on the federal government. In coping with this burden, the federal government has necessarily entered the realm of big enterprise. Many factors have contributed to the growing importance of the government sector of the American and Western European economies.[6] With the industrialization and urbanization of the United States came many new problems, such as the regulation of big business, the improvement of education and health services, the preservation of natural resources, environmental protection, and urban renewal.

Since 1945, the disturbed international situation, the new concern with environmental protection, the need for new collective services, and the demands of the space age

[6] Solomon Fabricant, "Factors Affecting the Trend of Government Activity," *The Trend of Government Activity in the United States since 1900*, New York: National Bureau of Economic Research, 1953, pp. 140–155.

Table 3–5
Sources of U.S. National Income, 1929 and 1973

Sectors	1929 National income		1973 National income	
	In billions of current dollars	In percent	In billions of current dollars	In percent
Government	5.1	5.8	162.9	15.5
Agriculture	8.1	9.2	37.8	3.6
Manufacturing	21.9	24.9	291.9	27.7
Other nonfarm private activities	52.7	60.1	561.7	53.2
Total national income	87.8	100.0	1,054.3	100.0

Sources: *U.S. Income and Output,* 1958; and *Statistical Abstract of the United States,* 1974.

have resulted in a further enlargement of the functions of government. In 1965, the Department of Housing and Urban Development was established and was followed by the Department of Transportation in 1967. Recently, there has been a growing public interest in the establishment of a Department of Consumer Affairs. It appears that the potential for government expansion is far from being exhausted. Many indications point to the probability of a further development of both government structure and functions in the coming decades.

One should note that no part of the private economic system is today responsible for the general functioning of the total economy. Private business enterprises, labor unions, farmers' organizations, and trade associations are all concerned with the problems of some particular industry, region, or sector of the economy. Organized business is out for larger profits, organized labor for better wages, and organized agriculture for higher farm prices and incomes. While all economic interest groups have some legitimate concern with profits, wages, or prices, not all groups can always make satisfactory evaluations of their own economic interests in relation to the national economic interest. They can aid the government in making such evaluations, but they themselves lack the overall view that is so essential for a satisfactory determination of what is in the national interest. This being the case, the federal government must carry the main burden of expressing what is in the national interest and of determining when sectional and national interests are incompatible.

In the simple competitive economy of the nineteenth century, dispersion of economic interests presented no special problems, since in seeking its own interest each business unit tended to promote the general economic welfare. No one gave much attention to the level and direction of the nation's economic activity, for the operations of the competitive market mechanism were supposed to take care of these matters. With the shift to a much more complicated economy after 1875, it soon appeared that if the economy was to be efficiently operated, the general level and direction of economic activity could not be left entirely to the free play of private market forces. Responsibility has fallen to a large extent on the federal government. Besides being an arbiter among conflicting economic units, the federal government now also acts as an agent to promote the general health of the nation's economy. Its responsibility is to "promote high levels of production and employment . . . to contribute toward achieving an expanding and widely-shared national income . . . and to facilitate adjustments necessary in a dynamic economy."[7]

The Evolution of the Capitalist Economic System

The capitalist system has passed through a long period of economic development during which the structure and functioning of this type of economic system have undergone substantial change. The era of competitive capitalism was ushered in by the industrial revolution of the late eighteenth and early nineteenth centuries. It reached the pinnacle of its development in the half century from 1825 to 1875 when industry was small-scale, producers were numerous, workers took little collective action, and consumers exercised considerable sovereignty in the market place. The era of competitive capitalism was followed by an era of large-scale or monopoly capitalism in the years 1875–1929. In this period, large-scale industry became well established in such key industries as the steel, oil, chemical, electrical, and automobile industries. Collective action by both workers and farmers became widespread, and consumers lost much of their market sovereignty.

The era of large-scale or monopoly capitalism was followed by the period of welfare capitalism in the 1930s and 1940s. The Great Depression, which began in 1929, marked the decline of laissez faire in the nation's economic affairs and the rise of interventionism. In the United States as well as in the major Western European countries, the government was no longer willing to allow market forces to dictate largely the levels of employment, production, and income as the economy passed through the various phases of the business cycle. Instead, governments in the major industrial countries adopted a new activist role in which they accepted the responsibility of providing for a satisfactory level of employment and general economic welfare.

Since the end of the Second World War, the welfare capitalism of the 1930s and 1940s has been transformed into regulated or directed capitalism. In the United States, the United Kingdom, France, and other capitalist countries, governments have found it necessary to intervene in economic affairs on an increasingly wider front. In all these countries, the government has established special economic councils or agencies; these bodies analyze economic trends and recommend economic policies for the achievement of full employment and sustained economic growth with as little inflation as possible. The form of regulated capitalism in the post–World War II period has varied widely among the Western industrialized nations. In the United States, the United Kingdom, West Germany, and Canada, regulated capitalism has not involved more than a limited degree of intervention. By contrast, in France, Belgium, the Netherlands, and Japan, intervention has been carried to the point where it can be described as national programming or planning. Thus the degree of intervention varies widely, from the limited interventionism of the United States to the indicative national planning of France.

The American Economy, 1961–1965

The recent development of American capitalism can be divided into four periods: 1961–1965, 1966–1968, 1969–1973, and since 1973. During the first period, which started with the recession of 1960–1961, the main concern was to put the economy back on a growth path, where the full potential of the economic system could be realized. In the preceding eight

[7] *Economic Report of the President,* 1957, p. iii.

years of the Eisenhower Administration, prices had been kept stable, but only at the cost of low economic growth and high unemployment. After 1960, the Kennedy Administration turned to the task of trying to achieve high economic growth with low unemployment and stable prices. The new economic policy approach was based on what was described as *gap economics*. This economics was concerned with raising the actual Gross National Product up to the level of the nation's potential GNP, which the administration defined as "the volume of goods and services that the economy would ordinarily produce at the interim target unemployment rate of 4 percent."[8]

In 1961, the disparity between the nation's actual and potential Gross National Product amounted to $50 billion. To eliminate this gap a sustained annual economic growth rate of around 4 percent was needed. This would take up the slack in the economy by reducing unemployment and raising industry's capacity utilization rate to an optimal level. To achieve this goal, stimulative fiscal and monetary policies were adopted. Tax increases were avoided, budgetary deficits were allowed to develop, and government purchases of goods and services were increased. On the monetary front, the Federal Reserve Board pursued an antirecession policy; this included providing additional bank reserves through the purchase of government securities and increasing the money supply in step with the increase in GNP. By 1965, the gap between actual and potential GNP had been reduced to $10 billion, and the unemployment rate, which had been 6.7 percent in 1961, fell to 4.25 by the end of 1965. In that year, the Johnson Administration looked forward to developing a stabilization program that would reduce the gap in GNP to zero and the annual unemployment rate to 4 percent.

The post-1961 recovery was accompanied by a new approach to fiscal policy that was designed to provide vigorous economic expansion. This new approach was part of the activist position that the Kennedy and Johnson administrations adopted after 1961. In the past, extensive reliance had been placed on built-in or automatic fiscal stabilizers to strengthen the economy's resistance to recession. These stabilizers include government purchases, transfer payments in the form of unemployment insurance benefits, and reduced tax collections as corporate profits and private incomes, including wages, decline. As recession develops, these built-in stabilizers are set in motion by maintaining or expanding government purchases, increasing unemployment benefit payments, and reducing tax collections from corporations and individuals. In this way, the federal tax-transfer system automatically draws less purchasing power out of the economy's private sector than is drawn out at higher levels of production and employment.

In the 1960–1961 recession, corporate-profits tax liabilities fell $2 billion, while unemployment benefits payments increased at the annual rate of $1.4 billion, and government purchases of goods and services rose by $8 billion. These automatic stabilizers, however, were not large enough to prevent a serious recession from developing in 1960–1961. What was needed was more emphasis on discretionary action with regard to tax cuts and increased government expenditures. After 1961, the federal government gave a larger place to discretionary fiscal action in its new activist antirecession approach.

The new post-1960 fiscal policy accepted budgetary deficits as long as the economy suffered from excessive slack and inadequate

---

[8] *Economic Report of the President*, 1966, p. 40. For a survey of the economic developments of the 1960s, see O. Eckstein, "Economic Policy in the United States," in E. S. Kirschen and Associates, *Economic Policy in Our Time*, Vol. II, Chicago: Rand McNally, 1964, pp. 1–88; and Andrew Shonfield, *Modern Capitalism*, Ch. XIV, "United States Policy in the 1960s," New York: Oxford University Press, 1965, pp. 330–357.

private demand. The budgetary surplus of $3.5 billion in 1960 was converted into a budgetary deficit of $3.8 billion in 1961. The new economic game plan called for budgetary deficits every year until full employment was reached. In 1961-1964, budgetary deficits resulted from various fiscal measures that kept federal government revenues below government expenditures. In 1962 private business was stimulated by tax cuts which resulted from the 8 percent investment tax credit and from the use of more liberal depreciation rules. At the same time, the economy was stimulated by increases in government purchases, larger social security benefits, and extended unemployment insurance benefit payments.

In the years 1961-1965, federal, state, and local government purchases increased in constant dollars by 21 percent. Recovery from the recession of 1960-1961 was delayed, however, by the small budgetary surplus of $700 million in 1963 which occurred because the Congress had delayed providing for a reduction in income taxes. To avoid this problem, the president in 1962 had requested stand-by authority to make prompt income-tax reductions, but the Congress refused to provide this flexibility in the nation's tax system. Eventually, however, the Congress came around to the administration's position with regard to the need for reductions in income taxes; and in 1964 and 1965 recovery was further stimulated when both personal and corporate income taxes were reduced.

In the period 1961-1964, demand management was carried out through the use of both fiscal policy and monetary policy. The Kennedy Administration started in 1961 with a policy of monetary ease, which was to continue as long as the economy remained below the full employment level. Investment in plant and equipment and in residential construction was stimulated by keeping long-term interest rates low. Both the Federal Reserve Board and the Treasury followed a program of federal debt management that kept long-term interest rates low to stimulate domestic investment and short-term rates high enough to keep short-term capital from moving to other countries.

Although there was considerable slack and excessive unemployment in the years 1961-1963, and although the federal government looked forward to removing this slack, there was an ever-present fear of the return of inflationary pressures as the economy rose to higher levels of employment and production. During the recession of 1958-1959, wage rates and prices in large-scale industries had continued to rise in spite of the recessionary condition of the economy. In the two recession years of 1958 and 1959, consumer prices had annually increased almost 2 percent, while average hourly earnings in durable-goods manufacturing had increased approximately 4 percent. Both the large corporate enterprises and the large labor unions had shown that they had the necessary market power to raise prices and wage rates even in the face of adverse general economic conditions in the nation.

As the economy recovered after 1961, opportunities would again arise for large business enterprises and labor unions to use their market power to achieve inflationary wage and price increases. In September 1961, the president called for restraint on the part of the major steel companies and the steel workers' union in making price and wage adjustments. Price and wage restraint in the steel industry was secured only with the aid of considerable ad hoc "jawboning" on the part of the president. Dissatisfaction with this jawboning approach to securing wage and price restraint led to the establishment of voluntary wage and price guidelines in early 1962.

Anticipating the development of inflationary pressures in the full employment economy once it was achieved, the Kennedy Administration prepared to meet the inflation problem by announcing wage and price guideposts in January 1962. These guideposts were designed to secure the cooperation of business and organized labor in a program to prevent inflationary wage and price increases. The wage guidepost recommended that wage-rate increases should be tied to improvements in output per man-hour. In general, this guidepost called for increases in average wage rates equal to the average increase in output per man-hour for the whole private economy. In stationary or declining industries, where the annual improvement in productivity was less than the average national productivity improvement, prices would be raised. But in progressive, expanding industries, where the annual improvement in output per man-hour was more than the average national improvement, prices would be lowered. Price increases and decreases would tend to cancel each other and would leave the general price level relatively stable. When the guideposts were announced in 1962, the amount that wage rates on the average were to be allowed to increase annually was 3.2 percent, which was equal to the average annual national productivity improvement in the five-year period 1957–1961.[9] No allowance was made, however, for any increase in the cost of living. During the years 1960–1964 consumer prices were quite stable, increasing only a little more than 1 percent a year. In the same period, average wage rates increased a little more than 3 percent a year. Since there was still considerable slack in the economy and the unemployment rate remained above 5

[9] This guideline changed whenever the average annual national productivity improvement in any five-year period changed. For a discussion of the determination of the annual wage guideline, see *Economic Report of the President,* 1965, p. 108, and also the same report for 1966, p. 92. An analysis of American wage-price policy is presented in David C. Smith, *Incomes Policies,* Ch. 4, "The United States Guideposts for Wages and Prices," Economic Council of Canada, Ottawa, 1966, pp. 73–93; and John Sheahan, *The Wage-Price Guideposts,* The Brookings Institution, Washington, D.C., 1967, pp. 33–78.

percent, organized labor did not challenge the wage-price guideposts with the threat of strikes to enforce larger wage demands.

The wage and price guidelines announced in early 1962 were not extensively used before 1965 because the economy remained low pressure, with considerable unused industrial capacity and a high rate of unemployment. As the economic indicators in Table 3-6 indicate, both wholesale and consumer prices were quite stable during the years 1960–1964. Unemployment was high during all these years, never falling below 5 percent per annum. The industrial production capacity utilization rate (82.3 percent average for the years 1960–1965) remained well below the 92 percent rate; this rate is regarded by the business community as a normal or full-employment rate of capacity utilization. In these circumstances, neither labor nor management was inclined to challenge the government's wage and price guidelines. Table 3-6 shows that real hourly earnings in manufacturing rose much less than the improvement in output per man-hour in manufacturing. Whereas output per man-hour in the years 1960–1965 increased on the average 4.3 percent, real hourly earnings increased on the average only 1.6 percent.

By the end of 1965, the gap between the actual and the potential Gross National Product was closed, and the economy was approaching the interim full employment rate of 4 percent. During the period 1961–1965, the annual economic growth rate was close to 5 percent; the unemployment rate was reduced from 6.7 to 4.5 percent; and the consumer price index increased annually only 1.3 percent. In manufacturing, unit labor costs fell because wage rates rose less rapidly than output per man-hour. Wholesale prices remained almost unchanged in the five years 1961–1965. These conditions were favorable to the expansion of American exports, which were large enough to produce very sizable surpluses in the nation's international account during the years 1961–1965.

Table 3-6
Selected U.S. Economic Indicators, 1960-1965

	Gross National Product (in billions of 1958 dollars)	Consumer price index (1967 = 100)	Wholesale price index (1967 = 100)	Average hourly earnings in manufacturing (in $'s)	Output per man-hour in manufacturing (1967 = 100)	Unemployment rate (in percent)	Industrial production capacity utilization rate (in percent)
1960	487.7	88.7	94.9	2.26	79.9	5.5	80.1
1961	497.2	89.6	94.5	2.32	81.8	6.7	77.6
1962	529.8	90.6	94.8	2.39	86.6	5.5	81.4
1963	551.0	91.7	94.5	2.46	90.1	5.7	83.0
1964	581.1	92.4	94.7	2.53	94.5	5.2	85.5
1965	617.8	94.5	96.6	2.61	98.3	4.5	89.0
Annual average increase 1960-1965	4.8%	1.3%	0.4%	2.9%	4.3%	5.5%[1]	82.3%[1]

[1] Annual average, 1960-1965.

Source: *Economic Report of the President,* 1972.

Around 1965, the American economy had been transformed from a low-pressure into a high-pressure economy with an entirely new set of economic problems. The economic statistics in Table 3-6 reveal that average hourly earnings in manufacturing and both retail and wholesale prices began to move up rapidly in 1965. In that year, a number of labor unions secured wage rate increases much above the government's wage guideline of 3.6 percent. These unions insisted on wage increases that covered both annual productivity improvement and an adjustment for the rise in the cost of living; these increases therefore exceeded the official wage guideline. By 1965, the federal government had succeeded in removing the gap between the actual and the potential Gross National Product, but only at the cost of developing an inflationary high-pressure economy. If the post–World War II pattern of economic fluctuations had been extended to the first half of the 1960s, a recession would probably have developed by 1965 or 1966. This pattern did not prevail, however, and recession was not to come until eight years after the 1960-1961 recession.

While very considerable progress was made in the years 1961–1965 in achieving high levels of production, three main deficiencies in the economic game plan for this period nevertheless appeared. The first was related to the failure to develop the flexibility of fiscal policy needed to cope with major economic problems. Changes in tax rates should have been made with less delay, and changes in government expenditures would have been more effective had there been more adequate advance planning of public capital improvement projects. The Commission on Money and Credit, established by the Committee for Economic Development, had recommended in 1961 that the president be given stand-by authority to make prompt changes in tax rates and in capital improvement expenditures as required by changing economic circumstances.[10] Congress, however, failed to follow these suggestions for the improvement in the use of fiscal policies. The second deficiency in policy making was the failure to develop a satisfactory wage-price or incomes policy. The federal government did not succeed in getting the support of business and organized labor for the new wage-price guidelines adopted in early 1962. Instead of attempting to improve upon these guidelines, the government allowed them to fall into disuse after 1965. This was an unfortunate development, since it is now widely conceded that an incomes policy forms a necessary part of the economic policy mix required for the successful guidance of an advanced industrial economy.

The third deficiency in the economic policy making of the period 1961–1965 was the failure to achieve an equilibrium in the nation's external accounts. While considerable progress was made in securing a favorable balance in the current international account, this balance was not large enough to provide for an equilibrium in both the current and capital accounts. Not enough attention was paid by the government in 1961–1965 to the need for establishing realistic exchange rates that would reflect the changes in the private and government transactions between the United States and other countries. Vigorous and effective action on the international front was delayed until the second half of 1971, when a realignment of foreign exchange rates was secured.

The High-Pressure Economy, 1966–1968

The economic upturn that occurred in 1965 heralded the beginning of a three-year period in which the economy was to become overheated and to experience an inflationary development; this eventually led to the price and wage explosions of 1968 and 1969. Apart from a minor setback in the first half of 1967, the period 1965–1968 meant high economic growth, low unemployment, and escalating prices and wage rates. In the second half of 1965, the demand management program called for a reversal of the stimulative fiscal and monetary policies of the previous four years. When government expenditures increased after mid-1965, as a result of the Great Society program and the stepped-up Vietnam military program, total demand became excessive, and the federal government initiated a number of restrictive fiscal measures. Payroll taxes were increased, automobile and telephone excise taxes were extended at their expiration dates, and the investment tax credit and accelerated depreciation rules were suspended. The government proposed in 1967 to supplement these restrictive fiscal measures with a 6 percent surcharge on personal and corporate income taxes, but the Congress failed to act on the presidential recommendation.

The massive budgetary deficit of $25 billion that was incurred in fiscal 1968 caused the Congress to change its position and to approve a 10 percent surcharge on income taxes in 1968. The long delay in increasing income taxes had the unfortunate consequence of placing an excessively heavy burden on monetary policy as a means of curbing the economy's strong inflationary pressures. The Federal Reserve Board began its restrictive monetary policy in late 1965, when the rediscount rate was raised from 4 to 4.5 percent. Later, the supply of credit was further restricted by reducing bank reserves through open-market operations and by raising the reserve requirements on time deposits from 4 to 6 percent. Member banks were strongly advised to use restraint in making loans to industry. The money supply, however, was allowed to increase in the years 1965–1968 at the same

[10] The Commission on Money and Credit, *Money and Credit, Their Influence on Jobs, Prices, and Growth*, Englewood Cliffs, N.J.: Prentice-Hall, 1961, p. 137.

rate at which the Gross National Product grew.

Although the Federal Reserve Board followed a program of credit restriction from 1965 to 1968, the demand for credit continued very strong, even though interest rates rose to their highest level in over a century. The high interest rates and the tight credit situation had uneven effects on the nation's economy. Credit was still available to large private enterprises that could afford to pay the high interest charges, but it was denied to those small businesses, home builders, and local governments that were unable to absorb high interest costs. Residential construction measured in 1958 dollars fell from $24.2 billion in 1964 to $20.4 billion in 1967. Projects high on the list of social need, such as public housing, school and hospital construction, mass transportation, and improved sewage disposal, were forced to bear much of the burden of credit restriction and countercyclical adjustment; at the same time, private business investment and personal consumption remained at high levels.

With fiscal policy insufficiently restrictive in the years 1965–1968, monetary policy, even though restrictive, was not able to prevent the serious overheating of the nation's economy. Table 3–7 shows that during 1965–1968 consumer prices annually increased on the average 3.3 percent, while average hourly earnings in manufacturing increased 4.9 percent per annum. With unemployment at a very low level, organized labor in manufacturing was in a strong position to bargain for large wage-rate increases. These increases (4.9 percent) were quite close to the annual improvement in output per man-hour (2.1 percent) plus the increase in the consumer price index (3.3 percent). Wage rates rose much faster than output per man-hour, until labor costs increased and were passed on to consumers in the form of higher prices. In the high pressure economy of these years, the unemployment rate fell from 4.5 percent in 1965 to 3.6 percent in 1968.

In the opinion of many economists, the 3.6 unemployment rate was well below the critical level at which the wage-price mechanism becomes explosive.[11] According to this interpretation, whenever the annual rate of unemployment falls below 4 to 4.5 percent in the mature American economy, the wage-price spiral accelerates and inflation becomes so cumulative that it eventually gives rise to an explosive situation; this occurred in 1968 when consumer prices increased 4.2 percent and average hourly earnings in manufacturing increased 6.4 percent.[12] At levels of unemployment above 4 to 4.5 percent, it is possible to make a tradeoff between unemployment and inflation. Less unemployment may be secured at the cost of more inflation, and more unemployment means less inflation. Below 4 to 4.5 percent unemployment, when an inflationary psychology has gripped the economy, the situation is quite different. The inflationary psychology is deeply embedded in the business system and cumulative inflationary expectations are very strong. These expectations can be eliminated by very restrictive fiscal and monetary policies that push the unemployment rate well above the 4 percent level. Or these expectations can be curbed by a temporary wage-price freeze, such as was adopted in August 1971, to break the cycle of inflationary expectations.

Clearly, the Johnson Administration was

[11] Otto Eckstein and Roger Brinner come to this conclusion in their study of the inflation process in the United States in the period 1965-1971. Their views on this matter are explained in Joint Economic Committee, *The Inflation Process in the United States*, Joint Committee Print, Feb. 22, 1971. See also James Tobin, "Inflation and Unemployment," *American Economic Review*, March 1972, pp. 1–18.

[12] In other words, the long-run Phillips curve becomes vertical below the 4 percent rate of unemployment; there is then no longer any tradeoff between unemployment and inflation. Above 4 percent, the Phillips curve slopes to the right and a tradeoff is possible between unemployment and inflation. For a discussion of this point, see *The Inflation Process in the United States*, pp. 33–34.

Table 3-7
Selected U.S. Economic Indicators, 1965-1968

	Gross National Product (in billions of 1958 dollars)	Consumer price index (1967 = 100)	Wholesale price index (1967 = 100)	Average hourly earnings in manu- facturing (in $'s)	Output per man-hour in manu- facturing (1967 = 100)	Industrial production capacity utilization (in per- cent)	Unemploy- ment rate (in percent)
1965	617.8	94.5	96.6	2.61	98.3	89.0	4.5
1966	658.1	97.2	99.8	2.72	99.9	91.9	3.8
1967	675.2	100.0	100.0	2.83	100.0	87.9	3.8
1968	706.6	104.2	102.5	3.01	104.7	87.7	3.6
Annual average increase 1965-1968	4.6%	3.3%	2.0%	4.9%	2.1%	89.2%[1]	3.7%[1]

[1] Annual average, 1966-1968.

Source: *Economic Report of the President*, 1972.

unable to develop an economic policy mix that would enable it to cope successfully with the problems that came after 1965. The ad- ministration was successful in achieving high levels of production and employment but not on a sustainable basis. The failure of the fed- eral government's economic program in the years 1965-1968 was basically the result of placing excessive demands upon the nation's expanding output of goods and services.[13] This output was not large enough to support all the programs of the Great Society as well as the military program in Southeast Asia.

The resulting overheating of the nation's economy could have been avoided by restric- tive economic policies that would have curbed both private consumption and invest- ment, as public consumption and investment expenditures for the Great Society and for the military program expanded. The federal gov- ernment, however, was not prepared to adopt the necessary restrictive fiscal and monetary policies in 1967 and 1968. In its annual re- view of economic policy developments in the United States for 1967, the Organisation for Economic Co-operation and Development pointed out that "It may, as in most countries, still be easier [in the United States] to change policy in a stimulative than a restrictive direc- tion, and fiscal decisions can still take more time than is appropriate for modern de- mand-management."[14] To cope with this problem the OECD recommended that seri- ous consideration should be given to the pro- vision of more discretionary power for the president with regard to tax changes and other fiscal policy decisions.

[13] What caused the growing inflation of 1966-1968 was excess demand. For an analysis of inflation in this period, see Robert J. Gordon, "Inflation in Re- cession and Recovery," *Brookings Papers on Eco- nomic Activity*, Washington, D.C., 1971, pp. 105-144.

[14] Organisation for Economic Co-operation and De- velopment, *OECD Surveys, United States*, Dec. 1967, p. 10.

Economic Developments in the United States, 1969–1973

In 1969, the Nixon Administration sought to curb the strong inflationary forces that had developed in the previous four years by "fine tuning" the nation's economic system. An anti-inflationary program was designed to curb the economy's strong inflationary tendencies without at the same time plunging the nation into a recession. In order to achieve this goal, the Nixon Administration felt it necessary to remove some of the heavy pressures of demand coming from both the private and public sectors. It was realized that while some increase in unemployment would have to be accepted, in a program of fine tuning, the unemployment rate should not be allowed to rise above a socially acceptable level. The feeling was that the low unemployment rate of 3.1 percent of December 1968 could be maintained only with serious inflation. The Nixon Administration did not specify the unemployment rate that would be an acceptable national goal and that could be maintained without serious inflation. The administration was prepared to accept a limited gap between the actual and the potential Gross National Product, because this gap was expected to reduce the overheating of the economy and to make it possible to eliminate the inflationary psychology that had gripped the nation since 1965.

In early 1970, the Council of Economic Advisers explained that "Such a gap places a downward pressure on the rate of inflation. Businesses find themselves selling in markets less receptive to price increases. This forces greater resistance to cost increases, including wage increases."[15] It was hoped that restrictive fiscal and monetary policies would curb inflation, lower unit labor costs, break the wage-price spiral and eventually create a balanced economy that would be sustainable in the long run. The new administration expected in the future to avoid the stop-go economic policies of the prior administrations that had been accompanied by recurring periods of boom and subsequent recession. In place of these stop-go economic policies, the Nixon Administration proposed "to introduce an era of steadiness in policy that could yield long-run stability in the economy."

The new Nixon economic game plan for 1969 and 1970 based its fine tuning of the economic system primarily on the use of restrictive fiscal and monetary policies. General rather than selective fiscal and monetary policies were employed, and wage-price controls were avoided. In 1969 and 1970, the Congress again imposed a ceiling on total federal government expenditures; the surcharge on personal and corporate income tax rates was preserved but lowered from 10 to 5 percent; the investment tax credit was abandoned; government purchases were reduced; and a surplus was secured in the federal fiscal budget. At the same time, the availability of credit was considerably curtailed. The Federal Reserve Board raised the rediscount rate from 5½ to 6 percent, curtailed the supply of bank reserves through open market operations, and raised the reserve requirements for demand deposits; in these ways it severely restricted the supply of money, which in the second half of 1970 grew only at an annual rate of less than 1 percent.

Unfortunately, these restrictive fiscal and monetary policies had a much stronger deflationary impact on the economic system than had been expected by the proponents of economic fine tuning. As Table 3–8 shows, the nation's real product flow was severely restricted: Gross National Product measured in constant dollars fell in 1970 below what it had

[15] *Economic Report of the President*, 1970, p. 58. See also "The 1971 Report of the President's Council of Economic Advisers," *American Economic Review*, Vol. LXI, Sept. 1971, pp. 517–537.

Table 3-8
Percentage Changes from Previous Year in Selected United States Economic Indicators, 1969–1974

	Gross National Product	Consumer prices	Wholesale prices	Average hourly earnings in manufacturing	Output per man-hour in manufacturing	Unemployment rate	Balance on current account (million dollars)
1969	2.7	5.4	3.9	6.0	2.1	3.5	−1,633
1970	−0.4	5.9	3.7	5.3	2.0	4.9	−324
1971	3.3	4.3	3.1	6.3	4.0	5.9	−3,817
1972	6.2	3.3	4.6	6.7	2.9	5.6	−9,807
1973	5.8	6.2	13.1	6.8	3.7	4.9	450
1974	−2.1	11.0	18.8	8.1	1.8	5.6	−4,971
1975	−2.0	9.2	9.2	9.1	1.8	8.5	11,697
Average annual increase, 1969–1973	3.5%	5.0%	5.7%	6.2%	2.6%	5.0%[1]	—

[1] Average annual rate, 1969–1973.

Source: *Economic Reports of the President*, 1969–1976.

been in 1969; the unemployment rate rose to 4.9 percent; and industry's production capacity rate declined to 74.5 percent—far below the generally accepted norm of 92 percent as a long-term goal of optimum use of capacity.

At the same time, consumer prices and average wage rates continued to rise excessively, while output per man-hour decreased. Rapid inflation continued during the 1970 recession, because in some cases union contracts required wage increases, while in other cases strong unions were successful in demanding higher wages. Also, the price structure was inflexible downward and reflected rising wage rates. Hence the phenomenon of "stagflation" or rising prices in a stagnant or depressed economy. In this situation, the credit crunch and the high interest rates adversely affected private and public residential construction and investment in essential public capital facilities.

Between 1968 and 1971, when population was annually increasing by one and a half million and the demand for public goods and services was rising, total home construction measured in constant dollars declined $2 billion, while total government purchases of goods and services were reduced by the same amount. Many individuals, business firms, and local governments found themselves excluded from credit markets, where both short and long-term interest rates were at times well above 8 percent. By mid-1971, the Nixon Administration accepted the fact that its program for economic fine tuning had been a failure. The administration then introduced its New Economic Policy in August 1971; this was a marked departure from the economic policies that had been followed up to that time.

Mandatory Wage and Price Controls

The New Economic Policy of August 1971 provided for a compulsory ninety-day freeze of prices, wages, and rents, the suspension of the conversion of dollars into gold, a temporary surcharge of 10 percent on imports, and a number of changes in the tax system that were designed to stimulate the economy.[16] The purpose of the wage-price freeze was to break out of the circle of inflationary expectations that had developed after 1965 by shocking the public into the realization of the need to curb inflation drastically. During the wage-price freeze it was hoped that preparations could be made for an orderly return to noninflationary conditions when these controls would be no longer needed. The Nixon Administration explained that the New Economic Policy was undertaken because the orthodox methods of curbing inflation, which were "more consistent with economic freedom than wage-price controls," had by August 1971 failed to achieve the desired goal, and "new measures ... designed to bring the nation to higher employment, greater price stability, and a stronger international position had to be adopted."[17] Although the Nixon Administration was prepared to adopt wage-price and other economic control measures that it had formerly rejected as being contrary to the welfare of the private enterprise system, clearly, its long-term objective was a state of affairs "in which reasonable price stability can be maintained without controls."

The program for wage and price controls was divided into three phases. Phase I, lasting from August 15, 1971, to November 13, 1971, was a period of general or overall wage and price control. Phase II was regarded as a transition from overall control to a period of selective mandatory wage and price controls, which would continue until both wage and price inflation were satisfactorily curbed. Phase III would be a period when all wage and price controls were removed, or when some kind of long-term voluntary program for wage and price surveillance would be established. With respect to Phase III, there was in the early 1970's widespread disagreement among economists, business people, and labor leaders as to whether or not some kind of wage-price or incomes policy should be made permanent.

The main features of the wage-price control program introduced in 1971 were as follows: annual wage rate increases were to be limited to 5.5 percent plus 0.7 percent for fringe benefits, except in unusual circumstances, such as when the wages of a group of workers had failed to move upward with wages in general. The price guideline stated that prices on the average should not increase across the whole economy by more than 2.5 percent a year. Firms could not increase their prices if they were at their maximum permissible profit margin, which was measured by the ratio of profits per dollar of sales. The maximum allowable profit margin for each firm in Phase II was the highest average annual ratio of profits per dollar of sales that prevailed in any two of the three fiscal years ending before August 15, 1971. A firm could pass on increased costs of production and increase its selling prices only if its profit margin was below its maximum allowable profit margin.

In order to reduce the amount of administrative work involved in carrying out the wage and price controls, only firms with annual sales of $100 million and over and those firms with five thousand or more employees had to secure approval from the Price Commission

---

[16] A survey and analysis of the new wage-price controls are presented in *Economic Report of the President*, 1972, Ch. 2, "Inflation Control under the Economic Stabilization Act," pp. 73-100.

[17] *Economic Report of the President*, 1972, pp. 3-4. See also "The 1973 Report of the President's Council of Economic Advisers," *American Economic Review*, Vol. LXIII, Sept. 1973, pp. 509-545.

and the Pay Board for all increases in selling prices and wage rates. Other price and wage increases were selectively monitored by the Internal Revenue Service and other government agencies. Various items were exempted from the general price freeze, including raw agricultural and seafood products, exports and imports, rents on small residential units, interest rates, prices of securities and financial instruments, and wage rates below the federal minimum wage rate.

In the first year following the general price and wage freeze of August 15, 1971, some easing of inflationary pressures occurred. Consumer prices, which had risen at the annual rate of 4.4 percent in the six months before the general freeze, increased only 3.5 percent in the year after the freeze was begun. The rate of wage-rate increases also declined after the general wage freeze. Whereas average hourly earnings in manufacturing increased 6.7 percent in the period July 1970–July 1971, in the year after the general wage freeze was lifted, these hourly earnings increased 5.4 percent. As the economy recovered during 1972, output per man-hour rose; and with the decline in the rate of wage increases, unit labor costs began to fall for the first time in over six years. One of the major problems in the period that followed the ninety-day general freeze arose in connection with the increases in food prices. With raw agricultural products exempted from price controls, the prices of meat and other foods rose considerably during 1972. The federal government attempted to hold food prices down by temporarily enlarging the quotas on imported meat and by reducing military purchases of meat and other food items. The government also imposed controls on the markups of all firms that processed agricultural products; after June 1972 all food processors were subjected to the same profit margin limitations that applied to manufacturing in general. The major test of the price-wage controls was to come in 1973 when a large number of trade union contracts were to come up for renegotiation.

A major adverse development occurred in March 1972, when four of the five labor members resigned from the Pay Board which administered the wage controls. These four labor members felt that the price-wage control system was not fair to workers and consumers. Inequities arose because there was a precise maximum limit for wage-rate increases, i.e., 5.5 percent, but no similarly precise limit for the control of profits. Under the profit margin guideline established by the Price Commission, which was based on the ratio of profits per dollar of sales, there was no specific control of profits as a rate of return on stockholders' equity or net worth in business enterprises. Labor wanted an excess profits tax that would tax away any windfall or excess profits that might be generated during the period of price and wage controls. Organized labor also argued that price and wage controls should be tied in with tax changes that would distribute the overall national tax burden more equitably. In the view of organized labor, the changes in the tax system made when the general wage and price freeze was adopted in August 1971 were too generous to business and hence unfair to both workers and consumers. The American Federation of Labor–Congress of Industrial Organizations in March 1972, took the position that the four labor members of the Pay Board who had resigned would not return until the Nixon Administration had made the wage-price control program more equitable for all interested parties.

On January 11, 1973, Phase III of the wage-price control program was adopted. This new phase provided for the substitution of voluntary wage and price controls for the mandatory controls of Phase II, except in the case of the food, health, and construction industries. In these industries, where inflationary forces continued to be very strong, the mandatory controls of Phase II were retained. In the food industry, while prices at the farm were not subject to controls, the prices of selected processed or distributed food products, such as red meat, were frozen at early 1973 levels, and later all food prices were frozen at the levels of June 13, 1973. In late July of that year, most controls on food prices were removed, because processors and distributors of food products were caught in a profit squeeze between uncontrolled prices at the farms and controlled prices of processed or distributed food products.

In Phase III, the wage, price, and profit guidelines of Phase II were preserved, but business firms were no longer required to notify the wage-price control authorities of any increases in their selling prices or wage rates. The government now relied upon the voluntary cooperation of the private sector to keep wage and price increases within the wage and price limits established during Phase II. While business firms were no longer required to receive previous government approval of price and wage increases, large firms (the approximately eight hundred firms with sales of $250 million or more and those firms with five thousand or more workers) were required to file quarterly reports of price and wage increases with the Cost of Living Council, which administered Phase III of the wage- and price-control program. Furthermore, although Phase III introduced voluntary self-administered wage and price controls, the government retained a "stick in the closet," which could be used in those cases where the voluntary control program broke down. When the Cost of Living Council found that a business firm had increased its selling prices and had exceeded its allowable profit margin, the Council could roll back the firm's selling prices. Also, if a firm raised wage rates above the 5.5 percent wage guideline, these rates could be rolled back. The Nixon Administration expected few flagrant violations of the voluntary wage and price controls, and hence little need for the use of these legal restraints. A labor-management advisory commission, which was acceptable to organized labor, was established to secure the cooperation of the trade unions in carrying out the new program of voluntary wage and price controls.

Although considerable progress had been made during Phase II in curbing wage and price inflation, and although organized labor was willing to go along with the new program for voluntary wage and price controls, many union leaders remained highly skeptical about the possibility of curbing inflation under the voluntary self-administered system of Phase III. Organized labor was particularly distressed by the elimination in Phase III of all federal rent controls. The reaction of business executives to the elimination of compulsory wage and price controls was more favorable than that of organized labor. Many business leaders believed, along with the Nixon Administration, that continued mandatory wage and price controls would have created serious distortions in the private enterprise system, and that a more flexible self-administered system could avoid many of these distortions. These business executives looked forward to the eventual termination of all price and wage controls and a return to what they described as the "discipline of the competitive market."

Although business in general favored the move towards voluntary wage and price controls, a number of business leaders remained pessimistic about the possibility of coping successfully with inflation under a system of voluntary controls. They tended to think that some form of wage and price control should be made permanent, especially in the area of large-scale business and trade union activity. It is now widely believed that what is described as *pressure-group* inflation cannot be successfully curbed unless the nation's major pressure groups are brought into some program for wage and price control.[18]

The External Sector and the End of Price Controls

While the Nixon Administration made considerable progress in curbing inflation in the years 1971-1972, little improvement was recorded in the nation's external foreign trade sector. On August 15, 1971, the United States suspended the dollar's convertibility into gold and adopted a floating rather than a fixed exchange rate for the dollar. Other countries soon followed the United States in abandoning fixed exchange rates for their currencies; and in December 1971, the Smithsonian Agreement was made by the ten major trading nations to maintain a balance among their floating currencies.[19] This agreement, however, was not followed by the desired improvement in the American export trade and in its current balance of international payments. In 1971, the United States imports of merchandise exceeded its merchandise exports for the first time since 1945; and the merchandise deficit of $1.7 billion in 1971 was followed by similarly large deficits in 1972 and 1974.

The deterioration in the United States foreign trade position after 1967 is recorded in the international trade statistics in Table 3-9.

[18] See, for example, George L. Bach, *The New Inflation*, Providence, R.I.: Brown University Press, 1973.

[19] An analysis of these international financial developments and an explanation of the Smithsonian Agreement is provided in the *Economic Report of the President*, 1972, pp. 142-164.

Table 3-9
U.S. Foreign Trade Merchandise Balance and International Current Account Balance, 1965-1974 (In Millions of Dollars)

	Merchandise balance[1]	Current account balance[1]
1965	4,951	4,287
1966	3,817	1,943
1967	3,800	1,544
1968	635	−962
1969	607	−1,633
1970	2,159	−324
1971	−2,722	−3,817
1972	−6,986	−9,807
1973	471	450
1974	−5,683	−4,971

[1] (−) indicates a deficit.

Source: *Economic Report of the President*, 1975.

As this table shows, the American current international payments account, which was in surplus up to 1967, was usually in deficit after that year, as there was no merchandise export surplus to offset the deficit in international payments. This meant that after 1970 there was a large outflow of United States dollars which tended to weaken the external value of the dollar as foreign countries accumulated dollars or dollar credits. A balance in the American current international account would contribute to the securing of a stable dollar in the international financial world. In order to avoid deficits in its current external account, the American economy needs to be competitive in the area of world trade. Inflation should be avoided as much as possible, since it results in excessive imports, reduced exports, and deficits in the international balance of payments. Now that the American dollar no longer has a fixed exchange rate, it should not be permitted to fall in relation to other currencies so as to increase exports and to curb imports excessively. Trading nations, including the United States, should adopt fiscal, monetary, and other economic policies that will stabilize the domestic economy and provide for cooperation among these nations in securing the desired balance among all floating currencies.

Phase III of the wage-price control program, which was adopted on January 11, 1973, proved to be unsatisfactory for curbing the economy's inflationary pressures. During the first six months of 1973, the consumer price index rose at the disappointingly high annual rate of 11 percent. In response to widespread public demands, the Nixon Administration froze prices on a temporary basis for sixty days in mid-1973; at this time the basis for Phase IV was laid. This phase, introduced in August 1973, provided for the temporary tightening of some price controls and also for the gradual decontrol of all prices in anticipation of the expiration of the Economic Stabilization Act on April 30, 1974. After August 1973, prices and wages were decontrolled on a sector-by-sector basis at an increasing rate. By April 30, 1974, when the legal basis for the mandatory control of prices and wages was abandoned, only 8.6 percent of consumer prices and 27.6 percent of wholesale prices were still subject to government control.

When price and wage controls were dropped, the Council on Wage and Price Stability was established to monitor price and wage developments, with the hope of securing voluntary restraint from the two sides of industry. Unfortunately, price and wage controls were abandoned in 1974, at the time when new inflationary pressures were soon to develop as a result of the worldwide scarcities of oil, other raw materials, and food supplies. The Nixon Administration took the position in 1973 and 1974 that mandatory wage and price controls were ineffective and that inflation could be curbed more readily with fiscal and monetary policies.[20]

Economic Developments in the United States since 1973

In common with other industrial nations, the United States in late 1973 entered a period of great economic difficulties. The oil embargo by the Organization of Petroleum Exporting Countries (OPEC) and the subsequent quadrupling of their oil export prices were followed by the worst recession since the depressed 1930s. As the statistics in Table 3-8 indicate, the decline in Gross National Product (−2.1 percent in 1974) and in industrial production (−0.6 percent in 1974) were accompanied by strong inflationary developments. In 1974, while output was falling off and unemployment was rising, the consumer price index increased 11 percent, and the wholesale price index 18.8 percent. Wage rates, however, failed to increase as much as consumer prices, with the result that workers' real wages on the average declined in 1974. Unemployment, which was at the annual average rate of 5.2 percent in January 1974, increased to 7.2 percent by the end of that year. Also during 1974, the favorable current balance of international payments of 1973 was

[20] For the views of the Nixon Administration on mandatory wage and price controls, see Chapter 3, "Inflation Control under the Economic Stabilization Act," *Economic Report of the President*, 1974, pp. 88–109, and Appendix A, *Economic Report of the President*, 1975, pp. 223–229. The Council of Economic Advisers came to the conclusion in 1974 that "There is much prior evidence that price and wage controls of the kind tolerated during peacetime in free societies cannot significantly restrain inflation under the supply and demand conditions experienced in 1973." *Economic Report*, 1974, p. 109. See also "The 1974 Report of the President's Council of Economic Advisers," *American Economic Review*, Vol. LXIV, Sept. 1974, pp. 523–527.

converted into an unfavorable balance of $4.9 billion, as American merchandise exports failed to pay for merchandise imports and a large trade deficit was incurred.

The recession that began in late 1973 was not recognized as being a serious problem by the Nixon Administration, which continued to direct economic policy mainly towards the control of inflationary pressures. During much of 1974, both fiscal and monetary policy were designed to curb inflation rather than to offset declining production and employment. The tight monetary situation depressed the housing industry and discouraged private business investment. New housing starts, which were over 2 million in 1973, fell to 1.3 million in 1974. Real private investment in plant and equipment, having increased 12.8 percent in 1973 over 1972, rose only 0.5 percent in 1974 over 1973. Because of the restrictive fiscal policy, government purchases of goods and services showed little increase during 1974.

In late 1974, the Ford Administration finally admitted that "The economy is in a severe recession" and took some steps to support the sagging economy.[21] These steps included providing for a $50 billion federal budgetary deficit for fiscal 1976 (later enlarged by the Congress to $68 billion), reductions in personal income taxes, increased investment tax credits for business from 7 to 10 percent, increased funds for public employment, lower interest rates and a less restrictive monetary policy, the extension of unemployment benefits to millions of workers not formerly covered (and the extension of such benefits from fifty-two to sixty-five weeks), and the granting of funds to state and local governments to finance public projects.

Critics of the Ford Administration's antirecessionary program asserted that it was not sufficiently aggressive to bring the recession to an early end. The statistics in Table 3-10, which summarize the views of the OECD with regard to American antirecessionary policy, show that the OECD did not expect any significant improvement in American economic conditions in 1975. It was estimated

[21] *Economic Report of the President,* 1975, p. 3.

Table 3–10
Demand and Output in the United States, 1973–1975

	1973 Billion dollars	Percent volume change from previous year		
		1973	1974	1975[1]
Private consumption	805.2	4.7	−1.5	0
Public expenditure	276.4	0.8	1.0	0
Private fixed investment	194.0	7.9	−6.25	−6.75
Residential	57.2	−4.1	−26.0	−12.5
Nonresidential	136.8	12.8	0.5	−5.5
GNP at market prices	1,294.9	5.9	−1.75	−2.0
GNP implicit price deflator		5.6	10.0	10.5
Industrial production		9.0	−1.0	−2.5
Consumer prices		5.5	11.5	11.0

[1] Estimated by OECD.

Source: OECD, *OECD Economic Outlook,* 16, Dec. 1974, p. 75.

that there would be no increase in public expenditures in that year, that private fixed investment and GNP would continue to decline, and that double-digit inflation would continue. The response of the Ford Administration to its critics was that more vigorous antirecessionary measures would overstimulate the economy and plunge it into an inflationary boom. The administration therefore preferred to adopt a cautious approach to overcoming the recession.

The Mature American Economy in Retrospect and Prospect

In the quarter century since the close of World War II, the mature American economy has generally been prosperous. In the twenty-five years from 1947 to 1972, the GNP increased 139 percent, or at the average annual rate of 3.7 percent. Per capita GNP, measured in 1971 dollars, increased from $3,043 in 1947 to $5,057 in 1971. Americans enjoyed not only the highest per capita GNP in the world, but also a per capita product that was much higher than that of most nations. By mid-1950, the standard of living of the majority of the population was so high as to lead some observers to describe the American society as an affluent society.[22]

This society had passed through the era of mass consumption, and by the mid-1950s had entered the new era of the affluent service economy. In spite of this general economic progress, the mature American economy has been far removed from the ideal model of the mature capitalist economy presented in standard economics textbooks. Five economic recessions have occurred since 1947. Economic growth has been highly irregular, fluctuating in the years 1947–1972 between a negative annual growth rate of 1.4 percent and a positive annual rate of 7.9 percent. Unemployment has varied between a low rate of 2.9 percent and a high rate of 6.8 percent. Since 1947, the American economy has exhibited a strong inflationary bias, with prices being flexible upward but not downward. The market power of various organized economic interest groups, such as conglomerate business enterprises, large industrial unions, and multinational corporations, has greatly increased. Even in recessions, both prices and wage rates have continued to rise. In the advanced industrial economy, with a rapidly changing technology, unemployment has become a structural as well as a cyclical problem. Unemployment rates tend to be low for highly skilled white male workers, but high for young unskilled white and black workers, as well as for women workers. Even in relatively prosperous times, the mature American economy has difficulty in providing employment for many of its unskilled workers.

In spite of the nation's generally high standard of living, a large part of the population remains below the poverty line. In 1960, 40 million individuals were below the poverty line, while in 1968 about 22 million were still living in households with incomes below the poverty line. In the United States the distribution of income and wealth remains highly unequal, and is sustained by a tax system that has limited progressivity and many tax loopholes. A major deficiency of the mature American economy has been its inability to develop a viable external economy with a satisfactory overall international balance. Through its gold and dollar outflow, the United States has supplied much of the liquidity required by the international trading system in the past quarter century; it has also permitted the dollar to function as an international monetary unit. At the same time, the United States has not coordinated its domestic and international economic policies so as to

---

[22] For a description of this society, see John Kenneth Galbraith, *The Affluent Society*, Second Revised Edition, Boston: Houghton Mifflin, 1969.

secure a satisfactory balance in its international account. Domestic instability has made it impossible to secure stability in the nation's external account.

Besides deficiencies relating to annual economic growth, employment, price stability, and the international balance of payments, the mature American economic system has been criticized regarding its long-range goals and national priorities. The 1970 Economic Report of the President explained that "We have learned that 1-year planning leads to almost as much confusion as no planning at all, and there is a need to increase public awareness of long-range trends and the consequences for future years of decisions taken now."[23]

Concern with the nation's long-term economic and social goals raises the question of the lifestyle that the people wish to achieve. The affluent American society has been criticized on the ground that not enough attention has been paid to the various purposes which affluence is supposed to serve. With the social costs of continued economic growth frequently ignored, the natural and social environments have undergone considerable deterioration. The overriding focus on profit growth during the post–World War II period has resulted in the serious pollution of the land, water, and air, the destruction of social amenities in the urban areas, and the elimination of a number of wilderness areas. These undesirable consequences of economic growth have arisen because the setting of national priorities has been influenced to a great extent by strong private lobbying interests, while at the same time the general public has been inadequately represented.

Improving the American Economy in the Short Run

Efforts to remove the discrepancies between the actual mature American economy and the

[23] *Economic Report of the President,* 1970, p. 3.

ideal model of this economy analyzed in Chapter 2 fall into short-term, medium-term, and long-term categories. Programs to improve the functioning of the mature industrial economy in the short run deal chiefly with eliminating the cyclical fluctuations in economic activity that are accompanied by short-run economic instability and imbalance. Eliminating these instabilities and imbalances requires improvements in short-run fiscal, monetary, and other economic policies. Short-run fiscal policy could be improved by making it more flexible than at present by giving the president the stand-by authority to increase or decrease personal and corporation income taxes as economic circumstances warrant, but within set limits and subject to later congressional approval. In addition, public-works projects should be planned well in advance of their being set in motion. It has been recommended that the president be given stand-by authority to begin these projects when the economy begins to sag. Monetary policy can be made more effective by bringing all banks, savings and loan associations, and other credit institutions under the control of the Federal Reserve System.

In both fiscal and monetary policies, more reliance should be placed upon selective policies. General fiscal and monetary policies, while still very useful in circumstances of excessive or inadequate total demand, are frequently too blunt in their impact on the economy. Only by combining general and selective fiscal and monetary measures is it possible to achieve the successful fine tuning of the economic system that has thus far eluded the federal government. The need to supplement general economic policies with selective policies arises from the changes that have occurred in the American economic system as it has matured. When the economy was small scale and flexible with regard to price and wage adjustments, general fiscal and monetary policies were effective because they had a wide impact and distributed the burden of adjustment over all sectors of the economy. Also, the economy was quick to respond to changes in these policies in the desired directions.

As the economy matured and small-scale industry was in large part replaced by large-scale industry, small labor unions by large unions, and unorganized farmers by organized farmers, the mature economy became quite inflexible with respect to price and wage adjustments. General fiscal and monetary policies now affect some sectors of the economy much more stringently than others; and the remaining competitive sectors of the mature economy respond more quickly to economic policy changes than do the noncompetitive, large-scale sectors.

An effective program for bringing an end to the stop-go economic programs that have been followed since 1945 would supplement fiscal and monetary policies with a more vigorous manpower policy and some form of wage-price or incomes policy. In the small-scale competitive economy of the nineteenth century, little need arose for selective manpower policies, for the economy was flexible, labor was unorganized, and the labor supply was fluid. Few bottlenecks occurred in the nation's labor supply, the needed variety of skills was readily supplied, and labor was free to move where it was most efficient and was able to maximize its wages. In the mature American economy of today, a highly selective manpower policy is necessary if we are to make the labor market more responsive to the requirements of a program for eliminating or reducing short-term economic instabilities and imbalances.[24]

This manpower policy should include setting up a centralized and computerized federal employment service, providing tax incentives to employers in order to stimulate on-the-job training and the employment of disadvantaged workers, altering the hiring practices of large business enterprises in order to increase the employment of minorities, and requiring the trade unions to open their membership to blacks and other minorities. If labor-supply bottlenecks are to be eliminated, creating a job bank should be supplemented by a job placement program that tells unemployed workers where jobs are available. An effective manpower policy would also aid workers who are in financial need to move to the localities where labor is in short supply.

As has already been explained, one of the most controversial issues in the area of economic policy concerns the role of a wage-price or incomes policy in any program to reduce short-run economic fluctuations and instabilities. With the industrial economy no longer inherently flexible and market power widely possessed by both organized business and organized labor, wage and price adjustments tend to be inflationary and to run counter to the national interest. The position of those economists who favor the adoption of a voluntary incomes policy is well summarized in the 1969 Economic Report of the President; it states that "The cooperation of labor and business in the observance of voluntary standards of price and wage behavior is an essential part of a full program to combine high employment and reasonable price stability. Such cooperation must be viewed as a supplement to appropriate fiscal and monetary policy and to measures for improving the efficiency of the economy."[25] The wage and price guideposts would not be used in the

---

[24] A detailed analysis of a selective manpower policy is given in C. C. Holt, C. D. MacRae, S. O. Schweitzer, and R. E. Smith, *The Unemployment-Inflation Dilemma: A Manpower Solution*, Washington, D.C.: The Urban Institute, 1971.

[25] *Economic Report of the President*, 1969, p. 120. For the cases for and against a wage-price policy, see George P. Shultz and Robert Z. Aliber, eds., *Guidelines, Informal Controls, and the Market Place*, Chicago: University of Chicago Press, 1966. For a favorable view of wage-price policy, see John Sheahan, *op. cit.*, pp. 196–204.

highly competitive agricultural, service, and small-scale industry sectors where market forces determine prices and wages in an impersonal fashion. These guideposts would be applicable only to those sectors of the economy where a large amount of discretionary market power exists, and especially to the industrial core of the mature industrial economy; here are found the few hundred large industrial enterprises and the large trade unions that dominate the economy.

Other policies recommended for the achievement of economic stability are those that would seek to limit the use of market power. Such policies are primarily designed to make product markets more competitive. Prominent among them are a more vigorous enforcement of the antitrust laws and a strengthening of foreign competition in domestic markets. The strong enforcement of the antitrust policy would aim at reducing the degree of monopoly in the American economy. Some economists believe that a vigorous enforcement of the antitrust laws could significantly reduce the high profit rates of the large oligopolistic industries that lead to labor's demands for excessive wage increases. These economists think that a strong application of antitrust policy could weaken the ability of large-scale business enterprises to pass wage cost increases on to consumers in periods of weak aggregate demand.[26] Other economists, however, doubt that antitrust policy could ever alone achieve these goals. These economists would add the increased competition from imported goods to a more vigorous enforcement of the antitrust laws as a means of limiting the market power of large business enterprises and labor unions. They would reduce much of the protection that industry now gets through tariffs, import quotas, "Buy American" programs, and other domestic policies that exclude or limit many foreign imports.

The Mix of Short-Term and Medium-Term Economic Policies

Considerable progress has been made since the depressed 1930s in developing an economic policy mix for dealing with economic instabilities and imbalances. An important problem is the application of this improved policy mix to the problems of the mature industrial economy. Two different approaches to this problem have been developed among the Western industrial countries: the interventionist and the national planning methods. Among the capitalist economies, the United States, the United Kingdom (under the British Conservative party), West Germany, Canada, and Australia use the interventionist approach; France, Belgium, Japan, and the Netherlands employ the planning approach, which is similar in its fundamentals to the national planning operating in socialist Norway and Sweden.

In the United States, the interventionist position received a major impetus in the depressed 1930s when laissez faire was largely abandoned and was replaced by a new welfare philosophy. Since the early 1930s, this interventionist approach has been strengthened in a number of ways. By passing the Employment Act of 1946, the federal government became officially committed to a full employment goal. The establishment of the Council of Economic Advisers in 1946 created an agency that could propose, evaluate, and coordinate the various economic policies that together comprise the government's expanding economic policy mix. In the 1960s, wage, price, and manpower policies were added to fiscal and monetary policies as major features

[26] The case for vigorous antitrust enforcement is developed in John M. Blair, *Economic Concentration, Structure Behavior and Public Policy,* New York: Harcourt Brace Jovanovich, 1972, pp. 614–620.

of the government's improved economic policy mix.

After 1946, projections of the GNP and of the level of employment in the coming year were made and became the point of departure for annual adjustments in fiscal, monetary, price, wage, and other economic policies. Also over the decades, attention was increasingly paid to longer-range aspects of national economic guidance and economic policy formulation. These longer-term concerns were the structural aspects of the labor market, resource conservation, the prevention of environmental deterioration, the provision of private and public housing, the improvement and expansion of health, education, and other public services, the improvement of transportation, urban renewal, and the fostering of research and development.

Although the scope of national economic guidance was widened in the 1950s and 1960s, not much was done to alter the institutional basis of the program for national economic guidance beyond setting up the Council of Economic Advisers. No permanent national economic council or council on national priorities with representatives from the nation's major economic interest groups was established to consider the nation's economic goals and priorities and to advise the Congress on these matters. The Congress made few improvements beyond the use of cost-benefit analysis in the traditional way in order to evaluate national goals and to appropriate funds for achieving these goals. No congressional committee on national priorities was set up to provide the Congress with an overall view of national needs. Recommendations regarding national goals and priorities continued to come in traditional piecemeal fashion from the president, advised by his cabinet, the chairpersons of the Federal Reserve Board and the Council of Economic Advisers, and the Director of the Office of the Budget (now the Office of Management and Budget). No annual or four-year national economic budgets were published for the guidance of the Congress and the public in their evaluation of the major competing consumption and investment claims on the nation's Gross National Product. In other words, intervention in the nation's economic affairs was never carried to the point where it evolved into the kind of democratic indicative national planning that is carried on in France, Belgium, the Netherlands, Japan, and the Scandinavian countries.

National Programming and the Coordination of Economic Policies

Dissatisfaction with the interventionist approach to economic policy formulation and national economic guidance has increased in recent years. One of the early attempts to provide for a better coordination of economic policies with the aid of national economic budgets was made in 1950 when the Council of Economic Advisers published a five-year national economic budget for the programmed period 1950–1954.[27] The economy's capacity to produce had in the early postwar years been built up so rapidly that by 1950 it exceeded the economy's capacity to consume. According to the recommendations accompanying the five-year national economic budget for 1950–1954, fiscal and monetary policies were to have been changed so as to curb private investment in plant, equipment, and inventories and to increase private and public consumption. Before the Congress could consider the 1950–1954 national economic budget and the policy recommendations of the Council of Economic Advisers, the Korean War broke out and a new economic situation developed. The coordination of economic policies on the basis of medium-term national economic budgets was

[27] *Economic Report of the President,* 1950, p. 85.

not again discussed in the Economic Reports of the President until 1970, when the Council of Economic Advisers presented in its report for that year a six-year national economic budget or projection of the Gross National Product and the consumption and investment uses of this product.[28]

The council's national economic budget for 1970-1975, as shown in Table 3-11, reveals that although the Gross National Product was projected to increase from $932.4 billion in 1969 to $1,201 billion in 1975, only $12 billion of GNP would be available in 1975 for new economic and social programs, if one assumed that the existing private and public expenditure trends of 1969 were to continue into 1975. In 1970, the Council of Economic Advisers explained that the potential probable demands on the projected 1975 GNP would absorb most of that product. Thus, if other new economic and social demands on the GNP were to be met, then some of the existing demands on this product would have to be sacrificed. In its 1971 annual report, the Council of Economic Advisers carried its six-year national economic budget up to 1976; it indicated that by that year unallocated GNP, or a social dividend of $19 billion, could be available for new programs, such as environmental protection, urban transportation, resource development, and health care. The council pointed out that the private and public consumption and investment claims on the nation's GNP during the 1970s would be very numerous; it recommended that thought should be taken in advance about the selection of national economic and social priorities for 1976 and the formulation of appropriate economic policies for the achievement of these priorities.

In the opinion of the council, what was required was "some new thinking if our economic system is to make its maximum contribution to national well-being." The council proposed that fiscal, monetary, price, wage and other economic policies should be formulated within the framework of five- or six-year national economic budgets in order to use the GNP in a way that would contribute the most to national well-being. This might entail, for example, reducing personal consumption expenditures and raising government purchases so as to increase the flow of public goods and services in relation to the flow of private

[28] *Economic Report of the President,* 1970, p. 79.

Table 3-11

U.S. National Economic Accounts for 1969 and a National Economic Budget for 1975 (In Billions of 1969 Dollars)

	1969 (actual)		1975 (projection)	
	Dollars	Percent	Dollars	Percent
Personal consumption	576.0	61.8	769	64.1
Gross domestic private investment	136.7	14.7	187	15.6
Government purchases	214.7	23.0	228	18.9
Net export surplus	5.0	0.5	5	0.4
Unallocated Gross National Product	0	0	12	1.0
Gross National Product	932.4	100.0	1,201	100.0

Source: *Economic Report of the President,* 1970, p. 79.

goods and services. This was also the position of the National Goals Research Staff in the Executive Office of the President; it concluded that an analysis based on five- or six-year projections of the nation's Gross National Product and the consumption and investment demands on this product is essential for developing a satisfactory policy for national economic guidance.[29]

Using both annual and four- or five-year national economic budgets as a basis for economic policy formulation provides for coordinating short-term and medium-term economic policies.[30] The national goals set forth in the medium-term national economic budget are approached by annual steps, laid out in the annual national economic budgets. If circumstances change substantially, medium-term goals can be altered by making annual adjustments. Since the annual and medium-term national economic budgets are constructed in close cooperation with business, organized labor, and other major economic interest groups, an opportunity is provided for the participation of the public in national economic policy formulation and national economic guidance, as is done in France, the Netherlands, and the United Kingdom. In these countries national economic councils form a liaison between private economic interest groups and the government.

At this point in the evolution of the advanced American economy, the effort to make it approach more closely the ideal model of the mature capitalist economy discussed in Chapter 2 may take any one of three directions. If the advanced American economy were to move along the path suggested by Milton Friedman and other members of the Chicago school, government intervention would be significantly reduced and efforts would be made to establish a more competitive economic system. If the American economy were to take the route recommended by the Keynesians, efforts would be made to increase and improve the scope of government intervention by making economic policies more flexible and more selective. In addition, intervention would be expanded by enlarging the economic policy mix to include a wage-price or incomes policy and other policies. This is the course of action that would today probably be proposed by the majority of economists. Other economists, such as John K. Galbraith and Gunnar Myrdal, would advocate going beyond interventionism to some kind of social management or national programming, which would seek to achieve national priorities with the aid of national economic budgeting and a reformed congressional system.[31]

Whatever policy for national economic guidance in the United States is adopted in the future, it will doubtless reflect the heavy pressure of events as determined by the course of never-ending scientific advance and technological change, and by the fluctuating condition of the economic system. The serious recession of 1973–1974 renewed interest in the possibility of a more specific guidance of the nation's economy. In mid-1974, Wassily

[29] National Goals Research Staff, *Toward Balanced Economic Growth: Quantity with Quality*, Washington, D.C., pp. 152 and 160.

[30] In this connection, see the proposals of Gerhard Colm in National Planning Association, *Long-Range Projections for Economic Growth: The American Economy in 1970*, Pamphlet No. 125, Washington, D.C., 1968.

[31] Galbraith's and Myrdal's views in this connection are summarized in Allan G. Gruchy, *Contemporary Economic Thought*, Clifton, N.J.: Augustus M. Kelley, 1972. For a more limited approach to national budgeting, see Charles L. Schultze and others, *Setting National Priorities: The 1971 Budget*, The Brookings Institution, Washington, D.C., 1970 (and subsequent annual publications of the same type); and Charles L. Schultze, *The Politics and Economics of Public Spending*, The Brookings Institution, 1968.

Leontief recommended the establishment of a national economic planning board to obtain "a clear, detailed picture of the entire [economic] system" and to "draw conclusions about the future course of [its] development."[32] Leontief's proposal was supported by the Initiative Committee for National Economic Planning, whose membership included a number of outstanding social scientists and business and labor leaders.[33] In August 1974, Senators Hubert H. Humphrey and Jacob K. Javits introduced the Balanced Growth and Economic Planning Bill; if passed, this bill would have established a national economic planning board.

Major Problems of the Mature American Economy

We may summarize our analysis of the development of the mature American economy in recent decades by calling attention to some of the major problems now confronting this economy. Among these problems are: reforming the tax system in order to secure greater equity, securing a more equitable pattern of income distribution, providing a guaranteed work program, eliminating the imbalance in the nation's external sector, restoring consumer sovereignty, eliminating discrimination in all its forms, and providing adequate environmental protection. These major problems may all be summarized as a matter of defining more precisely the content of our national economic and social goals and priorities. Some progress in this direction has been made recently as the public has come to realize that an affluent society does not automatically achieve a lifestyle of high quality. Opinion is growing that a program for national economic and social guidance is needed to ensure that affluence is accompanied by excellence in the emerging postindustrial society in America.[34]

The many problems now facing the mature American economy come to a head in proposals for zero population and economic growth. These proposals are made on the ground that current population and economic growth, if not curbed in the future, will result in so much human congestion, pollution, and use of irreplaceable natural resources that the preservation of the human race will be in doubt. Both population and economic growth are examples of exponential or compounded growth. For example, in a country where population is increasing at an annual rate of 3 percent, the population doubles every 23 years. India, with a current population of approximately 500 million that is growing at the annual rate of 2.5 percent, will have a population of over 1 billion in the year 2000 if its present growth rate continues. The United States, with a more than trillion dollar Gross National Product in 1973, will double this product by 1985, if GNP continues to increase at the annual rate of 5 percent. The proponents of zero population and economic growth assert that under present population and growth trends, certain disaster is the inevitable outcome of these trends. A recent study of population and economic growth trends for the Club of Rome, an international group concerned with the future of mankind, concluded that within one hundred years the world will

---

[32] Wassily Leontief, "What an Economic Planning Board Should Do," *Challenge*, July–August 1974, p. 36.

[33] The Initiative Committee For National Economic Planning, "For a National Economic Planning System," *Challenge*, March–April, 1975, pp. 51–53.

[34] For an introductory statement of this problem, see the U.S. Department of Health, Education, and Welfare, *Toward a Social Report*. See also Gunnar Myrdal, *Beyond the Welfare State*, New Haven: Yale University Press, 1960; Lester C. Thurow, "The American Economy in the Year 2000," *American Economic Review*, Vol. LXII, May 1972, pp. 439–443; and Daniel Bell, ed., *Toward the Year 2000*, Boston: Houghton Mifflin, 1968.

probably not be able to support its expanding population in tolerable living conditions.[35]

At present, the highest rates of population growth are found in the less developed countries which usually have the lowest per capita economic growth rates. In the United States in the past decade, population has annually grown at the rate of 1.75 percent and per capita Gross National Product 3.4 percent; in India, the respective rates were 2.5 and 1 percent. Where the annual rate of growth of per capita Gross National Product falls behind the annual rate of population growth, as in India, the country is getting worse off economically instead of better. At present, the major portion of the world's raw materials is absorbed by the rich, developed nations, which account for only 400 million of the world's total population of 3.8 billion. Clearly any attempt by the world's less developed nations to duplicate the living standards of Western Europe and the United States would fail because of the lack of available raw materials. Furthermore, any effort by these nations to reach the high living standards of the Western industrial nations would cause the international environment to suffer severe deterioration, if current methods of production and of waste disposal were followed by these developing nations.

In the United States, the proposals for zero population and economic growth have come at a time when the nation's goals and priorities are being subjected to widespread criticism. Many critics of the affluence produced by the advanced industrial economies assert that affluence has been achieved at the expense of excellence, that too many gadgets of little real social utility are now being marketed, that leisure is being sacrificed to unnecessary work, and that it is time to accept a lower, if not zero, annual economic growth rate as a national goal. The youth movement, with its antagonism to economic success and competitive norms of economic behavior and its espousal of a simpler life or "backpack existence," has given much support to the proposals for zero population and economic growth.[36]

Various environmentalist groups have espoused the programs for the control of population and economic growth, and have pointed to the environmental crisis that has appeared on both the domestic and international fronts. Barry Commoner, a leading environmentalist, has explained in *The Closing Circle* that while in the United States population has grown 143 percent and Gross National Product 203 percent since 1945, pollution has increased 1,000 percent.[37] He believes that the rapid increase in pollution has been largely a post–World War II phenomenon, which can be attributed to technological progress and the marketing of many new products. Technological developments have in recent decades upset the world's ecological balance

---

[35] Donella H. Meadows and others, *The Limits to Growth*. The public's attention was called to the impending population crisis in 1968 when Paul Ehrlich published *The Population Bomb*, which was a call to prevent world overpopulation. To further his cause, Ehrlich helped to organize an activist group called Zero Population Growth. Its program includes demands for legalized abortion, a maximum of two children per family, tax incentives for smaller families, and government support of birth control programs. Not all economists agree with the authors of *The Limits to Growth*. Some critics of the latter's conclusions assert that social change and technological advance will nullify the pessimistic predictions of the Club of Rome. See H. S. D. Cole and others, *Models of Doom, A Critique of the Limits to Growth*, New York: Universe Books, 1973.

[36] The proposals of the youth movement are in line with Charles A. Reich's "Consciousness III," which in Reich's opinion is the next stage in mankind's evolution. This is a stage in which a transformed society would stress a dedication to a lifestyle based on simplicity, love, and comradeship. See Charles A. Reich, *The Greening of America*, New York: Random House, 1970.

[37] Barry Commoner, *The Closing Circle, Nature, Man, and Technology*, New York: Alfred A. Knopf, 1971, p. 146.

by introducing into the environment harmful elements in the form of fertilizers, pesticides, herbicides, detergents, thermal pollution, nondegradable synthetic fibers, leaded gasoline, and rubbish from industrial packaging. New production technologies with adverse impacts on the natural environment have displaced the old but less destructive technologies; consequently, the counter-ecological pattern of economic growth has given rise to a serious environmental crisis. This crisis has now been extended to the international environment of land, water, and air. The origins of this universal phenomenon lie in a worldwide industrial technology that has engulfed economic systems of widely varying ideologies.

If the population and environmental crises are to be handled successfully, there must arise a new planetary environmental ethic that will foster a benign rather than a destructive industrial revolution. This new revolution would minimize the pollutive and biocidal side effects of population and economic growth, and would provide for a global management that would recycle industrial waste and protect the natural environment. As a step in this direction, the United Nations Conference on the Human Environment, held at Stockholm in June 1972, proposed establishing a World Heritage Trust to preserve the world's natural and cultural areas and sites of unique value, and an Earth Watch to monitor and assess the pollutive effects of technological change.

The postindustrial mature American economy is suffering from, in essence, a crisis of values or national priorities. In the mature Western economies, scientific and technological progress has outstripped progress on the economic and social fronts. Our institutional and value patterns have not changed as rapidly as have our scientific and technological knowledge and procedures. A cultural lag has developed, in which old institutional arrangements and value patterns appropriate to the small-scale industrial society of a century ago have lingered on in a world where knowledge and technological explosions demand new institutional arrangements and new values, if social well-being is to be enlarged and a lifestyle of high quality is to be secured. Evidently, plans must be made to overcome this cultural lag. A viewpoint with a longer time horizon is needed; this would enable the people and the government to assess the consequences of scientific and technological advance as they relate to social and economic well-being.

In 1971, the Subcommittee on Urban Affairs of the Joint Economic Committee recommended that the Council of Economic Advisers construct a ten-year full-employment projection of the economy which would be updated annually. The work of the council would be supplemented by the activities of a National Resources Planning Commission, with representatives from business, labor, agriculture, and consumers, whose duty would be to recommend programs for the development of physical and human resources and to consider national priorities over a ten-year period.[38] In this way, the nation's major economic and social problems would be analyzed by the commission from the perspective of a long-term time horizon.[39]

Fortunately, some evidence exists that the affluent American society is becoming more oriented towards the future than it has been up to the present. The National Commission on Technology, Automation, and Economic Progress in 1966 concluded its report with the

[38] Subcommittee on Urban Affairs of the Joint Economic Committee, *Restoration of Effective Sovereignty to Solve Social Problems*, Joint Committee Print, Washington, D.C., Dec. 6, 1971, p. 10.

[39] For an example of this approach to economic policy formulation, see the Report of the President's Task Force on Economic Growth, *Policies for American Economic Progress in the Seventies*, May 1970, Washington, D.C.

observation that "Ours, like most modern societies, is becoming 'future-oriented.' We have become increasingly aware of the multiple impacts of social change—of which automation, one of the concerns of this Commission, is a prime example—and in so doing we realize that we have to plan ahead. We have to anticipate social change. We need to assess its consequences. We have to decide what policies are necessary to facilitate—or inhibit—possible changes."[40]

The Future of the Mature American Economy

Since the end of the Second World War, groups of social scientists have been organized in the United States, the United Kingdom, France, and other advanced industrial countries in order to analyze future long-term scientific, social, and economic trends. In the United States, the Commission on the Year 2000 was established "to indicate now the future consequences of present public policy decisions, to anticipate future problems, and to begin the design of alternative solutions so that our society may have more options and can make a moral choice, rather than be constrained, as is so often the case when problems descend upon us as unnoticed and demand an immediate response."[41] Economists and other social scientists associated with these groups studying the future of Western societies generally agree concerning the probable overall shape of the American economy in the year 2000. Population is expected to continue to grow at a rate that will increase the number of people in the United States to around 310 million by the year 2000.

[40] National Commission on Technology, Automation, and Economic Progress, *Technology and the American Economy*, Vol. I, Washington, D.C., 1966, p. 105.
[41] Daniel Bell, *op. cit.*, p. 1.

The strong economic growth trend of the past quarter of a century is also expected to continue. If the American Gross National Product were to grow at the annual rate of 4 percent, measured in 1971 dollars it would increase from $1,046 billion in 1971 to $3,266 billion in the year 2000. Per capita GNP would rise from $5,056 in 1971 to $10,535 in 2000.

The tendency in the advanced industrial nations in recent decades has been to preserve private industry as the main source of supplies of goods and services. Socialist governments in the Scandinavian countries, the United Kingdom, and West Germany have shown no interest in liquidating the private enterprise system on a large scale. Instead, the trend in these countries, as in the United States, has been to preserve the private business system but to subject it to an expanding system of regulation and control. This trend is expected to continue in the next quarter of a century and beyond. In these decades, however, the institution of private property will probably change in important ways. Family-owned business firms in the United States as in the industrialized West European countries will continue to disappear through the merger process. The decline in the number of family-owned business firms is expected to bring the separation of the ownership and control of private corporate wealth very close to completion by the year 2000.

It is widely accepted among economists and other social scientists concerned with the study of future economic and social trends that the private enterprise system will continue to fill an important role in the affairs of the Western democracies for many decades to come. Social scientists disagree, however, regarding the extent of the power and influence that private business may have in the United States by the end of the current century. John K. Galbraith, Daniel Bell, Robert L. Heilbroner, Herman Kahn, and others see the importance of private business declining very considerably in the next few decades, as our "business" civilization is converted into an "intellectual" or "science" civilization.[42] This trend may be strengthened as the center of creativity and innovation is shifted from the business world to the nation's universities, nonprofit research agencies, and government departments.

These social scientists believe that while private business will undoubtedly continue to play a large role in the postindustrial society, this role will probably decline significantly as the educational and scientific elite assume more responsibility for national economic and social guidance. According to this view, when the possession of scientific knowledge and technological know-how becomes more crucial than the possession of corporate assets, the scientists, educators, and civil servants will increasingly displace business people as the national leaders who shape to a considerable degree the values that give direction to the nation's economic and social trends.

Other economists assert that Galbraith and others overstate the case for the decline of the large business corporation as the central institution in the industrial society of the future. Shonfield argues that the large business enterprise will continue to occupy a "commanding position" in the advanced industrial economies because in the Western democracies people are no longer interested in enlarging the boundaries of state or public enterprise. Furthermore, the technology of management based upon the use of the computer as a tool of business decision making will, in Shonfield's opinion, favor the expansion of big private business.[43]

Leonard Silk follows Shonfield in believing that the large business enterprise will continue to have a major role in the postindustrial society. According to Silk's interpretation, the private business system, by absorbing the technologists and converting them into business leaders, is adapting so as to preserve its leadership role in the advanced industrial economy.[44] Both Shonfield and Silk argue that the advocates of the thesis of the decline of private business enterprise as the central institution in the Western democracies greatly underestimate the flexibility and adaptability of the private business corporation. The large business enterprise in the United States, the United Kingdom, and other industrial countries is becoming increasingly sensitive to the pressures created by consumers, organized labor, and government. Consequently, some important alterations in the structure and functioning of the private business system will take place over the next half century.

For example, the managerial structure may become less authoritarian as consumers and workers are given representation on the boards of directors of large industrial corporations. Pressures for new forms of public accountability may in the future cause business enterprises to take more account of the social costs of private production and to prevent the deterioration of the natural and social environments. Private business is expected in the next few decades to find it worthwhile to cooperate with the government and nonprofit organizations in coping with the complex problems that will emerge in the final quarter of the current century. These efforts to

---

[42] See, for example, Zbigniew Brzezinski, "America in the Technetronic Age," *Encounter*, Vol. 30, No. 1, Jan. 1968; and also Robert L. Heilbroner, *The Limits of Capitalism*, New York: Harper and Row, 1966. The latter states that "Thus it seems to me that the trends of the present, which are far from halted, fostered a continuation of the general elevation of non-business elites and a general compression of the influence of business leadership itself" (p. 54).

[43] Andrew Shonfield, "Business in the Twenty-First Century," in *Perspectives on Business, Daedalus*, Winter, 1969, p. 191.

[44] Leonard S. Silk, "Business Power, Today and Tomorrow," *Perspectives on Business, Daedalus*, Winter, 1969, pp. 181–182.

"socialize" the private business enterprise, however, are not expected by Shonfield, Silk, and other economists to produce any far-reaching radical changes in the private enterprise system and its power position in the next three or four decades in the United States.

Only time can settle the arguments among investigators of future economic and social trends as to the probable role of the large private business enterprise in the postindustrial society. These investigators agree that the outcome of these trends as they relate to the private business system will probably vary considerably among the Western democracies. In some of the Western European countries, such as the United Kingdom, Sweden, and Norway, the role of private business in national guidance may decrease significantly if national planning programs are expanded. In other countries, such as the United States, West Germany, and Canada, the decline in the power and influence of private business may be much smaller. In both cases, however, one may reasonably expect private business to continue as an important institution in the Western world in the final quarter of the twentieth century and even well into the twenty-first century.

While one may find it difficult to envision the nature of government-business-labor relations in the American economy of the year 2000, one can indicate probable trends in the evolution of these relations. Although the American bias against any form of national planning along the French or Swedish lines will doubtless remain very strong, it is reasonable to anticipate that in the American economy of the next quarter century more rather than less collective action will be taken in the field of economic policy formulation. The economic trends since the close of the Second World War suggest that in the future more collaboration will take place among government, business, labor, and other economic interest groups for the development of policies for the achievement of economic stabilization and growth. The logic of economic development appears to point in the direction of more "collaborative guidance" of the nation's economic system than has existed up to the present.[45] Furthermore, collaboration within the United States will be accompanied by collaboration between the United States and other nations in the search for what Gunnar Myrdal has described as the "world welfare state."

[45] Council of Economic Advisers, *First Annual Report to the President,* Dec. 1946, p. 21.

Selected Bibliography

BACH, GEORGE L. *The New Inflation.* Brown University Press, Providence, 1973.

BELL, DANIEL, ed. *Toward the Year 2000.* Houghton Mifflin Company, Boston, 1968.

BLAIR, JOHN M. *Economic Concentration, Structure Behavior and Public Policy.* Harcourt Brace Jovanovich, Inc., New York, 1972.

COLE, H. S. D., and others. *Models of Doom, A Critique of the Limits to Growth.* Universe Books, New York, 1973.

COLM, GERHARD. *Long-Range Projections for Economic Growth: The American Economy in 1970.* National Planning Association, Washington, D.C., 1959.

COMMISSION ON MONEY AND CREDIT. *Money and Credit, Their Influence on Jobs, Prices, and Growth.* Prentice-Hall Inc., Englewood Cliffs, N.J., 1961.

COMMONER, BARRY. *The Closing Circle.* Alfred A. Knopf, New York, 1971.

ECKSTEIN, OTTO. "Economic Policy in the United States." In *Economic Policy in Our Time,* edited by E. S. Kirschen and Associates, Rand McNally and Company, Chicago, 1964.

———, and ROGER BRINNER. *The Inflation Process in the United States.* Joint Economic Committee, Washington, D.C., 1971.

FABRICANT, SOLOMON. "Factors Affecting the Trend of Government Activity." In *The Trend of Government Activity in the United States since 1900.* National Bureau of Economic Research, New York, 1953.

FEDERAL TRADE COMMISSION. "Economic Report on Corporate Mergers." In *Hearings, Economic Concentration,* Part 8A, Washington, D.C., 1969.

GALBRAITH, JOHN KENNETH. *The Affluent Society,* 2d ed. Houghton Mifflin Company, Boston, 1969.

HEILBRONER, ROBERT L. *The Limits of Capitalism.* Harper and Row Publishers, Inc., New York, 1966.

HOLT, C. C., C. D. MACRAE, S. O. SCHWEITZER, and R. E. SMITH. *The Unemployment Inflation Dilemma: A Manpower Solution.* The Urban Institute, Washington, D.C., 1971.

INITIATIVE COMMITTEE FOR NATIONAL PLANNING. "For a National Economic Planning System." *Challenge,* March–April 1975, 51–53.

JOINT ECONOMIC COMMITTEE. *Restoration of Effective Sovereignty to Solve Social Problems.* Washington, D.C., 1971.

LEONTIEF, WASSILY. "What an Economic Planning Board Should Do." *Challenge,* July–August 1974.

MUELLER, WILLARD F. *A Primer on Monopoly and Competition.* Random House, Inc., New York, 1970.

NATIONAL COMMISSION ON TECHNOLOGY, AUTOMATION, AND ECONOMIC PROGRESS. *Technology and the American Economy,* I. Washington, D.C., 1966.

ORGANISATION FOR ECONOMIC CO-OPERATION AND DEVELOPMENT. *OECD Surveys, United States,* 1976.

PRESIDENT'S TASK FORCE ON ECONOMIC GROWTH. *Policies for American Economic Progress in the Seventies.* Washington, D.C., 1970.

REICH, CHARLES A. *The Greening of America.* Random House, Inc., New York, 1970.

SCHULTZE, CHARLES L. *The Politics and Economics of Public Spending.* The Brookings Institution, Washington, D.C., 1968.

———, and others. *Setting National Priorities: The 1971 Budget.* The Brookings Institution, Washington, D.C., 1968.

SHEAHAN, JOHN. *The Wage-Price Guideposts.* The Brookings Institution, Washington, D.C., 1967.

SHULTZ, GEORGE P., and ROBERT Z. ALIBER, eds. *Guidelines, Informal Controls, and the Market Place.* University of Chicago Press, Chicago, 1966.

SLICHTER, SUMNER. *The American Economy.* Alfred A. Knopf, New York, 1950.

SMITH, DAVID C. *Incomes Policies.* Economic Council of Canada, Ottawa, 1966.

THUROW, LESTER C. "The American Economy in the Year 2000." *American Economic Review,* LXIII (May 1972), 439–443.

Chapter 4
The Mature British Capitalist Economy

Among the major Western European industrialized nations, the United Kingdom is closest to the United States in its structure and functioning. Like the United States, the United Kingdom has resisted the strong trends towards increasing government intervention and planning. Ever since the industrial revolution of the early nineteenth century, the United Kingdom has displayed much stronger laissez faire tendencies than have France, the Netherlands, and the Scandinavian countries. During two intervals since 1945, the British Labour party has tried to turn the nation away from its laissez faire course, but these efforts have not greatly altered the British capitalist system. In the first interval, 1945-1951, the Labour government succeeded in nationalizing a number of basic economic activities including the national health service; but in the second interval, 1964-1970, the Labour government did little to change the structure and functioning of the British private enterprise system.

"The Middle Way"

The capitalism that the Conservative party set about restoring after 1951 was described by Harold Macmillan, a prominent member of the Conservative party and Conservative Prime Minister from 1957 to 1963, as "the Middle Way" between the laissez faire economic system of the last century and the socialist system of the Labour party. The twentieth-century capitalism of the Conservative party accepts a limited area in which public enterprise is permissible, proposes to guarantee full employment and a certain minimum of income for each family, and seeks to combine efficiency and freedom in the dominant private sector of the economy. Attention is paid to meeting certain minimum welfare needs of the general population, but securing high levels of consumer and occupational freedom in an efficient economic system is given the chief priority. The main reliance is upon the free-market mechanism as an allocator of economic resources and a distributor of goods and services in accordance with individual consumer preferences.

Restoring the capitalist system meant to the leaders of the Conservative party substituting for the planned economic system of the Labour government the free market system as the main determinant of the direction of economic activities. Although the Labour government did not eliminate the free market mechanism, it imposed upon this system many controls and restraints unacceptable to private business interests and the Conservative party. The restored capitalism of the Conservatives emphasizes "incentives" and "freedom," as against the "welfare" and "planning" of the Labourites. Both parties are concerned with personal incentives, freedoms, and welfare and government planning; but the "welfare socialism" of the Labour party is separated from the "middleway capitalism" of the Conservative party by the different ways in which these important objectives are combined and emphasized.

According to one measure, shares of the world's industrial production, the United Kingdom ranks fourth among the Western world's industrialized nations, being surpassed only by the United States, West Germany, and Japan. According to per capita income, the United Kingdom now stands fourteenth. It has succeeded in developing a highly productive economy, even though its natural resources are very limited. In addition to its total civilian labor force of 25 million, the United Kingdom's limited natural resources consist of 30 million acres of arable land, large coal deposits, limited reserves of low-grade iron ore, sizable natural gas and oil deposits in the North Sea, and an abundance of fish in coastal waters. Until electricity can be generated in large amounts from nuclear-energy plants, the British economy will have to continue to derive most of its electric power from coal and oil. British agriculture remains small scale, with the great majority of holdings below the optimum size of four hundred acres. Having very few natural resources, the United Kingdom must depend upon a large export-import trade, just like West Germany, the Scandinavian countries, France, and the Netherlands. The United Kingdom's annual exports and imports are each equal to about 25 percent of Gross National Product. If it is to achieve a satisfactory level of economic performance, the United Kingdom must remain internationally competitive with the United States, major Western European countries, and Japan.

The Structure of the Mature British Economy

As in the case of the other Western industrialized countries, in the United Kingdom, industry contributes a very large share of the nation's gross domestic product. Table 4-1 shows that manufacturing accounts for 27.2 percent and agriculture for only 2.5 percent of gross domestic product—a contribution that is less than that of agriculture in West Germany and the United States. In both France and Japan, agriculture contributes much more to total output than it contributes in the United Kingdom.

While the structure of the British industrial sector is very similar to that of the United States, the total size of the British industrial sector is much smaller than that of the United States. In 1973 the United States accounted for 41.1 percent of total world manufacturing, whereas the United Kingdom provided only 5.6 percent. Like the United States and the other major Western European industrialized countries, the United Kingdom has a sizable

Table 4-1
Gross Domestic Product by Kind of Economic Activity in the United Kingdom and Selected Countries, 1973

	France (1972)	United Kingdom (1972)	West Germany	Japan	United States
Agriculture	6.2	2.5	2.9	5.9	4.5
Mining	—	1.4	3.5[1]	0.6	1.5
Manufacturing	36.2	27.2	40.4	37.8	25.2
Electricity, gas, and water	—	2.7	8.1	1.5	2.3
Construction	9.8	5.6	—	8.3	4.8
Domestic trade and commerce	—	9.1	12.4	18.7	17.4
Transportation and communications	47.8	7.8	5.7	7.9	6.3
Other activities	—	43.7	27.0	19.3	38.0
Gross domestic product	100.0	100.0	100.0	100.0	100.0

[1] Includes construction.

Source: United Nations, *Monthly Bulletin of Statistics*, Vol. XXIX, May 1975.

core of large industrial enterprises, surrounded by many middle-sized and small-scale firms. The fifty largest British industrial enterprises account for approximately one-third of the total employment in industry. While the size of the British industrial sector is much smaller than that of the United States, the degree of concentration in the major industries is very similar in both countries.[1] Using an index of concentration based on the number of employees accounted for by the three (in the United Kingdom) or four (in the United States) largest firms in each industry investigated, a study revealed that in the United Kingdom 14 percent and in the United States 12 percent of the business firms studied had concentrations of over 70 percent; in both countries, 15 percent of the firms investigated had concentrations of between 50 and 69 percent.[2]

The very large British industrial firms are found in the iron and steel, chemical, electrical machinery, transport equipment, petroleum, food, and tobacco industries. There are no giant companies in the apparel, lumber, furniture, and leather product industries, and very few in the textile, printing, and stone, clay, and glass industries. Of the three hundred largest industrial companies outside the United States (in 1972) only Japan has more (seventy-five) than the United Kingdom.[3] West Germany is third, with forty-four

[1] An analysis of industrial concentration in the United Kingdom and other industrialized nations is given in the Hearings before the Senate Subcommittee on Antitrust and Monopoly, *Economic Concentration*, Parts 7 and 7A, Washington, D.C., April 1968.

[2] P. Sargant Florence, *The Logic of British and American Industry,* London: Routledge and K. Paul, 1953, pp. 130–135. See also P. E. Hart, M. A. Utton, and G. Walshe, *Mergers and Concentration in British Industry,* National Institute of Economic and Social Research, London, 1973.

[3] "Fortune's Directory of the 300 Largest Industrials outside the United States," *Fortune,* Vol. LXXXVI, No. 2, Aug. 1972, p. 152.

companies, while France is fourth with thirty-one companies. The largest three of the three hundred industrial enterprises outside the United States are British (Royal Dutch Shell, Unilever, and British Petroleum), while nineteen of the one hundred largest firms outside the United States have headquarters in the United Kingdom.

British industry is highly organized, with each major industry well represented by a trade association. In the larger industries, federations of employers have been established to deal with problems in the field of industrial relations. British industry has as its general spokesman the powerful Confederation of British Industry, with a membership of thirteen thousand companies and over two hundred trade associations and employers' federations. This confederation represents industry in all important discussions with the government concerning economic policies that relate to business affairs. It also provides representatives on councils and committees where the two sides of industry are brought together for the consideration of the government's economic proposals and programs.

In the United Kingdom, banking is highly concentrated. The banking system is dominated by nineteen large banks with fourteen thousand branches, which account for two-thirds of the total deposits in the nation's commercial banks. Among these banks, the eleven London Clearing Banks have a unique position, since they play the major role in the money market and are closely associated with the central bank, the Bank of England, in the determination of credit policy.

Unlike the Continental European countries where the trade union movement is concentrated in a small number of large unions, the United Kingdom still has many remnants of the craft union movement of the nineteenth century. At present, the 326 British trade unions have a membership of approximately 11.5 million. Almost three-quarters of this membership, however, is found in the 21 largest unions, and 60 percent of the total membership belongs to the 11 unions, each of which has a membership of over 250,000. The trend in the British trade union movement in the past decade has been towards the reduction of the number of unions through amalgamation and merger. The nation's major unions are united in a confederation, the Trades Union Congress, which represents 112 trade unions, with a combined membership of approximately 10 million. While the Trades Union Congress has much less control over its member unions than similar confederations in the Netherlands and the Scandinavian countries, it does speak for organized labor on all economic policy matters. Likewise, the National Farmers' Unions in England, Scotland, and Ireland provide leadership in all matters that affect agriculture and the welfare of the 734,000 people engaged in the agricultural sector and who provide one-half of the United Kingdom's food supply.

A special feature of the British economy is its large public sector, considerably expanded in the early post–World War II years when the British Labour government nationalized the steel, railroad, trucking, gas, electricity, aviation, and communication industries, along with the Bank of England and the nation's health service. Apart from the trucking industry, the nationalized sector remains as it was established by the Labour government in 1945–1951. The end result of the nationalization program was a further concentration of British industry, when the many small coal-mining and steel companies were combined to form the large public coal and steel corporations. No large private industrial company approaches in size the National Coal Board, which has 450,000 employees.

The structure of the mature British economy places a great deal of power in the hands of the few hundred leaders of a small number of large industrial enterprises, trade unions, and banks, and of organizations such as the Confederation of British Industry and the Trades Union Congress that represent these various powerful economic interest groups. All post–World War II governments in the United Kingdom have consulted with these various private groups and organizations when economic policies and programs were being developed or altered. Evidently, no government program for stabilizing the economy at a high level of employment and production can be successful in the long run unless it secures the cooperation of the two sides of industry and the various organizations representing these two sides. Thus far, little progress has been recorded in the development of a collaboration among the government, business, and labor that could lead to a stabilized, noninflationary economy.

The Functioning of the Mature British Economy

In the years since the end of the Second World War, the British economy has not performed as well as the majority of the Western European industrialized economies. On the economic front, the United Kingdom has done poorly when compared with France, West Germany, the Netherlands, and the Scandinavian countries; it has not been a member of what is described as the "growth league."[4] A comparison of the average annual increases in per capita Gross National Product since 1965, presented in Table 4–2, shows that, whereas West Germany, France, the Netherlands, and the Scandinavian countries have had annual increases in per capita Gross National Product ranging from 3 to 4 percent, the increase in the United Kingdom's per capita GNP has

[4] Angus Maddison, *Economic Growth in the West, Comparative Experience in Europe and North America*, New York: The Twentieth Century Fund, 1964, p. 29. Maddison divides the Western industrialized countries into the fast-growing and the slow-growing groups, the latter of which includes the United Kingdom, the United States, and Canada. While there are special factors to account in part for the rapid postwar economic growth of France, Italy, and West Germany, such as the postwar reconstruction and the flight from agriculture, it is widely conceded that the United Kingdom's growth in the past three decades has been sluggish.

Table 4–2

GNP Per Capita (1972) and Average Annual GNP Per Capita Growth Rate (1965–1972) in the United Kingdom and Selected Countries

	GNP per capita 1972 (in U.S. dollars)	GNP per capita growth rate 1965–1972 (in percent)
United States	5,590	2.0
Sweden	4,480	2.5
Canada	4,440	3.2
France	3,620	4.8
West Germany	3,390	4.1
United Kingdom	2,600	2.0
Japan	2,320	9.7
Italy	1,960	4.3
U.S.S.R.	1,530	5.9

Source: International Bank for Reconstruction and Development, *World Bank Atlas*, 1974.

been only 2 percent. It is quite clear that since 1960 the United Kingdom has been suffering a decline in relation to other industrialized countries. Whereas during 1961–1971 total world industrial production increased at the average annual rate of 5.7 percent and for the 6 members of the European Common Market 5.6 percent, industrial production in the United Kingdom increased at the annual rate of only 2.8 percent.

The failure of the British economy to keep up with its industrial partners in Western Europe has had adverse effects on Britain's international trade position. The recent decline in the international competitiveness of the British economy is measured by the fall in the United Kingdom's share of total world exports of manufactured goods. Table 4–3 shows that while the Netherlands, West Germany, Italy, and Japan increased their shares of these exports, the share of the United Kingdom, like that of the United States, suffered a decline. The United Kingdom's share of world exports of manufactured goods declined from 16.5 percent in 1960 to 8.8 percent in 1974. In the same period, Japan increased its share from 6.9 to 14.2 percent, and Italy from 5.1 to 6.9 percent. Much smaller increases were recorded for West Germany, the Netherlands, and Canada, while France's share fell from 9.6 to 9.0 percent.

During the years when the United Kingdom's industry was performing at a low level and was losing its competitive position abroad, recurring crises in the balance of international payments made it impossible to build up an adequate reserve of gold and foreign currency. The chronic need to subordinate domestic economic policies to external policies aimed at safeguarding the pound contributed to the poor overall performance of the nation's economy. During most of 1960–1972, unemployment remained at a low level in spite of the generally poor functioning of the economy. Output per man-hour in the United Kingdom since 1960 increased much more slowly than output per man-hour in neighboring industrial countries. In these countries, output per man-hour increased at an average annual rate of 6 or more percent, whereas in the United Kingdom the annual rate of improvement in industrial productivity was only 3.6 percent.

The combination of low productivity improvement and strong inflationary pressures arising from rapid increases in prices and wage rates in the past decade resulted in the United Kingdom's increasingly pricing itself out of the world's trade markets. During 1963–1972, British export prices increased at an average annual rate of 4.7 percent, whereas the rate in West Germany was only 0.8 percent and in Japan 1.1 percent. With these adverse developments, it was inevitable that the

Table 4–3
The United Kingdom's and Selected Countries' Shares of Total World Exports of Manufactured Goods, 1960–1974 (In Percent)

	United Kingdom	West Germany	France	Japan	Italy	United States
1960	16.5	19.3	9.6	6.9	5.1	21.6
1966	13.4	19.3	8.6	9.7	6.9	20.1
1970	10.8	19.8	8.7	11.7	7.2	18.5
1974	8.8	21.7	9.0	14.2	6.9	19.1

Source: National Institute of Economic and Social Research, *National Institute Economic Review,* Feb. 1975.

British economy would become the weak one among the major Western European industrialized economies.

The Reaction to Britain's Postwar Economic Problems

Both the Conservative and Labour parties have recognized the need to tackle the problem of energizing the sluggish British economy. In their party manifestoes, these parties have stressed the importance of achieving the goal of a vigorous economy with sustained and high economic growth and reduced inflationary pressures.[5] Both parties have proposed measures to curb restrictive business and labor practices, to devote more resources to industrial research and development, to get industry to take advantage of technological advances, and to modernize industry with the aid of a high level of private investment. While both parties agree regarding the goal of a modernized British economy, they hold very different views about the policies and programs that should be followed to achieve it.

The British Labour party has since 1945 proposed to improve the performance of the British economy with the aid of a national planning program that would be similar to the planning program now being carried on in Sweden and Norway. In these Scandinavian countries, medium-term (four- or five-year) national economic budgets, based on projections of Gross National Product and its uses for private and public consumption and investment, are the framework within which national economic policies and programs are constructed. With the aid of economic controls, the Swedish and Norwegian governments curb private consumption and expand both private and public investment. The general aim is to secure a high-investment economy that will direct an adequate flow of resources to the export industries and to the domestic industries that support the export industries. In this democratic national planning program that still relies primarily on private industry to turn out the bulk of the nation's gross national product, the government calls upon both business and organized labor to cooperate with it in the planning program to increase total output, improve labor productivity, and curb inflationary tendencies. The British Labour party's national planning program, while democratic and indicative in nature, requires an activist government that is prepared to intervene extensively in the nation's economic affairs.

The economic policies and programs of the British Conservative party are directly opposed to those of the Labour party. All Conservative governments since 1951 have stressed the desirability of achieving a better performance of the British economy by strengthening the free private enterprise economy. The economic program of the new Conservative government that took office in June 1970 was based on a view of the economic system similar to that which underlies the idealized model of the mature industrial economy discussed in Chapter 2. The main reliance for the good functioning of the economy is on the private business system. The Conservative government's program includes providing new incentives to saving, reforming the tax system and reducing the burden of taxation, and liberating industry from what is held to be unnecessary government intervention. The leaders of the Conservative government believe that if government controls are reduced, if organized labor can be induced to take a more responsible attitude toward unofficial strikes and work stoppages, and if business leaders can be encouraged to

---

[5] See, for example, the British Labour party's political manifesto for the 1964 general election, *The New Britain*, Part 2: "Planning the New Britain," pp. 8–13.

invest more extensively, a large increase in production will result, offsetting the economy's strong inflationary pressures.

In the Speech from the Throne of July 2, 1970, the Conservative government declared that its "first concern will be to strengthen the economy and curb inflation" with the aid of "rising production and a steadily growing national income."[6] The Conservative government emphasized that "vigorous competition is the best safeguard of the consumer," opposing any effort to plan the nation's economic activities as recommended by the Labour government in 1964–1970. Instead, the emphasis after June 1970 was on reducing the role of government in these activities and giving more weight to the operations of the supply and demand forces of the free market system to produce a balanced and efficient noninflationary economy.

The Conservative Party and Private Enterprise

The Conservative party election victory of October 1951 led to a restoration of the unplanned private enterprise system in the United Kingdom. The fairly narrow margin of their political victory caused the Conservative government to move slowly in making the transition from the planned economy of the Labour government to the post-1951 free private enterprise system. Although the British economy of the 1950s is best described as a free enterprise system, it was in some ways more regulated than similar systems in the United States and Canada. It was only by 1960 that most of the Labour government controls were abandoned. The main economic control preserved from the Labor government period

[6] House of Commons, *Parliamentary Debates* (Hansard), Fifth Series, Vol. 803, Session 1970–71, H.M.S.O., London, July 2, 1970, pp. 46–47.

was the control of sales of foreign exchange and of capital movements abroad. A second major carry-over from the Labour government's regime was the large area of nationalization. The Conservative government made no move to put the nationalized industries back into private hands—except for the iron and steel industry and long-distance trucking, which were denationalized. Other carry-overs were the national health service and rent control. In general, however, the Conservative government persistently moved forward after 1951 in restoring and advancing a regulated but unplanned private enterprise system.

In the industrial field, the Conservative government eliminated direct price controls, industrial raw-material rationing, and the allocation of industrial output. Business enterprises became free to import raw materials and other industrial items, to pursue their own capital-investment plans, and to price their output as they wished. Issues of company stocks and bonds were no longer regulated by the Capital Issues Committee, and the building licensing system under which factory construction was controlled prior to 1951 was abolished. Credit was no longer rationed to business enterprises by the commercial banks in accordance with directives issued to them by the Bank of England and with the backing of the Chancellor of the Exchequer. With the elimination of all export controls, British business enterprises were free to export their output to whatever markets they believed to be the most profitable.

Whereas British industrial markets were opened to vigorous competition from domestic and international sources, the British domestic agricultural markets remained highly protected. The Conservative government abandoned the system under which the government purchased all the output of the major agricultural products at controlled prices, and then resold these products to processors and wholesalers, and eventually to the consuming public at controlled retail prices. Under the Conservative government's agricultural program, farmers sold their output on the protected domestic markets for whatever price it would freely bring. At the same time, the government and the National Farmers Unions agreed on what were called "standard" or fair prices for each major farm product. When prices in the free domestic markets fell below "standard" prices set by the annual agreements (longer term for animal products), the government made up the difference by giving the farmers "deficiency payments."[7] Standard price guarantees and deficiency payments were used in connection with such major farm products as livestock, milk, eggs, wool, cereals, potatoes, and sugar beets. The production of crops was still controlled in order to prevent the accumulation of unsalable surpluses. Deficiency payments were also supplemented by "production grants" calculated to improve the efficiency of British agriculture. These production grants, which were subsidies, were given to farmers to encourage the ploughing-up of grassland, the use of fertilizers and lime, and the improved breeding and rearing of cattle. Production grants were also given under the post-Labour agricultural program to improve farm buildings and other capital facilities.

The Conservative governments after 1951 also widened the area of free private enterprise in the United Kingdom's external economy. All state or government trading, except for the stockpiling of strategic raw materials, was eliminated. The government no longer imported major raw materials and foodstuffs. Free commodity markets for cotton, lumber, tin, rubber, tea, and other major imports were re-established. The Conservative governments of Winston Churchill, Anthony Eden, and Harold Macmillan emphasized the importance of placing British foreign trade on a private, multilateral basis. State trading, government controlled commodity markets, bilateral trade agreements, and detailed foreign exchange controls had no permanent place in the international trade program of the Conservative government. The free enterprise markets of the domestic economy were combined with the free markets of the external economy.

The welfare aspects of the unplanned capitalism espoused by the postwar Conservative party did not involve any major advance beyond the position taken by the Labour party. The social service system inherited by the Conservative government of 1951 remained largely unchanged. The Conservative government made no move to make any major alterations in the Labour government's national health service. The only modification called for new or larger charges for various health services, so that a smaller financial burden was imposed on the Treasury after 1951. The postwar Conservative governments reduced housing subsidies, as well as subsidies on various foods, including bread and milk. They also curbed public-house building and enlarged the proportion of total annual house construction taken up by private house construction. Local government authorities, which under the Labour government secured low interest loans for the construction of municipal apartment buildings, were required to borrow at prevailing money market rates for construction purposes.

After 1951, the Conservative governments substituted free real estate markets for the highly regulated markets of 1945–1951. The Labour government's incremental land value or betterment tax program was abolished. The Town and Country Planning Act of 1953 abolished development charges (incremental

---

[7] The Central Office of Information, *Agriculture in Britain*, London, H.M.S.O., 1962, pp. 18–24.

value taxes), and left land owners free to realize the development value of their land, provided they could get the necessary permission from the local town and country zoning and land-use planning authority.[8] The Conservative government, under the Rent Act of 1957, provided for the decontrol at once of more than 800,000 houses, and on others controlled rents were increased.[9] After 1957, rent control did not apply to formerly rent-controlled houses that became vacant and were re-rented, or on houses coming up for rent for the first time and on new houses. The Conservative government's policy of progressive relaxation of rent control was pursued for two reasons. First, the freezing of rents at prewar levels allegedly so reduced landlords' investment returns that landlords were unwilling to do the necessary maintenance work. Consequently, many rented houses deteriorated into slum houses. Second, rent control led to an uneconomic use of housing accommodations. Security of tenure at low rent made many people unwilling to release houses that were too big for their needs, as in the case of old people whose families had grown up and left them.

The Performance of the British Capitalist Economy, 1951–1963

When the Conservative party took over the direction of the British economy in late 1951, prewar per capita levels of personal consumption had been restored. Industrial production was about 50 percent above its 1938 level; the volume of exports had reached the target of 75 percent above prewar; and the United Kingdom had demonstrated its ability to secure a favorable balance of payments in its external economy. The Conservative party started off in 1951 with an economy that, even though it was still very vulnerable to adverse developments from abroad, was in a generally sound condition. The years 1951–1962 were on the whole quite prosperous years for the British people. No prolonged serious recessions took place. Total national production continued to expand, and the nation's standard of living continued to improve. Apart from brief periods in 1952 and 1958, there was full employment. As production increased, consumption rose, and a new era of mass consumption was introduced in the area of durable goods, such as cars and television sets. However, although prosperity continued, some major economic problems persisted. Industrial production and exports expanded at much slower rates than in most of the Continental European countries. Also, the unfavorable balance of international payments continued to be a serious problem and prevented the United Kingdom from building up adequate reserves of gold and foreign exchange. Although much was accomplished by the Conservative governments during the 1950s, after about a decade in power there existed even among Conservatives a strong undercurrent of dissatisfaction with the performance of the British economy and its prospects for the 1960s.

Considerable light is thrown upon the performance of the British economy by an analysis of the distribution of the Gross National Product in Table 4-4. These statistics reveal that the Conservative governments were more concerned with developing a high-investment, limited-consumption economy than was the Labour government. Private consumption as a percentage of Gross National Product averaged 70.4 percent during the years 1948–1951 under the Labour government, and only 65.9 percent during 1952–1961 under Conservative governments. Gross

[8] The Central Office of Information, *Town and Country Planning in Britain*, London, H.M.S.O., 1962, pp. 6–7.
[9] The Central Office of Information, *Housing in Britain*, London, H.M.S.O., 1960, pp. 30–31.

Table 4-4
The Percentage Distribution of the United Kingdom's Gross National Product in Selected Years, 1948–1962

Distribution	1948	1951	1954	1957	1962
Private consumption	71.6	68.9	66.6	64.7	65.2
Public consumption	14.8	16.7	17.6	16.6	17.4
Gross domestic fixed investment	12.2	13.1	14.3	15.5	16.3
Change in inventories	1.0	3.9	0.3	1.7	0.3
Export surplus (+) or import surplus (−)	0.4	−2.6	1.2	1.5	0.8
Gross national product	100.0	100.0	100.0	100.0	100.0

Source: Organisation for Economic Co-operation and Development, *General Statistics*, Jan. 1962, and May 1964.

domestic investment in plant and equipment averaged 12.7 percent of Gross National Product in 1948–1951, and 15.1 percent in 1952–1962. The Conservative governments, while not reducing private consumption in absolute terms, were able to reduce private consumption and to increase capital investment as proportions of GNP. The Conservative governments altered fiscal and monetary policies in favor of private business companies as against private households. The tax system was adjusted so as to stimulate private investment in industrial plant and equipment and to curb private consumption. Higher purchase (sales) taxes and restrictive hire-purchase (installment buying) arrangements were used to direct the flow of economic resources away from private consumption and towards private investment. This was in line with the Conservative party's position that economic policy should stress the role of private investment as a factor in economic expansion. If the free market mechanism was to be revived as the major determinant of the direction and level of economic activity, it had to be supported by adequate private investment.

Public consumption made about as heavy a demand on the nation's total output under the Conservative governments as under the Labour government. Public consumption annually absorbed about 16 percent of Gross National Product in the Labour years 1948–1951 and about 17 percent in the Conservative years 1952–1963. Defense, education, health, and other social service needs continued to be about as important after as before 1951.

Various aspects of the performance of the United Kingdom's economy during 1953–1963 are revealed by the statistics relating to selected economic indicators given in Table 4–5. The major features of the United Kingdom's domestic economic development in 1953–1963 were a slow, but continuous, expansion and a very low rate of unemployment. The average annual increase in the United Kingdom's Gross National Product in those years was 2.6 percent, which was very low compared with the average annual economic growth rate in the six Common Market countries (5.6 percent), France (4.6 percent), and West Germany (7.1 percent).

The main reason for the slow annual increase in the United Kingdom's total national output was the low annual increase in its industrial production. During these years, British industrial production increased half as fast as French industrial production and much more slowly than German industrial production. All seventeen European members of the

Table 4-5
Selected British Economic Indicators, 1953–1963 (1953 = 100)

Year	Gross National Product	Per capita Gross National Product	Industrial production	Output per man-hour in manufacturing	Hourly earnings in manufacturing	Wholesale prices	Consumer prices	Volume of exports	Rate of Unemployment
1953	100	100	100	100	100	100	100	100	1.7
1954	104	104	107	102	107	100	102	104	1.4
1955	107	106	113	107	116	103	106	112	1.1
1956	110	109	113	106	123	107	112	118	1.2
1957	112	110	115	109	133	111	116	120	1.5
1958	113	111	114	110	137	111	119	115	2.2
1959	117	114	120	115	142	112	120	119	2.2
1960	122	118	128	121	155	113	121	125	1.7
1961	124	120	130	121	164	116	125	128	1.5
1962	125	119	131	124	171	119	131	131	2.0
1963	129	122	135	131	178	121	134	138	2.5
Average annual increase: 1953–1963	2.6%	2.0%	3.1%	2.7%	5.9%	2.0%	3.0%	3.3%	1.7%[1]

[1] Annual average.

Sources: OECD, *General Statistics*, Jan. 1964, and National Institute of Economic and Social Research, *National Institute Economic Review*, May 1964.

Organisation for European Economic Co-operation increased their industrial production in 1953–1960 at the annual average rate of 6.5 percent, while British industrial production rose at the average annual rate of only 3.1 percent. British industrial production increased at a relatively slow annual rate, even though the United Kingdom continued to raise the level of investment in industrial plant and equipment. In many years, the United Kingdom never succeeded in securing a full use of its industrial productive capacity. During these years, the Conservative government's main concern was with securing a favorable balance in the United Kingdom's external economy and not with securing a high rate of economic growth. When boom conditions appeared after 1951 and imports tended to become excessive, the government increased interest rates and taxes and reduced its spending in order to curb boom conditions, reduce imports, and protect the country's gold and foreign exchange reserves. Time and again economic expansion was cut off for mainly financial reasons. In these circumstances, both industrial production and GNP increased at low annual rates.

In spite of low annual economic growth, the British average annual rate of unemployment of 1.7 percent was one of the lowest in Western Europe. Two special factors account for this very low unemployment rate in the United Kingdom. Employers, when faced with a national economic slowdown, put their workers on a short work week in order to keep their work force intact. Also, many women and older workers, who lost their jobs in slow periods, left the work force and did not return until the next upswing. They did not therefore appear among the unemployed. The nation was thus faced with the paradox of retarded economic growth and a very low unemployment rate.

Although 1953–1963 was a period in which the United Kingdom had a relatively slow rate of economic growth and also had considerable slack in its economy, nevertheless, strong inflationary pressures were at work in these years. British wholesale prices, while not rising as rapidly as French wholesale prices, increased much more than did West German, Italian, and Dutch wholesale prices. Over the period 1953–1963, the average annual increase in British wholesale prices was 2 percent, whereas the annual rate of increase of West Germany's (Britain's main European competitor) wholesale prices was only a little more than one-half of 1 percent. Since import prices of raw materials fell during these years, the United Kingdom's inflationary pressures were generated by domestic factors. The main factor leading to domestic inflation was of a cost-push and not a demand-pull nature.

The Conservative governments of the period after 1951 made no attempt to change the system of free collective bargaining which was carried on in a very decentralized manner.[10] The typical annual wage development took the form of a wage round in which a few large trade unions, usually in high-productivity industries, secured wage increases, which then became the bargaining targets of unions in low-productivity industries. This spilling over of wage increases from high-productivity industries into lower-productivity industries caused the average hourly wage increase to rise faster than overall national productivity. Table 4-5 shows that wage rates on the average increased twice as fast as did output per man-hour in manufacturing. For the period 1953–1963, average hourly earnings in manufacturing increased 5.9 percent a year, while output per man-hour in manufacturing rose only 2.7 percent a year. Higher unit labor costs were passed on to consumers by business enterprises in the form of

---

[10] Organisation for European Economic Co-operation, "Wage Determination in the United Kingdom," *The Problem of Rising Prices*, Paris, 1961, pp. 419–447.

higher retail prices. Higher consumer prices then stimulated further wage demands. Since no one was prepared to break the wage-cost-price cycle, the wage-price spiral continued upward in 1953–1963.

Weaknesses of the Domestic Economy

The weaknesses of the United Kingdom's domestic economy in the years 1952–1963 were particularly significant in relation to the country's external or international economy. Retarded industrial production at home meant a correspondingly slow growth of British exports. These exports after 1951 increased at the same low rate (3.1 percent a year) as did industrial production. From 1953 to 1963, the volume of total goods exports of the United Kingdom increased at the average annual rate of 3.3 percent, whereas the average annual rate for all six European Common Market countries was 11.9 percent. West Germany, Britain's major European competitor, increased its volume of exports during these years at the average annual rate of 14.3 percent; France's annual rate was 9.8 percent. The sluggish behavior of the British export trade contrasted strongly with the vigorous export activity of most West European countries.

The failure of British exports to expand rapidly after 1951 created major problems in the United Kingdom's external economy, which had very adverse repercussions on its domestic economy. After 1951, the United Kingdom found it very difficult to build up its gold and foreign exchange reserve and maintain the international or external value of the British pound. The Conservative government started its new term of office in late 1951 with an inadequate gold and foreign exchange reserve equal to $1.958 billion United States dollars. This reserve was equal to the value of only three months' imports. It had been estimated that the United Kingdom's gold and foreign exchange reserve should at a minimum be equal to six months' imports if the government was to have adequate room in which to maneuver financially with the aim of offsetting the impact of adverse fluctuating economic conditions on the gold and foreign exchange reserve and on the international value of the British pound. According to this financial rule-of-thumb, the United Kingdom's official gold and foreign exchange reserve, which was the equivalent of approximately $2 billion in 1952, should have been approximately $4 billion at that time.

During 1953–1963, the United Kingdom was unable permanently to build up its gold and foreign exchange reserve. As the statistics in Table 4-6 reveal, this reserve never increased substantially after 1951 (except during the years 1960–1962) and stood at about the same level in 1963 as it had been ten years earlier. The gold and foreign exchange reserve, which was £909 million ($2.5 billion) in 1953, was £949 million ($2.6 billion) in 1963. During this decade, the United Kingdom's gold and foreign exchange reserve reached a maximum of $3.3 billion, but it was not possible to maintain this level for an extended period of time or to move beyond it. Although the United Kingdom in most years exported more goods and services than it imported and so had a favorable current balance on its international account in all years from 1953 to 1963 (except for 1955 and 1961), nevertheless it was unable to accumulate an adequate gold and foreign exchange reserve. The surpluses on its current international account were too small; and in addition, there were large drains on its international capital account in the form of investments in, and loans and grants to, Commonwealth countries.

The inability of the United Kingdom to build up adequate gold and foreign exchange reserves was strikingly different from the experience of West Germany and France in this

Table 4-6
The United Kingdom's Balance of Current International Payments, Volume of Exports, and Gold and Foreign Exchange Reserve, 1953-1963

Year	United Kingdom			West Germany's gold and foreign exchange reserve (million U.S. $)	France's gold and foreign exchange reserve (million U.S. $)
	Volume of exports	Balance of current international payments (million U.S. $)	Gold and foreign exchange reserve (end of year) (million U.S. $)		
1953	100	414	2,546	1,956	829
1954	104	350	2,798	2,636	1,261
1955	112	−437	2,156	3,076	1,912
1956	118	580	2,272	4,291	1,180
1957	120	605	2,374	5,644	645
1958	115	958	3,105	6,322	1,050
1959	119	592	2,750	5,015	1,720
1960	125	722	3,239	7,199	2,070
1961	128	−28	3,324	6,541	2,939
1962	131	285	3,311	6,447	3,610
1963	138	339	2,657	7,102	4,457

Sources: OECD, *General Statistics*, Jan. 1964; and National Institute of Economic and Social Research, *National Institute Economic Review*, May 1964.

area. West Germany's gold and foreign exchange reserve valued in United States dollars, approximately $2 billion in 1953, had increased to $7.1 billion in 1963. In the same period, France's reserve increased more than five times, rising from $829 million in 1953 to $4.4 billion in 1963. Both France and West Germany were able to increase their gold and foreign exchange reserves very considerably after 1953 because they had large surpluses on their current international accounts which were not offset by capital movements to the outside world.

British Economic Policy, 1951-1963

British economic policy during the 1950s had five major goals: (1) full employment, (2) reasonably stable prices, (3) adequate and sustained economic growth, (4) an international payments surplus on current account, and (5) adequate gold and dollar reserves. Although all five economic goals were very much desired, special importance was attached to maintaining full employment, securing reasonably stable prices, and achieving a favorable balance of international payments. Lower priorities were in practice assigned to securing adequate economic growth and building up larger reserves of gold and dollars. The British Conservative governments followed, for political reasons, the Keynesian policy of maintaining full employment at all costs. A full-employment policy, coupled with costly practices in wage negotiations, created a scarcity of labor and a tendency for wage rates to rise more rapidly than output per man-hour; this resulted in rising prices, large consumer-disposable incomes and a big demand for imported consumer goods or raw materials going into consumer goods. Since the United Kingdom at the same time had a relatively low rate of economic growth and a slow expansion of its volume of exported commodities, the rate of increase of merchandise imports tended to rise faster than the rate of increase of merchandise exports.

The main difficulty facing the British economy in the years 1952–1963 was the recurring disequilibrium in its external sector. With inadequate gold and dollar reserves and small export surpluses of goods and services, the British government had little room to maneuver in as it attempted to work out economic policies for dealing effectively with this persisting disequilibrium. Being one of the world's bankers, the United Kingdom had to give the highest priority to preserving the international value of the pound, even at the cost of inadequate economic growth. The British Labour government had endeavored before 1951 to meet the same problem with the aid of many direct economic controls. The British Conservative government abandoned these controls and attempted to cope with the problem of preserving the international value of the pound and the nation's gold and dollar reserves largely with the aid of indirect economic controls.

In the decade following the end of the Korean War (1953), the British economy passed through three major economic periods: the boom period of 1954–1957, the recession of 1958–1959, and the period of recovery and renewed expansion from 1960 to 1963. The boom period from 1954 to 1957 was accompanied by rapid increases in wage rates and in wholesale and retail prices and by adverse balances on current account in the international sector. The gold and foreign exchange reserve fell from approximately $2.8 billion in 1954 to the dangerously low level of $2.1 billion in 1955, continuing at this low level until 1958. The Conservative government's anti-inflationary program included a wide variety of measures designed to put a damper on economic expansion. In the monetary area, interest rates, including the Bank of England's discount rate, were sharply increased; the Chancellor of the Exchequer had informal talks with the London bankers concerning the need to curb credit expansion; hire-purchase (installment credit) controls were reintroduced; and the Capital Issues Committee placed additional restrictions on new security issues.

In the fiscal area during the boom period, the government increased the rates of purchase taxes and of taxes on distributed profits. Personal saving was encouraged by selling premium bonds that gave their owners the chance of winning annual drawings and by reducing the tax on the interest earned on small amounts of savings. Investment spending by businesses was discouraged by suspending initial depreciation allowances that permitted very large depreciation chargeoffs in the first year of any industrial equipment's use. Investment allowances, which permitted businesses to deduct a certain percent of any new investment from their annual tax bill, were also dropped. Special efforts were made to curb government spending for investment purposes. The capital investment programs of the nationalized industries were reduced, and local government authorities were asked by the central government to reduce their capital expenditures. These various anti-inflationary measures were effective in curbing imports and putting an end to the drain on the gold and foreign exchange reserves. However, wage rates and prices continued to rise from 1955 to 1957. Also, equilibrium was restored in the nation's external economy, but only at the price of industrial stagnation. Total industrial production was almost stationary in the three years 1955–1957, and very little increase in Gross National Product was recorded in the same period. The strong anti-inflationary measures not only curbed domestic production, but also slowed down the expansion of the volume of exports.

The recession years of 1958 and 1959 were accompanied by the reversal of the anti-inflationary measures adopted in 1955–1957. The credit squeeze was eliminated; taxes such as purchase taxes and taxes on distributed profits were reduced; and government capital spending was increased. With the return to more prosperous conditions after 1959, various anti-inflationary measures, such as increases in required reserves for commercial banks, higher central bank discount rates, and new hire-purchase controls, were adopted. During the years 1960–1962, the United Kingdom's internal economy was stagnant. Both industrial production and Gross National Product increased very little in these three years, even though wage rates and wholesale and retail prices underwent large annual increases. Inflationary wage and price developments in the boom years 1954–1957 could be attributed to the excess total demand that existed in those years.

The same explanation for inflationary developments could not be applied to the years 1960–1962, when industry had excess capacity, the unemployment rate had risen from the 1 percent of the boom years in the mid-1950s to 2 percent in 1962, and total demand was not excessive. Much of the price inflation of the years 1960–1962 was the consequence of wage inflation. Since wage rates increased faster than labor productivity, unit labor costs rose and were passed on by business enterprises in wholesale and retail price increases. Rising wage rates and domestic prices introduced the prospect of a new disequilibrium in the United Kingdom's external economy, since they led to higher export prices and a less competitive position for the United Kingdom in the world economy.

With improving economic conditions in 1960–1962, the value of the United Kingdom's imports of goods and services increased more rapidly than did the value of its exported goods and services. As national income rose, business people expanded inventories of imported goods and raw materials, and consumers increased their demand for imported products. In both 1960 and 1961, the United Kingdom had an adverse balance of international payments on current account. The import surplus led to a drain on the nation's gold and foreign exchange reserve. By 1963, this reserve of $2.6 billion was below what it had been in 1954 ($2.8 billion). In 1962, the Conservative government decided that a new approach to the United Kingdom's economic problems was necessary if the recurring problems of the 1950s were not to reappear during the 1960s. This new approach was to give special attention to improving industrial productivity, to raising the annual rate of economic growth, to developing a national incomes policy in order to curb inflationary developments, and to increasing the volume of exports in order to secure a favorable balance of international payments on current account.

The Development of a National Incomes Policy

The inflationary developments in the British economy and their adverse effects upon the rate of economic growth and the volume of exports raised the question of the need for a national incomes policy that would lead to more price stability and adequate economic growth. In March 1956, the British government issued a White Paper on "The Economic Implications of Full Employment," which called attention to the close association between full employment and rising prices. The White Paper pointed out that there was in the United Kingdom, to a greater extent than in many other Western European countries, "a continuing tendency for prices to rise as incomes increase faster than output."[11] The government had to ensure a high level of total domestic demand for goods and services in order to maintain full employment. But a high level of total domestic demand meant a strong demand for labor and a sellers' market at home for business people. In these circumstances, wage rates and profit margins increase more than is warranted by productivity improvements, if the prosperous economic conditions are fully exploited by trade unions and private business enterprises.

The White Paper of 1956 declared that "The solution lies in self-restraint in making wage claims and fixing profit margins and prices, so that total money income rises no faster than total output." The principle governing wage-rate adjustment should be the equalizing of average wage-rate increases and average improvement in national productivity. National productivity is measured by the amount of Gross National Product per man-hour per employed worker. If this output or product per man-hour annually increases 2.5 percent, wage rates on the average should increase no more than 2.5 percent a year. Wage rates in some industries where labor is in short supply may increase more than 2.5 percent a year in order to attract additional labor. In those industries with an annual productivity improvement considerably below the national average of 2.5 percent, the White Paper of 1956 stated that it may be necessary to grant wage-rate increases above the annual productivity improvement actually achieved in the industry in order to preserve "labor solidarity" or harmonious industrial relations. But in general annual average wage-rate increases should approximate the annual average improvement in Gross National Product per man-hour per employed worker.

[11] The Prime Minister, *The Economic Implications of Full Employment*, London, H.M.S.O., 1956, Cmnd. 9725, p. 5.

The price guideline enunciated in the White Paper of 1956 called for price reductions in those industries in which productivity rose more rapidly than the average productivity for the whole economy. In industries with less than average annual productivity improvement, prices could be increased where wage rates increased more than the productivity improvement in the industry. Price increases would be offset by price decreases so that prices in general would be stable. The government did not suggest any means of securing these wage and price objectives, except through an appeal for self-restraint on the part of the two sides of industry. When the government's appeal fell on deaf ears in the period 1956–1957, and both wage rates and prices continued to rise in the United Kingdom more than in such major foreign trade competitors as West Germany, France, Italy, and the Netherlands, the government appointed the Council on Prices, Productivity, and Incomes in August 1957 to keep price and wage developments under review and to make recommendations with regard to wage and price policy.

After studying the United Kingdom's price and wage problems for four years, the council did not go much beyond the 1956 White Paper on "The Economic Implications of Full Employment" in making proposals for securing noninflationary wage and price-profit adjustments. The council was extremely vague with respect to measures for achieving price stability. It was aware that businesses could easily increase prices in order to maintain or expand profit margins in a situation in which total demand was excessive and a sellers' market prevailed. The council also realized that even when total demand was not excessive and a sellers' market did not exist, business people who followed a "cost plus" or administered pricing policy could also attempt to raise prices with the aim of preserving or expanding profit margins. The two recommendations of the council for curbing excessive profits were that the government should prohibit business agreements involving price maintenance and that import duties should be lowered to make the home markets more competitive.[12] Lower prices in the United Kingdom's domestic market would induce British business enterprises to seek better markets abroad and to increase the volume of exports.

The Council on Prices, Productivity, and Incomes pointed out that a national wage policy tying average wage-rate increases to average national productivity improvement could not be successfully pursued until excessive wage increases at the local factory level were eliminated. It was at the local factory level that wage drifting (the payment of wage rates above the level agreed upon by employers and trade unions) took place. If wage drifting was to be reduced or prevented, more attention would have to be given at the local level to adjustments in wage rates originally determined on a national or industry-wide basis. Wage policy also would not be successful until the "annual rounds" of wage increases at the national level, in which low-productivity industries demanded the same wage increases as high-productivity industries, were also eliminated.

While the work of the Council on Prices, Productivity, and Incomes did not produce many concrete suggestions for improving wage and price policies, it did make very considerable progress in other directions. In its fourth and final annual report, the council stated that wage and price policies would not be successfully carried out until the United Kingdom could be assured a high and sustained annual rate of economic growth comparable to that of other countries such as France, Sweden, and West Germany. The council went on to explain that "there are three areas on which it [economic policy] must be brought to bear. The first contains all the forces that make for higher productivity, and those that shelter inefficiency or obstruct growth and change. The second contains those that generate the pressure of excess demand. In the third are the procedures through which rates of pay and profit are arrived at—the pricing decisions that fix profit margins, and bargaining on incomes both nationally and locally. In all three areas the aim of policy must be to provide a setting in which the forces making for growth are strengthened, and money incomes do not outrun production."[13]

The council further pointed out that labor productivity in the United Kingdom could be improved by increasing labor's skills and by providing adequate capital investment per laborer. Neither manpower nor investment needs should be left to the uncoordinated production and investment intentions of individual business enterprises. Instead, there should be government projections of manpower and investment requirements for the whole economy and for the various sectors of the economy. A "certain rate of growth in the rest of the economy" would have to be assumed, and projections of manpower and investment requirements would be adjusted to the estimated or projected rate of growth of the whole economy. In this manner, the labor-hiring and capital-investing intentions of business enterprises could be coordinated under government direction in order to avoid excessive or inadequate demands upon the country's labor and capital supplies. The expansion programs of separate business enterprises could be collected and collated in a national projection or program. The council pointed out that this was already being done in the British iron and steel industry, where the Iron and Steel Board coordinated the

---

[12] The Council on Prices, Productivity and Incomes, *Fourth Report*, London, H.M.S.O., July 1961, pp. 25–26.

[13] *Ibid.*, p. 19.

production and investment plans of all the private iron and steel companies in order to meet the steel needs of the expanding British economy.

It was also called to the government's attention that national programming or projecting of the labor, raw material, and investment requirements for the whole economy was being done by the Plan Commission in France with considerable success. The council believed that national programming had imparted a stimulus to France's economic growth since it was adopted in 1948. Where national programming had resulted in a high and sustained economic growth, there was a corresponding reduction in labor's fear of redundancy and an increase in its willingness to accept the consequences of technological progress. In these economic circumstances, it was much easier to develop and carry out a national incomes policy.

National Economic Development Council

In March 1962, the Council on Prices, Productivity, and Incomes was replaced by the National Economic Development Council, with twenty members representing the Treasury, the Board of Trade, the Ministry of Labour, the Trades Union Congress, private business, and the general public. The new council was assigned the tasks of examining "the economic performance of the nation," uncovering the "obstacles to quicker growth," and securing agreement on ways of increasing the "rate of sound growth."[14] A "target rate" of economic growth of 4 percent a year was set up for the period 1962-1966, and a five-year projection was made of the uses or distribution of gross domestic product. The implications of the 4 percent average annual increase in gross domestic product were worked out for a large cross section of British industry to indicate the manpower and investment needs for a 4 percent average annual economic growth in 1962-1966.

Table 4-7 shows the projection of the total available supply of goods and services for 1966 and their estimated or projected uses in that year. Total supply was projected to increase at the average annual rate of 4 percent, but personal and public consumption were projected to grow only 3.5 percent a year. Meanwhile, gross domestic investment in plant and equipment was projected to increase at the much higher average annual rate of 5.3 percent. The objective of economic policy was to curb private and public consumption in favor of a higher rate of public and private investment than prevailed prior to 1962. In this manner, the retarded economic growth rate of the 1950s was to be replaced by a higher and more adequate growth rate. In addition, during 1962-1966, the export of goods was projected to increase more rapidly (at an average annual rate of 5 percent) than the import of goods (at an average annual rate of 4 percent). In this manner, the export surplus would be a source of an expanding supply of gold and foreign exchange which could be used to build up the United Kingdom's reserve of gold and foreign exchange.

The National Economic Development Council drew attention in its report on The Growth of the United Kingdom Economy, 1961-1966 (1963) to the factors leading to a retarded rate of economic growth from 1953 to 1963. These factors included inadequate measures to increase the mobility of labor; a failure by business enterprises to introduce quickly new industrial techniques, processes, and raw materials; inadequate use of newer management techniques; and too low a level of capital investment per worker. The council listed a number of proposals in its report on Conditions Favourable to Faster Growth (1963) that could in its opinion lead to a

[14] National Economic Development Council, Growth of the United Kingdom Economy, 1961-1966, London, H.M.S.O., 1963, p. viii.

Table 4–7
Actual Uses of the Total Supply of Goods and Services in the United Kingdom in 1961 and Projected Uses in 1966

Goods and services	1961 Actual (million £)	1966 Projected[1] (million £)	Increase percent per annum
Total supply of goods and services			
Gross domestic product	26,491	32,230	4.0
Imports of goods	4,006	4,870	4.0
Net imports of services	70	95	—
Total	30,567	37,195	4.0
Uses of total available supply			
Personal consumption	17,336	20,590	3.5
Public consumption	4,570	5,440	3.5
Gross domestic investment	4,798	6,225	5.3
Exports of goods	3,863	4,940	5.0
Total	30,567	37,195	4.0

[1] At 1961 prices.

Source: National Economic Development Council, *Growth of the United Kingdom Economy, 1961–1966*, 1963, p. 32.

higher rate of economic growth.[15] Attention was directed to the following needs: larger expenditures on scientific and management education and on retraining; the forward planning of labor requirements to improve labor mobility and to reduce labor redundancy; a regional development program; a permanent improvement in the balance of international payments; and a tax program that would stimulate investment and economic growth. The council also emphasized the need for wage, price, and profit policies that would prevent inflationary developments in the full-employment or high-pressure economy that was the objective of the government's new economic program.

In November 1962, the government established a National Incomes Commission that was given the task of "keeping the rate of increase of the aggregate of monetary incomes within the long-term rate of increase of national production."[16] Disagreements between employers and trade unions over wage adjustments were to be referred to the commission, which would make public reports on how wage problems should be settled if inflation was to be avoided. In the 1962 wage dispute in the Scottish building trades, the commission recommended average wage increases of 3 percent a year, which were equal to the average annual increase in national productivity in recent years.

By the end of 1964, the proposals for employing national economic planning in the United Kingdom as a basis for constructing economic policies and measures designed to increase the nation's rate of economic growth had not borne much fruit. The political developments of 1963—1964 were not conducive

[15] National Economic Development Council, *Conditions Favourable to Faster Growth*, London, H.M.S.O., 1963, pp. 1–43.

[16] The National Incomes Commission, *Report on the Scottish Plumbers' and the Scottish Builders' Agreements of 1962*, London, H.M.S.O., 1963, Cmnd. 1994, p. iii.

to much experimentation in the area of economic policy. Further progress along these lines could not be made until political uncertainties were eliminated by the general election of late 1964. The United Kingdom's rate of economic growth in 1962 and 1963 continued to be much below the National Economic Development Council's target rate of 4 percent a year. The annual increases in gross domestic product for 1962 and 1963 were 0.2 and 3.0 percent respectively.[17] If national economic programming was to be the means of coping successfully with the United Kingdom's problem of a retarded rate of economic growth, there was by 1964 no clear indication as to how national programming could bring about this desired result. In 1963, the British government could say only that "Success in achieving a higher rate of economic growth will depend, to a large extent, on the way in which the Government, management and unions carry out their respective functions and on a new spirit of co-operation between them to make a reality of the agreed common objective."[18] Seven years were to pass before the Conservative party would be given the opportunity to try out a new policy of government, business, and labor cooperation; for it lost the general election of 1964 and was not returned to office until 1970.

The Conservative Party's Economic Program, 1970–1974

When the Conservative party took over the government again in June 1970, it was faced with an increasingly serious inflation problem. In the six months before the election, wage rates in manufacturing had risen at the average annual rate of 13 percent and retail prices at the rate of 8 percent. The inflation was not primarily due to the pressure of excess total demand, since economic growth had been retarded and unemployment was rising. The wage-price spiral was in large part the result of the exercise of market power by large business enterprises and large trade unions. Wage-rate increases far above the annual increase in output per man-hour secured by major trade unions initiated wage rounds; these in turn led less powerful unions to demand wage-rate increases much in excess of productivity improvement. These large wage-rate increases were then passed on to consumers in the form of price increases. A particularly disturbing consequence of the wage-price spiral was the increase in export prices that exceeded the increase in these prices in West Germany, France, Japan, and other nations competing with the United Kingdom in world markets.

The Conservative government planned to deal with the growing inflation problem after 1970 by reducing the gap between increases in incomes and in productivity. Several steps were taken to raise the productivity of industry and to curb wage increases at the same time. The fiscal policy of the new Conservative government called for curbing government spending and making adjustments in the tax system that would stimulate individual effort and efficiency. Personal income taxes were reduced; and private industry was to be stimulated by a reduction of the tax on company income, by making provision for more liberal depreciation rules, and by providing tax credits or allowances on investments in new plant and equipment. The overall fiscal aim was to shift resources from the public to the private sector, where private investment was counted on to spur economic growth.[19]

[17] Her Majesty's Treasury, *Economic Report, 1963*, London, H.M.S.O., March, 1964, p. 7.
[18] National Economic Development Council, *op. cit.*, p. 52.
[19] The long-term policy aimed at reducing the public sector's claim on the nation's economic resources was explained in the White Paper on *New Policies for Public Spending*, Cmnd. 4515, H.M.S.O., London, Oct. 1970. See also *Public Expenditures 1969-70 to 1974-75*, Cmnd. 4578, H.M.S.O., London, Jan. 1971.

The Conservative government's monetary policy in 1970–1974 was also designed to curb inflation without curbing economic growth and the expansion of exports. This policy sought to restrict the total amount of credit by placing a ceiling on the total credit supply and on the credit extended by individual financial institutions. The ability of the large London clearing banks to extend credit was restricted by having them place special deposits with the Bank of England and by the sale by the Bank of government bonds to the nonbank sector. At the same time that bank reserves and the money supply were curbed, the private banks were advised by the government to ration their supply of credit in a manner that would favor private investment in the export and export-supporting industries.

The Conservative government was not in favor of direct intervention on the price and wage fronts. It was not willing to go beyond the general pronouncement that "it is an essential condition of price stability that increases in incomes should not exceed increases in productivity."[20] The government did not propose to establish any specific or detailed wage and price guidelines on the ground that such guidelines had not been used successfully in the past.[21] The new policy with regard to prices and wages was to be based on a tougher stand which the government would take towards wage demands coming from government employees and workers in the nationalized industries. The government declared that it was prepared to sit out strikes in the public sector if it was necessary to achieve its wage increase goals, and that it would not intervene in private wage negotiations to secure compromises involving what it took to be excessive wage claims. The government expressed the hope that private business enterprises would also take a stronger stand against excessive wage demands. It was convinced that in the long run this stiffer approach would break the wage-price spiral and greatly reduce the inflationary pressures.

In 1970 and 1971, retail prices and wage rates continued to increase; they reached an explosive situation in 1971 when retail prices increased 7.7 percent and hourly earnings in manufacturing 13.3 percent. Private investment in plant and equipment did not respond favorably to the tax concessions that had been made by the government, and economic growth slowed down. Unemployment rose and reached the highest level (3 percent) since the end of the Second World War. Two years of slow economic growth in 1971 and 1972 created a sizable gap between the actual and the potential gross domestic product. One favorable development in these years was the continued high level of exports and the achievement of a large surplus in the current balance of international payments. The domestic inflation, however, was leading to higher export prices, which were eventually to reduce the United Kingdom's merchandise exports and by 1973 to result in a large deficit in the economy's external sector.[22]

When it became evident in 1971 that the domestic economic program was not working successfully, the Conservative government turned to a more active price-incomes policy. It proposed that business and organized labor should voluntarily adopt wage-price

[20] *Parliamentary Debates (Hansard)*, Vol. 883, 1971–72, p. 758.

[21] An analysis of the pre-1970 price-incomes policy is given in Lloyd Ulman and Robert J. Flanagan, *Wage Restraint: A Study of Incomes Policies in Western Europe*, Berkeley: University of California Press, 1971, pp. 11–47. The authors are inclined to the view that the adoption of some kind of price-incomes policy with specific guidelines is inevitable in the United Kingdom. See also David C. Smith, *Incomes Policies, Some Foreign Experiences and their Relevance for Canada*, Ottawa, Queen's Printer, 1966, pp. 95–119.

[22] The decline in the United Kingdom's external position is analyzed in some detail in G. F. Ray, "Labour Costs and International Competitiveness," *National Institute Economic Review*, Aug. 1972, pp. 55–56.

guidelines that would set definite limits to wage and price increases. The members of the British Confederation of Industry agreed to limit price increases to a maximum of 5 percent during the year ending July 31, 1972. Organized labor was asked to set up a similar guideline for wage increases. It refused to do so, but did agree to take the 5 percent price guideline into consideration during wage negotiations.

After two years of low economic growth (1970–1971), during which the annual unemployment rate increased from 2.1 to 3 percent, the government adopted an expansionary program. With the aim of stimulating demand, the fiscal budget for 1971–1972 increased personal income-tax concessions, reduced purchase (sales) taxes, provided for rapid depreciation on all new investments in machinery and equipment, increased tax allowances on industrial buildings, and reduced the tax rates on some capital gains. Also, the restrictions on the total supply of credit were relaxed, and the money supply was permitted to grow at a much faster rate than that of 1971. Although the rate of price and wage increases declined in the first half of 1972, British export prices continued to increase faster than these prices in competing countries. In the face of a deteriorating balance-of-international-payments situation, the government in June 1972 abandoned the fixed exchange rate for the pound and replaced it with a floating exchange rate in order to stimulate exports.

The efforts made in 1972 to reduce unemployment and to improve the economy's growth rate with the aid of stimulative fiscal and monetary policies prepared the way for new inflationary developments. To meet this problem, the Conservative government again turned in mid-1972 to a consideration of a voluntary price-incomes policy. It sought to enlist the cooperation of the Confederation of British Industry and the Trades Union Congress in developing this policy. The government suggested that the 5 percent price guideline of the Confederation of British Industry be continued after July 31, 1972, and that a wage guideline that limited weekly wage-rate increases to a maximum of two pounds a week be accepted by the Trades Union Congress. Some further adjustments in wage rates would be made if the retail price index rose above 6 percent in the next 12 months. When organized labor rejected the government's proposals, the tripartite discussions on price-incomes policy were stopped. On November 6, 1972, the government announced a ninety-day freeze on wages, prices (except for fruits, vegetables, meat, fish, and imported products), rents, and dividends.[23]

The standstill was continued until April 1973, when the second phase of the wage-price control program was begun. In this phase, manufacturers were not permitted to raise their prices except to take account of unavoidable cost increases resulting from wage adjustments or higher import prices. Ceilings were placed on both dividends and profits. Profits could not exceed the best profit margin (net profits as a percentage of sales) in the previous five years. Dividends were limited to a 5 percent annual increase, while wage-rate increases could not exceed 7 percent a year. An upper limit of £250 (approximately $600) a year was placed on all pay increases. All large business firms had to secure prior approval for price increases from the newly established Price Commission, and wage increases had to be approved by the Pay Board.

The major objective of the Conservative government's counter-inflation program was to prevent inflation from exceeding 5 percent annually. It was expected that at some point in

[23] Details of the wage-price standstill arrangements are given in *A Programme for Controlling Inflation: the First Stage*, Cmnd. 5125, H.M.S.O., London, Nov. 1972.

the future the second stage of the compulsory wage and price controls would be replaced by a voluntary price-incomes policy. The Heath price-incomes policy adopted in 1972 was similar in its essentials to the Wilson policy adopted in 1966. The latter policy temporarily curbed price and wage inflation, but it did not provide any long-term solution to the problem of inflation. It was widely believed that the Heath counter-inflation program of 1972–1973 would be no more successful than was the Wilson program.

In its analysis of the experiences of the United Kingdom with incomes policies, the Organisation for Economic Co-operation and Development pointed out that British incomes policies have been only "mildly beneficial."[24] During price and wage freezes in the United Kingdom in the past, stresses have been built up which have led to a rebound of wages and prices after the freeze has been lifted. The general belief is that price-incomes policies cannot be successful in the United Kingdom until certain attitudinal and institutional changes have been made. Less militant and more cooperative attitudes on the part of business and organized labor are necessary, as well as a more responsible centralized collective bargaining system that will keep the national welfare in mind. The Confederation of British Industry and the Trades Union Congress are not now in a position to establish the centralized collective bargaining system that has had considerable success in the Netherlands and the Scandinavian countries. What is needed for a successful working out of a price-incomes policy is a coordinated strategy for price and wage adjustments by the large industrial enterprises and trade unions within a framework that takes account of both private and public interests.

The Organisation for Economic Cooperation and Development, which made an analysis of the inflation problem in its twenty-one member countries, concluded in its 1970 report, *Inflation, The Present Problem*, that where large economic interest groups compete for shares of the national income without adequate overall national economic guidance, the resulting incomes race necessarily leads to the development of strong, inflationary pressures. The Organisation for Economic Co-operation and Development asserts that "the search for some form of price-incomes policy cannot be abandoned. If this is accepted, past experience seems to indicate that a broader, longer-term and less immediately ambitious approach may have to be adopted . . . it nevertheless seems likely that an effective policy will require guide lines of greater or less precision as to what increase in money incomes and price behaviour would, in the prevailing circumstances, be consistent with the collective interest."[25]

Furthermore, the Organisation for Economic Co-operation and Development explains that some fundamental changes in employer-employee attitudes and collective bargaining institutions will have to be made before an effective price-incomes policy can be established. This is especially true of the United Kingdom where organized labor and private business are frequently uncooperative and the collective bargaining system is highly decentralized. The National Economic Development Council as early as 1963 emphasized the need for a "new spirit of co-operation" in any program for curbing inflation and achieving high and sustained economic growth.[26] A decade later, unfortunately, there was no evidence that any such new spirit

[24] Organisation for Economic Co-operation and Development, *OECD Economic Surveys, United Kingdom*, Nov. 1970, p. 25.

[25] Organisation for Economic Co-operation and Development, *Inflation, The Present Problem*, Paris, Dec. 1970, p. 11.

[26] National Economic Development Council, *Conditions Favourable to Faster Growth*, 1963, p. 52.

of labor-business cooperation had been achieved.

The British Economic Crisis, 1973–1974

In June 1973, the Heath government entered the fourth year of office with the expectation that the economic upturn of early 1973 would be followed by continued prosperity. The economic indicators in Table 4–8 show that 1970–1972 were poor years with low economic growth rates and rising unemployment accompanied by considerable price and wage inflation. During these years, however, some strengthening of the pound sterling occurred; this resulted from a favorable balance between exports and imports after 1969. During 1970–1973 the average annual increase in gross domestic product was close to the long-term average of 2.8 percent. Annual consumer price increases of 8 percent were higher than the increases over the decade of the 1960s (about 5 percent). In 1970–1973, average annual wage-rate increases in the manufacturing industries of 13.7 percent about equaled the average annual improvement in output per worker (4.6 percent) and the increases in consumer prices (8 percent). The wage and price explosions did not come until 1974.

In the upturn of 1973, the gross domestic product and industrial production increased at the rates of 5.3 and 7.3 percent, respectively, and the unemployment rate in that year declined from 3.8 to 2.6 percent. The 1973–1974 fiscal budget that was adopted in April 1973 was described as being "broadly neutral" in its effect on the nation's economy. It was constructed in order to secure a 5 percent increase in total national output; this increase was to be led by increasing exports accompanied by wage and price controls under Stage Two of the counter-inflationary program.

Table 4–8
Percent Changes over Previous Years in Selected British Economic Indicators, 1970–1974

	Gross domestic product	Consumer prices	Wholesale prices[1]	Hourly earnings[2]	Output per man-hour[2]	Unemployment rate[3]	Current balance of payments (mil. £s)
1970	1.5	6.4	5.3	15.2	1.0	2.6	460
1971	1.8	8.4	4.6	11.8	5.0	3.4	698
1972	2.3	7.1	4.4	14.0	7.0	3.7	1,052
1973	5.3	9.2	32.3	13.1	5.4	2.6	82
1974	−0.5	16.1	48.9	20.1	−2.4	2.6	−1,117
Average annual change, 1970–74	2.1%	9.6%	19.1%	14.8%	3.2%	3.0%	—

[1] Prices of basic materials.
[2] In manufacturing.
[3] Annual rates.

Sources: National Institute of Economic and Social Research, *National Institute Economic Review*, Feb. 1975; Central Statistical Office, *Economic Trends*, April 1975; and International Monetary Fund, *International Financial Statistics*, June 1975.

The Heath government's 1973 program for orderly economic expansion was undermined by the worldwide commodity inflation that gripped all industrial nations during 1973.

In late 1973, this program was disrupted further by the oil crisis that followed the Arab-Israeli conflict of October 1973. The energy crisis in Great Britain was greatly exacerbated by the industrial strife that accompanied Stage Two of the wage-price control program, which had never received the endorsement of the Trades Union Congress or the trade unions. During 1973, the gas, automobile, and hospital workers, the longshoremen, and some branches of the civil service went out on strike, while other workers such as the coal miners, railwaymen, and power-station engineers banned all overtime work and reduced production by working slowly according to rule. The energy crisis then worsened, and the foreign trade deficit reached alarming proportions as increases in import prices greatly exceeded increases in export prices. The government on November 13, 1973, declared a national emergency for the fifth time since 1970 and assumed the power to regulate the supply and distribution of food, gas, oil, and electricity. A number of additional measures were taken to cope with the worsening economic situation. On December 13, 1973, the government ordered a three-day work week in order to conserve the use of all forms of energy and reduced the supply of electric power going to the assembly-line industries by 35 percent.

The emergency fiscal budget of December 17, 1973, reduced proposed government expenditures by £1,200 million ($2.7 billion) and increased taxes on personal incomes over $11,500 by 10 percent. It also tightened monetary policy by raising commercial-bank, base-lending rates to their highest level since 1914 (10 percent)—by increasing the reserve requirements for the London banks, and by severely restricting consumer installment credit.

On February 5, 1974, the National Union of Mineworkers, which had rejected a wage increase of 16.5 percent, called for a strike. The government refused to bargain with the coal miners and was in the midst of a serious confrontation with them when it lost the general election of February 28, 1974.

By early 1974, the prospect for an increase in Britain's gross domestic product was nil. Unemployment was rapidly increasing, and both retail prices and wage rates in industry were rising at explosive rates. The current balance of international payments, which had been favorable from 1969 to 1972, was projected to be in greater deficit than it had been in 1973. Many of the critics of the Heath government asserted that it was much too inflexible in its unwillingness to bargain with the coal miners and other workers in the nationalized industries. More serious than this failure to enter into collective bargaining in the public sector was the underlying hostility between organized labor and the government, which increased as international developments greatly weakened the United Kingdom's external position. Even if domestic circumstances had been much more favorable than they were in 1973–1974, it is highly probable that the United Kingdom would have experienced very serious difficulties in its efforts to cope with the international developments of those years.

Table 4-9, which shows the increases in consumer prices in the United Kingdom and eight other industrial countries, reveals that all these countries, with the exception of West Germany, had much higher inflation rates in 1974 than in 1973. The United Kingdom, Italy, and Japan experienced much higher rates of inflation than the other six selected countries, and also than the twenty-four OECD members taken as a group. The severe inflation that afflicted the United Kingdom and other industrial countries was accompanied by widespread declines in their rates

Table 4-9
Consumer Price Inflation in the United Kingdom and Selected Countries (In Percent), 1962-1974

	1962-1972	1973	1974
Italy	4.3	10.8	24.5
Japan	5.7	11.7	21.9
United Kingdom	4.9	9.2	19.1
France	4.4	7.3	15.2
United States	3.3	6.2	12.2
Sweden	4.7	6.7	11.6
Norway	5.1	7.5	11.3
Netherlands	5.4	8.0	10.9
West Germany	3.2	6.9	5.9
OECD average	3.9	7.9	14.2

Source: International Monetary Fund, *International Financial Statistics*, June 1976.

of economic growth. Table 4-10 presents the rates of real economic growth in the United Kingdom and other industrial countries from 1959 to 1974, with estimates for 1975. The United Kingdom, the United States, and Japan had negative growth rates in 1974, while France, West Germany, Italy, and Canada grew more slowly in 1974 than in 1973. According to the OECD estimates for 1975, growth rates in industrial countries will continue to be much below their long-term level.

The course of domestic events since February 1974, when the new Labour government came into office, does not suggest that this government will have much more success than did the previous Conservative government in making the British economy viable. Neither the Conservative party nor the Labour party is prepared to cope successfully with the United Kingdom's long-standing economic problems. By mid-1975, it appeared to many leaders in the Western industrial countries that the 1974-1975 recession had reached its bottom and that in the second half of 1975 an upturn might occur. It was still doubtful, however, that the United Kingdom would be a member of any high-growth league in the second half of the 1970s.

Supply Management in the British Economy

Demand management in the British economy is primarily concerned with the short-term financial aspects of the program for economic stabilization. Under demand management, fiscal and monetary policies have been used primarily to influence the course of private and public demand in the immediate future. Demand management, however, is not alone sufficient for the achievement of noninflationary economic stability and growth. Securing the good performance of an industrialized economy requires combining demand-and-supply management. In the latter type of management, attention is directed towards the supply side of the nation's economic activities where there may be major obstacles to the achievement of high levels of efficiency and productivity. In order to be competitive in world markets, the United Kingdom must have an efficient economic system, with highly productive workers. Much of the failure of the United Kingdom to be competitive in the international sector can be attributed to deficiencies in industrial and market organization and to inefficiencies in the use of labor.

Various British studies have pointed out a number of factors said to be responsible for much of the inefficiency and low productivity of British industry.[27] These studies conclude

---
[27] For an analysis of the productivity problems of British industry, see National Economic Development Council, *Conditions Favourable to Faster Growth* and *Growth of the United Kingdom Economy to 1966*, 1963. An American view of the same problems is presented in Richard E. Caves and Associates, *Britain's Economic Prospects*, Washington: The Brookings Institution, 1960. See

Table 4–10
Average Growth of Real Gross National Product in Seven Major Countries (In Percent), 1959–1975

	1959–1960 to 1971–1972	1973	1974	1975[1]
United States	4.1	5.9	−1.75	−2.0
France	5.8	6.0	4.75	3.0
West Germany	4.9	5.3	1.0	2.5
Italy	5.5	6.0	4.75	−0.25
United Kingdom	3.1	5.3	−0.5	1.75
Japan	11.0	10.2	−3.25	2.0
Canada	5.0	6.8	4.5	3.5
Total of above countries	5.5	6.5	−0.25	0.25
Total OECD	5.4	6.3	0.25	0.5

[1] Estimated by OECD.

Source: OECD, *Economic Outlook*, 16, Dec. 1974.

that too many industries in the United Kingdom outside of the steel, chemical, machinery and other large-scale industries, have excessive numbers of small-scale producing units with many product lines and production runs that are too short. Many investigators call for an active merger program that would concentrate output in a smaller number of more efficient firms with a larger scale of operation. British industry also suffers from a failure to use the most advanced management techniques, to spend enough on research and development, to introduce promptly advanced industrial processes, and to cope with the scarcity of scientists and engineers. The Robbins Report of 1964 analyzed a number of the deficiencies of the British educational system that adversely affect the efforts of business enterprises to improve their productivity. The report emphasized the importance of expanding business education and improving the education of engineers. The available information suggests a close correlation between larger expenditures on research and development and the improvement of labor efficiency and industrial productivity.

In recent decades, the output of the science-based industries in the United Kingdom has been growing twice as fast as the output of manufacturing industry as a whole. A need now exists to shift resources from basic science to applied research and development and to move resources into the research-intensive industries. Too much of British foreign trade is with the less developed countries, which have little demand for the output of the science-based industries with their very sophisticated technology of production.[28] If the United Kingdom is to

---

also C. F. Pratten, "The Reasons for the Slow Economic Progress of the British Economy," *Oxford Economic Papers*, Vol. 24, No. 2, July 1972, pp. 180–196.

[28] This point is developed in F. V. Meyer, D. C. Corner, and J. E. S. Parker, *Problems of a Mature Economy*, London: Macmillan, 1970, Part IV, "Overseas Trade," pp. 451–496.

compete with the research-oriented industries of West Germany, the Netherlands, and the Scandinavian and other continental countries in the Western European, American, and Canadian markets, British management must develop scientific and technical awareness and more interest in taking advantage of the contributions of industrial research and development. Both the British educational system and the national science policy need to be altered so that they may contribute more than in the past to the productivity of industry.[29]

Labor also raises major obstacles to the improvement of the productivity of British industry. Restrictive shop-floor practices constitute serious barriers to increased labor efficiency. The greater prevalence of craft unionism in the United Kingdom results in considerable resistance to the introduction of new production techniques and to the continued employment of superfluous labor. Labor productivity is reduced by the tendency of British firms to hoard skilled labor in an economy where this labor is frequently in short supply. While considerable progress has been made in recent years in improving manpower policies in the United Kingdom, much remains to be done to improve further the supply and mobility of skilled labor. In 1970, manpower shortages occurred in several branches of engineering and in the chemical and allied industries at the same time that there was considerable unemployment in the mining, shipping, and construction industries. In Southeast England in 1969 and 1970, the unemployment rate was only 1.5 percent as compared to the rate of 4 to 5 percent in Northern England and Scotland.[30] British manpower policies would have to undergo much improvement before they could compare favorably with these policies as they have been developed in the Scandinavian countries.[31]

Demand Management in the United Kingdom

Improving the efficiency and productivity of a nation's industrial system is in many ways a long-term problem. Whereas demand management is in large part concerned with economic stability and growth in the immediate future, supply management takes account of developments that may occur over a number of years. Altering the structure of an industry, improving the level of business management, fostering industrial research and development, and enlarging the supply of skilled personnel involve the use of a long-time horizon.[32] No nation can substantially improve the productivity of its industry on a lasting basis in a short period of time. This problem is made all the more difficult to deal with successfully where there is no widespread agreement on the kind of economic system that should be the national goal. Over the past quarter of a century, the four post–World War II British Labour and Conservative governments have been so occupied with altering and realtering the general shape of the nation's economic system and with coping with periodic short-term economic crises that they have been forced to give less than adequate

[29] For a critical analysis of the role of management in British industry, see Rex Malik, *What's Wrong with British Industry?* Baltimore: Penguin Books, 1964; and Michael Shanks, *The Stagnant Society*, Baltimore: Penguin Books, 1961.

[30] Organisation for Economic Co-operation and Development, *Economic Surveys, United Kingdom*, Nov. 1970, p. 13.

[31] A survey of Swedish manpower policies is given in Andrew Shonfield, "Manpower Planning: Sweden," *Modern Capitalism*, New York: Oxford University Press, 1965, pp. 199–211.

[32] In other words, in many circumstances, the demand situation is more volatile than the cost situation. The buyer with liquid resources can change his or her demand pattern on very short notice. The reaction of suppliers to the demand situation is much slower because of supply bottlenecks, long-term contractual relationships, and various institutional arrangements that prevent the quick adjustment to variations in demand.

attention to the underlying and persisting problem of how to improve the productivity of the United Kingdom's economy so as to make it more competitive in the international markets.

It is now widely conceded that the United Kingdom's main long-term problem is to secure a stable growth of its economy at an agreed-upon annual growth rate. As long as business people expect the United Kingdom's growth rate to be highly irregular from year to year and to stay at an overall low level, they will continue to make investments in plant and equipment on a piecemeal basis. They will tend to refrain from making large investments with the aim of replacing old plants with new modern plants. Low rates of investment and of economic growth will continue to foster a lack of interest in improving production and managerial techniques and in raising the level of expenditures on industrial research and development. The United Kingdom is in a "vicious circle," in which expectations of poor medium-term performance of the nation's economy result in a low rate of investment which in turn contributes to further expectations of poor economic performance. The crucial factor in this adverse circle of economic development is the expectations of business people with regard to the economy's future expansion. This circle can be broken only by securing several years of sustained and high economic growth which will lead business people to have confidence in the future, and which will induce them to invest in plant and equipment at a higher level and on a broader scale than in the recent past.

In the opinion of the Organisation of Economic Co-operation and Development in 1972, an opportune time for such a development would be when the United Kingdom joined the European Common Market.[33] In 1972, there was considerable slack in the United Kingdom's economy, which was moving into the upswing phase of the business cycle. Circumstances were also favorable for the United Kingdom to experiment with production and managerial techniques that could lead to the achieving of a high sustainable annual economic growth rate.

The National Institute of Economic and Social Research, a British nongovernmental research organization, has shown how projections of the nation's gross domestic product could be used as the basis for a program for sustained economic growth and for a more effective program for supply-and-demand management. The Institute's four-year (1972–1975) projection of the United Kingdom's gross domestic product and its consumption and investment uses presented in Table 4–11 was constructed on the assumption that this product would grow at the average annual rate of 4.9 percent.[34] What the Institute proposed as a national goal was a high-private-investment, low-public-expenditure economy that would favor the nation's export industries. In the 1972–1975 gross domestic product projection, public consumption and investment expenditures were limited to an average annual growth rate of 2.75 percent, while private fixed investment expenditures were projected to increase at a rate of 6.5 percent. This high level of private investment would be necessary to sustain the large annual increase in gross domestic product of approximately 5 percent.

The Institute's medium-term gross domestic product projection indicated the contributions to total national output that would have to be made by the electric power, coal, steel and other industries if the medium-term growth goal was to be achieved. The next step would be to show how this projection could

---

[33] Organisation for Economic Co-operation and Development, *OECD Economic Surveys, United Kingdom*, 1972, p. 30.

[34] National Institute of Economic and Social Research, "Medium-Term Forecasts Reassessed," *National Institute Economic Review*, No. 62, Nov. 1972, p. 42–43.

Table 4-11

The Gross Domestic Product and Its Uses in the United Kingdom for 1971 (Actual) and 1975 (Projected) in £ Million, 1963 Prices

	1971 National economic accounts (actual)	1975 National economic budget (projected)	Percent change 1971-1975
Private consumers' expenditures	24,080	29,830	5.5
Public consumption and investment expenditures	9,000	10,000	2.75
Private fixed investment expenditures	3,970	5,120	6.5
Increase in inventories	—	330	—
Net export surplus	125	−375	—
Gross domestic product	37,175	44,905	4.9

Source: National Institute of Economic and Social Research, *National Institute Economic Review*, Nov. 1972.

be employed as the basis for the construction of the government's demand-and-supply management policies. This is done in Sweden, Norway, and France, where published medium-term gross domestic product projections have been used since 1945 as the point of departure for the construction of a sustained economic growth program and its associated demand and supply management policies.

The second requirement for the successful adoption of a program for sustained economic growth is to provide a way in which all the nation's major economic interest groups may participate in the construction and execution of any such program. Before this program can be successful, it must secure the cooperation of all concerned parties that have enough market power to influence significantly the course of economic events. This is especially true of business and labor, which are highly organized in the Western industrialized countries. This means that in the United Kingdom the Confederation of British Industry and the Trades Union Congress have very important roles to play in any program for securing sustained economic growth.

A beginning was made in this direction when the National Economic Development Council in 1964-1970 discussed economic policies and programs with the Department of Economic Affairs. Much more could be done by having the National Economic Development Council, with representatives from management, the trade unions, and the public, cooperate with the government in the construction, publication, and carrying out of medium-term programs for sustained economic growth.[35] All major economic interest groups could then see how their interests would be affected by the medium-term program for economic stabilization and sustained economic growth. Such a development, as has already been explained, would require some fundamental changes in the attitudes of business and organized labor, which until now have displayed little willingness to cooperate with the government in its efforts to place the nation on a path of sustained economic development.[36]

[35] For arguments in favor of moving in this direction, see Thomas Wilson, *Planning and Growth*, London: Macmillan, 1965, pp. 55-61; "Political and Economic Planning," *Growth in the British Economy*, 1960, pp. 24-25; and Andrew Shonfield, *Modern Capitalism*, New York: Oxford University Press, 1965, pp. 171-172.

[36] The lack of enthusiasm of the Trades Union Congress for collaboration with governments on price-incomes, planning, and other economic policies has been longstanding. The situation is not different in

The United Kingdom and the European Economic Community

On January 1, 1974, the United Kingdom, along with Denmark and Ireland, became a member of the European Economic Community. In the view of the Conservative government, membership would improve the efficiency of British industry for a number of reasons. The Community would provide a large trading area with a population of 255 million and a Gross National Product equal to about two-thirds of the American product valued at $1.152 trillion. British membership is expected to raise the pressure for business efficiency, to reduce restrictive trade union practices, and to remove the diseconomies of scale that arise from the excessive product differentiation in the home market. Offsetting the gains from a more efficient industry will be the higher prices paid for agricultural products by British consumers. These higher prices will result from the integration of British agriculture with the community agriculture under the Common Agricultural Policy and from the loss of cheap agricultural imports from New Zealand, Australia, and other areas. It is expected, however, that there will be a net gain from the integration of both British industry and agriculture with the economies of the eight other members of the Community.[37] The size of the gain to be secured from Britain's entry into the European Common Market remains a subject of considerable dispute among economic experts.[38]

Business is much more favorably disposed towards membership in the Common Market than is organized labor. The antipathy of the labor movement towards domestic business is extended to business in the European Common Market, which is considered by a large section of organized labor to be run by foreign bankers and business people. Much of the opposition of the labor movement to British membership stems from its view that a socialist Britain would be dominated by the capitalist EEC members. Both the Trades Union Congress and the left wing of the Labour party are actively opposed to the Common Market because they consider it unrealistic to try to integrate the members both economically and politically. They are also disturbed by the higher farm prices that will result from the Common Agricultural Policy, the restriction of trade with the British Commonwealth and less developed countries, the weakening of the Atlantic alliance with the United States, and the large cost budget imposed on the United Kingdom by the Common Market's budget. The British trade unions are much more aggressive than trade unions in a number of the EEC countries, and they are fearful that they will lose much of their independence in a European Common Market. In spite of the antipathy of a large section of the labor movement to British membership in the EEC, the Labour governments since 1964 have favored this membership. Harold Wilson and the majority of his cabinet thought that this membership would be an aid in the effort to achieve a viable economy.

While it is widely believed that EEC membership will redound to the United Kingdom's benefit, it is also felt that the benefits from this membership will be quite limited and will be

---

industry. As one study of the problem puts it, "But, as in the case of union co-operation, little hope can be entertained of the success of such a policy if private industrialists retain their present desire for independent decision on development policy." "Political and Economic Planning," *Growth in the British Economy,* London: George Allen and Unwin, 1960, p. 25.

[37] Richard E. Caves, *Britain's Economic Prospects,* p. 18, and Lawrence B. Krause, "British Trade Performance," *Ibid.,* pp. 227–228. See also the British White Paper, *Britain and the European Communities: An Economic Assessment,* Cmnd. 4829, Feb. 1970. The European Economic Community is also known as the European Common Market.

[38] See for example G. D. N. Worswick, "Trade and Payments," *Britain's Economic Prospects Reconsidered,* pp. 92–100.

secured only in the long run. Britain's entry into the Common Market will have little to do with removing the ideological antipathies between business and labor, with strenthening the national as against the local trade union leadership, or with removing the negative attitudes of both business and labor towards active cooperation with the government in the effort to place the British economy on a permanently sound basis. Changing economic and political attitudes is a very slow process. For this reason, it should not be surprising if Britain takes many years to find the road to a viable economic system on a sustained basis.

The Search for a Viable British Economy

In the opinion of much of the world, the United Kingdom is now the "sick man" of Western Europe. The sluggish British economy has continued for a number of decades to experience an "entrepreneurial gap," resulting from managerial reluctance to be experimental in business matters, to adopt new organizational forms, and to be aggressive in the use of marketing techniques. Emphasis is all too frequently on routine management rather than on getting over the "developmental hump."[39] Many studies have been made of the failure of Britain to become a member of Europe's "growth league." These studies have generally been inconclusive, as is evidenced by the conclusions arrived at by two recent in-depth analyses of the causes of the sluggish performance of the British economy.[40]

Efforts to uncover the roots of Britain's economic difficulties have frequently concentrated upon a single or a few factors such as poor management, restrictive labor practices, a failure to be aggressive in foreign markets, or the lack of cooperation between business, labor, and the government. Each of these factors may contribute to the United Kingdom's postwar economic problems; but some analysts believe that these problems result from a wide range of economic, social, and political factors that comprise the nation's social climate. If Britain's economic sluggishness is due to its social climate, the government cannot do much to improve the nation's economic performance, since the social climate determines the powers and policies of the government.[41] It has also been argued that the British people prefer the relaxed way of living that goes along with a low rate of economic growth. As the Brookings report on Britain's economic prospects puts the matter, it may be that the British society is one in which "don and docker alike prefer tradition, leisure, and stability" to growth and change.[42] This view, however, is not widely held by many trade union and business leaders, who believe that the British public in general is very much interested in improving its standard of living.

Making the British economy viable on a lasting basis will be a very difficult task, because it would mean reversing many of the adverse economic trends of the past half century. A comparison of the United Kingdom and eleven other democratic industrial nations shows that the British economy has slipped badly since the close of the Second World War. In 1958, the United Kingdom, surpassed only by the United States, Canada, Switzerland, and Sweden, held fifth place in

---

[39] F. V. Meyer, D. C. Corner and J. E. S. Parker, *op. cit.*, pp. 131 and 133.

[40] See the Brookings report, *Britain's Economic Prospects* (1968), and the British reply, *Britain's Economic Prospects Reconsidered* (1971).

[41] Sir Alec Cairncross, "Concluding Reflections," *Britain's Economic Prospects Reconsidered*, London: George Allen and Unwin, 1971, pp. 231–232.

[42] *Britain's Economic Prospects*, p. 495. See also Anthony Sampson, *The New Anatomy of Britain*, New York: Stein and Day, 1972, pp. 655–673.

terms of Gross National Product per capita when compared with the United States, Canada, Japan, and nine West European countries. At that time, the United Kingdom was ahead of West Germany, France, Italy, and Japan. By 1973, it had fallen to the eleventh place among these countries and is now behind West Germany, France, Belgium, Holland, Austria, and Japan, surpassing only Italy among the major democratic Western European industrial nations.[43] Compared to these other eleven countries, Great Britain has a low-investment, high-consumption economy.

The statistics in Table 4-12 show that high economic growth rates tend to be associated with high investment rates. Japan, whose annual growth rate has usually been about four times that of Great Britain, in 1968-1972 invested 32.1 percent of its Gross National Product in plant and equipment, whereas Great Britain invested only 16.1 percent. Among the Western European industrial nations, France, West Germany, Sweden, Holland, and Denmark have higher investment ratios than the United Kingdom. These industrial nations of the West with higher growth rates than the United Kingdom have also had a higher investment ratio than that country.

A high ratio of investment to Gross National Product does not alone account for high levels of economic growth and prosperous economic conditions. If a nation is to have a high growth rate, low labor costs per unit of production, and competitive international prices, it must have adequate investment in plant and equipment, accompanied by progressive business management, considerable labor-management cooperation, an aggressive foreign trade program, and a government that is prepared to facilitate the economy's expansion. With regard to these matters, the United Kingdom has been significantly deficient in recent decades. Unless it can remove these

[43] *Business Week,* "Why Nothing Works in Britain," Feb. 10, 1975, pp. 50-60.

Table 4-12
Gross Fixed Investment as a Percent of Gross National Product in the United Kingdom and Selected Countries, 1968-1972 Average (In 1963 Prices)

	Percent of GNP		
	Gross fixed investment	Plant and equipment	Residential construction
Japan	38.7	32.1	6.6
France	26.3	19.8	6.5
West Germany	25.9	20.7	5.2
Netherlands	25.3	19.6	5.7
Denmark	23.6	19.0	4.6
Sweden	23.1	18.1	5.0
Italy	19.8	13.9	5.9
United Kingdom	19.6	16.1	3.5
United States	17.0	13.5	3.5

Source: OECD, *OECD Economic Surveys, Norway,* Appendix, *International Comparisons,* Jan. 1975.

deficiencies in the coming decades, there can be little prospect of making the British economy sound and viable in a lasting way.

In spite of the efforts of private industrial groups, research organizations, and government departments to have these deficiencies corrected, not enough has been accomplished along these lines to prevent what the British Secretary of State for Industry described in 1975 as "the trend to contraction of British manufacturing industry," which, if not corrected, would close down 15 percent of British manufacturing capacity between 1970 and 1980.[44] It appears that the economic situation in the United Kingdom, after years of drift and poor economic performance, now calls for some drastic remedies. The answer to Britain's economic problems may lie in a form of national economic guidance similar to that now used in France, Holland, and the Scandinavian countries.

[44] British Information Services, *Survey of Current Affairs*, April 1975, p. 158.

Selected Bibliography

BRITISH INFORMATION SERVICES. *Survey of Current Affairs.*

BRITISH LABOUR PARTY. *The New Britain,* London, 1964.

CAIRNCROSS, SIR ALEC. *Britain's Economic Prospects Reconsidered.* George Allen and Unwin, London, 1971.

CAVES, RICHARD E., AND ASSOCIATES. *Britain's Economic Prospects.* The Brookings Institution, Washington, D.C., 1960.

CENTRAL OFFICE OF INFORMATION. *Housing in Britain.* H.M.S.O., London, 1960.

———. *Town and Country Planning in Britain.* H.M.S.O., London, 1962.

CMD. 9725. *The Economic Implications of Full Employment.* H.M.S.O., London, 1956.

CMND. 4515. *New Policies for Public Spending.* H.M.S.O., London, 1970.

CMND. 4829. *Britain and the European Communities: An Economic Assessment.* H.M.S.O., London, 1970.

CMND. 5125. *A Programme for Controlling Inflation: The First Stage.* H.M.S.O., London, 1972.

FLORENCE, P. SARGANT. *The Logic of British and American Industry.* Routledge and K. Paul, London, 1953.

MADDISON, ANGUS. *Economic Growth in the West, Comparative Experience in Europe and North America.* The Twentieth Century Fund, New York, 1964.

MALIK, REX. *What's Wrong with British Industry?* Penguin Books, Baltimore, 1961.

MEYER, F. V., D. C. CORNER, AND J. E. S. PARKER. *Problems of a Mature Economy.* Macmillan and Company, London, 1970.

NATIONAL ECONOMIC DEVELOPMENT COUNCIL. *Conditions Favourable to Faster Growth.* H.M.S.O., London, 1963.

NATIONAL INSTITUTE OF ECONOMIC AND SOCIAL RESEARCH. "Medium-Term Forecasts Reassessed." *National Institute Economic Review*, No. 62 (Nov. 1972).

ORGANISATION FOR ECONOMIC CO-OPERATION AND DEVELOPMENT. *Inflation, The Present Problem,* Paris, 1970.

———. *OECD Economic Surveys, United Kingdom.* Paris, 1970 and 1972.

ORGANISATION FOR EUROPEAN ECONOMIC CO-OPERATION. "Wage Determination in the United Kingdom." *The Problem of Rising Prices.* Paris, 1961.

POLITICAL AND ECONOMIC PLANNING. *Growth in the British Economy.* George Allen and Unwin, London, 1960.

 PRATTEN, C. F. "The Reasons for the Slow Economic Progress of the British Economy." *Oxford Economic Papers,* 24 (July 1972).

RAY, G. F. "Labour Costs and International Competitiveness." *National Institute Economic Review,* Aug. 1972.

SAMPSON, ANTHONY. *The New Anatomy of Britain.* Stein and Day, New York, 1972.

SHANKS, MICHAEL. *The Stagnant Society.* Penguin Books, Baltimore, 1961.

ULMAN, LLOYD, AND ROBERT J. FLANAGAN. *Wage Restraint: A Study of Incomes in Western Europe.* University of California Press, Berkeley, 1971.

WILSON, THOMAS. *Planning and Growth.* Macmillan and Company, London, 1965.

Chapter 5

West Germany's Social Market Economy

Among the post–World War II capitalist countries of Western Europe, none has attracted more attention than West Germany. Whereas the United Kingdom economy has performed rather poorly since 1945, the West German economy has been noted for its excellent performance. Other Western European countries, such as France, the Netherlands, Belgium, and the Scandinavian countries, have enjoyed prosperous economies, but they have achieved this goal with the aid of national economic planning. Without such planning, West Germany has led the economic growth league of Western Europe, in considerable contrast to those countries that have turned to national economic planning. Per capita Gross National Product in West Germany now exceeds per capita Gross National Product in France and the United Kingdom. As recent events have shown, the West German deutsche mark is among the strongest of international currencies. Although West German annual economic growth rates are now considerably lower than they were in the 1950s and early 1960s, and although West Germany is now beset with economic problems that did not exist before 1963, it continues to enjoy an unusually strong export position, a very low unemployment rate, and a prosperous economy.

The Development of the West German Economy since 1948

The West German economy has passed through three phases of development since the close of the Second World War. During the first period, 1948–1955, the war-devastated economy was reconstructed and the nation's standard of living restored to the level enjoyed by other Western European industrialized countries. In these early postwar years, there occurred a strong adverse reaction to the bureaucratic government planning and intervention of the Hitler years. This reaction led to the effort to establish the free competitive social market economy, based on the principle that economic activity should be left very largely to the uncontrolled operation of free market forces, with government intervention kept to a minimum.

In the second period, from 1955 to the end of the Adenauer government in 1963, the West German economy continued to expand and consolidated its position as one of the world's major exporters of manufactured goods. In these years, the so-called German economic miracle (*Deutsches Wirschaftswunder*) attracted worldwide attention. In this period, efforts were made to curb the growth of monopoly, to encourage owner-entrepreneurs, to foster the widespread ownership of private property, and to establish a legal and social order that would give support to the official goal of a competitive exchange economy.

The third period covered the decade 1964–1975, during which there was a considerable erosion of the official goal of a free competitive economy. In the 1960s, the pattern of West German economic activity was gradually transformed so as to duplicate the pattern of the mixed economy found in other Western industrialized nations. In the early 1960s, West Germany shifted from a low-pressure to a high-pressure economy, when new problems of wage and price inflation, economic fluctuations, and labor unrest made their appearance. During the 1960s, acceptance of the official goal of the competitive social market economy was gradually weakened, and the need for more government intervention in economic affairs along Keynesian lines was more widely accepted. While West Germany continued to have large export surpluses and a generally prosperous economy, the trend towards greater concentration in industry and the acquisition of increased market power by major economic interest groups pointed in the direction of a much less competitive mixed economy; the latter was significantly different from the competitive social market economy accepted as the official government goal in the 1950s and early 1960s. After the 1966 electoral defeat of Ludwig Erhard, a strong advocate of the social free market economy, there was a much greater acceptance of government as an important factor in national economic guidance. By 1971, when the socialist Social Democratic Party of Willy Brandt took over the reins, the West German economy was far removed from the competitive free enterprise economy advocated by the proponents of the social market economy.

The Post–World War II West German Economy

The Federal Republic of Germany (West Germany) has a land area (99,200 square miles) that is a little more than half the area of prewar Germany and somewhat more than the land area of the United Kingdom (94,214 square miles). The German Democratic Republic (East Germany) occupies the mainly agricultural areas of prewar Germany, while West Germany inherited the main coal-bearing, industrialized part of prewar Germany. West Germany has a population of 62 million (1975) and a total labor force of approximately 27 million. This labor force turns out a Gross National Product valued at 209 billion (1972), as compared with Gross National Products in France and the United Kingdom of $187 billion and $145 billion respectively. GNP per head in West Germany in 1973 was $5,320, which was 86 percent of the 1973 United States Gross National Product per head of $6,200. West Germany is very much like the United Kingdom from the point of view of resource endowment and economic structure. It is thickly populated (637 persons per square mile in West Germany, as compared with 590 in the United Kingdom) and highly industrialized, its main resources being the land, large coal reserves, and a skilled population.

Like the United Kingdom, West Germany derives very little of its gross domestic product from agriculture. As the statistics in Table 5-1 indicate, agriculture accounted for 12 percent of the West German gross domestic product in 1950, but its contribution to this product had fallen to only 3 percent by 1972. Industry's relative contribution to the gross domestic product remained almost unchanged during the twenty-year period. The sector of the economy that expanded in relation to other spheres was the private and public service industries. The changes in the origins of West Germany's gross domestic product in recent years are reflected in changes in the national employment pattern, which are presented in Table 5-2. Between 1962 and 1972 the number employed in agriculture declined 1.4 million, or 42.3 percent, while the number employed in the service industries (wholesale and retail trade, transportation and communications, and other services) increased 643,000 or 13.2 percent. In West Germany, as in other Western European countries, the flight from agriculture has coincided with the development of the service economy. By 1972, 42 percent of total employment in West Germany was found in the wholesale and retail trade, transportation and communications, and the various private and public service industries.

Having no extensive natural resources besides land, coal, and iron ore, West Germany must import a large part of its raw materials and foodstuffs, which are paid for by manufactured exports. West Germany's imports of goods and services constitute 28 percent of its Gross National Product, while its exports of goods and services amount to 25 percent of this product. Like most major Western European countries, West Germany relies upon an extensive foreign trade to maintain high levels of output and employment, and is vitally interested in the expansion of world trade and the economic integration of Western Europe.

Industry and Banking in West Germany

West Germany's industrial pattern is similar to that of the United States and the other major Western European industrialized countries, which show a high degree of overall

Table 5-1

The Origins of the West German Gross Domestic Product in 1950, 1960, and 1972 (In Percent)

	1950	1960	1972
Agriculture	12	6	3
Industry	46	47	45
Construction	7	7	9
Wholesale and retail trade	10	15	12
Transportation and communications	8	6	6
Other services	17	19	27
Gross domestic product	100	100	102[1]

[1] Includes statistical discrepancy.

Source: United Nations, *Statistical Yearbook*, 1954 and 1973.

Table 5-2

The Distribution of Total Employment in West Germany in 1962 and 1972

	(In thousands)		Percent change between 1962 and 1972
	1962	1972	
Agriculture	3,383	1,953	−42.3
Mining and quarrying	710	323	−54.5
Manufacturing	9,954	10,435	4.8
Construction	2,041	2,038	−0.1
Public utilities	211	183	−13.2
Commerce	3,712	3,955	6.5
Transportation and communications	1,497	1,530	2.2
Services	4,874	5,517	13.2
Total employment	26,382	25,934	−1.7

Source: International Labour Office, *Year Book of Labour Statistics*, 1975.

industrial concentration as well as considerable concentration within major individual industries. In the industrial core of the West German economy are 400 large industrial enterprises, which account for 70 percent of total industrial sales, and which are surrounded by almost 100,000 firms of diminishing size. The statistics in Table 5-3 show that in 1968, 1,152 large business enterprises, each with 1,000 or more workers, employed 3.1 million, or 38.2 percent of all industrial workers. Out of the total of 99,783 firms, 2,713 accounted for 41.2 percent of total industrial employment. The 86 percent of all industrial firms with less than 100 workers per firm employed only 20 percent of all industrial workers.

Not much information on trends in industrial concentration is available, but what is known indicates a movement towards further concentration. A study of industrial concentration for 1959–1965 by the Federal Cartel Office found that the share of total industrial sales accounted for by the 100 largest industrial companies had increased from 37 percent in 1959 to 45.6 percent in 1966. In the same period the four largest companies in the petroleum, motor vehicle, electrical equipment, chemical, shipbuilding, and rubber products industries had increased their shares of the total sales of their respective industries.[1] The eight largest companies in each of these industries accounted for more than 50 percent of their total sales. These and other large enterprises are the driving force behind the powerful Federation of German Industries (*Bundesverband der Deutschen Industrie*), which speaks for the West German business community on all important economic issues. These were industrial trends that ran contrary to official government policies of preventing the development of "market dominating positions" by large-scale industrial enterprises and fostering the growth of medium-sized and small business.

West German industry is organized on a much larger scale than industry in most other Western European countries. Before the Second World War, German industry was dominated by nine large cartels which integrated

[1] United States Subcommittee on Antitrust and Monopoly, *Hearings on Economic Concentration*, S. Res. 233, Part 7, April 1968, pp. 3490–3491.

Table 5-3
The Firm Sizes, Number of Firms, and the Number of Workers in West German Industry in 1968

Firm size	Number of firms	Number of workers
1–9	43,298	162,826
10–49	32,183	771,753
50–99	10,050	704,966
100–199	6,567	921,184
200–499	4,672	1,438,376
500–999	1,561	1,073,453
1,000 and over	1,152	3,137,499
Total	99,483	8,210,057

Source: Statistiches Bundesamt, *Statistiches Jahrbuch für die Bundesrepublik Deutschland*, 1970.

the iron and steel, coal, and chemical industries. These large combines were in turn serviced by three large banks. The deindustrialization and decartelization programs begun by the Allied occupation authorities were never carried out as far as had been originally planned. However, the nine large combines were dissolved and replaced by fifty-four separate iron and steel and coal and coke enterprises. The three large banks were also "deconcentrated" and replaced by nine smaller banks.[2] The deindustrialization and decartelization programs were not carried far enough to alter the basic large-scale nature of West Germany's key industries. The law on cartels enforced since January 1958 prohibits cartels except where special approval is obtained from the Cartel Office.

As in the prewar era, the major West German industries, such as the iron and steel, machinery, chemical, and electrotechnical industries, remain highly concentrated. These industries are heavily involved in West Germany's export trade, since about 85 percent of all merchandise exports consist of finished goods, the bulk of which is made up of machinery and other capital or investment goods. West Germany's social market economy does not call for the pulverization of big industry. On the contrary, large-scale industry with its low unit costs is accepted as an essential feature of West Germany's economic system. However, large industrial enterprises are expected to operate in a competitive manner. Price fixing and other restrictive or monopolistic practices are forbidden by law. West Germany's highly concentrated industries have to contend with stiff competition in the international field. Their domestic markets are no longer protected by cartels and other business arrangements. In order to increase competition in its domestic markets, the West German government has pursued a policy of reducing tariff duties on imported manufactured goods, a policy that was formalized after the establishment of the European Common Market.

There is a considerable nationalized sector that includes the railroads and most local

[2] Alfred Grosser, *The Colossus Again*, New York: Frederick A. Praeger, 1955, pp. 94–100.

transportation, a large part of the public utilities, the communications system and broadcasting, the savings banks, and some industrial enterprises. The federal government, with its financial control of 60 percent of the nation's building and construction activity, can easily alter the flow of investment. In the large key private industries, which include the iron and steel, engineering, coal, and chemical concerns, business and government cooperation is close. The highly centralized private banking system fosters informal cooperation among private economic groups and between business groups and the federal government.

Competition is more prevalent among the small-scale producers of consumer goods and other light-industry products and in the retailing field. However, even in these fields, there exist strong tendencies towards joint action through trade associations which limit the impact of competitive forces. Competition in retailing has recently increased as the result of the invasion of the retailing field by large chain or multiple unit retailing organizations. West German membership in the European Economic Community has also opened the doors to strong competitive influences. As in all other highly industrialized capitalist countries, in West Germany a constant struggle has been waged to preserve the competitive features of the largely private enterprise economic system.

A special feature of the West German economy is the close working relations between the government, business, and the private banks in economic affairs. Originally, the private banks tended to be one-purpose commercial, savings, cooperative credit, or mortgage banks, but since 1945 they have become all-purpose institutions that offer a wide variety of banking services. Although the private banks compete on a service basis, the banking system is highly concentrated, with the three major banks (the Deutsche Bank, the Dresdner Bank, and the Commerzbank) holding approximately 50 percent of total private bank assets, and having extensive branch banking systems throughout the country.[3]

The number of private banks was 2,000 in 1928, but had fallen to 240 at the end of 1958. A West German business company typically has financial relations with only one bank, which is prepared to hold securities issued by the company and to participate in floating its stock and bond issues. West German banks, unlike the British banks, have close relations with the stock exchanges, vote stocks held by their individual customers, and place representatives on the supervisory boards of directors of business enterprises. The Federal Central Bank maintains a close relation with the nation's major banks and conveys to them the federal government's position on various economic policy issues. Since the large West German private banks are closely associated with the steel, coal, chemical and other major industries, and since they also have close relations with the federal government and the Central Bank, the situation is favorable to the development of joint consultation and action among the government, the large business enterprises, and the major banks. The private banks also work closely with the federal government's Reconstruction Loan Corporation (*Kreditanstalt für Wiederaufbau*) and the Ministry of Economics in securing public funds for investment in those industries and

---

[3] H. W. Auburn, *Comparative Banking*, London: Waterlow and Sons, 1960, pp. 39–47; and R. G. Opie, "Western Germany," in R. S. Sayers, *Banking in Western Europe*, Oxford: Clarendon Press, 1962, pp. 53–123. In 1968, the president of the West German Cartel Office stated that the "degree of concentration in banking is still high," even though there has in recent years been some increase in the competition to provide various banking services. See the U.S. Senate Hearings, *Economic Concentration*, Part 7, p. 3471.

regions that are not able to obtain funds from the private capital markets.[4]

Agriculture and Labor in West Germany

West German agriculture presents a marked contrast to West German industry. The major portion of West Germany's domestic agricultural products comes from small-scale, high-cost family farms. Like other Western European countries, West Germany has undergone a postwar "flight from agriculture," as agricultural labor has moved in large numbers to the higher-productivity industrial sector. In 1950, agriculture produced 12 percent of West Germany's gross domestic product, but by 1972 it was turning out only 3 percent. The agricultural census of 1964 revealed that 90 percent of all the farms had an average acreage under cultivation of less than fifty acres per farm. With the average farm size in West Germany being only twenty-five acres, agriculture is operated on a much smaller scale than in France and the United Kingdom, where the average farm sizes are respectively 60 and 170 acres. The consolidation of small farms into larger and more economic units since 1954 has not been carried far enough to alter the basic structure of West German agriculture with its reliance on the small-sized family farm. West Germany's farm policy is similar to that of other Western European countries, seeking to guarantee to farmers an average annual income per farmer that is roughly comparable to an average industrial worker's income. The number of farmers who will be protected and guaranteed an adequate income is fixed by the amount of agricultural raw materials and foodstuffs that West Germany has decided to obtain from domestic rather than foreign sources. By 1965, West Germany was meeting 78 percent of its food requirements from domestic sources.

As the agricultural program of the European Economic Community is further developed, West Germany will have to adjust its agricultural objectives to the overall objectives of the community. Since West German agriculture is at a competitive disadvantage compared with other sectors of the economy, steps have been taken to offset this disadvantage and to protect agriculture from the effects of competition.[5] Measures to aid West German agriculture have included protecting the main domestic farm markets (especially the markets for wheat, meat, milk and dairy products, and sugar beets) from the competition of imports and from the effects of any price fluctuations arising from fluctuations in domestic production. Subsidies of various forms to supplement earned farm incomes have also been used. The government regulates the supply of agricultural products by intervening in the domestic markets when necessary and by controlling the flow of agricultural imports. In addition, guaranteed prices are applied to such major crops as grain and sugar beets. The West German farmers are expected to rationalize farm production as much as possible in return for the price protection and income guarantees supplied by the government.

West German agricultural policy has slowed somewhat the transfer of agricultural labor to industry, and consequently has preserved considerable underemployment in the agricultural sector. Other countries, such as

[4] For a discussion of the role of the large private banks in the West German economy, see Andrew Shonfield, *Modern Capitalism, The Changing Balance of Public and Private Power*, pp. 253–264 and 277–282.

[5] Under the West German Agricultural Act of 1955, an annual Green Plan is prepared to show what subsidies and fiscal measures will have to be provided in order to improve the economic situation of agriculture. The details of the West German agricultural policy are presented in Organisation for Economic Co-operation and Development, *Agricultural Policies in 1966, Europe, North America, Japan*, Paris, 1967, pp. 259–278.

France and Sweden, have been more aggressive in shifting labor from agriculture to industry. By 1956, West Germany had reduced agricultural employment 19 percent below its 1939 level; by this time, France had reduced such employment 32 percent and Sweden 36 percent. Among the European Common Market countries, West Germany has been the most reluctant to adopt a common agricultural policy that would adversely affect its high-cost agriculture. West German governments have been unwilling to antagonize the still sizable farm vote by exposing West German agriculture to the competition of France and other Western European countries with a lower-cost agriculture than that experienced in West Germany.

In West Germany, as in other advanced industrialized countries, workers are well organized, although not as extensively as in the United Kingdom and the Scandinavian countries.[6] In 1971, 36.6 percent, or 8.3 million of the 22.6 million wage and salary earners, were members of trade unions. The main trade union organization is the German Federation of Trade Unions (*Deutscher Gewerkschaftsbund*), whose sixteen member unions have a total membership of 6.7 million. Several unions have memberships of over 400,000, with the largest union, the Metal Workers' Union, having a membership of approximately 2 million. Separate unions exist for civil servants (710,000 members) and office employees (471,000 members). In general, the West German trade union movement has been conservative in outlook and action, and labor-management relations have been quite free from serious conflicts since the end of World War II. The trade unions have adopted a pragmatic Keynesian approach to economic problems and government intervention. They have accepted the view that private "entrepreneurial activity is indispensable"; they have voted for the prohibition of cartels in industry; they have cooperated with consumers' cooperatives; and, in recent years, they have played down the demands for the nationalization of key industries and for national economic planning.[7]

A number of factors have contributed to industrial peace in West Germany. Organized labor cooperated with management in the task of reconstructing the economy after 1948 and accepted postwar economic policies, even though these policies at times favored management more than labor. German workers have historically emphasized order and discipline rather than economic advancement. Furthermore, they have been protected by one of the most advanced social security systems in Western Europe. The codetermination (*Mitbestimmung*), movement which gained momentum after 1950, has fostered a high level of labor-management cooperation. This movement has taken two forms: setting up works councils in factories and placing worker representatives in the top management of business enterprises.

The interest in works councils, whose members are chosen by the workers, has led to the creation of these councils in all operating plants.[8] These councils cooperate with

[6] Material on the West German trade union movement is presented in Adolf Sturmthal, *Contemporary Collective Bargaining in Seven Countries*, Ithaca, N.Y.: Cornell University Press, 1957; and "Labor Movements and Collective Bargaining in Europe," *International Encyclopedia of the Social Sciences*, Vol. 8, pp. 523-533. See also Martin Schnitzer, *East and West Germany: A Comparative Economic Analysis*, New York: Praeger Publishers, 1972.

[7] Hans-Joachim Arndt, *West Germany, Politics of Non-Planning*, Syracuse, N.Y.: Syracuse University Press, 1966, pp. 77-79.

[8] Adolf Sturmthal, *Workers Councils: A Study of Workplace Organization on Both Sides of the Iron Curtain*, Cambridge: Harvard University Press, 1964. For an evaluation of the current status of codetermination in West Germany, see Heinz Hartmann, "Codetermination in West Germany," *Industrial Relations*, Feb. 1970, pp. 137-147.

employers in carrying out collective bargaining agreements and in promoting the welfare of the business enterprises. Under the Codetermination Law of 1951, labor was given equal representation with management on the supervisory boards of the steel, coal, and mining companies; provision was also made for putting one labor member on each of these companies' management or executive boards.[9] In other industries, labor representation under codetermination makes up one-third of the membership of the supervisory boards, which appoint and supervise the managing boards in all major industries. The aim is to establish a form of economic democracy in which the workers would have an important role in the private industrial decision-making process.

The West German trade union movement has been much less aggressive than similar movements in the United Kingdom, the United States, and the Scandinavian countries. For example, in the five-year period 1967–1971, the number of working days lost through strikes per 1000 workers per year was 330 in the United Kingdom, but only 39 in West Germany.[10] Like the British Trades Union Congress, the German Federation of Trade Unions does not carry on centralized collective bargaining and can do little to influence the behavior of member trade unions, each of which bargains separately with employers in its own industry. German employers' associations, which are strong and well-disciplined, are combined in one central confederation of employers, the Federation of German Employers' Associations (*Bundesvereinigung der Deutschen Arbeitgeberverbande*).

In recent years, the peaceful industrial scene has changed significantly, for both employers and workers have come to display a new militancy which has resulted in an upsurge of strikes and lockouts. In 1971, the number of working days lost because of strikes (4.5 million) exceeded the total number of days lost for this reason in the entire previous nine years (3.1 million). The prolonged prosperity in West Germany since the early 1950s has had a disruptive impact on the West German trade union movement. The unions have suffered from a lack of support among young workers, from the growing number of white collar and professional employees who have elected not to join trade unions, and from a decrease in class consciousness among the workers. As a result of these developments, trade union membership has been stationary in the past decade at approximately one-third of the total number of wage and salary earners. The center of gravity of many unions has shifted from the union headquarters to the local plants, where unauthorized strikes have become more frequent. At the same time, the need to secure a larger place for organized labor in the national economic decision-making process and in the formulation of an incomes policy emphasizes the importance of developing a strong centralized union leadership. Two conflicting tendencies thus operate in the West German trade union movement, and at present there appears to be no easy solution to this contradiction, which is also found in other industrialized countries.

---

[9] German industrial companies have two boards of directors: an outside supervisory board (*Aufsichtrat*), which is responsible for general company policies, and an inside executive board (*Vorstand*), which deals with day-to-day management problems. The functions of the two boards are kept separate. For a discussion of these institutions, see Andrew Shonfield, "Organized Private Enterprise: Germany," *Modern Capitalism*, pp. 246–254.

[10] A good summary of the reasons for the docility of the West German trade union movement up to the early 1960s is given in Arthur M. Ross and Paul T. Hartman, *Changing Patterns of Industrial Conflicts*, New York: John Wiley and Sons, 1960, pp. 95–100.

West Germany's Foreign Trade

With regard to foreign trade West Germany, like Japan, has been the envy of many of the world's trading nations. The strong recovery of the West German economy after 1948 laid the foundation for a rapid expansion of foreign trade in the 1950s. By 1960, West Germany was producing more steel than each of its major competitors, the United Kingdom, France, and Japan. In 1950, West Germany produced only 2 percent of the world's output of motor vehicles, but by 1960 this share, much of which was exported (51.5 percent in 1964), had been increased to 12 precent. As the statistics in Table 5-4 show, West Germany is today the world's second largest trading nation and the world's largest exporter of manufactured goods. It accounts for 20.3 percent of the export of these goods, while the United States accounts for 17.7 percent and the United Kingdom for 9.3 percent.

The most rapid expansion of West German foreign trade occurred in the years 1948–1960. Since 1960, West Germany has maintained its share of the world's export of manufactured goods, while the shares of both the United States and the United Kingdom have recorded sizable declines. West Germany's rate of progress in the world of international trade has lain somewhere between that of countries like Japan and Italy—which have recorded very rapid advances in this area—and the United Kingdom and the United States—whose foreign trade performances have been comparatively poorer. In the decade of the 1960s, West Germany increased its exports of manufactures 200 percent; Japan 400 percent; the United States 110 percent; and the United Kingdom 91 percent.

Not only has West Germany developed a large export trade since 1948, but it has also managed to curb imports, with the result that a net export surplus of goods and services has been almost an annual occurrence. This export surplus has gone in large part into the building up of West Germany's international

Table 5-4
Foreign Trade Performance in West Germany and Selected Countries

	Shares of world export of manufactures (in percent) 1975	Changes in shares of world export of manufactures (in percent) 1955–1971	Increases in exports of manufactures (in percent) 1960–1970	Total merchandise exports (bil. U.S. dollars) 1975
United States	17.7	−26.5	110	106.2
West Germany	20.3	+29.0	200	91.6
United Kingdom	9.3	−45.5	91	43.8
France	10.2	−4.3	165	52.2
Italy	7.5	+52.1	310	34.8
Japan	13.6	+60.2	400	55.8
Others	21.4	+3.1	—	403.8
Total	100.0			788.2

Sources: Organisation for Economic Co-operation and Development, *Main Economic Indicators;* National Institute of Economic and Social Research, *National Institute Economic Review;* and U.S. Council on International Economic Policy, *The United States in the Changing World Economy,* Vol. II.

financial reserves (including gold, foreign exchange, Special Drawing Rights, and reserve position with the International Monetary Fund); these reserves were approximately $2 billion in 1953, $7 billion in 1963, and $32.4 billion in 1974. As we shall see, West Germany's outstanding success in the international trading area has created some special problems for its domestic economy and some serious problems for other nations that have been unable or unwilling to duplicate West Germany's domestic and external economic achievements.

The Model of the Social Market Economy

The basic principles of the social market economy (*Soziale Marktwirtschaft*) were first enunciated by Walter Eucken and Franz Böhm, two prominent members of the Freiburg school of neoliberal economists which was established in the early 1930s.[11] These principles were used by Ludwig Erhard, A. Müller-Armack, and other post–World War II advocates of the social market economy to construct a model of the private-enterprise economy along the lines of a competitive exchange economy. In this economy, the allocation of economic resources was to be regulated by the free forces of supply and demand, while the government was responsible for the development of a legal and social order that would foster competition. The social market economy was viewed as an expression of people's capitalism in which most individuals owned company stocks and possessed savings accounts. The ideal type of business person was the small owner-entrepreneur who possessed no market power and who was strongly opposed to national planning and bureaucratic intervention. In the social market economy where competition prevailed there would be no strong economic interest groups with market power. The social market economy would be "just" or "fair" to all people. When the market forces did not provide individuals with what the community regarded as fair or sufficient incomes, the government could intervene, as in the case of agriculture, to provide price supports and subsidies that would assure the receipt of normal competitive incomes.

In the model of the social market economy, the exchange economy was held to possess immanent tendencies that worked towards equilibrium. The achievement of this equilibrium, however, required a positive economic policy on the part of the government. It was at this point that the model of the social market economy differed from the model of the laissez faire competitive economy. The latter model recognized no need for a positive economic policy, since it was assumed that the unfettered forces of competition would automatically create a competitive order. In the model of the social market economy, government intervention was permitted in order to create what was regarded to be a truly competitive order. This intervention, however, must be compatible with the market mechanisms of the exchange economy.

In the model of the social market economy that guided West German economic policy formulation from 1948 to the early 1960s,

---

[11] A statement of these principles is found in Walter Eucken, *The Foundations of Economics*, Chicago: University of Chicago Press, 1951. An account of the origins of the concept of the social-market economy is given in M. MacLennan, M. Forsyth, and G. Denton, *Economic Planning and Policies in Britain, France, and Germany*, Ch. 2, "Germany: The Competitive Order," pp. 34–50. For a further explanation of the social market economy, see Ludwig Erhard, *The Economics of Success*, London: Thames and Hudson, 1963, pp. 7–10; Hans-Joachim Arndt, *op. cit.*, Ch. III, "The 'Social Market' Model," pp. 33–46; and Gustav Stolper and others, *The German Economy 1870 to the Present*, Ch. VII, "Social Policy in the Social Market Economy," New York: Harcourt, Brace and World, 1967, pp. 277–295.

permissible intervention included measures to prevent the growth of monopoly, to eliminate restrictive business practices, to reduce the social costs of economic growth, to provide social welfare for those who truly needed it, and to liberalize foreign trade and other measures that would create a desirable legal and social order. Intervention to provide a sound monetary system had a prominent place among permissible interventionist measures. The aim of monetary policy was to make the monetary system a stabilizing factor by altering the supply of money so as to prevent the growth of inflationary or deflationary tendencies. When the goal of a stabilized economy was achieved with the aid of monetary policy, there would then be no need to use fiscal policy as an anticyclical device.[12] Public expenditures could then be designed to meet social needs rather than to offset business booms and recessions.

The model of the social market economy that guided West German political and business leaders in the 1950s and early 1960s made no place for either the nationally planned economy or the regulated Keynesian economy. The main thrust of the social market economy of the years 1948–1963 was microeconomic rather than macroeconomic. In the social market economy, the government could control the economy in order to improve or preserve its competitive nature; but it was not to manipulate such aggregates as total output, investment, and consumption with the aim of achieving a full-employment economy at a high and sustained level of economic growth. According to the interpretation of the neoliberal proponents of the social market economy, the state should be concerned with enforcing the general rules of law, and should avoid trying to influence the aims of the economic system by issuing special administrative orders. This government approach would reduce the uncertainty with respect to government action, and individuals would then be free to use the state machinery according to their own private economic purposes.

The model of the economy that underlies the concept of the social market economy looks forward to the establishment of what is described in West German government circles as "workable competition." The official government position is that "concentration becomes objectionable economically if it leads to or strengthens market dominant positions. Workable and efficient competition belongs to the basic elements of the social market economy, because only under such conditions could prices fulfill their functions of steering production and distribution in a manner which is satisfactory from an economic and social viewpoint.... This implies a multitude of efficient, free, and independent entrepreneurs."[13] To achieve this goal of an economy of workable competition the West German advocates of the social market economy not only secured the enactment of the Cartel Law of 1957 that prohibits cartels, but also pursued a "middle class" (*Mittelstandspolitik*) policy of fostering the middle stratum of small and medium-sized business firms. These firms in the 1950s and early 1960s were aided by special subsidies, tax concessions, low-cost credit, preferences in the placing of public contracts, and other measures designed to stimulate small holdings of private property. Advocates of the social market economy believe that a vigorous attack on business monopoly and an active program to stimulate small and medium-sized

---

[12] When the West German advocates of the social market economy assigned the primary role to monetary policy and a secondary role to fiscal policy, they became anti-Keynesian. Their views with regard to economic policy and the primacy of monetary policy have been borrowed by Milton Friedman and other members of the Chicago school.

[13] Statement of Dr. Eberhard Gunther, President, West German Federal Cartel Office, *Economic Concentration*, Part 7, p. 3472.

business can restore competition in the West German economy to the point where it will become "workable and efficient."[14]

The Performance of West Germany's Social Market Economy, 1953–1963

The performance of the West German economy in the decade of the "economic miracle" after 1952 attracted worldwide attention.[15] Gross National Product, industrial production, and exports of goods increased at annual rates that exceeded those of all other major Western European countries. West Germany's Gross National Product during the years 1953–1963 increased at an average annual rate of 6.7 percent, whereas the rates for France and the United Kingdom were 4.7 and 2.7 percent respectively. In the same period, West German industrial production, as Table 5-5 shows, increased at the annual rate of 7.5 percent compared with rates of 7.2 and 3.1 percent for France and the United Kingdom, respectively. During these years German exports of goods increased four times faster than British exports. The comparison of basic economic indicators for West Germany, France, and the United Kingdom for the period since the end of the Korean War is particularly unfavorable to the United Kingdom.

Two factors that contributed greatly to the rapid and continuous expansion of the West German economy were the large additions to the supply of manpower from East Germany and the very high rate of investment in industrial plant and equipment. In addition, the long West German work week (forty-eight hours), the advances in industrial technology, and the industry of the German workers made significant contributions to West Germany's economic growth. In both the United Kingdom and France, shorter work weeks (forty-five hours), very limited increases in employment in manufacturing, and lower levels of investment in industrial plant and equipment restricted economic expansion. Before 1958, West Germany had a larger labor supply than it could profitably use. In 1953, when France and Great Britain had unemployment rates below 2 percent, the West German unemployment rate was 7.5 percent. Not until 1960 was West Germany able to reduce its unemployment rate below 2 percent. After 1960, with the labor supply from East Germany cut off, West Germany experienced overfull employment, with the unemployment rate in 1962 falling to 0.7 percent.

What was especially unique about West German economic expansion from 1953 to 1960 was that no significant inflationary pressures were developed as the economy expanded. Wholesale prices in West Germany were almost stationary during the 1950s. The wholesale price index for the period 1953–1963 shows an average annual increase of only 0.7 percent. West German consumer prices, largely in response to rising domestic farm prices, showed more increase (2 percent a year) than did wholesale prices. West Germany kept its prices below those of its main export competitor, the United Kingdom, and much below prices in France, which experienced strong inflationary pressures after 1957. Unlike France and Great Britain, West Germany did not have to contend with recurring rounds of wage adjustments that increased wage rates much faster than labor productivity. In most of the 1950s, West Germany's labor supply was excessive, unemployment was

---

[14] M. MacLennan, F. Forsyth, and G. Denton, "Germany: The Competitive Order," *op. cit.*, pp. 62–68.

[15] The German economic miracle (*Wirtschaftswunder*) is explained in Jossleyn Hennessy, "The German 'Miracle,'" in *Economic 'Miracles,'* London: Institute of Economic Affairs, 1964, pp. 1–73; Henry C. Wallich, *Mainsprings of the German Revival*, New Haven: Yale University Press, 1955; and Knut Borchardt, "The 'Economic Miracle,'" in *The German Economy 1870 to the Present*, pp. 219–298.

Table 5-5
West German Economic Indicators, 1953–1963 (1953 = 100)

Year	Gross National Product	Industrial production	Wholesale prices	Consumer prices	Average hourly wage rates in industry	Average hourly earnings in industry	Output per man-hour in industry	Unemployment rate
1953	100	100	100	100	100	100	100	7.5
1954	107	112	98	100	102	103	105	7.0
1955	120	129	101	102	108	109	112	5.1
1956	128	139	102	105	117	119	116	4.0
1957	135	147	103	107	126	132	126	3.5
1958	139	152	103	109	132	141	133	3.5
1959	149	162	102	110	137	148	144	2.4
1960	162	180	103	112	146	163	156	1.2
1961	173	190	105	114	157	180	163	0.8
1962	180	199	106	118	174	201	174	0.7
1963	187	206	107	122	185	211	186	0.8
Annual average increase 1953–63	6.5%	7.5%	0.7%	2.0%	6.4%	7.8%	6.4%	3.6%[1]

[1] Average annual rate, 1953–63.

Sources: Organisation for European Economic Co-operation, *Twelfth Annual Economic Review*, 1961; OECD, *Germany, Economic Surveys by the OECD*, 1963; and OECD, *General Statistics*, Jan. 1964.

high, and the trade unions were not powerful enough to lead their members through numerous rounds of wage increases that were larger than increases in output per man-hour.

In the period 1953–1963, average West German hourly wage rates in industry moved very closely with improvements in labor productivity in industry. Table 5-5 shows that for the whole period 1953–1963 both average hourly wage rates and output per man-hour in industry increased at the same average annual rate of 6.4 percent. Since wage rates moved closely with improvements in labor productivity, unit labor costs were stable and business people had no reason to increase their wholesale prices. The limited increase in unit labor costs that did result from wage drifting was offset by sufficient economies from other sources to keep wholesale prices, and hence export prices, quite stable. In both France and Great Britain, strong inflationary pressures resulted from the tendency of wage rate increases to outstrip annual improvements in output per man-hour.

West Germany's success in enlarging its volume of exports and once again becoming a major world trading nation was phenomenal. With a stable domestic wholesale price level in a world in which prices were generally increasing, West Germany was particularly well situated to compete for larger export markets. German export industries had the advantage of recently installed low-cost capital equipment, stable unit labor costs, and government aid in various forms.[16] Following government policy, the German banks were careful to make credit more available to export than to domestic industries. A comprehensive system of export credit insurance eliminated many of the risks encountered by West German exporters. West German exporters also received special tax privileges. They did not have to pay turnover or sales taxes on exported goods; they were able to reduce their taxable income by an amount equal to 3 percent of export sales; they were permitted to postpone payment of part of their income tax; and they were relieved of the obligation to pay taxes on negotiable instruments. West German exporters were permitted to sell a part of the foreign exchange that they earned at premium exchange rates. They were also allowed to retain a part of the foreign exchange that they earned and to use it to meet their import needs. Exports became the "sacred cow" of German economic policy.

In the period 1953–1963, the average annual increase in the volume of West German exports, as Table 5-6 reveals, was 11.8 percent, whereas a sluggish economy, such as the British economy, increased the volume of its

[16] L. Erhard, *Germany's Comeback in the World Market*, London: George Allen and Unwin, Ltd., 1954, pp. 225–228. For an analysis of West German economic policy in the years 1949–1961, see H. Besters, "Economic Policy in Western Germany 1949–1961," *Economic Policy in Our Time*, Vol. III, Country Studies, Chicago: Rand McNally, 1964, pp. 389–482.

Table 5-6

West Germany's Volume of Exports, Balance of International Payments on Current Account, and Gold and Foreign Exchange Reserve, 1953–1963 (1953 = 100)

Year	West German volume of exports	British volume of exports	French volume of exports	U.S. volume of exports	West German balance of current international transactions (mil. U.S. $)	West German gold and foreign exchange reserve (mil. U.S. $)
1953	100	100	100	100	970	1,956
1954	122	104	115	97	914	2,636
1955	142	112	133	98	641	3,076
1956	165	118	110	117	1,266	4,291
1957	188	120	131	123	1,741	5,644
1958	194	115	137	107	1,864	6,322
1959	217	119	164	104	1,686	5,015
1960	249	125	192	120	1,797	7,199
1961	264	128	202	120	1,612	6,541
1962	273	131	205	124	439	6,446
1963	303	138	223	133	1,151	7,102
Annual average 1953–63	11.8%	3.3%	8.4%	2.9%	—	—

Sources: OEEC, *Twelfth Annual Economic Review*, Sept. 1961; OECD, *General Statistics*, May 1964; and International Monetary Fund, *International Financial Statistics*, Aug. 1964.

exports in the same period at the low average annual rate of 3.3 percent. The more active French economy had an average annual rate of increase of 8.4 percent in the volume of its exports. In the years 1953–1963, the West German government never had an adverse balance of payments in its current international account. Export surpluses in West Germany's current international account annually averaged $1.4 billion during these years. The favorable balance on current international account and the high interest policy which attracted foreign funds made it possible for Germany to build up its gold and foreign exchange reserve from $274 million in 1950 to $7.2 billion ten years later. West Germany's foreign trade expansion was so successful that it became embarrassing to it and to its trading customers. Too many countries found themselves developing adverse balances of international payments with West Germany. These adverse balances led to excessive gold movements from various countries to West Germany, which could have done a better job than it did of offsetting these gold inflows by investing more abroad and giving more loans and grants to underdeveloped countries. Fewer restrictions on imports into West Germany, especially on agricultural imports, and fewer curbs on domestic private consumption would also have contributed to a better balance in West Germany's external economy.

A summary view of West Germany's economic performance after 1950 can be obtained by examining the ways in which its Gross National Product was annually used or distributed. Table 5–7 shows that after 1950 private consumption took up a declining share of Gross National Product, while gross domestic investment absorbed a rising proportion of GNP. As the West German economy expanded, private consumption increased in absolute terms, but not as a proportion of total national output. Private consumption was deliberately curbed by various economic policies in order to stimulate private investment. The postwar tax system reduced the fiscal burden on investment and increased the burden on consumption. Heavy indirect taxation was combined with a relatively uneven distribution of income to restrict private consumption and to expand private investment. Private consumption, which took up 63.6 percent of West Germany's Gross National Product in 1950, was absorbing only 57.4 percent of this product in 1962. The progressive decline in the relative share of Gross National Product taken up by private consumption was accompanied by a large increase in the relative share of GNP going into gross domestic

Table 5–7

The Percentage Distribution of West Germany's Gross National Product in Selected Years, 1950–1962

	1950	1954	1958	1962
Private consumption	63.6	60.0	58.5	57.4
Public consumption	14.8	14.5	13.5	14.9
Gross domestic fixed capital formation	19.0	20.9	22.1	25.4
Change in inventories	3.8	1.1	1.9	1.2
Export surplus (+) or import surplus (−)	−1.2	3.5	4.0	1.1
Gross National Product	100.0	100.0	100.0	100.0

Source: OECD, *General Statistics*, May 1964.

investment in plant and equipment. Whereas in 1950 gross domestic investment amounted to 19 percent of GNP, it accounted for 25.4 percent in 1962. After more than a decade of rapid economic growth, the investment-oriented pattern of GNP use in the high-investment economy of West Germany was markedly different from that of France and the United Kingdom. Comparative GNP statistics for these three countries are given in Table 5-8. Both France and the United Kingdom allocated about 65 percent of their GNPs to private consumption—compared with West Germany's 57 percent. In France and the United Kingdom, gross domestic fixed investment took up from 17 to 18 percent of Gross National Product as compared with West Germany's 25 percent. Both the French and British economies could be described as consumption-oriented economies when compared with West Germany's investment-oriented economy. France was much less concerned than West Germany with maintaining stable prices and securing a large export surplus. Unlike Germany, France did not have large reserves of unemployed manpower. Consequently, its high-pressure planned economy with its very low unemployment rate generated strong inflationary pressures which gave rise to an extended wage-price spiral. Both private consumption and imports were much less rigorously curbed in France than in West Germany. In the United Kingdom's low-pressure unplanned economy, a very strong trade union movement was aggressive enough to keep wage rates rising and the relative share of Gross National Product going into private consumption at a much higher level (65 percent) than in West Germany (57 percent), where the trade union movement was quite weak.

From Neoliberalism to Interventionism

The publication of the first annual survey of economic trends by the West German government in 1963 marked an important transition from the neoliberalism or noninterventionism of the 1950s and early 1960s to a new era of Keynesian interventionism. In the high-pressure West German economy that developed after 1960, there was the prospect of the growth of strong inflationary pressures, rising production costs, higher export prices, and a declining export surplus. The new Erhard Administration that replaced the Adenauer Administration in 1963 recognized the need to be prepared to deal with future fluctuations in the level of business activity.

Table 5-8
The Percentage Distribution of the 1961 Gross National Products of West Germany, France, and the United Kingdom

	West Germany	France	United Kingdom
Private consumption	56.9	65.7	64.6
Public consumption	14.1	14.6	17.2
Gross domestic fixed investment	25.1	17.8	16.9
Change in inventories	1.7	0.9	1.0
Export surplus	2.2	1.0	0.3
Gross National Product	100.0	100.0	100.0

Source: OECD, *General Statistics*, Jan. 1962.

In 1964, national economic guidance in West Germany was further strengthened by establishing the Council of Economic Exports, which was given the responsibility of issuing an annual report on the nation's economic trends and prospects.[17] The council has a membership of five economic experts who are independent of the federal government. It indicates alternative ways of achieving the nation's economic and social priorities, but it does not make any specific policy recommendations. When the council's annual report is published, it is accompanied by the federal government's comments on the council's analysis of the country's economic trends. The purpose of the council is to make available to the federal government an independent assessment of the nation's economic trends and prospects. On occasion, the interpretations and suggestions of the council and the government have been widely apart. In its 1965 and 1966 reports, the council asserted that domestic price stability could not be secured as long as there were fixed exchange rates and large export surpluses. According to the council's interpretation of West Germany's economic trends, domestic price stability required floating exchange rates which would prevent the undervaluation of the deutsche mark and the growth of large export surpluses from exercising their strong inflationary impact on the domestic price level. The federal government disagreed with this analysis of the domestic price problem and continued to maintain a fixed exchange rate for the deutsche mark until 1970.

The efforts to develop an effective contracyclical economic program in the period 1961–1966 did not turn out to be successful. The business boom of the years 1965–1966 was followed by a recession in late 1966 and 1967. The fiscal and monetary measures adopted in 1966 to curb the boom were too strong; consequently, business became excessively depressed, the real gross domestic product in 1967 registered no increase over 1966, and the unemployment rate increased from 0.7 percent in 1966 to 2.2 percent in 1967.

In this situation, the Council of Economic Experts suggested that the federal government's anticyclical policy be strengthened by developing a program for concerted action (*Konzertierte Aktion*) by the Ministry of Economic Affairs, the Council of Economic Exports, the Central Bank, and representatives of private business and the trade unions. Such a program was initiated under the Law for Promoting Stability and Growth in the Economy which was adopted in June 1967. This law calls attention to the four overall goals of West German economic policy: stable prices, high employment, external equilibrium, and adequate economic growth. If any one or more of these national economic goals are in danger of not being realized, then concerted action meetings of government, business, and labor representatives are held with the aim of securing the overall coordination of economic action needed for achieving the endangered goals. Participation by the various private economic interest groups in these concerted action meetings is voluntary. No votes on issues or programs are taken, and no specific policy recommendations are made at these meetings. The purpose of the concerted action is to inform the major private economic interest groups about the nation's economic problems, and to lay a foundation for some form of united action with respect to these problems.[18]

The Stability and Growth Law of 1967 provided for a number of improvements in the

---

[17] A discussion of the work of the council is presented in Gerhard Colm, "Comments on the German Economic Report," *Weltwirtschaftliches Archiv*, Band 95, Heft 1, 1965, pp. 1–6.

[18] For an assessment of the value of concerted action, see Otto Schlecht, "The Role of the 'Concerted Action' Program in the Economic Policy of the Federal Republic of Germany," *The German Economic Review*, Vol. 8, No. 3, 1970, pp. 255–260.

methods of coping with fluctuations in economic activity. As required by this law, the federal budget is now drawn up within the framework of a five-year financial plan that rolls forward each year. This financial plan relates the projected development of federal revenues and expenditures over a five-year period to the nation's economic and social priorities in this period. The five-year financial plan is accompanied by five-year macroeconomic target projections made by the Ministry of Economic Affairs and other ministries. These economic projections establish targets for the average annual increase in real gross domestic product, the unemployment rate, the increase in price level, the size of the net surplus of goods and services, and the shares of profits and wages in the national income.

Table 5-9 shows the medium-term target projections for each of the six five-year periods during the years 1966-1976. In the sixth five-year projection for the years 1971-1976, the average annual increase in real Gross National Product is projected to be above the 4.0-4.5 percent level; the unemployment rate is projected to be between 0.7 and 1.2 percent; the general price level is expected to rise 3.2 percent annually; and the net export surplus is projected to be between 1.5 and 2.0 percent of the country's Gross National Product.[19]

The West German government's five-year macroeconomic projections also indicate how it would like to see the consumption and investment uses of the Gross National Product change during the five-year projection period. The projected changes in these uses during the years 1971-1976 are presented in Table 5-10, which shows the West German national economic accounts for 1971 and the projection of these accounts in the form of a national economic budget for 1976. The uses or distribution of the Gross National Product in this table reveal that the federal government looks forward in 1971-1976 to a relative decline in private consumption expenditures and a relative increase in public consumption expenditures in order to meet the growing demands for additional public services. No detailed breakdown of the various consumption and investment components of the nation's Gross National Product is published, as is done in

[19] Organisation for Economic Co-operation and Development, *OECD Economic Surveys, Germany*, June 1972, p. 44.

Table 5-9
Official West German Medium-Term (Five-Year) Macroeconomic Projections, 1966-1976

Five-year periods	Average annual growth rate of real GNP	Average annual unemployment rate	Average annual change in the domestic price level[1]	Net export surplus as percent of GNP[2]
1966-1971	3.6	0.8	1.5-1.6	1.0
1967-1972	4.4	1.0	1.5	2.0
1968-1973	4.2	1.0	1.8	2.0
1969-1974	well above 4-4.5	0.7-1.2	2.2	1.5-2.0
1970-1975	well above 4-4.5	0.7-1.2	2.4	1.5-2.0
1971-1976	well above 4-4.5	0.7-1.2	3.2	1.5-2.0

[1] Measured by the GNP price deflator.
[2] Target refers to the final year of the projection period.
Source: OECD, *OECD Economic Surveys, Germany*, June 1972.

Table 5-10
The West German National Economic Accounts for 1971 and the National Economic Budget for 1976 (In Percent, 1971 Prices)

Components of the GNP	1971 National economic accounts (actual)	1976 National economic budget (projection)
Private consumption	54.2	53.2
Public consumption	17.0	18.0
Gross fixed investment	26.8	26.1
Increase in inventories	0.4	1.0
Net export surplus	1.6	1.7
Gross National Product	100.0	100.0

Source: Organisation for Economic Co-operation and Development, *OECD Economic Surveys, Germany*, June 1972.

France, Norway, and Sweden, where national economic planning is well established. Macroeconomic projections are used in West Germany only to provide guidance for the government's intervention program and to inform the public about this program, and not to lay a foundation for anything like a national economic planning program. While West German political parties are today prepared to use a Keynesian macroeconomic interventionist program, they are not ready to propose a national economic planning program similar to the French and Scandinavian indicative planning programs.

A comparison of the West German federal government's five-year macroeconomic target projections and actual economic developments in the years 1967-1972 shows considerable discrepancy between actual and projected economic developments. The unemployment rate, which averaged 1.2 percent in the years 1967-1972, was equal to the top range of the projected official target. The net export surplus of goods and services fell within the projected range of 1.5 to 2.0 percent of the Gross National Product. Although the five-year projections made allowance for some inflation, the actual inflation after 1969 was much above what was projected. Whereas the projected annual inflationary increase was 3.2 percent for the years 1970-1972, the actual increase was 6.9 percent. Also, while the actual annual average increase in real GNP in the years 1968-1972 was about the same as the projected rate of 4.5 percent, there were large fluctuations in the annual increases in real GNP. The most disturbing economic development in the 1967-1972 projection period was the wage and price explosion of the years 1971 and 1972, which pushed prices and wages far above the levels projected by the government.

West German Economic Performance, 1963-1972

The domestic performance of the West German economy in the 1960s was below that of the 1950s. Economic growth was slower and more irregular. Whereas the annual average increase in Gross National Product was 6.5

percent in the years 1953–1962, the annual increase was 4.5 percent in the years 1963–1972. The selected economic indicators in Table 5–11 also show that the annual economic growth rate became increasingly irregular after 1963. In the years 1963–1972, this rate fluctuated between the maximum of 8.1 percent in the boom year 1968 and the minimum rate of 0.2 percent in the recession year 1967. Although there were sizable fluctuations in the nation's growth rate in the years 1963–1972, the unemployment rate remained quite stable at around 1 percent, except for the recession year 1967, when the rate rose to 2.2 percent. Some of the fluctuations in employment were absorbed by the large contingent of workers from foreign countries, who numbered over 2 million in 1971. The major adverse development in the years 1963–1969 was the recession of 1966 and 1967, when economic growth stopped and the unemployment rate reached a new high level.

During the years 1963–1969, inflationary pressures were not allowed to get out of hand. The average annual increase in the consumer price index for this period was 2.5 percent, which was below the average annual increases in France, the United Kingdom, and other competitors of West Germany in international markets. In the years 1963–1969, wage rates in manufacturing increased moderately. The average annual increase in hourly wage rates in manufacturing was 6.3 percent, which was about the same as the average annual improvement in output per man-hour in manufacturing. Since the wage-rate increase of 6.3 percent was equal to the improvement in output per man-hour and made no allowance for the 2.5 percent annual rise in consumer prices, real wages in manufacturing did not rise as much as the improvement in productivity. With real wages rising less than the improvement in output per man-hour in industry, a wage lag developed. This development—adverse from labor's point of view—was largely responsible

Table 5–11
Selected West German Economic Indicators, 1963–1972 (Annual Percent Changes)

Year	Gross National Product	Consumer prices	Hourly wages in manufacturing	Output per man-hour in manufacturing	Unemployment rate
1963	3.1	3.0	6.0	6.3	0.9
1964	6.6	2.3	8.8	10.0	0.8
1965	4.4	3.4	7.0	2.7	0.7
1966	2.3	3.5	7.4	2.6	0.7
1967	0.2	1.4	5.3	8.6	2.2
1968	7.2	1.5	5.3	8.8	1.5
1969	8.1	2.7	6.4	5.1	0.8
1970	5.5	3.7	12.6	2.1	0.7
1971	2.7	5.4	13.6	4.1	0.8
1972	4.5	5.8	10.9	2.6	1.0
Average annual change 1963–1972	4.5	3.3	8.1	5.3	1.0

Sources: Organisation for Economic Co-operation and Development, *OECD Economic Surveys, Germany*; and National Institute for Economic and Social Research, *National Institute Economic Review*.

for the wage explosion that occurred after 1969.

After 1969, economic developments in West Germany followed a disturbing course. After two very prosperous years, when the economy became seriously overheated, West Germany experienced a wage and price explosion for the first time since the end of World War II. The annual average increase in consumer prices, which had up to 1969 been around 2.5 percent, more than doubled in 1970-1972. The annual increase in consumer prices almost reached the 6 percent level in 1972. A similar development occurred on the wage front. The annual average increase in hourly wage rates in manufacturing, which had been around 6 percent in 1963-1969, doubled in the years 1970-1972. In 1971, average hourly wage rates in manufacturing increased 13.6 percent, three times the improvement in output per man-hour.

This wage explosion was the result of a number of developments. In 1968 and 1969 the West German trade union movement became much more militant than it had been in prior years. An indication of the new trend in industrial relations is given by the fact that the printing workers after avoiding strike action for twenty years went out on strike in April 1973 to enforce their demand for an 11 percent increase in wage rates. The new trade union militancy was expressed in part through an upsurge of wildcat strikes that the old-line trade union leaders could not prevent. Also as already explained, a wage lag had developed in the years 1966-1969, when wage-rate increases failed to cover both productivity improvements and the increases in consumer prices. Wage explosions in other countries stimulated a similar development in West Germany. As a result of the wage explosion in West Germany in 1970-1972, large increases in labor costs per unit of output were recorded and were passed on by employers in higher selling prices both at home and abroad. West German wholesale export prices, which had increased 1.2 percent a year in the period of 1963-1968, increased 4 percent a year in the period 1969-1972. Exports were adversely affected, and the net surplus of exports which was $2.7 billion in 1968 fell to $131 million in 1971.

The wage and price explosions were followed by the recession of 1971; and like other advanced industrial countries, West Germany experienced both a rapid increase in prices and retarded economic growth. The wage explosion of the years 1970-1971 resulted in a squeeze on profit margins and a marked shift in income distribution to the advantage of wage and salary earners. Whereas in 1968 wages and salaries accounted for 55 percent of national income, by 1971 they absorbed 58 percent of national income. Income from property and entrepreneurship, which was 31 percent of national income in 1968, fell to 27 percent in 1971.

Since 1972, there has been some reduction in the price and wage inflation, and efforts have been made to restore profit margins. As with other industrialized countries, West Germany has since 1969 found it difficult to achieve a satisfactory degree of price stability. As long as there are large fluctuations in annual economic growth, it will continue to be hard to secure the desired price stability. In its 1972 report on West Germany, the Organisation for Economic Co-operation and Development concluded that "In the long run achievement of a satisfactory degree of price stability may also be difficult. . . . Experience of recent years suggests that a steadier growth of activity than previously will probably be an essential condition for improving price performance, both because it would cause less distortions in income distribution and because it would facilitate the operation of an incomes policy."[20]

An examination of the distribution or uses of the West German Gross National Product in

[20] *Ibid.*, p. 54.

the years 1963–1973 throws some light on recent economic trends in West Germany. The statistics in Table 5-12 reveal that West Germany has continued since 1963 to be a high-investment, low-consumption economy. Although national output has increased and the standard of living has continued to rise, the distribution of the national income continues to favor investment over consumption. Over the years 1963–1975, the general trend has been to keep the share of Gross National Product going to personal consumption limited as compared with the share going to public consumption and gross fixed investment. The distribution of Gross National Product in the years 1967–1971 shows that approximately one quarter of GNP was taken up by gross fixed investment, which includes investment in plant, equipment, and housing. The gross fixed investment pattern in West Germany is very similar to that of France, Sweden, Norway, the Netherlands, and Japan, which allocate much more of their Gross National Product to fixed investment than do the United States and the United Kingdom. The relatively limited amount of personal consumption in West Germany (approximately 55.5 percent of GNP in 1975) is offset by a sizable amount of public consumption (21.3 percent of Gross National Product in 1975), which is the basis of a large social-welfare program. In 1975, gross fixed investment, which took up 21.1 percent of Gross National Product, was somewhat under the investment trend of the 1960s.

Some critics of West German economic policy assert that the large public expenditures are made to reduce public resentment of the low level of per capita private consumption.[21] Private consumption has been more effectively restricted in West Germany than in other Western European countries, such as the United Kingdom, France, Belgium, and Denmark, where personal consumption absorbs 62 percent of Gross National Product, as compared with 55 percent in West Germany. If the Social Democratic party remains in office a number of years and the militancy of the labor movement in West Germany continues to grow, efforts may be made to alter the distribution of Gross National Product in the direction of relatively more personal consumption, less private investment in industrial plant and equipment, and a smaller net surplus of exports. Greater efforts may in the future be made to secure more of the "fair sharing" of national income that is so much

[21] Frederick G. Reuss, *Fiscal Policy for Growth without Inflation, The German Experiment*, Baltimore: Johns Hopkins Press, 1963, p. 278.

Table 5-12

The Distribution of the West German Gross National Product in 1963, 1967–1971, and 1975 (In Percent)

	1963	1967–1971 (annual average)	1975
Personal consumption	57.2	55.5	55.5
Public consumption	15.7	16.1	21.3
Gross fixed investment	25.2	24.7	21.1
Change in inventories	0.6	1.3	−0.3
Net export surplus	1.3	2.4	2.4
Gross National Product	100.0	100.0	100.0

Source: Organisation for Economic Co-operation and Development, *OECD Economic Surveys, Germany*, 1965–1974.

the concern of the British trade union movement. Also more attention may be paid to increasing public expenditures on pollution control, urban transportation, scientific research, and education. Smaller net export surpluses, which in some years considerably exceed the official goal of 1.5 percent of Gross National Product, would make it possible to shift resources from the external to the public sector where social or collective wants and aspirations have in recent years been assuming a growing importance.[22]

[22] As the Organisation for Economic Co-operation and Development puts it, "The authorities should be encouraged to ... highlight the financial implications of longer-term trends in the provision of collective goods needed to sustain the future rise in public welfare." *OECD Economic Surveys, Germany,* June 1972, p. 55.

West Germany's External Sector

Since the end of World War II, West Germany has maintained a strong export position. In the 1950s West Germany rapidly expanded its exports of manufactured goods and by 1960 was exporting one-fifth of the world's total export of manufactured goods. Since 1963, as Table 5–13 shows, West Germany has expanded the volume of exports at the average annual rate of 11 percent. During the 1960s, West Germany continued along the course that in the 1950s had resulted in securing a strong international trade position. In most years, export prices were kept at favorably low levels. In 1963–1968, the average annual increase in wholesale export prices was only 1.2 percent.

Table 5–13
West German External Financial Indicators, 1963–1974

	Annual % increase in volume of exports	Annual % change in wholesale export prices	Current balance of international payments (mil. U.S. dollars)	International financial reserves (mil. U.S. dollars)	Net export surplus as % of GNP
1963	12	0.0	255	7,650	1.3
1964	11	2.0	116	7,882	1.3
1965	9	3.0	−1,518	7,429	−0.1
1966	12	1.9	105	8,029	3.3
1967	9	0.0	2,359	8,153	3.3
1968	16	−0.9	2,726	9,948	2.4
1969	12	4.7	1,556	7,129	1.6
1970	8	5.4	666	13,610	1.4
1971	7	4.3	131	18,392	0.7
1972	9	1.6	1,041	23,785	0.8
1973	16	6.4	4,576	33,147	2.7
1974	13	17.0	9,358	32,899	3.9
Average annual increase 1963–1972	11.1%	3.8%	—	—	1.8%

Source: International Monetary Fund, *International Financial Statistics.*

For the whole period 1963–1974 these export prices annually increased 3.8 percent. In the same period, there was usually an annual surplus in the current balance of international payments; this was not as large, however, as the annual surplus had been during the 1950s.

During the 1960s, the nation's international financial reserves fluctuated around the $8 billion level. Toward the end of the 1960s, strong speculative movements from the dollar into the deutsche mark forced the West German central bank to purchase large quantities of U.S. dollars to preserve the fixed exchange rate and to prevent what the government took to be an excessive upvaluation (revaluation) of the deutsche mark. Between 1969 and 1974, West German international financial reserves (primarily holdings of gold and dollar exchange) increased from $7.1 billion to $32.9 billion. The increase consisted primarily of dollar exchange with the gold reserve remaining around the $4 billion level. This very large increase in West Germany's international financial reserves (363 percent) was more a measure of the consequences of the breakdown of the international financial system than of a spectacular improvement in West Germany's foreign trade.

Apart from the years 1969–1971, when West German exports were reduced because of rapidly rising labor costs and higher export prices, West Germany had enjoyed an enviable export record. A number of factors have contributed to this outcome, which has been duplicated by France, Italy, and Japan. Like the latter countries, West Germany has been able to keep its export prices low as a result of the large annual improvements in output per man-hour in industry and the small increases in labor costs per unit of industrial output. Also, West Germany, until it adopted a floating exchange rate for the deutsche mark in 1971, tended to undervalue its currency. The fixed exchange rate from 1948 to 1971 was infrequently revalued or upvalued; the result was to make West German exports cheaper than would have been the case had larger and more frequent revaluations of the deutsche mark been made.

Now that the West German trade union movement may be more aggressive in seeking wage increases, that labor costs per unit of industrial output may rise more than in the past, and that the floating exchange rate may prevent the undervaluation of the deutsche mark, it may be more difficult in the future for West Germany to duplicate the very successfull export program of the 1950s and 1960s. To the extent that West Germany's successful export program has been attributable more to the financial weaknesses of its competitors than to the inherent efficiency of the West German economy, a world trade pattern that was more favorable to West Germany's competitors would be a desirable international goal. When a sound international financial system is established in the future, it is to be expected that a more satisfactory world trade pattern would emerge.

West German Fiscal Policy

In West Germany, as in all advanced industrial countries, fiscal policy plays an important role in the control of economic activities. The general tax burden in West Germany is heavy, since total government revenues amount to 38 percent of Gross National Product. While the tax burden, as Table 5-14 reveals, is lower in West Germany than in Sweden (51 percent) and Norway (45 percent), where the social welfare programs are more advanced than in West Germany, this burden is considerably higher than in the United States (31 percent). Like other Western European countries, West Germany, as contrasted with the United States and Sweden, relies heavily on indirect taxes, which amount to 70 percent of total direct taxes. This heavy dependence on indirect taxes as a source of government revenue makes it possible to shift the tax burden away

Table 5–14
The Tax Burden and Sources of Tax Revenue in West Germany and Selected Countries

	Total taxes as percent of GNP 1969–1971	Ratio of indirect to direct taxes 1965–1967	Ratio of indirect to total taxes 1965–1967
Sweden	50.8	51%	34%
Norway	45.2	73	42
United Kingdom	39.2	88	47
West Germany	37.9	70	41
France	37.8	83	45
Italy	33.0	75	43
United States	31.2	48	33

Sources: Organisation for Co-operation and Development, *OECD Economic Surveys, Germany,* 1972; and United Nations, *Yearbook of National Accounts Statistics,* 1971.

from private business enterprises and to encourage investment in plant and equipment, especially in the export industries. The West German tax system has also been employed to develop the "social" features of the social market economy. It supports a large social security system that absorbs about 30 percent of all federal government expenditures. Another use of the West German tax system has been the encouragement of a "people's capitalism" by reducing taxes on small savings and by giving favorable tax treatment to home owners.

During the 1950s, as has already been explained, fiscal policy in West Germany was dominated by the views of the neoliberals, who held that fiscal policy should be neutral in its impact on the economy.[23] Alterations in tax rates and other fiscal arrangements were to be made as infrequently as possible so that private business would not have to take account of numerous fiscal changes in developing its production, investment, price, and other business policies. A relatively inflexible fiscal policy was to be accompanied by a flexible monetary policy. The nation's tax system was to be used primarily to secure equity in the distribution of the tax burden; it was not to be employed to cope with the short-term fluctuations in the level of business activity. These fluctuations were to be handled instead with the aid of monetary policy. The neoliberal approach in post–World War II West Germany favored a balanced fiscal budget and was therefore anti-Keynesian in outlook. The fiscal budget was not to be used as a balancing factor which would be in deficit in years of recession and in surplus in boom years. Whatever countercyclical measures were needed were to be largely monetary in nature. Interest rates and the money supply (currency plus demand deposits) could be quickly altered in accordance with the need to stabilize the economy.

The real test of West German fiscal policy

[23] The limitations of West German fiscal policy in the 1950s and early 1960s are analyzed in Bent Hansen, *Fiscal Policy in Seven Countries, 1955–1965,* Paris: Organisation for Economic Co-operation and Development, 1968, pp. 209–274. See also Andrew Shonfield, *op. cit.*, pp. 284–289; M. MacLennan, M. Forsyth, and G. Denton, *op. cit.*, pp. 187–196; and Walter Heller and others, *Fiscal Policy for a Balanced Economy,* Ch. II, "Germany," Organisation for Economic Co-operation and Development, Paris, 1968, pp. 43–49.

did not come until after the economic miracle was over in the early 1960s, and boom years were followed by years of recession. The neoliberal fiscal and other economic policy measures proved to be unable to contain the business expansion in the years 1964–1965 or to prevent the recession of 1966–1967. By 1966, it was accepted in government and business circles that a more active countercyclical fiscal policy was needed to cope with fluctuations in business activity. In 1966, the Erhard Administration, which was neoliberal in outlook, was replaced by the Kiesinger Administration, which was prepared to use fiscal policy more actively as a countercyclical weapon. The Kiesinger Administration's Stability and Growth Law of 1967 was a major step forward in making fiscal policy more flexible and hence more effective in dealing with business fluctuations. At this time, the federal government abandoned its neoliberal goal of a balanced budget and turned to a more Keynesian approach in fiscal matters, which accepted budgetary deficits in years of recession.

The Stability and Growth Law of 1967 gave the West German government the authority to vary personal and company income taxes by 10 percent up or down; to introduce special depreciation allowances on industrial plant and equipment; to freeze federal, state, and local government borrowing for one year, and to establish an anticyclical reserve fund into which could be placed three percent of annual tax revenues in boom years. This fund was to be drawn upon in years of recession to curb deflationary developments. The 1967 law also created a Council for Anticyclical Policy, with representatives from the federal government, the ten states (*Länder*), the local governments, and the central bank. This council coordinates fiscal policies and programs at all levels of government so that these policies and programs may be more effectively used to deal with fluctuations in economic activity. As has already been explained, the federal government is also required to construct its annual fiscal budget within the framework of a five-year financial plan.

Since 1967, the West German federal government has used a wide variety of fiscal arrangements to offset fluctuations in economic activity. In boom years, repayable surcharges of up to 10 percent have been placed on personal and company income taxes; tax payments have been speeded up, the anticyclical reserve funds of the federal and state governments have taken up increasing amounts of current tax revenues; government expenditures have been postponed; and private investment in plant and equipment has been curbed as the result of the application of less favorable depreciation allowances and the imposition of special taxes on new investments in industrial equipment. In recession years, these fiscal measures have been reversed with the aim of stimulating the economy. Along with other antirecession measures, the tax surcharges imposed in the boom years have been repaid, and funds have been released from the contracyclical reserve fund to finance federal and state spending on public projects. As the financial statistics in Table 5-15 show, sizable federal budget deficits have been recorded in such recession years as 1967 and 1968. It is widely conceded that since the adoption of the Stabilization and Growth Law in 1967, West German fiscal policy has been altered in ways that have made domestic demand management much more effective than it had been in the early 1960s. Since this policy has become more flexible and more selective, it is now a much more effective countercyclical weapon.

West German Monetary Policy

The recent interest in West Germany in developing a more active fiscal policy as a countercyclical device has not reduced the reliance upon monetary policy in the effort to

Table 5-15
West German Financial Indicators, 1963-1974

	Federal fiscal budget surplus (+) or deficit (−) (in bil. DM)	Central bank discount rate	Annual increase in money supply (in percent)	DM-U.S. dollar exchange rate (DMs per U.S. dollar)
1963	−3.14	3.0	6.3	4.000
1964	−0.56	3.0	8.7	4.000
1965	−1.55	4.0	7.5	4.000
1966	−2.52	5.0	1.8	3.977
1967	−8.27	3.0	10.1	3.999
1968	−3.90	3.0	8.4	4.000
1969	1.68	6.0	6.0	3.690
1970	−0.57	6.0	9.7	3.648
1971	−1.36	4.0	12.7	3.268
1972	−3.65	4.5	22.8	3.202
1973	−10.10	7.0	0.1	2.703
1974	−2.85	6.0	12.1	2.409

Source: International Monetary Fund, *International Financial Statistics*.

control the fluctuations in economic activity. As has already been discussed, West Germany's large commercial banks work closely with the federal government and the Central Bank in the application of monetary and credit measures that are designed to curb booms or to stimulate the economy in years of recession. In the boom conditions of 1969 and early 1970, the Central Bank's discount rate rose to 7.5 percent, which was the highest rate reached since 1948. At the same time, the rediscount quotas of the private banks at the Central Bank were reduced by 3.5 billion deutsche marks, and the reserves behind demand and time deposits were increased. From 1963 to 1969, West German monetary, fiscal, and other economic measures were accompanied by moderate price and wage increases. Since 1969, both price and wage inflation have been much more serious than they were before that year. The failure of the authorities to curb inflation adequately in those years is measured in part by the changes in the nation's money supply that are presented in Table 5-15. Whereas the money supply had increased at an average annual rate of 8.5 percent in the years 1966-1970, in 1971, the money supply increased 12.7 percent and in 1972, almost 23 percent. Clearly, the price and wage explosions of 1971 and 1972 were accompanied by increases in the money supply that were not sustainable and that supported excessive inflationary developments.

West German monetary policy has been greatly influenced by developments in the country's external sector. The recurring net export surpluses have had a strong domestic inflationary impact. As a result of these surpluses, West Germany has accumulated a large gold and foreign exchange reserve; export concerns have in many cases had large liquid assets; and the banking system has had considerable free reserves. In addition, export surpluses have reduced the supplies of goods in the domestic markets. A further factor that has contributed to the growth of inflationary pressures since 1968 has been the movement of speculative foreign funds into West Germany in anticipation of the revaluation of the deutsche mark. As has already been explained, one of the aims of West German monetary policy has been to insulate the domestic economy from the inflationary impact of recurring export surpluses and inflows of speculative funds. The inflow of foreign funds was discouraged in the currency crises of 1968 and 1971 by eliminating interest payments on nonresidents' deposits in West German banks, by requiring these banks to have special permits to open new deposit accounts for nonresidents, and by increasing the required reserves behind these deposits up to 100 percent. The purchase of West German securities by nonresidents has been discouraged by placing special taxes on these purchases. Also, borrowing by West German business firms from foreign banks has been curbed in recent years by requiring these firms to make interest-free deposits in the Central Bank equal to variable percentages of the amounts borrowed.

West Germany is now well equipped with both flexible fiscal and monetary policies, and can experiment with a balanced mix of these policies as needed. Whether or not this mix is achieved depends, as the OECD 1971 survey of the West German economy points out, on "political will and determination to act."[24] The danger is always present, however, that monetary and fiscal restraints may prove to be excessive and may push the economy into a recession, as happened in late 1966 and early 1967. There is a strong tendency to place too much of the burden of demand management on monetary policy, which, if carried too far,

curbs private investment excessively and retards economic growth.[25] The outcome of demand management, with the aid of a mix of monetary and fiscal policies, has up to the present been a stop-go program with a highly irregular annual rate of economic growth. Some government and business circles now realize that even improved fiscal and monetary policies are not enough to cope with the incomes race that develops in boom years and with the "stagflation" (rising prices and wages and declining output in recession years) that is encountered in a period of recession. In the opinion of some critics of West German economic policy, what is needed in order to achieve sustained economic growth without serious inflation is some combination of flexible fiscal and monetary policies and an active wage-price or incomes policy. Thus far, the West German federal government has been unable to achieve an effective policy mix of this kind.

West German Incomes Policy

The failure to curb inflation successfully in West Germany has called attention to the need to supplement fiscal and monetary policy with an incomes or wage-price policy. Interest in an incomes policy was relatively late in developing in West Germany because the labor supply was large and wage rates increased only moderately up to the 1960s. When additions to the labor supply from East Germany were cut off after 1961 and the labor market became tight, concern with an incomes policy then made its appearance. In their annual report for 1965, the Council of Economic Experts recommended that

---

[24] *OECD Economic Surveys, Germany,* June 1971, p. 41. See also Organisation for Economic Cooperation and Development, *Monetary Policy in Germany,* Paris, 1973.

[25] The 1967 OECD survey of the West German economy explained that the restrictive monetary and fiscal policies of 1966 "overshot the mark. The growth of activity has been depressed substantially below the growth of capacity." *OECD Economic Surveys, Germany,* March 1967, p. 5.

a productivity-oriented wage policy be adopted. According to the council's argument, "If the cost level is not to rise, nominal wages under certain conditions—especially monetary and external equilibrium—may not rise more than the (average) percentage increase in productivity per man-hour in the economy."[26] The adoption of a productivity wage guideline was to be accompanied by programs that would curb inflation and provide for an equitable distribution of the national income. The underlying premise of the council's wage policy was that the responsibility for the good performance of the nation's economic system was to be shared equally by the government, management, and labor.

The West German federal government has since 1967 accepted the view that wage increases should be related to productivity improvement. The government, however, has no intention of interfering with the collective bargaining process and the independent setting of wage rates. Instead, the government has annually provided employers and workers with "orientation data," which explain recent economic developments and probable future economic trends. The government has hoped that the concerted action meetings of employer, trade union, and government representatives, when supplied with this orientation data, would be better able to understand the economic implications of decisions relating to wage-rate increases. Under the program for concerted action that was inaugurated in 1967, the government's annual forecast projects a rate of real economic growth and also in some years recommends a wage norm for the guidance of collective bargaining. In the years 1968 and 1969, the trade unions, in working out their wage-rate agreements, accepted the government's wage norms of a 4 to 5 percent average wage-rate increase for 1968 and 5.5 to 6.5 percent for 1969. Since the government's forecasts of the real growth of Gross National Product proved to be too low in those years, its wage norms were also too low; thus real wage-rate increases did not keep up with annual improvements in output per man-hour.

As a result of these developments, as has already been explained, a wage lag was created. After 1969, the trade unions no longer accepted the government's wage norms, and wage settlements were made much in excess of the annual average productivity improvement in industry. In their effort to remove the wage lag and to enlarge their share of the national income, the leading West German trade unions started a round of wage increases that resulted in an average wage-rate increase in manufacturing of 12.6 percent in 1970 and 13.6 percent in 1971. In the latter year, the trade unions rejected the government's wage guideline because of the lack of more specific guidelines for profits and prices. After 1969, the West German trade union leadership was no longer enthusiastic about concerted action as a preliminary to collective bargaining. The incomes policy that was initiated in 1967 and that had some success up to 1969 was seriously weakened by the course of events in the years 1970 and 1971. More favorable wage developments were expected in 1972 and 1973 not because of a better working of the incomes policy but because of the disciplinary effects of the floating and the upvaluing of the deutsche mark and the easing of demand pressures in labor and other markets as inflationary pressures declined.

The West German trade unions have emphasized that an incomes policy should take account of the distribution of national income. The unions favor a distribution of income that increases personal consumption, while business leaders call for a distribution that favors private investment. In 1965, the Council of Economic Experts stated that the share of national income going to employees, which was

[26] Organisation for Economic Co-operation and Development, *Inflation, The Present Problem*, Paris, 1970, p. 80.

then 55.5 percent, should be accepted as a norm of income distribution in any formulation of incomes policy. This proposal was unacceptable to the trade unions who saw their share of national income rise, as Table 5-16 shows, from 55.5 percent in 1965 to 59.3 percent in 1971.

In the same years, the share of national income accounted for by income from property and entrepreneurship fell from 30.2 percent in 1965 to 26.7 percent in 1971. In 1965-1971, the compensation of employees increased at an annual rate of 9.7 percent, whereas the income going to property and entrepreneurship increased at the rate of only 6.3 percent. The shift in income distribution in favor of labor did not occur until the wage explosion of 1970-1971, when wage income increased much more rapidly than income received by property and entrepreneurship. By this time, organized labor was unwilling to accept an incomes policy that would nullify the relative wage-income gains of 1970-1971, while business looked forward to reducing the profit squeeze. The basic problem in any incomes policy is to reconcile these two conflicting views with regard to the distribution of national income.[27]

The experience of West Germany with an incomes policy has been quite similar to that of other Western industrial nations. In periods of excess demand, West German incomes policy has usually deteriorated. When the federal government proved to be unable to curb inflation, and labor's share of the national income appeared to be declining in relation to other nonlabor income shares, the West German trade unions objected to specific wage norms

[27] In this connection, see Hellmuth Wagner, "Incomes and Stabilization Policy in the Federal Republic of Germany," *Incomes Policy*, General Confederation of Italian Industries, Rome, 1967, p. 116.

Table 5-16
Shares of West German National Income Received by Employees, Property Owners, and Entrepreneurs, 1965-1971

	Compensation of employees			Income from property and entrepreneurship		
	DM billions in current prices	Annual change in percent	Percent of national income	DM billions in current prices	Annual change in percent	Percent of national income
1965	230.0	—	55.5	125.3	—	30.2
1966	247.6	7.6	55.8	129.5	3.3	29.4
1967	247.9	0.0	56.1	127.2	−1.8	29.0
1968	266.3	7.4	55.2	150.6	18.4	31.2
1969	300.1	12.7	55.6	159.0	5.5	29.5
1970	353.2	17.6	58.1	173.1	8.9	28.5
1971	400.0	13.2	59.3	179.9	3.9	26.7
Annual average 1965-1971	—	9.7	—	—	6.3	—

Source: Organisation for Economic Co-operation and Development, *OECD Economic Surveys, Germany*, 1972.

on the ground that no similar norms were established for profits and other nonwage incomes. Unless the unions are convinced that all economic groups are being treated equitably under the program for the adjustment of income growth to productivity growth, they find ways of repudiating or evading the official wage norms. These ways include sizable additional pay benefits in the form of profit-sharing arrangements, year-end bonuses, compensation payments for shorter working hours, and holiday allowances. The wage and price explosions of 1971 and 1972 led to the proposal that mandatory wage and price controls be adopted similar to those in the United States and the United Kingdom. There is, however, no widespread enthusiasm in West Germany for mandatory wage and price controls. The trade unions are very much opposed to wage controls. Also, the Free Democratic party, which supports the Social Democratic government, and which draws much support from West German industrialists, is not enthusiastic about price controls. The Social Democratic party, which has controlled the West German federal government since 1969, is unwilling to run counter to the widespread public antipathy towards formal wage and price controls. In early 1973, when strong upward pressures on prices and wages developed, the socialist Brandt Administration turned to restrictive fiscal and monetary measures rather than to wage and price controls in its effort to reduce the overheating of the economy.[28] Nothing was done then to try to develop a more effective incomes policy.

[28] A recent study of West German incomes policy concludes that "the German government has generally been reluctant to take the lead in formulating a [wage-price] policy," and that the events of 1969–1971 greatly reduced the potential for administering an incomes policy through the West German collective bargaining institutions. See Lloyd Ulman and Robert J. Flanagan, *Wage Restraint, A Study of Incomes Policies in Western Europe*, Berkeley: University of California Press, 1971, pp. 198–199.

West German Antirecession Policy, 1973–1975

The pattern of West German economic development of the late 1960s and the early 1970s was considerably altered by the energy crisis that began in late 1973. This crisis occurred when the West German domestic economy was in a deep slump. In the first half of 1973, West Germany's Gross National Product increased at a 9 percent annual rate. Strong measures taken to curb the boom included raising corporate and personal income taxes, curbing government expenditures, raising interest rates and restricting credit supplies, and revaluing the deutsche mark. After mid-1973, the domestic nonexport sector of the economy became stagnant and the restrictive fiscal and monetary policies of the first half of the year had to be reversed. This policy reversal, however, was not able to prevent the domestic, nonexport sector from remaining in a depressed state in 1974, in marked contrast to the export boom in the economy's external sector. When the oil crisis developed in late 1973, West Germany had a large "non-oil" surplus on its current international account and a high level of foreign exchange reserves. When the export boom continued into 1974, West Germany had no difficulty in absorbing the price effects of the oil crisis.

In August 1973, the German government approved an energy program that reduced the consumption of imported oil and placed greater reliance on coal, coke, and nuclear power as sources of energy. Special measures were taken to cope with the energy crisis without resorting to price controls or rationing of petroleum products. Arrangements were made to construct an oil refinery in Iran with German financial aid; to import seven hundred tons of enriched uranium from the Soviet Union; to extend oil and natural gas pipelines from Czechoslovakia and East Germany that carried Soviet oil and gas; and to provide subsidies to the steel, electricity, and other industries that replaced oil with more expensive coal and coke. Higher prices for gasoline and other petroleum products reduced the demand for these products in the private sector.

With the aid of these measures and the continued export boom, West Germany was able to maintain a large merchandise trade surplus and an overall favorable balance on its current international account, in spite of the quadrupling of the price of imported crude oil. In 1974, the favorable current account balance was $9 billion, and for 1975 it was estimated to be $6 billion.[29] A part of this favorable balance was the result of capital goods back-flows from the oil exporting countries. These back-flows were purchases by the oil-producing countries of West German machinery and equipment which were financed by the higher prices for crude oil exported from Iran and other OPEC countries.

Higher prices for petroleum and petroleum products in West Germany were not accompanied by any large increase in the level of consumer prices. Table 5-17 shows that the West German consumer-price index, which increased 5.5 percent in 1972, rose 7 percent in both 1973 and 1974, when double-digit inflation was being recorded in France, the United Kingdom, Sweden, Italy, and Japan. In 1974, West Germany had one of its worse production records since the economic miracle of the 1950s. In that year, gross domestic product, which since 1960 had increased at an average annual rate between 4 and 5 percent, increased only one percent, while industrial production fell one percent. With production stagnant and unemployment rising to its highest level since 1960, the trade unions in 1974 accepted the government's orientation wage guideline that recommended an increase in basic hourly rates of not much more than 9 percent. With private business accepting some diminution in its profit margins and

[29] West Germany's handling of its oil problem is analyzed in OECD, *Economic Surveys, Germany,* May 1974 and *Economic Outlook,* 16, Dec. 1974.

Table 5-17
Percent Changes over Previous Years in Selected West German Economic Indicators, 1971-1974

	Gross domestic product	Consumer prices	Wholesale prices	Hourly earnings in manufacturing	Output per man-hour	Unemployment rate[1]
1971	5.9	5.3	4.3	11.0	5.0	0.8
1972	2.9	5.5	2.6	9.0	5.7	1.1
1973	5.3	7.0	6.6	10.4	7.2	1.2
1974	1.0	7.0	13.4	10.2	5.0	2.6
Average annual change, 1971-1974	3.8%	6.2%	6.7%	10.1%	5.7%	1.4%

[1] Annual rates.

Sources: United Nations, *Monthly Bulletin of Statistics;* and International Monetary Fund, *International Monetary Statistics.*

the trade unions showing considerable restraint in their wage demands, inflation in 1973-1974 was much less serious in West Germany than among its foreign competitors.

While West Germany was successful in dealing with its oil problem, it could not insulate its economy from the impact of the worldwide recession of the years 1973 and 1974. When the domestic economy became depressed after mid-1973, the government sought to raise the levels of employment and production in the nonexport sector without at the same time expanding the economy's inflationary pressures. This was done by allowing the surcharges on corporate and personal income taxes to lapse and by abolishing the 11 percent tax on new business investment, by lowering bank reserve requirements, and by increasing the flow of public expenditures. The government's aims were to raise the level of private consumer spending, to increase the level of investment in the housing industry and in the nonexport sector, and to bring the whole economy close to its potential growth rate of 4.5 percent.

Table 5-18 indicates that the government failed to prevent the West German economy from sliding into a serious domestic slump in 1974. Real private consumption, which had increased 2.9 percent in 1973, did not increase in 1974. At the same time, private residential and nonresidential investment suffered large declines in that year. While public consumption and investment increased considerably in 1974, they did not rise enough to offset the large declines in private consumption and investment; thus the real GNP increased only one percent in 1974. The statistics in Table 5-18 also show the West German government's economic expectations for 1975, which included an upturn of the economy, a sizable increase in industrial production, and an increase of 2.5 percent in real GNP.

The years 1973 and 1974 were a severe test for the West German government's stabilization and growth policies. Had there been no

Table 5-18
Demand and Output in West Germany, 1973-1975

	1973 Billion DM	Percent change from previous year		
		1973	1974	1975[1]
Private consumption	496.8	2.9	0.0	3.0
Public consumption	168.7	3.8	3.0	2.75
Fixed investment	230.0	1.1	−6.75	−2.25
Public	31.3	−3.2	7.75	2.25
Private residential	58.8	1.9	−12.0	−5.25
Private nonresidential	139.9	1.7	−8.0	−2.25
Change in inventories	9.6	0.7	−1.5	0.75
Net export surplus	25.3	2.0	3.75	0.0
GNP at market prices	930.4	5.3	1.0	2.5
Industrial production		7.5	−0.5	2.25
Consumer prices		7.0	7.5	7.0

[1] OECD estimates.
Source: OECD, *OECD Economic Outlook*, 16, Dec. 1974.

export boom in those years, West Germany, like the United Kingdom, the United States, and Japan would probably have suffered a negative growth rate. This leads to the conclusion that no economy can be effectively insulated from the effects of a worldwide recession. Various domestic measures may be used to soften the adverse impacts of such a recession, but these measures are no substitute for worldwide economic and financial cooperation among nations to prevent the occurrence of international recessions.

The Future of the West German Social Market Economy

The extent to which the West German economy of the 1970s deviates from the competitive model envisioned by the postwar neoliberals remains a matter of considerable disagreement among economists. Some economists believe that the good performance of the West German economy can be largely attributed to the government's emphasis upon achieving "effective competition." Other economists dispute this interpretation, asserting that West German economic policies and programs have in essence been a "massive interference" with competition. The first group of economists stresses the importance of free market coordination, while the second emphasizes the significance of the extramarket coordination provided by the government, the banks, and the large industrial enterprises.[30] On a matter so difficult as determining the relative importance of competition and intervention in accounting for the good performance of the West German economy since 1948, probably no general agreement can be reached. Economists of a neoliberal persuasion tend to emphasize the importance of competition and market coordination, while economists of a Keynesian persuasion will give greater weight to intervention and nonmarket coordination.

What is above argument, however, is that during the 1950s in West Germany a popular reaction against government intervention and planning occurred, and a widespread interest in establishing a free enterprise economy arose. It is also beyond argument that since the early 1960s there has been in West Germany a greater willingness to accept more government guidance of the nation's economic affairs. Now (1976) that the socialist Social Democratic party is in control of the federal government, one may reasonably expect more and not less government intervention as long as this party remains in office. Economists with the Keynesian approach to economic problems accept the conclusion that the West German economy of today is far removed from the model of workable competition considered by Ludwig Erhard and other neoliberals in the 1950s and 1960s to be the ideal economy.

In the decade 1963–1972, the Keynesian model of the West German economy that emerged as a guide for economic policy making made a place for an activist federal government that was prepared to identify national economic and social goals, and to indicate what should be done to achieve these

---

[30] For the views of the first group, see Egon Sohmen, "Competition and Growth—The Lesson of West Germany: Reply," *Economic Concentration*, pp. 4138–4142; and for the views of the second group, see Karl W. Roskamp and others, "Competition and Growth—The Lesson of West Germany: Comment," *Economic Concentration*, pp. 4130–4137. The 1964 West German official *Report on the Result of an Investigation into Concentration in the Economy (Bericht über das Ergebnis einer Untersuchung der Konzentration in der Wirtschaft,* Bonn, Deutscher Bundestag, Drucksache IV/2320, 1964) has been variously interpreted with regard to the issue of competition versus nonmarket coordination. MacLennan, Forsyth, and Denton find that the report supports the view that banker coordination does not seriously interfere with market coordination, while Shonfield comes to the opposite conclusion. See MacLennan, Forsyth, and Denton, "Is the Economy Planned by the Banks?," *op. cit.*, pp. 68–72; and Shonfield, "Co-ordination by Banker," *op. cit.*, pp. 253–255.

goals. This post-neoliberal model of the economy also took account of the large economic interest groups whose extensive market power has enabled them to have important roles in the wage-price determining process. The Federation of German Industries, the German Employers' Association, the Federation of German Trade Unions, and the Farmers' League represent powerful interest groups with which the federal government must come to terms. The government consults with these groups when it formulates economic policies and adopts measures to handle major economic problems.

As yet, however, no very satisfactory method of securing the cooperation of the government, business, labor, and the farmers with the aim of coping with economic and social problems has been worked out. This is particularly true with respect to the problem of developing an effective incomes policy. Many of the problems with which the West German economy is now faced are common to other advanced industrial economies, such as the United States, the United Kingdom, and Canada; these countries have rejected national planning along the French, Japanese, and Scandinavian lines, and have instead accepted regulation or intervention as the basic principle of national economic guidance. The interventionism in West Germany, as we have seen, stops short of national planning. It seeks instead to achieve a regulated but not a formally planned economy.[31]

The West German economy is today one of the world's most prosperous economies; and there is the good prospect that it will continue to be an efficient and prosperous economy with a major world trade position. In the past quarter century, the structure and functioning of the West German economy have undergone considerable change, and the outlook is for more change. Two recent developments could have much to do with shaping West Germany's economic and social future: (1) the coming to power in 1969 of the first post–World War II socialist government, and (2) the new activism of the German labor movement. While the Social Democratic party has abandoned its Marxist image, it remains a non-revolutionary socialist party. If it remains in office long enough, it may combine with a militant trade union movement and alter many of the nation's economic and social priorities. From now on, organized labor in West Germany will probably have a larger role to play in the formulation of national economic policies. If this turns out to be the case, one can expect in West Germany a distribution of national income that will be less favorable to business and more favorable to the workers, small farmers, and consumers than the past distribution. A socialist government and an active labor movement would doubtless over time pay more attention to the reduction of the social costs of economic growth than was given in the 1950s and 1960s. More of the nation's resources could also be devoted to the provision of social services and the improvement of its infrastructure. The Social Democratic party seeks to achieve these goals without losing the electoral support of the "new center" in the nation's political middle ground.

It is also clear to West Germany's political and economic leaders that their country's future will be greatly influenced by developments in the European Economic Community. There is a widespread realization that many of West Germany's economic and social problems can be handled successfully only in cooperation with the other eight members of

---

[31] The general direction of German economic policy towards regulation rather than national planning is shown in Organisation for Economic Co-operation and Development, *The Industrial Policies of 14 Member Countries*, Ch. I, "Germany," Paris, 1971, pp. 9-48. In Germany's well-disciplined social market economy, where business and labor tend to accept direction from the government, there is no need for formally established national planning. See Frank Vogl, *German Business after the Miracle*, New York: Macmillan, 1973, pp. 191-214.

the community. This applies particularly to such problems as inflation, international financial stability, the balance of world trade, and environmental protection. As community cooperation develops, the structure and functioning of the West German economy will necessarily reflect the constraints imposed by the difficulties of coordinating nine different national economies, which range in nature from capitalist to socialist.

Selected Bibliography

ARNDT, HANS-JOACHIM. *West Germany, Politics of Non-Planning.* Syracuse University Press, Syracuse, 1966.

BESTERS, H. "Economic Policy in Western Germany 1949–1961." *Economic Policy in Our Time,* Country Studies, III, Rand McNally, Chicago, 1964.

COLM, GERHARD. "Comments on the German Economic Report." *Weltwirtschaftliches Archiv,* Band 95, Heft 1, 1965, 1-6.

ERHARD, LUDWIG. *Germany's Comeback in the World Market.* George Allen and Unwin, Ltd., London, 1954.

———. *The Economics of Success.* Thames and Hudson, London, 1963.

EUCKEN, WALTER. *The Foundations of Economics.* University of Chicago Press, Chicago, 1951.

GROSSER, ALFRED. *The Colossus Again.* Frederick A. Praeger, New York, 1955.

HANSEN, BENT. *Fiscal Policy in Seven Countries, 1955–1965.* Organisation for Economic Co-operation and Development, Paris, 1968.

HARTMANN, HEINZ. "Codetermination in West Germany." *Industrial Relations,* Feb. 1970, 137-147.

HENNESSY, JOSSLEYN. "The German 'Miracle.'" In *Economic 'Miracles,'* Institute of Economic Affairs, London, 1964.

MACLENNAN, MALCOLM, MURRAY FORSYTH, and GEOFFREY DENTON. *Economic Planning and Policies in Britain, France, and Germany.* Praeger Publishers, New York, 1968.

Organisation for Economic Co-operation and Development. *Agricultural Policies in 1966, Europe, North America, Japan.* Paris, 1967.

———. *Monetary Policy in Germany.* Paris, 1973.

———. *OECD Economic Surveys, Germany.* Paris, 1967, 1971, 1972, and 1974.

———. *The Industrial Policies of 14 Member Countries.* Paris, 1971.

Report on the Result of an Investigation into Concentration in the Economy (Bericht über das Ergebnis einer Untersuchung der Konzentration in der Wirtschaft). Deutscher Bundestag, Drucksache IV/2320, Bonn, 1964.

REUSS, FREDERICK G. *Fiscal Policy for Growth without Inflation, The German Experiment.* Johns Hopkins Press, Baltimore, 1963.

ROSKAMP, KARL W., and others. "Competition and Growth—The Lesson of West Germany: Comment." *Hearings on Economic Concentration,* U.S. Subcommittee on Antitrust and Monopoly, 1968.

ROSS, ARTHUR M., and PAUL T. HARTMAN. *Changing Patterns of Industrial Conflicts.* John Wiley and Sons, New York, 1960.

SCHLECHT, OTTO. "The Role of the 'Concerted Action' Program in the Economic Policy of the Federal Republic of Germany." *The German Economic Review,* 8, No. 3 (1970), 255–260.

SCHNITZER, MARTIN. *East and West Germany: A Comparative Economic Analysis.* Praeger Publishers, New York, 1972.

SOHMEN, EGON. "Competition and Growth—The Lesson of West Germany: Reply." *Hearings on Economic Concentration,* U.S. Subcommittee on Antitrust and Monopoly, 1968.

STOLPER, GUSTAV, and others. *The German Economy 1870 to the Present.* Harcourt, Brace and World, New York, 1967.

STURMTHAL, ADOLF. *Contemporary Collective Bargaining in Seven Countries.* Cornell University Press, Ithaca, 1957.

———. *Workers Councils: A Study of Workplace Organization on Both Sides of the Iron Curtain.* Harvard University Press, Cambridge, 1964.

VOGL, FRANK. *German Business after the Economic Miracle.* Macmillan Company, New York, 1973.

WALLICH, HENRY C. *Mainsprings of the German Revival.* Yale University Press, New Haven, 1955.

Chapter 6
The French Planned Economy

In the period since the close of the Second World War, the French economic system has attracted worldwide notice, because France is the only major Western European capitalist country that has pursued a well-defined program of national economic and social planning. This planning has been continuous since 1947, and now appears to have become a more or less permanent part of the national policy system. Although the national planning program was initiated by the socialist and communist parties in the early postwar years, it has since the late 1940s been adopted by the nonradical political parties and has received strong support from the nation's large business interests. When the middle-of-the-road Gaullist party, the Union for the New Republic, came to dominate French politics in 1959, the government found the program of indicative national planning to be an essential feature of what is described as the "new society." This is also true under the current d'Estaing administration. Although the French planned economy is in part the product of special national circumstances, its successful operation has raised the question as to whether or not some of its features could be profitably borrowed by other countries. The United Kingdom, whose economic performance since 1945 has lagged much behind that of France, has been faced with this issue. This question led to the establishment of the British National Economic Development Council in 1962 with the hope that some kind of planning program could be substituted for the unsuccessful stop-go economic program.

Since the close of the Second World War, the French economy, like the Japanese economy, has been generally dynamic and prosperous. In the past quarter century, France has been transformed from a closed, cartel-ridden, low-growth economy into a much more open, internationally competitive, high-growth economy. Since the early 1950s,

France has forged ahead of the United Kingdom in terms of per capita Gross National Product. By 1973, France's per capita GNP ($4,540) was larger than that of the United Kingdom ($3,060) but lower than West Germany ($5,320). In 1960–1973, France had an annual growth rate of per capita GNP (4.7 percent) that was higher than that of West Germany, Sweden, the United Kingdom, the United States, and Canada. Not only has France had a high growth rate since 1945, but it has also been able to achieve a sustained high growth rate, something which most major Western industrial nations have not been able to secure. Unlike many other Western industrialized nations, France, has been generally free from recessionary developments, although it has at times suffered from strong inflationary pressures. Consequently, France had no serious unemployment problems prior to 1973.

France eliminated the Malthusian pessimism (*Malthusianisme économique*) that made it the "sick man" of Europe in the interwar years 1919–1939.[1] Since 1958, France has taken the lead in developing the European Common Market and has been active in liberalizing foreign trade in industrial products in Western Europe. The new French dynamism has resulted in the restructuring of its industry and the expansion of such high-technology industries as the automobile, chemical (plastics), machinery, and electric (electronic) industries. While French national planning has led to considerable economic progress, it has also been accompanied by severe social and political strains, as evidenced by the student-worker disturbances of May–June 1968.

The highly centralized, hierarchical French society was poorly prepared to contend with the high social costs of rapid industrialization and economic growth in the 1950s and 1960s. The French planners failed to cope satisfactorily with urban congestion, environmental deterioration, inadequate transportation and telecommunication systems, poor housing, an overburdened and outmoded educational system, and widespread regional inequalities. In preparing the national plan for 1976–1980 (Plan VII), the planning authorities expect to pay much more attention to social indicators and the construction of what former Premier Jacques Chaban-Delmas envisioned as the *new society*.

The economic development of France since 1945 may be divided into five periods. The first period, 1945–1950, was one of postwar reconstruction and a return to a peacetime economy. The objectives of the socialist-dominated governments in these early postwar years were to restore the economy as rapidly as possible to pre–World War II levels and to set the economy on the path of high and sustained growth. The new growth program was inaugurated in 1947 with the adoption of the first of the seven medium-term programs that France has constructed since the end of the Second World War. In the second period, 1951–1958, national economic planning became more sophisticated and was accompanied by rapid domestic expansion and high economic growth. Economic progress was marred by a high level of domestic political instability and a failure to develop a strong external economy.

Both of these deficiencies were greatly reduced in the third period (1959–1968) when Charles de Gaulle in 1959 began a decade of strong political and economic leadership. The 1960s were the decade of the French "economic miracle," during which an average annual growth rate of 5.7 was achieved, unemployment was reduced to a very low level, and

---

[1] A good survey of France's economic progress is presented in "Pompidou's France, An Economic Survey," *The Economist*, Vol. 245, No. 6745, Dec. 2, 1972, pp. 1–46. See also Andrew Shonfield, "The Etatist Tradition: France," *op. cit.*, pp. 71–87.

large exports enabled the government to increase its gold and foreign exchange reserve from $2 to $6 billion. During 1959-1968, many of the postwar controls were relaxed, foreign trade was liberalized, and more reliance was placed on the private market system within the framework of planned national economic guidance.

When de Gaulle withdrew from political activity in April 1969, the fourth and current period in France's postwar economic development began. Although France had enjoyed political stability and economic prosperity under de Gaulle, the final year of his presidency was disrupted by widespread student revolts and workers' strikes. In the 1960s, the government's economic and social programs had paid inadequate attention to such needs as improving the nation's social infrastructure, developing a less centralized social and political system, preventing environmental deterioration, and providing what workers and farmers believed were fair shares of the national income.

In 1969, Georges Pompidou replaced de Gaulle as the nation's political leader and proposed to meet France's serious economic and social problems by carrying out programs that would lead to the "new society." Pompidou's administration emphasized more participatory democracy, in which students and workers would have more influence on the nation's decision-making processes. The new program also stressed improving housing, transportation, and telecommunications, preventing environmental deterioration, providing for more regional autonomy, preserving the urban amenities, and improving the economic lot of the aged, the handicapped, and other disadvantaged groups. In the Sixth Plan (1971-1975), special emphasis was placed on providing the collective goods and services required by the new society, while at the same time continuing the modernization of French industry and the effort to make it more competitive in the world economy. It remains to be seen whether or not the government's plans for achieving these twin goals and improving the quality of life enough to satisfy the French people will be successful under Valéry Giscard d'Estaing, who succeeded Pompidou in May 1974.

Major Features of the French Economy

France is the least densely populated of the major Western European countries and the third largest industrialized country in Western Europe. Its total civilian labor force of 21.2 million turned out a Gross National Product of $187.4 billion in 1972, as compared with $209 billion for West Germany and $144.9 for the United Kingdom. In 1973, France's per capita GNP ($4,540) was 73 percent of the United States' per capita GNP ($6,200). With regard to the production of manufactured products, France falls behind both West Germany and the United Kingdom. The statistics in Table 6-1 show that while France and West Germany have maintained their relative positions among the world's producers of manufactured goods, both the United States and the United Kingdom have suffered significant relative declines. France, which was fifth among the noncommunist industrial nations in 1963, was fourth in 1974. The most spectacular industrial development in these years occurred in Japan, which by 1974 had surpassed all major Western European industrialized countries, becoming the world's second largest noncommunist producer of manufactured goods.

France is well endowed with natural resources. It has a favorable climate and geographical location and a land area that supports a highly diversified agriculture. France's industrial resources include extensive iron-ore deposits and large reserves of low-grade

Table 6-1
Relative Importance of Manufacturing Output in Selected Noncommunist Countries, 1963 and 1974

	Relative Importance	
	1963	1974
World output of manufactured goods	1,000	1,000
United States	452	372
West Germany	89	94
United Kingdom	73	48
France	51	69
Italy	36	36
Japan	55	103

Sources: United Nations, *Monthly Bulletin of Statistics;* and National Institute of Economic and Social Research, *National Institute Economic Review.*

coal, as well as deposits of bauxite and phosphate. The mountainous regions of France are a source of large amounts of hydroelectric power. France is deficient in nonferrous metals, petroleum, coke, and textile raw materials; like other Western European countries, it relies upon a large export trade to secure the necessary supplies of raw materials. France is Western Europe's largest producer of iron ore and aluminum and the second largest producer of steel—after West Germany but ahead of the United Kingdom. While agriculture is a major economic activity in France, accounting for 6 percent of gross domestic product, manufacturing is responsible for about 40 percent of France's gross domestic product. The French economy is a highly industrialized economy, over 60 percent of whose exports are manufactured products.

Like other Western European countries, France has made large changes in the structure of its economy since 1945. The two major structural developments have been the decline of agriculture and the rise of the service industries. The statistics in Table 6-2 show that between 1960 and 1973 employment in agriculture fell 38.9 percent, whereas employment outside agriculture and industry increased 36.3 percent. As is seen from Table 6-3, agriculture, which accounted for 9 percent of France's gross domestic product in 1960, accounted for only 5 percent in 1974. Young workers have tended to go into the private and public service activities, which are the low-productivity activities, rather than into the high-productivity domestic and export industries. This trend, which the government finds disturbing, has been fostered by the traditional educational system which pays inadequate attention to education along scientific and technological lines.

Under Plan VI (1971–1975), in which the development of the high-technology industries was emphasized, the government sought to reduce the flow of workers into the service sector. This was done by revamping the educational system so as to emphasize training in scientific and technological fields, by increasing the funds assigned to industrial research and development, and by developing a manpower policy that fostered the progressive high-technology industries. All these programs are designed to increase productive investment (*l'investissement productif*), i.e.,

Table 6-2
Civilian Employment by Sector in the French Economy, 1960 and 1973

	1960		1973		Percent change 1960 to 1973
	In 1,000s	In percent	In 1,000s	In percent	
Agriculture, forestry and fishing	4,193	22.4	2,560	12.2	−38.9
Industry	7,070	37.8	8,243	39.3	16.6
Other	7,449	39.8	10,151	48.5	36.3
Total employment	18,712	100.0	20,954	100.0	10.7

Source: OECD, *OECD Economic Surveys, France,* 1970–1975.

investment that results in more production, especially of exports.[2]

Like the United Kingdom and West Germany, France derives more than one-third of its gross domestic product from the manufacturing industries. Although the size of the contribution of French industry to GNP (approximately 40 percent, as indicated in Table 6-3) has not changed significantly in the past two decades, substantial qualitative changes have occurred in industrial output. In order to compete with the world's trading nations, France has had to direct its efforts towards the development of the electronics, automobile, plastics, aerospace, and other high-technology industries. In recent years much concern has also been voiced about the possible invasion of these industries by foreign multinational enterprises, and steps have been taken to prevent or to curb this penetration of French industry.[3]

Unlike the United States, the United Kingdom, West Germany, and Japan, France has been slow to establish multinational companies. In 1970, France accounted for only one of the thirty-two largest United States and European firms in the automobile, electrical, chemical, and petroleum industries that are the source of many of the large multinational companies. Thirty of the world's largest firms in these four industries had headquarters in the United States, West Germany, the United Kingdom, and Italy.[4]

The French economy, like the British economy, has a large nationalized sector, which includes the coal, gas, and electricity industries; communications; the railroads; some of the transatlantic marine transportation and most of the air transportation; the Bank of France and four major commercial banks; the bulk of the insurance industry; the aircraft industry; and the Renault automobile firm.[5] In addition, the French government

---

[2] La Documentation Française, *Le Sixième Plan,* Paris, 1971, p. 94. Investment in housing, schools, hospitals, and other social capital is not considered to be "productive," since it does not increase directly the supply of marketable domestic and export products.

[3] This issue was brought to the public's attention in France in 1968 with the publication of Jean Jacques Servan-Schreiber's *The American Challenge,* New York: Atheneum, 1968.

[4] The European Economic Community, *Multinational Corporations: Problems Confronting Europe,* European Studies, 16, 1973, p. 2.

[5] M. Einaudi, M. Bye, and E. Rossi, *Nationalization in France and Italy,* Ithaca: Cornell University Press, 1955, pp. 81–86. For a review of the French economy, see John Sheahan, *An Introduction to the French Economy,* Columbus, Ohio: Charles E. Merrill, 1969. See also W. C. Baum, *The French Economy and the State,* Princeton: Princeton University Press, 1958.

Table 6-3
Origins of the French Gross Domestic Product, 1960–1974 (In Percent)

	1960	1974
Agriculture	9	5
Industry	40	36
Construction	8	10
Wholesale and retail trade	12	17
Transportation and communications	5	5
Other service industries	25	27
Gross domestic product	99	100

Source: United Nations, *Statistical Yearbook;* and *Monthly Bulletin of Statistics,* Aug. 1976.

holds a part of the share capital of many private enterprises. In 1961, the French government held 30 percent or more of the share capital of 496 private enterprises of an industrial and commercial character. Approximately 20 percent of the productive capacity of French industry is government owned.

The French government plays major roles in the labor and capital markets. The government hires about 25 percent of the nation's nonagricultural labor force. Civil servants and employees of the nationalized industries constitute about one-quarter of the nonagricultural labor force. Being the largest single employer, the government is in a strong position to influence the level of wage rates. The central government, along with the local governments and the nationalized industries, accounts annually for about one-half of the nation's gross domestic fixed investment. The French capital market is much less well developed than similar markets in the United Kingdom and West Germany. The French investing public prefers to hold government securities and savings deposits rather than the capital shares of private business enterprises. The weak French capital market has forced the government to finance the public and private sectors in part by selling treasury bills and bonds to the public and loaning the proceeds to nationalized and private business enterprises. The government's Economic and Social Development Fund lends treasury funds to both public and private enterprises. Special government-owned or government-controlled credit institutions receive deposits from savings banks and also sell bonds. They then lend the proceeds on a medium or long-term basis, or purchase capital shares of private business enterprises. The major portion of the financing of home construction is provided directly or indirectly by the French central and local governments.

French agriculture, like that of all other Western European countries, is small scale and favorable to the continuance of the single-family farm. French agricultural policy has the same general aims as agricultural policy in other Western European countries. Domestic farm markets are protected by tariffs and other restrictive arrangements; the prices of major farm products are fixed by agreement between the government and the farmers' organizations; farm production is regulated so as to curb overproduction; and farm prices and subsidies are adjusted in order to bring about parity between the annual incomes of farmers and industrial workers. Because of the advantages of soil fertility and a favorable climate, France can produce cereals and other major farm products more cheaply than can other Western European countries; it consequently exports considerable amounts of these products to Western European markets.

The French banking system is similar to the banking systems of other continental countries—having commercial, savings, agricultural, and special purpose banks, which make medium and long-term loans to industry and various public bodies. Banking in France is not as highly centralized as it is in West Germany, the United Kingdom, and other Western European countries. The 361 French commercial banks have a network of 3,800 bank branches, and the five leading deposit banks account for over 50 percent of the total assets of all deposit banks. The two unique features of the French banking system are the government ownership of a significant portion of the nation's banking system and the extensive role of the government in the nation's banking affairs.

Besides owning the central bank and four of the largest deposit (commercial) banks, the government controls a number of important private banks by appointing key members to their boards of directors. In addition to deposit, investment, and savings banks, there are specialized credit institutions, either government owned or controlled, which have an active role in France's national economic planning program. These institutions, such as the State Deposit and Consignment Bank (*Caisse des Dépôts et Consignations*) and the National Bank of Agricultural Credit (*Caisse National de Crédit Agricole*), play important roles in the agricultural, industrial, home construction, and foreign trade sectors of the French economy. Their sources of funds are loans from the Treasury; the accumulated funds of savings banks, pension plans, and the social security system; and proceeds from the sale of debentures to the public. These funds are loaned by the specialized credit institutions to private industries, nationalized industries, cooperatives, and local government authorities in such a manner as to further the objectives of the five-year national plans. Loans from the Treasury and from government-owned or controlled specialized credit institutions must be approved by the Economic and Social Development Fund.

This fund, originally called the Modernization and Equipment Fund, has representatives from all the major economic ministries of the government, the Bank of France, and some of the specialized credit institutions. Its function is to approve all the investments in the national and regional plans which receive government financial support. The National Credit Council, with representatives from the government, the Bank of France, public and semipublic credit institutions, industry, trade, and agriculture, advises the government with respect to short-term credit policy. The Capital Issues Committee, with representatives from the Ministries of Finance, Economic Affairs, and Industry and Commerce, the Bank of France, and the General Plan Commission, controls the supply of long-term credit by licensing the issuance of private bonds.

France has a large foreign trade sector, but is not as dependent on foreign trade for the efficient functioning of its economy as are the United Kingdom, West Germany, and other Western European countries. In 1973, France's exports were equal to 19.3 percent of its Gross National Product, whereas exports in the United Kingdom were equal to 27 percent and in West Germany to 23 percent of GNP. France's major export markets are found in Western Europe among the members of the European Common Market and its former colonies.

French National Planning

The functioning of the French economy since 1945 cannot be adequately explained without reference to the role of national planning in French economic life.[6] By 1972, France had operated under national economic plans for twenty-five years. All the evidence points to the probability that national planning has become a permanent feature of French economic life. National planning is no longer the special concern of any one of the political parties. Although French national planning originated as a program that was strongly supported by the Socialist party, this planning has evolved so as to secure political support from nonsocialists as well as socialists. After a quarter century of experience with planning, the French people appear to have accepted planning as a necessary part of their way of making a living.

Both historical and cultural factors have contributed to secure wide popular support for national planning. France was one of the first major European countries to be unified politically; this unification was accompanied by a high degree of centralization in the nation's economic and political activities. The philosophy of laissez faire never secured the widespread acceptance in France during the nineteenth and early twentieth centuries that it did in the United Kingdom and the United States.[7] In addition, the political unification of France was accompanied by the development of a civil service that was prepared to play a highly efficient role in a very centralized society. The wide gap between "business" and the "civil service" that developed in more laissez faire economies never made its appearance in France. One of the reasons for the successful execution of national planning in France since 1945 has been the presence of a reliable and efficient civil service that carries on successfully in spite of the frequent changes in governments.

French national economic planning is in many ways a special product of the French postwar environment. Although it was originally in large part the product of socialist theorizing, after 1948 this planning lost its ideological connection with the socialist movement. French planning has drawn considerable support from most major economic groups. Big business is favorably disposed towards national planning because its affairs are closely connected with those of the government. It is clearer to big business than to small business that the high economic growth rates set forth in the five-year national plans are crucial for the welfare of the private business system. It is not surprising that criticism of French national planning comes more from small business and farmers than from big business. Unlike the national planning of the Scandinavian countries and of the United Kingdom (when the Labour party is in power), national planning in France is not a product of the French labor movement. Although it was very active in its support of national planning in the early postwar years, the French trade union movement since 1948 has not played the dominant role in French planning. Organized labor in France has usually not controlled the government of the day, nor has it occupied key positions in the nation's plan organization. Trade union representatives have always been in a minority position on the various planning commissions associated with the national planning program. From the

---

[6] For a review of the development of French planning, see Yves Ullmo, "The National Context, France," in Jack Hayward and Michael Watson, *Planning, Politics, and Public Policy, the British, French and Italian Experience.* Cambridge, U. K.: Cambridge University Press, 1975.

[7] S. B. Clough, *France, A History of National Economics, 1789-1939*, New York: Charles Scribner's Sons, 1939.

ideological point of view, French planning is neither "right" nor "left," but rather "center" in terms of French politics. Supported enthusiastically by neither the extreme right nor the extreme left, French planning has commanded enough support from the middle of the political spectrum to continue to be a major feature of French economic life since 1947.

In many of its essentials, French national planning is very similar to Scandinavian national planning. In both cases, similar planning techniques are employed. Four- or five-year national plans are constructed as frameworks for annual economic plans. In both cases, national economic budgets are constructed and projections are made of the Gross National Product and its private and public consumption and investment components. In both French and Scandinavian national planning, the projected annual growth of GNP is the key concern of the whole national plan. After the projected growth rate has been decided upon, the plan then turns to the distribution of the total national output. As in the case of Scandinavian and British Labour party planning, in French planning, the plan is executed with the aid of various economic controls and inducements.

The most significant difference between French and other Western European forms of national planning lies in the extent to which private business participates in the construction and execution of the national plans. In Scandinavian national planning, business people, trade unionists, and farmers play no direct role in the construction of the national plans. In Norway and Sweden, the planning authorities usually consult separately and informally with business, labor, and farm groups when new national plans are being drawn up and when these plans are being carried out. But consultation does not go beyond these informal arrangements.

The Organizational Structure of French Planning

French national planning is unique with respect to the way in which it provides for the participation of private business, labor, consumers, and agriculture in the construction and execution of the annual and five-year national plans.[8] The role of the private business system in national planning can be best explained by inquiring into the general scheme of the French plan organization, which is presented only in major outline in Figure 6-I. Although it was not true of the first three national plans, these plans are now approved by the National Assembly before they are put into operation. The broad outlines of the national plans are determined by the prime minister and his cabinet. They decide what major objectives and national priorities are to be incorporated in the five-year national plans. The general task of constructing the plan and of implementing it is assigned to the General Plan Commission (*Commissariat Général du Plan*) which, formerly attached to the Ministry of Finance, is now responsible to

[8] For general surveys of French planning, see Stephen Cohen, *Modern Capitalist Planning: The French Model*, Cambridge, Mass.: Harvard University Press, 1969; Pierre Bauchet, *Economic Planning: The French Experience*, London: Heinemann Educational Books, 1964; John and Anne-Marie Hackett, *Economic Planning in France*, Cambridge, Mass.: Harvard University Press, 1963; John S. Harlow, *French Economic Planning: A Challenge to Reason,* Iowa City: University of Iowa Press, 1966; and Vera Lutz, *French Planning*, Washington, D.C.: American Enterprise Institute, 1965; and *Central Planning for the Market Economy, An Analysis of the French Theory and Experience*, London: Longmans, Green, 1969. French views on planning are presented in C. Gruson, *Origine et espoirs de la planification française,* Paris: Dunod, 1968; Yves Ullmo, *La Planification en France*, Cours de l'Institut d'Etudes Politiques, Paris, 1971–1973; and Atreize, *La planification française en pratique*, Paris: Les Editions Ouvrières, 1971.

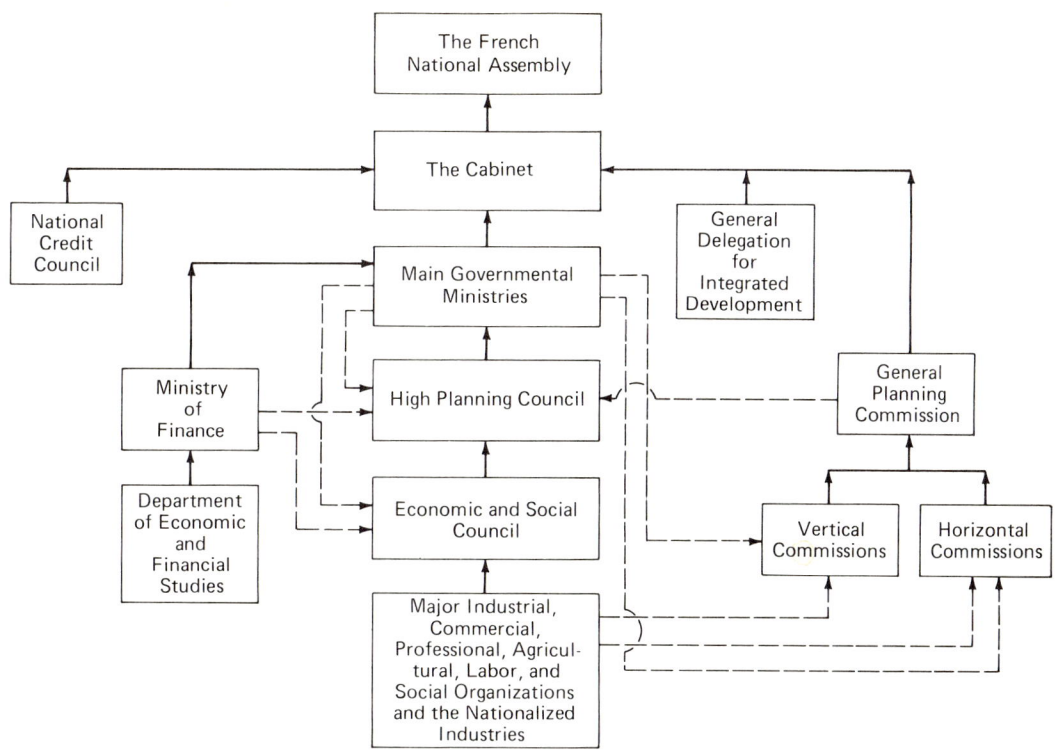

Figure 6-1
The French National Economic Planning Organization, 1975

the Prime Minister's Office. This planning office supervises the construction of the five-year national economic plans, and acts as a liaison among all the government ministries and agencies concerned with national planning.

The High Planning Council, with the prime minister as its chairman and sixty members representing the economic departments of the government as well as all major private economic interests, gives an opinion on the final draft before the national plan is submitted to the government and the Economic and Social Council. In addition, it analyzes the execution of the national plan and suggests appropriate measures to the government as needed. The General Delegation for Integrated Development, associated with the General Plan Commission and with seventy-five representatives from the government and labor and business organizations, investigates the prospects for the country's development over the long term. Associated with the Minister of Finance are the Economic and Financial Research Service, which constructs annual plans within the framework of the five-year national plan, the Economic and Social Development Fund, and the Regional Committees. The fund invests or lends public funds in support of the national plan, while the twenty-one regional committees advise the government on the drafting of regional development plans. The national plan, after it is approved by the prime minister and his cabinet, is then sent to the National Assembly for its approval.

The public participates in French national planning activity in two ways: through the Economic and Social Council and through the modernization committees. The Economic and Social Council brings together representatives of all the major national interests including the government. The membership of the council includes representatives of government ministries, major industries, confederations of trade unions, national farmers' unions, agricultural cooperatives, the nationalized industries, the professions, and various social organizations. Pierre Massé, Chairman of the General Plan Office, explained in 1961 with reference to the construction of the Fourth Plan (1962-1965) that "Before deciding between these [plan] alternatives, however, the Government consulted the . . . Economic and Social Council, an assembly of representatives of all the main national interests. This is a new development in economic democracy. Its value lies in providing those who are often unfairly called technocrats [government officials concerned with economic planning] with broader points of contact. It is highly desirable that the nation should be consulted through its political institutions not only when the Plan is approved, but also at the earlier stages when the Plan is being pieced together."[9] The Economic and Social Council is only advisory in nature. Its main purpose is to enable the government to secure the reaction of the private economic and social groups to its planning proposals, and to provide these groups with a means of influencing the government when it is constructing the national plans.

The modernization commissions, which include vertical and horizontal commissions, furnish a more important means for the nation's major private economic interests to influence the construction of French national economic plans. These commissions, established at the same time (1946) as the General Planning Office, were set up in order to enable the private economic groups to participate in the construction of the plans. These modernization commissions are tripartite bodies with representatives of industry, the workers, and the government. They are of two kinds: the twenty-five vertical commissions and the five horizontal commissions. The vertical commissions represent all important sectors of the economy, such as the chemical, steel, and manufacturing industries; transportation; and the social areas of housing, culture and the arts, and public health. The five horizontal commissions, which cut across all sectors and areas of the economy, deal with economic and financial matters of interest to the government and to private economic groups. The five horizontal commissions are concerned with manpower, productivity, regional planning, scientific and technical research, and general economic and financial matters. Each vertical and horizontal commission has representatives on it from each of the government ministries interested in the work of the commission.

Working in cooperation with the General Plan Office, each vertical commission analyzes the impact of the proposed five-year national plan upon its area of the economy. The overall national plan is reduced to a detailed program for each industry and sector. Working with an input-output table that relates to the whole plan, each vertical commission estimates its sales to and purchases from the other vertical commissions. For example, the forty-member steel commission analyzes the proposed five-year plan in terms of the output of the steel industry that is sold to other areas of the economy, and in terms of its input needs for coal, iron ore, coke, and various chemicals. All this analysis is made in

---

[9] Political and Economic Planning, *Economic Planning in France*, Vol. XXVII, No. 454, London, Aug. 14, 1961, pp. 216-217. See also Pierre Massé, "French Methods of Planning," *Journal of Industrial Relations*, Vol. XI, Nov. 1962.

terms of the annual rate of growth of Gross National Product assumed in the five-year national plan. Each steel firm participating in the work of the steel commission can determine its future manpower, capital, and financial needs in terms of the planned, expanding national economy. In this manner, each major private economic activity is represented during the plan construction so that it can be determined how it will fit into the plan, and how its interests can be defended within the broader framework of the national interest. The business and labor leaders in each industry are not only informed of the value of the plan to them, but they are also given an opportunity to cooperate with the government in requesting the support of the public for the plan.

The Theory of French National Planning

While French national planning was to some extent developed pragmatically as a response to France's early post–World War II economic and social problems, it has nevertheless been guided by certain theoretical considerations. According to the theorists of French planning, the advanced industrial economy no longer possesses sufficient self-correcting forces to ensure its good performance.[10] The modern industrial economy, with its unplanned collective action in control of individual action and its price, wage and other inflexibilities, suffers from highly irregular economic growth and recurring periods of financial crisis and high unemployment. If the modern industrial economy is to perform satisfactorily, it must be supplemented by some form of national economic guidance that goes beyond private market guidance.

The French planners explain that their four- or five-year plans are applied to what is fundamentally a private-market economy (*une économie de marché*).[11] Under their planning, private economic decisions are placed within a framework that, if all economic units play the game, assures not only a high and sustained level of total national output, but also adequate supplies for all industries and adequate markets for their outputs. In this situation, the role of the government is to stimulate and to support the private economy; to prevent the growth of supply bottlenecks and to maintain full employment; and to provide incentives and controls that lead employers and workers to realize the nation's full growth potential.

According to the theory guiding French national planning, the advanced industrial economy has, along with a public sector, two private sectors, one monopolistic and oligopolistic and the other competitive. In the large-scale sector, prices and wages are largely administered, whereas in the small-scale sector prices and wages are flexible and responsive to changing market conditions. In an unplanned economy, these two sectors are not well coordinated or meshed. The oligopolistic sector exploits the competitive sector by placing the burden of adjustment to fluctuating economic conditions largely on the small-scale competitive firms. The efforts of all sectors to protect what they consider to be their legitimate economic interests lead to the development of strong inflationary pressures, an incomes race, and recurring recessions with financial crises. In the opinion of French

---

[10] Pierre Bauchet, Director of Studies at the École Nationale d'Administration and adviser to the Commissariat du Plan, concludes that "the Plan entails a transformation of the structure of French capitalism which is so radical that people are beginning to wonder whether the system still deserves that name." *Economic Planning: The French Experience*, p. xv. François Perroux finds that national planning is the solution to the "crisis of capitalism." *Le Capitalisme*, Paris: Presses Universitaires De France, 1962, pp. 87–106.

[11] *Le Sixième Plan*, p. 3.

planners, only a program of national economic guidance can cope successfully with the problems of the advanced industrial economy.

The public sector includes the nationalized industries as well as the various government agencies or departments dealing with defense, education, health, transportation, environmental protection, housing, and other national concerns. In the unplanned private enterprise economy, the interrelations between the public sector and the two private sectors raise the basic question of how the nation's economic resources will be divided among them. There is a tendency for a disproportionately large share of resources to go into the private sectors, so that there will be an oversupply of private goods and services and an undersupply of public goods and services, such as schools, hospitals, public health services, and environmental protection.

French planners substitute for the unplanned market economy the planned or modified market economy.[12] The economic model that guides their economic proposals lies between the classical laissez faire model, in which the market allocates all resources, and the command model, in which all resources are allocated by a central planning authority. The latter model is associated with imperative national planning, in which there are no democratic individual freedoms. In the intermediate position between the pure market and pure command models of the economy is a wide area of regulation, intervention, and planning in which the pure market model is replaced by a modified market model. The modification of the pure market model varies from country to country.

The modified market economy of the French planning authorities is described as a *concerted economy (une économie concertée).*

[12] The concept of the modified market model is discussed in Stephen Cohen, *Modern Capitalist Planning: The French Model*, pp. 18–20.

Pierre Massé, formerly chairman of the General Plan Commission, has called the French economic system a "collective enterprise" in which close collaboration occurs between government, business, labor, and the farmers, and in which the economic system is guided by a program of indicative national planning.[13] A concerted economy is not one in which the government and the major economic interest groups are equals. On the contrary, the government has the special role of providing an overall guidance to ensure the economy's satisfactory performance. The indicative national planning applied to the concerted economy with its annual and medium-term national plans indicates only the national economic and social goals or priorities that should be achieved. Behind and supporting this planning is a system of incentives and controls that is used by the government to guide the economy towards the plan's goals.

French indicative planning explains how private enterprise and private economic decision making will benefit from the operations of the plans; and it offers fiscal and monetary inducements to individuals and private enterprises to work along with these plans. When necessary, however, the government is prepared to withhold economic advantages from those business enterprises that do not support the national plan; it is also ready to impose fiscal, monetary, and other economic controls in order to move the economy towards the national goals approved by the French Parliament and incorporated in the national plans. The emphasis in the modified market model of the French planners is on securing the voluntary cooperation of all private economic groups with the government,

[13] Pierre Massé in Political and Economic Planning, *Economic Planning in France*, Vol. XXVII, No. 454, London, 1961, p. 212. In *Le Sixième Plan*, it is explained that the national plan is the fruit of a wide collaboration (*une large concertation*) between many private and public groups (p. 3).

but at all times some elements of direction or coercion remain.[14]

The Performance of the French Planned Economy, 1953–1963

During the decade 1953–1963, France had a high sustained rate of economic growth which was accompanied by a number of adverse financial developments. The general goal of a 4.5 percent annual increase in Gross National Product, which was incorporated in the Second and Third Plans, was achieved. The statistics in Table 6-4 show that France had an average annual increase in Gross National Product of 4.9 percent and in industrial production of 6.9 percent for the period 1953–1963. From 1953 to 1957 large increases in hourly wage rates were offset by similar increases in output per man-hour. Both wholesale and retail prices were quite stable in those years. Although the volume of exports grew rapidly, imports increased much faster during the boom years 1956 and 1957, and an adverse balance of international payments on

[14] The question as to how far the French national plans are "voluntary" or "coercive" remains unsettled. For different views on this issue, see MacLennan, Forsyth, and Denton, *op. cit.*, pp. 102–106; Vera Lutz, *French Planning*, pp. 7–12; Andrew Shonfield, *op. cit.*, pp. 145 and 150; and Pierre Bauchet, *op. cit.*, pp. 47–59.

Table 6-4
Selected French Economic Indicators for the Years 1953–1963

Year	Gross National Product index	Industrial production index	Wholesale price index	Consumer price index	Hourly manufacturing wage rate index	Unemployment rate	Volume index of merchandise exports	Gold and foreign exchange reserves (in mil. U.S. $)
1953	100	100	100	100	100	1.4	100	829
1954	105	109	98	100	106	1.7	115	1,261
1955	111	117	98	101	114	1.5	133	1,912
1956	116	128	102	103	124	1.1	119	1,180
1957	123	139	108	106	133	0.9	131	645
1958	126	145	121	121	149	1.0	137	1,050
1959	129	150	127	129	158	1.4	164	1,720
1960	137	167	130	134	169	1.3	192	2,070
1961	143	175	132	138	183	1.1	202	2,939
1962	152	185	136	144	198	1.2	205	3,610
1963	161	194	141	152	215	1.5	223	4,457
Average annual increase 1953–1963	4.9%	6.9%	3.5%	4.3%	8.0%	1.3%[1]	8.3%	—

[1] Average annual rate.

Sources: OECD, *General Statistics*, May 1964; and OECD, *Manpower Statistics, 1950–62*, 1963.

current account developed. Between 1955 and 1957 France lost two-thirds of its gold and foreign exchange reserve. Prices were kept stable only with the aid of extensive price controls.

In 1957 and again in 1958, the French franc was devalued; price controls were largely eliminated; and more reliance was placed on monetary and fiscal measures for controlling the inflationary pressures generated in the high-pressure, low-unemployment French economy. After the devaluation of the franc in December 1958 France had something of an "economic miracle." Gross National Product continued to increase at an average annual rate of about 5 percent, and even though the French economy was plagued with rapidly rising wage rates and prices, exports expanded rapidly. The volume index of French merchandise exports, which was 137 in 1958, rose to 223 in 1963. This was equivalent to an average annual increase in the volume of French merchandise exports of 10.2 percent for the years 1958–1962. The current balance of international payments after 1958 was quite favorable, with the result that the French gold and foreign exchange reserve increased from $645 million in 1957 to $4.45 billion in 1963. The only disturbing aspect of French economic activity after 1957 was the strong inflationary pressure that showed no sign of declining.

While the period from 1958 to 1963 was prosperous, it was not a period of uncontrolled boom and very large excess demand. Investment in plant and equipment continued at a high level, so that many firms had some unused capacity. Because labor was short in supply and unemployment very low, the French labor market continued to import labor from foreign countries and to draw labor from the rural areas of France, where much underemployment existed. Considerable progress was made in raising the standard of living. In the decade 1954–1963, real wages in manufacturing increased at the average annual rate of 3.5 percent. The very rapid expansion of the output of passenger cars, television sets, and household appliances enabled France to move further into the stage of high mass consumption. Between 1954 and 1962 the annual output of passenger cars increased from 437,000 to 1,278,000, and the annual output of television sets from 84,000 to 991,000.

The inflationary pressures in the French economy before 1963 were generated in large part by the strong pull of excess total demand, especially in the boom years 1955–1957. After 1957, wage rates rose more rapidly than output per man-hour, with the result that unit labor costs were also increased and were passed on by producers to buyers in the form of higher wholesale and retail prices. Larger price supports in the agricultural sector led to higher farm prices, which combined with rising prices in the service sector to raise the consumer price index. Whereas prices had been relatively stable from 1953 to 1957, wholesale and retail prices rose rapidly after 1957, as is shown by the wholesale and retail price indices in Table 6-4. In the years 1958–1963, wholesale prices increased at an average annual rate of 4.6 percent and consumer prices at a rate of 6.2 percent. Government aid to exporters helped to maintain French exports in spite of the large increases in wholesale prices. By 1962, stringent measures were taken to curb the growth of inflationary pressures in the French economy.

French national economic planning in the years 1953–1963 was more concerned with securing a high rate of economic growth and a low unemployment rate than with achieving a stable price level. Under the first four national plans, the private consumption component of Gross National Product was reduced in relation to the other components, while the public consumption and the gross domestic fixed investment components were expanded. Table 6-5 gives the percentage distribution of France's GNP in the period 1949-1962. During these years, private consumption declined from 69 to 65 percent of Gross National Product, whereas gross domestic fixed investment increased from 16.8 to 19.6 percent of the GNP. The proportion of GNP going into capital investment in France, however, has been much less than in West Germany, Norway, and other Western European countries.

Nevertheless, France has maintained a high rate of economic growth. Much of France's economic growth has resulted from the modernization of industry and agriculture and from the shift of workers from low-productivity agriculture and retailing to higher-productivity industries. Government planning authorities were successful in achieving the increases in GNP and the distribution of this product projected as goals in the annual and longer-term national plans. They succeeded in controlling the real flow of goods and services as called for by the national plans. However, the government planning authorities were much less successful in the area of financial planning, one major objective of which was price stability. The General Plan Commission did not succeed in coordinating or integrating the French economy's real product and income-expenditure flows so as to achieve a high degree of price stability.

Performance of the French Economy, 1964-1972

The performance of the French economic system before 1963 was undermined by the Indochinese and Algerian conflicts and by the political instability that accompanied the numerous weak governments that came to office after 1945. Both of these disturbing factors were eliminated in the 1960s by the ending of the seven-year Algerian war of independence in March 1962 and the establishment of the Fifth Republic in September 1958, which ushered in a period of political stability such as France had not seen since the close of the Second World War. A further factor affecting the functioning of the French economy in the 1960s was the establishment of the European Economic Community in 1958. Much of France's economic progress during the 1960s can be attributed to the impetus of the Common Market and the need to modernize French industry in order to be competitive in that market.

Table 6-5
The Percentage Distribution of France's Gross National Product in Selected Years, 1949-1962

	1949	1953	1957	1962
Private consumption	69.0	67.7	67.0	65.0
Public consumption	12.4	16.0	15.2	13.3
Gross domestic fixed investment	16.8	15.8	18.9	19.6
Change in inventories	2.5	0.7	0.9	1.5
Export surplus (+) or import surplus (−)	−0.7	−0.2	−2.0	0.6
Gross National Product	100.0	100.0	100.0	100.0

Source: OECD, *General Statistics*, Jan. 1962, and May 1964.

The decade of the 1960s, like that of the 1950s, was a prosperous one, in which a high economic growth rate was sustained, and a low level of unemployment was achieved. Table 6-6 shows that for the period 1963-1972 the average annual growth rate of the nation's GNP was 5.7 percent, a rate which fluctuated only between a low of 4.7 percent (1965) and a high of 7.4 percent (1969). Some sizable fluctuations in industrial output, however, did occur between boom and recession years. The declines in industrial production were not permitted to reduce the economy's overall growth rate. Under the government's national planning program, steps were taken to sustain the economy's overall performance by increasing investment in the nationalized industries, by activating public works programs, and by encouraging private consumption. The net effect of these public policies was to prevent long declines in industrial production and to maintain high levels of overall production and employment. According to the French method of calculation, the unemployment rate, which annually averaged 1.6 percent in the years 1963-1972, fluctuated between 1 and 2 percent in these years.[15]

During 1964-1967, after the Stabilization Plan of 1963, France enjoyed a period of relative price and wage stability. After 1967, the

[15] According to the unemployment concept used by the United States Bureau of Labor Statistics, the French annual unemployment rate for 1960-1969 was 2.3 percent, whereas the United States rate was 4.8 percent. OECD, *OECD Economic Surveys, France*, April 1971, p. 52.

Table 6-6
Selected French Economic Indicators, 1963-1972

	Annual percentage changes						
	Gross National Product	Industrial production	Consumer prices	Wholesale prices	Hourly earnings in manufacturing	Output per man-hour	Rate of unemployment
1963	5.8	4.1	5.3	4.2	8.7	2.8	1.1
1964	6.6	8.0	3.0	2.0	7.0	7.0	1.2
1965	4.7	0.9	2.9	1.0	10.7	3.7	1.5
1966	5.6	7.3	2.8	4.1	5.3	8.1	1.7
1967	5.0	2.6	2.8	−0.9	6.6	5.1	1.5
1968	5.0	5.0	4.5	−1.6	12.5	7.3	1.7
1969	7.4	12.7	6.0	11.6	7.7	11.3	1.8
1970	5.9	5.6	5.7	7.4	12.4	6.1	1.6
1971	5.0	5.3	5.9	2.2	12.1	6.4	2.0
1972	5.5	7.5	6.8	4.6	11.8	8.0	2.2
Average annual change 1963-1972	5.7	5.7	4.6	3.5	9.5	6.6	1.6[1]

[1] Average annual rate.

Sources: International Monetary Fund, *International Financial Statistics;* and National Institute of Economic and Social Research, *National Institute Economic Review.*

price-wage situation changed radically when, as in other Western European countries, a price-wage explosion occurred. Whereas consumer prices had increased at an average annual rate of 2.9 percent during 1964–1967, this rate jumped to 5.8 percent during 1968–1972. Wage rates followed a similar inflationary path. Whereas hourly earnings in manufacturing increased at the average annual rate of 7.4 percent in 1964–1967, they rose at the average annual rate of 11.3 percent in 1968–1972. A number of factors contributed to the wage explosion that began in 1968. The growth of real consumer spending power had been restricted by increases in the value-added tax and in the charges of public utilities, and by lower social security reimbursement rates. Organized labor strongly condemned these restrictions on the expansion of workers' real buying power. The economic situation deteriorated in 1967 when industrial production suffered a recessionary decline and unemployment increased. Also, the university crisis of early 1968 coincided with labor disturbances which affected large areas of manufacturing industry and construction as well as the transport, communications, and other service industries.

The large wage increases that followed the student revolts and worker strikes of May–June 1968 resulted in large increases in the labor cost per unit of manufacturing output, higher domestic and export prices, and an adverse balance in international payments. The gold and foreign exchange reserve, which was $6.1 billion in 1967, was reduced to $3.8 billion in 1969 as confidence in the French franc declined, and funds were transferred into stronger currencies such as the Swiss franc and the German mark. In August 1969, the French government devalued the franc 11.1 percent and took steps to tighten demand management. To prevent excessive price increases after the devaluation, a temporary general price freeze was adopted, and both fiscal and monetary policies were made more restrictive. The strong measures taken to restore confidence in the French franc coincided with the speculative movement against the U.S. dollar, which culminated in the severing of the connection between gold and the dollar in August 1971.

Although since the devaluation of the French franc in 1969, both consumer prices and wage rates have continued to increase at the high rates first recorded in 1968, the French economy has in general performed very well. Both total national output and industrial production have increased at rates close to the goals set forth in the national plan; the current balance of international payments has been favorable; and the gold and foreign exchange reserve increased to $8.5 billion by the end of 1972. An unfavorable development has been the continued slow rise of the rate of unemployment among young workers (under twenty-five years), which by 1974 reached 4.9 percent, as compared with 1.4 percent for workers twenty-five to forty-nine years of age.

French Economic Performance, 1973–1975

In common with the other industrial countries of Western Europe, France suffered the adverse consequences of the worldwide recession that began in late 1973. While it did not experience in 1974 the negative economic growth of the United Kingdom, the United States, and Japan, France had a large drop in the rate of growth of total national output; this was accompanied by strong price and wage inflation. The boom that overheated the French economy in 1973 continued through the first half of 1974, but a major turnaround occurred in the summer and was followed by a deceleration of economic activity.

During the boom years, a strong anti-inflationary program was established. The main burden of controlling inflation was put on monetary policy. Interest rates were raised; bank reserve requirements behind demand and time deposits were increased; ceilings were placed on the annual increases in total bank credit; heavy progressive penalties in the form of additional reserves were imposed on banks that exceeded these ceilings; the increase in the money supply was restricted to the increase in nominal gross domestic product (14.5 percent for 1974); and special qualitative controls were placed on loans for such items as automobiles and second homes.

Fiscal policy during the boom period of 1973 was also very restrictive. The government's fiscal budget was shifted from a deficit to a surplus. Tax revenues were increased by raising corporate and personal income taxes; depreciation allowances were made less liberal; and public expenditures were reduced. Price controls were tightened by adopting new annual price agreements between the government and business enterprises which limited price increases. A new provisional levy (*prélèvement conjoncturel*) was introduced in December 1974 for the purpose of taxing any increases in profit margins above previously established profit norms. According to this levy, a firm's profits were not to increase faster than nominal gross domestic product; and if they did increase faster a levy equal to one-third of the excess profits was to be imposed. In this manner, inflationary profits led to higher taxes on profits, which acted as a deterrent to the development of further inflationary pressures.

Table 6-7 shows that while gross domestic product was increasing much more slowly in 1974 than in 1973, both consumer prices and wage rates in manufacturing were rising much faster. Wage rates were rising fast enough to cover both the annual improvement in worker productivity (4 percent) and the increase in consumer prices (9.6 percent). The French economy did not reach the bottom of the recession until 1975, when gross domestic product decreased 2 percent. The recovery of the French economy from the depressed conditions of 1974-1975 has been greatly influenced by the rate at which world trade has recovered. France's recovery also depends

Table 6-7
Percent Changes over Previous Years in Selected French Economic Indicators, 1972-1975

	Gross domestic product	Industrial production	Consumer prices	Wholesale prices	Hourly wage rates[1]	Output per man-hour[1]	Unemployment rate[2]	Current balance of payments[3]
1972	6.1	7.7	5.8	4.6	11.3	8.6	2.2	284
1973	6.1	7.1	7.3	14.7	12.4	7.0	1.9	−677
1974	3.8	3.3	13.7	29.8	18.6	5.0	2.1	−5,980
1975	−2.0	−9.7	11.7	−6.0	17.1	−4.7	2.8	330
Average annual change 1972-1975	3.5%	2.1%	9.6%	10.7%	14.8%	4.0%	2.1%	—

[1] In manufacturing.
[2] Annual rates.
[3] Million U.S. dollars.

Sources: OECD, *Main Economic Indicators*, April 1975, and *OECD Economic Surveys, France*, Jan. 1975; and International Monetary Fund, *International Financial Statistics*, July 1975.

upon the rapidity with which the restrictive fiscal and monetary policies of 1974 are relaxed. France, like the other industrial nations, is faced with the twin problems of curbing inflationary price and wage pressures, while at the same time restoring the pre-1974 levels of output and employment.

While France suffered negative economic growth in the 1974–1975 recession, it also had reversals in its external economy. The merchandise trade surplus of 1970–1973 was replaced by a large deficit in 1974. With the prices of imported oil and raw materials rising much more rapidly (51 percent in 1974) than the prices of French exports (26 percent in 1974), the terms of trade turned against France, and a large deficit on the current international account was recorded. Table 6–7 reveals that the small current-account deficit of $677 million in 1973 became a $6 billion deficit in 1974, with a large deficit of $4.7 billion for 1975. Having large foreign exchange reserves and the ability to borrow abroad as needed, France had no difficulty in coping with the financial problems associated with these adverse and unfavorable foreign trade developments.

At the end of 1974, it appeared that the French government was more concerned with holding down inflation and securing a better external balance than with raising the level of domestic economic activity. Continued low levels of employment and production could make households more cautious and inclined to increase their rate of saving at the same time that business enterprises might be induced to postpone investment projects. If world trade were to prove to be weaker than anticipated in 1975 and later, French exports could show less improvement than expected by government forecasters. Much of the success of French national planning has been based upon the government's ability to achieve an annual economic growth rate of around 5 percent on a sustained basis, and on its ability to convince both households and private business enterprises that this would actually be the outcome. The recession of 1974–1975 was more than an ordinary recession, for it appeared to be accompanied by the need for major industrial structural changes as nations adjusted to permanently higher oil and raw material prices, and to new economic and financial relations between the developed and the less developed countries.

In these circumstances, the French government may find it increasingly difficult in the coming decades to assure the nation a high and sustained rate of economic growth, such as was experienced prior to 1974. The OECD has drawn attention to the need for a "fresh impetus" in French national planning if the problems arising from the 1974–1975 recession are to be handled successfully. This fresh impetus would be concerned with a restructuring of industry; it would deal with the decline of some industries, such as the automobile industry, and the transfer of capital and labor to other areas, such as alternative forms of energy and capital goods. The process of industrial conversion made necessary by the unique turn of international events after 1973 is to be the special concern of a newly established French planning agency, the Superior Planning Council (*Conseil Supérieur de Planification*).[16]

Demand and Supply Management and National Planning

French supply-and-demand management and national planning are interrelated at the annual, medium-term, and long-term levels.[17] At

---

[16] An evaluation of France's reaction to the 1974–1975 recession is given in OECD, *OECD Economic Surveys, France,* Jan. 1975, pp. 55–62.

[17] Supply-and-demand management is sometimes referred to as *economic management*. In both cases, attention is drawn to the supply-and-demand factors that have an impact on the level of Gross National Product. These factors may be related to three time horizons: short-run, medium-term, and long-term.

the annual or short-term level, economic and social policies and programs are formulated and carried out within the framework of the annual national economic budget and the annual fiscal budget. As has already been explained, the former budget shows the prospective Gross National Product for the coming year and its distribution between private and public consumption and investment uses. The annual national economic budget looks toward the future, incorporating the government's goals for the next year's increase in total national output, and dividing this increase or "social dividend" among the nation's expanding social and economic needs. The correlate annual fiscal budget is designed to aid the government in achieving the annual goals set forth in the economic budget. Direct and indirect taxes, public expenditures, and government saving through budget surpluses are annually altered and adjusted so as to secure the government's annual policy goals. Other policies, such as monetary, price, wage, and foreign trade policies, are combined with fiscal policy to achieve the objectives presented in the annual national economic budget.

At the next level, medium-term supply-and-demand management is related to five-year national economic budgets and five-year projections of the national fiscal budget. Many supply-and-demand factors can have their full impact on the economic system only after four or five years have elapsed. These factors, such as manpower, plant and equipment investment, health and educational programs, housing, urban renewal, and environmental protection, can at times be altered successfully only over several years. Medium-term goals are presented in the five-year economic budgets; and five-year projections of the fiscal budget are made to show how the tax and public expenditure systems may be adjusted to meet the fiscal needs of the five-year economic budgets. All such projections are tentative, and are designed to reveal the magnitudes of the problems with which medium-term supply-and-demand management may have to cope.

Supply-and-demand factors are also considered from the long-term view, which frequently relates to a twenty- or twenty-five-year plan period. These factors are influenced by long-term steps taken to encourage industrialization, to advance scientific research and technological development, to alter the pattern of foreign trade, to redirect the educational system, to modernize the politicoeconomic decision-making process, or to encourage greater public participation in this process. This type of planning is described as *perspective planning*. While a twenty- or twenty-five-year national economic budget may be constructed to indicate the consequences of long-term economic and social developments in quantitative terms, such a budget has no operational significance. It is rather a technical device that aids the planning authorities and the public to grasp more readily the significance of long-term developments.

Short-Run Demand and Supply Management, 1963–1973

Short-run demand-and-supply management is aimed at achieving domestic and external equilibrium at high levels of employment and production without inflation. What is unique about French short-run demand-and-supply management is that it revolves around annual national plans. The objectives which are specifically stated include (1) next year's increase in real gross domestic product; (2) the distribution of this product between private

---

John Sheahan makes a distinction between "supply-specific planning" and planning final demand or the uses of national income. See his "Planning in France," *Challenge*, March–April 1975, pp. 19–20.

and public consumption and investment; (3) the increase in the general price level in the coming year; and (4) the estimated size of the surplus or deficit in the current balance of international payments. For example, the 1973 annual plan projected a 6 percent increase in real gross domestic product, an increase in the general price level of 5.75 percent, and annual increases in the private and public consumption and investment components of gross domestic product, as shown in Table 6-8. Private consumption and gross fixed private and public investment are major factors in keeping total national output close to its potential. The net export surplus, which was approximately 2 percent of gross domestic product in 1972, was expected to remain at the same level in 1973.

A program for the management of demand and supply in 1973 was announced by the government in December 1972. The fiscal measures adopted for 1973 were designed to curb inflation and to restrict consumption. These included reductions in value-added taxes and the sale of long-term government bonds to absorb excess consumer liquidity. The monetary measures adopted included the imposition of ceilings on the amount of bank credit to be extended in 1973 and an increase in interest rates on savings bank accounts to encourage personal saving. The government also recommended to management and labor that wage-rate increases in 1973 be kept within the limit of 6 percent. With these and other fiscal and monetary measures, the government hoped to keep prices from rising no faster than in competing countries. Domestic price and wage restraint would, if successful, enable France to have a favorable current balance of international payments and to secure a sizable net export surplus. On the supply side, the 1973 management policy was designed to reduce unemployment by increasing real total national output. It was calculated that a 6 percent increase in this output would provide approximately 150,000 additional industrial jobs.

French Price Policy

France has developed a complex system of short-run policies and controls that can be used in attempting to achieve domestic and

Table 6-8

The French National Economic Budget (Annual Plan) for 1973

	1972 national economic accounts (in billions of 1972 francs)	1973 national economic budget (in billions of 1972 francs)	Projected percentage increase over 1972
Private consumption	556.0	588.0	5.75
Public consumption	111.2	115.6	4.0
Gross fixed investment	252.9	269.3	6.5
Change in inventories	28.6	31.0	0.25[1]
Net export surplus	18.6	21.4	0.0[1]
Gross domestic product	967.3	1,025.3	6.0

[1] As a percentage of GDP in the previous period.
Source: *OECD Economic Surveys, France*, 1973.

external equilibria. When necessary, temporary general price freezes on industrial and agricultural products can be imposed, as occurred after the devaluation of the franc in August 1969. Since general price freezes tend to create distortions in price relationships and at best are only temporary, the French government's price policy has in recent years emphasized achieving price stability through "concertation" or agreements between the government and sellers.[18] In the manufacturing area, the government enters contracts with enterprises under which these enterprises agree not to raise prices more than a fixed amount in the next twelve months. Similar contracts stabilize percentage markups in the distributive trades. Where firms do not enter these programme or planning contracts (*contrats de programme*), they must give the price-control authorities prior notice of any proposed price increases and must secure approval for any such increases. In the service sector, the government seeks to control price increases through a policy of consultation. At present, some 85 to 90 percent of industry is covered by programme contracts, but much smaller proportions of the distribution and service sectors operate under contracts.

The French economy is particularly vulnerable to inflation. A comparison of price movements in France and other Western countries shows that during 1950-1970 the average annual increase in retail prices in France was 4.2 percent and only 2.68 percent on the average in seven other major industrialized countries. For wholesale prices, the comparative rates of increase were 3.25 percent for France and 1.59 percent for the other seven countries.[19] Several factors have contributed to France's strong inflationary pressures. European Economic Community price supports, as well as domestic efforts to maintain parity between agricultural and urban incomes, have raised food prices. In industry, structural rigidities, bottlenecks, and restrictive business practices have played an important part. Additions to the labor force have tended to go into the service trades with low productivity rather than into manufacturing with higher productivity. Since wage rates tend to advance at the same rate in both sectors, the movement of labor into the service trades tends to be inflationary. One of the long-term objectives of French demand-and-supply management is to have young workers move into industry rather than the service trades. A further factor that makes it difficult to curb short-run price instability in France's high-pressure economy is the strong competition among business enterprises for the limited supply of skilled labor.

Short-Term Monetary Policy

The French government relies very heavily on monetary policy in its program to achieve short-run economic stability and to curb inflationary tendencies.[20] The two general aims of monetary policy have been to adjust

---

[18] Recent developments in French price policy are outlined in Organisation for Economic Co-operation and Development, *Non-Wage Incomes and Price Policy*, Paris, 1966, pp. 143-150; and *Present Policies against Inflation*, Paris, June 1971. See also John Sheahan, "Growth and Prices," in *An Introduction to the French Economy*, pp. 93-106; Andrew Shonfield, "The Example of Price Control," in *Modern Capitalism*, pp. 148-150; and MacLennan, Forsyth, and Denton, "Prices, Incomes and the Labour Market," in *Economic Planning and Policies*, pp. 275-278.

[19] OECD. *OECD Economic Surveys, France*, Feb. 1972, p. 12.

[20] For an analysis of the role of monetary policy in French planning, see MacLennan, Forsyth, and Denton, "Monetary and Credit Policy," *Economic Planning and Policies*, pp. 158-168; Pierre Bauchet, "Control of Credit and Self-Financing,'" *Economic Planning*, pp. 103-107; and John Sheahan, "Monetary Management and the Tax Structure," *An Introduction to the French Economy*, pp. 83-91. See also Organisation for Economic Co-operation and Development, *Monetary Policy in France*, Paris, 1974.

the money supply to the growth of total national output, and to direct the flow of credit in such a way as to achieve the investment goals set forth in the annual and medium-term plans. In addition to the traditional monetary-policy instruments—such as changes in bank reserve requirements and interest rates and open-market operations—special monetary controls include ceilings or limits on total credit, compulsory reserves on bank loans, and selective rediscounting of commercial paper by the Bank of France.

In periods of strong inflationary pressures, the National Credit Council imposes limits or ceilings on the total credit to be supplied by banks and other financial institutions. The level of the ceilings depends upon the need for credit restriction. A bank that exceeds the credit ceiling assigned to it is penalized by being required to deposit an amount equal to any excess above its ceiling in a noninterest bearing account with the Bank of France. In 1969, the credit ceiling permitted no expansion of credit during the year; and commercial credit, which was 214.2 billion francs in 1968, totalled 214.9 billion francs in 1969. Since 1967, special compulsory reserves up to 50 percent on bank loans have been used to curb the increase in the credit supply. When these special reserves are imposed, a bank must deposit from 10 to 50 percent of any new loans in a noninterest bearing account in the Bank of France. Credit can also be restricted by the bank by reducing its rediscount lines with the commercial banks. The specialized public or state banks also reduce the number of loans that they are willing to endorse for rediscount purposes.

In the short run, efforts are made to direct credit towards industries which contribute the most to the growth goals of the annual and medium-term plans. While much of the credit rationing by the banks reflects the impact of the uncontrolled forces in the private-market system, the government nevertheless has an influential role in this rationing. The three large government-owned commercial banks work closely with the National Credit Council and the Bank of France. The Bank of France makes short-term loans to business enterprises that are considered to be important for the achievement of plan goals but which cannot be obtained from other banks. The Bank also follows a selective policy in deciding upon the rediscount lines that will be made available to private industry. Special consideration is given to priority discounting for the export industries. At times, preferential low rediscount rates are made available on short-term export credits. Interest subsidies are also made available on loans to business enterprises that are willing to invest in underdeveloped regions. When necessary, consumer credit is adjusted up or down. If the household savings rate is too low and private consumption is exceeding the goal provided in the annual plan, installment credit is then made more restrictive.

While French monetary policy has had a considerable impact on the amount and use of short-term bank credit, and has succeeded in imposing considerable credit restraint on the economy, it has nevertheless not measured up to the government's expectations. Total credit ceilings have frequently been exceeded.[21] Credit restrictions apply to only between one-half and two-thirds of total lending to the private sector. These restrictions do not apply to "back to back deals" or direct loans between business enterprises. Nor do they apply to the self-financing from the retained earnings of private firms that pay for almost three-quarters of their new investment from

[21] The Organisation for Economic Co-operation and Development observes that "The total outstanding credit subject to the general restrictions seems to have constantly exceeded—sometimes by significant amounts—the ceilings laid down in the various periods over which the restrictions were extended." *OECD Economic Surveys, France,* April 1971, p. 27.

this source.[22] Banks have also gotten around the domestic credit restrictions by borrowing in the Euro-currency market. Table 6-9 shows that in the period 1963-1972 the money supply increased at the average annual rate of 9 percent, while the Gross National Product increased at the rate of 5.7 percent. In the boom year 1971 the money supply increased at the rate of 11.1 percent, or more than twice the economic growth rate, and commercial short-term bank loans at the rate of 26 percent. In spite of high interest rates and restrictive credit measures, the nation's banking system continued to finance the inflationary high-pressure economy of 1969-1973.

Foreign Exchange Policy

Since France exports close to one-fifth of its Gross National Product, vital to the good performance of its economy is the maintenance of a high level of exports of goods and services. This in turn depends in large part upon having an exchange rate that does not overvalue the franc in relation to other currencies. Planning for French exports and imports and adjusting the exchange rate of the franc as circumstances require is a regular part of French

[22] One of the main financial problems in French national planning is to find some means of controlling private self-financing. For a discussion of this problem, see Pierre Bauchet, *op. cit.*, pp. 103-107.

Table 6-9
Selected French Domestic and External Financial and Economic Indicators, 1963-1972

	Average annual percent change in money supply	Bank of France discount rate	Annual percent change in volume of exports	Current balance of international payments (in mil. U.S. dollars)	Gold and foreign exchange reserves (in mil. U.S. dollars)	France's share of world exports of manufactures
1963	14.5	4.00	8.7	488	4,457	9.0
1964	8.3	4.00	7.0	83	5,105	8.7
1965	9.4	3.50	11.2	494	5,459	8.8
1966	7.8	3.50	5.0	42	5,745	8.6
1967	4.8	3.50	5.6	205	6,108	8.5
1968	8.0	6.00	12.1	−855	4,200	8.2
1969	0.4	9.00	15.5	−1,475	3,833	8.7
1970	10.9	7.00	15.2	68	4,789	8.9
1971	11.1	6.50	8.1	525	7,402	8.8
1972	14.9	7.50	14.1	284	8,585	9.3
Average annual percent change 1963-1972	9.0	—	10.4	—	—	8.7[1]

[1] Annual average share.

Sources: International Monetary Fund, *International Financial Statistics;* and National Institute of Economic and Social Research, *National Institute Economic Review.*

planning. The French government has been prepared to make use of a variety of foreign trade and foreign exchange regulations with the aim of preserving the franc as a strong currency. Whenever the franc has become overvalued, as in 1957 and 1958 and again in 1969, it has been devalued. When the United States and other major industrialized countries abandoned their fixed exchange rates in 1971, France did likewise.

On August 23, 1971, a two-tier foreign exchange market was introduced, in which there are two floating franc exchange rates, one for "commercial" francs and one for "financial" francs. The purpose is to protect French exports and at the same time to discourage an inflow of speculative foreign money while the franc is floating. The commercial franc exchange rate gives French exporters more francs per dollar, while the financial franc exchange rate gives speculators who plan to buy francs fewer francs per dollar. In this way, exports are protected or stimulated, and speculative runs on the franc are discouraged.

When international financial crises involve the franc, the French government quickly turns to additional foreign exchange controls, as in 1968 and 1971. When imports exceed exports or speculators sell francs and the franc exchange rate needs to be sustained, foreign exchange travel allowances to residents may be decreased, curbs may be placed on the amount of French bank notes that may be taken abroad, and transfers of funds for industrial investments abroad may be restricted. When the crisis subsides, these exchange controls are relaxed or lifted. In general, since the late 1950s, the French franc has been a strong international currency unit, with the only serious run on the franc taking place in 1968 and 1969 after the period of student-worker strife. In 1969, France's gold and foreign exchange reserves fell from $6.1 billion to $3.8 billion as speculative funds moved out of France. Recovery was quick, however, and in 1971 these reserves amounted to $7.4 billion. As Table 6-9 indicates, France has since 1963 increased its real volume of exports at a high average annual rate of more than 10 percent; apart from 1968 and 1969 it has had favorable current balances of international payments. These favorable developments have placed the French franc among the world's few strong or hard currencies.

Short-Run Fiscal Policy

French fiscal policy has an important role to play in the annual program to achieve financial and economic equilibrium.[23] In the short run, the primary objective of fiscal policy is to contribute to economic stability by using budgetary restraint to curb books and budgetary stimulation to avoid recessions. Short-term fiscal policy is designed to achieve a balance among private and public consumption and investment expenditures that will support the planned rate of economic growth without excessive inflationary pressures. With the aid of various fiscal devices, the Ministry of Finance can stimulate or restrict private and public consumption and investment as circumstances warrant. Domestic consumption may be curbed by tax increases in order to make goods available for export; private investment may be stimulated by liberalizing depreciation rules or by making investment tax credits available to private industry; or an economic slowdown may be prevented by increases in spending by the government and the nationalized industries.

---

[23] For an analysis of French fiscal policy, see Walter Heller and others, *Fiscal Policy for a Balanced Economy*, Ch. II, "France," Paris: Organisation for Economic Co-operation and Development, 1969, pp. 36–42; Bent Hansen, *Fiscal Policy in Seven Countries, 1955–1965*, Ch. 4, "France," Paris: Organisation for Economic Co-operation and Development, pp. 149–207; MacLennan, Forsyth, and Denton, "Fiscal Policy," in *Economic Planning and Policies*, pp. 196–203; and Pierre Bauchet, "Means of Enforcement," *Economic Planning*, pp. 76–99.

The French fiscal system has two unique features: one is the importance of indirect taxes and the other is the role of the government in national saving. Indirect taxes are a much more important source of revenue than are direct taxes. In the 1973 consolidated budget for the central and local governments, indirect taxes contributed 39 percent of total current revenues, while direct taxes contributed only 18 percent. Since the main source of indirect taxation is the value-added tax, which is paid by business enterprises and not by consumers, this tax can be altered without having an adverse effect on personal consumer incentives.

The second special feature of the French fiscal system is that the Treasury is a large source of national saving. Under the national plans, the Treasury is called upon to give financial aid to nationalized industries, to private industries that make important contributions to economic growth, and to various regions and localities in need of special financial assistance. Since France's capital market is poorly developed, the Treasury does more saving and investing than is done by governments in other Western industrialized countries. In France, the central and local governments and the nationalized industries account for about 28 percent of gross domestic capital formation, which is financed through government saving and borrowing. Because it directly and indirectly accounts for a large part of the nation's saving and investing, the central government is in a very strong position to influence the current flow of funds and the investing process.

Fiscal policy is the primary responsibility of the Minister of the Economy and Finance. He or she must combine securing economic and financial stability with achieving the economic and social priorities incorporated in the annual and five-year national plans. While the Ministry of Finance and the General Plan Commission work together in coordinating the annual fiscal budgets and the national plans, adapting the French economy to the vagaries of the business cycle and to the long-term needs of the planning program is not always a smooth process. The Ministry of Finance is primarily interested in economic stabilization policy, whereas the planning authorities are more concerned with long-term economic and social developments.

At times, the interest of the Minister of Finance in curbing government spending programs conflicts with the planners' interest in expanding housing, school building, urban renewal, and other high-priority national goals. The suggestion has been made to improve the coordination of short-term and long-term economic policies by overhauling the government administrative machinery and curbing the power of the Ministry of Finance.[24] Short-term economic policy is the main concern of the various ministries, which are eager to protect their special prerogatives. This situation limits the extent to which the General Plan Commission can effectively coordinate the mix of short-term economic policies.

French short-term fiscal policy during 1963–1973 followed the Keynesian practice of incurring stimulative budgetary deficits in periods of slowdown and restrictive budgetary surpluses in years when the economy was overheated. In the boom year 1969, when restraint was called for, the central government curbed its purchases of goods and services, stepped up company tax payments, reduced depreciation allowances, abolished investment tax-credit allowances, and permitted the heavy tax payments of the boom year to run ahead of government expenditures in order to create a budgetary surplus. A large volume of

---

[24] Pierre Bauchet, *op. cit.*, p. 100. "The first step towards the fulfillment of the Plan would be to overhaul the State machinery, for the better coordination of its activities... The trouble with the *State organization* is that the conditions governing economic conditions are chaotic, and the Ministry of Finance has too much power." See also MacLennan, Forsyth, and Denton, *op. cit.*, pp. 237–243.

authorized government spending was blocked and transferred to a newly established Fund for Contracyclical Action (*Fonds d'Action Conjoncturelle*).[25] These blocked funds were to be released in future years when an expansionary fiscal budget was adopted. In 1973, when an economic slowdown was anticipated, the expansionary fiscal budget provided for a small surplus on current account, increased government spending for goods and services, the release of funds from the Fund for Contracyclical Action for government projects, increases in equipment subsidies for nationalized industries, and reductions in the value-added taxes on manufactured goods and food products. By stimulating private consumption and increasing government expenditures in 1973, the central government expected to achieve the planned annual growth goal of 6 percent without any worsening of inflationary pressures.

Short-term French fiscal policy has been more successful in encouraging sustained economic growth and high employment than in contributing to domestic price stability and export-import equilibrium. The tax system has been manipulated so as to secure a balance between saving and investing that not only supports high and sustained growth, but also approximates the distribution of total national output projected in the annual national plans. The main deficiency of French short-term fiscal policy has been its inability, along with other short-term economic policies, to prevent the growth of strong inflationary pressures in prosperous years.

French Incomes Policies

Although both short-term monetary and fiscal policies have made important strides towards achieving economic and financial stability,

[25] OECD. *OECD Economic Surveys, France*, March 1970, p. 13. These funds were released in 1970, 1971, and 1972 when the budget turned expansionary.

these goals have not always been reached because of disagreements among business people, workers, and farmers over prices, profits, and wages. These disagreements have resulted in an incomes race among the major economic interest groups with which monetary and fiscal policy cannot deal effectively.[26] Since the early 1960s, the government has been keenly aware of the need to supplement monetary and fiscal policies with an incomes policy. In the 1950s, when the main domestic problem was demand-pull inflation, the government attempted to influence the development of money incomes with temporary stop-gap measures, such as price freezes and wage pauses. In 1959–1963, the new de Gaulle Administration turned to the "exhortative approach" and requested workers and business people to exercise restraint in raising wage rates and prices. The aim was to establish a policy under which, once price stability was attained, wages would be constantly adjusted to changes in average productivity and the resulting growth in national income.[27] Because of the lack of cooperation of both the trade unions and the employers the exhortative approach to incomes policy was a failure. In the Interim Plan for 1960–1961, a 4 percent guideline was announced for annual wage-rate increases, but the actual increases were far above this guideline rate.

In 1963, the government decided to go beyond the simple guideline approach and to

[26] On French incomes policy, see J. E. S. Hayward, "Interest Groups and Incomes Policy in France," *British Journal of Industrial Relations*, July 1966; and "State Intervention in France," *Political Studies*, Vol. XII, Sept. 1972, pp. 289–294. See also J. Lautman and J.-C. Thoening, *Planification et Administrations Centrales*, Paris, Copédith, 1966.

[27] The French Embassy, Press and Information Division, *The First Five Years of the Fifth Republic of France, January 1959–January 1964*, 1964, p. 52. Surveys of French incomes policy are found in Eric Schiff, *Incomes Policies Abroad*, Part II, Washington, D.C.: American Enterprise Institute, 1972, pp. 5–16; David C. Smith, *Incomes Policies*, pp. 175–182; and Lloyd Ulman and Robert J. Flanagan, *Wage Restraint*, pp. 147–170.

develop an incomes policy that could cope with the cost-push variety of inflation. At conferences on incomes, held in 1963 and 1964, with representatives from the government, employers' associations, trade unions, industry, commerce, and agriculture, proposals were made for the integration of incomes policy with national planning. These proposals included incorporating in the five-year plans value planning that would indicate the desired balance among the major aggregates of incomes and the desirable rate of increase of each category of income. In addition, an independent Commission for the Study and Evaluation of Incomes (*Collège d'Étude et d'Appréciation des Revenues*) was to be established for the study of the functioning of the incomes policy, and to assess whether or not upward or downward deviations from the government's income recommendations were warranted.[28]

The proposals of the conferences on incomes were turned down by organized labor and the business community. The leading labor organization, the communist-dominated General Confederation of Labor, asserted that an incomes policy would eliminate free collective bargaining, and would control wages but not profits. The National Council of French Employers was prepared to accept wage control but not profit control. Since the reaction of both labor and business to the incomes conference proposals was predominantly negative, the efforts by the government to establish a "contractual" incomes policy, under which the government and the labor market parties would agree on wage, price, and profit guidelines, were abandoned. The government then turned to an "indicative" incomes policy, under which annual wage, profit, and price guidelines were incorporated in the five-year plans only as government recommendations. After 1964, the government also included wage and price guidelines in the annual national plans prepared by the National Accounts and Economic Budget Commission. These wage, price, and profit guidelines have been made ineffective by the wage and price explosions of 1968 and the continued strong inflationary pressures since that time. Actual wage and price increases during 1968–1972 were far above the government's recommended guidelines.

As the experiences of other countries demonstrate, the failure of the French government to develop a workable incomes policy is not unique. The French experience with an incomes policy has been duplicated in most industrialized countries. Fortunately, the wage-rate increases in France above the government's recommended guidelines have been offset to a considerable extent by large annual improvements in output per man-hour, which averaged 7 percent per year for the period 1963–1972. These large annual improvements in labor productivity have curbed the increase in labor costs per unit of output in manufacturing, and have enabled France to continue to be competitive in international markets. The short-term economic policy mix, in spite of its limitations, has resulted in enough economic and financial stability to enable France to achieve a high and sustained economic growth rate, low unemployment, and a strong currency unit, and at the same time to approximate the economic and social goals of the medium-term national plans.

Medium-Term French Planning

French national planning has had both strong and weak features. The planning for the main aggregates, such as total output, consumption,

---

[28] OECD, *OECD Economic Surveys, France*, 1964, pp. 36–37. The prior Toutée Report of 1963 also recommended a joint management and labor board, periodic consultation between the government and the trade unions concerning productivity statistics, and joint wage boards in the nationalized industries. For a further discussion of French incomes policy, see Jacques Delors, "Incomes Policy in France," in Confederation of Italian Industries. *Incomes Policy*, Rome, 1967, pp. 75–102.

and investment, as well as for the big sub-aggregates relating to the basic industries has been in the main successful. The weak features concern the nonbasic manufacturing industries, inflationary developments, and the foreign trade sector. One close observer of French planning in the period 1947–1962 concluded that "expansion during the past fifteen years has conformed fairly closely to the forecasts given in the plans. . . . Delays or advances on the forecasts were slight, and partial disturbances, such as inflation, foreign trade deficits and regional disequilibrium never brought expansion to a halt or caused serious unemployment."[29]

The French planning authorities draw a distinction between plan objectives or goals (*objectifs*) for basic nationalized and non-nationalized industries and plan estimates or anticipations (*prévisions cohérentes*) for nonbasic industries such as the apparel, textile, home furnishings, and furniture industries. Unlike the plan objectives, the plan estimates are not serious targets, for the government is not prepared to devote considerable resources to their achievement. The plan estimates for the nonbasic small-scale industries (*industries de transformation*) are merely guidelines that fit in with the general pattern of the national plan.[30] A much more serious limitation of French planning relates to the difficulty of planning France's role in the international economy. The planning authorities can react to international economic developments, but they cannot control them. For this reason, French medium-term national planning is kept flexible, and is adjusted to changing international situations with the aid of annual national plans.

The four medium-term national plans that were used to guide French economic policy after 1962 emphasized maintaining a high economic growth rate, achieving a surplus in the external sector large enough to finance investments abroad, diverting a larger proportion of the annual increase in total national output to the low-income and disadvantaged classes, and securing a better regional balance. Although the Fourth Plan (1962–1965) approximated its overall annual growth goal of 5.5 percent and succeeded in raising the rate of investment in housing, public works, and communications, the plan failed to achieve the desired price stability and a favorable current balance of international payments. In 1962 and 1963, both consumer prices and wages increased at rates that could not be continued without serious damage to the nation's domestic and external economies. Strong inflationary pressures came also from the agricultural sector, where farm incomes were raised by increasing farm prices, and from the rapid increase in population that resulted from the massive movement of French citizens from Algeria where the war of independence had ended in 1962.

To cope with the growing inflation the government interrupted the Fourth Plan by adopting a Stabilization Plan in September 1963. This temporary plan introduced a price freeze on all industrial and agricultural products, postponed planned increases in public utility rates and rents, and provided for very restrictive fiscal and monetary policies.[31] The main purpose of the 1963–1964 Stabilization Plan was to eliminate the inflationary psychology that had been building up since 1958. The plan had considerable success in this sphere, for consumer prices remained below the 3 percent level from 1964 to 1967. The

---

[29] Pierre Bauchet, *op. cit.*, p. 189. For a less favorable view of French planning in these years, see Vera Lutz, *French Planning*, pp. 65–76.

[30] This point is discussed in Andrew Shonfield, *op. cit.*, pp. 136–137. See also Bernard Cazes, *La Planification en France et le Quatrième Plan*, Paris: L'Epargne, 1962, p. 84; and Jean-Jacques Bonnaud, "Planning and Industry in France," in *Planning, Politics and Public Policy*, pp. 93–110.

[31] For a discussion of the Stabilization Plan and its effects, see *OECD Economic Surveys, France,* Aug. 1964, pp. 27–31.

anti-inflationary plan for 1963–1964, however, had the adverse effect of curbing the growth of industrial production. This unfavorable consequence was offset by stepping up government spending on public works and increasing the number of new housing starts so that there was no major decline in the economy's overall growth rate.

The Stabilization Plan provided only temporary relief from the problems of inflation and economic disequilibrium. The Organisation for Economic Co-operation and Development noted that "The next question is how far the Stabilization Plan has struck at the root causes of rising prices in France, how far it has created conditions in which price stability can be reconciled with an expansion in keeping with France's production potential...."[32] One of the root causes of inflation that the Stabilization Plan did not deal with effectively was the incomes race among farmers, workers, and business people. This race is the major factor in the inflationary spiral that has been so conspicuous a feature of postwar French economic activity.

The Fifth Plan (1966–1970) adopted a number of innovations calculated to restrict the growth of inflationary pressures. These innovations took the form of value planning

[32] *Ibid.*, p. 30.

(*programmation en valeur*).[33] Up to 1965, the planning authorities had been mainly interested in real or volume planning, which is concerned with the growth of real gross domestic product and its distribution among consumption and investment uses. Not much attention was given in the published plans to prices, costs, and incomes, saving and investing, and other financial relationships. By 1965, the planning authorities agreed that the main problem lay not in the economy's productive machinery, but instead in its price-cost-income relationships. In the fourth and earlier plans, nonsustainable price-cost-income relationships had undermined both the domestic and external equilibria. The value planning introduced in the Fifth Plan sought to avoid the development of nonsustainable financial relationships by integrating the real or volume plans and the financial or value plans. This was to be done by incorporating financial guideposts and various warning signals in the five-year national plans.

The financial guideposts of the Fifth Plan

[33] Value planning is explained in *Le Cinquième Plan* (pp. 179–191), where a distinction is drawn between "volume" and "value" projections. The integration of the volume and the value planning is the work of the General Economy and Finance Commission. The use of value planning is analyzed in MacLennan, Forsyth, and Denton, *op. cit.*, pp. 93–99.

Table 6–10
Implementation of the Fifth Plan, 1966–1970

	Annual percent change, 1969–1970	
	Planned	Actual
Personal consumption	4.6	5.2
Public consumption	6.5	3.2
Business investment	5.0	8.4
Government investment	7.9	6.6
Gross domestic product	5.0	5.9

Source: *OECD Economic Surveys, France,* April 1971.

dealt with price, income, and savings trends and goals. The guidepost for prices projected a 1.5 percent annual increase in the general price level. The guideposts for incomes projected a 4.8 percent annual real increase in farm incomes and a 3.3 percent annual real increase in wage rates and the profits of individual nonfarm entrepreneurs. The savings guideposts indicated the projected increases in the real savings of households, businesses, and government that would be balanced by investments by these three groups in the years 1966-1970. The primary objective of the savings guideposts was to assure enough saving to finance a rate of private and public investment that would make it possible to achieve the Fifth Plan's overall annual economic growth rate of 5 percent. The warning signals or indicators of alert (*clignotants*) incorporated in the Fifth Plan were designed to detect in advance areas of potential disequilibrium in the economy. These indicators revealed the tolerable variations up or down in prices, exports, total output, productive investment, and unemployment. When these limits of tolerance were passed with regard to any one indicator, steps were to be taken to eliminate the deviation from the indicator goal.

The Fifth Plan had both successes and failures. The statistics in Table 6-10 show that in spite of domestic and external difficulties, the overall annual economic growth goal of 5 percent was more than fulfilled. The high annual growth rate of 5.9 percent made possible above-plan increases in private consumption and business investment, particularly in the latter component of gross domestic product, which increased at the actual annual rate of 8.4 percent instead of the planned rate of 5 percent. The high rate of business investment was achieved in part by failing to reach the planned annual rates of increase of public consumption and public investment, as indicated by the statistics in Table 6-10.

The failure of the Fifth Plan to conform with its allocations for public consumption and investment continued the tendency of French planning to overemphasize private consumption and investment at the expense of public consumption and investment. This development, strongly criticized by organized labor on the left, was largely responsible for the severe social disturbances of 1968.

Table 6-11
Planned and Actual Public Investment during the Fifth Plan (1966-1970)

Public capital investment	Percent of plan goal fulfilled
Facilities for cultural activities	97.6
Post and telecommunications	96.7
Health and welfare	85.3
Rural capital facilities	84.2
Schools and universities	82.7
Urban areas	81.1
Roads and transport	74.9
Scientific research	68.1

Source: *Rapport d'éxecution du Ve Plan annexé au projet au Loi de Finances pour 1971.*

The French planned economy

The Fifth Plan also failed to achieve both price stability and favorable current balances in the external sector. In spite of the price and wage guideposts and indicators of alert incorporated in the Fifth Plan, the last two years of the plan were accompanied by severe price and wage explosions, with annual increases in consumer prices and wage rates in manufacturing going above 5 and 12 percent respectively. In 1968 and 1969 the large deficits in the current balance of international payments led to the devaluation of the French franc.

The Sixth Plan (1971–1975) proposed to maintain the high 6 percent annual growth rate but at the same time to give more attention to improving the quality of life and the lot of the low-income and disadvantaged classes. The statistics in Table 6–12 show that during the plan period there was to be a very limited increase in private consumption, a drop in the rate of business investment, and increases in the rates of both public consumption and public investment. It remains to be seen whether the government can successfully combine a high rate of economic growth with a program for improving urban amenities, protecting the environment, and providing for social welfare in a way that will meet the demands of the general public for a lifestyle of high quality.

The changes in the distribution or uses of the nation's GNP in the past decade do not indicate that the business-dominated French government has been prepared to trade off much economic growth for improvements in the nation's lifestyle. The statistics in Table 6–13, which show the relative changes in the use of France's Gross National Product in 1962–1974, reveal that the relative shares of GNP going into public consumption and public investment remained unchanged at approximately 15.5 percent. In the same period, 1962–1971, industrial investment increased from 19 to 22.4 percent of GNP, while private consumption as a share of GNP registered a moderate relative decline. The large social and economic disturbances of 1968 do not yet appear to have greatly altered the national priorities as reflected in the distribution of the nation's total national output.

Medium-Term French Demand and Supply Management

Whereas the Ministry of Finance and other ministries are concerned with securing an equilibrium between total demand and total supply in the short run, the General Plan

Table 6–12
Main Projections of the Sixth Plan (1971–1975)

	Percentage annual changes	
	1960–1970 (actual)	1971–1975 (projected)
Private consumption	5.2	5.6
Public consumption	3.2	4.6
Business investment	8.4	7.4
Government investment	6.6	7.2
Gross domestic product	5.9	6.0

Source: *OECD Economic Surveys, France,* April 1971.

Table 6–13
The Percentage Distribution of France's Gross National Product, 1962, 1966, 1969, 1971, and 1974

	1962	1966	1969	1971	1974
Private consumption	61.6	60.3	59.1	59.0	59.4
Public consumption	13.0	12.4	12.3	12.3	11.8
Gross fixed asset formation:					
Government investment	2.8	3.3	3.2	3.9 ⎫	26.2
Industrial investment	19.0	21.5	21.7	22.4 ⎭	
Changes in inventories	2.8	2.1	4.2	2.3	1.9
Net export surplus	0.8	0.3	−0.5	0.8	0.7
Gross National Product	100.0	100.0	100.0	100.0	100.0

Source: *OECD Economic Surveys, France.*

Commission is primarily interested in obtaining a balance between total demand and total supply during the five-year plan period. The major objective of the five-year or medium-term demand-and-supply management is to finish up the plan period with the Gross National Product and its distribution among investment and consumption uses as projected for the fifth year of the plan period. The medium-term demand-and-supply management supplements and facilitates the private enterprise system, which accounts for the bulk of the nation's total output.[34] On the supply side, the problem is to make available the productive equipment, manpower, and raw materials required for the planned increase in gross domestic product over the five-year plan period. Medium-term supply planning deals with such matters as the prevention or elimination of supply bottlenecks, providing adequate supplies of skilled labor, restructuring outmoded industries, assuring supplies of scarce raw materials, improving managerial practices, improving labor productivity, and stimulating research and development. Medium-term demand management works primarily through monetary and fiscal policies that influence private and public consumption and investment expenditures during the five-year plan period. These policies are constructed with the aim of assuring the amount of medium-term investment needed to support the five-year planned growth rate.

Medium-Term Monetary and Fiscal Management

The General Plan Commission, the Treasury, the Economic and Social Development Fund, the specialized credit institutions, the National Credit Council, and the Bank of France have important roles in the steering of medium-term economic development with the aid of monetary policy. The government is in a strong position to use medium-term credit as a means of influencing the economy's development for two reasons. Since the French capital market is poorly developed, many private firms must turn to one of the government's financial agencies to obtain credit. Also, since the government is directly responsible for one-quarter of all fixed investment

[34] Problems of medium-term supply and demand management are analyzed in Bernard Cazes, "French Planning"; in John T. Dunlop and Nikolay P. Fedorenko, *Planning and Markets*, New York: McGraw-Hill, 1969, pp. 21–46; and Andrew Shonfield, "Planning: Britain and France Compared," *Modern Capitalism*, pp. 151–175.

and owns three of the largest banks, it is in a good position to direct credit towards the industries and regions that are high on the national priority list. In the field of public investment, which includes investment by government agencies and nationalized industries, the Economic and Social Development Fund controls all publicly financed investment according to the requirements of the national plans. The fund, which is under the direction of the Ministry of Finance, works closely with the General Plan Commission and the Bank of France, in guiding public investment. The Treasury finances the fund through the sale of three- to five-year government bonds which private banks are required to hold up to a certain limit, and which the investing public strongly prefers over privately issued bonds and stocks. The Treasury controls the timing of all new private bond issues.

Much of the medium-term financing of private firms is done by official specialized credit institutions, such as the *Crédit National* and the *Crédit Foncier,* whose extensions of credit to private industry must be approved by the Bank of France, the Treasury, and the General Plan Commission. Loans at reduced rates, with preferential terms regarding their duration and deferred payment, and subsidized loans are made to private firms by government agencies to aid the grouping of those firms or their merger, or to induce them to establish plants in France's underdeveloped western and southern regions.

While the ability of the government to influence medium-term plant and equipment investment expenditures is quite extensive, this ability is weakest where private firms are not chronically short of capital and can finance much of their investment from their retained earnings. This has been the situation in the automobile and oil industries which have been quite profitable in the postwar period. Other industries that have been chronically short of capital, such as the steel and textile industries, have had to turn to government-controlled financing. The recent efforts to improve the private capital market by having investors shift from government securities to private securities, if successful, will make it more difficult for the planning authorities to manage the medium-term demand for credit.

In France, as in other Western industrialized nations, considerable controversy has arisen over how neutral should be the impact of the tax system on the economic system. Jacques Rueff, the leading French opponent of national planning, and other exponents of economic liberalism argue for a tax system that in their opinion would strengthen competitive market forces.[35] By contrast, the planning authorities hold the view that the tax system should be adapted to the needs of the national plans.

This interventionist view of the role of the tax system was especially strong before the establishment of the Fifth Republic under de Gaulle in 1958. Although the Fifth Republic took a conservative turn under de Gaulle and Pompidou, it has not accepted the neutralist view of the role of the nation's tax system. Consequently, the French tax system has continued to be used as one of the major medium-term devices for steering the economy in the directions called for by the national plan. The tax system has been employed to achieve the total output, total consumption, and total investment that would sustain the planned medium-term growth. The tax burden in France, as measured by total taxes as a percent of Gross National Product (38 percent), falls between the 31

---

[35] Rueff and other neoliberals advocate "complete freedom" as opposed to the planners' "controlled freedom." Jacques Rueff and others, *Les fondaments philosophiques des systèmes économiques,* Emil Claasen, ed., Paris: Payot, 1967, p. 474. See also Vera Lutz, *Central Planning for the Market Economy,* pp. 28–32; and Andrew Shonfield, *op. cit.,* pp. 131 and 148.

percent burden in the United States and the 51 percent burden in Sweden. As has already been explained, the French indirect tax burden is among the highest in the Western world: close to one-half of total taxes in France are indirect. Since private consumption is much less volatile than private investment, French medium-term fiscal policy is primarily concerned with adjusting the tax system to secure the desired private investment during the five-year plan period.

Disincentives to investment have been removed by substituting the value-added tax for the old traditional sales tax that penalized the late stages of production. Also, depreciation rules have been altered to reflect current inflated values, and accelerated depreciation has been increased according to the length of life of new capital. Medium-term investment incentives have been improved with the aid of fiscal contracts (*contrats fiscaux*), which assure the continuity of preferential fiscal treatment of private industry over a number of annual budgetary periods. Tax relief under these contracts is given to firms that agree to make capital investments or to conduct industrial research and development along lines that support the national plans.

Fiscal discrimination is used to stimulate exports and regional development. Exporters have been relieved of the duty of paying value-added taxes; and firms that have been willing to establish plants in the underdeveloped southern and western regions of France have been relieved of the payment of the distributed profits tax up to 5 percent on new capital issues. Exporters who have reached fixed export goals have been given export cards (*carte d'exportateur*), which have entitled them to favorable depreciation provisions, to exemptions from increases in the domestic value-added tax, and to priority access to the capital market. The preferential fiscal treatment for firms willing to invest in France's underdeveloped regions has been joined with programs to establish growth centers or poles in these regions.[36] These growth centers are planned to provide the social capital infrastructure and the coordinated private industries that are needed to place regional economic growth on a self-sustaining basis.

Medium-term French fiscal policy provides special incentives for the restructuring and modernization of industry, which are designed to reduce the highly fragmented nature of French industry, and to make it more competitive in the European Common Market. Special tax relief is given to small and medium-sized firms that form industrial groups or associations, to mergers acquiring land and buildings, and to holding companies whose subsidiaries pay profits taxes. Such tax relief has been more effective in the concentrated steel and chemical industries than in the machine tool and other small-scale industries, where the National Confederation of Small and Medium-Sized Enterprise has traditionally been hostile to state intervention. It is widely believed that foreign competition, especially from the other European Common Market countries, has been a greater stimulus to the restructuring and modernization of French industry than have been selective fiscal measures.

Demand and Supply Management and Long-Term French Development

As has already been explained, French demand-and-supply management is also carried on within a framework of long-term economic and social analysis, which deals with such matters as population growth, urban and

[36] The concept of polarized growth is associated especially with the work of François Perroux, *L'Economie du XXe Siècle*, Paris: PUF, 1961. See also J. R. Boudeville, *Problems of Regional Economic Planning*, Edinburgh: Edinburgh University Press, 1966.

rural development, the restructuring of industry, changes in the labor force and its productivity, evaluation of household consumption, and advances in science and technology.[37] The first long-term study of the French economy, *Réflexions pour 1985*, which was published in 1968, analyzes probable economic and social developments during 1960–1985.[38] This study discusses the major options with respect to long-term national priorities. In the next twenty-five years, France will become much more urbanized, agricultural employment will continue to decline as the service industries expand, industry will become larger scale, and exports will increasingly reflect the expansion of the high-technology industries. Between 1960 and 1985, France's population is expected to increase from 46 to 57 million; the work week may decline to 40 hours; and all workers may have a one-month paid holiday. It is estimated that the gross domestic product could increase in the period 1960–1985 at the average annual rate of 4.7 percent. By 1985, the gross domestic product, which was 244 billion francs in 1960, would at this rate of growth be 769 billion francs (measured in 1960 prices).

The view of the French society in 1985 presented in *Réflexions pour 1985* is a composite of what is described as the probable and the desirable. This future society will be an urban, mass-consumption society with considerable leisure time available to its members. In order to achieve what the 1985 study group referred to as "une économie et une société nouvelles," decisions must be made regarding the division of the 1985 GNP between private- and public-consumption and investment uses; these decisions will reflect long-term national priorities.

The national economic budget for 1985 presented in Table 6–14 summarizes the options considered by the 1985 study group. A comparison of the actual uses of the national output in 1960 and the prospective uses in 1985 shows that private consumption is expected to undergo a relative decline as public consumption and gross fixed investment increase. In the society of 1985, more of the total national output would be taken up by such collective needs as urban renewal, improved transportation and telecommunications, and more technical education. Also, more of the national output would be allocated to new industrial investment and the program for research and development with the aim of furthering France's industrialization. The 1985 national economic budget incorporates the long-term changes in demand and supply that can be anticipated as the consequences of the national priorities chosen for 1985. For example, consumers can be expected to spend relatively less on food and clothing and more on education, health, transportation, amusement, and culture. Manpower policy will emphasize the need to enlarge the supply of managers, engineers, and skilled workers; and regional development will increase employment opportunities more rapidly in the regions outside the Paris region. High-technology industry will be stimulated by scientific research and technological advance. Long-term analysis will also be applied to land use and regional growth.

The 1985 study group explains that their

---

[37] The restructuring of French industry and related structural problems are considered in Organisation for Economic Co-operation and Development, *The Industrial Policy of France*, Paris, 1974; and *The Industrial Policies of 14 Member Countries*, Ch. VI, "France," Paris, 1971, pp. 177–196.

[38] Le Groupe 1985, *Réflexions pour 1985*, Paris: La Documentation Française, 1964. This study was made by an ad hoc committee (Le Groupe 1985). In 1963, long-term analysis and planning was formalized by establishing the National Commission for Integrated Development, which works closely with the General Plan Commission. See also Bernard Cazes, "The Use of Long-Term Studies in Planning," in *Planning, Politics and Public Policy*, pp. 424–444.

Table 6-14
The French National Economic Budget for 1985 (In Billions of 1959 Francs)

	1960 national economic accounts (actual)	1985 national economic budget (projection)
Private consumption	170 (69.7%)	523 (68.0%)
Public consumption	13 (5.3%)	45 (5.9%)
Gross fixed investment	49 (20.1%)	176 (22.9%)
Change in inventories	6 (2.45%)	10 (1.3%)
Net export surplus	6 (2.45%)	15 (1.9%)
Gross domestic production	244 (100.0%)	769 (100.0%)

Source: La Documentation Française, *Réflexions pour 1985*, Paris, 1968.

long-term analyses do not provide a detailed map of the routes to the future. Although the future remains highly uncertain, it is worthwhile to consider the probable dimensions of the future society in which individuals will be faced with problems of mobility, obsolescence, participation, leisure, and aesthetic values. The twenty-five-year national economic budget has no expectational or operational significance. It is only a device to show how national priorities may in the long run become claims on the Gross National Product and affect the distribution or use of this product. The perspective planning associated with the twenty-five-year national economic budget provides a background for the five-year national plans which in turn supply a framework for the annual plans. The coordination of long-term, medium-term, and short-term supply-and-demand management requires the cooperation of the National Commission for Integrated Development, the General Plan Commission, and the Ministry of Finance. As the critics of French national planning have pointed out, there is much room for improvement along this line.[39]

[39] Pierre Bauchet, "General Conclusions," *op. cit.*, pp. 247-253; and John and Anne-Marie Hackett, *op. cit.*, pp. 357-370.

The Concerted Economy in Retrospect and Prospect

A survey of the performance of the French concerted economy since it was established in the early postwar years reveals that this performance has in economic terms been very good.[40] France has been foremost among the industrialized Western European countries that have achieved sustained and high economic growth rates. A recent OECD study shows that in 1955-1972 France came much closer to securing its potential gross domestic product than did West Germany, the United Kingdom, Italy, and the United States. Table 6-15 indicates that the average gap between actual and potential gross domestic product

[40] While French planning has been criticized on a number of grounds, many analysts believe that France has had a net gain from its national planning. For views about French planning, see John Sheahan, "Planning in France," *Challenge*, March-April, 1975, pp. 15-20; Vera Lutz, "Conclusions," *French Planning*, pp. 95-99; Pierre Bauchet, "General Conclusions," *Economic Planning*, pp. 247-253; MacLennan, Forsyth, and Denton, "Conclusions," *Economic Planning and Policies*, pp. 399-419; and Michael Watson, "Conclusion, A Comparative Evaluation of Planning Practice in the Liberal Democratic State," *Planning, Politics and Public Policy*, pp. 445-483.

Table 6-15
Average Half-Yearly Deviations of Actual from Potential Gross Domestic Product in France and Selected Countries, 1955-1972.

	GDP gap In percent of potential GDP
Norway	−0.4
France	−0.6
Sweden	−0.8
West Germany[1]	−1.1
United Kingdom	−1.4
Italy	−2.0
Canada[1]	−2.9
United States[1]	−3.3

[1] GNP

Source: OECD, *OECD Economic Outlook, Occasional Studies, The Measurement of Domestic Cyclical Fluctuations*, Paris, July 1973.

measured as a percent of the latter was smaller for the planned economies of France, Norway, and Sweden than for the unplanned Western industrialized economies.[41]

France has also had a low unemployment rate that compares favorably with the rates of other West European industrialized countries. In the international area, France has maintained its share of the expanding world trade in manufactured goods, has accumulated a large reserve of gold and foreign exchange, and has succeeded in maintaining the franc as one of the world's few strong currencies. The high-pressure economy that has been created as the result of efforts to keep actual gross domestic product close to its potential has contributed to strong inflationary pressures. The government's anti-inflationary program, while not eliminating these pressures, has curbed them enough to keep France competitive in international markets.

[41] OECD, *OECD Economic Outlook, Occasional Studies, The Measurement of Domestic Cyclical Fluctuations*, Paris, 1973.

France has also succeeded in developing a strong position in the European Economic Community. Considerable progress has been made in recent years in restructuring French industry so as to make it more competitive in both the EEC and world markets.

One of the main criticisms of French national planning is that it has placed too much emphasis on economic growth, and has given inadequate attention to improving the lifestyle of the average citizen. France has suffered in a less extreme form from the Japanese problem of rapid economic growth with inadequate attention to the social costs of this growth. France continues to have serious deficiencies in housing, mass transportation, educational facilities, telecommunications, urban renewal, and environmental protection. Wide differences in per capita regional incomes exist, as well as wide variations in the educational and cultural advantages available in the country's twenty-one regions. The student-worker strife of 1968 led to a reevaluation of national priorities and a declaration by the Pompidou Administration that in the future more emphasis would be placed on programs for the improvement of social welfare.

The Labor Movement and French Planning

The prospects of reaching this national goal would be better if France had a strong labor movement comparable to that of the United Kingdom and the Scandinavian countries. In the latter countries, the well-organized trade unions are in a strong position to influence national priorities. This is not the case in France, where only 15 percent of the total work force holds union membership, and where the labor movement is weakened by competing Catholic, socialist, and communist trade unions and union confederations. While the French trade union movement is weak at the factory level, it has considerable strength at the national political level. The socialist and communist political parties, with strong union backing, usually occupy one-fifth or more of the seats in the National Assembly, and generally refrain from close cooperation with the other political parties.[42] For this reason, organized labor has a relatively small role in the construction and execution of the national plans which are the primary concern of the dominant centrist trade union, the Gaullist Union of Democrats.[43]

French national planning has undergone considerable change since it was inaugurated in 1947. The first three plans were primarily concerned with the modernization of the nation's economy. They were plans for production rather than for consumption and were designed to secure the support of the conservative business community, which was at first not strongly in favor of national planning. By the end of the Third Plan (1958–1961), it was evident that the future success of national planning required that more attention be paid to the democratic and social aspects of planning. This was to be achieved by reordering national priorities in order to raise the standard of living of the low-income and disadvantaged classes, and to devote more of the nation's resources to investments that were less productive of exports such as housing, transportation, educational facilities, urban renewal, and regional development. Also, the National Assembly and the organized labor movement were to be given a larger role in the formulation of the national plans. Beyond submitting the five-year national plans to the National Assembly for its approval and making modest increases in public consumption and investment, the government did not achieve much along these lines before the student-worker strife of 1968.

Efforts to democratize and socialize French national planning have drawn attention to the question of the role of the labor movement in national planning. Up to 1968, the coalition of centrist-right political parties, with the strong support of the conservative National Council of French Employers, had restricted organized labor to a very minor role in the national planning program. In the first four plans, labor had only 10 percent of the membership of the important Vertical Commissions, whereas private business had 39 percent. It was realized that organized labor could not speak effectively for the workers as long as the trade unions were very weak at the factory level. A number of steps have been taken to remedy this situation.

In 1967, the de Gaulle government sought to advance the program for greater labor participation by requiring all firms with more than one hundred employees to adopt a

[42] In the elections of May 1973, when the Gaullist party was on the decline, the socialist and communist parties won 35.7 percent (175) of the seats in the National Assembly.

[43] In November 1967, the original Gaullist party, the Union for the New Republic (UNR) was reorganized as the Union for Democrats (UDR).

profit-sharing program. Legislation was also passed to establish a program of "mensuralization" under which blue-collar workers are paid on a monthly basis and are given all the fringe benefits enjoyed by white-collar workers. In 1968, legislation was enacted that required employers to recognize trade unions, to allow their representatives on the factory premises, to permit workers to devote some of their working time to union matters, and to refrain from persecuting workers because of prounion activities. The Pompidou government was active in substituting negotiation for confrontation in industrial relations, and in getting the National Council of French Employers to meet more regularly with the trade unions. The Catholic French Democratic Federation of Workers (CFDT) has been favorably disposed towards these closer employer-employee relations. The Marxist General Confederation of Workers (CGT), however, has attacked all programs for worker participation on the ground that they would weaken class warfare. Since the CGT accounts for about one-half of all French trade union members, the prospect of developing a strong program for industrial participation or codetermination in the concerted French economy is not good. Furthermore, the enthusiasm of the recent French governments for worker participation has not been duplicated in private business circles.

Economic Interest Groups and French Planning

The French political and economic power structure is today dominated by a strong etatist or centralistic tradition, which nourishes close working relationships between the government and the large private business enterprises. Support for the government's economic policies, and especially for the national planning program, comes primarily from the large business enterprises and not from small manufacturers, retailers, farmers, or trade unions. Many of the nation's political and business leaders are products of the two main graduate schools, the École Polytechnic and the École National d'Administration. These graduates, who frequently make their mark early in their careers as outstanding civil servants (*inspecteurs des finances*), provide an informal communications system that brings government and business close together. Large private business firms in France usually have a director whose main function is to keep in close contact with the various government ministries, and to be informed about government policies and how they may affect private enterprise.

Making the French planned economy work is simplified by the presence of an unusually strong and coherent government-business elite.[44] This elite has been willing to make some concessions in recent years that have improved the collective bargaining process, enabled the workers to share in the nation's economic progress, and improved the social security program. These concessions, however, have not significantly altered or weakened the conservative political and economic power structure which is the main support of what is described as "gaullism" and "pompidolism."

An important problem not yet resolved by French planners is the role of economic interest groups in the planning process. There is wide disagreement concerning how much economic interest groups should be allowed to influence the construction and execution of the national plans. The trade unions are in

[44] *L'Expansion*, a French business monthly, has recently claimed that one hundred business and government leaders are behind most important economic decisions in France. This question of the role of the government-business elite is discussed in *The Economist*, "Pompidou's France, An Economic Survey," 1972, p. 21. See also Andrew Shonfield, "The Etatist Tradition: France," *op. cit.*, pp. 71–87.

favor of an equirepresentative method, which would give labor an equal voice with business in the deliberations of the modernization commissions and other planning bodies where labor and business have important roles to play. This is the method usually followed in the United Kingdom, the Netherlands, and the Scandinavian countries, where the trade union movement is strong and aggressive. In the French national planning program, the policy has been for the government to appoint members of the various planning bodies in their individual capacities and not as representatives of any interest group.[45] Since these planning bodies do not settle issues by voting, conflicts between economic interest groups are not highlighted. French planners have avoided developing a system of corporative government in which individuals regard themselves as representatives of their respective groups. The planners have kept the influence of various economic groups to a minimum, and have left the ultimate control of the planning program to the two Chambers of the Parliament. Since organized labor is not well represented in the Parliament, it has refrained from approving the national plans; national planning has thus become more the concern of big business than organized labor. Leaving ultimate control of the plans to the Parliament means that organized labor is largely excluded from the planning process, and that national planning is mainly a product of the power structure supporting the center-right political parties in the Parliament.

Planning in the New Society

The Pompidou government in 1969–1974 was active in sponsoring the development of what is called "the new society." Former Prime Minister Chaban-Delmas and other leaders in the Pompidou government concluded that national planning cannot make much further progress until the hierarchical, sectional French society (*la société bloquée*) has been replaced by a "new society" in which the national interest is recognized as being of paramount importance. It is widely agreed among the proponents of French national planning that the establishment of the new society requires a number of institutional, political, and ideological changes.[46] Among the institutional innovations would be a change in the nature of private property and private profit making, which would permit more public control of corporate self-financing and capital gains from private investment. Without some alteration along these lines, there can be no hope of developing a satisfactory incomes policy, because workers will not accept wage controls unless controls are also placed on the accumulation of private profits and capital gains.

Political changes are needed to increase public participation and to emphasize the importance of securing group collaboration; the latter would reduce the disruptive effects of intersectional rivalry. It would also be desirable to have the French Parliament play a more active role in determining the broad directives which guide the national plans. The advocates of the French planned economy call for a new ideological approach that will give "political and philosophical content" to the plan, and will provide a basis for the determination of national priorities.[47] These advocates support the substitution of a new

---

[45] For a discussion of the political control of the French plans see Pierre Bauchet, "Who Should Have Control," *op. cit.*, pp. 116–120.

[46] See, for example, the proposals of Pierre Bauchet, *op. cit.*, pp. 247–253; and John and Anne-Marie Hacket, *op. cit.*, pp. 357–370. See also Jack Hayward, "Planning and the French Labour Market," in *Planning, Politics and Public Policy*, pp. 173–174. The concept of the highly sectionalized society (la Société Bloquée) is developed in Michel Crozier, *La Société Bloquée*, Paris, 1970.

[47] Pierre Bauchet, *op. cit.*, p. 252.

solidaristic ideology for the excessively individualistic ideology that is still dominant in French politics.

The de Gaulle and post–de Gaulle governments have endeavored to foster the development of a new solidaristic or nonradical, neocollectivist ideology in several different ways. A program has been launched to make France an industrial power commensurate with its resources. The fruits of the second industrial revolution are to be shared by the workers through a program of industrial participation; the poor and underprivileged classes are to receive special consideration in the form of higher minimum wages and an improved social security program; the farmers are to be assured parity with the industrial workers; and regional planning is to reduce economic and cultural inequalities and to decentralize much of the national planning. France is to become less self-sufficient and nationalistic, and more prepared to enter joint consortia that emphasize economic benefits rather than international prestige.

As has already been explained, the solidaristic ideology and the economic and social development under the six national plans reflect the centrist-right position that has dominated French politics since 1948. This middle-of-the-road political thrust has called for no radical change in the national patterns of wealth and income distribution. The workers have shared in the nation's economic growth but without any significant change in the nation's wealth or income distribution. The tax system continues to place an excessive burden on expenditures and not enough on personal incomes. Regional inequalities continue to be large. Organized labor has a much smaller role in the setting of national priorities and guiding the economic system than is the case in many of the other Western industrialized countries. Nevertheless, more than most of these countries, France with its concerted economy has drawn attention to one of the most pressing problems now facing the world's advanced industrialized nations: that is, the problem of taking collective account of the nation's economic and social priorities and the role they play in providing national economic and social guidance.

It is impossible to determine how much France would have progressed after World War II without national planning. In the quarter century since the end of that war Western Europe has generally been prosperous. France would doubtless have shared in this prosperity even if it had had no national planning program. The question arises as to whether or not its rate of economic growth would have been as regular without national planning. The main benefit of this planning has been to provide a method of taking stock of the nation's economic and social priorities, and evaluating the consequences of long-term changes in these priorities. Much remains to be done to alter France's power structure so that all of the nation's economic interest groups may participate more fully in the planning process; but the development of a way—national planning—by which national priorities may be more satisfactorily analyzed and evaluated places France in a good position to deal with the most pressing problem of the last quarter of the twentieth century. This is the problem of achieving national priorities that contribute to a lifestyle of high quality.

The model of the French planned economy is far removed from the model of workable competition that dominates American economic policy making. The difference between the models is that between indicative national planning and inadequately coordinated government intervention. In many ways, the two models reflect the basic historical, cultural, and psychological differences between the United States and France. French national planning was devised to overcome the obstacles to economic growth in a hierarchical, cartel-ridden, and highly sectionalized country. The American concept of workable competition with its uncoordinated government intervention was developed to tame a dynamic private enterprise system that was beginning to show a need for more social control of large business enterprises. Recent economic developments seem to suggest that the planned French economy could profitably pay more attention to the decentralization of its planning program, while the regulated American economy would do well to be more concerned with long-term economic and social development and the setting of national priorities.

Selected Bibliography

BAUCHET, PIERRE. *Economic Planning: The French Experience.* Heinemann Educational Books, London, 1964.

BAUM, WARREN C. *The French Economy and the State.* Princeton University Press, Princeton, N.J., 1958.

BOUDEVILLE, J. R. *Problems of Regional Economic Planning.* Edinburgh University Press, Edinburgh, 1966.

CAZES, BERNARD. *La Planification en France et le Quatrième Plan.* L'Epargne, Paris, 1962.

COHEN, STEPHEN. *Modern Capitalist Planning: The French Model.* Harvard University Press, Cambridge, 1969.

CROZIER, MICHEL. *La Société Bloquée.* L'Epargne, Paris, 1970.

DUNLOP, JOHN T., and NIKOLAY P. FEDORENKO. *Planning and Markets.* McGraw-Hill Book Company, New York, 1969.

The Economist. "Pompidou's France, An Economic Survey." No. 6745 (Dec. 2, 1972), 1–46.

EINAUDI, MARIO, MAURICE BYE, and ERNESTO ROSSI. *Nationalization in France and Italy.* Cornell University Press, Ithaca, 1955.

GENERAL CONFEDERATION OF ITALIAN INDUSTRIES. "Incomes Policy in France." *Incomes Policy.* Rome, 1967.

GRUSON, C. *Origine et espoirs de la planification française,* Dunod, Paris, 1968.

HACKETT, JOHN and ANNE-MARIE. *Economic Planning in France.* Harvard University Press, Cambridge, 1963.

HARLOW, JOHN S. *French Economic Planning: A Challenge to Reason.* University of Iowa Press, Iowa City, 1966.

HAYWARD, J. E. S. "Interest Groups and Incomes Policy in France." *British Journal of Industrial Relations,* July 1966, 165–200.

———. "State Intervention in France." Political Studies, XII (Sept. 1972), 289–294.

HAYWARD, JACK, and MICHAEL WATSON, eds. *Planning, Politics and Public Policy, The British, French and Italian Experience.* Cambridge University Press, Cambridge, England, 1975.

LAUTMAN, J., and J.-C. THOENIG. *Planification et Administrations Centrales.* Copédith, Paris, 1966.

Le Groupe 1985. *Réflexions pour 1985.* La Documentation Française, Paris, 1964.

LUTZ, VERA. *Central Planning for the Market Economy, An Analysis of the French Theory and Experience.* Longmans, Green, London, 1969.

———. *French Planning.* American Enterprise Institute, Washington, D.C., 1965.

MASSÉ, PIERRE. "French Methods of Planning." *British Journal of Industrial Relations,* XI (Nov. 1963).

Organisation for Economic Co-operation and Development. *Monetary Policy in France.* Paris, 1974.

———. *Non-Wage Incomes and Price Policy.* Paris, 1966.

———. *OECD Economic Surveys, France.* Paris, 1964, 1970, 1971, 1972, and 1975.

———. *The Industrial Policy of France.* Paris, 1974.

PERROUX, FRANÇOIS. *Le Capitalisme.* Presses Universitaires De France, Paris, 1962.

———. *L' Economie du XXe Siecle.* PUF, Paris, 1961.

Political and Economic Planning. *Economic Planning in France.* London, 1961.

RUEFF, JACQUES, and others. *Les fondaments philosophiques des systèmes économiques.* Emil Claasen, ed., Payot, Paris, 1967.

SCHIFF, ERIC. *Incomes Policies Abroad,* II. American Enterprise Institute, Washington, D.C., 1972.

SHEAHAN, JOHN. *An Introduction to the French Economy.* Charles E. Merrill, Columbus, 1969.

ULLMO, YVES. *La Planification en France.* Cours de l'Institut d'Etudes Politiques, Paris, 1971–1973.

Chapter 7
The Capitalist Economies: In Retrospect and Prospect

The wide range of Western capitalist economies that lies between the regulated American economy at one extreme and the planned French economy at the other may be divided into three groups. In the first group are such countries as the United States, Canada, Australia, and the United Kingdom (when the Conservative party is in office). While government policy in these countries may be called interventionist, nevertheless, strong laissez faire tendencies operate within the dominant business community. Regulation of the economy is tolerated, but there is much opposition to anything associated with national planning. Labor-management cooperation is not a major feature of these economies; and intervention by the government is not accompanied by much collaboration by government, business, and organized labor.

Italy, West Germany, Denmark (when the Conservative-Liberal coalition is in office), and Finland constitute the second group. Here, economic tendencies are much less laissez fairist than in the first group; intervention and regulation are more extensive; more collaboration between economic interest groups and the government exists; and the government tends to be much more activist than in the United States and the United Kingdom. In this group, West Germany provides the leading example of a regulated but unplanned industrial country.

In the third group are France, the Netherlands, Norway (when under a nonsocialist coalition), Belgium, and Japan. The chief distinguishing characteristic of these capitalist economies is their national planning with the aid of annual and medium-term national economic budgeting. In these countries a higher degree of coordination of economic policies exists than in the other two groups of capitalist economies. In the economies of all three groups, the dominant private economic interest is the business interest, with organized labor playing a secondary role.

The Emergence of the High-Pressure Economy

Although there is much diversity among capitalist nations, they have, nevertheless, developed a basically similar pattern of operations, which may be described as that of a high-pressure economy. This type of economy is the result of the efforts of advanced industrial economies since 1929 to achieve full employment. The adverse developments during the depression years of the 1930s resulted in the establishment of the welfare state in one form or another in all the advanced industrial economies. The principal feature of the welfare state is the commitment of the government to a policy of full employment. After 1945, nation after nation either formally or by informal action accepted full employment as a national goal of the highest priority. The majority of the Western European industrial nations have had very low unemployment rates since the close of World War II. The statistics in Table 7-1 reveal that for the period 1960-1969 the average annual unemployment rate in these countries was about 2 percent. Since 1969, unemployment has increased in the United Kingdom, West Germany, and Sweden, but it still remains much below the American and Canadian unemployment levels, which were 4.8 and 5.1 respectively in the years 1960-1969. The Scandinavian countries, Japan, and West Germany have usually been able to get unemployment below two percent. In some countries, such as the Netherlands, West Germany, and France where unemployment has been very low, it was necessary up to 1973 to import workers from Greece, Turkey, and Yugoslavia to fill low-paying jobs.

The result of the efforts to achieve full employment on a lasting basis in the Western world has been to create the *high-pressure economy*, i.e., one with little slack, since labor and equipment are fully used. Full employment results in a generally high and sustained rate of economic growth, which in turn requires high levels of investment and supports a rising standard of living. In a country like Japan, where gross fixed investment takes up 39 percent of the nation's Gross National

Table 7-1

Unemployment in Percent of Civilian Labor Force in Selected Industrial Countries, Average Annual Rates, 1960-1969

	National concepts	Concepts of the U.S. Bureau of Labor Statistics
United States	—	4.8
Canada	—	5.1
Italy	3.4	3.7
United Kingdom	1.9	2.9
Belgium	2.2	—
France	1.5	2.3
Sweden	1.7	1.7
Japan	1.3	1.3
Netherlands	1.1	—
West Germany	1.0	0.6

Source: OECD, *OECD Economic Surveys, France*, April 1971.

Product, the standard of living, although improving, has been held back by a tradeoff that has favored private investment against private and public consumption. Among the Western European industrial countries (1972), Norway has the highest ratio of gross fixed investment to GNP (29 percent). In the Netherlands, West Germany, and France, where growth rates are high, the investment-output ratio fluctuates between 24 and 29 percent. This ratio in the United Kingdom and the United States, which have lower growth rates, has ranged between 16 and 18 percent.

In the high-pressure capitalist economies, a marked contrast appears between the open, internationally competitive, high-technology export industries and the sheltered domestic industries, which include small-scale manufacturing, the various service industries, and agriculture. The export industries, a number of which are multinational in scope, set the pace. Since these economies in Western Europe export from one-fifth to one-third of their Gross National Products, they are very dependent upon the good performance of their high-technology, large-scale industrial enterprises. These enterprises are frequently favored by tax arrangements that enable them to retain large profits for investment purposes. They possess very considerable economic and political power, and work closely with the government in the formulation and execution of fiscal, monetary, and other economic policies.

Whereas the internationally competitive large-scale industries in a high-pressure economy secure large profits, wield considerable economic and political power, and are in a strong position to influence government policy, the situation is quite different with respect to the sheltered domestic industries. In the domestic sector, returns on investment are smaller, average personal incomes are lower, workers are less well organized, and there is much less economic and political power. This sector of the high-pressure economy is called upon to make many adjustments that are felt by small producers, retailers, and poorly organized or unorganized workers to be destructive of their best interests.

As the high-pressure economy has developed, it has become necessary to shift resources from the inefficient service trades, small-scale manufacturing, retailing, and agriculture into the higher productivity, high technology export and export-supporting industries. Governments have sponsored modernization and rationalization programs designed to reduce the number of small producers, retailers, and farmers. In some cases, where organization has been strong, as in the case of farmers and some groups of skilled workers, the government has encountered considerable opposition to its programs to shift resources out of the low-productivity industries. In spite of this resistance, since the early 1950s there has been in all the high-pressure economies a significant flight from agriculture and a merging of small manufacturing units into larger ones.

Short-Run Problems of High-Pressure Western Economies

The problems that have accompanied the development of high-pressure economies since 1945 have placed a heavy burden on the central governments of the Western industrial nations. Among the most pressing short-run problems have been curbing inflation, developing an incomes policy, and securing an external equilibrium. Since the high-pressure economy has little slack in its supplies of labor, plant, and equipment, it is subject to strong inflationary pressures. Aggregate demand tends to exceed aggregate supply, and employers find it easy to pass on wage increases in the form of higher prices. In this situation, employers offer little resistance to workers' demands for higher wages. Even in periods of limited economic contraction, cost-push, supported by strong employer and employee organizations, continues to move wage rates and prices upward.

An analysis of price and wage changes in the United States, Canada, Japan, and five Western European industrial countries in 1963–1972 shows that all these countries have experienced considerable inflation. The average annual increase in consumer prices in these eight countries was 4.3 percent. For 1968–1972, the inflation was stronger, the average annual rate being 5.3 percent. An analysis of the inflationary developments in the eight industrial countries shows that inflation reached higher levels in the planned economies of Japan, France, the Netherlands, and Sweden than in the unplanned economies of West Germany, Italy, Canada, and the United States. The only exception to this observation was the United Kingdom, whose inflation was about the same as that of the four planned economies.

Although all Western industrial economies suffered from serious inflation after 1963, for the most part they did not have prolonged, recurring periods of external disequilibrium. The only important exceptions to this development were the United Kingdom and the United States. The reason for this development is that these Western industrial nations have usually curbed their inflation enough to remain competitive in international markets. Wholesale prices rose more slowly than consumer prices, and, in addition, special efforts were made to control the increases in export prices. To keep these prices down, special tax concessions were given to exporters. Also, at times exporters accepted reduced profit margins in order to curb export price increases. In Italy, where consumer prices increased at the average annual rate of 3.9 percent in 1960–1970, export prices rose only 0.8 percent. In Japan, where consumer prices in the same years increased at the annual rate of 5.8 percent, export prices rose only 0.5 percent a year.

The pattern of the inflationary developments of the 1960s was abruptly broken in the early 1970s when raw material, food, and oil scarcities created strong inflationary pressures in all major Western industrialized countries. The statistics in Table 7–2 show that after 1972 prices began to rise rapidly and reached their highest level in 1974. For the whole Western world, consumer prices in 1974 were on the average more than twice what they had been in 1971 and 1972. There were large price increases but at different rates in the United States, the United Kingdom, France, Italy, and Japan. Both planned and unplanned Western capitalist countries have had the same experience with the recent serious inflation, as is shown by the experience of both planned France and Japan and unplanned United Kingdom and Italy. Differentiation in types of economic systems in the Western countries has presented no barrier to the inroads of strong inflationary developments coming from external sources. As has already been explained, West Germany was the only exception to the strong inflationary trends of the early 1970s. By early 1975, these trends began to subside in the Western nations, with the exception of the United Kingdom, where consumer prices reached levels in early 1975 that were higher than those of 1974.

Incomes Policy and National Priorities in Industrial Economies

All Western industrial nations have tried some kind of incomes policy. Their experiments have included the use of wage and price guidelines, wage and price pauses and freezes, prior notification by industrial enterprises and trade unions of proposed price and

Table 7-2
Changes in Consumer Prices in Selected Western Countries since 1971[1]

	1971	1972	1973	1974	1975
World	5.9	5.9	9.6	15.1	13.4
United States	4.3	3.3	6.2	11.0	9.1
France	5.5	5.9	7.3	13.6	11.7
West Germany	5.2	5.5	6.9	7.0	6.0
United Kingdom	9.4	7.1	9.1	15.9	24.2
Italy	4.8	5.7	10.8	19.1	16.9
Japan	6.3	4.8	11.8	22.7	12.1

[1] Includes Japan.

Source: International Monetary Fund, *International Financial Statistics*, July 1976.

wage increases, and government requests for wage and price restraint. But no industrial nation has as yet developed a satisfactory incomes policy. In some countries like the Netherlands, Norway, and Sweden, where organized labor is strong and in the habit of cooperating with the employers and the government, and collective bargaining is highly centralized, an incomes policy has helped to delay wage and price increases, but has not in the long-run prevented wage and price inflation. Where a nation's domestic price level does not rise more rapidly than the price levels of its international competitors, no strong pressure is exerted to search for an effective incomes policy.

The need for an active government in the high-pressure economy extends far beyond the problems of curbing inflation, preventing an external disequilibrium, and developing an incomes policy. The government is called upon as an active agent to enlarge the social security program, to act as the employer of last resort, to remove regional inequalities and stimulate regional development, and to give expression to national priorities. The high-pressure capitalist economy is characterized by an increase in the scope of collective action as economic interest groups organize to defend their interests. The advanced industrial economies have their confederations of industry, trade associations, confederations of employers and of trade unions, separate blue-collar and white-collar unions, farmers' organizations, and consumers' organizations. Organized labor is exhibiting a new militancy as it seeks a place in the councils of private industry. Likewise, the new consumerism is going beyond the market place to inquire into the social costs of economic growth and their impact on the quality of life. Regional groups are demanding a larger share of the national prosperity. In this situation, the governments of the Western industrial countries must respond to the sometimes conflicting demands of many pressure groups. Their response raises the overall questions of what the national priorities should be, and how the various economic and social groups should contribute to the setting of these priorities. The need then arises for the government to provide appropriate national economic and social guidance.

Governments in the Western industrial countries have coped with this need in a variety of ways. Some, like the United States,

Canada, and the United Kingdom, have been hesitant about enlarging the role that government plays in national guidance. Nevertheless, in spite of their opposition to increased intervention, they have found it necessary to adopt wage and price freezes, to establish wage and price guidelines, to manipulate floating exchange rates, and to impose export controls. Other countries, like West Germany, Italy, Denmark, and Finland, have been more likely to expand the government's interventionist role and to foster the cooperation of private economic and social interests with the government in the setting of national priorities. Still other countries, such as the Netherlands, France, Belgium, and Japan, have turned to democratic indicative national planning as the best way to provide national economic and social guidance. In all such countries, from the somewhat unstructured welfare capitalism of the 1930s and 1940s has evolved the more structured and directed capitalism of the 1960s and 1970s.

The Performance of the Western Capitalist Economies

The three decades since the end of the Second World War were up to 1973 a period of considerable growth and prosperity for the Western capitalist economies. In the noncommunist world, overall real Gross National Product in the period of 1960-1970 increased at an average annual rate of 5 percent.[1] The rate of growth for the developed industrial countries of Western Europe, the United States, Canada, and Japan during this decade was 4.8 percent, while for the less developed countries it was 5.7 percent. The latter countries were growing faster than the developed industrial countries in terms of total national output, but since population was growing faster in the less developed countries, per capita GNP increased much more slowly than in the developed industrial countries. During 1960-1970, per capita output increased at an average annual rate of 3.9 percent in the Western developed countries and only 2.8 percent in the less developed Third World countries.[2]

Although the Western developed nations in general shared the economic growth of the postwar decades, they varied considerably in the extent to which they participated in the postwar expansion. As the statistics in Table 7-3 show, during the 1960s most Western developed countries had economic growth rates between 4 and 6 percent. Japan had the highest growth rate (11.1 percent), and the United Kingdom the lowest (2.8 percent). Unlike the less developed countries, whose economic expansion was on the whole fairly stable, the developed industrial countries were subject to considerable economic fluctuation. In the years 1968-1972, the average annual increase in the real Gross National Product of the Western industrial countries varied from the high rate of 5.7 percent in 1968 to the low rate of 2.5 percent in 1972. These annual variations in growth were recorded for the United States, Canada, West Germany, Italy, the United Kingdom, France, and Japan. Among these nations, the only one to have an actual annual decline in real total national output during 1968-1972 was the United States, which had no economic growth in 1970. The country with the smallest deviation between its highest and lowest annual growth rates was France.

[1] International Monetary Fund, *Annual Report*, Washington, D.C., 1973.

[2] Council on International Economic Policy, *The United States in the Changing World Economy*, Volume II, Background Material, Washington, D.C.: U.S. Government Printing Office, 1971, Chart 59.

Table 7-3
Growth of World Output, 1960–1972 (Percentage Changes in Real GNP)

	Annual average			Changes from preceding year				
	1960–1970	1960–1965	1965–1970	1968	1969	1970	1971	1972
Industrial countries	4.8	5.2	4.5	5.7	4.8	2.5	3.5	5.5
United States	4.0	4.8	3.2	4.7	2.7	−0.4	3.2	6.1
France	5.8	5.8	5.8	5.0	7.7	5.9	5.0	5.7
West Germany	4.8	5.0	4.6	7.3	8.2	5.8	2.7	2.9
Italy	5.7	5.3	6.1	6.4	5.7	4.9	1.6	3.2
United Kingdom	2.8	3.4	2.2	3.3	2.2	2.4	1.6	2.2
Japan	11.1	10.1	12.1	14.2	12.1	10.3	6.2	9.2
Canada	5.2	5.6	4.8	5.9	5.3	2.6	5.8	5.8
Other countries	4.8	5.0	4.6	4.7	6.3	5.2	3.2	3.9
Primary producing countries	5.7	5.6	5.8	5.9	7.0	6.4	5.6	5.9
More developed countries	6.4	7.1	5.6	5.1	7.2	5.7	5.2	5.4
Less developed countries	5.5	5.1	5.8	6.2	6.9	6.6	5.7	6.1
World[1]	5.0	5.3	4.7	5.7	5.4	3.5	3.9	5.6

[1] International Monetary Fund member countries plus Switzerland.

Source: IMF, *Annual Report,* 1973.

After 1972, the real economic growth pattern of the 1960s in the Western capitalist countries was altered by the worldwide recession of 1974–1975. Table 7-4 shows the growth pattern of seven major capitalist countries for the years 1974–1976. Most of these countries, which had economic growth rates above 5 percent in 1973 and above 4 percent in the 1960s, had a low or negative growth rate in 1974 or 1975. Japan, with a growth rate of 10.9 percent in the 1960s, had a negative rate of 1.8 percent in 1974. The United States, the United Kingdom, West Germany, and Italy suffered large declines in their growth rates during the recession years. Since most of the industrialized capitalist countries have strong economies, their return to a more normal growth pattern in the second half of the 1970s decade can be anticipated if no further major shock to the international economic system occurs.

A comparison of the performances of the Western industrial nations (including Japan) of the free world and the communist nations of Eastern Europe reveals a wide gap between these two groups. Table 7-5 indicates that per capita output in the Western capitalist countries in 1972 ranged from a high of $5,590 for the United States to a low of $1,960 for Italy. In the Eastern communist countries per capita output ranged from a high of $2,180 for Czechoslovakia to a low of $530 for Albania.

Table 7-4

Growth of Real GNP in Seven Major Capitalist Countries, 1974-1976

	Average 1959-1960 to 1972-1973	From previous year		
		1974	1975	1976[1]
Canada	5.1	2.8	−1	4¼
United States	4.2	−2.1	−3	5¾
Japan	10.9	−1.8	1¼	4¼
France	5.9	3.9	−2	3
Germany	4.9	0.4	−3¾	3¼
Italy	5.6	3.2	−4½	1½
United Kingdom	3.3	0.1	−2¼	0
Total of above countries	5.5	−0.6	−2¼	4¼
Total OECD countries	5.5	−0.1	−2	4

[1] OECD estimates.

Source: OECD, *Economic Outlook*, 18, Dec. 1975, p. 13.

Among these communist countries, only East Germany and Czechoslovakia compared favorably with the bottom two of the nine Western industrialized nations.

When the performance of the Western industrial countries is measured in terms of per capita Gross National Product as a percentage of the United States per capita product, considerable variation also appears. The statistics in Table 7-6 show the changes in per capita output in selected industrial countries as a percentage of the United States per capita output. In the decade 1960-1970, in all these countries except the United Kingdom, per capita output increased faster than the American per capita output; and the gap between these countries and the United States was reduced. The improvement in the position of Japan was particularly impressive, the Japanese percentage of the American per capita output rising from 16 in 1960 to 39 in 1970. By 1970, the top three nations in per capita output rank were the United States, Sweden, and Canada. Since the comparisons up to 1970 were made on the basis of fixed exchange rates, they reflected the overvaluation of the United States dollar.

The fourth column in Table 7-6 shows the per capita GNP comparisons when the floating exchange rates of June 28, 1973, are used as the basis of these comparisons. According to this calculation, by mid-1973 both Sweden (108 percent) and Germany (102 percent) exceeded the United States level of per capita output. The June 1973 comparison takes account of the fact that the overvaluation of the United States dollar was eliminated after 1971 by the adoption of floating exchange rates, which are a better measure of the relative purchasing powers of the various national currencies. It is possible that the United States dollar is currently undervalued, in which case the 1973 comparisons in Table 7-6 may have overcorrected for the earlier overvaluation. Nevertheless, the trends in the development of the major Western European industrial nations seem to indicate that in the near future a number of the industrial countries such as the United States, Canada, Sweden, West Germany, and France—and in the not too distant

Table 7-5
Per Capita GNP in Nine Western Capitalist Countries and Nine Eastern Communist Countries, 1972

	1972 GNP per capita (U.S. $)	GNP per capita average growth rate (1960–1972)		1972 GNP per capita (U.S. $)	GNP per capita average growth rate (1960–1972)
Western Countries[1]			*Eastern Countries*		
United States	5,590	3.0	Czechoslovakia	2,180	3.4
Sweden	4,480	3.2	East Germany	2,100	3.4
Canada	4,440	3.6	Soviet Union	1,530	6.4
France	3,620	4.7	Hungary	1,520	3.9
West Germany	3,390	3.7	Poland	1,500	3.7
Netherlands	2,840	4.1	Bulgaria	1,420	5.9
United Kingdom	2,600	2.3	Romania	810	7.7
Japan	2,320	9.4	Yugoslavia	810	4.8
Italy	1,960	4.4	Albania	530	4.6

[1] Includes Japan.

Source: The World Bank, *World Bank Atlas*, 1974.

future Japan—may be clustered around the United States level of per capita total national output.

This does not mean, however, that the standards of living in all the advanced industrial nations will be the same. A nation's institutional background and national priorities have much to do with the uses of its GNP and how these uses affect its standard of living. Some countries assign a significant part of

Table 7-6
Per Capita GNP in Selected Industrial Countries as a Percentage of U.S. Per Capita GNP, 1960–1973

	1960	1965	1970	1973[1]
United States	100%	100%	100%	100%
Sweden	69	74	79	108
West Germany	48	55	63	102
Canada	66	67	73	85
France	47	57	60	84
United Kingdom	49	51	45	62
Japan	16	25	39	51

[1] As of June 28, 1973.

Source: *Washington Post*, July 2, 1973. For different calculations see *World Bank Atlas*, 1975, p. 7.

their total national output to military and space exploration expenditures, while other countries do little in these areas. In 1970, the military burden, measured as the percent of GNP taken up by military expenditures, was 10 percent in the Soviet Union, 8 percent in the United States, and 4.8 percent in the United Kingdom, but only 2.7 percent in Italy and 0.8 percent in Japan.[3] Americans consider leisure an important item in the standard of living, but the Japanese put much less value on it. In the United States, the five-day week has been the standard work week since 1945, but in Japan the five-and-a-half-day work week prevails. Comparative GNP statistics do not take account of this difference, since leisure does not show up in the national economic accounts. Where a nation assigns a large portion of its GNP to investment, as in Japan and Norway, in order to achieve a high growth rate, its personal consumption level and standard of living will be lower than with less investment; in the long run, however, the continued high investment will make a high standard of living possible in the future.

Apart from differences in the levels of personal consumption among the world's major industrial countries, there will always be differences in the ways in which these countries choose to spend their incomes. Americans place a much higher value on education than do many other countries. The proportion of young people pursuing higher education is almost four times as large in the United States as in West Germany. All the industrial countries of Western Europe spend much more on social welfare than does the United States. In West Germany, France, Italy, and Sweden, social security expenditures absorb from 15 to almost 18 percent of GNP, whereas in the United States these expenditures take up only close to 5 percent.[4]

Long-Term Trends in the Western Capitalist Economies

As economic historians have pointed out, the competitive capitalism of the first three-quarters of the nineteenth century was followed by the large-scale capitalism of the period 1875–1929. This phase in the evolution of the capitalist system was followed by the welfare capitalism of the 1930s and 1940s and the rise of the welfare state. Since the close of the Second World War, the knowledge explosion and the technological revolution have quickened the pace of institutional, attitudinal, and value changes. The computer, automation, the television set, thermonuclear energy, and rapid transport have altered the lives of individuals throughout the world, and have made a significant impact on all types of economic systems. The postwar knowledge explosion and technological revolution have had a special importance for the Western capitalist countries, because their scientific research and technological development have been largely responsible for the rise of the computerized society. At the same time, this scientific and technological advance has raised issues relating to national priorities, the quality of life, worker participation in business affairs, the social responsibility of industrial enterprises, and environmental protection; these matters receive much less attention in the communist world and the Third World of the less developed countries.

The issues of zero economic growth and zero population growth have attracted little attention outside the Western capitalist nations. Not surprisingly, the less developed

---

[3] Bureau of Economic Affairs, U.S. Arms Control and Disarmament Agency, *World Military Expenditures, 1971*, Washington, D.C., 1972, pp. 26–27.

[4] International Labour Office, *The Cost of Social Security, 1964–1966*. Geneva, 1966.

countries of the world show little interest in coming to terms with the growth race, when they suffer from very low levels of per capita output and consume a small part of the world's economic resources. The mature and rich capitalist nations are concerned about zero economic and population growth for two reasons. First, they have come to question the values of the affluent society that make a virtue of continued economic growth and the forty-hour work week, without considering such issues as equity, the exhaustion of resources and the quality of life. Secondly, these nations have become alarmed at the specter of a world in which many poor nations aspire to the high standards of living of the few rich Western nations; in such a world, if the poor nations succeed, they will add to the drain on the finite supply of natural resources and greatly worsen pollution. It is not surprising that the Club of Rome's report on *The Limits To Growth* was prepared by a research team in the United States and not by a team in the Soviet Union, India, or the People's Republic of China. These nations have little time and few resources to devote to the problem of zero economic growth in a world of finite natural resources.

Western industrial nations are becoming increasingly "future-oriented."[5] Instead of dealing with economic and social problems by reacting to them, they are shifting to the stage of anticipating them. The knowledge explosion and the technological revolution of the past three decades have provided the new tools and techniques that are needed to assess the future. Computerized information systems, computerized modeling of complex economic and social systems, systems analysis, "futures" research, and economic and social indicators are now employed in Western capitalist nations to analyze complex problems and to provide a basis for private and public, economic and social decision making. In a general way, the Western industrial nations have since 1945 entered a *plan age*—an age of technological, economic, and social assessment—in which they have become increasingly aware of the impacts of economic and social change and the need to assess the consequences of this change. They have come to understand the importance of anticipating technological and other changes and of planning ahead in order to direct the course of these changes so that they may contribute to an enlargement of social well-being.

The Unfinished Business of the Capitalist Economies

The anticipatory way of dealing with technological, economic, and social problems in the Western industrial nations is of such recent origin that only a beginning has been made in applying this new approach to the major problems of these nations. As illustrations of the unfinished business confronting the Western capitalist nations, we may turn to the problems of continued population and economic growth, industrial democracy, multinational corporations, and national priorities. The United States Commission on Population Growth and the American Future has emphasized the importance of the population problem by observing that the time has now come for each industrialized country to ask what should be its optimum population level.[6] The commission concluded in its 1971

---

[5] As the National Commission on Technology, Automation, and Economic Progress has explained, "Ours, like most modern societies, is becoming 'future-oriented.' We have become increasingly aware of the multiple impacts of social change.... We have to anticipate social change." *Technology and the American Economy,* Vol. 1, Feb. 1966, p. 105.

[6] Commission on Population Growth and the American Future, *Population Growth and America's*

report to the president that the United States can no longer afford the uncritical acceptance of the population growth ethic that "more is better." At some point in the future, the finite earth will not be able to accommodate more human beings satisfactorily. The problem is to achieve a balance between the size, growth, and distribution of the population and the quality of life desired by the nation. The commission asserted that no substantial benefits would result from the continued growth of the nation's population. It recommended that the United States and other industrial nations should seek to achieve a stabilized population by limiting families to two children on the average. For the United States, this would mean that its total population by the year 2000 would be about 270 million. It also urged the establishment of a Council of Social Affairs to monitor the growth of population and its impact on the quality of life.

Closely associated with the population-growth ethic is the economic-growth ethic, which asserts that more output is always good, and economic growth is a good index of progress. According to many critics of Western industrial nations, both ethics should be abandoned. Continued population and economic growth lead to increasing demands for scarce natural resources. At present, the United States imports 15 percent of its raw material and fuel requirements. Long-run projections made before the 1973–1974 energy crisis, indicated that by the year 2000 the United States would probably have to import from 30 to 50 percent of its mineral requirements and a greatly increased proportion of its oil. Even with raw material recycling and resource conservation, it is quite probable that the United States will make very large demands on the world's scarce resources by the year 2000.

Future, An Interim Report to the President and the Congress, Washington, D.C.: U.S. Government Printing Office, 1971, p. 1.

Since other nations by that time will want to import more raw materials, more costly sources of these materials will have to be exploited. A continuation of present growth trends in world population, industrialization, pollution, food production, and resource depletion will, in the opinion of the authors of *The Limits to Growth,* within the next one hundred years bring an end to growth on this planet and a sudden and uncontrollable decline in both population and industrial capacity.[7] The authors of *The Limits to Growth* call upon the mature industrial nations to abandon the growth ethic, and to establish a global equilibrium state in which both population and industrial production would be stabilized at some agreed-upon levels.

No Western capitalist nation is now prepared to adopt programs for zero population and economic growth. Some of the critics of the conclusions reached in *The Limits to Growth* argue that the authors of this study are too pessimistic about the consequences of exponential growth, that their predictive model of the world system is excessively mechanical, and that it pays inadequate attention to social factors.[8] Criticisms of the Malthusian and technocratic aspects of the predictive world model of the authors of *The Limits to Growth* are not intended to downgrade the importance of the problems of resource scarcities and environmental deterioration that would accompany the continued growth of

---

[7] Donella H. Meadows and others, *The Limits to Growth, A Report for the Club of Rome's Project on the Predicament of Mankind,* New York: New American Library, 1972, p. 29. For a similar view, see *The Ecologist,* "Blueprint for Survival," Vol. 3 Jan. 1972, pp. 2–5, in which the argument is presented that the industrial way of life is not sustainable. This argument is criticized as an overstatement in *Nature,* "The Case Against Hysteria," Vol. 235, Jan. 14, 1972, pp. 63–65.

[8] Criticisms of the conclusions of *The Limits to Growth* are presented in H. S. D. Cole and others, *Models of Doom, A Critique of the Limits of Growth,* New York: Universe Books, 1973.

the advanced industrial nations and the efforts of the less developed countries to reduce the gap between them and the rich nations. These are very serious problems whose consequences should be assessed and made the subject of advanced planning. Both business and organized labor in the industrial nations, however, are opposed to the adoption of a program for zero economic growth. Business asserts that such a program would depress economic activity and lead to both business and scientific stagnation. Organized labor fears such a program on the ground that it would result in large-scale unemployment. The proponents of zero economic growth assert that these problems could be avoided by joint national planning for a stable equilibrium society with zero economic and population growth.[9]

Industrial Democracy in the Western Industrial Countries

Since 1945, a strong movement has arisen in West Germany, France, the Netherlands, and the Scandinavian countries to establish *industrial* or *economic democracy*.[10] This movement seeks to enlarge the role of the workers in the decision-making processes of the companies in which they work. A number of factors have contributed to the emergence of this movement. In spite of the very considerable rise in their standard of living since 1945, workers have become alienated from the private enterprise system. This is especially true of the young workers who have been influenced by the demands of the youth movement which has flourished since the early 1950s. As private companies have merged, become larger, and in some cases turned multinational, workers have felt increasingly powerless in a world of big business and big government. They have resented the computerized assembly line, the dullness of large-scale production, and the lack of a voice in deciding how much overtime shall be worked, who should be dismissed because of worker redundancy, how supervisors shall be selected, where plants shall be relocated, and which plants shall be closed. When the future of a plant is determined by the board of directors of a multinational corporation with its headquarters in some other country, workers are increasingly disturbed by their exclusion from the decision-making process. As the workers' educational levels have risen in recent decades, they feel better prepared to understand the issues and to participate in business comanagement.

In recent years, a number of countries in Western Europe have adopted or are in the process of adopting the German system of codetermination. Since 1971, the Netherlands has required all firms employing more than one hundred workers and with capital and reserves of at least 10 million guilders (approximately $4 million) to appoint workers to

---

[9] The authors of *The Limits to Growth* point to the need for "concerned international measures and joint long-term planning . . . to reach a rational and enduring state of equilibrium" (pp. 197–198). Similar views are spreading throughout the EEC, where the dedication to continued high economic growth is beginning to be questioned on the ground that it leads to a decline in the quality of life. Sicco L. Mansholt, President of the European Communities Commission has deplored the overemphasis in the EEC on Gross National Product and has suggested that more attention be given to "gross national welfare." Raymond Barre, the Vice President of the European Communities Commission, has explained that society's well-being is too subjective to be measured by GNP.

[10] A review of this movement is presented in John Robinson, "Giving the Workers a Say in Running the Firm," *European Community*, March, 1973; and Thomas Barry-Braunthal, "Labor vs. Management in Europe," *European Community*, No. 156,

May 1972, pp. 14–16. For recent developments in Sweden, see "When Workers Become Directors," *Business Week*, No. 2297, Sept. 15, 1973, pp. 188–196.

their supervisory boards. The workers, however, comprise less than one-third of the board members. In 1972, legislation was enacted in Sweden to require all companies with at least one hundred employees to have two employees on their boards of directors. Because Sweden, unlike West Germany, does not have the two-tier supervisory and management board system, the worker-directors will be directly involved in the managerial decision-making process. This is not a new experience for Sweden, as a number of companies in the automobile, shipbuilding, wood products, and industrial equipment industries had voluntarily appointed worker representatives to their boards of directors before 1972. The Swedish industrial associations, while supporting the legislation requiring codetermination, would have preferred to keep it on a voluntary basis. The trade unions in Sweden look forward to enlarging worker-director participation to include independent worker company audits, negotiation in the choice of supervisors, and a voice in determining who shall be laid off.

The Swedish experiment with codetermination, which is to last three years, is being closely watched by organized labor and business leaders in Britain, Norway, and Denmark, because the Swedish program, if successful, could very well spread to these and other countries. Unlike German codetermination, which was established in the face of a weak trade union movement, Swedish codetermination is supported by one of the world's strongest and most aggressive trade union movements. Traditionally, in countries where trade unions are strong and well organized, they have not been much interested in worker-director participation. In Italy and France, many of the unionists have actively opposed the introduction of this kind of participation. With the growing dissatisfaction and alienation of many workers in the industrial society of today, both private business and organized labor have felt a need to find some way of reducing worker dissatisfaction. For this reason, in all major Western capitalist nations, steps are being taken to improve working conditions and to enlarge the role of labor in the private economic decision-making process. Before 1939, worker participation and industrial democracy were primarily the concern of the socialists. Since 1945, private business and nonsocialist trade unions have increasingly accepted worker participation and other forms of industrial democracy, but within a private-enterprise, capitalist framework.

In addition to codetermination, experiments are being conducted in Sweden, the United Kingdom, the United States, and other countries to humanize the computerized production assembly line. These experiments include introducing team work on the assumbly line, rotating workers in different jobs on and off the assembly line, enlarging the scope of the works councils to include personnel problems, and in other ways enabling workers to feel responsible in part for important decisions that affect their welfare.

The issue of codetermination has recently assumed new significance because of the plan to make provision for European companies (Eurocompanies) which would operate across national boundaries in the European Economic Community.[11] The draft articles of association of these Eurocompanies, published by the commission in 1970, provide for a uniform system of workers' representation and two-tier supervisory and management boards of directors in Eurocompanies with over five hundred workers. Worker-director representation would not exceed one-third of the membership of the supervisory board.

These proposals for worker-participation in

[11] For a discussion of the problems associated with the Eurocompany idea, see Brian Childs, "Workers, Bosses Clash on Eurocompany Plan," *European Community*, March 1973.

the proposed Eurocompanies have not been enthusiastically received by either employers or workers. The EEC employers' association has rejected all proposals involving worker participation in the Eurocompany structure. The communist trade unions in France and Italy reject the whole idea of the Eurocompany on the ground that it favors the formation of multinational enterprises. The moderate socialist and nonsocialist unions disapprove of the minority "watchdog" role proposed for workers' representatives on the supervisory board of the Eurocompany. They advocate instead a three-sided board structure, with one-third representing shareholders, one-third, workers, and one-third, the general public interest. The Confederation of British Industry and the British Trades Union Congress, while not approving the specific proposals for worker participation in the Eurocompany, accept the need for full consultation at all levels between the management and the workers. It is clear that unless some acceptable arrangements are made for joint management-labor consultation in the European Economic Community, there will be the danger of serious industrial strife.

While the need for more industrial democracy in the Western private enterprise economies is widely recognized today, achieving this goal at a satisfactory level will be very difficult. Employer opposition to anything more than token codetermination continues to be very strong. Many trade union leaders are not convinced that codetermination is desirable, since they believe that it may weaken the trade union movement. They insist that workers cannot be equally loyal to their companies and their unions. Those labor leaders who do support the worker-participation movement want more than a minority watchdog role for labor on the company board of directors. They want parity codetermination for labor and management; this is most unacceptable to the latter. Many labor leaders argue that the place to strengthen worker participation is at the shop or factory level in the works councils, where the workers may influence matters that involve them daily. After worker participation at this level is improved, it may then move upwards to the company board level. Up to the present, the experience with works councils in the United States, the United Kingdom, France, Italy, and Belgium has been generally unsuccessful. More success in this sphere has been achieved in West Germany and the Scandinavian countries. All the signs appear to indicate that the spread of industrial democracy in the Western private enterprise economies will at best be a slow and difficult development.

Western Industrial Nations and Multinational Corporations

Another problem that has arisen among the Western industrial nations in recent decades is the large transnational or multinational corporation (MNC).[12] The MNC is not a new development, for the location of subsidiaries in other countries goes back at least one hundred years. But since 1945, changes in technology and marketing have fostered the growth of these international corporations on a large scale in the high-technology industries, such as the petroleum, automobile, electrical, chemical, and machinery industries. Since these are the industries that require

---

[12] The term *multinational corporation* is used in a broad sense to cover all enterprises which control assets such as factories, mines, and sales and other offices in two or more countries. For a comprehensive survey of the problem of multinational corporations, see United Nations, Department of Economic and Social Affairs, *Multinational Corporations in World Development*, New York, 1973. See also Raymond Vernon, *Sovereignty at Bay; The Multinational Spread of U.S. Enterprises*, New York: Basic Books, 1971; and Frederic G. Donner, *The World-Wide Industrial Enterprise; Its Challenge and Promise*, New York: McGraw-Hill, 1967.

large outlays on capital equipment to exploit new industrial techniques and to acquire large markets, the major MNCs are large-scale industrial enterprises.

Up to the early 1970s, the expansion of the multinational companies was dominated by American business enterprise. In 1972, the world's MNCs had gross sales of $350 billion, which accounted for 10 percent of the world's production of goods and services. Sixty percent of the output of MNCs was provided by American MNCs. Since 1950, foreign investment abroad by United States MNCs has increased from $12 to $90 billion. In 1970, of the thirty-two largest American and European MNCs in the petroleum, automobile, electrical, and chemical industries, sixteen were American, six German, five British, three Italian, one French, and one Dutch. The pacesetters of the multinational corporate business are the United States giants, such as General Motors, Ford, Standard Oil, General Electric, International Business Machines, DuPont, and Union Carbide. One may expect that the trend towards multinational business enterprise will accelerate in the next few decades, with Western European countries and Japan competing more actively with the United States. The Western European countries will probably import fewer foreign workers and will export industrial capital to Spain, North Africa, and other less developed areas, as Japan does in Malaysia, Taiwan, and the Philippines.

The rapid spread of the MNCs throughout the world since 1945 has created many problems in the host countries—both developed and developing. Since the large multinational corporation is a global enterprise, it adopts a global rather than a national strategy in its operations. In pursuing its global strategy, the MNC transfers assets and funds from one country to another, bargains with different countries over various concessions, manipulates profits through the use of transfer prices, and takes advantage of lenient tax laws wherever they are found. At times, this corporate global strategy may be contrary to the host country's national strategy. The host country's efforts to achieve full employment or a balance-of-payments equilibrium may be made difficult by the closing of branch plants, a reduction in the MNC's investment program, or by the transfer of its funds ("hot money") to other countries in order to avoid foreign exchange losses or to make foreign exchange profits. Organized labor in the host country finds it difficult to bargain with a large MNC that can close plants and shift production to other countries. In countries with planned economies, such as France, the Netherlands, and Sweden, foreign MNCs are not encouraged unless they are prepared to operate in conformity with the medium-term national plans. In countries like the United Kingdom, where there is no medium-term national planning, foreign MNCs have found entry less difficult than in the planned Continental countries.

The MNCs contribute to the expansion of world trade by transferring technological know-how and industrial capital from the developed to the less developed countries. No nation has a monopoly on scientific and technological advance, and all countries, including the United States, in which Western European MNCs have considerable investment, stand to gain from the free movement of industrial technology and investment. Since no international law governs the behavior of the MNCs, a strong movement has developed in the host countries to eliminate the unacceptable practices of the MNCs and make them more socially responsible. The European Economic Community is developing a code of behavior for the MNCs that operate among the nine EEC members. Proposals have been made for establishing an International Trade Organization under United Nations auspices to register MNCs and to enforce a broad international code of conduct with respect to them. This organization could monitor the operations of MNCs to prevent transfer pricing, tax evasion, market sharing, and other monopolistic practices.[13]

The economic and political power of the large MNCs has been challenged not only by the host countries but also by organized labor in these countries. On February 9, 1973, the socialist-oriented trade unions, representing 28 million workers from fourteen European countries, created the European Confederation of Syndicates. This confederation regards itself as an international counterforce of free and democratic trade unions against the expanding worldwide concentration of industrial enterprise and its influence on European economic integration. The European trade unions are prepared to coordinate their responses to the MNCs in Europe and to work out joint programs for worker participation, manpower planning, and social security. Individual trade unions, such as the automobile and chemical workers' unions, have organized on an international level to deal with MNCs in the automobile and chemical industries. Strong unions in the home countries are now prepared to give aid to weak unions in host countries. In some cases, trade unions have set up international committees to deal with specific firms, such as Ford, General Motors, General Electric, and Westinghouse. These developments in unionism all point in the direction of an expansion of international collective bargaining.[14]

National Priorities and Directed Capitalism

The economic and social developments in Western Europe and the United States since 1945 clearly indicate that the Western capitalist economies are undergoing a significant transformation. The basic problem as it is now seen in these economies is to combine the market economics of the private sector and the nonmarket economics of the public sector. What is rational from the viewpoint of the individual producer or consumer in the private sector may not always appear so in the eyes of those who make decisions in the interest of the entire nation. Private economic decisions that result in environmental deterioration or the waste of finite economic resources may seem rational to the private decision-maker, but such behavior may be judged irrational from the social point of view. Less than maximum efficiency by individual government departments that fail to take account of the whole range of national needs and overemphasize the importance or value of individual government programs—such as defense, highway construction, or space exploration to the neglect of education, health, and resource conservation—may likewise be judged irrational from the social point of view.

Under the stimulus of critics such as John K. Galbraith, Ezra J. Mishan, and Barry Commoner, the need for a social rationality is becoming understood in the United States; this rationality transcends both the private and public sectors, and applies to the areas of both market and nonmarket economics. Evidence of the search for this higher social rationality is found in the recent criticisms of Gross National Product as a measure of social well-being.[15] These criticisms appear to lead to the

[13] For an analysis of the problem of how to domesticate the MNCs, see *Multinational Corporations in World Development*, Chapter IV, "Towards a Programme of Action," pp. 75–103.

[14] Commission of the European Communities, *Multinational Corporations: Problems Confronting Europe*, European Studies, 16, 1973, pp. 3–4.

[15] See for example, Arthur M. Okun, "Should GNP Measure Social Welfare?," *The Brookings Bulletin*, Vol. 8, No. 3, Summer, 1971, pp. 4–7; and William Nordhaus and James Tobin, "Is Growth Obsolete?," in *Fiftieth Anniversary Colloquium* V, National Bureau of Economic Research, Columbia University Press, New York, 1972. Nordhaus and Tobin propose adjustments to GNP so that it would include the services of consumer capital, leisure, and the product of household work. A correction would be made for some of the disamenities of urbanization. GNP would then be a more meaning-

conclusion that there can be no adequate quantitative full measure of social well-being. Nevertheless, the quantitative and qualitative aspects of social well-being can be combined in a judgmental way, as is done in all democratic countries when parliaments approve of national goals and priorities. The Western free enterprise nations are experimenting with different ways of making socially rational decisions about national priorities.

In the United States, the Congress is considering fiscal budget reform that would create multiyear fiscal budgets. These three- or five-year budgets would enable the Congress to take an overall view of all federal government spending and revenue collecting so as to reconcile all national needs. The recent establishment of the Environmental Protection Agency and the Office of Technology Assessment contributes to a more socially rational approach to environmental problems. The current interest in developing social indicators, in establishing a Council of Social Advisers, and in creating a Department of Consumer Affairs points in the same direction. The subcommittee on Urban Affairs of the Joint Economic Committee has recommended the creation of a National Resources Planning Commission with representatives of all major economic interest groups. This Commission would prepare ten-year plans for the development of physical and human resources in cooperation with the Council of Economic Advisers, which would construct ten-year full-employment projections of the economy.[16]

Other nations, such as the United Kingdom, Norway, and France, have created Departments of Consumer Affairs or Environmental Protection. The United Kingdom, West Germany, and France have adopted multiyear fiscal budgets which provide a better view of the impact of these budgets on the nation's goals and priorities. The coordination of the accumulated interventions of the past three or four decades is becoming an accepted strategy for national economic guidance. As has already been explained, this coordination of public and private economic policies does not follow the same format in all the Western industrial nations. In all cases, however, there exists the same fundamental aim of securing a more effective guidance of the nation's economy. The problems associated with improving this guidance revolve around the setting and achieving of national economic and social priorities. These problems raise such questions as the nation's power structure and its impact on national guidance, the social responsibility of private corporate enterprise, incomes policy and the distribution of national income, and the control of both population and economic growth. These problems are related more to the distribution and use of national output than to its increase. The directed capitalist economies in the next half century will be faced with the challenge of doing as good a job in controlling, distributing, and using their total output as they did in enlarging this output in the past century.

The directed capitalism of the last quarter of the current century will be more collective than the earlier welfare capitalism, because it will be under pressure to bring additonal interest groups into the nation's economic decision-making process. The new consumerism is pressing for more consumer representation on the boards of directors of the large financial and industrial enterprises and on governmental regulatory bodies. Organized labor is asking for a larger role in corporate decisions relating to personnel, manpower, industrial

---

ful Measure of Economic Welfare (MEW). Elementary economics textbooks now go beyond GNP to Net Economic Welfare (NEW). See Paul A. Samuelson, *Economics*, Ninth Edition, New York: McGraw-Hill, 1973, pp. 195–196.

[16] Report of the Subcommittee on Urban Affairs of the Joint Economic Committee, *Restoration of Effective Sovereignty to Solve Social Problems*, Dec. 6, 1971, pp. 9–11.

relocation, and the introduction of new machinery. In Great Britain, the Trades Union Congress wants to place representatives on the managerial boards of all nationalized industries. It is now widely accepted that incomes policies will not be successful until collective bargaining is more centralized and more cooperation goes on among business, labor, and the government. Furthermore, not much progress can be made in improving national economic and social guidance until all economic and social interest groups are in a position to contribute to this guidance. This is clearly the lesson to be learned from the experiences of France, the United Kingdom, the Netherlands, and the Scandinavian countries in the area of national economic and social guidance. These various developments in Western Europe and the United States suggest that the directed capitalism of the future may very well become a more collective capitalism.

Selected Bibliography

BARNET, RICHARD J., and RONALD E. MÜLLER. *Global Reach, The Power of the Multinational Corporations.* Simon and Schuster, New York, 1975.

BARRY-BRAUNTHAL, THOMAS. "Labor vs. Management in Europe." *European Community,* 156 (May 1972), 14–16.

BUREAU OF ECONOMIC AFFAIRS, U.S. Arms Control and Disarmament Agency. *World Military Expenditures, 1971.* Washington, D.C., 1972.

BUSINESS WEEK. "When Workers Become Directors." 2297 (Sept. 17, 1973), 188–196.

CHILDS, BRIAN. "Workers, Bosses Clash on Eurocompany Plan." *European Community,* March 1973.

COMMISSION OF THE EUROPEAN COMMUNITIES. *Multinational Corporations: Problems Confronting Europe.* European Studies, 16, 1973, 3–4.

COMMISSION ON POPULATION GROWTH AND THE AMERICAN FUTURE. *Population Growth and America's Future, An Interim Report to the President and the Congress.* Washington, D.C., 1971.

COUNCIL ON INTERNATIONAL ECONOMIC POLICY. *The United States in the Changing World Economy, II,* Washington, D.C., 1971.

DONNER, FREDERIC G. *The World-Wide Industrial Enterprise: Its Challenge and Promise.* McGraw-Hill Book Company, New York, 1967.

INTERNATIONAL LABOUR OFFICE. *The Cost of Social Security, 1964–1966.* Geneva, 1966.

INTERNATIONAL MONETARY FUND. *Annual Report.* Washington, D.C., 1973.

MEADOWS, DONELLA H., and others. *The Limits to Growth, A Report for the Club of Rome's Project on the Predicament of Mankind.* New American Library, New York, 1972.

NATIONAL COMMISSION ON TECHNOLOGY, AUTOMATION, AND ECONOMIC PROGRESS. *Technology and the American Economy.* 1 (Feb. 1966), 105.

NATURE. "The Case Against Hysteria." 235 (Jan 14, 1972) 63–65.

NORDHAUS, WILLIAM, and JAMES TOBIN. "Is Growth Obsolete?" In *Fiftieth Anniversary Colloquium* V, National Bureau of Economic Research, Columbia University Press, New York, 1972.

OKUN, ARTHUR M. "Should GNP Measure Social Welfare?" *The Brookings Bulletin,* 8, No. 3 (Summer 1971), 4–7.

REPORT OF THE SUBCOMMITTEE ON URBAN AFFAIRS OF THE JOINT ECONOMIC COMMITTEE. *Restoration of Effective Sovereignty to Solve Social Problems.* Dec. 6, 1971.

ROBINSON, JOHN. "Giving the Workers a Say in Running the Firm." *European Community*, 163, March 1973.

SAMUELSON, PAUL A. *Economics*, 9th ed. McGraw-Hill Book Company, New York, 1973.

THE ECOLOGIST. "Blueprint for Survival." 3 (Jan. 1972), 2–5.

UNITED NATIONS, DEPARTMENT OF ECONOMIC AND SOCIAL AFFAIRS. *Multinational Corporations in World Development*. New York, 1973.

VERNON, RAYMOND. *Sovereignty at Bay: The Multinational Spread of U.S. Enterprises*. Basic Books, New York, 1971.

Part Three
The Democratic Socialist Economies

8
The Model of the Democratic Socialist Economy

9
The Norwegian Socialist Economy

10
The Swedish Socialist Economy

11
The British Socialist Economy

12
The Mature Democratic Socialist Economies: In Retrospect and Prospect

Chapter 8
The Model of the Democratic Socialist Economy

An important development in the field of comparative economic systems has been the emergence of the democratic socialist economy. During the 1930s, socialist governments were established in Norway and Sweden and, except for brief periods, have remained in office since then. Socialist governments have also been in power at various times since 1945 in the United Kingdom, Denmark, Holland, West Germany, and France. In both the United Kingdom and Denmark, the socialists are well entrenched in the political system, and all indications are that they will play major political roles in the future. In 1969, the socialist Social Democratic party under the leadership of Willy Brandt established a coalition government in West Germany. One may reasonably assume that the German Social Democratic party will become a still more important factor in German political life in the next half century. Among the less developed nations, India provides the outstanding example of a country that has adopted the democratic parliamentary socialism of Western Europe. In those Western European countries where the socialists have not in recent years taken over the reins of government, such as France, Italy, and Belgium, the socialist parties have been very active in an opposition role.

Socialism in Western Europe has passed through three stages in the past century.[1] After 1870, the socialism that appeared in the United Kingdom and on the Continent was largely Marxist. In June 1881, Henry M. Hyndman established the Democratic Federation (after 1884 called the Social Democratic Federation) in Great Britain with the aim of organizing a British socialist working-class movement along Marxist lines. Hyndman's

---

[1] For the development of socialism after 1870, see Harry W. Laidler, *A History of Socialist Thought*, New York: Thomas Y. Crowell, 1927; and G. D. H. Cole, *A History of Socialist Thought*, New York: St. Martin's Press, 1953.

platform called for the eventual full socialization of the British economic system along Marxist lines. On the Continent, in Germany, France, and the Scandinavian countries, the early Marxist socialist parties were more militant than in Great Britain, emphasizing the importance of class warfare and the elimination of the capitalist system.

After the first development of Marxist socialism in the 1870s and 1880s, the socialist movement became less militant and more prepared to move in a gradualistic, parliamentary direction. In the United Kingdom, the trade union movement supported the socialism of the Fabian Society, which was established in 1884. Much less militant and revolutionary in its proposals than the Social Democratic Federation, the Fabian Society recommended the adoption of socialism by "practical steps."[2] Private industry was to be nationalized only as rapidly as could be conveniently managed by society. Eventually, however, all land and industrial capital would be nationalized and the capitalist system would disappear. In the final decade of the nineteenth century and the early decades of the new century, the Fabian type of socialism became well established in England and later in the Scandinavian countries. Sympathy for Marxian socialism lingered on among the workers in the Scandinavian countries until the end of the depressed 1930s. After World War II, each Scandinavian socialist party ceased to be a class party *(klasseparti)* and became instead a people's party *(folkeparti)*, drawing support from the middle class as well as from workers, farmers, and fishermen.[3]

[2] Margaret Cole, *The Story of Fabian Socialism*, London: Heineman Educational Books, 1961, p. 5. The fundamentals of Fabian Socialism are presented in this volume.

[3] The goal of the Scandinavian socialists was still a socialist transformation of society but not in the Marxist sense of a "liberation of the exploited classes." The Swedish Social Democratic Labor Party, *The Programme of the Swedish Social Democratic Labor Party*, Stockholm, 1945, p. 3.

The third stage in the evolution of democratic socialism in Western Europe came after the Second World War. The Fabian or parliamentary socialism advocated before the Second World War was democratic full socialism. It recommended the nationalization of all important means of production, including the land, and the elimination of all incomes except wages. When the British, Norwegian, Danish, and Swedish socialist parties came to power after 1945, their goal was partial democratic socialism rather than full democratic socialism. They no longer called for the nationalization of the land and all means of production, the elimination of private profits, rents, and interest, and the immediate equalization of pay for men and women in the same work. Full Fabian socialism became so truncated in practice in England and the Scandinavian countries that it is best described as partial or limited democratic socialism. Socialism in West Germany has followed the same path. After shedding its Marxist traditions and coloration in the 1960s, what the Social Democrats of West Germany came to advocate is essentially the partial democratic socialism of Great Britain and the Scandinavian countries. In the third and current stage of its evolution, Western European socialism has become reformist rather than revolutionary. It is now designed to appeal to farmers, civil servants, and middle-class liberals as well as trade unionists. In the view of this reformist socialism, any transformation of the private enterprise society should be accomplished very slowly and only with the approval of a large mass of voters.

The Marxian Socialist Model

The Marxian socialist model that failed to win the allegiance of the major part of the working classes in Western Europe, as the standard of living of these classes improved after 1885, is derived from Karl Marx's economic and political theories and proposals. According to Marx's interpretation, the contradictions within the capitalist system would inevitably lead to its demise.[4] They would result in the further concentration of industry and the ownership of the means of production, the increasing severity of the business cycle, a declining rate of profit, a growing army of the unemployed, and the increasing misery of the masses. Eventually, the condition of the masses would become so intolerable that they would rise in revolt and overturn the capitalist system. Capitalism would be replaced by socialism as a transitional stage, eventually followed by the final stage, communism. Socialism as a transitional stage would preserve some of the features of the capitalist system, such as the private ownership of consumer goods and wage differentials based on productivity differentials. The communist society that would be finally established after an unspecified time would dispense with all forms of private property and with payments of wages according to productivity. The communist society would be an ideal society, without a political government, in which individuals would lead a communal existence, and would draw upon the community's income according to need and not according to ability to produce.

In his *Capital* and other works, Marx devoted most of his analysis to the deficiencies of the capitalist system.[5] He gave much less attention to socialism than to capitalism and much less attention to communism than to socialism. Since the communist society would be achieved only in the distant future, Marx's views on the eventual coming of communism had no operational significance. The socialist society, however, that preceded the communist society could, in the opinion of Marx and his ardent followers, lie just around the corner. For this reason, the Marxian model of the socialist society was operational, for it sought to guide those who would overthrow capitalism and establish socialism. In this model, the exploitative capitalist government would be replaced by a one-party dictatorship of the workers, which would direct the transition from capitalism to socialism and would negate all efforts to restore capitalism. After the overthrow of capitalism, the workers' state would take over the land, the factories, the mines, and all other means of production. Personal property in the form of consumer goods, however, would be preserved, as would the money and accounting systems. All private incomes except wages would be eliminated, and wages would be paid according to ability to produce. All forms of sexual and racial discrimination would be ended, and production would be for use and not for profit.

The socialist economy that Marx envisioned would be a planned economy. The production and distribution of goods and services would be planned by the economic division of the state, and production and distribution would be carried on by state enterprises. Workers would no longer be exploited, since they would receive as wages the surplus value that they created, less whatever was reserved for social saving. Although Marx did not inquire into many of the aspects of this transitional socialist society, he did give enough details to provide considerable guidance for the Marxists who overthrew capitalism in Russia, Central Europe, and Asia after World Wars I and II.

The Marxist socialist model has been variously interpreted by those who followed Marx. Lenin, Stalin, Khrushchev, Tito, and Mao Tse-tung have each in their turn made their interpretation of Marx's views on

---

[4] Marx-Engels-Lenin Institute, *Karl Marx, Selected Works*, Vol. I, Moscow: Co-operative Publishing Society, 1935, pp. 204–205.

[5] Karl Marx, *Capital: A Critique of Political Economy*, Chicago: Charles H. Kerr and Co., 1906; and Karl Marx and Friedrich Engels, *Manifesto of the Communist Party*, New York: International Publishers Co., 1937.

socialism. Stalin saw Marx as approving a highly centralized socialist state, whereas Khrushchev viewed Marx as favoring a more decentralized economy. Tito has found no contradiction between Marx's socialism and a market socialism that opens the door to considerable consumer sovereignty. Mao Tsetung considered the Soviet interpretation of Marx to be faulty on the ground that it postpones arriving at the communist society indefinitely. Mao would shorten Marx's socialist transition from capitalism to communism as it has been viewed by Stalin, Khrushchev, Kosygin, and Brezhnev, and would hasten the arrival of the communist society. While there are thus various interpretations of Marx's vision of the socialist society, all the interpretations in the communist world have common features which together constitute the Marxist socialist model. These features include a one-party political system, public ownership of the means of production including land, personal ownership of consumer goods, collectivized agriculture, the elimination of all private incomes except wages, the payment of wages according to ability to produce, and a planned economic system. While variations of this model exist in different parts of the communist world, all such variations are deviations from a basic Marxian model.

The Fabian Socialist Model

The Fabian model of the socialist society is the model that still influences much of socialist thinking in the Western democratic nations.[6] Although the socialist thought that today dominates the operations of socialist governments in Western Europe is in many ways far removed from the pure Fabian socialism of the 1890s and later, when present-day Western socialists think of the next stage in the evolution of their socialism they revert to the purer form of socialism as expressed by Fabianism. Unlike the Marxian socialists, the Fabian socialists did not accept Marx's view of the class struggle and did not advocate the revolutionary overturn of capitalism. Socialism was to be established gradually by the votes of the people; and the democratic political system with its variety of political parties was to be preserved. Political parties with occupational rather than geographical representation were preferred. In other respects, the Fabian socialist model was quite similar to the Marxian socialist model. The land and most of the means of production were to be nationalized without compensation. All unearned incomes in the form of profits, rent, and interest were to be eliminated, since the only source of income was to be labor. Each citizen was to be guaranteed a national minimum standard of living. What the individual secured above this minimum would be determined by his personal capabilities.

The nation's economic surplus above the consumption needs of the population would be used for the common good. This surplus would be employed to meet the investment needs for economic growth, to provide adequate social services, to meet the cultural and recreational needs of the people, and to provide for scientific and technological advance. The Fabian socialist model was based upon a planned economy, which would coordinate all the large nationalized and remaining small-scale private industries.

Since the Fabian socialists did not accept the Marxian theory of the development of capitalism with its inherent contradictions, they had to stress the need to work for the

[6] The Fabian Society was established in England in 1884 by a group of middle-class intellectuals with the aim of providing the British trade union movement with an alternative to Marxian socialism. The essentials of Fabian socialism were presented in *Fabian Tracts*, Nos. 1 to 126, published by the Fabian Society from 1884 to 1906. A number of Fabians also collaborated on *The Fabian Essays in Socialism*, Boston: Ball Publishing Co., 1908.

establishment of socialism. For this reason, they emphasized the importance of educating the working class for the tasks that lay ahead with the aid of lectures, instructional classes, pamphlets, and other published materials. The Fabians favored the setting up of farm cooperatives, the municipalizing of local industries, the taking over of local governments, and the infiltration of the Liberal party. The British Labour party, which was organized in 1906, incorporated the fundamentals of Fabian socialism in its constitution. While it did not advocate the immediate adoption of full Fabian socialism, the British Labour party before 1939 thought in terms of moving eventually to the Fabian view of a socialist society.

The Model of a Partial Democratic Socialist Society

When the British Labour party won the 1945 election with a landslide victory, it turned to the task of constructing a socialist society. It did not, however, view this job as one of inaugurating full democratic socialism. On the contrary, the approach of the first majority Labour government, as of the later Labour government of 1964–1970, was very limited and pragmatic. The Labour party political manifesto of 1945, *Let Us Face the Future*, on the basis of which the election was won, imposed a rigorous system of economic controls on an essentially private enterprise system.[7] Only key industries, such as coal, steel, transportation, power, gas, and communications, were nationalized, with compensation paid to their former private owners. All the remaining private industries were supervised in order to eliminate restrictive business practices and to fit these industries into the national plan. Neither urban nor farm land was nationalized, but any increase in the value of land was taken up by the state through taxation. Since the economic system was to be basically private, all forms of private incomes were preserved.

In two major spheres, the model of partial democratic socialism differs from the model of private capitalism: (1) national planning and (2) the enlargement of the system of economic controls. An overall national plan is drawn up with a number of subplans for industry, agriculture, manpower, foreign trade and other sectors. The annual and medium-term plans incorporate goals for the increase in the nation's Gross National Product and its distribution among private and public consumption and investment uses. The national plans are accompanied by an extensive system of economic controls, which include price, rent, building, credit, foreign exchange, and other controls. These controls are employed in order to achieve the priorities of the national plans.

While the model of partial democratic socialism that gives direction to British, Scandinavian, and Continental parliamentary socialism does not eliminate the private enterprise system, it does substantially alter the disposition of the nation's total output of goods and services. The model shifts much of the nation's economic surplus from the upper-income groups to the lower-income groups. This is accomplished through such devices as the heavy taxation of large income receivers and wealth owners, the establishment of a national health service, the opening of higher education to the lower classes, more public housing with rent control, an expanded social security system, and extensive subsidies to farmers and other low-income economic groups.

The three major issues to which the model of partial democratic socialism pays limited attention are the establishment of industrial

---

[7] The Labour Party, *Let Us Face the Future, A Declaration of Labour Policy for the Consideration of the Nation*, London, 1945.

democracy, the elimination of class distinctions, and the elimination of concentrated private wealth and power. When the socialist parties gained political control after the Second World War in the United Kingdom and the Scandinavian countries, they did not move forward vigorously on these fronts. Some efforts were made to enlarge industrial democracy by providing for the establishment of joint industry councils in all major private industries. These councils, with equal representation from management and labor, were to discuss all major matters of interest to both sides.

The movement to establish joint industrial councils has not proved successful. Private business has in general been unsympathetic to these councils; and organized labor has felt poorly prepared to function on them. The British Trades Union Council has explained that "Past efforts in the direction of securing for working people a greater degree of participation in the decisions which affect them have largely been ineffective, partly because of the low priority that unions have accorded to these activities, partly because of the limits set by employers and the Government in their respective fields."[8] In the United Kingdom after 1945, the setting up of joint industrial councils, which was voluntary at first, was made compulsory. These councils were abolished after 1951 when the British Conservative government replaced the Labour government. In Norway, joint industrial councils have not done much to improve industrial democracy. In recent years, efforts have been made to improve industrial democracy by placing workers on the boards of directors of business enterprises.

In the United Kingdom, the Labour government hoped after 1945 to reduce class distinctions by altering the educational system. It was proposed to establish "common schools" that would combine the public vocational and general schools and eventually absorb the private schools. It was hoped that this homogenization of the school system would lay the foundation for a more democratic and less class-ridden society. But after being in office from 1945 to 1951, the Labour government had succeeded in establishing very few common schools. The plan for common schools was abandoned by the Conservative government in 1951, but was revived by the Labour government in 1964. Thus far, the radical reorganization of the school system envisioned by the British socialists has not been achieved.

In Sweden, where class distinctions remain firmly established, the Social Democratic government has been disturbed by the failure of the lower-income groups to achieve more upward mobility. Recent efforts have been made to meet this problem by providing financial grants which enable rural students to take advantage of higher education.

Since 1945, the socialist governments have been concerned about the continued high concentration of private wealth. Some reduction in this concentration has been achieved through increased taxation but not enough to alter the pattern of the national distribution of wealth significantly. The failure to nationalize land and the preservation of the bulk of the private enterprise system have meant that private wealth continues to be owned in large part by a relatively small part of the total population in the United Kingdom, the Scandinavian countries, and on the Continent. The possession of private wealth in countries dominated by socialist governments preserves a social stratification that is deplored by the left wings of the socialist parties in these nations. Many socialists assert that the continued concentration of private wealth in relatively few hands is a major hindrance to

---

[8] The Trades Union Congress, *Economic Development and Planning*, report of the T.U.C. General Council presented to the T.U.C., Brighton, England, Sept. 1963, p. 16.

placing socialism on a firmer basis. In the United Kingdom and the Scandinavian countries, many of the newspapers and other communications media are controlled by private interests that represent concentrated private wealth. Up to the present, this situation has been tolerated by the Scandinavian and British socialist governments; consequently, the private Establishment has continued to wield considerable power.

The Model of Partial Democratic Socialism in Transition

During the quarter century after the Second World War, the socialist governments adhered closely to the model of partial democratic socialism discussed above. It was a new experience for these governments in the United Kingdom and the Scandinavian countries to be in a position to carry out a socialist program; thus they proceeded cautiously. Much of what they did in the economic and social fields would probably have been done by nonsocialist governments. The socialist governments concentrated on establishing a planned economy, achieving stable economic growth, and securing a more equitable distribution of the national income. Radical institutional changes, as has already been explained, were for the most part avoided. During 1945-1975, the extreme left wings of the socialist parties called for much more radical changes than were proposed by the socialist governments, but the left wings were not strong enough to challenge the middle-of-the-road position that dominated these governments.

In recent years, Western socialist parties have been challenged from within and without. The British Labour government went down to defeat in 1970 after six difficult years of trying to bolster the sagging British economy. In recent elections, both the Norwegian and Swedish socialist parties, although managing to stay in office, have lost considerable voter support. The nonsocialist parties have benefited from a popular yearning for "decentralization," relief from a heavy tax burden, and a "Green Wave" that would lead to a greater regard for environmental protection and a less urbanized life.

As the planned economy has expanded in the Scandinavian countries, a mixed collection of young people, low-income workers, and alienated citizens in urban areas have protested against the expanding bureaucracy, and the lack of a sense of contact with and control over the planning authorities. In the late 1960s and early 1970s, the Swedish socialist government's hitherto good record in the field of industrial relations was marred by unofficial strikes in the state-owned iron mines and by strikes of government workers and school teachers. It was alleged in both cases that the government was insensitive to the problems of the workers.[9] To some extent, this dissatisfaction with socialist policies and programs is a reflection of a more generalized dissatisfaction with the industrialized society and its values. Some critics of social democracy in Scandinavia have posed the question as to whether or not this type of socialism has passed its peak.

The reaction of the Scandinavian and British socialists to widespread criticism has been to take the offensive and to move their parliamentary socialism further to the left. This shift in emphasis involves some modification of the model of partial democratic socialism that guided socialist thinking

---

[9] Nils Kellgren, "Trade Unions and Social Policy in Sweden," *Sweden in Europe, 1971*, The Swedish Institute, Stockholm, 1971, pp. 69-70. Contrary to the postwar trends in Swedish industrial relations, the doctrine of nonintervention by the state had to be abandoned in the spring of 1971 when negotiations between the state and its professional workers broke down. This raised the question of a possibly new trend in Swedish industrial relations.

in the past quarter century. The first modification is a proposal for an extension of the state ownership of industry. The 1973 annual conference of the British Trades Union Congress approved the extension of state ownership to include the shipbuilding, aircraft, machine tool, pharmaceutical, and road transport industries. In addition, the congress proposed the nationalization of absentee-owned farmlands and the production of offshore oil and gas.

The Swedish Social Democratic party has advocated the use of surplus social security funds to purchase the stock of private companies, a proposal that has also been sympathetically received by the British Labour party. Government ownership of private-company stock would enable the government to supervise private business more closely and make it more compatible with socialist ideals. The new programs for socialism would more effectively curb speculation in company stock, commodity, and real estate markets. The British Labour party's 1964 general election manifesto, *The New Britain*, recommended setting up Crown Land Commissions that would end the competitive scramble for building land by buying up this land and controlling its use for future urban development.[10] All these proposals would enlarge very considerably the portion of the economy under state management. They would further reduce the concentration of private ownership in industry and the power that goes along with private wealth.

A further modification of the model of partial democratic socialism relates to the proposals to enlarge economic or industrial democracy. The workers in the advanced industrial countries have become increasingly alienated from the computerized assembly lines of the large industrial enterprises, and have expressed a desire for more control over working conditions. The socialists have become increasingly disturbed by the growth in the size of the business unit, whether in the form of private or public ownership. The leaders of British socialism have pointed out that "Desirable as these trends [towards bigness in industry] may be on economic grounds, they all carry with them the overtones of threats to the democratic process. One of the purposes of trade unionism is to protect and enlarge the freedom and dignity of the individual worker. In a complex industrial society big organizations threaten this dignity. It will therefore be of growing importance for trade unions to find ways of influencing decisions which are made by business organizations and by Government."[11]

In recent years, the socialists in Western Europe, while not prepared to advocate workers' control of industry, have become interested in developing codetermination or comanagement. Improvement in living conditions and security has turned the interest of the individual worker towards other aspects of the job than merely the pay and other benefits. Workers are now concerned about a better work environment and more satisfaction on the job. In Sweden, the socialist government in 1972 proposed a number of changes in the working environment that would give the workers more control over their jobs. Industrial democracy in Sweden is to be expanded by giving the workers a larger voice in deciding how the assembly line shall be operated, how supervisors shall be chosen, who shall be laid off in a situation of redundancy, and what plants shall be closed or relocated. In the late 1960s, the British Labour government sought to achieve the same goals by setting up Economic Development Committees with labor and management representation in all major industries.[12] The British and Scandinavian

[10] The British Labour Party, *Let's Go with Labour for the New Britain*, London, 1964, p. 14.

[11] Trades Union Congress, *op. cit.*, p. 15.

[12] Department of Economic Affairs, *The Task Ahead*, London, 1969, pp. 108–113.

socialists seek to expand worker participation at the factory level so as to reach the final goal of "equality between work and capital" in private industry.[13]

The dynamics of the Western democratic socialist movement point in the direction of more and not less socialism. Many of the socialist proposals, such as codetermination, consumer protection, a national health service, and national planning, have now been approved of and taken over by the nonsocialist parties. Unless the socialists move further to the left, they may have little that is new to offer the voters and may lose out to the nonsocialists. How to cope with this issue has created a major split between the right and left wings of the socialist parties in the United Kingdom and the Scandinavian countries. The conservative wing of the socialist movement argues that adopting a radical socialist program will alienate many liberal voters who are not members of the socialist party, and will make it difficult to win elections. The radical wing of the socialist movement points out that socialism has to offer something more than is advocated by the nonsocialist political parties if it is to win elections. For this reason, the leadership of the socialist movement in Great Britain, Norway, and Sweden is now proposing to move along a much more radical path than was followed during 1945–1975. When recommending more radical programs, the socialist leaders have found it necessary to modify considerably the model of partial democratic socialism that guided their thinking and action in the early post–World War II decades. The new model will tend to make Western democratic socialism less "partial" and more "full," but still less full than was envisioned by the socialist theoreticians of the nineteenth century. Western socialism will always be less than full socialism as long as industrial enterprise remains to a considerable extent in private hands. This seems to be the prospect for some time to come.

[13] Andre Thiria, Swedish Confederation of Trade Unions, "Labor's Voice Joins the Corporate Board," *Viewpoint*, Swedish Information Service, New York, May 29, 1973, p. 5.

Selected Bibliography

BRITISH LABOUR PARTY. *Let Us Face the Future. A Declaration of Labour Policy for the Consideration of the Nation.* London, 1945.

———. *Let's Go with Labour for the New Britain.* London, 1964.

COLE, G. D. H. *A History of Socialist Thought,* I–V. George Allen and Unwin, London, 1925–1927.

COLE, MARGARET. *The Story of Fabian Socialism.* Heineman Educational Books, London, 1961.

DEPARTMENT OF ECONOMIC AFFAIRS. *The Task Ahead.* London, 1969.

FABIAN SOCIETY. *Fabian Essays in Socialism.* Ball Publishing Co., Boston, 1908.

FABIAN SOCIETY. *Fabian Tracts,* Nos. 1 to 126. Fabian Society, London, 1884–1906.

KELLGREN, NILS. "Trade Unions and Social Policy in Sweden." In *Sweden in Europe, 1971.* The Swedish Institute, Stockholm, 1971.

LAIDLER, HARRY W. *A History of Socialist Thought.* Thomas Y. Crowell, New York, 1927.

MARX-ENGELS-LENIN INSTITUTE. *Karl Marx, Selected Works,* I. Co-operative Publishing Company, Moscow, 1935.

MARX, KARL. *Capital: A Critique of Political Economy.* Charles H. Kerr and Co., Chicago, 1906.

———, and FRIEDRICH ENGELS. *Manifesto of the Communist Party.* International Publishers Co., New York, 1937.

SWEDISH SOCIAL DEMOCRATIC LABOR PARTY. *The Programme of the Swedish Social Democratic Labor Party.* Stockholm, 1945.

THIRIA, ANDRE. "Labor's Voice Joins the Corporate Board." In *Viewpoint,* Swedish Information Service, New York, May 29, 1973.

TRADES UNION CONGRESS. *Economic Development and Planning.* Report of the T.U.C. General Council presented to the T.U.C., Brighton, England, Sept. 1963.

Chapter 9
The Norwegian Socialist Economy

Norway and Sweden, like France, have formally planned economies, but their economies, unlike that of France, are dominated by socialist governments. In all three countries, the economic systems rely primarily upon private enterprise for the production of goods and services. The difference between the Norwegian and Swedish economies, on the one hand, and the French economy on the other, lies not in planning techniques and procedures, but instead in the classes that direct economic and social developments. Whereas the goals of the planned French economy are greatly influenced by the business class and the nonsocialist government, the Norwegian and Swedish economic aims are very largely determined by the trade union movement and the socialist government. The French economy is a planned capitalist economy; the Scandinavian economy is a planned socialist one. While they have much in common, there exist also major differences in ideology, power distribution, and national objectives.

Although strong socialist movements flourish in many of the Western European countries, in Norway, Sweden, and Denmark this movement has reached its highest level of development. This is particularly true of Norway and Sweden, where the socialist parties have controlled the government almost continuously since the early 1930s. Since that time, the private-enterprise system in Norway and Sweden has been significantly altered along Western socialist lines. In both countries, a number of important industries, such as power, communications, railroad, munitions, aviation, and television, have been nationalized, an extensive welfare system developed, and a formally planned economy established. The best example of a partial or limited democratic socialist economy appears in Norway, where the labor or socialist government has usually held a majority of the parliamentary seats since the early 1930s, and has vigorously pursued its socialist aims. In Sweden, where the socialist governments have usually been minority governments with reliance on coalition parties, socialist objectives have been advocated less vigorously.

The Pattern of the Scandinavian Economies

The economies of the Scandinavian countries follow a common pattern.[1] All of them except Iceland are highly industrialized, with manufacturing employing approximately one-third of the total number of workers and accounting for somewhat more than one-quarter of the nation's gross domestic product. Table 9-1 shows the origins of gross domestic product by industry in Norway, Sweden, and Denmark. Agriculture, which in these countries is small scale and of declining importance, accounts for only from 5 to 8 percent of gross domestic product. It is, however, efficient and well organized.

[1] Surveys of the Scandinavian economies are presented in the *OECD Economic Surveys* for Norway, Sweden, and Denmark, which are periodically made by the Organisation for Economic Co-operation and Development.

In recent decades the expanding sector of the Scandinavian economies has been the sector that includes the private and public service industries. All Scandinavian economies export a large part of their gross domestic product (Norway, 37 percent; Sweden, 24 percent; and Denmark, 27 percent); they are thus very dependent upon international trade for imports of food, raw materials, fuel, and other essentials. In spite of a lack of natural resources, such as coal, oil, and various minerals, the Scandinavian countries enjoy high standards of living. As Table 9-2 indicates, Sweden, Denmark, and Norway have per capita GNPs that place them among the world's top eight nations, ranked in size of per capita GNP. After the United States, Sweden is second, Denmark fifth, and Norway sixth.

A special feature of the Scandinavian economies is their high degree of collective action. Employers, workers, farmers, and fishermen are well organized in cooperatives, trade unions, and employers' associations and in various confederations of these collective organizations. These organizations, which are represented by a number of different political parties, usually cooperate in dealing with economic and social problems. They also work closely with the central government,

Table 9-1
Gross Domestic Product by Industry of Origin in Norway, Sweden, and Denmark, 1974

	In Percent		
	Norway	Sweden	Denmark
Agriculture[1]	6	5	8
Manufacturing[2]	27	32	28
Construction	8	7	9
Services	59	56	55
Gross domestic product	100	100	100

[1] Includes forestry and fishing.
[2] Includes mining, electricity, gas and water.

Source: United Nations, *Monthly Bulletin of Statistics*, Aug. 1976.

Table 9-2
Gross National Product Per Capita (1973) and Average Annual Per Capita Growth Rate (1960-1973) in the United States and Selected Western European Countries

	1973 GNP per capita (U.S. dollars)	1973 GNP per capita (in percent)	1960-73 average annual per capita growth rate (in percent)
United States	$6,200	100	3.1
Switzerland	6,100	98	3.0
Sweden	5,910	95	3.0
Canada	5,450	88	3.7
West Germany	5,320	86	3.7
Denmark	5,210	84	3.9
Norway	4,660	75	4.0
France	4,540	73	4.7

Source: World Bank, *World Bank Atlas*, 1975.

when there is a need for public action in coping with these problems. Political activity in the Scandinavian countries, being conducted on the basis of proportional representation, leads to a politics of compromise.[2] Political compromise and collective action in economic and social matters in all Scandinavian countries result in a great deal of political stability and freedom from industrial strife.

Norwegian Economic Trends, 1945-1973

The Norwegian economy has undergone major structural changes since 1945.[3] Before World War II, Norway had a high-consumption, low-investment economy, with 76.7 percent of net national product going into private consumption and only 12.2 percent being taken up by net domestic investment in plant, equipment, housing, and inventories. After 1945, the Norwegian economy was converted under the labor government's guidance into a low-consumption, high-investment economy. The Labor government sought to lay a foundation for a high standard of living in the future by first investing in the plant and equipment required for a high level of industrialization. By 1951, private consumption took up only 66.9 percent of net national product, whereas net domestic investment then absorbed 20.9 percent of net national product. After World War II, a very large flight from agriculture began, as labor was absorbed in increasing numbers in the postwar recovery and reconversion programs and later in the further industrialization of Norway. By 1963, one-fifth of Norway's total civilian labor force was still employed in the

[2] Dankwart A. Rostow, *The Politics of Compromise*, Princeton: Princeton University Press, 1955, pp. 226-237.

[3] Structural developments in Norway since 1945 are discussed in Sigurd Ekeland, *Norway in Europe, An Economic Survey*, Oslo: Royal Ministry of Foreign Affairs, 1970; and Arne Haarr, *The Industrial Policy of Norway*, Oslo: Royal Ministry of Foreign Affairs, 1970.

primary industries of agriculture, forestry, and fishing with about one-quarter employed in manufacturing. It is estimated that by 1990 only 7 percent of Norway's total employment will be in agriculture, forestry, and fishing.

The Norwegian plan for 1970–1990 looks forward to a large decline in agricultural employment and a large increase in employment in the private and public service industries. Table 9–3 shows that employment in agriculture, forestry, and fishing is projected to decline from 20 percent of total employment in 1963 to only 7 percent in 1990.[4] While employment in manufacturing is projected to remain at about 25 percent of total employment, services of all types, which accounted for 46 percent of total employment in 1963, would take up 63 percent of this employment in 1990. By 1990, if the years 1970–1990 are peaceful and prosperous, the planned Norwegian economy would be a well-developed service economy with a high standard of living.

The trends in the development of the Norwegian economy since 1945 are revealed by an analysis of the distribution or uses of Norway's gross domestic product. The statistics, in Table 9–4 indicate that from 1950 to 1974 private consumption absorbed a declining portion of the nation's gross domestic product, as public consumption and public and private investment together accounted for a relatively larger share of gross domestic product. In the twenty-year period, 1970–1990, the Norwegian Labor party, if in office, would continue the trend towards a welfare state with expanding programs for education, health, environmental protection, and regional development. The Norwegian twenty-year program projects an increase in public consumption to 22 percent of gross domestic product, while private consumption would fall to 44 percent and gross domestic investment would be 35 percent. Between 1970 and 1990, gross domestic product is projected to increase at an average annual rate of 4 percent. With this rate of economic growth, per

[4] Royal Norwegian Ministry of Finance, *Perspektivanalyser, Skisser For Utviklingen Fram Mot 1990, Vedlegg til St. meld. nr. 55 (1968–69), Langtidsprogrammet 1970–1973*, Oslo, Norway, p. 13.

Table 9–3

Employment by Industry in Norway in 1963 (Actual) and 1990 (Projected)

	In percent	
Industries	1963 (Actual)	1990 (Projected)
Agriculture, forestry, and fishing	20.2	7.0
Processing of primary products	7.5	4.2
Manufacturing	26.4	25.4
Commerce	12.0	16.8
Other private services	16.6	18.9
Foreign shipping	3.5	3.2
Public services	13.8	24.5
Total employment	100.0	100.0

Source: Royal Norwegian Ministry of Finance, *Perspektivanalyser, Skisser For Utviklingen Fram Mot 1990*, Oslo, Norway, 1969.

Table 9-4
The Norwegian Gross Domestic Product and Its Uses in 1950 (Actual), 1974 (Actual), and 1990 (Projected)

	Percentage distribution		
	1950	1974	1990
Private consumption	60.5	52.3	43.9
Public consumption	8.9	16.4	21.6
Gross domestic investment	35.4	33.8	34.6
Net export surplus	−4.8	−2.5	−0.1
Gross domestic product	100.0	100.0	100.0

Sources: OECD, *OECD Economic Surveys, Norway*; and Royal Norwegian Ministry of Finance, *Perspektivanalyser, Skisser For Utviklingen Fram Mot 1990*; UN, *Monthly Bulletin of Statistics*, Aug. 1976.

capita real private consumption would increase even though private consumption as a percentage share of gross domestic product would decline. Much of the annual increase in this product would be in the form of collective goods and services rather than private goods and services.

The Planned Norwegian Economy

Norway, like France, has since the early post–World War II years planned its economy with the aid of national economic budgets.[5] These budgets have been used from the point of view of three time horizons: annual, medium-term, and long-term. Immediately after the war, annual and medium-term (four-year) national budgets were constructed and used as a basis for the formulation of the government's economic policies. The four-year national economic budget became the central factor in the whole national planning program.[6] It served as the starting point for the projection of the nation's expanding gross domestic product and its distribution among private and public consumption and investment uses. The four-year national economic budgets provided an overall framework for the guidance of the annual economic budget.

Planning in Norway with a time horizon longer than four years deals with the development of the nation's economy over two or three decades. In this time period, major changes can occur in the structure and functioning of the economic system. Norwegian long-term planning aims to indicate the

[5] The early development of national planning in Norway is analyzed in Alice Bourneuf, *Norway, The Planned Revival*, Cambridge: Harvard University Press, 1958. For the later progress of Norwegian national planning, see Petter J. Bjerve, *Planning in Norway, 1947–1956*, Amsterdam: North-Holland Publishing Co., 1959. The role of labor in Norwegian planning is discussed in Mark W. Leiserson, *Wages and Economic Control in Norway, 1945–1956*, Cambridge: Harvard University Press, 1959.

[6] A discussion of the role of the national economic budget in Norwegian national planning is presented in Appendix I, "Concepts and Method in National Budgeting," *The National Budget of Norway, 1966*, Royal Norwegian Ministry of Finance, Oslo, Norway, 1965, pp. 67-86. See also Bank of Norway, "National Budgeting in Norway," *Economic Bulletin*, Vol. XXXVII, No. 3, Oslo, Norway, Sept. 1966, pp. 114-120.

alternatives available in such areas as industrialization, urbanization, increased economic growth, the increase in leisure-time activities, and the preservation of the national environment. It is also the objective of the long-term national planning to reveal the economic and social consequences of choosing among different alternatives. In 1969, the problems of long-term planning in Norway were for the first time formally presented to the public in the form of a report on prospective economic and social developments up to the year 1990. This report paid particular attention to the expanding role of the public sector and the problems of education, health services, transport and communications, and the energy supply in the period 1970–1990.[7]

Table 9–5 presents the Norwegian national economic budget for the four-year plan period 1974–1977. This budget summarizes in quantitative form the government's medium-term economic objectives for this four-year period. It shows that Norway plans to maintain its high-investment, low-private-consumption economy. Approximately one-third of Norway's total available domestic supply of goods and services is to be devoted to gross private and public investment, while private consumption is to be kept close to only one-half of the total available supply of goods and services. The growth goal for the plan period 1974–1977, is projected at 4.5 percent a year, which is very close to what was actually achieved annually from 1963 to 1973. The major economic objectives of Norway's seventh four-year national plan include: (1) securing a high rate of economic growth, (2) coming close to a balance in the external economy, (3) curbing private consumption, and (4) expanding public consumption in line with the annual growth rate of the nation's economy.

The annual plans are used in Norway to move year by year towards the goals set forth in the four-year national economic plans.

[7] Finans- og tolldepartementet, *Perspektivanalyser, Skisser For Utviklingen Fram Mot 1990, Vedlegg til St. meld. nr. 55 (1968-69), Langtidsprogrammet, 1970–1973*, 1969. This report appears as an appendix to the four-year plan for 1970–1973.

Table 9–5
The Norwegian National Economic Accounts for 1973 and the National Economic Budget for 1977 (Million Kroner in 1971 Prices)

Components of gross domestic product	National economic accounts 1973 (actual)	National economic budget 1977 (projected)	Average annual % increase 1973–1977
Private consumption	55,100 (50.2%)	64,500 (49.3%)	4.0
Public consumption	15,000 (13.7%)	17,600 (13.4%)	4.1
Gross fixed investment	37,150 (33.8%)	44,500 (34.0%)	4.7
Increase in inventories	400 (00.3%)	1,200 (00.9%)	0.6[1]
Net export surplus	2,150 (02.0%)	3,100 (02.4%)	0.4[1]
Gross domestic product	109,800 (100.0%)	130,900 (100.0%)	4.5

[1] Increase as a percent of GDP.

Source: Norwegian Ministry of Finance, *Norwegian Long Term Programme, 1974–1977*, Parliamentary Report No. 71, 1972–1973, Oslo, 1973.

The annual plans are also employed to make adjustments in economic policies and plan objectives that may be made necessary by unexpected domestic or international developments. Through its annual plans the Norwegian Labor government secures the flexibility required in a rapidly changing economic world. Table 9-6 presents the Norwegian annual plan for 1975. The major economic objectives of this plan year are: (1) a 6.2 percent increase in Gross National Product, (2) a faster growth of personal consumption, (3) a considerable increase in public expenditures on education, research, communications, and social services, and (4) a sizable increase in the rate of private and public investment. The increased private investment is projected to go into ships, machinery, and equipment, while the public investment is allocated to highways, hospitals, communications, and defense. The 1975 annual national plan makes no change in the goal of the high private-investment, high public-investment, and low personal-consumption economy that Norway has maintained in the past two decades. Private consumption continues to take up only a little more than one-half of the nation's total output of goods and services, while private and public investment absorb more than 30 percent of total output.

An overall view of the Norwegian planning structure is presented in Figure 9-1.[8] The central body in Norway's national economic planning activity is the prime minister's cabinet, made up of the leading members of the Norwegian Labor party, which is responsible for the government's general economic program. The Cabinet relies upon the Central Statistical Office for the statistical information that must be available in any discussion of the problems of national economic planning. The Cabinet is also assisted by an Economic Committee of the Cabinet to which major economic issues are referred for consideration before the whole Cabinet makes any final decisions with regard to these issues. The Ministry of Finance plays a key role in the actual

[8] The organization of national economic planning in Norway since 1945 is reviewed in Hermod Skånland, "Current Problems in Norwegian Economic Planning," Institut für Weltwirtschaft, *Weltwirtschaftliches Archiv*, Band 92, Heft 1, Hamburg, 1964, pp. 94–110.

Table 9-6

The Norwegian National Economic Accounts for 1974 and the National Economic Budget for 1975 (Million Kroner in 1973 Prices)

Components of gross domestic product	National economic accounts 1974 (actual)	National economic budget 1975 (projected)	Percent increase in 1975 over 1974
Private consumption	60,890 (52.8%)	64,360 (52.5%)	5.7
Public consumption	18,765 (16.2%)	19,320 (15.8%)	3.0
Gross fixed investment	35,300 (30.6%)	36,700 (30.0%)	4.0
Increase in inventories	1,600 (01.4%)	1,100 (00.9%)	−0.5[1]
Net export surplus	−1,155 (−01.0%)	1,020 (00.8%)	1.8[1]
Gross domestic product	115,400 (100.0%)	122,500 (100.0%)	6.2

[1] Increase as a percent of GDP.

Source: Norwegian Ministry of Finance, *The National Budget of Norway, 1973*, Parliamentary Report No. 1, 1972-1973, Oslo, Norway, 1973.

Figure 9-1
Structure of the Norwegian Planning Organization, 1976

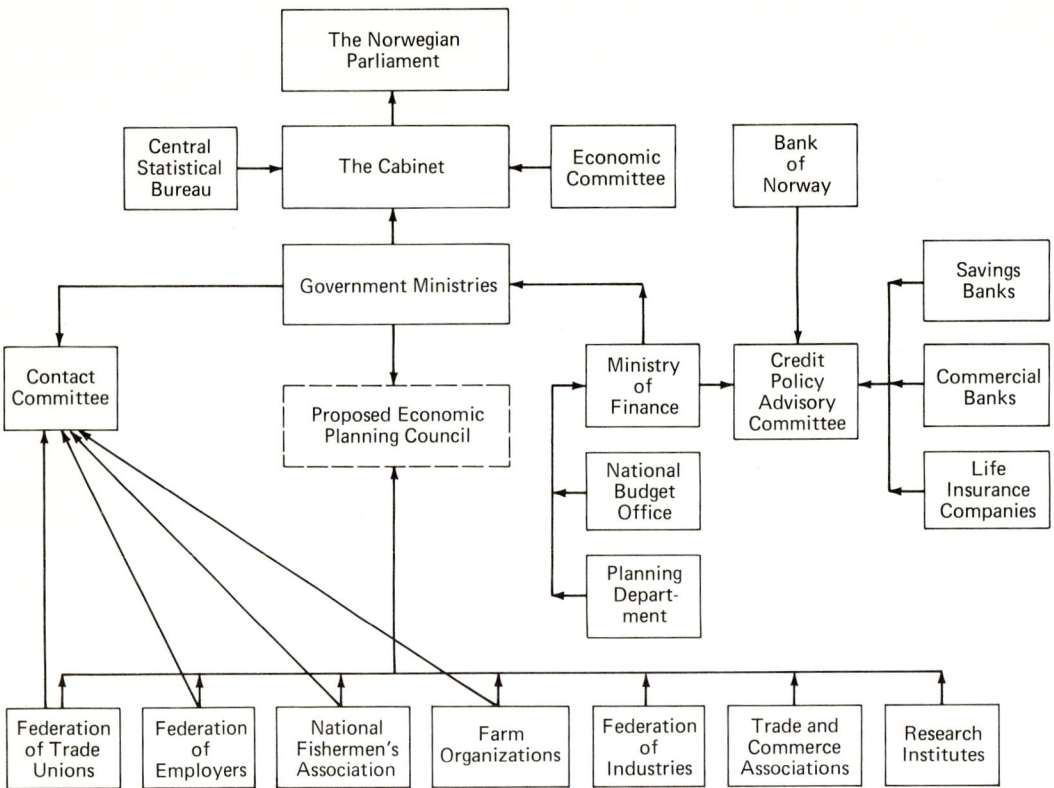

construction of the annual national economic plans and also in the construction of the recurring four-year national economic plans whose general features are determined by the Cabinet. The National Budget Office of the Ministry of Finance is responsible for the work of constructing the annual plan which when completed is sent to the Cabinet for its final consideration. Upon the endorsement of the annual national plan by its Economic Committee, the Cabinet approves the plan for publication and presents it to the Parliament.

The four-year plans are constructed by the Planning Department of the Ministry of Finance and are handled in the same manner as the annual plans. Norwegian national economic planning on the financial side is carried on with the aid of the Credit Policy Advisory Committee, which has representatives from the Ministry of Finance, the Bank of Norway, the commercial and savings banks, and the life insurance companies. This committee discusses monetary and credit policies for the coming year that will supplement the national economic plan. Finally, there is the Contact Committee with representatives from the government, the trade unions, the employers, and the farmers' and fishermen's associations. This committee makes proposals for wage and farm price adjustments in order to secure noninflationary increases in these areas. It also seeks a fair sharing of the national income by all economic groups with the aid of an incomes policy.

In recent years, it has been proposed that an Economic Planning Council be established, with representatives from the government, labor, industry, commerce, agriculture, and various economic and social research institutes. This council would enable private economic interests to be formally consulted by the government during the construction of both annual and four-year national economic plans. Its nature would be simply advisory and informational. The Economic Planning Council could perform not only the very important function of securing the support of the private economic interests for the national economic plans, but, in the government's opinion, it could also broaden the general public's understanding of the nature and role of Norwegian national economic planning.

The Performance of the Norwegian Economy, 1963–1972

Norwegian economic development since 1945 falls into four periods.[9] The first period, which included the first national plan for the years 1949–1952, was one of recovery from the war-time destruction and the conversion from a war-time to a peace-time economy. During these years, the war-time economic controls were largely maintained in order to cope with the scarcity of raw materials, skilled labor, and capital equipment. The second developmental period covers the years of the second national plan (1954–1957) and the third (1958–1961) national plan; during this period many war-time controls were relaxed or eliminated, foreign trade was liberalized, and the private market system was widely restored. The Norwegian labor government continued to provide a considerable amount of economic and social guidance; but after the early 1950s it increasingly emphasized indirect rather than direct controls, coupled with persuasion and exhortation.

The period of the second and third Norwegian national plans, 1954–1961, was one of continued economic growth without any serious recession. From 1953 to 1963, Gross National Product increased at an average annual rate of 3.7 percent; unemployment was very low; the volume of exports continued to grow at the average annual rate of 7 percent; and the reserves of gold and foreign exchange were doubled. The full-employment, high-pressure Norwegian economy developed strong inflationary tendencies during the 1950s and early 1960s, but these were no stronger than were similar tendencies abroad. In spite of inflationary developments, Norway continued to be competitive in the world's freight and commodity markets. Average annual increases of 6.4 percent in wage rates in manufacturing were offset by large increases in output per man-hour. Centralized collective bargaining reduced strikes and losses of workdays to a very low level.

The third period in Norway's postwar economic development extended from 1962 to 1969. As the selected Norwegian economic indicators in Table 9-7 reveal, the economic trends of the 1950s and early 1960s continued up to 1969, when Norway, like other Western European countries, suffered from disturbing price and wage explosions. From 1963 to 1969, Norway enjoyed a sustained average annual economic growth rate of almost 5 percent. The annual increases in consumer and wholesale prices and in industrial wage rates were in line with the increases in these items in the previous decade, 1953–1962. Price and wage-rate increases during these years left Norway competitive in the world's trading

[9] Economic developments in Norway since 1945 are analyzed in Petter J. Bjerve, *op. cit.*; Alice Bourneuf, *op. cit.*; Per Kleppe, *Main Aspects of Economic Policy in Norway since the War*. Oslo: Royal Ministry of Foreign Affairs, 1968; and J. Eaaland, "Economic Policy in Norway, 1949 to 1961," *Economic Policy in Our Time*, Vol. II, Country Studies, Chicago: Rand McNally, 1964, pp. 155–224.

Table 9-7
Selected Norwegian Economic Indicators, 1963–1972

	Annual percent change					
	Gross domestic product	Consumer prices	Wholesale prices	Average hourly earnings in manufacturing	Output per man-hour in manufacturing	Unemployment rate
1963	5.2	2.5	1.0	5.3	6.4	1.6
1964	5.5	5.7	3.9	6.2	4.8	1.4
1965	5.2	4.3	2.8	6.8	4.7	1.2
1966	4.4	3.2	1.8	7.1	3.3	1.1
1967	5.6	4.4	1.8	7.6	4.7	1.0
1968	4.0	3.5	0.9	8.1	7.5	1.4
1969	4.4	3.2	3.5	9.6	7.6	1.3
Annual average 1963–1969	4.9	3.8	2.2	7.2	5.6	1.3
1970	3.5	10.6	7.6	12.0	3.4	1.0
1971	5.0	6.2	4.7	12.4	4.7	1.0
1972	4.0	7.2	3.1	9.6	5.6	1.1
Annual average 1970–1972	4.1	8.0	5.1	11.3	5.3	1.0
Annual average 1963–1972	4.7	5.1	3.1	8.5	5.3	1.2

Sources: OECD, *OECD Economic Surveys, Norway* and IMF, *International Financial Statistics*.

markets. The volume of exports was maintained at a high level in most years. When, however, this volume declined, as in 1965 and 1967, total national output and employment were sustained by government programs that stimulated building and construction and by private programs that added to inventories in the export industries.

The fourth and most recent period in Norway's economic development covers the years since 1969. These were years of international boom, recession, and serious inflationary developments. Like other Western European countries, Norway in 1970–1972 experienced very large increases in prices and wages. In 1970, consumer prices rose 10.6 percent and wage rates in industry 12 percent. Consumer prices, which had increased at the average annual rate of 3.8 percent in 1963–1969, rose at the rate of 8 percent in 1970–1972. The price and wage explosions in Norway resulted from a number of domestic and external developments. At home, the introduction of a 20 percent value-added tax in 1970 and the slow growth of real wage income in the late 1960s led to unusually large wage demands from organized labor. Poor harvests and heavier demands for raw materials abroad made Norwegian imports much more costly after 1969 and were a further factor contributing to Norway's price and wage inflation. With higher labor costs, Norway's export prices rose at the same time that the annual increase in the volume of exports fell much below the usual increase of around 10 percent.

A number of steps were taken to curb inflation. General price freezes in 1971 and 1972 were accompanied by restrictive fiscal and monetary policies. Tax increases were combined with a reduction in government purchases of goods and services, and limits were placed upon the increase in the supply of credit. As a consequence of these anti-inflationary policies, consumer prices and wage rates increased much less rapidly in 1972 than in 1970; but they were still rising at an annual rate that was well above the trend rates of 1963-1969. By 1973, the volume of Norwegian exports was again expanding at the normal annual trend rate of around 10 percent. In 1973, inflation in Norway remained a serious problem, because it was at a level that was well above that of the past two decades. This situation led the OECD Economic and Development Review Committee to conclude in early 1973 that "experience in the past two years suggests a disquieting departure from past trends."[10] The committee also pointed out that Norway had come through the international recession of 1970-1971 without serious unemployment or retardation of growth. As Table 9-7 indicates, unemployment in these years continued at the very low rate of one percent, and the annual increase in gross domestic product never fell below 3.5 percent.

[10] OECD, *OECD Economic Surveys, Norway,* Jan. 1973, p. 5.

The Performance of the Norwegian Economy since 1972

Norwegian economic performance after 1972 was influenced by a number of factors: namely, the boom in world trade that continued until 1974; the oil crisis of late 1973 and 1974; and the bringing into production of the oil fields on Norway's continental shelf and in the North Sea. These oil fields contain estimated reserves of 3 billion barrels of oil and 100 billion cubic meters of natural gas. By the end of 1975, Norway's offshore oil and gas production was expected to match its total domestic oil and natural gas consumption. After 1975, Norway would soon become Western Europe's first net oil exporter.

The statistics in Table 9-8 summarize Norway's economic performance in the period 1972-1975. The strong expansionary trends of 1972-1973 were accompanied by a 4 percent annual economic growth rate, low unemployment, strong price and wage inflation, large annual increases in the volume of merchandise exports, and a manageable deficit in the current balance of international payments. Like other industrial countries, Norway suffered from the contractionary impact of the large 1973 increase in the price of crude oil. Both industrial production and total national output increased at lower than normal rates, the volume of merchandise exports in 1975 fell 1.6 percent, and a larger than usual deficit in the external account (14,492 million kroner) was recorded. At the same time, the annual increases in both consumer prices and wage rates in manufacturing reached new high levels as the result of a tight labor market, a large upward wage drift, and higher farm prices. Hourly wage rates in manufacturing increased almost 20 percent in 1975 as workers sought to recover the loss in real wages in 1972 and 1973. Consumer prices were kept below a 10 percent increase in 1974 only by

Table 9-8
Norwegian Economic Indicators, 1972–1975

	Percent change over previous year						Current balance of payments (mil. kr.)	Unemployment rate
	Gross domestic product	Industrial production	Consumer prices	Hourly wage rates[1]	Output per man-hour[1]	Volume of exports		
1972	4.0	2.9	7.1	8.9	4.3	13.8	−387	1.0
1973	4.2	5.6	7.4	10.6	3.5	10.4	−2,010	0.8
1974	3.5	3.6	9.4	17.8	3.6	−1.6	−5,560	0.7
1975	4.0	−1.7	11.6	19.5	3.0	−1.6	−14,492	0.8

[1] In manufacturing.

Sources: OECD, *OECD Economic Surveys, Norway*, Jan. 1975; Norges Bank, *Economic Bulletin*, 1975; and IMF, *International Financial Statistics*, Sept. 1976.

increasing domestic food subsidies. The prospect for 1976 includes somewhat lower wage and price inflation, a decline in the balance-of-payments deficit, but with a high rate of economic growth of 5 percent, supported by inventory accumulation and increased production in the shipping and oil sectors. Unlike many other industrial countries, Norway did not have a major decline in its gross domestic product as a result of the 1973–1974 oil crisis.

Like other Western industrialized countries, Norway has had to adjust to the worldwide inflation and recession that came after 1972. A recent OECD survey of the Norwegian economy concludes that "Norway has absorbed the contractionary demand impact and the inflationary price effect of the oil crisis rather more smoothly than most other countries."[11] Norway has been able to succeed along these lines for three reasons. First, its large supply of electric power has made Norway less dependent on oil imports than many other industrial countries. Second, its

North Sea oil exports have stimulated an investment boom in the nonoil sector, and will eventually free Norway from the adverse consequences of higher world oil prices. Third, Norway has taken steps to plan the relations between its oil and non-oil sectors so that the impact of the international recession will be greatly reduced.[12]

As Norway's exports have declined since 1973, a number of measures have been adopted under its annual national plans to sustain total demand, output, and employment. These measures have aimed at stimulating domestic private consumption, home construction and public works, accumulation of export inventories, and private business investment. A special effort has been made since 1973 to increase the share of gross domestic product taken up by private households. In 1973, real private consumption increased only 1.9 percent over 1972, whereas

[11] Organisation for Economic Co-operation and Development, *OECD Economic Surveys, Norway*, Jan. 1975, p. 38.

[12] The implications of its oil sector for the Norwegian economy are analyzed in OECD, *OECD Economic Surveys, Norway*, March 1974, pp. 19–20 and 31–36. See also the Norwegian Parliamentary Report, No. 25, 1973/74, *Petroleumsvirksomhetens plass i det norske samfun (The Place of the Oil Activity in the Norwegian Society)*, Oslo, 1973.

in 1974 the increase was 4.2 percent; the 1975 annual plan anticipated a 5.7 percent increase over 1974.

Special fiscal measures were used in 1974 to enlarge private consumption. Personal income taxes on lower-income groups were reduced; social security payments made by employers and employees were lowered; pension payments and children's allowances were increased; and subsidies on food products were enlarged in order to limit the rise in the cost of living. Private business investment was encouraged by making monetary policy less restrictive. Bank credit was made more available for inventory accumulation and investment in new plant and equipment, especially in the export and export-supporting industries. Bank reserve requirements were reduced in 1974; the Norwegian central bank increased its loans to private banks and its purchases of government bonds in the open market; and the government increased its ceiling on total credit available to all borrowers. Much emphasis was placed on financing inventory accumulation as a means of sustaining economic activity in sectors faced with declining export sales. To a limited extent, the central government was prepared to make supplementary appropriations for selected public-works projects as private economic activity fell off.

The Norwegian short- and medium-term planning strategy is to mesh the activities of the nation's oil and non-oil sectors so that a balanced economic growth may be achieved. By 1980, the level of production from the Cod Ekofish, Frigg, and Statfjord oil fields is to be stabilized at approximately 200,000 barrels per day (70 million barrels per year); and future oil discoveries are to be used to maintain production at this level beyond 1980. By 1977, foreign exchange earned from oil and gas exports is expected to exceed net freight earnings and to be equal to more than half the earnings from traditional exports.

The revenue from the Norwegian government's participation in oil and natural gas production through its nationalized oil enterprise, Statoil, is expected by 1977 to be the equivalent of 13 percent of the 1974 total tax receipts. The Norwegian government is taking special steps to prevent the new oil sector from disrupting activities in the nation's non-oil sector by attracting excessive amounts of labor and capital from agriculture, fishing, forestry, and traditional industry. Already by 1974, 13 percent of Norway's domestic total annual fixed capital investment was being placed in oil exploration and production. Labor market and investment policies will provide for some resource allocation to the new oil industry, but not enough to alter excessively Norway's existing industrial structure. Much reliance is to be placed upon imported labor and capital to develop the Norwegian oil fields so as to contain the pressure on the nonoil sector to release its supplies of labor and capital to the new oil industry. The government's oil revenues are to be used for the following purposes: to lower the private tax burden; to increase expenditures on housing, various public projects, and social services; to support regional development; to protect the nation's natural environment; and to aid the less developed countries. According to the Norwegian planning strategy, the private market system is to have much less influence in Norway's oil sector than it has in the oil sectors of the United States and other unplanned countries.

Private Business in the Planned Norwegian Economy

As in other Western European countries that have turned to national planning, Norway must adapt its private enterprise system to the requirements of the national four-year plans. Since around 85 percent of the employment and production is accounted for by the private enterprise system, national planning in Norway largely consists of securing the cooperation of the private enterprises, farmers, and trade unions, and of supplementing and guiding the private market system. Subsequent sections of this chapter deal with how the planning authorities fit private business, agriculture, and the trade unions into the framework of the annual and medium-term national planning programs.

The basic way in which private business enterprise has been fitted into Norwegian national planning has been by providing it with general guidelines in the form of the broad economic goals of the annual and four-year national economic plans. After the planning authorities have set goals for total output and its division between consumption and investment, private business is invited to cooperate in the securing of these economic goals. Although private business in Norway does not play any direct role in the determination of the broad features of the country's national plans, it is consulted by the planning authorities at many points in the construction of these plans. Large business enterprises, industry organizations, commercial associations, and farm organizations are frequently consulted concerning their role in the coming year's national economic plan. National planning at the industry level is very much of a cooperative affair, since the government wants the advice and the understanding of private industry's technical experts; at the same time, each industry seeks to protect its own interest as far as it is affected by the national planning program. Both sides to the planning program believe that they can benefit from these mutual relationships that are so important a feature of Norwegian national economic planning. No specific annual production targets are set for each individual firm within an industry, but each industry can readily calculate its success in meeting the output goal proposed for it by the annual national plan, and also its total capital, manpower, and raw material needs in relation to this planned output goal.

After the annual national economic plan has been constructed and private industry's place in this plan indicated, the next step in adjusting private business to the national plan is to use certain strategic economic controls, where necessary, to guide private industry towards the plan's goals. In the early postwar years from 1945 to 1951, the system of economic controls imposed on the private business system was quite complex. With the return to a situation of greater equilibrium after 1951, many economic controls, such as individual price controls, industrial rationing, and quantitative import controls, were abandoned, while others were relaxed. Today, the five basic economic controls applied to the private business system are the fiscal, monetary, price, building, and foreign exchange controls. These are the minimum controls that the Norwegian Labor government believes to be necessary if it is to retain the power of guiding the Norwegian economy towards the goals set forth in its annual and longer-term national economic plans.

It is the government's objective to permit the private business system to operate without the imposition of economic controls as long as private business functions in such a way as to contribute to the goals of full employment, sustained growth, stable prices, and an equilibrium in Norway's external economy. For example, although the government has the power to control prices, most prices are today not regulated by the government. Before increasing their prices, large private business enterprises may discuss the proposed price increases with the Price Directorate of the Ministry of Wages and Prices in order to obtain the government's view on a price rise. If agreement about proposed price changes can be secured, the government will then not find it necessary to use its power to control prices by issuing a price regulation.

As a result of many years of cooperation with the government authorities during and after World War II with regard to economic controls, private business now works closely with the government in those areas where controls may still be imposed. Such procedures reduce the need to impose controls officially. Many of the problems that arise in fitting the private business system into the Norwegian national plans are settled through consultation and discussion and not through the imposition of economic controls. Norwegian national economic planning is best described as "strategic" planning. The government intervenes with its controls only at strategic points in the economic system. Much of the private economic decision making is free from governmental controls, just as it is in the Western capitalistic countries.

Two devices used to fit private industry into the Norwegian national economic plans are the joint industrial council and the joint production committee. The "Common Program," approved by all major Norwegian political parties in June 1945, recommended the establishment in each major industry of a joint industrial council with representatives from management, labor, and the public. The purpose of these councils is to promote cooperation between the employers and their workers in each major industry and between the industry and the government in the effort to solve the industry's pressing problems. The joint industrial councils analyze problems relating to markets, industrial research, supplies of raw materials and skilled labor, technical progress, and industrial rationalization. Their general function is to advance the efficiency and the progress of the industries in which they are located.

At first, the government suggested that the joint industrial councils should be set up voluntarily. In most industries, the employers were opposed to the joint industrial council because they felt that copartnership or comanagement was an undesirable invasion by labor of the field of the private management of industry. When joint industrial councils failed to materialize after 1945, the government then turned to the mandatory establishment of these councils. Legislation was enacted in June 1947 to give the government the power to set up joint industrial councils when either side of industry requested such a council. Thus far, only fourteen joint industrial councils have been organized in the textile, boot and shoe, canning, diesel motor, electrical, brick, sawmill, pulp and paper, confectionery, fish-product, and foundry industries. Up to now, many of the joint industrial councils have remained rather inactive in spite of the government's high expectations. Private business enterprises have remained skeptical about the value of these councils and so have not put their weight behind the movement to encourage them. Although organized labor has always supported the plan to establish these councils, it has found that the lack of education and training prevents many workers from being effective representatives on the joint industrial councils. The Norwegian Labor government is disappointed with the limited progress up to the present of the joint industrial councils. It continues, however, to look forward to further advances in the effort to develop Norway's industrial democracy with the aid of the joint industrial council. The new problems arising from the automation of industry and the economic integration of Western Europe will increase the need for more workers' participation in industrial affairs and may lead to more interest in developing joint industrial councils.

In December 1945, the Norwegian Federation of Trade Unions and the Norwegian Employers' Association entered into an agreement that provides that all companies having more than fifty employees and being members of the association must set up joint production committees. These committees seek to foster in the workers a feeling of personal responsibility for the production level in the plant or workshop and a desire to cooperate with management in improving this level. The size of the joint production committee reflects the size of the industrial plant; but in all cases management and labor are equally represented on the committee. In 1975, close to a thousand joint production committees were found scattered throughout the Norwegian industrial system. The joint production committees have been most successful in large industrial plants where workers have been trained by their own unions for membership on these committees. Both management and the unions are for the most part favorably disposed towards joint consultation at the plant level. The Norwegian Employers' Association has found that joint production committees are a very useful device for getting workers to understand the reasons for rationalizing industry.

Likewise, the Norwegian Federation of Trade unions supports the joint consultation movement at the plant level, since the workers' income can be improved in the long run through the rationalization of industry. One of the duties of the joint production committees is to work for a sound and correct rationalization of production. New methods of production must be introduced, time and motion studies made, and piece work adjusted to the new production methods. Where workers cooperate with management through the joint production committee, the streamlining of production is accomplished with less friction. Since Norway's long-term economic prosperity depends so much upon improving productivity throughout the economy, the joint production committee has a vital role to play in the nation's economic affairs.

Private Investment in the Planned Norwegian Economy

In the postwar Norwegian economy, which has assigned a high priority to investment, both private and public, one of the most important concerns of economic policy is the level and direction of private investment in plant, equipment and inventories. Private investment in Norwegian industry, agriculture, forestry, mining, and other economic activities accounts for about three-quarters of total annual domestic gross investment. The one-quarter of total annual domestic investment that is public is about evenly divided between central government and local government investment. Since private industry is the mainspring of the Norwegian economy, the flows of private saving and private investment are major factors determining the general functioning of the economy. Private saving and investment are the result of decisions made by many individuals and private organizations in a mixed economy in which the government intervenes to a considerable extent.

The Norwegian Labor government is unwilling to allow the capital market to function as freely as it does in some Western European countries and the United States. While the Norwegian Labor government does not attempt to control in any detailed way the saving and investment decisions of private business enterprises, it does supply a general framework within which private saving and investment decisions must be made. This framework provides a system of priorities for the guidance of both public and private saving and investment and is derived from the total investment budgets that are incorporated in the annual and four-year national plans.

When constructing its annual national economic plan, the government indicates the proportion of the coming year's Gross National Product that it would like to see taken up by total gross investment. Furthermore, the government draws up a total gross domestic investment budget that shows the projected division of total investment between private and public investment; it also includes the projected or planned distribution of the coming year's fixed investment among such major economic categories as agriculture, forestry, manufacturing, shipping, electric power, dwellings, hospitals, and other government projects. Table 9-9 indicates actual gross fixed investment for 1973 and 1974 and projected investment for 1975. In 1974, total domestic fixed investment increased 6.4 percent over 1973 because of large increases in investment in oil exploration, oil and gas production, other industries and communications. The national plan for 1975 called for 4 percent increase in total fixed investment with declines in investment in oil exploration and production, but with increases in the ship-building, power, and manufacturing industries. The volatile items in the annual national investment budget are the investments in oil exploration and production, ship building, and export industries.

Annual projections of total gross investment and its three main categories are constructed on the basis of detailed projections of gross investment in Norway's various industries. Each private industrial association works with the Ministry of Industry in gathering information concerning the coming year's investment plans of the individual firms within the various industries. In most of the postwar years, private industry in Norway has wanted to invest more than the annual investment plans of the government have permitted. Each year before the construction of the annual plan, the Ministry of Industry makes a survey of the

Table 9-9
Allocation of Norwegian Gross Fixed Investment by Industry, 1973-1975

	Million 1973 kroner			Percent change	
	1973 (Actual)	1974 (Actual)	1975 (Projected)	1974 over 1973	1975 over 1974
Agriculture	1,216	1,190	1,205	−2.1	1.3
Forestry	150	152	152	1.3	—
Fishing	442	450	450	1.8	—
Production of oil and gas	2,440	3,150	1,900	32.0	−37.6
Other mining	369	357	303	−3.3	−15.1
Industry	3,965	4,956	5,452	25.0	10.0
Power supply	1,897	2,000	2,280	5.4	14.0
Building and construction	615	664	717	8.0	8.0
Oil exploration	550	1,400	1,330	154.5	−5.0
Commerce	1,726	1,795	1,885	4.0	5.0
Commercial building	801	881	969	10.0	10.0
Shipping	4,893	3,630	4,860	−25.8	33.9
Other communications	1,740	1,955	1,965	12.4	0.5
Other business	810	850	901	4.9	6.0
Housing	5,868	6,015	6,256	2.5	4.0
Public capital projects	5,701	5,855	6,075	2.7	3.8
Total domestic fixed investment	33,183	35,300	36,700	6.4	4.0

Source: Finans- og tolldepartementet, *Nasjonalbudsjettet 1975*, St. meld. nr. 1, Oslo, 1974, p. 43.

investment plans of Norwegian industry for the coming year. These surveys of the investment intentions of private industry are used as a basis for budgeting private investment and for formulating economic policies concerning private investment. For example, the survey of private industrial investment plans for 1973 made by the Central Bureau of Statistics in May 1972 indicated that private business enterprises that were surveyed had planned to increase their investments in plant and equipment by 8 percent in 1973. Since the government's annual national plan for 1973 was constructed with the goal of only a 7 percent increase in private fixed investment, the annual plan called for restrictive monetary policies and smaller construction quotas.

Major decisions, such as whether to stimulate investment in the export industries or in the purely domestic industries, are made by the government. Also, the decision as to whether to expand a nationalized industry at the expense of private industry can be made only by the government. Within the private sector, investment decisions, although initiated by private business enterprises, are somewhat influenced by government officials and by private financial agents such as banks and other credit institutions. These agents cooperate with the government in regulating the flow of private investment in accordance with the government's annual investment plan. Regulating or controlling the saving and investment processes in Norway is a continuous activity that moves from one annual plan to the next. The investment planning for any one year is but an extension of the planning of the preceding year, with adjustments made for changes in the level of economic activity.

The Control of Private Investment

Investment in private industrial buildings and construction is controlled by a quota system for building permits. No new firm can be established until it secures a license to construct the buildings it needs, nor can an established firm expand its industrial plant until it obtains the necessary building permit. Each year the government incorporates in its annual plan a building quota or budget which allocates building licenses to industry, agriculture, and local county government authorities who issue licenses for local government building and construction. The building quota applies only to what is described as "regulated building activity."[13] In recent years, building restrictions have been greatly relaxed, so that much home building and nonresidential construction involving limited financial outlays are no longer regulated through the building license system.

The control of building and construction through the building license system enables the government to direct private fixed investment into those economic activities and geographical areas that it believes will contribute the most to the welfare of the Norwegian people. Industry at times is directed away from the congested area around Oslo; when feasible, it may be required to locate in the underdeveloped northern counties where year-round employment is scarce and the standard of living is lower than in the more populous areas to the south. Tax concessions and availability of credit are also used to induce private business enterprises to locate their industrial plants in the northern areas of Norway. While some progress has been made in establishing fish-processing plants and iron and steel mills and in expanding mining activities in these areas, the economic disadvantages of locating in the northern counties have thus far prevented extensive industrialization.

Private investment in industrial building and construction is also controlled on the

---

[13] The Royal Norwegian Ministry of Finance, *The National Budget of Norway, 1973*, pp. 72-73.

financial side. Where industrial building is financed externally, either long-term mortgage loans are secured from commercial and savings banks and insurance companies or bearer bonds are sold in the nation's capital market. In both cases, the supply of long-term credit is controlled by the government according to its annual financial plan. The annual physical quota for regulated building is accompanied by financial planning which seeks to ensure that the projected industrial, agricultural, and local government building and construction are adequately financed. Control of the long-term financing of industrial building and construction is secured through the cooperation of the Ministry of Finance, the Bank of Norway, and the country's private lending institutions.

Private investment in producers' equipment, such as machinery, transportation equipment, and ships, is also subject to considerable control under the Norwegian annual planning programs. As in the case of industrial plant, the government's survey of private business investment plans throws considerable light on private plans for investment in machinery and equipment. These private investment plans usually exceed the total investment in machinery and equipment that is set forth as an investment goal in the government's annual projected investment budgets. Consequently, in most of the years since 1945 the Norwegian government's investment policy has been designed to restrict the flow of private funds into producers' equipment. A number of regulatory measures have been adopted to control the flow of private investment in producers' goods. The main device used is the rationing of bank credit for the purchase of machinery and equipment. The government, through the Credit Policy Advisory Committee, requests the commercial and savings banks to ration intermediate credit in the light of the requirements of the machinery and equipment investment goals set forth in the annual national plan. When planned private investment in producers' equipment in a boom period exceeds the level of investment regarded by the government as adequate for sustained economic growth, special taxes may be levied on new investment in equipment to restrict this type of investment.

Norwegian Price Policy

Like other Western European countries, Norway is very much interested in achieving price stability.[14] The price problem is important internally because the program for achieving a fair or reasonable sharing of the nation's income is made very difficult where prices are rapidly increasing and all major economic groups are struggling to increase their share of the country's expanding real national income. Intergroup struggles over shares of national income lead to further increases in prices and a weakening of Norway's international trade position. Since prices in Norway, as in most countries in the postwar period, have continued to rise, a major effort has been directed towards curbing inflation and preventing Norway's export prices from rising faster than the export prices of other countries. In the latter objective, Norway has generally been successful.

Norway entered the postwar period with an extensive system of price controls, which was maintained relatively intact during the years 1945-1949. After 1949, when supplies became more abundant, many detailed price controls were abandoned. Norway did not, however, return to the free market price system that now operates in some other Western European countries and in the United States.

[14] Norwegian price policy is reviewed in Organisation for Economic Co-operation and Development, *Non-Wage Incomes and Prices Policy*, Paris, 1966, pp. 156-160; and in the *Economic Bulletin*, the quarterly publication of the Bank of Norway.

The Norwegian Price Control Act of 1953 gave the government the power to: (1) regulate prices and profits, (2) control cartels and restrictive business arrangements, and (3) impose dividend limitations in the form of maximum rates of dividends that can be paid on company shares. Both goods and services are subject to regulation under the Price Control Act, which also empowers the price-control authorities to regulate the prices of enterprises operated by the state and the municipalities.[15] Under this new price control legislation, the control of prices is assigned to the Price Directorate, assisted by a Price Council with both government and private business representatives. Major decisions with regard to price policy are made by the Ministry of Prices and Wages or, if thought desirable, by the Parliament itself.

Since the Price Control Act went into operation in 1954, price control in Norway has not taken the form of setting maximum prices for many individual commodities and services. In the manufacturing and service or trade areas, individual prices are in most cases no longer controlled by establishing maximum prices for individual commodities. The main efforts of the government have been directed at restoring competitive supply-and-demand conditions so that prices will be free from restrictive business practices. All cartels and trade associations or other groups that act collectively in the business world are required by law to register with the price-control authorities. The government has reduced the number of restrictive business practices by prohibiting horizontal price agreements among members of trade associations or business "rings." It has also placed a ban on price fixing by individual manufacturers and suppliers; they can no longer enter into agreements with individual wholesalers and retailers which require them to sell at fixed prices. Suppliers may indicate or propose to dealers resale prices for their commodities, but dealers are free to sell at any price above or below a supplier's suggested list price. While suggested prices are legal, the Price Directorate can prohibit the use of suggested prices at any time if there is ground "to assume that the activity leads to excessive prices or markups, or otherwise works against an effective competition." Since 1953, the Norwegian government has also relaxed import restrictions and increased the flow of imports in order to stimulate more competitive pricing in Norway's domestic markets.

When prices have increased at an alarming rate, as they did in 1970, the government has turned to a general price freeze, during which the prices and profit margins of many goods and services cannot be increased without the prior approval of the Price Directorate. Such drastic measures have been used infrequently and only when Norway's external equilibrium has been threatened. In recent years, price subsidies have been extensively used to hold down the prices of milk and dairy products, but they have not played as important a role in other sectors of the economy and none at all in the manufacturing sector.

Price developments in Norway clearly show that the government's price-control policy has not prevented inflation but has only curbed it. The success or failure of the government's price-control policy must be judged in the light of the goal set for this policy. Since 1945, the Norwegian government has placed a much higher priority on full employment and adequate sustained economic growth than on stable prices. Where a high-pressure economy is made the prime goal, as in Norway, price stability is to some extent sacrificed. This was made very clear when Norway's Labor Prime

---

[15] The Nordic Economic Cooperation Committee (Det Nordiske Økonomiske Samarbeidsutvalg). *Nordic Economic Cooperation, Special Part, Problems of Economic Cooperation,* Vol. 3 (*Nordisk Økonomisk Samarbeid, Spesiell Del Økonomiske Samarbeidsproblemer,* Oslo, 1957), pp. 185–195.

Minister stated that "The development of prices and wages becomes an important problem only when it jeopardizes the economic growth of our nation. A stable price and wage level is desirable, but it is not a goal in itself. For the Government the main goals are: to induce an ever better exploitation of natural resources, to expand production, and to assure a socially equitable distribution of income. To reach these goals we shall have to resort to a number of tools that will help to increase efficiency, strengthen our competitive position, and maintain full employment."[16]

Norwegian Organized Labor

The development of national economic planning in Norway has raised the important question of the role of organized labor in a democratically planned economy. Trade unions first appeared as a means of defending and promoting the interests of the workers in a largely unplanned economic situation in which each major economic interest in the nation sought to maximize its share of the national income. The methods and purposes of the labor movement were adjusted to the needs of a highly competitive struggle over shares of the nation's total output. Aggressive labor leadership was prepared to enforce its demands by resorting to work stoppages whenever necessary. In general, these leaders in the early years of the labor movement were more concerned with the special interests of their own particular group than with the overall national interest.

Although many of the harsh features of the industrial relations system had been eliminated by the early 1930s, and both organized labor and organized business had by this time come to appreciate the advantages of regularized procedures and restraint in collective bargaining, the trade unions were still essentially aggressive organizations *(kamporganisasjoner)*: their leaders were fighting for the welfare of a "protectionist" or "special" interest and not for the national welfare. Even though the Norwegian labor movement was both an economic and a political movement after 1880, its political aspirations did not interfere with its economic class objectives so long as the trade unions did not control the party with a majority in the nation's Parliament. When the Norwegian Labor party took over the government in the 1930s, the trade unions began to reconsider their role in an economy in which they were to play a major if not dominant role. But no extensive national economic planning was carried on before 1939. Only when the Norwegian Labor party embarked upon a comprehensive national economic planning program after 1945 was organized labor forced to reconsider its role in the new planning era.

An important part of Norwegian national planning is the planning of the use or distribution of the nation's supply of workers. This part of the planning program is carried out with the aid of annual and four-year manpower budgets that show how the labor supply may be adjusted to the needs of the expanding total national output. Since Norway's population increases at the low annual rate of 0.8 percent, the annual addition to the total work force of 1.7 million is small, and the annual increase in gross domestic product of approximately 4.5 percent requires an efficient use of whatever labor supply is available. The manpower budgets are designed to show the trends in the use of labor and how labor may be efficiently distributed over the economy during the plan period. Table 9-10 summarizes the manpower projection for the plan period, 1974-1977. In this four-year plan period, total employment is projected to increase by 43,000 or 2.7 percent. This

[16] The Norwegian Information Service, *News of Norway*, Vol. 16, New York, Jan. 29, 1959.

Table 9-10
Employment by Industry in the Norwegian Economy, 1973 (Actual) and 1977 (Projected)

Industries (thousand man-years)	1973 (Actual)	1977 (Projected)	Annual growth rate in percent, 1973–1977
Agriculture and forestry	156	134	−3.8
Fishing	30	26	−3.6
Mining and manufacturing	408	408	—
Construction	137	151	2.5
Electricity, gas, and water	15	16	1.6
Wholesale and retail trade	211	225	1.6
Water transport	51	45	−3.1
Other transport and communications	103	107	0.9
Financial institutions	38	40	1.3
Government services	102	108	1.4
Other service industries	313	347	2.6
Commercial buildings	3	3	—
Total employment	1,567	1,610	2.7

Source: Royal Norwegian Ministry of Finance, *Norwegian Long Term Programme, 1974–1977*, Parliamentary Report No. 71, 1972–1973, Oslo, 1972, pp. 61–62.

additional labor supply is projected to be taken up mainly by construction, the wholesale and retail trade, government services, and other service industries. In addition, workers are projected to move in considerable numbers out of agriculture, fishing, and water transport; these areas are expected to lose 32,000 workers, while construction and the public and private services gain 68,000 workers. These changes in the employment pattern during the plan period 1974–1977 would continue the trends at work since 1950.

Collective Bargaining in Norway

Somewhat more than one-half of Norway's 1,654,000 wage earners are members of trade unions. In all Scandinavian countries, the degree of union organization is very high. Workers are considerably more organized in Norway than in the United Kingdom and much more than in the United States. Since in all major industries—forestry, mining, manufacturing, building, and transportation—almost all the workers belong to unions, no need is felt by organized labor for closed or union shops. The Norwegian trade union movement is one of the most centralized union movements in the Western world. The Norwegian Federation of Trade Unions, with its membership of 648,000 workers, accounts for 96 percent of all the nation's unionized workers with membership in independent trade unions. The fifteen large industrial unions are the mainstay of the Norwegian Federation of Trade Unions: they account for 85 percent of the Federation's membership. The remaining 15 percent of the membership belong to twenty-three national craft unions.

The Norwegian Federation of Trade Unions has much more power over the activities of its member unions than do the Danish and Swedish federations. It established itself as a strong central body at the time of its founding (1899) when it took over the operation of the member trade unions' central strike fund. With this control in its hands, the Norwegian Federation of Trade Unions took an active role in both labor disputes and in politics; socialist and union leadership were very close in the latter area. The supreme authority of the federation is the Congress of three hundred union delegates, which meets once every four years. Between sessions of the Congress, the National Council of 135 members meets annually to approve the general principles that guide the federation in negotiations concerning collective bargaining agreements. The center of power in the federation is its Executive Council of fifteen members, which meets weekly and handles all immediate problems. This council is in effect a general staff with a strong influence over the federation. While each member union of the federation maintains a great deal of control over its internal affairs, the external affairs of member unions are subject to a high degree of centralized control.

The constitution of the Norwegian Federation of Labor states that one of the aims of the federation is: "To promote the establishment of common principles for all unions, in order to be able . . . to create unity and strength in the work for promoting and consolidating the professional, economic, social, and cultural interests of the wage-earners." This unity is achieved by giving the federation's Executive Council extensive control over the collective bargaining activities carried on by the federation's member unions. No member union may terminate a wage agreement or put forward a demand for a new wage agreement unless such action is first approved by the federation's Executive Council. No union may initiate a strike unless the sanction of the Executive Council has been procured. In the event of a strike involving more than one union, the council assumes active leadership of the dispute; none of the participating unions may settle their dispute without the council's permission. The federation is always represented in government mediation and arbitration proceedings; if more than one union is involved, the federation through its representatives conducts the proceedings for the unions. If any member union acts contrary to the demands of the Executive Council, it loses the moral and financial (strike benefits) support of the federation and may be expelled from the federation by the Executive Council. In the postwar period, 1945–1975, Norwegian unions rarely acted against the general principles governing union contract negotiations or without the sanction of the federation's Executive Council. Since World War II the federation has increasingly tended to take command over industry-wide contract negotiations.

Norwegian employers, like their workers, are well organized and are united in the field of industrial relations through membership in a highly centralized employers' association. The Norwegian Employers' Association, like the Norwegian Federation of Trade Unions, is organized for the most part along industrial lines. Employers in forty-one industries are organized in industrial associations, which, along with many of the large individual firms, constitute the membership of the association. The approximately 8,500 member firms of the Norwegian Employers' Association have a total labor force of about 250,000 workers. Although some of the large industrial associations in the major export industries remain outside the association and conduct their labor contract negotiations independently, the general principles of negotiation laid down by the Norwegian Employers' Association are accepted by all employers. The General Meeting of the association, with its 250 delegates, holds an annual congress to determine broad policy lines in the field of industrial relations. The Central Board of forty-seven members deals with more immediate matters. The Executive Committee of eight members directs the labor contract negotiations carried on by the industry associations with the trade unions and the Executive Council of the Federation of Trade Unions. Effective policy making is undertaken by the Central Board and the Executive Committee of the Employers' Association. These two bodies are responsible for creating a united front among the nation's employers, and for doing all they can to ensure that this front is not weakened during contract negotiations.

Unity among Norwegian employers is obtained by giving their association a high degree of control over labor contract negotiations. The association determines all the general principles with respect to the contents of the collective agreements that are acceptable to the organized employers. Such agreements generally cover whole industries. No employer or industrial association holding membership in the association may enter into a collective labor agreement without the advance approval of the association's Executive Committee. All lockouts by employers must receive the prior sanction of the Executive Committee. Any Norwegian employer who continues to work despite a directive to close his or her plant, or who signs a separate agreement during a general strike, is subject to a heavy fine. Any employer who does not abide by the directives of the association's Executive Committee is deprived of strike or lockout benefits which the association pays out of its accumulated fees. In addition, he or she may be fined and is open to future economic reprisals from other members of the association. In recent decades there have been very few employer members who have not accepted the discipline required by the Norwegian Employers' Association of its members.

The centralization of control in Norway's employer and employee national organizations has exerted much influence on the development of collective bargaining. With all large employers and trade unions represented in their respective central bargaining organizations and tight reins being held over all major collective bargaining negotiations and industrial disputes, collective bargaining in Norway has become a highly rationalized process. Every possible arrangement is made and every possible step taken to reduce the areas of disagreement and to conclude agreements without recourse to work stoppages. The original labor contract terms are prepared by the national unions and the industrial associations, and then are submitted to the appropriate central organization. Each organization works with its members in developing basic policies with respect to wages and other work conditions. Both the Norwegian Federation of Trade Unions and the Norwegian Employers' Association evaluate the bargaining demands of their members to see if they are in line with the general policies developed by each organization. The central organizations trim excessive demands before they reach the bargaining table. Even so, both sides realize that contract demands as originally presented are usually maximum proposals which are open to bargaining.

Collective bargaining contracts in Norway usually run for two or three years, are industry wide in application, and, in the case of the contracts for the major industries, terminate in the first six months of the same year. Since all the major contracts are renegotiated at about the same time and determine the bargaining trends for all Norwegian industry, the Executive Council of the Federation of Trade Unions is in a very good position to evaluate the overall impact on the Norwegian economy of the combined wage demands of the trade unions. The council then can propose adjustments in wage demands to meet the needs of national policy. While theoretically the council's contract proposals are not binding on the affiliated unions, most unions are unwilling to fight for wage increases not approved by the council. Only on very infrequent occasions since 1945 have member unions been unwilling to bargain for the contract terms approved by the Executive Council. Employers have less autonomy with respect to contract terms, since they must bargain for those terms that have been approved by the Central Board of their association.

Many of the provisions of collective bargaining agreements have been standardized by a Basic Agreement made by the Federation of Trade Unions and the Employers' Association in 1935. This agreement makes provision for the settlement of disputes with regard to contracts, the duties of shop stewards, worker lay-offs, the admission of new members to the employers' and employees' central organizations, methods of voting on collective agreements, and other matters of common interest. All disputes arising from the interpretation of collective agreements must be submitted to the Labor Court, which was established by the Labor Disputes Act of 1915. In all disputes stemming from collective agreements, the decisions of the Labor Court are final. The small case load of this court reveals that employers and employees prefer to try to settle their disputes about contracts without calling upon the court for a decision.

If collective bargaining fails to give rise to a collective agreement, the dispute goes to the State Mediator. Under Norway's mediation system, which was set up in 1915, all unsettled industrial disputes must be submitted to mediation before recourse to a strike or lockout. If the State Mediator cannot settle the dispute in a "cooling off" period of eighteen days, both sides are free to stop work. Mediation is frequently used in Norway; in some years, more contracts between employers and employees are concluded through mediation than through the ordinary process of collective bargaining. Where mediation fails to bring contract negotiations to a successful conclusion, compulsory arbitration may be used by the government if it feels that a strike or lockout would seriously affect the nation's economy. The Norwegian government still resorts to compulsory arbitration in emergency situations; in such cases, the government appoints special wage boards, whose rulings on wage disputes are mandatory.

As in the other Scandinavian countries, a very low proportion of Norwegian industrial employees are involved in strikes, and the annual loss of working time per employee is very low. In the seven-year period 1965–1971, work stoppages averaged only eight a year: only 1,340 workers out of a total of over 1 million workers were on the average involved each year; and the average annual number of working days lost was only 15,759. The reduction in industrial strife in Norway can be attributed to, among other factors: (1) the strength and stability of the trade union movement; (2) the mature pattern of industrial relations, which has given Norway a highly rationalized collective bargaining system, and (3) the close relations between the Federation of Trade Unions and the Norwegian Labor party.

In recent decades, the Norwegian labor movement has been free from internal conflicts of an ideological or jurisdictional nature, and its membership has been very stable. Labor and business, under their "basic agreement" of 1935, have recognized each other's right to organize and have developed highly refined bargaining procedures. With the Labor government in office in most years since 1945, the Norwegian labor movement has had to accept much of the responsibility for preserving industrial peace. It is not surprising that the strike as an industrial weapon has lost much of its importance in Norway; for the past twenty-five years there has been a strong and secure union movement, a well-developed and highly centralized system of collective bargaining, and a political situation that has caused labor to emphasize the importance of avoiding industrial conflict.

Norwegian Wage Policy

Unlike prices and other economic factors, wage rates in postwar Norway have never been subject to direct governmental controls. Since the Norwegian economy is still largely a private enterprise economy and is subject to a limited number of controls, wage rates are still the product in large part of relatively free economic forces at work in the nation's private markets. Employers and employees are free to bargain over wage rates in the unionized sector of the economy, which includes only one-half of the nation's workers. Wage rates in the large nonunionized sector of the economy are still very much under the influence of competitive supply-and-demand factors, although it is the unionized sector that sets in motion the basic wage trends of the whole economy. Government wage policy in Norway consists of intervening at various strategic points in the process of wage determination with the aim of indirectly guiding this process so that wage movements will serve rather than obstruct the national welfare. The government is in frequent contact with both the Norwegian Employers' Association and the Norwegian Federation of Trade Unions for the purpose of explaining how it believes wage rates should be changed if the national interest is to be preserved. This consultation has been fairly effective in bringing both sides of industry around to accepting voluntarily the broad outlines of wage policy laid down by the government in the years since the end of the Second World War.[17]

[17] Lars Aarvik, "Labor Relations and Wage Policy in Norway," *Scandinavia Past and Present, Five Modern Democracies*, Arnkrone, Denmark, Edvard Henriksen, 1959, pp. 812-816.

Norwegian wage policy contains the following features. Wage-rate increases should bear some relation to the annual improvement in productivity or output per man-hour, and some allowance should be made for any rise in consumer prices. Wage-rate increases should not be so large as to result in large increases in wage costs per unit of output, which would make Norwegian exports less competitive in the world's trading markets. Furthermore, following the principle of solidarity, trade unions in high-productivity industries should share their productivity improvement with workers in low-productivity industries. This is done by giving special consideration during collective bargaining to increases in wage rates in low-productivity industries. Norwegian wage policy also calls for the reduction of wage differentials within individual industries and between them. Wage differentials between skilled and unskilled, old and young, and male and female workers should be reduced wherever possible. Business firms that cannot remain profitable with rising wage rates should be eliminated and their workers should be absorbed by the more successful enterprises. In an expanding economy, labor should move from the low-productivity to the higher-productivity industries in order to obtain a more equitable share of the annual increase in the gross domestic product.

These principles of wage policy were widely applied in Norway in the years after the Second World War. Much of the gap between average wages in agriculture and the extractive industries and average wages in manufacturing was reduced. Wage differentials between skilled and unskilled and male and female workers in the same industry were also lowered. The large demands for labor in all sectors of the high-pressure Norwegian economy eliminated former areas of high unemployment with their depressed wages. In addition, the solidaristic wage policy of the

Norwegian trade unions and the Norwegian Labor party has contributed to a reduction of wage differentials between and within industries. However, considerable wage differentials among Norwegian workers remain in effect, largely as a result of the considerable wage drifting that leads employers to pay wages above the negotiated wage rates called for by labor contracts. Wage drifting occurs mainly among skilled workers in short supply; it constitutes an important means of attracting workers into the nation's high-priority and high-productivity industries.

From 1963 to 1969, wage developments did not undermine the government's program for achieving sustained and adequate economic growth. The annual average increase in wage rates in manufacturing of 7.2 percent was largely offset by an annual improvement of output per man-hour of 5.6 percent. While wage costs per unit of output increased in Norway in these years, they did not increase more rapidly than in many other Western European countries, so that Norway remained competitive in the world's export markets and continued to have large annual increases in the volume of its exports. Norway's favorable wage developments came to an end, however, in 1970 when a wage explosion occurred; hourly earnings in manufacturing in that year rose 12 percent and were followed by an increase of 12.4 percent in 1971. After a pause in 1972–1973, large wage increases were again secured in 1974 and 1975, the increase in the latter year being 19.5 percent.

Agriculture in the Planned Norwegian Economy

Norwegian agriculture suffered severely during the depressed 1930s when the decline in national income greatly restricted the domestic market for agricultural products. During the Second World War, when imports were largely unobtainable and domestic demands were at a high level, agriculture improved its economic status in relation to the nation's other economic activities. When the Norwegian Labor party was returned to office after the war, with a great deal of its political support coming from the country's small farmers, it incorporated in its planning program measures for the preservation of the prosperity of the agricultural sector of Norway's economy. The economic status of the average farmer was to be raised to that of the average industrial worker so that the nation's farmers would be able to get a reasonable share of the expanding Gross National Product.

The postwar agricultural plan of the Norwegian Labor government had four major goals: (1) the expansion of agricultural income in equal step with nonagricultural income; (2) the equalization of agricultural incomes between "rich" and "poor" areas within the agricultural sector; (3) the achieving of established production goals for animal and cereal products; and (4) the maintenance of low food prices so that both the cost of living and wage rates tied to the cost of living could be kept down. All these agricultural policy objectives were to be sought after within the general framework of the annual and long-range national plans presented to the Norwegian Parliament.[18]

The income objectives of Norwegian agricultural policy are closely associated with the concept of the "national farm." According to this concept, all of Norway's farms are viewed for policy purposes as being parts of one large national farm. An account is drawn up each year for this national farm that shows the total gross income, total expenditures or costs, and total net earnings of all Norwegian

[18] Organisation for European Economic Cooperation, *Further Problems in Agricultural Policy, 4th Report on Agricultural Policies in Europe and North America*, Paris, 1960, pp. 143–165. See also OECD, *Agricultural Policy in Norway*, Paris, 1975.

agriculture. By observing changes in the gross income and expenditures of the "national farm," i.e., in the aggregate account of Norwegian agriculture, the government can uncover changes in the total net-income position of all Norwegian farmers. As agricultural costs go up, the aim of agricultural policy is to make appropriate adjustments in farm prices and subsidies to maintain the farmers' net income or share of national income. Also, as agricultural productivity rises, this productivity improvement is reflected in rising farm incomes.

If the total account of the "national farm" shows that total farm expenditures or costs are increasing faster than total farm receipts and that total net farm labor income is declining, the agricultural agreements relating to agricultural prices and subsidies are renegotiated to restore farmers' net labor income. Also, when new wage agreements increase industrial wage rates, the maximum or ceiling prices of liquid milk and dairy products are likewise increased in new agricultural agreements in order to preserve the income position of the nation's farmers relative to that of industrial wage earners. Agricultural agreements are usually made in the first half of the year after wage agreements in the economy's major industries have been negotiated. Negotiations concerning agricultural prices and subsidies then can take into account the terms of wage agreements and their impact on the cost of living and agricultural costs.

The core of postwar Norwegian agricultural policy lies in the agreements negotiated by the Norwegian government and the two major farmers' organizations, the Norwegian Farmers' Union and the Norwegian Farmers' and Smallholders' Union. These agreements, started in 1947 and formalized by the General Agreement of 1950, recognize the need for the regulation of the supplies of agricultural products, for measures to secure an equitable income for the agricultural population, and for close cooperation between the government and the various farmers' organizations in the formulation of agricultural policy. Under these annual, two-year, and three-year agreements, price agreements are made for cereals, dairy products, wool, vegetables, and fruits. These agreements include fixed prices for grains and maximum prices for milk and dairy products. The government enforces price and market regulation measures, as called for by the agricultural agreements, while the farmers agree not to follow any agricultural practices that are contrary to the provisions of the agricultural agreements. During any agreement period, if economic conditions change significantly, both sides to the agreement may ask for a reconsideration of the agreement, which must in all cases be approved by the Parliament before being put into operation.

Norwegian farms vary widely in income earning capacity, from the prosperous areas of southern and central Norway to the poor areas of western and northern Norway. The Norwegian government has used its price and subsidy programs to give special financial support to Norway's low farm income areas. The Cereal Monopoly, a division of the State Grain Corporation, pays special premiums above the fixed price for barley grown by farmers in less favored mountain and fjord regions in western and northern Norway. The Feed Monopoly, also a division of the State Grain Corporation, sells animal-feeding stuffs at low subsidized prices on a rationed basis that benefits the small farms more than the large farms. State milk subsidies vary according to the size of the farm and also from region to region. Small farms and farms in poor areas benefit most from milk subsidies, which increase the prices received for milk in poor areas by from 4 to 30 percent over the prices received in the more favored areas of the country. Farmers in northern Norway and in the mountain and fjord regions also receive for the production of potatoes special payments per hectare (2.47 acres) that are not given to farmers in other regions.

In order to increase agricultural productivity, agricultural agreements for a number of years have provided for subsidies in the form of price reductions on all types of fertilizers and agricultural lime, and low transport charges on these farm needs. Additional price reductions have been made for farms of less than twenty acres. These fertilizer and transport subsidies have been covered in part by allocations from the general revenues of the State Treasury and in part by special levies imposed on some domestically produced fertilizers. Other subsidies which have tended to raise the incomes of the small farmers in poor regions are state grants from the Farm House Fund to modernize farm buildings and to rationalize farm work, and subsidies for the purchase of high quality seeds, silo construction, and for grain drying and storage.

Norwegian agricultural policy has met with success in some areas but not in others. The government's program for raising the productivity of Norwegian agriculture has been quite successful. Improvements in agricultural practices and the extensive mechanization of Norwegian agriculture have resulted in an average annual increase in output per man-year that since 1953 has exceeded the average annual increase in output per man-year in industry. In spite of the large increase in total agricultural production, there has been no accumulation of large unsalable agricultural surpluses in Norway. The various private agricultural marketing associations, such as the Milk Producers' Association and the Norwegian Egg Pool, have successfully taken on the burden of making certain that, in general, supply is adjusted to demand. The government's program for securing a favorable relationship between farmer and factory worker incomes has had some success. Real incomes of farmers, while not equal to those of factory workers, have since 1950 increased more rapidly than the real incomes of industrial workers so that the gap between farmer and factory worker incomes is being reduced.

On the debit side, the Norwegian agricultural program has been very costly. Government subsidies supply from 35 to 40 percent of annual agricultural income. These subsidies have annually absorbed about 15 percent of the central government's total revenues. It is difficult to reduce agricultural subsidies, since any such reductions increase the cost of living and result in trade union demands for increases in wage rates. A second deficiency of the postwar Norwegian agricultural policy has been its failure to lead to the creation of larger and more efficient farms. In spite of the very large movement of labor out of agriculture since 1945, the number of farms in Norway has decreased very little, and there has been no significant change in the size of the average farm. Norwegian agricultural policy has increased the cost of food and agricultural raw materials to domestic buyers by preventing the importation of cheaper foreign agricultural products. The law of comparative advantage has not been permitted to work itself out freely in the trade relations between Norway and other countries so as to bring to Norway the benefits of low foreign agricultural prices. However, the Norwegian Labor government is well aware of these limitations of its agricultural program and has accepted them as the price of bringing stability and security to the agricultural sector of the Norwegian economy.

The External Sector

Norway's international economic relationships place it in a very delicate balance with respect to the rest of the world, especially with Western Europe, which takes three-quarters of Norwegian commodity exports.

Since Norway's exports and imports of goods and services each constitute approximately 40 percent of its Gross National Product, the country is faced with the perennial problem of maintaining exports at a high enough level to pay for large imports. About two-thirds of Norway's exports consist of wood and paper products, base metals, chemicals, fish and fish products, and other raw materials; one-third consists of ships, machinery, and other manufactured goods. Norway has had a vigorous export-import trade since the Korean War. In the period 1963–1972, the volume of Norwegian commodity exports annually increased at an average rate of 8.4 percent. This export experience compares favorably with that of Sweden, Denmark, and France and is much superior to that of the United Kingdom.

Norway usually has an unfavorable commodity balance of trade. Commodity exports pay for only about one-half of Norway's commodity imports. The remaining half of Norway's commodity imports is paid for mainly by the exporting of freight service. Since 1952, Norway's merchant fleet has more than doubled in size and is now the world's third largest fleet. Norway's heavy reliance upon the export of shipping services to pay for its commodity imports places it in a dangerously exposed economic position. Not only is international shipping a highly competitive industry, but freight rates are very sensitive to changes in world prosperity. A decline in world economic activity very quickly leads to lower freight rates and unchartered ships. Norway must therefore be prepared to take action quickly to offset any sizable decline in its revenues from shipping.

Since Norway is less affluent when compared with the major Western European countries and has capital needs that are beyond what its domestic saving can finance, it must borrow from other countries to finance a part of the expansion of its extractive industries and its merchant fleet. Foreign capital has been used to finance in part the aluminum, chemical, oil production, and shipping industries. In most years since 1953, Norway has had an import surplus. However, if the net import of ships is excluded from total imports, Norway's exports of goods and services are usually sufficient to pay for all other imported goods and services.

Not having a large gold and dollar reserve, Norway must keep a close watch on its current balance of international payments. This balance tends to become adverse in prosperous times when imports of consumer goods, raw materials, and producers' equipment expand more rapidly than Norway's exports. The main economic danger that Norway faces is a tendency for imports to increase more rapidly than exports, especially in boom periods when rising personal incomes result in an increasing demand for imported goods. Commodity exports are at times slow to increase, because severe competition abroad makes it difficult to expand foreign markets. Before 1958, external deficits were kept within satisfactory limits by means of foreign exchange control supplemented by fiscal, monetary, price, and wage policies. Since 1958, when foreign exchange control was greatly relaxed, more use has been made of fiscal, monetary, and other economic policies to curb consumer and business demand for commodity imports in boom periods. Sales taxes have been increased on imported goods or on goods using imported raw materials; increased income taxes have curbed personal and business disposable incomes; and wage restraint has restricted domestic price increases. This combination of domestic economic policies has enabled the Norwegian Labor government to prevent the development of large deficits in its external economy—deficits which otherwise would have seriously reduced the nation's gold and dollar reserves or led to excessive borrowing abroad.

In the near future Norway's external sector will probably undergo significant changes. The prospective rapid rise in oil revenues from Norway's North Sea oil fields after 1980 should greatly ease its foreign trade problems. At first much of this increase in revenues will be needed to repay loans used to finance Norway's oil exploration and production program. Eventually, however, Norway could be a large exporter of oil and gas with a large surplus in its current balance of international payments. It would then be in a very favorable position to pay for its imports of goods and services and to develop a strong creditor position with regard to the rest of the world.

The Norwegian Tax System

The distinguishing feature of the Norwegian tax system is its heavy reliance on personal and company income taxes, which along with property taxes account for 38 percent of total general government revenue. Municipal personal income taxes have a maximum rate of 20 percent, and the national personal income tax has a maximum rate of 73.5 percent. Norwegian corporate income is taxed at the rate of 30 percent.[19] Contributions to the national insurance scheme account for 24 percent of general government revenue, while indirect taxes supply 38 percent of this revenue. The main source of indirect taxation is the value-added tax of 20 percent, which replaced the 13 percent general sales tax in 1970, and which applies to 72 percent of private consumption. The total tax burden in Norway, measured by the ratio of total taxes to gross domestic product, is one of the heaviest among Western industrialized nations. In 1973, this burden was 48 percent for Norway, 33 percent for the United Kingdom, and 29 percent for the United States.

As the welfare state in Norway has expanded, the tax burden has increased. The tax burden, which was 30.1 percent in 1955-1957, increased to 38.7 percent in 1967-1969. The low-income classes in Norway are relieved of much of the tax burden through social security transfer payments, such as children's allowances and other welfare payments, and also through subsidies to low-income farmers and fishermen. Social security payments and other transfers to household accounts take up approximately 30 percent of general government expenditures, while subsidies, primarily to agriculture and fishing, account for about 12 percent of these expenditures. A major feature of the Norwegian fiscal system is its large government saving and investment. The central government and the municipalities provide about one-fifth of the annual investment in fixed capital.

The short-term objective of fiscal management is to achieve economic stability by adjusting the fiscal system to cyclical variations in the level of economic activity. In boom periods, such as 1972-1973, the Norwegian government has adopted a restrictive fiscal program. This program includes increasing taxes—especially indirect taxes (value-added taxes)—reducing government expenditures, and securing a fiscal budget surplus. Private business enterprises are encouraged to place some of their profits in tax-free investment reserves, while individuals are stimulated with tax concessions to increase their personal savings.[20] Also, the government loans to the

---

[19] The details of the Norwegian tax system are presented in the Royal Ministry of Finance and Customs, *A Survey of the Norwegian Tax System in 1970*, Oslo, Norway, 1970.

[20] A Norwegian business enterprise may take a tax-free deduction of up to 25 percent of its annual net income which is placed in a blocked account in the Bank of Norway. These deposits may be released as an antirecession measure at the government's discretion for investment in plant and equipment or to cover the expenses of market development abroad and research related to the taxpayer's business activity.

state banks are reduced so as to curb the financing of home building and municipal construction. In periods of economic decline, such as 1969-1971, the government reverses these restrictive fiscal programs.

Fiscal Planning and Long-Term National Objectives

The government's medium-term and long-range fiscal planning has three main objectives: (1) maintaining a high level of public and private saving and investing; (2) securing a more equitable distribution of income; and (3) guiding the distribution of the nation's gross domestic product so as to maximize social welfare.[21] A prime goal of Norwegian fiscal planning has been to curb private consumption in order to expand both private and public investment. The statistics in Table 9-11 show that Norway assigns a larger percent of its gross domestic product to private and public investment than do most Western industrialized countries. Norway's average investment ratio (ratio of total fixed investment to gross domestic product) for 1953-1969 was 28.6 percent, as compared with 16.2 percent for the United Kingdom and 16.8 percent for the United States. Other nations, such as Sweden, West Germany, and France, have lower investment ratios than Norway but higher annual economic growth rates. This results from the lower investment productivity in Norway. Norwegian output per investment or capital unit is lower because much of Norway's investment provides communications and electrical power to remote parts of the country, or is made in the low-productivity industries of agriculture, forestry, and fisheries.[22]

[21] Both fiscal and monetary policy are parts of the larger Norwegian industrial policy that is designed to fit private enterprise into the framework of the national plans. Industrial and related economic policies are explained in Organisation for Economic Co-operation and Development, *The Industrial Policies of 14 Member Countries*, Ch. IX, "Norway," Paris, 1971, pp. 233-256.

[22] The incremental capital-output ratio (ICOR) for Norway in the years 1953-1969 averaged 1:0.2 whereas this ratio was 1:0.3 for the major OECD countries. OECD, *OECD Economic Surveys, Norway*, Jan. 1973, p. 9.

Table 9-11
Growth of Gross Domestic Product and Investment Ratios in Norway and Selected Countries, 1953-1969

	GDP growth percent average 1953-1969	Investment ratio percent average[1] 1953-1969
Norway	4.0	28.6
Sweden	4.3	22.4
Germany	6.3	24.2
Japan	10.0	28.2
France	5.5	21.0
Italy	5.5	20.4
United Kingdom	2.8	16.2
United States	3.4	16.8

[1] The investment ratio is the ratio of total fixed investment to gross domestic product.
Source: OECD, *OECD Economic Surveys, Norway*, 1972.

Table 9-12
Net Tax as a Percent of the Pretax Income for Various Income Groups of Norwegian Families with Two Children in 1958

Pretax income groups, annual income in kroner	Direct taxes	Sales tax	Excise taxes	Social security contributions	Price subsidies	Social security benefit payments	Net tax
4,000– 7,999	3.9	6.9	4.8	8.5	−3.4	−15.3	5.4
8,000–11,999	6.6	6.9	4.9	6.8	−3.4	−5.9	19.9
12,000–15,999	8.9	6.9	4.7	5.7	−3.4	−3.6	19.2
16,000–19,999	9.6	7.0	5.4	4.8	−3.0	−2.6	21.2
20,000–23,999	12.0	7.0	6.8	3.9	−2.6	−2.2	24.9
24,000–31,999	15.6	7.0	7.4	3.1	−2.0	−1.6	29.5
32,000–39,999	20.8	6.7	7.5	2.4	−1.6	−1.2	34.6
40,000 and over	27.7	7.7	10.3	1.7	−1.5	−0.5	45.4

Source: Norwegian Ministry of Finance, *The General Lines of the Norwegian Tax Policy*, 1961.

Norway maintains its high investment ratio by making appropriate adjustments in its tax system. Excessive wage-rate increases are prevented from expanding private consumption as a percent of gross domestic product by increasing indirect taxation. Although wage rates increased very considerably from 1970 to 1975, private consumption continued to take up only approximately 50 percent of the nation's gross domestic product, and gross fixed investment, one-third. Not only can the government curb consumption by increasing taxes, but it can also increase the prices of services provided by the government-owned railroads, telephone system, and power plants.

Government financial planning has also been used in Norway to bring about what the Labor party considers to be a fairer distribution of national income. Three methods have been used to redistribute incomes. First, progressive income and property taxes have passed much of the tax burden on to the upper-income groups. Second, subsidies to farmers, fishermen, and low-income industrial workers have been considerably increased since 1938. In that year, total government subsidy payments amounted to 1.4 percent of privately-earned income, but by the late 1950s these payments had increased to 6.2 percent of privately-earned income. In the same period, social security and other transfer payments, such as child allowances and old-age pensions, increased from 4.5 to 7.8 percent of privately-earned income. The distribution of the tax burden among wage and salary earners and self-employed persons (farmers and fishermen excluded) is presented in Table 9-12.[23] In this table, the net tax paid by the taxpayer in each income group is the sum of his direct and indirect taxes and social security contributions, minus the price subsidies and social security payments to his benefit. Direct taxes are highly progressive, while excise taxes are less progressive and sales taxes are proportional. Social security payments and price subsidies reduce the tax burden greatly for the families at the bottom of the income scale.

[23] Norwegian Ministry of Finance, *The General Lines of the Norwegian Tax Policy*, (Parliamentary Report No. 54, 1960–61), Oslo, 1961, p. 3.

Recent studies of income distribution show that the bottom tenth with the lowest personal income in Norway in 1970 received 2.6 percent of total post-tax personal income, while the top tenth received 27.7 percent. In France, by contrast, the bottom tenth received only 1.4 percent and the top tenth 30.4 percent of total post-tax personal income. These studies also show that Norway, like Sweden, continues to be among the nations recording the lowest degree of inequality of post-tax income distribution, whereas France, Italy, and the United States have the most unequal post-tax income distribution. The Atkinson technique of measuring post-tax income inequality takes .100 as an average measure of inequality, with deviations below .100 measuring less inequality and deviations above .100 measuring more inequality. According to this measure of post-tax inequality of income distribution, Norway and Sweden in 1970 had .079 and .077 measures of inequality respectively, while France, Italy, and the United States had measures of inequality of .141, .130, and .122 respectively.[24]

The tax, social security benefit, and price-subsidy program of the Norwegian Labor government has been constructed to curb the consumer expenditures of the upper-income groups and to enlarge these expenditures of the lower-income groups. As we have seen, total consumer expenditures are restricted to about 50 percent of total national output. With total consumer expenditures rather severely restricted in order to increase investment expenditures, the Norwegian government wants to be sure that the restricted amount of consumer goods is fairly evenly distributed over the total population. This is the general objective of the extensive price subsidy and social security benefit program, which is in accordance with the priorities established in the annual and four-year national plans.

Government expenditures in Norway are projected over the four-year plan periods with the aim of achieving the national priorities as set forth in the medium-term plans. Table 9-13 shows the projected central government expenditures on goods and services and social security payments for the period 1970-1973. This plan emphasizes the importance of increasing these expenditures on family and consumer affairs, art and cultural purposes, research and other aids to manufacturing, regional development, aid to developing countries, and environmental protection. Projecting the central government's expenditures over the 1970-1973 plan period was part of the new program for medium-term fiscal budgeting that was first adopted in 1963. When the four-year national economic budget is now prepared, a related four-year fiscal budget is also constructed.[25] The planning authorities explain that "By preparing a long-term budget it is possible to make a broad evaluation of the future developments and take a tentative position regarding the allocation of resources so that there is a better basis for the work connected with the annual budget.[26] The four-year fiscal budget concentrates on national economic and social goals, alternative methods of achieving these goals, and the cost effectiveness of these alternative methods.

Monetary and Credit Policy

Monetary and credit planning in Norway is the primary responsibility of the Bank of Norway working in cooperation with the Ministry of Finance. Closely associated with the government authorities in this planning is

---

[24] OECD Economic Outlook, *Occasional Studies, Income Distribution in OECD Countries*, Paris, July 1976, pp. 14-17.

[25] The genesis and development of long-term fiscal budgeting is explained in *Norwegian Long Term Programme, 1970-1973*, pp. 108-109.

[26] *Ibid.*, p. 109.

Table 9–13
Central Government Expenditures on Goods and Services and Transfers by Program Areas in 1969 (Actual) and 1973 (Projected)

	Million kroner, 1969 prices		
Program area	1969 (Actual)	1973 (Projected)	Percent change 1969–1973
Aid to developing countries	200	450	125
Consumer affairs	22	41	86
Interest on government debt	638	1,130	76
Manufacturing research	164	271	65
Nature preservation	9	13	44
Cultural purposes	88	113	28
Manpower measures	140	167	19
Internal transportation	2,185	2,586	18
Health services	600	700	17
Education	2,028	2,360	16
Defence	2,460	2,734	11
Social measures	1,407	1,531	9
Administration	598	625	4
Agriculture including subsidies	1,030	1,046	2
Other expenditures	2,653	2,823	6
Total government expenditures	14,222	16,590	17

Source: Norwegian Ministry of Finance, *Norwegian Long Term Programme, 1970–1973*.

the consultative Credit Policy Advisory Committee.[27] While the activities of this committee place no formal obligations on the private financial institutions, they are expected to follow the government's monetary and policy recommendations. The basic purpose of these recommendations is to adjust the money and credit supply to the needs of the annual and four-year plans. Monetary and credit policies are formulated so that they contribute to achieving the private- and public-consumption and investment goals set forth in the annual and four-year national economic budgets. When these budgets are constructed, credit sub-budgets are also drawn up. These sub-budgets show the total credit supply available in the plan period to the private sector and the municipalities as well as the contributions of the various financial institutions to this supply. The credit supply sub-budget for 1975 is presented in Table 9–14. This

---

[27] The Credit Policy Advisory Committee was preceded by the Joint Consultation Council (1951–1965), which provided for formal annual and five-year credit agreements between the government's financial agents and the private financial institutions. After the nonsocialist coalition government came to power in 1965, these institutions objected to the formal procedures of the council and in 1970 accepted in its place the informal purely advisory committee. The functions of the committee are discussed in Norges Bank, "The Monetary and Credit System in Norway," *Economic Bulletin*, Vol. XLIV, No. 1, March 1973, pp. 28–41.

Table 9-14
The Norwegian Credit Supply (Actual) for 1974 and Credit Budget (Projected) for 1975

	Million kroner		
	1974 (actual) credit supply	1975 (projected) credit budget	Credit increase in 1975 over 1974
Credit from abroad	6,500	6,500	0
Domestic credit supply			
Commercial banks	2,800	3,200	400
Savings banks	2,300	2,700	400
State banks	4,200	4,900	700
Private financial companies	250	300	50
Insurance companies	950	1,050	100
Bond market	2,400	2,600	200
Share market	700	900	200
Other credit supply	1,200	1,850	650
Total credit supply to private individuals and municipalities	21,300	24,000	2,700[1]

[1] Total increase in credit supply in 1975 over 1974 (projected).

Source: Finans- og tolldepartementet, *Nasjonalbudsjettet, 1975*, St. meld. nr. 1, (1974–75), p. 65.

budget reveals the actual sources of credit for 1974 and the projected sources for 1975. It was designed to keep the availability of credit and the money supply in line with the domestic economy, which was projected to expand at the rate of 4.5 percent in that year. The planning authorities' main problem is to allow the total credit supply to expand, without its becoming excessive and a source of new inflationary pressures.

The government annually fixes a limit or ceiling on the total amount of credit of all types, with each financial institution assigned a portion of the total credit to be made available during the year. The credit supply is rationed by the financial institutions in accordance with the consumption and investment goals presented in the annual national economic budget. Bonds are issued only under permits issued by the Ministry of Finance. To assure a market for government bonds, the banks, insurance companies, and pension funds are required to invest in these bonds a certain proportion of the annual increase in their total resources. The liquidity of the banking system is adjusted to a limited extent through the Bank of Norway's open-market operations and mainly through changes in bank reserve requirements. In periods of excessive boom, the Bank of Norway sells government securities and raises the primary bank reserve requirements (ratio of cash, deposits with the central bank, and Treasury bills to a bank's total deposits), and the secondary bank reserve requirements (ratio of government and government-guaranteed bonds to a bank's total deposits). If a further restriction of credit is needed, supplementary reserve requirements are added to the primary and secondary reserve requirements. If banks exceed their credit ceilings, they may be required to provide special supplementary reserves up to 50 percent of the excess loans. Consumer credit is regulated by increasing or decreasing down payments and the periods of repayment.

The Norwegian monetary and credit planning seeks to make the targets for the allocation of credit consistent with the goals for the allocation of real resources, industrial capacity utilization, and exports and imports as set forth in the national economic budgets. Any deviations from these targets are corrected by appropriate counter measures.[28] When adjusting the credit supply to changing business conditions with the aid of these counter measures, the Norwegian government makes little use of changes in interest rates; and the Bank of Norway very infrequently changes its discount rate. Between 1945 and 1972, the Bank's discount rate was changed only twice. The Bank's policy has been to keep interest rates on long-term government bonds low and to ration credit so that it would be available for high priority, public- and private-investment projects. In this manner, the government places very definite limits on the operations of the private money market in Norway.

The Control of Borrowing Abroad

Monetary and credit planning applies to borrowing from abroad, as well as from domestic sources. In the annual plans, ceilings are placed on the amounts that can be borrowed abroad by private enterprises and municipalities. The order of priority among the various projects to be financed by foreign borrowing is decided by consultation between the Bank of Norway and the ministries dealing with the private sector and the municipalities. The highest priority is accorded borrowing abroad to finance additions to Norway's merchant marine, which is the largest single source of Norway's export earnings. The government also controls the amount of domestic banks' borrowing from foreign banks and the amount of deposits of nonresidents that may be accepted by Norwegian banks. The control of borrowing abroad and the inflow of short-term funds is a part of the program to curb inflationary developments that achieved considerable success during the 1960s. The monetary and credit planning during the years 1963–1969 kept the annual increase in the money supply close to the average rate of 8 percent. Deficits on the current balance of international payments were small enough to be financed abroad without any difficulty; the Norwegian crown was a stable monetary unit; and the nation's reserve of gold and foreign exchange was doubled. The statistics in Table 9-15 show that the good financial record of the 1960s was not duplicated in the early 1970s.

The oil crisis of 1973 and the widespread recession of 1974–1975 created serious problems in Norway's external economy, to which the planning authorities could react but which they could not prevent. Since 1970, Norway's external sector has closely followed international economic developments. Boom years, with large increases in exports and low deficits in the current balance of international payments, have been followed by recession years, with exports failing to increase and large deficits on current account. Export prices, which had increased from 1963 to 1972 at the average annual rate of 2.3 percent, rose 31 percent in 1974 and 15 percent in 1975,

---

[28] Norges Bank, Annual Report, 1972, pp. 2–3. The working out of monetary and credit planning annually is discussed in the annual reports and monthly bulletins published by the Bank of Norway. See, for example, *Norges Bank,* "Monetary and Credit Policy in 1972," *Annual Report, 1972* pp. 3–11.

Table 9-15
Selected Norwegian Financial Indicators, 1963–1975

	Annual percent changes			Gold and foreign exchange reserves (mil. U.S. $)	Current balance of international payments (mil U.S. $)
	Money supply	Volume of exports	Export prices		
1963	5.4	9.3	−1.0	354.0	−180
1964	6.7	16.1	3.1	387.0	−74
1965	5.5	5.1	4.0	476.0	−101
1966	7.7	9.0	1.0	527.7	−150
1967	7.2	6.4	−1.0	677.1	−200
1968	15.0	12.6	−2.9	702.5	152
1969	8.3	11.2	2.0	712.5	134
1970	12.6	4.8	8.7	813.4	−181
1971	11.4	0.9	4.4	1,154.4	−363
1972	16.3	12.0	1.9	1,325.0	−60
1973	11.0	10.4	9.7	1,574.8	−353
1974	11.1	−1.6	31.0	1,928.5	−1,104
1975	16.8	−1.6	14.2	2,236.7	−2,588

Source: International Monetary Fund, *International Financial Statistics*, Sept. 1976.

when world trade was falling off extensively. Import prices followed a similar path. The Norwegian government countered these developments by curbing the overall increase in the money supply, easing credit to support the accumulation of inventories of export goods, and borrowing abroad to finance the large deficit on current account. The projected balance of exported and imported goods and services for 1975 revealed that another large deficit was anticipated on the nation's current account. A return to a more normal external balance would have to wait upon a general recovery from the international recession.

The Norwegian Labor government's fiscal and credit planning have been quite effective in a selective way. They have enabled the government to achieve its planned distribution or use of Norway's total output of goods and services. While there have been some deviations from the consumption and investment goals presented in the annual and four-year national economic plans, these goals have, on the whole, been quite accurately met. Private consumption has been restricted according to plan by the use of selective monetary and fiscal measures. With the aid of transfer payments and progressive taxation, the government has succeeded in redistributing income to the extent that redistribution has been considered desirable; the restricted supply of consumer goods and services has been widely shared by the general population. Furthermore, the government has succeeded in having the economy generate the large savings required for the high level of private and public investment that has been a major goal of Norwegian national economic planning. Where deviations from the consumption and investment goals have occurred, they have usually been in the direction of exceeding the investment goals and not quite reaching the consumption goals of the annual and four-year national plans.

Price and Incomes Policies

A prominent part of Norwegian financial planning is the program to curb inflationary price and wage developments with the aid of an incomes policy. The broad aims of the Norwegian incomes policy have been to maintain the international competitiveness of Norway's export prices, while at the same time achieving an equitable sharing of the national income by the nation's economic interest groups. Norwegian incomes policy is designed to do more than curb inflationary wage and price developments. It also seeks to achieve what can be accepted by a majority of the voting population as a fair sharing of the national income. Unlike other countries, Norway has not developed a formal incomes policy accompanied by established or fixed wage, profit, and price guidelines. In its approach to the problems of an incomes policy, the government has relied upon centralized collective bargaining and other institutionalized arrangements, and on close contacts with business enterprises, trade unions, and other economic interest groups. The main burden of working out the Norwegian incomes policy is placed on the Contact Committee, established in 1962 as a means of developing a more effective incomes policy.[29]

The government has an active role in the work of the Contact Committee when wage rates, farm prices, and fishermen's subsidies are being discussed before any final agreements on these matters. The government explains the current condition of the Norwegian economy, its prospects in the near future, and the need to use restraint in raising wage rates and prices. It also gives its position on price subsidies, family allowances to low-income families, social policy, and taxation.

The wage agreements between the employers and the industrial workers' unions set the pattern of income settlements for all other groups. These wage-rate increases which make provision for increases in the cost of living, are kept as close as possible to improvements in labor productivity in order to curb increases in wage costs per unit of output and in prices. After industrial wage-rate increases have been agreed upon, farm prices, farm subsidies, and subsidies to fishermen are then settled. The aim is to achieve a "reasonable" parity of income among workers, farmers, and fishermen. This means that as a matter of principle the "standard farm" of twenty-five acres should provide its owner with an income for labor input at least equal to the average income of industrial workers. Income parity is approached with the aid of subsidies given to low-income farmers and fishermen, and by family or children's allowances given to low-income industrial workers and other low-income groups. The incomes of pension recipients are kept in line with the growth of national income through automatic cost-of-living adjustments.

In Norway, industrial workers, farmers, and fishermen accept government guidance of income settlements, because profit, rent, and

---

[29] The work of the Contact Committee and an evaluation of its effectiveness are discussed in *OECD Economic Surveys, Norway*, Jan. 1971, Annex A, "The Institutional Framework of Incomes Policy," pp. 39–44. The Contact Committee is assisted in its analysis of wages and prices by a Technical Expert Group, which estimates the likely effects on prices, incomes, and income distribution of alternative wage settlements. An econometric price-income model is used by the Technical Expert Group in its work of projecting the economic consequences of different increases in wage costs.

interest incomes are also brought within the scheme for national guidance. Domestic prices and profit margins are subject to government control, and when necessary, may be subject to price and profit margin freezes. Norway's export prices are not subject to government control; but the profits of the export industries and the income of their owners come under control through the tax system, which for personal incomes is highly progressive. The members of Norway's trade unions are very much concerned with after-tax wages, and are willing to exercise wage restraint because they feel that the tax burden is equitably distributed among all economic classes. No incomes policy can be successful unless it is related to the nation's tax system, and unless after-tax income shares are felt to be equitably determined. Since 1962, income settlements in Norway have been made without frequent recourse to compulsory arbitration or price freezes. These income settlements have been made without endangering Norway's international competitive position.

In 1971, after evaluating the impact of the incomes policy in Norway, the Organisation for Economic Co-operation and Development concluded that "The merits of the Norwegian incomes policy, besides being an instrument in income distribution, lie in the fact that it has enabled the Government to keep the use of productive resources on a very high level throughout postwar years. While the average increase in prices and production costs does not differ much from developments in most countries, unemployment has usually been lower than the European average, and economic growth has been rapid and steady. With persistently strong pressures on resources, un-coordinated wage and incomes policies could easily have led to wage and price inflation."[30] This favorable evaluation was followed by the wage explosions of 1970 and 1971, when wage rates in each year increased more than 12 percent and exceeded increases in other Western European countries. An analysis of these inflationary wage developments by the government revealed that they arose chiefly from the mutually incompatible fiscal goals of the nonsocialist coalition government and the trade unions.[31] The government enlarged the income share of the inactive population by increasing pension payments, but this was done at the expense of the real income of the active population which grew very little in the years 1969–1971. The trade unions were not opposed to providing a fair share of the national income to pension recipients; in this case, however, they felt that the government had gone too far in enlarging the real income of the inactive population and in holding down the real income of the workers. The trade unions attempted to neutralize the government's policy of increasing the real incomes of pensioners by demanding unusually large increases in their wages that would protect the relative level of their real earnings.[32]

[30] *OECD Economic Surveys, Norway,* 1971, p. 44.

[31] In his 1972 annual address, the Governor of the Bank of Norway drew attention to the mutually incompatible fiscal goals of the government and the trade unions, and emphasized the importance for incomes policy of securing agreement between the government and the trade unions with regard to tax policy and tax goals. *Norges Bank*, Annual Report, 1972. Appendix A, "The Economic Situation," pp. 97–99. The need for new institutional arrangements and more precise guidelines is stressed in Norges Bank, "Fresh Approach to Prices and Incomes Policy," *Economic Bulletin*, Vol. XLIV, No. 3, Sept. 1973, pp. 116–126.

[32] This attempt to neutralize the government's transfer payments policy through "tax shifting" was accomplished in large part through a wage drift that increased the wage incomes of the more skilled workers. The OECD has pointed out that the impact of the wage drift of 6 percent a year in 1970 and 1971 was to widen the differential between the workers and pension recipients. OECD, *OECD Economic Surveys, Norway,* 1973, pp. 17–21.

In 1974–1975 Norway experienced a very rapid rise in wages, the increase in hourly earnings in manufacturing being 17.8 percent in 1974 and 19.5 percent in 1975. As the statistics in Table 9–16 show, the trade unions suceeded in increasing their real wages by securing large increases in nominal or money wages to offset the rapid rise in consumer prices that resulted from large increases in import prices. During 1974–1975 the average annual increase of 4.8 percent in real hourly earnings in manufacturing was slightly above the average annual increase of 4.4 percent in output per man-hour in manufacturing. The rapid rise in wages and consumer prices during these years made it necessary to increase Norway's export prices. This made it difficult for Norway to secure adequate exports of goods and services. To meet this problem and to curb wage inflation the Norwegian government is now offering the workers reductions in their taxes in return for more moderate demands for wage increases. It is hoped that this new approach in incomes policy will curb wage and price increases and enable Norway to continue to be competitive in the world's trading markets.

Income developments in Norway since 1970 have demonstrated again the importance of securing public support for any reforms that require income sacrifices from the trade unions or any other part of the population. What is needed is a further development of the arrangements governing income settlements that have already been developed since 1962. It has been recommended that the Contact Committee be replaced by a Council for Prices and Incomes Policy with a broader membership, which would include the Federation of Norwegian Industries, the Federation of Norwegian Commercial Associations, and the Cooperative Union and Wholesale Society. The main limitation of the Contact Committee is that it does not deal with overall

Table 9–16
Consumer Prices, Money and Real Hourly Earnings, and Output Per Man-hour in Manufacturing in Norway, 1970–1975

	Annual percent change			
	Consumer prices	Money hourly earnings in manufacturing	Output per man-hour in manufacturing	Real hourly earnings in manufacturing
1970	10.6	12.4	6.4	1.8
1971	6.3	13.0	4.0	6.7
1972	7.1	7.9	4.8	0.8
1973	7.5	10.6	4.6	3.1
1974	9.4	17.8	3.5	8.4
1975	11.6	19.5	3.0	7.9
Annual average 1970–1975	8.7	13.5	4.4	4.8

Sources: United Nations, *Monthly Bulletin of Statistics*, Aug. 1976; International Monetary Fund, *International Financial Statistics*, Sept. 1976, and International Labour Office, *Yearbook of Labour Statistics*, 1976.

price policy or with tax policy. The council would be expected to deal with all issues relating to incomes such as wages, prices, profits, tax rates, subsidies, and other price supports. The main concern of the council, which would be only advisory, would be to develop guidelines, "covering an integrated system of wages, social security payments, tax rates, prices, and subsidies."[33]

These reforms are designed to bring the government and the two sides of industry closer together in the construction of an incomes policy. Their cooperation would be a normal part of the collaboration that has already been developed in connection with the construction of the four-year national economic and fiscal budgets. This cooperation would perpetuate the freedom of action of both the employers and workers, and would not lead to any government-dictated incomes policy such as exists in the Eastern communist countries.

The Norwegian Planned Economy: An Evaluation

A survey of major economic indicators reveals that the postwar Norwegian economy has performed very well. Norway's economic growth rate has been high and sustained enough to place it among the affluent industrialized nations, with one of the lowest rates of unemployment in Western Europe. In addition, Norway has been able to curb its inflationary tendencies enough to remain competitive in the world's export markets and to avoid balance-of-payments crises. In most years, the volume of exports has increased; the Norwegian international reserves have continued to grow; and the Norwegian crown has continued to be a strong currency. In the postwar decades, centralized collective bargaining has resulted in considerable wage restraint, accompanied by widespread industrial peace. The well-rounded social security system has provided many financial supplements to the earnings of families with limited incomes, and has considerably increased the level of national pension payments. A number of the objectives that have guided Norwegian economic policy since 1945 have not differed from those pursued in other Western countries. These aims include sustained economic growth, full employment, a reasonable degree of price stability, external financial equilibrium, a fair sharing of the national income, and adequate social security.

Like other Western economies, the Norwegian planned economy is a market economy that depends very heavily upon the good performance of the private enterprise system. In the period since 1945, Norway's mixed economic system has had an excellent record. The Organisation for Economic Co-operation and Development, after reviewing Norway's economic development since the Second World War, concluded in 1972 that "Viewed against the background of the main policy objectives and considering the inherent trade-offs between the various objectives the authorities can certainly claim to have had a large measure of success."[34] The OECD goes on to point out that since 1945 Norway has never had a prolonged recession nor any serious unemployment. Costs and prices have generally been kept in line in spite of the strong inflationary pressures of a full-employment economy and solidaristic wage settlements. The distinction between the planned Norwegian economy and unplanned Western economies, such as West Germany, the United Kingdom (under the Conservative government), the United States, and Canada

---

[33] "Fresh Approach to Prices and Incomes Policy," p. 24.

[34] *OECD Economic Surveys, Norway,* 1972, p. 8.

lies in the Norwegian emphasis upon the importance of national economic and social guidance. The socialist government of Norway has held the view that economic and social forces can be successfully regulated and controlled according to social and egalitarian principles. The reconstruction of the economy along these lines requires a great deal of joint effort on all levels of decision making and also long-term considerations of economic and social developments. Norway's medium and long-term planning has been designed to achieve a society with both affluence and excellence.

The quest for such a society has turned the nation's attention to the problem of controlling the process of industrialization so as to develop a life style of high quality. This has meant that considerations and objectives of a primarily noneconomic nature have at times been placed ahead of purely economic concerns; more of this will probably be done in the future. Illustrative of the willingness to subordinate economic growth to noneconomic considerations are the goals of checking the growth of large urban agglomerations to avoid the loss of social amenities, the maintenance of population in areas with a low level of industrialization, protection of the natural environment, and maintenance of a certain degree of self-sufficiency in some agricultural products. Norway is prepared to sacrifice some economic gains to the larger purpose of increasing human welfare. Like France, Belgium, the Netherlands, and other countries with planned economies, Norway is convinced that achieving a lifestyle of high quality is done more effectively with national planning than without it.

At the same time, major differences exist between the goals of planned capitalist countries like France, Belgium, and the Netherlands and planned socialist countries like Norway, Sweden, and the United Kingdom under a Labour government. The Norwegian economy is a laboristic economy in which the center of economic and political power has shifted from the business enterprises to the trade unions. The socialist government in Norway has aimed at an egalitarian society in which ultimate power would be possessed by the labor movement, but all economic interest groups would be in a position to defend and advance their special interests. The egalitarian society is an open forum in which all interest groups can express their preferences; and consideration is given to all such preference when governmental decisions are made in a democratic manner.

Critics of National Economic Planning

The criticisms of indicative national economic planning that come from private economic groups in Norway emphasize the issue of personal freedom under planning. Business people, bankers, and others assert that the Norwegian Labor government's planning program has interfered excessively with consumer and business freedoms. All parties agree that there has been no diminution of the political freedoms for which Norway and the other Scandinavian countries are well known. Critics of Norwegian national planning assert that consumer freedom has been reduced in a number of ways. They allege that investment takes more of the total national production than is necessary for the current rate of economic growth, and that therefore total private consumption is excessively restricted. They also argue that consumers, if left free to choose, would prefer more private goods and services and fewer public goods and services. If fewer resources were put into public investment and public consumption, both the size and mix of private consumption could be changed. More consumer goods could be produced at home and imported from abroad.

Furthermore, the private service trades, whose expansion has been curbed by building, financial, and other restrictions, would be freer to cater to private demands.

Likewise, it is asserted that business freedoms have been seriously restricted under Norwegian national planning. The licensing of building and construction; the rationing of credit; the control of security issues, imports, prices, interest rates, and rents; and the rationing of foreign exchange create a web of controls from which private business was largely free before World War II. The private business groups believe that the efficiency of the economic system would be improved if many of these controls were eliminated. They argue that the controls imposed on private business could be reduced in a number of ways if excess total demand were eliminated. The business groups assert that the government's own economic policies and programs contribute much to the creation of excess total demand, which in turn necessitates the use of an extensive system of economic controls in the private business sector. The business groups explain that if the government would eliminate many subsidies, reduce its purchases of goods and services, curb its loans to the state banks, and not push for such a low level of unemployment, total demand would be better balanced with total supply. A less progressive tax system would also encourage more personal saving and thus reduce the pressure on prices. Business groups believe that with these different economic arrangements there would be much more slack in the economy and hence much less need for the imposition of economic controls on the private business system.

Business frequently asserts that even more economic progress would be achieved if Norway's private capital market were to be freed from the current governmental controls. The private business interests argue that government planning of private investment results in a less-than-optimum allocation of private investable resources. Private critics of the Norwegian government's investment policy urge that the marginal productivity of private capital would be higher if it were free to seek the most profitable investment outlets, without governmental restraint or direction. In their view, too much of the nation's savings is put into public rather than private investment, with the result that consumer preferences are not satisfactorily met. These critics argue that consumers prefer more private and fewer public goods and services than are now being produced in Norway. In the opinion of the private business interests, a capital market largely freed from governmental controls would better serve consumer interests and thus enlarge economic welfare. The Norwegian Labor government counters with the assertion that the uncontrolled capital market would enlarge private investment at the expense of public investment; that it would not pay adequate attention to investment for collective wants, such as health and education; and that it would in some cases serve less urgent private wants (luxuries) to the neglect of more urgent or high-priority private wants (necessities). Since 1945, enough of the Norwegian people have accepted the Norwegian Labor party's views on the need to control the volume and direction of private investment to keep the party in office through most of the postwar period.

In reply to these criticisms of its national planning program the Norwegian Labor government concedes that this program has restricted consumer choices at the upper-income levels. However, the government states that the redistribution of national income has increased consumer freedom by placing more income in the hands of the low-income and less-privileged groups and by enlarging the area of their consumer choices. In its opinion, a net gain in consumer freedom has occurred, because the increase in the consumer freedom of the lower-income groups outweighs the loss of consumer freedom on the part of the upper-income groups. Concerning the loss of business freedoms, the government argues that its system of economic controls is essential to the achievement of the priorities set forth in the annual and longer-term national economic plans. Since these priorities are approved by the citizens who keep the Norwegian Labor party in office, the Labor government asserts that the system of controls applied to the private business system, which is an alternative to the nationalization of private industry, is necessary to secure the economic objectives of the national planning program on the basis of which the government appeals to the nation's voters.

It should be pointed out in any evaluation of Norwegian national economic planning that any one of the major nonsocialist political parties, if it had been in office in the postwar years, would probably have been able to achieve a high rate of economic growth and a low level of unemployment, since the postwar years in Norway for the most part have been quite prosperous. A survey of Western European countries since the end of the Korean War shows that most of them, irrespective of the type of government in office, enjoyed steady economic progress and high levels of production and employment until the energy crisis of 1973.

The egalitarian Norwegian society is still being constructed, and the fitting of private business into this society is far from completed. Although they accept the major economic goals of the Norwegian Labor party, private business groups in Norway have offered some resistance to the socialist reconstruction of Norwegian society. After participating for a number of years in the work of the Economic Coordination Council, along with organized labor and other economic and social interest groups, the business representatives withdrew from the council, which was then dissolved in 1957. In recent years, the Labor government has proposed to reestablish the council with a different format, but private business has been reluctant to participate again in such collaborative activities. The Norwegian banks and other private financial institutions have also objected to the controls imposed on the nation's financial system by the Labor government. When the Labor government fell in 1965 and was replaced by a nonsocialist coalition government, banks and other financial institutions succeeded in abolishing a number of the controls imposed on them by the Labor government.

The question arises as to how much further the Norwegian Labor party can go in building a socialist society. If current trends in the expansion of public expenditures and the enlargement of the social security program continue, by 1985 the tax burden as measured by the ratio of total taxes to gross domestic product could be 51 percent, as compared with 48 percent in 1975.[35] There appears to be a growing consumer resistance to further increases in the national tax burden and in the transfer of income from the active to the inactive class. Some groups of workers, such as school teachers and government employees, feel that the differentials between blue-collar and white-collar workers have been narrowed too much. In the prosperous Norwegian society, the Labor party is finding it difficult to follow a middle course between its left wing, which calls for more socialism now, and its right wing which does not wish to press for more socialism. In recent years, the Labor party has been weakened by defections of its members

[35] *OECD Economic Surveys, Norway,* 1975, p. 60.

who are opposed to membership in the North Atlantic Treaty Organization and in the European Economic Community. The Labor Party, which received 46.9 percent of the total votes in the 1969 election, received only 35.5 percent in the 1973 election, and has been kept in office only by the support of the splinter socialist and communist parties. Similar developments in Sweden and Denmark have raised the question as to whether or not the tide is running against the social democracy which has been such a prominent feature of Scandinavian life since the 1930s. The Norwegian Labor party leaders are convinced that recent developments in Norway reflect only a pause in the movement towards a more socialist society.

Selected Bibliography

BANK OF NORWAY. "National Budgeting in Norway." *Economic Bulletin*, XXXVII, No. 3 (Sept. 1966), 114–120.

BJERVE, PETTER J. *Planning in Norway, 1947–1956.* North-Holland Publishing Company, Amsterdam, 1959.

BOURNEUF, ALICE. *Norway, The Planned Revival.* Harvard University Press, Cambridge, 1958.

BUKDAHL, JORGEN, AND OTHERS, EDS. *Scandinavia: Past and Present*, Arnkrone Publishers, Copenhagen, 1959.

EIDE, LEIF. *The Norwegian Monetary and Credit System*, Norges Banks Skriftserie, No. 1, Oslo, 1973.

EKELAND, SIGURD. *Norway in Europe, An Economic Survey.* Royal Ministry of Foreign Affairs, Oslo, 1970.

FAALAND, J. "Economic Policy in Norway, 1949 to 1961." *Economic Policy in Our Time*. Country Studies, II. Rand McNally, Chicago, 1964.

FINANS- OG TOLLDEPARTEMENTET. *Perspektivanalyser, Skisser For Utviklingen Fram Mot 1990, Vedlegg til St. meld. nr. 55 (1968–69), Langtidsprogrammet 1970–1973.* Oslo, 1969.

HAARR, ARNE. *The Industrial Policy of Norway.* Royal Minstry of Foreign Affairs, Oslo, 1970.

KLEPPE, PER. *Main Aspects of Economic Policy in Norway since the War.* Royal Ministry of Foreign Affairs, Oslo, 1968.

NORDIC ECONOMIC COOPERATION COMMITTEE (Det Nordiske Økonomiske Samarbeidsutvalg), *Nordic Economic Cooperation, Special Part, Problems of Economic Cooperation,* 3 *(Nordisk Økonomisk Samarbeid Spesiell Del, Økonomiske Samarbeidsproblemer).* Oslo, 1957.

NORGES BANK. *Economic Bulletin.* Oslo.

———. *Reports and Accounts for the Year.* Oslo.

NORWEGIAN INFORMATION SERVICE. *News of Norway.* Washington, D.C.

NORWEGIAN MINISTRY OF FINANCE. *The General Lines of the Norwegian Tax Policy.* Parliamentary Report No. 54, 1960–61, Oslo, 1961.

NORWEGIAN PARLIAMENTARY REPORT. *Petroleumsvirksomhetens plass i det norske samfun (The Place of the Oil Activity in the Norwegian Society).* No. 25, 1973/74, Oslo, 1973.

ORGANISATION FOR ECONOMIC CO-OPERATION AND DEVELOPMENT. OECD, *Agricultural Policy in Norway.* Paris, 1975.

———. *Non-Wage Incomes and Prices Policy.* Paris, 1966.

———. *Occasional Studies, Income Distribution in OECD Countries*, Paris, July 1976.

———. *OECD Economic Surveys, Norway.* Paris, 1971 to 1975.

ORGANISATION FOR EUROPEAN ECONOMIC COOPERATION. *Further Problems in Agricultural Policy, 4th Report on Agricultural Policies in Europe and North America.* Paris, 1960.

ROSTOW, DANKWART A. *The Politics of Compromise.* Princeton University Press, Princeton, 1955.

ROYAL MINISTRY OF FINANCE AND CUSTOMS. *A Survey of the Norwegian Tax System in 1970.* Oslo, 1970.

ROYAL NORWEGIAN MINISTRY OF FINANCE. "Concepts and Method in National Budgeting." *The National Budget of Norway, 1966,* Appendix I. Oslo, 1965.

———. *The National Budget of Norway, 1973. Parliamentary Report No. 1, 1972-73.* Oslo, 1973.

SKÅNLAND, HERMOD. "Current Problems in Norwegian Economic Planning." *Weltwirtschaftliches Archiv,* Band 92, Heft 1, Instituts für Weltwirtschaft, Hamburg, 1964, 94-110.

Chapter 10
The Swedish Socialist Economy

Among the nations that have adopted a program of partial democratic socialism, Sweden has been the most successful from the economic point of view, for Sweden is next to the United States in Gross National Product per head, among Western industrialized nations. In 1974, Sweden had a per capita GNP of $6,720, which was 101 percent of per capita GNP in the United States. With relatively limited natural resources, Sweden has nevertheless developed a highly productive and efficient economic system, with a concomitant extremely high standard of living. As the comparative statistics in Table 10–1 indicate, Sweden enjoys a much higher standard of living than the other major industrialized countries of Western Europe. In Gross National Product and private consumption per head, as well as expenditure on education as a percent of GNP, Sweden is considerably ahead of West Germany, France, the United Kingdom, Norway, and the Netherlands. Sweden also runs ahead of these nations in terms of passenger cars, television sets, telephones, and other material measures of living standards.[1]

This economic advance has been accomplished in the past forty-four years, during which the Social Democratic party was in office almost without interruption (the Social Democrats lost the Sept. 19, 1976 election by a narrow margin). In these four decades, the Swedish socialist government has pursued a program of limited or partial socialism. The Social Democratic party has frequently had to rely upon the political support of nonsocialist parties, such as the Center (Agrarian) and Communist parties, to stay in office. It has also drawn considerable electoral support from low-income farmers, government workers,

---

[1] These comparative data are at best only crude measures of differences in national living standards, since they take no account of institutional and other cultural differences. Furthermore, many aspects of standards of living cannot be readily quantified.

Table 10-1
Indicators of Living Standards in Sweden and Other Countries

	GDP per head 1972	Private consumption per head, 1972	Education expenditures, % of GNP, 1970	Per 1,000 inhabitants		
				Passenger cars 1971	Television sets 1972	Telephones 1972
United States	$5,643	$3,494	5.4[1]	443	474	628
Sweden	5,092	2,737	7.8	290	333	576
Denmark	4,257	2,430	7.0	231	282	377
Norway	3,860	2,035	5.9	206	241	320
Canada	4,852	2,794	8.6	321	349[2]	499
West Germany	4,177	2,255	4.0	239	293	268
France	3,792	2,263	4.7	260	237	199
Netherlands	3,472	1,944	7.3[1]	211	243[2]	299
Japan	2,778	1,455	4.1[1]	100	225	315
United Kingdom	2,759	1,754	5.5	219	305	314
Italy	2,165	1,399	4.3	209	202	206

[1] 1969.
[2] 1971.

Source: Organisation for Economic Co-operation and Development, *OECD Economic Surveys, Norway, Basic Statistics: International Comparisons*, Jan. 1975.

and middle-class liberal groups. Because it has found it necessary to appeal to an electorate much broader than the strongly socialist elements among the trade unionists, the Social Democratic party has since 1945 moved forward slowly in constructing a socialist society.

The Swedish Welfare State

Unlike the British Labour party of the late 1940s, the Swedish Social Democratic party did not after the Second World War turn enthusiastically to a program for the widespread nationalization of industry. Rather, Swedish industry is today almost entirely privately owned. More than 90 percent of the industrial labor force works for nongovernment enterprises, while 6 percent are employed by state enterprises. Publicly owned industry is mostly engaged in mining, where the state company accounts for about 80 percent of the national iron-ore output, and in electric-power generation, where public enterprise provides a 40 percent share of the total national-power output.[2] Public enterprise also includes the operation of the national health system and the railway, postal, telephone and telegraph, broadcasting, and television services, as well as the tobacco and liquor monopolies and the production of war material. While industry has been largely left in private hands, it has been placed within the framework of a national planning program. The Swedish Social Democrats have also left private agriculture undisturbed and have made no effort to nationalize the land.

[2] The Swedish Institute, *Swedish Industry*, 1970, p. 4; and *The Swedish Economy*, Stockholm, 1971, p. 2.

The main concern of the Social Democrats since they came into office in 1932 has been to establish a strong welfare state in which national income would be equitably shared by individuals, classes, and regions. The main features of the Swedish welfare state as it has developed since the end of the Second World War are as follows. The unemployed, handicapped, and retired workers who suffer from interruptions in the receipt of income or from inadequate income receive social security benefits in the form of unemployment, old-age pension, child allowance, maternity benefit, rent supplement, and other payments. The welfare program also provides for an approach to parity incomes for farmers and industrial workers. Farm subsidies in various forms are designed to raise the income of a farmer with a standard-sized farm close to the average income of an industrial worker. Also, the welfare program of the Swedish Social Democrats provides for less inequality of income between the well-to-do southern industrialized counties and the poor northern forest counties. Special financial arrangements are made to induce private industry to locate in the areas of high unemployment in the central and northern counties.

Sweden has directed a large part of its usual annual 4 percent increase in Gross National Product to improving its welfare state. This has been accomplished chiefly through the nation's tax system, which places a heavy burden on the population in general. Sweden has a heavier tax burden (measured by the ratio of total taxes and social security contributions to GNP) than all other major Western European countries (except Norway), Japan, and the United States. In 1970, Sweden's tax burden was 40.8 percent, in contrast to the United States figure of 29.9 percent.[3] In addition Sweden relies more heavily on personal income taxes as a source of tax revenue than do most Western industrialized nations. In 1970, direct taxes on individuals in Sweden were 19.3 percent of GNP, but only 14.4 percent in the United States and 8.8 percent in West Germany. A 1968 comparison of Swedish and American personal tax burdens reveals that a family of four with a $20,000 income paid an income tax of $9,200 (46 percent) in Sweden and $3,428 (17 percent) in the United States.[4]

Although Swedish tax policy and welfare measures have exerted a strong leveling and equalizing effect on after-tax personal incomes, they have not greatly altered the distribution of wealth ownership. The Swedish tax records show a high correlation between large incomes and large wealth ownership. However, the incomes from wealth account for a very small share of total after-tax national income. Income inequality in Sweden, as far as it exists, arises primarily not from differences in wealth ownership but from differences in hours worked and market evaluation of jobs. In the Swedish welfare state, when the government finds that the actual distribution of income is not compatible with its goal for income distribution, personal income-tax rates are altered in order to bring the current income distribution closer to the desired pattern of income distribution.[5]

When the Swedish Social Democratic party and the trade unions presented their postwar program in July 1944, they proposed to achieve a number of short-run and long-run

---

[3] Ministry of Finance, *The Swedish Budget 1973/74*, Stockholm, 1973, p. 140.

[4] Joint Economic Committee, *Guaranteed Minimum Income Programs Used by Governments of Selected Countries*, Paper No. 11, Washington, D.C., 1968, p. 60. It should be noted that some of Sweden's taxes are used to finance a national health service and other social services that are financed by private individuals in the United States.

[5] In recent years, greater tax uniformity or equality has been achieved by increasing the average marginal tax rate from 12.5 percent in 1966 to 20.5 percent in 1970 and to 25 percent by 1975. Swedish Ministry of Finance, *The Swedish Economy 1971–1975 and the General Outlook up to 1990*, SOU 1970:71, Stockholm, 1971, pp. 187–188.

goals.[6] The more immediate goals called for full employment, higher living standards, and a fair distribution of national income. The longer-term goals were of a decidedly socialistic nature; they included the nationalization of important natural resources and private enterprises, more industrial democracy through worker representation in industry, and the abolition of class distinctions. A review of Swedish economic and social developments since 1945 shows that not much progress has been made in achieving a socialist organization of industry and a classless socialist society. Industry remains largely in private hands, wealth ownership remains highly concentrated, and class distinctions are still well established. What the Swedish socialist governments have achieved since 1945 are a much fairer sharing of national income, a very extensive welfare state and a nationally planned economy. Similar goals have in large measure been fulfilled by nonsocialist governments in the Netherlands, Belgium, and France.

After forty-four years in office the Swedish Social Democratic party appears to have reached a critical point in its development. Although the party was not put out of office in the 1973 general election, it suffered a considerable loss of parliamentary seats and electoral votes; and the nonsocialist Liberal, Moderate (Conservative), and Center (Agrarian) parties won half the parliamentary seats. In recent years, the popularity of the Social Democratic government has declined as citizens protested the rising tax burden; consumers were disturbed by severe inflation; and, for the first time in twenty-five years, the government was forced to intervene to end strikes and lockouts. The mild socialism of the Social Democrats appears now to be on dead center and to be losing out both with the nonsocialist sections of the public and with the left-wing of the trade union movement that calls for more rapid progress towards a fully socialist society. The recently adopted plan to use the state pension fund to purchase the shares of Swedish private companies, which was given parliamentary approval in May 1973 over strong nonsocialist opposition, has been interpreted as a move by the Palme government to extend state control over private industry, and to move away from the current mixed economy towards a more truly socialist economy.

The Swedish Industrialized Economy

Since 1945, the Swedish economy has developed in directions similar to those of the other industrialized nations of Western Europe. Employment in agriculture, forestry, and fishing and the percentage contribution of these activities to total national output have undergone large declines. In 1950, Swedish agriculture accounted for 21 percent of total national employment; by 1974 it accounted for only 6.7 percent. As the statistics in Table 10-2 reveal, agriculture, forestry, and fishing contribute only 4.6 percent of the nation's gross domestic product. Industry accounts for

Table 10-2
Output and Employment in Sweden, 1974 (In Percent)

	Gross domestic product	Employment
Agriculture[1]	4.6	6.7
Industry[2]	38.9	37.0
Services	56.5	56.3
Total	100.0	100.0

[1] Includes forestry and fishing.
[2] Includes mining, manufacturing, construction, electricity, gas, and water.
Source: United Nations, *Monthly Bulletin of Statistics*, Aug. 1976 and International Labour Office, *Yearbook of Labour Statistics*, 1975.

---

[6] The Social Democratic Labor Party and the Swedish Trade Union Federation, *The Post-war Programme of Swedish Labour, Summary in 27 Points and Comments*, Stockholm, July 1944.

38.9 percent and private and public services for 56.5 percent of total national output. Like other Western European countries, Sweden has become a highly industrialized country with a large and expanding service sector. Among the services, the public services required by the expanding welfare state have grown most rapidly since 1945. Although agriculture in Sweden has in recent decades declined a great deal in relation to other economic activities, it continues to meet 90 percent of the nation's food needs.[7] Farming is still conducted on a small-scale basis with the average farm (of all farms over five acres) having only forty-six acres. At the same time, farming has become highly mechanized, and with the application of fertilizers, average yields per acre are in line with yields in other Western European countries.

Although farming in Sweden is small scale, the farmers are highly organized in cooperatives and professional bodies. Eighty percent of farm output is sold through farm cooperatives. In 1971, the federation of farm cooperatives and the Swedish Farmers' Union combined to form the Confederation of Swedish Farmers. This confederation enables the 162,000 farm owners to exercise an important influence on agricultural policy, and also provides much political support to the Center (Agrarian) party, which made a strong showing in the 1973 general election.

As the industrial revolution did not occur in Sweden until after 1850, the country was spared the adverse consequences of that revolution, which took place earlier in the United Kingdom. In Sweden, more environmental protection was provided, slums did not develop, and less industrial strife broke out than in the United Kingdom. Up to 1900, Swedish industry exploited the natural resources of mineral ore and forests for steelmaking and the production of wood products. It has become largely oriented to export markets, with 40 percent of Swedish industrial production now being exported.

Since the end of the Second World War, among the major industrial trends, there has occurred a shift from the wood products, textile, and apparel industries towards such capital-intensive industries as the metalworking, pulp and paper, chemical, and engineering areas. New workers have tended to go not into industry but into the service sector. In recent decades, strong tendencies towards industrial concentration have emerged. As the statistics in Table 10–3 point out, the one hundred largest industrial companies account for close to one-half of all industrial output. Nearly two-thirds of the total value added by manufacturing is contributed by two hundred large private companies, twenty state-owned firms, and the large consumer-owned Cooperative Union and Wholesale Society. A wave of mergers, which began in the early 1960s, has increased industrial concentration in the industries that have met strong competition in the European Common Market and other export areas. The metal products, machinery, and chemical industries have been active in establishing subsidiaries abroad. In 1969, these subsidiaries employed 200,000 workers abroad as compared with 1.1 million workers at home.

Swedish industry has long been known for its aggressive sales tactics and concern for research and development. Government research grants to private industry now amount to 1.5 percent of GNP. The government's Board for Technical Development finances research in private industry, while the Swedish National Development Company

---

[7] The Swedish Institute, *Agriculture in Sweden*, Stockholm, 1970, p. 2. Agricultural problems and policy are discussed in the Ministry of Agriculture, *Swedish Agriculture*, Stockholm, 1968; Sveriges Lantbruksförbund, *Agricultural Cooperation in Sweden*, Stockholm, 1969; and Hans Linden and Erik Swedborg, *Policy for Swedish Agriculture in the 1970's*, Falköping, 1969.

Table 10–3
Shares on Value Added in Swedish Industry, 1969

	Share of value added
The 100 largest privately owned companies	46%
The next 100 large companies	6%
State-owned companies	6%
The Cooperative Union and Wholesale Society	2%
Farming and lumbering cooperatives	3%
Other companies (12,500)	37%

Source: The Swedish Institute, *Swedish Industry*, 1970.

underwrites research in such matters of public interest as environmental protection and regional development. Private research and development are concentrated in the large firms in the electrical, chemical, transport equipment, machinery, pharmaceutical, and aircraft industries. In spite of the enlargement of the Swedish welfare state, private industry has remained vigorous and internationally competitive. Since company income taxes are relatively low, providing only a small amount of total tax revenue (only 4 percent), the large Swedish industrial enterprises have been free to devote much of their earnings from exports to industrial research and development and new investments.

Like all other sectors of the Swedish economy, the private industrial and commercial sectors are highly organized. The main industrial organization is the Federation of Swedish Industries, which represents industry to the government and the general public. The Federation has a membership of close to 5,000 companies in 26 lines of industry, which employ approximately 700,000 workers. The Federation deals with all matters of general interest to private industry, and collaborates with the Swedish Employers' Confederation, which is concerned only with management-labor relations. The two private-industry organizations have established the Industrial Institute for Economic and Social Research, which along with other private research organizations provides much of the factual information used by the government in the construction and carrying out of its five-year and annual national plans. Other private business organizations provide information, foster rationalization, and in general promote the interests of the private sector. These organizations include the trade associations in the various industries and the General Export Association of Sweden, the Federation of Swedish Wholesale Merchants and Importers, and the Swedish Retail Federation with their private research institutes.

A unique feature of the post–World War II Swedish economy is its freedom from industrial strife. Since 1945, collective bargaining has been carried on with very little resort to strikes or lockouts. Before the Second World War, the very considerable industrial strife of the 1930s was brought to an end by the Saltsjöbaden Agreements of the late 1930s between private business and organized labor, which gave rise to the Basic Agreement concerning trade union contracts and their enforcement. In the decade 1930–1939, the annual average number of workdays lost from strikes and lockouts was 1,537,349. In the decade 1950–1959, the number of workdays lost annually fell to 114,126; and in the decade

1960–1969 this number was only 51,697. Among the Western industrialized countries, Sweden has the best record with regard to workdays lost from strikes. Sweden along with West Germany and the Netherlands has much less industrial strife than most of the advanced industrialized countries, as the statistics in Table 10-4 show.

Much of the credit for this industrial peace goes to the efforts of the Swedish Employers' Confederation (SAF) and the Swedish Confederation of Trade Unions (LO). The operations of both of these organizations are highly centralized. The Employers' Confederation has 43 affiliated industry associations, with 24,000 member firms that employ 1,250,000 workers. The Trade Union Confederation represents 29 national trade unions, with 2,700 locals and 1,700,000 members, who constitute 90 percent of all blue-collar workers. White-collar and professional employees have their own organizations: the Central Organization of Salaried Employees (with 660,000 members) and the Confederation of Professional Associations (with 108,000 members). Both the employers' and workers' confederations control their members by threatening to withdraw financial aid in times of strikes or lockouts, and by threatening to expel member firms or unions that do not accept the proposals of the executive committees of their respective federations.

Collective bargaining in Sweden is carried on in the same general manner as in Norway at the national and industry levels.[8] At the national level, the two sides of industry bargain on wages and working conditions and arrive at "frame" agreements that provide a ceiling on annual average wage-rate increases during the two- or three-year agreements. The individual unions in each industry bargain with their employers on an industry-wide basis, but within the frame agreement agreed upon by both sides of industry. If no agreement can be reached even with the aid of government mediators, the dispute may be submitted to the Labor Market Council, which was set up in 1936 with seven union and seven employer members and an independent chairman. If both sides agree to submit their wage dispute to the Council, they agree to abide by its decision. There is no provision for any government-enforced compulsory arbitration such as is used in Norway. Apart from a five-month conflict in the metal industry in 1945 and a five-week dispute in 1953, Sweden enjoyed a remarkable period of industrial peace after the Saltsjöbaden Agreement of 1936.

Table 10-4
Number of Workdays Lost through Strike Action per 1,000 Population, 1959–1968, in Selected Countries

	Average annual workdays lost per 1,000 population
Sweden	15
West Germany	20
Netherlands	37
Norway	116
United Kingdom	262
France	312
Denmark	404
Canada	784
Italy	1,088
United States	1,114

Source: International Labour Office, *Yearbook of Labour Statistics,* 1973.

[8] T. L. Johnston, *Collective Bargaining in Sweden,* Cambridge, Mass.: Harvard University Press, 1962. See also Walter Galenson, *Trade Union Democracy in Western Europe,* Berkeley: University of California Press, 1961, pp. 68–86; Arthur M. Ross and Paul T. Hartman, *Changing Patterns of Industrial Conflict,* New York: John Wiley, 1960, pp. 107–112; and Andrew Shonfield, "Manpower Planning: Sweden," *Modern Capitalism,* New York: Oxford University Press, 1965, pp. 199–211.

Since the winter of 1969, however, some new elements of dissatisfaction have appeared in the field of industrial relations. In December 1969 and early 1970, a rash of unofficial strikes occurred in the state-owned iron mines in Northern Sweden, among the longshoremen at Göteborg, and among the workers in the Volvo and Saab automobile plants. While the number of workers on strike was not statistically significant, the wildcat strikes emphasized the need to pay more attention to contacts between employers, union officials, and workers at the local level. Another adverse development, in the early months of 1971, was the strike of 47,000 civil servants, teachers, and railway workers, who were protesting the failure of the government to maintain the differential between white-collar and blue-collar workers' wages. For the first time since the end of the Second World War, the government was forced to intervene in the collective bargaining process, and found it necessary to enact emergency legislation that banned strikes and lockouts in the public service and nationalized industries for six weeks. The split between white-collar and blue-collar workers was widened when the Confederation of Trade Unions supported the government's move to ban strikes and lockouts in the nonprivate sectors of the nation's economy.

The Financial System

The Swedish financial system, which in its broadest definition includes both the private money and credit system and the government fiscal system, has as its main function the collecting of the nation's supply of investable funds and the distributing of these funds among their various users. In performing this function, the financial system contributes to the matching or balancing of the real flow of goods and services and the financial flow of incomes and expenditures. Sweden's private- and public-credit system makes possible the credit-financed demands coming from individuals, business enterprises, and government authorities for consumer and producer goods. These demands financed by credit are added to the demands financed out of current income to make up the total demand for goods and services. In any one year, the objective is for total demand and total supply to be in balance; at the same time, the aim is for total demand to be composed of the kinds of consumption and investment demands that will meet the needs of national welfare determined by the annual and five-year national economic budgets.

Sweden's financial system is one of the most well developed in Western Europe. A wide variety of financial institutions has grown up to meet the financial needs of individuals, business enterprises, and the central and local governments. Sweden's capital market very efficiently collects the nation's available investable funds and makes them available to various private and public borrowers. The Swedish private financial system is similar in its basic structure to the private financial systems of other Western European countries. The main private financial institutions include the commercial banks, the savings banks, the specialized private mortgage institutions and the insurance companies. Commercial banking, which is highly concentrated, is in the hands of 14 banks with over 1,100 branches. Sweden's savings-bank system is much less concentrated, with its 440 savings banks, which are a major source of long-term bank credit. The nation's savings banks have their own private central bank, the Bank for Savings Banks (*Sparbankernas Bank*), which, among other things, accepts deposits from and makes loans to the savings banks. Thus cooperation among the many savings banks is highly developed. The commercial and savings banks encounter strong competition in the rural areas from the 581 private agricultural credit associations that conduct a general banking business. These agricultural credit associations, like the savings banks, have a central organization, the Bank of Agriculture.

In addition to the commercial and savings banks and the agricultural credit associations, a number of credit institutions specialize in long-term or mortgage lending. The ten rural and thirty-seven urban mortgage associations obtain funds by selling bonds in Sweden's capital market. These funds are then loaned out on a long-term basis to finance real estate purchases. A few private mortgage banks, which also raise funds by issuing their own bonds on the capital market, extend long-term credit to shipping and various industries. Long-term credit is also supplied by Sweden's insurance companies. Like commercial banking, the life insurance business is highly concentrated, twenty insurance groups doing 90 percent of the life insurance business.

The Swedish government occupies an important place in the country's banking system. It owns the Bank of Sweden, the nation's central bank, which functions as a bankers' bank and performs all the functions ordinarily associated with a country's central bank. The government also operates the Post Office Savings Bank and the Postal Cheque Service, which together account for approximately 20 percent of all deposits in Swedish banks. The government also owns the third largest commercial bank, the Credit Bank of Sweden. In addition, the government has established special state lending institutions for the support of agriculture, housing, small industry, and shipping. These lending institutions provide credit that cannot ordinarily be obtained from private credit institutions. The government also is involved indirectly or on a joint basis in a number of other credit institutions. Along with a few leading commercial banks, it jointly operates the Industrial Credit Bank, which makes loans to small firms unable to use the nation's capital market. The government also guarantees the capital and appoints the chairman of the central institutions of the rural and urban mortgage associations, which account for 15 percent of all housing loans.

The Swedish private financial system is highly organized. In some cases, such as in commercial banking, urban and rural mortgage banking, and the life insurance business, financial activity is in relatively few hands. In other cases, such as in savings banking and agricultural credit-association banking, there are several hundred small institutions in the field. In these cases, coordination and cooperation are obtained through the establishment of central institutions, which perform as central banks. In addition, the commercial banks, savings banks, and insurance companies are organized through their own private associations. In carrying out its monetary and credit policies, the government can very easily maintain contact with all branches of the private credit system. Financial policies and programs can be worked out readily through the collaboration of the Bank of Sweden, the Ministry of Finance, and representatives of the various private credit institutions.

Much of the functioning of Sweden's private financial system is in response to decisions made by private borrowers and lenders. The private credit institutions finance business enterprises that are meeting the needs of Sweden's private domestic and international markets. The government, however, is prepared to intervene in Sweden's capital market in two important ways. First, the government provides overall direction or guidance for the private saving-investing process. This guidance does not take the form of directly intervening in the lending and borrowing activities of individuals or private business and financial organizations: intervention is carried out on a much higher and more general level. In following its annual economic plans, the government may endeavor to retard the flow of credit into nonstrategic domestic industries and to stimulate this flow into high-priority domestic or export industries. Or the government may curb the use of credit by consumers in general, so that more credit may be available for the construction of homes.

Second, the government may intervene to restrict the flow of private investment in order to enlarge public investment. In this situation, the private financial system is required to direct private savings into government rather than private-investment outlets. This is done by having the private financial institutions purchase government or government-guaranteed bonds rather than privately issued bonds. Decisions as to how much of the nation's private savings should go into the public sector and how much into the private sector are collective, nonmarket decisions. They are made by the government on the assumption that it represents the public and is therefore able to express the public's preferences concerning the division of total investment between private and public investment.

The Planned Swedish Economy

The beginnings of Swedish national planning are found in the government's annual calculations of the coming year's various private and public demands for goods and services and of the expected available total supply of goods and services; these calculations were first made in 1943.[9] The government initiated this policy during the war years in order to determine the extent to which total demand would exceed total supply, unless appropriate anti-inflationary policies were adopted to curb demand in various sectors. This practice of planning for the removal of inflationary gaps was continued until national planning on a broader basis was adopted in 1947 by the Social Democratic government.

The main features of the structure of the Swedish national planning organization are presented in Figure 10-1. The major responsibility for drawing up Sweden's annual and five-year national economic plans lies with the Cabinet. Annual national economic plans are given their general shape by the Cabinet, which in September of each year lays down the broad lines that the coming year's national economic plan is to follow. The actual construction of the plan is done by the Economic Division of the Ministry of Finance. This ministry is assisted in the work of constructing the next year's national economic budget by the National Institute of Economic Research and the Research Council. The institute, a government agency organized in 1937, analyzes past economic developments and future economic trends and provides much of the statistical analysis required in the work of plan construction. The Research Council, made up of representatives from government agencies, including the institute and private industrial, commercial, agricultural, and trade union research groups, advises the Ministry of Finance with respect to the coming year's national economic budget. After the national economic budget has been constructed by the Economic Division of the Ministry of Finance, it is then approved by the Cabinet and presented to Parliament at the time that the fiscal budget is presented.

In the early postwar years there was considerable "central coordination" by the government planning authorities of private and public annual spending plans. As economic

---

[9] Planning procedures in Sweden are discussed in Jan Wallander, "Experiences of Long-Term Planning in Sweden," *Quarterly Review*, Vol. 37, No. 2, April 1956, pp. 50-58; Ingvar Ohlsson, "The Swedish National Budget," Skandinaviska Banken, *Quarterly Review*, Vol. 38, Oct. 1957, pp. 100-107; Ingvar Svennilson and Rune Beckman, "Long-Term Planning in Sweden," *Quarterly Review*, Vol. 43, 1962, pp. 71-79; Karl Jungenfelt, "The Methodology of Swedish Long-Term Planning," *Quarterly Review*, 1964:4, pp. 111-115; and Ingvar Svennilson, "Swedish Long-Term Planning—The Fifth Round," *Quarterly Review*, 1966:2, pp. 37-43.

Figure 10-1
Structure of the Swedish Planning Organization, 1975

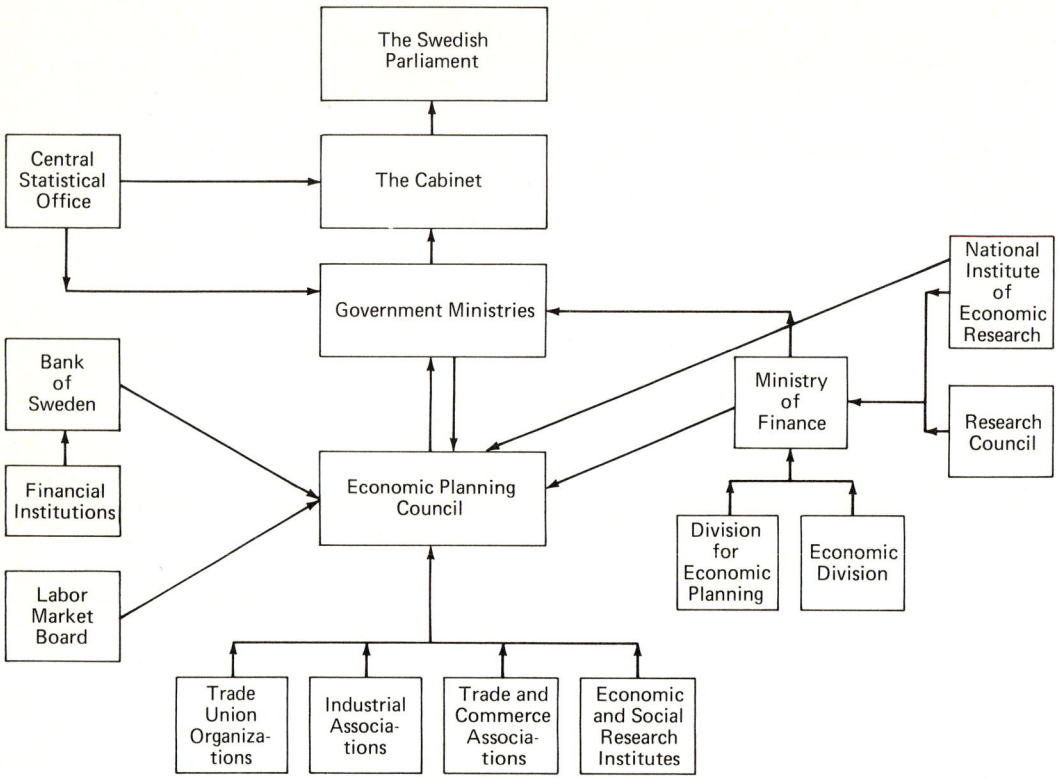

controls were relaxed, the elements of central coordination were reduced in number and scope. Decentralized private and local government expenditure intentions have been accepted more frequently as final plans during the construction of the annual national economic budgets by the central government planning authorities. Gösta Rehn, Chief of the Economic Division in the Swedish Ministry of Finance in 1962, explained that "Initially, the National [Economic] Budget contained pronounced elements of central coordination, but it has subsequently to an increasing extent become a statistical summary of decentralised [expenditure] intentions. However, these are also governed by a severe law—'the dictatorship of circumstances'; taken altogether, they must find room within the framework of our combined resources (i.e., total supply or gross national product)."[10] In other words, the national economic budget provides an "overall view" of economic conditions in the coming year. Within this scheme, the total of all expenditure intentions or plans does not exceed the available total supply, and the total available supply of goods and services is distributed among private and public investment and consumption in accordance with priorities established partly by individual consumers and partly by the central and local governments. In the establishing of priorities in

[10] Gösta Rehn, "The National Budget and Economic Policy," *Quarterly Review*, Skandinaviska Banken, Vol. 43, No. 2, 1962, p. 41.

the use of goods and services, private households and business enterprises are permitted to go only as far as is consistent with the expansion of national economic welfare, as defined by the government.

The Swedish Economic Planning Council was established in 1962 to place medium-term planning on a more regularized basis than previously. The council has representatives from the Ministries of Finance, Commerce, and Interior, the Bank of Sweden, the Labor Market Board, the National Institute of Economic Research, private industrial, commercial, and trade union organizations, and nongovernmental economic and social research institutes. Its function, which is purely advisory, is to secure the support of all major private economic interests for the Cabinet's medium-term national economic planning proposals. The council analyzes the medium-term trends of the Swedish economy and suggests remedies for the problems that appear during the effort to secure a balanced expansion of the economy. It is assisted in its work by the Division for Economic Planning in the Ministry of Finance, which now has the responsibility for the construction of Sweden's five-year national economic plans and national economic budgets.

The Labor Market Board deals with the problems of labor allocation and unemployment and supervises the investment of unemployment insurance funds and private tax-free investment reserves on deposit in the Bank of Sweden. Financial planning is largely the responsibility of the Ministry of Finance, which correlates the annual fiscal and national economic budgets, and of the Bank of Sweden, which informally works out annual monetary and credit agreements with the commercial and savings banks and other financial institutions. The "financial" planning of the Ministry of Finance and the Bank of Sweden is calculated to aid the government in securing the goals of its "real" national economic planning program. The Ministry of Finance plays a key role in this coordinating or meshing of "real" and "financial" national planning in Sweden, as does the Ministry of Finance in Norway.

Like Norwegian and French planning, Swedish national planning is of an indicative nature. No targets are established for separate industries or individual firms. Each firm is free to develop its own investment, production, pricing, and sales programs. Private business in Sweden is free to respond to international economic developments, and is subject to the usual efficiency tests of private domestic and international markets. It operates, however, within a framework of national economic guidance provided by the annual and five-year plans or programs. The central government sets a goal for the division of output between the private and public sectors. It also determines objectives for such public needs as education, health, defense, social services, and the nationalized industries; private consumption makes a residual claim on the nation's economic resources. Although few direct controls are applied to private enterprise in Sweden, fiscal advantages and financial aids are given to those private enterprises that cooperate with the government in the effort to achieve the nation's economic and social priorities.[11]

The Performance of the Swedish Economy, 1963–1972

In the 1960s, the performance of the Swedish economy was on the whole quite good. The selected economic indicators in Table 10–5 show that from 1963 to 1969 gross domestic product increased at the average annual rate of 4.3 percent; the average annual increase in

[11] Lars Th. Hellström, "The Credit Market Calculations of the National Budget," *Quarterly Review*, 1964:2, pp. 52–57.

Table 10-5
Selected Swedish Domestic Economic Indicators, 1963-1972

	Percent change over previous year						
	Gross domestic product	Industrial production	Consumer price index	Wholesale price index	Hourly earnings in manufacturing	Output per man-hour in manufacturing	Unemployment rate
1963	5.1	6.3	3.1	3.2	7.5	6.0	1.4
1964	6.4	10.0	3.0	4.4	6.0	12.5	1.1
1965	4.1	7.3	5.8	4.2	11.3	7.8	1.2
1966	2.7	3.3	6.4	2.9	7.6	6.3	1.6
1967	2.9	2.4	4.3	0.0	9.5	7.9	2.1
1968	4.1	5.6	1.7	1.1	6.5	8.6	2.2
1969	4.6	7.6	2.4	3.9	8.1	9.5	1.9
1970	4.9	6.3	7.1	6.7	13.1	7.5	1.5
1971	0.0	−0.7	7.4	3.0	7.7	7.6	2.5
1972	2.2	2.6	6.2	4.8	14.4	7.8	2.7
Average 1963-1969	4.3	6.1	3.8	2.8	8.1	8.4	1.6
Average 1970-1972	2.4	2.7	6.9	4.8	11.7	7.6	2.2

Sources: *International Financial Statistics, United Nations Monthly Bulletin of Statistics;* and *OECD Economic Surveys, Sweden.*

consumer prices of 3.8 percent was not out of line with inflationary developments in the rest of Western Europe; hourly earnings in manufacturing did not increase much faster than labor productivity improved; and the rate of unemployment was very low. Export prices did not increase excessively, and Swedish exports remained competitive.

Considerable annual fluctuations in total national output and exports occurred during 1963-1969. Merchandise exports fell off severely in 1964 and 1965, and there were sizable declines in total national output during the recession years 1966 and 1967. These fluctuations in output and exports indicate how exposed the Swedish economy is to international economic developments. However, years of recession and contraction were sufficiently offset by years of prosperity and expansion to make the period from 1963 to 1969 one of good performance on the average. During these years, Sweden's economic performance enabled it to preserve its position as a country with a very high per capita Gross National Product.

The performance of the Swedish economy after 1969 did not turn out to be as satisfactory as it had been in general in 1963-1969. The statistics in Table 10-5 show that in 1970-1972 the average annual rates of growth of gross domestic product and industrial production were cut in half, while the average annual rates of increase in consumer and wholesale prices were approximately doubled. The average hourly earnings in manufacturing increased from 8.1 percent in the years 1963-1969 to almost 12 percent in 1970-1972, while unemployment became widespread. The years since 1969 have been quite disturbing to those who are responsible for the guidance of the Swedish economy. An unusually strong wage-price spiral began in 1970, which was a year of high economic growth and very low unemployment.[12] The wage-price spiral continued into 1971 and 1972 in the face of rising unemployment and declining Gross National Product, industrial production, and merchandise exports. Factors contributing to the wage-price spiral were the large wage drift caused by the scarcity of skilled workers, high import prices, and increases in value added taxes which were passed on in consumer prices.

For the first time since the end of the Second World War, the Swedish economy in 1971 and 1972 entered a period of near stagnation with a considerable rise in unemployment. As the statistics in Table 10-6 indicate, one of the largest deficits in the current balance of payments was recorded in 1970. Sweden's international reserves fell to nearly their lowest level since 1963. Steps were taken in 1972 and 1973 to return the nation to its normal growth path. Private investment was stimulated by the provisions for the rapid depreciation of investment in machinery and equipment, the special tax allowances for research and development investment in private industry, the use of tax-free investment reserve funds for the construction of factories, and the maintenance of an easy credit policy. Policies to increase employment in the construction

[12] For an analysis of the inflation-unemployment dilemma in Sweden, see Lars Jacobsson and Assar Lindbeck, "Labor Market Condition, Wages and Inflation—Swedish Experiences, 1955-67," *The Swedish Journal of Economics*, Vol. LXXI, June 1969, pp. 64-95; and Rudolf Meidner, "Active Manpower Policy and the Inflation Unemployment Dilemma," *The Swedish Journal of Economics*, Vol. LXXI, Sept. 1969, pp. 161-183.

Table 10-6

Selected Swedish External Economic Indicators, 1963-1972

| | Percent change over prior year | | | Current balance of payments (in million U.S. dollars) | Gold and foreign exchange reserves (in million U.S. dollars) |
	Volume of exports	Import prices	Export prices		
1963	8.7	1.0	1.0	51	3,891
1964	1.0	3.8	3.0	66	4,929
1965	0.9	1.9	3.9	−178	4,944
1966	12.5	1.8	0.9	−168	5,235
1967	4.0	0.0	0.9	−46	4,230
1968	8.4	0.0	0.0	−113	4,137
1969	12.0	2.7	3.7	−207	3,410
1970	9.4	7.8	8.0	−301	3,624
1971	3.5	5.6	4.9	189	5,065
1972	5.6	1.5	3.9	252	7,320
Average 1963-1972	6.6	2.6	3.0	—	—

Sources: *International Financial Statistics* and *OECD Economic Surveys, Sweden.*

industry included the abolition of restrictions on nonpriority building and the speeding up of public relief works. By 1973, the near stagnation of Sweden's economy was overcome, and the official forecast for the increase in the gross domestic product for that year was between 4.5 and 5 percent.

The near stagnation of the Swedish economy in 1971 and 1972 raises the question as to whether or not some new trends in Swedish economic development have made their appearance. In recent years, there has been an increase in the structural component of unemployment, with the result that unemployment has been swollen by a rising number of long-term unemployed persons.[13] Increasing numbers of women are seeking employment at the same time that there appears to be a certain saturation in residential construction and related infrastructural investments. Sweden's technological advantage over its Western European competitors may be on the decline as these competitors, like West Germany and Japan, close the technological gap between themselves and Sweden.[14] If this is true, there will be a need for more rapid structural adjustments in Swedish industry in the future if exports are to be maintained. The recent trend of young workers to prefer employment in the service industries rather than in manual labor in industry underlines the necessity of attracting workers into industry by "adaptations of working conditions, remuneration methods, and decision-making processes" that make blue-collar work more attractive.[15]

There also appears to be some question as to the effectiveness of Sweden's incomes policy. Centralized collective bargaining has been successful in reducing labor strife, but it has had inflationary consequences because the workers in the various industries try to preserve their wage differentials. Other groups in the community, such as the farmers, small business people, and retired workers, also try to protect or improve their relative positions in the pattern of income distribution. The 1973 OECD Economic Survey of Sweden states that "It would seem that, in this situation, a closer co-operation between the various trade union organizations as well as the other parties on the labour market could play an important role to ensure less inflationary adjustments of wage differentials to desired structural shifts in the economy."[16] The unofficial Swedish incomes policy is not well suited to dealing with the situation of relative deprivation in which certain economic groups feel inferior as compared to other groups, and so seek to preserve or restore wage or other income differentials. In the new economic era that Sweden may be entering, the current unofficial incomes policy may prove to be inadequate to deal with the problems of structural change and income distribution. For these and other reasons, future developments in the Swedish planned economy are difficult to predict.[17]

Swedish Economic Performance, 1973–1975

Although 1973 was for Sweden a year of economic recovery from the recession of 1971–1972, the economic upturn did not reach the level forecast by the planning authorities.

---

[13] An extensive analysis of the Swedish unemployment problem is made in *OECD Economic Survey, Sweden*, June 1973, pp. 15–21.

[14] This problem is discussed in "Slower Rise in Productivity: Serious Problem or Temporary Phenomenon?", *Quarterly Review* 2/1972, pp. 55–60; and Bengt Rydén, "Concentration and Structural Adjustment in Swedish Industry during the Post-War Period," *Quarterly Review*, 1967:2, pp. 51–58.

[15] OECD, *OECD Economic Surveys, Sweden*, June 1973, p. 33.

[16] *Ibid.*

[17] For a critical review of recent economic developments in Sweden, see "Sweden: A Business Survey," *The Economist*, Nov. 17, 1973, pp. 77–82.

Domestic demand was weaker than anticipated because personal saving was much higher than expected; residential construction and local government investment remained at low levels; and the central government pursued a cautious fiscal policy because of the public's strong resistance to higher taxation. By 1973, the Swedish tax burden (measured by the ratio of total tax revenue to Gross National Product) of 42 percent was one of the highest in Western Europe. A more active fiscal policy to enlarge domestic demand would have required increases in taxes that the government was unwilling to recommend. The emphasis of the government's demand management program was on two priorities: namely, achieving a good price performance and an improvement in the balance of international payments. It did not seek to enlarge domestic demand. Concerning these two priorities, the government experienced some success. A price stop or freeze was imposed on basic foods, wood products, and building materials. In the light of controls on prices of basic foods and tax concessions in the form of lower income and value-added taxes, organized labor was willing to accept smaller wage increases in 1973 than in 1972. The increase in consumer prices from 6 to 7 percent in 1973 was below the increases in a number of other industrial countries. The large increase in the volume of exports in 1973 (16.5 percent) was accompanied by a large surplus in the balance of international payments.

The oil crisis of late 1973 hit the Swedish economy when it was experiencing an upswing that continued in spite of the oil shock. Table 10-7 shows that economic growth continued on its upward course in 1973 and 1974 without the large consumer price and wage-rate increases experienced in other industrial countries.[18] The government could not prevent the economy from moving into a deficit

[18] The performance of the Swedish economy in 1973 and 1974 is analyzed in OECD, *OECD Economic Surveys, Sweden*, July 1975.

Table 10-7
Selected Swedish Economic and Financial Indicators, 1973–1975

	Percent change over previous year					Balance of payments (mil. U.S. $)	Gold and exchange reserve (mil. U.S. $)
	Gross domestic product	Consumer prices	Hourly earnings in manufacturing	Unemployment rate[1]	Volume of exports		
1971	0.5	7.0	7.8	2.0	4.0	−177	1,110
1972	2.5	6.5	14.8	2.0	4.8	−255	1,575
1973	3.3	7.0	7.8	1.9	16.5	−1,149	2,528
1974	4.1	9.0	11.0	1.5	3.1	−999	1,735
1975	0.5	9.1	14.9	1.6	−12.8	−1,599	3,077
Annual average 1971–1975	2.2	7.7	11.3	1.8	3.1	—	—

[1] Annual rate.

Sources: United Nations, *Monthly Bulletin of Statistics*, Aug. 1976; and International Monetary Fund, *International Financial Statistics*, July 1976.

position in its balance of international payments, but measures were taken to offset the contractionary domestic demand impact of higher oil import prices. The 1974 expansionary fiscal policy included reductions in the value-added tax on consumer goods, special allowances to pensioners, families with children, and students, larger transfer payments to municipalities, and increased subsidies on basic foods. The price freeze was extended and included a larger number of basic consumer products. With organized labor showing some restraint in its wage demands, both wages and prices rose much less in Sweden in 1974 than in other industrial countries. This is borne out by Table 10-8, which compares changes in GNP, consumer prices, and balances of international payments in Sweden and nine other industrial countries in 1973 and 1974. These comparative statistics indicate that all ten industrial countries have been adversely affected by the oil crisis. Their economic growth slowed down, and in most cases they incurred large deficits in their balances of international payments to pay for the high-priced oil imports from the oil producing countries. Among the ten countries, France, Holland, Sweden, Norway, and Denmark tended to have less disruption of their growth trends than the other countries.

While Sweden was able to maintain good levels of output and employment during the oil crisis, its balance of payments in 1974 reversed the favorable position of 1973 and showed a billion-dollar deficit in 1974. This payments deficit, however, presented no special financing problems. The upturn of the Swedish economy had gone far enough in 1974 to require more restrictive monetary and fiscal policies. These policies included raising the discount rate of the Bank of Sweden, increasing the reserve requirements of the commercial banks, and reducing the deficit in the central government's 1975 fiscal budget. Sweden's forecast for 1975 was a 3 percent increase in gross domestic product and a 7 to 8

Table 10-8
Production, Prices, and Balances of International Payments in Sweden and Other Industrial Countries, 1973–1974

	Gross domestic product		Consumer prices		Balance of payments (bil. U.S. $)	
	1973	1974	1973	1974	1973	1974
Sweden	3.1	3.5	6.7	10.0	+1.1	−1.0
Norway	4.2	4.2	7.5	9.5	−0.3	−1.0
Denmark	3.9	2.0	9.3	15.25	−0.5	−1.0
West Germany	5.3	0.5	6.9	7.0	+4.5	+9.5
France	6.0	4.0	7.3	13.5	−0.7	−6.0
United Kingdom	5.3	−0.25	9.2	16.0	−3.1	−9.0
Holland	4.4	2.25	8.0	9.5	+1.8	+1.75
Italy	5.9	3.75	10.8	19.0	−2.4	−7.5
United States	5.9	−2.25	6.2	11.0	+0.5	−1.5
Japan	10.2	−3.5	11.7	24.5	−0.1	−4.5

Source: Danmarks Nationalbank, *Beretning og regnskab*, 1974, Copenhagen, p. 8.

percent rise in consumer prices. These forecasts proved to be overly optimistic since in 1975 gross domestic product increased only 0.5 percent and consumer prices rose 9.1 percent. While 1976 may show some improvement in Sweden's external sector, Sweden will probably have considerable difficulty in reaching the total demand and output goals set forth in the 1973-1977 national plan.

The early 1970s were a period of increasing problems for the Swedish planning authorities who found it difficult to forecast accurately the country's annual economic growth rate. Personal consumption was much more volatile than had been anticipated on the basis of pre-1970 trends in personal saving. The two new phenomena of consumer-spending reluctance and widespread resistance to tax increases made short-run demand management much more uncertain than it was in the 1950s and 1960s. Discretionary consumer spending is very hard to estimate in an economy subject to large shocks from the outside world. Also, even in a rich nation like Sweden it becomes increasingly hard to raise the tax burden on the working population in order to transfer income to the nonworking population and to the nation's underdeveloped regions. It should not be surprising if Swedish annual planning in the 1970s becomes much more controversial than it was in the years 1950-1969.[19]

Short-Run Demand and Supply Management

Short-run demand-and-supply management in Sweden confronts the same basic issues as does this management in other industrialized countries. Its primary objective is the achievement of short-run internal and external economic equilibrium with the aid of fiscal, monetary, price, wage, and other economic policies. This means that in boom periods, restrictive economic policies are used to curb inflationary developments, and in recession periods, economic policies are made expansionary so as to bring the economy closer to its output potential. In the prosperous years 1968-1970, the Swedish government sought to curb excessive pressure on the nation's economic resources by increasing indirect taxes, cutting government expenditures, increasing bank reserve requirements and restricting the credit supply, calling for restraint in raising prices and wages, and directing manpower into industries where skilled labor was in tight supply.[20] Private enterprises were induced to place excess profits in tax-free investment reserve accounts with the Bank of Sweden, the supply of building permits was reduced, and private bond issues were controlled.

In the recession years 1971-1972, on the other hand, local and central government expenditures were increased; an easy credit policy was adopted; business investment was stimulated by releasing tax-free investment reserve accounts for spending on plant, equipment, and inventories; and very liberal depreciation on new equipment was allowed. Special grants up to 75 percent of the cost of business investment to protect the environment were also made. Tax concessions to private business were given for investment in research and development. An active manpower policy was pursued in order to retain

[19] For a discussion of related issues see Erik Dahmén, "The Present Economic Situation and the Future Prospects," *Skandinaviska Enskilda Banken Quarterly Review*, 1/1975, pp. 21-35.

[20] Details of these programs are found in OECD, *OECD Economic Surveys, Sweden*, 1969-1970. For fiscal policy, see Walter Heller, *Fiscal Policy for a Balanced Economy*, Ch. II, "Sweden," OECD, Paris, 1968, pp. 55-62; and Bent Hansen, *Fiscal Policy in Seven Countries, 1955-65*, Ch. 7, "Sweden," OECD, Paris, 1969, pp. 339-400.

workers and to move them from the areas of high unemployment.[21]

Sweden's annual plans recommend fiscal, monetary, and other economic policies designed to help accomplish the various goals set forth in the annual national economic budget. Table 10-9 shows the Swedish national economic accounts for 1973 and the national economic budget for 1974. For the plan year 1974, the gross domestic product was projected to increase 4.5 percent, while private consumption was estimated to increase at the same rate and public consumption at the lower rate of 3 percent. Gross fixed private and public investment as a percent of real gross domestic product were projected to remain almost unchanged, while there was to be a considerable buildup in business inventories. Both exports and imports of goods and services were projected to increase so that the net export surplus of goods and services would be the equivalent of 2.5 percent of the 1974 Gross Domestic Product. The 1974 national plan emphasized achieving a high level of output and employment, allocating increased output to private and public consumption and inventory replacement, and maintaining a sizable net export surplus.

In some years, annual national economic guidance, with the aid of annual plans, has been quite successful; and estimates or projections of the coming year's economic developments have been close to the actual outcomes. At other times, large discrepancies between projected annual plans and actual outcomes have occurred. The outcomes of annual demand and supply management in 1970 and 1971 are presented in Table 10-10. In 1970, which was a boom year, the government's national economic estimates or projections were largely met. The actual or realized volumes of personal consumption and merchandise exports, business investment expenditures, and gross domestic product were very close to the government's estimates for the year 1970. The main deviations

[21] OECD, *OECD Economic Surveys, Sweden,* 1971–1972. See also Tord Ekstrom, "Swedish Manpower Planning," *Planning and Markets,* 1969, pp. 301–312.

Table 10-9

Swedish National Economic Accounts for 1973 and National Economic Budget for 1974 (In Million Kroner, 1973 Prices)

	National economic accounts 1973	National economic budget 1974	Percent change from 1973 to 1974
Private consumption	115,100	120,300	+4.5
Public consumption	52,000	53,600	+3.0
Gross fixed investment	47,000	46,900	−0.2
Change in inventories	−2,800	900	0.4[1]
Export of goods and services	61,000	64,900	+6.4
Import of goods and services	−54,700	−59,200	+8.2
Gross domestic product	217,600	227,400	+4.5

[1] Percent of 1974 GDP.

Source: Swedish Ministry of Finance, *The National Budget, 1974.*

Table 10-10
Swedish Short-Run Demand and Supply Management in 1970 and 1971

	1970 (In 1969 prices)		1971 (In 1970 prices)	
	National economic budget estimates	Actual outcome	National economic budget estimates	Actual outcome
	Percentage change over previous year			
Personal consumption, volume	2.8	2.2	3.0	−0.2
Business investment expenditures	2.9	2.6	8.5	2.2
Residential construction expenditures	−5.0	−2.6	−2.0	−5.6
Local government investment expenditures	0.3	9.8	2.0	−10.9
Merchandise exports, volume	9.5	9.8	8.5	3.5
Gross domestic product	4.3	4.9	2.8	0.3

Sources: Swedish Ministry of Finance, *Preliminary National Budget* for 1971 and 1972.

from government estimates were the volume of residential construction, which did not decline as much as was expected, and the volume of local government expenditures, which were estimated to increase only 0.3 percent in 1970 but which actually increased 9.8 percent. This latter development underlines one of the weaknesses of Swedish national planning: that the central government does not have much control over the size of local government expenditures.

The planning experience in the prosperous year 1970 and the demand-and-supply management associated with it were quite different in the recession year 1971. In the latter year, wide discrepancies appeared between the government estimates of and actual changes in the volumes of personal consumption, merchandise exports, and residential construction, the size of business investment and local government expenditures, and the annual increase in gross domestic product. Instead of increasing 3 percent as expected in 1971, the volume of personal consumption expenditures actually declined 0.2 percent; real business investment expenditures increased only 2.2 percent, instead of the estimated 8.5 percent; the volume of merchandise exports increased only 3.5 percent, instead of the expected 8.5 percent; and local government expenditures declined almost 11 percent, instead of rising 2 percent as anticipated. Also, residential construction expenditures fell off much more than the government had estimated for 1971. Real gross domestic product, which was projected in the annual plan to increase 2.8 percent, rose only 0.3 percent. Similar large discrepancies between annual forecasts and actual outcomes for the recession year 1975 were recorded.

The inadequacies of annual demand-and-supply management stemmed from a number of factors. The rate of personal saving remained much higher than the government had forecast, local government expenditures declined much more than the government had estimated, and business investment expenditures did not respond favorably to the government's efforts to increase them. The poor performance in annual supply-and-demand management can be attributed in large part to the government's overly cautious 1971 antirecession policy. This policy was the result of the government's fear of continued strong inflationary pressures, even though the economy's growth potential was not being realized and unemployment was increasing. The government also saw the prospect of a large deficit in the current balance of international payments for 1971, which was expected to result from the declining international competitiveness of Swedish industry. With the return of more domestic and external balance in the Swedish economy in 1973 and 1974, the prospect of large discrepancies between the government's annual economic projections and actual outcomes was greatly diminished for those years.

Medium-Term Demand and Supply Management

As in Norway and France, the framework for Swedish annual planning and short-run demand and supply management is provided by the five-year national plans or "surveys."[22] The general objective of these economic surveys is to project the growth of the nation's gross domestic product and its distribution among private and public consumption and investment uses over the coming five-year period. A number of alternative projections are made so that "some foundation for choosing a strategy for economic policy during the coming five years" may be provided.[23] The general strategy followed since the close of the Second World War is shown by the statistics in Table 10–11, which compare the distribution of Sweden's gross domestic product among private and public consumption and investment uses in 1950 and 1970. During this twenty-year period, economic policies have had as their objectives major changes in the uses of the nation's gross domestic product. These changes include a large decline in private consumption as a share of gross domestic product (from 66.3 percent in 1950 to 52.6 percent in 1970), and a large increase in public consumption from 13.9 to 23.4 percent of gross domestic product. At the same time, gross private and public investment increased from 19.2 to 22.8 percent of this product. In the quarter century after World War II, the six five-year plans were used to direct resources

[22] The five-year Swedish plans have been called "programs," "long-term perspectives," and "economic surveys." In recent years, the tendency has been to avoid the term "national plan," and to point out that the five-year economic surveys provide a number of "alternative lines" of economic development. The 1971–1975 Economic Survey states that "The results presented here are not to be taken as proposals for the coming five-year period, either for the economy as a whole or for the government sector" (p. 8). Clearly, the government regards one of the alternative lines of economic development as the "basic calculation," which dominates its economic policy formulation during the five-year survey or plan period. Assar Lindbeck declares that "The long-term reports in Sweden may be regarded mainly as forecasts, rather than plans." See his "Theories and Problems in Swedish Economic Policy in the Post-War Period," *American Economic Review*, Vol. LVIII, June 1968, p. 58.

[23] The Swedish Ministry of Finance, *The Swedish Economy, 1971–1975*, Stockholm, 1971, p. 37.

Table 10–11
Distribution of the Swedish Gross Domestic Product in 1950 and 1970 (In Percent, Current Prices)

	1950	1970
Private consumption	66.3	52.6
Public consumption	13.9	23.4
Gross investment	19.2	22.8
Change in inventories	−0.2	2.1
Net export surplus	0.8	−0.9
Gross domestic product	100.0	100.0

Source: Swedish Ministry of Finance, *The Swedish Economy, 1971–1975*.

increasingly into the public sector. The national health system, housing, the improved educational system, regional development, increased environmental protection, and enlarged social services have over the years absorbed increasing amounts of labor, raw materials, and capital. Whereas in 1950, public consumption, public investment, and housing absorbed 24 percent of the nation's gross domestic product, by 1970 these three components accounted for 37 percent of this product.

The 1971–1975 Swedish five-year national plan continued the economic trends of the 1950s and 1960s. Table 10–12 presents the national accounts for 1970 and the national economic budget projections for 1975. Gross domestic product is projected to increase at the annual rate of 3.8 percent during the five-year plan period. Private consumption is projected to grow at a slower rate (3.3 percent), and public consumption at a faster rate (4.5 percent), than gross domestic product. Investments in housing and in government projects are to be curbed in order to permit an expansion of private business investment. Since Sweden's labor supply is expected to grow very little in the years 1971–1975, the improvement in labor productivity must come largely from improved worker skills and more capital per worker. Additional reasons for increasing the amount of capital per worker will be the expected decline in the length of the work week, and the need to restructure Swedish industry in order to maintain or improve its international competitiveness. The objective of securing a surplus on the current balance of international payments equal to 1 percent of gross domestic product by 1975 will require sizable structural changes in the Swedish export industries.

The Division for Economic Planning constructs its five-year economic projections in the light of the government's primary and secondary goals. The primary goals include full employment, rapid economic growth, a more equal distribution of national income, reasonably stable prices, and balanced international payments. Among the secondary goals are environmental protection, regional balance, job satisfaction, equal rights for women in the labor market, adequate housing, improved education, and other items contributing to human well-being. These goals are derived from interpretations of "existing political valuations."[24] The problem is to plan

[24] *The Swedish Economy, 1971–1975*, p. 28.

Table 10–12

The Swedish National Economic Accounts for 1970 and National Economic Budget for 1975 (In Million Kroner, 1959 Prices)

	1970 national economic accounts	1975 national economic budget	1970–1975 annual percent change
Private consumption	56,600	66,600	3.3
Public consumption	18,400	23,000	4.5
Gross investments	23,300	27,700	3.5
Change in inventories	2,900	2,400	—
Net export surplus	−300	1,800	—
Gross domestic product	100,900	121,500	3.8

Source: Swedish Ministry of Finance, *The Swedish Economy, 1971–1975*.

the use of the nation's resources so as to achieve the nation's collective and private economic and social goals and to maximize personal well-being. The Swedish planning authorities admit that many aspects of human welfare are omitted from the contents or composition of gross domestic product, and that "The national [economic] accounts were not, and do not claim to have been designed to measure the development of welfare in the widest sense."[25] These accounts, the Swedish government planners explain, give inadequate attention to the "qualitative" aspects of economic and social development such as the environment, health, security, and other items of well-being. The concept of gross domestic product is useful for analyzing from a quantitative point of view productive capacity and the resources available for future consumption, capital formation, the scope for aid to developing countries, and the goal for the surplus on the current balance of international payments. The Swedish planning authorities explain that gross domestic product "can only serve as a starting point and frame of reference when it comes to the welfare and other qualitative aspects of economic and social development."[26]

When the Swedish government goes beyond measurable gross domestic product in its program for enlarging human welfare, it moves away from the quantitative to the qualitative aspects of social welfare. It then turns to "intuitive methods as a basis for decisions" concerned with maximizing national priorities. These methods involve making judgments as to the relative marginal social utilities of various government expenditures on defense, health, education, agricultural protection, environmental conservation, regional development, and other national objectives. Guidelines for judgments made by the planning authorities with respect to these national priorities are settled in the political sphere, and are passed on by the government to the Economic Planning Division of the Ministry of Finance. It should be pointed out, however, that the national goals and their mutual priority are not specified in great detail, so that the Planning Division is in a position to consider a variety of alternative combinations of national goals. Working with the valuation guidelines supplied by the government, the division makes intuitive decisions as to what "basic" combination of public expenditures will maximize social utility, and hence social welfare. The Swedish prime minister and his cabinet may accept, reject, or modify the conclusions of the Planning Division but, since the division takes its original valuation guidelines from the Ministry of Finance and other cabinet members, the national priorities and expenditures as proposed in the five-year published economic survey are very close to the priorities recommended by the government.

A methodological innovation adopted in the 1971–1975 medium-term economic survey was the use of an econometric model of the Swedish economy as an aid in improving the analytical basis of Swedish national economic planning.[27] This model makes it possible to calculate the consequences of distributing or allocating resources in different ways, and also to study how the pattern of economic development is influenced by different assumptions as to the economic situation at home and abroad. On the basis of this econometric model are worked out the various alternative lines of economic development. In each alternative, the quantitative relationships between the components of total

[25] *Ibid.*, p. 18.

[26] *Ibid.*, p. 19. For a further development of this point, see Anders Östlind, "Some Personal Observations on Homo Sapiens, Happiness and Equality," *Quarterly Review*, 4/1972, pp. 140–149.

[27] A description of this model is given in Section 1.5–1.52 of *The Swedish Economy, 1971–1975*, pp. 31–37.

demand and total supply are clearly indicated. The various alternatives are not forecasts, but are rather illustrations of the consequences of different combinations of domestic and external circumstances and goals of economic policy. The Swedish planning authorities are careful to point out that the econometric model does not supply answers to judgmental problems relating to choices among national priorities. No econometric model can evaluate the relative social marginal utilities of different public expenditures. This model can only explain or illustrate the future consequences for the Swedish economy—for exports, imports, industrial production, employment, wages, prices, taxes, and the like—of alternative ways of endeavoring to maximize collective or social utility and hence social welfare. Collective value judgments concerning national priorities have to be fed into the econometric model, which can then provide some quantitative measurements of the consequences that may follow upon accepting these value judgments.

In the plans of the late 1940s and 1950s, the quantitative aspects of human well-being were emphasized to the neglect of its qualitative aspects. In the 1960s and early 1970s, more interest was expressed in the negative effects of rapid economic growth. This growth has been achieved only at the cost of increased pollution and a lower quality of life. It has shifted the population from the rural northern counties to the industrial southern counties; and in the opinion of some workers, the quality of life in the congested industrial centers of the south is lower than in the less congested northern counties.

The increased computerization of the assembly line has lowered the level of job satisfaction at the very time that workers are becoming better educated. The desire for a shorter work week raises the question of the extent to which economic growth should be sacrificed to increased leisure. Insofar as these developments have increased the importance of the qualitative aspects of social welfare, national planning has become more difficult. The 1971–1975 Economic Survey points out that "the problem has been that intuitive methods have had to be used for adding and balancing the various items [national priorities] without the help that can be derived from quantifying their importance."[28] Some members of the Swedish Center (Agricultural) and Liberal parties would find the solution to these problems by returning to a more simple, rustic way of living. The Social Democratic party recommends accepting the necessity of the modern industrial system, but making certain that it serves the needs of human well-being rather than narrow economic goals.

As has already been explained, the Swedish five-year economic surveys are not presented as national plans that receive government approval. The government has explained that "Planning in Sweden is not concerned with individual economic units [private firms], nor does it involve revising their plans to conform with an integrated national perspective. It is expected that private enterprises and sectors will adapt themselves to changes on the market. It is, however, a function of planning to reduce the element of uncertainty represented by the authorities' future policy and actions, as well as the unknowns inherent in economic growth, the large share of foreign trade in Sweden's GNP, etc."[29] Although Sweden has had no official five-year national plans, its medium-term demand-and-supply management has achieved the broad national goals established for its guidance. In the past quarter century, economic growth has been maintained at an average annual rate of 4 percent and private consumption has been

---

[28] *Ibid.*, p. 19.
[29] The Swedish Ministry of Finance, *The Swedish Budget, 1973/74*, Stockholm, 1973, p. 117.

curbed, while both public consumption and gross investment have increased in relation to private consumption. While there have been some discrepancies between the five-year macroeconomic projections and the actual outcome, these discrepancies have not been major deviations from the government's economic goals.

The statistics in Table 10-13 show the economic projections for 1965-1970 and the actual outcomes for that period. Private consumption developed in line with the projections, but public consumption increased more rapidly than projected. The main discrepancy was in gross investments, which increased more slowly than projected, because both private fixed investment and residential construction were weaker than anticipated. Whereas gross fixed investments were projected to increase at the average annual rate of 5.1 percent, they actually increased at the rate of only 3.4 percent. The actual annual increase in gross domestic product was close to the projected annual goal of 4.1 percent. The medium-term economic surveys have projection periods that are long enough to provide for some flexibility in policy formulation. In each five-year period, the government can take those policy steps that are necessary to prevent major deviations from the macroeconomic goals presented in the medium-term economic surveys. Although large discrepancies between the estimates of annual national plans and actual outcomes have occurred in some years of recession, the record for the five-year national plans has been much better, and discrepancies between projections and outcomes have been much smaller than in annual plans.

Sweden's 1973-1977 Economic Survey

The Swedish practice has been to review each five-year economic survey at its midpoint to see whether the economic trends in the remaining years will follow the lines originally projected for the first year of the survey. If significant changes in economic trends are found, the economic survey is then revised to take account of these changes. In the years 1955-1970, the mid-period reviews did not reveal any changes in economic trends that were substantial enough to warrant issuing revised five-year economic surveys. When, however, the 1971-1975 survey, was reviewed in 1973, it was decided that the

Table 10-13
Projections of the 1965-1970 Swedish Economic Survey and the Actual Outcomes

	Projected annual percent increases 1965-1970	Actual annual percent increases 1965-1970
Private consumption	3.4	3.4
Public consumption	4.5	5.2
Gross fixed investments	5.1	3.4
Gross domestic product	4.1	3.9

Source: *The Swedish Economy, 1971-1975*, p. 16.

economy would probably not follow the pattern of development as outlined in this survey. Consequently, a new 1973–1977 survey was constructed to cover the second half of the 1971–1975 survey and the next two years.[30]

The economic trends that had not been anticipated when the 1971–1975 survey was constructed have already been mentioned in the discussion of the Swedish economy's performance in the years 1971–1975. These trends include the high rate of personal saving, the decline in residential construction, the very low level of local government investment, and the impact of the oil crisis on Sweden's external economy. Table 10–14, which compares the economic trends underlying the 1971–1975 and 1973–1977 surveys, reveals that the latter survey differs from the former in a number of important ways. What the 1973–1977 survey looks forward to is a reallocation of the nation's total output as it expands at a projected rate of 4.2 percent. Relatively more output is projected to go into the private-consumption and local-government investment components of gross domestic product, and less into central-government investment and residential construction. The claims on gross domestic product of public consumption and private investment will remain substantially as they were projected for 1971–1975. Private investment will support the export and export-supporting industries,

[30] The new medium-term economic survey is presented in Finansdepartementet, *Svensk Ekonomi Fram Till 1977* (The Swedish Economy to 1977), Statens Offentliga Utredningar, 1973: 21, Stockholm, 1973. A brief analysis of this survey is found in OECD, *OECD Economic Surveys, Sweden*, July 1974, pp. 30–36.

Table 10–14
Economic Trends in the Swedish 1971–1975 and 1973–1977 Economic Surveys

Use of GDP	Percent annual changes projected	
	During 1971–1975	During 1973–1977
Private consumption	2.6	4.4
Public consumption	3.8	4.0
Central government	3.2	3.5
Local government	4.2	4.3
Gross investment	2.1	2.5
Housing	−1.0	−0.6
Public investment	1.4	2.9
Central government	4.0	1.7
Local government	0.6	3.4
Private investment	3.5	3.4
Exports of goods and services	6.7	7.1
Imports of goods and services	5.2	7.3
Gross Domestic Product	3.1	4.2

Source: Finansdepartementet, *Svensk Ekonomi Fram Till 1977*, SOU 1973:22.

and the achievement of an equilibrium in Sweden's external account is projected for 1977.

The economic uncertainties that led to the revision of the 1971–1975 economic survey also raise some questions as to the feasibility of securing the goals of the 1973–1977 survey. This survey raises the annual economic growth rate from 3.1 percent in the earlier survey to 4.2 in the current survey. With annual economic growth averaging only 2.2 percent in 1971–1975, some observers of the Swedish economy express considerable doubt that it can achieve a 4.2 percent growth rate in the years 1973–1977. Neither the labor inputs nor the worker productivity required for this growth rate may be forthcoming, because total hours worked may continue to decline, and labor may also continue to move into low-productivity activities such as private and public services.

Long-Term Supply and Demand Management

Long-term supply-and-demand management in Sweden is based upon considerations relating to plan periods that vary from ten to twenty years. These longer-term economic plans make it possible to consider wider alternatives than do five-year plans with respect to the growth and uses of gross domestic product within the framework of possible economic and social developments. They throw light on the restructuring of the nation's economic system that may be required in the long run by the effort to achieve the nation's changing priorities.[31] Since the assessment of internal and external developments over twenty years necessarily contains a large element of uncertainty, long-term supply-and-demand management should present clear alternatives and be highly flexible.

On the supply side, long-term national management deals with the prospects for economic growth as indicated by trends in the availability of manpower and in the improvement of labor productivity. In 1970–1990, population is expected to grow very slowly, while the labor participation rate of men is projected to decline as the rate for women rises. Three-quarters of the increase in the Swedish labor force is expected to come from the immigration of workers from Nordic countries, largely from Finland.

As Table 10–15 shows, between 1970 and 1990 employment is projected to decline relatively in all sectors except in the public service sector, where it will rise from 17.6 to 37 percent of total employment. Production in many forms of economic activity will become increasingly capital intensive. With shorter working hours, there will be more shift work in order to obtain a more efficient use of the nation's capital supply. Further urbanization and a greater relative importance of the service industries will create more attractive job opportunities for women and will raise their labor participation rate. The annual increase in gross domestic product in the 1970s is projected to be about 4 percent, with a lower rate of around 3.5 percent for the 1980s, when employment will be shifted increasingly into the low-productivity service industries. Over the twenty-year period, the total national output is expected to be doubled.

On the demand side, long-term Swedish national management is concerned with shifts in the distribution of the nation's expanding output between the three categories of capital formation, public consumption, and private consumption. For the 1980s, the planning authorities present six alternative patterns of output use or demand for gross domestic

---

[31] Torsten Carlsson, "Structural Rationalisation in Swedish Industry," *Quarterly Review*, 1964: I, pp. 1–6; and Erik Lundberg, "Productivity and Structural Change—a Policy Issue in Sweden," *Economic Journal*, Vol. 82, March 1972, pp. 465–485.

Table 10–15
The Distribution of Swedish Employment, 1970–1990 (In Percent)

Sectors	1950 (actual)	1970 (actual)	1980 (projected)	1990 (projected)
Agriculture and forestry	21.3	8.1	4.3	2.0
Mining and manufacturing	42.9	42.7	37.9	30.5
Private services	27.9	31.6	32.2	30.5
Public services	7.9	17.6	25.6	37.0
Total employment	100.0	100.0	100.0	100.0

Source: Ministry of Finance, *The Swedish Economy, 1971–1975 and the General Outlook up to 1990*, p. 320.

product. These alternatives have different annual growth rates, varying from a low of 2.9 to a high of 4.6 percent, and also different consumption-investment ratios. Two of the 1980–1990 patterns of total output use are presented in Table 10–16. The 1980–1990 Alternative Pattern I is a high private-consumption, limited-investment pattern, whereas the Alternative Pattern II is a low private-consumption, high-investment pattern. Although, as has been explained, the Economic Survey for 1971–1975 does not recommend the adoption by the government of any particular pattern of output use, nevertheless it describes Pattern I as "our principal alternative."[32] As Table 10–16 indicates, Pattern I for the 1980s very closely follows the pattern of output use projected for the 1970s.

The main guidelines for economic development in the years 1970–1990 suggested by the long-term Economic Survey include the following. Private consumption is expected to grow relatively slowly, because much of the rise in the standard of living will

[32] *Ibid.*, p. 323.

Table 10–16
Sweden's Uses of Total Output, 1970–1990, as Percentages of Gross Domestic Product (1959 Prices)

	Average 1970–1975	Average 1975–1980	Average 1980–1990	
			Pattern I	Pattern II
Private consumption	54.8	54.3	54.1	46.9
Public consumption	18.9	19.1	20.0	20.2
Gross fixed investment	22.8	24.0	23.4	30.3
Change in inventories	2.0	1.3	0.8	1.0
Net export surplus	1.5	1.3	1.7	1.6
Gross domestic product	100.0	100.0	100.0	100.0
Average annual increase in GDP	3.8%	4.3%	3.6%	4.1%

Source: Ministry of Finance, *The Swedish Economy, 1971–1975 and the General Outlook up to 1990*, pp. 314–315.

be taken in the form of increased leisure. Increased efforts to curb environmental deterioration will slow down economic growth and reduce the potential growth of private consumption. Swedish aid to the less developed countries is projected to amount to 1 percent of the nation's gross domestic product in 1980 and to 2 percent in 1990. In 1970–1990, the volume of imports is projected to rise rapidly from one-third to one-half of gross domestic product. This development will require a rapid expansion of export capacity if external balance is to be maintained. Furthermore, the restructuring of industry that contributed to the rise in production in the 1960s will have to be speeded up even more in the 1970s and 1980s.

The long-term Economic Survey for 1970–1990 emphasizes that the economic integration process in Western Europe will probably continue in the 1970s and 1980s. The links between Sweden and other countries will be strengthened, and labor and capital will move more freely over national boundaries. This will promote the international division of labor, and reduce the differences in economic conditions and standards of living among the Western European countries. Increased integration will present many difficult problems. Governments will have less freedom to pursue separate national economic policies. Structural changes in Sweden and other countries will have to be gradual and controlled. Multinational corporations will become more important, and Sweden will have to join with other nations to protect their national interests by placing more controls on these corporations.[33] World trade can be expected to continue to rise.

Sweden and other advanced industrial countries will be expected to remove trade barriers against the less developed countries, which will then be in a better position to participate in achieving an optimum global division of labor. What all this means for Sweden in the next twenty years is that as standards of living rise in the less developed countries, there may be a slowdown in the rise of Sweden's standard of living. The General Outlook for 1970–1990 concludes that "It is not entirely inconceivable that the affluent countries [including Sweden] for a time may have to accept an unchanged level of living standards," if the gap between the poor less developed countries and the rich mature countries is to be reduced.[34]

Trends in Swedish Incomes Policy

Sweden, like Norway, has not adopted a formal incomes policy.[35] The government has made no effort to establish any fixed wage guideposts which could be used to restrain wage-rate increases. The official position is that "The Swedish government has little confidence in the usefulness of a direct incomes policy as an instrument of price stabilization, irrespective of whether this policy be executed by exhortation or by a special machinery set up for the purpose."[36] Instead, the government has limited its role in the wage-determining process very largely to providing background information on the general state of the economy to the two sides

---

[33] This issue has been raised in Lars Otterbeck, "Multinational Companies and International Site Selection," *Quarterly Review*, 3/1973, pp. 86–94.

[34] *Ibid.*, p. 325.

[35] For analyses of Swedish incomes policy, see Lloyd Ulman and Robert J. Flanagan, *Wage Restraint, A Study of Incomes Policies in Western Europe*, Berkeley: University of California Press, 1971, pp. 88–115; David C. Smith, *Incomes Policies, Some Foreign Experiences and their Relevance for Canada*, Ottawa: Queen's Printer, 1966, pp. 151–173; and Eric Schiff, *Incomes Policies Abroad*, Washington, D.C.: American Enterprise Institute, 1971, pp. 25–33.

[36] Swedish Ministry of Finance, Secretariat of Economic Planning, "Inflation and Economic Development" (mimeo.), Stockholm, July 1965, p. 6.

of industry in the collective bargaining process. On occasion, the government has expressed its opinion on an appropriate general wage development in the light of the probable economic conditions in the coming year. Instead of an official incomes policy, Sweden has had an unofficial voluntary incomes policy, under which the Swedish Employers' Association and the Swedish Confederation of Trade Unions have concluded "frame" agreements; the latter have provided for general or average wage increases. From 1945 to 1965, this unofficial incomes policy worked quite well, and wage settlements were made with little recourse to strikes or lockouts. Wage-rate increases were not so large as to cause large increases in unit labor costs, serious inflation was avoided, and a favorable balance of international payments was usually achieved. In those years, the record for economic growth and employment was very good.

Since 1965, the unofficial incomes policy has deteriorated somewhat.[37] This deterioration culminated in the wildcat strikes of 1969 in a number of major industries, the wage explosion of 1970, and the strike of fifty thousand civil service workers in 1971, which closed the railroads, the law courts, and the schools. The wildcat strikes of 1969 indicated a certain grass-roots dissatisfaction with the highly centralized system of collective bargaining. A more serious issue is the inflationary impact of the sizable wage drifting that has taken place in Swedish industry. The efforts of the Swedish Confederation of Trade Unions to apply the principle of solidarity in collective bargaining have been largely frustrated by the wage drifting that has maintained the wage differentials between workers in low-productivity and high-productivity industries.[38] The attempts of individual unions to preserve their interindustry wage differentials contributed to domestic inflation in the years 1969–1972, when there were no strong inflationary pressures coming from abroad.

Since 1972, increases in wage rates have weakened Swedish industry's international competitiveness and have created interest in proposals to lower personal income taxes in return for the trade unions' agreement to restrain their wage demands. With moderate increases in wage rates and reductions in personal income taxes, the workers could be assured of a given increase in their real disposable wage incomes. Such arrangements would lower industry's wage costs per unit of output and would make it more competitive in the world's export markets. Prior to the March 1975 collective wage bargaining, the government announced cuts in income taxes with the hope that these reductions, to come into effect in 1976, would have a restraining impact on the trade unions' initial wage claims.

A further complication has been the dissatisfaction of white-collar and professional workers in recent years with the collective bargaining process. The Swedish Confederation of Trade Unions has favored a policy of reducing wage-rate differentials throughout the economy. This has coincided with an upgrading of the nation's educational system and an increase in the supply of white-collar and professional workers; these developments have tended to reduce the wage differentials between blue-collar and white-collar workers. The Central Organization of Salaried Employees (TCO) and the Swedish Confederation of Professional Associations (SACO) have

[37] Steven D. Anderman, "Central Wage Negotiation in Sweden: Recent Problems and Developments," *British Journal of Industrial Relations*, Vol. V, Nov. 1967, pp. 322–337.

[38] In recent years, more than half of the total increase in hourly earnings in manufacturing has come from wage increases over and above the negotiated or contractual increases. This problem is analyzed in Sture Eskilsson, "The Wage Drift," *Quarterly Review*, 1966:I, pp. 8–15.

in recent years separated their bargaining activities from those of the Swedish Confederation of Trade Unions and have become more aggressive in demanding that established differentials between blue-collar and white-collar wages should be preserved. When these demands have not been met, the white-collar unions have in recent years exhibited a new militancy which has resulted in considerable labor-management strife. After a bitter strike and lockout of teachers and headmasters in the schools and universities in 1971, SACO obtained an average pay increase of 17 percent for its white-collar members, whereas the trade unions secured only a 5–7 percent wage increase for their blue-collar members.

In 1967, the Swedish Employers' Association recommended the adoption of a more formal incomes policy than had been followed until that time.[39] It was proposed that future wage increases be based on a joint calculation by two expert employer representatives and two expert representatives from the blue-collar and white-collar workers. The proposed wage increase would make allowance for three items: probable wage drift, new fringe benefits, and a negotiated wage residual. The size of these items would be related to jointly agreed targets for economic growth and improvement in labor productivity and to jointly made assumptions with regard to inflation and other economic developments. In the event of disagreement among the four experts, the scope for wage increases would be determined by a board of arbitration representing labor and management. The aim of the proposal of the Swedish employers was to make the collective bargaining process more systematic and to assign a larger role to technical experts. This proposal was turned down by the Swedish Confederation of Trade Unions on the grounds that the proposal would weaken the unions' traditional collective bargaining function, and that it did not provide for enough government participation. Up to the present, no major changes have been made in Sweden's unofficial voluntary incomes policy. The difficulties of 1969–1972 were handled without any major injury to the established collective bargaining process. As long as Sweden can maintain high levels of production and employment and a satisfactory balance in its external economy, it is doubtful that major changes will be made in the nongovernment or voluntary incomes policy that has been developed since the late 1930s.

Disagreement has frequently arisen concerning the size of subsidies to farmers, the proper level of wage rates, and the squeezing of business profits; but when the international competitiveness of Sweden's economy has been seriously endangered, the government has forcefully explained the situation to all income claimants, and has succeeded in harmonizing income claims sufficiently to prevent inflation from seriously weakening Sweden's international competitiveness. Income claims on all sides have been moderated enough under government guidance to keep the Swedish price level from getting out of line with the price levels in other industrial countries. Also, the national pattern of income distribution that has resulted from the application of the government's unofficial incomes policy has thus far received enough public approval to assure a high level of social harmony and to make possible an efficient and prosperous economy.

Industrial Democracy in Sweden

One of the major unsettled problems of the Swedish economy is how to achieve industrial

---

[39] This proposal is analyzed in Gösta Edgren, Karl-Olof Faxén, and Clas-Erik Odhner, "Wages, Growth, and the Distribution of Income," *Swedish Journal of Economics*, Sept. 1969. See also Karl-Olof Faxén, "The Swedish Cost Problem and the Range of Action for a Swedish Incomes Policy," *Quarterly Review*, 1967:3, pp. 71–78.

democracy. While the principles of democracy have become well established in political life, similar progress has not been made in the working life of blue-collar and white-collar employees. In Swedish private enterprises, the use of manpower is still mainly a prerogative of business management. The Swedish Confederation of Trade Unions believes that the sole right of employers to decide matters of manpower management should be replaced by an obligation to make these matters a concern of employer-employee negotiation. Most collective bargaining agreements at present do not give employees much voice in manpower management. At its 1971 congress, the Swedish Confederation of Trade Unions emphasized that union members should acquire a real degree of joint influence over the private enterprises for which they work. What the trade unions seek is a system of codetermination to cover all matters affecting the worker in his daily work.

The increasing concentration and rationalization of industry in Sweden has improved labor productivity and raised workers' incomes at the same time that job satisfaction has declined. This decline has occurred because work on the assembly line has become more mechanized, isolated, and clocked. The Swedish Confederation of Trade Unions has pointed out that "Demands are being raised for a better work environment and more satisfaction on the job, while at the same time mechanization and streamlining of production make it more difficult to meet these demands."[40] While the unions agree that the policies of the Social Democratic government have improved workers' economic conditions in general, their working conditions or job environments are said to have remained largely unchanged.

A recent report of the Swedish Employers' Confederation concludes that the auto, refrigerator, and television factories of the 1980s must differ significantly from those of the 1950s and 1960s "if we are to find people who are willing to work in these factories . . . we cannot anticipate that, during this century, such factories will be populated by industrial robots, other than to a very limited extent. We must therefore intensify our efforts on the purely technical plane to find alternative lines of progress for the arrangement of industrial work."[41] In recent years, Swedish employers have experimented with various ways of reducing the adverse consequences of assembly-line production such as high absenteeism and the large turnover of personnel. The traditional or classical assembly-line production system, with its specialized work positions, is now being abandoned in favor of a "positionless" work organization, with work groups or teams in place of separate and isolated individual workers.

In the shipyards, automobile factories, and other assembly-line enterprises, workers are now organized in teams in which they become trained in many tasks, and continuously learn more parts of the assembly work. Piece-rate wage systems have been dropped in favor of monthly wages, with bonuses determined by team output rather than by individual output. In this way, the work organization becomes more fluid and adaptable; assembly lines are designed to make the work roles of individuals more attractive; workers undergo continuous training and development; and account is taken of the views and preferences

---

[40] Andre Thiria, International Secretary, the Swedish Confederation of Trade Unions, "Labor's Voice Joins the Corporate Board," *Viewpoint*, Swedish Information Service, New York, May 29, 1973, p. 1.

[41] Rolf Lindholm, *Advances in Work Organization, Four Swedish Cases*, Swedish Employers' Confederation, Stockholm, 1973, pp. 18–19; and Richard B. Peterson, "The Swedish Experience with Industrial Democracy, *British Journal of Industrial Relations*, Vol. VI, July 1968, pp. 185–203.

of all employees. It is realized that some reduced efficiency will result from a lower degree of division of labor and assembly-line specialization. It is expected, however, that this lower efficiency will be outweighed by the other advantages of team work, so that the total productivity of the new "positionless" assembly line will be higher than that of the old conventional "box" assembly-line with its isolated workers.

While the Swedish trade unions are prepared to cooperate with employers in the effort to humanize work conditions, they feel that improving job satisfaction requires more than better working conditions. They take the position that the dependent status of the worker must be eliminated by making employers and employees partners in industry, and by achieving "equality between work and capital."[42] This equality can be secured, according to trade union leaders, only when the workers can influence company decision making at all levels. For this reason, the Swedish Confederation of Trade Unions called upon the government to require private enterprises to place workers' representatives on their boards of directors.

A law passed in 1972 now requires all Swedish business corporations with one hundred or more employees to allow two representatives to sit as board-of-director members, if this is requested by the trade union local in the respective firm. The worker-directors have the same responsibilities as other corporate board members, with the exception that they are barred from board decisions concerning labor-management negotiations and related matters. The law is expected to apply to about 2,300 Swedish companies which employ 1.2 million workers. It will enable the Swedish labor movement to place about four thousand representatives on company boards of directors, where they will have the opportunity to influence corporate decision making. Being represented on company boards will enable the workers to deal with issues such as closing one or more divisions of a company because of insufficient profitability, curbing pollution, or dealing with Swedish multinational companies which may establish branch plants abroad and so reduce the demand for labor in Sweden.

The placing of worker-directors on company boards is regarded by the trade unions as only one further step in the democratization of private industry. It has already been proposed that the trade unions should have the right to nominate accountants to participate in corporate accounting, so that the workers and their representatives may keep themselves better informed about their firms' economic situation. Although a few major Swedish firms, such as the Volvo auto company and the Uddevalla and Götaverken shipyards, had voluntarily appointed worker-directors before 1973, the Swedish Employers' Confederation opposed the 1972 legislation requiring the appointment of worker-directors. The business spokesmen regarded worker representatives on company boards as threatening industrial secrecy and competitive advantage, and as opening the door to policies that would not be to the advantage of the companies or their stockholders.

These disagreements with regard to co-determination and other ways of improving industrial democracy raise the question of how far it is possible to go in democratizing private industry, and yet maintain the private nature of industry. The radical elements in the Social Democratic party are pressing for measures that will "extend society's and of course the labor movement's influence and stake in the business world."[43] Strong pressure

---

[42] Andre Thiria, op. cit., p. 5.

[43] Rune Johansson, the Swedish Ministry of Industry, *Industrial Democracy through Legislation*, Swedish Information Service, New York, Jan. 1973, p. 2.

is now being exerted on the Social Democratic government to invest a part of the assets of the National Insurance Pension Fund, which has total assets now equal to 30 percent of the nation's Gross National Product, in the shares of private companies. Up to now, the funds of the National Pension Fund have been largely invested in government bonds and in housing, agricultural, and municipal loans. If the fund were to invest heavily in private company shares, the government would be in a strong position to influence private company decision making. The fund is also able to influence the course of economic activity through loans made directly to private business enterprises, and through the purchase of bonds issued by the government investment bank established in 1967. Since the labor movement controls the Swedish government, developments along these lines could be used to achieve more industrial democracy.

Up to the present, the Swedish Social Democratic party has moved slowly in enlarging industrial democracy. Now that it remains in office with the help of the Swedish Communist party, there may be more pressure to enlarge labor's role in industrial production. At the same time, the decline in recent years in the political strength of the Social Democratic party may be interpreted as a sign that the people do not want more socialism or an extension of the welfare state. These problems arise in all countries where a socialist government relies heavily on a private enterprise system to provide the bulk of the nation's goods and services. In these countries, there are always strong ideological pressures to restrict private enterprise and to expand the socialist program. At the same time, where the mixed socialist-private-enterprise economy supports an affluent society, as in Sweden, strong pragmatic reasons exist not to alter greatly the structure and functioning of the mixed economy.

Environmental Protection

Environmental protection policy in Sweden is based on the premise that there is a body of environmental assets, including land, air, water, health, and the urban environment, from which the nation enjoys a flow of benefits, and which need to be maintained and improved upon as is done in the case of private and public capital in the form of residential construction, plant, machinery, and other forms of equipment.[44] The land includes not only rural and urban land, but also wilderness areas, areas of historic interest, objects of scenic beauty, and coastlines. The quality of life is improved by securing the optimal flow of psychic benefits from the available stock of environmental assets. This flow of environmental benefits may be decreased when individuals and private enterprises dump wastes of various types on the land or into the air and water. Similarly, municipalities and counties decrease the flow of environmental benefits when they dump inadequately treated sewage into rivers, lakes, and seas, or fail to remove the litter from streets and other areas. The flow of benefits can be increased by taxing polluting emissions, by enlarging wilderness areas, by protecting coastlines, and by investing more funds in devices to purify water and to dispose of solid wastes without adding to

[44] In the words of the Swedish Economic Planning Division, "there is a capital stock of clean water, which is reduced by the emission of pollutants but increased by improved purification. Corresponding capital stocks can be said to exist for clean air, dwelling environments, health and so on, these being affected favourably or unfavourably by different factors involved in economic development and measures taken in connection with this. This capital is tied in part to the present generation but in part it represents the heritage of coming generations (clean water, unspoiled countryside and so on)." *The Swedish Economy, 1971–1975*, p. 18.

air pollution.[45] In Sweden, the question of environmental protection has been given increasing attention in recent years, and access to a good environment is now widely accepted as a national goal of economic policy.

Concern with environmental care has raised the difficult questions of the aims and costs of this care. Concern with the aims of environmental policy has led to efforts to establish environmental goals in the form of minimal levels of purity for water and air and of noise.[46] The National Environmental Protection Board, supported by the Environment Advisory Committee with representatives from all major economic and social groups, is responsible for establishing minimum levels of environmental care. While some of these levels can be quantified, other goals such as the desirable number of wilderness areas and national parks, and the choice of coastlines to protect from commercial development, do not lend themselves to quantitative measurement. Since the benefits to consumers that flow from the environment do not have market prices on them, it is difficult to assess the valuation placed on these benefits by citizens.

The social utility of a further improvement in environmental protection must be weighed against the social utilities of the alternative goals that would have to be abandoned in order to achieve a given improvement. The ideal policy is to carry out the improvement in environmental care as long as its social utility exceeds the social utility to be obtained from some alternative goals. If the central and local governments allocate 25 percent of Gross National Product to public projects, the aim is to spread this portion of the GNP over a wide range of public purposes, including environmental care, so that the social utility derived from all these local and central government projects may be optimized. Since the social utilities to be derived from environmental care and other public objectives are not readily quantified, the governments at the local and national levels must make intuitive judgments as to what disposition of public funds for environmental care and other public purposes would be approved by the voting public. The only conclusion that the Swedish government feels certain about is that measures for environmental care will in the future place expanding claims on the annual increment in the nation's income.

In 1964, Sweden adopted the Nature Conservancy Act to provide for setting aside land as national parks or wilderness areas, to regulate the use of the coastlines, and to protect areas of natural beauty. The Environment Protection Act of 1969 controls the polluting emissions of communities and industries such as the pulp and paper, iron and steel, and chemical industries. Substantial appropriations are made by the central government for research in the area of environmental protection. Also, the government makes grants to local government and industries to cover partially (30 to 50 percent) the cost of constructing municipal plants for sewage purification, and partially (up to 25 percent) the cost of private investment in devices to reduce water, air, or noise pollution. In years of recession, these grants have been increased to cover up to 75 percent of private investment costs as a further stimulus to adopt environmental protection measures and in order to increase employment.[47] By 1975, local governments are

---

[45] For one approach to this problem, see Karl-Göran Mäler, "Environmental Control and Economy," *Quarterly Review*, 1971:3, pp. 63–68.

[46] Sweden's program for environmental conservation is presented in Royal Ministry for Foreign Affairs, "Steps to care for the environment in Sweden," *Sweden's Reply to the United Nations Enquiry in Connection with the Preparations for the United Nations Conference on the Human Environment*, Stockholm, 1970, pp. 25–38. See also the Swedish Institute, *Environmental Protection in Sweden*, Stockholm, Nov. 1969.

[47] *The Swedish Economy, 1971–1975*, p. 192.

expected to be devoting 24 percent of their total investments (excluding housing) to construction and equipment for environmental care of all types.

Regional Development Policy

The problem of regional development has attracted increasing attention in recent years in Sweden.[48] Before 1965, limited consideration was given to the consequences of rapid economic growth, such as major sectoral and geographical changes in the structure and functioning of economic activities. The sectoral changes involved the decline of agriculture and forestry in relation to mining, manufacturing, and the service industries; the latter industries expanded very rapidly. The geographical changes resulted in the decline in the small-scale and middle-size industries in the northern and central counties and the swift expansion of industries in a few areas of the southern counties.

Today, about one-half of Sweden's population of 8,129,000 is concentrated in the four southern industrial areas of Stockholm-Lake Mälaren, Östergötland, Göteborg, and Western Skåne (the Malmö area). During the 1960s, the three major urban areas (Stockholm, Göteborg, and Malmö) accounted for approximately two-thirds of the total population increase, while 80 percent of the municipalities with less than ten thousand inhabitants had a drop in population. A further migration of the population from the sparsely populated northern and central counties is expected in the 1970s. The six regions into which Sweden is divided by the planning authorities vary widely as to labor productivity, wages, job opportunities, employment of women, and social services. The sparsely settled northern and central counties suffer from unemployment above the national average, underemployment of much of the working population, low labor productivity, and inadequate public services.

It is widely agreed that the problems of regional development should not be settled by the spontaneous forces of an unregulated market system. The first approach to the problem of declining economic regions was to adopt a number of measures that were primarily concerned with reducing unemployment. In the declining counties, road construction and other public projects were put in motion in order to provide relief work; funds were transferred from the expanding counties to the contracting counties with the aid of tax equalization grants; and subsidies were paid to firms that would operate in the sparsely populated counties. Manpower programs were established to retrain workers and to assist their removal to the expanding counties.

Following the adoption of the Provincial Planning Act (1967) and the Regional Development Act (1970), the central government took a new approach to the problem of securing a "balanced expansion and balanced contraction."[49] Under this policy, the rate and direction of structural change in industry are dictated not by the demands of private-business efficiency, but by concern for overall social welfare. Current regional policy calls for avoiding excessively rapid regional contraction and expansion, curbing the industrial expansion of the three major cities, establishing growth centers outside of these cities, providing financial aid only to industries in the northern and central counties that will be viable in the long run, and decentralizing central-government administrative activities

[48] For a survey of recent developments in this area, see Office of International Affairs, Department of Housing and Urban Development, *Urban Growth Policies in Six European Countries*, Washington, D.C., Nov. 1, 1972, pp. 52–59.

[49] Recent developments with regard to regional development policy are analyzed in *The Swedish Economy, 1971–1975*, Section 3.10, "Regional Development," pp. 164–173.

as much as possible. The government is taking measures to improve conditions for economic growth in selected regions that have good export potentials. Also, emphasis is being placed on influencing the location of private industry to a greater extent than was done in the past. To avoid a drastic reduction in productivity, there will be only a gradual check on the industrial expansion of the Stockholm, Göteborg, and Malmö areas, and only a limited number of new growth centers as alternatives to major cities will be established in the future.

The efforts to provide guidance for structural change in industry and regional development in Sweden have raised the question of the consequences of regional policy for the nation as a whole. The 1971–1975 Economic Survey points out that these consequences are extremely difficult to evaluate, because they involve issues of costs and benefits, many of which cannot be satisfactorily measured or quantified. The Swedish planning authorities make extensive use of the cost-benefit approach to regional problems, which relates the costs of regional development to its benefits. While this approach is helpful, it has its limitations because the costs and benefits of regional development are frequently difficult to evaluate. A more serious problem is that little agreement exists on what should be the benefits or goals of regional development. The Swedish people have yet to decide to what extent they are prepared to sacrifice economic growth and increased personal incomes to a slower pace of industrialization that would give more attention to the "demand for security of employment and [individual] preferences for places of work and residence."[50]

The 1971–1975 Economic Survey explains that making further progress in the area of regional development is being delayed by the fact "that we do not know enough about what people desire in such matters." Until more is known about "the ultimate aims of our economic activities," the planning authorities will continue to assign high priority to improving the efficiency of the Swedish economy. There is no immediate prospect that Sweden will substantially curb economic growth or alter current economic trends in order to achieve a variety of noneconomic goals and to emphasize different aspects of social well-being.[51]

The Critics of Swedish National Economic Planning

National economic planning in Sweden has been criticized by a number of Sweden's leading economists on the ground that it leads to an overheated and inefficient economy. Erik Lundberg, Bertil Ohlin, Bent Hansen, and other critics argue that organized labor's aspirations concerning the appropriate employment level are too high.[52] With very little unemployment, and hence little slack in the economy, these critics believe that strong inflationary pressures develop, resources are poorly allocated, and economic inefficiencies arise. They assert that with a less ambitious full-employment aim, the market system could function more efficiently, and national income would be larger than with an excessively high employment level. Hence the unplanned economic system, if it operated this

[50] *Ibid.*, p. 49.

[51] This problem is analyzed in Ulrich Herz, "Towards the Saturation Society?", *Quarterly Review*, 1964:4, pp. 105–110.

[52] The views of these critics are presented in Assar Lindbeck, "Theories and Problems in Swedish Economic Policy in the Post-War Period," *American Economic Review*, Vol. LVIII, No. 3, Part 2, Supplement, June, 1968, pp. 1–87. See also Erik Lundberg, *Business Cycles and Economic Policy*, London: George Allen and Unwin, 1957; and Bertil Ohlin, *The Problem of Employment Stabilization*, New York: Columbia University Press, 1949.

way, would not be detrimental from a welfare point of view. The critics of Swedish national planning argue that the active manpower policy supported by the government and the trade unions leads to excessively high wages, which squeeze profits and reduce the ability of private firms to maintain a high investment level. Lundberg observes that "As a direct result of the squeezed profit margins and deteriorated profitability, the companies' capacity for the self-financing of investment expenditures . . . has been strongly curbed since 1959."[53] Without adequate profits, private firms are said to be unable to maintain a high enough ratio between investments and GNP to support the desired annual economic growth rate.

The critics of Swedish postwar economic policy and national planning call for fewer direct economic controls, and more reliance on general than selective economic policies. General economic policies leave it to the market system to be selective in the allocation of resources. The government would then not be required to try to develop criteria for the application of selective economic policies and controls. For example, the critics of Swedish postwar economic policies recommend that attempts by the government to ration credit among specific industries should be abandoned in favor of only general monetary policies that work their way out through the unrationed credit system. Lundberg advocates putting more weight on monetary than fiscal policy in any economic stabilization program designed to restore macroeconomic equilibrium. Intervention would be reduced to a minimum, and there would be no excessive concentration of power in the public sector. Bertil Ohlin proposes that round-table conferences between the government, the opposition political parties, industry, agriculture, and labor be held in order to seek agreement on stabilization policy and moderation in the struggle over shares of the national income. Bent Hansen opposes the solidarity principle of organized labor under which efforts are made to keep the wages of low-productivity workers in line with wages in higher-productivity industries.[54] In his opinion, the application of this principle leads to wage-cost inflation accompanied by wage drifting and the squeezing of profits, and to inadequate business saving and investment in the long run.

Thus a wide gulf concerning economic policy lies between the critics of Swedish national planning and its advocates in the trade unions and the Social Democratic party. The latter are proponents of an extremely high level of employment and an active labor mobility policy. As long as Sweden remains at or very near the top among the world's industrial countries with respect to per capita Gross National Product, the socialist government will continue to plan for a high level of employment and will accept whatever inefficiencies accompany a very tight, high-pressure economy. The advocates of democratic indicative national planning in Sweden admit that this planning results in some economic rigidities and inefficiencies. They argue, however, that Swedish national planning is flexible enough to prevent these rigidities and inefficiencies from undermining what is widely regarded as an internationally competitive and highly productive industrial economy.

The Swedish and Other Mixed Economies

If one compares the Swedish mixed economy with various nonsocialist mixed economies, certain prominent differences emerge. In the

---

[53] Jaak Järv and Erik Lundberg, "Profits and Investments in Swedish Industry," *Quarterly Review*, 1964: I, p. 11.

[54] Assar Lindbeck, *op. cit.*, p. 23.

private sector of the Swedish economy, it is generally agreed that capital and labor are equal partners in a well-developed, highly centralized collective-bargaining process, which is not duplicated in the United Kingdom and various nonsocialist, mixed economies. Closely associated with the Swedish industrial relations system is a manpower or labor-market mobility policy that is much more "active" than similar policies in many of the other industrialized countries. This is what one would expect in an economy dominated by trade unions and a socialist political party. Also in Sweden, as in Norway, the welfare system is more extensive and more experimental than in other Western countries. In Sweden and the other Scandinavian countries the view is widely accepted that the social welfare system really pays for itself in economic terms, because it makes for happier, healthier, and more efficient workers in the long run. This position is not, however, widely held in other Western countries, where much of the population regards social-welfare expenditures as largely a necessary evil. Also, it is not surprising that national economic and social planning should constitute such a major feature of the Swedish mixed economy, since the socialist parties have always been strong advocates of this planning. The same enthusiasm for planning is not found in many of the nonsocialist mixed economies.

A major difference between the Swedish mixed economy and other mixed economies relates to the different potentials for further economic and social change in these economies. The Swedish economy could very well be on the verge of turning in directions that are not likely to be followed closely in other Western mixed economies, at least for some considerable time to come. The first new direction relates to the expansion of industrial democracy. This could be achieved by enlarging the role of organized labor in the internal affairs of Swedish private business enterprises far beyond the role played today by organized labor in the United States, the United Kingdom, and other Western European countries.

Another direction in which the Swedish economy may move ahead of other mixed economies relates to the role of government in private business affairs. If the Swedish Social Democratic government decides to purchase company shares with the large funds of the national pension system, it could come to have a major influence on decision making in the private-business sector. Considerable control of the nation's business system could be achieved in this manner without resort to the outright nationalization of industry. As of now, however, it is not possible to predict with any accuracy in what direction the Swedish Social Democratic party may move in this area. The conservative elements in the Swedish labor movement argue that the majority of the voters do not now wish to push the Swedish economy further along the socialist path. In contrast, the left wing of the labor movement asserts that this movement has lost much of its momentum, and that in order to arrest the recent decline in its voter support there should be a greater emphasis on changing "the organisation of our economy in a socialist direction."[55] This argument can be settled only by the course of events over the coming decades. No matter how the disagreement is eliminated, it is probably safe to say that the Swedish and Norwegian mixed economies will in many important ways continue to be significantly different from the

---

[55] The Swedish Social Democratic Labor Party and the Swedish Trade Union Federation, *The Postwar Programme of Swedish Labour*, Stockholm, 1944, p. 31. Much of the discussion by Swedish economists of this problem and its ideological issue is not very penetrating, and it usually avoids the discussion of economic and political power and its distribution in the Swedish economy. See, for example, the analysis of "Liberalism or Socialism" in Assar Lindbeck, *op. cit.*, pp. 78–79.

American and other Western nonsocialist industrial economies.

The nonsocialist Center, Conservative, and Liberal party coalition government that came to power on Sept. 19, 1976 will probably not make any major changes in Sweden's domestic or international economic policies. This is what occurred in Norway when a nonsocialist coalition government was briefly in power from 1968 to 1971. The new nonsocialist coalition government in Sweden will not move the nation further along the path towards a socialist system. While it is not likely to alter Sweden's welfare state and planned economy in any major way, the new coalition government will change the nation's goals somewhat by placing more emphasis on curbing the expansion of the public sector, by limiting the expansion of the welfare state, and by emphasizing individual freedom in the modern society. Even with a political change it would be quite surprising if Sweden did not continue to be the challenging social and economic laboratory that it has been during the past half century.

Selected Bibliography

DAHMÉN, ERIK. "The Present Economic Situation and the Future Prospects." *Quarterly Review*, Skandinaviska Enskilda Banken, 1, 1975, 21–35.

FINANSDEPARTEMENTET. *Svensk Ekonomi Fram Till 1977 (The Swedish Economy to 1977)*. Statens Offentliga Utredningar, 1973: 21, Stockholm, 1973.

GALENSON, WALTER. *Trade Union Democracy in Western Europe*. University of California Press, Berkeley, 1961.

HERLITZ, NILS. *Sweden, A Modern Democracy on Ancient Foundations*. University of Minnesota Press, Minneapolis, 1939.

JACOBSSON, LARS, and ASSAR LINDBECK. "Labor Market Condition, Wages and Inflation—Swedish Experiences, 1955-67." *Swedish Journal of Economics*, LXXI (June 1969), 64–95.

JOHNSTON, T. L. *Collective Bargaining in Sweden*. Harvard University Press, Cambridge, 1962.

JOINT ECONOMIC COMMITTEE. *Guaranteed Minimum Income Programs Used by Governments of Selected Countries*. Paper No. 11, Washington, D.C.

JUNGENFELT, KARL. "The Methodology of Swedish Long-Term Planning." *Quarterly Review*, 4, 1964, 111–115.

LINDBECK, ASSAR. "Theories and Problems in Swedish Economic Policy in the Post-War Period." *American Economic Review*, LVIII, No. 3, Part 2 (June 1968), 1–87.

LINDBECK, ASSAR. *Swedish Economic Policy*. University of California Press, Berkeley, 1973.

LINDÉN, HANS, and ERIK SWEDBORG. *Policy for Swedish Agriculture in the 1970's*. Falköping, 1969.

LUNDBERG, ERIK. *Business Cycles and Economic Policy*. George Allen and Unwin, London, 1957.

MEIDNER, RUDOLF. "Active Manpower Policy and the Inflation Unemployment Dilemma." *Swedish Journal of Economics*, LXXI (Sept. 1969), 163–183.

OHLIN, BERTIL. *The Problem of Employment Stabilization*. Columbia University Press, New York, 1949.

OHLSSON, INGVAR. "The Swedish National Budget." *Quarterly Review*, 38 (Oct. 1957), 100–107.

ORGANISATION FOR ECONOMIC CO-OPERATION AND DEVELOPMENT. *OECD Agricultural Policy Reports, Agricultural Policy in Sweden*. Paris, 1974.

ORGANISATION FOR ECONOMIC CO-OPERATION AND DEVELOPMENT. *OECD Economic Surveys, Sweden*. Paris, 1969 to 1975.

PETERSON, RICHARD B. "The Swedish Experience with Industrial Democracy." *British Journal of Industrial Relations*, VI (July 1968), 185–203.

ROSS, A. M., and PAUL T. HARTMAN. *Changing Patterns of Industrial Conflict*. John Wiley and Sons, New York, 1960.

RYDÉN, BENGT. "Concentration and Structural Adjustment in Swedish Industry during the Post-War Period." *Quarterly Review*, 2, 1967, 51–58.

SOCIAL DEMOCRATIC LABOR PARTY AND SWEDISH TRADE UNION FEDERATION. *The Post-War Programme of Swedish Labour, Summary in 27 Points and Comments*. Stockholm, July 1944.

SVENNILSON, INGVAR. "Swedish Long-Term Planning—The Fifth Round." *Quarterly Review*, 2, 1966, 37–43.

SVENNILSON, INGVAR, and RUNE BECKMAN. "Long-Term Planning in Sweden." *Quarterly Review*, 43, 1962.

SVERIGES LANTBRUKSFÖRBUND. *Agricultural Cooperation in Sweden*. Stockholm, 1969.

SWEDISH CONFEDERATION OF TRADE UNIONS. *Economic Expansion and Structural Change*. George Allen and Unwin, London, 1963.

SWEDISH MINISTRY OF FINANCE. *The Swedish Economy 1971–1975 and the General Outlook up to 1990*. SOU 1970:71, Stockholm, 1971.

The Economist. "Sweden: A Business Survey." 249, No. 6795 (Nov. 17, 1973), 77–82.

WALLANDER, JAN. "Experiences of Long-Term Planning in Sweden." *Quarterly Review*, 37, No. 2 (April 1956), 50–58.

Chapter 11
The British Socialist Economy

The development of British socialism since 1945 presents a marked contrast to the development of Norwegian and Swedish socialism. Whereas the Norwegian and Swedish socialists have maintained political control in their respective countries almost without interruption since 1945, the situation has been quite different in the United Kingdom, where the control of the government has moved back and forth between the Labour and Conservative parties. The Labour party was in office from 1945 to 1951 and again from 1964 to 1970. In 1974, the Labourites were returned to office, but only as a weak minority government. In the thirty years since the close of the Second World War in which they have had political control, the Norwegian and Swedish socialists have had the opportunity to lay the foundations of a socialist society. In the twelve years that the British Labour party has been in office, it has had little chance to make a significant beginning in the construction of a socialist society, in part because of extraordinary postwar economic problems.

No basic differences in socialist theory or proposals for action distinguish British socialism from Scandinavian. In all its essentials, British Fabian socialism duplicates the socialism of the Danish, Norwegian, and Swedish socialist parties. The failures of the British Labour Party stem from its inability to cope successfully with the United Kingdom's major postwar economic problems. With the British Conservative party no more successful in meeting these problems, the electorate has merely shifted governments periodically without finding one that can secure full employment and high and sustained economic growth with a favorable balance of international payments. The situation has been quite different in Norway and Sweden, where high employment and sustained economic growth have been achieved without recurring financial crises in their external economies.

British Socialism, 1945–1964

The British socialism espoused by the first majority Labour government, which came into office in August 1945, was very different from the socialism of the Fabian Society organized in 1884. The Fabian socialists of the late nineteenth century looked forward to the establishment of "full socialism" by parliamentary means.[1] They were not Marxian socialists, for they did not believe in the revolutionary overthrow of capitalism, and they did not regard socialism as a transitional stage between capitalism and communism. Like the Marxian socialists, the Fabians advocated the adoption of a planned economy, the nationalization of all land and industry, the elimination of all unearned income, the provision of a national minimum income for all members of society, and the use of the economy's surplus for socially useful purposes. The Fabian goal of full socialism was to be achieved only gradually by first establishing municipal socialism and then moving on to the national scene.

Between 1884 and 1945, the Labour party's socialism underwent some major changes. Less was heard of the eventual goal of full socialism. More concern was expressed for taking over the national government and making the first steps towards a socialist society. The Labour party leaders, realizing that the British public was not yet ready to accept full socialism, offered a program of "partial socialism." In the 1945 Labour party election manifesto, *Let Us Face the Future*, no mention was made of nationalizing either rural or urban land; the proposed nationalization of industry was limited to key industries, such as steel, coal, transportation, communications, gas, and electricity; and unearned income, although it was to be heavily taxed, was not to be eliminated. During 1945–1951, the Labour government gave particular attention to improving housing, education, health, and various social services. A major gap in the social security system was removed by establishing the National Health Service in 1948. Attention was also paid to town and country planning, regional development, and planning for agriculture. Consumer welfare was enlarged through rationing of essential goods and services, price and rent controls, improved quality controls, and extended consumer education. In these ways, the structure of the welfare state was enlarged and improved.

Although much was done to advance the welfare state and to lay the foundations of a socialist society, after 1945 the main concern of the Labour government was with moving from a wartime to a peacetime economy and with making the economy competitive in the world market. In the period 1945 to 1951, the Labour government retained most of the wartime economic controls and only gradually restored the working of the free price mechanism.[2] While the private market system was relied upon to a great extent to meet domestic and foreign consumers' preferences, the new planning system provided considerable national economic guidance.[3] The British

---

[1] The essentials of Fabian socialism are discussed in Margaret Cole, *The Story of Fabian Socialism*, London: Heinemann Educational Books, 1961; George B. Shaw and others, *The Fabian Essays in Socialism*, Boston: Ball Publishing Co., 1908; and R. H. S. Crossman, *New Fabian Essays*, London: Turnstile Press, 1952. For a further discussion of Fabian socialism see Ch. 8, pp. 244–245.

[2] For a review and analysis of developments in the British economy from 1945 to 1951, see A. A. Rogow, *The Labour Government and British Industry, 1945–1951*, Oxford: Basil Blackwell, 1955; G. D. N. Worswick and P. H. Ady (eds.), *The British Economy, 1945–1950*, Oxford: Clarendon Press, 1952; Robert Brady, *Crisis in Britain*, Berkeley: University of California Press, 1950; and Francis Walker, *Socialist Britain*, New York: Viking Press, 1945.

[3] British national economic planning is analyzed in James E. Meade, *Planning and the Price Mechanism*, London: George Allen and Unwin, 1948; Ben W.

planning program, which in its essentials was similar to the programs adopted in France, the Netherlands, Norway, and Sweden, was not as vigorously executed nor as successful in its operation as were the planning programs in these other countries. Compared with them, the British economy's program was sluggish. Its economic growth rate over 1945–1951 was close to 3 percent, whereas in the other Western European planned economies this rate varied between 4 and 9 percent. The British annual plans to curb private consumption and expand gross domestic investment were not successful. While it was planned to reduce private consumption to approximately 65 percent of gross domestic product, this consumption remained at about 70 percent. The plan to increase gross domestic investment to approximately 18 percent of GNP fell short of its goal, with this investment reaching only 14 percent on the average in 1949–1951.

In spite of the limited success with its national planning, the Labour government was able to make considerable progress in curbing imports and expanding exports. By late 1949, the United Kingdom achieved an overall balance in its external economy, but it was not able to place the pound on a firm foundation. Speculative runs against the pound and the demand for United States dollars in place of the pound reduced the United Kingdom's already inadequate gold and foreign exchange reserve to a dangerously low level. The devaluation of the pound in September 1949 from $4.03 to $2.80 was followed by another external financial crisis in 1951 when the Labour government was replaced by a Conservative government.

Lewis, *British Planning and Nationalization*, New York: Twentieth Century Fund, 1952; Arthur W. Lewis, *The Principles of Economic Planning*, London: Dennis Dobson, 1949; and Gilbert Walker, *Economic Planning by Programme and Control in Great Britain*, London: William Heinemann, 1957.

Criticism of Labour's Postwar National Planning

The national economic planning of the postwar Labour government aroused a great deal of criticism. Critics such as Hugh Gaitskell and Harold Wilson sought to improve Labour party planning, while other critics such as Roy Harrod and John Jewkes would have preferred to abandon socialist national planning and to replace it with a regulated private enterprise system. The record of the early postwar years makes it clear that the Labour government was not well prepared to execute a national plan under peacetime circumstances. Planning machinery that worked well under the pressures of war before 1945 did not function well after the war.

Labour government planning in 1945–1951 remained somewhat primitive and poorly organized. Annual plans were never supplemented with well-developed long-range plans as was done in Norway, Sweden, and other planned economies. No mathematical techniques, such as input-output analysis or linear programming, were used to incorporate a certain amount of sophistication into the national plans. The number of government experts engaged in planning was very small, and the supply of information was far from adequate. Although improvements were made in the nation's planning machinery after 1947, they were never carried far enough. Instead of establishing a separate ministry of planning on a permanent basis, the government subordinated planning to the work of the Treasury, which was overburdened with fiscal matters.

A more serious criticism of Labour government planning was that it was too ambitious, and that it was endeavoring to maintain levels of consumption and investment that the British economy was not capable of supporting without foreign aid. By 1948, the Labour government became more aware of the strains that it was placing on the economy, and it began to pare down its investment program. The housing program was cut; and the long-term reconstruction of basic industries was delayed to enable industry to make short-term investments that would quickly increase production for domestic and export markets. The government could have reduced the pressures on the economy further by reducing the ratio of private consumption to GNP as was done in Norway, Sweden, and other planned countries, but it was unwilling to increase the austerity already imposed on the general population.

Critics from the right attacked the Labour government's national planning program on the grounds that it was less efficient than programs carried out by private enterprise, and that it did not allocate resources in accordance with consumer preferences as much as was desirable. They proposed that the national planning program be abandoned in favor of an economic program that would make more use of the free price mechanism. Roy Harrod severely criticized the Labour government's planning program and argued that its difficulties arose primarily from an attempt "to do too much."[4] Harrod's remedy for the adverse economic developments of the early postwar years was to limit the capital investment program severely by cutting down expenditures on housing, school buildings, and other public facilities. Only essential consumer goods were to be rationed, rent controls were to be removed, and wherever possible other controls were to be eliminated. Harrod held that if enough slack in the economy could be created, inflationary pressures would disappear. In his opinion, the elimination of industrial bottlenecks, improved worker productivity, and greater business efficiency would mean not less but more GNP than if the Labour government's planning program with its many controls were to be maintained.

In spite of its failure to place the economy on a firm foundation in the early postwar years, the Labour party, after its defeat in the 1951 election, continued to believe in the efficacy of a planned economy. In place of abandoning its national planning program as recommended by its critics, the Labour party, when it was out of office from 1951 to 1964, sought to strengthen the national planning that it would reintroduce when it regained control of the Parliament. This was to be done by establishing a ministry of economic planning that would be independent of the Treasury, and a national economic council that would bring business, labor, and the government together in the planning activity. After the loss of the 1959 election the Labour party abandoned its efforts to expand the nationalization of industry beyond what had already had been nationalized. Nationalization was then no longer a main issue in Labour's program for the operation of the mixed economy. By 1964, when the Labour party resumed its control of the government, it was much more concerned with making the mixed economy function well than with enlarging the boundaries of the socialist society. The late 1950s and the early 1960s were relatively prosperous years in which the Labour party could no longer appeal for votes on the ground of eliminating mass unemployment, extreme poverty, substandard housing, and inadequate social services. It was necessary for the party to explain to the voters how it would manage the economy in the new era of mass consumption and technological change.

The British Socialist Economy, 1964–1970

The primary objective of the new 1964 Labour government's economic program was

[4] Roy Harrod, *Are These Hardships Necessary?*, London: Rupert Hart-Davis, 1947, p. 123.

to modernize the British economy so that it could take advantage of the scientific revolution of the twentieth century and put it to work with the aim of achieving a sustained economic growth rate of from 4 to 5 percent a year. The main indictment by the Labour party of the prior thirteen years of Conservative government was that the Conservatives had slowed up Britain's rate of industrial expansion. The Labour party's 1964 election manifesto pointed out that if the United Kingdom had had a 5 percent annual economic growth rate during the years 1951–1963 when the Conservative Party was in office, instead of the actual growth rate of about 2 percent, the United Kingdom's national income in 1963 would have been one-third or $22 billion (in constant 1963 dollars) larger than it actually was in 1963. The main thrust of the Labour government's economic program was to achieve a high economic growth rate by creating a "dynamic, just and go-ahead Britain." The 1964 election manifesto of the Labour party, *The New Britain*, declared that Britain could secure this goal "provided that it resolutely wills three things: the mobilization of its resources within a national plan; the maintenance of a wise balance between community and individual expenditure; and the education of all its citizens in the responsibilities of this scientific age, not merely a small section of them."[5]

The 1964 government proposed to secure the goal of a revitalized, highly productive Britain by means of "purposive planning." When reorganizing his cabinet in late 1964, the Labour prime minister, Harold Wilson, created two new ministries: namely, the Ministry of Economic Affairs with Regional Planning Boards, which had "the duty of formulating, with both sides of industry, a national plan"; and the Ministry of Technology, whose objective was "to guide and stimulate a major national effort to bring advanced technology and new processes into industry." Wilson's national planning, like French national planning, was to use modern mathematical planning techniques, such as input-output analysis and electronic computer calculations. Outstanding economists, such as Thomas Balogh of Oxford University and Nicholas Kaldor of Cambridge University, who in 1963 had advised the Labour party on the structure of the proposed new Ministry of Economic Affairs, were called in to advise the government on economic problems.

Economic planning was to be carried out on the basis of both annual and four-year national economic plans. These plans were to relate to three levels of economic activity—national, regional, and industrial. Each industry, working through management and worker representatives, was to have its own plan for investment, production, employment, and exports that would fit into the general national plan. Likewise, the plans for agriculture and the various regions of the country, such as Northern Ireland, Scotland, Wales, and northern England, were to be meshed with the overall national plan. Wilson's version of national planning would involve a "deliberate and massive effort to modernize the economy; to change its structure and to develop with all possible speed the advanced technology and the new science-based industries with which our future lies."[6] New ways of injecting modern technology into British industries included having the government establish new industries, either by public enterprise or in partnership with private industry. The government would stimulate industrial research by using "research and development contracts" for civilian projects. It would also introduce more extensive labor training and retraining schemes and would increase worker

[5] The Labour Party, *The New Britain*, London, 1964, p. 1.

[6] *Ibid.*, p. 3.

mobility by providing for the full transferability of workers' private pension rights. A national plan for all transport services was to be developed to eliminate the lack of coordination in this area and to aid both regional and community development.

On the financial side, the tax system was to be altered to encourage the new science-based industries and the export industries to increase their investment and to expand their production. The Monopolies Commission was to be strengthened by giving it the power to control industrial mergers and to review price increases. Most importantly, an effort was to be made by the Labour government to work out a "fair national incomes policy" that would relate the growth of all personal incomes to the annual growth of production. Beyond stating that it planned to consult with union and employer organizations about its national incomes policy, the Labour government said little specifically about how it would develop a satisfactory national incomes policy. In order to make its incomes policy more acceptable to the low-income groups, the Labour government planned to overhaul the tax system by taxing capital gains, by closing loopholes in the tax system, and by transferring a larger part of the burden of public expenditures from the local governments to the central government.

In 1964, Prime Minister Harold Wilson, the chief architect of the Labour government's program for national renewal, was more concerned with the need for economic growth than with the possibility of achieving a more egalitarian socialist society. He explained in *The New Britain* that the first task was to achieve "the sustained expansion we need"; and it was only after this goal was reached that "We must ensure that a sufficient part of the new wealth created goes to meet urgent and now neglected human needs." The United Kingdom first had to secure a lasting favorable balance in its external economy and a high and sustained rate of economic growth before it could adopt a more liberal national pension scheme, achieve an annual housing goal of 400,000 new houses, accelerate slum clearance, and embark on an ambitious hospital building program. Being a professionally trained economist, Wilson did not have a utopian approach to the problem of bringing into being the New Britain to which his party aspired. As a representative of the new managerial class among British socialists, Wilson was not prepared to sacrifice securing a modern British economy by assigning a higher priority to removing social inequalities than to removing economic inefficiencies throughout the nation.

The Labour government's proposals for national planning, which were announced in 1965, were soon set aside to deal with the more immediate and pressing problems of low economic growth, inflation, and deficits in the nation's external account.[7] The new Labour government soon became preoccupied with the problem of maintaining the pound sterling as a major international medium of exchange. For the next six years, the Labour government devoted most of its efforts to trying to make the British economy viable on a sustained basis. Before the government could turn to the reconstruction of the British society along socialist lines, it was necessary to place the nation's economy on a sound, self-sustaining basis.

The course of economic events during the Labour government's term of office from October 1964 to June 1970 can be divided into

[7] An extensive account of economic developments and related economic policies for the years 1964–1970 is presented in Richard E. Caves and Associates, *Britain's Economic Prospects*, Washington D.C.: The Brookings Institution, 1968; and the companion volume by Sir Alec Cairncross (ed.) *Britain's Economic Prospects Reconsidered*, Albany: State University of New York Press, 1970.

three periods.[8] In the first period, from October 1964 to July 1966, the Labour government relied upon the voluntary cooperation of business and labor in the effort to curb wage and price inflation and to enlarge exports. In the second period, from July 1966 to July 1967, the Labour government introduced mandatory wage and price controls along with very restrictive fiscal and monetary measures. The third period ran from August 1967 to June 1970, when the Labour government was replaced by the Conservatives. In this final period, mandatory wage and price controls were abandoned in favor of voluntary controls. After the devaluation of the pound in late 1967, a surplus was secured in the balance of payments but at the cost of low economic growth and high unemployment.

Short-Term Demand and Supply Management

In the first period, October 1964 to July 1966, the Labour government proclaimed as its objective a 3 percent annual increase in gross domestic product, a curbing of wage and price inflation so as to make the United Kingdom more competitive in international markets, and a surplus in the current balance of international payments large enough to build up the nation's international reserves and to enable the United Kingdom to be a net exporter of capital. In the period October 1964 to July 1966, short-run demand-and-supply management was concentrated on fiscal, monetary, foreign exchange, manpower, and incomes policies. The Labour government was forced to turn to the same deflationary, stop-go policy that had been reluctantly used by the Conservative government in the 1950s and early 1960s.[9]

The fiscal budgets for 1965 and 1966 introduced a number of very restrictive measures. Personal and corporate income taxes, excise taxes, the capital gains tax, and social security contributions were increased. At the same time, public expenditures, including military expenditures to maintain armed services abroad, were drastically reduced. A similarly restrictive monetary policy was adopted in these years. The Bank of England's discount rate was raised to 7 percent, and a ceiling was placed upon the total amount of credit that could be extended by the banks and other financial institutions. Credit was further curbed by requiring the London clearing banks to deposit 1 percent of their total deposits in special accounts in the Bank of England. Also, the banks were asked by the government to be more selective in their lending policies so that credit would be directed towards the export and export-supporting industries. Consumer expenditures were reduced by requiring larger down payments on automobiles and household equipment.

Stringent control measures were also applied to foreign trade and foreign exchange. A 15 percent surcharge was imposed on one-third of the nation's imports in November 1964. Stricter foreign exchange controls reduced foreign travel allowances, prohibited United Kingdom residents from selling or purchasing foreign securities and property abroad, required exporters to repatriate their export receipts promptly, curbed private investment outside the Sterling Area, and limited what foreigners could borrow in the Sterling Area. Exports were stimulated by giving

---

[8] For a running account of economic developments in the United Kingdom during these years, see OECD, *OECD Economic Surveys, United Kingdom*, 1965–1971.

[9] This stop-go policy for the period 1950–1966 is analyzed in Richard A. and Peggy B. Musgrave, "Fiscal Policy," *Britain's Economic Prospects*, pp. 42–44.

exporters tax rebates, by providing tax concessions to the export and export-supporting industries, and by making bank credit readily available to these industries.

A third feature of the Labour government's short-run demand-and-supply management related to manpower policy. Steps were taken to expedite the movement of workers from agriculture, mining, inland transportation, and the textile and clothing industries to the machinery and electrical-product industries, other manufacturing, public administration, and other essential services. The Selective Employment Tax, which was introduced early in 1966, was a payroll tax imposed on all employers. The tax discriminated against construction, nonexport manufacturing, and nonessential services, for it was refunded to export and export-supporting industries. Government training centers wer expanded, and training and retraining programs were adjusted to the needs for skilled labor in the expanding industries.

A fourth feature of the Labour government's short-run demand-and-supply management program was its incomes policy.[10] Shortly after coming to power in October 1964, the new Labour government turned to the formulation of a wage-price policy which was to supplement the fiscal, monetary, and other economic policies for the control of inflation.

In a Joint Statement of Intent adopted in December 1964, the trade unions and employers' associations formally accepted the government's basic view that the rise in money incomes should be kept in line with the improvement in productivity. They also pledged themselves to cooperate with the government in setting up machinery to keep the movement of prices and incomes under review. Under this machinery, the government could require an advance notice of thirty days before a wage settlement or price change could become effective. Within this period, the government could refer the proposed settlement or change to the National Board for Prices and Incomes, whose recommendations were not mandatory. The compulsory "early warning system" was thus accompanied by a voluntary acceptance of the incomes policy.

When applying its incomes policy in 1965 and 1966, the government adopted a wage guideline which would permit wage rates on the average to rise 3.5 percent a year.[11] Prices were to be increased only when increases in costs (as in the case of higher prices for imports) could not be absorbed, and were to be reduced where unit costs were falling. Incomes of self-employed persons were to be determined by the same principles that were applied to wages and salaries. Incomes of farmers and landlords were already limited by farm-price programs and rent controls. Company profits were to be controlled through the regulation of prices with attention being given to the rate of return on net investment.

The Failure of Short-Run Demand and Supply Management

The Labour Government's short-run demand-and-supply management fell far short of its

---

[10] For an account of the development of the British incomes policy see David C. Smith, "Attempts to Develop an Effective Incomes Policy in the United Kingdom," *Incomes Policies*, Oct. 1966, pp. 95–127; Lloyd Ulman and Robert J. Flanagan, "The United Kingdom," *Wage Restraint*, 1971, pp. 11–47, and Eric Schiff, "United Kingdom," *Incomes Policies Abroad*, 1971, pp. 3–14. See also Aubrey Jones, "Prices and Incomes Policy," *Economic Journal*, Vol. LXXVIII, Dec. 1968, pp. 799–806; J. F. Pickering, "The Prices and Incomes Board and Private Sector Prices: A Survey," *Economic Journal*, Vol. 81, June 1971, pp. 225–41; and R. J. Liddle and W. E. J. McCarthy, "The Impact of the Prices and Incomes Board on the Reform of Collective Bargaining," *British Journal of Industrial Relations*, Vol. X, Nov. 1972, pp. 412–435.

[11] The details of the Labour government's incomes policy are given in *Machinery of Prices and Incomes Policy* (Cmnd. 2577, Feb. 1965) and *Prices and Incomes Standstill: Period of Severe Restraint* (Cmnd. 3150, Nov. 1966), London: H.M.S.O.

goals in the period from October 1964 to July 1966. Total national output and industrial production were well below their potentials. Consumer prices and wage rates continued to increase excessively, with adverse consequences for the nation's external sector. While large deficits in the current balance of international payments were avoided, exports did not increase enough to provide a surplus on current account that could be used to pay off the debts incurred in the effort to avoid the devaluation of the pound. The government's incomes policy did not prove to be effective in keeping wage-rate increases close to the guideline of 3.5 percent a year. The statistics in Table 11-1 show that collective bargaining and wage drifting increased average hourly earnings in manufacturing 8.2 percent in 1965 and 7.7 percent in 1966. These annual wage-rate increases were more than double the annual improvement in output per man-hour in manufacturing, which was approximately 3.5 percent per annum. With unit wage costs rising faster in the United Kingdom than in West Germany, France, Japan, the United States, and other competing nations, the United Kingdom was unable to improve its international competitive position.

In July 1966, the voluntary incomes policy was abandoned, and mandatory price and wage controls were established under the Prices and Incomes Act. Wage rates and prices were frozen from July 1966 to August 1967, with six additional months of severe restraint. During this period of one year, wage rates were increased only in hardship cases, and where the wage increase was offset by an improvement in productivity. Prices could be raised only when wage increases could not be absorbed or the cost of imports rose. During the year of price and wage standstill and severe restraint, price and wage increases were very moderate, with consumer prices increasing 2.9 percent and hourly wage rates in industry 2.8 percent. When the period of severe restraint was abandoned after August 1967, there was a return to the pre-1966 incomes policy. This meant the reestablishment of the wage guideline of 3.5 percent, the "advance warning" system, and the delay of price and wage increases during their review by the National Board for Prices and Incomes. These voluntary controls proved to be as ineffective in curbing wage and price inflation as they had been before the price and wage standstill of July 1966. As the statistics in Table 11-1 indicate, inflationary pressures reached new high levels in the years 1968-1970, with the average annual increase in consumer prices being more than 5 percent, and the increase in hourly earnings in manufacturing being close to 8 percent.[12]

In 1967, according to Table 11-2, the United Kingdom again recorded a large deficit in its current balance of international payments as the result of its failure to keep its export prices in line with those of West Germany, Japan, and the United States, and because of the general decline in the growth of world trade. The volume of merchandise exports, which had been projected to increase in 1966 and 1967 at the annual rate of 5.5 percent, increased only 3.5 percent. Instead of increasing after 1965, the United Kingdom's gold and foreign exchange reserves fell to the very inadequate level of $2.4 billion. These low international reserves necessitated large borrowings from foreign central banks with the hope of preserving the exchange value of the pound. The Labour government's monetary measures failed to curb bank loans as much as planned, with the result that the

---

[12] The OECD concludes that "the effectiveness of prices and incomes policies during the sixties is not readily ascertained.... Prices and incomes policies may thus have had some mild restraining effect on prices in the medium term," OECD, *Inflation, The Present Problem,* Paris, Dec. 1970, p. 87. See also F. W. Paish, *How the Economy Works,* Ch. 8, "Rise and Fall of Incomes Policy," London: Macmillan, 1970, pp. 179-231.

Table 11-1
Selected United Kingdom Economic Indicators, 1963–1970

	Percent change over the previous year				
	Gross domestic product	Consumer price index	Hourly earnings in manufacturing	Output per man-hour in manufacturing	Unemployment rate
1963	3.3	1.8	3.8	5.4	2.5
1964	5.9	3.3	6.9	6.3	1.7
1965	2.7	5.0	8.2	3.7	1.5
1966	1.0	3.8	7.7	3.1	1.5
1967	1.6	2.5	4.1	3.5	2.4
1968	3.9	4.5	7.8	6.1	2.4
1969	2.1	5.3	7.7	2.0	2.5
1970	1.9	5.4	13.2	2.7	2.5
Annual average 1965–1970	2.2	4.4	8.1	3.5	2.1

Sources: *National Institute Economic Review; International Financial Statistics,* and *OECD Economic Surveys, United Kingdom.*

money supply annually increased twice as fast (4.2 percent) as the gross domestic product (2.1 percent) in the years 1966–1970. In these years, the commercial banks frequently exceeded the total credit ceiling annually posted by the government, and very restrictive measures had to be taken in 1968 and 1969 to curb bank lending.

By late 1967, the Labour government concluded that the pound was overvalued in relation to other currencies; consequently, on November 18, 1967, the pound was devalued 14.3 percent, from $2.80 to $2.40. Devaluation was accompanied by a further tightening of monetary and fiscal policies. The Bank of England's discount rate was increased from 6.5 to 8 percent; no increase was permitted in the ceiling on bank credit; taxes were increased to enlarge the fiscal budget surplus; public expenditures were cut further; and the government's power to defer price and wages increases for a maximum of twelve months was extended to December 1969.

A very large deficit in the current balance of international payments in 1968 led the Labour government to take more restrictive measures to curb the growth of domestic demand and imports. In November 1968, an import deposit scheme was adopted to curb imports. Under this arrangement, importers had to deposit up to 50 percent of the cost of planned imports in noninterest bearing accounts before the imports would be permitted. The money supply, which had increased 4 percent in 1968, increased only 0.2 percent in 1969, and the bank rate was raised to the new crisis level of 8 percent. In 1969, the government adopted the concept of "domestic credit expansion" (DCE) which linked bank lending, the fiscal budget surplus, and the current balance of international payments.[13] According to this concept, when this balance

[13] OECD, *OECD Economic Surveys, United Kingdom,* Dec. 1969, pp. 27-28. The DCE concept is explained in OECD, *OECD Economic Outlook,* No. 5, July 1969, p. 81.

Table 11–2
Selected United Kingdom Financial and External Economic Indicators, 1963–1970

	Percent change over the previous year				Current balance of payments (mil. £)	Gold and foreign exchange reserves (bil. U.S.$)
	Export prices	Exports in volume	Imports in volume	Money supply		
1963	3.0	5.3	3.2	0.3	124	2.7
1964	1.9	3.0	11.0	4.9	−376	2.3
1965	3.0	5.8	0.0	3.8	−52	3.0
1966	3.8	3.6	2.7	−0.1	83	3.1
1967	1.0	3.5	−6.1	7.6	−298	2.7
1968	7.3	2.6	27.1	4.0	−288	2.4
1969	3.4	15.0	0.7	0.2	440	2.5
1970	7.4	3.6	5.8	9.4	579	2.8
Annual average 1965–1970	3.9	5.3	5.6	3.8	—	—

Sources: *National Institute Economic Review; International Financial Statistics; OECD Country Surveys, United Kingdom;* and *United Nations, Statistical Yearbook.*

turns out worse than expected, bank credit is reduced; when this balance is better than expected, bank credit may be allowed to increase more rapidly. Reduced borrowing by the government from the banks in 1969 permitted more bank lending to the private sector within the overall limits imposed by the government's ceiling on total bank credit.

By 1969, the favorable consequences of the devaluation of the pound had time to make themselves felt. Combined with an improvement in world trade, these consequences enabled the United Kingdom to achieve a large surplus of £444 million in its external account in 1969. By that year, however, the government's incomes policy was no longer effective, and the prospect was for rapid increases in prices and wages which would in time eliminate the surplus on external account. In June 1970, the Labour government was replaced by a Conservative one. In that year, the consumer price index reached its highest level since 1963, and hourly earnings in manufacturing increased at the explosive rate of 13.2 percent. While the Labour government had succeeded after five difficult years in achieving a turnabout in the nation's external sector, it did not appear in 1970 that this turnabout would be sustained for long.

Medium-Term Demand and Supply Management

When the Labour government came to power in October 1964, it had expected to cope successfully with the export problem and to achieve a surplus in the current balance of international payments within a relatively short period of time. It therefore laid plans for the medium-term and long-term development of the British economy, which involved some fundamental changes in the structure and functioning of this economy. What was necessary, in the opinion of the Labour government, was "a deliberate and massive effort to modernize the economy; to change its structure and to develop with all possible speed the advanced technology and the new-science based industries with which our future lies."[14] What was needed for these purposes was a national plan and a plan organization. The plan organization that the Labour government established after October 1964 called for a considerable modification of the governmental system.

[14] *The New Britain*, p. 8. A discussion of the plan and its organization is provided in John and Anne-Marie Hackett, *The British Economy, Problems and Prospects*, London: George Allen and Unwin, 1967, pp. 127–158.

Figure 11-1 presents the basics of the machinery for national planning as it was developed in its final form by early 1966. Two new ministries, the Ministry of Technology and the Department of Economic Affairs (DEA), were added to the Ministry of Labour, the Board of Trade, and the Treasury, which were the main old-line ministries concerned with economic problems and policies. As already explained, the Ministry of Technology was responsible for stimulating technological advance and its application to private industry. The main responsibility for national planning was assigned to the DEA, which worked closely with the National Economic Development Council (NEDC). To the latter organization, the Trades Union Congress (TUC) and the Confederation of British Industry

Figure 11-1
The British Planning Organization, 1964–1970

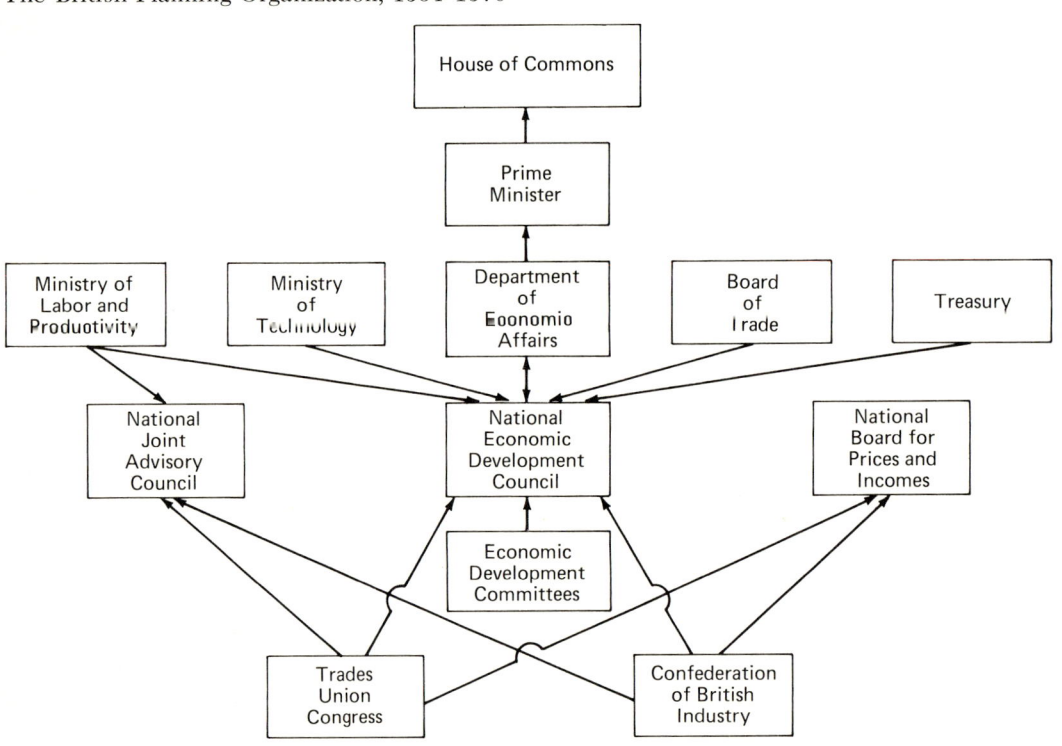

(CBI) each sent six representatives. The NEDC, with representatives from the five main economic ministries, from business, and from labor, and with the Minister of the DEA as its chairperson, had been originally set up in 1962, and was continued by the Labour government after October 1964. Economic Development Committees (EDCs), with representatives from management and labor, were organized by the Labour government in twenty-one major manufacturing industries to analyze the problems of each of these industries, and to work closely with the NEDC in fitting private industry into the national plan.

The DEA had four divisions: the Economic Planning Division, concerned with the construction of the national plans; the Regional Planning Division, dealing with the economic problems of the nation's eight regions; the Industrial Policy Division, working with the various private industries and their respective EDCs; and the Economic Coordination Division, handling problems of prices and incomes and the coordination of all economic policies. After constructing the national plan with the close collaboration of the NEDC and the other economic ministries, the DEA would have the plan approved by the prime minister and his cabinet, and then passed on to the House of Commons for its consideration. This plan, incorporating the views and goals of the Labour government, was not formally voted upon by the House of Commons. It was designed only to inform the House of Commons and the nation of the direction in which national economic guidance was expected to move. The national plan was constructed on the assumption that there would be very close working arrangements among the various economic ministries led by the DEA, the NEDC and its EDCs, the TUC, and the CBI. This would apply to the carrying out of the plan as well as its construction.

Two additional bodies involved in British national planning were the National Joint Advisory Council (NJAC) and the National Board for Prices and Incomes (NBPI). The NJAC, with representatives from the TUC and the CBI and with the Minister of Labour as its chairperson, dealt with problems of mutual interest to labor and management. The NBPI was an independent body with representatives acceptable to the TUC and the CBI. The NBPI was created in 1965 by the Labour government to investigate wage and price increases. The board examined these increases when they were referred to it by the government, and then recommended their approval or rejection by the government. The DEA was especially interested in wage and price problems, since the success of its planning activities would depend in large part upon how effective the government would be in curbing the development of inflationary pressures.

In September 1965, the DEA published its five-year National Plan, which was constructed on the basis of close cooperation with the representatives of industry and the trade unions and with the National Economic Development Council. The National Plan was described as a "guide to action" by the government, private industry, and the trade unions. The theory underlying the plan was that the main constraint on economic growth was not the shortage of capital and labor but rather the low level of aggregate demand. The way to secure sustained economic growth on a high level was to reduce uncertainty and to increase business confidence in a future high level of demand. Quantitative national planning or programming could contribute to the solution of this problem by establishing a high growth rate as a national goal, which would inject a degree of optimism into the business community. Individual business firms would then have a clear picture of the potential growth of the economy five years ahead, and would then base their investment decisions on a "long-term view." No specific output or investment targets would be set for individual firms or industries. It was hoped that the plan would encourage industry and labor to support the quantitative projections incorporated in the plan.

Table 11-3 shows the quantitative goals of the National Plan which it was hoped would be achieved in the five years, 1966-1970. Gross National Product was projected to increase at the average annual rate of 3.8 percent. The general strategy was to curb the growth of private and public consumption and to switch resources to private and public investment. Over the period 1966-1970, private consumption was projected to increase at the annual rate of 3.2 percent, whereas private investment was projected to increase at a much higher annual rate: 7.6 percent. Public consumption was expected to increase at a 4 percent annual rate, whereas public investments were projected to increase at rates varying from 4.5 to 9.7 percent. The objective of the Labour government was a low-consumption, high-investment economy, which would release resources to the export industries and lay the foundation for a sustained surplus in the balance of international payments. The goal was to increase this surplus by £50 million a year until it would amount to £500 million by 1970. This large surplus would enable the government not only to pay off the large debts incurred in defending the pound, but

Table 11-3
The Planned Increase in the United Kingdom's Gross National Product and Its Component Items, 1964-1970

	£ million, 1964 prices		Average annual percentage increase 1964-1970
	1964 (actual)	1970 (planned)	
Personal consumption	21,334	25,790	3.2
Public consumption	3,481	4,405	4.0
Gross fixed investment	5,802	8,015	5.5
Of which:			
Manufacturing	1,351	2,090	7.6
Other private	1,298	1,620	3.8
Nationalized industries	1,145	1,490	4.5
Housing	1,209	1,595	4.8
Roads	194	340	9.7
Other public investment	605	880	6.5
Defense	1,930	2,045	1.0
Inventory increase	526	530	—
Net export surplus	−226	275	—
Gross National Product	32,847	41,060	3.8

Source: Department of Economic Affairs, *The National Plan*.

also to increase the nation's gold and foreign exchange reserves and its export of capital to foreign countries.

The National Plan and the Action Program

The National Plan was accompanied by a proposed action program, designed to aid in the achievement of the plan's 1970 goals.[15] Industrial efficiency was to be improved by standardizing output and reducing its variety, by enlarging the size of business firms and encouraging mergers that promoted efficiency and international competitiveness, and by encouraging the interest in management education. The Economic Development Committees in all the major industries were expected to uncover ways in which industrial efficiency could be improved, aid could be given to exporters, and a more balanced regional development of industry could be secured. The action program looked forward to a large increase in investment in the manufacturing industries that would provide capacity for additional exports and for import replacement. This program also called for an active manpower policy that would increase employment by 800,000 by 1970, and would raise the level of the workers' technical skills. The regional policy was to make a fuller use of manpower in the less prosperous regions. Government spending was to be reallocated so as to divert research and development expenditures from defense to civilian uses, to improve training and retraining facilities at all levels, and to speed the application of modern technology to British industry. It was also explained that the plan would be kept under regular review in the light of developments, and that periodic reassessments of the plan would be made.

After the National Plan was adopted in September 1965, a number of steps were taken to carry it out. The Industrial Reorganisation Act of 1967 set up the Industrial Reorganisation Corporation to promote the rationalization and modernization of industry by making loans to private firms or by purchasing some of their capital shares. The Economic Development Committees made surveys of the nation's major industries and submitted reports on methods of improving industrial efficiency and of enlarging exports. New facilities were provided for the education of industrial managers. Cash grants stimulated private investment in high priority industries. Regional development was promoted through favorable fiscal and credit arrangements for firms that established plants in areas of excessive unemployment. Labor mobility was encouraged by setting up additional Industrial Training Boards and by enlarging the capacity of the government training centers. Workers were encouraged to leave low-productivity industries by giving them generous redundancy payments, and were assisted in moving to new jobs by the provision of travel grants. Mergers among small-scale business enterprises were encouraged with loans or stock purchases by the Industrial Reorganisation Corporation. The government encouraged exports by expanding export credit insurance facilities at reduced cost, by refunding sales taxes to exporters, and by providing financial assistance for promotional activities abroad. The Bank of England called upon the major banks to facilitate the expansion of the high priority industries. Special efforts were made under the Distribution of Industry Act to induce private industry to locate in the depressed development areas of the northwest and the northeast.

Whatever progress was made in restructuring British industry and laying the foundation

---

[15] This action program is summarized in Department of Economic Affairs, *The National Plan*, London, 1965, pp. 5–21.

for a more internationally competitive economy in the years 1965–1970, it was not enough to enable the Labour government to achieve the goals set forth in the 1965 National Plan. Since the plan was itself set aside in 1966, when the price-wage standstill was adopted, no periodic reviews of the plan were made. The government failed to achieve the growth goal in the plan for the years 1965–1970; it was unable to curb private consumption as much as it had hoped; and it did not succeed in expanding fixed investment at the high annual rate set forth in the plan. The comparative statistics in Table 11–4 show that the annual economic growth rate of 2.2 percent fell far short of the plan goal of 3.8 percent; personal consumption increased excessively at the rate of 4.1 percent instead of the planned 3.2 percent; the actual rate of unemployment was 2.5 percent in 1970 rather than the projected or planned rate of 1.4 percent; and gross fixed investment increased at the rate of 3.2 percent instead of the planned 5.5 percent. On various occasions in the years 1965–1970, the Treasury projected annual increases in the gross domestic product of from 3 to 3.5 percent, but the actual outcomes were usually well below these figures. The failure of the Labour government's national planning for the years 1965–1970 was climaxed by the failure to secure a sizable favorable balance of international payments before 1969.

The Economic Assessment for 1969–1972

With the restoration of a large favorable current balance of international payments in 1969, the Labour government proposed another experiment with national planning. The second planning document, *The Task Ahead: Economic Assessment to 1972*, was prepared by the Department of Economic Affairs and published in February 1969. The document stated that "This is a planning document, not a plan. That is to say, the document provides a basis for a further stage in the continuing process of consultation between Government and both sides of industry

Table 11–4
The National Plan Goals and the Actual Outcomes, 1964–1970

	Annual planned percentage increases 1964–1970	Annual achieved percentage increases 1964–1970
Personal consumption	3.2	4.1
Public consumption	4.0	1.9
Gross fixed investment	5.5	3.2
Gross national product	3.8	2.2[1]
Rate of unemployment	1.4[2]	2.5[2]

[1] Gross domestic product.
[2] Planned and actual rates of unemployment for 1970 only.

Sources: Department of Economic Affairs, *The National Plan* and OECD, *OECD Economic Surveys, United Kingdom.*

about major issues of economic policy."[16] Like the National Plan of 1965, the second planning document made medium-term projections of the growth and uses of the gross domestic product. The second plan was more flexible, however, since it projected a "wedge" or "range" of economic growth rates over the period 1967 to 1972 between a little less than 3 percent and 4 percent.

After discussing four possible lines of economic development, the DEA adopted what it described as the "basic case" or plan projection for the year 1972, which is presented in Table 11-5. The five-year national program for 1968-1972 looked forward to a further shift of resources from personal consumption and defense expenditures into private investment in plant, equipment, and inventories and into public investment in transportation, health, educational, and other public capital facilities. Over the plan period 1968-1972 gross domestic product was projected to increase at an annual average rate of 3.2 percent, fixed private industrial investment at the rate of 5.3 percent, and personal consumption at the rate of 2.4 percent. By 1972, the surplus in the current balance of international payments was expected to be £920 million ($2.2 billion), or 2 percent of the nation's gross domestic product.

The second Labour planning document emphasized the need for consultations among the government, the employers, and the workers "at the early stages in the formation of new policies and for the exchange of views about longer-term issues."[17] It was also explained that the whole country would have to

[16] Department of Economic Affairs, *The Task Ahead: Economic Assessment to 1972*, London: H. M. S. O., 1969, p. 1. See also Central Office of Information, *Britain 1971, An Official Handbook*, London: H.M.S.O., 1971, pp. 234-236.

[17] *Ibid.*, p. 108.

Table 11-5
Projected Uses of the United Kingdom's Gross Domestic Product, 1967-1972 (Basic Case)

	1967 National economic accounts (£ million, 1967 prices)	Increase 1967-1972 (£ million, 1967 prices)	Increase 1967-1972 average annual percentage
Personal consumption	25,323	3,130	2.4
Public consumption	4,746	1,000	3.9
Defense	2,317	−380	−3.5
Investment			
Private industries	3,056	890	5.3
Nationalized industries	1,530	−40	−0.5
Housing	1,464	150	1.9
Public services	1,095	480	8.0
Stockbuilding	130	460	—
Net exports of goods and services	−568	920	—
Gross domestic product	39,093	6,610	3.2

Source: Department of Economic Affairs, *The Task Ahead: Economic Assessment to 1972*.

become much more adaptable to the rapid changes in the economic and technological fields, if it was to become more internationally competitive. Bilateral discussions between the government and the Confederation of British Industry and the Trades Union Congress, and tripartite discussions within the National Development Economic Council, were expected to "form the beginning of a continuing process in which the forecasts [projections of the gross domestic product] and subsequent consultations are rolled forward regularly on whatever lines prove by experience to be the most useful to industry and to the Government."[18]

In October 1969, the Department of Economic Affairs was dissolved; its planning function was taken over by the Treasury, which in May 1970 published a new economic assessment entitled *Economic Prospects to 1972—Revised Assessment*. The revised assessment assumed that the annual increase in gross domestic product from 1968 to 1972 would be 3 percent, which was in keeping with the trend in the nation's production potential. Within a month after the revised assessment of the United Kingdom's economic prospects was made, the Labour party was out of office, and the incoming Conservative government put an end to the national planning program.

The Third Labour Government and the British Economy, 1974–1975

The third post–World War II Labour government was returned to office in February 1974 after three years of Conservative party administration that ended in the economic and financial crisis of late 1973 and early 1974. The new Labour government was faced with two major tasks. The first was to overcome the national emergency that had been precipitated by the strike of the National Union of Miners against the Heath government. The second task was to adjust the British economy to the contractionary impact of the oil crisis that began in October 1973. Both tasks came together in the efforts to control wage and price inflation, to expand exports, and to maintain the value of the British pound.

Both 1974 and 1975 were very difficult years for the British economy as can be seen from the behavior of the economic indicators in Table 11-6.[19] In spite of the efforts of the Labour government to offset the adverse impact of the higher prices for imported oil, gross domestic product, which had increased 5.3 percent in 1973, was almost stationary in 1974 and decreased 1.75 percent in 1975. In the economy's external sector, the adverse balance of payments, which was $8.4 billion in 1974, was $3.8 billion in 1975. While there were some prospects of a slightly better performance of Britain's economy early in 1976, these prospects were soon reversed when a widspread loss of confidence in the British pound reduced its dollar value from $2.00 in March 1976 to $1.63 in October of that year. Some improvement in performance could be anticipated from the repeal of the Industrial Relations Act of 1971, an act which was vigorously opposed by the trade unions, and from the approval of Britain's membership in the European Economic Community by the British public referendum of June 1975.

In July 1974 the Labour government abolished the mandatory wage controls inherited from the prior government, and replaced them with a "social contract" between the government and the Trades Union Congress. Under this contract, the unions were not supposed to seek wage increases larger than the annual

[18] *Ibid.*, p. 113.

[19] Economic developments in the United Kingdom in 1974–1975 are analyzed in OECD, *OECD Economic Surveys, United Kingdom*, March 1975; and *Economic Outlook*, 15 and 16, July and Dec. 1974.

Table 11-6
The United Kingdom's GDP and Its Uses, 1973-1975

	1973 million £	Percentage changes over previous year		
		1973	1974	1975
The uses of GDP				
Private consumption	44.9	4.6	0.25	−0.25
Public consumption	13.3	3.7	2.0	2.50
Fixed investment	13.9	4.8	−4.0	−0.75
Public	5.5	0.4	2.0	—
Private residential	1.7	7.6	−23.5	—
Private nonresidential	6.7	8.0	−4.5	—
Change in inventories	0.5	1.3[1]	−1.25[1]	−2.50
Net export surplus	−1.9	−0.5[1]	1.0[1]	0.5
Gross domestic product	70.2	5.3	−0.5	−1.75
Industrial production		7.2	−1.5	
Consumer prices		8.6	14.75	21.25

[1] Change expressed as a percentage of GDP in the previous year.

Source: Organisation for Economic Co-operation and Development, *Economic Outlook*, 16, Dec. 1975, p. 89, and *OECD Economic Surveys, United Kingdom*, Feb. 1976, p. 32.

increase in the cost of living, which was then about 20 percent. Prices were less rigorously controlled in order to avoid a profit squeeze. Both fiscal and monetary policies were kept very restrictive, but special arrangements were made for aiding low-income groups and the export industries. In the 1974 and 1975 fiscal budgets, social security benefits were enlarged, larger subsidies on basic goods were increased, value-added taxes on consumer goods were lowered, and taxes were increased on upper-income groups and private companies. Credit was tightened by raising interest rates, increasing bank reserve requirements, and keeping the growth of the money supply below the growth of nominal gross domestic product. Although a ceiling was placed upon the expansion of the credit supply, the banks were called upon by the government to ration credit on a selective basis and to make it available to industry to finance productive investment, especially in the export and export-supporting industries.

The Labour government's program for controlling inflation and restoring the economy to its full growth potential proved unsuccessful. A number of powerful trade unions ignored the social contract and secured annual wage increases well above the 20 percent recommended by the contract. By mid-1975, wage inflation and higher prices for oil and other imports resulted in price inflation at an annual rate of 47 percent. With the value of the British pound falling, and the external account deficit remaining at an unsustainably high level, the Labour government in July 1975 sought to curb inflation by re-establishing mandatory wage controls. With the backing of the Trades Union Congress, the government announced a ceiling of £6 ($13) per week on all wage and salary increases; this amounted to an increase of approximately 10 percent of average industrial wages. It was hoped that the new wage controls along with the existing price controls would enable the government to bring inflation down to 10 percent within a year and below that by the end of 1976.

Under the wage controls, employers who increased wages more than 10 percent were not allowed to pass on any excess wages in increased prices. Both local governments and nationalized industries were also barred from increasing prices to pay for wage increases above the established ceiling. While the majority of trade union members supported the government's wage controls, some of the strong unions remained unsympathetic to these controls. The experience with mandatory wage controls in the United Kingdom since 1945 casts considerable doubt on the feasibility of this new effort to control wage inflation. At best, statutory wage and price controls are only temporary devices for dealing with wage and price inflation. Experience with these controls in Norway, Sweden, Denmark, and Holland seem to indicate that in the long run only voluntary controls are workable. With this approach to controls in mind, Prime Minister Wilson in May 1975 suggested that inflation could be successfully attacked in a sustained manner only when the government, business, and labor could voluntarily agree on an allocation of income between wages and profits that would bring an end to the inflationary incomes race.[20]

While most of the energy of the Labour government after February 1974 was absorbed in trying to make the British economy more viable, some attention was nevertheless given to furthering socialism in the United Kingdom. The 1974 Labour party manifestoes, "Programme for Britain" and "Britain Will Win with Labour," declared that it was the party's aim to provide for the more democratic control of industry, and "to bring about a fundamental and irreversible shift in the balance of wealth and power in favour of working people and their families." Nationalization was to be expanded to include the North Sea oil and gas resources, shipbuilding and repairing, marine engineering, the aircraft and pharmaceutical industries, and urban land required for housing. More importantly, the government was to purchase minority equity interests in the twenty-five leading private companies so as to be in a better position to monitor their activities. Social justice was to be extended by imposing special taxes on private wealth. Class distinctions were to be reduced by expanding the comprehensive school system and ending the eleven-plus, two-track educational system that separated academically and vocationally oriented students. Under this educational system children were all tested at the age of eleven and were then separated into two different groups, one going on for academic education and the other for vocational education.

The Labour government entered on its program for expanding socialism in Britain by passing the Industry Act in February 1975.[21] The purpose of this act is to provide a "closer, clearer and more positive relationship between government and industry." The act establishes a National Enterprise Board which may enter into plan agreements with major strategic business enterprises in key sections of manufacturing. These agreements, which are drawn up by the board in close cooperation with the firms and their trade union representatives, cover the capital investment

---

[20] Central Office of Information, *Survey of Current Affairs*, Vol. 5, June 1975, p. 238.

[21] The government's explanation and defense of this act is given in its White Paper on *The Regeneration of British Industry*, Cmnd. 5710, Feb. 1975.

plans of the individual enterprises over a three-year period and are to be rolled forward annually. These agreements seek to assure that private enterprise is taking steps to improve the efficiency and competitiveness of British industry by enlarging the amount of investment per worker.

At the time of the passing of the Industry Act, it was pointed out that capital investment per industrial worker in the United Kingdom was less than half that in France, Japan, and the United States, and well below what it was in West Germany and Italy. The Labour government felt that it had to take an active part in assuring that private industry was prepared to do the investing in productive equipment required for a high level of economic growth. The National Enterprise Board was to have £1 billion ($2 billion in January 1976) available for lending to private firms in need of financial aid to carry out their plan agreements. When this financial aid was given to private companies, the government was empowered to acquire equity interests in them.

The plan agreements, which provide a new and improved framework for cooperation between the government and Britain's leading industrial companies, are regarded by the Labour Party as a step forward in enlarging the program for industrial democracy. These agreements would open up the hitherto undisclosed investment plans of the private companies to their employees, and would enable the latter to have a role in the decision making with regard to these plans. In this manner, private industry would be further democratized. These plan agreements would expand public ownership on a limited basis into the profitable areas of industry, and would strengthen the government's hand in its planning for the British public-private or mixed enterprise economy. It remains to be seen if the Labour government stays in office long enough after 1976 to establish the system of plan agreements on a firm foundation.

British National Planning: An Evaluation

The Labour government originally intended that a national planning program would be initiated with a five-year plan which would be annually evaluated and rolled forward until the next five-year plan was adopted. National planning would then be on a permanently rolling basis. Each year, an annual plan would be published within the framework of the five-year medium-term national plan. Annual plans had been published in the years 1947–1951, but no five-year plan. No annual plans were published in 1965–1970, and no public assessments were made after 1965 of the 1965 National Plan. Outside of government circles, national planning had no role to play when the Labour government was in office. While the government made projections of the growth of the gross domestic product and its uses for private and public consumption and investment purposes, these projections were for internal use only in the formulation of governmental economic policies and so were not published. Consultations between the government and the two sides of industry in the years 1966–1968 were carried on without reference to any published annual or medium-term national plans. The same applied to the work of the National Economic Development Council and the twenty-one Economic Development Committees. In late 1964 and 1965, and again in 1969 and 1970, steps were taken to develop a program of indicative national planning, as has already been explained, but in both cases the planning efforts failed to take root. In the first case, the pressure of events turned attention away from the projected goals of the national planning program; and in the second case, the Labour government was out of office (in June 1970) before it could do much about carrying out its second five-year plan.

While the Labour government failed to place indicative national planning on a firm foundation in the United Kingdom, as was done in France, the Netherlands, Norway, and Sweden, its efforts in this direction were not entirely fruitless. As has already been discussed, the action program of the 1965 National Plan was continued even though many of the plan's economic goals were abandoned. This program has incorporated both macroeconomic and microeconomic qualities. The macroeconomic aspect concerned the government's short-term, medium-term, and long-term economic policies and programs dealing with the functioning and structure of the whole economy. These policies and programs emphasized what the government could do to secure sustained economic growth, full employment, and a favorable balance of international payments.

The microeconomic aspect of the action program dealt with the efforts of individual firms and industries to improve labor productivity, industrial efficiency, and the ability to enlarge exports. Although the Labour government did not succeed in establishing a national planning program in the years 1966–1970, the action program of the plan did serve a useful purpose in emphasizing how much the improvement in the performance of the nation's economy depended upon the good performance of the microeconomic producing units. Furthermore, the Labour government did succeed in underlining the need for an effective coordination of economic decision making at both the macro- and micro-levels, if the British economy was to become viable on a sustained basis.

The planning efforts of the Labour government also called attention to the need to improve the ways in which national economic guidance is provided. The essence of this guidance is to make the micro-decisions of individual firms mutually consistent with the general growth of the economy. Those economists who find some value in indicative national planning assert that this planning at the aggregative level makes it possible for the micro-decisions of individual firms to be based on the best available evidence of the general growth of the economy.[22] A recent critic of the National Plan, Michael Posner, conceded that the plan was a failure, but agreed with many other economists that the general notion of indicative planning could serve a useful purpose. As he put it, "Nevertheless, I remain of the view that a general notion of the way in which the authorities envisage the course of aggregate demand developing over the coming five years (on a 'rolling forward' basis) can serve a useful purpose in providing a common 'key' into which the projections of [private] corporate planners can be fitted."[23] This same critic concluded that although British national planning in the 1960s failed, "I would venture the unfashionable remark that planning, in the sense of making rational expectations mutually consistent for a chosen growth rate, will have to be resuscitated one day soon."[24]

The British Socialist Economy: In Retrospect and Prospect

The economic policies of the Labour government during 1964–1970 did not end the

---

[22] R. E. Caves, "Second Thoughts on Britain's Economic Prospects," in *Britain's Economic Prospects Reconsidered*, p. 216.

[23] Michael V. Posner, "Industrial Policies and Growth," in *Britain's Economic Prospects Reconsidered*, pp. 155–156. For the opposite view that the government should not make macroeconomic projections at all, see Vera A. Lutz, *Central Planning for the Market Economy*, London: Institute of Economic Affairs, 1969; and Political and Economic Planning, *Economic Planning in Britain, France and Germany*, London, 1968.

[24] Michael V. Posner, *op. cit.*, p. 155. See also P. D. Henderson, "Planning and the Machinery of Policy," *Economic Growth in Britain*, London: Weidenfeld and Nicolson, 1966, p. 222.

sluggish performance of the British economy—sluggish, that is, as compared with the German, French, Swedish, and other Western industrial economies. As the comparative statistics in Table 11-7 indicate, while the United Kingdom, like other advanced industrial economies, experienced considerable price and wage inflation in 1965-1970, it did not achieve the higher economic growth rates of those economies. On the average, these rates were about twice as high as the British growth rate. Compared to other Western industrial economies, the British economy was a low-investment one. In the period under review, the United Kingdom allocated 15 percent of its Gross National Product to gross fixed investment, while the other Western industrialized countries allocated about 20 percent of GNP.

The unsatisfactory development of the British economy during 1964-1970 had adverse effects upon the nation's external economy. Whereas the West German, French, Italian, and Japanese economies increased or maintained their export market shares in 1964-1970, the United Kingdom's market share continued to decline. The British share of the value of the world's exports of manufactured goods, which was 14.2 percent in 1964, fell to 10.8 percent in 1970. Over these years, the Labour government was unable to achieve a sustained surplus in the current balance of international payments, and was unable to build up its international reserves.

The statistics in Table 11-7 reveal that the British official international reserves amounted to only 13 percent of total merchandise imports in 1970. In the same year, France's reserves were 26 percent and West Germany's reserves 45.6 percent of 1970 total merchandise imports. While important measures were taken by the Labour government to improve industrial productivity, and while these measures had some favorable effects, nevertheless the British productivity path rose less steeply than the American, the German, and the Swedish. It is estimated that output per employee in industry in the United States was at least two and a half times as high as in the United Kingdom in the 1960s.

The Labour government adopted the position in the 1960s that economic growth could be accelerated under government auspices with the aid of a national planning program. Other countries, such as France, the Netherlands, Norway, Sweden, and Japan, had enjoyed some success along these lines. The Labour government, however, was unable to place national planning on a sustained basis. Even if it had done so, it would still have had to demonstrate that it could duplicate the success of other Western planned economies in achieving 4 to 5 percent growth rates. No widespread agreement exists concerning the factors that have contributed to the poor performance of the British economy. This situation has stemmed from a combination of economic, social, and political variables that has not yet been woven into a generally accepted theory of growth.[25] It is clear, however, that setting high economic growth goals and seeking to achieve these goals with macroeconomic policies are not in themselves enough to eliminate the sluggishness of an economy like that of Britain. Many other attitudinal and institutional changes must be made if indicative national planning is to be successful. Employers and workers must substitute cooperation for conflict; and both sides of industry must be prepared to collaborate

---

[25] For different interpretations of the causes of the slow rate of economic growth in the United Kingdom see John Knapp and David Lomax, "Britain's Growth Performance," *Lloyds Bank Review*, Oct. 1964; N. Kaldor, *The Causes of the Slow Rate of Economic Growth of the United Kingdom*, Cambridge: Cambridge University Press, 1966; E. F. Denison, *Why Growth Rates Differ*, Washington D.C.: The Brookings Institution, 1967; and Samuel Brittan, *Steering the Economy: The British Experiment*, LaSalle: Open Court Publishing Co., 1971.

Table 11-7
Comparative Economic Indicators for the United Kingdom and Selected Countries, 1965–1970

	United Kingdom	West Germany	France	United States	Sweden	Japan
Gross National Product, average annual increase, 1965–1970	2.4[1]	4.6	5.8	3.2	3.9[1]	12.1
Gross fixed investment as % of GNP 1966–1970 (average)	15.1	19.9	19.3	13.2	17.9	30.1
Consumer prices, average annual increase, 1965–1970	4.6	2.7	4.3	4.3	4.4	5.5
Hourly earnings in industry, average annual increase, 1965–1970	6.7	7.4	9.2	5.3	8.9	14.7
Gains or losses of export market shares, 1960/61–1970/71 (average)	−2.9	1.0	1.0	−2.1	−0.1	7.9
Current balance of payments, as % of GNP, 1966–1970 (average)	0.2	1.0	−0.4	0.1	−0.6	0.9
Official reserves at end of 1970 as % of imports in 1970	13.0	45.6	26.0	36.3	10.9	35.5

[1] Gross domestic product.

Source: OECD, *OECD Economic Surveys, United Kingdom,* "Basic Statistics: International Comparisons," Jan. 1973.

with the government in the execution of a national planning program. In addition, both sides of industry must be well organized and disciplined, and must be willing to put their weight behind the planning program.

It has been suggested that a comparison of British and Swedish economic experience would throw some light on the difficulties encountered by the Labour government in its efforts to plan the economy. The success of Swedish national planning appears to be associated with a number of human factors not found in the United Kingdom. It has been observed that "The level of education in Sweden is high, and the Swede attaches great importance to the qualifications to be attained through it. By the same token, he brings to the task of administration and design a thoroughness of reasoning and vigour of imagination that he combines with readiness to follow in practice the course they mark out. In the same way he combines a disciplined acceptance of decisions reached collectively with a strong sense of individual responsibility: the cohesion of the employers' association in collective bargaining does not sap the competitive drive of management."[26] The cohesion of the Swedish workers' Confederation of Trade Unions, which is not duplicated among British trade unionists, also contributes significantly to the good performance of the

[26] E. H. Phelps Brown, "Labour Policies: Productivity, Industrial Relations, Cost Inflation," *Britain's Economic Prospects Reconsidered,* p. 112.

Swedish socialist economy. It appears that the British socialist economy will probably not perform very well as long as current attitudes among employers and workers and existing economic institutional arrangements remain unchanged.[27]

E. H. Phelps Brown concludes that much of the slow growth of the British economy in 1964–1970 arose from the fact "that the culture of British managers and workers was generally less propitious to change and development than, in their different ways, the cultures of those other countries [such as Sweden and West Germany]."[28] Lloyd Ulman reaches the same conclusion and attributes the low growth of the British economy in part to "the bloodymindedness of British labor" and "the backwardness of British management."[29] As long as these unfavorable attitudinal and institutional factors are present, the Labour government cannot hope to plan the nation's economic and social affairs successfully.

In May 1975, Prime Minister Wilson recognized the need for new attitudes on the part of employers and workers and new institutional arrangements in the economic system when he recommended a program for dealing with England's economic difficulties, which is very similar to the planning programs followed in Norway and Sweden.[30] He called upon the Confederation of British Industry and the Trades Union Congress to join with the government in adopting a national plan that would project the GNP over a four- or five-year period. Agreement would be sought with regard to the division of the national product among private consumption and investment and public expenditures. Adequate provision would be made for capital investment and exports, and joint consultation would be carried out with respect to wage and profit incomes. There would be annual consultations by the government with business and labor; and the planning program would be evaluated at quarterly intervals. To curb inflation, spur investment in private industry, and enlarge exports there would be required a continuous monitoring of the economy against a background of joint consultation or determination. Thus far, Wilson and his successor James Callaghan have been unable to put any such program into operation, because neither the Confederation of British Industry nor the Trades Union Congress has been willing to give it full support.

Many critics of the Labour government's economic program assert that it gives inadequate attention to encouraging growth through an increase in efficiency.[31] In the opinion of these critics, more attention should

---

[27] Both socialists and nonsocialists have for a long time been aware of the importance of securing these attitudinal and institutional changes. For a nonsocialist view, see Political and Economic Planning, *Growth in the British Economy*, London: George Allen and Unwin, 1960, p. 241. A more recent statement of this problem is presented in Richard Lecomber, "Government Planning, With and Without the Cooperation of Industry, Reflections on British Experience," *Economics of Planning*, Vol. 10, No. 1–2, 1970.

[28] E. H. Phelps Brown, *op. cit.*, p. 121.

[29] Lloyd Ulman, "Collective Bargaining and Industrial Efficiency," *Britain's Economic Prospects*, p. 331.

[30] British Information Service, *Survey of Current Affairs*, June 1975, p. 238.

[31] The non-British authors of *Britain's Economic Prospects* concluded their study of the British economy in 1968 by stating that "Our analysis and policy recommendations may fly in the face of fashion by encouraging growth via increase in efficiency rather than encouragement to investment or aggregate demand" (p. 494). Similar views are expressed in *Britain's Economic Prospects Reconsidered*. See especially Sir Alec Cairncross, "Concluding Reflections," pp. 217–236. E. H. Phelps Brown concludes that Britain's poor economic performance has been due to personal qualities and interpersonal relations and not due to the inadequacy of broad flows of input and output which the government can act upon by fiscal and monetary measures. E. H. Phelps Brown, "The Brookings Study of the Poor Performance of the British Economy," *Economica*, Vol. XXXVI, Aug. 1969, pp. 235–252.

be paid by the Labour government to improving the organization of business enterprises and the use of the labor force. A more vigorous attack should be made on the overuse of labor and the underutilization of capital in British industry. There should be less piecemeal investment that merely adds small amounts of new equipment to old and inefficiently organized plants. The diseconomies of small-scale operation that arise from a high level of product differentiation should be ended by encouraging large-scale investment projects designed for longer and more standardized production runs.[32] Also, inadequate attention is given to the shift of resources from basic science to industrial research and to the development of research-intensive industries. In addition, more effort should be made to transfer labor and other scarce resources from the low-productivity domestic industries to the high-productivity export industries.

Other critics of the Labour government's economic program assert that the main deficiency of this program is not primarily its failure to improve industrial efficiency, but rather its failure to provide for expectations on the part of the government and private business of high economic growth.[33] These critics believe that the chief cause of growth is the expectation of growth. The Labour government has never been able to stimulate private business enterprise by raising growth expectations to the 4 to 5 percent level and actually achieving this level on a sustained basis. Instead, during the Labour party's tenure of office, growth expectations have been around 2.8 percent, with the result that investment and production have remained low. While it is important to consider the economy from the supply side and to be concerned with raising the efficiency of industry, it is more important, in the opinion of some critics of Labour government policies, to view the economy from the demand side, and to emphasize the role of high-growth expectations. Many economists would doubtless say that the Labour government should be more involved with both the supply-and-demand sides of the problem of making the British economy more viable. Clearly, any further reconstruction of the British society along socialist lines will require an economic system on a firm foundation—a goal that the Labour party has been unable to achieve. The party's proposals to tax away much private wealth and to give the government greater equity participation in industry with the aim of advancing socialism will probably attract little public support, if the party continues to be unable to achieve a stable and prosperous economy.

---

[32] West Germany's experience in this connection is worth investigating. The number of large plants has been increasing a great deal faster in West Germany than in Britain; also, in West Germany, large plants are more concentrated in the export industries than they are in Britain. See National Institute of Economic and Social Research, "The Size of Plant: A Comparison," *National Institute Economic Review*, No. 38, Nov. 1966, pp. 63–66.

[33] For a discussion of this approach to the Labour government's economic problems, see W. Beckerman, "The Determinants of Economic Growth," *Economic Growth in Britain*, pp. 78–81; and W. Beckerman and Associates, *The British Economy in 1975*, Cambridge: Cambridge University Press, 1965, pp. 64–69. For a similar view, see Nicholas Kaldor, "Conflicts in National Economic Objectives," *Economic Journal*, Vol. 81, March 1971, pp. 1–16. Kaldor calls for export-led growth rather than consumption-led growth which, however, is preferable to stagnation, as he explains in *Causes of the Slow Rate of Economic Growth in the United Kingdom*, Cambridge; Cambridge University Press, 1966.

Selected Bibliography

BECKERMAN, WILFRED, ed. *The Labour Government's Economic Record: 1964–1970.* Gerald Duckworth and Co., London, 1972.

———, and ASSOCIATES. *The British Economy in 1975.* Cambridge University Press, Cambridge, 1965.

BRADY, ROBERT. *Crisis in Britain.* University of California Press, Berkeley, 1952.

BRITISH LABOUR PARTY. *The New Britain.* London, 1964.

BRITTAN, SAMUEL. *Steering the Economy: The British Experiment.* Open Court Publishing Co., LaSalle, Ill., 1971.

CAIRNCROSS, SIR ALEC, ed. *Britain's Economic Prospects Reconsidered.* State University of New York Press, Albany, New York, 1970.

CAVES, RICHARD E., and ASSOCIATES. *Britain's Economic Prospects.* The Brookings Institution, Washington, D.C. 1968.

COLE, MARGARET. *The Story of Fabian Socialism.* Heinemann Educational Books, London, 1961.

CROSSMAN, R. H. S. *New Fabian Essays.* Turnstile Press, London, 1952.

DEPARTMENT OF ECONOMIC AFFAIRS. *The National Plan.* London, 1965.

———. *The Task Ahead: Economic Assessment to 1972.* London, 1969.

HACKETT, JOHN and ANNE-MARIE. *The British Economy, Problems and Prospects.* George Allen and Unwin, London, 1967.

HARROD, ROY. *Are These Hardships Necessary?* Rupert Hart-Davis, London, 1947.

HENDERSON, P. D. *Economic Growth in Britain.* George Weidenfeld and Nicolson, London, 1966.

KALDOR, NICHOLAS. *Causes of the Slow Rate of Economic Growth of the United Kingdom.* Cambridge University Press, Cambridge, 1966.

LEWIS, ARTHUR W. *The Principles of Economic Planning.* Dennis Dobson, London, 1949.

LEWIS, BEN W. *British Planning and Nationalization.* Twentieth Century Fund, New York, 1952.

MEADE, JAMES E. *Planning and the Price Mechanism.* George Allen and Unwin, London, 1948.

ORGANISATION FOR ECONOMIC CO-OPERATION AND DEVELOPMENT. *OECD Economic Surveys, United Kingdom.* 1965–1971.

PAISH, F. W. *How the Economy Works.* Macmillan and Company, London, 1970.

POLITICAL AND ECONOMIC PLANNING. *Economic Planning in Britain, France and Germany.* London, 1968.

———. *Growth in the British Economy.* George Allen and Unwin, London, 1960.

ROGOW, A. A. *The Labour Government and British Industry, 1945–1951.* Basil Blackwell, Oxford, 1955.

SHAW, GEORGE B., and OTHERS. *The Fabian Essays in Socialism.* Ball Publishing Co., Boston, 1908.

WALKER, FRANCIS. *Socialist Britain.* Viking Press, New York, 1945.

WALKER, GILBERT. *Economic Planning by Programme and Control in Great Britain.* William Heinemann, London, 1957.

WILSON, THOMAS, *Planning and Growth.* Macmillan, London, 1965.

WORSWICK, G. D. N., and P. H. ADY, eds. *The British Economy, 1945–1950.* Clarendon Press, Oxford, 1952.

Chapter 12

The Mature Democratic Socialist Economies: In Retrospect and Prospect

Democratic partial or limited socialism, although well established only in Sweden and Norway, has had a considerable impact in the United Kingdom, West Germany, France, and the Netherlands. In the United Kingdom, the socialists have taken over the government four times since the end of World War II. In Denmark, the Social Democratic party has been in office six times since 1945 and has left a deep imprint on the Danish economic system. In France and the Netherlands, where the socialists have usually been out of office since 1945, the socialists have had a large following, and have exerted considerable influence on the shape and direction of national economic policies. In West Germany, the Social Democratic party became strong enough by 1969 to challenge the nonsocialist Christian Democratic Union successfully and to take over the reins of government in that year. Although the socialist parties in the advanced Western industrial nations have played influential political and economic roles in these countries, only in Sweden, Norway, and Britain have they been in a position to reconstruct society along democratic socialist lines. In many ways, the socialist experiments in Sweden and Norway have had considerable success, whereas much less progress has been made in Britain.

The Performance of the Democratic Socialist Economies

The statistics in Table 12–1 provide a comparison of economic indicators in three socialist planned economies and three nonsocialist planned economies; these statistics constitute a rough measure of the superior performance of the Swedish and Norwegian economies as compared with the United Kingdom. Economic growth rates in Sweden and Norway were approximately twice the rate in Britain during the 1960s. Per capita

Table 12-1
Comparisons of Economic Indicators in Six Planned Economies

	Average annual percent increase in per capita GNP, 1960-72	Per capita GNP 1970, (U.S. $)	Average investment ratio,[1] 1953-1969	Average annual percent change in unit labor costs, 1965-1971	Earnings per hour in industry as a % of U.S. earnings (U.S. = 100%) 1972	Tax burden[2] 1972
Socialist planned economies						
United Kingdom	2.3	2,600	16.2	4.9	42	38.0
Sweden	3.2	4,480	22.4	3.3	89	40.8
Norway	4.0	3,340	28.6	5.9	—	40.9
Nonsocialist planned economies						
Netherlands	4.1	2,840	24.2	3.9	67	40.3
France	4.7	3,620	21.0	3.1	53	36.1
Japan	9.4	2,320	28.2	2.3	42	19.9

[1] Investment ratio is calculated as gross fixed asset formation in relation to gross domestic product (percent of GDP).
[2] Total taxes and social security contributions in relation to Gross National Product (percent of GNP).

Sources: IRBD, *World Bank Atlas*, 1974; USDL, *Productivity and the Economy*, 1973; and OECD, *OECD Economic Surveys, Norway*, 1972.

Gross National Product, which in Sweden in 1973 was $5,910, was 48 percent less in Britain ($3,060), while Norway's per capita output was 52 percent larger than that of Britain. In general, high economic-growth rates are associated with high-investment ratios (gross fixed investment as a percent of gross domestic product). This relationship is indicated by the comparative statistics in Table 12-1; they show that in 1953-1969 the annual investment ratio in the United Kingdom was 16.2 percent, whereas it was over 20 percent in both Sweden and Norway. Although hourly earnings in industry in Sweden are more than twice what they are in Britain, Sweden has been more successful than Britain in curbing the rise in unit labor costs of production. This is because the annual rate of improvement of output per man-hour in manufacturing in Sweden is double that of Britain.

A comparison of the three socialist planned countries—the United Kingdom, Sweden, and Norway—and the three nonsocialist planned countries—the Netherlands, France, and Japan—shows that the economic performance of Sweden and Norway compares favorably with the performance of the three nonsocialist countries. The annual growth rates of Sweden, Norway, the Netherlands, and France in the decade of the 1960s were in the range of 3.2 to 4.7 percent. Among the six planned countries, Japan had the highest annual economic growth rate (9.4 percent) and an investment ratio that was larger (28.2 percent) than that of all the other planned countries except Norway. With low hourly earnings in industry (42 percent of United States earnings) and a very large annual increase in output per man-hour (11.5 percent), Japan was able in the period 1965 to 1971 to curb the increase in unit labor costs of production more effectively than the other five planned economies. This cost development was the basis for Japan's large exports and rapidly increasing share of the world's exports of manufactured goods. Although Japan's per capita GNP has increased steadily since 1945, by 1970 it was still only 52 percent of Sweden's per capita output.

The tax burden in all the Western planned economies is high because of their extensive social-welfare systems. The exception among the planned countries is Japan, which has a tax burden that is about one-half of the burden of the Western planned economies. Besides having a less well developed social security system than the other planned countries, Japan allocates a larger portion of its GNP to industrial investment than do most of the Western planned countries.

An OECD study of economic growth prospects and problems in the 1970s shows that the major policy problem of this period will not be to find the means to increase the rate of economic growth. The statistics in Table 12-2 reveal that in most of the major countries of Continental Europe the growth of national output has been in the range of 4.5 to 6 percent per annum, with rates of growth of productivity running from 3.5 to 5 percent a year.[1] The only exception to this observation was the United Kingdom, which had an annual growth rate of national output of only 2.7 percent in 1960-1970. The OECD growth projections for 1970-1990 show some improvement for the United Kingdom, a slowing down of the growth rate of Sweden, and a continuation of generally high growth trends for most Continental European countries, the United States, and Japan. The 1970 OECD study of economic growth and its problems concludes that there will be two major problems in the 1970s. The first will be to realize the potentialities for the growth of national output without endangering internal or external financial stability. The second problem will be to achieve a better guidance of the growth process so that the extra national output created is used to meet national priorities, while at the same time the damaging side effects of economic growth are prevented.

The OECD growth study explains that short-term demand management can be improved by combining fiscal and monetary policies with an incomes policy, an active manpower policy, regional policies, and, where necessary, exchange-rate adjustments. It is further pointed out that "action in the field of short-term demand management needs to be decided within the framework of medium and longer-term prospects and policies."[2] Concentration on short-term problems of economic stabilization results in "stop-go" cycles, which have undesirable consequences. The growth of demand and output in the 1960s in many countries was excessively uneven; the forward planning of productive investment was made more difficult; fluctuating pressures in the labor market inhibited the development of an effective incomes policy; and attention was diverted from the longer-term objectives of economic and social policy.

What is needed, in the opinion of the Economic Policy Committee of the OECD, is the development of methods of economic projecting or programming "which will make it possible to foresee the need for action sufficiently far in advance to enable policy to anticipate, rather than follow, the course of events."[3] In

[1] OECD, *The Outlook for Economic Growth, A Summary Report on Experience, Prospects, and Problems of Policy, 1960–1980*, Paris, May 1970, p. 9.

[2] *Ibid.*, p. 24.
[3] *Ibid.*

Table 12-2
Projections of Output and Productivity in Selected Western Industrial Economies and Japan, 1970–1980

	Actual gross domestic product, 1960–1970	Projected gross domestic product, 1970–1980	Projected output per man-hour, 1970–1980
United Kingdom	2.7	3.2	2.9
Norway	4.7	4.4	4.1
Sweden	4.5	3.6	3.2
France	5.6	6.0	5.4
West Germany	4.7	4.6	4.4
Italy	5.7	5.6	4.8
Netherlands	5.1	4.6	3.5
United States	4.2	4.7	3.0
Canada	4.9	5.4	2.7
Japan	11.3	10.0	9.0

Source: OECD, *The Outlook for Economic Growth*, 1970, pp. 15 and 16.

an era of rapid technological change and economic advance, governments will find themselves increasingly concerned with the use made of the annual social dividend created by enlarging the nation's total output of goods and services. This concern will require governments to establish national priorities and to open them up for public discussion and guidance. Attaining these priorities will require long-term projections of output and expenditures as guides to action in making economic decisions.

The OECD report on economic growth points out that governments that have used national programming have usually made four- or five-year projections of increases in output and expenditures, and that the focus of these medium-term projections has been on the rate of increase in national output. While five-year projections clearly play an important role in policy formulation, they also obviously have important limitations. Their main limitation relates to their short time horizon. The changes in resource allocation required by the policies and programs to deal with the problems of economic growth and the improvement of the quality of life can be made only over a period of years. Consequently, many policies and programs should be considered in terms of a substantially longer-term horizon than that used in five-year projections. Also, these projections should focus not on increases in the rate of economic growth, but instead on the social goals or priorities which economic growth makes possible. These priorities should be translated into programs with claims on the nation's GNP. Quantifying national priorities as claims on the nation's total output provides a focus for the public discussion of national priorities and helps to create what the OECD report on economic growth describes as a "more general sense of social purpose."

The policy recommendations of the OECD report on economic growth resemble what is already being done in the planned Norwegian and Swedish economies, and what the British Labour government had hoped to do in the period 1964–1970. As we have already seen, short-term demand-and-supply management in Norway and Sweden has been placed within the framework of four-or five-year national plans. In recent years, medium-term (four- or five-year) plans have been supplemented by long-term or fifteen-year plans. An examination of economic indicators shows that both the Norwegian and Swedish economies have performed very well when compared with other Western industrial economies. Gross domestic product has grown at an annual rate between 4 and 5 percent; unemployment (adjusted to United States concepts) has been less than half the rate in Britain, the United States, and Canada; and inflation, while serious, has not been so out of line with inflationary developments in other Western economies as to create serious balance of payments difficulties. As has already been explained, the Norwegian and Swedish crowns have been stable currencies; and international gold and foreign exchange reserves have been large enough to cope successfully with international financial problems.

As the statistics in Tables 12–3 and 12–4 reveal, Sweden and Norway have enjoyed highly stable economies in the postwar period. The statistics in Table 12–3 indicate that Sweden, Norway, France, and Italy in 1953–1969 had high and sustained annual increases in gross domestic product. Other countries, such as West Germany, the United States, and Canada had good but fluctuating growth rates. The United Kingdom had a stable but low economic growth rate.

The situation is similar with regard to the annual growth of export volume. Table 12–4 shows that in 1953–1969, Norway, Sweden, and Denmark had a high and sustained growth in their volume of exports. Other nations, such as West Germany, France, Canada, and the United States, had large but more variable growth in the volume of their exports. The United Kingdom had a stable volume of exports but at an undesirably low level in 1953–1969. In 1970–1975, Norway was more successful than Sweden and the United Kingdom in sustaining its growth, employment, and volume of exports. The generally high and sustained levels of economic growth, employment, and export volume in both Norway and Sweden since the 1950s have been major goals of the national planning programs that have been so prominent a feature of the economic activity of these two countries. In successfully attaining these goals, both Norway and Sweden have avoided the stop-go economic policy that has so adversely affected the performance of the British, American, and Canadian economies.[4]

The British, Norwegian, and Swedish Socialist Economies: A Comparison

A number of factors account for the poor performance of the British socialist economy and the relatively much better performances of the Swedish and Norwegian socialist economies. In both Norway and Sweden, the political situation, as already explained, has been more favorable to the success of partial democratic socialism than in the United Kingdom. Both the Norwegian and Swedish socialist governments have had long periods of political dominance in which to experiment with a planned socialist economy. Matters have been quite different in the United Kingdom, where socialist planning has been abruptly ended, as in 1951 and 1970, after relatively short periods of economic experimentation.

More fundamental explanations stem from attitudes and institutions. Both Norway and

---

[4] Erik Lundberg, the well-known Swedish economist, explains that Sweden has never been forced to adopt a stop-go policy. Erik Lundberg, "Productivity, and Structural Change—A Policy Issue in Sweden," *Economic Journal*, Vol. 82, March. 1972; p. 465.

Table 12-3
Growth and Variability of Gross Domestic Product in Selected Industrial Economies, 1953–1969

	GDP growth, percent annual average, 1953–1969	Variability of GDP growth, 1953–1969[1]
United Kingdom	2.7	1.3
France	5.3	1.4
Italy	5.6	1.4
Sweden	4.2	1.5
Norway	4.1	1.6
Netherlands	4.9	2.3
Denmark	4.2	2.4
United States	3.7	2.6
West Germany	5.9	2.7
Canada	4.1	3.1

[1] Variability is defined as the standard deviation of the percentage changes from year to year over the period considered.
Source: OECD, *OECD Economic Surveys, Norway,* Jan. 1972, p. 10.

Sweden, being industrialized much later than the United Kingdom, avoided the harsher features of the pre-1850 industrialization in the United Kingdom, which laid the foundation for much class distrust and antagonism. Consequently, business and labor leaders in Norway and Sweden have been more prepared to collaborate on solving economic problems than in the United Kingdom, where class suspicions linger on. A major difference between the Scandinavian and the British economies is institutional. When the socialist governments in Norway and Sweden call upon organized business and organized labor to discuss economic problems and to make proposals for their solution, they deal with highly organized and disciplined employers' associations and confederations of trade unions that have the "habit of positive discussion." T. L. Johnston has pointed out that "The habit of positive discussion which these Basic Agreements [between employers and trade unions] have fostered can again be awarded a high rating on an international perspective. It is broadly accepted that one of the main problems of industrial relations is that of effective communications. To have achieved the kind of rapport which now exists at all levels of Swedish labour relations . . . is clearly an efficient outcome, even if it cannot be quantified."[5] The habit of positive discussion and the positive outlook of business people, farmers, and workers that are found at the level of industry affairs also appear on the national level where economic policy formulation and economic guidance are carried on.

The situation is quite different in Britain. When the British Labour governments in the 1950s and again in the 1960s turned to organized business and organized labor for cooperation in handling major economic

[5] T. L. Johnston, *Collective Bargaining in Sweden,* Cambridge: Harvard University Press, 1962, p. 119.

Table 12-4
Growth and Variability of Export Volume in
Selected Western Industrial Economies, 1953–1969

	Export volume growth, average annual percent, 1953–1969	Variability of export volume growth, 1953–1969[1]
Denmark	7.1	2.3
Norway	8.1	2.5
United Kingdom	4.2	2.8
Sweden	6.3	3.0
Netherlands	8.3	3.4
Italy	14.2	4.4
Canada	6.2	4.8
West Germany	11.3	5.4
France	8.2	6.1
United States	6.3	6.3

[1] Variability is defined as the standard deviation of the percentage changes from year to year over the period considered.

Source: OECD, *OECD Economic Surveys, Norway,* Jan. 1972, p. 11.

problems, they found employer and trade union associations that were organizationally deficient and poorly disciplined by Norwegian and Swedish standards. Cooperation between business and labor in setting up organizations like the National Economic Development Council, the National Incomes Commission, and the National Board for Prices and Incomes was somewhat grudgingly provided, especially by organized labor.[6] The Confederation of British Industry and the Trades Union Congress are less effective than their counterparts in Norway and Sweden in

[6] When the NEDC was established in 1962, some powerful labor leaders were opposed to any form of collaboration with business and the government. The TUC refused to send representatives to the National Incomes Commission, which was set up in 1962 to monitor wage increases. See Andrew Shonfield, *Modern Capitalism,* New York: Oxford University Press, 1965, pp. 153 and 155.

persuading their member firms and trade unions to accept the policies proposed by the national executive boards of the CBI and TUC.

Both British business and labor leaders appear much less informed about national economic needs and issues than are Norwegian and Swedish leaders in these fields. It has been pointed out that "A great deal of the undoubted Swedish success in seeking to progress through discussion must be ascribed to a healthy respect for education. If the education manifested itself only at the level of the LO [Confederation of Trade Unions] and SAF [Swedish Employers' Association] leaders and their research staffs there would be an obvious danger that an *élite* of technocrats would come to dominate collective bargaining. The emphasis on skilled manpower at the LO, SAF, and union levels of activity is of course remarkable in itself, and undoubtedly an eye-opener in an international context."[7] Not only are the business and labor communities in Sweden well informed about domestic and international economic conditions, but they are also willing to work with the government in an effort to develop policies and measures that are acceptable to all interest groups.

In both the Norwegian and Swedish socialist economies, national economic and social planning have been given a well-established institutional basis. During the thirty years in which this planning has been in operation, there have been established various bodies such as the short-term and long-term planning divisions in the Ministry of Finance; interministerial committees; joint consultation committees or councils for the discussion of wage, price, and credit problems; and national economic councils with representatives from all major economic interest groups. These planning organizations have become so well developed since 1945 that they continue to function even with a change of government. When the nonsocialist coalition led by the Center (Agrarian) party took office in Norway in the years 1968-1971, it left the planning organization intact and continued to develop economic policies within the framework of annual and four-year national plans. It is generally agreed that the nonsocialist parties that won control of the government in Sweden in late 1976, will also leave the planning machinery basically unchanged. Obviously, planning by the British Labour party has suffered greatly from its failure to develop an effective planning machinery. When the Department of Economic Affairs was established in 1964, it was heralded as an essential link in the nation's plan organization. Yet in 1968, the DEA was abolished and its functions were taken over by an already heavily burdened Treasury office. This was a repetition of what occurred in 1948 when the Ministry of Economic Affairs, which had been established as an independent ministry of planning in 1947, was absorbed by the Treasury office. In both cases, the new arrangement in the United Kingdom did not result in creating an effective planning machinery.

The Future of British Socialism

The British Labour party's political influence has in recent decades been weakened by the increase in the proportion of total wage and salary earners classified as white-collar workers. By 1966, only 51 percent of British workers were classified as production-process workers. Professional, technical, and administrative workers accounted for 13 percent of the total economically active population.[8] These white-collar workers were prone to organize their own unions and not to affiliate with the Trades Union Congress, which is dominated by blue-collar workers. In 1966, workers in the service trades accounted for 36 percent of the nation's total work force. The Labour party has in recent years experienced considerable difficulty in its efforts to attract white-collar workers into the socialist movement. It claims to be a party of "workers by hand and brain," but there was a growing danger in the 1960s and 1970s that the party would cease to be a "mirror of the nation at work."

In the decade from 1952 to 1961, the Labour party developed a new program that emphasized social ethical goals rather than economic goals.[9] With economic issues on the way to being settled, the Labour party under

---

[7] T. L. Johnston, *op. cit.*, p. 342.

[8] International Labour Office, *1973 Year Book of Labour Statistics*, Geneva, 1973, p. 270.

[9] G. D. H. Cole, *World Socialism Restated*, The New Statesman and Nation, London, 1956, p. 43.

the leadership of Hugh Gaitskell turned to a consideration of "social equalitarianism." The party of the future was to emphasize the need to equalize cultural as well as economic opportunities and to construct a society in which privilege and class distinction no longer existed. The two main objectives of the party, as outlined in *The Future Labour Offers You* (1958) and *Signposts for the Sixties* (1961), were to eliminate disparities in the ownership of private wealth and class distinctions. Questions of economic efficiency and growth were not to be ignored, but they were no longer of primary importance in the further progress of British socialism. All that the Labour party could assert in this connection was that they, in their opinion, would be more effective than the Conservative party in achieving adequate and sustained economic growth.

Before 1951, the Labour party had emphasized the need to redistribute national income more equitably, but had paid little attention to inequalities in the distribution of private wealth. The statistics of income distribution for 1938 and 1949 given in Table 12–5 show that a very considerable leveling of personal incomes had been achieved by 1949.

Table 12–5

The Percentage Distribution of Post-Tax Personal Income in the United Kingdom, 1938 and 1949, at 1938 Prices

	1938	1949
Wages	37	47
Salaries	23	22
Armed Forces' Pay	2	3
Mixed Income	12	10
Property Income	20	10
Social Income	6	9
Total personal income	100	100[1]

[1] Original statistics do not add to 100.

Source: D. Seers, *The Levelling of Income since 1938*, 1951, p. 55.

Not much more was to be gained by leveling personal incomes still further by increasing the marginal rates of the personal income tax.

A 1976 study of personal income distribution in ten industrialized countries by the Organisation for Economic Co-operation and Development reveals that the United Kingdom and other countries such as Norway and Sweden with strong socialist political parties have much less post-tax income inequality than do such capitalist countries as the United States, France, and West Germany. The statistics in Table 12–6 show that the lowest tenth (decile) of the households in the United Kingdom in 1973 received 2.4 percent of total post-tax personal income, whereas this decile received only 1.4 percent in France in 1970. The top decile in the United Kingdom received 23.9 percent of total post-tax personal income, while in France this decile received 30.5 percent. In the United Kingdom, Norway, and Sweden the more equal distribution of personal income after taxes has been achieved in large part by means of transfer payments for social services to the lower-income groups from funds obtained by taxing the upper-income groups. Among the West European nations, Sweden is the one that has done the most to reduce income inequality. As a result of the application of a very progressive income tax system and a large transfer payment system which supplements the incomes received by the low-income groups, the top tenth of households in Sweden in 1972 received only 18.6 percent of total post-tax personal income as compared with slightly more than 30 percent going to the top tenth of households in France (1970) and West Germany (1973).

Although great inequalities in personal income had been eliminated by 1950, there were still large inequalities in the distribution of personal wealth. In 1950, 1 percent of persons over twenty-five owned 50 percent of all private capital in England and Wales, while

Table 12-6
Size Distribution of Post-Tax Personal Income Based on Standardized Household Size in Selected Countries

Country	Year	Deciles									
		1	2	3	4	5	6	7	8	9	10
United Kingdom	1973	2.4	3.7	5.3	6.9	8.5	9.9	11.1	12.9	15.4	23.9
Sweden	1972	2.6	4.7	6.3	7.8	9.0	10.0	11.6	13.1	16.4	18.6
Norway	1970	2.4	4.2	5.7	7.3	8.7	10.2	11.7	13.0	15.0	21.9
Japan	1969	2.7	4.4	5.7	6.7	7.8	9.0	10.1	11.6	14.1	27.8
France	1970	1.4	2.8	4.2	5.5	7.4	8.8	9.7	13.1	16.6	30.5
Germany	1973	2.8	3.7	4.6	5.7	6.7	8.2	9.8	12.1	15.7	30.6
United States	1972	1.7	3.2	4.6	6.3	7.9	9.6	11.4	13.2	16.0	26.1

Source: OECD, *OECD Economic Outlook, Occasional Studies, Income Distribution in OECD Countries,* July 1976, p. 19.

61 percent owned only 5 percent.[10] By 1968, the top 1 percent of the population still owned 41 percent of the nation's private wealth. The tendency of inheritance taxes to reduce inequalities of wealth ownership had been offset by the expanding capital gains received by the owners of private companies.

Since the possession of large amounts of private wealth confers much economic power on those owning this wealth and preserves class distinctions, the Labour party now proposes to eliminate large differentials in wealth ownership by increasing inheritance taxes, increasing taxes on capital gains, and putting an end to income tax avoidance. Inheritance taxes would be paid by transferring company securities to the state. The state would then receive all further gains in capital values which could be used to finance local and central government expenditures. With the elimination of large amounts of private wealth, the concentration of economic power in private hands, resulting from the ownership and control of the six hundred large privately-owned firms that dominate the private sector of the British economy, would disappear. Also, the whole economic basis of class distinctions would be removed since educational privileges based upon "public school" (private school) class education could no longer be purchased by wealthy classes. This is why the Labour party has in recent years assigned a very high priority to educational reform and the elimination of "class education" and "educational privilege."[11]

The "new look" of the Labour party does not satisfy many members of the party who feel that a change in the location of economic and political power from private to public hands is not enough. These critics assert that the Labour government has assisted in the creation of a managerial society that threatens to destroy personal freedoms. Central planning and the extension of public ownership are alleged to have created a "new despotism," which is accompanied by despotism in the affairs of large private oligopolies and

---

[10] K. Langley, "The Distribution of Capital in Private Hands," *Bulletin of the Oxford University Institute of Statistics,* Dec. 1950 and Feb. 1951. See also Edward V. Morgan, *The Structure of Property Ownership in Great Britain,* Oxford: Clarendon Press, 1960.

[11] *Signposts for the Sixties,* p. 31.

large trade unions.[12] Voters, consumers, workers, and trade union members are finding it increasingly difficult to engage actively in the affairs of the Labour party and its local branches, of nationalized industries, and of trade unions.

Critics within the Labour party assert that a socialist society should keep the door open to responsible participation by all citizens. The Labour party, like the Conservative party, is in danger of developing into a party oligarchy which values party discipline above free political criticism. Nationalized industries have failed to overcome their workers' feeling of frustration with regard to their influence on industry affairs. The consumers' councils have also never quite fitted into the operations of the nationalized industries. The apathy of workers and consumers is matched by that of trade union members who do not attend local union meetings and who feel remote from their national union executives. Today, many thousands of trade union members are affiliated with the Labour party through their trade unions not because they actively support socialism, but because they have not bothered to disassociate themselves formally from the Labour party. Collective membership in the Labour party through trade unions may strengthen the party financially, but it does make for an indifferent party membership.

According to the interpretation of the members of the Socialist Union, a group of Labour party members organized in 1951 to restate the principles of British socialism, too many socialists have in the past acted on the assumption that "given only the right sort of machinery—in government, industrial organisation and in social life generally—the good society would come into being."[13] The Socialist Union believed that the Labour party could no longer afford to act on this assumption. What was needed above all was an education that was designed to nourish the "will for responsible participation." The Socialist Union concluded that "We could content ourselves with full employment, social security and a minimum standard for all, supplemented by more refrigerators and television sets. The very fact that men are not content with this alone points to the pent-up indealism within them. Socialism has in its trust the key which will release the great creative energies still so often dormant in humanity." The Labour party is playing a big gamble in assuming that the majority of the British voters are now prepared "to end the social inequalities and educational anomalies" of the current British society and to call for the planned, classless society promised in Labour's 1974 political manifesto, *Let Us Work Together—Labour's Way Out of the Crisis.*

The Nature of Scandinavian Socialism

Unique among the Western European socialist movements, Scandinavian socialism has found a more successful political expression than has the socialism of the United Kingdom, West Germany, France, Italy, and other Western European countries. In these countries, the socialist parties have not yet succeeded in becoming a major political force with the ability to take over the reins of government for extended periods of time, as has been the case in Norway, Sweden, and Denmark. Socialist governments have been in power in both Norway and Sweden almost continuously since the early 1930s; they have had considerable success in winning governmental control in Denmark in the same period. Although the Scandinavian socialist

---
[12] R. H. S. Crossman, *Socialism and the New Despotism*, Fabian Tract 298, London, The Fabian Society, 1956, pp. 5–7.
[13] The Socialist Union, *Socialism, A New Statement of Principles*, London, Lincolns-Prager (Publishers) Ltd., 1952, p. 62.

parties usually have not enjoyed clear parliamentary majorities, except in Norway, they have been strong enough politically to wield great influence and to succeed in reshaping significantly the social and economic structures of the Scandinavian countries. These countries cannot yet be described as fully socialist, since they continue to preserve many of the basic features of the private enterprise system. However, Norway, Sweden, and Denmark have been altered enough under socialist direction to be described as socialist rather than capitalist in essence. This is especially true of both Norway and Sweden.

It is the experimentation with democratic partial or limited socialism that makes the Scandinavian countries the object of great interest today. The experiment is of significance for a number of reasons. First, it shows how different democratic socialism is in theory and practice. What is now developing in Norway, Denmark, and Sweden is far removed from the full socialism written and dreamed about by the socialist theoreticians of the late nineteenth and early twentieth centuries. Second, many new nations, such as India, Sri Lanka, Israel, and some of the new African nations, show a deep interest in a moderate and limited form of socialism. Such nations may find much that is useful in the Scandinavian experience with national economic planning as they seek to develop their own economies. The third reason why current Scandinavian economic experimentation is significant derives from the fact that the Scandinavian economies have preserved much of the private enterprise system. Consequently, some of their experimentation may indicate new ways of handling the problems of a capitalist system like the American economic system. Capitalist nations of the West, which show little evidence of becoming socialist, may still learn something from the Scandinavian experiment about the ways of coordinating private and public economic policies with the aim of achieving sustained economic growth and full employment with price stability. Since economic experimentation shows no sign of coming to an end in the Scandinavian countries, it would not be surprising if these countries continue for some time to be a unique economic and social laboratory of worldwide interest.

Scandinavian socialism has for many years emphasized the importance of noneconomic goals and of the need to open the door to a larger share of the nation's cultural benefits for the working population.[14] Now that socialism in Norway, Sweden, and Denmark has succeeded in providing the people with a widely shared economic prosperity and that there is reason to believe the standard of living will continue to rise in the future, interest in socialist circles is turning from economic to noneconomic problems, especially to the task of creating a cultural democracy that is solidly based on both economic and political democracies.

Scandinavian socialists point out that the betterment of the material conditions of the working population has never been the main goal of socialism, even though it was the leading problem in Scandinavia from 1880 to 1939. The ultimate goal of socialism is the political, economic, and cultural emancipation of humanity. Today, this broad goal of human emancipation calls for a new appraisal of where the emphasis should be placed in the effort to create a truly socialist society. The outcome of this appraisal by the leading Scandinavian socialist theoreticians is that a truly cultural democracy can be secured only by providing an education that will give to each individual a personal sense of joint responsibility for the efficient functioning of society and an opportunity to develop up to

[14] C. Christiansen, "The Cultural Demand of Social Democracy," *The Way to Democracy and Socialism (Vejen Til Demokratie og Socialisme)*, Copenhagen, 1945, pp. 239-245.

the limits of his personal capacities. As it has been expressed by Torolf Elster, a well-known Norwegian socialist theoretician:

The only alternative is then the mobilizing of all intellectual powers. . . . The task is to create a higher grade of consciousness such that we can cooperate in freedom to solve our problems. This is socialism . . . to organize society so that it stimulates all to develop themselves, and it creates in them a sense of personal responsibility . . . to secure for all a general and technical education up to the limit of their personal capacities. In this manner we shall effectively break down class divisions. Today it is education . . . that draws the deepest lines between individuals. It is around education that the question of human rights and human value is concentrated. . . . This leads to the same thing: education which is the central consideration in the socialism of our times. . . . Thus the two main tasks fuse together the technical and the cultural revolutions. This becomes the content of socialism in our time.[15]

The technological revolution of the twentieth century is giving Scandinavia a highly complicated society. There is a great danger that the individual worker will become what the Norwegians call a *fagidiot,* i.e., a technically competent person who, however, lacks any adequate social vision, sense of social responsibility, or awareness of his role in society and so is not a truly free individual. The big problem of the future, in the opinion of present-day leaders of Norwegian socialism, will be to combine freedom and order in the planned socialist society. Unless great care is taken, the complicated economy of the future may reduce people to mere "means of production" who are not responsible for the management of the nation's economy and who do not as a group control its future development. The ultimate task is to combine individual freedom and social solidarity so that the gains of collective action may be achieved without losing the freedom of the individual to choose his way of life, his occupation, and his cultural goals.[16]

What will make the union of personal freedom and social solidarity possible in the opinion of the Norwegian socialists is an improved and extended educational system which will not only remove the barriers between manual workers and the academic and technical elite, but will also provide both general and technical educational opportunities for individuals at all levels of personal capacity. In the cultural democracy envisioned by the Norwegian socialists, education will provide the link between freedom and social order or solidarity. Education will enable the individual to work out his own way of life and, at the same time, play a vital role in the people's control of Norway's economic and social development.

Scandinavian socialism was strongly Marxian in outlook when it was established early in the third quarter of the nineteenth century. Since the Scandinavian socialist parties soon became dominated by a reformist majority, it was not long before they became gradualist and constitutional in outlook and in action. By the late 1920s the aim of Scandinavian socialism was no longer to convert Scandinavia into a working-class state but rather into a "people's home." The goal of the socialists was still a socialist transformation of society, but not in the sense of a "liberation of the exploited classes."[17] In making this significant change in its approach to the problems of capitalism and its reconstruction, each Scandinavian socialist party has ceased to be a class party *(klasseparti)* and has become instead a people's party *(folkparti),* which draws its support from members of the middle

---

[15] T. Elster, *Socialism before the Year 2000 (Socialismen Foran År 2000),* Oslo, The Norwegian Labor Party, 1956, pp. 12-14.

[16] The Norwegian Labor Party, *A Cultural Program for Debate (Et Kulturprogram Til Debatt),* Oslo, 1956, pp. 7-10.

[17] The Swedish Social Democratic Labor Party, *The Programme of The Swedish Social Democratic Labor Party,* Stockholm, 1945, p. 3.

class as well as from workers, farmers, and fishermen.

The Future of Scandinavian Socialism

Scandinavian socialism appears for the time being to have reached something of a plateau in its evolution. Looking back over several decades, one can see a long period of development from the time when the Social Democrats were a militant minority party in the 1880s to the present day in which the Social Democratic party is the dominant single political organization in the Scandinavian countries. The prospect for the immediate future is that the Scandinavian Social Democrats will continue to be the main single political force in Denmark, Norway, and Sweden, but that they will probably not move forward to a much stronger political position than the one they now occupy. It will be difficult in prosperous economic circumstances to expand the membership of the Social Democratic party, which originated as a party of economic and social protest. Now that the major political and economic problems in the Scandinavian countries have been solved or reduced to tolerable proportions, much of the early enthusiasm associated with Scandinavian Social Democracy as a reform movement has disappeared. The dry rot of success presents grave problems to the Scandinavian Social Democrats, as it does to any reformist group that has succeeded in coping with many of the major problems that once aroused the enthusiasm of the group's members in the early period of the reform movement. The Scandinavian Social Democrats are finding it increasingly difficult to hold the interest and allegiance of young voters who until recently knew nothing but the prosperity of the period since the end of the Second World War. A society in which the number of blue-collar workers is growing less rapidly than the number of white-collar workers presents serious organizational problems to both the trade union movement and to the Social Democratic or Labor party. The programs of the Scandinavian Social Democratic parties that remain to be carried out are the very ones that would tend to reduce class consciousness and quite possibly to make the "labor class" much less of a vigorous political and economic force than it has been up to now in the Scandinavian countries.

The left wing of the Scandinavian socialist movement seeks to bring new life to this movement today by emphasizing the need to make further advances in the areas of industrial and cultural democracy. It is recommended that efforts be made to democratize private industry still further by devising ways of giving labor a more effective voice in the management of private industry. This means going beyond the joint production committees in the factories to establish some kind of joint industrial councils that would enable organized labor to exert more influence on the general functioning of private industry. Of equal concern to the more militant Scandinavian socialists is the need to come closer to a cultural democracy in which individuals would have more opportunities to share in the nation's cultural advantages. From the point of view of the left wing of the Scandinavian socialist movement, one of the main defects of the present-day Scandinavian social system is the preservation of a class system based upon inherited wealth, social position, and unequal educational opportunities.

Like all European countries, but to a lesser degree than most of them, Denmark, Norway, and Sweden have what is called *the Establishment*. This is a section of the population that enjoys inherited cultural, economic, and political advantages that are not available to the bulk of the population. One of the major factors that contributes to the preservation of class differences in the Scandinavian and other Western European countries is inequality of educational opportunities. Children of low-income families, especially those living in remote rural areas, frequently do not have the educational opportunities available to the children of higher income urban families. While much has been done under the social welfare programs of the Scandinavian countries to make secondary and university education more available to the children of low-income rural families, educational opportunities are still unequal enough to make it possible for class distinctions and class advantages to constitute a major cultural problem in the eyes of many Scandinavian Social Democrats.

In the years 1963–1976, there has been a considerable decline in the voters' support of the Swedish Social Democratic party.[18] The statistics in Table 12-7 show that the voter support of this party fell from 48.5 percent in 1964 to 43.6 percent in 1976. The Center (formerly Agrarian) party in the same period increased its voter support from 15.0 to 24.6 percent of the total votes. The latter party has taken advantage of a growing dissatisfaction with trends in the Swedish industrial society. With its "Big is bad" approach, the party champions small business and the "little urban person." The Center party, which formerly drew its main strength from farmers, is now receiving much support from salaried workers and small business people in the towns and villages of the rural districts, which are losing their industries to the large urban centers in southern Sweden. It is also receiving support from the liberals and members of the middle class who deplore the decline of rural Sweden.[19]

[18] Anthony Howard, "Sweden: The Fading Dream," *New Statesman*, Vol. 81, June 4, 1971, pp. 756–757; and Thomas Munch-Petersen, "Sweden's Lost Consensus," *New Statesman*, Vol. 86, Sept. 7, 1973, pp. 307–308.

[19] For a discussion of the changing Swedish electorate, see Bo Särlvik, "Sweden: The Social Bases of the Parties in a Developmental Perspective," in Richard Rose (ed.) *Electoral Behavior: A Comparative Handbook*, New York: Collier Macmillan, 1974, pp. 389–399. For similar developments in Norway, see Henry Valen and Stein Rokkan, "Norway: Conflict Structure and Mass Politics in a European Periphery," Richard Rose, *op. cit.*, pp. 332–335; and Sven Groennings, "Patterns, Strategies, and Payoffs in Norwegian Coalition Formation," Sven Groennings, E. W. Kelley, Michael Leiserson (eds.), *The Study of Coalition Behavior*, New York: Holt, Rinehart and Winston, 1970, pp. 60–79.

Table 12-7
Swedish Political Party Voter Support, 1964 and 1976

	Percent of total votes		Parliamentary seats	
	1964	1976	1964[1]	1976[2]
Parties:				
Social Democratic Labor Party	48.5	43.6	113	152
Center (formerly Agrarian) Party	15.0	24.6	35	86
Moderate Union (formerly Conservative) Party	13.7	15.7	32	55
Liberal Party	18.0	11.2	42	39
Communist Party	4.8	4.9	11	17
Totals	100.0	100.0	233	349

[1] Lower house only.

[2] Both houses now one unit (unicameral).

Sources: *The Europa Year Book, 1976*, Europa Publications; and *Current Sweden*, The Swedish Institute.

The Center party appeals to the nation's youth who display a growing aversion to industrial work, to low-income unskilled workers who resent the dehumanizing environment of large-scale industry and the over-centralization of trade union activity, and to the alienated citizens living in high-rise apartments in cities or in communities on the fringes of these cities. The Center party recommends the decentralization of the government and industry, lower taxes, and the support of a "green wave" that would bring people closer to nature. It is not clear how this party would reverse the trends in government and industry in order to give the people a greater sense of contact and control over those who rule them. Nevertheless, the populism of the Center party makes a growing appeal to the large and growing section of the population that is unhappy with the tensions of the modern industrialized society.

Similar trends have appeared in the political and economic activities of Norway and Denmark. In the 1973 election in Norway, the Labor party polled 25 percent less than its usual one million votes, and managed to remain in office only with the votes of the radical Socialist Election League, which includes a few communist representatives. The dissatisfaction with the industrial state led the Norwegian voters to repudiate the proposal to join the European Common Market. In Denmark, the Social Democrats were swept from office in December 1973 by a coalition of small parties whose only unifying principle was widespread dissatisfaction with current industrial and government trends.

The reaction of the Scandinavian socialists to their loss of public favor in the past decade has been to take account of the prevailing wind that is blowing in the direction of more concern with the feelings, protection, and welfare of the individual. More decision-making power is to be given to workers by enabling them to have representatives on company boards of directors. Work is to be humanized by giving workers more control over work conditions. The Swedish Confederation of Trade Unions (LO) at its 1971 Annual Congress made the improvement of the working environment one of its principal concerns and emphasized the growing importance of job satisfaction, security, and safety. There is a new concern among Scandinavian socialists with regard to the protection of the individual from the overorganized and overconcentrated social system. Consumer protection is to be enlarged by establishing the office of Consumer Ombudsman, as was done in Sweden in 1971. Laws are being passed to protect personal privacy by curbing the use of data banks. The Social Democrats in the Scandinavian countries are becoming more concerned about what the people actually want from their economic system. What they currently want appears to be less organization and less concentration. More attention is also being paid to regional development and preservation of the natural environment.

Since the 1950s, the Social Democrats have accepted the industrial trends that have depopulated rural regions and concentrated industry in a few urban areas without much critical review of these developments. These economic trends have been rather uncritically and blindly accepted because they have contributed to greater economic efficiency and labor productivity. Now that a growing section of the population outside of the supporters of the socialist parties has come to question the consequences of continued industrialization, the socialists have become concerned, because they have lost the floating or marginal voters in large numbers.[20]

---

[20] If the politics of compromise is to be successful from the point of view of the socialists, they must not antagonize marginal voter groups as they have been doing in recent years. See Herbert Tingsten, "Stability and Vitality in Swedish Democracy," *Political Quarterly*, Vol. XXVI, April 1955, pp. 140-151; Nils Stjernquist, "Sweden: Stability or Deadlock," in Robert A. Dahl, *Political Oppositions in Western Democracies*, New Haven: Yale

The socialists in Norway, Sweden, and Denmark hope to offset these adverse political trends by paying more attention to the welfare of the individual in the planned economy.

At the same time that the Scandinavian socialists have responded to the need to reduce voter alienation by attacking some of the adverse consequences of the process of industrialization, they have also felt a need to enlarge their control of the nation's economy. Unlike their British counterparts, the Scandinavian socialists are not much interested in the further nationalization of industry. Emphasis has been placed instead upon extending the public control of private industry by having the government acquire shares in major private companies with funds taken from the national supplementary pension scheme.

Consideration is also being given, as in Norway, to the taking over by the government of the private banking system. A more effective control of the allocation of bank credit would greatly increase the government's ability to provide guidance of the private business system, since credit could be more effectively rationed in accordance with the goals of the national plans. A stricter control of private business and banking could very well lead to a strengthening of the bureaucratic centralization and concentration tendencies that have been deplored with considerable success by the nonsocialist parties in recent years. The Scandinavian socialists are confronted by the dilemma that arises from the fact that more socialism opens the door to the possibility of greater concentration of government and economic activity accompanied by possibly greater citizen alienation.

The Swedish socialists have also responded to their loss of voter support by emphasizing the need to secure greater economic equality.

University Press, 1966, pp. 142–146; and Leon D. Epstein, *Political Parties in Western Democracies*, New York: Praeger, 1967, pp. 285–288.

A government official commission set up in 1971 reported that one-third of the working population and 60 percent of the retired workers were below what was considered by the government to be the poverty line.[21] This study pointed up the fact that Sweden is still far from being a genuine egalitarian society and is not the classless paradise sought by Swedish socialism. Olof Palme, the new leader of the Swedish Social Democratic party after 1969, launched an equality crusade which asked the middle- and top-income receivers to hold back in their claims for higher incomes, while workers at the lower-income levels were brought up. It was felt that this was necessary because the social security system benefits in Sweden have not yet eliminated poverty.

While Sweden's national income has continued to expand, the proportion going to the classes at the bottom of the income scale has remained too small, in the opinion of many members of the Social Democratic Labor party. The attempt on the part of the Palme government to reduce income differentials and to create more equality was unfavorably received by many white-collar and upper-income blue-collar workers, who objected to the further paring down of income differentials, and who wished to preserve a hierarchical income distribution that is not acceptable to much of the socialist leadership. The effort of the Social Democrats to retain or to win the support of the low-income groups with the campaign for "increased equality" could very well result in the loss of support among middle-income voters.

Democratic Socialism and the Welfare State

The democratic socialist countries have played a prominent role in the establishment

[21] Anthony Howard, *op. cit.*, p. 757.

of the modern welfare state, which antedates the taking over of their governments by the Social Democratic parties in the 1930s. Before 1929, Liberal parties in a number of Western European countries under pressure from the trade unions began to lay the foundations of the welfare state with early forms of pension and unemployment systems. Before World War I, the United Kingdom and Sweden had introduced national pension plans, while the United Kingdom and Norway had adopted unemployment insurance plans on a national basis. The main thrust towards the welfare state, however, was not to come until the 1930s, when unemployment insurance, pension, health, and children's allowance systems were widely installed by both socialist and capitalist countries.

After 1929, the Social Democratic parties became major factors in the political systems of Sweden, Norway, and Denmark and introduced a new era in the development of the Scandinavian welfare state.[22] This new era was marked by a shift from providing on a charitable basis for the harsh consequences of private economic activity to adopting a more preventive approach that attempted to remove the causes of poverty, poor family living conditions, and other types of human distress. Working in coalition with Liberal and Agrarian parties, the Social Democratic parties embarked upon a program for the reconstruction of capitalism that was expected to eliminate many of the deficiencies of that system.

Since 1945, the Scandinavian welfare state has been enlarged within the framework of a full-employment, national-planning program. Now that the problem of maintaining full employment has been met to a large extent, the Scandinavian social welfare program has emphasized three goals: (1) the maintenance of an adequate flow of income to individuals and families in all circumstances; (2) the prevention of human distress and inadequacies such as illness and limited personal development; and (3) the rehabilitation of the incapacitated and the victims of technological unemployment. These three goals are now being achieved by measures in the following fields: (1) family welfare; (2) workers' protection and welfare; (3) social housing policy; (4) health, old age, and disability insurance; and (5) social assistance.

Family welfare is one of the major concerns of the Scandinavian welfare state, since it is in this field that measures can be readily taken to prevent individuals from becoming social and economic liabilities to the community. The objective of the family welfare policy is to get the family to function in such a manner that all its members will have an equal opportunity to develop their potentials to the fullest. Family and worker welfare is closely associated with the program to provide acceptable housing for all individuals. This program emphasizes: (1) making an adequate supply of dwelling units available to all income levels; (2) constructing dwelling units with enough rooms to house large families; (3) reducing land and building costs; (4) planning of building sites and exterior design; (5) making dwelling units more livable by adhering to interior space standards; (6) making adequate funds available through a loan-subsidy system to finance the social housing policy; and (7) providing satisfactory housing for the aged and for the disabled.

The Scandinavian countries have made very considerable progress in meeting their housing problems. The obligation to house all people decently is now widely accepted as a

---

[22] The evolution of the Scandinavian welfare state is traced in the Ministries of Social Affairs in Denmark, Finland, Iceland, Norway, and Sweden, *Freedom and Welfare, Social Patterns in the Northern Countries of Europe*, Copenhagen, 1953; Wilfrid Fleisher, *Sweden, the Welfare State*, New York: John Daly, 1956; and Henning Friis, *Scandinavia between East and West*, Ithaca: Cornell University Press, 1950.

national goal, which is incorporated in the five-year and longer-term national plans. Since the 1930s, slums have been eliminated. Annual housing quotas supported by financial priorities have been established, and high exterior and interior construction standards have been rigorously enforced. The livability of houses has been considerably increased, and building costs and rents have been kept within reasonable family budgetary limits. In spite of this progress, however, the Scandinavian housing problem persists. Overcrowding is still very much of a problem in the large cities as the flight from the rural areas continues to swell the urban population. Also, rising real incomes have led to increased demands not only for more dwelling units but also for larger units.

The Scandinavian countries are noted for their well-developed national health insurance and pension schemes, which provide medical and hospital care from birth to death, income maintenance during sickness, and security against poverty for the aged and the disabled. The five major features of the Scandinavian national health insurance schemes are: (1) sizable financial contributions by the insured members; (2) public hospitals; (3) freedom of doctors to remain in private practice; (4) local control and administration of the system by self-governing health insurance societies under general central-government supervision; and (5) cash benefits to sustain the family income during sickness.

A number of factors have contributed to the popular acceptance of the Scandinavian public-health insurance schemes. Since the medical profession from the first was deeply involved in both government-sponsored medical service and the activities of the private nonprofit sickness benefit societies, no strong opposition to the establishment of national health insurance schemes came from the medical profession. The fact that government intervention in the provision of medical care has not impaired the excellence and worldwide renown of Scandinavian medical service has served to strengthen public acceptance of compulsory health insurance. Medical research has been generously supported by government and private agencies, and hospitals have generally set high standards of performance. As a result, the Scandinavian infant-mortality rates are among the lowest in the world (9.2 per 1,000 live births in Sweden in 1974), and the average duration of life is among the longest in the world (71.9 years for males in Sweden in 1972). The major deficiencies of the Scandinanvian public-health insurance schemes are inadequate dental care and insufficient hospital facilities for psychiatric and alcoholic treatments.

Old-age pension schemes have had an important role in the Scandinavian social security systems since the early years of the present century. In the 1960s, the Scandinavian countries instituted benefits which supplemented their basic national pension plans. Sweden led the way in reforming its pension system by adopting a supplementary pension scheme in January 1963, which is financed entirely by employers. The sum of the two pension payments is equal to about two-thirds of the average yearly income earned by a worker. This is a considerable improvement over the national pension benefits, which before 1963 gave a single pensionor only about 25 percent of an average worker's income, and a married couple about 40 percent. Sweden's progress in reforming its old-age pension scheme aroused a great deal of interest in Norway and Denmark, where similar but less generous supplementary pension schemes have been adopted.

The Scandinavian welfare state has set an example that has been widely followed in the capitalist Western countries since 1929. France, West Germany, Holland, and other Continental countries, which had begun to construct their social security systems early in this century, followed the Scandinavian countries in enlarging the scope and benefits of their social security systems.[23] The United States, which was a latecomer in the area of welfare capitalism, did not provide for a national unemployment insurance system until 1935; in that year a national pension scheme was also inaugurated. It still lags badly in the area of national health service. In 1965, a national health insurance system was established to provide free hospitalization only for pensioners age 65 and over, with other medical services covered only under a voluntary health insurance program financed by pensioners. Unlike many Western European countries, the United States has no children's allowance program. Japan's national social security program was developed mainly after World War II, except for a national health insurance scheme that was established in 1938. A Japanese national pension system was adopted in 1941 and an unemployment insurance system in 1947. Like the United States, Japan has no national children's allowance program. In spite of its low social security expenditures and congested urban living conditions, Japan has one of the lowest infant-mortality rates (11.3 in 1973) in the world. Table 12–8 shows that Sweden and the Netherlands are among the countries with the lowest infant-mortality rates and the longest life expectancies.

In the advanced industrial societies, welfare expenditures take up a large and growing part of Gross National Product. Table 12–8 shows that in Sweden and the Netherlands 21.8 percent of Gross National Product is absorbed by social security expenditures, which include expenditures for pensions, unemployment insurance, work-injury payments, health insurance, family allowances, and public welfare assistance.[24] France, West Germany, Belgium, and Canada are not far behind, with expenditures of this type between 18 and 19 percent of GNP. The United Kingdom, the United States, and Japan are far behind, with social security expenditures of only 12.5, 10.8, and 5.9 percent respectively. Low expenditures in these countries are attributable in part to low benefit payments (the United Kingdom), the lack of children's allowances (the United States and Japan), and limited health insurance (the United States).

The capitalist economies have felt it necessary to compete with the democratic socialist economies in providing protection from the insecurities of the private enterprise system. A major factor in preserving the capitalist system in France, West Germany, Holland, Belgium, Canada, and Italy has been the welfare systems, which have been greatly improved since 1929.[25] Today in the advanced capitalist economies, as in the industrialized democratic socialist economies, workers are generally provided with a basic minimum of protection from the insecurities of economic life. Even so, much remains to be done in both types of economies to assure workers a life of high quality. This problem far transcends the problem of providing economic and social security.

---

[23] The welfare programs of these and other countries are summarized in U.S. Department of Health, Education, and Welfare, *Social Security Programs throughout the World*, Washington, D.C., 1973.

[24] U.S. Department of Health, Education, and Welfare, *National Expenditures on Social Security in Selected Countries, 1968 and 1971*, Research and Statistics Note No. 29, Washington D.C., Oct. 18, 1974, p. 2.

[25] Welfare programs, including housing, are analyzed in Joint Economic Committee, *Economic Policies and Practices, Guaranteed Minimum Income Programs Used by Governments of Selected Countries*, Paper No. 11, Washington, D.C., 1968; and U.S. Department of Housing and Urban Development, *Urban Land Policy: Selected Aspects of European Experience* (1969) and *Urban Growth Policies in Six European Countries* (1972), Washington, D.C.

Table Table 12-8
Social Security Expenditures, Life Expectancy, and Infant Mortality Rates in Selected Countries

	Social security expenditures as % of GNP, 1971	Life expectancy at birth, males	Infant mortality per 1,000 live births, 1972
Sweden	21.8	71.9 (1967)	11.1
Netherlands	21.8	70.7 (1970)	11.4
West Germany	18.7	67.6 (1966–1968)	22.5
France	18.7	67.6 (1969)	16.0
Canada	18.6	68.8 (1965–1967)	17.5
Belgium	18.3	67.6 (1963–1966)	19.8
United Kingdom	12.5	68.6 (1968–1970)	17.2
United States	10.8	67.1 (1970)	18.5
Japan	5.9	69.1 (1968)	12.4

Sources: U.S. Department of Health, Education, and Welfare, *Research and Statistics Note*, No. 29, 1974; United Nations, *Demographic Yearbook*, 1971, and *Population and Vital Statistics Report*; and World Health Organization, *World Health Statistics Report*.

The Western Planned and Unplanned Economies: An Evaluation

A number of important observations can be made on the basis of an analysis of the economic indicators relating to the nine Western industrial nations and Japan which are presented in Table 12-9. These countries may be classified either as capitalist and democratic socialist or as planned and unplanned countries. Since all but two of the ten nations have capitalist economies, a more useful comparison may be made between the planned and the unplanned economies. A comparison of the planned economies of France, Japan, Netherlands, Norway, and Sweden and the unplanned economies of Canada, Italy, United Kingdom, West Germany, and the United States reveals the following developments in these countries.

In the decade of the 1960s, per capita economic growth in the five planned economies, as Table 12-9 shows, averaged 5.2 percent a year and 3.4 percent a year in the five unplanned economies. The annual increase in the volume of exports in the planned economies was 11.6 percent, and 9.4 percent in the unplanned economies. The only significant differences in the economic experiences of the planned and unplanned economies in the period 1960–1970 related to unemployment and inflation. Since the planned economies tend to be of a more high-pressure nature than the unplanned economies, it would be expected that unemployment would be lower and inflation would be higher in the planned economies than in the unplanned economies. The economic indicators in Table 12-9 support these expectations. The average annual unemployment rate in 1960–1970 in the five planned economies was 2.0 percent, as compared with 3.9 percent in the five unplanned economies. In the same period, consumer prices increased annually 4.5 percent in the planned countries and 3.5 percent in the

Table Table 12-9
Economic Indicators in Ten Democratic Unplanned and Planned Countries, 1960-1970

		Average annual growth rate in percent					
	Per capita GNP (1970) in U.S. dollars	Per capita GNP	Consumer prices	Hourly earnings in industry	Output per man-hour in manufacturing	Volume of exports	Unemployment rate
United States	4,760	3.2	3.0	4.7	3.0	6.6	4.7
Canada	3,700	3.6	2.8	5.6	4.2	10.8	5.6
West Germany	2,930	3.5	2.9	9.4	5.8	11.0	0.8
United Kingdom[1]	2,270	2.2	4.1	7.4	3.6	5.3	4.6
Italy	1,760	4.6	4.6	11.1	6.1	13.2	3.7
Sweden	4,040	3.8	4.4	10.2	7.3	8.3	2.2
France	3,100	4.6	3.9	9.5	5.7	10.2	2.5
Norway	2,860	4.1	4.6	8.1	5.6	9.3	2.1
Netherlands	2,430	3.9	4.3	11.9	6.7	12.1	2.2
Japan	1,920	9.6	5.1	14.3	10.8	17.8	1.2

[1]The United Kingdom is included among the unplanned countries because national planning was never well established there in the 1960s.

Sources: IMF, *International Financial Statistics*, May 1974; and United States Department of Labor, *Monthly Labor Review*, Nov. 1973.

unplanned countries. An examination of wage-rate increases and unit labor cost developments shows that, as would be anticipated, in the five high-pressure planned economies hourly earnings and unit labor costs in industry increased at higher annual rates than in the five low-pressure unplanned economies.

As a group, all ten countries except the United Kingdom enjoyed a good economic performance in the decade of the 1960s. The United Kingdom suffered from low economic growth and high unemployment, along with considerable inflation and relatively poor exports. The Japanese economy performed very well, with a per capita GNP growth rate close to 10 percent, a very low unemployment rate of 1.2 percent, and an annual increase in its volume of exports (17.8 percent) that was double the average annual increase in the volume of exports of the nine planned and unplanned Western industrial economies. Japan had considerably more inflation of consumer prices (5.1 percent) than did the Western industrial economies (average rate of 3.8 percent). In spite of this domestic inflation, Japan remained highly competitive in the world's export markets. The socialist economies of Norway and Sweden performed about as well as the planned capitalist economies of France and the Netherlands, and somewhat better on the average than the four unplanned capitalist economies of the United States, Canada, West Germany, and Italy.

In the early 1970s, there was increasing evidence that the performance of the ten Western and Japanese industrial economies might not be as good as it had been during the 1960s. In 1970-1973, strong inflationary trends in these countries were accompanied by a tendency for economic growth rates to decline. In West Germany, Sweden, Italy, the United Kingdom, and Japan, the annual increases in Gross National Product in 1970–1973 were lower than in the 1960s. The United States, which had been growing at the annual rate of 4.5 percent in the 1960s, grew at the rate of 2.9 percent in the years 1970–1973. In the same years, the Japanese annual economic growth rate fell from 11.1 percent to 8.5 percent, while the Swedish annual growth rate declined from 4 percent in the 1960s to 2.4 percent in 1970–1973. In the ten industrial economies analyzed in Table 12–9, consumer prices, which had increased at an average annual rate of 3.9 percent in the decade of the 1960s, increased at the rate of 8.7 percent in the early 1970s. In the same countries, hourly earnings in industry that had risen at an average annual rate of 9.2 percent in the decade of the 1960s increased at the annual rate of 15.1 percent in 1970–1973.

Also, in these ten countries, the price and wage inflation of the early 1970s, which was in part due to the world scarcity of food supplies, was worsened in 1974 by the large increases in the price of crude oil posted by the Middle East and other oil-producing areas. A number of the developed countries, such as the United Kingdom, France, Italy, and Japan, and many less developed nations soon suffered large deficits in their current balances of international payments because of their large expenditures for imported oil. The international monetary system, which had become seriously deranged before the 1974 oil crisis, was plunged into further difficulties in that year. By 1976, it was quite clear that both the unplanned and the planned Western industrial economies would have to develop some new economic and financial arrangements, if the world's major economic and social problems of the final quarter of the twentieth century were to be dealt with successfully.

If the economic growth rates of the 1960s in the advanced industrial countries were to be projected into the future, per capita gross domestic product in Japan, Sweden, and the Soviet Union would overtake per capita gross domestic product in the United States in sixteen, twenty-nine, and forty years, respectively. Economic growth has been particularly rapid in recent decades in Japan. By 1971, output per man-hour in the Japanese iron and steel industry was approximately the same as in the United States. Table 12–10 shows that in the years 1964–1971 Japan, as the result of the widespread use of oxygen furnaces, outstripped both West Germany and France in enlarging output per man-hour in its iron and steel industry and in catching up with the United States; the United Kingdom during this period showed almost no relative progress.

The United States continues to lead the world in expenditures on research and development and in both computer installations and the use of numerically controlled machine tools. In 1971, the United States had one electronic digital computer in use for each 2,353 of its population, whereas there was one computer for each 10,489 of the population in Japan, for each 7,952 in the United Kingdom, and for each 7,569 in West Germany.[26] Supporting this new capital equipment are the much larger research and development expenditures in the United States. In 1969, these expenditures in the United States were $130 per person; they were $50, $45, and $15 in West Germany, Canada, and Japan, respectively.[27] Much of the progress in other countries depends upon borrowing the

[26] Bureau of Labor Statistics, *Productivity and the Economy,* Washington: U.S. Government Printing Office, 1973, p. 55.

[27] National Science Foundation, *National Patterns of R & D Resources, Funds and Manpower in the United States, 1953–1972,* Washington: U.S. Government Printing Office, 1971, p. 3.

Table 12-10
Relative Output per Man-hour in the American, Japanese, British, French, and West German Iron and Steel Industries, 1964–1971

	Index of output per man-hour: 1964 = 100		Relative output per man-hour: U.S. = 100[1]	
	1964	1971	1964	1971
United States	100	108.6	100	100
Japan	100	234.2	43–54	93–116
United Kingdom	100	110.6	46–50	47–51
France	100	147.6	48–51	65–70
West Germany	100	137.0	54–63	68–80

[1] The data for Japan and the Western European countries are presented in terms of ranges, with high and low estimates because of data gaps and limitations.

Source: Bureau of Labor Statistics, USDL, *Productivity and the Economy*, 1973, p. 14.

industrial technology that is developed in the United States. In general, large-scale industries and large countries with rich resource endowments are in a better position than other countries to devote resources to scientific and technological advance. The European Economic Community could go far to improve the competitive position of its nine member countries with respect to technological advance, if it could more effectively combine the science policies and resources of these countries.

The Dynamics of Partial Democratic Socialism

The democratic socialist economies of Western Europe have evolved in response to such factors as scientific advance and technological change, which affect many different types of economic systems, and also in response to more specialized factors, such as ideological preferences. Although both the Western capitalist and socialist economies are subject to the same basic technological and economic trends, reactions by various economic interest groups to these trends reflect ideological choices. A government dominated by big business and the middle class, as in the United States, the United Kingdom when the Conservative party is in office, and France, will not take the same position on major economic and social issues and their future development as would a government strongly influenced by organized labor and low-income voters, as in Norway, Sweden, and the Netherlands. Some analysts of the Western mixed economies seek to avoid ideological issues, asserting that it is fruitless to discuss whether an economy of the Swedish or Norwegian type is capitalistic (liberal) or socialistic.[28]

Those who adopt this position fail to view the mixed economy as a developing process whose future may be greatly influenced by ideological preferences. For example, the

---

[28] See, for example, the views of the Swedish economist Assar Lindbeck, presented in *Svensk ekonomisk politik, Problem och teorier under efterkrigstiden* (*Swedish Economic Policy, Problems and Theories during the Postwar Period*), Stockholm: Bokforlaget Aldus/Bonniers, 1968, pp. 194–195.

strong trends towards social and economic equality with an emphasis on eliminating wide disparities in wealth ownership, political power, and educational opportunities, which one now sees in Norway, Sweden, and the United Kingdom under the Labour party, are not duplicated in the United States, France, and other capitalist countries. The Western capitalist and socialist economies are similar in many respects, such as having a large public service sector, a strong interventionist economic policy, and private dominance on the production side; nevertheless, this convergence between the two types of mixed economies does not eliminate wide ideological differences. These differences are especially important in dealing with such questions as: where are the current economic and social trends going, and how should the nation endeavor to direct them? The exponents of democratic socialism in Western Europe deny that ideology is dead or that we have seen "The End of Ideology."[29] To the contrary, they assert that ideologies will continue to have a very important role to play in the dynamics of Western industrialism.

In Western advanced industrial economies, technological trends appear to favor the growth of big government, big business, big labor and the possible alienation of the "little urban person." The planned capitalism of France, the Netherlands, and Belgium, like the planned socialism of Norway, Sweden, and the United Kingdom, must cope with the same problem of protecting the individual from the bureaucratic controls of the highly centralized state. Even those countries that are not planned in any formal way, such as the United States, Canada, West Germany, and Great Britain under the Conservative party, must deal with the same issue. The Western democratic socialists are confronted with the additional question of how far the private enterprise system can be controlled or planned, and yet continue to function as a private system motivated by private profit seeking. In order to differentiate themselves from all the nonsocialist parties, the socialist parties in Britain, Norway, and Sweden are currently prepared to push further along the socialist path.

Where these efforts will lead, however, is not clear. As yet, the Western socialists do not advocate full socialism. Being less ideological than the socialists in Eastern Europe, the Western socialists are more prone to be pragmatic about the future of socialism. They do not believe that the dynamics of their socialism points inevitably in the direction of full socialism. Some of the extreme radical elements in the Western socialist parties do say that the ultimate goal should be full socialism and that these parties should energetically work towards this goal. The great majority of the members of the Western socialist parties, however, do not propose to work actively towards this goal. They appear to be willing to wait until events push them further along the socialist path, as events seem to have done in the United Kingdom, Norway, and Sweden in recent years.

The dynamics of socialism place heavy pressure on Western democratic socialists to secure a more equitable distribution of income and wealth. In the United Kingdom and the Scandinavian countries, the socialists have until now tolerated considerable inequalities in income and wealth distribution on the ground that high economic growth requires rewards in the form of these inequalities. Critics of British and Scandinavian socialism have declared that thus far the socialists have

---

[29] Daniel Bell, *The End of Ideology*, Glencoe, Ill.: The Free Press, 1960. Bell's title is poorly chosen, since he really meant to say that the exhaustion of old ideologies has led to a hunger among the young for new ones not yet formulated. For an explanation of this point, see Daniel Bell, *The Coming of Post-Industrial Society*, New York. Basic Books, 1973, p. 34 fn.

been more successful in developing "managerial capitalism" than genuine socialism.[30] The challenge to democratic socialism is to achieve economic growth with greater equality than now prevails in the United Kingdom, Norway, and Sweden. The question in the opinion of some socialists is: "Can the Labour movement now identify a progressive combination of growth and greater equality? It is the key question for this generation of socialists."[31] The quest for such a combination could very well induce Western democratic socialists to move much further along the socialist path than they have gone up to now.

The dynamics of democratic socialism raises issues that transcend the long-standing equity problem. The democratic socialist economies of the future will be called upon to give consideration to issues that up to now have been largely neglected. These include the failure of young people to fit into the elaborate "over-organized [socialist] society," the inadequate concern for women's rights, the excessive power that goes with concentrated private wealth, the elitist quality of higher education that delays the achievement of an egalitarian society, the growing job dissatisfaction in automated industries, and the lack of agreement among economic interest groups about the role of income differentials in a socialist society.[32]

Sweden's recent experience with the youth movement illustrates the problems that affluent socialist societies may have to meet in the future. Young people in Sweden have expressed deep concern about the growing materialism of their country and the excessive interest in high economic growth, the political power of large-scale private enterprises, their advertising practices, and their sales to nations with unacceptable race policies such as South Africa. Young people in Norway have pressed for a greater appreciation of the need for an environmental or ecological ethic that would prevent industrialism from lowering the quality of life. They were in part responsible for Norway's rejection of membership in the European Economic Community on the ground that the community overemphasized the values of an industrial society, and gave inadequate attention to the impact of industry on the natural and social environments. It remains to be seen how the Western democratic socialist societies will cope with these problems that are common to all affluent societies, and that were not anticipated by socialist theoreticians before the rise of the postindustrial society.

---

[30] John Hughes, "The Increase in Inequality," *New Statesman*, Vol. 76, Nov. 8, 1968, p. 626.

[31] *Ibid.*

[32] Socialist Sweden's problems are critically reviewed in Eli Ginzberg, "Sweden: Some Unanswered Questions," *The Public Interest*, Fall 1970, pp. 158–166.

Selected Bibliography

BELL, DANIEL. *The End of Ideology.* The Free Press, Glencoe, Ill., 1960.

CHRISTIANSEN, C. "The Cultural Demand of Social Democracy." *The Way to Democracy and Socialism (Vejen Til Demokratie og Socialisme),* Copenhagen, 1945.

COLE, G. D. H. *World Socialism Restated.* The New Statesman and Nation, London, 1956.

ELSTER, T. *Socialism before the Year 2000 (Socialismen Foran År 2000).* The Norwegian Labor Party, Oslo, 1956.

EPSTEIN, LEON D. *Political Parties in Western Democracies.* Praeger Publishers, Inc., New York, 1967.

FLEISHER, WILFRID. *Sweden, The Welfare State.* John Daly, New York, 1956.

FRIIS, HENNING. *Scandinavia between East and West.* Cornell University Press, Ithaca, 1950.

GINZBERG, ELI. "Sweden: Some Unanswered Questions." *The Public Interest,* Fall 1970, 158–166.

GROENNINGS, SVEN. "Patterns, Strategies, and Payoffs in Norwegian Coalition Formation." In *The Study of Coalition Behavior,* edited by Sven Groennings, E. W. Kelley, and Michael Leiserson. Holt, Rinehart and Winston, Inc., New York, 1970.

JOINT ECONOMIC COMMITTEE. *Economic Policies and Practices, Guaranteed Minimum Income Programs Used by Governments of Selected Countries.* Paper No. 11, Washington, D.C., 1968.

LINDBECK, ASSAR. *Svensk ekonomisk politik, Problem och teorier under efterkrigstiden (Swedish Economic Policy, Problems and Theories during the Postwar Period).* Bokforlaget Aldus/Bonniers, Stockholm, 1968.

Ministries of Social Affairs of Denmark, Finland, Iceland, Norway, and Sweden. *Freedom and Welfare, Social Patterns in the Northern Countries of Europe.* Copenhagen, 1953.

MORGAN, EDWARD V. *The Structure of Property Ownership in Great Britain.* Clarendon Press, Oxford, 1960.

NORWEGIAN LABOR PARTY. A Cultural Program for Debate *(Et Kulturprogram Til Debatt).* Oslo, 1956.

ORGANISATION FOR ECONOMIC CO-OPERATION AND DEVELOPMENT. *The Outlook for Economic Growth, A Summary Report on Experience, Prospects and Problems of Policy, 1960–1980.* Paris, May 1970.

SÄRLVIK, BO. "Sweden, The Social Bases of the Parties in a Developmental Perspective." In *Electoral Behavior: A Comparative Handbook,* edited by Richard Rose. Collier Macmillan, New York, 1974.

SWEDISH SOCIAL DEMOCRATIC LABOR PARTY. *The Programme of the Swedish Social Democratic Labor Party.* Stockholm, 1945.

U.S. DEPARTMENT OF HEALTH, EDUCATION, AND WELFARE. *National Expenditures on Social Security in Selected Countries, 1968 and 1971.* Research and Statistics Note No. 29, Washingtonp D.C., Oct. 18, 1974.

———. *Social Security Programs throughout the World.* Washington, D.C., 1973.

VALEN, HENRY, and STEIN ROKKAN. "Norway: Conflict Structure and Mass Politics in a European Periphery." In *Electoral Behavior: A Comparative Handbook,* edited by Richard Rose.

Part Four
The Communist Economies

13
The Four Models of the Communist Economy

14
The Soviet Economy

15
The Soviet Economy (continued)

16
The Communist Economies of the Comecon Bloc

17
The Yugoslav Socialist Market Economy

Chapter 13
The Four Models of the Communist Economy

In the study of the economies of the communist countries, special attention attaches to the Soviet economy because the Soviet Union was the first major country to adopt a communist program for rapid economic development. While other communist countries have in recent decades deviated considerably from the Soviet economic model, nevertheless, much of this model is still found in the Eastern European communist countries, the People's Republic of China, and communist countries in other parts of the world. The Soviet economic model has itself undergone considerable change since the first five-year plan was inaugurated by Stalin in 1928. The first version of this model was the Stalinist version of the years 1928–1953, when the Soviet Union was operated as a highly-centralized planned economy. The second and current version of the Soviet economic model is the post-Stalinist or reformed version which has been taking shape since Stalin's death in 1953. Like the economies in the various Eastern European communist countries, the Soviet economy has in recent years undergone extensive economic reform.

For the purposes of our study, we shall draw special attention to four basic types of communist economies that are currently found in the communist world: (1) the mobilized communist economy; (2) the orthodox or Stalinist command economy; (3) the reformed command economy; (4) and the decentralized market-oriented communist economy. They are summarized in Table 13-1. This fourfold division of communist economies provides a spectrum running from economies with a large element of mobilization or centralized administration to economies with a large element of decentralized market orientation. While various communist economies may be placed at specific points on the spectrum today, it should be observed that some of them have moved along the spectrum to the right over the years and will probably

Table 13-1
The Spectrum of Communist Economies

Major features	The mobilized command economy	The orthodox command economy	The reformed command economy	The decentralized market-oriented economy
Political system	Utopian, totalitarian monoparty	Dictatorial monoparty	Authoritarian monoparty	Monoparty with democratic bureaucracy
Organization of economic system	Hierarchical	Hierarchical	Hierarchical	Polycentric with institutional pluralism
Type of national planning	Highly centralized	Highly centralized	Centralized, but with some devolution	Decentralized with little centralization
Economic development strategy	Utopian; new communist man (or woman) with high economic growth	Rapid unbalanced growth; emphasis on heavy industry	High, but more balanced economic growth	High balanced growth; market oriented
Industry	Emphasis on large-scale; small-scale tolerated	Emphasis on large-scale	Emphasis on large-scale	Scale determined by market conditions
Workers' self-management	No	No	No	Yes
Markets and prices	Centrally controlled	Centrally controlled	Centrally controlled, but some concern for consumer demand	Trend towards uncontrolled market prices

Table 13-1
The Spectrum of Communist Economies—(cont.)

Major features	The mobilized command economy	The orthodox command economy	The reformed command economy	The decentralized market-oriented economy
Managerial latitude	Little	Little	Considerable	Much
Worker incentives	Largely noneconomic	Mainly economic	Mainly economic	Mainly economic
Occupational freedom	Greatly curbed	Greatly curbed	Little curbed	Extensive
Consumer freedom	Little	Little	Some	Much
Tolerance of private enterprise	Low	Low	Medium	High
Macroeconomic policy	Active budget policy; passive monetary policy	Active budget policy; passive monetary policy	Active budget policy; less passive monetary policy	Active budget and monetary policies
Trade unions	Passive role; school of communism	Passive role; command transmission belt	Passive role; no real independence	Some independence; defends workers' rights
Agriculture	Highly collective; rural communes	Collective; no private farms tolerated	Collective; some private farming	Both collective and private farms
Foreign trade	Largely with other communist countries; autarkic tendency	Largely with other communist countries; autarkic tendency	Foreign trade monopoly weakened; more trade with noncommunist world	Trend towards open economy with multilateral foreign trade

The four models of the communist economy

continue to do so at different rates in the future. Movement to the right on the spectrum can be impeded or accelerated by historical circumstances as well as by the exigencies of leadership.

While the world's communist countries are at different stages of economic development and have liberalized their economies to varying degrees since 1960, they share, nevertheless, certain common elements. They all profess to accept the Marxist-Leninist ideology.[1] They officially accept Marx's view that labor creates all value, and that the surplus value above the value measured by wages (present labor) and depreciation (past labor) is available under socialism for new investment or increased consumption. The official ideological position in all communist countries is that capitalist development will inevitably lead to the demise of the capitalist system. This will occur, according to the Marxists, because under capitalism the development of the economic system will lead to a concentration of industry and its ownership, a declining rate of profit, an increasing severity of the business cycle, a growing misery of the masses, and an increasing army of the unemployed.

All these contradictions will result in the overturn of the capitalist system. With the separation of the capitalist society into the declining bourgeoisie and the expanding proletariat, and the transfer of surplus value from the proletariat to the bourgeoisie, the workers will eventually revolt and destroy the capitalist system. Capitalism will then be followed by a transitional period of socialism in which the dictatorship of the proletariat will consolidate the socialist victory and prepare the way for the final stage of communism. In this final stage, for which no fixed timetable is given, the political state will wither away; the community's economic activities will be coordinated by some central administration; wages will be abolished; and individuals, while producing according to ability, will be recompensed according to need. Private property in producers' and consumers' goods will be eliminated, and all property will be owned communally.

In addition to this common ideological basis, all communist countries share certain elements that relate to their economic and political organization. They are all currently in what they consider the transitional stage of socialism. The Soviet Union, the Eastern European communist countries, Mainland China, and the other Asiatic communist countries have essentially monoparty political systems. These countries have state ownership of the land and the nation's industries, with a limited tolerance of private enterprise in the service and craft industries. Agriculture is organized to varying degrees on a collective basis.

With the aim of achieving rapid industrialization, all communist countries have planned economies, in which annual and five-year plans are used to coordinate the nation's economic and social activities. These plans relate to microeconomic activities at the enterprise level and to macroeconomic activities at the regional and national levels. Labor, with some restriction, is free to move from one job to another; and consumers are free to spend their wages on whatever limited supplies of consumer goods are available. All communist countries have financial systems with units of currency, banks, taxes, wage differentials, and related financial arrangements. In all communist countries, some use is made of the elements of a market system, such as prices, costs, and sales contracts. The physical or supply planning is coordinated with financial planning, which deals with problems of inflation, price reform, credit rationing, and

---

[1] "Despite these differences, Marxist ideology remains one of the ties which bind Eastern Europe together. . . . The new Marxism is not radically new." Richard T. De George, *The New Marxism*, (New York: Pegasus, 1968), p. 6.

capital investment plans. The national planning also coordinates the trade relations between the communist countries, and between them and the non-communist world.

The Spectrum of Communist Economies

Although all communist countries possess the common features discussed above and are to some extent derived from a common Soviet mold, at the same time they are in many ways highly diversified between the theoretical extremes of a pure command economy and a pure socialist market economy. A comparison of Stalinist Albania and Maoist China with decentralized, market-oriented Yugoslavia and Hungary highlights the broad spectrum on which the world's communist countries of today may be placed. Specialists in the field of comparative economic systems have tried in a variety of ways to develop a systemic typology for the analysis of different communist economic systems. All typologies or classificatory systems accept the broad distinction between the ideal or theoretical types of command and market economies, but a number of these classifications make further typological refinements.[2] Whereas Jan S. Prybyla, Oleg Zinam, and others construct their systemic typologies within the command-market framework, Karl C. Thalheim uses the threefold classification of "conservative," "compromising," and "progressive" communist economies. John M. Montias divides these economies into four basic types: the "mobilization system," "the centralized" and "decentralized administered systems," and "market socialism." Carmelo Mesa-Lago has constructed a continuum of six static types or models of communist economies that lie between two poles: namely, the utopian mobilized communist economy, and the pragmatic, market-oriented communist economy.

Some of these typological schemes are static in their approach, while others emphasize the dynamic nature of the different evolving communist systems. Mesa-Lago's typology classifies the Soviet Union, Mainland China, Cuba, Czechoslovakia, and Yugoslavia as of mid-1968. With the use of a dynamic approach, such as Montias' typology, a communist economy can be placed in different categories at different times. For example, the Soviet economy between 1917 and 1974 moved along the typological spectrum from a mobilization war economy in the years 1917–1920 to a highly centralized administered economy from 1928 to 1953; it returned briefly to a market-oriented economy in the period of the New Economic Policy (1921–1927); and since 1953, it has been a reformed command economy. Likewise, the Yugoslav communist economy, which started as a highly centralized command economy in 1946, is now a highly decentralized, market-oriented economy. Other Eastern European communist economies have undergone considerable reform of their command economies, which were established in the early post–World War II years.

A survey of economic and political developments in the world's communist countries since 1960 indicates a general movement

[2] These typological refinements are discussed in Jan S. Prybyla, "Meaning and Classification of Economic Systems," *Comparative Economic Systems*, New York: Appleton-Century-Crofts, 1969, pp. 9–18; Oleg Zinam, "The Economics of Command Economies," *Ibid.*, pp. 19–46; Karl C. Thalheim, "Conclusion: Is There a Congruence?", in L. A. D. Dellin and Hermann Gross (eds.), *Reforms in the Soviet and East European Economies*, Lexington, Mass.: D. C. Heath, 1972, pp. 141–153; John M. Montias, "Types of Communist Economic Systems," in Chalmers Johnson (ed.), *Change in Communist Systems*, Stanford: Stanford University Press, 1970, pp. 117–134; Carmelo Mesa-Lago, "A Continuum Model to Compare Socialist Systems Globally," in Morris Bornstein, *Comparative Economic Systems*, Homewood: Richard D. Irwin, 1974, pp. 511–529; and Alexander Eckstein, *Comparison of Economic Systems, Theoretical and Methodological Approaches*, pp. 1–23.

The four models of the communist economy

along the typological spectrum or scale towards a less centrally planned type of economy. There is nothing inevitable or teleological about such a movement, since historical occurrences or the idiosyncrasies of leaders can at any time delay or reverse the evolutionary process. But an inherent cultural logic does operate to create a dynamics of change favorable to continued economic and political evolution. This logic suggests that as the communist economies become more industrialized, as they become structurally and functionally more complicated, and as their standards of living rise, these economies will tend to move away from the orthodox command economy towards the decentralized market-oriented economy.[3]

The pressures of this cultural logic in the communist sphere have given rise to the wave of "economic reform" that has swept over the communist countries in recent years. This reform has not stemmed from any specifically planned program on the part of the ruling communist elites. Rather, it has been largely the pragmatic result of unplanned reactions to economic and social pressures, which in turn reflect the maturing of the industrialization process through which the communist countries have been passing in the past twenty years.

The Mobilized Command Economy

Representative of the somewhat utopian mobilized type of communist economy are the Soviet Union during the period of War Communism (1918–1920), Mainland China today, and Castro's Cuba.[4] What is common to these underdeveloped economies is their mobilization on a wartime footing. Their basic aim is to establish a classless, egalitarian society by moving as rapidly as possible from capitalism to the goal of full-fledged communism. The ideological thrust of this type of communist economy is highly utopian, with its emphasis upon creating the "new communist man [or woman]". Such a person would be motivated by nonmaterial or "moral" incentives that emphasize curbing the self in favor of community welfare. The new communist man (or woman) is not to be an individualist, since he (or she) is to function within a collectivistic framework. The mobilization communist economy has strong populist tendencies, and emancipation from capitalism and the capitalist mentality is to be a collective not an individual emancipation.[5] This mobilization ideology is based upon ideas taken from the "young Marx," Trotsky, Mao, Guevara, and Castro. The advocates of the mobilized communist economy condemn the materialism of both the capitalism of the West and the state socialism of Eastern Europe. They attack the self-seeking, the alienation, and the inequalities found not only in the Western capitalist countries, but also in the Soviet

---

[3] As Lowenthal expresses it, "Our argument, then, suggests the existence of a long-term trend toward the victory of modernization over utopianism: as Communist-governed developing societies approach the level of advanced industrial societies, the arbitrary reshaping of their social structure by ideologically guided political power—in Marxist terms, the reshaping of their 'basis' by their 'superstructure'—becomes increasingly difficult and ultimately impossible." Richard Lowenthal, "Development vs. Utopia in Communist Policy," in Chalmers Johnson (ed.), *Change in Communist Systems*, Stanford: Stanford University Press, 1970, p. 54.

[4] The analysis of the mobilized command economy presented here applies with special force to Mao's China and Castro's Cuba, which have operated on a wartime basis but in a period of peace. The War Communism of the Soviet Union of the years 1917–1921 had little opportunity to develop its utopian features, since it was laboring under the severe constraints of actual warfare. Consequently, Chinese and Cuban communism are better examples of a mobilized command economy than is Soviet War Communism.

[5] For an analysis of the Chinese communist view of the new "Maoist man [or woman]," see the articles of Stuart R. Schram, Arthur A. Cohen, and various commentaries in "Maoism: A Symposium," *Problems of Communism*, Sept.-Oct. 1966, Vol. XV, pp. 1-23.

Union and the industrialized Eastern European communist countries.

The mobilization command economy is characterized politically as a highly authoritarian economy with a charismatic dictatorship such as would be provided by a Lenin, a Mao, or a Castro. The leader of the monoparty dictatorship is supported by a tightly organized communist party, which supplies both political and economic leadership. Although the organization of the mobilization economy is hierarchical, and considerable reliance is put on commands handed down from the top, nevertheless, much reliance is placed on initiative and cooperation at the bottom. As in the People's Republic of China, in all mobilized economies there is much emphasis on the "self-reliance" of the general population, guided, however, by the vanguard Communist party. The mobilization effort requires participation by all sectors of the economy and especially by the peasants and urban workers. This means that the Communist party at the local level is very active in the mobilization of peasants and workers with the stated aim of building up an advanced industrial society on an egalitarian base.

Since the mobilization economy is strongly anti-free market, economic coordination is achieved through planning at national, regional, and local levels. This planning is primarily physical or supply planning, with a minimum use of financial planning. A money and credit system is used, but its role is largely passive. Prices of producer and consumer goods are arbitrarily fixed by the planning authorities, and widespread use is made of rationing on the basis of priorities determined by the central authorities. Wage differentials and monetary bonuses are sparingly employed. Emphasis instead is on non-economic rewards and such practices as socialist emulation, shock work, and "volunteer" or unpaid work in such activities as road repair, canal and other construction, and crop harvesting. No role is left in the mobilization economy for private enterprise, except to a limited extent, in the handicrafts, the retail trade, and agriculture.

The leaders of the mobilized command economy exercise a tight control over the nation's cultural and ideological developments. They believe that a strong ideological leadership is needed to maintain the people's revolutionary fervor. They also believe that their ideological goals can be achieved in the long run only by exporting the social revolution and changing the external world along Marxist-Leninist lines. The development strategy of the mobilization economy has been described as "teleological," in the sense that it emphasizes the early achievement of the ultimate objective of full communism.[6] At times, economic efficiency is sacrificed to a revolutionary "morality" that plays down the economic and material sphere. In the mobilization economy, economic development is to take place, but it is always to be ideologically guided. There must be repeated revolutions from above because forced economic development, unless rigorously controlled, is accompanied by spontaneous changes, such as the emergence of a privileged managerial class and the desire on the part of the workers for material rewards, which run counter to the utopian communist vision of the leaders of the mobilized economy.[7]

In the mobilized command economy, economic development is cyclical rather than linear. It zigzags between periods of rapid economic growth, with weak revolutionary fervor and periods of low growth, with strong revolutionary fervor. In the long run, as the original revolutionary leaders die off and are replaced by men and women who never experienced the shift from capitalism to

[6] John M. Montias, *op. cit.*, p. 125.
[7] Richard Lowenthal, "Development vs. Utopia in Communist Policy," Chalmers Johnson (ed.), *Change in Communist Systems*, p. 47.

socialism, it is quite conceivable that economic efficiency and modernization will win out over revolutionary utopianism. For the time being, however, the mobilization economies of the underdeveloped communist countries, such as Mainland China and Cuba, present a marked contrast to the reformed command economies of the industrially advanced Soviet Union, East Germany, and Czechoslovakia. The model of the mobilized command economy continues to appeal strongly to the world's underdeveloped economies which have plenty of manpower but few other economic resources.

The mobilized command economy is to be distinguished from the reformed command and the decentralized market-oriented communist economies of the Soviet Union and Eastern Europe by the fact that it repudiates the consumer society, large wage differentials, and reliance on the free market system. It emphasizes instead maintaining permanent revolution, developing a communist mentality, creating an egalitarian society, and approaching socialism and communism at the same time. For the followers of Mao, Guevara, and Castro, "the struggle is happiness." The spiritualized people should act as if the revolution is permanent. In the mobilization economy, technological progress and economic advance are acceptable goals, but primarily for the purpose to provide aid to people in the struggling underdeveloped countries and to support the movement towards world communism. The leaders of the Chinese and Cuban mobilization economies attack the economic reform movement of recent years in the Soviet Union and the Eastern European communist countries on the ground that it substitutes a capitalist mentality and morality for a communist mentality and morality and delays the movement towards world communism.[8]

[8] This line of criticism is presented in Ernesto Che Guevara, "Socialism and Man in Cuba," in Rolando

The Orthodox Command Economy

The orthodox centralized command economy, which was widespread in the communist world in the late 1940s and 1950s, was the product of Soviet economic experience in the period between the start of the first five-year plan in 1928 and Stalin's death in 1953. Some of the main features of the orthodox Stalinist command economy have been abandoned in the communist sphere in recent years; and in its orginal Stalinist form, this type of communist economy is now found only in such backward communist countries as Albania, Outer Mongolia, and North Korea. Even the Soviet Union has now moved quite a distance away from the rigid Stalinist model towards an economic system that is more flexible and more concerned with economic rationality and consumer welfare, although it remains far behind the progressive Hungarian and Yugoslav economies. Although the orthodox Stalinist command economy professed to adhere to the Marxist goal of a classless, egalitarian communist society, its main concerns in practice were rapid industrialization and the building up of a strong military state. Success along these lines depended upon achieving a high level of forced economic growth through massive doses or injections of capital and labor, with little regard for optimal or balanced national planning, or for plant and worker efficiency. The emphasis was on pushing out the extensive margin of economic development to convert a backward economy into an advanced economy as rapidly as was possible.

In order to grow rapidly, the ultra centralized command economy concentrated attention on the accumulation of capital in the

E. Bonachea and Nelson P. Valdes (eds.), *Selected Works of Ernesto Guevara,* Cambridge: MIT Press, 1969, p. 21; and Martin Kenner and James Petras, *Fidel Castro Speaks,* New York: Grove Press, 1969, p. 327.

heavy industries, such as the steel, coal, power, chemical, and machinery industries. Consumers were kept at a low standard of living, while the nation's expanding resources were largely directed towards the expansion of heavy industry, which was operated according to the principle of "one-man management." Agriculture was sacrificed to industry by using the agricultural surplus for industrial development; and manpower was deployed arbitrarily according to the priorities of the central planning authorities. Directives from the top were enforced with the aid of a system of organized terror. Both consumer and occupational freedoms were severely limited, and trade with the capitalist world was kept to a minimum. In the traditional command economy up to the 1950s, the planning was mainly "from above."

The techniques of planning included centrally determined prices, rationing of important commodities, material incentives in the form of large wage differentials and money bonuses, and the maintenance of a sellers' market in which the demand for goods and services always exceeded the supply of these items. Since the centrally administered command economy was not market oriented, financial planning played a very limited role in the national planning program. Long-term investment was rigorously controlled by means of direct allocations from the fiscal budgets, with the state bank passively adjusting the supply of short-term credit to the plan goals of the central authorities.

In the traditional Stalinist model that was widely adopted in the communist sphere in the 1940s and the 1950s, a harmonious relationship existed between the nation's economic base and its economic and political superstructure. The rigorously planned system of production at the bottom supported a highly authoritarian economic and political superstructure. The Communist party and the government bureaucracy were interested in maintaining the command economy, for it enabled them to preserve a monopoly of political power. The authoritarian command economy could be successfully maintained only as long as the population was poorly educated, the standard of living was low, and not much contact with the noncommunist world was permitted. The Stalinist command economy was self-defeating, because its own success would eventually create a literate population, a substantial improvement in the standard of living, and a desire by the workers for more economic and political freedom. Although Stalin and his associates in the years before 1953 could delay the transition to a more decentralized economy that would have considerable economic and political freedom, the time was bound to come when there would be strong pressures to make substantial changes in both the structure and functioning of the command economy.

The Reformed Post-Stalinist Command Economy

The post-Stalinist reformed command economy is the dominant economic model in the communist world today.[9] It is found in the

[9] In the flood of literature dealing with the economic reform movement in the Soviet Union and Eastern Europe the following items provide a good coverage: Kurt London (ed.), *Eastern Europe in Transition*, Baltimore: The Johns Hopkins Press, 1966; M. C. Kaser (ed.), *Economic Development for Eastern Europe*, New York: Macmillan, 1968; Michael Gamarnikow, *Economic Reforms in Eastern Europe*, Detroit: Wayne University Press, 1968; Ljubo Sirc, *Economic Devolution in Eastern Europe*, New York: Frederick A. Praeger, 1969; Michael Kaser and Janusz G. Zielinski, *Planning in East Europe*, London: The Bodley Head, 1970; L. A. D. Dellin and Hermann Gross (eds.), *Reforms in the Soviet and East European Economies*, Lexington, Mass.: D. C. Heath, 1972; Radoslav Selucky, *Economic Reforms in Eastern Europe*, New York: Praeger Publishers, 1972; Morris Bornstein (ed.), *Plan and Market, Economic Reform in Eastern Europe*, New Haven: Yale University Press, 1973; and Robert W. Campbell, *The Soviet-Type Economies*, Boston: Houghton Mifflin, 1974.

The four models of the communist economy

Soviet Union, and in all Eastern European communist countries, except Albania, which is still Stalinist, and Hungary and Yugoslavia, which have moved in a progressive way beyond the other Eastern European communist countries. By the early 1950s many signs had appeared that the highly centralized command economy in the Soviet Union and Eastern Europe was becoming increasingly inadequate for the achievement of an advanced industrial society. Planning and management methods that were useful in an earlier and less developed economy were proving to be inefficient and wasteful in a complicated, more industrialized economy. With an increase in the number of basic wants of consumers provided for after 1953, a shift from a sellers' market to a limited buyers' market took place.

Before 1953, state enterprises had not been motivated to satisfy consumer preferences; thus where physical output rather than sales or profitability was the main success indicator, unwanted consumer goods accumulated in involuntary sellers' inventories. The first stage in the dismantling of the Stalinist command economy after 1953 was the elimination of the terrorist police state and the curtailment of the power of the secret police. The first stage, however, did not fundamentally change the nature of the functioning of the orthodox command economy. The second stage in the dismantling process resulted in some qualitative changes in planning and management techniques, which called for a considerable decentralization of the former orthodox command economy.

The basic aim of the post-Stalinist economic reforms of the 1960s has been to make the Soviet-type economic model more efficient without changing the party-state bureaucracy power structure. The central authorities still make the decisions concerning the rate of economic growth, the division of Gross National Product between total investment and total consumption, the total wage bill of state enterprises, the allocation of scarce raw material supplies, and the prices of producer and consumer goods.

At the microeconomic level, managers have been given considerable latitude in the operations of their enterprises. They have more freedom in purchasing inputs, fixing the size of the work force, and determining what to produce. New success indicators emphasize reducing costs, introducing new production processes and new products, and increasing profitability calculated as a percentage of the fixed and working capital used by the enterprise. Enterprise managers are also encouraged to produce goods that satisfy consumer preferences. Under these economic reforms, prices are brought closer to full costs, which now include a charge for the use of capital and rent for the use of natural resources. Both consumer and occupational freedoms are enlarged by increasing the supply of goods and services available to consumers, and by guaranteeing workers the right to move freely from job to job. Workers, however, in the reformed Soviet and East European command economies have little opportunity to participate in decision making at the enterprise level, since no provision has been made in these economies for workers' self-management. Trade unions continue to have no real independence of action and so are not able to defend what they take to be the workers' rights. Also, foreign trade continues to be very much of a state monopoly.

The conservative regimes in the Soviet Union and most of the Eastern European communist countries have been unwilling to carry economic reforms to the point where they would weaken the power position of the party and the state administrative apparatus.[10] For this reason, the freedom of action of state-enterprise directors and plant managers,

[10] See, for example, Alec Nove, "The U.S.S.R.: The Reform That Never Was," *Reforms in the Soviet and East European Economies*, pp. 19–37.

while enlarged over what it was before 1953, has nevertheless continued to be quite limited. This has also been true of consumer freedom. The freedom of the enterprise directors to decide what inputs to purchase and what output to sell is still greatly restricted by organizations that intervene between the central ministries or state committees at the top and the enterprises at the bottom of the planning hierarchy.[11] These intermediate planning organizations in the form of industry branch associations or industrial centrals have in recent years been established in East Germany, Czechoslovakia, Rumania, and other Eastern European countries, but not in the Soviet Union.

In the latter country, there have been horizontal groupings (*firmy*) of relatively small state enterprises and other experiments with combines, trusts, and intermediate administrative organizations (*glavky*); but the Soviet Union has not moved as far in the direction of cartelization as have a number of the smaller Eastern European countries.[12] Also, in the reformed command economies, price reform has not been carried very far and prices are still fixed by the central authorities. Prices are frequently not set at equilibrium levels that equate supply and demand without the use of turnover taxes, nor are they adjusted frequently to new cost and other market conditions. As a consequence of this somewhat reluctant approach to economic reform in recent years, the reformed command economy occupies a middle position between the highly administered Stalinist command economy, which has now largely disappeared in practice, and the highly decentralized and more market-oriented economy as now found in Hungary and Yugoslavia.

Extensive and Intensive Development in the Orthodox and Reformed Command Economies

The difference between the orthodox and the reformed command economies lies in the contrast between extensive and intensive economic development.[13] In extensive development, unused or underused factors of production are employed to extend the margin of operations outward and to increase industrial output; in intensive development, the emphasis is on making the current system more efficient by employing factors of production more efficiently at the intensive or internal margin of operations of the various state industrial enterprises. The basic difference between these two types of economic development is found in the distinction between the widening (extensive development) and the deepening (intensive development) of industry. Before World War II, the orthodox Stalinist command economy required for its economic development massive doses or injections of capital and labor to expand the industrial system. Less interest was expressed in the efficient internal operation of the many thousands of individual industrial plants. Usually, where extensive development is the

---

[11] East Germany has been a leader in the experiment of "reformed centralism," which has favored the further concentration of industry and has moved in the opposite direction to Hungarian reform. For a discussion of East Germany's reformed centralism and its New Economic System, see Michael Keren, "Concentration and Devolution in East Germany's Reforms," *Plan and Market, Economic Reform in Eastern Europe*, pp. 123–151. See also J. F. Brown, "Rumania Today, I: Towards Integration," *Problems of Communism*, Jan.–Feb. 1969, pp. 8–17.

[12] This problem of industrial integration in the period of economic reform since 1960 is analyzed in Michael Kaser and Janusz G. Zielinski, *Planning in East Europe*, pp. 93–106; and Michael Gamarnikow, *op. cit.*, pp. 96–111.

[13] It is not surprising that economists in highly industrialized Czechoslovakia should be concerned in the 1960s with intensive rather than extensive economic development. This matter is discussed in John M. Montias, "East European Reforms in Retrospect." Joint Economic Committee, *Economic Concentration*, p. 3790.

main concern there are unused or underemployed manpower and other resources. Rapid extensive development of the economy is secured in two ways: (1) by employing unused labor such as women's labor; and (2) by shifting labor and capital from old low-productivity industries to new high-productivity industries. This occurred in the extensive development of the Soviet economy in the years 1924–1953, and has taken place in Mainland China since 1949.

In the reformed command economies of industrialized East Germany, Czechoslovakia, and the Soviet Union, the time for extensive economic development has largely passed. Women have already entered the labor force in large numbers; the collective farms have released much labor; and new plants have been widely established in the steel, power, machinery, chemical, and other high-technology industries. While room still exists for some more extensive economic development in the advanced communist economies, much more interest is now expressed in intensive development and in the more efficient use of scarce labor and capital.

This interest arises not only from the pressure to use scarce resources more efficiently, but also from the new concern in the reformed command economy for consumer welfare. Where extensive development is the dominant aim, quantity rather than quality of output is the main success indicator, as was the case in Stalin's command economy. In the current Chinese mobilization economy, extensive development stresses the importance of increasing total output rather than the variety and quality of consumer goods and services. Where intensive economic development is a major concern, increased interest in consumer welfare calls for a larger variety of high-quality goods and services from the existing industrial plant and equipment. This is the situation today in the Soviet Union, East Germany, and Czechoslovakia, where efforts are being made to improve the work incentives of apathetic and frustrated consumers by improving the quality and variety of the output of the consumer goods industries. Such a development has profound implications for the course of economic and political liberalization, since an advance towards consumer freedom sooner or later raises the question of progress towards political freedom.

The interest in intensive economic development in the Soviet Union and the Eastern European communist countries in the past decade has also resulted in a concern for economic science that is not found in communist countries where the main issue has been or is extensive economic development. During the years 1924 to 1953, Stalin was very critical of economic science as it had been developed in the Western capitalist countries; and he opposed the efforts of some Soviet economists to make use of Western economic theories and concepts, such as interest and rent charges, opportunity costs, marginal pricing, and optimal planning. The party leaders in the mobilization and orthodox command economies cling to a Marxian economics that is of little help in providing guidance of the industrialized communist economy.

Likewise, in Communist China and Cuba, where emphasis is put on the extensive development of an underdeveloped economy and "redness" is elevated above "expertness," there is a very limited interest in theoretical developments in the field of economic science. When a communist country turns to intensive economic development, the problems of optimal planning, plant and worker productivity, price reform, full costing, equilibrium prices, and similar matters come to the fore. It is then discovered that the Marxian concepts of value, socially necessary labor, surplus value, and social product do not supply answers to many of the problems that arise in macroeconomic and microeconomic planning.

The reformed command economy is to be distinguished from both the mobilization command and the orthodox command economies by the interest of its party leaders in the economic concepts and theories of the school of mathematical economists, represented by such thinkers as Leonid Kantorovich, V. V. Novozhilov, and V. S. Nemchinov in the Soviet Union. They proposed major changes in the existing system of macroeconomic and microeconomic planning on the basis of more modern economic concepts than were acceptable to the leaders of the orthodox Soviet command economy in the years 1924–1953.[14] All these modern economic concepts are directly or indirectly related to the concept of the equilibrium free price system, which has not yet been fully accepted by the leaders of the reformed command economy in the Soviet Union and most of the Eastern European communist countries. This means that this economy is a halfway station between the orthodox command economy, which was hostile to Western market economics, and the decentralized, market-oriented communist economy, such as the Yugoslav economy, which is favorably disposed towards Western economies.

The Decentralized, Market-Oriented Communist Economy

The fourth type of communist economy is the decentralized, market-oriented economy, which is further away from the traditional or orthodox model than is the current reformed Soviet-type economy. This fourth type operates today in Yugoslavia and Hungary, and was the goal of the Czechoslovakian economic reformers before the invasion of Czechoslovakia by the Soviet Union and other Warsaw Pact countries in August 1968. The advocates of this progressive kind of communist economy find the current Soviet-style economy unacceptable, because the latter is opposed to workers' self-management, full price reform, and free-trade relations with the outside, noncommunist world.

The theoretical justification for the market-oriented communist economy has been developed by such liberal communist theoreticians as Oskar Lange, Ota Sik, and Branko Horvat. They have recommended the substitution of market socialism for the administrative socialism still operative in the Soviet Union and most of the Eastern European communist countries.[15] In the opinion of these advocates of market socialism, administrative socialism leads to overcentralized state socialism, which is more responsive to the aims of the leaders of the communist party and government bureaucrats than to the goals of the mass of consumer-citizens. The most significant feature of market socialism is that it combines economic and political liberalization, and thus underlines the need to shift

[14] An analysis of the development of mathematical economics in the Soviet Union since 1960 is provided in John P. Hardt and others, *Mathematics and Computers in Soviet Economic Planning*, New Haven: Yale University Press, 1967.

[15] The economics of market socialism is presented in Oskar Lange, *Political Economy*, Vols. 1 and 2, Oxford: Pergamon Press, 1971; Branko Horvat, *An Essay on Yugoslav Society*, White Plains, N.Y.: International Arts and Sciences Press, 1969, and *Towards a Theory of a Planned Economy*, Beograd: Yugoslav Institute of Economic Research, 1964; and Ota Sik, *Plan and Market under Socialism*, White Plains, N.Y.: International Arts and Sciences Press, 1967, and *Czechoslovakia: The Bureaucratic Economy*, White Plains, N.Y.: International Arts and Sciences Press, 1972. For Western views on market socialism, see Jaroslav Vanek, *The General Theory of Labor-Managed Market Economies*, Ithaca: Cornell University Press, 1970; Abram Bergson, "Market Socialism Revisited," *Journal of Political Economy*, Vol. 75, Oct. 1967, pp. 663–665; Benjamin Ward, "Marxism-Horvatism: A Yugoslav Theory of Socialism," *American Economic Review*, Vol. 57, June 1967, pp. 509–523; and Paul R. Gregory and Robert C. Stuart, *Soviet Economic Structure and Performance*, New York: Harper and Row, 1974, pp. 301–327.

power from the party and the state to the workers at the bottom of the social hierarchy. These workers would then determine the nation's priorities and the path of economic growth.

The main features that distinguish the decentralized, market-oriented economy from the reformed Soviet-type command economy are described in the following discussion.[16] Under the program for a decentralized economy, planning at the center is largely abandoned. The central ministries of the government are abolished or reduced in number, and their planning functions are largely transferred to regional, district, or local planning agencies. The central government continues to plan large macroeconomic aggregates, such as total output, total consumption, and total investment, and to be concerned with the long-term development of the nation's economy. It no longer becomes involved in physical or supply planning in any detailed way.

The key economic institution in the decentralized, market-oriented economy is the workers' self-managed cooperative or collective, which elects its own management and functions without detailed, direct controls from the top. The managers of the working collectives are also free to compete on a price basis; the main success indicator for both managers and workers is profitability, which ultimately determines both incomes (profit shares) and bonuses. The working collectives are allowed to export what they produce and to import raw materials and equipment. The investment needs of the collectives are financed out of enterprise profits and by loans from the national, regional, or local banks. State enterprises are no longer largely financed by budgetary allotments, which are under central government control, but instead by loans from a largely independent banking system. Market prices, which are calculated to bring about an equilibrium between supply and demand, cover all costs including interest charges on capital and rents for natural resources. The decisions of the managers of the workers' collectives with respect to investment, production, and sales are market tested; and collectives that do not make a profit may be removed through bankruptcy.

The decentralized, market-oriented communist economy is to a considerable extent an open economy, in which domestic production technologies, costs, and prices are compared with world technologies, costs, and prices. Strong pressures exist to make domestic and export prices full-cost, rational prices, to maintain realistic foreign exchange rates, and to increase the use of imported, advanced industrial technology. Relatively free trade promotes cooperation with producers in Western, noncommunist nations in joint investment ventures. At the same time, the creation of an open, market-oriented economy has given rise to major economic problems similar to those found in the Western, market-oriented economies. These problems include increased unemployment, price inflation, monopolistic business practices, increasing income inequalities, balance-of-international-payments difficulties, and economic instability arising from fluctuations in the level of economic activity. These problems, however, are accepted as the price of developing a democratic market-oriented economy.

The decentralized communist economy has reached its highest level of development in Yugolsavia; it is, however, far from having

---

[16] The essentials of a decentralized, market-oriented economy are presented in Ota Sik, "On the Economic Problems in Czechoslovakia," *Economic Concentration*, Part 7A, pp. 4509–4530. See also Ota Sik, "The Economic Impact of Stalinism," *Problems of Communism*, Vol. XX, May–June 1971, pp. 1–10; *Plan and Market under Socialism*, 1967; and *Czechoslovakia: The Bureaucratic Economy*, 1972.

achieved its final form. The authorities have been reluctant to close down unprofitable industrial plants for fear of increasing unemployment. Many producer-good prices and prices of staple consumer goods are still fixed by the central government rather than by the market system. Also, limited progress has been made in developing a competitive capital market where working collectives would compete for investment funds. There is also a question as to how effective workers' self-management can be in a complicated, advanced industrial society. The individual workers' collective, which is usually a specialized unit in a particular industry, is frequently not in a good position to gather information with respect to domestic and external economic trends. This problem raises the issue as to how far decentralization can go in an industrial economy where problems of research and development, technological progress, and long-range investment are beyond the purview of the small and medium-size industrial enterprises. In spite of all these unsettled issues, Yugoslavia has made more progress towards a decentralized, market-oriented economy than any other communist country.

Economic reform that includes adopting workers' self-management, providing for free market prices, and enlarging consumer welfare also brings up the question of the kind of political structure that would be compatible with extensive economic liberalization. The economic reforms of the late 1960s in Czechoslovakia led to an interest in the establishment of a "pluralistic socialism," in which the monopoly of economic and political power held by the Communist party would be eliminated. The socialist pluralism of the Czechoslovakian reformers would have created an uncensored press and would have required the acceptance of different points of view within the communist political system.

In other words, if the reform movement in Czechoslovakia had succeeded, there would have been a democratization of the communist political system that would have resulted in the establishment of a participatory, pluralistic communist state.

In Yugoslavia, the political consequences of economic liberalization have not yet been worked out fully. Local Communist party representatives have been given a larger role in the party's decision-making process; provision has been made for a more frequent turnover in party office holding; and ideological dogmatists opposed to economic reform have been curbed. The one-party political system, however, is still dominant, and the Yugoslav League of Communists is still the main center of political power. Also, considerable uncertainty still exists about the role of trade unions in an economy based on workers' self-management. In large industrial enterprises, where a number of separate plants are operating, workers at times find it difficult to influence management at the top. They then turn to the trade unions to defend their interests when the work force is reduced or unprofitable industrial plants are closed; on occasion, they have engaged in unofficial strikes. At present, the role of the trade unions in Yugoslavia remains poorly defined.

The connection between economic and political liberalization raises the issue of the relations between the nation's economic base and its institutional superstructure. According to the Marxian interpretation, a fundamental change in the mode of production creates a contradiction between the new economic system and the old political superstructure that can be eliminated only by creating a new political structure. Reformers such as Ota Sik and Milovan Djilas believe that the time has already come to establish a participatory pluralistic communist society on the foundation of the new economic system. According to this interpretation, the decentralized market-oriented economy, with workers' self-management, competitive pricing, and free-trade relations with the external world, constitutes a basic change in the nation's production relations. This change makes it necessary to construct a society in which the means of production would be socially owned, but citizen-consumers—not the Communist party—would be the final arbiters in all economic, social, and political matters.

In other words, in the decentralized market-oriented communist economy, the Communist party would guide the economy, but would not direct it as is done today in the Soviet Union and all other Comecon countries.[17] Yugoslavia has made considerable progress in this direction, but conflicts among the six federated republics appear to be a major obstacle to further progress along this line. Among the Comecon countries, progress in establishing a more democratic society will depend very largely upon the attitude of the Soviet Union towards economic and political reform.[18] Up to now, Soviet policy has succeeded in greatly curtailing this reform; but the future direction of Soviet influence is subject to a wide variety of interpretations. These interpretations range from those held by Western observers of the Soviet Union, who see the Soviet system becoming a petrified directed system, to interpretations that expect the Soviet system to move towards a system of "institutional pluralism."[19]

The Future of Communist Economic Reform and Development

We can summarize this analysis of the spectrum of communist economic models by pointing out that the thrusts or emphases of the three different models of major significance today are quite different. In the mobilization command economies of China and Cuba, the emphasis is on struggle and permanent revolution; in these countries, utopia consists of finding happiness or fulfillment in the struggle to create a classless egalitarian society. In the reformed command economies of the Soviet Union and the Eastern European communist countries, the stress is placed on economic rationality or efficiency; and utopia is taken to be a society in which all share a high standard of living but without full political and cultural freedoms. In the decentralized market-oriented communist economies of Yugoslavia, Hungary, and Czechoslovakia of 1968, emphasis is not on permanent revolutionary struggle or economic rationality, but on the building of a free society on a sound economic base. In this type of economy, utopia is viewed as a condition of economic, cultural, and political freedom supported by an efficient and productive economic system.

The question may be asked: How stable are these three contending types of communist

---

[17] By 1974, the Council for Mutual Economic Assistance (CMEA or Comecon) had been in operation for twenty-five years. It was created by Stalin in January 1949, with representatives from the Soviet Union, Poland, Czechoslovakia, Hungary, Romania, and Bulgaria in order to coordinate the economic policies of the Soviet Union and these satellite countries. Albania joined in 1950, but withdrew in 1961; East Germany joined in 1950, Outer Mongolia in 1962, and Cuba in 1972. Both Yugoslavia and Finland have cooperative arrangements with Comecon but are not full members. Comecon has a role in Eastern Europe somewhat similar to that of the European Economic Community in Western Europe.

[18] John P. Hardt, "East European Economic Development," *Economic Developments in Countries of Eastern Europe*, Joint Economic Committee, Washington, D.C., 1970, pp. 26–40.

[19] In this connection, see Jerry F. Hough, "The Soviet System: Petrification of Pluralism?", *Problems of Communism*, 2, March–April, 1972, pp. 25–45.

economies? Are they likely to persist indefinitely as alternative ways of organizing economic, social, and political activities in communist countries? The proponents of the mobilized and the reformed command economies in Mainland China and the Soviet Union are in a strong position to support their economic and political objectives with all the power that a major nation possesses. The situation is quite different with the decentralized communist economy advocated by minor nations such as Yugoslavia and Hungary. However, economic developmental trends may in the long run be more favorable to Yugoslavia, Hungary, and suppressed Czechoslovakia than to Mainland China and the Soviet Union. This raises the question of a possible progression from the mobilized economy to the decentralized economy through which communist economies go as they become increasingly industrialized, and as they achieve higher standards of living. Is there a logic of economic development that points to this progression, which may be deflected for a time by historical accidents or by a cult of personality, but which in the long run pushes all communist countries towards the model of a decentralized and democratized economy? If such a logic is at work among the communist countries, their future could lie more with the economic and political experiments being conducted today in Yugoslavia and Hungary, and tried briefly in 1968 in Czechoslovakia, than with what is now going on in the Soviet Union and the Peoples' Republic of China.

If economic reform has very disturbing political implications for entrenched party ideologues and government bureaucrats, the question may be asked: why did the ruling elites in the Soviet Union and its communist satellites tolerate the economic reforms of the 1960s to the extent that they did? The answer appears to be that there was no choice in this matter. In the 1960s, the old command economy was proving to be wasteful, inefficient, and unable to cope with the complications of the industrialization process at work in the communist countries. In these countries, rates of economic growth were declining; production efficiency was falling; exports were increasingly unable to compete with the products of the noncommunist Western countries; technological progress was slow; prospects of catching up with and surpassing the advanced Western economies were fading away; and consumers whose primary wants were now met were not spending their discretionary income on shoddy, low-quality goods, which were accumulating in unwanted inventories.[20]

To improve the efficiency of plant and enterprise management and worker incentives, it was necessary to modify the old orthodox Stalinist command economy in a number of important ways. Where the Communist party leadership is cautious, as in the Soviet Union, East Germany, Bulgaria, and Rumania, the objective of the economic reform program has been to make the economy more efficient without seriously weakening the monopoly of power held by the party leaders and state bureaucrats. Enterprise directors and managers could be given more leeway in the operation of their enterprises, and more consideration could be given to enlarging consumer welfare; but there was to be no workers' self-management, no free competitive pricing of goods and services, and no free development of foreign trade. In the final analysis, the reformed command economy was to remain in essence an administratively run economy.

[20] The annual percentage increase in per capita GNP in Czechoslovakia for 1955–1960 was 5.4 percent, but for 1960–1967, only 2.4 percent. The respective statistics for East Germany were 5.8 and 3.0 percent. In Poland, economic growth was low in the whole period, 1955–1967. Thad P. Alton, "Economic Structure and Growth in Eastern Europe," *Economic Developments in Countries of Eastern Europe*, p. 47.

Socialism in the Soviet Union and the other Comecon countries is today much more "administrative" than "market" socialism. Robert W. Campbell concludes that "after the experience of the Sixties, the prospects for market socialism do not seem very bright. Only one country has succeeded in making this transition, and it is a discouraging reminder of how precarious this commitment is in socialist countries to find both political and economic liberalism under attack in Yugoslavia in the early Seventies."[21]

If, in the long run, the Soviet Union and Eastern Europe continue their poor economic performance and fail to meet the people's rising expectations, one can anticipate renewed pressures to abandon the reformed command economy and to substitute for it a decentralized market-oriented economy. As one Kremlinologist has put it, "The root problem that will have to be faced by Soviet and East European leaders is the necessity to replace rather than modify the Stalinist system."[22] The replacement rather than the modification of the command economy requires a new comprehensive theory of a decentralized and democratized communist economy that has not yet been worked out fully.

However, something of a common pattern of economic reform has already emerged. Despite the many differences of approach, emphasis, and economic circumstances found among the Eastern European communist countries, all reform programs agree on the need to operate the communist economies more rationally. All such programs agree on the importance of price reform, plan decentralization, improved enterprise and plant management, more effective harnessing of individual incentives, and more concern for consumer welfare. This pattern of economic reform largely reflects pragmatic reactions to concrete economic problems rather than scientific theorizing about the emerging post-Stalinist communist economy. Theorizing about this new economic model has been hindered by the widespread acceptance of the inherited Stalinist interpretation of Marxism-Leninism, which supports the Stalinist command economy and its reformed version. The logic underlying economic and political liberalization in the communist countries points towards an erosion of the outmoded Stalinist interpretation of Marxism-Leninism and its eventual replacement by a more scientific and humanistic interpretation of Marxism-Leninism. To the extent that this latter interpretation gains acceptance, one can anticipate a growing interest in communist countries in the establishment of a decentralized and democratized market-oriented economy.

---

[21] Robert W. Campbell, *The Soviet-Type Economies, Performance, and Evolution*, p. 239.

[22] John P. Hardt, "East European Economic Development," *op. cit.*, p. 40.

Selected Bibliography

BORNSTEIN, MORRIS, ed. *Plan and Market, Economic Reform in Eastern Europe.* Yale University Press, New Haven, 1973.

CAMPBELL, ROBERT W. *The Soviet-Type Economies.* Houghton Mifflin Company, Boston, 1974.

CHE GUEVARA, ERNESTO. "Socialism and Man in Cuba." In *Selected Works of Ernesto Guevara,* edited by Rolando E. Bonachea and Nelson P. Valdes. The MIT Press, Cambridge, 1969.

DE GEORGE, RICHARD T. *The New Marxism.* Pegasus, New York, 1968.

DELLIN, L.A.D. and HERMAN GROSS, eds. *Reforms in the Soviet and East European Economies.* D.C. Heath, Lexington, Mass., 1972.

GAMARNIKOW, MICHAEL. *Economic Reforms in Eastern Europe.* Wayne University Press, Detroit, 1968.

GREGORY, PAUL R., and ROBERT C. STUART. *Soviet Economic Structure and Performance.* Harper and Row, New York, 1974.

HORVAT, BRANKO. *An Essay on Yugoslav Society.* International Arts and Sciences Press, White Plains, N.Y., 1969.

———. *Towards a Theory of a Planned Economy.* Yugoslav Institute of Economic Research, Beograd, 1964.

JOINT ECONOMIC COMMITTEE. *Economic Developments in Countries of Eastern Europe.* Washington, D.C., 1970.

KASER, M.C., ed. *Economic Development for Eastern Europe.* Macmillan, New York, 1968.

———, and JANUSZ G. ZIELINSKI. *Planning in East Europe.* The Bodley Head, London, 1970.

KENNER, MARTIN, and JAMES PETRAS. *Fidel Castro Speaks.* Grove Press, New York, 1969.

LANGE, OSKAR. *Political Economy,* 1 and 2. Pergamon Press, Oxford, 1971.

LONDON, KURT, ed. *Eastern Europe in Transition.* The Johns Hopkins Press, Baltimore, 1966.

MESA-LAGO, CARMELO. "A Continuum Model to Compare Socialist Systems Globally." In *Comparative Economic Systems,* edited by Morris Bornstein. Richard D. Irwin, Inc., Homewood, 1974.

MONTIAS, JOHN M. "East European Reforms in Retrospect." *Economic Concentration,* p. 3790.

———. "Types of Communist Economic Systems." In *Change in Communist Systems,* edited by Chalmers Johnson. Stanford University Press, Stanford, 1970.

PRYBYLA, JAN S. "Meaning and Classification of Economic Systems." In *Comparative Economic Systems,* edited by Jan S. Prybyla. Appleton-Century-Crofts, New York, 1969.

SELUCKY, RADOSLAV. *Economic Reforms in Eastern Europe.* Praeger Publishers, New York, 1972.

SIK, OTA. *Czechoslovakia: The Bureaucratic Economy.* International Arts and Sciences Press, White Plains, N.Y., 1972.

———. *Plan and Market under Socialism.* International Arts and Sciences Press, White Plains, N.Y., 1967.

SIRC, LJUBO. *Economic Devolution in Eastern Europe.* Frederick A. Praeger, New York, 1969.

VANEK, JAROSLAV. *The General Theory of Labor-Managed Market Economies.* Cornell University Press, Ithaca, 1970.

WARD, BENJAMIN. "Marxism-Horvatism: A Yugoslav Theory of Socialism." *American Economic Review,* 57 (June 1967), 509–523.

Chapter 14
The Soviet Economy

In the development of the communist world since World War I, the Soviet Union has occupied a unique position. As the first country with an official communist ideology, the Soviet Union has been a leader in the development of the communist strategy for rapid industrialization and economic growth. Having the world's second largest land area and being richly endowed with mineral and other natural resources, the Soviet Union has the necessary foundation for a high level of industrialization. Because the Soviet Union is the first major nation to pursue national planning within a communist framework, its leaders have had to experiment with different economic policies and programs.

This experimentation has been carried on under the influence of Karl Marx's analysis of capitalist development and his views regarding the future of socialism and communism. Since Marx devoted most of his analysis to capitalism and its problems, he did not give much attention to the economics of socialist planning. While the Soviet leaders have tried to work within Marxian economic concepts, they have been forced to take account of the real economic world in a pragmatic fashion. Much of what they have done in building a planned socialist economy and in working out a strategy for rapid economic growth has arisen more from the Soviet Union's economic circumstances since 1917 than from any effort to adhere to pure Marxist-Leninist ideology. Nevertheless, the impact of this ideology on economic developments in the Soviet Union since 1917 has been quite large. Its influence has been especially important in the political sphere, where an authoritarian or totalitarian state has been established.

The Soviet Union is a federation of fifteen republics with a one-party government.[1] The

---

[1] For the details of the Soviet political system, see Merle Fainsod, *How Russia Is Ruled*, Cambridge: Harvard University Press, 1963; Alec Nove, *The Soviet Economy*, 2nd rev. ed., New York: Frederick

1936 constitution provides for a president, a dual legislative body known as the Supreme Soviet, a prime minister, and an administrative body—the Council of Ministers. The latter corresponds to the prime minister's cabinet in the Western democracies and carries on the daily government activities. While the Soviet political system resembles on paper those of Western countries, a shadow government behind the constitutional government in practice runs the country. This shadow government is provided by the Communist party of the Soviet Union, with a membership of 15,694,000 (1976) in a total population of 256 million.

In theory, the policies and programs of the Communist party are determined by the Congress of the party which meets every five years. In fact, the party is run by the sixteen (1976) members of the Politburo at the top and by the Central Committee of the party; this is a standing committee responsible for the functioning of the party between the Congresses. The leadership of the party, concentrated in the Politburo and the Central Committee, spreads throughout the constitutional political system. It occupies all the important positions in the government and effectively controls both the political and economic systems. For this reason, the Soviet economy has been described as "totalitarianism harnessed to the task of rapid industrialization and economic growth."[2] From this point of view, there are three major entities: the political state or government; the Communist party, with a monopoly in Soviet affairs; and a supercorporation or production apparatus under a single management, which is responsible for operating the economy in accordance with centrally determined national goals or priorities.

The Evolution of the Soviet Economy

In the more than half a century since the Bolshevist Revolution of 1917, the Soviet Union has undergone major economic changes. Lenin's New Economic Policy of 1921–1927, which provided for a restoration of private farming and marketing but the retention of state enterprise in the key industries, constituted only a pause in the movement towards a socialist society. During these years, the advocates of balanced economic growth, who would have paid more attention to consumer preferences and would have placed more reliance on the free functioning of the market system, lost out to the advocates of unbalanced growth, whose aim was the forced and rapid industrialization of the Soviet economy.[3] In 1924, the private capitalist sector of this economy accounted for 23.7 percent

---

A. Praeger, 1969, pp. 66–110; Leonard Shapiro, *The Communist Party of the Soviet Union*, 2nd ed., New York: Random House, 1970; John A. Armstrong, *Ideology, Politics, and Government in the Soviet Union*, New York: Frederick A. Praeger, 1962; and Robert J. Osborn, *The Evolution of Soviet Politics*, Homewood, Ill.: The Dorsey Press, 1974.

[2] Robert W. Campbell, *The Soviet-Type Economies, Performance and Evolution*, Boston: Houghton Mifflin, 1974, p. 3.

[3] The economic development of the Soviet Union in the 1920s was accompanied by a very extended debate over what path to follow in order to construct a socialist society as rapidly as possible. The industrialization debate of the 1920s gave rise to three different views as to how the Soviet Union should be developed. E. A. Preobrazhensky and other members of the left wing of the Bolshevik party followed Marx closely and advocated an unbalanced growth strategy that would sacrifice agriculture and light industry to heavy industry. Lev Shanin and other members of the right wing of the party favored an unbalanced growth program that would elevate agriculture over industry in a free-market environment. Nikolas Bukharin, another member of the right-wing group, advocated a balanced growth program, in which all sectors of the economy would be developed simultaneously; this had been done to some extent during the period of the New Economic Policy (1921 to 1927). The Soviet industrialization program put into operation by Stalin after 1927 followed Preobrazhensky's

of gross industrial output, whereas the socialist sector accounted for 76.3 percent.[4] By 1937, after two of Stalin's five-year national plans, the elimination of the New Economic Policy, and the forced and widespread collectivization of agriculture, the private capitalist sector was all but eliminated—it provided only 0.2 percent of gross industrial output. By 1937, Stalin had completed the transition from a mixed private-public-enterprise economy to a mainly public-enterprise or socialist economy.

The transformation of the Soviet economy after 1928 was accompanied by rapid economic growth and significant changes in the structure and functioning of this economy. According to official Soviet statistics, which are not fully acceptable to Western analysts, gross industrial output increased sixty times in the years 1913 to 1965, at an average annual rate of about 8.2 percent.[5] Some indications of the pace of economic growth are given in Table 14-1, which shows large increases in the output of major industries in the years

pro-heavy-industry proposals, but added the program to collectivize agriculture. The wholesale collectivization of agriculture was designed to force the peasants to produce an economic surplus that could be invested in heavy industry. For a discussion of the Soviet industrialization debate, see Alexander Erlich, *The Soviet Industrialization Debate, 1924–1928*, Cambridge, Mass.: Harvard University Press, 1960; Nicolas Spulber, *Soviet Strategy for Economic Growth*, Bloomington: Indiana University Press, 1964; and Nicolas Spulber (ed.), *Foundations of Soviet Strategy for Economic Growth*, Bloomington: Indiana University Press, 1964.

[4] These and related statistics are taken from A. Yefimov, *Soviet Industry*, Moscow: Progress Publishers, 1968, p. 11.

[5] The main difficulties encountered in using Soviet economic statistics are the following ones. Soviet statisticians often employ concepts that have an ideological rather than an analytical appeal. A good example is the concept of "material production," which excludes many services, to measure aggregate output rather than the Western concept of GNP. Another limitation of Soviet official statistics is that there are strong pressures to create statistics that exaggerate output. Factory managers exaggerate output by producing large quantities of low-quality products. There is also the index number problem, which concerns the attempts to measure economic progress over time or to compare the performances of two or more economies. This problem arises in connection with the choice of the base year of the index, and also with the reliability of price as

Table 14–1
The Expansion of Selected Industrial Outputs in the Soviet Union, 1928–1970

Industrial outputs	1928	1940	1945	1960	1970
Electric power (billions of kilowatt-hours)	5.0	48.3	43.3	292.3	740.0
Steel (millions of tons)	4.3	18.3	12.3	65.3	116.0
Petroleum (millions of tons)	11.6	31.1	19.4	147.9	352.6
Gas (billions of cubic meters)	0.3	3.4	3.4	47.2	199.6
Coal (millions of tons)	35.5	165.9	49.3	509.6	624.1
Cement (millions of tons)	1.8	5.7	1.8	45.5	95.2
Metalworking machine tools (thousands of units)	2.0	58.4	38.4	155.9	202.3
Motor vehicles (thousands of units)	0.8	145.0	75.0	523.6	916.1
Tractors (thousands of units)	1.3	31.6	7.7	238.5	459.0
Chemical fertilizers (millions of tons)	0.1	3.2	1.1	13.9	55.4

Source: Joint Publications Research Service, *State Five-Year Plan for the Development of the USSR National Economy, 1971–1975*, p. 5.

1928-1970. In 1928, the Soviet economy was but little advanced over its position in 1913. The big upsurge in economic growth took place after the Second World War.

In the years since 1917, major changes have occurred in the structure of the Soviet economy. In 1913, when the Russian economy was largely agricultural, 52.8 percent of the total number of industrial workers were employed in the light and food industries, and 14.4 percent in the engineering and metalworking industries. In 1965, only 26.3 percent of the workers were employed in the light and food industries, and 34.1 percent were employed in the heavy industries. Although today the Soviet Union is one of the world's major industrialized countries, a comparison of national income by sector of origin in the Soviet Union and the United States reveals some very significant economic differences between these two large industrialized countries.

As the statistics in Table 14-2 indicate, agriculture is a much larger sector in the Soviet economy than in the United States economy. Whereas 21 percent of Soviet national income originated in the agricultural sector in 1969, only 3 percent of the U.S. national income came from this sector. Also, the service sector is much larger in the United States than in the Soviet Union. This sector accounted for 57 percent of the United States national income, but for only 32 percent of the Soviet national income. An analysis of the composition of fixed investment in the United States and the Soviet Union shows that the Soviet Union invests relatively more heavily in industry and agriculture and less in housing, trade, education, transportation, communications, and other services than does the United States.

The American economic system is a mature industrial economy with the world's highest standard of living. In 1973, per capita GNP in the United States was $6,200, as compared

---

a measure of real cost. It is well known that in Soviet-type economies prices tend not to be good measures of real resource costs or of the relative worth of different commodities at any one time. In this connection, see Vladimir G. Treml and John P. Hardt (eds.), *Soviet Economic Statistics*, Durham, N.C.: Duke University Press, 1972; Abram Bergson, "Reliability and Usability of Soviet Statistics," *American Statistician*, Vol. 7, June–July, 1953, pp. 19–23, and *The Economics of Soviet Planning*, New Haven: Yale University Press, 1964, pp. 207–208; and Nicolas Spulber, *The Soviet Economy*, rev. ed., New York: W. W. Norton, 1969, pp. 145–159.

Table 14-2

U.S. and U.S.S.R. National Income by Sector of Origin (Percentages of Total)

Sectors	U.S. 1970	U.S.S.R. 1969
Industry and mining	29	37
Construction	5	9
Agriculture	3	21
Transportation and communications	6	11
Domestic trade	17	6
Other services	40	16
Total national income	100	100

Source: Robert W. Campbell, *The Soviet-Type Economies*, Boston: Houghton Mifflin Co., 1974, p. 101.

with $2,030 in the Soviet Union.[6] The Soviet GNP in 1972 was estimated to be $580 billion; the American GNP was $1,118 billion. With a larger population (247.5 million) than that of the United States (209 million) and GNP estimated to be a little more than one-half (51.8 percent) that of the United States, the Soviet Union had a much lower standard of living. According to the findings of the International Bank for Reconstruction and Development, per capita GNP is considerably higher in many of the Western European countries than in the Soviet Union.[7] Furthermore, the Soviet Union's per capita GNP is much smaller than that of East Germany and Czechoslovakia but larger than that of most of the other Eastern European countries as well as the Asiatic communist countries.

The American economy can be described as a high-consumption, low-investment economy, whereas the Soviet economy is a low-consumption, high-investment economy. The statistics in Table 14–3, which present the distribution or use of the GNP in the United States and the Soviet Union, show that private and public consumption take up 72 percent of this product in the former and only 56 percent in the latter. The situation is reversed regarding investment. Private and public investment use 17.8 percent of GNP in the United States; these investments absorb 33 percent of the Soviet GNP. Both nations devote a sizable part of their output to national defense.

Since 1917, the economic gap between the Soviet Union and the United States has been closing. The Soviet Union has borrowed the industrial technology of the West, increased its supply of engineers and technicians from 310,000 in 1941 to 2,554,000 in 1965, organized a total work force of 128 million, and established a large-scale industrial system. In 1913, according to Soviet calculations, the output per industrial worker in Russian industry was one-ninth that in the United States, but by 1968 this labor-productivity gap was reduced to one-half.[8] By 1968, 5.5 percent of all industrial enterprises employed 42 percent of all industrial workers, and accounted for 56 percent of total gross industrial output. In 1970, the Soviet Union claimed to have surpassed the United States in the level of output for coal, coke, iron ore, pig iron, lumber, cement, wheat, cotton, and wool.

[6] IBRD, *World Bank Atlas*, 1975, p. 7.
[7] *Ibid.*

[8] A. Yefimov, *op. cit.*, p. 66.

Table 14–3
Distribution of U.S. and Soviet GNP by End Use, 1970

End uses	Share in total GNP in percent	
	U.S.	U.S.S.R.
Consumption	72.0	56
Defense	7.2	10
Investment	17.8	33
Government administration	3.0	1
Gross National Product	100.0	100

Source: Robert W. Campbell, *The Soviet-Type Economies*, Boston: Houghton Mifflin Co., 1974, p. 100.

The Ninth Five-Year Plan states: "If we assume that the United States develops in the 1971–1975 period at the same rate as in the 1966–1970 period, in 1975 the national income produced in the USSR will constitute 80 percent of the level in the United States, industrial output will constitute 85 percent of the level in the United States, and with respect to agricultural output the USSR will approximately reach the level of the United States."[9] Even if these total goals were reached in 1975, the per capita gap between the two countries would still be large, since the Soviet Union's population exceeds that of the United States by approximately 39 million. A factor favoring the Soviet Union has been its higher annual economic-growth rate. According to the statistics of the Joint Economic Committee, industrial production in the Soviet Union increased at the annual rate of 6.7 percent in the years 1960–1971; in the United States the growth rate was 4.7 percent. While higher growth rates in the Soviet Union have helped in the past to narrow the economic gap with respect to the United States, the reduction of this gap may be more difficult in the future. In the past decade, the industrial growth rate has been declining in the Soviet Union as the movement from low-productivity to higher-productivity economic activities has slowed down, and also as labor has moved into the lower-productivity service industries. If these economic trends continue, the Soviet Union will find it increasingly difficult to reduce the Soviet-American per capita output or national income gap.

In spite of the increasing concern with consumer welfare in the Soviet Union since 1953, the Soviet economy remains a high-investment, low-consumption economy. Table 14-4 shows the trends in the allocation of Soviet GNP during the years 1928–1965. In these years, private consumption as a share of GNP decreased from 64.7 to 46.2 percent, while public consumption increased from 5.1 to 9.9 percent. Total private and public consumption, which accounted for 69.8 percent of GNP in 1928, continued to decline after 1928, until in 1965 total consumption was 56.1 percent of GNP. Defense, which took up only 2.5 percent of GNP in 1928, had increased to 11.3 percent by 1965. Total investment, which absorbed 25 percent of GNP in 1928, accounted for 30.4 percent in 1965. Although total private consumption declined as a relative share of GNP during the years 1928–1965, absolute per capita private consumption rose, because total private consumption was a declining relative share of a GNP that was increasing in absolute size. The statistics on the trends in per capita consumption show that this consumption increased after 1944 but at a declining average annual rate.[10] There is no evidence of any significant change in these trends since 1965. The Soviet society is still far from being a consumers' society, and no prospect of any major change in this direction appears likely in the near future.

The Soviet Planned Economy

The Soviet Union, the first communist country, has become the prototype after which all other communist economies have been largely patterned. This Soviet model shows us an economy operated as a huge single enterprise with the Politburo of the Communist party functioning as its board of directors. The Soviet Union, with the aid of a 125 million workers and a vast system of factories, mines, and farms on the world's largest land area,

[9] Joint Publications Research Service, *State Five-Year Plan for the Development of the USSR National Economy for the Period, 1971–1975, Part II*, Washington, D.C.: U.S. Department of Commerce, 1972, p. 350.

[10] Stanley H. Cohn, *Economic Development in the Soviet Union*, Lexington, Mass.: D. C. Heath, 1970, p. 73.

Table 14–4
Trends in the Distribution of the GNP, 1928–1970

End use	Percent of total GNP						
	1928	1937	1940	1950	1955	1965	1970
Private consumption	64.7	52.5	51.0	51.0	50.6	46.2 ⎫	56.5
Public consumption	5.1	10.5	9.9	8.0	8.2	9.9 ⎭	
Investment	25.0	25.9	19.2	23.0	25.3	30.4	30.2
Defense	2.5	7.9	16.1	13.3	13.0	11.3 ⎫	13.3
Government administration	2.7	3.2	3.8	4.7	2.9	2.4 ⎭	
Gross National Product	100.0	100.0	100.0	100.0	100.0	100.0	100.0

Sources: Stanley H. Cohn, *Economic Development in the Soviet Union*, p. 71; and Abram Bergson, *Prospects for Soviet Economic Growth in the 1970s*, p. 27.

turns out a GNP of around $865 billion (1975), which is the world's second largest total national output. The size and nature of this output reveal the overriding influence of the central planning authorities. The rate at which the Soviet annual national output grows, the kinds of products turned out, and the manner in which the output is distributed among various claimants are determined in the final analysis by the central planners. This kind of national planning differs greatly from the national planning carried on in democratic socialist countries such as Norway, Sweden, Israel, and India. While Russian and Western national planning have certain features in common, the two types of planning reflect profound ideological differences.

The Soviet Union was the first country in modern times to embark on the task of planning an entire economy. In 1928, when the Soviet Union began its planning experiment on an overall national basis, no other nation was attempting to plan its affairs on a large-scale basis. In the Western world, national economic planning outside the Soviet Union was not to take hold until after World War II, when the United Kingdom, France, the Scandinavian countries, and Holland inaugurated national economic planning programs. In the same years, national planning programs were established in Poland, Czechoslovakia, Yugoslavia, and other Eastern European communist countries and in China and other Asian countries. National planning has also been instituted since World War II in India and other underdeveloped nations. Unlike these many latecomers to national planning, the Soviet Union had no domestic or foreign experience to draw upon in developing its system of national planning before 1928. The writings of Marx, Engels, and Lenin provided no significant guidance with regard to the details and requirements of constructing a workable system of national planning. What the Soviet Union has produced in this area is the result of concrete experience molded by whatever analysis of the situation has come from Soviet leaders, administrators, and economists, all of whom have been constrained in their economic and political thinking by the monolithic heritage of Marxism-Leninism.

Although Soviet national planning reveals the birthmarks of its Marxist-Leninist origins, it should be noted that national economic planning wherever it is found follows a certain inner logic which is independent of ideology and cultural background. All systems of national economic planning, whether democratic or totalitarian, have three basic features in common. In any system of national planning there must be a central planning body or organ whose function is to deal with the problems of national planning. Second, some kind of national plan must be constructed by the central planning body. Third, a number of arrangements or controls are necessary in order to carry out the national plan. National planning varies widely as to ideological underpinning and the manner in which plans are constructed and executed. This becomes quite clear when one compares the national planning carried on in democratic Scandinavia and France and the type of planning in operation in totalitarian Russia, its satellites and China. However, we shall see that many of the problems met by the Soviet planners are also found in democratically planned countries.[11]

The goals of Soviet national planning include a high rate of industrial growth, an expanding military program, the exploration of space, and improved living standards. Under Stalin, the two major goals were the industrialization and the militarization of the Soviet Union. The improvement of standards of living did not have a high enough priority as a national goal to interfere much with the securing of a high rate of industrialization and a strong military position. Since Stalin's death in 1953, the establishment of priorities among Soviet national goals has become a much more complicated process than before that year. Securing industrial growth and an adequate military posture is no longer largely a matter of developing the steel, coal, iron, and power industries. In recent years, there has been a need to shift from the traditional complex of heavy industries to new industries of the space age, which include the electronic, petrochemical, chemical, and missile-support industries. Both the aerospace and strategic military force programs make heavy demands upon these technologically advanced industries. Sustained high industrial growth also requires a changeover from the steel-coal-power complex to the new industries of the second half of the twentieth century and a modernization of the industrial process.[12]

Since Stalin's death in 1953, more attention has been paid by the Communist party leadership to improving the Soviet standard of living. This has meant a shift of economic resources towards the goals of improved housing, more durable consumer goods, improved transportation, and a better diet. When the Seven-Year Plan was inaugurated in 1959, a high priority was attached to improving living conditions. However, progress in this direction has been delayed by recurring readjustments of priorities, which have subordinated enlarged consumer welfare to more space exploration and larger strategic military budgets. The recent efforts of the Soviet government to advance on all four fronts—industrial growth, more extended space exploration, improved living conditions, and enlarged strategic military forces—have at times led to an overcommitment of the nation's economic resources. Whenever an overcommitment has occurred, both agricultural and consumer welfare goals have been subordinated to industrial growth, aerospace, and military goals.

The determination of national goals in the Soviet Union is not a popular democratic process in which the welfare of the individual is the ultimate concern of the goal-making

[11] A. Kursky, *The Planning of the National Economy of the U.S.S.R.*, Moscow: Foreign Languages Publishing House, 1949, pp. 9–15.

[12] John P. Hardt, "Strategic Alternatives in Soviet Resource Allocation Policy," *Dimensions of Soviet Economic Power*, 1962, p. 15.

process. Goals in the Soviet Union are said to be determined according to the principle of "democratic centralism." This doctrine, which originated before the revolution of 1917, was introduced by Lenin as the governing principle of the Communist party. It was considered the correct method of arriving at decisions that were binding upon the entire party membership. When transferred to the broader realm of government activity and national planning, the principle of democratic centralism meant that the choice of national goals was based upon free discussion by both the Communist party leadership and the general population. However, once the decisions were freely made, they were to be followed by completely united and disciplined action in carrying them out. In other words, the popularly made decisions were to have the force of law.

An official statement of the fundamentals of Marxism-Leninism explains that "The economic activity of the socialist state rests on Lenin's principles of *democratic centralism.* This means that planning proceeds not only from the top downwards but also from the bottom upwards. Centralised state planning is combined with socialist democracy, with the initiative and spontaneous activity of the working masses."[13] On the surface, this statement appears to make Soviet planning a thoroughly democratic process. In fact, however, the situation is otherwise. Decisions about national goals are made by the top of the Communist party hierarchy, with discussions of these goals by the underlying population limited to the means by which they may be achieved. In the application of the principle of democratic centralism to national goal determination in the Soviet Union, the emphasis is on centralism and not on democracy. The Communist party rule that "the decisions of higher bodies are obligatory for lower bodies" has been extended to the general functioning of the entire Soviet Union.[14] The goals of Soviet national planning, unlike national goals in Norway, Sweden, France, and other democratic planning countries, are determined in the final analysis not by the Soviet people but by their Communist party leaders.

Although the party leadership is mainly responsible for the determination of the Soviet Union's national goals, the military establishment is to some extent independent of party control. The military group is in a more strategic position than the party leaders to determine an effective military program. Clearly the party cannot impose its control over the military establishment to the point of seriously reducing the military program's effectiveness. Whatever balance between party control and military effectiveness is achieved, such a balance must give the military forces an independence that continues to be a constraint upon the party in the allocation of economic resources.

The monolithic control of the Communist party over the use of the Soviet Union's economic resources is also watered down to some extent by a need to cater to the wishes of the underlying population for improved living conditions. The party leadership can provide adequate work incentives only by offering the workers a larger per capita supply of goods and services. Also, since the Soviet government has abandoned the terroristic methods of the Stalin regime and is now paying more attention to seeking the consent of the general population, a higher priority must be attached to improved living conditions as a national goal. The effort of the Soviet government to improve the world image of the Soviet system requires that the government deliver on their

---

[13] *Fundamentals of Marxism-Leninism,* Moscow: Foreign Languages Publishing House, 1961, p. 708.

[14] *Rules of the Communist Party of the Soviet Union, Adopted by the 22nd Congress of C.P.S.U.,* Oct. 31, 1961, Moscow: Foreign Languages Publishing House, 1961, p. 14.

"claim that more 'goulash and ballet' are hallmarks of the Soviet brand of Communism."[15]

The Soviet Union finds itself in a difficult position in attempting to reach the goals of rapid industrial growth, extensive space exploration, adequate military strength, and improved living conditions. Traditional Stalinist planning methods, with their emphasis upon "campaigning" and "storming" towards national goals, are no longer suitable for meeting the Soviet Union's needs. Hence the party leadership has had a great interest in recent years in finding methods of improving and refining the planning process with the aid of mathematical and electronic planning techniques. As the Soviet Union matures, reaching national goals becomes more and more a matter of efficiently squeezing more output from a given or a slowly increasing supply of economic resources.

The Administrative Apparatus of Soviet National Planning

The detailed blueprint planning of the economic activities of 250 million people and many hundreds of thousands of economic enterprises in the world's largest country requires a very extensive administrative system and highly complicated procedures. The Soviet planning authorities must coordinate the activities of 41,014 state industrial enterprises, 33,600 collective farms, 14,994 state farms (all statistics for 1970), and many thousands of construction sites, repair and service stations, warehouses, and retail trade establishments. In addition, there is a vast network of transportation units, financial institutions, foreign-trade organizations and scientific, cultural, and educational establishments. The planning of the affairs of all these organizations, enterprises, and establishments is shared by a large number of planning agencies on the national, republic, regional, provincial, district and local levels.

A general idea of the present system of planning and management in the Soviet economy is presented in Figure 14-1.[16] The overall body or agency responsible for planning and management is the administrative arm of the governmental system, which consists of the All-Union Council of Ministers and the fifteen Union Republic Councils of Ministers. The All-Union Council is made up of seventy-seven ministries, state committees, departments, and banks. The main planning agency is the U.S.S.R. State Planning Committee (Gosplan), below which the government planning apparatus broadens through a number of *staff* and *line* administrative layers at the national, republic, regional, provincial, district, city, and local levels. At each lower level, the planning activity is spread over a larger number of planning organizations until the bottom of the hierarchical pyramid is reached, where are found the planning departments of many thousands of operating plants and other establishments. As planning moves down from the apex of the planning apparatus, its general nature changes. At and

---

[15] John P. Hardt, *The Future Role of the Soviet Central Planner*, McLean, Virginia: Research Analysis Corporation, 1964, p. 17.

[16] A description and an analysis of Soviet planning are given in I. A. Yevenko, *Planning in the U.S.S.R.*, Moscow: Foreign Languages Publishing House, 1961; and Abram Bergson, *The Economics of Soviet Planning*, New Haven: Yale University Press, 1964. See also the discussion of Soviet planning in Howard Sherman, *The Soviet Economy*, Boston: Little, Brown, 1969; Paul R. Gregory and Robert C. Stuart, *Soviet Economic Structure and Performance*, New York: Harper and Row, 1974, pp. 113–178; Konstantin Lukyanov and Boris Tsvetkov, *How the USSR Plans Its National Economy*, Moscow: Novosti Press Agency Publishing House, 1973, pp. 37–59; Michael Manove, "A Model of Soviet-Type Economic Planning," *American Economic Review*, Vol. 61, June 1971, pp. 390–406; and Michael Ellman, "The Consistency of Soviet Plans," *Scottish Journal of Political Economy*, Vol. 16, Feb. 1969, pp. 50–74.

Figure 14-1
The Soviet Government Administrative Organization

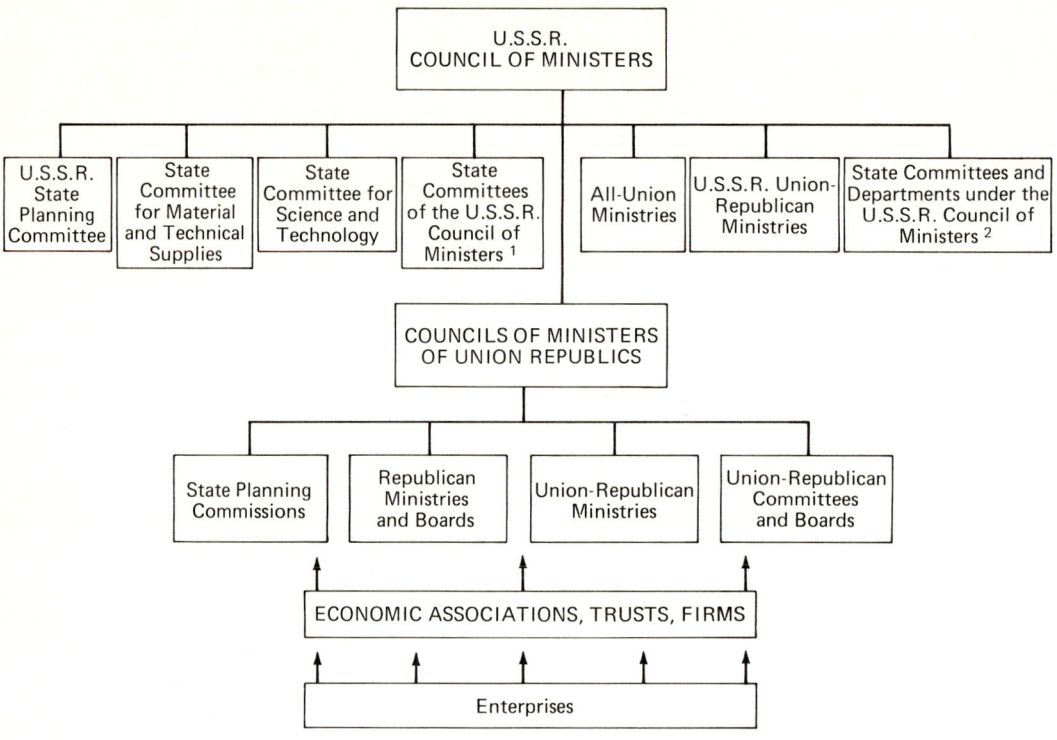

[1] Building
Labour and Wages
Foreign Economic Relations
Farm Purchases
Press
Radio and Television
Cinematography
Vocational Education
Soyuzselkhoztekhnika Organisation

[2] Central Statistical Board
Bank of Construction
Atomic Energy
Standards, Measures and Measuring Instruments
Inventions and Discoveries
Commission for Mineral Resources
Hydrometeorological Service

Source: A. Yefimov, *Soviet Industry*, p. 230. For a more detailed organizational chart see Central Intelligence Agency, *Central Economic Administrative Structure of the USSR*, Washington, D.C., 1972.

near the top of the planning structure, planning (which is of a staff nature) is concerned with the construction of national plans in accordance with the general directives coming down from the Politburo of the Communist party down through the U.S.S.R. Council of Ministers.

The two highest administrative layers of the planning apparatus—the national or all-union and republic levels—are mainly interested in the broader or staff aspects of national plan construction. The several layers of the planning apparatus below the all-union and republic staff layers are primarily involved in *line planning*, or seeing that the national plans are being executed in accordance with the general directives coming down from the apex of the planning structure. Line planning is essentially a matter of monitoring the execution of the national plans by the producing units at the bottom level of the planning structure.

In Soviet national economic planning, special attention is directed to the planning of industry, construction, agriculture, transportation, and foreign trade. Specialized planning organizations have at various times been established at the national, republic, and regional levels for the planning of these major sectors of the Soviet economy. Industry, including mining and the production of power, has been singled out for special consideration, since it is this sector that produces the major portion of Soviet national output. The core of the annual and medium-term economic plans is found in the planning of the industrial sector. Construction is likewise a very crucial factor in the development of the Soviet economy. Special planning bodies have therefore been set up to meet the construction needs of the expanding Soviet economic system. Agriculture has been a major obstacle to successful planning in the Soviet Union since the inauguration of the first Five-Year Plan in 1928. It has been selected for particular attention by the Soviet planning authorities, especially since 1953 when continuing efforts have been made to give more consideration to the needs of consumers.

Each planning agency, such as the U.S.S.R. State Planning Committee and the State Committee for Material and Technical Supplies, has a major planning task assigned to it and devotes its energies primarily to the accomplishment of the assigned task; a great deal of cooperation, nevertheless, goes on among the many planning and other government agencies at all levels of the national planning apparatus. When the U.S.S.R. State Planning Committee is drafting a five-year plan, it draws heavily upon the work of the state committees for agriculture, construction, scientific research, automation, and electronics; on ministries for such matters as transportation, foreign trade, and finance; on the Central Statistical Administration; and on many other government agencies that are in a position to contribute to the construction of medium-term national economic plans.

Similarly, the State Planning Committee, when constructing an annual national plan, relies heavily for information and advice upon a large number of government organizations at various levels. All planning agencies are contributing to the planning of one single large enterprise, the Soviet economy. Also, these agencies are responding to one will—that of the Politburo of the Communist party, whose directives provide the general shape of the annual and longer-term national economic plans. For this reason, Soviet national planning is a gigantic cooperative effort that seeks to fuse the activities of a vast complex of planning organizations on a number of levels, from the Council of Ministers on the highest level to the planning departments of the state enterprises at the bottom producing level.

Soviet economic planning is a combination of sectoral and territorial planning. Sectoral planning includes the planning of the enterprises in the major sectors of the economy, such as industry, agriculture, transportation, communications, foreign and domestic trade, and construction. Territorial planning is concerned with the geographical interrelationships of the industrial enterprises in the nineteen economic regions of the Soviet Union. Figure 14-2 provides an overall view of sectoral and territorial planning. The plans of all the industrial enterprises at the bottom of the planning pyramid are fitted into the overall state or national plan in two ways. Sectoral planning flows from the ministries responsible for various industries to the industrial associations, firms, combines, and trusts and then down to the individual enterprises in these industries. Territorial planning runs from the republics to the regions and districts

Figure 14-2

The Soviet Planning Pyramid

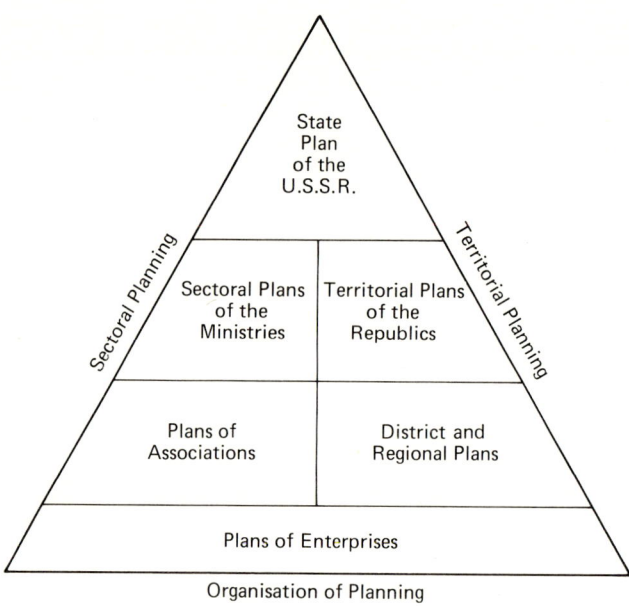

Source: A Yefimov, *Soviet Industry*, p. 241.

within the republics and then down to the industrial enterprises. At the same time, there is a reciprocal flow of planning activity from the enterprises at the bottom, through the upper layers of planning, to the State Planning Committee at the top. In this manner, the individual producing unit or enterprise at the bottom of the planning pyramid develops its ties with other enterprises in an industrial center or economic region and also in other sectors of the economy. The State Planning Committee at the top of the pyramid meshes the sectoral and territorial planning in one overall national plan.

The Three Types of Soviet Plans

Soviet national plans fall into three categories: long-term "comprehensive" plans covering more than five years; medium-term "perspective" plans relating to five-year plan periods; and "operational" annual or current plans. Comprehensive plans with a ten- to twenty-year coverage are concerned with long-term trends in population growth, labor supplies, technological progress, changes in industrial structure, resources availability, and regional development. In constructing long-term national economic development plans, the State Planning Committee (Gosplan) cooperates with the State Committee for Science and Technology and other state committees, the central ministries, the planning bodies at the republic level, and other agencies such as scientific centers of the U.S.S.R. Academy of Sciences.

Currently, scientific centers of the U.S.S.R. Academy of Sciences are working on long-term projections for individual industries and

426   Comparative economic systems

various sectors of the national economy. These projections have been made for the development of the transportation, oil, and petrochemical industries, land reclamation and the application of chemicals in agriculture, the nation's fuel balance, the development and location of the key branches of the Soviet economy, and the comprehensive development of the Union republics up to the year 1980.[17] On the basis of its long-term projections of economic trends, Gosplan works out the best alternative (or variant) for the development of the country's economy. The individual ministries and republics then construct drafts of long-term plans for the development of industries and other economic activities within the framework of this national alternative. This ten- to twenty-year variant serves as a framework within which the five-year plans are constructed. For example, Gosplan completed the work on the 1970–1980 long-term plan in time for the planners working on the Tenth Five-Year Plan for 1976–1980 to take the projections of this long-term plan into account.

While the Soviet government has always been involved in some long-term planning, in the past decade special emphasis has been placed on such planning. The Report of the Central Committee of the Communist party to the twenty-fourth Congress of the party in 1965 emphasized that the task of planning for an advanced communist economy made it necessary to broaden the horizons of economic planning, and to pay more attention to the long-range problems of determining national priorities and identifying the range of issues to be handled.[18] In the Stalinist era, when a base for rapid industrialization was being established, the main concern was with medium-term and annual planning. Now that the emphasis is on efficiency and the quality as well as the quantity of output, long-term considerations of scientific advance and technological progress, environmental protection, personal incentives, regional development, and foreign economic relations make it imperative to work out a long-range economic and social development plan.

The five-year plans are described by the Soviet planners as the "basic" form of planning. Like the long-term comprehensive plans, they are not operational, and do not closely guide the daily economic activities of the Soviet Union. However, having the perspective of a five-year plan period, the medium-term plans are closer to the annual plans of the industrial and agricultural enterprises than are the comprehensive, long-term plans. The medium-term plans provide a framework for the annual plans. They set production targets for the various economic activities, while at the same time taking account of the impact of long-term economic trends during the five-year plan period. Each enterprise develops its own annual and five-year plans in the light of the medium-term target set for the branch of the economy to which the enterprise belongs. Since the medium-term plans cover five-year plan periods and are broken down into five annual plans, flexibility can be obtained by making annual adjustments as required by changing circumstances.

Unlike the five- and ten-year plans, the annual plan is operational in nature. It is designed to provide day-to-day guidance for the operations of all of the nation's economic activities. Each factory, farm, and mine has an annual production schedule assigned to it by the planning authorities. Each enterprise is expected to adhere to its planned schedule (or to surpass it) and thereby to make its contribution to the production targets presented in the annual national plan. The annual national plan is much more detailed in its construction

[17] Progress Publishers, *Soviet Economy Forges Ahead, Ninth Five-Year Plan, 1971–1975*, Moscow, 1973, p. 225.

[18] Progress Publishers, *op. cit.*, p. 113; and A. Yefimov, *op. cit.*, p. 245.

than are the medium- and long-term plans, and therefore comes closer to being a blueprint for the guidance of economic activity than do the other plans.

It should be kept in mind that national economic planning in the Soviet Union is a continuous process. Plans for the next five-year plan period are drawn up long before the last year of a five-year plan period. Also, annual planning is a never-ending process. In annual plan periods, planning for the following year is always underway. Since planning of some sort—short run or long run—is always being carried on, there is a constant movement of planning activity from the top of the planning hierarchy down to the bottom, and from the bottom up to the top level. Annual or medium-term directives are frequently being sent down to the republics and state enterprises; at the same time, preliminary lower-level plans are being sent up from the state enterprises to the republic state planning committees and then on to the economic ministries, specialized state committees, and to the U.S.S.R. State Planning Committee at the highest planning level.

In this situation, relations among thousands of planning bodies and departments at all levels are well established and a gigantic pattern of plan relationships has emerged. Government officials, planning authorities, and plant managing and working personnel acquire years of planning experience. Both the art and the science of national planning have been widely cultivated in the Soviet Union for the past half-century. While Soviet national planning contains much inefficiency, the cruder aspects of early planning have been eliminated, and much thought has been given over the years to ways in which planning may be improved. The continuous process of national planning provides a laboratory in which experimentation with new planning methods can be carried on. The Soviet leaders are still far from satisfied with the existing national planning procedures and performance, for they have frequently resorted to changes in plan organization and procedures over the years.

The construction of Soviet five-year plans, which is the main responsibility of the U.S.S.R. State Planning Committee, is carried out in several stages. The first stage is the definition of the main economic tasks to be achieved during the five-year plan period. This is done by the Communist party; in its deliberations about the goals of medium-term national planning, the Central Committee and the Politburo have a dominant position. In the final analysis, the select core of the Communist party leaders determines the broad objectives of the perspective or medium-term national economic plans. These party leaders determine the key economic tasks of the coming medium-term plan and the directions of Soviet economic development.

The second stage in the construction of the five-year national plan is the preparation of a concrete plan on the basis of the general directives from the Communist party Politburo. At this point, the U.S.S.R. State Planning Committee steps into the picture and, with the cooperation of the many other planning agencies and government organizations described in an earlier section of this chapter, proceeds to construct the medium-term plan. The committee first makes a study of the preceding five-year plan to determine the position of the Soviet economy at the beginning of the new plan period. Having ascertained the current levels of production in the various sectors of the national economy, the State Planning Committee can then indicate how to achieve the broad economic goals established by the party leaders. At this point, the committee works out the *control figures* of national economic development. These control figures are rates of growth for the various sectors of the Soviet economy that together show the proportional development of the economy during the plan period. The control figures set targets for the national plan, which, if achieved, will bring about the proportional development of the economy that is called for by the directives of the Communist party leadership.

From the broadest point of view, when the State Planning Committee drafts a five-year plan, it makes what in Western terminology would be described as a national economic budget for the final year of the plan period. This budget shows the total national output projected for the last year of the five-year plan period; the budget also indicates how this output is to be distributed among private and public consumption and various government investment uses. All the production plans of state factories, state and collective farms, construction sites, and other producing units are brought together in a national economic balance or budget for the plan period.

The main feature distinguishing Soviet national planning from planning in Western democratic countries is the detailed and extensive system of targets that is set up to guide Soviet economic development during the plan period. As has already been explained, these targets are established in the light of the economic, cultural, and political tasks assigned to the national plans by the Communist party Politburo. These targets are presented in either physical or value terms. For example, the iron, steel, oil, and housing long-term goals are measured in tons, or square meters, while the gross output, capital investment, and national income targets are measured in rubles.

Industrial Subplans

Behind the system of plan targets is a number of subplans which cover major sectors of the economy. The economic sector that is the primary concern of the State Planning Committee is industry. When drawing up the national plan for Soviet industry, the State Planning Committee designs a number of major subplans, which cover the spheres of industrial production, capital investment, the location of industry, labor productivity, and the introduction of new technology. Since from the Soviet point of view, the industrial sphere or sector is the principal sector of the national economy, industry is the key consideration in the Soviet medium-term national plan and is the point of departure in working out all the other targets of the national plan.

Associated with the State Planning Committee's medium-term production plan are its capital investment and construction plans. Changes in the Soviet economy's production pattern necessitate changes in its capital structure that are of both a quantitative and a qualitative nature. Every billion-ruble increase in Soviet industrial production requires more plant and equipment of various types. If there were no change in the make-up of Soviet industrial production during the plan period, the capital problem would merely be one of enlarging the existing supplies of plant and equipment. But, as already discussed, Soviet long-term national planning at times involves radical changes in the composition of industrial production. Consequently, the five-year production and investment plans must be closely coordinated so that the planned changes in capital structure mesh with the planned changes in industrial production.

The labor and technical subplans of the Soviet five-year national plans have as their objectives: (1) creating an adequate supply of labor equipped with the kinds of skills required by the national production plan; (2) improving the productivity of labor; and (3) introducing new methods of production and new products. Population trends indicate to the planning authorities the probable size of the total work force during the plan period.

The five-year labor plan takes account of the future labor needs of industry, agriculture, construction, and other economic activities and also distributes the expanding work force.

The technical plan visualizes an extensive mechanization and automation of production processes in the plan period. Mechanization will reduce the need for manual labor in many branches of industry, agriculture, and transportation. The automation program emphasizes the objective of organizing fully automated factories in which widespread use will be made of computing machine techniques. It has been projected that the measures for the overall mechanization and automation of production and for the development of regional specialization and cooperation in industry will improve labor productivity by almost 40 percent in the plan period 1971–1975.

Other subplans or *principal tasks,* as they are described by the Ninth Five-Year Plan, are the subplans for agriculture, foreign economic relations, and consumer welfare. The subplan or program for agriculture "calls for a further substantial increase in the output of all agricultural products and fuller satisfaction of the population's growing needs for foodstuffs and industry's growing needs for raw materials."[19] This agricultural plan goal is to be achieved through projected increases in such basic outputs as grain, cotton, wool, meat, milk, and eggs. For example, the Ninth Five-Year Plan projects for the years 1971–1975 an annual increase of 3.1 percent in grain, a 4.3 percent increase in meat, and a 2.1 percent increase in cotton. The national plan provides for measures to strengthen the material and technical base of agriculture. These measures, which require more investment in agriculture, have as their objective the further mechanization of agriculture, land reclamation and improvement, the chemicalization of agriculture through the more extensive use of fertilizers, pesticides, and herbicides, and the introduction of advanced agricultural technology.

The foreign economic relations subplan provides for a balance between the exports and imports of goods and services at rising levels of foreign trade. During the plan period 1971–1975 an increase of 33 to 35 percent in foreign trade was expected. The emphasis was to be on expanding trade with the socialist countries of Eastern Europe that belong to the Council for Mutual Economic Assistance. Beyond this, the foreign economic relations program seeks to expand trade relations with the less developed countries of Asia, Africa, and Latin America, and also with the industrially advanced capitalist countries.

The subplan for the improvement in consumer welfare or for "a further rise in the material and cultural standard of living," as the Ninth Plan expresses it, has become of increasing importance in the past decade as efforts have been made to improve worker incentives and to raise labor productivity. In order to increase the flow of consumer goods, the emphasis has shifted from the heavy to the light consumer-goods industries, and for the first time since five-year planning started in 1928 the Ninth Plan projected a higher annual increase in consumer goods output than in heavy goods output. The subplan for improving consumer welfare includes measures to enlarge the supplies of scarce consumer goods such as meat, household chemical products, housing, and personal services. The expanding output of consumer goods is to be matched by a continued growth of the real income of the population.

In the plan period 1971–1975, the projected increase in the average monthly wage of workers was from 122 rubles in 1970 to 149.3 rubles in 1975. In the same period, substantial

---

[19] *State Five-Year Plan for the Development of the USSR National Economy for the Period, 1971–1975,* Part I, p. 168. The large 1975 grain purchases by the Soviet Union from the United States indicate that these agricultural plans were far from being fulfilled.

annual increases in per capita private and public consumption and retail trade turnover were anticipated. A recurring concern of the subplan for enlarging consumer welfare is the gap between the urban and rural standards of living. The consumer welfare program of the Ninth Plan stated that particular attention would be given to taking "an important new step in consistently overcoming the substantial differences between the city and rural areas."[20]

The Unity of Soviet Planning

The Soviet planning theorists carry on their work in accordance with what they call the "principle of unity of scientific and technical, economic and social planning."[21] They point out that problems of social development are now increasingly prominent in the five-year plans. During the construction of the Ninth Five-Year Plan, much attention was paid to such social problems as raising the living standards of low-income families, improving the status of women, and eliminating the distinction between town and country. Comprehensive long-term plans combine both economic and social planning, and increasingly embody the principle of unity referred to above. The Soviet planning authorities look forward to "the setting up of a single system of optimal management and planning," which will extend from the individual enterprises at the bottom up to the top planning and management bodies. They believe that this is possible by using mathematical methods of optimal planning and modern electronic computer techniques. In order to achieve this aim, the Soviet government is in the early stages of developing a nation-wide automated system of data collection and processing for use in planning and managing the nation's economy. The optimal plan, if achieved, would then combine comprehensive long-term, perspective medium-term, and operational current plans in one continuing planning process.[22]

A serious question, which the Soviet planners tend to ignore, is the role of the general population in determining the national priorities that would guide the optimal planning. The wide employment of economico-mathematical methods and the use of electronic computer techniques can improve the efficiency of planning; they do not, however, provide any answers to the question of what national purposes lie behind this efficiency.[23] Thus far, the Politburo's preferences have largely prevailed over the citizen-consumers' preferences; thus the latter group has not had much to do with the determination of the Soviet Union's economic and social goals.

The Balance Method of Soviet Annual National Planning

Any national economic plan that is operational, i.e., is used to guide the nation's

---

[20] *Ibid.*, Part II, p. 295. The execution of the Ninth Plan up to 1975 indicated that these consumer goals were far from being achieved.

[21] Progress Publishers, *op. cit.*, p. 226.

[22] An optimum or "best" plan would be chosen from among several consistent plan variants; it would require the least inputs of scarce resources to achieve the goals of the national plan. The best plan would thus avoid the misallocation of scarce resources, providing for the most efficient allocation of these resources so as to achieve the nation's goals. For a further discussion of optimality in planning, see Nicolas Spulber, *op. cit.*, pp. 197–233; and Paul R. Gregory and Robert C. Stuart, *op. cit.*, pp. 137-138.

[23] When discussing the work of the "new" mathematical economists, Campbell explains that "in general, the new theoreticians have tried to minimize any political, ideological, or institutional interpretations of their work. They all claim to be good Marxists.... They are also very careful to steer away from the issue of goals—their technical apparatus is value-free, and they have no quarrel with the right of the leadership to set goals for the society." Robert W. Campbell, *op. cit.*, p. 198.

production, investment, and consumption activities, must be internally consistent if the planning is to be successful. Internal consistency in a plan is achieved when all the parts of the plan are in balance. In this situation, the necessary input requirements exist for meeting the plan's production targets. For each unit of planned output, an adequate supply of materials, equipment, and labor will be available to produce that output. If the plan is successful, planned output and planned input will balance. If the planned economy is an open economy that carries on international trade, the national plan will also call for a balance between the export and the import of goods (including gold as a commodity) and services. These various balances are real balances that are concerned with balancing physical inputs of materials and equipment to secure the planned physical output. They relate to the real product flow of the economy, in which various physical inputs are converted into different kinds of physical output.

The economy also has an income-expenditure flow, which must be planned when an annual national plan is constructed. Since materials, equipment, and labor are bought and sold, firms must be supplied with cash or credit to make the necessary purchases. In addition, workers must be supplied with cash and credit to purchase the supply of consumer goods. Real plans must therefore be supplemented with financial plans. Real balances must be accompanied by financial balances that will balance the sales and purchases of producers' and consumers' goods in the nation's markets.

In a free market economy, real and financial balances are created by the forces operating within the free market. This is most clearly seen in a purely competitive market, where the interactions among many thousands of sellers and buyers tend to establish balances between the supplies of and demands for various types of commodities, equipment, and labor. The function of the free market system is to provide these various balances without the intervention of the government or any other extra market agency. In a planned economy, such as the Soviet economy, where the free market system is not in operation, the planning authorities themselves have to perform the functions of a free market by constructing the necessary balances. In the Soviet Union, real planning or the construction of material balances is much more important than financial planning. This is because outside the consumer sector of the Soviet Union, no free market exists for goods and services; and even in the consumer sector, the market is in some ways severely restricted.

On the surface, the marketing of industrial supplies is apparently carried on in much the same way in the Soviet Union as in Western democracies. A Soviet enterprise "buys" its needed input materials from a producing enterprise at prices stipulated by commercial contracts and, under the same contract system, "sells" its output to other purchasing state enterprises. However, there is a major difference between Soviet and American industrial purchasing. In the Soviet Union, the enterprise or firm does not buy its input materials on an open market, where materials are freely acquired if the purchase price can be met. Instead, all important input materials and equipment are centrally distributed by all union or republican planning agencies. In order to secure the necessary major input materials, the Soviet enterprise must not only have the money, but also a government-approved authorization (*fond*) to acquire the materials from other producing enterprises. Since providing the enterprise with the necessary cash or credit presents no difficulties, the major Soviet planning problem is distributing the rights to acquire input materials and making certain that supplies of these materials will be available when needed to honor these rights. Securing balances between various kinds of inputs and outputs is achieved through the "balance method of planning," the basic method used in Soviet annual national planning.

The balances used in Soviet annual national planning are of three general types: material, labor, and financial.[24] The material balances are balances of industrial raw materials and supplies, such as ores, metals, chemicals; agricultural raw materials, such as grain, cotton, hides, and wool; building materials; fuel and electric power; raw materials for consumer goods and food processing industries, such as flour, meat, vegetables, oil, and sugar; and equipment, such as machine tools, motor vehicles, agricultural machinery, and building equipment. The labor balance shows the balance between the supplies of various types of labor and the demands for these labor supplies. The financial balances are of three kinds: the cash, credit, and consumer-income balances. These three financial balances constitute the nation's annual financial plan, which goes along with the annual real product or output plan.

Of the three types of balances—material, labor, and financial—the most crucial for Soviet annual planning are the material or supply balances. The main concern in Soviet annual national planning is the output of material producers' and consumers' goods. This output requires a vast supply of raw materials, industrial and agricultural supplies, and equipment. The planners must be prepared to provide this large input of materials at the right places and at the right times. The "primary task" of Soviet planning is therefore "drafting plans of material supply," which are the "most laborious section of the state plan," for they require about six months of concerted work by the management of the state enterprises and the various planning agencies.[25]

A material balance is, in essence, a balance statement of the supply of and demand for a given product. The central planning organ of the Soviet Union constructs material balances in the annual plans for from eight hundred to one thousand important centrally allocated commodities; it shows in these balances the available supplies and the various demands expected in the plan year for each of these commodities. Table 14-5 presents the constituent elements of a typical material balance. Most of the total supply of a material, often as much as 95 percent, comes from the enterprises of the republics and the all-union ministries which produce the material. The small remainder comes from imports, other sources such as scrap, and possibly a decrease in the stocks of the material held by supply or sales organizations. The bulk of the material is used to meet the production and operation needs of state enterprises of the republics and all-union ministries, the construction industry, and the market for consumers' goods (market fund). Some of the output of the material may go into the state reserves held as a protection against national disasters and into the reserves of the Council of Ministers, which are used to meet the needs of enterprises that overfulfill their production targets or fail to get input materials because of supply failures.

The crucial problem in materials balance planning is how the imbalances between the preliminary planned output and the planned uses of a material are eliminated in the construction of the final draft of the annual national economic plan.[26] If the preliminary

[24] I. A. Yevenko, *Planning in the U.S.S.R.*, Moscow: Foreign Languages Publishing House, 1961, pp. 171-182.

[25] *Ibid.*, pp. 83-88.

[26] Herbert S. Levine, "The Centralized Planning of Supply in Soviet Industry," Joint Economic Committee, *Comparisons of the United States and Soviet Economies*, Part I, Washington, D.C., 1959, pp. 160-161. See also R. W. Davies, "Planning a Mature Economy in the USSR," *Economics of Planning*, Vol. 6, 1966, pp. 138-153; Gertrude Schroeder, "Recent Developments in Soviet Planning and Managerial Incentives," in Joint Economic Committee, *Soviet Economic Prospects for the Seventies*, Washington, D.C., 1973, pp. 11-38; and Paul R. Gregory and Robert C. Stuart, *op. cit.*, pp. 128-138.

Table 14–5
Soviet Material Balance for Product X in Plan Year Y

Sources	Uses or distribution
1. Production of state enterprises in republics or ministries.	1. Production and operation needs of user state enterprises in republics or ministries.
2. Imports	2. Construction
3. Other sources	3. Market fund
4. Stocks of suppliers at the beginning of the plan year.	4. Exports
	5. Increase of State Reserves
	6. Increase of Reserves of Council of Ministers
	7. Stocks of suppliers at end of plan year.

Source: H. S. Levine, "The Centralized Planning of Supply in Soviet Industry," *Comparisons of the United States and Soviet Economies*, Part I, 1959.

planned supply of steel proves to be less than the preliminary planned uses of steel, how is this imbalance removed? Usually, the material imbalance arises because the planned uses of the material exceed its planned supply. In this situation, the industrial department of the planning agency that is concerned with the material works on its supply, while the appropriate summary or distribution department of the planning agency works on its uses or distribution.

These two departments of the planning agency, working closely together, strive to eliminate the imbalance. The basic principle generally followed is that the demand for the material is not to be reduced to the level of the available supply, since this means that the output dependent upon the use of the material will also have to be curtailed. On the supply side, steps are taken to increase the supply of the deficit material by drawing upon stocks held by suppliers, by increasing imports, and, more commonly, by increasing current production of the material. This latter goal may be achieved through a better use of equipment or by installing new equipment earlier than planned. At the same time, the summary department of the central planning agency attempts to reduce the demand for the deficit commodity by having enterprises operate more efficiently and economize in the use of the deficit material without reducing the output target for which the material is used. In some cases, nondeficit materials may be substituted for the deficit material. In this balancing of supply of and demand for the deficit material, adjustments are made, if necessary, in the low-priority (usually consumer) sectors which may have their allocations of the deficit material cut or which may be required to use substitute materials.

Where the imbalance is corrected by increasing the output of the deficit material, materials planning could become very complicated. If the planned output of steel is increased beyond what the plan originally called for, related adjustments must be made in the production of all the inputs required for the production of more steel; and further adjustments must be made in the production of those materials required to increase the inputs originally required to produce more steel. In this manner, enlarging the output of a deficit material requires additional increases in outputs of various kinds in a series of steps which, mathematically, would be infinite in number. However, since the adjustments at each step of rebalancing get smaller in volume, the adjustment or rebalancing process is usually stopped after a few rounds of adjustments have been made. In Soviet annual materials planning, it is not the practice to go beyond three or four rounds of adjustments in tracing out the effects or consequences of increasing the supply of a deficit material; even this is done only where the consequences of rebalancing are readily distinguished.

Thus far, the Soviet planners do not appear to have extensively used input-output techniques and high-speed computers in their annual planning of material balances, but research is being actively carried on with this aim in view. At present, removing materials imbalances is done largely by avoiding second-round effects when making adjustments between the demand for and the supply of input materials. With regard to the use of a deficit material, user enterprises are pressured to economize in the use of the scarce material by improving their input norms. Only as a last resort is the supply of the deficit material increased by reducing current inventories or by reducing the supply available to low-priority users of the deficit material.

Soviet Real and Financial Planning

The Soviet annual and five-year plans are real or physical plans, which are constructed in terms of constant or base-year ruble prices. They measure real changes in the output of enterprises, industries, and the total economy, and in national and per capita income, labor productivity, total investments, and related items. Soviet national planning also deals with the financial or value aspects of economic activities in terms of financial proportions or balances. If expenditures for consumer and producer goods are not in balance with the supplies of these goods, imbalances may result in the appearance of inflationary pressures in consumer-goods markets or in supply bottlenecks in producer-goods markets. The planning authorities concerned with financial balances use four instruments in order to secure the right financial proportions or balances. These are the cash plan, the credit plan, the personal wage fund, and the fiscal budget. By coordinating these four financial instruments, the planning authorities are able to construct various financial plans that support the annual and five-year real plans.

The cash plan is designed to maintain balance between the supply of and demand for consumer goods. Wage income before taxes usually exceeds the value of the available supply of consumer goods, because this income is earned in producing both consumer and producer goods. If annual wage income amounts to 200 billion rubles and the supply of consumer goods is valued at 150 billion rubles, consumer demand could exceed consumer supply by 50 billion rubles if there was no personal saving. The usual practice in the Soviet Union is to secure a consumer-goods, supply-demand balance by imposing turnover taxes (sales taxes) to absorb whatever excess wage income there is.

This cash plan is accompanied by a credit plan which contributes towards a financial balance between the supply of and demand for producers' goods. These goods can be purchased by drawing upon enterprises' depreciation funds, investing retained profits, and securing bank loans. If the available supply of producers' goods amounts to 100 billion rubles, a balance must be struck so that no more than 100 billion rubles is made available from various sources to purchase the supply of producers' goods. The Soviet banks and the Ministry of Finance, which constructs the fiscal budget, play important roles in the construction of the balance between the supply of and the demand for producers' goods. The banks influence the demand for producers' goods by rationing the credit supplied to enterprises.

The fiscal budget taxes the profits of some enterprises, and provides budgetary grants to other enterprises for the purchase of producers' goods. Government revenues from turnover taxes, profits taxes, and personal income taxes are used to finance expanding and new industries, government administration, social and cultural programs, and the defense and space exploration programs. The annual fiscal budgets seek to provide financial support for the achievement of the national goals set forth in the annual plans.

Financial or value planning in the Soviet Union also involves manipulation of the total personal wage fund by the State Committee on Labor and Wages. By controlling the size of this wage fund and its distribution among the various industrial branches, the planning authorities can then control the cash flows of private households and the demand for consumer goods. Soviet financial planning also meshes the financial plans of individual enterprises and the overall national plan. The microplans of the individual enterprises, which make provision for depreciation funds and total profits, are coordinated with the macroplans of the total economy for securing a balance between total saving and total investment.

Soviet financial planning comes to a head in the overall planning for the use of the national income, which consists of a consumption fund and an accumulation or investment fund. The consumption fund is used for personal and public consumption; the accumulation fund is employed for investment in plant, equipment, and additions to inventories. In Soviet financial planning, a balance is secured between the national income and its consumption and investment (accumulation) components. Table 14-6 shows the distribution of the actual national income in 1970 and the projected or planned national income for 1975. In 1970, 74.1 percent of the national income was spent for consumption purposes and 25.9 percent for investment purposes. During the years 1971–1975, national income was projected to increase by 107 billion rubles, or at an annual rate of 6.8 percent. No major changes in the distribution of the national income between consumption and investment expenditures were projected for this plan period. Between 1960 and 1970 a significant increase in the consumption-fund component of national income occurred, but this trend weakened after 1970.[27] In 1975, Soviet financial planning was expected to provide for consumption expenditures of 286 billion rubles (74.5 percent of national income) and investment expenditures of 98 billion rubles (25.5 percent of national income).

Soviet Annual Planning

The annual national plans, which are organic parts of the five-year plans, largely predetermine the successful fulfillment of the whole five-year plan. Each annual plan is a step towards the goals set forth in the final year of the five-year plan. Some of the major goals of the 1972 annual plan are presented in Table 14-7. This plan outlines the essential shifts in the structure of industry. Special attention was given in this annual plan to securing faster rates of development in the consumer-goods industries. Also, substantial increases in the resources allocated to agriculture were projected. During 1972, it was anticipated that new equipment would be put into operation in the electric-power, petroleum, coal, chemical, knitwear, and leather-footwear industries.

[27] During the years 1960–1970, the percent of national income spent on consumption increased from 72.1 to 74.1. See Keith Bush, "Is the Ninth Five-Year Plan Consumer-Oriented?", *Prospects for Soviet Economic Growth in the 1970s*, p. 84.

Table 14-6

The Distribution of the Soviet National Income in 1970 and 1975

Expenditures	1970 (Actual) In billions 1970 rubles	1970 (Actual) In percent	1975 (Projected) In billions 1970 rubles	1975 (Projected) In percent
National income used for consumption	205	74.1	286	74.5
National income used for investment	72	25.9	98	25.5
National income	277[1]	100.0	384[1]	100.0

[1] Estimated.

Source: *State Five-Year Plan for the Development of the USSR National Economy, 1971–1975*, Part I, pp. 71–77.

The 1972 annual plan emphasized that the success of the 1971–1975 five-year plan depended very largely on the "unconditional fulfillment of plans for capital construction."[28]

Table 14–7 also shows the 1976 state annual plan which is much less ambitious than the 1972 state annual plan. By 1975 it was accepted by the Soviet government that there had been a permanent slowdown in the economy's growth. Whereas national income had been projected to increase 6.2 percent in 1972, the planned increase in national income for 1976 was only 5.4 percent. Also by 1976 the effort to increase the supply of consumers' goods faster than the supply of producers' goods was abandoned. The statistics in Table 14–7 show that the planned increase in Group A or producers' goods for 1976 was 4.9 percent, but the planned increase in Group B or consumers' goods was only 2.7 percent.

The planning authorities reported some shortcomings in economic activity in 1971

[28] *State Five Year Plan* (1971-1975), Part I, p. 50.

Table 14-7

The Soviet 1972 and 1976 Annual State Plans

Main plan targets	Planned percentage increases in 1972 over 1971	Planned percentage increases in 1976 over 1975
National income	6.2	5.4
Industrial output	6.9	4.3
Group A goods (producers')	6.8	4.9
Group B goods (consumers')	7.1	2.7
Freight turnover	5.0	5.7
Volume of capital investments	5.7	5.1
Labor productivity in industry	6.1	3.4
Retail trade turnover	7.7	3.6
Real per capita income	5.2	3.7

Source: *State Five-Year Plan for the Period 1971–1975*, Part I, p. 49; and Central Statistical Administration, Moscow, Jan. 1976.

that they hoped would not be repeated in 1972. These shortcomings included a drop in the growth rate of industrial output, a failure to complete and place in operation many production facilities, and a failure to plan for the creation and introduction of new equipment in a number of industries. Also, the assignments for the production of certain consumer goods were not being fulfilled. The planning authorities observed that the annual national plans were suffering from the fact that "many business executives have unfortunately taken a lenient attitude toward failure to fulfill these plans, particularly at construction sites of the light and food industries. It is a question of honor for all builders to complete work on all construction projects slated for construction in 1972, so that they begin operation on schedule."[29]

The economic reforms instituted in 1965 will have been in effect for one decade by the end of the Ninth Plan. The Soviet government expected during the Eighth and Ninth Plans to reverse the trend towards a lower economic growth rate that had begun in the early 1960s. While some progress has been made in improving the system of planning and management and the incentive system, a number of Western analysts think that labor productivity has not risen enough to improve the Soviet Union's growth record during the years 1965-1975.[30] National planning has not yet benefited much from the 1965 economic reforms, because the original purpose of these reforms—to enlarge the freedom of the enterprise directors—has not been realized. Ministries and planning agencies have seized the initiative in the application of the economic reforms; they have imposed on the state enterprises a new maze of norms, rules, and guidelines that has greatly curbed the freedom and spontaneity of the state enterprises. Consequently, the modus operandi of planning and management has changed very little since 1965. The result is that the obstacles to improved planning, such as "a still rising volume of unfinished construction, gross waste on every side, perverse incentives, foot-dragging on introduction of new technology, poor quality of products, and shortages of both consumer and producer goods," are said by some Western economists to continue to plague the work of the Soviet planners.[31]

The Ninth Five-Year Plan, 1971–1975

The first five of the five-year plans, covering the Stalinist period 1928–1953, emphasized extensive planning, in which economic growth was achieved by increasing labor and capital inputs. Stress was placed upon securing plan fulfillment without much regard for efficiency or rational economic decision making. Stalin's antipathy towards the economics of the Western world made it difficult for Soviet economists to underline the importance of using economic science in order to maximize the output from a given supply of scarce resources. During the years 1953–1964, between Stalin's death and Khrushchev's removal from office, an interest developed in a kind of planning that would pay more attention to the intensive and efficient use of labor and capital. Not much was accomplished during the Malenkov-Khrushchev era (1953–1964) to make planning more rational and efficient. Much of Khrushchev's concern was focused on the agricultural problem, which had been badly neglected by Stalin. During

---

[30] See Robert W. Campbell, *op. cit.*, p. 115; Gertrude E. Schroeder, "Economic Organization and Management as Factors in Soviet Economic Growth in the 1970s," in M. Yves Laulan, *Prospects for Soviet Economic Growth in the 1970s*, Brussels, 1971, p. 151; and Abram Bergson, "Toward a New Growth Model," *Problems of Communism*, March–April, 1973, p. 8.

[31] See, for example, Gertrude E. Schroeder, *op. cit.*, p. 151.

the Sixth Five-Year Plan (1956–1960), abandoned in 1958, and the Seven-Year Plan (1958–1965) planning and management techniques were not much improved; considerable advance, however, was made in the universities and research centers of the U.S.S.R. Academy of Sciences in mathematical economics and its theoretical implications for planning and management.

The Eighth Five-Year Plan, which began in 1966, drew attention to the new era in Soviet planning, in which intensive rather than extensive planning would be emphasized, and the traditional methods of planning would undergo considerable modification. The economic reforms introduced by Brezhnev and Kosygin in 1965 were calculated to improve greatly the planning and management system. While these reforms have not been as effective as their originators asserted they would be, nevertheless, they represent a marked improvement over the economic decision making carried on by planners and enterprise directors during the Stalin era. In spite of the setbacks experienced by the Brezhnev-Kosygin reforms, Western analysts generally agree that the reform movement in the Soviet Union is by no means dead. One critic commented: "Perhaps we should not discount the prospects for significant change in the Soviet domestic economy."[32] The Ninth Five-Year Plan continued the effort "to provide further improvement of the planning system, to continue to pursue a rise in the scientific substantiation and the accuracy in the balancing of plans, and optimum combination of branch, territorial, and combined planning."[33]

The Ninth Five-Year Plan (1971–1975) was the second plan to be carried out since the end of the Khrushchev era. Like the Eighth Plan (1966–1970), the Ninth Plan was designed to cope with a declining economic growth rate at a time when the national goals emphasized the importance of enlarging consumer welfare as well as securing a high economic growth rate. The report of the Central Committee of the Soviet Communist party to the 24th party Congress in 1971 stated that "The main task of the five-year plan is to ensure a substantial rise in the material and cultural standard of living [of the workers and employees] on the basis of high rates of development of socialist production, a rise in production efficiency, scientific and technical progress, and a faster growth of labor productivity."[34] Whether or not the Soviet planning authorities achieved a significant rise in the general population's standard of living during the plan period 1971–1975, they intended to maintain high growth rates for national income and industrial production. High economic growth is essential for industrial progress and the support of the military and space exploration programs.

Some of the major targets of the Ninth Plan are listed in Table 14–8, which shows the breakdown of the five-year plan on an annual basis. National income, officially reported as growing at an annual rate of 7.1 percent in the plan period 1966–1970, was expected to increase at the annual rate of 6.8 percent in the years 1971–1975. Industrial output, having increased at the average annual rate of 8.5 percent, according to the Eighth Plan, was estimated to increase at a rate of 8 percent in the Ninth Plan. For the first time in Soviet planning experience, consumer goods were projected in the years 1971–1975 to increase at a faster rate (8.3 percent) than producer goods (7.9 percent). With real per capita income rising at an average annual rate of 5.6 percent and the flow of consumer goods enlarged,

[32] John P. Hardt, "Summary," *Soviet Economic Prospects for the Seventies,* 1973, p. XVII.

[33] "Compilation of the Ninth Five-Year Plan in Gosplan USSR," *State Five-Year Plan for the Development of the USSR National Economy for the Period 1971–1975,* Part II, p. 462.

[34] *State Five-Year Plan* (1971–1975), Part I, p. 1.

Table 14–8
Selected Major Targets of the Soviet Ninth Five-Year Plan, 1971–1975 (1970 = 100)

Planned targets	1971	1972	1973	1974	1975	Annual % increase 1971–1975
National income	106.1	113.0	121.0	129.0	139.0	6.8
Industrial output	106.9	115.4	124.4	135.1	147.0	8.0
Group A (producer goods)	106.7	115.3	124.1	134.7	146.3	7.9
Group B (consumer goods)	107.4	115.7	125.1	136.0	148.6	8.3
Labor productivity in industry	105.9	113.0	120.3	129.0	138.8	6.8
State capital investments	106.5	112.8	124.0	132.5	139.6	6.9
Freight turnover	105.3	111.6	118.3	126.0	135.1	6.2
Retail trade turnover	106.4	114.6	123.3	132.3	141.8	7.2
Real per capita income	104.7	111.0	117.3	123.8	131.0	5.6

Source: *State Five-Year Plan for the Development of the USSR National Economy, 1971–1975*, pp. 22 and 57.

some positive steps could have been taken in the years 1971–1975 to improve the general population's standard of living.

A major feature of the Ninth Plan was the projection of a large annual improvement in labor productivity. This productivity in industry was projected to increase at an annual rate of 6.8 percent and was to be accompanied by an annual increase in capital investment at the rate of 6.7 percent. Earlier five-year plans had secured high economic growth by making use of large inputs of labor and capital into the economy. The Soviet planners can no longer depend upon securing large increases in the supply of labor, because the rate of population growth has been falling; also, the possibility no longer exists of any large-scale shifts of labor from the agricultural to the industrial sector.

Furthermore, although large supplies of capital are still made available to industry, capital as a growth factor is suffering from the fact that in recent decades its productivity has been declining. The marginal productivity of capital in industry has been declining, as each additional unit of capital has been accompanied by a smaller increment to Gross National Product. With the labor force growing less rapidly and the productivity of capital investment declining, economic growth in the Soviet Union since 1950 has been slowing down; during the same period, other nations have experienced greater success in maintaining their growth rates.[35]

During the Ninth Plan, the Soviet planners hoped to maintain a high economic growth rate by improving labor productivity and raising the marginal productivity of capital. Labor productivity was to be improved during this plan by introducing "a broad program for hastening scientific and technical progress, technical reequipment of the national economy, improvement of the structure of production, and the creation and introduction of new types of machines, equipment and materials."[36] The planners looked forward to reducing the capital-output ratio by eliminating

[35] An analysis of the Soviet Union's economic growth problem is provided in Stanley H. Cohn, *Economic Development in the Soviet Union*, pp. 57–58. See also Robert W. Campbell, *The Soviet-Type Economies*, pp. 83–115.

[36] *State Five-Year Plan* (1971–1975), Part I, p. 71.

a number of practices that have lowered the efficiency of capital investments. The Ninth Plan emphasized that in all branches of the nation's economy, investment funds had to be concentrated on capital facilities near completion; construction periods and costs had to be reduced; existing enterprises had to be modernized; new plants had to be brought up to rated production capacity as soon as possible; and the plan for the mechanization and automation of production had to be "unconditionally fulfilled."[37] It was the failure to follow these practices that accounted for much of the declines in the productivity of capital investments and in the economic growth rate in recent years.

Major Ninth-Plan Targets

The Ninth Plan presented control figures or targets for industry, agriculture, personal consumption, and other sectors of the economy. A number of these targets are listed in Table 14-9. Besides the usual increases in such basic outputs as steel and electric power, the industrial targets showed large planned increases in the output of oil and natural gas and a very limited increase in coal, which is losing out to oil and gas. The changes in the fuel industry are accompanied by major changes in the chemical industry, where the output of plastics and synthetic resins was planned to increase at an annual rate of 16.1 percent; this rise was well above the rate of expansion of steel, electric power, oil and other basic raw materials.

A 10.2 percent annual increase in the output of chemical fertilizers was planned to provide for sizable annual increases in meat, grains, milk, eggs, and other food products. The comprehensive plan for agriculture proposed a redistribution of national income to the advantage of the agricultural sector. This meant that agriculture during the years 1971-1975 was to receive larger supplies of machinery, fertilizers, herbicides and other chemical products. Output per one hundred hectares of land was projected to increase one-third. The output of meat measured in kilograms per person per year was planned to increase from forty-eight in 1970 to fifty-nine in 1975. These improvements in agricultural output were expected to contribute significantly to a higher standard of living.

Further improvements in the standard of living were to be achieved by raising per capita consumption from 815 rubles in 1970 to 1,083 rubles in 1975 (measured in 1965 prices). The light industry was to increase the supply of scarce consumer goods and improve the quality of consumer goods in general. The supply of household chemical products was projected to rise at the very high annual rate of 13.4 percent. The amount of total floor space per urban resident was planned to go from 11 square meters in 1970 to 11.9 in 1975. The supply of domestic services, such as dry cleaning, laundering, and car repairing, was projected to double during these years, while the annual output of passenger cars was planned to rise from 513,000 in 1970 to 1,260,000 in 1975. If these consumer goals had been achieved by 1975, the Soviet society would not yet be a consumer society, but considerable progress would have been made in raising the nation's standard of living.

Performance under the Ninth Plan, 1971-1975

Although the Soviet government hailed the Ninth Five-Year Plan at the Twenty-fifth Congress of the Communist party, February 24, 1976, as a major contribution to stable economic progress, it was conceded that a number of production targets had not been

[37] *Ibid.*, p. 15.

Table 14–9
Selected Targets for Individual Products in the Ninth Soviet Five-Year Plan, 1971–1975

Targets	1970 (Actual)	1975 (Projected)	% Increase in 1975 over 1970
Steel (million tons)	115.9	146.4	4.8
Hydroelectric power (billion kilowatt-hrs.)	124.4	165.0	5.8
Coal (million tons)	624.1	694.9	2.7
Crude oil (million tons)	352.6	505.0	7.5
Natural gas (billion cubic meters)	198.0	320.0	10.1
Plastics and synthetic resins (thousand tons)	1,673.0	3,533.0	16.1
Chemical fertilizers (million tons)	55.4	90.0	10.2
Meat (kilograms per person)	48.0	59.0	4.3
Per capita consumption (in rubles, 1965 prices)	815.0	1,083.0	5.8
Retail trade turnover (billion rubles, 1970 prices)	153.7	218.0	7.2
Floor space of housing per urban resident (square meters)	11.0	11.9	8.1
Household chemical products (million rubles)	152.43	286.33	13.4
Passenger cars (thousands)	513.00	1,260.00	19.7

Source: *State Five-Year Plan for the Development of the USSR National Economy, 1971–1975*, pp. 5 and 26.

met by 1975 and that much of what was produced was of poor quality and not the desired assortment.[38] The statistics in Table 14–10 reveal that the slowdown in the Soviet Union's overall economic growth rate continued during the years 1971–1975. National income, which had been projected to increase 38.6 percent over the five-year plan period, increased only 28 percent or at an average annual rate of 5.1 percent instead of the planned 6.7 percent. An analysis of the statistics in Table 14–10 shows that the production of consumers' goods was curbed in favor of producers' goods; the increase in real per capita income fell much below its planned goal; agricultural production was far below its target; and the production of steel, oil, and gas while impressive was below targeted goals.

The Soviet government attributed the inadequate performance of the Soviet economy to a number of factors which included the wasteful use of raw materials, poor industrial management, a slowness in adapting technological advances to industry, bottlenecks in the supply and contract system between industrial enterprises, deficient economic planning procedures, and delays in completing new investment projects.[39] It should be pointed out that while the Soviet Union suffered an economic slowdown during 1971–1975, it was spared many of the economic dislocations that were visited upon the advanced Western economies during the recession of 1974–1975.

[38] For a discussion of the execution of the Ninth Plan, see Robert C. Stuart, "The Soviet Economy: Problems and Prospects in the 1970's" *Current History*, Oct. 1975, pp. 129–132 and 145.

[39] For a discussion of the deficiencies of the Ninth Plan see "Brezhnev's Report to the Congress," *The Current Digest of the Soviet Press*, March 24, 1976, pp. 1–33; and "Kosygin's Report on the Five-Year Plan," *The Current Digest of the Soviet Press*, April 7, 1976, pp. 1–10.

Table 14-10
Results of the Soviet Ninth Five-Year Plan, 1971–1975

Targets	1970 = 100 1975 planned increase over 1970	1975 actual increase over 1970[1]
National income	138.6	128
Industrial production	147.0	143
Group A (producers' goods)	146.3	145
Group B (consumers' goods)	148.6	137
Real per capita income	131.0	124
Average worker's wage	122.4	120
Collective farmer's income	130.6	122
Agricultural production[2]	121.7	113
Total investments	141.6	141
Steel (mil. tons)	146.4	142
Oil (mil. tons)	505.0	489
Coal (mil. tons)	695.0	700
Gas (bil. cu. meters)	320.0	285

[1] Includes estimates of Western Soviet analysts.
[2] Five-year average.

Sources: *The Current Digest of the Soviet Press,* March 24, April 7, and May 12, 1976; Alec Nove, "Moderate targets in Russia's five-year plan," London: *The Times,* Jan. 5, 1976, and Moscow: *Pravda,* Dec. 4. 1975.

One of the factors that has been a drag on the performance of the Soviet economy since 1970 has been the fluctuating level of grain output. The Ninth Plan projected an average annual output of 195 million metric tons of grains in 1971–1975. The grain output which fell to 167 million tons in 1972, increased to 222.5 million tons in 1973; in 1975, however, it again fell to an estimated 140 million tons. In an exceptionally good year like 1973, a part of the harvest has been lost because of inadequate transportation, storage, and other facilities. In a poor harvest year like 1972, the rationing of products like meat, poultry, and dairy products has been made necessary. In order to offset the adverse developments in the Soviet Union's agricultural sector, deliveries of farm equipment from the heavy industries have been speeded up; supplies of chemical fertilizers have been increased; pools of spare parts have been established on the collective and state farms; and, in some cases, factory workers have been drafted to increase the supply of farm workers.

As a consequence of these efforts to bolster the agricultural sector, output has been transferred from the heavy industry sector, which in turn has drawn resources from the consumer goods sector. As has been explained, the Ninth Plan had proposed to reverse the pre-1971 trends and to increase the supply of consumer goods at a faster annual rate than the supply of producer goods. After the disastrous 1972 crop year, there was a reversion to the pre-1971 program of favoring the supply of producer goods over that of consumer goods.

The Tenth Five-Year Plan, 1976–1980

In June 1975, the Soviet Council of Ministers met and examined the draft of the basic directions in the construction of the Tenth Five-Year Plan for 1976–1980.[40] The Council instructed the State Planning Committee to pay particular attention to the following matters in their further work on this draft. The development of the economy during this five-year period is to be based on accelerated technological progress, increased labor productivity, and improved quality indices. The increased effectiveness of capital investment is to be achieved through the modernization and reequipment of existing industrial enterprises, increasing capacity at these enterprises, and accelerating the process of putting new plant and equipment into operation and bringing them up to their full output potentials.

In this plan, special attention is to be given to the discovery of additional resources of metals and to the production of equipment for the metallurgy, chemical, and electrical engineering industries. Fuel production is to be enlarged, and special steps are to be taken during the plan period to conserve the use of fuel resources. The material and technical base of the agricultural sector is to be strengthened further in order to increase agricultural output. The people's standard of living is to be raised further by ensuring high growth rates of consumer goods, expanding consumer services, and improving the quality of both consumer goods and services. No mention was made by the U.S.S.R. Council of Ministers of increasing the supply of consumer goods at a rate faster than that of producer goods. In general, the Tenth Five-Year Plan appears to continue the basic directions that guided the Ninth Plan.

The statistics in Table 14–11 show a number of the planned targets of the Tenth Soviet Five-Year Plan, described as "the five-year plan of efficiency and quality," which was set in motion in January 1976. It is clear from these statistics that the Tenth Plan is much more modest than the Ninth Plan. National income is projected to increase during 1976–1980 at a slower rate than during 1971–1975. Also, there is a return to the traditionally higher rate of growth of producers' goods than consumers' goods due to the shortages and bottlenecks in the supplies of basic industrial materials, especially fuels, and to the expanding military burden. Under the Tenth Plan, major investments are to be made in western Siberia in order to increase the output of oil and gas. Special attention is also to be given to the improvement of agriculture, which will take 33 percent of total investment in the years 1976–1980.

The success of the Tenth Plan will depend very much upon the improvement in labor productivity in the various branches of the economy, since the labor supply will increase less than 4 percent. During the Tenth Plan, the improvement in labor productivity is projected to provide 90 percent of the increase in industrial output and all the increase in agricultural output in the plan period. Such a large improvement in labor productivity will require rapid advances in industrial management, economic planning, and the application of technological advances to industry. These are advances that many Western Soviet analysts do not believe will be forthcoming. It is their view that too much of the traditional overcentralized planning system survives in spite of economic reforms to prevent the needed 5 percent annual overall increase in

---

[40] *The Current Digest of the Soviet Press*, Vol. XXVII, No. 23, p. 15.

Table 14-11
Selected Major Targets of the Tenth Soviet Five-Year Plan, 1976-1980

Targets	1975 actual output (bil. rubles)	1980 planned output (bil. rubles)	Planned annual percent increase in 1980 over 1975
National income (1973 prices)	362	456	4.8
Industrial output (1967 prices)	523	720	6.6
Group A (producers' goods)	380	532	7.0
Group B (consumers' goods)	143	188	5.6
Agricultural production	91	105	3.0
Oil (mil. tons)	489	630	5.3
Gas (bil. cu. meters)	285	418	8.0
Steel (mil. tons)	142	165	3.0
Coal (mil. tons)	700	800	2.7
Retail trade turnover	—	—	5.1
Average worker's wage	—	—	3.2
Collective farmer's income	—	—	4.6
Labor productivity	—	—	4.9

Source: *The Current Digest of the Soviet Press*, Vol. XXVIII, April 7, 1976, p. 3.

labor productivity if the Tenth Plan is to be successful.

The Deficiencies of Soviet Annual Materials Planning

The numerous complaints regarding the availability of input materials that appear in the Soviet press, official reports, and policy statements indicate that Soviet annual materials planning suffers from some very serious deficiencies. These deficiencies arise from three sources. First, Soviet annual planning can be described as very "tight" planning that results in a national economy with very little slack, inadequate reserve stocks or inventories, and very tight production-delivery schedules. Miscalculations with regard to the supply of or demand for input materials cannot be easily rectified if there is no slack in the economy (or very little) that can be used for this purpose. In view of this situation, deficiencies in the supply of input materials can be eliminated only to a great extent by cutting down the demands of the low-priority sectors. This explains in large part why the plans for raising the cultural and economic levels of the general population are frequently not carried out as originally projected.

The second reason for deficiencies in materials planning is the poor operation of the very extensive and complex bureaucratic organization set up to construct the annual plan for materials and to carry it out. The timing of the plan construction on occasion proves to be faulty, and annual plans are sometimes not completed before the beginning of the planned year. Output and input plans frequently lack coordination, in large part as a result of the many changes made in the plans before and after they are completed. In addition, the completing of the production-delivery schedules is a very difficult task in an economy the size of the Soviet economy. In this extremely complicated system of planning for production and deliveries, where the central planning agency substitutes for the market system of a free enterprise economy, inputs frequently are not delivered on schedule or in the amounts and assortment ordered by the consuming enterprises. Where the emphasis is on plan fulfillment and overfulfillment, meeting production targets takes precedence over meeting delivery schedules of the "right" kinds of goods at the right time. Nor is there adequate concern with spreading technological progress and producing new and more economical materials, since introducing innovations in the production process tends to reduce production and to interfere with deliveries.

The third deficiency in Soviet materials planning lies in the planning procedure itself. The method of balancing the production and distribution of the material input needs of a large and highly industrialized economy, without the aid of a free market system and without the use of well-developed input-output techniques, must necessarily be primitive in many important respects. Many Soviet economists have recognized this deficiency of Soviet annual materials planning and are proposing to improve it by a more widespread use of input-output techniques and high-speed computers.

Input-Output Planning in the Soviet Union

Soviet planners have in recent years become very much interested in seeing how their planning might be improved by adopting input-output and other mathematical techniques.[41] The input-output technique is a statistical method of determining interindustry material balances, which is a substitute for the trial-and-error method of working out material balances. Considerable progress has been made in the Soviet Union in constructing input-output or interindustry tables, which are of two types. Accounting or *ex post tables* are based on some past year and reveal the interrelations among the nation's major industries in that year. Planning or *ex ante tables* are projections of accounting tables which are used as a basis for constructing the annual and five-year plans. These input-output projections make adjustments for the impact of technological progress on the interrelations among industries.

Table 14-12 presents a reconstructed version of the 1966 Soviet input-output table with fifty-five producing sectors.[42] The fifty-five rows show the material outputs of each producing sector and the purchases of this output by each of the fifty-five producing sectors. The fifty-five columns in Table 14-12 show the total outlays of the fifty-five producing sectors for the inputs required by their outputs. Total outputs (sales) and total inputs (outlays) of the fifty-five producing sectors each amounted to 258,509.9 million rubles in 1966.

The reconstructed 1966 Soviet input-output flow table also shows the total final demand

---

[41] For a discussion of this development, see John P. Hardt and others, *Mathematics and Computers in Soviet Economic Planning,* New Haven: Yale University Press, 1967; and Michael Ellman, "Introduction: The use of mathematics in Soviet economics—an historical survey," *Planning Problems in the USSR,* Cambridge: Cambridge University Press, 1973, pp. 1–17.

[42] The 1966 Soviet input-output table was constructed in physical terms for 237 commodities and in value terms for 110 producing sectors. The reconstruction of this table from Soviet data is explained in Vladimir G. Treml, Barry L. Kostinsky, and Dimitri M. Gallik, "Interindustry Structure of the Soviet Economy: 1959 and 1966," *Soviet Economic Prospects for the Seventies,* pp. 246–269.

for the gross outputs of the fifty-five producing sectors, which is valued at 223,000.9 million rubles. This total final demand consists of private and public consumption, gross investment primarily in the public sector, and the export-import balance. All the interindustry relations of the fifty-five producing sectors as well as the total final demand for outputs, are summarized in Table 14-13. This table shows that total inputs or outlays (481,510.8 million rubles) for material and other inputs, depreciation, wages, profits, turnover taxes, bonuses, agricultural income-in-kind, social security payments, and miscellaneous elements of net income are balanced by total outputs or sales (481,510.8 million rubles). This total input-output balance for the whole economy is made up of separate balances for each of the 55 producing sectors. For example, the electric- and thermal-power industry (sector) in Row 9 in Table 14-12 produced a gross output valued at 7,527.3 million rubles, of which 5,683.3 million rubles were distributed to the fifty-five producing sectors. The remaining 1,889 million rubles of the power industry's output were distributed in the form of final demand to private and public consumers and investors. In order to produce a gross output valued at 7,527.3 million rubles, the electric- and thermal-power industry had to purchase inputs of the same total value from the fifty-five producing sectors. Table 14-14 shows this separate balance for the electric- and thermal-power industry.

A projection of an accounting (*ex post*) input-output table to some future year, such as the final year of a five-year plan period, would show an increased total gross output and increases in the separate gross outputs of the various industries or producing sectors contributing to the total gross output of the plan year. Each additional billion kilowatt-hours of power would require more coal, labor, transportation, and so on. If the plant and equipment of the power industry were fully utilized at the time that the accounting table was constructed, further investment in plant and equipment would be necessary to meet the demand for additonal power in the future plan year. The industries that supply inputs to the power industry would in turn require larger inputs from other industries, and so on in many rounds of interindustry adjustments. The problem then would be to secure a balance among all the industries supplying direct and indirect inputs to the power industry. The same would hold for all the other industries or producing sectors that contribute to the economy's total gross output.

If an adequately detailed input-output table were to be constructed, it would then be possible to uncover the material input requirements for any given output. For example, the interindustry relationships of the input-output table will show how much coal, steel, electricity, nonferrous metals, and other material inputs are required for the production of a given number of motor trucks. The 1959 Soviet input-output table indicated that the production of one motor truck required directly and indirectly 3.6 tons of steel, 10.1 tons of coal, and 5,309 kilowatt hours of electricity. By developing similar input-output ratios (called *technological coefficients of production*) for other types of output, it is possible to determine the input requirements for as many different kinds of output as are brought within the scope of the input-output table. The more detailed the table, the more numerous are the technological coefficients or ratios between output and input requirements that can be established. These ratios then become the basis for the construction of material balances. By combining the material input requirements information from the input-output table and information relating to the available production of these materials, one can then construct material balances for hundreds of output items if the input-output table has a large enough number of product sectors. The

Table 14-12
Reconstructed 1966 Soviet Input-Output Table: Flow Matrix

Sector no.	Sector title	Ferrous ores and metals (1)	Electric and thermal power ...(9)	...(21)
1	Ferrous ores and metals	2218.3	10.3	649.1
2	Nonferrous ores and metals	1009.8	.0	80.2
3	Coke prod. and refractory mat.	746.6	1.8	18.2
4	Industrial metal products	55.6	6.7	39.4
5	Coal	447.0	1542.4	8.9
6	Oil extraction and refining	124.8	461.6	22.6
7	Gas	211.3	444.1	14.4
8	Peat and oil shales	3.5	208.0	.5
9	Electric and thermal power	278.7	11.5	92.1
10	Energy and power M + E	1.8	13.1	3.1
11	Eltech M + E and cable products	35.6	11.5	74.8
12	Metalworking M + E	2.6	.0	10.9
13	Tools and dies	4.6	1.0	24.1
14	Precision instruments	4.5	3.6	7.0
15	Mining and metallurgical M + E	119.9	.0	.0
16	Pumps and compressors	2.3	.9	5.8
17	Specialized M + E	.8	.0	.2
18	Hoist-trans. and construction M + E	7.6	.3	.3
19	Transportation M + E	3.8	.2	.3
20	Automobiles	9.4	1.2	51.8
21	Tractors and agricultural M + E	2.5	.0	898.1
22	Bearings	6.9	.7	82.0
23	Other machine-building	60.5	23.1	98.1
24	Other metalworking	22.9	2.6	48.2
25	Metal structures	1.2	.0	.0
26	Repair of M + E	107.2	40.1	7.3
27	Abrasives	13.2	.5	9.3
28	Mineral chemistry products	4.3	.5	.1
29	Basic and other chemistry prod.	133.5	14.0	8.9
30	Aniline dye products	.3	.1	3.6
31	Synthetic resins and plastics	3.4	3.0	3.1
32	Synthetic fibers	.5	.0	.0

Inter-industry use	Private consumption	Public consumption	Other final demand	Total final demand	Gross value of output	Sector no.
... (56)	(57)	(58)	(59)	(60)	(61)	
11123.0	4.6	487.0	605.4	1097.0	12220.0	1
8324.0	.0	342.3	−99.3	243.0	8567.0	2
1720.7	.0	.0	98.9	98.9	1819.6	3
1175.2	15.4	71.5	−60.1	26.8	1202.0	4
5709.1	153.4	685.1	181.4	1019.9	6729.0	5
7728.2	167.0	778.4	1483.6	2429.0	10157.2	6
1433.2	128.3	66.2	2.3	196.8	1630.0	7
494.6	.0	92.3	−23.0	69.3	563.9	8
5638.3	1156.4	684.1	48.5	1889.0	7527.3	9
577.8	.0	.0	908.2	908.2	1486.0	10
4198.3	765.9	201.7	1642.1	2609.7	6808.0	11
108.4	.0	.0	1118.7	1118.7	1227.1	12
373.7	.0	24.6	167.7	192.3	566.0	13
503.4	622.4	41.4	1612.8	2276.6	2780.0	14
498.9	.0	.0	2201.1	2201.1	2700.0	15
299.9	320.1	55.2	1124.8	1500.1	1800.0	16
317.4	120.3	.3	1001.6	1122.2	1439.6	17
380.1	.0	.0	1448.9	1448.9	1829.0	18
377.0	.0	40.6	3382.4	3423.0	3800.0	19
2482.0	960.9	157.8	1764.3	2883.0	5365.0	20
2770.3	.0	.0	1989.7	1989.7	4760.0	21
437.1	.0	9.1	101.8	110.9	548.0	22
4081.1	1659.1	536.4	4723.4	6918.9	11000.0	23
2457.3	1034.7	342.2	466.8	1843.7	4301.0	24
661.6	.0	.0	24.3	24.3	685.9	25
1483.8	.0	28.2	6714.0	6742.2	8226.0	26
369.9	.0	.0	5.0	5.0	374.9	27
396.3	.0	.0	26.7	26.7	423.0	28
4353.0	585.8	696.5	542.7	1825.0	6178.0	29
261.0	4.6	1.7	17.0	23.3	284.3	30
1342.4	.0	27.1	−137.5	−110.4	1232.0	31
1261.7	.0	.0	−110.7	−110.7	1151.0	32

Table 14-12 (cont.)
Reconstructed 1966 Soviet Input-Output Table: Flow Matrix

Sector no.	Sector title	Ferrous ores and metals	Electric and thermal power	Tractors and agricultural M + E
		(1)	... (9)	... (21)
33	Organic synthetic products	6.9	.6	4.1
34	Paints and lacquers	6.2	2.2	29.8
35	Rubber and asbestos products	38.4	3.0	179.9
36	Logging	18.2	.8	2.7
37	Woodworking	24.9	2.9	50.8
38	Paper and pulp	4.5	.7	5.1
39	Construction materials	17.0	3.3	4.0
40	Glass and porcelain	5.3	1.2	3.5
41	Textiles	17.1	2.8	14.1
42	Other light industry products	52.4	6.4	21.2
43	Fish products	.0	.0	.0
44	Meat and dairy products	16.3	2.1	6.2
45	Sugar	.0	.0	.3
46	Bread, flour, and confections	.2	.0	.0
47	Other foods	7.1	3.3	1.7
48	Industry, n.e.c.	29.8	18.6	25.8
49	Construction	.0	.0	.0
50	Crops	.8	.0	.1
51	Animal husbandry	.3	.0	.1
52	Forestry	.0	.0	.0
53	Transportation & communications	1168.1	4.1	302.1
54	Trade and distribution	281.8	.4	36.2
55	Other branches of material prod.	192.3	.8	16.5
56	Material purchases	6082.6	2852.1	2626.3
57	Total purchases	7532.5	2856.6	2964.6
58	Depreciation	860.4	1159.4	
59	Wages	1524.1	836.4	833.4
60	Other net income	2303.0	2674.9	773.0
61	National income	3827.1	3511.3	1606.4
62	Total outlays	12220.0	7527.3	4760.0

Source: Joint Economic Committee, *Soviet Economic Prospects for the Seventies*, 1973, p. 268.

Inter-industry use ... (56)	Private consumption (57)	Public consumption (58)	Other final demand (59)	Total final demand (60)	Gross value of output (61)	Sector no.
1600.3	.0	9.5	72.2	81.7	1682.0	33
1339.1	9.5	144.9	−57.5	96.9	1436.0	34
2534.0	73.8	344.3	662.9	1081.0	3615.0	35
5232.8	167.1	467.5	−921.4	−286.8	4946.0	36
6559.3	2365.7	222.6	−.5	2587.8	9147.1	37
1540.5	.0	96.6	15.9	112.5	1653.0	38
12264.6	163.1	393.9	678.4	1235.4	13500.0	39
1270.5	424.7	43.8	13.0	481.5	1752.0	40
26885.8	10966.6	704.1	−703.5	10967.2	37853.0	41
4314.7	15895.2	647.8	−1380.7	15162.3	19477.0	42
2170.6	2309.5	215.4	278.5	2803.4	4974.0	43
6523.0	14970.0	1205.3	860.7	17036.0	23559.0	44
3174.7	4621.4	202.9	−136.0	4688.3	7863.0	45
5138.4	13908.1	451.1	−129.6	14229.6	19368.0	46
9579.9	23899.0	239.0	245.1	24383.1	33963.0	47
3543.2	7077.3	986.1	198.8	8262.2	11805.4	48
.0	.0	.0	43360.0	43360.0	43360.0	49
31784.9	7800.0	230.0	5895.1	13925.1	45710.0	50
22993.6	13300.0	510.0	836.4	14646.4	37640.0	51
221.2	.0	.0	215.3	215.3	436.5	52
19000.0	.0	.0	.0	.0	19000.0	53
16150.0	.0	.0	.0	.0	16150.0	54
1350.1	1565.7	299.9	24.3	1889.9	3240.0	55
223359.9						56
258509.9	127215.6	12784.4	83000.9	223000.9	481510.8	57
21658.5						58
92799.6						59
108542.8						60
201342.4						61
481510.8						62

Table 14-13
The Total Input and Output Flows of the Soviet Economy in 1966

(In millions of rubles)

Total inputs (outlays)		Total outputs (sales)	
Interindustry outlays	258,509.9	Interindustry sales	258,509.9
Depreciation	21,658.5	Sales to private consumers	127,215.6
Wage payments	92,799.6	Sales to public consumers	12,784.4
Profits, taxes, etc.	108,542.8	Sales to investors and net exports	83,000.9
Total inputs (outlays)	481,510.8	Total outputs (sales)	481,510.8

Source: Joint Economic Committee, *Reconstructed 1966 Soviet Input-Output Table*, 1973.

input-output table also throws light upon the labor and equipment inputs as well as the material inputs required for the production of a given output. For example, input-output tables can be used to reveal the amounts of labor, plant, and equipment required to produce a ton of steel or coal.

The state planning agency can show the Soviet leaders the economic consequences of selecting any one of a number of different sets of national goals. The economic impacts, in terms of needed raw materials, labor, and equipment, of making different decisions with regard to defense policies, foreign aid programs, and domestic industrial development can be readily revealed with the aid of input-output techniques and high-speed electronic computers. With the real cost of any national program quickly revealed by "planometrics" or input-output planning, the Soviet leaders are in a better position to decide whether or not any proposed national program is both feasible and desirable.

When the Soviet Union's national economic goals in the form of total final demands for private and public consumption and investment have been established by the planning authorities for some future plan year, the planning input-output tables can be used to indicate the output level required for each industry. If the required total of output levels for all industries is not feasible because of production capacity limits in some industries, or because of some overall constraint or

Table 14-14
Input and Output of the Soviet Electric and Thermal Power Industry[1] in 1966

Inputs (outlays)		Outputs (sales)	
Total purchases from other industries	2,856.6	Total sales to other industries	5,638.3
Depreciation	1,159.4	Private consumption	1,156.4
Wages	836.4	Public consumption	684.1
Profits, bonuses, taxes, etc.	2,674.9	Gross investment and net exports	48.5
Total inputs (outlays)	7,527.3	Gross value of total output	7,527.3

[1] Producing sector no. 9 in the reconstructed 1966 Soviet input-output table.

Source: Joint Economic Committee, *Reconstructed 1966 Soviet Input-Output Table*, 1973.

bottleneck such as an inadequate supply of skilled labor, then the planners investigate alternative combinations of final demands based upon different coefficients of production. The aim is to uncover what the planners believe to be the best alternative total final demands for consumption and investment purposes that are consistent with the capacity and other constraints on the output levels of the various industries. It is possible to investigate feasible alternative combinations of final demands very rapidly with the aid of high-speed electronic computers. In this situation, balancing supplies and demands with the aid of input-output tables could theoretically be used to replace the more primitive trial-and-error balancing with the aid of material balances.[43]

Although Soviet planners have investigated the applications of input-output techniques to their planning programs, and have constructed input-output tables of increasing size and complexity, they have made very little progress in substituting input-output planning for materials balance planning. Western analysts have concluded that:

"Impressive as the efforts and accomplishments of the advocates of new techniques may be, the fact remains that after eight to nine years of experimentation and exploration, after construction of two large ex-post, nine large planning, and twenty-three regional tables, input-output techniques have neither replaced the planning apparatus nor been integrated with it. It is probably safe to conclude that by now most ideological obstacles have been overcome, that the shortage of cadres of mathematically trained economists has been somewhat alleviated, and that Soviet computer hardware and data processing facilities have improved. Nevertheless, as both the advocates and the opponents of the new techniques testify, 'input-output analysis remains in an experimental stage.' "[44]

Also, Soviet economists have reported that "input-output techniques have been sufficiently perfected but are not being used in actual planning."[45] Clearly a substantial gap still exists between the potential employment of input-output techniques and the actual possibility of applying them in Soviet national planning.

Soviet leaders are still reluctant to substitute "electronic" planning for "campaign" planning. If it were to be revealed that electronic computers were making many of the planning decisions rather than the whole hierarchy from party to state enterprise, it would be difficult to maintain the sense of mission that has up to now pervaded at least the top levels of Soviet national planning activity. What appears to be developing is that electronic or input-output planning is being perfected not as a substitute for the current method of constructing national plans, but as a means of aiding or strengthening the latter. Behind the scenes and within government planning bodies, input-output techniques will probably be used more and more in the future to construct national plans more scientifically; as far as the general public is concerned, however, the impression will continue to be conveyed in the Soviet Union that national plans are being constructed with much human effort and with widespread participation on the part of the general population. The "discovery" by Soviet economists that input-output techniques were used in the Soviet Union by state planning agencies during the 1920s has removed the bourgeois stigma attached to these techniques. But the Soviet leaders are not prepared to do away with

[43] In this connection, see Herbert S. Levine, "Growth and Planning in the Soviet Union," in Wayne A. Leeman (ed.), *The Soviet Economy in Theory and Practice*, Columbia, Mo.: University of Missouri, School of Business and Public Administration, 1964, pp. 67-94; and Michael Ellman, "The Consistency of Soviet Plans," *Scottish Journal of Political Economy*, Vol. XVI, No. 1, Feb. 1969, pp. 50-74.

[44] Vladimir G. Treml, "Input-output Analysis and Soviet Planning," in John P. Hardt and others, *op. cit.*, pp. 101-102.

[45] *Ibid.*, p. 102.

much of the ritual of national planning, accumulated since the inauguration of the first five-year plan in 1928, which is so essential to the Marxian view of national economic development.

Efficiency in Soviet National Planning

Efficiency in national economic planning requires more than securing a balance between the inputs and output needed to produce a projected final bill of goods and services or Gross National Product. Input-output economics is only a balancing technique that takes no account of many of the problems associated with the best allocation of resources and the most efficient methods of investment and production. Input-output analysis does not deal with the most efficient substitution of one input for another, such as aluminium for steel in the making of machinery, or oil for coal in producing electric power. Although input-output economics may make use of planning tables that incorporate technological progress and new production methods, this kind of economics does not deal explicitly with how alternative production techniques may be considered in order to choose the techniques that maximize output. This type of analysis is the concern of another mathematical technique, known as *linear* and *dynamic* (nonlinear) *programming*.

Linear programming is a method of securing the best result by choosing from among a number of processes or combinations of scarce economic resources the process or combination that will minimize cost or maximize gain. Government officials and private business in Western countries are frequently faced with complex problems, such as how to select from many possible ingredients the lowest-cost combination of ingredients in making a commodity, how to transport goods between a number of producing plants and many scattered customers in such a manner as to minimize the costs of transportation, or how to select from a number of inventory systems the one that will reduce inventories to a minimum. Linear programming solves these problems mathematically, according to the minimax principle, so that gains are maximized or costs are minimized in accordance with the nature of the problem that is presented. Linear programming was actually developed earlier in the Soviet Union than it was in the United States. L. N. Kantorovich did pioneer work in linear programming in the late 1930s, but was unable during Stalin's regime to interest Soviet planners in the application of his work to the problems of economic planning. In recent years, Soviet economists have come to appreciate the importance of Kantorovich's work in linear programming for the improvement of national planning techniques.[46]

Since the late 1950s, Soviet planners have broadened their application of linear programming from a consideration of limited production problems to the much broader question of the most efficient plan for the whole economy.[47] In their search for such a plan, they have customarily worked out a large number of plan variants according to different alternative uses of economic resources; they have then selected the variant that makes the best use of these resources. In applying linear programming to the whole economy, Soviet planners employ two criteria. The first is the minimization of inputs so as to secure a given level of Gross National Product or national income; the second is the

[46] For an analysis of Kantorovich's contributions, see Robert W. Campbell, "Marx, Kantorovich and Novozhilov: Stoimost' Versus Reality," *Slavic Review*, Vol. 20, No. 3, Oct. 1961, pp. 402–418.

[47] Benjamin Ward, "Linear Programming and Soviet Planning," *Mathematics and Computers in Soviet Planning*, pp. 147–200.

maximization of GNP or national income during a given plan period. The most efficient plan thus maximizes national income or GNP by providing for the most balanced and efficient use of the nation's scarce resources.

Developing the most efficient plan possible, with the aid of input-output economics, linear and dynamic (nonlinear) programming, and other mathematical techniques, has not yet proved practical. Both theoretical and practical problems remain. One of the main obstacles to Soviet plan optimization has been the unavailability of information in a form suitable for optimal planning. Besides collecting and processing data in forms not adapted to optimal planning, the Soviet planners still lack a sufficiently well-developed network of computers. In addition, in view of some Western economists, it is not feasible to construct a fully mathematicized and computerized optimal plan, because the economic model underlying such a plan would always diverge significantly from the real economic world.[48] Furthermore, a *computopia* (described by Egon Neuberger as a highly cyberneticized economic system) would fail to cope with some of the basic problems of the Soviet economy, such as the quality of output, the rate of application of new technological innovations, the unreliability of data, and improving worker incentives. Thus far, the Soviet government has settled for much less than a complete computopia, and has adopted instead a relatively centralized version of the planned economy, in which "planning by computers and models, assisted by a comprehensive network of information centers, is combined with limited autonomy for primary economic units [enterprises], guided mainly by incentives.[49]

Although the application of linear programming, input-output analysis, and other mathematical techniques to Soviet economic problems has not yet resulted in the development of the most efficient plans possible, the analysis and application of mathematical planning techniques has profoundly affected Soviet economic theory and the course of Soviet economics since the late 1950s. This impact appears in such problems as the determination of rational prices, capital investment, and the location of industry. The Marxian labor theory of value, which dominated Soviet economic theorizing until the late 1950s, inadequately treats the problems of scarcity and opportunity costs.[50] The labor theory of value asserts that value is determined by the amount of embodied past and present labor. This theory assigns no surplus-creating productivity to capital and land, and ignores the opportunity costs associated with both factors of production. Linear programming emphasizes the basic ideas of resource scarcity and opportunity cost. It stresses that value or price is an index or measure of scarcity, and that the allocation process is one of using scarce resources in such a way as to minimize opportunity costs and to maximize values.

In Soviet planning, the linear programmers regard the optimal plan as a basis for determining rational prices. Each resource should

---

[48] On this issue, see Egon Neuberger, "Libermanism, Computopia, and Visible Hand," *American Economic Review*, Vol. LVI, May 1966, pp. 131–144; and Alec Nove, "Planners' Preferences, Priorities and Reforms," *Economic Journal*, June 1966, pp. 267–277.

[49] Egon Neuberger, *op. cit.*, p. 143. See also Michael Ellman, *Soviet Planning Today*, 1971, pp. 14–20; and *Planning Problems in the USSR*, Cambridge: Cambridge University Press, 1973, pp. 169–175.

[50] For an analysis of the Marxian labor theory of value and Marxian economic theory in general, see E. Preobrazhensky, *The New Economics*, Oxford: Clarendon Press, 1965, pp. 43–76; Alec Nove, "Concepts and Ideas," *The Soviet Economy*, 1969, pp. 284–324; and Nicolas Spulber, "Social Accounting and Finance," *The Soviet Economy*, 1969, pp. 132–159.

be used according to the optimal plan so as to relate the relative significance or value of the resource to the fulfillment of the plan. In other words, under linear programming each resource must have a price that covers all its costs of production, including wages, a charge for capital (interest), and a differential rent charge. Account must also be taken of the *opportunity cost* of each resource; this cost is the output or production forgone by not using the resource in other ways. In recognizing the scarcity value of resources, linear and dynamic (nonlinear) programming open the door to the concept of marginal analysis or the diminishing rate of marginal substitution. It then becomes clear that what is important in determining price is marginal rather than average cost. Also, linear programming finds a place for the concepts of demand and consumption, since the ultimate end of optimization is not production but consumption. When outputs are maximized, they are maximized in terms of relative usefulness to consumers. Resources should be allocated in a manner that not only minimizes opportunity costs but also maximizes social utility.

The Soviet planning authorities have not accepted all the recommendations of the new generation of mathematical economists concerning price determination, capital investment, and the location of industry; but they have acquiesced in some of the dictates of the new Soviet economics. Price reforms have already been carried out that call for more adequate charges for depreciation and for the use of capital, and for differential rent charges in the case of such scarce resources as oil and coal. Prices for scarce resources are now much more rational than they were in the Stalin era, since they now cover a wider range of costs. With prices more rational, opportunity costs are more meaningful, and enterprise managers can not only more efficiently choose among alternative inputs, but they can also price their outputs more rationally.

When prices are more rational, both input-output analysis and linear programming—which employ prices as value indices—become more rational and useful to planners. The same applies to capital investment and the location of industry. Now that capital has an interest cost, Soviet planners can deal more effectively with the problem of capital allocation. When capital was interest free under Stalin, there was a tendency to waste capital by putting too much in large capital projects such as hydroelectric power plants. Power could have been obtained more cheaply by investing less capital in smaller thermal-power plants. Now that capital carries a charge, planners will have to take this charge into account when comparing alternative investment plans. Unwarranted capital intensity can then be avoided, and the supply of capital can be spread more rationally and more efficiently over a wider range of projects. Similar considerations influence the development of transportation systems and the location of industry in the various economic regions.

The Future of Soviet Planning

The success of the Ninth Five-Year Plan depended very much upon improving the management of state industrial enterprises and collective farms. The economic reforms of 1965 proposed to improve the management system in three ways: (1) by cutting down the number of central controls imposed upon enterprise managers, thus giving them more freedom to operate their enterprises; (2) by having enterprises make more use of such mathematical techniques as linear programming and systems engineering; and (3) by increasing the incentives of managers and workers to take advantage of technological progress, to reduce costs, and to operate profitably. Economic progress in the Soviet Union during the 1970s will depend very much upon the success of the 1965 reforms.

As we shall see in our analysis of Soviet industry and agriculture in Chapter 15, Western analysts generally agree that these reforms have not been nearly as successful as their originators had expected. Bergson points out that "the planning reform initiated in 1965 had diverse aims, but clearly a cardinal one was to accelerate the increase in factor [labor and capital] productivity and so provide a basis for rapid growth of output other than the inordinate capital stock inputs required under the Soviet [Stalinist] model. The reforms were modest, and according to all indications so, too, were any successes achieved."[51] This view of the progress of the 1965 economic reforms led the participants in the 1971 North Atlantic Symposium on "Soviet Economic Growth in the 1970s" to conclude that the Ninth Five-Year Plan was too optimistic. The participants agreed that the annual improvement in labor productivity for the whole economy would be 2 percent or less rather than the implied goal of 3 percent as calculated by Western analysts, and that the overall annual economic growth rate would be between 4 and 5 percent rather than the implied goal of 5.8 percent.

Progress in improving Soviet national planning has been delayed by the reluctance of many bureaucrats and party theorists to expedite the application of the new mathematical-economic techniques to planning problems. The bureaucracy in the State Planning Committee, the State Committee for Material and Technical Supplies, and other government agencies have offered considerable resistance to changing planning methods.[52] Both the bureaucratic planners and the party theorists, whose importance could be diminished in a planning program based on the new mathematical-economic techniques, prefer the status quo in the area of planning.

After the construction of the 1966 input-output table in value terms, the Council of Ministers directed the State Planning Committee to use these tables in preparing the draft of the 1971–1975 national plan. From what information is available, it does not appear that input-output techniques were fully integrated with the other planning tools in the construction of the 1971–1975 five-year plan. The evidence available to Western analysts supports the view that the State Planning Committee continues to construct national plans to a considerable extent with the aid of traditional planning methods. In spite of the claims of the state planning authorities, Western specialists have concluded that while input-output tables have been used for a variety of purposes, "with few exceptions these studies [based on input-output tables] appear to have remained on the periphery of the Soviet administrative planning and management system, and there is little evidence that any of the results were linked directly to the decision-making process [of the planning system]."[53]

It will take some time to make it clear to Soviet planning authorities that planning technicians and top-level decision makers have different roles to play. The decision makers should be concerned with the nation's goals as claims on the output of the economy,

---

[51] A. Bergson, "Part III: Conclusions," *Prospects for Soviet Economic Growth in the 1970s*, p. 31. For a similar evaluation of the consequences of the 1965 economic reforms, see Gertrude E. Schroeder, "Organization and Management as Factors in Soviet Economic Growth in the 1970's," *Prospects for Soviet Economic Growth in the 1970s*, pp. 149–150.

[52] For an analysis of the low esteem in which input-output planning techniques are held by officials in the influential State Committee for Material and Technical Supplies, see Gertrude Schroeder, "The Reform of the Supply System in Soviet Industry," *Soviet Studies*, Vol. XXIV, No. 1, July 1972.

[53] Vladimir G. Treml, Barry L. Kostinsky, and Dimitri M. Gallik, *op. cit.*, p. 249.

i.e., the claims of consumption, investment, defense, net export surplus, and foreign aid. When these goals have been agreed upon, then the planning technicians, with the aid of input-output tables and other planning techniques, should be called in to explain the implications of these national goals for the growth of the steel, oil, power, chemical and other industries. After these goals have been settled on, the determination of how much steel or coal to produce or whether to expand the coal or oil industry, is a technical supply problem and not a consumers' preference problem. To attain a more effective planning system, the Soviet Union needs an economic system in which the central government is prepared to decentralize the planning system more than at present, and in which producing units are freer to respond to consumers' preferences.

Clearly, Soviet national planning in the past decade has deviated somewhat from the unbalanced Stalinist type of planning with its excessive emphasis on "heavy" as compared with "light" industries. It is likely that this trend away from the Stalinist command planning model will continue, and that a more balanced kind of economic growth will be achieved. Although considerable erosion of the Stalinist planning model has already occurred, the future direction of Soviet planning remains uncertain. Always present is the possibility that new pressures may arise from a failure to reach the desired level of economic efficiency or to cope with rising consumer expectations. Such pressures may lead to a genuine market-oriented reform and to the "market socialism" that many Western economists thought was being introduced by the economic reforms of 1965. The achievement of this type of socialism is a goal that must wait upon the further evolution of the Soviet economic system.

We may conclude our investigation into Soviet national economic planning by pointing out that in some important respects, this planning has been quite successful, while, in other ways, it has done poorly. The planning of a large industrialized nation without the aid of a free market system would be a most difficult task even if all the most recent advances in planning procedures and techniques were to be employed. Although Soviet national planning is in many ways still cumbersome, nevertheless, the high-priority needs of the Soviet Union, as determined by the Politburo of the Communist party, are usually met. The national planning has been successful enough to make possible a very rapid rate of industrialization, a high level of scientific progress, and a strong military force. From the viewpoint of the Politburo, the fact that the Soviet consumer has not up to now fared very well by Western standards is not as yet a matter of great moment. In the authoritarian Soviet Society, consumers can raise few objections to what they may well regard as the undesirable consequences of Soviet national planning.

Selected Bibliography

ARMSTRONG, JOHN A. *Ideology, Politics, and Government in the Soviet Union.* Frederick A. Praeger, Publisher, New York 1962.

BERGSON, ABRAM. *The Economics of Soviet Planning.* Yale University Press, New Haven, 1964.

COHN, STANLEY H. *Economic Development in the Soviet Union.* D. C. Heath and Co., Lexington, Mass., 1970.

ELLMAN, MICHAEL. *Planning Problems in the USSR.* Cambridge University Press, Cambridge, England, 1973.

ERLICH, ALEXANDER. *The Soviet Industrialization Debate, 1924–1928.* Harvard University Press, Cambridge, 1960.

FAINSOD, MERLE. *How Russia Is Ruled.* Harvard University Press, Cambridge, 1963.

Fundamentals of Marxism-Leninism. Foreign Languages Publishing House, Moscow, 1961.

GREGORY, PAUL R., and ROBERT C. STUART. *Soviet Economic Structure and Performance.* Harper and Row Publishers, New York, 1974.

HARDT, JOHN P. *The Future Role of the Soviet Central Planner.* Research Analysis Corporation, McLean, Virginia, 1964.

———, and others. *Mathematics and Computers in Soviet Planning.* Yale University Press, New Haven, 1967.

JOINT ECONOMIC COMMITTEE. *Comparisons of the United States and Soviet Economies.* Washington, D.C., 1959.

———. *Dimensions of Soviet Economic Power.* Washington, D.C., 1962.

———. *Soviet Economic Prospects for the Seventies.* Washington, D.C., 1973.

JOINT COMMITTEE ON SLAVIC STUDIES. *Current Digest of the Soviet Press.* Washington, D.C.

JOINT PUBLICATIONS RESEARCH SERVICE. *State Five-Year Plan for the Development of the USSR National Economy for the Period, 1971–1975.* U.S. Department of Commerce, Washington, D.C., 1972.

KURSKY, A. *The Planning of the National Economy of the U.S.S.R.* Foreign Languages Publishing House, Moscow, 1949.

LAULAN, M. YVES, ed. *Prospects for Soviet Economic Growth in the 1970s.* Brussels, 1971.

LUKYANOV, KONSTANTIN, and BORIS TSVETKOW. *How the USSR Plans Its National Economy.* Novosti Press Agency Publishing House, Moscow, 1973.

NOVE, ALEC. *The Soviet Economy,* 2d rev. ed. Frederick A. Praeger, Publisher, New York, 1969.

Progress Publishers. *Soviet Economy Forges Ahead, Ninth Five-Year Plan, 1971–1975.* Moscow, 1973.

SHAPIRO, LEONARD. *The Communist Party of the Soviet Union,* 2d ed. Random House, New York, 1970.

SHERMAN, HOWARD. *The Soviet Economy.* Little Brown and Co., Boston, 1969.

SPULBER, NICOLAS. *Soviet Strategy for Economic Growth.* Indiana University Press, Bloomington, Indiana, 1964.

———. *The Soviet Economy,* rev. ed. W. W. Norton and Co., New York, 1969.

TREML, VLADIMIR, and JOHN P. HARDT. *Soviet Economic Statistics.* Duke University Press, Durham, 1972.

———, and ROBERT FARRELL, eds. *The Development of the Soviet Economy: Plan and Performance.* Frederick A. Praeger, Publisher, New York, 1968.

Chapter 15

The Soviet Economy (Continued)

The Soviet industrial system is managed very much as though it were a huge holding company with many operating units, each having an independent legal existence, but, at the same time, dominated by the general purposes of the overriding parent organization. A state enterprise may take the form of a single plant or establishment; it may be a group of such establishments organized horizontally as a trust; or it may appear as a combine composed of vertically integrated firms—coal and iron mines, iron and steel plants, or machinery building plants. The state enterprise, which is a legal entity that can sue and be sued, is autonomous within the general framework established by the Soviet annual and longer-term national economic plans.

The size of Soviet industrial enterprises reflects the influence of a number of different factors such as technical requirements, regional markets, and political considerations. The emphasis on large-scale rather than small-scale production has been an enduring feature of Soviet planning. In some industrial branches, such as steel, power, and chemical production, a number of large enterprises are found, while in branches that meet regional and local needs many middle-sized and small firms are in operation.

As the statistics in Table 15–1 indicate,

Table 15–1

Distribution by Size of Soviet Industrial Enterprises in the Early 1960s

Number employed	Percentage of	
	Enterprises	Employed
Up to 100	29.8	2.7
101–500	45.8	19.8
501–1,000	12.7	15.7
Over 1,000	11.7	61.8
Total	100.0	100.0

Source: Ya. Kvasha, *Voprosy ekonomiki*, No. 5, May 1967, p. 27.

approximately 30 percent of all industrial enterprises with workers numbering less than one hundred accounted for only 2.7 percent of all employed workers in the early 1960s. At the top of the scale, only 11.7 percent of all industrial enterprises each of which employed over one thousand workers accounted for 61.8 percent of total industrial employment. The top 5.5 percent of all industrial enterprises in 1968 accounted for 55.9 percent of total gross industrial output.[1] Under Stalin up to 1953, the emphasis was upon building large plants, which at times went beyond the point of maximum economies of scale. This interest in gigantic plants declined considerably under Khrushchev, who showed more interest in determining the size of enterprises in accordance with the goal of optimum efficiency. Small-scale industrial production in the Soviet Union has in many cases been absorbed into large industrial enterprises and combines where it continues to produce spare parts or materials under the form of subsidiary or auxiliary production.

The chief executive of a state industrial enterprise is the director, who is appointed by either a ministry or a local authority, depending on the type of enterprise. The director is solely responsible for the operation of the enterprise within the limits set down by higher governmental authorities. This principle of "one-person command" does not exclude checking on the director's managerial activities by local Communist party representatives, trade union leaders, and representatives of various government agencies, including the State Bank and the Ministry of Finance. However, the enterprise director remains solely responsible for any losses incurred or profits made. The main task of the director is to fulfill and, if possible, to overfulfill the production plan for the enterprise as provided by the annual national plan. In this work of plan fulfillment or overfulfillment, the director relies very heavily upon the entire personnel, from senior associates at the top managerial level down to the brigade leaders and workers at the bottom.

The activities of each state industrial enterprise are governed by its technical-industrial-financial plan (*tekhpromfinplan*), which is worked out during the construction of the annual national plans. This plan consists of a set of programs relating to such matters as output, use of productive capacity, technical progress, labor productivity, cost reduction, capital construction, supply procurement, personnel and wages, and the financing of the enterprise's yearly activities. The key plan within the complex of technical, industrial, and financial plans is the enterprise's output plan. At the beginning of the year, the enterprise "is supposed to know *what* it will produce (output plan), by what *means* (utilization of capacity, technical development, and capital construction programs), at what *cost* (procurement, payroll, and cost plans), for *whom*, and at *what prices* (sales plan)."[2] If Soviet planning worked smoothly and effectively, these annual objectives of each state industrial enterprise would be realized without much trouble by its director. However, since there are considerable discrepancies between Soviet planning in theory and in practice, the state enterprise encounters many difficulties in its endeavor to fulfill its plan obligations.

The Annual Output Plan

The annual output plan of the state industrial enterprise indicates the enterprise's annual production targets in both value and physical terms. The enterprise is expected to reach a planned level of gross value of output that will

[1] A. Yefimov, *Soviet Industry*, Moscow: Progress Publishers, 1968, p. 184.

[2] Nicolas Spulber, *The Soviet Economy*, New York, W. W. Norton and Company, Inc., 1969, p. 58.

be a planned percentage above the gross value of last year's total production. Each industrial enterprise is expected to make a contribution to the Soviet economy's annual increase in total gross industrial output. Since a high annual rate of economic growth is one of the top priorities of Soviet national planning, much pressure is placed upon the individual industrial enterprise to exceed the gross value of output target set forth in the enterprise's annual output plan. This pressure to overfulfill the gross value of output target leads enterprises at times to produce an output mix that is overweighted with high-priced articles or items that can be produced in abundance.

Similar problems arise in connection with the meeting of physical output goals.[3] The enterprise's annual output targets expressed in physical terms cannot specify all the different assortments of products that might be needed by the user industrial enterprises. All that the annual enterprise output plans can do is to set forth physical targets in broad categories according to number of pieces, sizes, weights, lengths, and the like. It is expected that more refined breakdowns of assortments will be the subject of negotiation between producer and user industrial enterprises. In order to meet, and if possible exceed, their physical output targets, industrial producer enterprises have tended to produce heavy items when the output target is expressed in tons, to turn out items light in weight and narrow in width when the output target is given in some linear measure, and to produce small items when the output target is given in numbers of units of output.

Since it is much easier to establish quantity indices than quality indices, the Soviet industrial enterprises have paid more attention to meeting quantitative goals than to meeting quality standards. Wherever quality can be slighted without serious consequences for the efficient working of the Soviet economy, as in the case of consumer-goods production, the state industrial enterprises have tended to yield to the pressure to give the highest priority to quantitative goals. In high-priority branches of industry, such as iron and steel, machinery, and chemical production, quality indicators or targets have usually been given considerable attention. But in low-priority, consumer-goods branches, low quality and defective goods have sometimes been produced in large quantities. In recent years, when more emphasis has been placed on the problem of raising the general population's standard of living, greater efforts have been made by the national, republic, and local planning authorities to require industrial enterprises to meet qualitative as well as quantitative output targets in the low-priority and nonpriority industries.

The production activities of the state industrial enterprises are closely associated with the supply system, by means of which each enterprise obtains the raw materials, fuels, and equipment that it needs to fulfill its production plans. Most material inputs are subject to control by national, republic, or regional planning authorities. These inputs are obtained by industrial enterprises that hold allocation certificates. These certificates specify the quantity and quality of raw materials and other production components to which a user enterprise is entitled according to the annual national plan; they also indicate the producing enterprise that is to supply the user enterprise. The use of allocation certificates gives rise to contracts between enterprises to sell or purchase specified quantities of output, which are to be delivered at precise dates. State enterprises have no right to enter free contractual relationships with one another, as is done in a free-enterprise economy. Instead, all state enterprises are tied closely together in a supply-allocation

---

[3] Alec Nove, "The Problem of 'Success Indicators' in Soviet Industry," *Economica*, Vol. XXV, No. 97, Feb. 1958, pp. 4–6.

system that is based on the allocation decisions of the supply departments of the national and republic planning agencies. State arbitration tribunals settle disputes between industrial enterprises and enforce the fulfillment of all contracts between enterprises. A few raw materials of local significance, such as sand and gravel, are not subject to allocation under the annual national plans.

The supply needs of each industrial enterprise are determined by the planning authorities by applying norms for the use of materials to the prospective planned annual output of the enterprise. These norms indicate the raw-material requirements for each unit of output. The planning authorities endeavor to lower these raw-material requirement norms in order to conserve scarce supplies of raw materials and to raise the utilization standards of the industrial enterprises. The directors of the industrial enterprises resist the lowering of the norms because of the ever-present possibility of inadequate raw material inventories.

The enterprise director is constantly concerned about the supply problem. This concern comes about because the supply-delivery system cannot be relied upon to deliver required raw materials and other supply components in the right form at the right time. The reactions of enterprise directors to the deficiencies of the planned supply system take various forms. In applying for allocation certificates, enterprise directors tend to overstate their supply or input requirements. There are also strong inducements to hoard inventories of raw materials. Some industrial enterprises set up their own workshops to produce supply components, such as tools and castings, in order to assure the availability of these items when needed. Enterprise directors turn to semilegal and illegal methods of coping with the discrepancies between what the supply contracts call for and what is actually delivered to the purchasing enterprise.

The personnel of industrial enterprises frequently include, under the cover of normal personnel categories, employees constituting a staff of "expediters," whose special task is to deal with the inadequacies relating to the assortment of supply components, as well as to their quantity, quality, and timing. These expediters or "pushers" *(tolkachi)* keep in touch with the supply departments of central-planning administrations and supply-delivery centers with the aim of expediting the delivery of needed materials.[4] They also make contacts with enterprises with surplus inventories that are willing to exchange a part of their surplus inventories for various considerations, including bribes. Enterprise expediters arrange for the swapping of authorizations for scarce raw materials and use whatever influence they can to secure the necessary supply inputs.

This semilegal system of influence and pressure (what the Russians call *blat*) overcomes the rigidities of the highly centralized Soviet supply plan. Since the supply planning is accompanied by many discrepancies and deficiencies, the enterprise directors must turn to unofficial devices to achieve the fulfillment or overfulfillment of the production plans. The Soviet enterprise director functions in a tightly planned economy that has very little slack and that suffers from all the adverse features of a chronic "sellers' market." The constant pressure of demand upon supply enables the producing enterprises to sell all their output, even though they do not meet all the specifications regarding supply laid down in the contracts between producer and user enterprises. As long as the Soviet economy continues to be a very high-pressure economy, the Soviet supply system

[4] Joseph S. Berliner, "Managerial Incentives and Decision Making: A Comparison of the United States and the Soviet Union," *Comparisons of the United States and Soviet Economies*, Part I, 1959, p. 361.

will present great obstacles to the enterprise director in his or her efforts to reach production targets and to comply with the ever-insistent demand from the top of the industrial pyramid for an economic growth rate that exceeds the rates of almost all other industrialized countries.

Soviet Industry and Economic Accountability

The Soviet industrial enterprise, like any corporation or company in Western countries, is expected to sell its output at prices that not only cover all costs, but also leave a profit. Functioning as autonomous financial entities with their individual profit-and-loss accounts, state enterprises are operated according to the principle of economic accountability *(khozraschet)*. The essence of economic accountability is "A method of planned operation of socialist enterprises . . . which requires the carrying out of state-determined tasks with the maximum economy of resources, the covering of money expenditures of enterprises by their own money revenues, the ensuring of the profitability of enterprises."[5]

Economic accountability for a Soviet industrial enterprise only superficially resembles this accountability for a Western industrial enterprise. The Soviet state enterprise, when it is first organized, is assigned its fixed capital by the Soviet government. The enterprise does not "own" this capital, since it continues to be regarded as state property, nor can the enterprise dispose of its fixed capital or use it for any purpose except that indicated by the annual national plans. The state industrial enterprise is also given its own working capital. Additions to this capital for seasonal or temporary purposes, such as financing the gap between production and sales are secured

[5] Alec Nove, *The Soviet Economy*, New York, Frederick A. Praeger, 1969, p. 32.

from the State Bank at an interest charge of 2 percent or less. The costs of production of a state industrial enterprise include the costs of materials and fuels, depreciation, wages and salaries, other costs such as interest charges on short-term loans from the State Bank, and, since 1965, an interest charge on the enterprise's fixed and working capital.

Wages and Salaries

Wages and salaries, like material and equipment prices, are centrally determined by the state. The All-Union Council of Ministers is responsible for the general features of Soviet wage policy. The general level of wage rates, basic and differential wage rates, and the total annual wage bill or fund are established by the U.S.S.R. Ministry of Finance and the State Committee on Labor and Wages. The Council of Ministers approves all final decisions relating to the Soviet economy's wage structure. The central determination of wages includes setting wage rates for different industries and geographical zones and for different grades of skill. All these matters constitute the national wage plan, which is carried down to the different industrial sectors and to the many enterprises operating in these sectors. The directors of industrial enterprises must handle their wage problems within the framework of the overall annual wage plan that comes to them from the higher levels of government above. Although all the important aspects of wage determination are beyond the control of the enterprise director, a considerable area exists within which he or she can adjust the centrally-determined wage system to the needs and realities of the situation at the enterprise level.

Annually, the central planning authorities determine the total amount to be paid out as wages and salaries. The size of this total wage bill is influenced by the number and grades of workers to be hired in the forthcoming year, the total available supply of consumers' goods on which wage incomes will be spent, and the level of retail prices at which these goods will be sold. Not only must wages act as a stimulant to output and higher productivity in all sectors of the economy, but they must also be kept in balance with the available supplies of consumer goods. After the total wage bill or fund for the coming plan year has been determined, it is then apportioned to the remaining all-union economic ministries and republics. Before the industrial reforms of 1957, the central industrial ministries played a major role in distributing the total national wage fund. The portion of the total annual wage fund allotted to each industry is further divided among the state enterprises in each industry. The share of the total wage bill or fund allotted to each enterprise is determined by the number of workers, their qualifications or grades, and the wage rates paid to each grade of workers in the coming plan year.

The classification of workers, the number of workers needed by the enterprise, and the wage schedule for the working personnel are determined by the central planning authorities. The official wage schedule provides for from eight to twelve grades, depending upon the industry. The unskilled worker at the bottom of the wage scale (grade one) receives a base wage rate, with all higher grades receiving multiples of this base wage rate. If a skilled worker is assigned a wage coefficient of 2, he then receives twice the wage of the grade-one unskilled worker. Base wage rates vary from industry to industry and within each industry, according to working conditions. More hazardous and unpleasant jobs and types of work assigned high priorities have higher base wage rates than do the less dangerous and low-priority types of work.

The carrying out of the industrial enterprise's annual wage plan would appear on the surface to be rather routine, since the state fixes both the wage rates paid by the enterprise and also its total annual wage fund. If workers in the Soviet Union were directed to their jobs by compulsion and the enterprise director had no problem in securing the labor required by his or her annual output plan, implementing the enterprise's annual wage plan would present no serious difficulties. But this is not the situation that confronts the directors of Soviet state enterprises. Although before 1956 workers were not free to leave their jobs in search of other types of employment, since that year there has been little government direction of labor in the Soviet Union. At present, only graduates of institutions of higher learning and members of the Communist party can be ordered to places of work. The enterprise director has to recruit in a relatively free labor market a large part of his or her work personnel, including all his or her ordinary factory workers and clerical help.

Since the Soviet economy is a tightly planned, high-pressure economy, the labor and wage plans of the individual enterprises are not carried out smoothly. The enterprise director finds that he or she must modify his or her annual wage plan in ways that are not always approved by the central planning authorities and the various government inspecting agencies. The enterprise director finds it very difficult to fit each worker into the appropriate grade according to his or her skills and other work qualifications; while the industry wage-schedule manual clearly states the qualifications of each grade of workers, it is not an easy task to determine and differentiate between the qualifications of from six to twelve grades of workers. Since skilled labor is usually in short supply, the enterprise's hiring authorities are strongly tempted to overgrade or upgrade the skilled worker in order to keep him or her on the payroll. Upgrading workers tends to distort the wage structure, since the lower grades of workers can be upgraded, but the skilled workers in the top grade cannot be paid more than the maximum multiple of the bottom grade set forth in the industry's centrally determined wage schedule. Upgrading thus tends to reduce wage-rate differentials between workers, which are necessary incentives to improve labor efficiency.

In order to hold or to secure workers, enterprise directors make other unofficial wage adjustments. Orders to enterprise directors to increase piecework norms, i.e., the number of "pieces" of work that an employee should normally turn out in an hour or a day, are in many cases not effectively carried out. Keeping piecework norms low enables a worker to overfulfill more easily his or her piecework norm and to receive higher piecework rates for all his or her output above the normal hourly or daily output. Failing to increase piecework norms is a disguised way of increasing a worker's money wages and keeping him or her in the enterprise's work force. These wage-rate adjustments, made necessary by the difficulties encountered by directors in carrying out their enterprises' annual wage plans in a somewhat free-labor market, tend to result in increasing an enterprise's total annual wage bill beyond the amount set by the central planning authorities.

In some years, even as late as the early 1950s, actual total annual wage bills have exceeded the planned wage bills by considerable amounts. The overpaying of wages has not been the only reason for excessive total wage bills, since the inflation of retail prices has also contributed to these bills. In recent years, the disparities between planned and actual total wage bills of industrial enterprises have been reduced; as long, however, as enterprise directors are caught between an authoritarian wage structure and a relatively free market for labor, actual total-wage payments will tend to exceed planned total-wage payments. Since it is more important for an enterprise director to fulfill, or if possible overfulfill, his or her production plan, he or she will be strongly tempted to attach a higher priority to securing an adequate labor supply than to achieving other targets, such as cost reduction, improved labor productivity, or the introduction of technological improvements. Some of the enterprise directors' unofficial wage adjustments, such as overgrading workers and failing to increase piecework norms, have forestalled planned cost reductions, since these adjustments sometimes result in the same or higher labor costs per unit of output. Evidently, the annual wage plans, with their state-determined wage schedules, in some cases hinder the enterprise director in his or her efforts to reduce production costs and to raise labor productivity.

The Wholesale Price System

The wholesale prices of Soviet industrial goods are determined by building up from below, i.e., by starting with the weighted average cost of production and then adding a margin for profit. In each industrial branch, the wholesale prices of products are determined according to the average cost-pricing principle. A planned average cost for a product is determined by the price-fixing authorities by averaging the unit costs of all the firms in the industry, or by establishing some "standard" cost for the product, or by using the average unit costs of the more progressive firms in the industry. No attempt is made to use marginal costs as a basis for price determination. After the planned average cost per unit of the product has been calculated, a planned profit margin is added to the planned average unit cost to arrive at the fixed wholesale price of the product. According to published Soviet sources, average profit markups in heavy industries should be added to average unit costs to provide total profits for these industries equal to from 5 to 10 percent of their total production costs. In each industry, some individual industrial enterprises will make total profits equal to more than 5 to 10 percent of their total production costs, while less efficient firms will incur losses.

This raises the question for the Soviet price fixer: how large should total profits or profit markups be? Since there are no markets for producers' goods, profit standards cannot be found in the market place. The guiding Marxian principle is that the profits of an industrial enterprise should be equal to the surplus value created by the labor power used in the enterprise or industry. Soviet economists are now working on the problem of how to measure the surplus value created by an industry and how to relate it to the profit markup of the industry. Thus far, no satisfactory theoretical answer to this problem has been found.[6] Since Soviet economists do not agree on how to use surplus value as a profit yardstick, determining the profit level of an industry remains an arbitrary procedure on the part of the Soviet price-fixing authorities. Arbitrarily determined profits constitute an additional obstacle to the development of a rational price system for Soviet industrial products.

The industrial enterprise plays no direct role in establishing the wholesale prices of its products, since price determination is a government-controlled activity. All prices except those in markets where peasants sell their surplus farm products are fixed by government authorities. The prices of key industrial products are established by the central planning authorities, with the final approval of the U.S.S.R. Council of Ministers. The prices of less important industrial products are set by the republic councils of ministers, except in the case of wholesale prices of local industries which are determined by local soviets. The directors of state industrial enterprises have no authority to fix selling prices, except in the case of goods made to special order for which no prices exist. The industrial reforms of 1957 decentralized the price-determining process to some extent. However, all decisions with regard to general price policy are still made by the U.S.S.R. Council of Ministers. Price determination in the Soviet Union continues to be far removed from the free market price determination found in many Western countries.

The Profitability of Enterprises

The annual financial plan of the state industrial enterprise is constructed on the basis of the planned costs and planned prices of industrial products. The major feature of the enterprise's financial plan is the calculation relating to the profitability of the enterprise in the forthcoming year. The profitability of enterprises within an industry will vary with the extent to which an enterprise has been mechanized and provided with the newest technological developments. Enterprises in an industrial branch vary over a wide range from the lowest-cost to the highest-cost firm. In the construction of the annual financial plans for the industrial enterprises, account is taken of the varying cost conditions among these enterprises and the planned total costs and total profits are adjusted for each firm. Although most enterprises are expected to achieve their planned total profits during the plan year, in some cases the annual financial plan of the enterprise anticipates a planned loss. A new enterprise in the early stages of its development may operate for a number of years with a planned loss, as may also a firm that has not yet been fully modernized. Where losses are planned, they are offset by transferring profits from other firms in the industry or by granting subsidies from the state budget.

If an enterprise's actual costs of production

---

[6] L. Turgeon, "Cost-Price Relationships in Basic Industries during the Plan Era," *Soviet Studies*, Vol. IX, No. 2, Oct. 1957, pp. 159–160.

are the same as its planned costs and it fulfills its production plan, its actual profits will then be equal to its planned profits. Only a small part of the planned profits, varying from 1 to 6 percent, are retained by the industrial enterprise. The bulk of the planned profits, when achieved, are taken as deductions by the state that owns the enterprise and is, therefore, entitled to share in enterprise profits. The profits retained by the enterprise are placed in three funds that are used for the benefit of the enterprise personnel as bonuses and investments in housing, and for improving the enterprise's productive facilities. Workers' incentives are more closely linked with unplanned (overplan) profits than with planned profits. If the director of the enterprise and his or her working staff succeed in reducing actual costs of production below planned costs, then unplanned or overplan profits in excess of planned profits are made. A much larger percentage of unplanned profits than of planned profits is placed in the enterprise fund. For example, whereas only 6 percent of planned profits in the iron and steel, coal, oil, and cement industries are diverted to enterprise funds, 50 percent of any unplanned or overplan profits are put into the enterprise funds of firms in these industries. When large overplan profits are made, the directors and their personnel receive larger bonuses, more adequate housing facilities, and various cultural amenities. However, a limit is placed on the extent to which the director and his workers can share any overplan profits by providing that the total enterprise fund in any one year cannot exceed 5 percent of the total amount paid out in wages and salaries.

Investment in Soviet Industry

The investment process in the Soviet Union has suffered from the Marxian ideological antipathy to the concept of interest as a charge for the use of capital, and from the lack of a freely operating capital market, in which the directors of industrial enterprises could compete for available investment funds. In the years before 1960, when the Soviet government did not accept interest as a legitimate charge for the use of capital, decisions still had to be taken as to when and where investments would be made in plant and equipment. It was necessary to make comparisons of the efficiency or returns on different investment proposals or variants. This problem was handled in the Stalin era by adopting a recoupment or payoff period as a device for preventing industrial enterprises from using scarce capital wastefully or inefficiently.[7]

For example, the recoupment period has been used in the electric-power industry to decide how far it should go in constructing capital-intensive, hydroelectric-power stations in preference to less capital-intensive, steam-power stations. A hydroelectric-power station requires a much larger fixed capital investment than does a steam-power station, but the annual operating costs of a hydroelectric station are less than those of a steam-power station with the same production capacity. The much larger capital investment in a hydroelectric-power station is economically justifiable only where the savings in annual operating costs are large. If these savings are small, it would be more rational to build steam-power stations and to invest the saving in fixed capital in other industries where the scarce capital would be more productive than it would be in the hydroelectric-power industry.

For the guidance of planners in the power

---

[7] For a discussion of the Soviet investment process, see Gregory Grossman, "Scarce Capital and Soviet Doctrine," *Quarterly Journal of Economics*, Vol. 67, No. 3, Aug. 1953, pp. 98–110; Alec Nove, *The Soviet Economy*, 1968, pp. 231–240; Abram Bergson, *The Economics of Soviet Planning*, Ch. 11, pp. 241–274, and Paul R. Gregory and Robert C. Stuart, *op. cit.*, pp. 214–231.

industry, the Soviet Academy of Sciences in the early 1960s recommended a standard recoupment period of ten years. The application of this investment standard would be made in the following manner. Let us assume that a hydroelectric-power station requires 100 million rubles more capital investment than a steam station of equal output capacity, and that the annual operating costs of the hydroelectric station are 10 million rubles less than those of the steam station. If the hydroelectric station is built, it will take ten years for its savings in annual operating costs to equal the extra capital investment of 100 million rubles required to construct this station. In other words, the larger capital investment in the hydroelectric station would be recouped in ten years; and the relatively greater efficiency or effectiveness of the hydroelectric station over the steam station would be .10 or 10 percent.[8]

If the annual saving in the operating costs made by choosing the hydroelectric station over the steam station is regarded as something earned in the sense of resources being saved for other purposes, then the extra capital investment of 100 million rubles annually earns 10 million rubles or 10 percent. According to the investment standard recommended by the Soviet Academy of Sciences, the extra investment in the hydroelectric station should not be made if the recoupment period exceeded ten years. For example, if the annual savings in operating costs made by choosing the hydroelectric station over the steam station were only one million rubles, it would take one hundred years to recoup the extra capital investment of 100 million rubles in the hydroelectric station. The rate of return on the extra capital investment would be viewed as being only 1 percent a year. Where the State Planning Commission prohibits a longer recoupment or payoff period than ten years, it is in effect saying that extra capital should not be invested in hydroelectric plants unless it earns at least 10 percent a year. The device of the recoupment period is then used to direct capital to those industries in which it will earn the highest returns.

Investment decision making has been improved in the Soviet Union in a number of ways since the late 1950s. Interest charges are now included among the costs of using capital; recoupment period norms have been standardized for all industries; and more rational procedures have been worked out for deciding how to allocate investments among different sectors of the economy. The 1969 rules governing investment decisions, which incorporated the "Standard Methodology for Determining the Economic Effectiveness of Capital Investments," made two advances over earlier rules. The new investment rules establish a uniform recoupment norm or criterion of relative effectiveness (CRE) of eight and three-tenths years to replace the variable industry recoupment norms formerly used for which there was no economic justification.[9]

---

[8] The relatively greater efficiency or effectiveness of the hydroelectric station over the steam station (CRE) is determined in the following manner where

K_a = the capital outlay on the hydroelectric station
K_b = the capital outlay on the steam station
C_a = the operating expenses of the hydroelectric station
C_b = the operating expenses of the steam station
CRE = the criterion or coefficient of relative effectiveness

$$CRE = \frac{C_b - C_a}{K_a - K_b} = \frac{50,000,000 - 40,000,000 \text{ rubles}}{500,000,000 - 400,000,000 \text{ rubles}}$$

$$= \frac{10,000,000 \text{ rubles}}{100,000,000 \text{ rubles}} = .10 \text{ or } 10 \text{ percent}$$

This formula states that for every additional ruble of capacity outlay on the hydroelectric station 1/10 or .10 ruble of operating expense would be saved over the operating expense of the steam station

[9] For recent developments with respect to the principles guiding the Soviet investment process, see P. Gregory, B. Fielitz, and T. Curtis, "The New Soviet Investment Rules: A Guide to Rational Investment

The 1969 standards for investment allocation also establish a criterion to guide intersectoral and interregional industrial investment. This criterion is described as a coefficient of absolute effectiveness (CAE) which measures the contributions of different investment outlays to net national income. Under this criterion, investments in different sectors of the economy are ranked according to the size of their returns or payoffs; those that have large payoffs measured in terms of contributions to net national income are selected over those with low payoffs. While this criterion of absolute effectiveness ranks investments according to their net national income or social payoffs, it does not indicate to the State Planning Committee how much investment should be allocated to each sector.

The criterion of relative effectiveness is used by the planning departments of the industrial enterprises in their choice of the most efficient new technological alternative to be financed by their retained profits. Allowing the industrial enterprise to make its own decisions concerning the use of the investment funds that it generates in the form of retained profits encourages the development of local technological evaluation, and avoids overcentralized control over the enterprise's investment activity from Moscow. The criterion of absolute effectiveness is used by the State Planning Committee when it allocates investment funds from the central fiscal budget to the various sectors of the nation's economy. While considerable progress has been made since the 1950s in developing more rational investment standards, these standards are not always followed by the planning departments of the industrial enterprises and the State Planning Committee. Political decisions by the party leaders with regard to the allocation of investment funds frequently override what would otherwise be accepted as economically desirable from the viewpoint of an efficient use of scarce resources in order to increase consumer welfare.

Industrial Management in the Planned Soviet Economy

Western Soviet analysts have found that considerable progress has been made in improving all levels of management in Soviet industrial enterprises since the early years after the revolution of 1917. Over the decades, the industrial managers, originally recruited from among the party members who were usually better known for their party loyalty and revolutionary fervor than for their managerial skills, have been replaced by a new generation of Soviet "organization men."[10] These new managers are products of technical schools and universities; although educated in communist ideals and loyal to the party, they are first of all technicians and engineers more interested in increasing industrial production than in dominating or directing Communist party affairs. Unlike many American managers who come to managerial positions with a background of legal, marketing, or financial experience, the Soviet managers at the higher levels are usually engineers and other specialists of extensive technical capac-

---

Planning?", *Southern Economic Journal*, Vol. 41, Jan. 1974, pp. 67–86; and Alan Abouchar, "The New Soviet Standard Methodology for Investment Allocation," *Soviet Studies*, Vol. 24, Jan. 1973, pp. 402–410.

[10] For an analysis of Soviet management, see David Granick, *The Red Executive*, Garden City, New York: Doubleday, 1960, and *Managerial Comparisons of Four Developed Countries: France, Britain, United States, and Russia*, Cambridge, Mass.: MIT Press, 1972; Barry M. Richman, *Soviet Management*, Englewood Cliffs, N.J.: Prentice-Hall, 1965; and Joseph Berliner, *Factory and Manager in the USSR*, Cambridge, Mass.: Harvard University Press, 1957, and "Managerial Incentives and Decisionmaking: A Comparison of the United States and the Soviet Union," in M. Bornstein and D. Fusfeld (eds.), *The Soviet Economy*, 3rd ed., Homewood, Ill.: Irwin, 1970, pp. 165–195.

ity. Since the Soviet engineer-manager is production oriented, he or she is usually not greatly concerned about the selling, marketing, legal, and financial aspects of his enterprise's activities.

The kind of Soviet manager who has risen to the top is the type favored by the production-minded party leaders and government planners. With the shift from the old overemphasis on mere production to efficient production (with some considerable concern about the quality of products), the need for competent management at all managerial levels from director down to foremen has quickened the interest of Soviet leaders in raising managerial capacities to still greater heights. Western Soviet analysts now generally agree that Soviet management compares very favorably with Western European and American management. The Soviet manager, who is assigned to a modern large-scale factory, performs about as well on the average as does his or her Western counterpart. He or she is a member of the high-income group in the Soviet Union, which earns five to six times as much as an average factory worker, and he or she enjoys a position of high prestige in Soviet society. On the income scale, Soviet managers have the same relative position as do American managers in relation to other workers in American corporations. The standard of living of the Soviet manager is lower, however, than that of his or her American counterpart, since the standard of living in general in the Soviet Union is lower than in the United States.

The competent Soviet manager functions very much as do successful American managers in those day-to-day activities that are also carried on by American corporations. The Soviet managers at all levels are motivated by much the same goals as are American managers. The Soviet manager is driven by the desire for a higher standard of living, prestige, and power, and by the urge to find creative expression through the organizing of well-run enterprises. But more immediately, he or she is interested in maximizing his or her monthly salary by pursuing those activities that will increase his or her monetary rewards. The motivation of the Soviet manager, as of the American manager, is a highly complex matter. What is different in the Soviet Union and in the United States is the manner in which managerial motivation leads to action in the business world. The Soviet manager functions in a rigorously planned, high-pressure economy which gives rise to widespread sellers' markets. The American manager, on the other hand, operates in a relatively unplanned, low-pressure economy that is characterized much of the time by buyers' markets. These contrasts in generally prevailing economic circumstances explain the differences in managerial practices and procedures in the two countries. Whenever American managers find themselves in an economic situation similar to the one in which Soviet managers operate—as they did during World War II, when a planned, high-pressure economy prevailed in the United States—they function very much as Soviet managers do in both wartime and peacetime.

The key to the explanation of Soviet managerial activity is the monetary bonus or premium system, which is a special feature of Soviet economic life. "A premium is essentially a bonus earned by a managerial official, over and above his fixed salary, for performance equal to or better than a plan target."[11] Salary premiums are of two major types, the basic and the special. The basic premium, which is paid to senior management and staff officials (directors and chief engineers), is calculated according to a scale that rises with the percentage of fulfillment of the monthly production plan. Special premiums, which are

[11] Joseph S. Berliner, *Factory and Manager in the USSR*, Cambridge, Harvard University Press, 1957, p. 27.

paid to managers below the senior management level, are for specific tasks, such as economizing in the use of raw materials, making consumer goods from waste materials, reducing costs, and improving the production process.

The special premiums earned by intermediate and junior managers enable them to secure monthly premiums that are comparable to those earned by senior managers. In addition to basic and special monthly premiums, there are annual bonuses paid out to managers from the incentive fund. These annual premiums, which are paid for excellence in general performance, are not as large as the monthly premiums directly associated with output and special tasks relating to the production process. Consequently, they do not play as important a role in providing managers with the incentive to increase production. Premiums in kind, such as tickets to vacation resorts and Red Banners won in socialist competition (getting the highest percentage of overfulfillment), are relatively less important as motivating factors. Unlike the Soviet manager, the American manager usually receives bonuses which are much less than half his or her annual salary, and what bonuses he or she receives are not so directly related to output as they are in the Soviet Union.

The basic premium is a powerful motivating factor in the world of Soviet managerial activity. Since a failure to fulfill his or her output plan may cost the Soviet manager 30 to 50 percent of his or her monthly salary, he or she is under a heavy strain to reach the output goal. The monthly premium method of compensation puts much more pressure on the Soviet manager than does the American method of managerial compensation. Soviet managerial prestige and status are measured in terms of premiums earned. A good manager is one who receives large premiums for output plan fulfillment and overfulfillment. Large monthly premiums are the main index of successful management. It may seem unusual that the Soviet system should place so much emphasis upon a system of compensation that makes almost a fetish of the monthly monetary bonus. Communism, in theory, relegates personal pecuniary gain to a low status compared with nonmonetary forms of compensation. The Soviet ideologist meets this apparent contradiction by explaining that personal monetary incentives will not disappear until after the period of communist construction, when there will be a general abundance of goods, differences between town and country will have been eliminated, and preferences for mental over manual labor will have disappeared.

Unofficial Managerial Practices

The Soviet system of managerial premiums, combined with the high-pressure, rigorously planned Soviet economy, accounts for many of the unofficial practices of managers. In their efforts to achieve the frequently unreasonably high production targets set by the central planners and to secure large monthly premiums, Soviet managers not only engage in practices that are not officially recognized by the government, but which, in some cases, violate officially approved managerial rules. The three main unofficial practices of Soviet managers are: (1) striving for a "safety factor" with regard to production; (2) adjusting output to give the appearance of fulfilling output targets; and (3) using influence and related devices to expedite the production process. A safety factor is obtained by understating productive capacity, securing an "easy" output plan that will be fulfilled much more readily than a larger output plan, creating hidden reserves of raw materials, and padding requests for new supplies of input items. An industrial enterprise that possesses hidden reserves of input items and productive capacity is in a better position to meet emergency demands for above-plan outputs. Such reserves are also very useful when new industrial techniques are being adopted and production lines are temporarily disrupted.

Adjusting production to give the appearance of fulfilling the output plan involves producing only that assortment of output that contributes most to plan fulfillment, economizing or shaving on quality, and indulging in overplan expenditures in order to secure the needed supplies of materials, equipment, and labor skills. In some situations, output targets are met only by *storming*, or speeding up the production process towards the end of the monthly, quarterly, or annual output plan periods, with less than the usual regard for costs of production, in order to reach plan fulfillment. In other situations, false reports are made and production is "borrowed" in the current plan period from the next plan period.

Using influence to assure receiving the necessary production inputs on time or to induce an inspector to overlook some violation of official managerial procedures appears to be a widespread Soviet managerial practice. The extent of these unofficial and, in some cases, criminal managerial practices is not known, since no on-the-spot investigation of Soviet managerial practices can be made. However, the frequent criticisms of these practices that appear in the newspapers, journals, and official speeches indicate that they are well established and of long standing.

The question might well be raised: why does the Soviet government tolerate managerial practices that run counter to its plan directives? It is true that not all unofficial managerial practices escape detection and that managers are sometimes heavily penalized for violations that fall in the criminal category. And yet there are strong forces at work to make the "real rules of managerial behavior" prevail over the "official rules of behavior." In the first place, the Soviet government attaches the highest priority to the fulfilling and overfulfilling of output targets. Even though Soviet managers violate official rules in achieving this goal, successful managers are not challenged as to procedures unless they flagrantly violate official procedures. The consequences of violating official managerial rules are only marginal. On the whole, output plans as constructed by the government are carried out. Soviet managers ignore official managerial rules primarily in connection with low-priority goods. The burden of any such managerial malpractices falls on consumers and not on government enterprises and agencies. This development was not a matter of major concern during the Stalin era when consumers came in for little consideration. However, the greater concern for consumer welfare since 1953 may have altered the government's view concerning what managerial malpractices to ignore and what malpractices to outlaw. However, there has been no sign of any letup in the maintenance of a high-pressure, full-blast economy in the Soviet Union.

The Soviet party leaders know that they are placing a very heavy burden on Soviet management to meet frequently unrealistic output targets, and they doubtless realize that unofficial Soviet managerial practices are a normal reaction in an overdemanding economic environment. Furthermore, violations of official managerial rules by Soviet managers have some consequences that are favorable to the good working of the Soviet economy. The striving for a safety factor in the form of concealed reserves reduces the heavy strain imposed on Soviet managers by offsetting the unrealistically high output targets set by the central planners. The reduction in managerial strain arising from availability of hidden reserves of raw materials and productive capacity permits the Soviet manager to pay more attention to such secondary goals as cost reduction, profitability, and quality control. Hidden reserves also improve the flexibility of the economy and permit the satisfying of emergency demands for increased output.

The adjusting of output to give the appearance of fulfilling an output target ensures that the shaving of quality will be more applicable to low-priority consumer goods than to high-priority producer goods. The use of personal influence or *blat* overcomes some of the rigidities of an economy rigorously planned according to a national blueprint.

If Soviet national plans were constructed without defects and if their implementation could be smoothly carried out, there would be no need for the "expediter" and *blat*. But such is not the case. Soviet national plans contain many discrepancies, especially with respect to the production and delivery of input materials and other supply components. The managers of Soviet industrial enterprises would suffer much more frustration than they now do if they were unable to coordinate the production process with the aid of "pushers" and personal influence. The situation has been neatly summarized with the observation that personal influence or "Blat is the grease in the gears of the economic system which serves to keep the mechanism running more smoothly and quietly."[12]

Unlike American corporate executives, who jealously guard their business secrets and shield their activities as much as possible from the scrutiny of other executives and public officials, Soviet executives live in an open business world. The associates of the Soviet enterprise director, such as the chief accountant and the chief engineer, are relied upon by the state to provide information about the way in which the enterprise is being operated. Representatives of the State Committee for Party-State Control, the State Committee for State Security, the Ministry of Finance, the State Bank, and other supervisory governmental agencies are constantly at work checking upon the performance of Soviet managers.

However, government supervision of Soviet management is never an all enveloping activity. The strictness of managerial supervision is held in check by the growth of a "family atmosphere," in which local Communist party secretaries, trade union representatives, and top-level managers find it to their interest at appropriate times to "look the other way" when managerial practices veer from what is officially approved. As long as the enterprise is successful in fulfilling its output plan, all these representatives of various interests are prepared in many situations to go along with the management and bask in the sunshine of success. Certain types of managerial problems can be met only by action on the part of the republic and central governments and not by a strengthening of the system of checking on the performance of Soviet managers. Soviet managers are shifted about in the economy much more frequently than are Western managers. Soviet managers who do not quickly produce good results are soon replaced by others, while successful managers are promoted to more challenging and rewarding positions.

The high mobility of Soviet managers leads them to emphasize short-run economic considerations. They are reluctant to introduce large-scale technological innovations, for a strong probability exists that plan fulfillment would be difficult to achieve in the early stages of extensive rebuilding of the industrial plant; also, the managers are far from certain of being associated with the enterprise when the technological innovations eventually pay off. Since the Soviet government cannot count on its enterprise managers to introduce technological developments, new designs, and other innovations as rapidly and as extensively as the central planners think they should be introduced, the government relies upon central or state committees of the U.S.S.R. to step up the rate of technological progress. The State Committees on Automation and Machine Building, Electronic

---

[12] Joseph S. Berliner, *op. cit.*, p. 327.

Technology, Chemistry, and Coordination of Scientific Research have the task of discovering whether or not industrial enterprise directors have been active in introducing technological innovations into their production processes. When directors lag in this managerial area, the state committees are supposed to take the necessary steps to secure a more rapid introduction of technological improvements.

New Directions in Soviet Management

Soviet economic development since the end of the Stalin era has not always been as fast as party leaders would have liked, even though many of the major obstacles that Stalin placed on the path to rapid economic growth have been removed. Many of the imbalances in the Soviet economy have been eliminated, economic incentives have been improved, and various deficiencies in the planning organization have been removed. As the Seven-Year plan (1959–1965) was being carried out, it became clear that the various reforms and reorganizations after 1953 had not succeeded in reconstructing the Soviet economy along the more efficient lines that had been envisioned. The reorganization of the central planning machinery, the abolition of most of the central economic ministries, and the setting up of regional economic councils in 1957 had not resulted in the greater "plan discipline" (adherence to plans), the better coordination of supply and demand, the greater efficiency in construction, the higher quality of manufactured products, the larger supplies of consumer goods, and the more favorable attitude towards innovation that had been expected by the Soviet leaders. The impact of the reforms and reorganizations of the years 1953–1957 on the managerial level of the Soviet industrial enterprises was not nearly as great as had been anticipated.[13]

The failure of industrial reforms and planning reorganizations of the post-Stalin period to raise the level of enterprise management to what had been expected by the early 1960s opened the door to some very critical analysis by Soviet economists of Soviet planning and production methods. Among the many proposals for improving the performance of Soviet industrial enterprises are those of Professor E. G. Liberman of the Kharkov Engineering-Economic Institute. Liberman proposed in a *Pravda* article of September 9, 1962 on "The Plan, Profits and Bonuses" that the main success indicator of the performance of industrial enterprises should be the profitability of the enterprise's annual activities and not the fulfillment of its annual output plan.[14] He asserted that enterprises' annual production plans are "as a rule far lower than their true potentials," because output plans are geared too much to "achieved levels" of production in previous years and not enough to possible higher levels in future years. According to Liberman's proposals, greater "freedom of economic maneuvering" would be given to enterprise directors by having the government assign to enterprises only plans for a fixed amount of output with a stated assortment of products and fixed delivery schedules. Enterprises would be free to make their own plans with respect to wages, labor, productivity, and costs. They would be stimulated to maximize output at minimum cost by an incentive system based on enterprise profitability.

Other Soviet economists have gone beyond Liberman to recommend that state industrial

---

[13] M. Kaser, "The Reorganization of Soviet Industry and Its Effects on Decision Making," *Value and Plan*, 1960, p. 230.

[14] E. G. Liberman, "The Plan, Profits, and Bonuses," *The Current Digest of the Soviet Press*, Vol. XVI, No. 37, Oct. 10, 1962, pp. 19–20.

enterprises should be allowed freely to buy and sell raw material and other input components, with the state planning only the final outputs of each industrial enterprise. Such a proposal, if carried out, would eliminate the cumbersome raw materials allocation system that is the object of so much criticism by the managers of state industrial enterprises.

The response of Khrushchev and other party leaders to the criticisms of Soviet methods of planning and improving the level of enterprise management was not to adopt the suggestions of Liberman and other Soviet economists. Khrushchev emphasized the need to make more use of profitability as a measure of managerial success and, in addition, he called for more "operative independence and initiative of enterprises." Instead of improving the indices of enterprise management and reforming the price system, Khrushchev in 1961 again reorganized the system by means of which the state attempted to plan and direct the activities of the state industrial enterprises. He reduced the number of regional economic councils from one hundred and four to forty-eight; created a new national economic council to supervise the forty-eight regional economic councils; transferred many of the powers of the regional economic councils to central or state industrial committees of the U.S.S.R. Council of Ministers; and split the Communist party into two parts, one to supervise industry and the other to supervise agriculture.

The decentralization of industry achieved in the late 1950s was thus followed by a recentralization in the early 1960s. It was found that the decentralization of industry had led to duplication, improper coordination of supply and demand, excessive attention to local needs, and insufficient interest in taking advantage of technological innovations and the rationalizing of industry. All such reorganization measures, however, merely redistributed the vast burden of national planning without getting at the roots of many of the difficulties that beset planning and management in the Soviet economy. If further steps were to be made in improving the management of Soviet industrial enterprises, more attention would have to be given to reforming the price system, improving enterprise-success indicators, devising better incentive systems, and giving enterprise directors more freedom at the operational level.

Writing in 1963, a well-known Western Soviet analyst concluded about the industrial reforms of the post-Stalin decade, 1953–1962, that

Certainly, with regard to one of the most crucial criteria of decentralization—the enhancement of the autonomy of the individual enterprise—the changes in the past decade have been minute. The Soviet enterprise is still closely and continuously directed and controlled from above. In fact, this virtual lack of autonomy at the enterprise level . . . has prompted increasingly frequent and vocal complaints, sometimes bordering on cries of desperation, on the part of managers and some economists.[15]

The Soviet Economic Reforms of 1965

The drive to improve the efficiency of economic planning and enterprise management which gathered momentum during the late 1950s and early 1960s culminated in the economic reforms that were adopted in 1965. The general object of these reforms has been to enlarge consumption without reducing the role of economic growth. The standard of living of the general population is to be improved by a more efficient use of labor and natural resources at both the macroeconomic and microeconomic levels. The 1965 economic reforms constitute another attempt to reorganize the Soviet economy in the hope

[15] Gregory Grossman, "The Soviet Economy," *Problems of Communism*, Vol. XII, No. 2, March–April 1963, pp. 39–40.

that its efficiency will be improved. Khrushchev's reorganization on the basis of regional economic councils had failed to improve the efficiency of the Soviet economic system and to halt the decline in the rate of economic growth. The economic reforms of 1965 involved a recentralization of the planning system and a partial return to the planning by central ministries which had prevailed for a quarter of a century before Khrushchev's decentralization program of the late 1950s.

The new plan recentralization of 1965 differed, however, from the centralization in effect before Khrushchev's time in one important way. In the centralized planning of the years 1928–1953 (the Stalin era) the state industrial enterprises had very little independence of operation. They were for the most part rigorously controlled by the central ministries in Moscow, which regulated the activities of these enterprises by imposing on them a large number of performance norms or indices. The new feature of the 1965 economic reforms is the greater independence of operation permitted in theory at least to the industrial enterprises. The economic reforms are based on "an optimum combination of centralised planning with wide economic initiative of enterprises on the basis of complete khozraschot [economic accountability]."[16]

This optimum combination of national planning and managerial independence is to be obtained by assigning special macroeconomic functions to the central planning authorities and special microeconomic functions to the state industrial enterprises. The central planners are to plan the overall economic growth rate, the division of the Gross National Product between consumption and investment, the rate of technological progress, and major trends in production and consumption. The state industrial and agricultural enterprises are to be concerned with reducing costs and improving labor productivity, modernizing and automating the production system, introducing new products, and improving the level of profitability.

As explained by Kosygin in September 1965, the economic reforms included the following: (1) a restoration of some central ministries and the creation of new state committees in Moscow; (2) some enlargement of the freedom to operate and innovate on the part of enterprise managers; (3) a change in the success or performance criteria for enterprises; (4) a revision of wholesale prices, which would include an interest charge on an enterprise's fixed and working capital; and (5) a reform of the industrial supply system, including the creation of a wholesale market for producer goods. In general, the central planning authorities and the state enterprises are to function at different levels and in different spheres of activity. The state is to interfere with enterprise activities as little as possible.

Some important ties, however, do exist between the central planning authorities and the state enterprises. The state still imposes on each enterprise various norms or indices of performance, but these have been reduced from forty to eight. The central ministries assign performance indices relating to volume and assortment of output, sales of output, total profits and profitability, labor productivity, size of total wage fund, and norms governing the rate of technological progress. In addition, the central planners fix wage rates and selling prices. The enterprises are left free to develop the structure of their labor forces, to accumulate orders from clients and to test consumer demand, to purchase raw materials and other inputs from the wholesale market, to develop a capital investment program involving modernization and automation, and to decide

---

[16] Novosti Press Agency Publishing House, *The Soviet Economic Reform, Main Features and Aims*, Moscow, 1966, p. 6. An enterprise is operating on a *khozraschet* basis when it "keeps account of all outlays which are to be covered by its income leaving also a margin of profit" (p. 6).

upon the introduction of new production techniques and new products. Much emphasis is placed upon increasing profits and profitability. As the profits of the enterprise increase, a larger portion of the profits is to be assigned to the enterprise's production development, material incentive, and social and cultural funds. The development fund sustains a capital investment program that reduces operation costs, while the incentive fund is used to increase worker and employee bonuses, and the social and cultural fund is used for improving social and cultural programs and housing.

The central planners under the 1965 economic reforms expect each enterprise to move towards its own local best performance at the same time that the central planners approach a national optimum on the macroeconomic level. Liberman has explained that "Seeking to reach the local optimum, each enterprise will find an efficient solution of technological and organizational problems of benefit to society and to its personnel. Moreover, fulfillment of this optimum at each enterprise also guarantees the fulfillment of the national optimum."[17] Under what Liberman describes as the *plan-khozraschet system,* what benefits the society is also supposed to benefit the worker, and the reverse is also true. The central planners assert that they achieve the same goal that a perfectly competitive private market is supposed to achieve under capitalism, but that this goal is secured under socialism without a spontaneous wasteful play of market forces. The Soviet planners believe that a free spontaneous market system leads to group conflict and exploitation. They propose to work out the planned guidance of the economy, instead of the spontaneous guidance found in the capitalist economies. Whatever freedom of operation they are prepared to accord to state enterprises, it does not include the freedom to compete for the consumers' rubles on the basis of price competition—a kind of competition that is found in the Western democratic nations.

The greater freedom of operation envisioned by the 1965 economic reforms for industrial enterprises led to some changes in the ties between these enterprises. Under the Stalinist centralized planning, the contracts to buy or sell between enterprises merely reflected the dictates of the central ministries in Moscow. Under the economic reforms of 1965, enterprises are now free to determine their own contracts with suppliers and purchasing clients. One of the aims of the economic reforms is to develop a wholesale market that will take the place of the centrally determined allocation of supplies by the Moscow planners. As these planners reduce the number of commodities allocated by the ministries in Moscow, enterprises will be free to purchase supplies in the expanding wholesale markets, which are supposed to be supported by adequate inventories.

Under the new economic reforms, the development of wholesale markets is to be accompanied by price reform. Before the profitability of an enterprise can be determined, prices must constitute accurate measures of costs, and must make adequate provision for profits. The price reforms since 1965 have included making provision for interest charges on capital, adequate reserves for depreciation, and, in the case of the extractive industries, differential rent charges according to location and natural conditions (such as the size and availability of mineral deposits). The amount of profit per unit to be added to the average unit costs of raw materials, labor, depreciation, interest, and rent is a matter of great concern to the individual enterprise. If profits are to be a stimulus to enterprise efficiency and worker productivity, they must

[17] Y. Liberman, "Plan, Direct Ties and Profitableness," *The Soviet Economic Reform,* p. 59.

be large enough to reward higher levels of manager and worker performance. In addition, profits must be high enough to meet a large part of the capital investment expansion of the nation's industrial system that is required by the annual and five-year plans.

The economic reforms of 1965 advanced the profitability norm to the front rank. This norm is of crucial importance, since it is a measure of the overall performance of the enterprise. Each industrial branch is expected to achieve an assigned rate of return on its productive or capital assets; this rate has been set at roughly 15 percent for industry as a whole. The average rate of profitability as measured by return on capital varies from 10 to 15 percent for heavy industry and from 30 to 35 percent for most light industry, with wide variations among individual enterprises within each industrial branch. If an enterprise exceeds its assigned profitability norm, special additional deductions from total profits are made and are paid into the enterprise's production development, worker incentive, and social, cultural, and housing funds. These deductions, however, decrease with each percent increase in the profitability norm or index. If the enterprise does not fulfill its profit plan, and so does not reach its profitability norm, the deductions from profits going into the three enterprise funds decrease.

Soviet Industrial Management since 1965

In spite of the Soviet efforts to improve industrial management with the aid of the economic reforms of 1965, industrial production (which had grown rapidly in the 1950s, but slowed down in the early 1960s), continued to grow at a declining rate in the years 1966–1972. Table 15-2 provides statistics relating to changes in industrial growth and labor productivity in these years. During 1966–1970,

Table 15-2

U.S.S.R. Average Annual Percentage Rates of Growth of Industrial Production, Factor Inputs, and Factor Productivity, 1951–1975

	1951–1960	1961–1965	1966–1970	1971–1972	1971–1975 (plan)
Industrial production	9.9	7.2	7.0	5.6[1]	8.0
Inputs					
Labor inputs (manhours)	2.4	3.0	3.3	2.1	1.3
Capital inputs	11.5	11.2	8.7	8.7	8.4
Labor and capital inputs	5.8	6.3	5.5	4.8	4.3
Productivity					
Labor productivity	8.0	4.1	3.6	3.5	6.7
Capital productivity	−1.4	−3.6	−1.6	−3.0	−0.4
Factor productivity	4.1	0.8	1.5	0.8	3.7

[1] Civilian industrial production. Statistics in this column are from R. V. Greenslade and W. E. Robertson, *Soviet Economic Prospects for the Seventies*, p. 275.

Source: James H. Noren and E. Douglas Whitehouse, "Soviet Industry in the 1971–75 Plan," *Soviet Economic Prospects for the Seventies*, 1973, p. 221.

industrial production grew at an average annual rate of 7 percent and continued the decline from the years 1951-1960, when the growth rate is estimated to have been close to 10 percent. In the years 1971-1975, the rate of industrial production is estimated to have fallen close to 6 percent, which was 2 percent below the goal for the 1971-1975 plan. Also, labor and capital productivity in the years 1971-1975 fell much below the targets for the 1971-1975 plan period. As Table 15-2 shows, the highly ambitious annual industrial production growth goal of 8 percent is dependent upon a very large annual increase in labor productivity of 6.7 percent. In the years 1966-1972, the annual improvement in labor productivity was close to 3.5 percent; Western Soviet analysts consider it very unlikely that this annual improvement will be close to the 1971-1975 plan goal of 6.7 percent. If developments in 1971-1975 are indicative of probable productivity trends, the labor productivity improvement rate will be somewhere between 3 and 4 percent in those years. Capital productivity will also improve less rapidly than the Soviet planners had anticipated for 1971-1975.

A survey of the implementation of these reforms as they relate to industrial management reveals why the goals of these reforms have apparently not been achieved.[18] By 1971, the Soviet government began to back away from the objectives of the 1965 reforms by curbing the freedom of enterprise managers and the incentives of workers. This was done in a number of ways. Being dissatisfied with the rate of technological progress in industry, the government increased the party control of the central ministries and put more pressure on these ministries to induce industrial enterprises to introduce improved industrial technologies and to enlarge the number of new products. The State Committee on Science and Technology and the ministries were required to construct new indices that would measure the technological performance of state enterprises.

The number of plan success indicators applied to these enterprises increased rather than declined as the 1965 reforms had proposed. Price fixing became more bureaucratic and complex, and the worker incentive system became increasingly complicated. When worker productivity failed to improve after 1965, the government returned to the old approach to management problems that stressed the need for "discipline."[19] Less attention was paid to material incentives and more attention to moral incentives, which rely on appeals to socialist pledges to greater thrift or efficiency, to the acceptance of shock work (free work time and overtime work), and to socialist emulation. All such appeals in recent years have not proved to be very successful. Khrushchev had used the same approach in the late 1950s and early 1960s without much success.

The 1965 economic reforms had also provided for a gradual transition to a system of wholesale trade in producers' goods, in which industrial enterprises would not need allocation certificates in order to purchase these goods. Very little has been accomplished in this direction because such a development would have meant the derationing of producers' goods by the central authorities; this dera-

---

[18] The consequences of the 1965 economic reforms are analyzed in Gertrude E. Schroeder, "Recent Developments in Soviet Planning and Incentives," pp. 11-38; James H. Noren and F. Douglas Whitehouse, "Soviet Industry in the 1971-75 Plan," pp. 206-245; and Rush V. Greenslade and Wade E. Robertson, "Industrial Production in the USSR," pp. 270-282, in *Soviet Economic Prospects for the Seventies*, 1973. See also Gregory Grossman, "Economic Reforms: A Balance Sheet," *Problems of Communism*, November-December, 1966, pp. 43-45; and Eugene Zaleski, *Planning Reforms in the Soviet Union, 1962-1966*, Chapel Hill: University of North Carolina Press, 1967, pp. 140-192.

[19] Gertrude E. Schroeder, "Soviet Economic Reform at an Impasse," *Problems of Communism*, July-August, 1971, p. 45.

tioning is opposed by many elements in the top Soviet administrative echelon.[20] A wholesale system requires considerable inventories for its good operation, and would work best where the planning is not very taut and enterprise managers have considerable autonomy with respect to investment in producers' goods. After the 1965 reforms, Soviet national planning continued to be very taut; the planning authorities have been unwilling to give up their control of the allocation of scarce producers' goods. Soviet planning has always been operated on the principle that its goals should be set at very high levels which cannot be achieved, but which put great pressure on lower-echelon administrative personnel and enterprise managers to secure as much national output as possible.

The New Industrial Associations

The failure to achieve the desired high levels of labor and capital productivity and technological progress in recent years has led the planning authorities to try a new organizational arrangement in the area of industrial organization. A party decree of April 2, 1973, declares that the production association will become the basic element of industrial organization.[21] According to this decree, a new organization will be established between the industrial enterprises and the central ministries that regulate and plan their activities. In the various industries, it has been usual to keep separate the complementary research organizations, design bureaus, and the operating industrial enterprises. Under this arrangement, there has frequently been a lack of coordination of these three branches of each industry; as a result, the industrial enterprises frequently have not taken advantage of the contributions of the research organizations and design bureaus. Perennial criticism has been voiced of the process of introducing new technology at the enterprise level.

The purpose of the 1973 decree is to stimulate technological research and its application to Soviet industry. Under this decree, production or industrial associations are to consolidate the enterprises in an industry in a single association, which will take over some of the powers of the ministries and assume responsibility for the management of the production, investment, and research activities of the individual enterprises. Clearly, substantial economies of scale can be achieved by these production associations, but it remains to be seen whether the ministries and enterprises will be willing to lose some of their independence of operation. It is also not clear how far the central planning authorities are willing to go in allowing the production associations to take over the allocation of scarce raw materials and producer goods. Meanwhile, the function of the production association is to apply the new indicators of technological progress to the industrial enterprises, to induce them to automate their productive processes, and to substitute new products for obsolete products. All of this would be in conformity with the general aim of the Ninth Five-Year Plan which is to improve efficiency at all levels, from the enterprises at the bottom to the planning authorities at the top, by monitoring the applications of technological advance.

The reaction of the Soviet government to the failures of the 1965 reforms has been to emphasize a number of other ways of improving labor and capital productivity. All capital

[20] A review of efforts to reform the supply system is presented in Gertrude E. Schroeder, "The 'Reform' of the Supply System in Soviet Industry," *Soviet Studies*, Vol. XXIV, No. 1, July 1972, pp. 97–119.

[21] For a discussion of the problems of the research-production associations, see *The Current Digest of the Soviet Press*, Vol. XXVI, No. 38, Oct. 16, 1974, pp. 6 and 13; and also Alice C. Gorlin, "The Soviet Economic Associations," *Soviet Studies*, Vol. XXVI, No. 1, Jan. 1974, pp. 3–27.

construction projects are to be finished before new projects are started. Until now, the productivity of capital has been kept low by the proliferation of unfinished construction projects. Also new project starts, when permitted, will be limited to the sectors that are lagging in the introduction of new productive capacity. In recent years, the Soviet government has also stepped up the importation of new industrial technologies and the products of high-technology industries from Western Europe and the United States. None of these measures is designed to make any major change in Soviet industrial organization.

Many Western analysts conclude that "the latest round of modifications in Soviet planning and incentives leaves the essentials of the system unchanged, but adds to the degree of centralization and to the complexity of administrative arrangements . . . the familiar malfunctions persist, and the problem of devising incentive schemes to remove them continues to defy solution."[22] The search for industrial microefficiency has apparently ended in the routinization of the innovative process and the greater bureaucratization of the production process. The prognosis is for the Soviet leadership to rely primarily on administrative methods of dealing with the problems of industrial organization. The "economic levers" that were supposed to foster technological progress seem to be contributing to the deficiencies common to all forms of administrative socialism, which has no real place for the free market system.

In the Soviet universities and research institutes, some academic economists continue to discuss far-reaching reforms that would introduce real markets, rationalize prices to the extent of taking account of the principle of marginal costing, and truly decentralize decision making at the enterprise level, as is done to some extent in Hungary and more extensively in Yugoslavia. No strong support exists, however, for the Hungarian type of economic reform or for the Yugoslav market approach, both of which are vigorously condemned by the Soviet government. The Soviet planners still cling to the position that the market system must remain subsidiary to the planning system. Their uncompromising view is that blueprint or target planning is decisive for the economy and that the market system must be employed only to support the centralized management of the economy. In Kosygin's own words, "Of course, we reject all kinds of erroneous ideas that would substitute markets for the guiding role of state centralized planning."[23]

Agriculture in the Soviet Economy

The most unique feature of the Soviet economy is its agricultural sector.[24] Many of the basic features of Soviet industrial enterprises are quite similar to the industrial enterprises found in the West. The organization and operational procedures of the typical Soviet industrial enterprise are duplicated to

---

[22] Gertrude E. Schroeder, "Recent Developments in Soviet Planning and Incentives," *Soviet Economic Prospects for the Seventies*, 1973, p. 38. See also Gregory Grossman, "Innovation and Information in the Soviet Economy," *American Economic Review*, Vol. LVI, No. 2, May 1966, pp. 117–130.

[23] Gertrude E. Schroeder, "Economic Organization and Management," in Norton T. Dodge (ed.), *Analysis of the USSR's 24th Party Congress and 9th Five-Year Plan*, Cremona Foundation, Mechanicsville, Maryland, 1971, p. 69.

[24] The development of the Soviet agricultural sector is analyzed in W. A. Douglas Jackson (ed.), *Agrarian Policies and Problems in Communist and Non-Communist Countries*, Seattle: University of Washington Press, 1971; Robert C. Stuart, *The Collective Farm in Soviet Agriculture*, Lexington, Mass.: D. C. Heath, 1972; Lazar Volin, *A Century of Russian Agriculture*, Cambridge, Mass.: Harvard University Press, 1970; Erich Strauss, *Soviet Agriculture in Perspective*, London: George Allen and Unwin, 1969; and James R. Millar, *The Soviet Rural Community*, Urbana: University of Illinois Press, 1971.

a large extent in the typical American corporate enterprise. The situation is quite different in Soviet agriculture. The collective farm of the Soviet Union represents a kind of agricultural enterprise found only in Soviet-type economies; it is, in fact, more common in the Soviet Union than in Eastern European communist bloc countries, such as Poland and Yugoslavia. The Soviet collective farm is the outcome of a clash between the strong ideological preferences on the part of Soviet leaders and the stern realities of the agricultural situation as it developed in the post-revolutionary years.

If the environment had been more favorable to the acceptance of the preferences of the Communist party leaders, private peasant farming would probably soon have been converted into state farming, with the farms organized and operated very much like state factories. Neither the attitudes of the Soviet peasantry nor the economic circumstances of the 1920s favored this turn of events in the Soviet Union's agricultural sector. A compromise was worked out by Lenin and Stalin in which some of the features of both state farming and peasant farming were combined to create the collective farm; this has remained substantially unchanged in its general features since it was widely established in the Soviet Union in the years 1928 to 1932.

The Soviet state farm or *sovkhoz* is a state enterprise with the same general features as those of a state industrial enterprise. The state farm is the property of the Soviet government and is administered currently by the agricultural ministry of the republic in which it is located. Before the middle 1950s, state farms were administered by the Ministry of State Farms in Moscow which was abolished under the program to decentralize the administration of the Soviet agricultural sector.

State farms vary widely in size, depending on the region in which they are located. State grain farms in the plains areas average 80,000 acres, while the largest state farms (those engaged in sheep raising), average 480,000 acres. Each state farm is managed by a director, with the help of his or her deputy and agricultural specialists, who are appointed by the republic ministry of agriculture. As in the case of the state industrial enterprise, the director of the state farm is solely responsible for his or her enterprise's performance. The work of the state farm is carried on by a number of functional and operational departments. The work force of the state farm is divided into a number of brigades, such as livestock and tractor brigades, under the direction of foremen or brigadiers, who assume responsibility for the performance of their brigades.

The operations of the 15,000 (1970) state farms are conducted in accordance with their annual plans, which are constructed within the framework of the annual and longer-term national economic plans. The state farm plans are produced by the cooperative efforts of the central and republic planning authorities, working together with the planning departments of the state farms. These annual state farm plans—which include output, labor, and financial plans—set forth the scheduled volume of production of various agricultural outputs; the delivery plans for these outputs; capital investments; labor expenditures for each type of product; the number of workers in each grade of skill; labor norms and planned cost reductions; and the interrelations among the state farm's income, expenditures, and tax obligations.

The primary objective of the state farm director is to achieve the farm's planned output and delivery goals. State farm workers are paid wages that reflect pay scales graded according to levels of skill and work norms based on an eight-hour work day. Both qualitative and quantitative norms are used in determining workers' wages. Managerial salaries are divided into two parts; 70 percent of the salary is paid monthly, with the remaining 30 percent being accumulated on an annual basis. The accumulated salary is paid only in proportion to the fulfillment of the state farm's output plan with financial penalties for underfulfillment. Where the output plan is overfulfilled, from 5 to 12 percent of overplan profits are distributed among the farm's working force. Each worker on a state farm is assigned a small garden plot, the output of which cannot be sold. As a further inducement to cut down labor turnover on the state farms, workers are provided special financial credits for the construction of houses.

The Soviet state farms have always been regarded as the ideologically superior type of farm organization in the Soviet Union.[25] The state farm appeals to the Communist party leaders because it is state owned, it represents the highest form of property, i.e., public property, and it operates like a state factory and not a producers' cooperative.

The Soviet state farms were slow to expand before the Second World War because they were found to be too large to be efficient; furthermore, working conditions were so unsatisfactory that labor turnover was extremely high. For years, the losses of state farms had to be covered by subsidies from the state budget. Since the death of Stalin in 1953, Soviet agricultural policy has been directed not only towards improving the efficiency of the state farms, but also towards enlarging their role in the Soviet economy's agricultural sector. The performance level of the state farms has been improved by increasing the number of managers with highly specialized agricultural training, by improving costing and pricing procedures relating to state farm products, and by reducing labor turnover by means of improvements in working and living conditions on the state farms.

The Role of Collective Farms

The collective farm (*kolkhoz*) is based on two economies, the communal or socialized economy and the private economy. The private economy relates to the farmer's work on his or her small personal household or garden plot on the collective farm. The tools used on these plots and their output are the personal property of the farmer and his or her family. The communal economy of the collective farm encompasses the main activities on the collective farm, which are carried on cooperatively over most of the farm's cultivated area. Each member of the collective farm shares in the collective output in accordance with his or her work contribution. The collective farm member and his or her family do both communal and private farm work and receive both a collective and a private income, since they participate in the activities of both the communal and private economies of the collective farm.

Each collective farm has a charter or constitution that determines its structural organization, indicates the responsibilities of members and elected functionaries, and provides guidelines for its operations. The collective farm land belongs to the state, but the collective has a right to the permanent use of the land. It cannot sell, buy, or lease land. Each peasant family on the collective farm has the right to a garden plot that varies in size in different regions from one quarter of one hectare to one hectare (2.47 acres). All the buildings, farm equipment, and other assets belong to the collective farm, except for the tools, buildings, and livestock on the garden plots, which are the personal property of the peasant family. Before 1958, heavy agricultural ma-

[25] Lazar Volin, "Reforms in Agriculture," *Problems of Communism*, Jan.-Feb. 1959, Vol. VIII, pp. 36–37.

chinery such as tractors, seeders, and harvester combines, were owned not by the collective farms, but by the Machine Tractor Stations, which, however, have been eliminated since 1958. Unlike the state industrial enterprise, the collective farm does not receive its capital equipment from the state free of charge. All collective farm machinery, which is classed not as public property, but as collective farm property, is purchased from state industrial enterprises.

Under the collective farm charter, the management of the collective is the responsibility of its members, who meet in a general assembly to elect officers and to make decisions with respect to such matters as membership, work rules, budgets, production plans, and income distribution. The general meeting of the collective farm members is, in theory, the highest authority on the collective farm. It elects a managing committee of from five to nine committeemen (depending upon the size of the farm), whose chairperson, also elected by the general meeting, is the highest official on the collective farm. The managing committee chairperson is the official who is responsible for the day-to-day operations of the collective farm. The members of the collective are organized for work purposes in brigades of from fifty to one hundred members under the direction of a foreman or brigadier. Many brigades are further subdivided into small work squads or links. Each brigade is assigned specific tasks and is equipped with the necessary machinery and livestock to perform these tasks.

While in theory the 33,600 (1970) collective farms are democratically organized and operated, in fact, they are controlled by the Communist party, whose local, district, and provincial committees closely supervise all important farm activities. The party is also influential in placing its members in all important positions on the collective farms. Collective farm government, like the government of the Soviet Union, is only a "paper" or "sham" government, behind which the Communist party operates in such a way as to achieve its major objectives. This is not to say that the official organization for the administration of the collective farms performs no useful functions. It mobilizes the labor force on the collective farms, provides an opportunity for the individual member to express his opinions, and keeps the members of the collective informed about the progress of the farm's annual and longer-term production plans.

However, on all crucial matters, the views of the Communist party and not those of the collective farm members prevail. The collective farm, like the industrial enterprise and the trade union, is operated according to the principle of democratic centralism, with the result that authority, originating in the Communist party, runs from the top down to the peasants at the bottom. Although recent agricultural reforms have tended to get collective farm members more deeply involved in the administration of their farms and to increase their incentives to produce, the collective farmers still have no real power to make decisions affecting the nature and direction of farm operations.

The annual output of the collective farms is disposed of in three ways. One part of the total farm output is sold to the state for use by the various nonagricultural state enterprises or for export. Another part of the collective farm's output may be sold to consumer cooperatives for resale in the retail market. The third part of the farm's output is taken up in the form of payments in kind to the workers on the collective farm. This three-fold division of the collective farm's output occurs only where the farm produces food crops or livestock products. Where the farm produces only an industrial crop, such as cotton, flax fiber, or sugar beets, contracts are made to deliver the whole crop to the state.

Collective farm sales to the state before the price reform of 1958 were of two kinds, the first being the compulsory deliveries of farm output at fixed low prices. These compulsory deliveries of produce from each farm were fixed at so much per unit of tillable land; they were determined by the state's needs for agricultural raw materials and food for the urban population, as set forth in the annual national economic plans. The compulsory delivery prices established by the state had no special relation to costs of production and frequently covered only a part of total average costs per unit of farm output. When the compulsory quotas had been met, above-quota sales by the collective farms to the state were made at higher prices.

Since 1958, this two-price system has been replaced by a single price system for most crops, with only one price paid to the collective farm for all sales of its product to the state. No longer are any premium or above-quota prices paid by the state. There are however, zonal variations in the prices paid by the state to collective farms for each farm product; these variations reflect different cost conditions in different regions. Each zonal price for an agricultural product is based on the weighted average per unit cost of production on the collective farms in the region, to this unit cost a small profit markup is added. What amounts to land rent is absorbed by the state, which pays low zonal prices in fertile areas and higher zonal prices in high-cost, less fertile areas.

Deliveries of output to the state by collective farms are no longer compulsory in a legal sense, but the rigorous implementation of the annual output plans of the collective farms has the same effect with regard to deliveries to the state as did the compulsory delivery plan in force up to 1958. Each collective farm is assigned sales quotas per unit of land, which it is expected to meet. These quotas are determined according to government plans. At present, the state continues to have first call on collective farm output and secures what it needs before any output goes to farm workers or urban consumers.

Sales of collective farm output to consumer cooperatives are now usually for resale on a commission basis at controlled prices in urban markets. Collective farms, in some cases, sell their surplus farm produce in urban free markets through their own retail outlets. Collective farm sales in urban free markets are usually at prices well above the prices paid by the state. Payments in kind to collective farm workers out of the farm's total output, as partial compensation for their services, are not supposed to exceed what is required to meet each peasant family's needs. If workers sell farm produce on the free markets of the urban areas, such produce is supposed to come from their small household or garden plots and not from the collective farm.

The Annual Revenues of Collective Farms

The annual gross cash revenues of the collective farms are used to cover current expenses, such as production and administration costs, taxes, and insurance; to build up capital investment and other funds; and to provide the farm workers with a share of the farm's net money profit. Of the annual collective farm expenditures, about 55 percent are taken up by expenses of production and contributions to reserves or funds. The most important fund is the capital fund or "indivisible fund," which contains the collective farm's retained profits to be spent for investment purposes. The government fixes the annual contributions out of gross cash revenues paid into the capital fund by each collective farm. Before the elimination of the Machine Tractor Stations in 1958, these contributions varied from 12.5 to 20 percent of each farm's gross cash revenues. The government has to fix the annual contributions to the collective farm's capital fund to prevent the peasants from taking up too much of the farm's cash income for personal consumption purposes. The annual contributions to the collective farm's capital or indivisible fund are spent for building materials, tools, trucks and machinery, and also for capital repairs. When all the expenditures have been met, the remainder of the gross cash revenues, along with the output reserved for payments in kind to the peasants, is available for distribution as annual income shares to the peasants. Until 1966, each worker on the collective farm shared in the farm's net income (measured in cash and in kind) in proportion to his contribution to the work of operating the farm. A worker's contribution was measured in terms of workday units or *trudodni*. All types of farm work were graded and assigned a number of workday units for a normal amount of work done in an eight-hour day.

At the end of the year, the number of workday units earned by the personnel on the collective farm was added up, along with adjustments in the form of workday bonuses; the total was divided into the amounts of money and produce available for distribution in order to determine the cash and produce value of each workday unit. For example, each workday unit might turn out to have a value of 3 rubles in cash, 2 kilograms of potatoes, and 1 kilogram of butter. A farm worker who had 300 workday units recorded to his credit during the year would then receive 900 rubles in cash and 900 kilograms of potatoes and butter.

The workday unit system of compensation had some objectionable features, such as the uncertainty of the value of the workday unit at the end of the work year, as well as the uncertainty of the annual income of each collective farm worker. While Khrushchev had removed some of these deficiencies of the workday unit system of compensation by reforming this system so as to guarantee each farm worker a certain minimum amount of monetary income on a monthly basis, Brezhnev later felt that the farm workers needed more definite monetary incentives. Consequently, in 1966 the workday unit system of compensating collective farm workers was abandoned, and collective farms were instructed to use the wage payment system developed in industrial enterprises and state farms. If a collective farm could not pay these wages, it could borrow from the State Bank until it was in a better financial position to meet the monthly wage levels of the state farms. All monthly wages going to collective farm workers are not paid in monetary form, since they receive some wages in kind, such as grain and fodder to be fed to the livestock on their private farm plots.

The Private Sector in Soviet Agriculture

The Soviet agricultural sector is divided into two parts: (1) the socialized sector, which includes the state and collective farms; and (2) the private sector, which includes the small farm plots cultivated by collective and state farm workers and by workers in factories and other urban enterprises.[26] The private household plots still play a very important role in the Soviet economy. They occupy only 3.3 percent of the Soviet Union's total sown land area, but are responsible for a large part of the total output of many major food items such as vegetables (40 percent), potatoes (65 percent),

---

[26] The role of the private agricultural plot is examined in Karl-Eugen Wädekin, *The Private Sector in Soviet Agriculture*, Berkeley: University of California, 1973, and "Private Production in Soviet Agriculture," *Problems of Communism*, Jan.–Feb. 1968, pp. 22–30.

meat and milk (35 percent), and eggs (50 percent). In 1956, 30 percent of the Soviet Union's total agricultural output came from the household plots. Output per acre on these plots is much higher than on the collective and state farms. Surpluses of food and livestock products from the garden plots are sold at unregulated prices in the urban markets and are a major source of income for the peasants. In some years, farm workers have received more income from their plots than from their collective farms.

Before 1958, peasant's plots were subject to compulsory deliveries to the state of farm produce at fixed low prices and also to high agricultural taxes ranging from 12 to 48 percent of the incomes from the plots. Since 1958, compulsory deliveries by cultivators of garden plots have been abandoned and the agricultural income tax considerably reduced. Sales of garden plot surpluses by peasants are a highly inefficient method of marketing food products. Peasants travel long distances to market their produce; the marketing is small scale; and the lack of a means of coordinating peasants' free market sales results in a very uneven national distribution of the output of the garden plots.

The attitude of the Soviet government is basically unfavorable to the "acre and a cow" or household plot farming in the private sector of Soviet agriculture. The small garden plots, which are a survival of private enterprise in the Soviet Union, are not ideologically acceptable to the Communist party leaders. These plots have been permitted to flourish only because they have filled certain gaps in the planned agriculture sector. Under Khrushchev's agricultural program, steps were taken to hasten the decline of the garden plot as a significant factor in Soviet agricultural life. State farm workers and urban industrial workers with garden plots were forced to sell their livestock to the state or to collective farms, and pressure was placed on collective farm workers to do the same with their livestock. Legislation was enacted to bring about a reduction in the size of collective farm private plots. Now that farmers' incomes have been enlarged as the result of increases in the prices paid to the collective farms by the government and collective farm members are paid wages similar to those of state farm workers, the Soviet government believes that there is much less reason for the preservation of the small private garden farmstead or plot system. Certainly, as the Soviet leaders view the situation, there is no place for small private plots in a situation in which the collective farms are becoming much more like state farms and collective farm members are called upon to devote all their efforts to improving the efficiency of their farms.

In the period of "communist construction," the Soviet leaders find the small private farm plot increasingly unpalatable. They look forward to the time when production on the collective farms "will achieve a level at which it will fully satisfy members' requirements. On this basis, supplementary individual farming [on private plots] will gradually become economically unnecessary. When collective production . . . is able to replace in full production on the supplementary individual plots," collective farm workers will give these plots up "of their own accord."[27] The realization of the Communist party's goal along this line depends not on ideological preferences, but on whether or not the party is able to pull Soviet agriculture out of the rut of inefficiency in which it has lain so long.

Soviet Agricultural Policy, 1953–1964

One of the major developments in the field of Soviet agricultural policy after 1953 was the reform of the cost-price structure as it related

---

[27] Programme of the Communist Party of the Soviet Union, *The Road to Communism*, 1961, p. 530.

to the prices paid by the state for deliveries of output from the collective farms.[28] Before 1958, the collective farms had not been operating on a basis of economic accounting or "business accountability." The collective farms concentrated on meeting the compulsory delivery quotas established for them by the central planning authorities and paid little attention to the costs of producing various crops. Farm labor, which was not paid wages, but received instead a share of the collective farm's annual net income, was regarded as a costless farm input and was widely wasted by the use of excessive numbers of workers on farm tasks. Also, there were no adequate means of determining the machinery costs of producing a crop, since the Machine Tractor Stations provided the heavy machinery and their charges for the use of this machinery were not based on strict economic accounting. Before 1958, collective farm chairmen were unable to calculate accurately the actual average costs of production per unit of their various crops. Cost records were incomplete, costing procedures were inadequate, and no satisfactory method existed for determining unit labor costs of output on the collective farms.

After 1958, steps were taken by the Soviet government to put collective farms, like state farms, on a strict accounting basis. In his report on agricultural developments in the years 1954–1958, Khrushchev declared that:

The [collective] farms cannot be operated any longer without profound and comprehensive study of production costs—without control by the ruble. Our [collective farm] managerial personnel . . . must have a perfect knowledge of the economics of agricultural production and must operate their farms economically and make better use of farm reserves and potentialities in an effort to reduce production costs.[29]

Measures were taken to apply the economic accounting (*khozraschet*) system or "control by the ruble" to collective farm operations. Farm labor was no longer regarded as costless, since it was assumed to cost as much as equivalent state farm labor, whose cost was measured in terms of monthly wages. After the elimination of Machine Tractor Stations, machine costs were more scientifically determined. Collective farms operated their own heavy agricultural machinery and charged annual depreciation as an appropriate cost of production. Efforts were also made to determine the total average unit costs of production for a variety of crops in order to maximize the collective farm's annual income by selecting the most profitable crops for cultivation—as the annual plans permitted.

Under Stalin, the very low prices paid by the state for compulsory collective farm deliveries were much below the actual costs of production. Under Khrushchev, state prices for collective farm products were raised until they were much closer to real costs of production. Zonal prices that were paid to all collective farms in the same zone were fixed by taking the average costs of production per crop unit and adding a markup for profit. Furthermore, an effort was made to adjust supply to demand. When crops were small, zonal prices were raised; when bumper crops were harvested, these prices were reduced.

Soviet agricultural policy has emphasized the importance of improving the efficiency of both state and collective farm operations. Khrushchev, in his speech early in 1958 to the Conference of Foremost Belorussian Agricultural Personnel, pointed out that the solution

---

[28] Jerzy Karcz and V. P. Timoshenko, "Soviet Agricultural Policy, 1953–1962," *Food Research Institute Studies*, Vol. 4, No. 2, May 1964; Roy D. Laird and Edward L. Crowley (eds.), *Soviet Agriculture: The Permanent Crisis*, New York: Praeger, 1965; and Nancy Nimitz, *Agriculture under Khrushchev: The Lean Years*, Santa Monica: Rand Corporation, March 1965.

[29] N. S. Khrushchev, Report on the "Results of the Development of Agriculture in the Past Five Years and Tasks of Further Increasing the Output of Farm Products," *The Current Digest of the Soviet Press*, Jan. 28, 1959, Vol. X, No. 51, p. 18.

of the agricultural problem would be found in an "unprecedented growth in labor productivity." The many deficiencies of Soviet agriculture at the end of the Stalin era (1953) were attributed by Khrushchev and other party leaders to a number of factors.[30] The best workers had been absorbed by industry with insufficient regard for the effect of their transfer on agriculture; the poor labor discipline on the farms allowed workers to put too much time on private garden plots; the state had not adequately encouraged agricultural research; the Machine Tractor Stations were not operated on a sound economic basis; material incentives for state and collective farm workers were much too small; and the guidance of collective farm work provided by the farm chairpersons and the foremen was very unsatisfactory. Out of 94,000 collective farm chairpersons in 1953, only 2,400 had had a higher agricultural education, and only 14,200 had had a secondary school education.

During the 1950s and 1960s a strenuous effort was made to improve the educational and financial position of collective farm chairpersons. The number of these chairpersons with higher and specialized education rose from 29.3 percent in 1955 to 69.6 percent in 1966.[31] As the educational status of collective farm chairpersons has improved, their wage differentials have widened. Whereas in the early 1950s the average collective farm chairperson earned little more than the average peasant, by 1970 he or she earned two to three times more, and in many cases four to five times as much.

The End of the Machine Tractor Stations

With the aim of improving farm efficiency, the Soviet government put an end to the Machine Tractor Station system in 1958.[32] The Machine Tractor Stations, first established in 1928, had served a very useful purpose in the 1930s when the collective farms were widely established and stood in need of good management. After the Second World War, these stations began to interfere with the smooth functioning of the now better managed collective farms. Khrushchev early in 1958 complained that "We have two masters on the same land—the collective farm and the MTS. And where there are two masters there can be no good management."[33] As the collective farms increased in size, each Machine Tractor Station, which had originally serviced a large number of small collective farms, in the 1950s serviced only a few large farms. The time had come when these stations could very easily be absorbed by the large collective farms. After March 1958, the Machine Tractor Stations were replaced by Repair Technical Stations, whose activities consist mainly of selling spare parts and repairing agricultural equipment. The heavy machinery of the Machine Tractor Stations was purchased by the collective farms, which had become large enough to make an efficient use of their own heavy machinery.

The failure to enlarge output through improvements in farm labor productivity caused the Soviet government to turn to "crash pro-

---

[30] N. S. Khrushchev, *Measures for the Further Development of Agriculture in the U.S.S.R., Report Delivered at a Plenary Meeting of the C.C., C.P.S.U., September 3, 1953*, Moscow, Foreign Languages Publishing House, 1954, pp. 9–13.

[31] Jerry F. Hough, "The Changing Nature of the Kolkhoz Chairmen," in James R. Millar, *op. cit.*, p. 104. See also Norton T. Dodge, "Recruitment and the Quality of the Soviet Agricultural Labor Force," in James R. Millar, *op. cit.*, pp. 180–213.

[32] Robert F. Miller analyzes the role of the Machine Tractor Stations in Soviet agriculture in *One Hundred Thousand Tractors, the MTS and the Development of Controls in Soviet Agriculture*, Cambridge, Mass.: Harvard University Press, 1970.

[33] N. S. Khrushchev, "Speech to the Conference of Foremost Belorussian Agricultural Personnel," Jan. 22, 1958, *The Current Digest of the Soviet Press*, Vol. X, No. 4, March 5, 1958, p. 13.

grams" for increasing farm production.[34] The "new lands program" of 1954 and 1955 increased grain production by bringing under cultivation 26 million hectares (64 million acres) of marginal land in Siberia and Kazakhstan. The 1955 "corn program" increased animal feedstuffs by substituting corn for oats and other low-yield crops. The "plough-up program" was Khrushchev's last proposal for increasing agricultural production. In 1961, he saw a "hidden reserve" in arable land in the 64 million hectares (30 percent of the cultivated land area in 1961) that were sown to grass or were lying fallow. Khrushchev proposed a change in the Soviet cropping system that would take uncultivated acres or acres temporarily assigned to grass in the crop rotation system and devote these acres to such crops as corn, sugar beets, peas, and field beans.

In 1962, 16 million hectares were shifted to cultivated crops under this "plough-up" program, which necessitated using much more mineral fertilizer and agricultural machinery than would have been the case if this land had been left fallow or in perennial grasses. Khrushchev's new lands, corn, and plough-up programs did not meet the basic problem of Soviet agriculture, namely raising the productivity of farm workers and increasing the yields per hectare. The great drawbacks to Khrushchev's crash programs were the low average annual yields resulting from frequent droughts in the marginal farm areas of the eastern and southeastern parts of the Soviet Union; the unsuitability, due to a short growing season, of much Soviet farm land for corn production; and the possible loss of soil fertility from the plough-up program and the abandonment of the grass land and clean fallow rotation system.

The Soviet Union made considerable progress in expanding total agricultural production after 1953, even though the overly ambitious agricultural goals announced by Khrushchev were not achieved. According to the estimates of Western Soviet analysts, in the period 1953–1961, total industrial production increased 104 percent and total agricultural production 56 percent. From 1953 to 1961, total agricultural production increased at an average annual rate of 5.7 percent, while population grew at an average annual rate of only 1.7 percent. The output of key food products, such as meat, milk, sugar beets, and grains, increased from 2.47 to 6 times as rapidly as total population. These increases in agricultural output gave rise to a gradual improvement of the national diet. It should be noted, however, that in the years 1950–1953 the per capita outputs of vegetables, meat, and milk were still somewhat below what they had been in the years 1926–1929.

Soviet Agricultural Policy since 1964

The last five years of the Khrushchev regime were years of poor agricultural performance in the Soviet Union.[35] Although Khrushchev continued to maintain a high level of inputs in the agricultural sector, as Table 15-3 shows, the productivity of labor and capital in agriculture failed to improve, and the average annual rate of growth of total agricultural output in the years 1961–1965 was little more than one-half what it had been in the years 1956–1960. While Khrushchev's farm programs had improved farm productivity and output in the second half of the 1950s, these programs were much less successful in the early 1960s.

[34] Lazar Volin, "Agricultural Policy of the Soviet Union," *Comparisons of the United States and Soviet Economies,* Part I, 1959, pp. 311–314.

[35] An analysis of Soviet farm output in the years 1950–1971 is presented in F. Douglas Whitehouse and Joseph F. Havelka, "Comparison of Farm Output in the US and USSR, 1950–1971," *Soviet Economic Prospects for the Seventies,* 1973, pp. 340–374.

Table 15-3
U.S.S.R. Average Annual Rates of Growth (Percent) of Total Agricultural Output, Total Inputs, and Factor Productivity

	1951-1955	1956-1960	1961-1965	1966-1970	1971-1972	1971-1975 (plan)
Total output	4.8	4.9	2.8	3.4	−1.9[1]	4.5[1]
Total inputs	3.1	2.0	2.8	1.3	2.0	1.9
Factor productivity	1.7	2.9	−0.4	2.1	−3.8	2.5

[1] Output for the terminal year only over the three-year average for the base year.

Source: D. B. Diamond and C. B. Krueger, "Recent Developments in Output and Productivity in Soviet Agriculture," in *Soviet Economic Prospects for the Seventies*, 1973, p. 318.

When Brezhnev took Khrushchev's place in 1965, he accepted Khrushchev's goal of increasing consumer welfare through an improvement in consumers' diets, and he assigned a high priority to the improvement of the agricultural sector in the eighth Five-Year Plan (1966-1970).[36] The new agricultural policy emphasized the importance of improving farm labor productivity by increasing investment in plant and equipment, making more skilled labor available, and enlarging the supplies of chemical fertilizers, pesticides, and herbicides. Brezhnev's farm policy reversed Khrushchev's policy of officially discouraging private garden-plot auxiliary farming, which accounted for about one-third of total farm production. The agricultural statistics in Table 15-3 show that while the annual rate of growth of agricultural production and the annual rate of improvement in factor productivity in the years 1966-1970 did not reach the levels of the 1950s, the performance of the agricultural sector in the Brezhnev years (1966-1970) was much better than in the Khrushchev years (1961-1965).

Brezhnev's agricultural policy as presented in the Ninth Five-Year Plan (1971-1975) was an ambitious scheme to stimulate farm production so that it would return to the high levels of the 1950s when it was increasing at an annual rate of close to 5 percent.[37] The achievement of the 1971-1975 agricultural goals was dependent mainly upon large increases in the availability of farm machinery and chemical fertilizers. The projected increase in the supply of farm machinery for the years 1971-1975 over the years 1966-1970 was 54 percent; this was to be accompanied by a two-thirds increase in the supply of chemical fertilizers. Two-thirds of the gain in total gross farm output in 1971-1975 was expected to result from the increased use of chemical fertilizers. The very ambitious farm program for 1971-1975 projected an annual increase in total farm output of 4.5 percent and an annual increase in factor productivity of 2.5 percent. Poor harvests in 1972 and in 1975 resulted in declines in both farm output and factor productivity. Many Western Soviet experts believe that it will take much more than increased inputs of machinery and fertilizers to prevent the Soviet Union's agricultural sector from being a heavy drag on Soviet economic progress. What the Soviet agricultural sector

[36] Roger A. Clarke, "Soviet Agricultural Reform since Khrushchev," *Soviet Studies*, Vol. 20, Oct. 1968, pp. 159-178; and Jerzy K. Karcz, "From Stalin to Brezhnev: Soviet Agricultural Policy in Historical Perspective," in James R. Millar, *op. cit.*, pp. 36-70.

[37] For recent Soviet agricultural developments, see Douglas B. Diamond and Constance B. Krueger, "Recent Developments in Output and Productivity in Soviet Agriculture," *Soviet Economic Prospects for the Seventies*, 1973, pp. 316-339.

Table 15-4
Soviet Urban-Rural Wage Differentials, 1952 and 1967

	Average annual wages in current rubles	
	1952	1967
Industry	917–100%[1]	1,344–100%[1]
State farms	494– 54%	1,007– 75%
Collective farms	164– 18%	647– 48%

[1] Percent of annual industrial wages.

Source: Paul R. Gregory and Robert C. Stuart, *Soviet Economic Structure and Performance*, 1974, p. 252 fn.

needs is a thoroughgoing systematic reorganization that will place more emphasis on independence for local economic decision making by collective farm managers and better incentives for farm workers.

One of the major developments in the post-Stalin era has been the very large improvement in the level of rural family incomes. The net effect of Soviet farm policy from 1953 to the late 1960s was to increase farm workers' incomes very significantly and to reduce the differential between rural and urban incomes. From 1953 to 1968, the total income of the agricultural population from farm wages and private plot returns more than doubled, while the number of farm workers declined more than 10 percent.[38] Table 15-4 shows that annual average collective farm wages, which were less than 20 percent of annual average industrial wages in 1952, had risen to almost half the latter wages fifteen years later. The very sizable reduction in the rural-urban wage differentials has been in line with the Soviet government's announced intention of reducing and eventually eliminating the financial, social, and cultural gap between town and country.

Agriculture in the Soviet Union and the United States

A comparison of agricultural performance in the Soviet Union and the United States shows that the former lags far behind the latter (see Table 15-5). The output per farm worker in the United States in 1970 was $7,746, whereas the output per Soviet farm worker was only $834 or 11 percent of the American output. These comparative statistics show that American farms were much better supplied with trucks and tractors; that they used much more chemical fertilizer per acre; that the yields of major crops per acre in the Soviet Union were on the average only 58 percent of the American yields; and that the Soviet livestock yields from cattle, milk cows, and hens were also much lower than the American livestock yields. With much more cultivated land and a much larger work force, Soviet agriculture is able to produce an output equal to only about 80 percent of the American total agricultural output.

The very low comparative productivity of resources in Soviet agriculture can be attributed to a number of factors. Poor natural conditions constitute a major cause. The Soviet Union compares unfavorably with the United States in terms of soil fertility, length of growing season, rainfall, and temperatures.[39] Low labor productivity on Soviet farms can be explained partly as the result of the failure of the planners to provide ample supplies of plant and equipment, fertilizers, and other

---

[38] The large improvement in rural incomes in the post-1953 period is discussed in David W. Bronson and Constance B. Krueger, "The Revolution in Soviet Farm Household Income, 1953–1967," in James R. Millar, *op. cit.*, pp. 214–258.

[39] Only one percent of the U.S.S.R. sown area is subject to an annual precipitation of over twenty-eight inches, as compared with 60 percent of the U.S. sown area. Keith Bush, "Conclusion of a note on Soviet Agriculture in the 1970s," *Prospects for Soviet Economic Growth in the 1970s*, 1971, p. 90.

Table 15-5
Economic Indicators in the U.S. and U.S.S.R. Agricultural Sectors, 1970

Indicators	U.S.	U.S.S.R.	U.S.S.R. as % of U.S.
Share of labor force employed in agriculture (percent)	4	31	775
Output per farm worker (dollars)	$7,746	$-834	11
Number of persons supported by one farm worker	46	7	15
Sown acreage per tractor (acres)	64	258	403
Trucks per 1,000 farm workers	665	34	5
Fertilizer nutrients applied to crops (pounds per acre)	93	45	48
Livestock yields			
Average live weight at slaughter: cattle (pounds)	953	681	71
Eggs per hen-year	218	166	76
Milk per cow per year (pounds)	9,388	4,652	50
Crop yields (bushels per acre)			
Spring wheat[1]	28	14	50
Winter wheat[1]	33	26	79
Corn[1]	69	35	51
Oats[1]	52	34	65
Potatoes	382	173	45
Sugar beets (metric tons per acre)	16	9	56

[1] Three-year average (1969/70/71).

Source: F. D. Whitehouse and J. F. Havelka, "Comparison of Farm Output in the US and USSR, 1950-1971," in *Soviet Economic Prospects for the Seventies*, 1973, p. 354.

chemical products, skilled workers, and funds for the advancement of agricultural science. Even if the Soviet Union enjoyed the natural agricultural advantages of the United States, considerable doubt exists that it would be able to achieve the high input-output rates of the United States under the current Soviet agricultural system.

Many Western experts feel that the Soviet Union could do much to improve its agricultural performance and could come much closer to performance standards characteristic of the world's advanced economies without abandoning its Marxist-Leninist ideological framework.[40] The Soviet agricultural sector needs a liberalization that will provide greater autonomy at the local farm management level as well as limited mobility of factors of production among farms. More autonomy could be achieved by permitting interfarm sales of feed and other crops. Collective farms could

[40] See, for example, the suggestions of Arcadius Kahan for the improvement of Soviet agriculture in "The Present State of Soviet Agriculture," Hearings, Joint Economic Committee, *Soviet Economic Outlook*, pp. 77-80.

carry crop specialization further; surplus labor and capital could be moved to farms where they would be more productive; and efforts could be made to establish farms of the most efficient size. The highly centralized agricultural policy in the Soviet Union prohibits interfarm sales of farm products and interfarm mobility of factors of production, thus reducing the incentives of both farm managers and workers to improve their efficiency. In other words, Soviet agriculture requires some fundamental organizational changes that the Communist party has not been willing to make.

In addition to improving Soviet agricultural productivity, enlarging investment in agriculture, improving workers' skills, and encouraging advance in agricultural science, the need exists for a further reform of farm prices. Supplies of meat and meat products remain insufficient to meet consumer needs, because at current prices it is more profitable to sell surplus grain to the state than to feed it to animals; it is also more profitable to produce grain for human consumption than fodder for animals. Consequently, with the current farm price system the planned targets for meat production are not usually met.

The 1980 agricultural goals of 176 pounds of meat and 2,200 to 2,640 pounds of grain per head appear to be too ambitious. The growth of agricultural output will probably continue to be slow. There will be no sizable transfer of trained labor from industry to agriculture. Some of the labor surplus in the lower Volga region, West Ukraine, Georgia, and the Central Asian republics may be transferred to the Eastern Ural region and Western Siberia. The Ninth Plan did not provide the large investment required for agricultural resettlement, an improved road network, and village reconstruction. Investment will continue to be used inefficiently because of the lack of trained workers or "mechanizers." It was estimated in 1970 that there was an overall 20 to 30 percent deficit of livestock and other production mechanizers and a need for three to four times as many agricultural specialists as were available at that time.[41] Among the kolkhoz production brigade leaders in 1970, only 1.2 percent had a university level training and 14.3 percent a secondary level professional training. The result was a deteriorating man-machine ratio. An additional factor contributing to low labor productivity in Soviet agriculture is the aging of the farm population. In 1959, 22 percent of the kolkhoz labor was over fifty years of age. By 1970, this percentage had risen to 30. Increasingly, the Soviet farm population tends to become old and female and not a good source of the young skilled mechanizers required by advanced agriculture.

Not much additional help in meeting agricultural plan targets can come from the private agricultural sector in the future because of the competition of the socialized agricultural sector. As personal incomes rise on the collective farms, less incentive exists to cultivate the highly productive small farm plots in order to supplement personal incomes. Also, now that farm workers have old-age pensions, there is less pressure to cultivate garden plots. Attempts to enlarge farm output through irrigation and improvement of acid or wet soils do not meet with much success, because these improvements in land use are very costly and contribute heavily to the high costs of farm production.

The final conclusion about Soviet agriculture in the 1970s is that it remains a stumbling block to rapid economic progress. In the 1960s and 1970s, the general trends in Soviet agriculture indicated very slow progress in meeting the "major goal of Soviet agriculture of the current period as the task of supplying

[41] Karl-Eugen Wädekin, "Agriculture and Economic Growth: The Soviet Situation Today," *Prospects for Economic Growth in the 1970s*, 1971, p. 96.

the population with an adequate and varied diet, with special emphasis on the supply of livestock products."[42] The Brezhnev agricultural programs since 1964 have not effected the transformation of Soviet agriculture necessary to raise it to the efficiency levels of American agriculture. Stepping up the inputs of capital and labor is not sufficient if the basic agricultural system still requires considerable modification for its efficient operation. As we have seen, increased inputs of equipment and other forms of capital have not been followed by the expected improvement in labor and capital productivity. Soviet agriculture suffers from overcentralized planning; the inefficient use of its human, land, and capital resources; inadequate attention to scientific advance in agriculture; a hostile attitude towards private auxiliary farming; and a general unwillingness to expand the social overhead capital in agriculture. In these circumstances, the existing personal incentive system is inadequate, and local decision making lacks independence and initiative.

The systematic change needed for the efficient operation of Soviet agriculture is yet to come. Such a change could result in a return to more private agriculture, as in Yugoslavia and Poland, or it could move in the direction of "agri-industrial" settlements, which would bring an urban and communist way of life into the countryside by resettling the rural population from dispersed small villages in large rural centers. With agricultural labor concentrated in the new rural centers, agriculture could become highly "industrialized," and the fields and livestock areas could be consolidated into larger and more efficient production units. Urbanizing and industrializing rural life and making it more attractive to young people might tend to stop the outflow of young skilled labor. There is no guarantee that increasing the scale of operations in the socialized agricultural sector would be economically superior to enlarging the scope of private agriculture. In many lines of agricultural activity in the Eastern communist countries, private agriculture still appears to be more efficient than the large state and collective farms. If Soviet agriculture becomes more "industrialized" and larger scale, the problem would remain of providing the personal incentives that would lead to an efficient operation of the new industrialized agriculture.

The development of agro-industrial settlements would be very costly. It would also, if successful, move industry away from the established urban centers. Stalin's program of exploiting the rural areas for the benefit of the urban areas would be reversed, and a more balanced national development would be achieved. The Ninth Five-Year Plan, however, did not propose a large step forward in creating a modern infrastructure throughout the countryside. In the next decade, little progress can be anticipated in achieving major systematic changes in Soviet agriculture. Such changes probably await what one Western analyst has described as "a change in the style and content of Soviet leadership."[43]

Although both Khrushchev's and Brezhnev's farm programs have not paid off very well in terms of improved efficiency, the past two decades have witnessed some basic changes in Soviet agriculture that constitute steps towards the ultimate goal of establishing a single form of state property and eliminating the differences between rural and urban areas. These steps have already led to a large increase in the number and importance of state farms and a decrease in the number of collective farms, a very large increase in state-paid prices for farm products, and a movement to bring the collective farmers' earnings to the level of that of state farmers. These trends can be expected to continue, so

---

[42] Arcadius Kahan, *op. cit.*, p. 77.

[43] Keith Bush, *op. cit.*, p. 90.

that before the end of this century there may be little difference between state and collective farms, and both may be merged in a single form of state agricultural unit. The trends are unmistakable. The only uncertain matter is how swiftly these trends may move towards a major reconstruction of Soviet agriculture.

Labor in the Soviet Economy

The Soviet total civilian labor force was estimated for 1973 at 119.1 million, of which 87.4 million were in industry and the services and 31.7 million in agriculture. During the years 1973-1980, the industrial labor supply is projected to increase at the low annual rate of 1.3 percent, while employment in the services will increase at the high annual rate of 3.5 percent. In the agricultural sector, employment is projected to decline at the low annual rate of −0.7 percent. Within agriculture, employment on state farms will increase, whereas employment on collective farms will decrease.

The major changes in the use of Soviet labor over the past twenty-three years are shown in Table 15-6. Between 1950 and 1973, the share of industry and the services in total civilian employment rose from 47 to 70 percent, while the share of agricultural employment fell from 53 to 30 percent. It is estimated that by 1980 agriculture will account for only 25 percent of total civilian employment; this is a much larger percentage than is found in the Western industrialized nations. Table 15-6 reveals that the major changes in the Soviet employment pattern have occurred in agriculture, not in the nonagricultural sectors. Between 1950 and 1973, state farm employment increased from 8 to 26 percent of total agricultural employment, whereas collective farm employment fell from 64 to 44 percent. During the

Table 15-6

U.S.S.R.: Estimates and Projections of Employment 1950 to 1980 (in percent)

	1950	1960	1973	1980
Total civilian employment	100	100	100	100
Nonagricultural employment	47	58	70	75
Agricultural employment	53	42	30	25
Nonagricultural employment	100	100	100	100
Industry	41	41	38	35
Services[1]	35	33	38	40
Other[2]	24	26	24	25
Agricultural employment	100	100	100	100
State farm	8	17	26	31
Collective farm	64	56	44	39
Private farm plots	28	27	30	30

[1] Includes trade, finance, health services, education, government administration, etc.
[2] Includes construction, forestry, transportation, communications, etc.
Source: Murray Feshbach and Stephen Rapawy, "Labor Constraints in the Five-Year Plan," *Soviet Economic Prospects for the Seventies*, 1973, pp. 520-521.

The Soviet economy (continued)

years 1973-1980, these trends in agricultural employment are projected to continue as collective farms are converted into state farms and farm labor shifts from the remaining collective farms to the state farms.

The pattern of employment in the nonagricultural sectors is much more stable than in agriculture. Employment in industry is expected to decline as a relative share of total nonagricultural employment, and the relative share of employment in the services will increase; but these changes are not large enough to indicate a major transformation of the employment pattern in these areas and in other activities, such as transportation, communications, and construction. The new additions to the nation's labor supply are more likely to be deployed to public services (as they are classified in the West) than to manufacturing. The Soviet Union will still be short, by Western standards, in the provision of personal services. Even by 1980, the Soviet Union will be far removed from the Western concept of a service economy, in which the consumer is free to purchase a wide variety of personal, recreational, amusement, and other services.

As in other types of economies, in the Soviet Union workers are organized in trade unions, whose functions are in many ways quite different from the functions of unions in the Western democracies.[44] The twenty-four Soviet trade unions, organized along industrial lines, usually represent most of the workers in each industry, since important economic benefits are derived from membership. The benefits include preferential treatment in the allotment of new apartments and in securing accommodation in rest homes and sanatoria. Soviet trade unions provide a "transmission belt" between the party and the workers that enables the party to dominate the workers. According to Lenin's interpretation, the trade unions are a "school of communism" as well as a "school of management" and a "school of labour discipline."[45] Besides indoctrinating the workers with the communist ideology, the trade unions guide the workers in meeting their output targets and maintain discipline in the production line.

The Soviet trade unions lack two of the important functions of Western trade unions: bargaining over wage rates and resorting to strikes. Although there is no legislation specifically prohibiting strikes, Soviet unions do not engage in them. As the recognized representative of the white- and blue-collar workers, the trade union committee in the factory enters into a collective labor agreement with the enterprise management. The union sees to it that this agreement conforms to the legislation and government directives relating to wage rates and working conditions. The Soviet unions are, in fact, an extension of the state bureaucracy and do little to differentiate themselves from the government administration. In essence, these unions are no more than company unions, with the state being the company.

The Soviet trade unions participate in factory management much more than Western trade unions. The tradition of union participation in factory management has its origin in the revolutionary and early postrevolutionary period, 1917-1921, when workers' soviets or councils operated the factories. Although the enterprise director now has the final responsibility for managerial decisions, he or she is kept aware of the workers' opinions and suggestions concerning the management of the factory. During the Stalin era, the fixing and revising of production norms for workers

---

[44] For an analysis of labor's role in the Soviet Union, see Paul R. Gregory and Robert C. Stuart, "Labor Allocation in the Soviet Union," *op. cit.*, pp. 193-214; Emily Clark Brown, *Soviet Trade Unions and Labor Relations*, Cambridge, Mass.: Harvard University Press, 1966; and Nicolas Spulber, Ch. 7, "Labor," *The Soviet Economy*, 1969, pp. 115-132.

[45] Isaac Deutscher, *Soviet Trade Unions, Their Place in Soviet Labour Policy*, London: Royal Institute of International Affairs, 1950, pp. 48-51.

became the sole concern of management. In 1956, the Soviet government issued new regulations that required managers to change output norms only in cooperation with the factory trade-union committee. The trade unions are now in a position to defend the workers' interests with respect to output norms. In any conflict, however, between the workers' desire for low norms and the state's desire for high norms, the Soviet unions apparently have no choice but to accept the view of the government authorities.

The remaining major area of trade union activity in the Soviet Union is the sphere of social and cultural affairs. The Soviet trade unions administer much of the social security system, allocate housing, and make provision for cultural, educational, and recreational activities. No counterpart to the omnipresence of the Soviet trade union exists in the Western democracies. The worker feels the union's pervading influence in his or her position as an employee in the industrial enterprise, an occupant of a union-built apartment, a customer in a community store, a patient in a rest home or sanatorium, or as a member of an amateur dramatics or sport society. From the time he or she joins the trade union as a youth until he or she retires to an old-age home, the worker is under the pervasive influence of the factory trade union committee. The Soviet trade union directs, disciplines, educates, stimulates, protects, and entertains the worker. It marshals the nation's labor force in the "great undertaking" of rapidly industrializing the Soviet Union.

The successful operation of state industrial enterprises and of the Soviet economy in general depends upon the cooperation and productivity of the Soviet industrial labor force of about 90 million industrial workers. The Soviet Union has been faced with some unique labor problems during the past third of a century, during which the world's second largest industrial system has been established. First came the problem of converting a mainly agricultural economy with its mass of unskilled workers into a highly industrialized economy with its millions of skilled workers. This was largely a technical problem of establishing factories, introducing the most modern methods of production, shifting workers from the rural to the urban areas, and providing the workers with the necessary skills. The second and more difficult problem was securing the cooperation and support of many millions of industrial workers in a highly planned economy in which worker freedom of the Western type was largely absent.

The Labor Plan

Soviet labor policy deals with the management of the nation's labor supply so as to make the most efficient use of labor in securing the goals of the annual and longer-term national economic plans. The purpose of Soviet labor policy is to devise methods of implementing the national labor plan, which is a part of the larger national economic plan. The labor plan is the framework within which Soviet labor policy is developed. This policy is concerned with three major subjects: (1) the size, distribution, and availability of the work force; (2) the productivity of the labor force; and (3) the work attitudes and incentives of the workers. The major features of Soviet labor policy are constructed by the U.S.S.R. Council of Ministers working in cooperation with such agencies as the State Planning Committee and the State Committee for Labor and Wages. The annual labor plan, by means of its various balances, shows the manpower available, its distribution by branches of the national economy at the beginning and end of the plan period, the number of workers available for interregional transfers, the number of young workers ready for training and work direction, the availability of technical specialists, and the utilization of the labor force with regard to labor time inputs and losses, and reserves of worktime.[46]

The implementation of the annual national labor plan presents a number of difficulties to the government since Soviet workers are no longer legally tied to their jobs and have been free, since 1956, to leave their current jobs and to seek work elsewhere. The compulsory recruiting of youths for enrollment in training schools has also been abolished. Ever since the First Five-Year Plan was carried out in the early 1930s, the Soviet government has had in operation an extensive recruitment program (*orgnabor*). In more recent years, resettlement administrations have been added to the earlier recruitment administrations. Soviet recruitment has been closely associated with the Soviet school system.

The national recruitment quotas established in the annual state economic plan are broken down into quotas for individual districts (*rayoni*, which are equivalent to a county in the United States). The recruiting organizations, acting as agents for particular industries, construction projects, or transportation agencies, conclude contracts with individual workers for periods of one to three years. Special inducements in the form of wage bonuses, free transportation, or housing accommodation are given to workers who are willing to move from the densely populated European section of the Soviet Union to sections east of the Ural Mountains. Short-term unpaid volunteers (*subbotnicks*) are also mobilized to spend "free time" after work and on weekends on harvesting, road and house building and repairing, and on civic improvement work.[47]

[46] M. S. Weitzman, M. Feshbach, and L. Kulchyka, "Employment in the U.S.S.R.: Comparative U.S.S.R.-U.S. Data," *Dimensions of Soviet Economic Power*, pp. 633–635.

[47] N. Antropov, *The Role of Trade Unions in the State Economic and Cultural Life of the U.S.S.R. (1917–1959)*, Moscow, Trade Union Publishing House, 1960, p. 9.

State labor-force management is accompanied by labor-supply management at the industrial enterprise level. Although the state planning authorities, school system, labor commissions, and recruiting and resettling organizations do much to direct the flow of labor into high-priority economic sectors, most of the new hiring is done by the individual state enterprises. Direct hirings, which are made from among the local labor supply, result in considerable labor turnover, since enterprises must frequently attempt to attract personnel from other local enterprises. Competitive bidding for workers tends to distort the planned wage structure and to inflate the total wage bill. Enterprises endeavor to attract workers by offering them "easy" work norms and by overgrading them. On-the-job training is widely used by state industrial enterprises to secure the needed supplies of skilled workers. Special purpose and professional-technical courses are made available to workers who wish to increase their skills.

Labor management has become an increasingly important concern of Soviet labor policy as the program for the rationalization of industry advances. Mechanization and automation result in large transfers of workers. This is particularly the case when the high labor-consuming auxiliary activities of industrial enterprises, such as freight handling, are mechanized. Schooling and training programs, under the direction of the Ministry of Higher and Secondary Specialized Education and the State Committee for Vocational-Technical Education, are being adjusted to the need for a highly flexible labor-management policy.

If the Soviet economy were completely planned and static in nature, labor management would consist simply of placing each worker in the appropriate job at the state-fixed wage rate. The national economic plan would provide a job for each worker to which he or she could be compulsorily assigned or directed. In fact, however, the Soviet economy is not as rigorously planned as this, nor is labor for the most part arbitrarily assigned to jobs. The dynamic, expanding nature of the Soviet economy limits the extent to which it can be planned in detail; and the need to enlist the support of the work personnel in the program for rapid industrialization makes the compulsory directing of workers no longer feasible. Therefore, the state management of the nation's labor force by administrative direction has had to be supplemented by a certain amount of reliance on the operation of partially free market forces. The planning authorities in the Soviet Union have been forced by circumstances to permit the emergence of a labor market in which workers have some freedom of movement and in which wage rates have responded to some extent to supply-and-demand forces. Consequently, Soviet economists have had to concern themselves with wage theory and have had to develop wage policies that would aid the carrying out of the program for a planned, rapid industrialization of the Soviet economy. The somewhat free Soviet labor market has had its ups and downs, having passed through a number of periods alternating between widespread acceptance (during the New Economic Policy, 1921–1927) and considerable hostility (during the Stalin era, 1928–1953). In the period of the "thaw" since 1953, the Soviet labor market has once more become a significant institution in Soviet economic affairs.

Microeconomic Aspects of Soviet Wage Policy

Soviet wage theory and policy have both microeconomic and macroeconomic aspects.[48] The former deals with the determination of

[48] With regard to Soviet wages and wage theory, see Leonard J. Kirsch, *Soviet Wages: Changes in Administration and Structure since 1956*, Cambridge,

individual wage rates, while the latter is concerned with the national or total wage bill. Soviet wage theory, like wage theory in the Western nations, directs attention to productivity as a prime factor in the determination of individual wage rates. In Soviet wage theory, variations in the productivity of workers account for differentials in wage rates. Very early after the 1917 revolution, the Communist party under Lenin laid down the rule that wages should be tied to productivity in a differential way. Some elements in the party proposed that wage rates should be equal, since wage inequality was "bourgeois" in origin and contrary to the egalitarian spirit of communism. Lenin vigorously attacked these "levellers" on the ground that wage differentials would stimulate production.

Stalin was strong in his opposition to wage leveling and other egalitarian trends. His wage reforms were designed to widen the differentials between the least productive and the most productive workers. However, although he argued in favor of basing wage rates on the individual worker's productivity, Stalin did not follow the Western principle of keeping wage rates in step with improvements in productivity. Soviet economists have uniformly proposed that wage rates should rise less rapidly than improvements in productivity or increases in output per man-hour. They argue that such a development will leave more of the expanding national output available to the state for investment in factories, mines, railroads, and other capital facilities.

Wage rates are centrally determined in the Soviet Union for each economic sector of the economy. Preliminary discussions about wage rates are carried on by the state planning

Mass.: MIT Press, 1972; Alec Nove, "Wages and Prices," *The Soviet Economy*, 1968, pp. 131–144; and Abram Bergson, Ch. 6, "Industrial Labor and Recruitment and Utilization," *The Economics of Planning*, 1964, pp. 93–157.

authorities, the State Committee for Labor and Wages, the central trade union organization (the All-Union Central Council of Trade Unions), and the central committees of the trade unions. Draft wage proposals are submitted to the trade union organizations and factory or local trade union committees for their consideration. Final wage proposals are submitted by the State Committee for Labor and Wages and the All-Union Central Council of Trade Unions to the U.S.S.R. Council of Ministers for its final approval. The trade unions have only a consultative role in this determination of wage rates.

Soviet wage rates are differentiated within and among industries and among geographical regions. Wage differentials, which are largely determined by market forces in Western economies, are centrally determined in the Soviet Union, but with the same general objectives: to encourage the creation of a supply of skilled workers, to attract workers to high-priority or high demand industries, and to direct the flow of labor into those geographical areas where labor is in short supply. In the 1930s and 1940s, the wage rates of skilled workers were from four to eight times those of unskilled workers. In recent years, as the level of education of the labor force has been raised and many unskilled jobs have been eliminated, the wage rates of top-level skilled workers have been two and one-half times those of unskilled workers.

High-wage industries include the coal, iron and steel, oil, chemical, and machine-building industries, whereas the low-paid workers are found in the woodworking, building materials, consumer goods, and food industries. The light industries have been continually at the bottom of the wage scale since the era of comprehensive national planning began in 1928. Regional wage differentials have been used to speed the industrialization of the Ural, central Asian, and Siberian regions. Special wage inducements in these areas have been combined with free transportation, tax exemptions, special housing facilities, and land grants in order to secure the planned migration of labor to the new expanding industrial areas of the eastern part of the Soviet Union.

Top-grade scientists are among the highest paid individuals in the Soviet Union, receiving in some cases as much as thirty times the monthly wage of an unskilled worker. Other high-paid occupations include heads of government agencies, opera singers, professors, and plant managers. Plant managers may receive as much as twenty times the monthly wage of the unskilled worker. Physicians and teachers, who are chiefly women, have salaries that are relatively low compared to those of skilled workers, technicians, and engineers.[49] The top-grade monthly salary of a physician is less than half that of a skilled worker and one-third that of an engineer. Salary and wage differentials in the Soviet Union in some industries have exceeded the differentials in the same industries in the United States.

Before 1958, Soviet administrators and plant managers had a strong preference for wages based on piece rates rather than time rates. At that time, most production workers were on a piece-rate basis, with time rates being reserved for office and managerial personnel. The policy after 1928 had been to extend piecework to as many industries as possible. By 1953, 77 percent of the workforce was on a piece-rate basis. After the wage reforms of 1958–1960, there was a substantial decline in the percent of workers paid according to piece rates. Between 1957 and 1961, this percent fell from two-thirds to one-third of all industrial workers. The trend since 1960

[49] For a discussion of the role of women in the Soviet economy, see Norton T. Dodge, *Women in the Soviet Economy: Their Role in Economic, Scientific, and Technical Development*, Baltimore: Johns Hopkins Press, 1966.

has been towards centrally determined basic time wage rates on a national basis supplemented by various bonus or premium schemes. Also, more attention has been given to the expansion of "social" as against "money" wages. The latter are increasingly supplemented by social wages, which include free medical service, free schools and universities, subsidized low-rent housing, free child care, and cost-free cultural amenities.

Soviet wage differentials between the high- and low-paid industrial workers in the period 1930–1950 were probably greater than in the United States. However, since the early 1950s Soviet wage differentials have been substantially narrowed, until they are now probably smaller than American differentials. In recent years, an effort has been made to introduce more equity in Soviet wage determination, but wage differentials still remain large.

The overall distribution of family incomes, is obviously much more equal in the Soviet Union than in the United States. The reason for this lies in the fact that property income in the Soviet Union goes mainly to the state rather than to private individuals. According to one estimate, the share of per capita family income (excluding per capita collective farm income) received by the top 10 percent of spending units in the Soviet Union in 1966 was approximately 4.5 times that of the lowest 10 percent.[50] In the United States in 1967, the top 10 percent of the family spending units received incomes that were 28 percent larger than the incomes received by the lowest 10 percent of family incomes.

Not only the disparity between low-paid and high-paid personnel in the same industry but also between workers in different parts of the country and between the incomes of peasants and industrial workers is to be reduced. The trend towards reduced wage differentials in the Soviet Union is not unique to that country. Similar trends have been operating in the Western democratic nations. Worker solidarity is not promoted by the existence of large wage differentials. The problem in both the Western democracies and in the Soviet Union is to find some acceptable middle position between solidarity with its egalitarian bias and productivity with its emphasis on wage differentials as an incentive to higher production. Communist theorizing favors the solidarity principle, the equalizing of wages, and the maintenance of consumption differentials according to need rather than ability to produce. Some communist purists assert that wage differential incentives should be replaced by nonmonetary incentives, such as honors and special privileges. The realists in the Communist party, such as Stalin and Khrushchev, vigorously fought against this egalitarian approach in the formulation of wage policy. They were willing to concede that at some future time when full communism was achieved, wage differentials would have outlived their usefulness; the realists in the communist camp, however, have clung to wage-rate differentiation as the proper principle of wage determination for the Soviet Union at its present level of development.

Macroeconomic Aspects of Soviet Wage Policy

The macroeconomic aspects of Soviet wage policy relate to total wages as a share of national income and as a source of expenditures on consumption, which is a major component of the demand for the total national product. The total wage bill is a real wage bill, and an increase in the planned wage bill is supposed to be accompanied by an increase in the volume of consumer goods. An increase in the

---

[50] P. J. D. Wiles and Stefan Markowski, "Income Distribution under Communism and Capitalism," *Soviet Studies*, Vol. 22, Nos. 3 and 4, January, April, 1971, pp. 244–369 and 487–511. See also Paul R. Gregory and Robert C. Stuart, *op. cit.*, pp. 397–399.

total wage bill without a corresponding increase in the supply of consumer goods must result in either inflation or the rationing of consumer goods. Since both the total wage bill and the volume of consumer goods are determined by the central planning authorities, the trade unions have no room for bargaining over the total wage bill. If the trade unions were to influence the size of the total wage bill, they would have to exert pressure for a larger total wage bill while the national plan was being constructed. Precisely what influence the trade unions have in this connection is not known. It is quite clear, however, that once the national plan is completed and the size of the total wage bill has been set, the trade unions can do nothing about it. No bargaining about wages is possible at the regional or enterprise levels.

The size of the total wage bill or fund reflects Soviet policy with regard to the ratio of consumption to investment. This policy seeks to keep total private consumption at as low a level as possible in order to maintain the high level of investment required for rapid industrialization. The policy of keeping annual wage-rate increases below annual labor-productivity increases goes hand in hand with the policy of restricting private consumption by limiting the size of the total national wage fund. Whereas France and the United Kingdom permit around 60 percent of their gross national product to go into private consumption, the Soviet Union allocates only 56 percent to this purpose. Limiting the size of the total national wage fund that is paid out to 90 million nonagricultural wage earners restricts the growth of both per capita money and real wages in the Soviet Union.

Trends in Soviet Labor Policy

Soviet labor policy since the early 1950s has shifted its emphasis from coercion to persuasion, accompanied by incentives. This change in labor policy trends can be attributed to two major developments: the changing character of the Soviet working class and the more complicated industrial system, which puts a premium on technological progress.

Before 1950, the bulk of the labor supply, which had come from the rural areas, was largely unskilled and unused to the routine of factory operations. In addition, industrial production methods and equipment in the 1930s were primitive in comparison with Western European and American industrial methods and equipment. In this situation, the Soviet government turned to coercive measures in the effort to maximize industrial production. More use was made of the "stick" than the "carrot" in managing the nation's labor supply. By 1940, the internal passport and the "labor book" or "work book," with its detailed record of the worker's job history, were used to keep a close check on workers' movements. Workers were tied to their jobs under an arrangement which permitted a worker to leave his or her job only with the permission of the management. The factory manager kept the worker's internal passport and labor book until he or she had permission to change his job. Young people about to enter the work force were compulsorily recruited for training programs and later assigned to jobs in factories. Severe penalties were imposed by the people's courts for absenteeism and recurring lateness. By the beginning of the Second World War, Stalin had put the nation's labor force in a straitjacket. Insofar as incentives were used from 1928 to 1940 to manage the Soviet labor supply, the emphasis was placed upon the shock worker and Stakhanovism (a movement named after Alexei Stakhanov who was reported in 1931 to have greatly exceeded his coal production norms), with the result that a premium was placed on physical effort and individual pacing on the production line.

By the early 1950s, the Soviet labor supply was no longer mainly recruited from the rural areas. The majority of new workers were then workers' children from the urban areas who readily acquired labor skills and adapted themselves to the factory routine. With this kind of worker, persuasion and indoctrination are much more effective devices for improving labor productivity than are coercion and pressure. But more important than the changing nature of the nation's labor force as a factor in the moderation in Soviet labor policy has been the technological progress of the past four decades. This has converted the Soviet industrial system from a primitive to a highly advanced production process. Interest in shock work and Stakhanovism, with their stress upon physical effort and production record-breaking, has been replaced by a concern for new techniques of production and automation. The shock worker or Stakhanovite is now being replaced by the leading worker or the innovator *(novator)* as the ideal type of worker whose image is to be kept constantly in the public mind. A labor policy that seeks to enlist the support of the "new" Soviet worker must be more relaxed and more moderate than the harsh Stalinist labor policy of the period 1928–1950.

The relaxation of Soviet labor policy began in 1951 with a government decree that provided for more lenient penalties for unexcused absences from work. The biggest step taken towards a more moderate labor policy was made in April 1956 when the decree "On abolishing court liability of wage earners and salaried workers for leaving the employ of enterprises and institutions without permission and for absence from work without valid reason" was issued. This decree put an end to tying the worker to his or her job, the compulsory transfer of workers from plant to plant, and the criminal prosecution of employees absent from work without valid reason. Since 1956, workers have been free to leave their jobs after giving two weeks' notice of their intentions to the management. This worker freedom, however, is more apparent than real. The Soviet government is very much opposed to "floating" labor or high labor turnover. Even though workers are legally free to move from job to job, the government thoroughly discourages the use of this freedom. Every change of job is recorded in the worker's "labor book" so that frequent job-changing is easily detected and discouraged by management. Floaters are branded as "disorganizers of production," and pressure arises in the trade union, the enterprise, and the Communist party to prevent labor turnover.

The more moderate Soviet labor policy of recent years has undoubtedly proved to be of some value in raising labor productivity in the Soviet Union. However, it will take many more years' experience with the new labor policy to see how fully effective it can be in improving labor productivity. In recent years, the annual rate of growth of industrial production has been declining as the result of the reduction of the work week from forty-seven to forty-one hours; the increase of investment in military production and space exploration; and the effort to introduce more diversification in output. Also, the labor supply has been adversely affected by the low birth rate during the years 1940–1945 and by the declining birth rate in recent decades.

As a consequence of these developments, much attention has been paid in recent years to methods of improving labor productivity, such as decentralizing industry so as to encourage more personal initiative on the enterprise level; a greater emphasis on introducing technological innovations; more participation by the trade unions in the management of industry; a reform of the wage structure; and, lastly, a labor management policy that substitutes persuasion for coercion. The relaxed labor policy was a part of the post-Stalin "thaw" that altered many features of the Soviet society. This policy is a recognition by the Soviet government that the worker's willingness to work is, in the final analysis, the most important factor contributing to the quality and quantity of his output.

The extent to which the average Soviet worker's freedoms have been expanded since the early 1950s is a matter of considerable disagreement among Western Soviet experts. Some analysts believe that the Soviet workers have gained considerably more freedom than they had before 1950; others see no significant change in the Soviet worker's position in the labor market. The only reliable observation is that the door is now open in the Soviet Union to the development of a labor management policy more appropriate to an economy in which a well-trained, literate labor force is better prepared to respond to persuasion than coercion. How far the Soviet leaders will go in enlarging labor freedoms and in stimulating the worker's willingness to produce remains to be seen.

The Soviet Manpower Problem

Soviet manpower policy has been greatly influenced since 1960 by the drying up of sources of increased labor supply in households and collective farms and by the decline in the rate of population growth. In the past quarter century the birth rate has declined from 27 to 18 per 1,000 population, and the annual rate of population growth in the same period has decreased from 1.7 to 0.9 percent.[51] Increasingly, the only source of additional labor is becoming the able-bodied individuals who have terminated their education on a full-time basis. The Ninth Five-Year Plan (1971–1975) projected an annual increase in industrial employment of only 1.3 percent, as compared with the 3 to 4 percent of previous plans. The plans prior to the Ninth Plan largely ignored the labor supply problem, but starting with the 1971–1975 five-year plan this problem has been receiving special attention. In 1967, a new State Committee on Labor Resources Utilization was established to find solutions to the Soviet Union's growing manpower problems.

To some extent, the Soviet labor shortage is artificially created by bad planning and industrial management practices. A study by the State Gosplan revealed that the need of industrial enterprise managers for labor was exaggerated by 1.9 million workers in the 1970 annual plan and by 1.3 million in the 1971 plan. Plant managers overestimate their labor requirements in order to be able to meet additional production assignments imposed during the plan by the central planning authorities, to have labor available for agricultural work at the peak of the harvest season and for building houses for the plant's workers, and to have the capability of *storming*. Storming involves working very intensively or overtime at the end of a plan period in order to meet the plan goal. The reason plant managers overestimate their labor needs is that the annual plans are so tightly constructed that little labor is available for unforeseen developments and emergencies. Cautious plant managers then seek to protect themselves by having "hidden" reserves of labor.

The reaction of the central planning authorities to the growing manpower problem has taken the form of many diverse efforts to enlarge the labor supply in industry.[52] These efforts include reducing the need for new workers by improving the productivity of the current labor force through the more extensive mechanization and automating of the production processes. Plans are also being carried out to reduce the labor norms used to determine the amount of labor required by a plant to meet its production goal; to improve recruitment procedures; to move labor surpluses from the Transcaucasus and the

[51] Frederick A. Leedy, "Demographic Trends in the U.S.S.R.," *Soviet Economic Prospects for the Seventies*, 1973, p. 431.

[52] A survey of these manpower policies is made in Murray Feshbach and Stephen Rapawy, "Labor Constraints in the Five-Year Plan," *Soviet Economic Prospects for the Seventies*, 1973, pp. 485–563.

Central Asian Soviet Republics; and to draw pensioners back into work. Other schemes seek to recruit more foreign labor from Bulgaria, North Korea, and Finland; to have people take on two jobs; to enlarge volunteer work especially in local government activities; and to put new plants in small cities where there are pockets of unemployment. Efforts are also being made to reduce the annual labor turnover, which is 20 percent for industrial workers and 33 percent for construction workers. To this end, special bonuses are paid to nonquitters who stay with one industrial enterprise. In recent years the government has stepped up its campaign against *parasites,* i.e., able-bodied workers between the ages of eighteen and fifty-nine who have not worked for four months.

Although the overall supply and demand for labor may be balanced in the annual and five-year plans, the shortages of labor show up in individual branches of industry, such as the construction, transportation, consumer goods, and food industries. There is frequently an overabundance of auxiliary (largely manual) workers and a scarcity of engineers, technicians, and other skilled workers. In Soviet industry, there are eighty-five auxiliary workers per one hundred basic (skilled) workers; in the United States, the ratio is thirty-five to one hundred. In the Soviet Union, auxiliary workers account for 50 percent of all workers in industry, for 60 percent in construction, and for 80 percent in agriculture. These workers constitute a "reserve" that the Ninth Plan expected to reduce considerably through the mechanization and automation of industry. The productivity of the Soviet auxiliary workers is very low, as a 1971 study of the State Gosplan shows. This study revealed that, according to Soviet statistics, the Soviet basic workers have a productivity that is from 70 to 75 percent of their United States counterparts, whereas the Soviet auxiliary workers have a productivity equal to only 20 to 25 percent of American auxiliary workers.

The reduction in the length of the Soviet work week in industry to five days and forty-one hours has placed additional pressure on the planning authorities to uncover ways of raising labor productivity. This accounts for the considerable interest in the experiment of the Shchekino Chemical Combine in reducing the total number of work personnel, while at the same time increasing total output. In 1967, the Shchekino Chemical Combine was allowed to use cost savings from labor force reductions in order to raise the wages of the remaining workers. It was hoped that this would encourage plant managers to eliminate excess staff and thus improve labor productivity. While the results of the Shchekino experiment were impressive, the experiment has not been widely followed by Soviet plant managers, because there are still many reasons for managers not to cut excess workers from their rolls. Surplus workers are retained in order to take care of additional production assignments that might be imposed by the central authorities during the plan year, and in order to maintain the capability of storming.[53] If the Soviet planners do not succeed in raising labor productivity significantly in the next decade, the annual and five-year plans will have to be adjusted to reflect this situation. This means that the government would have great difficulty in curbing the decline in the overall economic growth rate that set in after 1958.

The Soviet Distribution System

The Soviet Union, like other types of advanced economic systems, has an extensive wholesale-retail distribution system. Soviet ideologists explain that wholesale-retail trade and market systems must be preserved under socialism, but that in the final stage of communism no goods and money will be

[53] See Murray Feshbach and Stephen Rapawy, *op. cit.,* p. 489; and Leonard Joel Kirsch, *op. cit.,* p. 147.

exchanged through trade. In the communist society of the future, there will be only "direct distribution" of abundant goods to consumers in accordance with their needs. Although in theory, the socialist form of exchange and distribution currently functioning in the Soviet Union is supposed to wither away and to be supplanted by direct communist distribution, in practice the Soviet wholesale-retail distribution system continues to play a very important role in the functioning of the Soviet economy.

The Soviet distribution system, while having much in common with the distribution system of Western countries, has important characteristics that are not duplicated in noncommunist countries.[54] In the Soviet Union, goods are distributed through two different networks: the material-technical supply system, which is concerned with the "allocating" of goods; and the wholesale-retail trade system, which deals with the "trading" or buying and selling of goods. The bulk of producers' goods are distributed through the former system, and most consumers' goods through the latter system. Under the material-technical supply system, scarce supplies and producers' goods are not marketed, but are allocated by the central and republic planning authorities. In the material-technical supply sector, no real change of ownership occurs, since goods owned by the state are distributed by allocation among state enterprises. In the sphere of "trading," as distinguished from "allocating," occur transfers of ownership of goods through purchases or sales, as well as many of the supply-and-demand phenomena usually associated with the concept of a market. Soviet commerce includes all sales of goods by state and cooperative retail outlets to private consumers; all sales by the government to producers' cooperatives (before they were nationalized and converted into local state industries in 1960), to consumers' cooperatives, and to collective farms; and also state and cooperative purchases of agricultural produce from the collective farms.

The Soviet consumer-goods market has three divisions: the state retail market, the cooperative retail market, and the collective farm or peasant market. The state retail market accounts for 68 percent of total retail sales, the cooperative retail market for 26 percent, and the collective farm or peasant market for 6 percent. The domestic trade sector, like all other sectors of the Soviet economy, is planned on both an annual and a long-term basis. The annual plan in its final form shows a balance between the total supply of consumer goods that will be available in the plan year and the expected demand for these goods arising from the total disposable income of the workers and from transfer incomes, such as social security benefits and old age pensions, that will be spent on consumer goods during the plan year. The amount of consumer goods available during the plan year depends upon central-government decisions with respect to the division of total national output between investment goods and consumption goods. These decisions, in turn, reflect the priorities established by the leadership of the Communist party.

The production of nonessential consumer goods has usually been given limited consideration by Soviet leaders, but since 1953, efforts have been made to enlarge the flow of a wider variety of consumer goods. The production of essential consumer goods, such as textiles, clothing, and shoes, is planned by the central government planning agencies, which also supervise the interrepublic deliveries

---

[54] For a discussion of the Soviet consumer sector, see Janet Chapman, "Consumption," in Abram Bergson and Simon Kuznets (eds.), *Economic Trends in the Soviet Union*, Cambridge, Mass.: Harvard University Press, 1963; M. I. Goldman, *Soviet Marketing, Distribution in a Controlled Economy*, Glencoe, Ill.: Free Press and Collier-Macmillan, 1963; and Alec Nove, "The Price System," *The Soviet Economy*, 1968, pp. 400–406.

of these commodities. Less essential consumer-goods production and distribution is planned by the republic planning agencies, working in cooperation with the regional and local trade administrations.

The major retail outlets, such as department stores and trade administrations of the local soviets in charge of retail stores in the cities, draft preliminary plans for retail sales in the coming year. These preliminary plans are passed up to higher state and cooperative trade organizations on regional and republic levels and, finally, to the national level, where they are combined with the central government's plans with respect to consumer goods production to create the annual state trade plan. This plan includes both physical and financial balances. Physical balances show the material, labor, and other inputs required for the planned annual output of consumer goods, while financial balances—which involve problems of turnover tax, price setting, currency circulation, and consumers' income-expenditure patterns—show the balance between total available supplies of all types of consumer goods and the total demand for these goods coming from workers, old-age pensioners, and others receiving social security benefits. The state trade plan for the whole consumer sector constructed at the top of the trade planning pyramid is, in effect, a summation of the many thousands of trade and financial plans (*torgfinplani*) of the wholesale offices and stores at the bottom of the pyramid. The *torgfinplan* of each trading enterprise is the counterpart of the *tekhpromfinplan* (the technical-industrial-financial plan) of each state producing enterprise.

The trade and financial plan of each retail enterprise sets forth annual goals relating to such matters as turnover of stock, reduction of costs of operation, and volume of retail trade to be handled. In line with the usual Soviet pattern of compensation, store managers and other personnel are given bonuses when actual sales exceed planned sales, but receive less than standard remuneration when sales do not reach the annual planned goal. Although retail-store personnel are stimulated to increase sales, the fact that they usually function in a sellers' market militates against improving their services to customers. In general, demand tends to outstrip supply in Soviet retail markets. Although a few goods, such as wool textiles, leather footwear, and clothing, have at times been in surplus in recent years, usually stocks of consumer goods other than necessities tend to be in short supply. Unable to purchase as much as they would like to, consumers have been forced into involuntary saving. No competition exists in the Soviet retail trade, since the state stores service primarily the urban areas and the cooperative stores the rural areas.

As the result of the failure of the Soviet government to direct enough investment into retail premises and equipment as the population has expanded, of the lack of competition in the retail markets, and of the existence of a sellers' market, the standards of performance in the sphere of Soviet retail trade are much below what they are in Western Europe and the United States. Soviet retail outlets are frequently small, very poorly equipped, and not well located. Storage facilities are inadequate, and refrigeration is frequently lacking. The variety of consumer goods is very restricted, many goods are of poor quality, and little packaging of goods is done. While there are some retail outlets in large urban centers classified as "progressive," with packaged goods for sale and with self-service, they are still a very small fraction of the total number of retail outlets. Installment selling of durable consumer goods and the use of automatic vending machines are not yet widely developed. Compared to the United States, the Soviet Union has a very small retail trade network which has to serve a much larger population.

The ratio of personnel employed in retailing and public catering to total population in the Soviet Union is one-fourth the American ratio.

Prices of Consumer Goods

Outside of the collective farm or peasant markets where farm produce is sold to individual buyers at uncontrolled prices, Soviet consumer-goods prices are not left to be determined freely by the market forces of supply and demand. These prices are fixed by the government planning authorities at the central, republic, or local levels, depending upon the importance of the consumer good. Prices of consumer necessities, such as food and clothing, are fixed by the central planning authorities. In the late 1950s, one-half of the total retail trade was carried on in commodities with prices that were fixed by the central government. The retail price for a consumer good is the end-product of a price-fixing process that stretches back to the industry producing the consumer good. In this process, prices are fixed at three levels: the industry level, the wholesale level, and the retail level. At each level, average costs per unit of production or per unit handled by a marketing organization are calculated and a profit markup is added to unit costs to arrive at the selling price.

The objective of the Soviet government's price-fixing program is to price consumer goods in such a way that total retail sales will just match consumer income available for spending, and also to price each consumer good in such a way that there will be no oversupply (excessive inventory) or undersupply (queuing for the commodity). Soviet trade planning and price fixing have frequently failed to achieve these two major goals. Excess consumer buying power can easily be removed by increasing the turnover taxes and, hence, the prices of consumer goods. But the Soviet government has been reluctant since 1954 to raise consumer prices, since this would conflict with the government's announced policy of keeping consumer prices stable and, in some cases, reducing them. The Soviet government increased meat prices 30 percent and butter prices 25 percent on June 1, 1962, in order to bring the supply of and demand for these products into better equilibrium and, at the same time, to reduce the purchasing power held by consumers. The urban population is reported to have reacted violently to these large price increases with a series of protest rallies and riots. The deficiencies of Soviet price fixing stem from the failures of the planning authorities to anticipate accurately enough changes in the demand patterns of consumers and to balance effectively the real flow of consumer goods and the financial flow of personal incomes and expenditures.

In the collective farm or peasant markets, prices are not fixed by any government authority; but the Soviet government can influence these prices by altering the supplies of food products that are available in the state retail stores. The peasants and others who are selling privately in the market stalls of the urban centers are free to charge whatever prices the traffic will bear. A main constraint on the free prices in the peasant markets is the prices of food products in the nearby state and cooperative stores. If food is relatively abundant in these stores, then prices in the peasant markets fall close to the level of the state and consumer cooperative retail prices. If certain food items are available only in the peasant markets, then the only limit to increases in the prices of these products is the size of the consumer demand. Although the peasant markets account for only 9 percent of all food sales, they are an important source of money income for the peasantry. Since the collective farm markets are a survival from the prerevolutionary period and would have no place in a communist society, the Soviet government hopes to eliminate these markets by stepping up the production of food and livestock products on the state and collective farms in the socialized farm sector.

Soviet consumer price policy since 1928 has passed through three major periods: the period from 1928 to 1939, during which real wages were kept down by inflating consumer prices; the second period from 1947 to 1954, during which the government raised real earnings by extensive reductions of consumer-good prices; and the third period since 1954, during which the official policy has been to stabilize the consumer price level with only occasional changes in the prices of luxury and semiluxury consumer goods.[55]

Official statistics of changes in retail price indices in the Soviet Union during 1960–1970 show that there was almost no inflation in those years. The official price statistics in Table 15-7 for the USSR, East Germany, Bulgaria, Hungary, and Poland reveal that retail prices changed very little in these countries, whereas there was serious inflation in Yugoslavia between 1960 and 1970. Although the official Soviet overall retail-price index has recorded hardly any inflation since 1955, other evidence tends to support the view that there has been considerable suppressed inflation in those years. In the collective farm markets, where prices are free to record supply-and-demand changes, inflation occurred at the annual rate of approximately 4 percent in the 1960s. An examination of official prices of individual food items in state retail stores for 1960–1969 shows that these food prices increased only 5.5 percent over the entire period. However, unofficial Western investigations of the prices of basic staple foods show that on the average these prices increased 35 percent over the same ten-year period, with the price of bread rising 70 percent and of meat and meat products 50 percent.

Prices have crept upward in the Soviet Union since Stalin's death because of both cost-push and demand-pull inflationary forces. Cost-push forces have been strengthened by the government's policies, which have raised urban minimum wages from 22 rubles in 1950 to 70 rubles in 1975, and which have raised agricultural prices very

[55] A discussion of inflation in the Soviet Union is presented in Norton T. Dodge, "Inflation in the Socialist Economies," in Gardiner C. Means and others, *The Roots of Inflation*, New York: Burt Franklin, 1975, pp. 211–238; Keith Bush, "Soviet Inflation," in M. Yves Laulan (ed.), *Banking, Money and Credit in Eastern Europe*, Brussels, 1973, pp. 97–105; and Morris Bornstein, "Soviet Price Theory and Policy," in Morris Bornstein and Daniel Fusfeld (eds.), *The Soviet Economy*, 4th ed., Homewood, Ill.: Richard D. Irwin, 1974, pp. 85–116.

Table 15-7
Change in Retail Price Indices in Six Communist Countries, by Five-Year Periods, 1950–1970

Period	U.S.S.R.	East Germany	Bulgaria	Hungary	Poland	Yugoslavia
	(Average annual rate of change in percent)					
1950–1955	−6.2	−17.3	7.0	9.7	10.4	−5.1
1955–1960	0.0	−1.9	0.1	0.2	2.3	2.4
1960–1965	0.2	0.0	−1.7	0.5	1.3	11.3
1965–1970	0.0	−0.2	−0.8	0.9	1.3	9.9

Sources: Based on data from the following statistical handbooks: *Narodnoe Khoziaistva SSSR*; *Statistiches Jahrbuch der Deutschen Demokratischen Republik*; *Statisticheski Godeshnik na Narodna Republika Bulgariia*; *Statisztikai Evkönyv*; *Rocznik Statystyczny*; and *Statistički Godišnjak Jugoslavije*.

considerably since 1953. The policy of raising minimum wages and reducing wage differentials tended to increase worker incomes faster than productivity in industry has improved, with the result that unit labor costs have increased. Higher labor costs have not always been passed on to consumers because turnover taxes on consumer goods have been reduced and subsidies have been given to agricultural and service producers. In their efforts to meet or to exceed production targets, managers have at times exceeded their total wage allocations for the plan period, have competed for scarce skilled labor, and have offered actual or disguised increases in wage rates. These policies have contributed further to the upward wage drifting or "wage creep" that has been observed in both socialist and capitalist countries. Furthermore, the wage creep has been strongest in the heavy producers' goods industries that do not produce consumer goods on which additional wage incomes might be spent.[56]

Demand-pull has forced up the retail price level since 1955 in the Soviet Union as the result of the government's programs for raising minimum wages, increasing collective farm family incomes, and enlarging pension and other social security payments. Also, upward wage drifting has placed increasing amounts of income in the hands of the consuming public. With an inadequate supply of consumer goods in the state and cooperative retail stores, consumers' discretionary income has moved into unofficial markets, such as farmers' markets, special and second-hand stores, private housing (second homes in the countryside), handicrafts, and modern art. Evidence of suppressed inflation is further supplied by the queuing for desirable consumer goods in short supply, the existence of black markets, and the trebling of savings deposits from 1966 to 1970 as consumer incomes rose. The experience of the Soviet Union with the combination of demand-pull and cost-push inflationary forces seems to suggest that the socialist countries of the East have in many ways the same problem of controlling inflation as do the capitalist countries of the West.

The Soviet stable consumer-price policy and the related wage policy can be maintained in the future only if the necessary priority is assigned to the production of consumer goods. If the economic incentives of the workers are to be improved and higher levels of productive efficiency are to be achieved with stable prices, more attention will have to be given in the future to maintaining the equilibrium between expanding consumer incomes and the increasing flow of consumer goods at stable prices.

Consumer Welfare in the Soviet Union since 1964

Consumer welfare was considerably enlarged under Khrushchev in the years 1956–1964.[57] Per capita consumption during those years increased at the annual rate of 4.8 percent. Khrushchev raised the minimum wage rate of urban workers by more than one-third and of rural workers by about one-half. Wage rates rose more rapidly in the low-income services sector of the economy than in the industrial sector, and most of the collective farm workers and their families were placed under a new

---

[56] Robert M. Fearn, "Controls over Wage Funds and Inflationary Pressures in the USSR," *Industrial and Labor Relations Review*, Vol. XVIII, No. 2, Jan. 1965, pp. 186–187.

[57] Consumer welfare in the Soviet Union is analyzed in David W. Bronson and Barbara S. Severin, "Soviet Consumer Welfare: the Brezhnev Era," in *Soviet Economic Prospects for the Seventies*, 1973, pp. 376–403, and "Consumer Welfare," in *Economic Performance and the Military Burden in the Soviet Union*, Washington, D.C., 1973; and Paul R. Gregory and Robert C. Stuart, "Consumer Welfare in the Soviet Union," *op. cit.*, pp. 400–406.

social security system similar to the one for nonfarm urban workers. Under Brezhnev's leadership, the Soviet war on poverty has been stepped up since 1964. Since that year, the average level of living in the Soviet Union has risen rapidly. Diets have been improved with more emphasis on meat and other quality foods and less on starches. The supply of consumer durables had become so large that by 1975 it was expected that most families would have the basic household appliances.

In spite of the large improvement in the Soviet standard of living since 1964, the gap between the Soviet and American standards remains large. In the Soviet Union, more so than in the United States, supplies of quality foods, housing, and personal services are still inadequate. The Soviet government is not yet able to provide the population with a high-quality diet and adequate housing. Consumer incomes have continued to increase faster than the supply of goods and services; some purchases have to be postponed because of scarcities; and queues for quality goods still occur in the market place. In 1972, the average monthly wage of Soviet workers (130.3 rubles) was less than two-thirds of what was considered to be necessary to support a family of four persons at the minimum standard. This situation accounted for the high participation of women in the labor force and also in part for the low birth rate in the urban areas. With official consumer prices remaining stable in the years 1965-1972, and wages and salaries rising at an annual rate of 7.6 percent, there was a rapid accumulation of personal savings that could not be spent because the supply of consumer goods fell behind the demand for these goods.

The patterns of consumption in the Soviet Union have changed very considerably since 1950, as is shown by the statistics in Table 15-8 on the average Soviet diet for the period 1950-1971. Much more meat, milk, dairy products, and sugar are now being consumed

Table 15-8

U.S.S.R. Average Diet Per Person in 1950, 1960, and 1971 (Kilograms Per Person Per Year)

Food item	1950	1960	1971
Meat	22.1	33.3	43.0
Fish	7.0	9.9	14.8
Milk	116.6	146.5	182.5
Fats and oils	9.1	15.6	20.5
Sugar	11.6	28.0	39.5
Grain products	172.0	164.0	149.0
Potatoes	241.0	143.0	128.0

Source: David W. Bronson and Barbara S. Severin, "Soviet Consumer Welfare: The Brezhnev Era," *Soviet Economic Prospects for the Seventies,* 1973, p. 382.

in place of grain products and potatoes. There has also been a shift from home-produced to purchased food, a greater availability of ready-made clothing and shoes, and much larger supplies of refrigerators, washing machines, and television sets—all of which were generally not available in 1950. By Western standards the supplies of automobiles, housing, and personal services are still extremely limited.[58] Nevertheless, considerable progress has been made in these areas. The supply of housing was doubled in the period 1951-1972, so that fewer people are living in each room. Other improvements are much more central heating, more retail sales personnel in relation to the total population, and more packaged goods. In recent years, buyers' markets have developed for all consumer manufactured goods, except for automobiles and for quality foods such as meat. There are no waiting lists except for housing and automobiles. In 1970, there were only 10

[58] For a discussion of the current housing situation in the Soviet Union, see Willard S. Smith, "Housing in the Soviet Union—Big Plans, Little Action," *Soviet Economic Prospects for the Seventies,* 1973, pp. 404-426.

cars per 1,000 population in the Soviet Union, whereas there were 432 cars per 1,000 population in the United States.

The Ninth Plan (1971-1975) did not call for any major change in national priorities as they relate to consumer welfare. The plan goals were to be a continuation of the movement initiated by Khrushchev and continued by Brezhnev to enlarge consumer welfare. The main efforts were to increase the supplies of personal services and durable consumer goods. By 1975, according to Soviet claims, of every one hundred families, seventy-two would have television sets and washing machines, sixty-four would have refrigerators, and eighty-five would have radios. It was estimated in 1970 that the Soviet Union would have about 3 million privately owned automobiles in 1975, almost three times the number in 1970, but still only about one automobile per one hundred people. Among the welfare measures projected for the plan period 1971-1975 were increases in the minimum wage from 60 to 70 rubles a month, reduced taxes for low-income workers, increases in pension payments, subsistence payments for the children of low-income families, and annual repayments on compulsory mass-subscription loans made during World War II and the 1950s.

A comparison of diets in the Soviet Union, the United Kingdom, and the United States shows that the British diet is superior to the Soviet diet in meat, meat products, eggs, sugar, and fats. The American diet is superior to both the British and Soviet diets in most of these items. Table 15-9 indicates that the per capita consumption of meat and meat products in the United States is twice that in the Soviet Union. Americans consume more eggs, fats, and sugar than Russians but less fish, milk, potatoes, bread, and flour products.

Soviet Foreign Trade

Foreign trade, like all other economic activities, is brought within the scope of the Soviet annual and five-year plans.[59] Subplans are

[59] For a survey of Soviet foreign trade, see Paul R. Gregory and Robert C. Stuart, Ch. 8, "Soviet Foreign Trade," *op. cit.*, pp. 272-297; Franklyn D. Holzman, *Foreign Trade under Central Planning,*

Table 15-9

Comparative Diets in the Soviet Union, the United Kingdom, and the United States, 1970 (In Kilograms Per Capita Per Year)

	Soviet Union	United Kingdom	United States
Meat and meat products	48	61	96
Fish and fish products	15.4	10	5
Milk and milk products	307	462	291
Eggs	9	15	19
Sugar	38.8	53	49
Vegetable oil and margarine	6.8	10	15
Vegetables and melons	83	58	125
Potatoes	130	98	48
Bread and flour products	149	87	74

Source: Philip Weitzman, "Soviet Long-Term Consumption Planning," *Soviet Studies,* Vol. XXVI, July 1974, p. 308.

drawn up to indicate the national goals that relate to exports and imports, and like all other subplans, the foreign trade subplan provides a ruble balance between total exports and total imports. Unlike the Western democratic nations, the Soviet Union does not trade freely with other nations so as to take full advantage of national specialization and the law of comparative advantage. Instead, foreign trade is looked upon as a way of getting rid of surplus goods and of importing goods to remove production bottlenecks, to import foreign technology, and to meet emergencies like bad harvests. Soviet state enterprises are not permitted to calculate whether domestic sales or foreign sales will maximize their profits, and then to choose the sales that are most profitable. Exports and imports are determined by the central planners who are primarily interested in securing balance in the national plan without much concern for the most rational export-import program. Soviet foreign trade is hampered by the lack of rational domestic prices and ruble foreign exchange rates. The exchange rates which are set by the government are unrealistic and bear no relation to purchasing power parities. Since the ruble cannot be imported and exported, there are no internationally quoted ruble exchange rates.

Ever since the establishment of the Soviet regime in 1917, foreign trade has been a state monopoly in the Soviet Union under the direction of the central Ministry of Trade. Following the instructions of the Minister of Trade, which are in line with the annual and five-year foreign trade plans, Soviet exporting and importing organizations purchase goods for export from the state industrial enterprises and sell imports to these enterprises at domestic prices. Foreign exchange earned abroad is used to pay for imports, with gold sales being used only infrequently to pay for any unusually large imports. Usually, bilateral trade arrangements are made with various countries so that the value of exports is balanced by the value of imports at prices determined on the world markets. Since world prices are used as norms in foreign trade, irrational Soviet domestic prices are no hindrance to this trade. What the irrational Soviet domestic prices do is prevent the Soviet government from determining its gain from foreign trade and maximizing it.

Under Stalin, foreign trade was kept to a minimum, since he fostered a program for self-sufficiency. Under Khrushchev in the years 1955–1964, Stalin's policy of economic autarky was somewhat weakened. The major new development in Soviet foreign trade did not come until the 1960s when an important shift away from autarky and towards greater participation in trade relations with the non-communist world occurred. At the 23rd Congress of the Communist party in 1965, it was declared that there was a need for an "international division of labor" and for "increasing substantially the volume of purchases in capitalist countries."[60] By the time that the Ninth Five-Year Plan was introduced (1971), it was clear that the Soviet Union had moved a long way from a policy of economic autarky. Much of the success of the Ninth Five-Year Plan and later plans will depend upon the extent to which the Soviet Union can develop its trade relations with the United States. The Soviet Union plans to increase its imports of American machinery and technological know-how. It is planning to develop its natural resources to earn the necessary foreign exchange with which to pay for the increased imports from the United States

---

Cambridge, Mass.: Harvard University Press, 1974; and Carl McMillan, "Some Recent Developments in Soviet Foreign Trade Policy," *Canadian Slavonic Papers*, Fall, 1970, Vol. 12, No. 3, pp. 243-272.

[60] Edward T. Wilson, "U.S.–Soviet Commercial Relations," *Soviet Economic Prospects for the Seventies*, 1973, p. 643.

which rose from $161 million in 1971 to over $500 million in 1973. The Soviet Union is now seeking extensive American credits and the application to its American trade of the most-favored nation clause. Reforms are now being proposed in the Soviet Union which would give more freedom to industrial enterprises to import and export goods. Any such reform would doubtless strengthen the trend towards more extensive trade relations between the Soviet Union and the West.[61]

The Soviet Union is not now heavily dependent on foreign trade, since total exports and imports each constitute less than 4 percent of its Gross National Product. The Soviet Union is a large importer of machinery and equipment and consumer goods, and an exporter of machinery and equipment, consumer goods, and raw materials. The statistics in Table 15-10 show that two-thirds of Soviet trade turnover (exports and imports) is with the communist countries of Eastern Europe. The remaining one-third is roughly divided between the developed West and the less developed countries. Among the Western nations, the United Kingdom, West Germany, France, and Italy, and in addition Japan, carry on extensive trade with the Soviet Union. Up to now, the Comecon countries of Eastern Europe have been the main Soviet trading partners. Larger commercial relations with the United States could bring much benefit to both the Comecon countries and the Soviet Union.

The Soviet Financial System

The Soviet economy is a money-using economy with a well developed financial system.[62] The Soviet currency system is based on

[61] For a discussion of the prospects and consequences of increased U.S.-U.S.S.R. commercial relations, see the statements of Steven Lazarus, Foy D. Kohler, and Gregory Grossman in Joint Economic Committee, Hearings, *Soviet Economic Outlook*, Washington, D.C., 1973, pp. 111-144.

[62] The financial system and its problems are analyzed in detail in the 1973 colloquium on monetary policies in the East European countries arranged by the NATO Directorate of Economic Affairs. See *Banking, Money and Credit in Eastern Europe*, Brussels, 1973.

Table 15-10
U.S.S.R.: Geographic Distribution of Trade, 1971 (in millions of U.S. dollars)

	1971	
	Exports	Imports
Total	13,806	12,479
Communist countries	9,018	8,177
Eastern Europe	7,241	7,257
China	78	76
Other	1,699	844
Free World	4,788	4,302
Developed West	2,710	2,860
Less developed countries	2,078	1,442

Source: Edward T. Wilson and others, "U.S.-Soviet Commercial Relations," *Soviet Economic Prospects for the Seventies*, 1973, p. 697.

a defined monetary unit, the ruble. Its banking system consists of a short-term credit bank *(Gosbank)*, a long-term credit or investment bank *(Stroibank)*, and savings banks; and its fiscal system involves taxes, public expenditures, and bond sales and redemptions. The Soviet Union officially operates a gold standard monetary system with a monetary unit, the ruble, containing 15.1 grains of gold nine-tenths pure. The U.S. dollar contains 11.4 grains of gold nine-tenths pure. However, the paper money is not redeemable in gold coin or bullion and cannot be legally exported or imported. Rubles are not bought and sold like other currencies in the world money markets since no supplies of rubles are available for sale or purchase. The official rate of exchange in the Soviet Union between the ruble and the dollar is determined by the legal or defined gold contents of the ruble and the dollar. Since the defined gold content of the ruble is equal to the defined gold content of $1.32 (U.S.), the official ruble-dollar exchange rate in the Soviet Union is 1 ruble for $1.32 (in 1976). However, this ruble-dollar ratio of 1:1.32 has nothing to do with the relative real purchasing powers of the ruble and the dollar and is used only internally in the Soviet Union. In the illegal black market in the Soviet Union the unofficial rate of exchange fluctuates around 2 rubles for 1 U.S. dollar. This unofficial exchange rate more realistically reflects the actual purchasing power of the ruble which is equivalent to around one-half a U.S. dollar. In all external financial or trade transactions, the Soviet Union uses foreign currencies at whatever exchange rates prevail in world financial markets or it pays for imports with gold sold at the prevailing world price ($115 per ounce in October 1976).

The money flow in the Soviet Union moves in two circuits, the enterprise circuit and the household circuit. In the enterprise circuit, money is basically an accounting unit, and enterprise activities are given monetary expression. The enterprise's production target, raw-material allocations, capital-investment plan, and labor allocation are expressed in both physical and monetary terms. The money that the enterprise receives from the sale of its products gives the enterprise no options or power to influence the production process, since the enterprise must carry out the physical planning instructions of the central authorities. The enterprise is not free to spend its profits as it wishes, but must instead follow the physical or real plan instructions handed down by the top-level planning authorities, which are stated in physical and monetary terms. Money thus becomes an instrument through which the enterprise is controlled by the central planners.

In the household sector, money does provide options, because the money received as wages, grants, pensions, and interest on savings accounts can be used to express consumer preferences or choices. The planners can control the overall output of consumer goods, but they cannot exactly determine how this output will be distributed among consumers. Although the consumer can dispose of his income as he wishes, his area of choice is very limited. He has no control over the division of output between consumption and investment, and since prices are not flexible, the consumer cannot influence the planners' decisions to supply consumer goods.

State enterprises, government agencies, and a limited number of individuals have accounts in the State Bank (Gosbank), into which funds are paid and later withdrawn. Payments between state enterprises and government agencies are made with checks on their respective accounts. Households are paid wages or salaries and grants from the state in cash, and most payments for goods and services are made with cash. Excess household funds are deposited in savings banks, where they earn 2 to 3 percent interest.

Local, republic, and the central governments receive income in the form of tax payments by state enterprises, collective farms, and individuals, and disburse funds to state enterprises, collective farms, individuals, and various governmental agencies. Government bonds are issued to individuals with surplus wage or salary incomes. The State and Investment Banks extend credit mainly to state enterprises, state farms, and collective farms for the purchase of plant, equipment, and raw materials. Individuals, who infrequently use credit, draw upon their savings for the purchase of automobiles and houses.

Nothing in the Soviet Union compares to the capital markets of the Western nations. There is no stock market, since state enterprises are owned by the state and do not issue securities. For the same reason, no bond market exists. All long-term loans are held by the Investment Bank, and government bonds held by individuals are not negotiable. Likewise, there is no market for short-term financial paper or bills of exchange, since the state enterprises do not use commercial paper or trade acceptances, and the central government does not issue treasury bills. The State Bank, like other central banks, issues currency, keeps accounts for state enterprises, and handles the financial business of government agencies. The State Bank does not regulate the financial system through changes in rediscount rates, bank-reserve requirements, or open-market operations (government-bond sales and purchases). Since there are no private banks in the Soviet Union and all banking affairs are concentrated in the government State and Investment Banks, there is no private banking system to be regulated or controlled as in the Western nations, where financial controls are imposed on private banks to offset booms and recessions. Private finance as it is known in the Western industrialized countries does not exist in the Soviet Union. There all finance is public finance and is fully controlled by the governments at the national, regional, and local levels.

The Real and Financial Flows

Like all other economies, the Soviet economy has two basic flows: the real flow of goods and services and the financial flow of incomes and expenditures. The real flow of goods and services is summarized in the five-year and annual national plans, which project the nation's total output or GNP and its distribution among private and public consumption and investment uses. The real flow is a production flow, which combines land, labor, and capital and creates a supply of goods and services. These goods and services are taken up by enterprises, collective farms, state farms, households, and government agencies. Associated with this real flow is a financial flow of incomes that are generated by the production of goods and services. State enterprises, collective farms, households, and government agencies receive incomes in the form of profits, wages and salaries, and taxes and in turn spend these incomes on goods and services.

In the case of the real flow of goods and services, the central planners are concerned with physical balances between inputs and outputs, which are in many cases regulated by means of the central allocations of raw materials and producer goods. As we have seen in the discussion of Soviet economic planning, this planning seeks to achieve physical balances between the supply and demand for raw materials, between producing and using enterprises, and between all sectors of the economy. The additional problem arises of securing financial balances between incomes earned and spent: this is the overall problem of correlating the financial and real flows.

In an unplanned competitive economy, the

nation's real and money flows are coordinated through the free market mechanism with the aid of a system of flexible prices. The free market system brings about balances between the supply and demand for goods and services and for the factors of production. Scarcities and bottlenecks are eliminated by changes in prices, which bring about a reallocation of scarce resources. In this manner, the real and financial flows are meshed or kept in balance. In the planned economy, the market mechanism does not provide the desired balance between these two flows; consequently, the central planning authorities attempt to provide the balance.

In the planned Western countries, such as France, the Netherlands, and the Scandinavian countries, the well-developed private-enterprise system can be relied upon to achieve much of the desired coordination of the real and financial flows. In the Soviet Union, where the private-enterprise system has been largely eliminated and the market mechanism is poorly developed, much of the coordination between the real and financial flows has to be provided administratively by the planning authorities. This coordination is secured through a set of balances, which combine both physical and financial items.

The real and financial balance of Soviet households is achieved through a currency or cash plan, which seeks to balance the cash incomes of households, less personal saving, and the supply of consumer goods and services. This is a matter of regulating the flow of wages, salaries, and grants to households so that consumer buying power does not exceed the available supply of consumer goods and services. The balance of the cash plan can be achieved by controlling the total wage and salary allowances of the state enterprises and by regulating the prices of consumer goods and services. The Ministry of Finance and the State Committee for Labor and Wages have much to do with the total amount of wages and salaries that is made available in the annual plans. The state is interested in keeping the total wage and salary bill as low as possible to curb consumption and expand investments. The workers aspire to a rising standard of living, which only rising wages can provide.

The real and financial flows within the state enterprises and collective farms are balanced with the aid of their annual technical-industrial-financial plans. The aim in fulfilling these annual plans is to balance the enterprises' total output and total sales with a profit to the enterprises. This balance is upset only when an enterprise's annual production plan is either underfulfilled or overfulfilled. Underfulfillment of annual production plans is not tolerated by the planning authorities, while overfulfillment is most acceptable to these authorities. When the latter occurs, adjustments are made in other enterprises' production plans in order to absorb the overfulfillment of output and to create an overall balance between the enterprises' real outputs and their sales of these outputs.

The State and Investment Banks also contribute to a balancing of the Soviet economy's real and financial flows with the aid of their short-term and longer-term credit plans. Each bank has a credit plan which is designed to aid the enterprises in their efforts to balance output and sales. The State Bank's credit plan provides short-term credit to the state enterprises and state and collective farms insofar as they need this credit in order to purchase some of the inputs required by their annual production plans. The Investment Bank's credit plan does the same for the longer-term investment needs of the state enterprises and state and collective farms. Both the State and Investment Banks provide credit as an aid in securing an overall balance of the real and financial flows in the activities of the state enterprises and the state and collective farms.

The State Fiscal Budget

The Soviet state fiscal budget is the closest approximation to an overall financial plan. The Ministry of Finance, which constructs the state fiscal budget, controls the financial affairs of households through the turnover and income taxes. It controls the financial activities of the state enterprises and collective farms by taxing the profits of these organizations. Also, the Ministry of Finance influences the banking system by depositing budgetary surpluses in the State and Investment Banks that limit the amount of bank credit to be extended to enterprises for the purchase of raw materials, plant, and equipment.

The state fiscal budget is also used by the Soviet government to give expression to its plans concerning the division of the national income between consumption and investment. The state fiscal budget redistributes about one-half of the Gross National Product, which is mainly assigned to capital investment in industry, agriculture, and other sectors and to collective consumption for cultural and social purposes.

Table 15-11, which presents the Soviet state budget for 1974, shows that the turnover tax on consumer goods and the tax on state enterprise profits both contribute approximately one-third of total state budget revenues. Taxes on collective farms contribute very little (approximately 3 percent) to total revenues, while personal income taxes account for only 9 percent of total revenues. Social security contributions are approximately 6 percent of total revenues, with the entertainment tax, custom duties, and local taxes and fees accounting for the remainder. Almost one-half of total revenues are used to finance investments in industry, agriculture, and other economic activities. Thirty-six percent of the 1974 total revenues were used to finance educational, health, and social welfare services. The only other large expenditure in 1974 was for defense, which, according to Soviet calculations, absorbed 9 percent of total revenues. As is usual, the 1974 state budget recorded a small surplus of 200 million rubles; this is not, however, a real surplus in the Western sense, since it is used to extend credits to industry, agriculture, or trade or as an addition to a central government reserve. Soviet state budgets do not have large surpluses or deficits to offset fluctuations in economic activities, as is the case in the Western industrialized countries. This is so because there are no large cyclical fluctuations in the highly planned Soviet economy.

Table 15-11
The Soviet State Budget for 1974

Revenues	Billions of rubles	%	Expenditures	Billions of rubles	%
Turnover tax	61.9	32	National economy	95.1	49
Profits tax on state enterprises	62.6	32	Social and cultural	70.3	36
			Defense	17.6	9
Personal income tax	16.7	9	State administration	1.9	1
Taxes on collective farms, social security contributions, etc.	53.1	27	Other expenditures	9.2	5
Total revenues	194.3	100	Total expenditures	194.1	100

Source: *The Europa Year Book 1976*, Vol. I, 1976.

Soviet economists have not yet developed a theory of planning that fully integrates their physical and financial balances. Some economists look forward to developing a consolidated balance that will serve as an umbrella over all the other balances. So far, any such master balance has eluded the Soviet economists, in part because the real and financial flows of the economy are not fully interconnected either conceptually or in practice. For the time being, the term "balance of the economy" refers to presenting only the various physical and financial balances that are not integrated into any fully developed master balance.

The Soviet banking and budgetary system is especially designed to support the administrative socialism that has dominated the Soviet financial scene since the first five-year plan was adopted (1928). Prices, incomes, profits, and taxes are all manipulated to preserve the bureaucratic control of the central planners. These financial manipulations are designed to prevent money and credit from giving options or choices to those enterprises and individuals who hold money or credit. In Hungary and Yugoslavia, the economic reforms have decentralized the banking system and introduced competitive prices, with the result that enterprises and individuals are able to choose among alternatives in purchasing goods and services. This has weakened the controls of the central planning authorities in these countries to an extent that is not acceptable to the Soviet planning bureaucracy. Economic reforms have not been permitted to enlarge to any great extent the independence of enterprise managers in the use of retained earnings and borrowed funds. In all fundamental matters, Soviet enterprise managers still have to follow the directions handed down by the central planners. Also, the Soviet economic reforms have not introduced free, competitive prices; thus consumer preferences are not allowed to replace planners' preferences. The financial planning carried on with the aid of the centralized banking and budgetary system continues to buttress an administrative socialism in which money, credit, and markets open the doors to little freedom on the part of producers and consumers.

The Performance of the Soviet Economy

The Soviet Union has made outstanding progress in the past half century, for it has moved up from a low level of industrialization to become the world's second industrial power. The Soviet Union has enjoyed a high rate of economic growth, has established an extensive social welfare program, and has raised the literacy rate from 44 percent in 1920 to 99.7 percent today. It has also spectacularly enlarged its stock of highly qualified manpower. Between 1950 and 1970, the number of employed natural scientists increased from 71,000 to 284,000, while the number of employed persons with degrees in engineering rose from 400,000 in 1950 to almost 2.5 million in 1970. The Soviet Union has built up a large complex of industrial enterprises, construction projects, state farms, collective farms, and other producing organizations, which together produce a total output valued at $865 billion in 1975. However, while the economic growth of the Soviet Union has been substantial, it has not been above that of a number of the Western European countries and Japan.

A comparative study of economic growth rates for the years 1958–1965, presented in Table 15-12, shows that the Soviet Union's average annual economic growth rate was a little below that of France, West Germany, and Italy, and much below Japan's growth rate. In the period 1965–1973, the Soviet

Table 15-12
Comparative Trends in the Growth of GNP and Labor Productivity in the Soviet Union and Selected Other Countries, 1958–1965

	Average annual rates	
	GNP	Labor productivity
Soviet Union	5.3	3.5
France	5.4	5.0
West Germany	5.8	4.6
Italy	6.1	6.5
United Kingdom	3.9	2.9
Japan	12.0	9.2
United States	4.4	2.6

Source: Stanley H. Cohn, *Economic Development in the Soviet Union*, 1970, p. 61.

Union's per capita GNP growth rate (3.6 percent) was below this rate for West Germany, France, Italy, Holland, Norway, and Japan. Since 1972, economic recession and the oil crisis have greatly reduced the growth rates of these latter countries, while the Soviet Union, largely insulated from international developments, will probably have less difficulty in maintaining a high economic growth rate.

Another measure of the Soviet economy's performance is the rate of improvement in its labor productivity. From this point of view, the Soviet Union has not done as well as many of the Western European countries and Japan. The statistics in Table 15-12 show that while the Soviet Union's overall average annual growth rate has been close to that of France, West Germany, and Italy, the average annual rate of improvement in its labor productivity has been much below the rate achieved in these Western European countries and in Japan. The Soviet Union has regularly increased its stock of industrial capital and its supply of workers at higher rates than those of the Western European countries, but it has continued to have a lower labor-productivity improvement rate than these other countries because the higher Soviet investment in labor and capital has not been accompanied by as high a rate of technological progress as has been experienced in the West.[63]

An adverse consequence of the large labor and capital inputs required to sustain the Soviet growth rate is the high cost in terms of consumer welfare that is exacted. If the Soviet Union were to achieve its high growth rate by using its labor and capital more efficiently, resources could be released for the production of consumer goods and services. During the Stalin era, the demands upon the economy for producer goods to support the high growth rate were so large that real wages and the standard of living actually fell, while high overall growth was achieved. Since 1953, real wages and the standard of living have slowly improved as more emphasis has been placed upon enlarging the supply of consumer goods. The Soviet planners seek to improve further the productivity of labor and capital so that more inputs of labor and capital can be devoted to the production of consumer goods. As yet, however, industrial labor productivity in the Soviet Union remains low, being only from 30 to 40 percent of American industrial labor productivity.[64] As long as the Soviet economy remains a high-investment, low-consumption economy, the standard of living in the Soviet Union will trail far behind the living standards in Western Europe and the United States.

Although the Soviet Union has demon-

[63] For an appraisal of the Soviet and East European economic systems, see Abram Bergson, "Development under Two Systems: Comparative Productivity Growth since 1950," *World Politics*, Vol. 23, No. 4, July 1971, pp. 579–607.

[64] Estimates of comparative industrial labor productivity in the Soviet Union and the United States vary considerably. In the late 1950s many Western analysts calculated that Soviet industrial labor pro-

strated no superiority over the Western economies with regard to the rate of economic growth, it does have a much more stable economy than do a number of the Western countries. This comparison is especially true with regard to the unplanned economies, such as the United States and Canada, where the annual rate of economic growth fluctuates between the high rates of boom years and the low rates of recession years. This comparison is less true of the planned economies of France, the Netherlands, Norway, and Sweden, which were able to achieve highly stable growth rates up to the crisis years, 1973-1975. Whereas the latter countries have not been able to maintain their high growth rates in the face of serious recession in the United States and the oil crisis, the Soviet Union has been able to maintain a high and stable, though slowly declining, growth rate.

The recession-proof Soviet Union has been in a position to provide its workers with a high degree of job and income security. Job security is accompanied by a social security system that provides free medical service and hospitalization and a pension for men and women at sixty, which averages out to 70 percent of wages at the time of retirement. Economic security in the Soviet Union, however, has been achieved under a highly centralized planning system, which, while providing a great deal of security, has done so at the cost of considerable economic and political freedom.

Not much information is available concerning the distribution of income in the Soviet Union. As would be expected in a fully socialist state, large inherited wealth has been abolished, and the extremes between low and high incomes observed in capitalist economies are not found in the Soviet Union. While personal incomes are more equitably distributed in the Soviet Union than in the United States and other capitalist countries, considerable differences still exist between top and bottom incomes in the Soviet Union, as revealed by the income statistics in Table 15-13. The span between the lowest and the highest incomes in this unspecified region of the Soviet Union in 1971 was 1:3.5 (600 to 2,100 rubles). Approximately two-thirds of the family members had annual incomes of over 600 rubles. Since 600 rubles per year is regarded as a basic living minimum, almost one-third of these family members were below the poverty level. Various studies of income distribution in the Soviet Union indicate that from 30 to 40 percent of workers are classified as poor by Soviet standards. While incomes may be more equitably distributed in the Soviet Union than in the Western

Table 15-13

Annual Per Capita Family Incomes in the U.S.S.R., 1971[1]

Annual income in rubles per person	Percentage of total members
Less than 600	32.6
601-900	31.2
901-1,200	17.7
1,201-1,500	9.1
1,501-2,100	7.1
More than 2,100	2.3
Total members	100.0

[1] In an unspecified region of the U.S.S.R.

Source: Zev Katz, "Insights from Emigrés and Sociological Studies on the Soviet Economy," *Soviet Economic Prospects for the Seventies*, 1973, p. 110.

---

ductivity was on the average one-third of American industrial labor productivity. See Abram Bergson, "Comparative Productivity and Efficiency in the Soviet Union and the United States," in Alexander Eckstein (ed.), *Comparison of Economic Systems*, Berkeley: University of California Press, 1971, pp. 180-181; and Gertrude Schroeder, "Soviet Industrial Labor Productivity," *Dimensions of Soviet Economic Power*, 1962, pp. 152-155.

capitalist countries, it is a low general income level that is equitably shared in the Soviet Union.

Soviet economic growth, like growth in the Western capitalist countries, has been accompanied by a serious problem of environmental deterioration. It has sometimes been asserted that environmental deterioration is a product of the capitalist system, and that no such problem would appear in a planned socialist economy because the planners would take full account of the social costs of rapid economic growth. This was the official Soviet position on this issue, which prevented the Soviet government from recognizing the seriousness of the environmental problem in the Soviet Union until recently.[65] Pollution was the main issue before a full session of the U.S.S.R. Supreme Soviet for the first time in 1972. Official recognition is now given to the facts that many lakes and rivers, such as Lake Baikal and the Volga River, are seriously polluted by the industrial wastes of state enterprises; that excessive irrigation has lowered the levels of the Aral and Caspian Seas to a dangerous point; and that the major industrial cities suffer from serious air pollution.

A number of factors have contributed to environmental deterioration in the Soviet Union. According to the Marxian interpretation, labor is the only source of value; the air, water, and land are treated as free goods. This approach, which led the Soviets to place no charges on the use of water and mineral resources, resulted in a wasteful use of these natural resources, with little regard for the risk of their exhaustion. In recent years, some economists have advocated the imposition of rental or royalty charges on all natural resources in order to use them as efficiently as possible and to conserve their supply. Soviet planners have contributed to the environmental problem by failing to insist that state enterprises make adequate allowances for the social costs of production in the setting of prices. Enterprise managers have been reluctant to take account of the social costs of their production because such an accounting would increase costs and lower profits. Part of the problem lies in the fact that in the Soviet Union, as elsewhere, it is difficult to measure social costs for pricing purposes. Furthermore, the Soviet planners are growth oriented and are very reluctant to devote investment to the production of equipment for purification and treatment purposes. All such investment detracts from rather than adds to total national output.

The Soviet Union has the same environmental problem as the United States and other capitalist nations because environmental deterioration is a consequence of the process of industrialization that is common to all types of economic systems.[66] In any large industrial system, the individual enterprises, whether privately or publicly owned, are not in a position to take account of all the externalities that are produced. Consequently, governments in all types of economic systems are called upon to deal with externalities or social costs that are communal responsibilities. Industrialization has also resulted in the sale of products that lead to serious problems of solid waste disposal. It has been accompanied by an urbanization that has led to congestion and the destruction of many urban amenities. Solutions to the problem of coping with environmental deterioration include setting up a super-coordinating body, upgrading antipollution technology and research, recycling various kinds of wastes, in-

[65] Marshall I. Goldman, "Pollution Comes to the U.S.S.R.," *Soviet Economic Prospects for the Seventies*, 1973, pp. 56-70.

[66] This thesis is developed in Erik Dahmén, "Environmental Control and Economic Systems," Peter Bohm and Allen V. Kneese (eds.), *The Economics of Environment*, New York: Macmillan, 1971, pp. 44-52; and Marshall I. Goldman, "The Convergence of Environmental Disruption," *Science*, Vol. 170, No. 3953, Oct. 2, 1970, pp. 37-82.

cluding sewage, setting limits to the extent to which the environment can be damaged, charging fees for environmental damages, and cooperating with other nations to preserve the world environment. There are no ideological barriers to a more effective prevention of environmental disruption. The Soviet Union, the United States, and other countries have a long way to go before their natural and social environments are adequately protected.

The limitations of the Soviet economy arise chiefly from its authoritarian nature. The Soviet people do not enjoy many of the political liberties found in the Western democracies. Associated with this lack of political freedom is the absence of economic, cultural, and scientific freedom. Although Soviet citizens do have some consumer and occupational freedom, they do not have much influence on national goals and priorities since these are largely determined by the Politburo. Obviously, the Soviet Union does not have a consumer-oriented economy.

Furthermore, literature and the arts are forced into a mold that serves the propagandistic purposes of the party more than the self-expression of the people. Prominent writers are kept from publishing their work or are expelled from the country. Outstanding artists and others defect from the Soviet Union in order to find free expression for their art. Even science suffers from the lack of intellectual freedom. While Soviet scientists have made much progress in spite of the lack of political and cultural freedom, there is some question as to the ability of these scientists to work effectively in the long run in an authoritarian society. Already a number of outstanding Soviet scientists have ceased to work at their scientific specialty or have migrated to the West. It may be difficult for the Soviet Union to close the technological gap between it and the West as long as the freedoms that are taken for granted in the West are denied to Soviet citizens.

The Soviet Union is now at a difficult point in its political and economic development, and appears to be uncertain as to what path to follow with respect to the question of personal freedoms. The "thaw" of the Khrushchev years marked a considerable advance in enlarging the freedoms of the Soviet people. Although there has been a reversal of the thaw to some extent since 1964, there has been no going back to the despotism of the Stalin era. The question now before the Soviet leaders is not freedom or no freedom, but how much freedom for the Soviet people. It is now widely admitted in the Soviet Union that its economy will not function well without considerable consumer and occupational freedom. The basic question today is how much more freedom of all kinds will be needed in order that the Soviet economy may reach the level of efficiency sought by the nation's planners.

Selected Bibliography

ANTROPOV, N. *The Role of Trade Unions in the State Economic and Cultural Life of the U.S.S.R., 1917–1959.* Trade Union Publishing House, Moscow, 1960.

BERLINER, JOSEPH. *Factory and Manager in the USSR.* Harvard University Press, Cambridge, 1957.

BROWN, EMILY CLARK. *Soviet Trade Unions and Labor Relations.* Harvard University Press, Cambridge, 1966.

DODGE, NORTON T. *Women in the Soviet Economy.* Johns Hopkins Press, Baltimore, 1966.

———. *Analysis of the USSR's 24th Party Congress and 9th Five-Year Plan.* Cremona Foundation, Mechanicsville, Maryland, 1971.

GOLDMAN, MARSHALL I. *Soviet Marketing, Distribution in a Controlled Economy.* Free Press and Collier-Macmillan, Glencoe, Ill., 1963.

GRANICK, DAVID. *The Red Executive.* Doubleday and Co., Garden City, New York, 1960.

———. *Managerial Comparisons of Four Developed Countries.* M.I.T. Press, Cambridge, 1972.

GREGORY, PAUL R., and ROBERT C. STUART. *Soviet Economic Structure and Performance.* Harper & Row, New York, 1974.

HOLZMAN, FRANKLYN D. *Foreign Trade under Central Planning.* Harvard University Press, Cambridge, 1974.

JACKSON, DOUGLAS, ed. *Agrarian Policies and Problems in Communist and Non-Communist Countries.* University of Washington Press, Seattle, 1971.

KASER, MICHAEL. *Soviet Economics.* George Weidenfeld and Nicolson, London, 1970.

KIRSCH, LEONARD J. *Soviet Wages: Changes in Administration and Structure since 1956.* M.I.T. Press, Cambridge, 1972.

LAIRD, ROY D., and EDWARD L. CROWLEY, eds. *Soviet Agriculture: The Permanent Crisis.* Praeger Publishers, New York, 1965.

LIBERMAN, E. G. *Economic Methods and the Effectiveness of Production.* International Arts and Sciences Press, White Plains, New York, 1971.

MILLAR, JAMES R., ed. *The Soviet Rural Community.* University of Illinois Press, Urbana, Ill., 1971.

MILLER, ROBERT F. *One Hundred Thousand Tractors, The MTS and the Development of Controls in Soviet Agriculture.* Harvard University Press, Cambridge, 1970.

NIMITZ, NANCY. *Agriculture under Khrushchev: The Lean Years.* Rand Corporation, Santa Monica, Calif., 1965.

NOVOSTI PRESS AGENCY PUBLISHING HOUSE. *The Soviet Economic Reform, Main Features and Aims.* Moscow, 1966.

RICHMAN, BARRY M. *Soviet Management.* Prentice-Hall, Inc., Englewood Cliffs, N.J. 1965.

SHARPE, MYRON E., ed. *The Liberman Discussion: A New Phase in Soviet Economic Thought.* International Arts and Sciences Press, White Plains, New York, 1966.

STRAUSS, ERICH. *Soviet Agriculture in Perspective.* George Allen and Unwin, London, 1969.

STUART, ROBERT C. *The Collective Farm in Soviet Agriculture.* D. C. Heath and Co., Lexington, Mass., 1972.

VOLIN, LAZAR. *A Century of Russian Agriculture.* Harvard University Press, Cambridge, 1970.

WÄDEKIN, KARL-EUGEN. *The Private Sector in Soviet Agriculture.* University of California Press, Berkeley, 1973.

YEFIMOV, A. *Soviet Industry.* Progress Publishers, Moscow, 1968.

ZALESKI, EUGENE. *Planning Reforms in the Soviet Union, 1962–1966.* University of North Carolina Press, Chapel Hill, 1967.

Chapter 16
The Communist Economies of the Comecon Bloc

The Comecon Bloc

The economies of Eastern Europe follow the model set by the Soviet Union. When they were brought under the Soviet wing after the Second World War, they uniformly adopted the type of highly centralized, authoritarian, planned economy that had been established by Stalin in his country. From 1945 to 1953, with the exception of Yugoslavia, which broke away from Soviet domination in 1948, all the Eastern European countries became parts of the monolithic communism that had Moscow as its center. Stalin envisaged the Eastern European countries as satellites supplying the Soviet Union with raw materials and taking Soviet finished products in return. Some industrial specialization was to be permitted in Czechoslovakia, which was highly industrialized before 1945, and in East Germany, which possessed a highly skilled work population; but Poland, Hungary, Romania, Bulgaria, Yugoslavia, and Albania were to remain largely sources of food, animal feedstuffs, oil, minerals, and other extractive products. Under these arrangements the Eastern European countries were to be welded into one large subeconomy closely tied both economically and politically to the Soviet Union. They were also to function as a buffer zone between the Soviet Union and the capitalist nations of the West.

Stalin's monocentric view of communism dominated Eastern Europe until his death in 1953. Since that time, Stalin's approach to communism has been replaced by a polycentric approach, which has weakened Moscow as the world's communist center and has nourished a number of different national paths to communism. At the same time that Moscow's dominance of the Comecon bloc has been reduced, two other trends, centrifugal in character, have contributed to the state of flux now found in Eastern Europe.[1] The first centrifugal trend found its roots in the strong nationalistic feelings long characteristic of the Eastern European countries. These feelings, suppressed by Stalin just as were the nationalistic urges of the many Soviet republics, fed the desire of the Eastern European countries to become industrialized states rather than mere suppliers of raw materials. In the 1950s and 1960s this powerful nationalist drive resulted in the satellite countries' shifting the emphasis in their national plans from producing raw materials to producing finished goods, which were largely exported to the Soviet Union and which eventually became something of a glut in the intrabloc markets.

The second centrifugal trend that weakened Moscow's hold on the Comecon countries after 1953 was the continuing association of these countries with Western Europe. Before the communizing of Eastern Europe in the late 1940s, the Comecon countries had strong cultural and commercial ties with West Germany, France, the United Kingdom, and other Western European countries. Although these ties were weakened during Stalin's regime under his program for Marxist-Leninist ideological purity, the relations between the Comecon countries and the West never reached the low level of the relations between the Soviet Union and the West. The Comecon countries in the 1940s and 1950s never became as autarkic as the Soviet Union. Their interest in the West was stimulated in the 1960s by the failure of the Soviet Union to reach the technological level of the West. This meant that the Comecon countries had to develop their trade with Western Europe if they were to import the advanced machinery and technical know-how of the Western nations. As long as they were tied to the Soviet Union, they would suffer from the same technological gap experienced by the Soviets.

Today the communist countries of Eastern Europe are in a state of flux. In the 1950s and early 1960s, they found the Soviet command economy to be an obstacle to their further economic and social development. They then turned to constructing economies that would be more efficient and better able to continue improving the people's standard of living. Yugoslavia is held up as an example of how successful a decentralized socialist economy can be in raising its economic growth rate, enlarging personal freedoms, and increasing the nation's standard of living. Reform movements in Poland and Hungary in 1956 and in Czechoslovakia in 1968 demonstrated the dissatisfaction with the imported Soviet command economy. The economic reform movement, which affected all the Eastern European countries except Albania, while not equally successful in all these nations, has nevertheless left its mark on the Comecon economies, and has placed some of them ahead of the Soviet Union in the task of restructuring the Soviet economic model. The détente between the Soviet Union and the United States should strengthen the pro-West proclivities of many of the Comecon countries. If the détente helps to close the technological gap between the Soviet Union and the United States, the Comecon countries will indirectly benefit from trade of a higher quality between them and the Soviet Union. These countries may also be encouraged to

---

[1] "Comecon" is the abbreviation for the Council of Mutual Economic Assistance, which was established as a common market for the Soviet Union and Eastern European countries in 1949. Comecon is also abbreviated CMEA or CEMA. Today the Comecon countries include the Soviet Union, East Germany, Poland, Czechoslovakia, Hungary, Romania, and Bulgaria. Yugoslavia never became a member of the Comecon bloc, and Albania now supports the People's Republic of China. For a discussion of the economic basis of the Comecon bloc, see Michael Kaser, *COMECON, Integration Problems of the Planned Economies*, 2nd ed. London: Oxford University Press, 1967; and Frederic L. Pryor, *The Communist Foreign Trade System*, Cambridge, Mass.: MIT Press, 1963.

develop closer ties of their own with Western nations.

The Soviet Union will, nevertheless, continue to hold a dominant position in the Comecon bloc for a long time to come. The Comecon bloc is different from the European Economic Community, because no single country can dominate the members of the latter. In the Comecon bloc, achieving higher levels of economic efficiency and intrabloc integration depends very much upon the views of the Soviet leaders with respect to these economic goals. Since the Soviet Union has been slower than a number of the Comecon countries in pushing the reforms that lead to greater efficiency, and also since foreign trade means much less to the Soviet Union than to the Comecon countries, the Soviet Union will probably continue to be an obstacle to the further marketization and integration of the Comecon countries. The adoption of the Brezhnev Doctrine, proclaiming Soviet dominance in the Comecon bloc, in 1968 is clear evidence that the Soviet Union intends to maintain a close surveillance over the economic and political development of the Comecon countries.

The six Eastern European communist countries (East Germany, Czechoslovakia, Poland, Hungary, Romania, and Bulgaria) are well endowed with agricultural resources, but are deficient in industrial raw materials. They have considerable reserves of coal, much of it of low quality, and limited supplies of iron ore and other metals. Only Romania is an important source of oil and natural gas. The Soviet Union is the main source of imported industrial raw materials. It provides the Comecon countries with 75 to 90 percent of their imports of iron ore, pig iron, lumber, and wheat and over 50 percent of their imports of coal, coke, and cotton. The total GNP of the six Comecon countries is one-sixth of the American GNP and one-third of the Soviet GNP. As the statistics in Table 16-1 show, there are wide variations in per capita GNP among the Comecon countries. Per capita GNP in Czechoslovakia and East Germany exceeds that of the Soviet Union and is much above per capita GNP in Hungary, Poland, Romania, and Bulgaria. Comparative studies of consumption levels show that in Czechoslovakia, the industrial hub of the Comecon bloc, consumers are significantly better off than in the Soviet Union and the other Comecon countries.[2] However, Czechoslovakian consumers are much less well off than consumers in the industrialized Western European countries. Per capita GNP levels in Czechoslovakia and East Germany are two-thirds to three-fourths of these levels in West Germany and France. Poland, Bulgaria, and Romania are below Italy but above Greece and Spain.

The Eastern European policy on personal consumption first followed the Soviet policy of the 1930s and 1940s, which was calculated to hasten the "building of socialism" by curbing consumption and expanding investment. After the East German riots in 1953 and the political upheavals in Poland and Hungary in 1956, the Eastern European governments began to pay more attention to consumer welfare. Since 1955, per capita consumption in Eastern Europe has increased as fast as GNP; direct rationing of consumer goods has decreased; and more attention has been given to consumer preferences. As in the Soviet Union, in the Comecon countries medical services and education are free, housing rents are fixed below maintenance and amortization costs, and the prices of basic foodstuffs and public services are relatively low. The prices of consumer durables and quality products are very high, even by Western European standards. Like the Soviet Union, the six

---

[2] Terence E. Byrne, "Levels of Consumption in Eastern Europe," Joint Economic Committee, *Economic Developments in Countries of Eastern Europe*, Washington, D.C., 1970, pp. 297–315.

Table 16-1
Total and per Capita GNP in the United States, the Soviet Union, and the Comecon Countries, 1973

	Total GNP[1] (billion U.S. dollars)	Per capita GNP	Percent of Soviet per capita GNP
United States	1,151.0	$6,200	305
Soviet Union	597.6	2,030	100
Czechoslovakia	40.8	2,870	142
East Germany	43.3	3,000	148
Hungary	19.3	1,850	91
Poland	54.2	2,090	103
Bulgaria	13.8	1,590	78
Romania	32.9	—	—

[1] In 1972.

Sources: Thad P. Alton, "Economic Growth and Resource Allocation in Eastern Europe," *Reorientation and Commercial Relations of the Economies of Eastern Europe,* 1974, p. 268; and World Bank, *World Bank Atlas,* 1975, p. 7.

Eastern European bloc countries have abandoned the policy of encouraging communal consumption rather than consumption by the individual.

In the 1950s, it was popular in communist circles to propose the development of the "socialist man [or woman]" by producing goods and services for communal rather than personal use. Communal dining and child care and public transportation were to take the place of personal services and the personal ownership of automobiles. Efforts to promote communal consumption have now been given up in the Comecon countries, as in the Soviet Union, in favor of incentive systems that emphasize personal consumption and personal ownership.[3] Household appliances and automobiles are now being made available to consumers in increasing volume. Television sets, refrigerators, and automobiles, which were extremely scarce in the 1950s, are now much more widely available.

The Structure and Performance of the Comecon Bloc

In the years since the end of the Second World War the Comecon countries have followed the same general pattern of rapid industrialization.[4] In all these countries, the

[3] Communal dining and caring for children are to be distinguished from social consumption, which includes government services, such as education, public health, and police protection. While efforts to expand communal consumption have now been largely ended, social consumption in the form of government services continues to be an important and large part of total consumption in the Soviet Union.

[4] The postwar East European industrialization has paralleled that of the Soviet Union. This similarity cannot be explained by referring to similarities in the level of development of these countries. Instead, it is to be attributed in large part to the ideological preferences of the party leaders in these countries, who have all stressed the importance of stimulating heavy industry, curbing total consumption, and underutilizing the foreign trade potential of the entire Comecon bloc. For a comparative analysis of the industrialization patterns of this bloc and Western countries, see Paul Gregory, *Socialist and Nonsocialist Industrialization Patterns,* New York: Praeger, 1970.

contribution of agriculture to the Gross National Product has declined very considerably, while industry, construction, transport, and communications have increased their contributions very significantly. In the period 1937-1967, industry in Czechoslovakia increased its contribution to GNP from 30.6 to 45 percent, while the agricultural sector's contribution fell from 28.9 to 12.4 percent.[5] In a less developed country like Bulgaria, industry and handicrafts in 1950 accounted for only 15.9 percent of GNP, while agriculture and forestry accounted for 41.3 percent. By 1972, the contribution of industry and handicrafts in Bulgaria had increased to 39 percent, and the contribution of agriculture and forestry had fallen to 21.1 percent.

Table 16-2 shows the distribution of employment in the various sectors of the Comecon countries. East Germany and Czechoslovakia are highly industrialized and have relatively small agricultural sectors. The Soviet Union, while having a large industrial sector, also has a large agricultural sector. Poland, Bulgaria, and Romania are much less industrialized and have large agricultural sectors.

[5] Thad P. Alton, "Economic Growth and Resource Allocation in Eastern Europe," Joint Economic Committee, *Reorientation and Commercial Relations of the Economies of Eastern Europe*, Washington, D.C., 1974, p. 256.

The contrast between Czechoslovakia and Romania is quite striking, with one-half of Czechoslovakia's work force finding employment in industry whereas only one-fifth of Romania's work force has employment in this sector.

Table 16-3 shows the changes in the origins of GNP in Czechoslovakia and Hungary during the years 1950-1972. While industry, construction, transportation, and communications expanded, the relative contributions of agriculture and housing declined, and trade and other services together remained in about the same relative position.

In the years 1960-1968 the Comecon countries had high GNP per capita growth rates which averaged from 5 to 6 percent a year. In the second half of the 1960s and the early 1970s, as Table 16-4 shows, GNP per capita growth rates in the Comecon countries fell quite considerably with a number of them having an annual average GNP per capita growth rate between 2.5 and 3 percent. It was this trend in economic growth rates in the latter part of the 1960s and early 1970s that led the Comecon countries to seek ways of improving the efficiency of their economic systems.

The statistics in Table 16-5 show that after 1950 there was a decline in the share of GNP

Table 16-2

Distribution of Employment in the Comecon Countries by Sectors, Latest Census or Estimate

Country	Agriculture	Industry	Services
East Germany	12.6	48.8	38.6
Czechoslovakia	16.4	48.0	35.6
Soviet Union	26.3	45.1	28.6
Hungary	24.5	43.6	31.9
Poland	38.6	34.4	27.0
Bulgaria	44.3	26.4	29.3
Romania	56.8	19.4	23.8

Sources: The national statistics of the seven countries.

Table 16-3
Composition of Gross National Product by Industrial Origin in Czechoslovakia and Hungary, 1950 and 1972 (in Constant Prices)

	Czechoslovakia		Hungary	
	1950	1972	1950	1972
Industry and handicrafts	34.8	47.7	25.3	37.3
Agriculture and forestry	23.9	11.7	29.7	17.1
Construction	6.7	7.2	6.2	8.7
Transport and communications	7.3	12.8	9.5	11.5
Trade	7.1	8.3	6.2	9.5
Housing	10.0	4.8	12.0	6.1
Government and other services	10.2	7.5	11.1	9.8
Total Gross National Product	100.0	100.0	100.0	100.0

Source: Thad P. Alton, "Economic Growth and Resource Allocation in Eastern Europe," *Reorientation and Commercial Relations of the Economies of Eastern Europe*, 1974, p. 256.

assigned to personal and public consumption and an increase in the share allotted to investment in the Comecon countries. At present, investment takes up around 40 percent of their GNP. Like the Soviet Union, the Comecon countries have achieved economic growth by using large inputs of labor and capital rather than by improving labor and capital productivity. Labor has been shifted from agriculture and the handicraft industries, while at the same time the growth of consumption has been held down. The growth strategy of the Comecon countries has led them into the same problems encountered by the Soviet

Table 16-4
GNP per Capita at Market Prices in 1973 and the GNP per Capita Annual Growth Rate, 1961-1968 and 1965-1973, in the Comecon Countries

Country	1973 GNP per capita amount (U.S. dollars)	GNP per capita growth rate (%) 1961-1968	GNP per capita growth rate (%) 1965-1973
East Germany	3,000	4.0	2.9
Czechoslovakia	2,870	3.7	2.6
Poland	2,090	5.5	4.2
Soviet Union	2,030	5.8	3.5
Hungary	1,850	5.2	2.7
Bulgaria	1,590	6.7	3.6
Romania	—	—	—

Source: World Bank, *World Bank Atlas*, 1970 and 1975.

Table 16–5
Gross National Product by End Uses in Czechoslovakia and Hungary in 1950 and 1967 (Percent of Total in Constant Prices)

	Czechoslovakia		Hungary	
	1950	1967	1950	1967
Personal consumption	52.7	44.1	55.8	50.6
Public consumption	17.4	14.6	11.1	9.2
Gross investment	29.9	41.3	33.1	40.2
Total GNP	100.0	100.0	100.0	100.0

Source: Thad P. Alton, "Economic Structure and Growth in Eastern Europe," *Economic Developments in Countries of Eastern Europe*, 1970, p. 59.

Union. Improvements in labor productivity have been negated by declines in the productivity of capital.[6] In all the Comecon countries except Czechoslovakia, capital productivity declined during the years 1960–1972. Much of the fixed capital is obsolete and should be eliminated by higher rates of scrapping.

What the Comecon countries needed in the 1960s was a new growth strategy that would shift attention from extensive growth to intensive growth. This was the same growth problem that had surfaced in the Soviet Union during the 1960s. Instead of stressing large infusions of labor and capital to achieve growth, the Comecon countries in the 1960s turned to methods of increasing the internal efficiency of the planning system and of enterprise management. Increasingly after 1960, more attention was paid to reforming the planning and management systems in order to raise the levels of both labor and capital productivity. What brought the interest in economic reform to a head in the early 1960s was the economic stagnation that appeared in Czechoslovakia, Poland, and East Germany. During the years 1960–1965, the average annual rate of growth of per capita GNP in Czechoslovakia was 1.3 percent, in Poland 2.8 percent, and East Germany 3.1 percent, while much higher growth rates were achieved in Bulgaria, Romania, and the Soviet Union.

The East and West of Europe since World War II have belonged to different worlds. Western Europe has been greatly influenced by the United States, and in adjusting to technological change has achieved rising levels of industrial efficiency. Eastern Europe, under Soviet influence, has suffered from a restrictive command economy and a lagging industrial technology. Before World War II, per capita output and efficiency were about the same in East as in West Germany, and not very different in Czechoslovakia and France or Belgium. Today, Czechoslovakia and East Germany are now operating with factor productivity about three-fifths of that of French and West German industry. The Eastern European countries have in some years achieved high rates of industrial growth but in an inefficient and costly manner.

The evidence suggests that the Eastern European countries are not "catching up" with Western Europe and are not closing the technological gap. In the heavy industries, the Eastern European countries use much more fuel and steel than do West Germany, Belgium, and Luxembourg to produce the same

---

[6] Laszlo Czerjak, "Industrial Structure, Growth and Productivity in Eastern Europe," Joint Economic Committee, *Economic Developments in Countries of Eastern Europe*, Washington, D.C., 1970, pp. 438–443.

amount of machinery and equipment. The industrial exports of Eastern Europe have become less competitive in Western markets, and the terms of trade have become increasingly unfavorable to the Eastern European countries. Inventory costs in the Comecon countries are higher than in Western Europe because of the inferior output mix and inefficient methods of enterprise operation. Capital and labor productivity are also much lower in the Comecon countries. A comparative study in 1967 showed that labor productivity in Czechoslovakia, East Germany, Hungary, and Poland averaged only 50 percent of labor productivity in West Germany.[7] Many Western analysts conclude that the Comecon countries have a long way to go and many major economic and political obstacles to overcome before they can catch up with Western Europe.

The Progress of Economic Reform in the Comecon Bloc

The economic reform movement in Eastern Europe has followed no single plan.[8] This movement in the six Comecon countries reflects differences in resource endowments, in reliance on the Soviet Union, in stage of industrial development, in historical background, and in quality of leadership. Among the Comecon countries, the three pacesetters in economic reform are Poland, Czechoslovakia, and Hungary. East Germany has not deviated far from the Stalinist economic model; and Romania and Bulgaria, although opening the doors to the discussion of much-needed economic reforms, have lacked the will to carry through these reforms, and so have been slow to reform their command economy. Among the reform pacesetters, Hungary has been outstanding, today ranking with Yugoslavia as a case of "market socialism." In both Poland and Czechoslovakia, the advanced blueprints for market socialism failed to develop permanent roots. In Poland, the bureaucratic Communist hardliners were able to abort the very liberal reform program that had been drawn up by the left wing of the Polish Communist party in 1956. In Czechoslovakia, the Soviet occupation of August 1968 put an end to the advanced economic reform program that in some respects went further than the Yugoslav experiment in the marketization of the command economy.

Poland pioneered in the 1950s with its blueprint for the Polish Economic Model. This blueprint provided for a far-reaching decentralization of the planning system and full independence of action for state enterprises.[9] These enterprises were to be self-governing organizations whose economic performance was to be measured by their profitability. Workers' councils, which were to be established in all state enterprises, would give the workers full rights of comanagement. State enterprises were to be largely self-financing;

[7] Edwin M. Snell, "Economic Efficiency in Eastern Europe," *Economic Developments in Countries of Eastern Europe*, 1970, p. 267.

[8] There is an extensive literature on the subject of East European economic reforms. Useful in this connection are the two studies of the Joint Economic Committee, *Economic Developments in Countries of Eastern Europe*, 1970, and *Reorientation and Commercial Relations of the Economies of Eastern Europe*, 1974. Also Michael Gamarnikow, *Economic Reforms in Eastern Europe*, Detroit: Wayne State University Press, 1968; Radoslav Selucky, *Economic Reforms in Eastern Europe*, New York: Praeger Publishers, 1972; and Morris Bornstein (ed.), *Plan and Market, Economic Reform in Eastern Europe*, New Haven: Yale University Press, 1973.

[9] For economic developments in Poland, see George R. Feiwel, *Poland's Industrialization Policy: A Current Analysis*, Vols. I and II, New York: Praeger, 1971; *The Economics of a Socialist Enterprise, A Case Study of the Polish Firm*, New York: Frederick A. Praeger, 1965; and "Economic Reform in Poland," *New Currents in Soviet-Type Economies*, Scranton: International Textbook Co., 1968; and John M. Montias, *Central Planning In Poland*, New Haven: Yale University Press, 1962.

all state subsidized production and distribution were to be eliminated; wage rates were to be tied to productivity; and prices were to be brought into line with real costs of production. The production plans of the industrial enterprises were to be based on detailed market analysis. The 1956 Polish blueprint for economic reform relied upon the free forces of the market mechanism to keep prices, production costs, and personal incomes in equilibrium. All of these reforms were designed to bring an end to the centralized command economy which had been established in Poland after the Second World War. When the orthodox communist bureaucrats returned to power in 1959, they recentralized the planning system, abolished the workers' councils, and abandoned wage and price reforms.

The second blueprint for economic reform, which was developed in 1964, again favored the more liberal elements in the Polish Communist party. This new reform program proposed a return to a decentralized planning system and an enlargement of the area of independent action for industrial enterprises. Although these enterprises are now free to make decisions with respect to self-investment, wage rates, employment, and internal organization, the central planners can still tell producing enterprises what and how much to produce. In 1969, twenty-eight large-scale industrial conglomerates were organized in the producer-goods industries to act as a buffer between the state enterprises and the central ministries. Similar industrial conglomerates or associations have been established in the consumer-goods industries. At present, the distribution of powers in this tri-level organization of the Polish economy is not clear. Although the Polish reform program is still highly experimental, evidently some progress has been made in decentralizing the economy and freeing enterprise management from many of the direct controls of the old command economy. In terms of economic reform, the Polish economy today lies between the still highly centralized East German economy and the decentralized and market-oriented Hungarian economy.

The Czechoslovakian Economic Reforms

The Czechoslovakian economic reform program was adopted in 1967–1968 in response to the economic stagnation that had occurred during the 1961–1965 plan period.[10] Whereas an annual economic growth rate of 7 percent had been achieved in the plan period 1956–1960, this rate fell to 1.8 percent in the years 1961–1965. Ota Sik and other Czechoslovakian economists attributed the poor performance of the economy to the stultifying effects of the outmoded Stalinist command economy. They introduced a reform program in 1967 that, if it had been successfully applied in practice, would have gone beyond the Yugoslav experiment in market socialism, and would have established in Czechoslovakia a truly socialist democracy.[11] The Czechoslovak economic reform program was a combination of central macroeconomic planning and industrial enterprise autonomy in microeconomic decision making. Under the decentralization program, the central government, ministries, and planning authorities were to

[10] For a survey of the course of economic reforms in Czechoslovakia, see George R. Feiwel, *New Economic Patterns in Czechoslovakia*, New York: Praeger, 1968; and "Economic Reforms in Czechoslovakia" in *New Currents in Soviet-Type Economies*, pp. 465–519. See also Ota Sik, *Czechoslovakia: The Bureaucratic Economy*, White Plains, N.Y.: International Arts and Sciences Press, 1972.

[11] The theoretical foundation of Sik's reform program is presented in Ota Sik, *Plan and Market under Socialism*, White Plains, N.Y.: International Arts and Sciences Press, 1967. The Czechoslovak economic reform program was never published, but a summary of it appears in Radoslav Selucky, *op. cit.*, pp. 86–87.

deal only with macroeconomic matters relating to growth rates, the ratio between total consumption and investment, structural changes in industry, sector development, technological progress, and long-term economic trends. The direct control of enterprises by central ministries was to be abolished, and enterprises were to enjoy autonomy in most of their operations. They were to be free to determine their own production plans, employment needs, wage scales, product mix, and prices for certain categories of consumer goods. These enterprises were to operate according to strict cost accounting; the profit motive was to guide their operations; and workers were to share the enterprise's profitability through a system of material incentives. Industrial associations or trusts, which enterprises could join voluntarily, were to provide services that were not available to individual enterprises. These associations were to carry on research and development, to uncover sources of raw materials, and to secure investment fund allocations for the individual enterprises from the State Bank. Unlike in East Germany, where the industrial associations in effect absorbed the state enterprises, in Czechoslovakia these associations were to be dominated by the member enterprises.

Novel features of the Czechoslovak reform program related to workers' councils and trade unions. The workers' councils that were established in 1968 were the foundation for what the reform program described as "self-management."[12] Under this arrangement, the workers chose their own managers and in effect became comanagers. Also, the Czechoslovak reform program restored the trade unions as truly independent institutions that would defend the rights of individual workers. The trade unions were no longer to be schools of communism and company unions. In the new autonomous state enterprises, three separate economic forces were to operate: the workers' councils, the management, and the trade unions.

An important feature of the 1968 Czechoslovakian economic reform was the reform of prices. Major price reforms were calculated to bring prices closer to full or real costs by taking account of adequate depreciation write-offs, interest charges on invested capital, capital levies on surplus profits, and allowance for reasonable profit margins. The price reform provided for a three-pronged pricing system of fixed, flexible, and free prices. Fixed prices were applied by the government to all essential raw materials, producer goods, and basic consumer goods. Flexible or limited movement prices, which could fluctuate between lower and upper limits set by the central planning authorities, were determined for less essential commodities and services. Free-market prices, which were determined by supply and demand and competition between state enterprises, applied to selected consumer goods. The plan was to upgrade the nonfree prices to the free-price category as soon as supply and demand permitted. The reformers hoped eventually to achieve a full operation of the market mechanism in which all prices would be free.

Other features of the Czechoslovakia reform program included diverse forms of property ownership and the elimination of the state monopoly of foreign trade. State ownership was to continue in all basic industries, banking, and transportation. In the mass consumption industries, there were to be self-administered industrial enterprises, subject to

[12] Much argument arose concerning the proper functions of workers' councils. The question was whether these councils were to be "organs of social control," with only consultative functions, or "enterpreneurial organs" that made basic decisions in matters of enterprise policy. For a discussion of these and related matters, see Vaclav Holesovsky, "Planning and Market in the Czechoslovak Reform," *Plan and Market*, pp. 329-338.

some macroeconomic controls by the central government, but enjoying autonomy in most operations. In addition, consumer and producer cooperatives and privately owned enterprises were to be free to compete with the self-administered industrial enterprises. Competition among industrial enterprises, cooperatives, and privately owned enterprises was to be stimulated by opening the Czechoslovakian economy to the competition of world trade. The state monopoly of foreign trade was to be abolished, and industrial enterprises were to be free to carry on importing and exporting. The free convertibility of the Czechoslovakian currency (koruna) into foreign currencies would bring the domestic price system into line with the world price level.

The "Prague Spring" of 1968, when the Czechoslovakian economic reform program was actually put into operation, was followed in August of that year by the Soviet invasion that put an end to much of the reform program. What caused the Soviet occupation was that the reform movement in the spring of 1968 gained a momentum that carried it beyond the limits of even the official reform program. The developments that the Soviet regime could not tolerate were the placing of enterprise control in the hands of the workers' councils, as in Yugoslavia; the transformation of the industrial associations from administrative supervisory organs, as in East Germany, to voluntary bodies performing functions assigned to them by industrial enterprises; and the emergence of free trade unions to represent the workers' interests and not those of the state.

The Soviet Union and many orthodox bureaucrats in the Comecon countries accused Alexander Dubcek and other Czechoslovakian reformists of the crime of "revisionism." These reformists had asserted that economic reform, to be successful, had to be accompanied by political reform. Dubcek and his followers wanted a simultaneous development of more democratic institutions within the existing political system. They did not call for a multiparty political system similar to the political systems of the Western European countries. Instead, they wanted a pluralistic and participatory democracy within the limits of the single Communist party system, which would be in accordance with the principle of socialist pluralism. The monocentric command economy, which had been introduced into Czechoslovakia from the Soviet Union after the Second World War, was based on the principle of socialist monism. This principle asserted that no conflict of interests among workers, managers, farmers, and government officials could exist in a Marxist society. There could only be a unity of interests. Since the Czechoslovakian reformers saw the possibility of a conflict between the interests of the state and the workers and between the managers and the workers, they recommended establishing workers' councils and free trade unions to protect the interests of the workers. The substitution of a conflict of interests for a unity of interests was regarded by orthodox Czechoslovakian bureaucrats as an unacceptable revision of Marxism-Leninism.

The Czechoslovakian reformers wanted to move beyond technocratic reforms that would only make economic decision making more efficient, and would only modify the planning and management system so as to improve managerial and worker incentives. Merely rational and pragmatic methods of planning and management, such as were adopted in East Germany, Romania, and Bulgaria, were not enough. What was necessary was a substitution of a humanistic Marxism for the dehumanized Marxism that had been developed in and exported from the Soviet Union since the late 1920s. The democratic socialism which was the goal of the Czechoslovakian reformers was "socialism with a human face."[13]

The Soviet invasion of August 1968 put an end to the political and economic liberalization that was begun in the Prague Spring. Following this invasion, came a rollback of economic reforms. The preponderant role of the central planners was restored, with the result that the autonomy of the industrial enterprises was greatly restricted and output targets were again imposed on industrial enterprises. The workers' councils were abolished, and enterprise managers assumed control of the day-to-day operations under the close tutelage of the appropriate central ministries. The trade unions lost their independence and returned to their previous role of elevating the state's interests over those of the workers. Wage controls from the center were restored, and prices were frozen. The three-tiered pricing system was suspended, with only a few consumer goods and services being left in the free-price category.

The postoccupation rollback of economic reforms did not return the Czechoslovak economy to the traditional command model of the 1950s. By 1968, the leaders in all the Comecon countries agreed that the inherited command economy needed considerable modification if its performance was to be improved. They were not willing, however, to move along the reform path recommended by Dubcek and his supporters. Since 1968, economic reform in Czechoslovakia has remained in a state of flux as the orthodox hardliners search for a new combination of the command and market economies that will be acceptable to the Soviet Union.

Hungarian Economic Reforms

The Hungarian economic reform program, introduced in 1968 under the slogan of the *New*

[13] Michael Gamarnikow, *op. cit.*, p. 187.

Economic Mechanism has succeeded where the Czechoslovakian economic reform failed.[14] The Hungarian program was adopted not long before the Soviet occupation of Czechoslovakia, and was designed to avoid the difficulties that beset the Czechoslovakian reformers. The very name of the Hungarian program suggested that it was more technological than political in nature. Although the Hungarian party leaders did not adhere to the monolithic concept of the solidaristic Marxian society that was espoused by the Soviet party leaders, they never openly carried their criticism of the Soviet command society so far as to open themselves to the criticism of being Marxian revisionists.

Janos Kadar and his Hungarian associates have successfully pushed the marketization of their former command economy further than any other Eastern European communist country except Yugoslavia. Under the New Economic Mechanism, the decentralization of the planning system included ending the control of industrial enterprises by the central ministries and planning authorities; the elimination of the industrial associations established in 1962–1963 to control the enterprises under their direction; and the abolition of annual planning, under which output and other binding criteria were imposed on the industrial enterprises. Under the New Economic Mechanism, each enterprise sets up its own production plan, which is based on an analysis of market demand. With central allocations of raw materials and producer goods abolished, the enterprise is free to enter contracts for raw materials and other supplies, to

[14] An analysis of the Hungarian economy is presented in Bela A. Balassa, *The Hungarian Experience in Economic Planning,* New Haven: Yale University Press, 1959; I. T. Berend and G. Ranki, *Hungary, A Century of Economic Development,* New York: Barnes and Noble, 1974; and "Economic Reforms in Hungary," in George R. Feiwel, *New Currents in Soviet-Type Economies,* pp. 519–534. See also William F. Robinson, *The Pattern of Reform in Hungary,* New York: Praeger, 1973.

determine its wage structure, and to set selling prices if the product being sold is in the free-price category.

In order to maintain full employment, the Hungarian reformers, unlike the Yugoslav reformers, did not give enterprise managers the right to discharge workers in order to reduce costs.[15] The Hungarian reform program did not follow the syndicalist line of the aborted Czechoslovakian program and so did not establish workers' councils. Instead, the enterprise directors are appointed by the government and are expected to emphasize the profitability of their enterprises' operations. While the Hungarian industrial enterprise has a great deal of autonomy, the power to make decisions concerning output, employment, investment, and credit needs is concentrated in the state-appointed enterprise director and not in the workers.

The managerial power of the Hungarian enterprise directors under the New Economic Mechanism is limited to some extent by a suspending veto given to the trade unions. The enterprise director is by law required to inform the local factory branch of the trade union of his or her various economic decisions. If the trade union objects to these decisions, it may appeal them to the appropriate central ministry but must comply with any decision made by the ministry. In effect, the trade union has no real independence and cannot effectively defend the workers against the enterprise management, as had been planned in Czechoslovakia, where the trade unions were to have become the free advocates of workers' interests.

By the terms of the New Economic Mechanism, the marketization of the Hungarian economy is being advanced in a number of ways. Prices are being reformed so that they reflect the costs of production including interest on invested capital. The three-tiered pricing system has been adopted in anticipation of an eventual free-price economy, where the forces of competition will keep all prices at their true market values. The 1966–1970 five-year plan placed heavy emphasis on the growth of industries serving the domestic consumer and the export markets. Foreign trade has been liberalized in order to increase imports, to increase competition, and to bring domestic prices in line with world prices. The New Economic Mechanism emphasizes the switch from extensive to intensive economic development. The earlier extensive development had concentrated attention on the heavy steel and machinery industries, with little concern for efficiency, full-cost pricing, and comparative international costs. The new intensive development alters the national priorities in favor of a more balanced economic growth, which gives more attention to the production of consumer goods and services and export goods that can compete in the world's trade markets.

The Hungarian industrial enterprises, which are expected to show a profit, have their annual profits divided in the following manner. After the state takes its tax on profits and interest on invested capital, the remaining profits are divided among four funds: the capital amortization, the investment, the profit and loss reserve, and the remuneration funds. The investment fund and loans from the State Bank take the place of the former state budgetary capital grants for investment purposes. Central controls over capital investment are reduced, and enterprise managers have more independence in setting up their own investment programs. The remuneration fund finances an elaborate profit-sharing scheme, which is designed to improve manager and worker incentives. This scheme, however, favors the upper-level management

[15] David Granick, "Variations in Management of the Industrial Enterprise in Socialist Eastern Europe," *Reorientation and Commercial Relations of the Economies of Eastern Europe*, 1974. Job security and full employment are high priority goals in all communist countries.

and is the cause of some dissatisfaction among the blue-collar workers, who tend to feel that the technocrats gain more from the economic reforms than they do. Managers and top assistants may receive salary supplements up to 80 percent of their regular yearly salaries, supervisory personnel and shop foremen up to 50 percent, and workers up to 15 percent of their wages. The wages of workers, however, are guaranteed by the state, whereas only 75 percent of top managerial salaries are guaranteed. The profit-sharing system is biased in favor of the managerial class in order to compensate it for the risks run in producing free-price consumer goods for which there are no state-guaranteed markets.

The Hungarian New Economic Mechanism applied to agriculture as well as industry.[16] Agricultural planning was decentralized by eliminating most of the central controls imposed on the collective farms. The compulsory indicators were reduced to only one, namely, the area sown to grains. Hungary gives more freedom of operation to its collective farms than do the other Comecon countries. Thus far, this reform has focused on improving farm efficiency in order to reduce costs of production. The government has been reluctant to increase procurement prices, because higher farm prices would increase the cost of living and would lead to demands for wage increases. The planning authorities have delayed the reform of farm prices, with the result that the disregard for full costing has led to distortions in land use. Livestock prices have failed to cover all costs, and domestic feed supplies have been inadequate. Hungary, Poland, Romania, and Bulgaria are net exporters of agricultural products, and they rely upon these exports to earn foreign currencies. If farm incomes are to be raised, adequate incentives provided to farm workers, the outflow of farm labor stopped, and agricultural exports increased, much more agricultural price reform must be carried out than has been done so far by Hungary and other Comecon exporters of agricultural products.

During the years 1969–1971, Hungary maintained a high economic growth rate; the rate of growth of agricultural output exceeded that of industry for the first time since the agricultural collectivization drive of the late 1940s; a favorable balance of trade was secured; and full employment was maintained. The supply of consumer goods was increased, and the standard of living of the general population was improved at an unprecedented rate. The number of retailed goods in the free-price category increased sharply. Also, the percentage of total industrial investment financed by the industrial enterprises under the arrangements for their increased independence of operation increased very considerably.

The prosperity of the early years of the reform program came to an end after 1971, when imbalances appeared. In the effort to cope with the pent-up consumer demand that was released after 1968, the consumer-goods industries overinvested in plant and equipment, shortages of skilled labor developed, and an unsustainable increase in the importation of consumer goods occurred. While the marketization of the Hungarian economy promoted rapid economic growth, it did not provide the market correctives that would have prevented the appearance of imbalances and disproportions. To cope with this situation, the Hungarian government after 1971 was forced to return to a system of controls to curb the investment expenditures of industrial enterprises and to restrict the importing of consumer goods. Since 1972, the evidence indicates a falling-off of the momentum of the economic reform.

---

[16] The application of Eastern European economic reforms to Hungary and the other Comecon countries is analyzed in Jerzy F. Karcz, "Agricultural Reform in Eastern Europe," *Plan and Market, Economic Reform in Eastern Europe*, 1973, pp. 207–243.

Two different reactions to economic developments in Hungary since 1971 have appeared. Although there seems to be considerable agreement that the new economic model introduced in 1968 has in general been successful, it is also agreed that this new model is itself in need of some reform if the problems of excessively rapid or unbalanced growth are to be met successfully.[17] The more conservative elements in the government recommend some degree of recentralization of the planning and management system. The advocates of full-fledged economic reform recommend meeting these problems by completing the dismantling of the command economy. This would be done by eliminating the remaining traces of the hierarchical pyramid of planning and management that prevents the enterprise directors from following a consistent market-oriented policy. At present, the general course of economic developments in the Comecon bloc appears to favor the more conservative backers of economic reform in Hungary. Considerable progress has been made in spreading the new economic model to all branches of the Hungarian economy, but no substantive reform of the nation's political system has taken place, and the leading role of the party remains unchallenged. Were the conservative wing of the party to gain control, the future of the New Economic Mechanism would be very uncertain.

Economic Reform in East Germany, Romania, and Bulgaria

Economic reform in East Germany is most aptly described as technocratic rather than market reform.[18] This reform was adopted in East Germany in 1963 at the suggestion of top-level technical experts, who proposed reforms to end the economic stagnation of the early 1960s. In the plan period 1956–1960, East Germany's annual economic growth rate averaged 8.1 percent; but from 1961 to 1963 it was only about 2 percent. The East German reforms of 1963 stemmed from a struggle between the technocrats and the government and party bureaucrats. The technocrats attributed the deficiencies of their economy to the political interference of the party bureaucrats in the day-to-day functioning of the industrial enterprises. The technocrats promised a smooth-running efficient economy in return for a share of the power to manage the economy.

The East German economic reform program that was constructed by the top-level technical experts and adopted in 1963 was imposed on the workers from above. It was mainly an organizational change, involving the establishment of ninety industrial associations patterned after the traditional German cartels. These specialized associations incorporated the industrial enterprises that produced the same or similar goods. The decision-making powers were transferred to these associations from the central ministries above and from the individual enterprises below. Since the technocrats wanted a rational economic system, their reform program provided for a partial marketization of the economy, which, however, was to act only as a supplement to the command economy. The price system was adjusted to reality by revaluing capital assets and insuring realistic depreciation write-offs, by eliminating subsidies to poorly run enterprises, and by imposing interest charges for the use of capital. Gross output was replaced by profitability as a performance indicator;

---

[17] A highly critical interpretation of the Hungarian reform program is given in Barnabas Biiky, "Hungary's NEM on a Treadmill," *Problems of Communism*, 5, Sept–Oct. 1972, XXI, pp. 31–39. A more favorable interpretation is presented in Charles Gati, "The Kadar Mystique," *Problems of Communism*, 3, May–June, 1974, Vol. XXIII, pp. 23–35.

[18] For the distinction between these two types of economic reform, see Radoslav Selucky, "The Alternatives of Reform," *Economic Reforms in Eastern Europe*, 1972, pp. 43–55.

and the individual enterprises were expected to operate according to strict cost accounting, to introduce modern technology, and to improve labor productivity. Material incentives were strengthened and income differentials maintained. All important economic decisions, including the setting of prices, were to be made by the industrial associations or supraenterprises rather than by the individual enterprises. Consequently, no large scope exists for the operation of free market forces. The industrial associations have effectively centralized the East German economy and prevented any substantial marketization of it.

The East German technocrats have succeeded in removing the irrational elements in the Stalinist system borrowed from the Soviet Union. Their aim is not to change the command basis of the economic system, but only to alter the internal makeup of the command economy in order to encourage intensive economic growth. They have introduced a cult of efficiency that has improved the performance of the East German economy with the aid of mathematical methods, automatic computers, and other advanced planning and management techniques. At the same time, no attempt has been made to introduce a participatory, socialist democracy. The technocratic reform has been based upon agreement between government, party bureaucrats, and the top-level experts—an agreement in which the general population has had no say.

Both Bulgaria and Romania have felt the winds of economic reform that have blown over the Comecon bloc since the early 1960s. In both cases, however, economic reform has made less progress than in the other Comecon countries. Bulgaria has been the Soviet Union's most reliable Comecon ally, and has duplicated much of the Soviet reform program. In the early years of its reform program, Bulgaria moved in the direction of plan decentralization and enterprise autonomy. Central ministries were abolished and replaced by industrial or enterprise associations. These associations were expected to serve as a link between the individual enterprises and the central planning authorities. The enterprises were to be operated according to the profit motive, and there was to be no state intervention as long as enterprise plans were in harmony with the central plan. Price reform was to duplicate the Hungarian three-category pricing system.

Although there was considerable theoretical discussion of the desirability of an extensive marketization of the Bulgarian economy, little actual progress was made in this direction. In 1971, a recentralization of planning and management occurred when the individual industrial enterprises were made subordinate to their respective industrial associations, and much of their decision-making power was transferred to these associations. A further recentralization took place in 1973 when the industrial associations were absorbed by superlarge economic complexes or vertical combines that incorporated interrelated industrial branches. Bulgaria began its reform activity with a reform blueprint modeled after Hungary, but ended with a highly recentralized economic system.

Among the Comecon countries Romania is the one in which economic reform has made the least progress.[19] In the early 1960s, Romania was in the takeoff phase of rapid industrialization. Up to that time it had been essentially an agricultural, raw-material producer. Like the other Comecon countries, Romania sought to attain some independence from the Soviet Union by industrializing its

[19] Romania's role in Comecon and its economic reforms are discussed in John Michael Montias, *Economic Development in Communist Rumania*, Cambridge, Mass.: MIT Press, 1967; and in "Rumania: Radicalism and Economic Traditionalism," in George R. Feiwel, *New Currents in Soviet-Type Economies,* pp. 563–587.

economy and becoming an exporter of manufactured products. Achieving independence is a matter of particular concern, because Romania is the only Comecon country that has developed a foreign policy not dominated by the Soviet Union. The pressure for economic reform came from the realization that Romania's independent foreign policy would be strengthened if its economy was industrialized and efficient enough to adapt to the highly competitive circumstances in the Western markets.

In 1967, Romania adopted a minireform program that provided for some decentralization of planning and some improvement in enterprise management. This decentralization took the form of setting up middle-management links in the shape of industrial centrals or enterprise associations, which have taken over some of the decision-making authority of the central ministries. Increased authority has also been given to enterprise managers, but not to the workers, whose factory-production committees have no real influence on enterprise decision making. In spite of the organizational changes, the central planning agencies continue to hold the decision-making authority relating to fundamental issues such as the rate of economic growth, the volume of investment and consumption, and the levels of prices and wages. The technocratic reform in Romania has been hampered by a lack of qualified technical experts and competent enterprise managers. Romania has had to maintain a tightly controlled economy for political reasons, which have set very definite limits on how far decentralization in planning and enterprise management would be tolerated. Whatever economic reforms are carried out in the future, they will probably be in the direction of a moderate and gradual technocratization rather than a democratization of the Romanian economy.

Comecon Economic Reform: In Retrospect and Prospect

Although economic reforms in the Comecon countries have followed a variegated path, it is possible to make some generalizations regarding these reforms. By the 1960s, the pressures for reform of the command economy coming from the workers for a higher standard of living, and from the technicians and enterprise managers for a more efficient economy, were so strong that it was inevitable that some kind of reform would be adopted sooner or later. The era of extensive economic growth was over, and the command economy was not an appropriate device by means of which to achieve intensive growth. The dismantling of the command economies of the Comecon countries then became an "historical necessity."[20] When the reform movement had succeeded in altering some of the major features of the command economy, the reform process became irreversible.

Although there were setbacks in Poland and Czechoslovakia, and more could occur in the future, there will probably be no return to the monocentric Stalinist economic model. The momentum of the economic reform movement is now so strong that the important issue is not whether reform should take place, but what kind of reform should be instituted. At this stage of the reform movement in the Comecon countries, it is not possible to predict the shape of the new economic model that will emerge in the coming decades. The unanswered question is how far economic reform will be permitted to alter the power

[20] Michael Gamarnikow, op. cit., p. 211. See also Zygmunt Bauman, "Twenty Years After: The Crisis of Soviet-Type Systems," Problems of Communism, 6, Vol. XX, Nov.–Dec. 1971, pp. 45–53. Bauman calls attention to the population's rising expectations, the new middle class, and the new industrial proletariat as forces generating demands for economic reform.

structures that now exist in the Comecon countries. The extent to which the new economic model will be allowed to marketize and democratize the command economy will depend upon the extent to which the ruling elites in the Comecon countries are prepared to relinquish their power to control the development of their economies.

The experience with economic reform up to the present indicates that the ruling groups in the Comecon countries will seek politically less challenging substitutes for the idealistic reforms proposed by the early Polish, Bulgarian, and Czechoslovakian reform programs. The government and party leaders, who accept the need for qualitative changes in the command economy, prefer to achieve these changes through industrial reorganization, middle-level industrial associations, more efficient management of industrial enterprises, improved production techniques, and the importation of modern industrial technology. They do not want a fully decentralized economy that would function in a highly interdependent world. They are also willing to leave many microeconomic decisions to enterprise managers, but they reserve for themselves the more important macroeconomic decisions. The ruling groups accept the need for price and wage reform and for market research as a guide to production plans, and they acknowledge the importance of the role of the market mechanism. They accept profitability as a major indicator of good enterprise performance, and they realize the importance of decentralizing the investment process so that much of the nation's investment may take place at the enterprise level. But they are not yet willing to embrace consumerism and allow the general population to determine the nation's economic and social priorities. Above all, most of the government and party leaders in the Comecon countries are unwilling to admit that the changes in the underlying industrial system or production relations of these countries, since the early 1960s, now require changes in the economic and social superstructure that point in the direction of a truly socialist democracy.

The Comecon Bloc and Economic Integration

The economic development of the Comecon countries has been greatly influenced by their membership over the past quarter-century in the Council for Mutual Economic Assistance. Stalin's original plan was to tie the Comecon countries both politically and economically to the Soviet Union. Moscow was to be the center of a large communist sphere, in which the loyal communist regimes of the Comecon countries would supply the Soviet Union with food and raw materials in exchange for Soviet manufactures. The Soviet ruble was to be the Comecon bloc currency; exchange rates between the ruble and Comecon currencies were to be favorable to the Soviet Union, and all trade was to be on a bilateral basis. Being the dominant member of Comecon, the Soviet Union would set terms of trade based upon ruble prices that would be favorable to itself. The Soviet Union's general aim in the Stalin era was to use Comecon trade relations as a means of exploiting the Comecon countries.

After Stalin's death in 1953, the Comecon countries turned to programs of rapid industrialization, more trade with the West, and more favorable terms of trade with the Soviet Union. World prices rather than Soviet prices were used as the basis of bilateral trade agreements, and more realistic rates of exchange between the Comecon currencies were established. Although the Comecon countries are very interested in trading with the West, two-thirds of Comecon foreign trade is still between the Soviet Union and other Comecon countries. The Soviet Union is the major source of raw materials imported by the

Comecon countries, which also use the Soviet Union as the main market for their exported machinery and equipment. Eastern European machinery and equipment are exported in large amounts to the Soviet Union because they are not competitive in Western markets.

The two problems that now face the Comecon countries are how to improve economic integration within the bloc and how to enlarge trade with the West.[21] The rapid industrialization of all the Comecon countries has resulted in the uneconomic development of heavy industries in some of the Comecon countries, and a failure to specialize along lines in which these countries are most efficient. An overabundance of machinery and equipment products ("soft" goods) exists, as well as a scarcity of raw materials ("hard" goods). Over the past twenty-five years, not enough attention has been paid to the economic integration and specialization of the Comecon countries that would have produced a better balance between the output of raw materials and manufactures.

In recent years, a number of steps have been taken to improve the integration of the Comecon bloc and to eliminate the duplication that resulted from the efforts of each country to industrialize rapidly. Interelektro, Interatomenergo, and Intertextilmas were established in 1973 to coordinate electricity production in the Comecon bloc, to organize cooperation for the production of nuclear equipment, and to oversee cooperation and production specialization in textile machinery. The Comecon International Investment Bank, established in 1971, and the International Bank for Economic Cooperation, founded in 1964, are prepared to finance joint ventures among the Comecon countries to enable them to specialize in the production of coal, cellulose, other raw materials, and parts of manufactured goods.

At the July 1971 session of the Council for Mutual Economic Assistance, a *Comprehensive Program* was adopted for the achievement of economic integration over the next fifteen to twenty years. This program includes proposals for improving the coordination of the five-year and long-term plans of the Comecon countries, the joint planning of individual branches of industry, and joint efforts relating to science and technology. While some progress has been made in these directions, the major obstacles to achieving a well-integrated Comecon bloc remain. Price reform has not yet been carried far enough in the Comecon countries so that their prices would reflect real market values. Hence no meaningful price comparisons can be made. Realistic exchange rates cannot be established until the Comecon currencies are freely convertible into one another. The bulk of trading is still carried on bilaterally. Without considerable multilateral trade, not much progress towards a high level of integration within the Comecon bloc can be achieved. Eastern European trade with the West will not expand much unless the Comecon countries can become more competitive in the Western markets and can earn the hard currency necessary to pay for the import surplus of machinery and equipment. The continued heavy reliance of the Comecon countries on the Soviet Union as a trading partner, and the failure of the economic reforms of the 1960s and early 1970s to make much progress, seem to suggest that the Comecon bloc is a long way from achieving a rational structuring of industry and a well-integrated regional economy.

---

[21] The difficulties met in achieving a rational, well-integrated economy in the Comecon bloc are analyzed in detail in J. T. Crawford and John Haberstroh, "Survey of Economic Policy Issues in Eastern Europe: Technology, Trade, and the Consumer," pp. 32–50 and Zbigniew M. Fallenbuchl, "East European Integration: Comecon," pp. 79–134, *Reorientation and Commercial Relations of the Economies of Eastern Europe,* 1974.

Selected Bibliography

BALASSA, BELA A. *The Hungarian Experience in Economic Planning.* Yale University Press, New Haven, 1959.

BAUMAN, ZYGMUNT. "Twenty Years After: The Crisis of Soviet-Type Systems." *Problems of Communism,* XX, No. 6 (Nov.–Dec. 1971), 45–53.

BEREND, I. T., and G. RANKI. *Hungary, A Century of Economic Development.* Barnes and Noble, New York, 1974.

BORNSTEIN, MORRIS, ed. *Plan and Market, Economic Reform in Eastern Europe.* Yale University Press, New Haven, 1973.

FEIWEL, GEORGE R. *New Currents in Soviet-Type Economics: A Reader.* International Textbook Company, Scranton, Pa., 1968.

———. *New Economic Patterns in Czechoslovakia.* Praeger Publishers, New York, 1968.

———. *Poland's Industrialization Policy: A Current Analysis,* I and II. Praeger Publishers, New York, 1971.

———. *The Economics of a Socialist Enterprise, A Case Study of the Polish Firm.* Frederick A. Praeger, New York, 1965.

GAMARNIKOW, MICHAEL. *Economic Reforms in Eastern Europe.* Wayne State University Press, Detroit, 1968.

GREGORY, PAUL. *Socialist and Non-Socialist Industrialization Patterns.* Praeger Publishers, New York, 1970.

JOINT ECONOMIC COMMITTEE. *Economic Developments in Countries of Eastern Europe.* Washington, D.C., 1970.

———. *Reorientation and Commercial Relations of the Economies of Eastern Europe,* Washington, D.C., 1974.

KASER, MICHAEL. *COMECON, Integration Problems of the Planned Economies,* 2d. ed. Oxford University Press, London, 1967.

MONTIAS, JOHN M. *Central Planning In Poland.* Yale University Press, New Haven, 1962.

———. *Economic Development in Communist Rumania.* M.I.T. Press, Cambridge, 1967.

PRYOR, FREDERIC L. *The Communist Foreign Trade System.* M.I.T. Press, Cambridge, 1963.

ROBINSON, WILLIAM F. *The Pattern of Reform in Hungary.* Praeger Publishers, New York, 1973.

SELUCKY, RADOSLAV. *Economic Reforms in Eastern Europe.* Praeger Publishers, New York, 1972.

SIK, OTA. *Czechoslovakia: The Bureaucratic Economy.* International Arts and Sciences Press, White Plains, New York, 1972.

———. *Plan and Market under Socialism.* International Arts and Sciences Press, White Plains, New York, 1967.

Chapter 17
The Yugoslav Socialist Market Economy

The Yugoslav economy since 1950 has been an object of great interest to economists and others because of the novel experiment which it has conducted. This experiment consists of combining social ownership of the means of production, workers' self-management, and a free market system. Yugoslavia provided for the abolition of the centrally planned Stalinist economy after 1950 by establishing a system of workers' self-management that introduced the syndicalist principle into Yugoslavian economic affairs. Under this arrangement, each factory or industrial enterprise became a working collective or producers' cooperative, whose assets are owned by society, but managed by the workers through an elected workers' council. Under the new system of market socialism, Yugoslavia has been transformed from an underdeveloped agricultural economy in 1939 to a moderately industrialized economy, which now rates in total industrial production ahead of Belgium, the Netherlands, Sweden, and about on the level of Spain.

The transformation that has occurred in the Yugoslav economy since 1950 has been rapid but somewhat irregular. Since no other country has attempted to combine workers' self-management with a free market mechanism, the Yugoslavian government has had to proceed experimentally and largely on an ad hoc basis. Experiments have been made with both extensive and limited price controls, with both detailed wage and personal income guidelines and very general guidelines, and with both the central direction of investment and the widespread freedom of the individual enterprises to decide their own investment policies. In the past quarter century, under the decentralized workers' self-management system, Yugoslavia has gone through a number of cycles of expansion and contraction, and has experienced much of the stop-go economic activity of the Western economies. Not having a clear view of the society of the future and being very pragmatic in its approach to economic, social, and political problems, Yugoslavia presents a challenge to individuals seeking to explain its operations and to place it in a precise economic category.

The Ideological Basis of Yugoslav Communism

In Yugoslavia, as in the Soviet Union, an official political and economic ideology provides a theoretical justification for the programs and policies adopted at the various levels of government. This official ideology, which has been developed by Josip Broz Tito and the Yugoslav Communist party's main theorist, Edvard Kardelj, is Marxist in its origins. The Yugoslav communists accept the Marxist view that capitalism will eventually disappear as society undergoes the revolutionary changes that make the coming of socialism and communism inevitable. However, the Yugoslav communists strongly objected to Stalin's position that the hostile relations between communism and capitalism would inevitably lead to a military conflict between these two systems. Long before Khrushchev came on the scene, the Yugoslav communists advocated a policy of "active coexistence" with the capitalist West.[1] The Yugoslav view was that the capitalism of the West would be gradually transformed into socialism and that during this transformation the communist countries could maintain peaceful relations with the West. The Yugoslavs objected to both the North Atlantic Treaty Alliance and the Warsaw Pact on the ground that these military blocs undermined any program for peaceful coexistence. This coexistence was held to be not only possible, but also necessary, if the ultimate stage of communism was to be achieved.

A main point of disagreement between the Yugoslav and Russian communists is the proper path of socialist development after the demise of capitalism. Stalin had asserted that there was only one path to communism—the one followed by the Soviet Union after the revolution of 1917. This meant that all countries in the Soviet orbit were expected to duplicate the Soviet Union's political and economic experiences of the years 1917–1948. The reaction of the Yugoslav communists to Stalin's position on this one route to socialism was to assert that there are "independent paths to socialism." Lenin had pointed out that capitalist countries had developed unevenly, some becoming ripe ahead of others for the transition to socialism. Likewise, according to the Yugoslav interpretation, socialist countries develop unevenly and must therefore create their own approach to socialism. This approach will reflect the special economic, political, and cultural conditions found in each emerging socialist country. No one nation should attempt to dominate other countries as they move along the various paths to communism. Far from aiding other countries to proceed along the route to communism, the Soviet Union, in the opinion of the Yugoslav communists, actually obstructs the socialist development of these countries when it asserts that it has found the only path to communism.

The Yugoslav path to socialism, and eventually to communism, leads to what the Yugoslav communists describe as *socialist democracy*. Tito's socialist democracy differs from Stalin's Soviet socialism in a number of important ways. These basic differences relate to the role of the state, the nature of property ownership, and the function of the Communist party. Soviet political theory accepts

[1] League of the Communists of Yugoslavia, *Yugoslavia's Way, The Program of the League of the Communists of Yugoslavia,* New York, All Nations Press, 1958, pp. 77–81.

the idea of the eventual withering away of the state, which was a prominent part of the Marxist interpretation of the course of events after the disappearance of capitalism. The Yugoslav comminists also accept this interpretation of the future course of political developments. However, they disagree with the Russian communists as to when the withering away process should begin. Stalin asserted that the state should grow stronger after the revolutionary overturn of the capitalist system and should not begin to wither away until socialism was well established. According to the Yugoslav communists, the withering away process should begin right after the transition from capitalism to socialism has been accomplished. If this does not occur, the great danger exists that an excessively powerful state will be created. The dictatorship of the proletariat will then degenerate into "state socialism" or "state bureaucratism"; and a cleavage between the general population and its socialist leaders will give rise to a state monopoly operated by a "bureaucratic caste" for its own ends and not for those of the people.

The Yugoslav interpretation of the role of the state is that the latter should begin to wither away very soon after the transition from capitalism to socialism, and continue to do so "throughout the entire epoch of transition from capitalism to communism." In this withering-away process, the decline in the powers and functions of the state will be accompanied by an increase in "social self-management" at the lower levels of collective action. Instead of being "state owned," property is "socially owned." Social self-management takes the form of operating factories and farms with the aid of workers' councils; carrying on local government by means of directly-elected people's committees; and conducting the affairs of various local social organizations, such as schools, hospitals, housing developments, and cultural centers, by means of locally elected boards. The central state will continue to perform only those functions that cannot be taken care of by social self-management at the local or district levels. These residual functions of the central state will include overall economic planning, the distribution of resources between consumption and investment, maintenance of public order, security, justice, and national defense. In the economic sphere, the state will not intervene in any direct detailed manner in the affairs of industrial and agricultural enterprises. Instead, the state will provide only general guidance for the national economy.

Yugoslav socialist democracy contains the following basic features. At the bottom is the producer or worker who is most directly concerned with production. These producers are united in *working collectives* or economic enterprises that coordinate the efforts of the individual producers. Above the working collectives is the *economic association* or *economic chamber* which in turn coordinates the activities of the various industrial enterprises or working collectives. The country is divided into between five hundred and six hundred *communes*, each of which is a "basic political-territorial and social-economic self-governing community of the working people." At the level of the commune, the bulk of social self-management is carried on. Associated with the communes and also at district and republic levels are many "socialist organizations" of a political, social, and cultural nature that satisfy the various needs of the citizens. At the top of this free society of producer-citizens is the state—in theory, of diminishing importance and becoming little more than an administrative organ concerned only with matters of national importance.

As the Yugoslav state withers away, the role

of the League of the Communists of Yugoslavia (formerly the Communist party of Yugoslavia) changes in fundamental ways. Where the state is a highly centralized and powerful body, as under Stalin, the Communist party plays the leading role and occupies the center of the nation's power structure. According to the Yugoslav communists, the Communist party—like the state—is slated to wither away, but more slowly. The withering away of the League of the Communists of Yugoslavia will be a lengthy process, and its power will gradually merge "into the direct power of the masses." The League of the Communists will continue to play a leading role, consisting of guiding the masses by education and propaganda. The final goal of this educational process is to develop the "socialist consciousness of the working masses" so that they can participate effectively in the new Yugoslav socialist democracy.[2]

The ultimate theoretical goal of Yugoslav communism is a socialist democracy, in which all class conflict will have been eliminated, the state and the League of the Communists will have withered away, and a direct, mass democracy will have been established. The Yugoslav direct, mass democracy would not be similar to Western democracies because there would be no multiparty political system. Since no class conflicts would exist, in the opinion of the Yugoslav communists, there would be no need for more than one political party, the Socialist Alliance of Working People of Yugoslavia. The Yugoslav socialist democracy woild function on the basis of the principle of self-management. In industry and agriculture, the workers' councils would be responsible for the operation of the state enterprises. In the commune, the basic political unit, self-management would find expression through "voters' meetings." Self-management would also operate with respect to citizens' councils that would watch over the administrative activities of the governing body of the commune, namely, the people's committee. Management boards composed of citizens would apply self-management to the affairs of all local organizations such as radio stations, hospitals, schools, and apartment houses. In this manner, self-management is supposed to fill in the gap left by the decentralization and withering away of the state and the League of the Communists of Yugoslavia.

The Yugoslav Political System

The Yugoslav political system resembles in many ways that of the Soviet Union and other communist countries. The usual communist political pattern includes a one-party political system and a government structure in which a national assembly, popularly elected, chooses a national executive council to carry on the administrative work of the government. The national assembly also elects a president who functions as the formal head of the political structure. The Socialist Federative Republic of Yugoslavia is a federation of six republics and two autonomous areas. Each republic, which has its own assembly, is divided into districts (75 for the whole country) and communes (566 for the whole country) which have their own elected "people's committee." There are two major variations from the Soviet Union's political system. The first is the provision for "councils of producers" at all government levels from communes to the national assembly. All assemblies (national and republic) and all district and communal people's committees are bicameral, made up of one council to represent the voters at large and one council to represent the workers in state enterprises of all kinds. There is thus a

---

[2] Ibid., p. 235. See also Branko Horvat and others, Self-Governing Socialism, White Plains, N.Y.: International Arts and Sciences Press, 1975; and M. J. Broekmeyer (ed.), Yugoslav Workers' Self-Management, Dordrecht, Holland: Reidel, 1970.

combination of occupational and geographical representation at all four levels of government. Since worker management at the enterprise level plays such an important role in Yugoslav economic and political theory, provision is made for worker representation through the councils of producers. These councils are especially important when economic legislation and policy are under consideration at the various levels of government.

The second main variation from the Soviet Union's political pattern is the Socialist Alliance of the Working People of Yugoslavia, which is an organization created out of the postwar People's Front. The League of the Communists of Yugoslavia, with its 1,146,984 members, works behind the scenes, while the Socialist Alliance, with its eight million members, openly represents the general public. All members of the league belong to the Socialist Alliance. In theory, the function of the League of Communists is to provide "general ideological leadership" and "political and educational work," while the Socialist Alliance nominates candidates for political office and deals with concrete political and economic questions. Since the League of Communists is in theory destined to wither away, eventually the remaining political body representing all the people would be the Socialist Alliance. Meanwhile, the alliance is a front for the league, which dominates the alliance and all other government bodies.

Both the League of Communists and the Socialist Alliance are organized like the Communist party in the Soviet Union, with congresses, central committees, executive committees, and district and local committees. As in the Soviet Union, in Yugoslavia all important government positions and the majority of the legislative seats are occupied by members of the League of Communists. The league in effect constitutes the real government of the country behind the constitutional facade. A trend towards a corporate type of society can be observed in the recent political development of Yugoslavia. As political power is constitutionally transferred from the national and republic assemblies to the 566 local communes, under the decentralization program started in 1950, a need is felt to provide some kind of general supervision of the people. This is done by enrolling almost all the voting population in the rather amorphous corporate body called the Socialist Alliance of the Working People. The corporate influence of this Alliance is designed to enable the government to keep the general population on the Yugoslav road to communism.

The Yugoslav Economy

Before the Second World War, the six Yugoslavian republics were unable to take advantage of their abundant natural resources to construct an industrialized economy. Although well endowed with nonferrous metals, large deposits of low-grade coal, and one of the largest hydroelectric power potentials in Europe, Yugoslavia was still an underdeveloped agricultural country in 1939. At that time, agriculture provided 75 percent of the nation's employment and accounted for 58 percent of its national income.[3] By 1974, the agricultural sector employed 48 percent of the labor force and contributed only 17 percent of the national income. Industry, which in 1939 had employed only 7 percent of the labor force and contributed 9.5 percent to the

[3] An excellent survey of the Yugoslavian economy since 1945 is presented in Joel B. Dirlam and James L. Plummer, *An Introduction to the Yugoslav Economy*, Columbus, Ohio: Charles E. Merrill Publishing Co., 1973. Current developments in the Yugoslav economy are analyzed in the OECD, *Economic Surveys, Yugoslavia*, which appear periodically. A good digest of economic and social developments is provided in Dusan Miljkovic, "Yugoslavia's Socio-Economic Development, 1947–1972," *Yugoslav Survey*, Feb. 1974, Vol. XV, No. 1, pp. 1–36.

national income, by 1974 employed 19 percent of the nation's work force and accounted for 42 percent of its national income. In the quarter century from 1945 to 1970, Yugoslavia was transformed into a moderate-sized industrial nation.

Yugoslavia does not enjoy a high standard of living. The statistics in Table 17-1 present comparative per capita GNP output and economic growth rates for Yugoslavia, the Comecon communist countries, and selected other countries. Yugoslavia, with a per capita GNP in 1973 of $1,010, was below all the other Eastern European countries except Albania ($460), and far below the United States ($6,200), the other Western European countries, and the Soviet Union. Although Yugoslavia has become rapidly industrialized since 1945 and now produces a wide variety of manufactured goods, it remains a largely underdeveloped country. Agriculture still provides about one-fifth of the nation's gross domestic product and employs 50 percent of the nation's labor force. This is in marked contrast to the United States, where agriculture provides employment for only about 7 percent of the economically active population. Like Poland, Yugoslavia never succeeded in largely collectivizing its agricultural sector. Eighty-five percent of Yugoslavia's agricultural land is held privately, with the other 15 percent being cultivated by state collective farms. The private farms produce largely livestock, wheat, tobacco, fruit, and vegetables, whereas the state farms produce the agricultural raw materials. The private farms have an average size of approximately nine acres, with the legal limit per farmer being twenty-five acres. Much of Yugoslav private farming is subsistence farming, with only 40 percent of its output going to the market. This private farming, although it

Table 17-1
Per Capita Gross National Product and Average Annual Growth Rates in Yugoslavia and Selected Countries

	Per capita GNP 1973	Average annual GNP per capita growth rate (%) 1960-1973
United States	$6,200	3.1
France	4,540	4.7
West Germany	5,320	3.7
East Germany	3,000	3.2
Czechoslovakia	2,870	2.4
Soviet Union	2,030	3.6
Hungary	1,850	3.2
Poland	2,090	3.9
Romania[1]	810	6.7
Bulgaria	1,590	4.7
Yugoslavia	1,010	4.3

[1] 1972 and 1960-1972.

Source: IBRD, *World Bank Atlas*, 1975.

provides for the nation's basic food needs, is highly inefficient because it is limited to an inefficient farm size, and is discriminated against in the purchase of farm machinery. Yugoslavia still officially looks forward to the substitution of collective farming for private farming in the long run.

The Yugoslav economy has a large socialized sector and a much smaller private sector. The socialized sector, which accounts for 98 percent paid employment (4,667,000 in 1975) and is occupied by the working collectives, produces the bulk of the nation's raw materials, semiprocessed goods, and manufactures. The private sector, which includes 13,750 private firms and has a total paid employment of 91,000, is strongest in handicrafts, personal services, catering, shoemaking, clothing, trucking, home construction, and repair work. Although the 1953 constitution states that "no one shall employ the work of others to gain an income," private firms are permitted to hire up to five employees. Clearly, the private sector fills the gap left open by the socialized sector, and would probably expand rapidly if the ceiling on the number of employees per firm were to be relaxed. A deterrent to any such relaxation is that private business in Yugoslavia has become a source of individual enrichment that is very embarrassing to the socialist state.

Industry in the Planned Yugoslav Economy

The Yugoslav state industrial or agricultural enterprise is a *working collective* or association of *free producers*. It is "nationally owned," and its assets are *social property*. Each state enterprise or working collective is an autonomous unit that is empowered to determine its own investment and production programs and the remuneration of its worker members, to fix the prices of the products it sells, and to draw up its own annual production plans. New enterprises are created by the public authorities at the federal, republic, and commune levels. All the enterprises in an industry belong to an industrial association which, while not intervening in the affairs of the member enterprises, coordinates their activities in such matters as markets, labor supplies, research, rationalization, and modernization. Economic chambers for industry, agriculture, building, transportation, and foreign trade provide coordination for state enterprises in major sectors of the economy.

The most unique feature of the Yugoslav state enterprises is their operation under a system of worker or self-management introduced in 1950. The first law on worker management, enacted on July 2, 1950, provided for the election by the workers in each enterprise of a workers' council with authority to manage the enterprise. According to this law, factories, mines, farms, and all other state enterprises are "in the name of the social community administered by their working staffs within the framework of the state economic plan."[4] The workers' council elects a management board, which approves the selection of a general manager by a special committee of the workers.

When a new state enterprise is established, it receives the necessary fixed and working capital in the form of a perpetual loan. A fixed charge of 6 percent on this capital is paid annually to the federal government by the enterprise. Established enterprises expand by investing their own accumulated earnings or by borrowing from the banking system. Long- and short-term credit is made available to various industries as recommended by the national financial plan. Within each industrial

[4] F. W. Neal, *Titoism in Action, The Reforms in Yugoslavia after 1948,* Berkeley: The University of California Press, 1958, p. 121.

category, individual enterprises bid competitively for the available credit supplies, with the credit going to those enterprises that are willing to pay the highest interest rates. Other factors such as the period over which the loan will be repaid and the profitability of the borrowing enterprise are also taken into consideration by the National Bank or the Investment Bank when it allocates credit.

State enterprises are required to cover all expenses and to secure a net income for distribution among the members of the working collective. Each enterprise is free to pay the prevailing market prices for labor and raw materials and, in the absence of price controls, to determine the prices of the products that it sells. A main problem of the Yugoslav government after 1950 was how to eliminate the distortions of the price system inherited from the previous period of highly centralized national planning. This problem was met by allowing state enterprises to fix their own prices in response to changing supply-and-demand conditions. The freedom of state enterprises to fix their own prices applies primarily to the markets for consumer goods. In the consumer sector, state enterprises compete extensively for the consumers' purchasing power; and successful enterprises are able to reward their workers with annual incomes that are frequently well above those earned in less successful enterprises. Competition in the consumer sector has been stimulated by permitting the entry of new firms whenever market conditions appeared to justify enlarging the number of competing enterprises.

The independence of action that has been given to state enterprises in Yugoslavia under the program for decentralizing national planning and restoring the free market economy should not be overemphasized. Although the typical state factory, mine, or farm is free from direct central government control, it is nevertheless subject to many indirect controls.

These controls are exercised by six different organizations: the State Secretariat of Finance, the National Bank, the local commune in which the enterprise is located, the Economic Chamber and the industrial association with which the enterprise is directly or indirectly associated, the trade union representing the workers in the state enterprise, and the League of the Communists whose local committees are in close touch with the affairs of all state enterprises.

Some of these organizations, like the Economic Chamber and the industrial association, were created to fill a gap left by the elimination of the federal ministries, which formerly coordinated the activities of all state enterprises. This coordinating function is now carried on by the various economic chambers and industrial associations, which have to some extent recentralized the Yugoslav economy. Other agencies, such as the State Secretariat of Finance and the National Bank, regularly inspect the state enterprises to see that they are meeting their contractual obligations and furthering the objectives of the government's annual and national economic plans. The communes, trade unions, and the League of Communists are in a position to put pressure upon the management boards and enterprise directors to follow the policy lines laid down by the Tito regime. Since the affairs of the state enterprises are always a matter of public record and the network of indirect controls and pressures is very extensive, the economic freedom of these enterprises is much less than that of business enterprises in the Western world.

Workers' self-management has been established in Yugoslavia for the purpose of transforming production relationships from "wage earning" into the free cooperation of "producers" in a working collective or state undertaking. The "emancipated producers" no longer receive "wages" or "salaries." Instead, they share in the residual net income of their state enterprise, which is described as "income" and not "profits." The enterprise has the right to dispose of its net income without interference by the public authorities, while the workers are entitled to share in the enterprise's residual net income. The worker is guaranteed a minimum income, but beyond this he shares the gains and risks of the state undertaking by which he is employed.

A state enterprise determines the amount of remuneration available for distribution among its workers by making a number of deductions from its gross receipts or sales.[5] Gross enterprise income is arrived at by deducting from gross receipts or sales all operating costs (excluding remuneration to workers), a fixed charge on capital, depreciation (fixed by the government), and turnover taxes. Net enterprise income is obtained by deducting from gross enterprise income the tax on gross income paid to the federal and local (communal) governments. Next, allocations to fixed and working capital, wage stabilization, and welfare funds are deducted from the state enterprise's net enterprise income to calculate the residual income to be shared by the workers. They share this residual income according to the amount of work done by each member of the working collective and the pay scales established for this work. In addition, a worker receives seniority payments, pay for overtime work, and various bonuses based on cost reductions or output above standard output norms. Finally, any surplus income remaining after all these payments is shared by all the workers in the form of a number of extra months' remuneration.

Although the state undertakings are legally free to determine how they will distribute their residual incomes among their workers, a number of indirect constraints prevent the state enterprises from paying excessive remuneration to their workers. The state imposes taxes on both the capital and the gross incomes of the state enterprises. In addition, it also determines how large the depreciation charges will be. Also, the enterprises must submit their proposed income distribution plans to the local council of producers and the trade union branch. If the proposed income distribution is held to be excessive, the council of producers and the trade union branch can "recommend" a different income distribution plan. The local commune can refuse to guarantee the investment loans of recalcitrant enterprises and can also levy special taxes on their residual incomes available for distribution to their workers. The prominent members of the local council of producers, who are appointed by the local industrial enterprises, and the local trade union leaders can put heavy pressure on state enterprises to accept their recommendations concerning income distribution among the workers.

The experience with the principle of state enterprise autonomy in income distribution has been that the enterprises as a whole have had a very high propensity to invest, and considerable restraint has been exercised by the workers' councils in distributing residual enterprise income. In recent years, however, with the new emphasis on raising standards of living the tendency has been for workers to pay themselves excessive amounts of personal income from the net profits of their enterprises. For this reason, a widespread need is now felt for some kind of incomes policy that would curb excessive payments of income to workers from enterprise profits.

When the communists took over Yugoslavia in the late 1940s, they followed the Soviet practice of establishing large manufacturing, mining, and other industrial enterprises. When the government developed a diversified industrial structure in most industries

[5] International Labour Office, *Workers' Management in Yugoslavia*, Geneva, 1962, pp. 208-242.

other than the handicrafts and wholesaling and retailing, a few large firms were established, and today most manufacturing industries must be classified as oligopolistic.[6] Eighty percent of the value of total sales are accounted for by only four firms in the natural gas, petroleum-products, iron and steel, nonferrous mining and smelting, iron-mining, machinery and equipment, building-materials, ceramics, and electrical-products industries. The 312 largest manufacturing and mining firms, or 12 percent of the total number of such firms in 1967, accounted for close to one-half of the assets of all firms in this sector; the largest 131 firms employed about 37 percent of all industrial workers; and 125 firms accounted for 40 percent of the net product created in industry and mining.[7] The trend towards industrial concentration continues to gather momentum in Yugoslavia because the government encourages mergers. The government takes the position that merged firms can better secure the economies of large-scale production, can more effectively carry on research and development, and can offer stronger competition in the world's trading markets.

The Yugoslav Monetary System

A further element of control is introduced into the Yugoslav economy by the banking system. Before Yugoslavia's planning system was decentralized in the 1950s, the banking system in Yugoslavia was similar to the highly centralized banking systems in the other Eastern European countries. The State or National Bank with its many branches dominated the nation's banking system and did most of the banking business. Since the early 1950s, the Yugoslav banking system has been decentralized, and now resembles the banking systems in the Western European countries. Today it includes the central National Bank, the federal Yugoslav investment, agricultural, and foreign trade banks, six republic banks, and a number of local or communal commercial and investment banks called "business banks." These business banks may establish branches or merge with other banks anywhere in Yugoslavia.

In 1960, there were 567 banks, but mergers have reduced this number to 74 with 465 branches. The Yugoslav National Bank now operates like the central bank in the Western countries and limits its activities to providing a supply of currency, performing financial functions for the federal government, and regulating the supply of money both by altering member bank reserves, which may be increased up to 35 percent of bank deposits, and by adjusting the rediscount policy. No well-developed capital market exists in Yugoslavia since state enterprises do not issue stocks and bonds, and the federal government has issued very few short-term or long-term bonds. Business banks, now 66 in number, are established by state enterprises and local government authorities, which contribute the banks' capital.

The banking system holds a unique position in the Yugoslav economy because the nation's capital market is very poorly developed, and monetary and credit policy have a very important role in the absence of an active fiscal policy. Before 1965, the nation's banks were under the control of the central and local government authorities, which provided the funds loaned out by the banks and also determined the directions of short-term and long-term credit. The federal government funneled tax revenues into its General Investment

---

[6] The evidence for the high concentration level in Yugoslav industry is presented in Senate Subcommittee on Antitrust and Monopoly, *Hearings, Economic Concentration,* Joel B. Dirlam, "Statement," Part 7, April 1968, pp. 3758–3785, and "Yugoslavia," Part 7A, pp. 4482–4506. See also Joel B. Dirlam and James L. Plummer, *op. cit.,* pp. 73–83.

[7] Joel B. Dirlam and James L. Plummer, *op. cit.,* pp. 79–80.

Fund, which then loaned these funds to the federal investment, agricultural, and foreign trade banks and to the republic and communal banks. The communal banks had a monopoly in their own areas.

The reform of the banking system in 1965 and 1966 decentralized the banking system by abolishing the General Investment Fund, transferring its funds to the three specialized federal banks, permitting state enterprises to establish banks, and requiring all banks to extend loans according to sound economic criteria and not political favoritism. One of the major weaknesses of the Yugoslav banking system is that it has been under strong pressure to extend credit to enterprises and regions possessing strong political power. Now that the large industrial enterprises can establish their own banks, there is also the danger of economically unsound collaboration between these enterprises and the banks. Such collaboration would remove the Yugoslav economy further from the open competitive market socialism that is supposed to be the objective of Yugoslav communism.

Labor in Yugoslavia

A unique feature of the Yugoslav economy is that the workers function both as producers and as employees. As producers, they are members of working collectives who share the net profits of the collectives at the end of the accounting year. As employees, they receive monthly wages and are free to move from one job to another. The labor market in Yugoslavia is imperfect, because workers do not respond only to established wage levels. Workers through their workers' councils invest some of the retained earnings of their enterprises and stand to gain profits in the future from these investments. Decisions to leave one enterprise and move to another take into account relative wage levels in these enterprises and their prospective profits. Since wage rates, but not earned profits, can be known in advance, workers are likely to be influenced in job seeking by significant differences between wage levels in various enterprises. The labor market functions to the extent that workers move from low-wage, low-profit enterprises to high-wage, high-profit firms. Wage differentials have also played a role in attracting workers out of private agriculture and into the tourist and other service industries.

The trade union has no clearly defined role in the Yugoslav economy. In theory, if workers' self-management worked perfectly, the trade unions would have no role to play. If all workers participated in the affairs of their enterprise, they would in effect be the managers of the enterprise and would be responsible for its performance. Those workers who disagreed with the majority management could move on to some other enterprise. Problems of worker discipline and worker grievances would be handled by arrangements set up by the members of the working collective. In fact, however, many workers do not actively participate in the management of their enterprises. Many are ill prepared to handle problems of enterprise management. Also, frictions have developed between enterprise managers and the workers. Enterprises with financial difficulties have at times failed to pay monthly wages, and workers have pressed the managers to seek financial aid from government sources.

In these circumstances, trade unions, which have branches in all factories, have found a role for themselves as defenders of the workers' interests. They train workers so that they can understand the managerial role; they review legislation that affects workers' welfare; and they are ready to play a part when conflicts arise between the workers and the managers over such matters as closing unprofitable plants and moving plants to new locations. Workers have gone out on strike to protest the failure of monthly wages to move up with the rising cost of living, the increasing unemployment, the division of enterprise profits between reserve investment funds and personal-income payments, and the slowness of the government in developing self-management relations. So far, the trade unions in Yugoslavia have not been active in providing leadership for workers out on strike. Much of what is done by trade union branches in factories could be done by the factory units of the Communist party, but the party units are more likely to represent the government's point of view than that of the workers.

Transformation of the Yugoslav Economy after 1945

The transformation of the Yugoslavia economy during the years 1945-1975 has greatly altered its foreign trade pattern. In these years, Yugoslavia has been transformed from an underdeveloped country with exports limited to a few primary products to an industrialized country with a well-diversified list of exports. Like other small industrialized nations, Yugoslavia is very dependent upon a high level of foreign trade for the smooth operation of its economy. Currently, Yugoslavia has exports of goods and services equal to about 20 percent of its gross domestic product, and imports equal to approximately 23 percent of this product. Yugoslavia is a large exporter of agricultural products, such as live animals, meat, cereals, raw materials including wood, semimanufactures including base metals, and finished manufactures, such as machinery and ships. Its imports include raw materials, such as textile fibers, high-grade coal, chemicals, and high-technology machinery and equipment. As the trade statistics in Table 17-2 show, one-half of Yugoslavia's commodity exports go to noncommunist countries and the other half to communist countries. Approximately three-quarters of Yugoslavia's commodity imports come from noncommunist countries and one-quarter from communist countries. Unlike the other Eastern European communist countries, Yugoslavia is oriented towards the West rather than the East.

Before 1952, the Yugoslav government, like other Eastern European countries, had a monopoly of foreign trade, with highly centralized controls emanating from Belgrade. Since then, foreign trade has been decentralized, and greater reliance has been placed on free market forces. Yugoslavia has joined

Table 17-2
Yugoslavia Commodity Exports and Imports by Area, 1975 (in Percent)

	Exports	Imports
OECD countries	35.7	60.8
Soviet Union	24.8	10.5
Other communist countries	22.4	14.3
Developing countries	17.1	14.4
Totals	100.0	100.0

Source: OECD, *Country Surveys, Yugoslavia*, 1976, p. 47.

Table 17-3
The Distribution of the Yugoslav Gross Domestic Product, 1964 and 1974 (Current Prices)

	1964		1974	
	Millions of dinars	Percent	Millions of dinars	Percent
Personal consumption	30,950	44.4	244,100	51.7
Public consumption	11,550	16.6	74,300	15.7
Gross domestic fixed investment	20,378	29.2	117,400	24.8
Change in inventories	7,289	10.5	57,800	12.2
Net export surplus	−1,671	−2.4	−41,000	−8.6
Residual error	1,174	1.7	20,000	4.2
Gross domestic product	69,670	100.0	472,600	100.0

Source: OECD, *Economic Surveys, Yugoslavia*, 1976, p. 77.

the International Monetary Fund and is an associate member of the General Agreement on Trade and Tariffs. The official goal is free importing and exporting by industrial and trading enterprises and full convertibility of the dinar. Recurrent commodity trade deficits have necessitated the maintenance of a number of trade and exchange controls. In 1961, the system of multiple exchange rates was replaced by a uniform exchange rate. In recent years, some imports have been placed on the free list, but the bulk of them remain subject to import controls. The Yugoslav Foreign Trade Bank, working with the industrial associations, allocates foreign exchange among the individual enterprises. Under a retention quota system, exporters are permitted to retain varying amounts of the foreign exchange that they earn. Because of the recurring large commodity-trade deficits and its inability to control domestic inflation, the Yugoslav government has been forced to devalue the dinar five times since 1950.

In line with its growth strategy, Yugoslavia has developed a high-investment, low-consumption economy, which allocates an unusually large proportion of its gross domestic product to fixed investment and inventory accumulation. The statistics in Table 17-3 reveal that more than 30 percent of the nation's total output is absorbed by investment in fixed plant and equipment and inventory accumulation. Yugoslavia normally has a net import surplus in spite of large earnings from tourism and workers abroad. In 1964, only 44.4 percent of the gross domestic product was taken up by personal consumption. However, much of the public consumption took the form of free health, education and other services. Between 1964 and 1974, personal consumption increased from 44.4 to 51.7 percent of gross domestic product as a result of the pressure placed on the government to raise the nation's standard of living. This development necessitated a decline in the relative share of the total output allocated to gross fixed investment at the very time that the government's program for intensive development called for a stepping up of the rationalizing and modernizing of industry through increased investment in plant, machinery, and equipment. The increase in personal consumption was made possible in large part in 1974 by having a large net import surplus (8.6 percent of GDP).

The Performance of the Yugoslav Economy, 1964–1975

The performance of the Yugoslav economy in the years 1964–1975 was marked by some outstanding achievements and also some conspicuous weaknesses. In those years, Yugoslavia achieved substantial economic growth, having a per capita GNP growth rate of 4.3 percent a year from 1960 to 1973. This was a rate that was higher than that of the Soviet Union and all other Eastern European countries except Bulgaria and Romania.

During the years 1964–1975, Yugoslavia reduced the relative importance of agriculture and increased that of industry and services, such as trade, catering, and tourism. Within the industrial sector, the handicraft, coal, and textile industries were curbed in favor of the more progressive electricity, petroleum-product, chemical, nonferrous metals, and machinery industries, which produced manufactured products for both the domestic and export markets. Special attention was given to the tourist industry, which contributed only $44 million to the current balance of international payments in 1963, but $700 million in 1974.

The economic indicators in Table 17-4 show that while Yugoslavia secured high rates of growth of gross social product and industrial production, this growth was highly irregular.[8] More than the other Eastern

[8] The problem of cyclical instability in socialist economic systems is analyzed in G. J. Staller, "Fluctuations in Planned and Free Market Economies," *American Economic Review*, Vol. 54,

Table 17-4
Percentage Annual Average Increases in Selected Yugoslav Economic Indicators, 1964–1975

Year	Gross social product	Industrial production	Consumer price index	Wages	Output per person in industry	Unemployment rate[1]
1964	12.6	16.2	11.9	29.0	8.8	6.3
1965	13.7	7.8	34.0	37.8	2.5	7.2
1966	6.8	4.1	22.4	37.2	5.2	7.4
1967	2.5	−0.2	7.3	12.8	0.7	8.2
1968	3.9	6.3	5.7	10.1	6.0	9.1
1969	10.5	1.2	7.5	3.4	7.1	8.5
1970	6.0	9.1	11.0	18.0	5.4	7.1
1971	8.8	10.4	15.3	21.1	1.7	7.2
1972	4.4	7.7	16.4	18.2	2.7	7.9
1973	5.0	6.0	19.4	16.0	2.3	9.3
1974	9.5	10.3	21.0	23.6	4.5	9.9
1975	4.0	5.7	24.0	22.5	−0.2	11.3
Average annual change 1964–1975	6.5	7.9	16.3	20.8	4.0	8.3

[1] Average annual rate.

Source: OECD, *Economic Surveys, Yugoslavia*, 1964–1976.

European communist countries, Yugoslavia has experienced wide cyclical movements in economic activity. Irregular economic growth has been a continuing feature of Yugoslavia's economic record ever since the early 1950s. As the statistics in Table 17-4 indicate, the annual rate of growth of gross social product fluctuated between a high of 13.7 and a low of 2.5 percent during the years 1964–1975. For industrial production, the relevant statistics are a high of 16.2 and a low of −0.2 percent. These fluctuations in Yugoslav economic activity are caused more by internal than external developments, and reflect Yugoslavia's inability to prevent sizable price and wage inflation and the heavy importing of raw materials, machinery and equipment, and consumer goods. Some of the economic instability has resulted from periodic reforms of the workers' self-management system that have removed or relaxed controls on prices, personal income payments by state enterprises, and imports; these reforms have then been followed by disruptive price and wage inflation and large increases in imports.

Economic development in Yugoslavia since 1950 has been accompanied by strong inflationary pressures. Over the period 1964–1975, the cost of living rose at an average annual rate of 16.3 percent, and wages per employed person in the social sector increased at an annual rate of 20.8 percent. A consumer-price explosion, which accompanied a high level of economic activity and inflationary price reforms in 1965 and 1966, resulted in a 34 percent increase in the consumer-price index in 1965 and 22.4 percent in 1966. Strong deflationary measures taken by the Yugoslav government reduced the annual consumer price increase to only 7.3 percent in 1967. Wages followed the same highly irregular pattern, rising 37.8 percent in 1965 and only 3.4 percent in 1969. During the period 1964–1975, the Yugoslav workers managed to obtain an increase in real wages equal to their productivity improvement by raising wages enough to cover both the increase in the cost of living and the improvement in output per person. In 1964–1975, the annual increase in wages of 20.8 percent just about equalled the 16.3 percent annual increase in consumer prices and the 4 percent annual increase in output per person in industry.

The decentralizing of the Yugoslav economy and the greater reliance on market forces have had the same effect in Yugoslavia as in Western Europe: to lead the government to resort to stop-go policies and measures. In order to curb the booms and reduce inflationary pressures in 1965–1966 and again in 1972–1973, the government has severely restricted money and credit and imposed very restrictive import controls. After a period of severe restraint, the monetary, credit, and import controls have been relaxed. In the periods of restraint, output has fallen to very low levels—industrial production actually declining in 1967—and unemployment has increased. Since 1964, the decentralized Yugoslav economy has had an annual unemployment rate fluctuating between 6 and 11 percent, a rate that would have been much higher if Western European countries had not absorbed nearly one million surplus Yugoslav workers.

In its external sector, Yugoslavia, while developing an extensive trade with the noncommunist world, has not yet secured a satisfactory equilibrium. Two unique features of Yugoslavia's foreign economic relations are the large tourist influx from the West and the large remittances sent to Yugoslavia by Yugoslavs working in foreign countries. The statistics in Table 17-5 reveal that workers' remittances, which increased from $59 million in 1963 to $1,644 million in 1974, in the latter

---

No. 4, June 1964, pp. 385–395. See also Branko Horvat, *Business Cycles in Yugoslavia*, White Plains, N.Y.: International Arts and Sciences Press, 1971.

Table 17-5
Yugoslavia's Current Balance of International Payments, 1963-1974
(Millions of U.S. Dollars)

Year	Commodity trade balance	Earnings from tourism	Workers' remittances from abroad	Current balance of payments
1963	−278	44	59	−80
1964	−433	55	52	−203
1965	−195	63	55	+70
1966	−351	82	63	−39
1967	−454	95	160	−75
1968	−532	136	191	−95
1969	−659	168	284	−63
1970	−1,195	144	544	−348
1971	−1,435	141	789	−357
1972	−992	219	1,049	+419
1973	−1,576	350	1,512	+434
1974	−3,737	368	1,644	−1,218

Source: OECD, *Economic Surveys, Yugoslavia*, 1976, p. 48.

year were close to one-half the year's commodity-trade deficit. Had Yugoslavia not had a large tourist influx and very sizable total workers' remittances in that year, it would have been unable to maintain the large importation of raw materials, machinery and equipment, and consumer goods. In almost all years, Yugoslavia has a deficit on its current balance of international payments, but this is normal since Yugoslavia is a developing country whose trade deficit is largely financed by private and public loans from abroad. On occasion, however, as in 1964 and 1970-1971, imports become excessive and an unsustainable deficit in the current balance of payments is created. This situation has been met with the imposition of more restrictive import licenses, increased foreign exchange controls, and reduced import quotas. For the first time since 1950, Yugoslavia achieved a surplus on its current balance of payments in 1965. Large surpluses were secured in 1972 and 1973, but only at the cost of low levels of economic growth. In 1974 and 1975 there were again very large deficits in the current balance of international payments.

Economic Planning in Yugoslavia

Like the other communist countries of Eastern Europe, Yugoslavia has had a planned economy since the end of World War II. Since 1950, the rigid centralized planning along Stalinist lines has been replaced by a type of planning that is closer to the indicative planning now carried on in France, the Netherlands, Norway, and Sweden. The current Yugoslav national plan for 1976-1980 is the sixth five-year plan to be constructed since Yugoslavia started on its independent path to communism in 1950. The national plan is constructed by the Federal Planning Office over a two-year period. The planning authorities receive the main directives or goals for the guidance of their plan construction from the Federal Executive Council, which is composed of the premier and his cabinet. In theory, all economic and socio-political units, such as individual enterprises, republic and local government agencies, and various self-managing organizations, participate equally in the elaboration of the plan. Internal consistency is achieved through close cooperation and consultation at all levels from the local and republican levels up to that of the federal government where the plan is completed. The final plan for the five-year period is approved by the Federal Executive Council before being submitted to the Federal Assembly for its approval.[9]

The 1971–1975 Economic and Social Plan

The 1971–1975 national plan had as its major goals increasing the efficiency of the economy, improving the living standard of the population, and reducing regional disparities in levels of development.[10] The plan emphasized rationalizing and modernizing the production process so that the overall efficiency of the economy would be improved. This goal was to be achieved by strengthening the competitive forces in the economy, securing a fuller integration of the domestic and foreign markets, and promoting scientific and technological advance. Also part of the national plan was the continued reduction of the role of the state in economic and social matters, and the expansion of the functions of workers' self-management. Although much has been done to reinforce the system of self-management, its role in an open socialist system has not yet been finally determined.

The Fifth Plan aimed at increasing average annual per capita income from the 1969 level of about $700 to $1,000 by 1975. This would have required an 8 percent annual increase in real social product (roughly gross domestic product). The reduction of regional disparities in development levels has been a longstanding objective in Yugoslavia. The 1971–1975 plan provided additional resources for this purpose.

The Fifth Plan also had ambitious goals for capital investment, employment of the expanding labor force, exports, and tourism. In the Fifth Plan as Table 17-6 shows, both private and collective consumption were projected to increase considerably more slowly than industrial production. The plan also anticipated an equilibrium in the current balance of international payments. Developments in the 1971–1975 plan period indicate that a number of the plan goals were overly ambitious. Instead of growing at the annual rate of 8 percent in the years 1971–1975 as planned, social product increased at the rate of 6 percent. Industrial production increased at the actual annual rate of 8 percent, instead of the planned rate of 9.5 percent. Private and collective consumption and gross fixed investment increased more slowly than planned. Also, the planned balance between exports and imports of goods was not achieved. The development of the oil crisis in 1973 and 1974 with its adverse effects on world trade and tourism made it all the more difficult for Yugoslavia to achieve its 1971–1975 plan goals.

[9] The methodology of Yugoslav national planning is discussed in OECD, *Economic Surveys, Yugoslavia*, 1962, pp. 13–17; *Yugoslavia*, June 1964, pp. 21–26; Joel B. Dirlam and James L. Plummer, *op. cit.*, pp. 165–167; and Jaroslav Vanek, "Economic Planning in Yugoslavia," Max F. Millikan (ed.), *National Economic Planning*, New York: National Bureau of Economic Research, 1967, pp. 379–407. See also George Masesich, *Yugoslavia: the Theory and Practice of Development Planning*, Charlottesville, Va.: University of Virginia Press, 1964.

[10] The 1971–1975 Yugoslav Five-Year Plan is analyzed in OECD, *Economic Surveys, Yugoslavia*, Nov. 1970, pp. 39–46.

Table 17-6
The Yugoslav 1966-1970 and 1971-1975 National Plans and Outcomes

	Annual percent changes at constant 1966 prices			
	1966-1970 Plan		1971-1975 Plan	
	Plan	Outcome	Plan	Outcome
Personal consumption	6.0	5.9	7.0	5.5
Collective consumption	2.6	5.5	6.5	5.0
Gross fixed investment	4.5	7.5	7.75	7.0
Exports (goods)[1]	10.0	10.2	—	5.0
Imports (goods)[1]	10.0	13.3	—	6.0
Social product[2]	6.0	5.4	7.5	6.0

[1] 1966-1969 outcome.

[2] Social product expressed in Yugoslav (Marxian) terms roughly approximates gross domestic product in Western terms.

Sources: OECD, *Economic Surveys, Yugoslavia,* November 1970, p. 43, and April 1976, p. 7.

Table 17-6 also shows the projections and outcomes of the 1966-1970 national plan. Although this five-year plan came close to achieving its economic growth goal of a 6 percent annual increase, both collective consumption and gross fixed investment grew at much higher rates than planned. Also, the balance between the exports and imports of goods planned for was far from being secured. Imports increased in 1966-1970 at the annual rate of 13.3 percent, while exports grew at the annual rate of only 10.2 percent. The excess of imports made it possible to increase collective consumption and fixed investment at much higher rates than planned. The 1966-1970 five-year plan exhibited the usual Yugoslav plan failures, namely, more imports of goods than planned and more collective consumption and fixed investment than planned. The 1971-1975 plan was better on these scores but failed to achieve the planned output goal.

Annual Planning in Yugoslavia

When Yugoslavia adopted the centralized planning method of the Soviet Union in the late 1940s, it accompanied the five-year plans with detailed annual plans that set forth the production and other targets to be met by the individual state enterprises in all sectors of the economy. The annual planning was an integral part of the five-year blueprint or target planning. Under the present relaxed indicative planning procedures, the detailed annual plans relating to the individual enterprises and branches of industry have been abandoned (as has been done in Hungary under its economic reform program). Now the Federal Planning Office makes only "annual Resolutions on Economic Policy" or forecasts, which indicate the expected macroeconomic trends in the economy during the coming year.[11]

Table 17-7 presents the annual resolution or forecast for the year 1974, the main emphasis of which was to increase the rate of real economic growth through an acceleration of consumer and especially investment spending. According to this 1974 forecast, only the rates of gross fixed investment and industrial production were expected to reach the rates

[11] The Yugoslav annual "Resolutions on Economic Policy" are analyzed in OECD *Economic Surveys: Yugoslavia,* 1966-1974.

Table 17-7
Yugoslav Government Forecast of Output and Expenditure and Outcome for 1974

	Percentage changes, volume					Average annual increase
	1971 Actual	1972 Actual	1973 Actual	1974 Forecast	1974 Outcome	1971-75 Plan
Expenditure						
Private consumption	9.0	5.0	2.5	5.25	8.0	7.0
Collective consumption	8.0	3.5	3.5	5.0	7.5	6.5
Gross fixed investment	6.5	3.5	4.0	7.5	9.0	7.0
Social product	9.0	4.5	5.0	6.0	9.0	7.5
Output						
Agriculture, forestry and fishing	8.0	−1.0	5.0	3.0	6.0	3.5
Industry and mining	11.0	7.0	6.0	8.0	11.5	8.0
Social sector of the economy	10.0	5.5	5.5	7.0	—	8.0
Social product	9.0	4.5	5.0	6.0	9.0	7.5

Source: OECD, *Economic Surveys, Yugoslavia*, April 1974, p. 6, and April 1976, p. 7.

set forth in the 1971-1975 plan. In both 1972 and 1973, the differences between planned and realized gross fixed investment and gross social production were substantial. Both 1972 and 1973 were years of low economic growth with weak consumer and business demand. While the forecast for 1974 was based upon the assumption of better levels of economic activity, it was clear in that year that many of the goals of the 1971-1975 plan as originally projected would not be fully achieved. The main reason why the goals of the 1971-1975 plan were not fully achieved was that the government decided to devote its efforts to curbing wage and price inflation, which reached explosive levels in the years 1971-1975, rather than to achieving high levels of economic growth and industrial production.

As the statistics in Table 17-7 reveal, the 1974 plan outcome was much better than had been forecasted for that year. Social product (total output) increased 9 percent instead of the planned 6 percent. Industrial production rose 11.5 percent rather than the planned 8 percent. Consumption and investment also increased much faster than forecasted. The favorable outcome in terms of employment and output in 1974 was due to an expansionary domestic policy stance which resulted, however, in continued high price and wage inflation and a very large adverse balance of international payments in that year. The large discrepancies between the 1974 plan projections or forecasts and the actual outcomes testify to the many difficulties met in planning the very volatile Yugoslav economy.

Short- and Medium-Term Supply and Demand Management

Unlike the other Eastern European communist countries, whose economies have highly centralized controls and do not experience large economic fluctuations, Yugoslavia has found it necessary to develop short-run demand management policies similar to those of the Western European countries and other Western nations. The basic aim of these short-run policies is to secure equilibrium in the commodity, capital, labor, and other markets, while at the same time maintaining high levels of production and employment and an income distribution acceptable to all parts of the community. Disequilibrium appears in the short run when inflation causes demand to outstrip supply, bottlenecks show up in the markets for raw materials and skilled workers, profits become excessive in relation to costs, wage differentials become unrelated to productivity, or when imports run ahead of exports. These disequilibria are associated with different phases of the economic cycle, through which all free market economies continually pass.

In Yugoslavia, the period from 1952 to 1965 was one in which the main recurring problem was excess demand in years of rapid economic growth with high levels of production, investment, and employment. The tendency was to find the causes of inflation and excess demand in excessive capital investment and government spending. Since 1965, when growth has been slower and demand has been less buoyant, inflation and disequilibrium have been attributed more to the behavior of enterprise management and the workers, which has resulted in wage-profit or cost-profit-push inflation.

Short-run demand management in Yugoslavia has used fiscal, monetary, wage, price, and related economic policies. Among these policies, up until recently, the most prominent were monetary, credit, and price policies. The Yugoslav government first employed the control of credit as the main way of stabilizing the economy and curbing strong inflationary pressures. When credit policy proved to be inadequate for the task, the government then turned to price controls and occasionally to price freezes. For the most part, fiscal policy has been passive and has had no large role in short-run demand management. Enlarging the area of price control and employing general price freezes ran counter to the long-run aim of establishing an open, competitive market economy. For this reason, the Yugoslav government has since 1965 become interested in developing an incomes policy as a supplement to credit, fiscal, and price policies in the struggle to control inflation and stabilize the economy.

Yugoslav Monetary and Fiscal Policies

In the course of developing the banking system into an instrument for the control of the decentralized Yugoslav economy, the government greatly altered the nature and functions of the banking system. In the centralized economy that existed before 1950, the control of commercial and investment credit was concentrated in Belgrade. The central planning authorities and the National Bank drew up a national credit plan as a part of the larger national plan. This national credit plan enabled the central government to apply quantitative and qualitative controls to the extension of short-term credit for working-capital purposes by banks at the federal, republic, and local levels. Also the credit plan permitted the government to control the extension of long-term capital investment loans by the General Investment Fund of the federal government, which received budgetary appropriations for this purpose.

After 1955, steps were taken to decentralize the banking system in line with the policy of enlarging the system of worker self-management. Local and republic banks were established and were assigned the short-term lending formerly handled by the National Bank and its various branches. It was hoped that these arrangements would make the banking system more flexible and more responsive to regional and local needs. The failure to apply sound economic criteria to both commercial and investment loans, the tendency to develop local and regional credit monopolies, and the subordination of sound credit policies to political considerations led to a wholesale reconstruction of the Yugoslav banking system in 1965.

The banking reforms of 1965–1966 took the federal government out of most of the banking business. The National Bank after 1965 no longer approved short-term loans to bank customers, and henceforth limited itself to applying only quantitative controls to the supply of short-term credit and money. In this way, the Yugoslav National Bank assumed the character and functions of a central bank as found in any of the Western noncommunist nations. Under the 1965 banking reform, local governments could no longer by themselves establish banks. Local banks are now established by industrial enterprises and local governments. It was hoped that the presence of industrial enterprises in bank managements would result in bank loans being extended according to more economically rational standards. The 1965 banking reforms removed the federal government from investment banking by abolishing the General Investment Fund. In the future, investment loans were to be made mainly by the local and republic investment banks. The hope was that these modifications of the banking system would result not only in a better control of the supply of money and credit, but would also bring about a more economically sound use of short-term and long-term credit.

The experience of Yugoslavia with monetary policy as an instrument of short-term demand management has been very unsatisfactory. With the maximum interest rate on commercial loans limited by law to 8 percent, there has been an excessive demand for bank credit. Having no interest-rate policy, the Yugoslav Banks are forced to rely upon credit rationing to restrict the credit supply. Pressures from enterprises and politicians to extend credit, combined with the policy of rarely allowing an enterprise to fail, have led banks not only to pay inadequate attention to sound bank-loan standards, but also at times to extend credit in excessive amounts. As a consequence of these unsound banking practices, the money supply has at times expanded excessively, and has contributed to the development of strong inflationary pressures. In the inflationary years 1972 and 1973, for example, the planned increases in the money supply were greatly exceeded. The planned increases for 1972 and 1973 were 12 and 15 percent, but the actual increases were 42.6 and 36.7 percent. The government also failed to control the growth of credit extended by some enterprises to other enterprises. This interenterprise debt, which was only 9 billion dinars in 1966, increased to 44 billion dinars by 1971. The OECD concluded in 1974 that "money and credit measures play a particularly important role in economic policy (in part due to a lack of an active fiscal policy), and monetary policy over the last two years has not been effective in controlling the money supply."[12]

Yugoslav fiscal policy, while modified like monetary policy to support the development of the workers' self-management system, has proved likewise to be an unsatisfactory instrument for effective short-term demand management. The fiscal changes since 1952 have very greatly reduced the role of the federal government in revenue collection and government spending. At present, the federal government collects and spends only 30 percent of total taxes, the remaining 70 percent being handled by the republic and local governments. Also, the federal government derives its revenues only from custom duties, sales taxes, and contributions from the republics. Personal income taxes are levied only by the republic and local governments.

[12] OECD, *Economic Surveys, Yugoslavia*, April 1974, pp. 28, 29, and 33.

Two factors make fiscal policy an unsatisfactory tool for short-term demand management: (1) the widely accepted view that all federal, republic, and local government budgets should be kept in balance, and (2) the failure to develop an effective progressive income tax system.[13] Although the public sector in Yugoslavia generally seeks a balanced budget, during the fiscal year the government may curb expenditures by instituting a budgetary freeze that limits the amount of the incoming revenues that can be spent. This was done in 1971, when the government sought to reduce inflationary pressures by limiting government spending to an increase of 14 percent over this spending in 1971. Any such surplus may be spent in a later year, when the economy may be in need of some stimulation, but the government cannot budget for a large deficit in any such year. The tax on the personal income paid out by enterprises is for most workers proportional (3 percent to the federal government and 7 percent to the republic and local governments), and becomes progressive only on incomes above 20,000 dinars—a level of personal income that excludes a large number of Yugoslav income recipients.[14] Since for most Yugoslavs the personal income tax is not progressive, it does not serve as an automatic stabilizer, taking a bigger tax bite when monetary incomes are high in boom years and a smaller bite when incomes are low in recession years.

Price Control and Incomes Policy

Since both monetary and fiscal policies have proved inadequate for short-term demand purposes, the Yugoslav government has been forced to turn to other instruments, such as the direct control of prices and rents in periods of economic overheating and disruptive inflation. In 1970, the Federal Executive Council met with the representatives of the communes and the economic chambers to discuss measures for dealing with the serious inflationary conditions. It was agreed to freeze rents for a year, to have the communal authorities exercise restraint in respect to public service charges, and to place ceilings on the margins of the distributors of basic foods. As a part of Yugoslavia's stabilization policy, frequent general price freezes have been imposed; and in December 1972, for the first time a wage freeze was applied to all government workers and workers in various private service industries. The number of workers whose wages were administratively controlled was equal to 30 percent of the labor force in the socialist sector.

Although the long-term aim continues to have price determination reflect competitive market conditions, short-term stabilization policy has in recent years strengthened direct price controls. Over the years, an extensive system of price control has been constructed. Under the Social Price Act of 1972, the federal government controls major agricultural prices and most industrial prices. The republics have responsibility for rail and bus services, electricity rates, and construction materials; and the price jurisdiction of the local governments covers rents, community utilities, and retail food prices. It is quite clear that the Yugoslav government plans to continue to exercise permanent price control over key commodities, and to retain the right to intervene on a broad price front when conditions require this intervention.

---

[13] J. Marcus Fleming and Viktor R. Sertic, "The Yugoslav Economic System," *International Monetary Fund Staff Papers*, Vol. IX, No. 2, July 1962, pp. 202-223.

[14] In 1968, the overall national pretax personal income was about 10,000 dinars. Up to 10,000 dinars, the federal income tax was 3 percent, 6 to 9 percent on incomes between 10,000 and 20,000 dinars, and 12 to 65 percent on incomes above 20,000 dinars. Berislav Sefer, "Income Distribution in Yugoslavia," *International Labour Review*, Vol. 97, No. 4, April 1968, pp. 371-389.

Price reform has played an important role in Yugoslavia's short-term demand management. One of the causes of rising prices has been that the prices of industrial and agricultural products have been increased so that they would more fully reflect cost conditions. Domestic prices had lost contact with world prices and also were distorted by arbitrary rules of pricing imposed by the price control authorities. As a result of the 1965 economic reforms, internal price imbalances between agricultural and industrial prices were removed, and domestic prices were brought into line with world prices. Since agricultural prices had been kept at an artificially low level, they were allowed to rise more than industrial prices. In this manner, a better pattern of relative prices was established. Yugoslav enterprises establish prices by determining the average per unit cost of a standard output and then adding a profit markup to arrive at the sales price. Average costs include wages, raw materials, depreciation, interest payments, and taxes. An interest charge of 6 percent on the net worth or invested capital of the enterprises was collected until 1971, when it was abandoned. Since the reforms of 1965, the Federal Price Office and other price regulating agencies have permitted increases in controlled prices as inflation has raised the costs of production. The aim of Yugoslav price reform is for prices to reach levels that would be established by an open-market system.

While direct price and wage controls are useful supplements to monetary and fiscal policy in coping with inflation, they do not reach the roots of this problem, which lie in the behavior of the workers in the industrial enterprises. Since the enterprises under the control of the workers can in key industries determine their own selling prices, and then use the profits earned to increase the workers' wages and personal income supplements at the end of the year, the behavior of the workers and the enterprise managers can lead to cost-push or wage-profit inflation. Since 1970, when consumer prices have risen at the high annual rate of 19 percent, even though the economy has been slack and there has been no overall excess of demand, the Yugoslav government has accepted the view that wage behavior is a major element in inflation.[15]

What has occurred since 1964 is a tendency to put less of the enterprises' net profits into their investment funds and to enlarge the portion of profits paid out as personal income to the workers. In 1964, the workers received 43 percent of total enterprise profits as personal income payments; but by 1970 they were receiving 72 percent, with only 28 percent going into the enterprise investment funds. To meet this problem, the government saw a need for an incomes policy that would constrain personal income payments to workers. By early 1973, the republic governments had agreed on the broad features of an incomes policy.

Under this new incomes policy, the republic governments negotiate social wage contracts with the enterprises and trade unions in each industry. These contracts are designed to maintain or increase the portion of profits retained in enterprise investment funds for expansion purposes. Each social wage contract fixes minimum and maximum wages in the industry, and requires an enterprise that pays wages above the average wages for the industry to retain a higher portion of earnings in the enterprise investment fund. Also, if an enterprise paying above average wages requests a

---

[15] The government has accepted the conclusion of considerable econometric research that enterprises with extensive monopoly market power, as well as public-service industries and other government agencies with similar monopoly positions, have created a wage-increase momentum that has spread throughout the economy, and has been the principal cause of inflation over the 1964–1973 decade. See OECD, *Economic Surveys, Yugoslavia*, 1973, pp. 15–16, and 1974, pp. 19–21; and Sofia Popov, "Intersectoral Relations of Personal Incomes," *Yugoslav Survey*, No. 2, 1972, pp. 63–80.

price increase, its request is not likely to be approved by the price-fixing authorities. The republic governments look forward to coordinating their social wage contracts so as to reduce the wage differentials among industries and to establish national average wages for different types of labor. If the social contracts succeed in keeping the wages of each enterprise close to national average wages, this would reduce the possibility of rapid wage increases in certain sectors, and would curb inflationary rounds of "catch-up" wage increases which occur when workers in an enterprise try to duplicate the high-wage payments in other enterprises. It is too early to tell whether or not the new incomes policy can be successfully applied and can make a significant contribution to the control of inflationary pressures.

Incomes policy in Yugoslavia is necessarily tied in with the problem of income distribution. One of the aims of short-term demand management is to prevent the economic instability and inflation that make prices an unjustified source of enterprise profits and worker incomes, and that distort the distribution of personal income. When centralized planning was abandoned, the emphasis was on moving towards equality in personal incomes; but since then, income differentials have been accepted as a means of rewarding productivity and stimulating economic development. At the same time, the objective is to prevent excessive interenterprise and intraenterprise wage differentials.

Some Yugoslav economists believe that the current wage differentials are too low to provide adequate personal economic incentives.[16] In 1968, the average personal incomes in the economy as a whole varied from an index number of 100 for unskilled workers to 247 for persons with a university-level education. The earlier policy of wage equality has not yet been sufficiently repudiated to permit the income differentials that some Yugoslavs believe are necessary to stimulate rapid economic development. Personal incomes still tend to cluster around the national average. In 1968, about 70 percent of all workers were in an income bracket ranging from 20 percent above the national average to 20 percent below it. The question arises as to whether or not this distribution of income provides adequate incentives. Yugoslavia's new incomes policy will have to face the issue of how far the nation should go in rewarding productivity differentials with wage differentials, and how far it should go in taking account of the equality principle by establishing minimum wages and providing income supplements to lower income groups in the form of children's allowances, rent subsidies, and other supplements.

Long-Term Supply and Demand Management

Short-term demand management is carried on within the framework of long-term demand management. In actual practice, there is no separation of these two types of management, since they are carried on simultaneously and are complementary to each other. The objectives of these two types of public management, however, are quite different. Whereas short-term demand management deals with the problems of economic stabilization, longer-term management is concerned with problems of growth and development, which are discussed in the five-year and longer-term national plans. Long-term management has to do with the structure of the economy and the various changes in it that are designed to improve its efficiency, to raise the nation's standard of living, and to achieve other objectives, such as ecological balance and a better lifestyle. Changing the structure

[16] Berislav Sefer, *op. cit.*, p. 212.

of the economy raises such questions as what industries to stimulate, what regions to develop, what foreign markets to cultivate, what research and development to conduct, and what manpower program to adopt. These problems constitute the center of attention in both medium-term and long-term planning.

The main concern in long-term supply and demand management is to achieve the most efficient allocation of capital or fixed investment resources. According to economically rational criteria, capital investment should go into those enterprises, industries, and regions where the highest economic return on the investment will be achieved. Under the pre-1952 centralized Yugoslav planning and management system, the amount and directions of capital investment were determined by the central planners in Belgrade. Since 1952, the investment process has been decentralized, until the bulk of capital investing has been done by enterprises and local and regional investment banks, with a limited amount being carried on by republican and local governments. Although banks making loans for fixed-investment purposes may establish branches anywhere in Yugoslavia, they tend to have strong local and regional attachments, which are magnified by local and regional political pressures. These attitudes and forces have inhibited the growth of a well-developed capital market that would increase the mobility of capital.

Since capital is not sufficiently mobile, the result has been considerable duplication of productive facilities in the Yugoslav processing industries that serve consumers. Insufficient capital investment has gone into agriculture, electricity production, and the basic raw-materials industries, such as coal mining and other extractive industries. As a result of this structural imbalance, the processing industries have had to rely upon large imports of raw materials and semiprocessed goods. A more balanced industrial structure would have provided some substitutes for these imported raw materials.

The decentralized capital investment process has permitted the expansion of *uncovered investments,* in which enterprises have begun fixed investment projects with working capital funds and without adequate long-term financing. After the uncovered capital investments have been begun, the investment banks are then called upon, under local or regional political pressures, and also in deference to the policy of never letting an enterprise go bankrupt, to provide the funds necessary to cover the originally uncovered investment. In these circumstances, it is impossible to achieve the best allocation of capital investment funds. A similar analysis applies to housing investment, which in recent years has gone into the construction of "weekend" houses in suburbs and the countryside rather than into urban housing, which would take care of more basic housing needs.

One of the adverse consequences of the unbalanced Yugoslav investment process has been what is described as *structural inflation.*[17] When investment in the agricultural sector is inadequate, the prices of agricultural products rise, as scarcities develop. In order to preserve their real position, the nonagricultural sectors react to increasing agricultural prices by raising their prices. If Yugoslavia had an open free economy, investment resources would flow into the agricultural sector, where higher returns can be secured than elsewhere. In the controlled Yugoslav economy, where capital is not very mobile, it is not free to move into the high-yield agricultural sector; thus the irrational investment pattern is preserved. Similar policy decisions have prevented the flow of capital into the

---

[17] OECD, *Economic Surveys, Yugoslavia,* 1974, p. 24 fn. The OECD survey draws attention to the "economically unwarranted investment" and the need to improve the "rationality of the structure of investment" (p. 41).

coal-mining industry, which needs modernizing. Some of the inadequacies of the Yugoslav long-term investment process stem from the strong nationalist movement that separates the relatively affluent northern Republics of Slovenia and Croatia from the poor southern Republics of Bosnia-Hercegovina, Montenegro, and Macedonia. The northern republics, with strong separatist tendencies, object to moving investment funds from them to the southern republics, even though considerations of capital mobility and rates of investment return would justify such a movement.

Yugoslavia's economically unwarranted investment program has adverse consequences for both research and development and manpower supplies. Research and development in economic activities are hampered when fixed capital is not directed to its economically optimal uses. Also, manpower does not reach the level of skills that it would if the emphasis were on modernizing and rationalizing industry so as to achieve the most efficient use of capital. While Yugoslavia has made much progress in decentralizing and rationalizing its investment mechanism, it is still hampered by attitudinal and institutional survivals from the predecentralization period, party bureaucrats, political influences, and strong centrifugal nationalist sentiments among the six republics.

The Yugoslav Economy: An Evaluation

An evaluation of the Yugoslav economy is difficult to make for three reasons: (1) observers of the Yugoslav scene disagree as to what is actually going on; (2) frequent changes in policy stances occur so that an observation that may be correct at one time may soon be incorrect; and (3) it is not possible to determine or measure the behind-the-scenes influences of government bureaucrats and party officials. As John M. Montias has pointed out, "It is symptomatic of the underdeveloped state of Yugoslav studies that radically divergent views can coexist on the economic system of Yugoslavia."[18] For example, one Western economic analyst described the Yugoslav economic system as a socialist market system guided by macroeconomic objectives; at the same time, however, a Yugoslav economist called it as "an ambivalent system, partly governed by the laws of imperfect competition and partly administratively controlled."

On the surface, Yugoslavia may appear to have a relatively open-market economy; but an analysis of the informal controls that result from agreement, collusion, or pressure, if it were available, could greatly modify this conclusion. Thus a study of the method by which enterprise managers are chosen in Yugoslavia indicates that the secretary of the local party committee and the president of the municipal assembly actually have the decisive word in selecting managers, even though they are not on the enterprise selection committee.[19] In spite of the very considerable disagreement as to the actual course of events in Yugoslavia, it is reasonable to agree with John K. Galbraith's conclusion after a visit to Yugoslavia that "the 'market' socialism of Yugoslavia is a going concern." This opinion was supported by knowledgeable analysts of Yugoslav affairs who believe that "Yugoslavia now has a workable and reasonably effective economy with high growth."[20]

In spite of Yugoslavia's progress in constructing a viable economy, some very difficult problems remain to be solved before it can be said that the Yugoslav experiment in

[18] John M. Montias, "Comment," in Max F. Millikan (ed.), *National Economic Planning*, p. 399.

[19] Paul Shoup, "Yugoslavia Today, The Evolution of a System," *Problems of Communism*, July–Aug., Sept.–Oct. 1969, p. 77.

[20] John Kenneth Galbraith, *Journey to Poland and Yugoslavia*, Cambridge: Harvard University Press, 1958, pp. 92 and 98.

combining social ownership and enterprise autonomy is a lasting success. A major unresolved issue is: how can economic coordination be combined with enterprise independence in producing, investing, and pricing? While there will probably be no return to the coordination of economic activity supplied by the old centralized planning system, the coordination now being provided by governments, economic chambers, and industrial associations has proved unsatisfactory. Local and republic interests still too frequently ignore national interests. In the rush to decentralize the economic decision-making process, not enough thought has been given to what new methods of overall coordination could be devised that would still be compatible with workers' self-management.

Another unresolved problem is the role of the manager in the self-managed society. In theory, worker self-management and director management have clearly defined and separate roles. The workers have the overall legislative function of basic business-policy decision making, and the directors have the executive function of day-to-day decision making. In actual practice, the danger exists of a growing "managerialism," in which a managerial class monopolizes the managerial function and reduces the workers to an inferior position, as in the capitalist system.[21] The trend towards managerialism, which is widely discussed in Yugoslavia, is supported by the failure of many workers to participate actively in the decision-making activities of their enterprises. There is even the danger that managerialism may, as Milovan Djilas has warned, give rise to a "new class" in economic and political circles that will undermine the self-management system.[22] It will be difficult to show that in the long run director management and worker self-management are compatible.

Another issue that will be of growing importance in the future is how feasible it is to combine foreign-equity investment in Yugoslavia with market socialism. Can there be joint ventures in the establishing of new industries in Yugoslavia in which workers' self-management would be combined with private foreign investment from abroad? The Yugoslav government has made it possible for foreign investors to control 49 percent of joint investment ventures, with the aim of attracting advanced industrial technology from the West.[23] So far, very few foreign investors have been induced to join fixed-investment ventures because of the restrictive legislation governing foreign investment and the low yield on such investments. Most of the foreign aid to Yugoslavia still takes the form of private and public loans from abroad. Large equity investments from the West have still to find their place in Yugoslavia's market socialism.

As a developing country that is trying to industrialize rapidly and at the same time fashion a new socio-economic system, Yugoslavia has not had much time to devote to issues that claim the attention of the Western world. Little attention is being paid to ecological problems, to the prevention of environmental deterioration, and to the preservation of urban amenities. The shallow Adriatic Sea is in danger of being polluted, and cities are being built without much regard for high standards of city planning. Political freedom, while more extensive than in the Soviet Union and the other East European countries, is not yet sufficiently well established to prevent the persecution of intellectuals, students, and political dissenters. These are problems

[21] Aleksander Bajt, "Management in Yugoslavia," in Morris Bornstein (ed.), *Comparative Economic Systems,* Homewood, Ill.: Richard D. Irwin, 1974, p. 199.
[22] Milovan Djilas, *The New Class,* New York: Frederick A. Praeger, 1957.

[23] Patrick J. Nichols, "Western Investment in Eastern Europe: The Yugoslav Example," *Reorientation and Commercial Relations of the Economies of Eastern Europe,* 1974, pp. 725–743.

that Yugoslavia shares with all other underdeveloped countries. Yet Yugoslavia has had enough success with its novel socio-economic experiment to suggest that the Yugoslav path to communism may very well be the path that other communist countries will take in the future.

The appearance of workers' self-management, or market socialism, in Yugoslavia has given rise to considerable controversy over precisely what is meant by the term "market socialism." Using Yugoslavia as a model, Western economists have constructed theoretical models of what they describe as *cooperative socialism,* or labor-managed or participatory economies.[24] According to an abstract view of cooperative socialism, the economy's firms would be managed and controlled by the workers; the firm's income would be shared by the workers; the firms would be owned by the state (which would levy a tax on each firm), and labor would be free to seek employment anywhere. In such a system, there would be a fully decentralized market economy, and economic planning would be of an indicative nature, with only indirect controls. This ideal cooperative socialism merely duplicates what was described in the nineteenth century by British socialist theorists as *democratic full socialism.* These early socialists were never able to explain satisfactorily how workers' control of industry would fit into a socialist society where the state was the ultimate authority and representative of the voting citizens, and where consumer interests might conflict with producer interests. These are matters that the present-day models of cooperative socialism, based as they are on a "rather abstract and generalized level" of analysis, do not handle satisfactorily.[25]

Clearly, the Yugoslav model of market socialism is still far removed from the abstract model of cooperative socialism with which Western economists have in recent years been concerned. As long as Yugoslavia continues to have a one-party government and considerable central government bureaucracy, the prospects of the Yugoslav economy closely approaching this model seem to be remote. It is widely agreed that Yugoslavia has moved far beyond the command or administrative socialism of the Soviet Union towards a more decentralized type of socialism. However, there is no way of predicting whether or not Yugoslavia will continue in the coming decades along the path towards democratic full socialism, or will remain indefinitely at a half-way station between authoritarian command socialism and democratic full socialism.

[24] For a discussion of cooperative socialism, see Benjamin Ward, "The Firm in Illyria: Market Socialism," *American Economic Review,* Vol. 48, Sept. 1968, pp. 566–589; and *The Socialist Economy,* New York: Random House, 1967; and Jaroslav Vanek, *The General Theory of Labor-Managed Market Economies,* Ithaca: Cornell University Press, 1970, and *The Participatory Economy,* Ithaca: Cornell University Press, 1971.

[25] Jaroslav Vanek, *The Participatory Economy,* p. 55.

Selected Bibliography

DIRLAM, JOEL B., and JAMES L. PLUMMER. *An Introduction to the Yugoslav Economy.* Charles E. Merrill Publishing Co., Columbus, 1973.

DJILAS, MILOVAN. *The New Class.* Frederick A. Praeger, Publisher, New York, 1957.

FARKAS, RICHARD P. *Yugoslav Economic Development and Political Change.* Praeger, New York, 1975.

FLEMING, J. MARCUS, and VIKTOR R. SERTIC. "The Yugoslav Economic System." International Monetary Fund Staff Papers, IX, No. 2 (July 1962), 202–223.

GALBRAITH, JOHN KENNETH. *Journey to Poland and Yugoslavia.* Harvard University Press, Cambridge, 1958.

HORVAT, BRANKO. *Towards a Theory of Planned Economy.* Yugoslav Institute of Economic Research, Beograd, Yugoslavia, 1964.

———, and others. *Self-Governing Socialism.* International Arts and Sciences Press, White Plains, N.Y., 1975.

INTERNATIONAL LABOUR OFFICE. *Workers' Management in Yugoslavia.* Geneva, 1962.

KOLAJA, JIRI THOMAS. *Workers' Councils: The Yugoslav Experience,* Praeger, New York, 1965.

LEAGUE OF THE COMMUNISTS OF YUGOSLAVIA. *Yugoslavia's Way, The Program of the League of the Communists of Yugoslavia.* All Nations Press, New York, 1958.

MILJKOVIC, DUSAN. "Yugoslavia's Socio-Economic Development, 1947–1972." *Yugoslav Survey,* XV, No. 1 (Feb. 1974), pp. 1–36.

NEAL, F. W. *Titoism in Action, The Reform in Yugoslavia after 1948.* University of California Press, Berkeley, 1958.

ORGANISATION FOR ECONOMIC CO-OPERATION AND DEVELOPMENT. *OECD Economic Surveys, Yugoslavia,* 1965–1975.

SHOUP, PAUL. "Yugoslavia Today, The Evolution of a System." *Problems of Communism,* July–Aug., 1969, 77–87.

STALLER, G. J. "Fluctuations in Planned and Free Market Economies." *American Economic Review,* 54, No. 4 (June 1964), 385–395.

VANEK, JAROSLAV. "Economic Planning in Yugoslavia." In *National Economic Planning,* edited by Max F. Millikan, National Bureau of Economic Research, New York, 1967.

———. *The General Theory of Labor-Managed Market Economies.* Cornell University Press, Ithaca, 1970.

———. *The Participatory Economy.* Cornell University Press, Ithaca, 1971.

WARD, BENJAMIN. *The Socialist Economy.* Random House, New York, 1967.

Part Five
The Less Developed Economies

18
The Model of the Less Developed Economy

19
The Chinese Communist Economy

20
The Indian Economy and the Third World

Chapter 18
The Model of the Less Developed Economy

Many economic systems do not have much in common with the mature Western capitalist systems, the well-developed Western democratic socialist systems, or the developed Eastern communist systems. Some investigators of comparative economic systems analyze them in terms of three different spheres: the capitalist world, the socialist or communist world, and the third world of the less developed countries.[1] The differences between the developed and the less developed economies are not ideological in any major sense.

From the ideological point of view, the less developed economies cover a wide range, from democratic India to the one-party socialist or totalitarian countries of Africa, Asia, and Latin America. Some less developed economies are based on highly advanced cultures, while others are on a primitive tribal level. The less developed economies are set apart from the developed economies not by their ideology or culture but by their stage of economic development. Economists may not agree as to the dividing line between less developed or developing and developed economies, but clearly, a large number of economies fall into these two categories; furthermore, the economies in each category have enough features in common so that a general economic pattern or model for each category can be constructed.

The International Bank for Reconstruction and Development (the World Bank) places 188 of the world's economies in five

---

[1] See, for example, Lloyd G. Reynolds, *The Three Worlds of Economics*, New Haven: Yale University Press, 1971, pp. 96–122. Gunnar Myrdal also analyzes the mixed economies of the West, the economies of the Soviet sphere, and the underdeveloped countries in the non-Soviet sphere. See his *Beyond the Welfare State*, New Haven: Yale University Press, 1960, pp. 220–225. Those who separate the mixed economies of the West into capitalist and democratic socialist mixed economies end with four types of economic systems and four spheres or orbits of influence.

Table 18-1
Population (mid-1973), GNP at Market Prices, and GNP Per Capita (1973) by Income Group

Income groups	Number of countries	Population (millions)	GNP (thousand millions in U.S. dollars)	Average GNP per capita (U.S. dollars)
Less than $200	43	1,151	136	120
$200 to $499	52	1,184	332	280
$500 to $1,999	53	531	530	1,000
$2,000 to $4,999	28	654	1,871	2,860
$5,000 and over	12	316	1,886	5,970

Source: World Bank, *World Bank Atlas*, 1975, p. 8.

categories with average GNP per capita ranging from $120 in the lowest category to $5,970 in the top category in 1973.[2] Table 18-1 shows the distribution of these 188 countries over the five categories with countries like India, Burma, Indonesia, and Kenya in the bottom category and the United States, Canada, Sweden, and West Germany in the highest category. The wide gap between the poor and rich nations is indicated by the fact that in 1973 the 43 nations with GNP per capita below $200 had 30 percent of the 188 countries' population but only 3 percent of their total GNP, while the 12 nations with GNP per capita of $5,000 and over had 8 percent of the population and 40 percent of the total GNP.

A survey of the major features of the forty-three countries in the lowest income group in Table 18-1, all of which had a GNP per capita below $200, shows that these economies have much in common. They tend to have inefficient one-party governments with poor public administration, large subsistence sectors with considerable underemployment, small public and private sectors, low productivity of the factors of production, underdeveloped natural resources, imperfect markets, low saving and capital accumulation, low per capita income, along with a very unequal distribution of income, a heavy dependence on the export of primary products and borrowing abroad, and, in many cases, low economic growth rates.

The Major Features of the Low-Income Developing Economy

The most striking features of the less-developed economies are their low per capita output and their poverty. In 1973, average GNP per capita in the developing Asiatic economies was only $200; in the developing African economies, it was $290. This was in marked contrast to average 1973 GNP per capita levels in Europe (excluding Southern Europe) of $2,990 and in North America (the United States and Canada) of $6,130. Not only is per capita output in less developed economies very small, but the gap between the developing and developed regions is widening.

An analysis of the per capita GNP statistics in Table 18-2 reveals that over the decade 1960–1970 all the world's developing regions had an economic growth rate (3.1 percent) only slightly more than that of the developed regions (2.8 percent). Some developing regions, Africa, Latin America, and Asia, however, grew less rapidly than the developing regions of the Middle East and Southern

[2] World Bank, *World Bank Atlas*, 1975, p.8.

Table 18-2
Gross National Product Per Capita by Regions, 1960 and 1970

	Countries included	GNP per capita in 1970 U.S. dollars		% annual increase, 1960–1970
		1960	1970	
Developing regions	79	185	250	3.1
Africa	31	145	180	2.2
Asia	14	100	125	2.3
Middle East	6	285	460	4.9
Latin America	21	435	560	2.5
Southern Europe	7	430	695	5.0
Developed regions	21	2,010	2,750	2.8
Japan	1	750	1,920	9.8
North America	2	3,820	4,660	2.0
Europe, excluding Southern	15	1,775	2,575	3.8
U.S.S.R.	1	1,160	1,790	4.4
Australia and New Zealand	2	2,090	2,800	3.0

Source: World Bank, *Trends in Developing Countries*, Table 2.5, 1973.

Europe. In the latter regions, the average annual GNP per capita growth rate was around 5 percent, whereas in the former regions it was close to 2.5 percent. Also, the developing economies in Latin America, Africa, and Asia grew at a much slower rate than did Europe (excluding Southern Europe), the Soviet Union, Japan, Australia, and New Zealand. The gap between the developing economies in Africa and Asia and the United States and Canada remained unchanged, since all these economies on the average grew about 2 percent annually.

A 1970 survey of the economic structure of one hundred countries at GNP per capita levels varying from $50 to $2,000 brings out the major features of the economies of the low-income or poor developing countries.[3] Table 18-3 shows the origins or composition of gross domestic product for economies at $50, $300, $800, and $2,000 levels of GNP per capita. Less developed economies at the $50 GNP per capita level derived almost 60 percent of their total output from agriculture, forestry, fishing and other primary industries. Industry contributed little more than 7 percent to total output. As the developing nations rise on the output or income scale, the origins of gross domestic product undergo major changes. Economies at the $300 GNP per capita level reduced the contribution of agriculture and related activities to 30 percent, and increased industry's contribution to close to 25 percent. These output trends continued until at the $2,000 GNP per capita level in the developed economies agriculture and other primary activities contributed only 10 percent of the total output, while industry contributed almost 40 percent. The service sector, while large in the low-income underdeveloped economies (approximately 35 percent), increased in importance until at the $2,000 level it contributed 51 percent to total output of

[3] Hollis B. Chenery, "Growth and Structural Change," *Finance and Development*, Vol. 8, No. 3, Sept. 1971, pp. 16–27.

The model of the less developed economy

Table 18–3
Origins of Gross Domestic Product of Economies at Selected GNP Per Capita Levels in 1965

Economic activities	Level of GNP per capita in 1964 U.S. dollars			
	$50	$300	$800	$2,000
Agriculture and other primary industries	58.1	30.4	18.6	9.8
Industry	7.3	23.1	31.4	38.9
Services	29.9	39.2	40.5	39.3
Public utilities	4.6	7.7	9.7	11.7
Gross domestic product[1]	99.9	100.4	100.2	99.7

[1] Not adjusted to total 100 percent.

Source: Hollis B. Chenery, "Growth and Structural Change," *Finance and Development*, Vol. 8, No. 3, Sept. 1971, p. 19.

goods and services. A survey of the origins or composition of the gross domestic products of the less developed countries in 1975 reveals that there has been no significant change in this composition in the decade 1966–1975.

The composition of gross domestic product in the low-income developing economies is correlated with the composition of the labor force in these economies. As the statistics in Table 18–4 reveal, in the low-income developing economies the great bulk of the labor force is employed in agriculture and other primary economic activities, with a very small part of the labor force at work in industry. For less developed economies at the $50 GNP per capita level, 75.3 percent of the labor force was in agriculture and related activities, and only 4.1 percent was in industry. In the case of less developed economies at the $300 level, the primary labor force fell to approximately half of the total labor force, and industrial labor increased to about one-fifth.

In the developed economies at the $2,000 level primary labor absorbed a little less than 10 percent of the total labor force, while industry took up almost 40 percent. The portion of the labor force taken up by the service industries continued to increase as the comparative survey moved into higher GNP per capita levels. Whereas the lowest-income underdeveloped economies had only one-fifth of the work force on the average in the service industries, the developed economies had over one-half of their labor force in this sector. Low-income developing economies are characterized by small urban populations, high birth rates, and high death rates. At the $50 level, only 7 percent of the total population in the low-income developing economies surveyed was in urban areas, as compared with 65 percent in the developed economies at the $2,000 level.

The low-income, less developed economies are also characterized by low rates of saving and investment, a small tax base, and a large unskilled work population. The statistics in Table 18–5 show that developing economies at the low GNP per capita level of $50 had savings equal to about 10 percent of their GNP, and domestic investment equal to about 11 percent of GDP. As output levels rose, both savings and investment continued to increase until at the $2,000 level both savings and investment were about 25 percent of Gross National Product and gross domestic product, respectively. In the low-income developing

Table 18–4

The Distribution of the Labor Force in Economies at Selected GNP Per Capita Levels in 1965 (in 1964 U.S. dollars)

Labor force	Level of GNP per capita in 1964 U.S. dollars			
	$50	$300	$800	$2,000
Agriculture and other primary industries	75.3	49.9	28.6	8.3
Industry	4.1	20.5	30.7	40.1
Services	20.6	29.3	39.2	51.6
Total labor force[1]	100.0	99.7	98.5	100.0

[1] Not adjusted to total 100 percent.

Source: Hollis B. Chenery, "Growth and Structural Change," *Finance and Development*, Vol. 8, No. 3, Sept. 1971, p. 19.

Table 18–5

Saving and Investment in Economies at Selected GNP Per Capita Levels in 1965

	Level of GNP per capita in 1964 U.S. dollars			
	$50	$300	$800	$2,000
Gross national savings as % of GNP	9.4	16.4	20.5	24.6
Gross domestic investment as % of GDP	11.7	19.7	23.0	25.4
Tax revenue as % of national income	9.8	19.5	28.0	28.0
School enrollment ratio	17.5	61.2	78.9	91.4
Adult literacy rate	15.3	65.0	85.4	93.0

Source: Hollis B. Chenery, "Growth and Structural Change," *Finance and Development*, Vol. 8, No. 3, Sept. 1971, p. 19.

economies, very low primary- and secondary-school enrollments and widespread adult illiteracy rates keep labor unskilled, poorly prepared to work with capital equipment, and low in productivity. At the $50 GNP per capita level, only 17.5 percent of the relevant school-age population was enrolled in school, and the adult literacy rate was 15.3 percent. At the $300 level, according to the comparative country survey, the school-enrollment ratio had increased to 61.2 percent and the adult-literacy rate to 65 percent. At the $2,000 level, these rates were 91.4 and 93 percent, respectively.

The ratio of exports to GNP reflects both the size and the GNP per capita levels of the less developed economies. In some small economies, such as the "oil," "copper," "banana," "cocoa," and "coffee" economies, this ratio exceeds 50 percent, while in the large Indian economy it is below 10 percent. The statistics in Table 18-6 show that in 1965 in the less developed economies at the $50 GNP per capita level, exports of goods and services were 9.9 percent of GDP, whereas for developed economies at the $2,000 level this ratio was almost 25 percent. The exports of the less developed economies consist very largely of primary products such as petroleum, copper, coffee, sugar, cotton, rubber and other agricultural, forestry, or mineral products. Among the low-income, less developed economies in 1965, primary exports were 89 percent of total exports, whereas among the developed economies at the $2,000 level these exports accounted for only 33 percent of total exports. Low-income, less developed economies, which import few primary products, import manufactured goods, industrial materials, and fuels. The primary-product exports of these economies vary widely from year to year because of fluctuations in foreign demand, world prices and crop yields.

The Model of the Less Developed Economy

The previous analysis of the structure and functioning of the less developed economies enables one to construct a generalized model of these economies. Table 18-7 presents a comparison of the Chinese, Indian, and LDC (less developed country) economic systems.[4] It is quite clear that the economic systems of the less developed countries are much closer to the Indian than to the Chinese economic system. With respect to the sixteen features of economic systems listed in Table 18-7, the Indian and LDC economic systems have ten that are similar, whereas the Chinese and LDC economic systems have only three features in common. These three features are

[4] For a discussion of the characteristics of less developed economies, see Walter Elkan, *An Introduction to Development Economics*, Baltimore, Md.: Penguin Books, 1973, pp. 13-27.

Table 18-6
Exports and Imports in Economies at Selected GNP Per Capita Levels in 1965

Trade	Level of GNP per capita in 1964 U.S. dollars			
	$50	$300	$800	$2,000
Exports of goods and services as % of GDP	9.9	18.0	21.8	24.8
Imports of goods and services as % of GDP	16.6	21.6	23.8	25.5
Primary exports as % of total exports	89	61	46	33
Primary imports as % of total imports	10	27	30	30

Source: Hollis B. Chenery, "Growth and Structural Change," *Finance and Development*, Vol. 8, No. 3, Sept. 1971, p. 19.

Table 18–7
A Comparison of the Chinese, Indian, and LDC Economic Systems

Features	Chinese Economic System	Indian Economic System	LDC Economic System
1. Ideological basis	Marxism-Leninism	Democratic socialism	Ideological mixture
2. Political structure	One party	Multiparty	One party
3. Population growth	Relatively low (1.8%)	High (2.3%)	High (2.8–3.0%)
4. Public sector	Large	Small	Small
5. Agricultural sector	Large	Large	Large
6. Per capita economic growth	Relatively high (2.6%)	Low (1.1%)	High (3.1%)
7. Type of economy	Public enterprise	Mixed economy	Mixed economy
8. Per capita income	Low	Low	Low
9. Savings ratio	High	Low	Low
10. Income distribution	Little inequality	Much inequality	Much inequality
11. Market system	Limited use	Used but imperfect	Poorly developed
12. Foreign trade	Very limited	Extensive	Extensive
13. Exports	Mainly primary	Primary and industrial	Primary
14. Inflation	Very little	Strong	Strong
15. Employment	Full	Less than full	Less than full
16. External public debt	None (long term)	Considerable	Considerable

The model of the less developed economy

one-party governments, high per capita economic growth, and exports consisting largely of primary products. All three types of economic systems differ with respect to their ideological basis and their reliance upon the market system. The ideological basis of the Chinese economic system is Marxist-Leninist, of the Indian system democratic socialism, and of the LDC system a mixture of African, Arab, and Asiatic socialist elements.[5] In the Chinese economic system, a strong bias operates against the free market system; in the Indian system no such bias exists, but the market system is imperfect; and in the less developed economic systems the market system is poorly developed.

The LDC and Indian economies have high population growth rates, small public sectors, mixed public-private-enterprise systems, low per capita income, low savings ratios, highly unequal income distribution, extensive foreign trade, strong inflationary pressures, less than full employment and much underemployment, and considerable external public debt. Like India, the less developed countries are active members of the international economy, and their levels of economic activity are closely associated with that of the world economy. In general, they do not duplicate the self-sufficient policy of the Chinese communists. Like India, these countries tend to adopt a neutralist position with regard to world affairs, and so do little to spread the doctrines of African, Arabian, or Asian socialism throughout the world.

Major Problems in the Less Developed Economies

In the past quarter century, the less developed nations of the Third World have made considerable progress on both the economic and social fronts.[6] While the economic growth of these countries has not equalled that of many advanced industrialized nations in Western Europe, it has nevertheless been substantial. As has already been explained, all developing nations in the period 1950–1970 had a per capita economic growth rate slightly higher than that of all the developed countries. Growth rates have varied widely among the less developed countries. In the twenty-year period, Iran (4.1 percent), the Philippines (3.1 percent), and Mexico (2.9 percent) had high per capita GNP growth rates, while Malaysia, Ghana, and Zaire had growth rates close to 2 percent. Other underdeveloped nations recorded little or no economic growth. In the same twenty-year period, Morocco's average annual growth rate was 0.1 percent, while Haiti reported no increase in GNP per capita over the entire period.

Rising GNP per capita in the less developed countries has been accompanied by considerable progress in improving their economic and social infrastructure and their quality of life. Roads, railways, other modes of transportation, and postal and other communications have been improved and extended. Banking systems and other financial

---

[5] African, Arabian, and Asiatic socialism seeks to establish an identity that separates it from Western socialism. It looks for this special identity in the historico-cultural roots of Africa, the Middle East, and Southern Asia that antedate the appearance of Western socialism. These roots include a reliance on communal or cooperative activities, an egalitarian society, and very little social stratification. Also, they include a bias against the materialistic individualism of the West and the formation of large economic and social organizations. These aspects of non-Western socialism are analyzed in William H. Friedland and Carl G. Rosberg, Jr., *African Socialism*, Stanford: Stanford University Press, 1964; Saul Rose, *Socialism in Southern Asia*, New York: Oxford University Press, 1959; and Abdel Moghny Said, *Arab Socialism*, New York: Barnes and Nobel Books, 1972.

[6] For a survey of this progress, see Lester B. Pearson, "Two Decades of Development: The Pearson Report," in Gustav Ranis (ed.), *The United States and the Developing Economies*, rev. ed., New York: W. W. Norton, 1973, pp. 33–54.

institutions have been established, and markets have been enlarged and improved. Colonial government administration has been replaced by indigenous administration. Schools, hospitals, and other public capital facilities, including public utilities, have been constructed. Very sizable advances have been made in the fields of health and education. Over the years 1950–1970, the death rate per one thousand population in seventy-nine less developed countries was reduced from twenty-four in 1950–1954 to fourteen in 1970–1974; and life expectancy in the developing world has increased from thirty to fifty years. Communicable diseases like malaria and smallpox have been largely eliminated, people's spirits and sights have been raised, the capacity to work has been increased, and the quality of living has been improved. The caloric intake in the developing countries has been greatly improved, although total protein availability remains too low; and in many of these countries the caloric intake is not far from the daily caloric standard developed by the Food and Agriculture Organization. Marked progress has been made in enlarging first- and second-level school attendance, which in seventy-nine developing countries was 26.5 percent of the relevant school age population in 1950 and 50.1 percent in 1970. Literacy rates of the population fifteen years and older have been raised until today they are 26 percent, 53 percent, and 76 percent in Africa, Asia, and Latin America, respectively.

In spite of the significant economic and social progress made by the developing countries since 1950, these countries are still faced with some very serious problems. Population continues to grow at too rapid a rate; underemployment and unemployment remain at high levels; their economies are still heavily dependent on a low-growth and irregular agriculture; wealth and income distribution continues to be highly unequal; exports are largely made up of primary products, which are subject to wide demand and price fluctuations; foreign economic aid continues to be inadequate; and the gap between the rich developed and poor developing nations is not closing.

The Growth Strategy of the Less Developed Economies

The less developed countries seek to move in a short period of time from a situation of little or no economic growth to a 4 or 5 percent annual increase in Gross National Product. These countries are frequently in the traditional pre-takeoff or early takeoff stage of development. Since economic development must be telescoped into a short time period, the typical less developed country must adopt policies and programs that seek to alter economic and social attitudes and institutions, to provide an adequate social and economic infrastructure, and to modernize the country's economic system. Until the current economic development program was adopted, such a nation's output went mainly into consumption, or, if an economic surplus existed, it was largely transferred out of the country by its top income class or by its former colonial administrators. The growth strategy of the less developed countries has been focused on curbing consumption, enlarging savings, and increasing investment in industry, agriculture, services, and public capital facilities. Since 85 percent of the investment in the less developed countries has been made possible by domestic saving, the main problem has been to increase the portion of the national income devoted to private and public saving. The assumption underlying much economic development strategy is that increased saving will find investment outlets that will increase the marginal efficiency of capital and labor and raise the rate of economic growth.

The economic model that guides growth strategy in many of the less developed countries is the Harrod-Domar type of model, which asserts that the rate of growth of national output is determined by the aggregate saving ratio, including government budgetary deficits financed out of new money and balance of payments deficits, and the incremental or marginal capital/output ratio.[7] In other words, when applied to less developed economies with a large labor supply, this model states that the rate of growth of GNP is determined by the rate of growth of the nation's plant and equipment. The higher the rate of saving the higher the rate of investment and capital creation, and consequently the higher the rate of economic growth. This model is useful in developed countries where there is a flexible and smooth movement from saving to investment because financial institutions and the market system are well developed. In the less developed economies where a backward traditional sector (agriculture and some services) exists alongside a modern industrial sector, without well developed capital and commodity markets, the Harrod-Domar and neoclassical types of growth model have very limited application.

In many less developed economies, accumulating savings is not enough, because of numerous barriers to the profitable use of these savings. In these developing countries, a bias operates against private enterprise and profit making, and frequently too much emphasis is placed upon wasteful private and public consumption—largely for ceremonial purposes.[8] Attitudes and institutions favor communal but not individual action. The environment is not favorable to private business experiment and innovation. If economic growth is to occur, inherited communal or tribal attitudes, values, and institutions must be replaced by those more favorable to the acceptance of change, experimentation, and innovation. To achieve these ends, the advocates of unbalanced growth in the less developed countries recommend an enlargement of the nation's infrastructure and investment in a few leading heavy industries; together, these measures should create favorable conditions for economic growth.

These conditions will then lead to further economic expansion and a cumulative upward movement of the whole economy.[9] The aim is to develop the industries that contribute the most to this upward movement or chain reaction through the exploitation of external economies. Certain industries will be found to have strong backward and forward linkage effects. Industries with backward linkages will create a demand for inputs from other domestic industries; new industries with forward linkages will stimulate other industries to use the output of the new industries. In an unbalanced or "big-push" growth strategy, stress is placed upon financing leading industries with high linkage effects.[10]

In India and other developing countries

---

[7] The Harrod-Domar model is based on the equation $G = s/k$, where G is the rate of growth of output, s is the saving ratio, and k is the capital coefficient or incremental capital/output ratio. If G is to be increased, s must be raised, given k, or k must be lowered, given s. In developing economies, economic growth can be raised either by increasing saving or by lowering the capital/output ratio. In a less developed economy, with abundant labor, the Harrod-Domar model suggests that the rate of growth of total output or GNP is determined by the rate of growth of the nation's capital stock. For a criticism of the applicability of this model to less developed economies, see Lloyd G. Reynolds, op. cit., pp. 106, and 268-274.

[8] Adamantios Pepelasis, Leon Mears, and Irma Adelman, Economic Development, New York: Harper & Brothers, 1961, pp. 101-102.

[9] For a discussion of the theory of unbalanced economic growth and its applicability to the less developed economies, see A. O. Hirschman, The Strategy of Economic Development, New Haven: Yale University Press, 1958; and Stephen Enke, Economics for Development, Englewood Cliffs, N.J.: Prentice-Hall, 1963, Ch. 17, "Unbalanced Industrial Growth," pp. 317-332.

[10] Robert E. Baldwin, Economic Growth and Development, 2nd ed., New York: John Wiley & Sons, 1972, pp. 82-94.

with much population pressure and a large labor surplus, two-sector growth models have been developed that have special application to these countries.[11] These growth models call for achieving growth by increasing the scope and importance of the public sector and by developing the heavy industries. The production of the required supplies of consumer goods would be obtained largely from labor-intensive household and handicraft industries. In agriculture, the necessary increases in production would come through land reform, community development, public credit, and cooperatives. Surplus labor would be absorbed by labor-intensive household industries and agriculture. As industrialization proceeded, labor would be shifted from the agricultural sector and household industries to the modern industrial sector. The main obstacle to the application of this growth strategy is the widespread and deep poverty found in most less developed countries.

Population Growth and Poverty

Although most less developed countries do not experience the population pressures felt by India, Pakistan, and Mainland China, they have both traditional agricultural and modern industrial sectors, with a labor surplus in the largely subsistence agricultural sector.[12] They are faced with the same problems of increasing savings, improving investment opportunities, pushing industrialization, and improving agricultural productivity. A main obstacle to raising the levels of output and income in the less developed countries is the high rate of population growth and the widespread poverty.[13] High population growth rates are found in the poor developing countries and low rates in the rich developed countries. Algeria, Kenya, Iraq, El Salvador, and Libya have rates above 3 percent, while most Western European countries have rates below 1 percent. Relative shares of the world's population are declining in Europe and North America and rising in Asia, Africa, and Latin America.

As the statistics in Table 18–8 show, in 1969, if the "poverty line" is defined as an annual income of $75, almost one-half of the 1.2 billion population in Latin America, Asia, and Africa were below the poverty line. Poverty was especially widespread in the less developed countries of Asia and Africa. A recent World Bank study of poverty and income inequality in the developing economies points out that the poor in these economies are disproportionately located in the rural areas, and are engaged in agriculture or allied rural occupations.[14] Estimates based on the 1960 world census suggest that today there are

---

[11] In India, two- and four-sector growth models were developed by P. C. Mahalanobis, Director of the Indian Statistical Institute and Statistical Adviser to the Prime Minister, as the foundation of the Plan Frame for the Second Five-Year Plan, 1956–1961. For a discussion of these growth models, see P. C. Mahalanobis, *Draft Recommendations for the Formulation of the Second Five-Year Plan, 1956–61*, New Delhi: Planning Commission, Government of India, March 17, 1955. Also A. H. Hanson, *The Process of Planning, A Study of India's Five-Year Plans, 1950–1964*, New York: Oxford University Press, 1966, pp. 125–130. For a criticism of Mahalanobis' growth model, see P. T. Bauer, *Indian Economic Policy and Development*, London: George Allen & Unwin, 1961, pp. 60–74.

[12] An analysis of some of the consequences of the uneven development of the less developed countries' modern and traditional sectors is presented in Hla Myint, *Southeast Asia's Economy, Development Policies in the 1970's*, New York: Praeger Publishers, 1972, pp. 39–41, and 165–166.

[13] The conflict between population growth and economic development is explained in H. Peter Gray and Shanti S. Tangri, *Economic Development and Population Growth A Conflict?*, Lexington, Mass.: D. C. Heath, 1970. In the less developed countries, economic development is held back by the very large number of people under fifteen years of age. Their dependency ratio (ratio of under 15 plus 65 and over to population 15 through 64) is 80.8 percent, compared to 57.5 percent in developed countries.

[14] Hollis B. Chenery and others, *Redistribution with Growth*, New York: Oxford University Press, 1975.

The model of the less developed economy

Table 18-8
Estimates of Population below the Poverty Line in Latin America, Asia, and Africa in 1969

Country	1969 GNP per capita (U.S. dollars)	1969 population (millions)	Population below U.S. $50 annual income		Population below U.S. $75 annual income	
			(millions)	% of total population	(millions)	% of total population
Latin America						
Average and total	545	244.5	26.6	10.8	42.5	17.4
Asia						
Average and total	132	872.0	320.0	36.7	499.1	57.2
Africa						
Average and total	303	83.8	23.8	28.4	36.6	43.6
Average and grand total	228	1,200.3	370.4	30.9	578.2	48.2

Source: Montek Singh Ahluwalia, "Income Inequality: Some Dimensions of the Problem," *Finance and Development*, Vol. 11, No. 3, Sept. 1974, p. 5.

more than 100 million smallholders in the developing countries operating farms of less than 5 hectares (12.35 acres). About half of these farm holdings are less than one hectare (2.47 acres).[15]

Poverty in the developing countries is accompanied by large inequalities in income and wealth distribution. A World Bank study of income inequality in 26 less developed economies, with GNP per capita no higher than $300, reveals that the lowest 40 percent of the population received 14 percent of total pretax income, the next 40 percent received 32.7 percent, and the top 20 percent received 53.3 percent. In half of the underdeveloped countries, income shares of the lowest 40 percent of the population averaged only 9 percent of total pretax income.[16]

As an illustration of the extreme inequality of income distribution we may take the case of Colombia in which, as Table 18-9 shows, the bottom one-tenth of the employed rural labor force in 1964 received only 1.4 percent of total personal income. At the same time the top one-tenth, which owned 75 percent of the agricultural land, received 51 percent of that income. In Colombia, as in most developing countries, poverty is mainly a rural problem which is made severe by a highly concentrated land ownership system. The statistics in Table 18-9 reveal that the inequality of income distribution found in the rural areas is also found in the urban areas. What made the future bleak was the fact that Colombia's income distribution had not changed significantly between the 1930s and the 1960s.

Poverty in the less developed countries is caused by a number of factors. Prominent among them is the existence side by side of a technologically advanced modern industrial sector and a technologically backward, traditional agricultural and handicraft sector. Income inequality increases as this dualism becomes more developed. Other causes of inequality are unemployment in the urban areas and underemployment in the rural areas, the higher birth rate of the lower-income groups, and the inadequate education of these groups. Many political leaders and members of the elite in the developing countries accept the

[15] Montek S. Ahluwalia, "Income Inequality: Some Dimensions of the Problem," *Finance and Development*, Vol. 11, No. 3, Sept. 1974, p. 8.
[16] Hollis B. Chenery and others, *op. cit.*

Table 18-9
Average Income, by Deciles, of Rural and Urban Workers in Colombia, 1964

Decile	Employed rural labor force		Employed urban labor force	
	Percent of total income	Average annual income per employed (pesos)	Percent of total income	Average annual income per employed (pesos)
1st	1.4	880	0.9	1,140
2nd	3.1	1,940	3.3	4,200
3rd	3.6	2,260	4.3	5,470
4th	3.9	2,450	5.0	6,300
5th	4.5	2,820	5.5	7,000
6th	5.5	3,450	7.0	8,910
7th	6.0	3,760	8.0	10,180
8th	8.0	5,020	11.0	14,000
9th	13.0	8,160	14.5	18,450
10th	51.0	32,000	40.5	51,530

Source: Miguel Urrutia M., "Income Distribution in Colombia," *International Labour Review*, Vol. 113, No. 2, March–April 1976, p. 208.

view that higher economic growth leads to less poverty. While this may be true in the very long run, it is not the case over quite a lengthy period of time.

Simon Kuznets has pointed out that in the early phases of industrialization in the underdeveloped countries income inequalities tend to widen before the leveling forces become strong enough to reduce these inequalities. As these countries seek to raise their savings ratio the tendency is to maintain, if not to increase, income inequality. This does not mean, however, that any extreme inequality has to be accepted by the general population. Measures can be taken to contain or lessen income inequality at the same time that the nation's savings ratio is being increased.[17] These measures include a more even distribution of land, rural public works to absorb some of the rural underemployment, improved rural primary education for both sexes, the emancipation of women, the expansion of industrial production to reduce urban unemployment, and the selection of development projects that benefit especially the low-income groups. These measures would require a considerable change in the less developed countries' power structures, which currently favor the top 20 percent of income receivers.

Not much success has yet been achieved in curbing population growth, in spite of efforts to popularize family planning. Estimates of population growth in the years 1970–2000 suggest average annual growth rates of 2.5, 2.8, and 3.0 percent for South Asia, Africa, and Latin America respectively. It is widely believed that not much success will be had in curbing population growth until the low

[17] For a discussion of these measures, see John H. Adler, "Development and Income Distribution," *Finance and Development*, Vol. 10, No. 3, pp. 2–5.

status of women in the less developed countries has been eliminated. High population growth will continue to require using scarce foreign exchange for food imports in bad crop years, to place heavy pressure on the educational system and other public facilities, and to contribute to rising levels of unemployment and underemployment.

The Future of the Less Developed Economies

The future of the less developed countries is clouded as a result of their continued reliance on exports of primary products. The industrialization that has occurred in these countries has been aimed more at reducing imports of machinery and industrial materials than at producing industrial products for export. Some progress in exporting manufactured products has occurred; but these amount to only 24 percent of total exports, while primary commodities constitute 76 percent of such exports. Since 1955, world exports of primary commodities (excluding petroleum) have grown at an annual rate of 3.7 percent, whereas world exports of manufactures have increased at a 10.7 percent rate.

The less developed economies are at a disadvantage in comparison with the developed economies, because they are dependent upon the low-productivity primary industries, whereas the developed countries are associated with the high-productivity, high-technology secondary industries. Unlike the developed economies, the less developed economies export primary products subject to wide fluctuations in output, demand, and prices. The oil-producing nations have in recent years overcome the difficulties of primary product producers by uniting to limit oil production and by raising its price from $3.21 per barrel in 1972 to $11.22 per barrel in 1974. The opportunities to apply similar tactics to other primary products such as copper, coffee, sugar, cotton, and rubber are not as good as they are for oil. The range of price fluctuations for internationally traded commodities (for example, sugar selling for 7.6 cents per pound in 1972, 25.3 cents in 1974, and 8.2 cents in 1976) that less developed countries experience makes it necessary to find ways of stabilizing these prices.

The less developed economies have not made much progress in reducing unemployment and underemployment. Underemployment in the agricultural sector has remained high because of the failure to curb population growth and to carry out land reforms and other agricultural policies that would improve farmers' incentives and raise agricultural productivity. Much of the financial aid given to agriculture benefits primarily the large landowners and upper-income farmers rather than the poor small farmers, who have little political influence in the rural areas. The Green Revolution, which led to large increases in wheat, rice, and corn as the result of the introduction of new "miracle" seeds, has benefited the large farmers more than the small farmers, who cannot afford to provide the fertilizers, equipment, and irrigation required by the new types of crops. The Green Revolution could easily convert many smallholders into landless laborers who drift to the urban centers only to add to unemployment there.[18]

The introduction of heavy industry into the less developed economies does not provide much wage employment because of the capital-intensive nature of this industry. Much underemployment in the agricultural sector could be eliminated if farmers were organized in off-season periods under government programs to engage in water conservation, irrigation, and reforestation projects,

[18] For an analysis of the consequences of the Green Revolution, see Clifton R. Wharton, Jr., "The Green Revolution: Cornucopia or Pandora's Box," Gustav Ranis, *op. cit.*, pp. 67–79.

as is done in Communist China. Such projects, including land reform, are more readily carried out by what Gunnar Myrdal has defined as a *hard state,* in contrast to a *soft state.*[19] The latter state is typical of the South Asian and other developing countries, in which there is a low level of social discipline, and in which government policies are often not enforced because the authorities are reluctant to place obligations on people, especially on upper-income people.

Industrialization and the failure to improve agricultural output have placed heavy burdens on the external sectors of the less developed economies. Exports have failed to pay for the imports of machinery and equipment, industrial raw materials, and food. The import of machinery and equipment has been financed largely by loans from governments and institutions, such as the International Bank for Reconstruction and Development, the International Development Association, and the International Finance Corporation. The external public debt of eighty developing countries increased from $37.4 billion to $66.7 billion between 1965 and 1970. Interest and principal payments on this large debt increased from $3.5 billion in 1965 to $5.9 billion in 1975.

Unlike Communist China and other less developed communist countries that have no long-term public debt, the noncommunist developing countries have gone into debt as an aid to their industrialization programs. While foreign debt supplements domestic saving as a source of investment funds, thus aiding industrialization, the accumulating annual interest and principal payments require a debt management program that ensures that loans from abroad are used for productive purposes, so that in the long run the external public loans are self-liquidating. Many less developed economies have not been successful in constructing workable debt management programs, and so have found the annual service payments on external debt to be a heavy burden on the current balance of international payments.

The prospects of the Third World are not bright. The concerted action of the oil-exporting nations led to a fourfold increase in the price of oil and a subsequent deep recession in the industrialized world. These events have created serious difficulties for the less developed countries. In these nations, the export demand for primary products has declined, imports have become more expensive, foreign exchange reserves have become depleted, and external debt has increased. The worldwide dislocation of the international monetary system and the economic recession have adversely affected millions of people in the less developed countries who, even in times of worldwide prosperity, live close to or under the poverty level. A recovery from the 1974–1975 worldwide recession would mean that many of the conditions that led to the recession would still prevail.

A well-known analyst of the problems of the less developed countries concludes that "the arithmetic of the situation is such that it is impossible to conceive of the gap [between the rich and poor nations] reducing in any significant manner if current trends, resulting from the present mix of policies and actions, continues into the future."[20] Population and economic growth trends from 1965 to 2000 indicate that, if current foreign aid policies and programs are not changed, by the year 2000 the gap between the rich and poor nations will be larger than it was in 1965. Based on the assumption of an annual GNP per capita growth rate of 2.85 between 1965 and 2000 in the less developed world and a

---

[19] Gunnar Myrdal, *Asian Drama, An Inquiry into the Poverty of Nations,* Vol. II, New York: Pantheon, 1968, pp. 895–900.

[20] Jagdish N. Bhagwati (ed.), *Economics and World Order from the 1970's to the 1990's,* New York: Macmillan, 1972, p. 9.

growth rate of 3.67 in the developed world, a widely accepted calculation shows that the GNP level in the less developed world will be further behind the GNP level in the developed world in the year 2000 than it was in 1965. Whereas the GNP level of the less developed world was 8.3 percent of the GNP level of the developed world in 1965, it would probably be around 6.3 percent in 2000, if the present mix of foreign aid policies and programs continues into the future to the year 2000. The statistics supporting these growth projections to the year 2000 are presented in Table 18-10.

Clearly, the long-run improvement in the economic and social welfare of the less developed countries depends not only upon an improvement in the functioning of their domestic economies but also upon an improvement in the international economic system. Better population control, land reform and a more productive agriculture, higher education levels, the emancipation of women, more effective tax systems, a more equitable distribution of income, and more sophisticated national planning could do much to raise the per capita incomes of the less developed countries.

In the international field, much could be done to reduce the gap between the rich developed nations and the poor underdeveloped nations. Since 1961, the net flow of official development assistance from the developed countries to the less developed countries has continuously declined. In 1961, this flow was 0.53 percent of the combined Gross National Product of the sixteen major aid-giving developed countries; by 1971, however, this flow had fallen to 0.35 percent of GNP. By 1974 the United States was giving official development aid equal to only 0.26 percent of its GNP. The United Nations has set 1 percent of GNP as an overall foreign aid goal for the industrialized nations, but as the recession deepened, the developed countries have moved still further from this goal. If the 1

Table 18-10

GNP Per Capita in 1965 and Estimates for the Year 2000 in Less Developed and Developed Areas

Regions	1965	2000	Annual rates of growth between 1965 and 2000
Less developed world			
Africa	144	281	1.95
Asia less Japan	118	324	2.95
South America	379	928	2.60
Total	145	388	2.85
Developed world			
Japan	866	8,656	6.80
North America	3,023	7,921	2.80
Oceania	1,641	3,344	2.05
Europe	1,377	5,087	3.80
Total	1,729	6,126	3.67
World total	646	1,769	2.90

Source: Jagdish N. Bhagwati (ed.), *Economics and World Order*, New York: Macmillan, 1972, p. 28.

percent development-assistance goal is to be reached, much will have to be done to improve the international economic system. The most desirable international planning would stabilize foreign exchange rates and provide for orderly changes in them as needed, provide for what both exporting and importing countries regard as fair prices for petroleum and other primary products, and take a long-range view of the world economy and the respective roles in it of the developed and the less developed economies.[21] In such an ideal situation, the latter economies could then more effectively combine the domestic and external sectors of their planning programs, and could look forward to moving more rapidly towards the goal of a developed economy.

[21] Isaiah Frank, "New Perspectives on Trade and Development," in Theodore Morgan and George W. Betz, *Economic Development*, Belmont, Calif.: Wadsworth Publishing Co., 1970, pp. 241-255.

Selected Bibliography

BALDWIN, ROBERT E. *Economic Growth and Development*, 2nd Ed. John Wiley and Sons, 1972.

BAUER, P. T. *Indian Economic Policy and Development*. George Allen and Unwin, London, 1961.

BHAGWATI, JAGDISH N., ed. *Economics and World Order from the 1970's to the 1990's*. Macmillan, New York, 1972.

ELKAN, WALTER. *An Introduction to Development Economics*. Penguin Books, Inc., Baltimore, 1973.

FEI, JOHN C. H. and GUSTAV RANIS, *Development of the Labor Surplus Economy*. Richard D. Irwin, Inc., Homewood, Ill., 1964.

FRIEDLAND, WILLIAM H., and CARL G. ROSBERG, JR. *African Socialism*. Stanford University Press, Stanford, 1964.

GRAY, H. PETER, and SHANTI S. TANGRI. *Economic Development and Population Growth, A Conflict?* D. C. Heath and Co., Lexington, Mass., 1970.

HANSON, A. H. *The Process of Planning, A Study of India's Five-Year Plans, 1950-1964*. Oxford University Press, New York, 1966.

HIRSCHMAN, A. O. *The Strategy of Economic Development*. Yale University Press, New Haven, 1958.

KAMARCK, ANDREW M. *The Economics of African Development*, Rev. Ed. Praeger Publishers, New York, 1971.

MORGAN, THEODORE, and GEORGE W. BETZ. *Economic Development*. Wadsworth Publishing Co., Belmont, Calif., 1969.

MYINT, HLA. *Southeast Asia's Economy, Development Policies in the 1970's*. Praeger Publishers, New York, 1972.

MYRDAL, GUNNAR. *Asian Drama, An Inquiry into the Poverty of Nations*, Vols. I, II, and III. Pantheon, New York, 1968.

———. *The Challenge of World Poverty*. Pantheon, New York, 1970.

RANIS, GUSTAV, ed. *Government and Economic Development*. Yale University Press, New Haven, 1971.

———. *The Gap between Rich and Poor Nations*. St. Martin's Press, New York, 1972.

REYNOLDS, LLOYD G. *The Three Worlds of Economics*. Yale University Press, New Haven, 1971.

ROSE, SAUL. *Socialism in Southern Asia*. Oxford University Press, New York, 1959.

SAID, ABDEL MOGHNY. *Arab Socialism*. Barnes and Noble Books, New York, 1972.

SHAFFER, HARRY G., and JAN S. PRYBLA. *From Underdevelopment to Affluence*. Appleton-Century-Crofts, New York, 1968.

Chapter 19
The Chinese Communist Economy

China and World Communism

In the communist sphere, the People's Republic of China has emerged since 1949 as a challenger to the Soviet Union and a candidate for leadership in this sphere. Much of the world's future history will doubtless depend upon the relations between these two major communist nations. In theory, they should work and live in harmony, since they are both communist countries officially following the Marxist-Leninist line. If they were to form a working partnership when Mainland China has become a superpower like the Soviet Union, they would be in a unique position to influence the course of world economic and political developments. At present, these two giants of the communist world are unfavorably disposed towards each other. Much of the friction between them undoubtedly arises from their long-standing antipathy that developed in the late nineteenth century as a result of Russia's policy of political aggression towards China. In addition, Communist China, like other developing countries, has nurtured a very strong nationalist feeling, which tends to stimulate political and economic independence. The role of nationalism is especially important in the affairs of the People's Republic of China because of the century of foreign domination from which it fully emerged only after 1949.

Other economic as well as political factors have created tensions between Mainland China and the Soviet Union. The two countries are at very different stages of economic development. The Soviet Union is now a well-developed and somewhat mature industrial country, whereas Communist China is an underdeveloped country, which has only recently passed beyond the takeoff stage of development. Mainland China is today where the Soviet Union was in the late 1920s and early 1930s, and in some ways, Mao Tse-tung duplicated the economic policies of Joseph Stalin and not those of Leonid Brezhnev. Like Stalin, Mao sought to create a self-sufficient economy that would have little need for foreign trade, would curb consumption severely in order to maximize the surplus available for rapid industrialization, would develop a strong military posture, and would isolate the population from the materialism of the West.

Much of this runs counter to the current plans and objectives of the Soviet Union. The Soviet Union no longer follows a policy of economic self-sufficiency, but is instead eager to expand its trade with the West and is making considerable progress in raising its standard of living. At the expense of investment, and while maintaining a strong military posture, the Soviet Union has shown some interest in détente and arms limitation. Since Khrushchev's time, the Soviet Union has accepted a program of peaceful coexistence and, as a member of the United Nations, has thrown its weight in favor of world stability. All this has meant that the Soviet Union has developed a live-and-let-live policy towards the capitalist West, which is still very fragile, and which may under different circumstances quickly disappear. But for the time being, it must be accepted that the Soviet Union has moved considerably away from the Stalinist distrust of the West that dominated the years 1924–1953.

In the opinion of the Chinese communist leaders, the Soviet Union has gone soft on capitalism and is now moving down the path of revisionism. The Soviets are said by the Chinese to have revised Marx and Lenin in unacceptable ways, and so have forfeited the right to be the leader of the communist world. The Chinese communist leaders believe that Brezhnev and Kosygin are betraying the 1917 revolution, and that they are failing to carry this revolution throughout the world. The Soviet leaders, according to the Chinese, are no longer true revolutionaries but instead have succumbed to the soft ideals of the United States and other rich industrial nations. In these circumstances, the Chinese communists are prepared to accept the role of world communist leader that they say the Soviet Union has abandoned.

In order to give substance to their claim of world leadership, Mao and his associates have since 1949 embarked upon a program of converting Mainland China from a somewhat primitive underdeveloped country into a powerful world state with a strong industrial and military base. At the same time, they have held up as their ideal the "new communist man [or woman]" who is selfless and committed to serving the welfare of the new China. What the Chinese leaders look to is a continuance of the worldwide revolution which began in the Soviet Union in 1917, faltered after 1953 when Stalin died, and now requires, in their opinion, a reinvigoration that only they can supply. In late 1957, Mao asserted that "The Chinese revolution has its own national characteristics and it is entirely necessary to take these into consideration. But in our own revolution and socialist reconstruction we have made full use of the rich experience of the communist party and the people of the Soviet Union."[1]

In recent years, China has felt a need to react affirmatively to the growing détente between the Soviet Union and the United States. It has opened its doors to a limited extent to the United States both diplomatically and otherwise, and has sought to strengthen its world position by developing friendly relations with the United States. While continuing its opposition to the Soviet Union, China has reversed much of its former anti-American stance and now looks with favor upon closer political and economic

[1] Leo Goodstadt, *China's Search for Plenty, The Economics of Mao Tse-tung*, New York: John Weatherhill, 1973, p. 18.

relations with the United States. The latter has in turn been willing to support Communist China which is now a member of the United Nations and is prepared to expand trade relations with it. At the current stage in its political and economic development, China now finds it worthwhile to curb its attacks on Western capitalism, and to offset Soviet power and influence by seeking the goodwill of the United States.

The Sino-Soviet conflict of recent years has frequently been interpreted as an ideological conflict. It is true that the Chinese communists claim that the Soviet communists are "revisionists," who are undermining world communism by falsely reinterpreting Marx and Lenin. In turn, the Soviet communists assert that the Chinese communists are "dogmatists," who have followed Stalin's incorrect interpretation of Marxism-Leninism and who have failed to interpret Marx and Lenin "creatively." The basic ideological argument is over whether or not the transition from capitalism to socialism in the noncommunist world can be peaceful. The Soviet communists declare that under "peaceful coexistence" the transition in the West and elsewhere can be achieved without revolutionary struggles and "wars of liberation." The Chinese communists assert the opposite. They claim that Lenin made it clear that war is the inevitable outcome of exploitation by capitalist systems and that therefore war between the United States and the communist camp is unavoidable.

A close examination of the Sino-Soviet conflict reveals that this conflict is ideological only on the surface. At bottom, the conflict is one between two great powers that are strongly nationalistic and that occupy very different international positions. The conflict is over what international policies to pursue. Ideology merely provides a medium through which more fundamental differences can be aired.[2] Mainland China is a "have-not" nation, whose communist revolution has been going only a quarter of a century, whereas the Soviet revolution has been over a half-century in the making and has brought the Soviet Union to the point of becoming a "have" nation. The Soviet Union, now controlling all the territory ever ruled by Moscow, is in a diplomatic equilibrium with the West. However, Communist China still has territorial claims, including Taiwan, that remain unsatisfied. It is led by "revolutionary leaders" still fresh from battle, whereas the Soviet Union is directed by "administrators," to whom actual revolution is a fast-fading memory. The central issue between the Soviet Union and Communist China is the worldwide role of the communist camp in the future. Should it be a closely knit, militant group of communist nations out to foment revolutionary wars, or should it be a loose organization in which each member is free to develop its own international position? The Soviet Union wants the latter type of international communist organization, while Communist China is calling for the former type.

Communist China as a Less Developed Country

Mainland China is not an ordinary underdeveloped country like many of the underdeveloped countries in Africa and Asia. It has an old and well-developed culture, is capable of turning out scientists of a very high caliber, and can feed and clothe adequately over 800 million people. Mainland China has constructed a huge industrial complex in its interior, has trained a first-class industrial work force, is conducting intensive scientific research and development, is producing ad-

[2] D. Floyd, *Mao against Khrushchev*, New York, Frederick A. Praeger, 1963, pp. 191–205.

vanced weapons and significant numbers of submarines, tanks, missiles, and jet aircraft, has detonated thirteen nuclear devices, and has launched two space satellites. In addition, Mainland China has provided considerable economic aid to other developing countries.

At the same time, the People's Republic of China is a poor country like many underdeveloped countries in Africa and Asia. If per capita GNP of $200 is taken as a dividing line between poor and less than poor developing countries, then Mainland China, as the statistics in Table 19-1 show, is above many African and Asian countries such as India, Pakistan, Nigeria, Tanzania, Burma, and Indonesia, but below Thailand, Egypt, South Korea, Cuba, and Iran. In 1952, Mainland China had a $59 billion GNP and per capita GNP of $104. By 1971, its GNP was $128 billion and its per capita GNP was $150.[3] The long-term rate of economic growth under the Chinese

[3] Estimates provided by Arthur G. Ashbrook, Jr., in "China: Economic Policy and Economic Results," in Joint Economic Committee, *People's Republic of China: An Economic Assessment*, Washington, D.C., 1972, p. 39. GNP and per capita GNP estimates vary widely among Western analysts, because very few economic statistics have been released by the Chinese government since 1961, and no reliable basis exists for these estimates. See Ashbrook, *op. cit.*, Appendix A, "Methodology for the Calculations of China's GNP," pp. 41-45.

Table 19-1
Economic and Population Growth Rates in Mainland China and Other Developing Countries, 1960-1973

Countries	Per capita GNP, 1973 (U.S. dollars)	Average GNP per capita growth rate, 1960-73 (percent)	Average annual population growth rate, 1960-73 (percent)
Brazil	760	3.6	2.9
Iran	870	6.4	3.2
Cuba	540	-1.0	2.0
Turkey	600	3.9	2.5
Algeria	570	1.7	3.2
South Korea	400	7.1	2.2
Egypt	250	1.5	2.5
Thailand	270	4.8	3.1
Mainland China	270	3.8	1.7
Nigeria	210	3.6	2.5
Sri Lanka	120	2.0	2.3
India	120	1.3	2.3
Tanzania	130	2.8	2.9
Pakistan	120	3.4	2.9
Afghanistan	90	0.3	2.2
Burma	80	0.7	2.2
Indonesia	130	2.4	2.0

Source: IBRD, *World Bank Atlas*, 1975.

communists since 1949 has averaged 4 percent a year or 2 percent per capita.

With per capita consumption $150 in 1971, a surplus of $45 per capita was available for industrial development. In other words, while GNP per head was rising from $104 in 1952 to $150 in 1971, personal consumption grew slowly, and the bulk of the annual GNP increase or economic dividend was allocated to investment in industry. The growth strategy for the period since 1949 has been one of holding back the increase in personal consumption in order to devote the nation's economic surplus to providing a strong industrial base for the development of a powerful military state. Underlying this growth strategy has been the Maoist ideology, which provides, as we shall see, an intellectual justification for the policy followed.

Communist China's basic economic problem is its poverty or low level of per capita real income. It has a large output potential for industrialization. However, with population increasing each year by 15 to 20 million, the current demands for consumption tend to leave limited real income for investment; and without high annual investment, no rapid industrialization can take place. Since large amounts of foreign economic aid (imports of machinery and industrial raw materials) are not available to Communist China, industrialization must be very largely financed from domestic sources. With the per capita real income very low, the bulk of the population unskilled, and little foreign economic aid available, any government in Communist China that would attempt to carry out a rapid industrialization program could only do so by imposing extreme hardships upon the general population. This is precisely what the government of Mao Tse-tung has been prepared to do. His personal experience as a revolutionary leader, his successful guerrilla campaign, and his special brand of Marxist-Leninist ideology prepared Mao well for launching and executing the program of forced-draught industrialization that has been imposed upon the people of Communist China since 1949. Mao's communism is a militant, authoritarian type of communism that is supported by a powerful spirit and loyalty on the part of the people. Mao's communism is not matched even by the hard-line communism of Stalin at the peak of its development.[4]

The Political Structure of Communist China

The political structure of Communist China duplicates that of the Soviet Union. The constitutional political pattern consists of a single national chamber, the National People's Congress with deputies representing twenty-one provinces, five autonomous regions, three municipalities, ethnic minorities, the armed services, and overseas Chinese. The Congress up to 1975 elected a President to act as head of state and a standing committee to function between sessions of the National People's Congress. The Congress also appoints the State Council, an executive body with thirty-two ministries and various commissions under its jurisdiction. The Premier, as the chairman of the State Council, administers the government of the country. Behind this front of constitutional government is the Chinese Communist party, also organized along the lines of the Communist party of the Soviet Union, with a Congress, a Central Committee, and a Politburo of twenty members at the top. Control of Communist China is centralized in the hands of the twenty members of the Politburo, of which Mao Tse-tung was the chairman until his death on September 9, 1976. The Chinese Communist party has a member-

[4] A. A. Cohen, *The Communism of Mao Tse-tung*, Chicago, The University of Chicago Press, 1964, pp. 193–202.

ship of twenty million. All important governmental and managerial positions are held by members of the Communist party. Since the eight other small political parties are pro-communist, Communist China, like all other communist countries, has, in effect, a one-party, proletarian political system.

The ideological basis of Chinese communism, as it has been developed by Mao Tse-tung, Liu Shao-chi, and other leading Chinese communists, shows the heavy imprint of its Marxist-Leninist origins. Mao accepted the basic theses of Marx and Lenin with respect to the inevitable demise of capitalism, the transition to socialism, and the eventual development of a communist society, or what the Chinese communists call the "world of Great Harmony." Mao took from Lenin the concept of the Communist party as an elite or vanguard with the function of instilling political consciousness in the proletariat. Mao also borrowed Lenin's concept of democratic centralism and his theory of imperialistic exploitation. The differences between Marxism-Leninism and Maoism are not mainly theoretical differences, but rather differences in views about how to handle the transition from capitalism to socialism and then on to communism. These differences stem largely from Mao's own personality and experiences and the special social and economic circumstances of China at the time of the revolutionary struggle to establish the People's Republic of China.

Mao had a strong anti-Western animus that caused him to regard Europe as a "burnt-out revolutionary hearth." In his opinion, the workers in Europe and the United States are hopelessly reactionary; unlike Khrushchev, Mao would put forth no effort to win over the workers of the West to communism. Unlike Lenin, who regarded nationalism as an obstacle to the development of world communism, Mao was a "revolutionary nationalist," who looked forward to securing for China the role in world affairs to which he believed it is entitled. Mao was much less cosmopolitan than was Lenin, who would tolerate nationalism only so long as it helped to achieve his goal of world revolution. Resenting European domination, Mao found nationalism to be an authentic value that would not disappear in the struggle to establish communism. This view of the value of nationalism leads some of the underdeveloped countries of Africa and Asia to look to Peking for leadership and not to Moscow.

Mao's experience as a successful practitioner of guerrilla warfare greatly influenced his views on how to carry on the struggle for communism. Mao was a militant communist, whose experience with guerrilla warfare caused him to look at economic problems in terms of "struggle and firmness of will."[5] Just as he won the war against the Chinese Nationalists under Chiang Kai-shek with few military resources, Mao proposed to convert China overnight into an industrial giant by relying very heavily upon the labor of the masses and their will to achieve the communist goal. There was a mood of impatience about Mao which led him to put politics above economics and to ignore the restraints placed upon human activity by the scarcity of economic goods and services. Mao's voluntarism and his emphasis on the importance of the "will-to-action" in the revolutionary struggle created blind spots in his view of the future of a Communist China.

Unlike Stalin, who was a good administrator, but who had little imagination, Mao was an effective leader who, however, had little interest in the routine tasks of constructing an efficient economic system. Mao was a successful revolutionary leader who turned out to be far from successful in coping with the more prosaic problems of socialist

[5] S. R. Schram, *The Political Thought of Mao Tse-tung,* New York, Frederick A. Praeger, Publisher, 1963, p. 82.

construction. His program for establishing rural communes, which destroyed peasants' incentives, and his "Great Leap Forward" program (1958–1960), which stimulated small-scale, inefficient "backyard" industries, took inadequate account of the realities of the economic situation of China in the late 1950s. As the transformation of the communist Chinese economy progressed during the 1950s, it became quite clear that what was needed was less of Mao's "redness" and more "expertness" from those who were responsible for guiding the Chinese economy.

The Chinese "way" to communism differed from the Soviet "way" in that it provided for a "democratic" phase after the overturn of capitalism.[6] In this early phase, the Chinese communists cooperated with those capitalists who were willing to accept the communist regime. The cooperating capitalists were incorporated in joint state-private enterprises, where they eventually lost their identity as capitalists and became communists. Mao's "creative development" of Marxism-Leninism in China also gave rise to the view that the rapid transformation of the Chinese economy could be secured through the mobilization of the energies of the masses and that it did not have to wait for the mechanization of the economy. Following this interpretation of Marxism-Leninism, Mao established rural communes in advance of the mechanization of agriculture. The Soviet leaders believe that these communes can be successfully organized only after agriculture has been fully mechanized. The lack of tractors and other agricultural equipment did not deter Mao from seeking to communize Chinese agriculture, since he felt that labor and willpower could be substituted for tractors.

Mao's early program for communizing Chinese agriculture as well as his program for rapidly expanding small-scale industry throughout the country so as to industrialize it quickly failed. These failures indicate that his militant and voluntaristic communism, with its urge to reshape both man and nature, can no longer cope with the problems of placing the Chinese economy on a rational basis. If it was not clear to Mao, it is now apparent to some of his younger communist leaders, led by the new Party Chairman Hua Kuo-feng, that politics cannot for long take precedence over economics if China is to develop an efficient and viable industrialized economy. The development of a more rational approach to the industrialization of China, if it takes place, will be the contribution not of Mao Tse-tung, the somewhat fanatical revolutionary leader of the "War of Liberation," but of his successors, who will be more like Lenin's "organization men."

The Structure of the Chinese Communist Economy

Mainland China is the world's third largest country (3.7 million square miles), with approximately one-quarter of the world's population, estimated to be over 800 million in 1976.[7] Having a huge population, a large skilled labor force, and abundant natural resources, China is destined to become one of

[6] *Selected Works of Mao Tse-tung*, "On the People's Democratic Dictatorship," Volume IV, Peking, Foreign Language Press, 1961, pp. 411–422.

[7] Analyses of the structure and functioning of the Chinese economy are presented in Donald P. Whitaker and others, *Area Handbook for the People's Republic of China,* Foreign Area Studies of The American University, Washington, D.C.: U.S. Government Printing Office, 1972; Audrey Donnithorne, *China's Economic System,* New York: Frederick A. Praeger, 1967; Jan S. Prybyla, *The Political Economy of Communist China,* Scranton: International Textbook Co., 1970; the Joint Economic Committee, *An Economic Profile of Mainland China,*1967, *People's Republic of China: An Economic Assessment,* 1972, and *China: A Reassessment of the Economy,* 1975; and Theodore Shabad, *China's Map, Regional and National Economic Development,* 2nd Ed., New York, Praeger Publishers, 1974.

the world's few superpowers. Its hydroelectric potential ranks first among nations; and its large deposits of coal and iron are capable of supporting an iron and steel industry that could compete on equal terms with that of the United States and the Soviet Union. China is today self-sufficient in crude oil and petroleum products, has large untapped oil reserves, and is a major producer of mercury, tin, and tungsten. It is deficient in the three alloying metals, chromium, nickel, and cobalt, and in rubber. It also has limited supplies of wood products as a result of the denuding of the land of its forest cover during recent centuries in order to provide fuel and to enlarge the area of farmland. Today, only from 5 to 10 percent of China is forested.

Of China's large land area, only about 11 percent, largely in the eastern third of the country, is suitable for cultivation. While China has large agricultural resources and a wide variety of soils, temperatures, and precipitation, and while multiple cropping can increase the output of the cultivated area by one-half, China finds it much harder to feed more than 800 million people than does the United States with its 213 million, and the Soviet Union with its 252 million. Before 1939, per capita cultivated land in China was only 0.45 acres, as compared with 2.01 acres in the Soviet Union and 8.04 in the United States. Since 1949, the land-population ratio has fallen still lower as population has continued to grow at the high annual rate of close to 2 percent; this increase adds more than 15 million to the total population each year. By 1976, China had greatly enlarged the small industrial base that it had inherited in 1949; but it is still an underdeveloped country in relation to its endowment of natural resources, its huge population, and the growth objectives of its political leaders.

Chinese agriculture is the most important sector of the economy, providing employment for 75 to 85 percent of the country's labor force of about 350 million and contributing one-third of the GNP. Much of the economy's surplus above consumption, which is available for investment, comes from the agricultural sector, which also provides a substantial part of the nation's foreign exchange earnings. Industry contributes an estimated one-half of the GNP, with the remaining 17 percent being contributed by transportation, communication, trade, and other services, including government service. In Asia, Mainland China is second only to Japan in GNP, having a product of $219 billion in 1973, compared with Japan's product of close to $393 billion.

The statistics in Table 19-2 show that Mainland China is far behind Japan and other industrialized nations in relation to per capita GNP. Whereas China's total GNP in 1973 was 56 percent of Japan's, China's per capita GNP was only 7 percent of Japan's per capita GNP; this disparity explains the wide gap between the living standards of these two Asiatic countries. The Soviet Union and the industrialized Western nations are much ahead of Communist China in both total GNP and per capita GNP. Also in the decade of the 1960s—a troubled one for China—the average annual economic growth rates of the Soviet Union and the major Western nations, except for the United Kingdom, were well above China's growth rate.

Mainland China has two quite different economies, the advanced modern economy and the inherited backward economy. The modern economy includes all the modern factories, with their up-to-date machinery and equipment, in the urban areas in the coastal and eastern regions of the country. It also encompasses the agricultural communes in the coastal and eastern parts of the country, where the best land is found and where the most advanced agricultural techniques are applied. Alongside the modern economy is the inherited primitive economy that includes small factories with obsolescent machinery and

Table 19-2
GNP and Economic Growth in Mainland China and Selected Industrialized Countries

	Total GNP, 1973 (billions of U.S. dollars)	GNP per capita, 1973 (U.S. dollars)	Average annual economic growth rate, 1960–1973 (percent)	Population, mid-1973 (thousands)
United States	1,304.5	6,200	3.1	210,400
West Germany	329.7	5,320	3.7	61,970
United Kingdom	171.4	3,060	2.4	56,000
Japan	393.0	3,630	9.4	108,350
Soviet Union	506.5	2,030	3.6	249,750
Mainland China	216.7	270	3.8	811,350

Source: IBRD, *World Bank Atlas*, 1975.

equipment in the urban and agricultural areas in the central and western parts of the country; here farming, transportation, and handicrafts are primitive and underdeveloped. The Chinese planners concentrate their investments in the high-productivity, capital-intensive modern economy rather than in the low-productivity, backward economy, which is labor intensive. Strict measures are taken to keep the surplus underemployed population in the backward economy from migrating to the urban areas, where the capital-intensive modern industries are able to absorb only a relatively small part of the total national labor force of 350 million.

The rapid industrialization of the Chinese economy has required a high level of investment. As the statistics in Table 19–3 reveal, close to one-quarter of China's gross domestic product is taken up by investment in plant and equipment in order to sustain a long-term growth rate of 4 percent. Japan, which has had

Table 19-3
The Chinese Gross Domestic Product by End Use, 1961, 1965, and 1970 (In Percent)

Uses	1961	1965	1970
Personal consumption	63	64	64
Government consumption	8	9	10
Fixed investment	19	23	23
Changes in inventory and statistical discrepancy	10	5	3
Export surplus	0	1	1
Gross domestic product[1]	100	102	101

[1] Percentages do not add to 100 because of rounding.

Source: Ta-Ching Liu and Kung-Chia Yeh, "Chinese and Other Asian Economies: A Quantitative Evaluation," *American Economic Review*, Vol. LXIII, No. 2, May 1973, p. 219.

a 10 percent growth rate, has allocated more than one-third of its GNP to investment. Close to two-thirds of China's total annual output has been absorbed by personal consumption which, when spread over more than 800 million people, provides a very limited per capita consumption.

The Decentralized Planned Chinese Economy

Like other communist countries, Mainland China has a highly planned economy. Before the decentralization program that took place after 1957, the Chinese planning system was essentially a reproduction of the highly centralized Soviet planning system. Many Soviet experts were involved in the construction of China's First Five-Year Plan (1953-1957).[8] This plan provided for the centralized control from Peking of all enterprises in China's twenty-one provinces and five autonomous regions. As in the Soviet Union, all important raw materials and capital goods were allocated by the central planners, who also closely supervised the economy's fixed investment program. By 1957, it was widely realized in China that the Soviet planning system with its emphasis upon the rapid expansion of heavy industry was not suitable for a country with relatively little capital but a huge labor supply. Consequently, Chinese planning underwent a transformation after 1957; as a result, the bulk of the plan construction and implementation was transferred from Peking to the provincial and local governments. Unlike the Soviet Union, which also decentralized its planning system after 1957, China did not abolish its central ministries in charge of the various industries; there ministries continued to draw up general plans for each industry, but left the execution of these plans to the provincial and local government planning departments.

Figure 19-1 shows the Chinese economic decision-making structure as it relates to the national planning program. The chairman and the other members of the Politburo pass down the general plan directives to the State Council, the administrative arm of the central government, whose planning department constructs the annual and five-year plans. These plans are then carried out partly on the national level by the economic ministries in Peking, and partly on the provincial and subprovincial levels by the planning departments of the twenty-one provincial and many thousands of subprovincial governments.

Under the new decentralized planning system, the central government planning authorities are concerned primarily with macroeconomic decisions relating to such matters as the nation's goals, its growth rate, the division of the Gross National Product between investment and consumption, and the balance between exports and imports. The central government keeps under its control the vital parts of the economy, i.e., the major heavy industries, electric-power stations, the production of military equipment, the technically complex branches of industry, experimental factories, the main railroad system, river conservation, the banking system, scientific-research institutions, foreign trade, state farms, and the enterprises of the People's Liberation Army. Apart from these specialized concerns, the rest of the economy falls within the planning jurisdiction of the provincial and local governments.

The planning activities of each provincial government cover the industrial, agricultural, and commercial activities of between 20 and

---

[8] For the details of Chinese national planning, see Yuan-li Wu, "Planning, Management, and Economic Development in Communist China," Joint Economic Committee, *An Economic Profile of Mainland China*, 1967, pp. 97-119; Dwight H. Perkins, "Plans and Their Implementation in the People's Republic of China," *American Economic Review*, Vol. LXIII, No. 2, May 1973, pp. 224-235; and Audrey Donnithorne, *op. cit.*, pp. 457-495.

Figure 19-1
China: Economic Decision-Making Structure, 1975

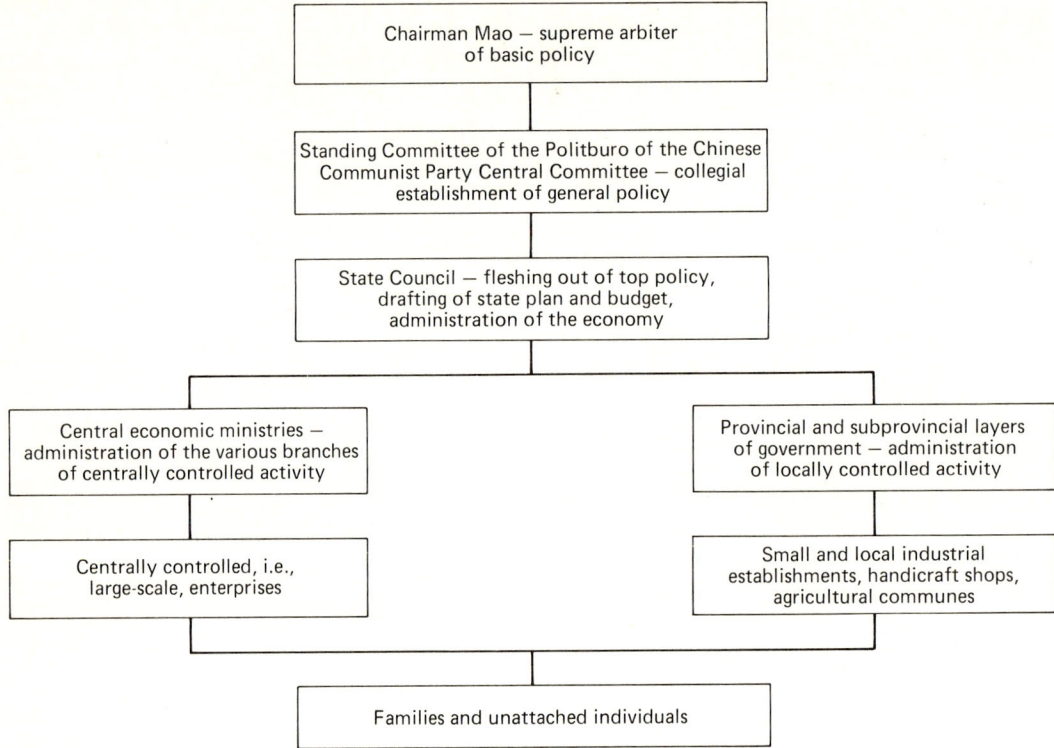

Source: Arthur G. Ashbrook, Jr., "China: Economic Overview," *China: A Reassessment of the Economy,* p. 48.

75 million people. Most of the industries secure their raw materials and sell their output very largely within their own province. Some need arises, however, to transfer grain, raw materials, and capital goods from surplus to deficit provinces. The heart of the planning in each province is a system of materials balances set in physical terms, under which the provincial planning authorities allocate scarce goods to individual enterprises within the province. Under the system of *transfer balances*, the central government transfers crucial scarce raw materials and finished goods from one province to another and outside of the country in return for imports. Within the provinces, each enterprise engages in annual and five-year planning. It passes on its plans to the local and provincial planners who coordinate the enterprise plans into an overall provincial plan; this provincial plan is then passed on to the central government planners in the State Planning Commission, who draw up annual and five-year plans for the whole country. The implementation of the plans falls primarily upon the enterprises and the provincial and local planning authorities.

Under the decentralization program, the flexibility of the individual state enterprises has been considerably increased by reducing the number of major plan targets for each enterprise from twelve to four, namely, output, cost reduction, profits, and labor productivity.

A major objective of the decentralized planning has been to develop the agricultural sector so that the nation can become self-sufficient in grains, have a large surplus to support the expanding industry in the urban areas, and provide exportable products that can earn foreign exchange. With the decentralization came a shift in national priorities. Under the First Five-Year Plan, the main emphasis was on developing heavy industry. The Second Five-Year Plan (1958-1962), which had the same objective, was abandoned in 1958 in favor of the decentralization program, which had as its objective *walking on two legs*, i.e., developing both agriculture and industry in a balanced manner. Decentralization has made it possible to use the abundant labor supply by developing new, labor-intensive, small-scale plants in the rural areas. While industry has not been neglected, it is called upon to make available to the agricultural sector more fertilizer, pesticides, and other chemical products, as well as machinery and equipment for small-scale industry. Besides utilizing the huge labor supply in the agricultural sector, decentralization has raised farm incomes and has helped to secure a more equitable distribution of income between the urban and rural areas.

When organized national planning was resumed in 1970 at the end of the Cultural Revolution, the Fourth Five-Year Plan (1971-1975) followed the same national priorities that had been established in the late 1960s. The new political ferment associated with the "anti-Confucius, anti-Lin Piao" campaign in 1973 resulted in attacks against reliance on material incentives, foreign technology, and the leadership of rehabilitated bureaucrats who had been downgraded during the Cultural Revolution.[9] In late 1974, the radical versus moderate confrontation was greatly reduced; and by early 1975, moderation in economic policy and an interest in increased production and improved technology once more became the emphasis of policy under Chou En-lai's direction. The nature of the Fifth Five-Year Plan (1976-1980) has not yet been revealed, but all indications are that this plan will be constructed by the moderates in the national leadership.

The Performance of the Chinese Economy since 1949

In the past quarter century, Communist China has made very considerable progress in restoring its economy from the ravages of a decade of warfare and placing itself well on the way towards the construction of a modern industrial nation. One Western analyst has described the results of this quarter century of communist rule of China as having been "mixed—striking economic successes, partial failures, and unfinished tasks. For the period as a whole, China's economic growth has been strong but erratic."[10] The erratic development of the Chinese economy has reflected the deep ideological differences between Mao and his followers, who have

---

[9] The radical elements in the Chinese Communist party in 1973-1974 attacked Confucianism as being highly authoritarian, in favor of class distinctions and preserving the status quo, and opposed to the creation of a classless proletarian-dominated society. Confucianism, which had a revival in China in the early 1960s, came under attack by the left wing of the Communist party; this wing is opposed to bourgeois tendencies, and wants to emphasize the importance of advocating perpetual revolution and periodic upheaval in order to prevent the possible restoration of capitalism. Lin Piao, the former Minister of National Defense and Mao Tse-tung's officially designated successor, led a plot against Mao in 1971 and perished in the effort. In 1970, Lin Piao opposed the mechanization of agriculture at the expense of the armed forces. He attempted to place military personnel in key positions in the Communist Party and to give the armed forces a larger role in the nation's government.

[10] Arthur G. Ashbrook, Jr., "China: Economic Policy and Economic Results, 1949-71," *People's Republic of China: An Economic Assessment*, p. 3. A very good summary of Chinese economic development during the years 1949-1971 is given on p. 4 and an extended analysis in pp. 15-36.

elevated "redness" over "expertness," and the more pragmatic communist leaders who have preferred "expertness" rather than "redness."

The post-1949 era of Chinese economic development falls into six distinct periods. The years 1949-1952 were devoted to recovery and rehabilitation of the nation's economy, while the years 1953-1957 were ones of rapid economic development under the First Five-Year Plan, which duplicated the Soviet plans. In the third period, 1958-1960, the Great Leap Forward was led by Mao, who hoped to speed up the industrialization process. This disastrous period of overstraining the economy was followed by a fourth period of economic readjustment and recovery, 1961-1965, during which the more pragmatic communists under Liu Shao-chi elevated concern for economic efficiency over ideological or revolutionary fervor and quickly achieved a balanced economy. In the fifth period, 1966-1969, a renewed attempt was made to return to the revolutionary Maoist method of operating the economy without the serious disruptions of the years of the Great Leap Forward. In the latest period of economic development since 1970, there has been a return to more normal economic policies and practices, and a resumption of systematic national planning.

After the recovery and rehabilitation of the years 1949-1952, the Chinese economy had a period of rapid and sustained growth during the First Five-Year Plan (1953-1957). Under Soviet direction a successful build-up of industry took place; a collectivization of agriculture in a number of stages also occurred. The economic progress achieved in the first five-year plan period is shown by the statistics in Table 19-4. During these years, the expansion of industry was stressed. Industrial production was doubled, while agricultural production was increased by only one-fifth. Steel production was quadrupled, and foreign trade, largely with the Soviet Union, increased at an annual average rate of 10.2 percent. Grain production increased more rapidly than the population, and living standards were stabilized at austere but improved levels.

China's economic momentum was lost during the Great Leap Forward, when an attempt was made to speed up the industrialization process by taking advantage of China's large

Table 19-4

The Achievements of the First Chinese Five-Year Plan, 1953-1957

	1949	1952	1957	Percent growth 1952-1957
GNP (billions U.S. $)	36	59	82	6.8
GNP per capita (U.S. $)	79	104	128	4.3
Industrial production index	31	51	100	14.4
Steel (million metric tons)	0.16	1.35	5.35	32.0
Agricultural production index	54	83	100	3.8
Grain (million metric tons)	108	154	185	3.8
Foreign trade (billions U.S. $)	0.83	1.89	3.06	10.2
Population (millions)	538	570	642	2.4

Source: Arthur G. Ashbrook, Jr., "China: Economic Policy and Economic Results, 1949-71," Joint Economic Committee, *People's Republic of China: An Economic Assessment*, 1972, pp. 5 and 46.

and underused labor force. The aim of the Great Leap Forward was to achieve an economic miracle in a few years. The Second Five-Year Plan (1958–1962) was discarded by Mao in its first year of operation on the ground that the Soviet system of planning was not applicable to the special circumstances of the Chinese economy. New large quotas were set for managers of industrial plants and hundreds of thousands of little backyard steel furnaces, fertilizer plants, and coal pits were opened. There was a very large but unsustainable increase in industrial production of almost one-third in the years 1958 and 1959, only to be followed by a precipitous decline of 35 percent in the two years 1960 and 1961. The establishment of the rural communes in 1958 was followed by three very poor crop years, which brought the population to a near-starvation level. The experimentation with *free supply*, or payment according to need, undermined peasant incentives, and led to major modifications in the rural commune system after 1961. The disasters on the industrial and agricultural fronts were combined with a loss of much-needed capital and raw material imports from the Soviet Union, which withdrew its technicians and economic aid after 1958.

The statistics in Table 19-5 reveal a considerable recovery in the years 1962–1965, when Mao was forced to give up control of the nation's economy. Under the direction of Liu Shao-chi, unprofitable small-scale industrial enterprises were abandoned; the rural communes were reorganized to place the burden of production on the production brigades and teams; material incentives were restored; and national priorities were changed to place more emphasis on developing a strong agricultural sector—although industry was still considered to be the leading sector. In addition, a major shift in foreign trade occurred, away from the Soviet Union and other communist countries to Japan, West Germany, and other Western countries. Living levels were restored to the spartan levels that existed before the Great Leap Forward. By 1966, industrial production surpassed the peak level reached in 1959 during the Great Leap Forward, and agricultural production had climbed back to the peak level of 1958. The recovery and readjustment of 1962–1966 were primarily concerned with regaining the ground lost during and after the Great Leap Forward.

Five-year national planning, which had been abandoned in 1958, was restored briefly in 1966 when the Third Five-Year Plan (1966–1970) was adopted by Liu Shao-chi and his technocratic supporters. By this time, however, Mao Tse-tung had regained control of the governmental apparatus, and he was disturbed by the planners' emphasis on economic efficiency and technical progress, which were of concern to the bureaucracy but influenced only a small part of China's population. In 1966, Mao initiated the Great Proletarian Cultural Revolution. This was calculated to contribute to his program of permanent revolution by challenging inherited beliefs, putting an end to outmoded institutions, and uprooting bureaucracies interested in preserving the status quo. Mao was committed to a revolutionary process and not to any fixed program or end.[11] He sought to engage the masses in putting the revolution back on the track, and to change China's political and economic course before it was too late.

For this purpose, Mao appealed over the heads of the party cadres and government bureaucrats to peasants, urban workers, and students to support the *Four Olds Movement*, against old customs, old habits, old thinking, and old ideology. Systematic planning under

[11] For a discussion of the Maoist model, see Edwin F. Jones, "Cultural Revolution: In Search of a Maoist Model," *People's Republic of China: An Economic Assessment*, pp. 52–58; and Leo Goodstadt, *China's Search for Plenty, The Economics of Mao Tse-tung*.

Table 19-5
Selected Economic Indicators of Chinese Communist Development, 1949–1974

Period and year	GNP (billions of 1973 dollars)	Population midyear (millions)	GNP per capita (1973 dollars)	Industrial production (1957 = 100)	Agricultural production (1957 = 100)	Steel output (millions of metric tons)	Grain output (millions of metric tons)
1949–1952, Rehabilitation							
1949	40	538	74	20	54	0.16	108
1950	49	547	89	27	64	.61	125
1951	56	558	101	38	71	.90	135
1952	67	570	117	48	83	1.35	154
1953–1957, 1st 5-year Plan							
1953	71	583	122	61	83	1.77	157
1954	75	596	125	70	84	2.22	160
1955	82	611	134	73	94	2.85	175
1956	88	626	141	88	97	4.46	182
1957	94	641	147	100	100	5.35	185
1958–1960, Great Leap Forward							
1958	113	657	172	145	108	11.08	200
1959	107	672	160	177	83	13.35	165
1960	106	685	155	184	78	18.67	160

1961–1965, Readjustment and Recovery						
1961	82	695	118	108	77	8	160
1962	93	704	133	114	92	8	180
1963	103	716	144	137	96	9	185
1964	117	731	160	163	106	10.8	195
1965	134	747	179	199	114	12.5	210
1966–1969, Cultural Revolution						
1966	145	763	190	231	116	15	215
1967	141	780	180	202	123	12	230
1968	142	798	178	222	116	14	215
1969	157	817	192	265	118	16	220
1970–1974, Resumption of Regular Planning						
1970	179	837	214	313	129	17.8	240
1971	190	857	222	341	134	21	246
1972	197	878	225	371	130	23	240
1973	217	899	241	416	138	25.5	250
1974 preliminary	223	920	243	432	141	23.8	255
Average annual increase, 1949–1974	7.2%	2.2%	4.9%	13.1%	3.9%	11.4%	3.5%
Average annual increase, 1957–1974	5.2%	2.2%	3.0%	9.0%	2.1%	9.2%	1.9%

Source: Arthur G. Ashbrook, Jr., "China: Economic Overview, 1975," Joint Economic Committee, *China: A Reassessment of the Economy*, 1975, p. 23.

The Chinese communist economy

the Third Five-Year Plan was abandoned as the Cultural Revolution went through three phases: (1) Red Guard student phase; (2) a military phase, when the People's Liberation Army stepped in to halt the decline in industrial production; and (3) a stabilization phase, when the army played an increasingly important role in restoring order and in participating in the management of government bureaus, factories, research institutes, and educational institutions at central, provincial, and local levels.

As Table 19-5 shows, the Cultural Revolution adversely affected both industrial production and economic growth for two years. In 1967, industrial production declined 12 percent and GNP almost 3 percent, according to Western estimates. Low levels of production continued through 1968, but when the Cultural Revolution came to an end in 1969, the pre-1967 growth pattern was restored. The living standards of the 85 percent of the population in the rural areas were not greatly altered by the Cultural Revolution, which did much less damage to the Chinese economy than the Great Leap Forward of 1958-1961. Although much of the party and government systems was disrupted during the revolution, some scholars believe that Mao did not achieve the restoration of the revolutionary spirit that he had expected. Except in the riot-torn urban areas, the economy continued to function about as it had before the Revolution and was soon able to recover from the disturbances of 1966-1968.

In the sixth period of China's economic development, which dates from 1970, China settled down once more to a period of sustained economic progress under the guidance of the pragmatic Premier Chou En-lai. There was a return to systematic planning under the Fourth Five-Year Plan (1971-1975), the objectives of which were basically the same as those of the Third Plan. In industry, the emphasis was on improving efficiency and technology and enlarging output; in agriculture, the aim was to make the rural areas more self-sustaining; in foreign trade, the objective was to exchange basic products for Western machinery and technology; in the field of labor the aim was some restoration of material incentives; and in the social area a gradual improvement in living standards was sought. The elimination of Marshall Lin Piao in 1971 may mean that the army is no longer needed to preserve discipline in the economy. Private plots have been permitted in the countryside. The small plants program in local areas, which has been further advanced, fits in with the development of giant industrial complexes in the nation's interior regions for the production of heavy industrial and military products. In his report to the National People's Congress held in January 1975, Chou En-lai reported large average annual increases in 1964-1974 in industrial production (11.3 percent), tractors (20 percent), petroleum (22.3 percent), chemical fertilizers (15.7 percent), and electric power (11.6 percent). The estimates of Western experts, given in Table 19-5, are that in the post–Cultural Revolution period from 1970 to 1974 Gross National Product increased at the average annual rate of 7.3 percent and industrial production at the rate of 10.3 percent.

Industry in the Chinese Communist Economy

Unlike the Soviet communists, the Chinese communists did not nationalize industry on a large scale after winning control of the country in 1949. The policy adopted towards industry was one of a slow transformation from private to state enterprise. The process of transformation was carried out in three steps: (1) utilization of private industry from 1949 to 1951; (2) restriction of private industry from 1952 to 1953; and (3) the final socialization of private industry from 1954 to 1957. When they took over the country in 1949, the Chinese communists divided capitalists into *bourgeois capitalists*, who had worked closely with the prior Nationalist Government and who would not accept communism, and *national capitalists*, who were prepared to cooperate with the new communist regime. The Chinese communists confiscated the property of the bourgeois capitalists, but did not treat the national capitalists in the same manner. The latter group of capitalists was willing to cooperate with the communists because they believed that some kind of private business sector might become a permanent feature of the new Chinese communist economy. Their hopes along this line proved to be groundless.

In the reconstruction stage from 1949 to the end of 1951, private businesspeople in industry and distribution were permitted to keep their enterprises intact and to manage them without direct government interference. The Chinese government needed the support of these businesspeople during the difficult period of postwar rehabilitation of the Chinese economy. The government increased output by placing orders with the privately owned factories. It also used the private stores as distribution outlets for the planned production. In the restriction stage, running from the beginning of 1952 to the end of 1953, the government adopted a policy of placing more restrictions upon private enterprise as the number of state factories and state stores increased. The private enterprises were drained of their working capital through a series of heavy fines imposed under the *5-anti campaign*, which accused the private businesspeople of tax evasion, bribery, cheating the government, and other "evils." Fines also absorbed much of the remaining net worth of the private industrialists, who were then forced to borrow from the nationalized state banks.

In the third stage of transformation of private enterprise into state enterprise—from 1954 to 1957—the government invested funds in the formerly private enterprises and established joint state-private enterprises in which the former owner-operators had only a secondary managerial role and received limited dividends upon their private capital. Finally, the owners of industrial enterprises were guaranteed 5 percent interest on their capital investment for a period of ten years, after which all private industrial property would become state property. The Chinese handicraft industries have undergone a somewhat similar transformation. The eight million independent craftsmen were first organized in supply and marketing groups under government direction. Next they were formally brought into supply and marketing cooperatives, in which they continued to use their privately owned equipment. Finally the handicraftsmen became members of producers' cooperatives, in which all equipment was collectively owned.

Urban communes were first set up in 1958 for the purpose of communizing the individual city worker's mode of life. The urban communes provide public mess halls and a number of public service centers that free women from household duties and enable them to become "productive" factory workers. Urban communes vary in size from 50,000 to 300,000 members. These communes have sprung up around the large state factories and mines in or near urban centers. They are also associated with local commune factories in urban areas that produce consumer goods. Urban communes have created much less resentment than the rural communes, because much of the normal pattern of independent city life can still be carried on. Members of the urban communes are not required to use the public mess halls and other common facilities as much as members of rural communes. Also, both men and women workers in urban communes are paid money wages, not wages in kind.

Since 1949, Mainland China has made significant progress in increasing the output of its major industries. By the early 1970s, China had the potential for the development of a fully modern and diversified manufacturing complex on a scale that would eventually be comparable to that of the United States and the Soviet Union. In 1974, China was the world's third largest producer of hard coal, with an estimated production of 430 million metric tons. In steel production, its output of 27 million tons placed it fifth among steel producing nations; it was surpassed only by the Soviet Union (136 million tons), the United States (132 million tons), Japan (117 million tons), and West Germany (53 million tons). Over the years 1949–1970, the average annual increase in China's industrial production was approximately 11 percent. A comparison of the increase in industrial production since the end of the Second World War shows that industrially both Japan (13.8 percent) and the Soviet Union (9.6 percent) have grown faster than China (6.4 percent); the latter has grown at about the same rate as India (6.7 percent).[12] China's industrial growth has been much more irregular than that of other industrialized countries because of the recurring Communist party conflicts over ideological issues.

The course of Chinese industrial development is indicated by the production statistics in Table 19–6. In the years 1949–1970, large modern installations were made in the steel, machine-tool, chemical, cement, and petroleum industries. In these years, steel production is estimated to have increased from 158,000 tons to 18 million tons. The output of machine tools rose from less than 2 million units to 50 million units. In some industries, such as the electronics industry, while China has made much progress, it still lags technologically far behind the United States, and has had to rely upon imports of advanced computers from Japan and Western Europe to keep up with the fast tempo of computer development in the West. The Chinese industrialization process has greatly altered the overall pattern of Chinese industry. Whereas in 1949 light consumer-goods industries accounted for 56 percent of total industrial output and heavy producer-goods industries 44 percent, by 1970 the percentage division was 29 and 71 percent. While the textile and other light industries grew slowly, the steel and

[12] Robert M. Field, "Chinese Communist Industrial Production," *An Economic Profile of Mainland China*, p. 278.

Table 19–6

Production of Selected Industrial Commodities in Mainland China, 1949 and 1970

Commodity	1949	1970
Coal[1]	32,430	300,000
Steel[1]	158	18,000
Chemical fertilizer[1]	27	7,400
Cement[1]	661	13,000
Electric power (million kilowatt-hrs.)	4,308	60,000
Machine tools (units)	1,582	50,000
Cotton cloth (million linear meters)	1,889	7,500

[1] Thousand metric tons.

Source: Robert M. Field, "Chinese Industrial Development," Joint Economic Committee, *People's Republic of China: An Economic Assessment*, 1972, p. 83.

other heavy industries grew much more rapidly.[13]

China has also been interested in altering the geographical distribution of its industries, which in 1949 were largely located in Northeast China (formerly Manchuria) and in eastern areas near the seacoast. Starting with the First Five-Year Plan, China began a policy of locating its new industrial installations in all parts of China. This was done for three reasons: (1) its natural resources are found in all of these areas; (2) industries would be less open to attack from abroad; and (3) the standard of living of the hinterland would be raised to bring it closer to that found in the coastal, eastern, and northeastern regions.

Agriculture in Communist China

The agricultural sector in Communist China, as in the Soviet Union, has proved the most difficult sector to adjust to the goals of the Communist party leaders. The agricultural problem has been rendered more difficult in China than in the Soviet Union by the attempt of Mao and other Chinese leaders to go far beyond the Soviet Union in radically altering the life pattern in the rural sector. The Soviet leaders were never forced to retreat from their goal of a collectivized agriculture, whereas the communist Chinese leaders have had to postpone their objective of a completely communized agriculture and to retreat to an agricultural system that in many ways is not very different from what prevails in the Soviet Union.

Mao's agricultural program for Communist China was carried out in three steps: (1) instituting land reform and distributing land to the peasants; (2) establishing agricultural cooperatives; and (3) setting up agricultural communes. Under the land-reform program that lasted from 1949 to 1952, the land of rich

[13] Philip D. Reichers, "The Electronics Industry of China," *People's Republic of China: An Economic Assessment*, p. 102.

farmers was confiscated and transferred to poor peasants as a reward for aiding the Chinese Communist party in its successful effort to win control of the Chinese mainland. In all, about 117 million acres of farm land were distributed among 300 million peasants under the land-reform program. Since each peasant was given only one-third of an acre of land, on the average, land reform did not improve agricultural productivity. Chinese agriculture continued to be an inefficient, small-scale type of agriculture, chronically short of capital for its improvement, and underemploying those for whom it provided work. As many peasants were forced to sell their small farm holdings, a class differentiation between poor and rich peasants soon reappeared.

In order to curb the further growth of "capitalism" in the rural sector, the Chinese Communist government turned to the second part of its agricultural program, the establishment of agricultural cooperatives. During the years 1952–1956, 96 percent of farm households were brought into agricultural cooperatives that were similar to the Soviet collective farms. At first, mutual-aid teams of a number of farm households were loosely organized to compensate for the shortage of draught animals and farm implements. When these mutual-aid teams failed to curb "capitalist" tendencies, "elementary" cooperatives were established throughout the rural economy. These proved to be so inefficient that they were followed by "advanced" cooperatives organized and operated like the Soviet *kolkhozi*. In theory, these cooperatives were democratically operated, but in fact, they were run by members of the Chinese Communist party. Each farmer entering the advanced cooperative gave up the ownership of his land and farm capital and was remunerated on a work-point basis in accordance with the amount and skill of his work as a member of a production brigade.

Under the "advanced cooperative" system, agricultural production did not increase significantly. Although the government claimed an average annual increase of agricultural production of 4.5 percent for the years 1952–1957, Western estimates place the annual increase as low as 1.7 percent. The cooperatives, suffering from a lack of managerial talent, were inefficiently operated. The peasants lost their work incentives and concentrated their attention on their small farm plots. Finally, in order to overcome peasant inertia and low farm production, Mao ordered the communization of the agricultural sector in the spring of 1958. Advanced cooperatives of around 150 farm households were replaced by large rural communes, each of which united about 5,000 farm households. These communes incorporated not only the agriculture in several townships, but also the industry, banking, retailing, education, and local government. The objectives of this communization of agriculture were to destroy the last vestiges of private property, to eliminate the family as an organizational unit, to increase the supply of labor by freeing women from household duties, and to extend political control over the countryside. Individual farm plots were abolished, family life was placed on a communal basis, peasants were converted into "agricultural workers," and commune operations were organized on a military basis. Remuneration was on a *free supply-wage basis*—with from 50 to 80 percent of the remuneration provided in the form of food, clothing, and other daily necessities. There was little or no consumer choice, and the free-supply remuneration was made available on the communist basis of need and not of work done. By late 1958, 90 percent of the farm households had been herded into 23,384 large communes, and 90 million women were released from domestic duties in peasant households for work in the fields.

Mao's fanatical effort to create the "new communist man [or woman]" turned out to be a colossal failure. The peasants, cut down from an inadequate daily per capita caloric intake of 1,830 units in 1956 to a starvation caloric level of only 600 units per day in 1961, indicated their strong discontent with the communization program through slowdowns at work, acts of sabotage, and attacks on commune management cadres. Three successive years of bad harvest (1959–1961), resulting in part from a series of natural calamities, such as floods and droughts, and in part from strong peasant resistance to the campaign to communize agriculture, were accompanied by a major retreat on the part of the Chinese communist leaders with respect to the program for the communization of the rural sector.

This retreat has taken the form of a decentralization program, which, while leaving the overall structure of the agricultural commune intact, has made the production brigades and teams the main operating units.[14] In 1971, there were about 74,000 farm communes with 750,000 *production brigades* subordinate to them. A production brigade is composed of several production teams, each of which is made up of from twenty to thirty households, and is coextensive with a village or hamlet. It is believed that breaking down the large commune labor force into smaller divisions of production brigades and teams on a village basis will get the peasants closer to the land and will raise their productivity. Agricultural communes, which were originally set up for collective living, have largely abandoned the collective-living barracks and dining halls, and are now mainly administrative units, concerned with the development of local industry, the provision of rural schools and health services, and the construction and main-

[14] For the development of the Chinese agricultural commune, see Shahid Javed Burki, *A Study of Chinese Communes, 1965*, Cambridge, Mass.: East Asian Research Center, Harvard University, 1969; and Frederick W. Crook, "The Commune System in the People's Republic of China, 1963–74," in *China: A Reassessment of the Economy,* 1975, pp. 366–410.

tenance of local roads and water-control facilities.

Under the decentralization program adopted after 1962, the production team, the lowest of the three administrative layers of the commune, is the basic collective land ownership and accounting unit. The crops that the production team produces are generally determined by the overall national five-year plan, but the production brigades and teams have some autonomy in making decisions regarding what crops to produce. Within this plan framework, the production team has accounting responsibilities that include the expenses of production and administration, the accumulation of reserve (investment and welfare) funds from the team's farm sales, the deliveries of grain and other staples to the state, and the payment of state and local taxes. From the gross annual income of the production team, various costs of production—including depreciation on capital equipment and contributions to reserve funds amounting to 20 percent of gross income—are deducted, leaving the net profit to be distributed among the members of the production team.

Those members of the production team families that are incapable of work are given free or subsidized payments; but all working members are paid "wages," which are shares of the team's net income. Each worker is graded for skill, strength, and attitude and is assigned to one of four grades which are worth from ten to forty points for a day's work. A team member in the lowest grade and working 25 days per month could be credited with 250 work points. Bonuses are sometimes added for performance above the prescribed norms. The value of each work point is determined by dividing the total number of team points into the team's annual net income and distributing the net income among the team members according to their individual contributions. Individual net incomes vary widely among the production teams because of the regional differences in productivity, state delivery assessments, and incentive plans. According to one estimate in 1969, the range of team member annual net income was from $32 to $102. Time of payment is after the harvest and is mainly in kind.

Team income is supplemented by income from private plots and handicrafts whose output may be sold in rural markets at uncontrolled, free prices; in contrast to the situation in the Soviet Union, these free prices do not vary much from the prices on the official controlled markets. The official attitude towards farm plots and sideline activities has fluctuated from abolition to limited permissiveness. With 5 percent of farm land taken up by farm plots, a sizable portion of farmers' incomes is from this source. Up to 20 percent of farmers' food requirements came from private plots in 1967.

Production teams are required to make sales of grain and other staple crops to the state at prices fixed at low levels below the free market prices. In addition, through the commune system, they pay an agricultural tax, mainly in kind; this tax is based not on the actual yield per acre, but on a calculated "normal yield." Compulsory grain deliveries are somewhat larger than the amounts collected as an agricultural tax; together they account for about half of the grain output. The state pays premium prices for over-quota deliveries of grain and other farm products.

China's Agricultural Prospects

The future of Chinese agriculture is dominated by the fact that the potential increase in arable land area is primarily limited to land that can be made usable for agricultural purposes through reclamation and irrigation.[15]

[15] For a discussion of the Chinese agricultural sector, see Owen L. Dawson, *Communist China's*

From 1952–1953 to 1975–1976 the cultivated land area is expected to increase only 5 percent, whereas population is projected to increase 50 percent. As Table 19–7 shows, the ratio of total population to total cultivated land area is expected to rise from 5.3 in 1952–1953 to 7.8 in 1975–1976. In general, the nation's water supply is adequate, but there is considerable uneven seasonal distribution and large periodical variability, which results in floods, waterlogging, and drought. Since China's land has been farmed for centuries and its fertility has been maintained without the use of chemical fertilizers, the land will require some special measures to improve its productivity. These include the application of chemical fertilizers and the use of improved varieties of plants to utilize the crop nutrients provided by the fertilizers. Since 1949, many improvements have been made in agricultural techniques, the selection of plants and animals, the control of plant and animal diseases, and the reduction of crop predators. In addition, there have been large increases in the number of tractors and the size of the farm labor force.

Thus far, however, even though agricultural

Agriculture, Its Development and Future Potential, New York: Praeger, 1970; Kang Chao, *Agricultural Production in Communist China, 1949–1965*, Madison: University of Wisconsin Press, 1970; and Dwight H. Perkins, *Agricultural Development in China, 1368–1968*, Chicago: Aldine, 1969.

Table 19–7
Communist China's Agricultural Development, 1952–1976

Agricultural indicators	1952–1953 (Estimated)	1957–1958 (Estimated)	1967–1968 (Estimated)	1975–1976 (Projected)	% Increase in 1975–1976 over 1952–1953
Cultivated area (mh)[1]	108	112	110	113	5
Crop area cultivated (mh)[1]	141	157	162.2	169	20
Population (millions)	578	637	754	869	50
Ratio of population to cultivated area	5.3	5.7	6.8	7.8	47
Food grain area (mh)[1]	119	121.9	128.5	136	14
Food grain production (mmt)[2]	170	185	214	245	44
Ratio of population to food grain production	3.4	3.4	3.5	3.5	3
Animal units (million head)[3]	102	133	148	163	60
Ratio of population to animal units[3]	5.6	5.7	5.2	5.3	−5
Gross chemical fertilizers (mmt)[2]	0.2	0.9	12.5	23–25	—
Tractors (thousands)	—	25	150	300	—
Farm labor force (millions)	—	263	301	346	—
Irrigated land (mh)[1]	30	38	39	45	50

[1] Mh: million hectares.
[2] Mmt: million metric tons.
[3] Animal unit: 1 large animal, 5 pigs, 7 sheep, and 100 chickens.

Source: Owen L. Dawson, *Communist China's Agriculture, Its Development and Future Potential*, 1970, p. 211.

production has increased two and one-half times since 1949, a satisfactory population-food balance based on domestic agricultural resources has not yet been secured. Table 19-7 shows that food grain production is estimated to increase 44 percent from 1952-1953 to 1975-1976, but population is estimated to increase 50 percent in those years (56.7 percent if the population is projected to rise to 900 million rather than 869 million by 1975-1976). The ratio of total population to total food grain production since 1952-1953 has remained almost stationary; the same is true of the ratio of total population to available total animal units. In order to keep the nation's population near the minimum adequate per capita caloric level of 2,150, considerable amounts of grain in years of poor harvests have had to be imported. In 1973, imports of wheat and corn were a record 7.7 million metric tons, or a little more than 3 percent of the estimated total domestic grain crop of 250 million tons of that year. In 1961-1975, China is estimated to have imported 78 million tons of grain, or one-third of a normal annual grain harvest—mainly from Canada, Australia, Argentina, France, and the United States.[16]

The Chinese Price and Wage Systems

The price and wage systems of the Chinese communist economy are more similar to the price and wage systems of the Stalinist era than to these systems observed in the Soviet Union today. Like Stalin, Mao Tse-tung and other Chinese communist leaders had a strong antipathy to the free market system of the capitalist countries, and so did not assign an important role to prices and wages as allocators of scarce resources. Even though the free market system plays no important role in the Chinese economy, nevertheless, price and wage formation have been of great concern to the Chinese planners.

Price fixing is the responsibility of the National Price Commission for major industrial and agricultural products and of the Provincial and District Price Commissions for other products. Prices are fixed at the factory, wholesale, and retail levels. At the factory level, prices are set on the basis of the average unit cost for the industry, to which is added a margin for profits. Average unit cost includes the cost of raw materials, wages, depreciation, and interest on borrowed working capital, but no allowance is made for interest on the enterprise's fixed capital. Since prices are not based upon full costing, nor do they take account of all costs (including interest on fixed capital), they are to some extent irrational and not optimal allocators of scarce resources. However, this does not mean that they do not reflect changing supply-and-demand conditions. On the contrary, as one Western Sinologist has put it, "The point here is that China's price structure probably reflected, at least to a degree, the underlying Chinese supply-and-demand conditions. The further the regime moved from the conditions at the time when prices were frozen, the less this was true."[17]

A turnover or industrial and commercial tax is added to the factory price. At the wholesale level, the expenses and profit of wholesaling are added to the factory price. The retail price is made up of the wholesale price plus the costs and profits of retailing including a commercial sales tax. In the case of retail prices, some account is taken of supply-and-demand conditions, and efforts are made to fix prices that will bring about a balance between supply and demand. Where it is felt that retail prices should be low, as in the case of cereals, cloth, and cooking oil, rationing is adopted to

[16] Alva Lewis Erisman, "China: Agriculture in the 1970's," in Joint Economic Committee, *China: A Reassessment of the Economy*, Washington, D.C., July 10, 1975, p. 343.

[17] Dwight H. Perkins, "Industrial Planning and Management," in Alexander Eckstein, Walter Galenson, and Ta-Chung Liu, (eds.), *Economic Trends in Communist China*, Edinburgh: Edinburgh University Press, 1968, p. 615.

provide for an equitable distribution of these low-priced goods. In the case of rents, which are very low and take only 5 percent of a worker's annual income, housing goes with the job.

A problem arises in connection with the determination of the size of an enterprise's profit margin. In the Chinese price calculations, profits are the equivalent of Marx's surplus value, but Marx provided no way of determining how large the profits in an industry should be. The profits in an enterprise may be set as a percent of the total wage bill of the enterprise, of its total costs of production, or of its net capital investment. The Chinese price fixers have an empirical approach to price fixing and cling to no one way of determining profit margins. The Chinese planners are not prepared to follow the Soviet economists by including a charge for interest on the firm's capital among its costs of production, and measuring the firm's performance by observing its net profits as a percent of its investment in fixed and working capital. Without the inclusion of interest charges on capital among costs of production, there can be no fully rational measure of an enterprise's profitability. The Chinese price fixers establish planned costs, profits, and prices for individual enterprises and are concerned about their profitability, but they do not use the definition of profitability employed in the Soviet Union and the Eastern European communist countries; there, interest on capital is accepted as a proper economic charge or cost of production. The Chinese price fixers are closer to Stalin, who felt that interest as a charge on capital was a bourgeois concept that had no place in a communist society. After analyzing Chinese price policy, one Western analyst concludes that "The overall impression is that empiricism and flexibility have had a larger part in Chinese price policy than in that of some other Marxist lands."[18]

[18] Audrey Donnithorne, *op. cit.*, p. 439.

While Chinese prices in general are stable, changes are made in relative prices as required by the planning program. Agricultural-procurement prices are altered to encourage the production of some crops and to discourage the production of others. Relative prices have also been altered to bring about a more equitable distribution of income. Agricultural prices since 1960 have been raised in order to close the gap between the average farmer's income and that of an unskilled urban worker. In order to prevent the emergence of excess demand for consumer goods at their fixed prices, the central planners control the size of the total wage bill. A balance is struck between total consumer income and the available supply of consumer goods at their prevailing prices. In the Soviet Union, producer goods tend to have relatively low prices and consumer goods high prices. The reverse is the case in China, where scarce capital goods are priced high in order to encourage the use of labor which is abundant.

Little connection exists between prices, profits, and capital investment in China. In a free market system, capital investment is made in those areas where prices of the output resulting from the investment give rise to maximum profits. Since there are no free markets in China for most commodities, and since capital investments are made to support the objectives of the planners, capital investment is not usually guided by considerations of profit maximization. Some evidence shows, however, that planners concerned with investment do take account of alternative uses of capital and varying rates of return on capital. They have followed a recoupment principle, according to which those capital investments are chosen whose costs can be recovered sooner than in the case of other investments. For example, thermal-power plants may be built in place of hydroelectric-power plants because the cost of thermal plants may be more quickly recovered.

The Chinese wage system has a number of

objectives. It is designed to keep wages low so that a surplus may be extracted from the workers and allocated to investment for the purpose of advancing the industrialization process. It is also geared to provide incentives for workers to increase production and to induce them to move into those industries and those geographic regions where the demand for labor is high. The Chinese wage system is in its essentials similar to that of the Soviet Union and other communist countries; some fundamental differences, however, appear. The main differences between the two systems relate to wage differentials, bonus payments, and nonmaterial incentives. The Chinese place much more reliance on nonmaterial rewards than on economic rewards as spurs to greater worker efficiency and higher labor productivity. This arises because Mao and other communist leaders hoped to prevent the growth of class distinctions and elitism based upon income differentials.[19]

Following the practice in other communist countries, China has a multiple wage-grade system in which wage scales in a factory are set up in eight grades, with workers in the highest grades being paid from 2.5 to 3.2 times what is paid in the lowest grades. Wages for men and women are the same in a given wage classification. Wage differentials apply between various industries; the coalminers receive the highest monthly wages and the textile workers the lowest. Both the intraplant and interplant differentials are smaller than in other socialist countries.[20] Some geographical and industrial differentials are designed to attract labor to developing industries and re-

gions. Bonuses are not an important item in the Chinese wage system. Ordinarily, workers' bonuses do not exceed 20 percent of the basic wage, while managerial bonuses have not normally been as large as in the Soviet Union and East Europe. In some factories, bonuses are not paid to the top managers, and in some cases the directors are paid less than the top-paid employee.[21] Average wages have risen as industrialization has proceeded, but not as much as labor productivity has improved. The "rational low wage" policy has been justified on the ground that rents and prices of consumer necessities are low, and workers pay no income taxes.

Labor enjoys no free movement in Mainland China. To change his or her job, a worker must have the permission of both the manager of his or her enterprise and the local party organization. Considerable upward mobility operates within each enterprise for those workers who make an effort to become more skilled and who display administrative abilities. Some horizontal mobility is achieved when the government transfers workers from established to newly opened enterprises—in some cases, in different geographical regions.

The Chinese have made much more use of nonmaterial work incentives than the Soviets, who have been criticized by the Chinese communists for putting too much emphasis on economic incentives. The Chinese Communist party plays an important role in emphasizing and encouraging nonmaterial incentives; but also involved are the trade unions, youth organizations, and lower political bodies. The Chinese believe that material incentives are a "bourgeois" survival, which eventually will be replaced by superior nonmaterial incentives.

These incentives emphasize cooperation rather than competition, and frequently involve mass participation or mass movements.

---

[19] For Chinese attitudes towards wealth, material gain, and self-interest, see Barry M. Richman, *Industrial Society in Communist China*, New York: Random House, 1969, pp. 309–321.

[20] According to one recent report, coalminers, in the highest-paid industry, earned 80 yuan (1 yuan = $0.425, Jan. 1973) monthly, while textile workers, in the lowest-paid industry, earned 55 yuan, the differential ratio being only 1:0.68. See Jan Deleyne, *The Chinese Economy*, New York: Harper and Row, 1971, p. 45.

[21] Barry M. Richmond, "Income and Ideology," *op. cit.*, p. 805.

Such incentives have both ideological and economic aims. The ideological aim is to aid in developing a communist society in which material incentives will be downgraded. The pragmatic aim of the nonmaterial incentives is to increase the productivity and output of the workers and peasants. While at the ideological level these incentives stimulate "revolutionary zeal," at the production level they increase output and make available a larger surplus for investment in the nation's expanding industries.

The Chinese Monetary and Fiscal Systems

Like all other communist countries, Mainland China has a complex financial system, based on a defined currency unit, the yuan or jenminpi, which has a rate of exchange fixed by the Chinese government at one yuan approximately equal to U.S. 50 cents. In addition there is a banking system made up of a variety of banks, and a fiscal system for the central, provincial, and local governments. This financial system supplements the real system of production that flows from producers to consumers. Since the real production system is planned by the government, the financial system must also be planned so that it supplements the production process and contributes to the achieving of the annual and longer-term plan goals.

Within the framework of the financial planning system, the functions of the fiscal and monetary systems are to finance the governments at all levels by collecting the necessary revenues and to regulate the supply of money and commercial and investment credit. The state budget, which is composed of the consolidated central, provincial, and local budgets, is a major financial-control mechanism. The revenues of this budget come from planned profits and depreciation funds transferred by industrial enterprises to the Ministry of Finance (65 percent of total budgetary revenues) and other tax collections (35 percent). The main taxes are sales or consolidated industrial and commercial taxes, imposed on the producing and retailing units, and the agricultural taxes, paid by production teams. Other important taxes are the salt tax and customs duties. The expenditures in the state budget include grants and loans to industry and agriculture for "economic construction" or investment purposes (60 percent of total government expenditures), expenditures for social services, culture, education, and science (12 percent), national defense (12 percent), government administration (5 percent), and loans to state agencies and local governments (11 percent).

By requiring state enterprises to transfer most of their profits and all their depreciation funds to the Ministry of Finance, and by collecting the surplus generated by industry and agriculture through sales or turnover taxes, the government maintains a strict control over the planned economy. Since three-fourths of all investments are financed through the state budget in the form of grants and loans to industry and agriculture, there is little independence of decision making with regard to investments on the part of the individual state enterprises. By means of budgetary controls, the central, provincial, and local governments can monitor the investment activities of all sectors of the economy to see how they conform with the annual and five-year investment plans. Since the Chinese industrial enterprises and rural communes have little control over the financial surpluses that they generate, they enjoy little of the autonomy of the Yugoslav state enterprises, which retain most of their financial surpluses, and do not rely upon budgetary grants or loans for investment purposes.

The Chinese government, like other communist governments, does not make use of budgetary deficit financing, since the economy does not suffer from the fluctuations observed in the Western democratic countries. The basic principle adhered to is balancing the budget at all governmental levels, with a small surplus ranging from 3 to 5 percent of total revenues for emergency purposes. Budgetary revenue goals are determined by the requirements for expenditure set down by the annual and five-year plans; thus no reason exists for any sizable discrepancy between state budget revenues and expenditures.

The banking system also plays an important role in China's financial planning and in the control of its economy. Following the pattern adopted in the Soviet Union, the People's Republic of China established the People's Bank of China as a central bank—which works closely with the People's Construction Bank (for investment loans)—the Bank of China (for handling foreign trade), the Agricultural Bank of China, the Joint State-Private Bank (for people's savings), and rural credit cooperatives. The key financial institution is the central bank, the People's Bank, which controls the money supply and the supply of short-term or working capital credit. The People's Bank is in a good position to ensure that the economy moves along according to plan. Since all state enterprises and government agencies are required to have accounts with the People's Bank and to make all payments through it, the bank is well informed through its 34,000 branches of how closely industrial enterprises are fulfilling their plans. It also oversees all payments of wages and bonuses to make certain that they do not exceed the planned total wage bill authorized by the annual plans for each enterprise. Like the Soviet State Bank, the Chinese People's Bank, which is the only issuer of bank notes, constructs cash and credit plans to regulate the supply of currency in circulation, to balance workers' incomes and the availability of consumer goods, and to balance the supply and demand for short-term and medium-term loans.

State enterprises are prohibited from extending short-term loans to one another.[22] While interest up to 4 percent is paid on bank deposits and interest from 2 to 2.5 percent is charged on short-term loans, the interest rate has no regulatory role in Mainland China. Since there are no fluctuations in the Chinese economy except those arising from changing harvest conditions or those induced by political developments, interest rates are stable. Chinese credit policy consists essentially of setting ceilings on the total amounts of working and fixed capital loans and of rationing these loans according to plan. The fixed capital grants to industry provided by the state budget are passed to industry through the People's Construction Bank. The Agricultural Bank controls the flow of credit to state farms, rural communes, production brigades and teams, and industrial enterprises in the rural areas. Through the cooperation of the Ministry of Finance in Peking, local budgetary authorities, and the specialized banks led by the People's Bank, a very extensive network of financial controls is imposed on the planned Chinese economy and is an effective part of the program to leave as little real income in the hands of the people as possible without reducing their incentives or their loyalty to the regime.

Mainland China's Domestic and Foreign Trade

Domestic trade, conducted as a monopoly by the central government, is used to achieve the national goals of the Chinese annual and five-year plans. These plans establish targets

---

[22] For a discussion of the cash and credit plans, see S. C. Tsiang, "Money and Banking in Communist China," *An Economic Profile of Mainland China*, pp. 330–339.

for the nation's producing, wholesaling, and retailing sectors. Within the framework of these plans, the aim is to assure adequate supplies of commodities at stable prices. The domestic trading system of Mainland China parallels the system employed in other communist countries. Under the Ministry of Commerce, a complex of government and commercial organizations operates at the central government, provincial, commune, and local levels. At the central government and provincial levels, the specialized internal trade corporations purchase and distribute the important goods that are subject to "planned purchase and planned supply"; these include grain, petroleum products, sugar, tobacco, textiles, coal, building materials, and machinery. The bulk of the wholesaling activity is carried on by these specialized corporations. In the urban areas, the department stores and other stores are operated by the municipal commerce departments. In the rural areas, supply and marketing cooperatives and the retail cooperatives meet the retail needs of the local population. Rural free markets provide an outlet in local and nearby urban areas for the produce of farm plots and the output of local handicrafts.

During the Great Cultural Revolution, city trade was carried on only with great difficulty. Much of the supervisory function of the Ministry of Commerce was taken over first by the People's Liberation Army and later by the revolutionary committees composed of representatives of the party, the army, and the retailing units. These revolutionary committees at the provincial, district, and municipal levels are now responsible for matters relating to the purchase, storage, and distribution of merchandise. Scarce commodities, such as cereals, cooking oil, meat, and cotton cloth, are rationed. Ample stocks of basic necessities are usually available; and the prices of food are low enough to enable low-income groups to secure a reasonably diversified diet.

Mainland China, being in the early stages of its economic development, has not been in a position to develop a large commodity export-import trade. In 1952, its total foreign trade turnover (commodity export-import trade) in terms of 1963 prices amounted to only $1.2 billion. As its export capabilities have improved, both exports and imports have increased until in 1974 they totalled $5.9 billion (in 1963 prices). The foreign trade statistics in Table 19-8 reveal that sizable fluctuations in Chinese foreign trade have occurred since 1950. This trade expanded rapidly in the 1950s and reached a peak in 1959 during the Great Leap Forward. In the early 1960s, when the economy was depressed, foreign trade declined, but was restored in the mid-1960s. During the Cultural Revolution, foreign trade again fell off; but since 1970, China's foreign trade has increased a great deal, as relations with the Western world, including the United States, have improved. Between 1969 and 1974, Chinese foreign trade in real terms grew at the average annual rate of 10.4 percent, which was well above the 7.3 percent rate of growth of GNP. The 1971–1975 Five-Year Plan emphasized allocating scarce investment resources to agriculture in order to increase rice exports, as well as to the young petroleum industry in order to enlarge the export of crude oil.

International trade in the People's Republic of China, as in all other communist countries, is a closely regulated state monopoly.[23] Chi-

[23] For an analysis of China's foreign trade and its future prospects, see A. H. Usack and R. E. Batsavage, "The International Trade of the People's Republic of China," in *People's Republic of China: An Economic Assessment*, pp. 335–370; Nai-Ruenn Chen, "China's Foreign Trade, 1950-74," pp. 617-652, and David L. Denny, "International Finance in the People's Republic of China," pp. 653–677, in *China: A Reassessment of the Economy*, 1975; Feng-Hwa Mah, *The Foreign Trade of Mainland China*, Edinburgh: Edinburgh University Press, 1972; and Arthur A. Stahnke (ed.), *China's Trade with the West*, New York: Praeger, 1972.

Table 19-8

Communist China's Foreign Trade, 1950-1974 (In Millions of U.S. Dollars)

Year	In current prices			In constant prices[1]		
	Turnover	Exports	Imports	Turnover	Exports	Imports
1950	1,210	620	590	—	—	—
1951	1,900	780	1,120	—	—	—
1952	1,890	875	1,015	1,800	795	1,005
1953	2,295	1,040	1,255	2,290	995	1,295
1954	2,350	1,060	1,290	2,275	930	1,345
1955	3,035	1,375	1,660	3,010	1,295	1,715
1956	3,120	1,635	1,485	3,115	1,560	1,555
1957	3,055	1,615	1,440	2,910	1,530	1,380
1958	3,765	1,940	1,825	3,765	1,940	1,825
1959	4,290	2,230	2,060	4,400	2,315	2,085
1960	3,990	1,960	2,030	3,990	1,920	2,070
1961	3,015	1,525	1,490	3,060	1,540	1,520
1962	2,675	1,525	1,150	2,765	1,585	1,180
1963	2,770	1,570	1,200	2,770	1,570	1,200
1964	3,220	1,750	1,470	3,120	1,685	1,435
1965	3,880	2,035	1,845	3,790	2,005	1,785
1966	4,245	2,210	2,035	4,070	2,155	1,915
1967	3,895	1,945	1,950	3,770	1,930	1,840
1968	3,765	1,945	1,820	3,655	1,920	1,735
1969	3,860	2,030	1,830	3,610	1,920	1,690
1970	4,290	2,050	2,240	3,755	1,865	1,890
1971	4,720	2,415	2,305	4,060	2,180	1,880
1972	5,920	3,085	2,835	4,685	2,570	2,115
1973	9,870	4,895	4,975	5,760	3,000	2,760
1974[2]	13,715	6,305	7,410	5,930	2,765	3,165

[1] In 1963 prices.
[2] Preliminary.

Source: Nai-Ruenn Chen, "China's Foreign Trade, 1950-1974," in Joint Economic Committee, *China: A Reassessment of the Economy*, 1975, p. 645.

na's external sector, like all other sectors, is planned with the aim of securing the imports that will contribute to the transformation of China into an advanced industrial nation. Communist China's foreign trade policy is governed by the requirements for the construction of a socialist society. The nation adheres to a policy of self-reliance; this means that it will use its own material and human resources as far as possible in carrying out its national plans. It does not mean, however, that self-reliance leads to a closed economy. On the contrary, the national plans use foreign trade as a supplement to the main task of building an industrialized society. At the same time, Chinese foreign trade policy makes no place for joint industrial ventures with foreign companies or for foreign investment in Chinese industrial enterprises, since these financial arrangements are held to violate the principle of self-reliance. Also, Communist China is not to become a market for consumer goods imported from abroad. Its imports are mainly limited to capital goods that incorporate the advanced technology needed for industrial development, important industrial materials—such as nonferrous metals, cotton, and rubber—and foodstuffs, including grains, only when domestic harvests are inadequate.

Chinese foreign trade policy is also influenced by foreign policy objectives. Much of China's foreign trade is carried on with the less developed countries of the Third World, which supply China with a large part of its imports of key raw materials. This trade with the Third World, supplemented by extensive economic aid, enables China to offset Soviet and Western influences in African and Asian countries.[24] From the communist Chinese point of view, its foreign trade is of mutual value to both itself and its trading partners, whereas capitalist foreign trade allegedly exploits the countries of the Third World, and Soviet foreign trade supposedly exploits the Comecon countries.

As far as it is possible, China's exports are expected to pay for its imports. Trade between China and the other communist countries is conducted on a balanced bilateral basis. Trade with the noncommunist countries is financed as much as possible through exports. Where these prove to be insufficient to pay for imports, as in the case of the importation of whole factories from Japan or West Germany, China has turned to six to eighteen month loans. Currently, China has no long-term foreign debt and so has no obligation to make large annual interest payments, as do many of the less-developed countries, which are heavily indebted to industrialized countries. China could borrow on a long-term basis, but refuses to do so.

The failure to use long-term credit is a severe restraint on the expansion of China's foreign trade, which has slowed down its industrialization process. Until recently, China could not expand its foreign trade very rapidly because its exports consisted largely of foodstuffs, crude industrial materials, textiles, and low-quality light manufactures, which were not much in demand among the developed countries. The commodities that these countries were willing to import, such as coal, petroleum, and metals, were in short supply in China itself and were needed for its own industrial expansion. Now that China has been able to exploit sizable oil deposits, and has potentially large onshore and offshore oil reserves, the structure of its commodity exports will probably undergo considerable change. Under the 1971–1975 national plan, a high priority was assigned to investment in the oil industry; crude oil production will therefore continue to grow at a rapid rate. The output of crude oil, which was 1 million metric tons a year in the early 1950s, increased to 65 million tons in 1974. China is now an important exporter of oil to Thailand, Hong Kong, Japan, the Philippines, and other countries in the Pacific Basin.

Up to 1960, the bulk of China's foreign trade was with communist countries, among which the Soviet Union was the largest trading partner. In 1959, 70 percent of China's

---

[24] For an analysis of Chinese foreign trade policy, see Young C. Kim, "Sino-Japanese Commercial Relations," pp. 600–616, and Carol H. Fogarty, "China: Economic Relations with the Third World," pp. 730–737, in *China: A Reassessment of the Economy*, 1975.

trade was with other communist countries and 30 percent with noncommunist countries. In 1974, 83 percent of China's trade was with noncommunist countries, with Japan and West Germany being major trading partners. Much of China's imported high-technology machinery, including whole factories, comes from Japan and West Germany. Whereas the Soviet Union was the main source of China's imported machinery and equipment before the break of 1959, today the Soviet Union engages in very little trade with China.

China's foreign trade is not a large part of its total economic activity. In 1973, its total foreign trade was only 4.5 percent of its GNP. The level of China's international trade can be expected to rise considerably in the next decade. China's more relaxed foreign policies of recent years have renewed the interest of Western businesspeople in Chinese export products and in the Chinese domestic market. China's trade with the United States, formerly negligible in amount, exceeded $1 billion in 1974. By developing more friendly relations with a number of countries, including the United States, China has recently laid the foundation for a substantial increase in its foreign trade; it remains to be seen, however, how far China is prepared to build on this foundation.

The Future of the Chinese Economy

Observers of the Chinese economy now generally agree that China has made very solid economic and social progress since the Liberation of 1949. China has the economic potential required for the creation of a major world power. Although the people's standard of living is not high by Western standards, they are much better off than they were in pre-1949 China. Although China's economic development has been quite erratic, as the result of ideological conflicts, it has been free from the large cyclical fluctuations that have been common in the West. For twenty-five years, China has fed, clothed, and housed its large population, has kept it in a healthy condition, and has educated most people. China has succeeded where India, Pakistan, and many underdeveloped countries have failed in providing a simple but adequate diet, full employment, and a wide range of social services.

As a result of the emphasis on limiting wage and salary differentials, the income distribution in China is more equal than in some of the communist countries, such as the Soviet Union, and in the Western industrialized countries. From the Western viewpoint, Mainland China is deficient with respect to consumer, occupational, and political freedoms. Consumers have a very limited selection of available consumer goods; young workers are subject to considerable government labor direction; population movements from rural to urban areas are controlled; and what is in effect a one-party political system greatly restricts the freedom of political expression.

One of the most outstanding features of Chinese economic and social development since 1949 has been the commitment to universal, nonelitist education. Mao Tse-tung gave Chinese education a practical, nonelitist emphasis that was lacking before the Cultural Revolution. His educational reforms reflect his propensity for short courses, students with work experience, a revolutionary faculty, a practical curriculum, and continuous political indoctrination. While such an educational system will meet the short-term needs of the expanding Chinese economy, some doubt exists that it will supply the highly trained personnel required in the long run to cope with the technological challenges of the future. The payoff of a highly practical educational system may not be an entirely satisfactory substitute for the payoff of the old pre–Cultural Revolution educational system, which emphasized "expertness" and the ability to perform as a scholar or scientist over "redness" and the willingness to serve a revolutionary cause.

China's low level of industrialization has enabled it to avoid much of the environmental degradation observed in the West. With four-fifths of its population located in rural areas, China has until recently stressed the importance of improving the health of the people and preserving the land. The program for industrial dispersal, which has favored the limitation of urban growth, the development of backward areas, and the spread of rural industrialization in small towns, has curbed the spread of industrial pollution. Since 1970, the greater concern for environmental protection led to the creation of the Chinese Office of Environmental Protection, which may do much to avoid the ecological problems of the Western capitalist nations.[25]

On other fronts, Mainland China has not been as successful as it would like. The rural commune, as originally established, proved to be unworkable, with the result that Chinese agricultural policy is today a compromise between the Maoist ideal of a highly organized rural society and one in which personal incentives play a large role. A second difficulty has been the inability to settle the issue between revolutionary purity and economic rationality. Chinese economic efficiency has suffered to some extent from the attempts to elevate ideology over economic efficiency. While China has decided not to follow blindly the economic growth ideal of the West, and is therefore prepared to place some noneconomic limits on the search for efficiency, it is not clear just what the Communist party leaders' policies with regard to these matters are. It is clear, however, that the Chinese economy is to be one without consumer gadgets.

A third major issue relates to motivation and the Maoist vision of a communist society. There is much question as to how far the Maoists have been able to go in substituting spiritual incentives for material incentives. In the foreseeable future this will not be a problem. Propaganda has been widely and steadily used to foster an acceptance of ideological commitment among the general population. While this propaganda has been quite successful up to now, one may well inquire how successful it will be now that Mao Tse-tung is gone and a more complex and affluent society may be achieved. The party leaders admit that many scientists and technicians do not support the official emphasis on nonmaterial motivation.

Another of China's unsolved problems is the population problem. Having the Marxian, anti-Malthusian bias against population control, the Chinese communists have only recently become concerned about limiting population growth.[26] Improvements in living conditions, rural health standards, and the services of thousands of "barefoot" doctors or paramedics have reduced the death rate at the same time that methods to control the birth rate have not had much success. Current Chinese population policy appears to be aimed at reducing the annual rate of population growth from 2 to 1 percent. If this goal were to be achieved, it would mean 100 million fewer people than otherwise in one decade. If the current rate of population growth continues to the year 2000, China's population could be over 1.5 billion.

The present campaign to control population

[25] A discussion of China's position with regard to ecological problems is presented in Leo A. Orleans, "China's Environomics: Backing into Ecological Leadership," in *China: A Reassessment of the Economy*, 1975, pp. 116-144. See also Jon Sigurdson, "Rural Industrialization in China," in *China: A Reassessment of the Economy*, pp. 411-435. Rural industries, which reduce industrial pollution, are complementary to medium- and large-scale urban enterprises in a balanced industrial structure appropriate for a developing country.

[26] Leo A. Orleans, "China's Population: Can the Contradictions be Resolved?", in *China: A Reassessment of the Economy*, 1975, pp. 69-80.

growth is a mixture of pressure for later marriages, contraceptive pills and devices, liberalized abortion and sterilization, and threats to eliminate welfare benefits for children beyond the second or third child. These measures will in time be supported by the higher level of education and the increased participation of women in economic and political activities. The success of any population-control program depends upon how vigorously the government is prepared to enforce its control measures. Thus far, the Chinese government has not been able to reduce significantly the 2 percent population growth rate, because it has not vigorously pursued its population-control program. In any event, this program at best has little impact on the very large rural population.

The future economic development of China remains uncertain for two reasons. If economic resources are increasingly devoted to an expensive military build-up, economic growth and the improvement of living standards will be curtailed. It is estimated that China now allocates 10 percent of its GNP to defense. Because of the conflict with the Soviet Union, China appears to be rapidly expanding its military production, and is becoming involved in expensive missile and nuclear weapons development programs. The prospect is for more and not less military production in a developing country that has a heavy demand on its surplus above private and public civilian consumption for the purposes of economic and social development.[27]

The second possible obstacle to China's economic development is ideological in nature. If the Maoist ideology remains strong in the future, the conflict between the "experts" and the "reds" may continue to disrupt the economic system and delay economic progress. From the Maoist point of view, periodically shaking up the economy in order to restore revolutionary fervor and thus perpetuate the revolution is well worth the cost in terms of lower economic growth. While the Maoists accept the need for efficiency and economic growth up to a point, they discourage the use of the profit motive in the allocation of resources, and they downgrade material incentives. The Maoists prefer an egalitarian society in which there is no high-consuming middle class, and which fosters plain and simple living and a commitment to helping others rather than to accumulating worldly possessions. If this view of the communist society meets strong opposition in the future, as it did in the 1960s, the conflict between the Maoists and the anti-Maoists could lead to a continuation of the erratic economic growth pattern of the years 1957–1970.

China's future economic development will depend very much upon how its ideological problem is solved in the long run. Many Western analysts are inclined to believe that in the long run, as the Chinese society becomes more technologically advanced and affluent, the "experts" will win out over the "reds"; the technological imperatives will be stronger than the ideological imperatives; and less pressure will be exerted for an egalitarian society. One Western analyst concludes that "The economy is steadily growing more complex. . . . As people acquire more education and work at more technical jobs, they presumably will expect commensurate increases in living standards. And they will respond increasingly to technocratic rather than ideological imperatives."[28]

---

[27] If China turns in the future from a ground-based People's Liberation Army to a more expensive modern defense establishment, its military burden could rise significantly. On this point, see Sydney H. Jammes, "The Chinese Defense Burden, 1965–74," in *China: A Reassessment of the Economy*, 1975, pp. 459–466.

[28] Arthur G. Ashbrook, Jr., *op. cit.*, p. 8. Audrey Donnithorne argues that modernization of the Chinese economy will continue, and that the growth of population and the spread of modern science and technology will create new methods of production that will be moulded by economic requirements and not primarily by political desire. See Donnithorne, *op. cit.*, p. 511.

Other Sinological analysts expect the Maoist experiment to have a permanent impact on the Chinese society. They point out that "Comunist China is not a paradise, but it is now engaged in the most interesting economic and social experiment ever attempted, in which tremendous efforts are being made to achieve an egalitarian development, an industrial development without dehumanization, one that involves everyone and affects everyone."[29] These analysts believe that the Maoist ideology with its new morality and the concept of the "universal man [or woman]" has its roots deep in Chinese history and culture, and represents a permanently new challenge to Western state welfare capitalism and its values. Other Western analysts conclude that it is premature to assume that the search for a Maoist model has ended, and that "Until a more stable regime appears, it is difficult to chart the pace and pattern of China's development."[30] Whatever the course of economic development in China, it would be difficult to believe that Maoism will not leave a permanent stamp on the Chinese economic system.

[29] John W. Gurley, "The New Man in the New China," *The Center Magazine*, Vol. III, No. 3, May 1970, p. 32.

[30] Edwin F. Jones, *op. cit.*, p. 58.

Selected Bibliography

BARTKE, WOLFGANG. *China's Economic Aid.* Holmes and Meier Publishers, New York, 1975.

BURKI, SHAHID JAVED. *A Study of Chinese Communism.* East Asian Research Center, Harvard University, Cambridge, 1969.

CHAO, KANG. *Agricultural Production in Communist China, 1949–1965.* University of Wisconsin Press, Madison, 1970.

COHEN, A. A. *The Communism of Mao Tse-tung.* University of Chicago Press, Chicago, 1964.

DAWSON, OWEN L. *Communist China's Agriculture, Its Development and Future Potential.* Praeger Publishers, New York, 1970.

DELEYNE, JAN. *The Chinese Economy.* Harper and Row Publishers, New York, 1971.

DONNITHORNE, AUDREY. *China's Economic System.* Frederick A. Praeger, Publisher, New York, 1967.

ECKSTEIN, ALEXANDER. *China's Economic Development.* University of Michigan Press, Ann Arbor, 1975.

FLOYD, D. *Mao against Khrushchev.* Frederick A. Praeger, Publisher, New York, 1963.

GARTH, BRYANT G., ed. *China's Changing Role in the World Economy.* Praeger Publishers, New York, 1975.

GOODSTADT, LEO. *China's Search for Plenty, The Economics of Mao Tse-tung.* John Weatherhill, New York, 1973.

JOINT ECONOMIC COMMITTEE. *An Economic Profile of Mainland China.* Washington, D.C., 1967.

———. *China: A Reassessment of the Economy.* Washington, D.C., 1975.

———. *People's Republic of China: An Economic Assessment.* Washington, D.C., 1972.

MAH, FENG-HWA. *The Foreign Trade of Mainland China.* Edinburgh University Press, Edinburgh, 1972.

MAO TSE-TUNG. *Selected Works of Mao Tse-tung.* Foreign Language Press, Peking, 1961.

PERKINS, DWIGHT H. *Agricultural Development in China, 1368-1968.* Aldine Press, Chicago, 1969.

———. "Plans and Their Implementation in the People's Republic of China." *American Economic Review,* LXIII, No. 2 (May 1973), 224–235.

PRYBYLA, JAN S. *The Political Economy of Communist China.* International Textbook Co., Scranton, 1970.

RICHMAN, BARRY M. *Industrial Society in Communist China.* Random House, New York, 1969.

ROBINSON, JOAN. *Economic Management, China 1972.* Anglo-Chinese Educational Institute, London, 1973.

SCHRAM, S. R. *The Political Thought of Mao Tsetung.* Frederick A. Praeger, Publisher, New York, 1963.

STAHNKE, ARTHUR A., ed. *China's Trade with the West.* Praeger Publishers, New York, 1972.

WHEELWRIGHT, E. L., and BRUCE MACFARLANE. *The Chinese Road to Socialism.* Monthly Review Press, New York, 1970.

WHITAKER, DONALD P., and others. *Area Handbook for the People's Republic of China.* Foreign Area Studies of The American University, Washington, D.C., 1972.

Chapter 20
The Indian Economy and the Third World

India is of great importance in the Third World of less developed countries because it offers a way of development markedly different from that of Communist China. Whereas the latter country has largely eliminated private enterprise, and has relied mainly on public enterprise within a nondemocratic political framework, India has retained much of the private-enterprise system and has developed a limited core of nationalized enterprise within a democratic political framework. China has accepted the Marxist-Leninist ideology as its official ideology and has allied itself with the communist sphere. India has rejected both the capitalist and communist ideologies and has adopted a neutralist stance towards the capitalist West and the communist East. Most of the less developed countries have also taken up a neutralist, nonaligned position with regard to the capitalist and communist countries.

In this connection, they find themselves close to India, which emphasizes that it is seeking its own path of economic and social development. In its five-year plans, India stresses "the need to take quick strides towards self-reliance" and independence from both the capitalist and communist nations.[1] While India is on the democratic socialist road of economic development, it points out that it is following its own special path to socialism; this path is adapted to India's particular circumstances and needs. The same can be said of the majority of the less developed countries of Asia and Africa; like India, these nations are seeking their own routes of economic and social development.

A major factor that India has in common with Communist China, but not with a number of the less developed countries, is its large population pressure. With an area about one-third of Mainland China, India in 1973 had a

[1] Government of India, Planning Commission, *Fourth Five-Year Plan, 1969-74*, Delhi: Government of India Press, 1970, p. 13.

population of 582 million, while China had 811 million. India's population density was 168 per square kilometer and that of Communist China 80. India has about three times the population of the United States and one-third its land. Although India suffers from a much greater population pressure than most less developed countries, the problems that arise in the course of its development are very similar to those of most of the less developed countries.

India has a variety of climates and soils; its agricultural activity is heavily dependent on the unreliable monsoon rains. It has excellent deposits of iron ore, mica, and manganese, along with large reserves of coal, bauxite, chromite, gold, and atomic-energy minerals. At the same time, India is deficient in a number of important minerals, such as tin, copper, nickel, lead, zinc, and oil. In relation to its population, India is not as well off in natural resources as are the United States and the Soviet Union. The two institutions that hold India back economically are the joint family and the caste system; the latter is illegal, but it still curbs upward economic and social mobility. When India achieved independence in 1947, it had a well-developed civil service and parliamentary government at the federal or union level and in the sixteen states.

The Ideological Basis of the Indian Economy

India is unique among the less developed countries because it has chosen the path of *democratic socialism* rather than that of authoritarian African, Arab, or Asiatic socialism.[2]

[2] Nehru describes Indian socialism as "democratic socialism" in the Foreword to Shriman Narayan's *Socialism in Indian Planning*, New Delhi: Asia Publishing House, 1964. While the Indian Constitution does not mention socialism, the Indian National Congress in 1955 adopted a resolution calling

Under the influence of Mahatma Gandhi and Jawaharlal Nehru, India developed a socialist program with a strong Fabian coloration. Gandhi moved in the direction of rural socialism, which emphasized mass participation in the development of a village society based upon a handicraft industry. Unlike Nehru, Gandhi had no interest in industrializing the Indian society. Instead, he looked back to the days of the old autonomous and self-contained village community, where there had been an automatic balance between production, distribution, and consumption. Gandhi advocated the establishment of a kind of simple democracy in which the people lived close to nature, the gulf between the rich and the poor was eliminated, and there was no concentration of economic or political power.[3] Gandhi condemned poverty, but at the same time he regarded the quest for an ever-rising standard of life as equally degrading and dehumanizing. In place of competition and the market-guided economy, Gandhi proposed to place cooperation and rural communalism. Labor was elevated as an activity worthwhile in itself, and economic progress was not synonymous with the multiplication of labor-saving devices. Individuals would realize their full potentialities only in a social framework that curbed the centralization of economic as well as political power. Gandhi's long-range program included the promotion of village industries on the basis of self-sufficiency, the reduction of the use of machinery and large-scale production to a

for a "socialistic pattern of society." The five-year plans, which were inaugurated in 1951, have accepted a "socialist pattern of society" as a goal of the country's program for social and economic development.

[3] Mohandas K. Gandhi's political and economic views are presented in *Indian Home Rule*, Ahmedabad: Navajivan Trust, 1946. See also J. J. Anjaria, *Essays in Planning and Growth*, Ch. XVII, "Gandhian Economic Thought," Bombay: Vora and Co., 1972, pp. 147–175.

minimum, the nationalization and state control of whatever industries must operate on a large scale, and greater equality in income distribution. The emphasis of Gandhi's program was on simplicity, decentralization, cottage industrialism, a classless society, self-denial, and cooperation.

Nehru, a disciple of Gandhi, accepted the latter's ethical approach to life and his condemnation of the caste system and other degrading features of Indian life. Like Gandhi, Nehru was opposed to the acquisitive society dominated by the private-profit motive and divided by class divisions and a wide gulf between the rich and the poor. There were, however, fundamental differences between the intellectual orientations of Nehru and Gandhi.[4] Nehru, unlike Gandhi, drew inspiration from his study of Marx and Lenin. He considered that Marx's general analysis of social development was a substantially correct one, although in need of adaptation to subsequent developments that followed the rapid growth of technology and advances in scientific knowledge. Following Marx, Nehru gave a much larger place in his economic thought to the industrialization of the economy and the importance of large-scale industry. Nehru accepted Gandhi's division between cottage industry and large-scale industry, but he reversed their importance. In Nehru's view of the future Indian society, the large-scale industrial sector was the economy's pivotal sector, and the traditional cottage industry sector was secondary. What Nehru found in Marx but lacking in Gandhi was a dynamics of change that would revolutionize society. In Nehru's opinion, India had been absorbed far too long by traditional habits of thought and action, and now needed new modes of thought and action that would lead to new horizons.

While Nehru drew much inspiration from the writings of Marx and Lenin, he was not a Marxian socialist. He was rather more of a Fabian socialist, who was greatly influenced by the policies and programs of the British Labour party. In his early years, Nehru adopted the basic tenets of Fabian socialism, which included the establishment of a planned economy; the nationalization of banking, industry, and the land; the elimination of all private incomes except wages; private ownership of consumer goods; equality of the sexes; a national minimum income for all independent of work done; and the use of the nation's economic surplus for the general welfare. After India won its independence in 1947, Nehru became less doctrinaire and more pragmatic. He regarded the program for India's economic and social development as a transitional one that would eventually lead to a fully socialist society. Meanwhile, the aim of India's socialist program was a mixed, public-private enterprise economy.

Nehru's model of the Indian socialist society, which has become the guideline for India's economic and social development, includes the following features. The core of the economy is to be made up of nationalized or state-owned heavy industries, including the steel, heavy-machinery, chemical, power, fuel, communication, and transportation industries. Private enterprise is to be tolerated, especially in the service and small-scale manufacturing industries, but is to be regulated in the public interest. In the agricultural sector, land reform is to be used to eliminate landlordism; large farms are to be broken up and distributed among the smallholders and landless rural workers. Agriculture is to be organized on a cooperative basis. In the external sector, some private trading is to be permitted, but the state is to play the major role in

---

[4] These differences are examined in Jawaharlal Nehru, *The Discovery of India*, New York: The John Day Co., 1946. See also his *Toward Freedom: The Autobiography of Jawaharlal Nehru*, New York: The John Day Co., 1941.

the conduct of international trade. Unemployment and underemployment are to be reduced by raising agricultural productivity, reorganizing village life with the aid of community development programs, developing a rural public-works program, stimulating labor-intensive industries in both the rural and urban areas, and curbing the growth of population.

Nehru's democratic socialism differs in important ways from both communism and such other forms of socialism as Southeast Asian, African, and Arabian socialism. For one thing, it is gradualistic and parliamentarian rather than revolutionary; it rejects the revolutionary principle of violence employed by the Soviet and Chinese communists. Instead, it followed a program of passive resistance in the preindependence era, and since 1947 has relied upon parliamentary procedures for the attainment of socialist goals. Unlike most less developed countries, Nehru's India has not turned to a one-party government such as was found in Nasser's "direct democracy," Nkrumah's "Nkrumahism," and Sukarno's "guided democracy." Nehru explained in "The Basic Approach" that the aim of Indian socialism is to serve the democratic freedoms of the individual, and also to improve "the quality of the individual and the dharma underlying it."[5] According to Nehru's interpretation, while India has much in common with the capitalist and communist countries, it has problems for which there are no parallels or historical precedents elsewhere. Consequently, while Western and Marxian economics are helpful, they have little bearing on India's present-day problems. His conclusion in 1958 was that "We have thus to do our own thinking, profiting by the example of others, but essentially trying to find a path for ourselves suited to our own conditions."[6]

Clearly, Indian socialism has been adjusted to India's prevailing economic, social, and political circumstances. Indian socialism of the 1930s and 1940s called for a more extensive social revolution than did the Indian socialism of the 1950s and 1960s. The transition from colonialism to full-fledged socialism was viewed by the preindependence socialists as being much quicker than the transition envisioned by the postindependence architects of the first five five-year plans. Since 1951, when the First Five-Year Plan was put into operation, a sizable gap has developed between socialist theory and socialist practice. Population growth has not been significantly reduced; land reform has made little progress; women remain largely unemancipated; the public sector, while it has expanded, remains quite small in comparison with the private sector—which still turns out 87 percent of the nation's net domestic product; and unemployment and underemployment continue to be serious problems. Instead of having a large public-enterprise, small private-enterprise economy, India after more than a quarter century of independence has a small public-enterprise, large private-enterprise economy. Extreme poverty remains widespread alongside of great income and wealth inequality. Nehru's socialism, like postcolonial India, has been "soft"; and a fundamental social revolution has not been mounted. Any such revolution would have to overcome the apathy of the masses and the economic and political power structure of the top 20 percent of the country's income recipients who have dominated the Congress party.

---

[5] Dharma is defined as the "the fulfilment of one's duty towards society with earnestness and devotion." Shriman Narayan, *op. cit.*, Foreword.

[6] Jawaharlal Nehru, "The Basic Approach," *Appendix A* in Shriman Narayan, *op. cit.*, p. 133.

The Indian Economy

Even though it has a growing industrial sector, the Indian economy is essentially a very poor agricultural economy. From 75 to 80 percent of the population of close to 600 million (1975) are dependent for their livelihood on agriculture and related activities. In 1973, GNP per capita was only $120, which was much below the communist Chinese GNP per capita of $270. Most of the other Asian and South Asian countries had a higher per capita GNP than India. In 1973, per capita GNP for other Asian countries was as follows: Republic of China (Taiwan), $660; Malaysia, $570; South Korea, $400; Philippines, $280; and Thailand, $270. In the 1972 list of seventy-five less developed countries with per capita GNP below $500, prepared by the World Bank, India placed 53rd from the top.[7] Of the seventy-five countries, only eighteen had a GNP per capita below that of India; and they included poor Middle East, Asian, and African countries such as Yemen, Indonesia, Afghanistan, and Ethopia.

Like other less developed countries, India is still largely an agricultural nation. As the statistics in Table 20-1 show, agriculture, forestry, and fishing account for close to one-half of the nation's total output of goods and services. Industry (manufacturing and mining) contributes only 15.3 percent of the gross domestic product, an amount that has remained unchanged over the past decade. Other major economic activities are construction, transportation, communications, and the wholesale and retail trades.

[7] The World Bank, *World Bank Atlas*, 1974, p. 7. When using GNP data as a basis for the comparison of developed and less developed countries, attention should be drawn to the difficulties of comparing countries with large subsistence sectors with countries without these sectors. Where large subsistence sectors exist, per capita GNP does not include a number of nonmarketable goods and services that are included in the GNP statistics of developed countries.

Further light is thrown on the nature of the Indian economy by examining the uses or distribution of its net domestic product. Like other less developed countries, India has a high-consumption, low-investment economy. The statistics in Table 20-2 reveal that 81 percent of India's net domestic product was taken up by private or household consumption in 1968 and only 10.2 percent by private and public net investment. With a very low per capita income, India was not able to generate a large amount of private and public saving. As with other poor developing countries, India was a debtor country with a net import surplus of goods and services. As its national income rises, India expects to reduce the relative share of private consumption and to increase the relative share of net investment. It was estimated that by the end of the Fourth Five-Year Plan (1969-1974) private consumption would take up only 77.6 percent of net domestic product, and net investment would increase to 13.1 percent. India's long-term program estimates that by 1981 private consumption will absorb a little less than three-fourths of net domestic product and investment almost 15 percent. Also, India expects to have a very small net export surplus. These estimates for 1981, like many of the planners' other estimates, appear to be overly optimistic in the light of international economic developments since the Fourth Plan was adopted in 1969. Furthermore, as long as India is unable to curb the growth of its population, it will be very difficult for her to move away from a high-consumption, low-investment economy.

Agriculture and Industry in the Indian Economy

With India seriously overpopulated and the bulk of the population tied to small farms, it is not surprising that India is a poor country.

Table 20-1

The Origins of India's Gross Domestic Product, 1973

Economic activities	In billion rupees	In percent
Agriculture	194.0	41.3
Mining	4.3	.9
Manufacturing	65.3	13.9
Electricity, gas, and water	4.8	1.0
Construction	23.2	5.0
Wholesale and retail trade	45.5	9.7
Transport and communications	20.6	4.4
Other	112.0	23.8
Gross domestic product	469.7	100.0

Source: United Nations, *Monthly Bulletin of Statistics*, Vol. XXX, No. 8, Aug. 1976.

According to the 1961-1962 agricultural survey, approximately three-quarters of the rural families had land holdings of less than five acres.[8] The lowest 10 percent of the families had 0.18 percent of the land held by all rural families. From this lowest 10 percent, agricultural labor is recruited. After independence was achieved, the Indian government took a number of steps to improve the lot of the peasants. The large class of absentee owners *(zamindari)*, originally created by the British, was abolished. Traditional rents of 50 percent of the crops were greatly reduced and the cooperative farming and marketing movement was encouraged. The government's community development project revived the village councils *(panchayats)* over the whole country to encourage villager participation in the agricultural development plans. Under the five-year plans, land was reclaimed, irrigation greatly extended, and credit and other financial aids were extended by the federal government to the peasants. The states passed laws to break up large land holdings by placing ceilings on the size of these holdings. Land above the ceilings was distributed among the landless rural workers. Fertilizer and chemical companies were established by the federal government to increase the

[8] Santikumar Ghosh, *The Economy of India*, Calcutta: The World Press Private, 1971, p. 18.

Table 20-2

The Percentage Distribution of India's Net Domestic Product, 1968-1981

NDP items	1968 (Actual)	1974 (Estimated)	1979 (Projected)	1981 (Projected)
Personal consumption	81.1	77.6	75.1	74.2
Public consumption	9.8	9.9	9.6	9.6
Net investment	10.2	13.1	15.1	15.9
Net export surplus	−1.0	−0.6	0.2	0.3
Net domestic product	100.0	100.0	100.0	100.0

Source: Planning Commission, *Fourth Five-Year Plan, 1969-1974*, 1970.

supplies of fertilizers, pesticides, and other chemical products used in the agricultural sector.

Considerable progress has been made in increasing food grains and other agricultural products in the quarter century since independence was gained. The total supply of food grains, which was 50.8 million metric tons in 1950–1951, increased to 107.8 million metric tons in 1970–1971. Over the twenty-year period, the average annual rate of growth of the supply of food grains was 3.8 percent. Three factors have, however, left India's food problem largely unresolved. The unreliable monsoons have subjected the country to devastating droughts. A population growth of 2.5 percent a year has allowed little room for the improvement of the typical peasant's diet. The states have been lax in enforcing the legislation reducing rents and limiting the size of landholdings. Widespread and deep apathy among the peasants and the survival in practice of the caste system have curbed peasant participation in community development programs and have delayed the modernization of Indian farming. When farming has been modernized and improved as the result of the Green Revolution and government financial aid, the well-to-do farmers have all too frequently benefited much more than the poor farmers.

India has undergone a considerable industrial transformation since the beginning of World War II. Between 1939 and 1975, India increased its crude steel output from 848,000 tons to 7,800,000 tons and in the same period more than doubled its output of coal. During the war, the British colonial policy of encouraging only light consumer-goods industries had to be abandoned in favor of more attention to heavy industries, which produced machinery, equipment, and war materiel. The development policy since 1947 has been to industrialize India as rapidly as possible with investment supported by domestic saving and foreign financial aid.

The Indian economy is divided into organized and unorganized sectors. The latter sector includes the cottage and handicraft industries, which cater largely to local village markets. The organized sector is the modern sector, which includes the private and government-owned industrial establishments that have national and international markets. All industrial enterprises with ten or more workers are placed in the nation's organized or modern sector. In 1972, this sector provided employment for 180.8 million in a total population of 563.5 million. The public part of the organized sector employed 113 million, and the private part 67.8 million.[9]

The Indian industrial system is still primarily a private-enterprise system. The private sector contributes 85 percent of the total national output, and the public sector the remaining 15 percent. This latter sector includes the nationalized railways, communication systems, airlines, public utilities, fourteen major banks, a large part of the insurance system servicing the public, three government-owned steel companies, the country's only atomic energy plant, and a number of companies producing machine tools, fertilizer, antibiotics, cables, and salt. The government's industrial policy has been to supplement rather than to nationalize the private sector, and to encourage the expansion of those industries that have an important role in India's development strategy. With this aim, the government has set up an atomic-power plant, aided industrial research and development, and stimulated the industries that produce import substitutes and nontraditional exports such as machinery, machine tools, cycle parts, railway equipment, pharmaceuticals, plastics, and other chemical products.

In 1975, India produced 7.8 million metric tons of steel and was seventeenth among the world's steel producers. Its steel output was only one-sixth of Mainland China's and the

[9] Indian Ministry of Information, India, *A Reference Annual*, 1974, p. 25.

United Kingdom's output. Although India has made considerable progress in moving from a largely subsistence, nonindustrialized economy in 1939 to an economy with a sizable industrial sector, it has as yet realized only a small part of its industrial potential. With regard to foreign trade, India is far behind the advanced industrial countries and many of the less developed countries. India's share of the world export market is still less than the shares of Sweden, Holland, and Belgium.

The Planned Indian Economy

Among the less developed Southeastern Asiatic and African countries, India stands out as an example of a country with a well-developed national planning program. Planning in most less developed nations does not usually get much beyond separate development projects with somewhat limited coordination.[10] These countries frequently lack the trained administrators and statistical information required for the construction and implementation of overall annual and medium-term national plans. Although Indian planning has at times suffered from a lack of adequate statistical information, India has nevertheless had enough well-trained economists and government administrators and statistical information to carry national planning far beyond the level achieved by most of the world's less developed economies. Since national planning is a cardinal feature of both Western and Eastern socialism, planning theory was well developed before the achievement of Indian independence on August 15, 1947. Both Fabian and Marxian socialism drew attention to the desirability of planning in economic and social affairs. As early as 1938, the Indian Congress party established a National Planning Committee with Nehru as its chairman.[11]

In 1944, a group of private industrialists had proposed the so-called *Bombay Plan*, which emphasized the industrialization of India and the quintupling of industrial production in fifteen years. This plan in some ways anticipated the later official five-year plans by assigning priority to the production of electric power and capital goods, making the fullest possible use of small-scale and cottage industries in the production of consumer goods, and avoiding the hardship of the masses by preventing inflation and increasing employment. In the same year, the Indian Federation of Labor promoted its *People's Plan*, which was quite different than the Bombay Plan. The former plan called for a socialist society with a much expanded public sector. It also criticized the Soviet pattern of economic development by asserting that consumer goods should have some priority over producer goods, that the collectivization of agriculture should be voluntary, and that, since India had no need for a large defense effort, it could devote more resources to agricultural development.

The proponents of the People's Plan criticized the Bombay Plan and the Soviet five-year plans on the grounds that they equated planning with industrialization and ignored the need to emphasize agricultural development. The Indian Federation of Labor also showed little enthusiasm for cottage industries, since they would make it difficult to raise the people's standard of living. The *Gandhian Plan*, also announced in 1944, was an unrealistic plan based upon local self-sufficiency, governmental decentralization, and the independent village community. Nevertheless this plan was important because

---

[10] A survey of economic and social planning in the less developed countries is provided in Albert Waterston, *Development Planning: Lessons of Experience,* Baltimore: Johns Hopkins Press, 1957.

[11] A history of the development of Indian planning up to the Third Five-Year Plan (1961–1966) is presented in A. H. Hanson, *The Process of Planning, A Study of India's Five Year Plans, 1950–1964,* New York: Oxford University Press, 1966.

of its emphasis on popular participation and the need to secure the willing cooperation of the ordinary villagers if democratic national planning was to be successful.

The new independent Indian government drew the broad outlines of the Indian economy of the future in its Industrial Policy Resolution of 1948, which raised the issue of public versus private enterprise and their respective roles in the independent Indian economy.[12] The resolution emphasized two points that have continued to be matters of great concern in all of Indian planning since 1947. It stated that "The nation has now set itself to establish a social order where justice and equality of opportunity shall be secured to all the people."[13] The means to achieve this goal of a new social order can be summed up as a "dynamic national policy," which seeks to increase production and provide for its equitable distribution. This resolution was not specifically socialistic in outlook. The wholesale nationalization of existing private industry was rejected in favor of a program in which the development of new heavy industry was to be mainly the government's responsibility, while private industry under government direction would continue to play a valuable role.

The resolution divided industry into four categories. The first two, defense and strategic industries including railway transport, were to be monopolized by the state. The other two, basic and key industries including iron and steel, coal, aircraft manufacture, and shipbuilding—were to be in the government controlled sphere. However, all new enterprises in these basic and key industries were to be government owned and operated. Twenty other important industries, including heavy chemicals, cement, machine tools, sugar, and textiles, were to be run by private enterprise but regulated by the state. Whereas some private key industries may be nationalized, these twenty important industries were not subject to the threat of nationalization. The residual industries were to remain in private hands but were to be open to state surveillance. Cottage industries were to have a distinct role in the national economy. They were to be developed along cooperative lines and were to be integrated with large-scale industries as far as possible.

The Construction of India's Five-Year Plans

Indian planning began formally with the setting up of the Planning Commission on March 15, 1950. It is a democratic, open process, in which there is wide political participation by the federal or union government, the governments of the sixteen states (which have responsibility for agricultural, educational, and social welfare policies and programs), and the governments of the ten territories. The five-year national plans incorporate the aspirations of the nation for economic and social advancement and a set of policy prescriptions for achieving these aspirations. Since India is not a homogeneous cultural entity, having a large variety of linguistic, cultural, and political groups, the national plans must provide for all these groups within the same plan framework. While the Planning Commission gives general guidance to the national economy, it must also function as a mediator among a wide variety of economic and social interest groups spread over a large land area.

The resolution that established the Planning Commission stated that one of its functions was to "make an assessment of the material, capital and human resources of the country including technical personnel, and

---

[12] The Directive Principles of this resolution are given in detail in Nabagopal Das, *The Indian Economy under Planning*, Calcutta: The World Press Private, 1972, p. 14.

[13] A. H. Hanson, *op. cit.*, p. 448.

investigate the possibilities of augmenting such of these resources as are found to be deficient in relation to the nation's requirements; [and to] formulate a Plan for the most effective and balanced utilisation of the country's resources."[14] The procedure followed by the commission is to use the *planning backward* approach.[15] The first step is to determine a growth target for the economy over the five-year plan period. A range of possible growth rates is set by extrapolating the past growth trend of the nation's GNP, and adjusting this trend on the basis of information concerning prospective economic developments. The average annual increase in India's gross domestic product since 1960 has been 3 percent. The annual growth target set by the Planning Commission has usually been around 5 percent, the hope being that setting a target growth rate above 3 percent would lead the nation to put extra effort into the program to achieve rapid economic development and a high growth rate.

The usual method of setting the five-year growth target for Net Domestic Product (Gross Domestic Product less depreciation) in the Indian plans has been to estimate how large net saving or new investment as a percent of NDP would be in each year of the five-year plan period, and also how much output this net saving or investment would add each year to total NDP. In the Fourth Plan the planning authorities in India estimated that new savings or investment each year would be 13.1 percent of NDP, and that this saving or investment would add 5.46 rupees of new output to each 100 rupees of NDP. In other words the estimated net saving or investment of 13.1 percent of Net Domestic Product would sustain an annual growth of this product of 5.46 percent.[16] Usually the Indian planning authorities have overestimated the productivity of net saving or investment so that the actual rate of growth of NDP has been nearer 3 than 5.5 percent a year.

After the five-year target growth rate has been set, the next step taken by the Planning Commission is to plan backward from the gross domestic product projected for the fifth year of the plan period.[17] This is done by constructing a national economic budget for the last year of the plan period, which shows the gross domestic product and its distribution among private and public consumption and private and public investment, including the net export surplus.

A provisional national economic budget for 1979, the last year of the Fifth Plan (1974–1979), is presented in Table 20-3. This national economic budget shows how the Indian planning authorities plan to use the net domestic product in order to achieve the

[14] H. K. Paranjape, *The Planning Commission, A Descriptive Account*, New Delhi: The Indian Institute of Public Administration, 1964, p. 11.

[15] Richard S. Eckaus, "Planning in India," in Max F. Millikan (ed.), *National Economic Planning*, New York: National Bureau of Economic Research, 1967, p. 312. See also R. Leela and N. Somasekhara, "Predictions of Mahalanobis and Performance of Plans," *Indian Economic Journal*, Vol. XX, Oct.–Dec. 1972, pp. 174-189.

[16] The calculation of the 5.46 percent NDP growth rate is as follows:

$$\frac{\text{Investment/Net Domestic Product ratio}}{\text{Incremental capital/output ratio}} = \frac{13.1\%}{2.4}$$

$$= \frac{13.1}{100} \times \frac{1}{2.4} = \frac{13.1}{240} = \frac{5.46}{100} \text{ or } 5.46\%$$

The investment/Net Domestic Product ratio indicates how much of this product is taken up by investment. In the Fourth Plan the planning authorities estimated that 13.2 percent of the NDP would be taken up annually by investment. The incremental capital/output ratio shows how many rupees of additional capital are required to add one more rupee to total national output or NDP. In the case of the Fourth Plan the planning authorities estimated that the incremental capital/output ratio for the plan period was 2.4 to 1, which meant that it would take 2.4 rupees of additional capital to add one more rupee of output to total national output or NDP.

[17] For a brief summary of Indian five-year planning, see Robert E. Baldwin, *Economic Development and Growth*, 2nd ed., New York: John Wiley, 1972, pp. 88-94.

Table 20-3
The Indian National Economic Budget for 1979 (Rs. 100 Crores at 1969 Prices)[1]

	1974 National economic accounts (estimated)		1979 National economic budget (projected)	
	In rupees	In percent	In rupees	In percent
Private consumption	324.9	77.6	428.8	75.1
Public consumption	41.0	9.9	55.0	9.6
Net private and public investment	55.0	13.1	86.2	15.1
Net export surplus	−2.3	−0.6	1.0	0.2
Net domestic product	418.6	100.0	571.0	100.0

[1] One crore is 10,000,000 rupees.

Source: Indian Planning Commission, *Draft Fifth Five-Year Plan, 1974–1979*, 1973.

national consumption and investment goals and priorities of the Fifth Plan. There is to be a considerable decline (2.5 percentage points) in private consumption as a relative share of the 1979 net domestic product, a very small decline in the relative share of public consumption (0.3 percentage points), a considerable increase (2 percentage points) in the relative share of net private and public investment, and a shift from an import surplus (−0.6 percent of net domestic product) to an export surplus (0.2 percent). The national economic budget for 1979 shows that the Indian government plans to curb private consumption in order to increase savings and investment, thus achieving a higher economic growth rate of 5.5 percent. If the Fifth Plan is no more successful than the earlier four plans, the growth rate actually achieved will be well below 5.5 percent.

The Planning Commission constructs an input-output table for each year of the plan period. This table shows the interrelations between all the economic activities that contribute to the GNP; it also gives the output and investment needed to achieve the annual planned increases in the various sectors of the economy, which must together be consistent with the annual planned increase in the GNP. Supply-and-demand balances are constructed for the major commodities such as steel, coal, power, heavy chemicals, and food grains, and for private and public investment, supplies of various types of labor, and imports and exports. The most important balance or subbudget is the investment subbudget, which shows the public and private investment estimated to be required to achieve the plan's projected annual growth rate. Table 20-4 shows that 90 percent of public investment and approximately 75 percent of private investment in the Fourth Plan are taken up by a few major types of investment in agriculture, irrigation, power, industry, transport, communications, education, health, and housing. The final step in the planning process is to select the investment projects in the public and private sectors that will be calculated to maximize labor productivity and total output.

Indian Financial Planning

The Indian five-year plans are drawn up in real terms, i.e., in constant prices. Real or physical planning is accompanied by financial

Table 20-4
The Investment Balance (Subbudget) of the Fourth Indian Five-Year Plan, 1969–1974 (Rs. 100 Crores at 1968–1969 Prices)[1]

	Planned investment expenditures			
	Public		Private	
	In rupees	In percent	In rupees	In percent
1. Agriculture	2,118	17.1	1,600	17.8
2. Irrigation	1,073	6.8	—	—
3. Power	2,448	15.4	75	0.8
4. Industry	3,298	21.0	2,000	22.3
5. Transport and communications	3,197	20.3	920	10.2
6. Education	278	5.2	—	—
7. Health	132	2.7	—	—
8. Housing	235	1.5	2,175	24.3
9. Others	876	10.0	2,210	24.6
10. Total investment	13,655	100.0	8,980	100.0

[1] One crore is 10,000,000 rupees.

Source: Planning Commission, *Fourth Five-Year Plan, 1969–1974*, 1970, p. 52.

planning, which seeks to equate public and private investment and public and private saving.[18] The objective of India's financial planning is to secure a balance between saving and investing. Not all of India's investments are financed from domestic public saving by the federal and state governments and private saving by individuals and companies. Both governments and private business enterprises may borrow abroad to finance a part of their domestic investment. The private sector can invest only to the extent that private domestic saving and funds borrowed from abroad are made available to private investors. The public sector's investments can be financed from a number of sources, such as current budget surpluses, profits of nationalized enterprises, sales of bonds to the public, financial assistance and aid from abroad, and borrowing from the central bank, i.e., the Reserve Bank of India. Financing public investments from current surpluses, from funds obtained by selling bonds to the public, and from foreign assistance and aid (which are used to import goods) is not inflationary when an increase in public spending is offset by a decline in private spending. When public spending for investment purposes is financed by borrowing from the central bank, and there is no offset in private spending, this public spending is inflationary.

The Fourth Plan (1969–1974) estimated public-sector plan expenditures for the five-year plan period to be Rs. 15,902 crores and private investment expenditures to be Rs. 8,980 crores. (Rs. is the abbreviation for the rupee, the monetary unit of India. A rupee is worth about 14 American cents; a crore is ten

[18] All Indian five-year plans have a section devoted to "Financing the Plan." See for example the *Fourth Five-Year Plan, 1969–1974*, Chapter 4, "Financing the Plan," pp. 71–92. See also B. B. Lal, "Rationalisation of Commercial Banks in India," *Indian Journal of Economics*, Vol. L, Oct. 1969, pp. 171–185.

million rupees.) It was expected that all but Rs. 30 crores of the private-investment expenditures would be financed by private household, cooperative, and corporate saving. The remaining Rs. 30 crores of private investment would be financed by a net inflow of foreign funds. More than three-fourths (78.2 percent) of the public-investment expenditures, totaling Rs. 12,435 crores, were expected to be financed from budgetary sources such as current budget surpluses, profits of nationalized companies, and bond sales.[19] Borrowing abroad and foreign assistance were estimated to finance 16.5 percent of total public-investment expenditures. The remaining 5.3 percent or Rs. 850 crores of public-investment expenditures, not provided for, would have to be financed by increasing taxes or borrowing by the government from the Reserve Bank. Since this type of borrowing tends to be inflationary, the Indian planning authorities in the Fourth Plan proposed to increase domestic saving from 8.8 percent of national income in 1969 to 13.2 percent in 1974 by increasing taxes and enlarging the current budgetary surplus or public saving. The increased public saving was to be used to reduce the deficit financing of the public-sector investment expenditures from 10.1 percent of these expenditures (in the years 1966–1969) to 5.3 percent (in the years 1969–1974). The much larger deficits in the Second and Third Plans were responsible for much of the strong inflationary pressure that had developed in the years 1956–1974.

India's Five-Year Plans, 1951–1979

India is currently (1976) carrying out its Fifth Five-Year Plan (1974–1979). National planning in India may be divided into three periods. The first period includes the first three five-year plans of the years 1951–1966;

[19] *Ibid.*, p. 78.

the second period runs from 1966 to 1968, when five-year planning was temporarily suspended after the failure of the Third Plan (1961–1966); and the third period covers the years 1969–1979, when five-year planning was resumed with the adoption of the Fourth Plan (1969–1974). The first Five-Year Plan (1951–1956) was a modest plan that achieved most of its targets and developed an atmosphere of optimism that carried over into the Second Five-Year Plan (1956–1961). The latter plan was much bolder than the First Plan. It formally approved a "socialistic pattern of society," called for an expansion of the public sector and a restriction of the growth of the private sector, and adopted the Soviet development model, which gave special attention to the expansion of heavy industries, such as the steel, heavy machinery, electric power, and chemical industries. The Second Plan also anticipated a 25 percent increase in national income, a large expansion of employment opportunities, a reduction of inequalities in income and wealth, and a more even distribution of economic power.[20] Much attention was to be given to land reform, the development of agricultural cooperation, community development, the improvement of village industries, and the extension of education and social services.

During the Second Plan, a number of serious problems emerged and have continued as obstacles to successful planning. Rising public expenditures were followed by rising consumer prices, especially the prices of food grains. Inflation was accompanied by imports much in excess of the planned imports. The federal and state governments failed to increase taxes to the level needed to finance the expanding development expenditures. India borrowed excessively from abroad, and had to

[20] The overly ambitious goals of the Second Plan are discussed in the Planning Commission, *Second Five-Year Plan, A Draft Outline,* Delhi, 1956, pp. 6–21.

be rescued from international balance-of-payments difficulties by special loans from foreign banks and governments. The Second Plan was far from being a complete success, as most key targets were from two-thirds to four-fifths fulfilled. However, enough success was achieved to convince the Planning Commission and the National Development Council that India could soon reach a level of "self-sustaining growth," which was a major objective of the Third Five-Year Plan (1961–1965).

The performance of the Indian economy during the Third Plan was very disappointing.[21] The major roadblocks to good performance were a series of bad harvests, military conflicts with Pakistan and China, the failure of the government to provide agriculture with the necessary inputs, and overly ambitious goals with respect to both financial and organizational resources. Bottlenecks appeared in transportation, power, and irrigation; and efforts to reduce income and regional inequalities slowed down economic growth. The poor performance of the Indian economy extended into the years 1966–1968, when five-year planning was replaced by annual planning. The economic stagnation of the years 1966–1968 led to a reappraisal of the goals of Indian national planning. The Indian government then decided to move away from the Soviet-style unbalanced growth strategy that had dominated the Second and Third Plans and to place more emphasis upon improving the agricultural sector by increasing employment and reducing underemployment. Also, the government turned to a less restrictive policy toward private enterprise.

The Fourth Five-Year Plan (1969–1974) incorporated three new strategies. The new agricultural strategy was to enlarge farm output by concentrating the Green Revolution on the farm areas with the largest output potential. Increased food grain output would remove the necessity of depending upon food grain imports for securing an adequate nutritional level. The new industrial strategy sought to achieve economic growth without increasing inflationary pressures. Inflation was to be controlled by financing development investment expenditures from increased public saving, resulting from increased taxes on the middle- and upper-income groups, rather than by means of deficit financing, which increased government borrowing from the Reserve Bank of India. The new foreign trade strategy was to eliminate the need for foreign financial aid by expanding nontraditional exports, such as machinery and equipment, synthetic fibers, plastics, pharmaceuticals, paper, and paper products. The overall goals of the Fourth Plan are summarized in Table 20–5, which shows the Indian national economic accounts for 1969 and the national economic budget for 1974, the final year of the 1969–1974 plan period. Between 1969 and 1974, the plan anticipated a relative decline in private consumption as a share of India's net domestic product, a considerable increase in the relative share of net private and public investment, and no change in the relative share of public consumption.

The 1969–1974 plan period was a time of growing economic difficulties. Abroad, the dislocation of the international monetary system, the worldwide inflationary development, the oil crisis, and the spread of recession adversely affected India's export markets. At home, the large deficit-financing program of the federal government, the food scarcities and sharp rise in consumer prices, the war with Pakistan, and the heavy financial burden of providing for the East Pakistan refugees disrupted the nation's economic activities. In these circumstances, the Fourth Plan proved too ambitious. Net domestic product, which

[21] A review of economic developments during the Third Plan is presented in Planning Commission, "Review of Economic and Social Situation," *Fourth Five-Year Plan, 1969–74*, Delhi, 1970, pp. 5–13.

Table 20-5

The Indian National Economic Accounts for 1969 and the National Economic Budget for 1974 (Rs. 100 Crores at 1969 Prices)

	1969 National economic accounts (actual)		1974 National economic budget (projection)	
	In rupees	In percent	In rupees	In percent
Private consumption	257.4	81.0	324.9	77.6
Public consumption	31.0	9.8	41.0	9.9
Net private and public investment	32.3	10.2	55.0	13.1
Net export surplus	−3.1	−1.0	−2.3	−0.6
Net domestic product	317.6	100.0	418.6	100.0

Source: Planning Commission, *Fourth Five-Year Plan, 1969–1974*, 1970, p. 32.

had been projected to increase 5.7 percent a year during the plan period, grew at a rate of only 3.7 percent; and industrial production, which was expected to rise at an annual rate of 7 percent, increased only 4.2 percent a year.

The Fifth Five-Year Plan (1974–1979) was constructed before the oil crisis and the recession of the years 1973–1974; it will probably record a performance of the Indian economy less satisfactory than that of the years 1969–1974. This plan has as its two main objectives the removal of poverty and the achievement of self-reliance in the area of foreign aid. The plan looks forward to the reduction of net foreign aid to zero by 1986. With regard to the ending of poverty, the plan anticipates raising the monthly per capita consumption of the lowest 30 percent of the population to Rs. 37.10 (approximately U.S. $4.75 at 1975 exchange rates). Removing poverty, however, requires a high economic growth rate. Table 20–6 shows that the Fifth Plan projects an annual growth rate of agricultural production of 4.7 percent, of industrial production of 8 to 10 percent, and of net domestic product of 5.5 percent—all of which are well above the rates actually achieved under the Fourth Plan in less difficult economic circumstances. With India's population growing at a rate of 2.3 percent annually and an estimated 20 million unemployed in 1974, the prospect of significantly reducing poverty in the near future in India is not very good.

The Performance of the Indian Economy, 1962–1970

The performance of the Indian economy since the early 1960s falls into two distinct periods. The first, from 1962 to 1970, was one of world-wide economic prosperity, in which the Indian economy made considerable but irregular progress. The second, 1971–1975, has been one of worldwide economic and financial dislocation, in which India's economic and financial problems have been greatly magnified. Burdened with a population of close to 600 million, a large part of which is usually close to the survival level, India has made little progress towards achieving a satisfactory standard of living on a sustained basis for its masses.

A survey of the performance of the Indian economy from 1962 to 1970 shows that the Indian economy grew at the average annual

Table 20-6
Major Targets of the Indian Fifth Plan, 1974–1979

Annual increases, 1974–1979, in:	In percent
Net Domestic Product	5.5
Agricultural output	4.7
Mining and manufacturing output	8.2
Exports	7.6
Cement	9.3
Coal	11.3
Finished steel	11.7
Food grains	4.3
Petroleum	9.0

Source: Indian Planning Commission, *Draft Fifth Five-Year Plan, 1974–1979*, 1973.

rate of 3.7 percent; this is low for a less developed economy with excellent natural resources and with an annual population growth rate of 2.5 percent. Both gross domestic product and industrial production increased at highly irregular rates. In the years 1962–1970, the annual changes in gross domestic product fluctuated between 9.8 and −5.3 percent; and the annual changes in industrial production were between 9.5 and −1.7 percent. Some of these fluctuations were caused by bad harvests, military conflicts, and international disturbances, while others resulted from the inadequacies of the national planning programs.

The statistics relating to changes in Indian economic indicators during 1962–1970 (presented in Table 20-7) reveal similar large fluctuations in consumer prices, the volume of exports, and the balance of international payments. After 1962, the Indian economy experienced strong inflationary pressures; these were caused in large part by recurring scarcities of food grains and by deficit financing of large public expenditures. Consumer prices rose during 1962–1970 at an average annual rate of 5.9 percent, with annual rates of price increases fluctuating between a high of 13 percent and a low of 1.9 percent. The volume of exports in this period increased at an average annual rate of 4.5 percent, which was far removed from the plan goal of 7 percent. Many developed Western European and less developed countries had much better export records than did India. The statistics in Table 20-7 show that India's poor export record was correlated with adverse current balances of international payments. The deficit in the current balance of payments was especially large during the years of poor plan performance from 1964 to 1968.

The Indian Economy, 1971–1975

In common with much of the rest of the world, India has passed through a difficult period since 1970. The worldwide recession of 1974–1975 was preceded by the Indian-Pakistani War of 1971, which placed a heavy military and refugee burden on an already weak economy. A declining rate of increase of gross domestic product after 1970 was accompanied by a rapid increase in domestic and import prices and a sizable increase in unemployment. Table 20-8 shows that in 1971–1974, the average annual increase in gross

Table 20-7
Annual Percentage Changes in Selected Indian Economic Indicators, 1962–1970

Years	Gross domestic product	Industrial production	Consumer price index	Volume of exports	Current balance of international payments (million U.S. $)
1962	2.7	9.5	3.2	7.2	−945
1963	5.3	8.7	3.1	12.4	−890
1964	7.6	9.0	13.0	6.0	−1,264
1965	−5.3	6.4	9.7	−6.6	−1,418
1966	1.2	1.7	10.5	3.0	−1,147
1967	9.8	−1.7	3.9	−4.0	−1,314
1968	1.7	6.9	2.6	13.2	−840
1969	4.9	7.3	1.9	−1.8	−463
1970	5.2	5.3	5.5	11.0	−607
Average annual % change 1962–1970	3.7	5.9	5.9	4.5	—

Sources: United Nations, *Monthly Bulletin of Statistics*; and International Monetary Fund, *International Financial Statistics*.

domestic product (1.6 percent) was less than the annual increase in population (2.3 percent) during those years, with the result that the real per capita GNP declined. Much of the limited increase in total output could be attributed to the recurring bad harvest years that resulted from the failure of the monsoons to provide a normal rainfall. A low volume of exports also contributed to the low national growth rate. At the same time that national output was low and unemployment was high, domestic prices rose rapidly, along with the high prices of imported food grains, oil, and manufactured products.

In 1974, the index of import prices increased 60.6 percent, while domestic consumer prices rose 21.1 percent and wholesale prices 26.8 percent. The world shortages of wheat and other grains and the quadrupled price of crude oil created balance-of-international-payments problems that prevented India from importing needed amounts of these commodities. As unemployment rose and food shortages developed, riots broke out in many parts of the country as the masses demanded work and food supplies at reasonable prices. A wave of strikes culminated in the strike of the workers of the national railway system and a general strike in 1974. While the government did much to provide public employment and to distribute food grains to famine-stricken rural areas, it did not succeed in preventing widespread criticism and political opposition. In 1975 the political situation worsened and government by proclamation replaced the usual democratic procedures. Since a democratic approach had not led to a solving of India's economic and social problems, the Indian government under Prime Minister Indira Gandhi turned to more authoritarian measures in the effort to make the Indian economy viable.

In the effort to curb the rampant inflation of 1973 and 1974, the Indian government turned to restrictive monetary and fiscal policies and to the control of the prices and distribution of wheat, rice, and other essential commodities. The takeover of the wholesale grain trade in 1972 had to be abandoned in 1974, because the government was unable to prevent widespread hoarding, price gouging, and black marketing in the grain trade. By 1975, domestic inflation was considerably reduced, but only at the cost of low levels of employment and production. The adverse foreign trade situation was eased by importing food grains from the Soviet Union and the United States and by arranging for oil imports on credit from Iran; the latter also invested surplus oil earnings in Indian iron-ore, steel, cement, paper, and chemical industries. By 1975, India's economic situation was considerably improved with the aid of good harvests, but at a level much below the level expected by those who constructed the five-year plan for 1974–1979.

Demand and Supply Management in the Indian Economy

National planning in India has been carried out with the help of a very extensive system of economic and financial controls. The general objective of these controls has been to establish a full-employment balance between supply and demand at the macroeconomic and microeconomic levels. Both fiscal and monetary policies have played a major role in India's demand management. Short-term fiscal policy has been constructed to aid in achieving economic stability. In the period of strong inflationary pressures since 1970, the federal government has increased taxes, required stricter enforcement of internal revenue measures, and slowed down public spending. The government's efforts in these directions in recent years have been largely unsuccessful, because of the continued widespread tax evasion and hoarding of undeclared wealth and the failure to hold down public spending adequately. This latter failure stemmed from the need to maintain a large military establishment and to provide relief to refugees and to drought-stricken areas. While the federal government has been able to secure surpluses on its current fiscal budget which includes current revenues and expenditures, its capital expenditures have usually exceeded its capital revenues; and the large borrowing for expenditures on public works and other public capital facilities has created inflationary capital budget deficits.

Fiscal policy has been used to curb consumption, increase domestic saving, and stimulate private investment. Tax concessions have been given in the form of exemptions from taxes on company profits in the case of newly established firms and from indirect taxes on exports. Heavy reliance is placed on indirect taxes in the form of customs duties, excise taxes, and sales taxes in the effort to curb private consumption. In 1974, 80 percent of the net revenue of the central government was obtained from indirect taxes and 20 percent from personal- and corporate-income taxes and taxes on wealth and real property. The tax programs of the federal and state governments are designed to limit private consumption to the 75 to 78 percent of the net domestic product set forth as national goals in the Fourth and Fifth Plans.

While it is to be expected that indirect taxation would be heavy in a less developed country like India, many Indian analysts believe that the upper-income classes do not bear a fair share of the tax burden in the form of direct taxes. The tax systems of most Western countries do more to redistribute income than does the Indian tax system. In 1965, the United Kingdom collected 16.1 percent of Gross National Product in direct taxes and the United States 18 percent, but India in 1967 collected only 2 percent of national income in direct taxes.[22] In agriculture, land ownership and land revenue taxes are much less progressive than urban personal-income taxes; and, as one Indian economist has put it, "It is a well established fact that the rural sector is comparatively under-taxed."[23] In the urban areas, much tax evasion takes place, and only a small part of the population pays any income tax. In 1972-1973 less than 1 percent (3,220,851) of the total population (563,490,000) paid any income taxes.

The Mahalanobis Committee set up in 1960 to inquire into taxation and income distribution concluded in its report that the Indian personal income tax had only a minor impact on income distribution. The top 20 percent of income recipients in urban areas, who had 57.6 percent of total pretax income, had 56.2 percent of aftertax income.[24] Although Indian personal income taxes are very progressive, with the maximum rate being 93.5 percent, there is so much tax evasion and poor tax collection that the high personal income tax rates are not very productive. The great inequality in income distribution and in sharing the national tax burden explains why the bottom 30 percent of the population takes up only 8 percent of total personal consumption, whereas the top 20 percent of the population takes up 40 percent of total personal consumption.[25]

Monetary and Other Aspects of Economic Management

India's short-term monetary policy has been designed to go along with its fiscal policy in the effort to curb inflation. In 1970-1974, the Reserve Bank of India's discount rate was increased from 5 to 9 percent; ceilings were placed on the total bank credit extended to private industry; this credit was rationed to essential industries to avoid speculation; the distribution of company dividends was limited to 12 percent of share values; and in 1974, 50 percent of the cost-of-living allowance due workers under their wage contracts was frozen for two years.[26] Table 20-8 shows that the rate of increase of the money supply was more than eight times the rate of increase of gross domestic product. Not until 1974, when drastic measures were taken to curb government spending and the expansion of bank credit, was the rate of increase of the money supply significantly reduced; both wholesale and retail prices then increased much less rapidly than in the early 1970s.

The activities of private industry are regulated in a number of ways. New industrial enterprises are controlled through a licensing system; stock and bond issues are regulated by a capital issues committee; supplies of scarce raw materials and equipment are rationed to business enterprises; and imports are regulated by foreign exchange controls. Government price control is widespread in the Indian economy. Under the Essential Commodities Act of 1955, the central gov-

[22] Angus Maddison, *Economic Progress and Policy in Developing Countries*, London: Allen and Unwin, 1970, p. 73.

[23] Alak Ghosh, *op. cit.*, p. 502. The problems of fiscal policy in the developing Indian economy are analyzed in "Fiscal Policy in a Developing Economy," *The Indian Economic Journal*, Vol. 23, Part II, 1975, pp. 51-271.

[24] Planning Commission, *Report of the Committee on Distribution of Income and Levels of Living*, Part I, Delhi, 1964 and Part II, Delhi, 1969.

[25] Nabagopal Das, *op. cit.*, p. 76.

[26] India's monetary policy is analyzed in the Reserve Bank of India, *Annual Report on the Working of the Reserve Bank of India and Trend and Progress of Banking in India*, 1970 to 1975.

Table 20-8
Annual Percentage Changes in Selected Indian Economic Indicators, 1971–1975

Years	Gross domestic product	Industrial production	Consumer prices	Wholesale prices	Money supply	Export prices	Import prices	Current balance of payments (mil. U.S. $)
1970	5.2	6.1	5.3	6.2	12.4	−1.0	−1.0	−392
1971	2.0	3.0	3.0	4.0	13.0	2.0	−1.0	−643
1972	1.0	7.0	6.8	7.7	12.3	9.8	2.0	−162
1973	2.9	0.6	16.4	19.6	17.3	21.4	30.7	−529
1974	0.5	1.8	21.1	26.8	9.3	25.0	60.6	—
1975[1]	2.4	4.4	6.1	2.4	6.7	—	—	—
Average annual % change 1971–1974	1.6	3.1	11.8	14.5	13.0	14.6	23.1	—

[1] Indian government estimates.

Sources: IMF, *International Financial Statistics*, Sept. 1976; and UN, *Monthly Bulletin of Statistics*, Aug. 1976.

ernment is authorized to control the supply, distribution, and prices of any commodities declared to be "essential." At different times, the prices of steel, nonferrous metals, coal, fertilizers, cotton textiles, sugar, and tea have been controlled. The government has also entered the food grain trade and has regulated both the supply and prices of food grains through rationing and the use of fair-price stores.

The government is very much concerned with preventing the growth of monopoly and the concentration of economic power in the private sector. The Monopolies Commission, established by the Monopolies and Restrictive Trade Practices Act of 1969, advises the government on matters relating to the expansion of existing industrial enterprises and proposed amalgamations of these enterprises.[27] In these and other ways, the government seeks to keep the demand coming from business enterprises as competitive as possible, and also in line with the general objectives of the national plans.

Supply management in the Indian economy is a matter of great concern because of the numerous scarcities and bottlenecks that have hindered the nation's economic development. The overly ambitious five-year plans have placed heavy burdens on the nation's transport system, and have made it necessary to ration supplies of imported industrial materials, machinery, and equipment. The continued high population growth rate and the recurring droughts have forced the government to enter the food grains trade so that it could assure supplies of these grains to high-scarcity areas.

To cope with these problems, the government has adopted a number of measures to increase the supplies of essential commodities. In the agricultural sector, the Fourth and Fifth Plans have taken steps to

[27] Alak Ghosh, *Indian Economy, Its Nature and Problems,* Calcutta: The World Press Private, 1973, p. 288.

increase agricultural productivity and output and to build up adequate buffer stocks of food grains. In industry, the government has supplemented the private production of steel, machine tools, fertilizer, and other essential commodities by establishing its own state-run enterprises. Industry has produced import substitutes in order to deal with the problem of import scarcities. The government has also given financial and other aids to industries producing nontraditional exports to take the place of such traditional exports as tea, jute, jute products, cotton textiles, and handicrafts, which meet stiff world competition. On a more general level, the government has sought to raise labor productivity by improving education and financing industrial and other research and development.

While demand management in India has enabled the planning authorities to achieve a number of their plan targets, three major criticisms have been directed against this management: (1) that it has failed to curb private consumption enough to create the desired domestic saving; (2) that it has resulted in strong inflationary pressures; and (3) that it has weakened personal and business incentives to produce more output. It is widely conceded that the impact of taxation has been much more severe on the urban and nonagricultural sectors than on the rural and agricultural sectors. It is alleged that the government continues to tax the rural sector lightly because there are many votes in the villages that are controlled by a small minority of well-to-do farmers.[28] The maldistribution of the tax burden and the considerable tax evasion by the upper-income groups have resulted in less tax revenue and public saving than anticipated in the national plans.

Inflation in the Indian economy has resulted in part from the failure of the monetary authorities to keep the increases in the money supply in line with the increases in the nation's total output. The Fifth Plan proposes to hold the government's deficit financing "down to the level at which the consequential increase in the money supply with the public will not exceed the requirement of the economy arising from growth in real terms, so as to avoid an inflationary bias in plan financing."[29] This prescription was not followed in 1962–1972 when gross domestic product increased at the annual rate of 3.2 percent, while the money supply grew at an excessive 11.2 percent annual rate. Less ambitious plan-investment goals and a more effective tax system would reduce the pressure to turn to deficit financing and unwarranted increases in the money supply.

Long-Term Demand-and-Supply Management and Structural Change

Much of India's inability to use short- and medium-term demand-and-supply management effectively is due to the inherited institutional structure that constitutes a major obstacle to the construction of an efficient and expanding economy. Until India modernizes its land tenure, educational, health, tax, and other systems, demand-and-supply management will be an ineffective tool for securing the national priorities incorporated in the five-year plans.[30] India's failure to achieve a high and stable economic growth rate with a rising standard of living during the five five-year national plans has resulted in restricting the private enterprise system still further and

---

[28] See, for example, Nabagopal Das, *op. cit.*, p. 75; and also Santikumar Ghosh, *op. cit.*, pp. 17–22.

[29] Alak Ghosh, *op. cit.*, p. 123. See also V. B. Ghuge, "Public Debt, Inflation and Economic Development in India," *Indian Journal of Economics*, Vol. L, Oct. 1970, pp. 117–127.

[30] For an exhaustive analysis of the deficiencies of the Indian economic and social structure, see Gunnar Myrdal, *Asian Drama, An Inquiry into the Poverty of Nations*, Vols. I, II, and III, New York: Pantheon, 1968.

enlarging the scope of the socialist sector. What this amounts to is a transformation of the Indian economy that looks in the direction of a more socialistic economic system.

The socializing process became accelerated after 1970 as India's economic and social problems became more serious. The long-term socialization plan is designed to increase the government's role in the nation's industrial heartland or core sector, by extending public ownership to the steel, coal, chemical, cement, and oil industries. In 1970, India's fourteen largest private banks were nationalized, and government importation was extended to sixty essential commodities. In 1972, India's only copper producer, the Indian Copper Company, the Indian Iron and Steel Company, the wholesale grain trade, and the entire jute trade were taken out of private hands. In 1973, 711 noncoking coal mines were nationalized; in the next year, 40 textile mills were nationalized, and plans were made to form a single holding company in charge of a public integrated steel, coal, iron ore, and managanese ore complex. This expansion of the socialist sector has been accompanied by a progressive *Indianization* program, under which all new foreign firms and extensions of old foreign firms are to have a maximum foreign-equity participation of 40 percent instead of the previously allowable 51 or more percent.

The socialization of the Indian economy is not being carried out in accordance with the requirements of a very specific long-term program. Rather this socialization is an ad hoc response to mounting economic and social problems. When the economy is prosperous, little new socialization is carried out; but when the economy is faced with major difficulties, socialization makes a greater appeal to the Congress party leaders. The same situation is found in the United Kingdom, where the serious economic problems of 1974 and 1975 led to the proposal to bring the nation's main industries under closer government control through the use of planning agreements between them and the government. In both India and the United Kingdom, the proposal to extend the government's influence over the private-enterprise system is supported by the arguments that private industry is not as efficient as it should be, is not investing enough to contribute to a high growth rate, and is curbing production and employment.

The Planned Indian Economy: An Evaluation

While India has moved a considerable distance along the path of economic development, it is widely felt that India has not realized as much of its potential for growth and development as it would have under a more vigorous leadership.[31] Analysts of India's economic problems agree that India is a "soft" state in which a dichotomy exists between ideals and reality, and in which "There is an unwillingness among the rulers to impose obligations on the governed and a corresponding unwillingness on their part to obey rules laid down by democratic procedures. The tendency is to use the carrot, not the stick. The level of social discipline is low compared with all Western countries—not to mention Communist countries."[32]

The softness of the Indian state can be attributed to the fact that India is in a state of

---

[31] See, for example, the conclusions reached by Wilfred Malenbaum in *Modern India's Economy, Two Decades of Planned Growth*, Columbus, Ohio: Charles E. Merrill, 1971, pp. 201–226.

[32] Gunnar Myrdal, *op. cit.*, Vol. I, p. 277. The analysis of India's economic and social problems presented in its five-year plans shows quite clearly that the Indian government knows what should be done to cope with these problems, but so far it has not been prepared to act forcefully along these lines. See especially the Indian Planning Commission, *Draft Fifth Five-Year Plan, 1974–1979*, New Delhi: Controller of Publications, 1973.

transition to a future society not yet clearly defined. Alak Ghosh has explained that the Indian economy is a mixed economy based upon what he describes as a "partnership capitalism," which the ruling Congress party expects at some future time to transform into democratic socialism.[33] The Indian economy hangs today somewhere between an abandoned private capitalism and a yet unborn full democratic socialism. Rejecting both regulated capitalism and Eastern communism, India appears to be pragmatically feeling its way towards some poorly defined socialist goal. Meanwhile, the power position of the Indian establishment—composed of the bureaucratic-military class, the big business group, and the entrenched rural gentry and well-to-do farmers—remains largely unchallenged. This upper-class elite sees to it that land reform is delayed, that taxation is evaded, that government-aid programs benefit the upper- rather than the lower-income groups, and that no vigorous attack is made on the problems of unemployment and underemployment. Instead of acting as a vehicle of reform, the ruling Congress party is dominated by a coalition of upper-income economic interest groups who tolerate Nehru's "soft" state, because in practice it is more responsive to the well-to-do urban elite than to the impoverished rural masses. Angus Maddison explains that while the intellectuals like the late Jawaharlal Nehru and his daughter Indira Gandhi provided the Congress party with formal leadership, the party has been controlled by an elite that is willing to accept reformist legislation as long as it is not effectively implemented.[34]

A comparison of Socialist India with Communist China brings out the deficiencies of the Indian development program. Communist China has constructed a highly egalitarian society in which large income differentials have been eliminated, full employment has been achieved, and underemployment has been greatly reduced by employing rural labor in the farming off-season on public works. In addition, education has been made available to the masses; inflation has been avoided; and development investment needs have been met without borrowing abroad. Corruption has been greatly reduced; and government administration has been improved. When policies are decided upon, they are enforced. The authorities are eager to place obligations upon the people, because such obligations give direction to the people's lives and develop in them a sense of loyalty to the ruling regime.

One may argue as to whether popular participation in Chinese economic and social affairs is a free response of the people to Mao Tse-tung's efforts to develop a "new communist man [or woman]," or is instead a fear-induced reaction to the demands of an authoritarian communist regime.[35] Like many Western states, China has been prepared to use forceful methods of achieving what is held to be good for society. Urban students have been sent upon graduation to the countryside; workers have been transferred to communes near the western and northern borders for defense reasons; and people have been prevented from moving from the rural areas to the cities. Education has been adjusted to the vocational and technical needs of the economy, and no class of "educated unemployed" has been allowed to emerge (as has been the case in India).

Indian economic development suffers from

---

[33] Alak Ghosh, op. cit., p. 289.

[34] Angus Maddison, *Class Structure and Economic Growth, India and Pakistan since the Moghuls*, New York: W. W. Norton, 1971, p. 87.

[35] Joan Robinson regards the Chinese situation as a spontaneous reaction of the Chinese people to the effort to build in China a genuinely new egalitarian, nonmaterialistic society. See her "Foreword" in E. L. Wheelwright and Bruce McFarlane, *The Chinese Road to Socialism*, New York: Monthly Review Press, 1970.

an *over-gradualist* approach, which is acceptable to those elements in the community that do not want effective social reconstruction. The whole emphasis of Indian planning is on avoiding force and on relying upon peaceful, nonviolent voluntariness. The democratic socialist view of the Indian society is one of a *self-reforming society,* in which the masses will respond to appeals to construct a classless egalitarian society. The Indian planners are against the use of force and negative controls, which they consider a retreat from democracy. Their emphasis has been upon developing self-government and cooperation, from the village level up to the urban centers. The government offers positive inducements to action, ranging from information, instruction, and advice to subsidies of many kinds. Such an approach works well in a country with a high literacy level and a well-functioning political system. Where the masses are noted for their apathy, educational and literacy levels are low, and local self-government is poorly developed, as in India, the concept of a self-reforming society has less effectiveness than in the well-developed Western countries. In a less developed country, the need is greater than in a developed country for the impetus towards social reform to come down from the top as well as from the bottom.

A "soft" state like India does little to remove the obstacles to successful national planning that are created by the conditions outside the narrowly defined economic sphere. Indian planning has too frequently been based upon simple models that have neglected the social forces outside the economic system. Too many government officials have clung to the view that investment would of itself generate economic development. Not enough attention is given in practice to changing the prevailing attitudes and institutions that act as barriers to economic development. Sustained economic development would be more assured if the Indian planners would take the necessary steps to change India's outmoded attitudes and institutions. Such steps should include a large-scale birth control program, an educational system geared to the vocational and technical needs of a less developed economy, the elimination of the remnants of the caste system, a vigorously enforced land reform and tenancy program, a more equitable tax system, a more rational agricultural policy, the elimination of corruption in government administration, and the mobilization of unemployed and underemployed labor for work on rural public projects and social capital. What is needed is not a series of small, gradual changes but rather a large and rapid alteration of attitudes and institutions, as has been suggested by Gunnar Myrdal.[36] Many analysts of the Indian situation would agree with Myrdal that a social, noncommunist revolution is called for to place India firmly on the road to successful economic and social development.

The revolutionary change that India needs for successful national planning includes a reformation of its religious system. Indian religion, rigid and resistant to change, constitutes a cause of economic and social inertia and an obstacle to sound national planning, because its sanction is basically irrational and opposed to a logical way of thinking. Hinduism, Islam, and other religions support a social and economic stratification that leads to "low social and spatial mobility, little free competition in its wider sense, and great inequalities."[37] National planning stresses the importance of rational behavior, which cannot be achieved so long as the life of the people is dominated by religious taboos, magic, and mysticism. Thus far, efforts to reform religion in India have had little success, in part because many progressive elements in the population have ignored religion rather than

[36] Gunnar Myrdal, *op. cit.*, Vol. I, p. 117 fn.
[37] Gunnar Myrdal, *op. cit.*, Vol. 1, p. 104.

attempt to modernize it. The caste system, segregation of women, child marriages, scorn for manual labor, the acceptance of poverty by the masses, and other institutional and attitudinal factors serve merely to continue a long-standing way of life that is inimical to the establishment of an egalitarian society with a rising standard of living. Clearly, until the religious superstructure in India is subjected to the modernizing effects of the dynamics of social and economic change, little hope can be held out for the achievement of successful national planning.[38]

The question may well be asked: What lessons can other less developed countries in the Third World derive from the Indian experience with economic development? First, not much can be accomplished before the population problem is solved—if population pressure is heavy. Second, pushing ahead with the development of heavy industry should be avoided until the agricultural sector is in a position to provide a sizable surplus capable of sustaining an expansion of heavy industry. Third, steps should be taken to make use of unemployed and underemployed labor, for this constitutes a national asset that should not be wasted. Fourth, national planning should not be limited to a narrow economic sphere, but should also take account of the many social factors outside the economic sphere that might be obstacles to economic development.

An unanswered question is: are economic development and democratic procedures compatible? Is there a tradeoff between democracy and economic development with more of one necessitating less of the other? For many Asian, African, and Latin American less developed countries, this issue is probably only of academic interest, since most of them, unlike India, did not have a strong democratic tradition at the time of achieving their independence. Their problem is to diminish authoritarian government and planning as economic development proceeds and standards of living rise. For India, the problem remains: to what extent can economic development and the democratic process go hand in hand? If India lags seriously behind Communist China in the next quarter century, it may have much difficulty in preserving its democratic procedures. As far as the Third World is concerned, the direction in which it moves in the next quarter century may be greatly influenced by the outcome of the competing methods of economic and social development in India and China.

[38] K. M. Panikkar, *Hindu Society at Cross Roads*, Bombay: Asia Publishing House, 1955.

Selected Bibliography

ANJARIA, J. J. *Essays in Planning and Growth.* Vora and Co., Bombay, 1972.

DAS, NABAGOPAL. *The Indian Economy under Planning.* The World Press Private, Calcutta, 1972.

GHOSH, ALAK. *Indian Economy, Its Nature and Problems.* The World Press Private, Calcutta, 1973.

GHOSH, SANTIKUMAR. *The Economy of India.* The World Press Private, Calcutta, 1971.

GOVERNMENT OF INDIA, PLANNING COMMISSION. *Fourth Five-Year Plan, 1969–1974.* Delhi: Government of India Press, 1970.

———. *Second Five-Year Plan. A Draft Outline.* Delhi: Government of India Press, 1956.

HANSON, A. H. *The Process of Planning, A Study of India's Five-Year Plans, 1950–1964.* Oxford University Press, New York, 1966.

MADDISON, ANGUS. *Class Structure and Economic Growth, India and Pakistan since the Moghuls.* W. W. Norton and Co., New York, 1971.

———. *Economic Progress and Policy in Developing Countries.* George Allen and Unwin, London, 1970.

MALENBAUM, WILFRED. *Modern India's Economy, Two Decades of Planned Growth.* Charles E. Merrill, Columbus, 1971.

MEHTA BALRAJ. *Crisis of Indian Economy,* Sterling Publishers, New Delhi, 1973.

MYRDAL, GUNNAR. *Asian Drama, An Inquiry into the Poverty of Nations,* Vols. I, II, and III. Pantheon, New York, 1968.

NARAYAN, SHRIMAN. *Socialism in Indian Planning.* Asia Publishing House, New Delhi, 1964.

NEHRU, JAWAHARLAL. *The Discovery of India.* The John Day Co., New York, 1946.

———. *Toward Freedom: The Autobiography of Jawaharlal Nehru.* The John Day Co., New York, 1941.

PANIKKAR, K. M. *Hindu Society at Cross Roads.* Asia Publishing House, Bombay 1955.

PANT, PITAMBAR. "International Development Strategy and Indian Perspectives; 1990–2000," in Jagdish N. Bhagwati, *Economics and World Order,* 1972.

PARANJAPF, H. K. *The Planning Commission, A Descriptive Account.* The Indian Institute of Public Administration, New Delhi, 1964.

REDDAWAY, W. B. *The Development of the Indian Economy,* Richard D. Irwin, Homewood, Ill., 1962.

SHENOY, B. R. *Indian Economic Policy,* Popular Prakashan, Bombay, 1968.

SWAMY, SUBRAMIAN. *Economic Growth in China and India, 1952–1970.* University of Chicago Press, Chicago, 1973.

WATERSTON, ALBERT. *Development Planning: Lessons of Experience.* Johns Hopkins Press, Baltimore, 1957.

Part Six
Conclusion

21
Economic Systems in the Crucible

Chapter 21
Economic Systems in the Crucible

The Static and Dynamic Aspects of Economic Systems

This study of the performance of many of the world's economic systems since the end of the Second World War underlines the need for analyzing both the static and dynamic aspects of these systems. Since the emphasis until now in the study of economic systems has been on their static features, many analysts currently believe that more stress should be placed on the dynamic features of these systems. Philip A. Klein has observed that "In the final analysis it is crucial to remember that the modern economy, like most man-made institutions, must be viewed dynamically. All the institutions which form a market-oriented economy need to be viewed and judged against the perspective of continual change in technology, in resources, in social objectives, and in expectations."[1] Similarly, Jan Tinbergen has pointed out that "Reality shows both [the command and the free economic systems] to be in permanent change."[2]

This approach to the study of economic systems contrasts markedly with the position of other analysts who stress the importance of static studies of parts of economic systems rather than the study of the entire economic system. Morris Bornstein differentiates between the *comparative-systems* approach, which includes the study of entire economic systems and the relationships among the various parts of these systems, and the *comparative-economics* approach, which compares the separate parts of economic systems, such as labor markets, industrial enterprises, the

---

[1] Philip A. Klein, *The Management of Market-Oriented Economies, A Comparative Perspective*, Belmont, Calif.: Wadsworth Publishing Co., 1973, p. 219.

[2] Jan Tinbergen, "Do Command and Free Economies Show a Converging Pattern?", *Soviet Studies*, Vol. XII, No. 4, April 1961, p. 333.

agricultural sector, and foreign trade.³ Bornstein states that these two approaches to the study of economic systems are complementary rather than conflicting; he proposes to combine them in a new synthesis that would be labelled *comparative economic studies*. He concludes that there is reason to believe that future research in the comparative economics field would be more fruitful if it dealt with static, partial studies rather than with broad "system-focused" studies.

No need exists, however, for any overall discipline known as comparative economic studies, because a proper grasp of the nature of the comparative-systems approach shows that it includes both dynamic and static studies and relates them to overall total systems. The trouble is that some comparative-studies analysts, who devote all or most of their time to wages, prices, national income, or similar matters in different economic systems, never get beyond the static aspects of their studies, and so fail to integrate them with dynamic studies of the total system. In this situation, comparative economics becomes little more than a taxonomic study of the parts of various economic systems.⁴

³ Morris Bornstein, "An Integration," in Alexander Eckstein (ed.), *Comparison of Economic Systems*, pp. 352–353.

⁴ This static approach to the analysis of economic systems makes this analysis nothing more than an extension of the static, orthodox approach to economics in general. See, for example, Paul A. Samuelson, who concludes his ninth edition of his *Economics* (New York: McGraw-Hill, 1973) with Chapter 43 on "Alternative Economic Systems," which is in essence only a taxonomic listing of various economic systems. In this chapter, Samuelson reproduces the static "What, How, and For Whom [goods and services are produced]" analysis of Chapter 2 on the "Central Problems of Every Economic Society," and then applies it to the Soviet system (pp. 877–880). Missing is any attempt to treat alternative economic systems as products of an ongoing process of industrialization, which has now extended into the Third World of less developed countries, and which imposes a certain uniformity of structure and functioning on countries at the same level of economic development.

Tinbergen's "permanent change" applies to mature industrialized countries as well as to the less developed countries. In some quarters, it is common to assume that the latter countries are subject to considerable change because they are in an early phase of industrialization, but that the mature industrial economies are subject to very little change since they are supposedly close to the end of the industrialization process. The evidence does not support this distinction between dynamic less developed economic systems and relatively static developed economic systems. A review of developments in the Scandinavian, West German, French, British, and American economies reveals already-developed economies moving from welfare capitalism to guided capitalism, from what Daniel Bell calls an industrial society to a postindustrial society, or from a high-growth economy with an unsatisfactory quality of life to a slower-growth economy with a higher quality of life.⁵ As Galbraith puts it, "Yet to suppose that the industrial system is a terminal phenomenon is, *per se*, implausible. It is itself the product, in the last sixty years of a vast and autonomous transformation . . . change is the law of economic life."⁶ This law applies equally well to the United States and the Soviet Union.

In the past several decades, the United States has been transformed from a predominantly laissez faire society to a welfare society; the prospect is for further significant structural and functional changes in the next few decades. Similarly, the Soviet Union has in the past half century changed from a rigidly planned command society to a much more decentralized, consumer-conscious society. In the case of the Soviet Union, the prospect is also for major institutional and attitudinal

⁵ Daniel Bell, *The Coming of Post-Industrial Society*, New York: Basic Books, 1974.

⁶ John Kenneth Galbraith, *The New Industrial State*, pp. 388-389.

changes in the next quarter century. All economic systems from the least developed to the most developed are operating in a world of widespread scientific, technological, and cultural ferment. Considerable resistance to this ferment will undoubtedly occur in many economic systems. Each system will react to this ferment in special ways, as dictated by historical, cultural, and geographical circumstances. None, however, will escape the universal impact of scientific and technological advances, for these impose a certain degree of uniformity on all societies that are in the process of becoming industrialized. All or almost all economic systems are now being transformed in a crucible of rapidly changing ideas and circumstances.

An analysis of the world's multifold economic systems leads to a number of generalizations. First of all, these systems share a number of common features. They all deal with the problem of scarcity and the need to use scarce resources in the most efficient manner. Efficiency, or getting the most from the least, is a universal concept that has as much validity in New York as in Moscow, and in London as in Peking. Problems of efficiency are associated with such matters as planning, management, pricing, income distribution, taxation, and welfare. At the same time, uniformity in economic activities is accompanied by considerable diversity. Some economic systems have primarily public ownership of the means of production, while others have primarily private ownership of these means. In some systems, the rule is highly centralized economic planning, collective profits, fixed prices, and little independence on the part of state enterprise management. In other economic systems, one expects decentralized planning, free market prices, private profits, and much independence in decision making by enterprise management.

Nicolas Spulber explains that the differences and similarities between economic systems are "multi-dimensional, continually evolving and hardly reducible to a simple and neat scheme."[7] He goes on to point out that in order to reach a broad understanding of an economy, the differences and similarities must be related not only to the economy but also to the political, social, and legal framework in which the economy functions. Such a view of the study of economic systems emphasizes the importance of an interdisciplinary approach that takes into account any data that illuminate how an economic system performs.[8] The interdisciplinary approach is especially significant when the question at issue is the possible convergence of economic systems. What appears to be convergence from the strictly economic point of view takes on a different import when account is taken of ideological and political factors as well as economic factors.

The Spectrum Model

The most widely used model in the study of economic systems is the static spectrum model; this envisions a spectrum of concrete economic systems lying between the two extremes of the pure command and the pure market-oriented economies. In some analyses, the polar extremes are defined as pure socialism and pure capitalism, both of

---

[7] Nicolas Spulber, *The Soviet Economy*, New York: W. W. Norton, 1969, p. 285. Morris Bornstein also observes that the forces influencing economic systems include the level of economic development, social and cultural factors, and the natural environment. See Morris Bornstein, *op. cit.*, p. 340.

[8] Morris Bornstein concludes that "Perhaps more than other branches of economics, the comparison of economic systems requires a multidisciplinary or—better still—interdisciplinary approach. Some aspects of the subject may need this approach to a greater extent than others. For example, the comparison of ideologies involves other disciplines much more than does the comparison of growth rates." See Morris Bornstein, *op. cit.*, p. 353.

which are theoretical or ideal types of economic systems.[9] Pure socialism differs from a pure command economy because pure socialism assumes that a democratic system prevails, and that the economic system is operated in accordance with consumer preferences. In a command economy, neither condition prevails. By definition, a command economy is undemocratic (in the Western sense of being democratic); and if account is taken of consumer welfare, this is only accidental, because what is good for those in command only happens to be also good for consumers. The spectrum model assumes that it is possible to measure how far a concrete economic system is from the pole of the pure command economy or of the pure market-oriented economy, so that it may be placed at some point on the systems spectrum. Systems analysts do not, however, agree as to what factors should be considered when placing a specific economic system on the systems spectrum. Even if consensus could be reached on the factors to be considered, such as centralized or decentralized planning, public or private ownership of property, and free or unfree markets, it would be very difficult to quantify these factors. In modern economic systems—in both the West and the East, where governments have large regulatory roles—clearcut distinctions between private and public ownership, free and unfree prices, and centralized and decentralized planning are difficult to make, let alone quantify.[10]

Another major deficiency of the spectrum model for comparing economic systems is its lack of dynamic analysis. The spectrum model tells us something about different economic systems at a point in time. It says little, however, about the different phases of growth through which economic systems pass, or about the factors that lead to the further development of these systems. In the comparative study of economic systems, nothing is more obvious than the fact that these systems are at different levels or phases in their development. The stage of development of Communist China, for example, matches that of the Soviet Union in the 1930s. In the Comecon area, Bulgaria and Romania are far behind East Germany and Czechoslovakia in their economic development. Among the mixed economies of the West, wide discrepancies exist between the United States, which is moving into the era of the postindustrial service economy, and many of the West European countries, which are still in the preservice, mass-consumption stage of economic development.

Systems analysts have paid inadequate attention to the factors that lead to the long-term development of economic systems. Theories of long-term economic development are especially important when concern is expressed about the shape that economic systems may have in the future. All such theories deal with the process of industrialization, which applies to all but the traditional, pregrowth-takeoff countries. The level of industrialization that a nation has reached is important because industrialization tends to bring with it a rising level of per capita output, a concentration of large-scale industry, a spreading urbanization, a rising level of education, and an expanding public sector.

As nations approach or reach a high level of industrialization, they exhibit a high degree of

---

[9] For a discussion of the spectrum model, see James R. Millar "On the Theory and Measurement of Economic Convergence," *Quarterly Review of Economics and Business*, Vol. 12, No. 1, Spring 1972, pp. 87–97.

[10] On the problems of identifying and quantifying features of different economic systems, see James R. Millar, *op. cit.*, p. 96. Balassa concludes that it is not possible to make a choice between economic systems on the basis of any success indicators, since individual preferences that vary so widely cannot be averaged to arrive at a consensus, and we cannot construct a preference scale for the whole community based on individual preferences. For this line of reasoning, see Bela A. Balassa, *The Hungarian Experience in Economic Planning*, New Haven: Yale University, 1959, pp. 5–24.

uniformity in economic structure, organization, and goals. Simon Kuznets believes that much of this uniformity derives from the industrial technology that is common to the developed countries. He points out that the variety in economic systems is probably greater among the less developed countries than among the more developed countries, because technology has a less influential role among the former than the latter countries.[11] Modern large-scale industrial technology is an imperative that has much to do with the structure and functioning of the mature industrialized countries. Gregory Grossman explains that the industrialization process and all that goes with it, such as urbanization, widespread education and technical expertise, and higher standards of living, "impose their stamp on outlooks, values, behavior patterns, and even forms of economic organization."[12] There is a kind of logic inherent in the process of industrialization that applies to all economic systems undergoing this process, and that carries them to higher levels of technological sophistication and economic complexity. John Kenneth Galbraith likewise assigns a role in the process of industrialization to what he describes as the imperatives of technology and large-scale organization.

Clark Kerr views economic systems as undergoing a great transformation as a consequence of the spreading industrialization process. He explains that no social or economic laws apply to this process, but that it does exhibit social and economic consistencies that stem from its inherent uniformities. The latter arise from the impact of the basic technology that underlies industrialism.[13] While Kerr sees much diversity among economic systems that results from cultural and environmental differences, he also observes beneath this diversity a basic uniformity that reflects "the pure logic of the industrialization process." Industrialization does not operate in a cultural vacuum, nor does the course of industrialization follow a single mould or pattern. Kerr explains that no two cases of industrialization can be expected to be the same in all respects, since nations have different characteristics and resources and start from varying levels of economic development.

These national differences may give direction to the inherent tendencies of industrialization in different ways, but all industrializing societies respond to the inherent logic of industrialization itself. For example, the industrial society is never static, because scientific and technological advances generate continual change in production methods and products, worker skills, managerial responsibilities, and occupations. The industrial society tends rather to have considerable mobility, for education plays a major role—as in the United States, the Soviet Union, and Communist China. It also has an elite class, managers and managed, urban areas, large-scale producing units, and a large role for government. Unlike the teleological Karl Marx, who saw the industrialization process as leading to a single stereotyped revolution and the eventual emergence of full communism, Kerr posits a "plural industrialism," which never reaches any final stage or equilibrium. According to Kerr and his associates, even after the conflicts generated by the class war, "the contest over private versus public initiative, and the battle between monistic and atomistic ideologies have been left far behind in the sedimentary layers of history, there will be no permanent settlement of the adjustment between the uniformity that draws on technology and the diversity that draws on individuality."[14]

[11] Simon Kuznets, *Modern Economic Growth: Rate, Structure, and Spread,* New Haven, Conn.: Yale University Press, 1966, p. 477–486.

[12] Gregory Grossman, *Economic Systems*, p. 111.

[13] Clark Kerr, John T. Dunlop, Frederick H. Harbison, and Charles A. Myers, *Industrialism and Industrial Man*, Cambridge, Mass.: Harvard University Press, 1960, pp. 33–46.

[14] *Ibid.*, p. 296.

The General Theory of Economic Systems

The problem of the general theory of economic systems can be treated from two points of view. Some students of economic systems think in terms of an overall theory of economic systems that would apply to all types of economic systems, very much as the theory of perfect competition provides a starting point for the analysis of economic activities in all standard economics textbooks. All economic systems have some common properties or aspects, such as scarce resources and their allocation, consumer preferences and commodity valuations, and contacts between producing and consuming units; but actual economic systems also have many diverse features that cannot be subsumed in a general theory of economic systems. Efforts to work out a general theory of economic systems in terms of one major economic system have so far not met with much success.

The second point of view in developing a theory of economic systems leads to a division of these systems between command economies at one end of the scale and free-market economies at the other end. Different actual economic systems are then placed at various points on the scale between the two poles of the command and the free-market economics, as has been explained in Chapter 1. These two theoretical poles do not exist in actual practice, since no pure command or pure market economies appear in the real world.

Placing economic systems on a scale between the poles of pure command and pure market economies for analytical purposes presents a number of difficulties. This approach to the study of economic systems, as has already been pointed out, is essentially a static approach, which takes account of economic systems only at a point in time. While this procedure does throw some light on the nature of economic systems, it is important to know whether an economic system is moving towards one end of the scale or the other, or is moving towards its center. This raises the question as to what kind of economic system would occupy the middle of the scale.

The concept of an evenly divided command and market economy does not have application to the real world. Actual economic systems usually lean towards either the command or the market economy, with certain deviations away from these pure theoretical types. The Soviet Union and the other Eastern European communist countries started out as thoroughly procommand economies, but in recent years have modified these economies by introducing elements usually associated with the free market economies. These free market economy elements include more independent decision making by the state enterprises, full costing to include interest and in some cases rent charges, market surveys to uncover individual consumer preferences, and, in a few cases (Czechoslovakia, Hungary, and Yugoslavia), limited free market prices for consumer goods. The United States and the democratic Western European countries, which before 1929 had very pro-free market economies, have since that year significantly altered their economies by introducing elements normally associated with the command economies. They have modified their free market economies by adopting programs for government intervention (as in the United States, West Germany, and the United Kingdom—when it has a Conservative government); programs for national planning (as in the case of France, Belgium, the Netherlands, Norway, Sweden, and the United Kingdom when it has a Labour government); and at times programs for wage and price control (as in the United States and the majority of the Western European countries).

If it is not feasible to construct a general theory of economic systems that is of much service in the analysis of the world's multifold concrete economic systems, there still remain two matters relating to economic systems about which considerable generalizing can be done. These two matters are: (1) the possible convergence of actual economic systems towards some middle-ground or uniform system; and (2) the logic of industrialization, which may apply to all actual economic systems at various stages as they move along the path of industrialization towards the model of a mature industrial system.

The Convergence of Economic Systems

Since the 1950s, a belief has flourished in some circles that certain nations have been moving away from their polar positions and have been converging towards a kind of middle ground, which would in effect constitute a new kind of economic system. In its simplest form, the convergence thesis states that economic systems are becoming more alike, and will eventually develop some kind of relatively uniform industrial system. Chancellor Konrad Adenauer had some such theory in mind when he is alleged to have said to Nikita Khrushchev: "My dear Mr. Khrushchev, in 100 years there will be no talk any more of capitalism and socialism."[15] The convergence theory is usually applied most frequently to the United States and the Soviet Union, which are examples of mature capitalist and communist countries.

In some quarters, the convergence theory is applied in a broader way to Western noncommunist nations and to Eastern communist nations. The Western nations, especially in Western Europe, have in recent decades adopted medium-term (four or five years) and annual national plans, price-control programs, and incomes policies, all of which are prominent features of communist economies. At the same time, since the early 1960s a wave of economic reform has swept over Eastern Europe, bringing in its wake considerable plan decentralization, greater independence in decision making for the directors of state industrial enterprises, and more attention to individual consumer preferences. These developments are interpreted by some systems analysts to mean that nations in the West and the East are on a path of convergence towards some common economic system.

A number of developments have contributed to the emergence of the convergence theory since the early 1950s. The death of Stalin in 1953, the more relaxed regime of Khrushchev, and his denial of the inevitability of military conflict between the Soviet Union and the United States introduced the possibility of a period of peaceful coexistence and possible convergence between the communist and capitalist worlds. The threat of nuclear war and the need to deal with the arms race made it imperative for the United States and the Soviet Union to develop a common policy with respect to nuclear weapons.

At the same time, the economic reform movement of the 1960s in the Eastern European countries was interpreted by analysts in the United States to mean that these countries were moving towards the capitalist free market economic model. The greater interest in Western economics in the Soviet Union in the 1960s, the acceptance of interest as a necessary charge for the use of capital, and the consumer-goods expansion in the Soviet Union convinced many observers in the West that the Soviet Union was also moving away from the model of the command economy towards the free market model. The emergence of Yugoslavia as an example of market socialism was interpreted by some systems

[15] Peter Wiles, "Will Capitalism and Communism Spontaneously Converge?", *Encounter*, Vol. XX, No. 6, June 1963, p. 84.

analysts in the East and West to mean that there was a middle position between the communist command economy and the capitalist free market economy towards which national economies were gravitating.

Evidence for a growing convergence of economic systems was not applicable only to the communist nations. In Western Europe, major modifications of the free market economy have been made since 1945. National planning has become well established in France, Belgium, the Netherlands, Norway, and Sweden, and less permanently in the United Kingdom. While this planning is much less centralized than the planning in the Soviet Union and other communist countries, it does mark a significant departure from the Western market-oriented economy. In Western Europe, and even in the United States, strong pressures have been exerted to develop wage and price or incomes policies that limit the area of free wage and price determination. Even the promarket governments of Richard Nixon in the United States and Edward Heath in the United Kingdom turned to mandatory price and wage controls in the 1970s. National planning, the development of incomes policies, and intervention to protect the natural environment have greatly increased the size and influence of the public sector in the Western economies. These developments have moved the Western economies away from the free market pole towards the middle of the scale, where some economists claim to see a new uniform industrial economy emerging.

In some quarters, the view still lingers that the capitalist and communist economies are inherently incompatible and that one or the other must disappear in the long run. This means that certain extreme apologists for capitalism believe that the Soviet economic system is unworkable in the long run and will eventually collapse of its own weight. A similar but opposite view is held by Soviet extremists, who assert that the convergence theory

is an outright ideological subversion, intended to confuse the people, to present the processes taking place both in the socialist and in the capitalist economies in a distorted light. Anti-communist propaganda is resorting to everything it can—gross falsification of the facts, slander against socialism, misinformation about the actual state of affairs in the capitalist system.[16]

The official Soviet position is that convergence is a bourgeois idea that is a myth both in theory and practice; the Soviets believe that in the long run the superiority of the communist system over the capitalist system will be demonstrated by the course of events. No specific timetable is provided for this development, but the 1974–1975 recession in the West is considered evidence of the long-run vulnerability of the capitalist system.

Interpretations of the Convergence Theory

Since the late 1950s, much discussion has occurred about the possible convergence of economic systems. Critical evaluations of the theory of convergence have eliminated much of the optimism that once accompanied the concept of peaceful convergence. Three positions are voiced about the theory of convergence. Some systems analysts assert that little prospect exists for any significant convergence; others see considerable convergence with respect to economic matters, but no prospect for any such development in ideological and political matters; and a third group of analysts is impressed by the amount of convergence that has occurred at the economic and noneconomic levels. The latter assert that "a basic convergence of the world's

[16] L. Leontiev, "Myth about the 'Rapprochement' of the Two Systems," *Reprints from the Soviet Press*, Vol. IV, No. 3, Feb. 9, 1967, p. 4.

economies toward certain common characteristics may reasonably be expected.... Something extremely important is happening in our time. After more than a century of implacable conflict, the extremist ideologies of individualism and collectivism have capitulated to one another."[17]

Peter Wiles argues that there are no internal developments in the Soviet Union and the United States that lead to what he describes as *strong convergence*.[18] On the contrary, he finds that in the Soviet Union the preference for computerized rational centralized planning is so powerful that there is little concern for free markets and consumer sovereignty. The modern computerized techniques of planning can be used, in the opinion of Soviet leaders, to introduce full communism without ever turning to the Western form of unplanned free markets and consumer sovereignty. Also, the ideologists in the communist countries seem determined not to allow the enterprise managers to become genuinely independent of the central planners. Wiles, in addition, points out that strong trends are present towards socialized rather than private consumption in many of the communist countries; such trends favor substituting public transportation for private transportation, apartments for single houses, public laundries for privately-owned washing machines, and public restaurants for home cooking.

Wiles sees little prospect of any major convergence of the Soviet and American economic systems. The trends in the United States are not in the direction of socialized consumption, nationalized property, or the use of modern mathematical techniques to establish central planning. Instead, these trends look towards preserving private consumption and private property, avoiding national planning, according much independence to the managers of private enterprises, and maintaining free markets, along with consumer sovereignty. Wiles agrees that there may be some *weak convergence* that may result from the need to cooperate in order to prevent nuclear warfare. Some form of world government may be necessary to establish an international inspection system for the control of nuclear weapons; and this may lead to what Wiles describes as weak or minor convergence. He concludes with the observation that "the systems will converge, if at all, through the sheer necessities of defense, and not through any internal evolution.[19]

Jan Tinbergen, who does not agree with Wiles on the convergence issue, finds that the changes in economic systems that result from trying to cope with their own weaknesses and being influenced by one another are in many respects "converging movements," and that these changes in the East and West are "tending toward the optimum order."[20] He sees the advanced Western capitalist nations and the Eastern communist countries moving towards an optimum pattern of organization. Tinbergen's optimum pattern or order is a "mixed order," which combines both public and private enterprise. In his public-private-enterprise economy, the public sector takes care of all activities showing external effects or indivisibilities of some importance (large-scale industry in general), while activities without these characteristics can be carried on by small and medium-sized enterprises in the private sector. Socio-economic policies are distributed over government authorities at different levels, while the regulation of total

---

[17] Cyril A. Zebot, *The Economics of Competitive Coexistence*, New York: Frederick A. Praeger, 1964, p. 146.

[18] Peter Wiles, *op. cit.*, p. 85.

[19] *Ibid.*, p. 90.

[20] Jan Tinbergen, *op. cit.*, p. 339; and H. Linneman, J. P. Pronk and Jan Tinbergen, "Convergence of Economic Systems in East and West," in Emile Benoit (ed.) *Disarmament and World Economic Interdependence*, New York: Columbia University Press, 1967, pp. 256-257.

demand, of the level of total investment, of unstable markets such as agricultural markets, and of income redistribution are among the tasks of the public sector.[21]

Tinbergen finds that the Eastern and Western economies deviate from the most efficient economic order but from the opposite sides of this order. For example, the Eastern communist countries have discovered that they should reduce the number of items that are centrally planned, and that they should permit the establishment of many more small enterprises, especially in the service industries, to supplement the large planned industrial establishments, because the small firms are frequently more efficient than large firms. The Eastern communist countries are coming to realize that they should grant more freedom to plant managers to make production decisions, that consumers want more quality and more output assortment, that freely determined prices in many cases do a better job than centrally planned prices, and that there should be more democracy in the Western sense.

In turn, the Western noncommunist countries are faced with such opposite issues as how far to carry the planning of their economies, how to deal with cost-profit push inflation, how to make education available to all as in the communist countries, how to deal with the capital gains from private enterprise, and how to secure more industrial democracy in industrial enterprises. Tinbergen explains that societies revealing deviations from the most efficient economic order will tend to converge towards this order. As he explains, "Clearly both Eastern and Western society deviate from the optimum as just sketched. As long as they do, we expect them to change. Since their deviations in most elements are on opposite sides from the optimum, a tendency for convergence can be expected."[22] Although Tinbergen finds that Eastern and Western economic systems are becoming more alike in various ways, the evidence favoring the doctrine of convergence that he presents is only economic evidence. He downgrades evidence of an ideological, political, or cultural nature on the ground that economic forces are the most fundamental.

Other systems analysts such as Gregory Grossman and Jan S. Prybyla, who take account of the role of noneconomic factors, tend to argue that while there has been considerable convergence on the economic front, there has been much less on the ideological and political fronts. If the political and ideological differences between economic systems are to be reduced, they will be reduced much more slowly than the economic differences. It is reasonable to conclude that for a very long time to come the ideological and political differences will remain large obstacles to further convergence between economic systems.[23] One can anticipate the continuation of considerable divergence between the planned socialism of Norway and Sweden and the regulated but unplanned capitalism of the United States, West Germany, Canada, and other Western democracies. Likewise, one can expect to see continued divergence between what appears to be an increasingly materialistic Soviet Union and a Communist China dedicated to a selfless new communist man or woman. Not many systems analysts see as much potentiality for the convergence of the United States, the Soviet Union, and other

[21] Jan Tinbergen, "The Theory of the Optimum Regime," in *Selected Papers*, Amsterdam: North-Holland Publishing Co., 1959, pp. 264–304; and "The Significance of Welfare Economics for Socialism," in *On Political Economy and Econometrics: Essays in Honour of Oskar Lange*, New York: Pergamon Press, 1965, pp. 591–599.

[22] H. Linneman, J. P. Pronk and Jan Tinbergen, *op. cit.*, p. 257.

[23] Jan S. Prybyla, "The Convergence of Western and Communist Economic Systems: A Critical Estimate," *The Russian Review*, Vol. 22, No. 1, Jan. 1964, p. 17; and Elliot R. Goodman, "Reflections on the New Soviet Party Program," *The Russian Review*, Vol. 21, No. 2, April 1962, p. 120.

mature industrial economies as do Cyril A. Zebot and P. A. Sorokin, who play down the ideological barriers to convergence.[24]

The Future of Economic Systems

As economic systems undergo changes in the crucible of world developments, they will all face a number of challenging economic, social, and political problems. The most basic concern will be to develop the attitudes and institutions that will enable the countries in the West, East, and South to cope with the kinds of social and economic problems that appear to be taking shape in the fourth quarter of this century. In the Western nations, we are seeing the end of an era—the era of the essentially directionless welfare mixed society—and the emergence of a new, guided or directed mixed economy. In this emerging era, society is more future oriented and anticipatory in its outlook on economic and social problems.[25] This approach leads, for example, to a "technology assessment" that anticipates the consequences of technological change, and takes steps to prevent any antisocial consequences. Behind this anticipatory outlook lies a new ethic based on an ideology that looks forward to the creation of a value system or lifestyle of high quality through various forms of democratic collective and individual action. Since the 1950s, we have not seen the "end of ideology," as Daniel Bell and Irving Kristol have said, but instead we have seen a shift from the outmoded ideology of the "middle way" for the middle-aged, which has turned off the young intellectuals, to a new postindustrial ideology that emphasizes what Galbraith has called the *civilized values*.[26]

The new ideology which is appropriate to the emerging postindustrial society repudiates the inherited middle-class hedonistic ideology, with its consumer's ethic leading to an affluent but suffocating society, and its technocratic ethic emphasizing superior performance in economic growth, technological innovation, and managerial efficiency. The emerging ideology places quality above quantity, creativity above conformity, and communion among individuals above extreme individualism. The postindustrial society that is arising in the United States and Western Europe is one in which economic considerations and criteria, once dominant in the previous industrial society, will be overshadowed by noneconomic concerns. In the postindustrial society in the West greater interest will be expressed in zero economic and zero population growth, the protection of the environment, the rebuilding of our inner cities as places to live in, an adequate guaranteed income for all, the reorganization of our universities to produce cultured individuals rather than technicians, and international cooperation to replace the chaos and disorder in the relations between nations.

---

[24] P. A. Sorokin, "Mutual Convergence of the United States and the USSR to the Mixed Socio-Cultural Type," *International Journal of Comparative Sociology*, Vol. 1, No. 2, Sept. 1960, pp. 143–176.

[25] As the National Goals Research Staff expressed this matter in its 1969 report, "We wish to shift from a reactive mode of dealing with problems that have forced themselves on us to an anticipatory mode in which we either attempt to prevent their occurrence or are prepared to deal with them as they emerge" (p. 31). *Toward Balanced Growth: Quantity with Quality, Report of the National Goals Research Staff*, Washington, D.C., July 1970.

[26] Daniel Bell and others have correctly diagnosed the 1950s as a decade in which the inherited hedonistic "bourgeois" ideology was repudiated by the nation's intellectuals, but he has erred in describing this development as "the end of ideology." There can be no end to ideology, since man in society lives by and with some kind of ideology. The ideology of the guided American society in the 1970s and 1980s that is emerging may not yet be well defined, but it is clearly taking shape. See Daniel Bell, *The End of Ideology*, Revised Edition, New York: The Free Press, 1965, pp. 393–407; and Daniel Bell and Irving Kristol (eds.), *Capitalism Today*, New York: Basic Books, 1971, p. 24.

A satisfactory postindustrial system in the West cannot be achieved without some kind of democratic social engineering. Our culture and our values should not only permit but also encourage some amount of social engineering.[27] It is unrealistic to contemplate dealing with the problems of zero economic and zero population growth, domestic and international environmental protection, the sharing of the world's natural resources, international financial stability, and aid to the less developed countries without some kind of domestic and international planning. What applies to Bell and other critics of industrial capitalism also applies to the New Left and all those new-generation intellectuals who disparage both the Old Left and the Old Right. The New Left is long on criticism of the capitalist system, but very short on the specifics of its proposals for remedying the economic and social situations that it so strongly deplores.[28]

---

[27] Daniel Bell, Irving Kristol, and other critics of corporate capitalism and contemplators of the new industrial society have no solutions for the resolution of the problems that they have so well analyzed. Bell states that our cultural crises and cultural changes "are not amenable to 'social engineering' or political control" (Daniel Bell and Irving Kristol, *op. cit.*, pp. 43-44). He asserts that our cultural crises are "manageable," and that cultural tensions can be relieved if political leadership is intelligent and determined. His optimism at this point, however, is supported by very few program specifics. The same lack of program specificity is found in Bell's *The Coming of the Post-Industrial Society*.

[28] The term *Old Left* refers to the old-style Fabian and Marxist socialists who came to the fore in the 1930s and 1940s. The *New Left*, a product of the post-World War II period with a strong Marxist tinge, has been spearheaded by the youth movement, which criticizes the Old Left on the ground that it failed to deal with such issues as personal alienation, lack of job satisfaction, environmental degradation, race and sex discrimination, the economic growth mania, and the evils of centralized national planning. The New Left's "Radical Economics" is analyzed in Martin Bronfenbrenner, "Radical Economics in America: A 1970 Survey,"

The No-Growth Society

One of the major problems with which the advanced industrial economies will have to deal in the future is curbing economic growth. Economists fall into two groups on this issue, some advocating a no-growth (ZEG) society and others a limited or restricted growth society.[29] Both groups agree that uncontrolled economic growth in a finite world cannot continue indefinitely. They also agree that if exponential growth in the material output of economic systems continues, a very large increase in pollution or in recycling must ensue. Environmental constraints will make it impossible to maintain current rates of economic growth throughout the world in the long run. Added to the probability of environmental limitations imposed by scarce natural resources is the widespread concern about the undesirable effects of economic growth on the "quality of life."

Where the disagreement arises is over the question of whether there should be no growth or limited economic growth. The advocates of no growth in the mature industrialized economies, such as the United States and the other Western industrialized nations, argue that in a rich society more growth does not add to the total of human welfare. Growth is said to be a false value, which induces people to buy gadgets they really do not want, or because they wish to emulate individuals

---

Journal of Economic Literature, Vol. VIII, Sept. 1970, pp. 747-766.

[29] For an analysis on both sides of this important issue, see Mancur Olson and Hans H. Landsberg (eds.), *The No-Growth Society*, New York: W. W. Norton, 1973. Both John K. Galbraith and E. J. Mishan may be classed as no-growth advocates, largely on the ground that economic growth fosters a materialistic social order that endlessly accumulates material gadgets, and is in itself an unbalanced and misdirected force in human affairs. See E. J. Mishan, "Ills, Bads, and Disamenities: The Wages of Growth," Mancur Olson and Hans H. Landsberg, *op. cit.*, pp. 63-87.

on a higher plane of living.[30] The advocates of limited growth argue against no growth for various reasons. Some are opposed to a no-growth society on the grounds that in such a society much conflict would arise over the distribution of income, the pioneering, innovative spirit would be unnecessary, and an excessive amount of government control would be called for. Others are opposed to the pursuit of a no-growth society because the need still exists for increased national output to raise the standards of living of low-income groups and to achieve other domestic tasks, as well as to contribute to the growth of the less developed countries abroad.

Two countries that have recently favored a limited growth policy are Norway and Sweden. As has already been explained in Chapters 9 and 10, both of these countries have decided to limit economic growth in order to improve the quality of life. They have adopted as a part of their national planning programs measures calculated to curb urban growth and to stimulate regional development, even though these measures will in the long run lower the nation's economic growth rate. Some growth in material output will be sacrificed in order to increase total national satisfaction by curbing the continued growth of large urban areas with their lack of social amenities, their congestion, and their personal alienation or lack of individual involvement. The goal of a lifestyle of higher quality is to be achieved in Norway and Sweden through democratic national planning, in which all interest groups are given the opportunity to discuss and improve upon the nation's goals and priorities. Unlike those proponents of a limited growth policy in the United States who say planning is not the answer, the Scandinavian advocates assert that democratic indicative planning provides a way of making collective decisions about growth policy that is not available where no planning is carried on.[31] National economic planning of the Scandinavian type creates an organized and orderly way for interest groups to come together to discuss such issues as zero economic and zero population growth. If curbing economic growth is to be attained in a democracy, it must become a national goal that receives the active support of the general population.

The Zero Population Growth Society

A matter that is equally as important as the issue of zero economic growth (ZEG)—if not more so—is the issue of zero population growth (ZPG). The world's population, which is approaching 4 billion, would, if present population growth rates continue, increase to 7 billion in 2000 and 13 billion in 2050. Where population grows at the annual rate of 3 percent, as in Ghana, Iran, and Cambodia, it doubles every twenty-four years. For the world as a whole, the issue is not whether to aim for zero population growth but when and how to do so. A distinction must be drawn between the maximum and optimum population. The former is determined by such factors as usable land area, soil fertility, and availability of mineral resources and water. The latter, which is always smaller than the maximum

---

[30] This approach to the growth problem takes account of the emulative "keeping up with the Joneses," or the Jones Effect which Thorstein Veblen commented upon as early as 1899 in his *The Theory of the Leisure Class*. See also Mishan on the "Jones Effect" in E. J. Mishan, *op. cit.*, pp. 84–85.

[31] Mancur Olson, not a planning advocate, states that "It won't do simply to say that 'planning' is the answer. The planning systems the world has had experience with have been designed to induce growth. . . ." See Mancur Olson, *op. cit.*, p. 11. As leaders in the planning movement, the Scandinavian countries are demonstrating that planning can be used for other purposes than continued high growth, such as protecting the natural environment, reducing urban congestion, and raising the quality of life.

population, is one that permits the optimum average well-being.[32] This well-being attains its most desirable level when the population is no larger than is necessary to provide the social, economic, and environmental diversity required to satisfy a wide variety of personal preferences.

The optimum population for a given country will depend upon existing social and technological conditions and will change with changes in these conditions. A country should adjust its population size to the prevailing technological and social conditions rather than hope that technology will improve enough to support what in the first place is too large a population. One environmentalist has estimated that the United States, with about 215 million people, has already exceeded its optimum population size under existing conditions.[33] Countries like China and India, with a combined population of around 1.5 billion, are far beyond their optimum population and are approaching their maximum population. Countries like India, China, and many of the smaller less developed countries need negative population growth (NPG), not zero population growth, until their best population level is established.

The main issue with regard to ZPG or NPG is how to develop a population policy that will achieve the desired goal. The main obstacle to constructing such a policy successfully is the widely held pronatalist view that reproduction is a basic human right with which the state should not interfere. People have a vague feeling that population numbers are excessive, but they do not see any immediate emergency with regard to these numbers; they are thus unwilling to accept effective population controls. They are the victims of outmoded values, which at one time placed no restraints upon reproduction, since high mortality rates kept population under control. Now that birth rates are high and death rates are low, new values with respect to reproduction freedoms and controls are needed. Few nations are prepared to go as far as Singapore, which suffers from an excessively large population on a small island; that country refuses free medical facilities and schooling after the third child, and is prepared to take more draconian measures if they are necessary to control the growth of population.

The prospect for adequate population control is not good. The World Population Conference, held in Bucharest in August 1974, failed to come to grips with the population problem. The prevailing view at this conference that population control was a matter exclusively within the national jurisdiction of each sovereign state made it difficult to deal with the global aspects of this problem. The unwillingness to consider compulsory methods of population control and the insistence upon voluntarism in this connection were indications of how far the world is from even considering an effective population-control policy. Consequently, in large areas of the world, excessive population will probably continue for an indefinite period to be a major obstacle to the good performance of many economic systems.

Economic Systems and International Planning

While the convergence of economic systems may be limited by ideological, political, and cultural factors, economic problems of worldwide impact will place a premium in the long run on joint action by the world's nations. These problems include stabilizing the international financial system, providing financial and economic aid to less developed countries,

---

[32] For the distinction between the maximum and the optimum population, see John P. Holdren, "Population and the American Predicament: The Case against Complacency," Mancur Olson and Hans H. Landsberg, *op. cit.*, pp. 39–41.

[33] John P. Holdren, *op. cit.*, p. 41.

sharing the world's finite supplies of natural resources, curbing population growth, and preserving the international environment. Meagre progress has as yet been made in coping with these problems, and the prospect for more effective action in the near future in dealing with them is not very good. The problem of international financial stability is largely limited to the noncommunist world, since the communist countries have a very extensive control of their foreign trade and their foreign exchange systems. It is the large Western nations, including the United States, that have in recent years failed to coordinate and stabilize their floating foreign exchange rates and to construct an acceptable world monetary unit.

As long as the international economy is subject to large inflationary and deflationary price movements, the less developed economies, which are heavily dependent on foreign trade, will find it very difficult to stabilize their economies. Their difficulties will be compounded by the failure of the rich developed countries to assure the poor developing countries a sustained and adequate flow of financial and economic aid. The future of these developing countries is tied to the problem of the availability of the world's finite mineral and other natural resources. The United States accounts for roughly one-third of the world's annual consumption of energy and of most industrial metals. The United States, the Soviet Union, Europe, Japan, and Australia together account for 85 percent of the world's consumption of energy, steel, and tin. It has been calculated that to supply the current world population with the average per capita consumption of industrial materials enjoyed by the ten richest nations would require more than sixty years' world production of these metals at the 1970 rate of production.[34]

[34] Harrison Brown, "Human Materials Production as a Process in the Biosphere," *Scientific American*, Vol. 223, No. 3, Sept. 1970, p. 206.

Rapid progress in the development of the poor countries may be possible only if the consumption of natural resources is stabilized in the rich countries. This means that the world's rich nations may have to consider moving into an era of reduced economic growth; at the same time, the world's poor nations should consider more effective ways of curbing the increase of their populations. A related problem is the protection of the international environment. Oil and chemical pollution, the dumping of industrial and other wastes, the destruction of wetlands and nesting grounds, and overfishing in international waters are serious threats to the international environment.

Strong pressures are being exerted on the world's economic systems to take joint international action to deal with these pressing problems. As the result of a lack of worldwide cooperation, nations or groups of nations are independently taking steps to maintain or improve their economic positions. Nations are extending their jurisdictions over fishing rights to the two-hundred-mile limit; the OPEC (Organization of Petroleum Exporting Countries) countries and others are uniting to control the production and sale of oil, bauxite, tin, and other scarce internationally traded commodities; and closely related groups of nations have formed blocs such as the European Economic Community and the Council of Mutual Economic Assistance. A new area of potential conflict is the extraction of minerals from the sea and ocean floors. Many of these developments have erected barriers to the construction of a world economic order that would benefit all countries in the West, East, and South. The result is that nations seek national solutions to problems when the only workable solutions are international or global in nature, as we have seen in the case of the multinational corporations.

The obvious solution is the one proposed by the Club of Rome in *The Limits to Growth*:

"We have no doubt that if mankind is to embark on a new course, concerted international measures and joint long-term planning will be necessary on a scale and scope without precedent. Such an effort calls for joint endeavor by all peoples, whatever their culture, economic system, or level of development."[35] The Club of Rome goes on to say that the major responsibility for initiating worldwide planning lies with the more developed nations, whose plateaus of economic development can be tolerated only if they are used as bases from which to secure a more equitable worldwide distribution of wealth and income. In doing this, the rich developed nations will be giving expression to a new social ethic that emphasizes man's harmony with nature instead of his exploitation of it. The creation of such an ethic would result in new lifestyles and a world society that would constitute challenges to the world's competing economic systems.

The belief is growing that international planning cannot be successful unless it has a solid basis in national planning. This view has received considerable support since the 1974–1975 economic recession, during which economists widely agreed on the need for a shakeup of "conventional economic thinking." As was explained in Chapter 4, a step was taken in this direction recently in the United States with the establishing on October 14, 1974, of the Initiative Committee for National Planning. The members of this committee, who are led by the well-known economist Wassily Leontief, call for the setting up of a national economic planning board to analyze the American economy and monitor its functioning in order to achieve balanced economic growth.

There is an increasing awareness in the United States, the United Kingdom, Canada, Australia and other unplanned countries that the Keynesian economics, first developed in the 1930s and expanded after the Second World War, is not adequate for dealing with the economic problems of the 1970s. Many Keynesian economists are now recommending the establishment of a "social contract" between management and organized labor, which would provide a foundation for an incomes policy. Since a social contract would require a high degree of collaboration among the government, business, and labor, some form of national planning would be helpful in encouraging such a contract. This planning presupposes that these three groups have developed enough joint consultation to make both national planning and an incomes policy workable.

What makes both national planning and the construction of an incomes policy very difficult is that these issues bring to the surface the problem of income distribution. This happens because the establishing of national priorities and the formulation of an incomes policy cannot avoid the question of how the nation's income will be distributed among a large number of different claimants. Undoubtedly, income distribution will be a key issue in the closing quarter of this century, not only within countries but also between them, as, for example, between the rich and poor nations of the world.

Clearly, the economy of the United States will continue to evolve in not entirely predictable ways. The only certainty is that change of some kind will occur. In France, Holland, and the Scandinavian countries, the national planning programs are undergoing major changes as organized labor challenges the probusiness government in France, as Holland seeks to find a more workable incomes policy, and as Norway and Sweden search for a better balance between white-collar and blue-collar workers and between the economically active and the economically inactive parts of the population in their

---

[35] Donella H. Meadows and others, *The Limits to Growth*, p. 197.

planned economies. In the communist world of the Soviet Union, the Central European communist countries, and the People's Republic of China, there is much disagreement about national goals, decentralized planning, the role of the market mechanism, and the proper limits of personal freedoms. Yugoslavia, Hungary, Poland, and Czechoslovakia are uneasy with their inherited Marxian dogma and are straining to move in novel economic and social directions. The nations of the Third World are feeling their way into the future with a great deal of uncertainty, as they contemplate the world's developed countries that are so absorbed with their own pressing problems that they appear to have little time for a consideration of the Third World's problems. Since these economic and social changes will profoundly affect our future, a study of economic systems can be truly useful only if it prepares us to deal with the coming stages in the evolution of these systems.

Selected Bibliography

BELL, DANIEL. *The Coming of Post-Industrial Society.* Basic Books, New York, 1974.

BRONFENBRENNER, MARTIN. "Radical Economics in America: A 1970 Survey." *Journal of Economic Literature*, VIII (Sept. 1970), 747–766.

GOODMAN, ELLIOT R. "Reflections on the New Soviet Party Program." *The Russian Review*, 21, No. 2 (April 1962), 109–120.

KERR, CLARK, JOHN T. DUNLOP, FREDERICK H. HARBISON, and CHARLES A. MYERS. *Industrialism and Industrial Man.* Harvard University Press, Cambridge, 1960.

KLEIN, PHILIP A. *The Management of Market-Oriented Economies, A Comparative Perspective.* Wadsworth Publishing Co., Belmont Calif., 1973.

KUZNETS, SIMON. *Modern Economic Growth: Rate, Structure, and Spread.* Yale University Press, New Haven, 1966.

LEONTIEV, L. "Myth about the 'Rapprochement' of the Two Systems." *Reprints from the Soviet Press.* Compass Publications, New York, IV, No. 3 (Feb. 9, 1967), 4.

LINNEMAN, H., J. P. PRONK, and JAN TINBERGEN. "Convergence of Economic Systems in East and West." In *Disarmament and World Economic Interdependence.* Columbia University Press, New York, 1967.

MILLAR, JAMES R. "On the Theory and Measurement of Economic Convergence." *Quarterly Review of Economics and Business*, 12, No. 1 (Spring 1972), 87–97.

PRYBYLA, JAN S. "The Convergence of Western and Communist Economic Systems: A Critical Estimate." *The Russian Review*, 22, No. 1 (Jan. 1964), 3–17.

SOROKIN, P. A. "Mutual Convergence of the United States and the USSR to the Mixed Socio-Cultural Type." *International Journal of Comparative Sociology*, 1, No. 2 (Sept. 1960), 143–176.

TINBERGEN, JAN. "The Significance of Welfare Economics for Socialism." In *On Political Economy and Econometrics: Essays in Honour of Oskar Lange.* Pergamon Press, New York, 1965.

———. "The Theory of the Optimum Regime." In *Selected Papers.* North-Holland Publishing Co., Amsterdam, 1959.

WILES, PETER. "Will Capitalism and Communism Spontaneously Converge?" *Encounter*, XX, No. 6 (June 1963), 84.

ZEBOT, CYRIL A. *The Economics of Competitive Coexistence.* Frederick A. Praeger, Publishers, New York, 1964.

Index

Administrative socialism, 412
Agriculture and agricultural policies
  in China, 615–619
  in India, 636–639
  in Norway, 277–279, 289
  in United States, 59
  in West Germany, 138–142
Albania, 402

Balance of international payments
  in France, 188, 191, 196
  in Sweden, 311, 314
  in United Kingdom, 347–349, 354
Balogh, Thomas, 343
Banking
  in China, 623
  in West Germany, 138–142
Belgium, 666, 668
Bell, Daniel, 95, 390n, 662, 672
Bergson, Abram, 457n, 459
Bhagwati, Jagdish N., 593n, 595
Bornstein, Morris, 11n, 661
Brezhnev, Leonid I., 244, 439, 492
Britain
  capitalism in, 99
  codetermination in, 232, 248
  inflation policy, 357
  socialism in, 247, 340, 358, 370–376
  as welfare state, 100
  see also United Kingdom
British Labour party, 104
  inflation policy and, 357
  national planning and, 341, 351, 359
  socialism and, 340, 358, 373–376
Bulgaria, and Comecon Bloc, 541

Capitalism
  in Britain, 99
  in Communist China, 612
  essence of, 32
  evolution of, 35, 69
  in France, 57
  hypothetical and actual, 42
  in Japan, 45
  long-term trends in, 228–236
  mature capitalism and, 49, 52
  model of competitive capitalism, 36, 47
  model of mature capitalism, 31, 44, 52
  national planning and, 54
  "partnership capitalism" and, 654
  planned capitalism and, 56
  pure capitalism and, 633
  regulated capitalism and, 49
  in the United States, 69

unplanned capitalism and, 670
  in West Germany, 57
Castro, Fidel, 400
Chenery, Hollis B., 590n
China, see Peoples' Republic of China
Chou En-lai, 612
Club of Rome, 20, 92, 229, 675
Codetermination
  in Britain, 232, 248
  in Sweden, 232, 330
  in West Germany, 231
  worker directors and, 232, 330
  workers' control and, 248
Coexistence, of communism and capitalism, 548
Comecon Bloc
  Bulgaria and, 541
  Czechoslovakia and, 402, 409, 535–543
  East Germany and, 402, 541
  economic integration of, 544
  economic reforms in, 411, 534–543
  Hungary and, 407, 410, 538–541
  Romania and, 541
  Stalin's view of, 527
  structure and performance of, 530–534
Command economy, 663, 666
  administrative socialism and, 412
  Albania, North Korea, and Outer Mongolia and, 402
  basic aims of, 404
  China and, 400–402
  East Germany and, 402
  nature of, 396
  permanent revolution and, 402
  reformed, 403–405
  Soviet Union and, 359, 402–405
  techniques of planning in, 402
  traditional Stalinist command model and, 402
Commoner, Barry, 93, 235
Communism
  Chinese, 596–598, 601, 629
  East European, 527–530
  humanistic Marxism and, 537
  ideology of, 401, 414
  Maoism and, 627–630
  Marxism-Leninism and, 398, 598
  models of, 395
  monocentric view of, 527
  Soviet, 402–405, 414
  spectrum of, 399
  Yugoslavian, 548–550
Communist China, see Peoples' Republic of China
Comparative economic systems, 24, 25, 661
Concerted economy, 186, 211–216

Consumer welfare, in Soviet Union, 512–514
Convergence theory
  economic systems and, 21, 667–671
  evaluation of, 668–671
  weak and strong convergence and, 669
Council of Economic Advisers, 77, 89, 90, 94
Council of Mutual Economic Assistance, 675
Council of Social Affairs, 230
Currency, revaluation of
  in France, 188, 191, 196
  in United Kingdom, 348
  in West Germany, 167
Cultural Revolution, 607, 624–627
Czechoslovakia, and Comecon Bloc, 402, 409, 535–543

de Gaulle, Charles, 175, 216
Democracy, industrial, 231–233, 246, 248, 328
Democratic socialism, 245
  in Sweden, 298
  and welfare state, 382
Djilas, Milovan, 409
Dodge, Norton T., 482n, 511n
Dubcek, Alexander, 537

East Germany
  and Comecon Bloc, 402, 541
  and command economy, 402
Economic growth policies, in France, 189
Economic indicators
  in France, 190, 198
  in India, 648–650
  in Japan, 367, 387
  in Norway, 260–263, 291
  in Sweden, 310, 313
  in United Kingdom, 110–124, 348, 362
  in United States, 73, 76
  in West Germany, 149–152, 155–159
Economic reforms, and Comecon Bloc, 411, 534–543
Economic systems
  classification of, 22
  Club of Rome and, 20, 675
  command economy and, 663, 666
  comparative economic studies and, 25, 661
  comparative systems approach and, 24, 661
  concept of, 4, 6
  convergence of, 21, 667–671
  Council of Mutual Economic Assistance and, 675
  definition of, 11
  Eastern and Western, 670
  European Economic Community and, 675
  future of, 671–677
  general theory of, 666

Economic systems *(cont.)*
  industrialization and, 665
  Initiative Committee for National Planning, 676
  international planning and, 674–677
  market-oriented economy and, 663–666
  no-growth society and, 672
  organization theory and, 7
  postindustrial society and, 671
  spectrum model of, 663–665
  static and dynamic aspects of, 9, 661
  theory of convergence and, 667–671
  theory of optimum system and, 670
  zero economic growth and, 92
  zero population growth and, 92, 673
Education, in India, 652
Environmental policy
  in the Soviet Union, 524
  in Sweden, 331
  in the United States, 93
Erhard, Ludwig, 146, 150n
Eurocompanies, 232
European Economic Community (EEC)
  economic systems and, 675
  Eurocompanies and, 232
  France and, 189, 196, 212
  international planning and, 675
  Norway and, 296
  United Kingdom and, 131
  West Germany and, 171–172

Fabian socialist model, 244, 339–340
Fabian Society, 242–245
Foreign aid, and India, 643, 645
Foreign trade
  in China, 623–627
  Japanese, 626
  in less-developed economies, 584
  in Soviet Union, 514–516
  in United Kingdom, 104, 112–114, 353, 360
  in West Germany, 145, 150, 168
  in Yugoslavia, 559, 561
France
  capitalism in, 57
  concerted economy of, 186, 211–213
  devaluation of currency in, 188, 191, 196
  economic and financial indicators (1963–1972) of, 198
  Economic and Social Council of, 184
  Economic and Social Development Fund of, 183, 207
  economic growth policy in, 189
  economic indicators of, 190, 198
  economic performance (1953–1975) of, 187–193
  European Economic Community and, 189, 196, 212

Fifth National Plan (1966–1970) of, 204–206
fiscal policy of, 192, 195, 199–201, 207
foreign exchange policy of, 198
General Plan Commission of, 183
Gross National Product distribution in, 189, 194, 207
horizontal commissions in, 184
incomes policy of, 201–204
inflation and price policy in, 188, 190, 193, 196, 203
main features of the economy of, 176–180
monetary policy of, 188, 192, 196–199, 207
National Credit Council of, 197, 207
national economic budget of, 195, 210
national planning in, 181–186, 202–206, 209–216
organized labor in, 191, 202, 213–215
state-controlled financial institutions of, 208
supply and demand management in, 193–209
theory of indicative national planning of, 185, 203, 214–216
vertical commissions in, 184

Galbraith, John K., 9, 26, 54, 85, 215, 662
Gandhi, Mahatma (Mohandas K.), 166, 633–636, 639
Germany, *see* East Germany; West Germany
Great Leap Forward, 602
Great Proletarian Cultural Revolution, 606, 612, 624, 627
Green Revolution, 638
Grossman, Gregory, 11, 23, 26, 475n, 670
Gross National Product
  in France, 201–204
  in Japan, 581
  in less-developed countries, 581–583
  in United Kingdom, 101, 109, 130
  in West Germany, 151, 169

Hansen, Bent, 334
Hardt, John, 421n, 456
Harrod, Roy, 342
Horvat, Branko, 407, 413
Hua Kuo-feng, 602
Hungary, and Comecon Bloc, 407, 410, 538–541

Ideology
  Chinese communist, 596–598, 601, 629
  Indian socialist, 636–639
  Marxist-Leninist, 398
  Soviet communist, 402–405, 414
  technology and, 629
  Yugoslavian communist, 548–550

Incomes policy
  in France, 201–204
  in Norway, 289–292
  in Sweden, 312, 326–328
  in United Kingdom, 115–118, 120, 346
  in United States, 79–84
  in West Germany, 164–167
  in Yugoslavia, 566–570
India
  agriculture in, 636–639
  Bombay plan of, 639
  Communist China and, 654–656
  dual economy of, 636–639
  economic indicators of, 648–650
  economic performance of, 646–649
  educational system in, 652
  financial planning in, 642–644, 653–656
  fiscal policy of, 649
  foreign aid and, 643, 645
  Gandhi, Mahatma, and, 633–636
  Gandhian plan of, 639
  ideological problems in, 633–636
  industrial policy in, 636–639
  inflation in, 647, 652
  land tenure in, 638, 652
  monetary policy in, 650–652
  monopoly control in, 651
  Myrdal, Gunnar, views on, 652
  nationalization program of, 653
  Nehru, Jawaharlal, and, 633–636
  planned economy of, 636–642
  population problem of, 636, 656
  private enterprise in, 638
  socialism in, 636–639
  structural changes in industry of, 652
  supply and demand management in, 649–653
  tax program in, 649, 650
Industrial democracy, 231–233, 246–248, 328–331, 358
Industrialization, 665
Industrial policy
  in China, 612–615
  in India, 636–639
  in Soviet Union, 470, 476, 479–481
  in Sweden, 328–331
  in Yugoslavia, 553–556
Inflation
  in Britain, 357
  in France, 188, 190, 193, 196, 203
  in India, 647, 652
  in Norway, 262
  in Sweden, 311
  in United Kingdom, 120, 123, 126, 345, 346
  in West Germany, 148, 157
  in Yugoslavia, 566

Initiative Committee for National Planning, 676
Japan
  capitalism in, 45
  Chinese trade and, 626
  economic indicators of, 367, 387
  income distribution in, 369
  market shares of, 361
  national planning in, 219, 367, 386–388
  per capita GNP in, 581
  social security expenditures in, 386
  world economic resources and, 675
Joint industrial councils, 246
Joint production committees, 265

Kadar, Janos, 538
Kaldor, Nicholas, 343
Kantorovich, L. N., 407, 454
Kerr, Clark, 665, 677
Keynes, John M., 43, 676
Keynesian policy, 153, 170
Khrushchev, Nikita, 243, 438, 460, 476
Klein, Philip A., 661, 677
Korea, *see* North Korea
Kornai, Janos, 8, 26
Kosygin, Alexei N., 244, 439, 482
Kuznets, Simon, 591

Labor, *see* Organized labor
Lange, Oskar, 407, 413
Lenin, Vladimir I., 243, 601, 634
Leontief, Wassily, 92, 413
Less-developed economies
  China as, 598
  comparative features of, 585
  distribution of labor force in, 581
  exports and imports of, 584
  future of, 592
  gross domestic product distribution in, 581–583
  growth strategy of, 587
  income inequality in, 591
  low-income developing economies and, 580
  major problems of, 586
  model of, 584–586
  population problems in, 589–592
  poverty in, 589–592
  regional per capita GNP and, 581
  saving and investment in, 581
  types of, 579
  World Bank and, 579, 593
Liberman, E. G., 475, 478
Lin, Piao, 607, 612
Liu Shao-chi, 601, 608
Lundberg, Erik, 334

Management, *see* Supply and demand management
Manpower policy
  in Norway, 272
  in Sweden, 324
  in United Kingdom, 346, 353
  in United States, 87
Maoism, 627–630
Mao Tse-tung, 400, 600, 609
Market-oriented economy, 407, 663–666
Marx, Karl, 9, 243, 598, 634
Marxism, humanistic, 537
Marxism-Leninism, 398, 598
Massé, Pierre, 186
Mishan, Ezra J., 235
Monetary policy
  in China, 622
  in France, 188, 192, 196–199, 207
  in India, 650–652
  in Norway, 263, 284–288
  in Sweden, 311–314
  in United Kingdom, 115, 120, 347, 353, 357
  in United States, 87
  in West Germany, 162–164
  in Yugoslavia, 566–568
Montias, John M., 8n, 399, 609
Multinational corporations, 232, 233
Myrdal, Gunnar, 9, 26, 54, 652, 655

National economic budgets, in France, 195, 210
National Economic Development Council, 118, 123, 350, 359
National planning
  in Britain, 341, 351, 359
  and capitalism, 54
  in China, 401, 605–612
  in France, 181–186, 202–206, 209–216
  in India, 642–644, 653–656
  in Japan, 219, 367, 386–388
  in Norway, 255–258, 292–296
  and socialism, 245
  in Soviet Union, 423–426, 431–436, 445, 454–456, 457, 461–464
  in Sweden, 307–309, 316, 320
  and Trades Union Congress, 363
  in United Kingdom, 341, 350–356, 359
  in Yugoslavia, 562–565, 572–574
Nehru, Jawaharlal, 633–636
Neoliberalism, 152–155
Netherlands, 340, 666, 668, 676
Neuberger, Egon, 455n
New and Old left, 672
New communist man (woman), 530, 597, 616, 654
No-growth society, 672

North Korea, 402
Norway
  agricultural planning in, 277–279, 289
  centralized collective bargaining in, 272–275
  Contact Committee in, 289
  credit budget in, 289
  Credit Policy Advisory Committee in, 284
  economic development of, 259
  economic indicators (1963–1975) of, 260–263, 291
  economic performance of, 259–263
  economic trends in, 253–255
  European Economic Community and, 296
  external sector of, 279–281, 287–289
  incomes policy of, 289–292
  inflation in, 262
  investment budget of, 267
  joint industrial councils in, 246
  joint production committees in, 265
  manpower budget of, 272
  monetary policy of, 263, 284–288
  national economic budgets in, 256
  national planning in, 255–258, 292–296
  oil crisis in, 261
  organized labor in, 273–276
  price policy of, 260, 264, 269, 278, 289
  private business and national planning in, 263–269
  socialism of, 249, 370–372, 376–382
  taxation in, 281–284
  wage policy of, 276, 289
  as welfare state, 383–385

Oil crisis, 168, 261, 313, 356
Optimum system theory, 670
Organization of Petroleum Exporting Countries (OPEC), 168, 675
Organization theory, 7
Organized labor
  in France, 191, 202, 213–215
  in Norway, 273–276
  in Soviet Union, 502
  in United States, 64
  in West Germany, 165, 171
  in Yugoslavia, 557
Outer Mongolia, 402

Peoples' Republic of China, 596–598
  agricultural sector of, 615–619
  banking system of, 623
  capitalism in, 612
  and command economy, 401, 403–405
  communes in, 613, 615–617
  communism of, 596–598, 601, 629
  Cultural Revolution of, 607, 624–627
  domestic trade of, 623–627

economic future of, 627–630
economic performance of, 607–612
economy of, 602–606
extensive and intensive development of, 405–407
fiscal system of, 622
foreign trade of, 623–627
Great Leap Forward of, 608–609, 612
gross domestic product distribution of, 604
ideological problems in, 596–598, 601, 629
and India, 654–656
industrial system of, 612–615
and Japan, 626
as a less-developed country, 598
material and nonmaterial incentives in, 609
mobilized command economy of, 400–402
monetary system of, 622
national planning in, 401, 605–612
National Price Commission of, 619
political structure of, 600–602
population problem of, 628
poverty problem in, 600
price system of, 619–622
"redness" over "expertness" in, 608, 629
Soviet Union and, 597
wage system of, 619–622
Plan Age, 229
Planning, *see* National planning
Poland, *see* Comecon Bloc
Pompidou, Georges, 176
Population
China's problem of, 628
India's problem of, 636, 656
in less-developed countries, 589–592
optimum, 674
zero population growth and, 90, 93
Postindustrial society
civilized values and, 671
quality of life in, 672
technology assessment and, 671
zero economic growth and, 672
zero population growth and, 673
Poverty, 589–592, 600
Preobrazhensky, E. A., 415n
Price policy
in France, 188, 190, 193, 196, 203
in Norway, 260, 264, 269, 278, 289
in Sweden, 312–315
in United Kingdom, 106, 346
in United States, 87
in Yugoslavia, 568–570
Prybyla, Jan S., 399, 670, 677

Rehn, Gösta, 308
Reynolds, Lloyd G., 23, 25n, 27

Robinson, Joan, 654n
Romania, and Comecon Bloc, 541

Scandinavian socialism, 245, 247, 249
Shonfield, Andrew, 96, 304n
Sik, Ota, 407, 409, 413, 539
Socialism
administrative, 407, 412
in Britain, 247, 340, 342–343, 358, 370–376
class distinctions and, 246
cooperative, 572
democratic, 245
dynamics of, 389–391
evolution of, 241
Fabian, 244, 340
independent paths to, 548
Indian, 633–639
industrial democracy and, 246–248
market, 407, 412
Marxian, 242–244
national planning and, 245
Norwegian, 249, 370–372, 376–382
parliamentary, 634
partial democratic, 245–249
pluralistic, 409
pure, 663
Scandinavian, 245, 247, 249
Swedish, 370–372, 376–382
in transition, 247
welfare state and, 382
workers' control and, 248
Social market economy, 146–148, 170
Social security
in Japan, 386
in United Kingdom, 107
Sorokin, P. A., 671
Soviet Union
administrative planning apparatus in, 423–426
agricultural policy of, 488–496
agriculture in, 482–496
annual planning in, 436, 461–464
balance method of planning in, 431–435
and China, 597
collective farms in, 485–487
command economy of, 395, 402–405
communism of, 402–405, 414
consumer welfare in, 512–514
control by the ruble (*khozraschet*) in, 489
deficiencies of planning in, 445
distribution system of, 507
economic performance (1971–1975) in, 441–443, 521–525
economic reforms of 1965 in, 476–482
efficiency of planning in, 454

Soviet Union (*cont.*)
  environmental policy, 524
  evolution of economy of, 415–419
  financial system of, 516–521
  foreign trade of, 514–516
  future of planning in, 457
  industrial associations in, 481
  industrial investment in, 468–470
  industrial management in, 470, 476, 479–481
  labor and incentives in, 497–509
  manpower problems in, 506
  mathematical planning techniques of, 454–456
  national planning in, 423–426, 431–436, 445, 454–456, 457, 461–464
  Ninth Five-Year Plan (1971–1975) of, 438–443
  profitability of enterprises in, 467
  real and financial planning in, 435
  role of trade unions in, 502
  sectoral and territorial planning in, 435
  state farms in, 483
  wage policy in, 501–506
  wages and salaries in, 464
  wholesale price system of, 466
Spulber, Nicolas, 663
Stalin, Joseph, 421, 438, 548, 618
  and Comecon Bloc, 527
Supply and demand management
  in France, 193–209
  in India, 649–653
  in Sweden, 315–326
  in United Kingdom, 126, 128, 345–354
  in Yugoslavia, 565–572
Sweden
  annual national planning in, 316
  balance of international payments of, 311, 314
  codetermination in, 232, 330
  democratic socialism in, 298
  econometric planning model of, 320
  economic indicators of, 310, 313
  economic performance (1963–1975) of, 309–315
  environmental protection in, 331
  financial system of, 305–307
  fiscal policy of, 311, 313–315
  gross domestic production distribution in, 318, 325
  incomes policy of, 312, 326–328
  industrial concentration in, 303
  industrial democracy in, 328–331
  industrialized economy of, 301–305
  inflation in, 311
  manpower policy in, 324
  monetary policy of, 311–314
  national economic budgets in, 316, 319
  national plan organization of, 307–309
  oil crisis in, 313
  price policy of, 312–315
  quality of life in, 321
  regional development in, 333
  socialism of, 370–372, 376–382
  supply and demand management in, 315–326
  Swedish Confederation of Trade Unions in, 304, 327–331
  Swedish Employers' Association in, 303, 328–331
  welfare state of, 299–301
  worker directors and codetermination in, 232, 330

Taxes
  in India, 649, 650
  in Norway, 281–284
Tito, Josip Broz, 243, 548
Trade, *see* Foreign trade
Trades Union Congress
  national planning and, 363
  United Kingdom and, 123
  wage policy and, 356, 363
Treml, Vladimir G., 459

United Kingdom (capitalist economy)
  British Labour party and, 104
  capitalism and, 99
  Confederation of British Industry in, 123, 363
  Conservative Party and, 106–108, 120–124
  Council on Prices, Productivity, and Incomes in, 117
  demand management in, 128
  economic crisis (1973–1974) of, 124–126
  economic growth of, 109, 122, 127–129, 132
  economic indicators (1953–1963) in, 110–124
  economic performance (1951–1963) of, 108–112
  economic policy (1951–1963), 113–118
  economic structure of, 100
  European Economic Community and, 129, 131–132
  export policy of, 112–114
  fiscal policy of, 114, 120
  gross national product distribution in, 101, 109, 130
  incomes policy in, 115–118, 120
  industrial production in, 109
  inflation problem of, 120, 123, 126
  "middle way" of, 99
  monetary policy of, 115, 120
  national economic budget of, 119, 124, 130
  National Economic Development Council of, 118–123
  National Institute of Economic and Social Research of, 129

postwar economic problems of, 105
price control in, 106
share of total world exports of, 104
social security system of, 107
supply management in, 126
Trades Union Congress and, 123
wage policy in, 111
wage-price freeze in, 122
United Kingdom (socialist economy)
annual national planning in, 359
balance of international payments in, 347-349, 354
British socialism in, 342-343
comparative economic indicators of, 362
criticism of national planning in, 341
devaluation of the pound in, 348
economic assessment (1969-1972) of, 354
economic growth of, 351, 363-365
economic indicators (1963-1970) in, 348
European Economic Community and, 131
evaluation of British socialism in, 359
export policy of, 353, 360
Fabian socialism in, 339
fiscal policy in, 345, 353, 357
gross domestic production distribution in, 352, 355, 357
incomes policy in, 346
industrial democracy in, 358
Industrial Reorganisation Act of, 353
industrial reorganization in, 353
inflation in, 345, 356
international reserves of, 347, 361
manpower policy in, 346, 353
monetary policy of, 347, 353, 357
national economic budget in, 352, 355, 357
National Economic Development Council of, 350, 359
National Plan (1966-1970) of, 351-354
national plan organization in, 350
national planning in, 350-356, 359
oil crisis in, 356
price policy of, 346
"socialist contract" and wage policy in, 356
supply and demand management, 345-354
Third Labour Government (1974-1976) in, 356
wage policy in, 346, 356-358
United States
agricultural sector of, 59
capitalism in, 69
economic indicators of, 73, 76
economic performance (1961-1973) of, 69, 74, 77, 81
environmental policy, 93
external sector of, 82

fiscal policy of, 74, 86, 92
future of, 95
high-pressure economy of, 74-76
incomes policy in, 79-84
industrial structure of, 61
Kennedy-Johnson Administration of, 70-76
life style in, 86
manpower policy of, 87
monetary policy of, 87
national economic budgets in, 89-92
national priorities of, 94
Nixon Administration of, 77-84
organized labor in, 64
Phillips curve in, 75n
role of government in, 67
wage and price policy of, 87
wage-price controls in, 79-83
and welfare state, 89
workable competition in, 44

Wage policy
in China, 619-622
in Norway, 276, 289
in Soviet Union, 501-506
and Trades Union Congress, 356, 363
in United Kingdom, 111, 346, 356-358
in United States, 87
in West Germany, 157, 165
Welfare state
Britain and, 100
democratic socialism and, 382
Norway and, 383-385
Sweden and, 299-301
United States and, 89
West Germany
agriculture and labor in, 138-142
anti-recession policy, 167-170
capitalism in, 57
codetermination in, 231
Council of Economic Exports, 153
economic indicators (1953-1963) in, 149-152, 155-159
European Economic Community and, 171-172
export policy of, 150, 168
external sector of, 159
financial indicators (1963-1974) of, 163
fiscal policy of, 151, 153, 160
foreign trade of, 145, 150
gross national product distribution in, 151, 169
incomes policy of, 164-167
industry and banking in, 138-142
inflation in, 148, 157
Keynesian economic policy in, 153, 170
monetary policy of, 162-164

Index

West Germany (*cont.*)
   national economic budget of, 154
   neoliberalism in, 152-155
   oil crisis in, 168
   organized labor in, 165, 171
   revaluation of the mark, 167
   social market economy, 146-148, 170
   Stability and Growth Law of 1967, 153, 162
   wage policy in, 157, 165
Wiles, Peter, J. D., 503n, 669, 677
Wilson, Harold, 343, 363
Worker directors in industry, 232, 330
Workers' councils, 536
Workers' self-management, 248, 547, 553-556
World Bank, 579, 593

Yugoslavia
   annual planning in, 564
   communism of, 548-550
   decentralized economy in, 561
   disequilibrium and decentralized investment in, 571
   economic associations in, 549
   economic fluctuations in, 560-562
   economic performance of, 562-565
   economic planning in, 562-565
   evaluation of planned economy of, 572-574
   fiscal policy of, 566-568
   foreign trade of, 559, 561
   income differentials and income distribution in, 570
   incomes policy in, 566-570
   industrial policy in, 553-556
   inflation (structural) in, 566
   labor and trade unions in, 557
   League of Yugoslav Communists, 409
   managerialism and the "new class" in, 573
   market-oriented economy of, 407
   monetary policy of, 566-568
   price controls and price policy of, 568-570
   Socialist Alliance of the Working People of Yugoslavia, 551
   supply and demand management in, 565-572
   withering away of the state of, 550
   workers' self-management in, 553-556

Zebot, Cyril A., 671
Zero economic growth, 20, 92, 672
Zero population growth, 20, 92, 672, 673